JET AIRLINERS OF THE WORLD 1996

compiled and edited by

Michael Austen, Lyn Buttifant, Chris Chatfield and Tony Pither

in collaboration with

Fred Barnes, Richard Church, Peter-Michael Gerhardt,
Terry Smith, Ray Turner, Reimar and Helga Wendt and Tony Wheeler

Published by: Air-Britain (Historians) Limited

Registered Office: 12 Lonsdale Gardens, Tunbridge Wells, Kent TN1 1PA, England

Sales Department: 5 Bradley Road, Upper Norwood, London SE19 3NT

Membership Enquiries: Dept JA, 36 Nursery Road, Taplow, Maidenhead, Berks SL6 0JZ

ISBN 0 85130 239 4

PHOTO CAPTIONS:

Front cover -

Airbus Industrie A321-131 CS-MAA c/n 0550 of Air Macau

Airbus Industrie A310-304 TU-TAC c/n 0571 of Air Afrique

Rear cover -

Airbus Industrie A330-322 F-WWKM/9M-MKC c/n 069 of Malaysia Airlines

Airbus Industrie A320-232 B-2340 c/n 0540 of Sichuan Airlines
(Airbus Industrie)

CONTENTS

Printed by Bell and Bain Ltd, Glasgow

INTRODUCTION

It is three years since the publication of the previous, fourth, edition of Jet Airliners of the World. The enthusiastic response to the last edition has prompted the publication of this, the 1996 edition of Jet Airliners.

Coverage has been extended from the 58 types of the previous edition to embrace 68 different aircraft types, from the first commercial jet transports to all those in current production, including for the first time production lists of military transports such as the Lockheed Starlifter and Galaxy and McDonnell-Douglas C-17, and jet maritime aircraft such as the British Aerospace Nimrod and Kawasaki C-1. Again, as complete production lists as possible of Soviet-built types have been included, with much more coverage than has heretofore been possible.

The basic format of the publication remains the same; aircraft are listed alphabetically by manufacturer, with the individual examples of each type being listed in constructor's number or serial number sequence. In response to a number of readers' requests Boeing line numbers have been included in the main production list, as they are for Douglas and McDonnell-Douglas types.

For each individual aircraft are listed the c/n or s/n, the current series, the identities (to March 1996) in chronological order with the latest identity last, the last known operator or lessee for leased aircraft (or owner where the operator is not known), and the fate where applicable. Previous identities shown in brackets are marks allocated but not officially taken up, and bracketed entries in the last known operator column indicate the then-named (generally airline) operator at the time the aircraft was written off or broken up. Dates of storage are generally those of the first report of the aircraft most recently being stored at the stated location.

Fate details have been expanded to indicate destroyed by fire or damaged beyond repair, as appropriate. In the latter examples, fuselages often remain extant at the fate location for several years. The country descriptions of fate locations are those of the country at the time of the accident. First flight dates for each type are quoted where known.

A major feature of this publication continues to be the Master Index registration-type-c/n (or s/n) cross-reference pioneered many years ago by Air-Britain in Business Jets International. This index lists in registration order by country prefix all registrations carried by or allocated to commercial jet aircraft, with this edition containing nearly 41,600 entries. We are indebted to Barrie Towey for the programming involved in producing the original Master Index and to Lyn Buttifant for all word-processing operations.

Contributors have been drawn from among Air-Britain's experts in commercial aviation history, and all of the information in this publication remains in the ownership of these contributors and Air-Britain and cannot be reproduced for publication elsewhere without the express prior written permission of Air-Britain and the appropriate contributor. Major contributors are listed on the title page, but particular thanks are due to Tony Pither for Boeing data and to the late George Stevens and to Terry Smith for data on Soviet-built aircraft, and to Michael Austen for the expansion into military transports. Credit is also due to the British Aviation Research Group for published information enabling the cross-checking of military-operated aircraft, to Scramble and to Soviet Airliners.

Updating of this publication can be achieved by reading the Commercial News section of Air-Britain News, our monthly magazine, all of whose correspondents must be warmly thanked for their indirect contributions to this Monograph. It is intended to follow this title with a second edition of Turboprop Airliners and Military Transports of the World in the not too distant future and, dependent upon sales, further editions will continue to be published on a regular basis.

While every effort has been made to ensure complete accuracy, the sheer volume of factual data in a publication of this nature means that occasional mistakes will get past even the most assiduous of proofreaders, and all those of you who can offer amendments or corrections are invited to do so to the address below, together with suggestions for improvements in future editions. To those who supplied factual data following the 1993 edition, we are particularly grateful, including John Burdett, J R Cain, Russ Carter, Jacques Chillon, Richard Church, Colin Frost, Heinz Kasmanhuber, Bernard Martin, J A Newton, John Pike, Tony Pither, Brian Print, Jon Proctor, Mark Reavey, Terry Smith, Ted Thompson and Tony Wheeler.

We hope that you will enjoy reading this Monograph and look forward to your views.

March 1996

Chris Chatfield
23 Woodcote Park Avenue
Purley
Surrey, CR8 3NL

ABBREVIATIONS

Abbreviations used in the text have the following meanings:

a/c	aircraft
Aerotpt	Aerotransport
AF	Air Force
A/L	Airlines
A/P	Airport
Ass	Association
A/W	Airways
Avn	Aviation
b/u	broken up
canx	cancelled
c/n	constructor's number
Corp	Corporation
c/s	colour scheme
cvtd	converted
dbf	destroyed by fire
dbr	damaged beyond repair
der	derelict
dest	destroyed
Eng	Engineering
Ent	Enterprise
Flt	Flight
fm	from
FSBU	First Security Bank of Utah
GECC	General Electric Credit Corp
Govt	Government
ILFC	International Lease Finance Corp
Inc	Incorporated
Inds	Industries
Inst	Institute
Int,Intl	International
LA	Lineas Aereas
Lsg	Leasing
Min	Ministry
Natl	National
Prod	Production
Rep	Republic
Sch	school
s/n	serial number
SOC	struck off charge
Svce	Service
Tpt	Transport
Trng	Training
UN	United Nations
wfs	withdrawn from service
wfu	withdrawn from use
w/o	written off
*	reservation

NOTES

The following comments apply to Soviet production:

1 When an incomplete sequence number (or construction number) is given, it indicates that only part of the number has been reported or that, by process of elimination, the s/n for the given aircraft is expected to fall in that order. As more and more information comes to light, more of the s/ns are completed, giving a more complete production listing.

2 Aeroflot now only appears when an aircraft has been wfs, preserved, w/o or wfu when the aircraft was last operated by the Aeroflot company; any survivor could still possibly be painted in the company colours and markings. The TU-104 and TU-124 have all been wfs or w/o etc whilst Aeroflot was the only Soviet airline carrier, and therefore the name appears in almost all cases.

3 A blank space is left in the Owner/Operator column when the operator is not known or confirmed, or if a recent sighting of the aircraft simply lists it as 'Aeroflot'. As Aeroflot only officially exists as Aeroflot Russian International Airlines and has a lot fewer aircraft and types than the number of aircraft reported as Aeroflot, we can only assume that many original Aeroflot aircraft are with other carriers who have not yet changed the logos or markings carried by the aircraft.

AIRBUS INDUSTRIE A300

C/n	Series	Last known Operator/Owner	Previous Identities/fate (where known)
01	(B1)	(Airbus Industrie)	F-WUAB F-OCAZ prototype; ff 28Oct72; final flight 31Aug74 Toulouse, France; b/u, parts at Paris-Le Bourget, France
02	B1	Trans European	F-WUAC OO-TEF wfu 25Nov90 and stored Brussels, Belgium
03	B2-103	NOVESPACE	F-WUAD (F-ODCX) F-WUAD F-BUAD
04	B2-1C	(Air Inter)	F-WUAA F-BUAE b/u Aug93 Montpellier-Frejourges, France
05	B2-1C	Air France	F-WVGA F-BVGA
06	B2-1C	Air France	F-WVGB F-BVGB wfs Montpellier-Frejourges, France
07	B2-1C	Translift Airways	F-WVGC F-BVGC EI-TL.
08	B2-1C	Air Inter	F-WNDB HS-VGD F-WNDB (F-BDHC) F-ODHC PH-TVL F-WNDB F-BUAF
09	B4-203	Grand Air Intl	F-WLGA (HS-VGF) F-ODCY D-AMAP G-BMNB F-GIJT RP-C8881
10	B2-1C	Air Inter	F-BVGD stored Mar96 Ardmore, OK
11	B2-1C	Air Inter	F-BVGE stored Mar96 Ardmore, OK
12	B4-103	Translift Airways	F-WLGC D-AMAX G-BMNC F-GIJU EI-TLB
13	B2-1C	Air Inter	F-BVGF stored 1995 Chateauroux, France
14	B4-2C	Korean Air	F-WLGB HL7218
15	B2-1C	Air Inter	F-WLGC F-BUAG
16	B4-2C	Korean Air	F-WLGB HL7219
17	B4-103	Holiday Air	F-WLGB OO-TEG (PH-TEV) OO-TEG SU-BBS D-AHLC F-GIJS TC-RAA
18	B4-2C	Korean Air	F-W HL7220
19	B4-203	Air France	F-BVGG stored Jun95 Paris-Le Bourget, France
20	B4-103	Translift Airways	(F-WLGB) D-AMAY F-BUAR EI-CJK
21	B2-1C	(Air Inter)	F-WNDA D-AIAA F-BUAM b/u Feb94 Paris-Orly, France
22	B2-1C	(Indian Airlines)	F-WNDC D-AIAB F-WZMB F-ODRD VT-ELV w/o 29Sep86 Madras, India
23	B4-203	Air France	F-WVGH F-BVGH
24	B4-2C	Korean Air	F-WNDD HL7221
25	B4-203	(Pakistan Intl A/L)	F-WNDA D-AMAZ SU-AZY D-AHLZ AP-BCP w/o 28Sep92 Kathmandu, Nepal
26	B2-1C	Indian Airlines	F-WNDB D-AIAC F-WZMJ F-ODRE VT-ELW
27	B2-1C	Air Inter	F-WLGB F-WLGC F-BUAH
28	B4-2C	Korean Air	F-WNDC HL7223
29	B4-102	Air Inter	F-WNDD HK-2057X HK-2057 F-ODJU F-BUAL
30	B4-2C	Korean Air	F-WNDB HL7224
31	B4-2C	Korean Air	F-WLGC F-WUAY F-WZEQ HL7238
32	B2K-3C	South African Airways	F-WLGA ZS-SDA
33	C4-203	Thai Airways Intl	F-WNDC HS-TGH HS-TAX HS-THH stored Nov95 Bangkok, Thailand
34	B2-1C	(Indian Airlines)	F-WLGB VT-EDV dbr 15Nov93 nr Madras, India
35	B4-103	Thai Airways Intl	F-WLGA HS-TGK HS-THK stored Nov95 Bangkok, Thailand
36	B2-1C	Indian Airlines	(F-WLGB) F-WUAT VT-EDW
37	B2K-3C	South African Airways	F-WUAU ZS-SDB
38	B2-1C	Indian Airlines	F-WUAV VT-EDX
39	B2K-3C	South African Airways	F-WLGB ZS-SDC
40	B2K-3C	South African Airways	F-WUAX ZS-SDD
41	B4-103	FSBU	F-WUAZ N201EA stored Jul95 Roswell, NM
42	B4-103	FSBU	F-WUAU N202EA stored Jul95 Roswell, NM
43	B4-103	FSBU	F-WUAT N203EA stored Jul95 Roswell, NM
44	B4-103	FSBU	F-WUAX N204EA stored Jul95 Roswell, NM
45	B4-2C	Air Charter	F-WNDA F-BVGI
46	B4-203	Grand Air Intl	F-WLGB F-WZER SX-BEB RP-C8882
47	B4-103	Air France	F-WUAX F-BVGJ stored Jun95 Paris-Le Bourget, France
48	B2-202	Air Inter	F-WNDB D-AIAD F-ODRF F-BUAO
49	B2-203	Alitalia	F-WUAV F-WZES F-ODHY F-GBNI N291EA I-BUSM
50	B2-1C	Air Inter	F-WNDB F-WZET F-GBEA
51	B2-203	Alitalia	F-WZEA F-ODHZ F-GBNJ N292EA I-BUSN
52	B2-1C	Air Inter	F-WNDC F-WZEB D-AIAE F-ODRG F-BUAP
53	B4-203	VIASA	F-WZEE D-AIBA YV-160C stored Jun95 Mobile, AL
54	B4-103	Thai Airways Intl	F-WZED HS-TGL HS-THL stored Nov95 Bangkok, Thailand
55	B4-103	Thai Airways Intl	F-WZEC HS-TGM HS-THM stored Nov95 Bangkok, Thailand
56	B4-203	Olympic Airways	F-WZEF SX-BEC Cancelled 25Oct94 on sale to USA
57	B4-2C	Air Inter	F-WZEG D-AIBB F-BUAQ
58	B4-103	Olympic Airways	F-WZEH SX-BED
59	B2-1C	Indian Airlines	F-WZEI VT-EDY
60	B2-1C	Indian Airlines	F-WZEJ VT-EDZ
61	B2-203	Iran Air	F-WZEK EP-IBR
62	B2-1C	Air Inter	F-BUAI
63	B4-103	Philippine Airlines	F-WZEL RP-C3001
64	B4-203	Pakistan Intl Airlines	F-WZEM D-AHLA(2) AP-BBM
65	B4-103	Air Alfa	F-WZEN F-GBNA N205EA N404UA HS-TAY V2-LDY OO-MKO TC-ALN
66	B4-103	Air Alfa	F-WZEO F-GBNB N206EA N405UA HS-TAZ OO-ING TC-ALS
67	B4-103	Alitalia	F-WZEP F-GBNC N207EA I-BUSP
68	B4-103	Alitalia	F-WZEA F-GBND N208EA N403UA I-BUST
69	B4-103	Philippine Airlines	F-WZEB RP-C3002
70	B4-203	(Air France)	F-BVGK dbf 17Mar82 Sana'a, Yemen
71	B4-103	Thai Airways Intl	F-WZEC HS-TGN HS-THN
72	B4-103	Thai Airways Intl	F-WZED HS-TGO HS-THO
73	B4-203	Carnival Airlines	F-WZEE 9M-MHA N224KW
74	B4-203	Air France	F-BVGL stored 1995 Chateauroux, France
75	B4-203	VIASA	F-WZEG D-AIBC YV-161C stored Jun95 Mobile, AL
76	B4-203	Iberia	F-WZEI D-AIBD G-BMZK EC-273 EC-EON
77	B4-203	Iberia	F-WZEJ D-AIBF G-BMZL EC-274 EC-EOO
78	B4-203	Air France	F-BVGM
79	B4-120	Conair	F-WZEN LN-RCA OY-CNA

AIRBUS INDUSTRIE A300

C/n	Series	Last known Operator/Owner	Previous Identities/fate (where known)							
80	B2-203	Iran Air	F-WZEO	EP-IBS						
81	B4-2C	Korean Air	F-WZEP	HL7246						
82	B2K-3C	Japan Air System	F-WZEQ	JA8464						
83	C4-203	Philippine Airlines	F-WZES	D-AHLB	EI-BZB	RP-C3007				
84	B4-103	Thai Airways Intl	F-WZET	HS-TGP	HS-THP					
85	B4-103	Thai Airways Intl	F-WZEC	HS-TGR	HS-THR					
86	B4-103	Onur Air	F-GBNE	N209EA	(N980C)	N14980	TC-TKA	N14980	TC-TKA	TC-ONK
87	B4-103	Onur Air	F-GBNF	N210EA	(N981C)	N29981	TC-TKB	N29981	TC-TKB	
88	B2-1C	Indian Airlines	F-WZED	VT-EFV						
89	B2K-3C	Japan Air System	F-WZEF	JA8465						
90	B2K-3C	Japan Air System	F-WZEG	JA8466						
91	B4-103	Akendiz Airlines	F-GBNG	N212EA	(N982C)	N16982	TC-TKC	N16982		
92	B4-103	Continental Airlines	F-GBNH	N213EA	(N983C)	N13983	stored Nov95 Los Angeles, CA			
93	B4-203	Carnival Airlines	F-WZEI	9M-MHB	N225KW					
94	B4-120	Corsair	F-WZEJ	SE-DFK	OY-CNK					
95	B4-203	Carnival Airlines	F-WZEM	9M-MHC	N226KW					
96	B4-203	Pakistan Intl Airlines	F-WZEP	AP-BAX						
97	B2-1C	Air Inter	F-BUAJ							
98	B4-203	Pakistan Intl Airlines	F-WZER	AP-BAY						
99	B4-203	Pakistan Intl Airlines	F-WZET	AP-BAZ						
100	B4-203	Air France	F-BVGN							
101	B4-203	Alitalia	F-WZEA	I-BUSB						
102	B2-1C	Holiday Air	F-GBEB	TC-RAB						
103	B4-103	Olympic Airways	F-WZEC	SX-BEE						
104	B2-1C	(Air France)	F-GBEC	dbr 26Dec94 Marseille, France						
105	B4-103	Olympic Airways	F-WZED	SX-BEF						
106	B4-203	Alitalia	F-WZEE	I-BUSC						
107	B4-203	Alitalia	F-WZEL	I-BUSD						
108	B4-103	Continental Airlines	F-GBNK	N215EA	(N984C)	N11984	stored Jul95 Los Angeles, CA			
109	B4-203	Air Jamaica	F-WZEM	PP-CLA	6Y-JMR					
110	B4-203	Japan Air System	F-WZEB	PP-CLB	JA8292					
111	B2-1C	Indian Airlines	F-WZEI	VT-EFW						
112	B2K-3C	Air Inter	F-BUAK	stored Aug94 Chateauroux, France						
113	B2-1C	Indian Airlines	F-WZEJ	VT-EFX						
114	B4-203	Pakistan Intl Airlines	F-WZEN	AP-BBA						
115	B4-203	(Egyptair)	F-WZEP	SU-BCA	w/o 21Sep87 Luxor, Egypt					
116	B4-203	Egyptair	F-WZES	SU-BCB						
117	B4-203	Continental Airlines	F-WZER	9V-STA	F-OGTB	N966C	N14966	stored Oct95 Marana, AZ		
118	B4-103	Alitalia	F-GBNL	N216EA	N401UA	I-BUSQ				
119	B4-103	Continental Airlines	F-GBNM	N217EA	(N985C)	N11985	stored Jul95 Los Angeles, CA			
120	B4-103	Alitalia	F-GBNN	N219EA	N402UA	I-BUSR				
121	B4-203	Continental Airlines	F-WZEK	9V-STB	F-OGTC	N967C	N15967	stored Oct95 Marana, AZ		
122	B4-120	(Malaysian A/L System)	F-WZEH	OY-KAA	w/o 18Dec83 nr Kuala Lumpur, Malaysia					
123	B4-203	Alitalia	F-WZET	I-BUSF						
124	B4-203	Channel Express	F-GBNO	N220EA	N407UA	N407U				
125	B4-203	Philippine Airlines	F-WZEO	RP-C3003						
126	B4-203	Continental Airlines	F-WZEC	9V-STC	F-OGTA	N974C	N968C	N13974	stored Marana, AZ	
127	B4-203	Air Jamaica	F-WZED	G-BIMA	6Y-JMJ					
128	B4-120	Sobelair	F-WZEE	SE-DFL	OY-CNL					
129	B4-203	Air France	F-BVGO							
130	B4-120	Iberia	F-WZEI	EC-DLE						
131	B4-203	Air Jamaica	F-WZEL	G-BIMB	6Y-JMK					
132	B2-1C	Air Inter	F-WZEM	D-AIAF	F-BUAN	stored Aug94 Chateauroux, France				
133	B4-120	Iberia	F-WZEB	EC-DLF						
134	B4-203	Qantas Airways	F-WZEJ	VH-TAA	D-AITA	P2-ANG	VH-TAA			
135	B4-120	Iberia	F-WZEA	EC-DLG						
136	B4-120	Iberia	F-WZEN	EC-DLH						
137	B4-203	Air Afrique	F-WZEP	TU-TAO						
138	B4-203	South African Airways	F-WZEQ	ZS-SDE	C-GIZJ	F-WWAG	ZS-SDE			
139	B4-203	Alitalia	F-WZES	I-BUSG						
140	B4-203	Alitalia	F-WZEF	I-BUSH						
141	B4-203	Thai Airways Intl	F-WZEH	HS-TGT	HS-THT					
142	B4-203	Alitalia	F-WZET	I-BUSJ						
143	B4-203	Air Jamaica	F-WZED	PP-VND	6Y-JMS					
144	B4-203	Pakistan Intl Airlines	F-WZEG	G-BIMC	AP-BBV					
145	B4-203	ZAS Airlines of Egypt	F-BVGP	SU-DAS						
146	B4-203	Pakistan Intl Airlines	F-BVGQ	AP-BEY						
147	B4-203	Air Maldives	F-WZMA	9M-MHD						
148	B4-103	Olympic Airways	F-WZMB	SX-BEG						
149	B4-203	Thai Airways Intl	F-WZMC	HS-TGW	HS-THW					
150	B4-203	Egyptair	F-WZMD	SU-BCC						
151	B4-203	Japan Air System	F-WZME	VH-TAB	D-AITB	VH-TAB	JA8263			
152	B4-203	Carnival Airlines	F-GBNP	N221EA						
153	B4-203	Air Alfa	F-GBNQ	N222EA	N14968	TC-ALP				
154	B4-203	APA International Air	F-GBNR	N223EA	(N986C)	N72986	OB-1631			
155	B4-203	Air Alfa	F-GBNS	N224EA	(N987C)	N72987	TC-ALR			
156	B4-120	Iberia	F-WZMF	EC-DNQ						
157	B4-203	Qantas Airways	F-WZMG	VH-TAC						
158	B4-203	Fleet National Bank	F-GBNT	N225EA	TC-JUY	N225GE	stored Smyrna, TN			
159	B4-220	Garuda Indonesia	F-WZMH	PK-GAA	wfs Jakarta, Indonesia					
160	B2K-3C	Japan Air System	F-WZMI	JA8471						

AIRBUS INDUSTRIE A300

C/n	Series	Last known Operator/Owner	Previous Identities/fate (where known)
161	B4-203	Fleet National Bank	F-GBNU N226EA TC-JUV N226GE stored Smyrna, TN
163	B2K-3C	Japan Air System	F-WZMJ JA8472
164	B4-220	Garuda Indonesia	F-WZMK PK-GAC wfs Jakarta, Indonesia
165	B4-220	Garuda Indonesia	F-WZML PK-GAD wfs
166	B4-220	Garuda Indonesia	F-WZMM PK-GAE wfs
167	B4-220	Garuda Indonesia	F-WZMN PK-GAF wfs
168	B4-220	Garuda Indonesia	F-WZMO PK-GAG wfs
169	B4-2C	Japan Air System	F-WZMP 9V-STD D-AHLJ G-BMNA D-AHLJ JA8276
170	B4-120	Iberia	F-WZMQ EC-DNR
171	B4-120	China Airlines	F-WZMR (EC-DNS) B-1812
173	B4-203	Alitalia	F-WZMS I-BUSL
174	B4-203	Japan Air System	F-WZMT 9V-STE D-AHLK JA8277
175	B4-203	ZAS Airlines of Egypt	F-BVGR SU-DAR
176	B2K-3C	Japan Air System	F-WZMU JA8473
177	B4-203	Air India	F-WZMV (G-BIMD) VT-EHN
178	B4-203	Japan Air System	F-BVGS JA8560
179	B4-220	China Airlines	F-WZMW (EC-DNT) B-1810
180	B4-203	Air India	F-WZMX (G-BIME) VT-EHO
181	B4-203	Indian Airlines	F-WZMY VT-EHC
182	B4-203	Indian Airlines	F-WZMZ VT-EHD
183	B4-203	Air Charter	F-BVGT
184	B4-103	Olympic Airways	F-WZMA SX-BEH
185	B2-203	Iran Air	F-WZMB EP-IBT
186	B2-203	(Iran Air)	F-WZMC EP-IBU shot down 03Jul88 over Straits of Hormuz, Persian Gulf
187	B2-203	Iran Air	F-WZMD EP-IBV
188	B4-203	Tunis Air	F-WZME TS-IMA
189	B4-103	Olympic Airways	F-WZMG SX-BEI
190	B4-203	Air India	F-WZMI (G-BIMF) VT-EHQ
192	B4-203	South African Airways	F-WZML ZS-SDF C-GIZL F-WWAN ZS-SDF SU-DAN G-BSZE ZS-SDF
193	B4-220	China Airlines	F-WZMM B-190
194	B4-203	Japan Air System	F-WZER PP-VNE JA8293
195	B4-203	Sempati Air	F-WZES N202PA PK-JIC
196	B4-203	Qantas Airways	F-WZET VH-TAD
197	B4-220	China Airlines	F-WZEP B-192
198	B4-203	Sempati Air	F-WZEQ N204PA PK-JIA
199	B4-203	Egyptair	F-WZMF (SU-BCD) SU-BDF
200	B4-203	Egyptair	F-WZMN (SU-BCE) SU-BDG
202	B2-203	VASP	F-WZMJ PP-SNL
203	B4-203	Philippine Airlines	F-WZMO RP-C3004
204	B4-203	Apollo Airways	F-GBNI N227EA N216PA V2-LDX OO-TJO OB-1596 SX-BFI
205	B2-203	VASP	F-WZMP PP-SNM
206		not built	
207	B4-203	Air Ops of Europe	F-GBNJ N228EA N14969 SE-DSH stored Oct95 Bristol-Filton, UK
208	B4-203	Apollo Airways	F-WZMQ N212PA SX-BAY
209	B2K-3C	Japan Air System	F-WZMH JA8476
210	B4-203	Apollo Airways	F-WZMK N213PA SX-BAZ
211	B4-203	TAESA	F-GBNV N229EA N14973 XA-SYG
212	F4-203	South African Airways	F-WZMS ZS-SDG C-GIZN ZS-SDG
213	B4-220	Garuda Indonesia	F-WZMT PK-GAH wfs Jakarta, Indonesia
214	B4-220	Garuda Indonesia	F-WZMU PK-GAI wfs Jakarta, Indonesia
215	B4-220	Garuda Indonesia	F-WZMY PK-GAJ wfs Jakarta, Indonesia
216	B4-203	APA International Air	F-GBNX N230EA (N988C) N72988 OB-1611
218	B4-203	Qantas Airways	F-WZMZ VH-TAE
219	B4-203	Philippine Airlines	F-WZMV RP-C3005
220	B4-203	Translift Airways	F-GBNY N231EA (N989C) N74989 SE-DSF
221	B4-220	China Airlines	F-WZMX B-194
222	B4-203	Philippine Airlines	F-WZMA 9V-STF ZS-SDH RP-C3006 stored Sep95 Manila, Philippines
223		not built	
225	B2-203	VASP	F-WZMB PP-SNN
226	B2-203	Iran Air	F-WZME EP-IBZ
227	B4-203	Carnival Airlines	F-WZMC N203PA N223KW
228		not built	
229		not built	(G-BIMG)
231		not built	
232	B4-220	China Airlines	F-WZMD B-196
234	B4-203	Philippine Airlines	F-WZMF N206PA F-OHPA
235	B4-203	Philippine Airlines	F-WZMG N211PA F-OHPB
236	B4-203	Carnival Airlines	F-WZMI N207PA F-WZMI N222KW
238	B4-203	Sempati Air	F-WZMN (G-BIMH) N210PA (F-WZMN) PK-JID
239	B4-203	Japan Air System	F-WZML SU-GAA JA8369
240	B4-203	Philippine Airlines	F-WZMM SU-GAB EI-CEB
242		not built	
243	B4-203	Air Afrique	F-WZMJ TU-TAS
244	B2K-3C	Japan Air System	F-WZMS JA8477
246		not built	
247	B4-203	Air Jamaica	F-WZMP N205PA VR-BNK N247JM
249	B4-203	Thai Airways Intl	F-WZMT HS-TGX HS-THX
250	B4-203	Hull 753 Corp	F-WZMU N970C N10970 stored Apr93 Mojave, CA
252	B4-622	Sudan Airways	F-WZLR F-ODTK
253	B2K-3C	Japan Air System	F-WZMX JA8478
255	B4-203	Egyptair	F-WZMY SU-GAC

AIRBUS INDUSTRIE A300

C/n	Series	Last known Operator/Owner	Previous Identities/fate (where known)						
256	C4-203	Japan Air System	F-WZMA	JA8237					
258		not built							
259	B4-203	APA International Air	F-GBNZ	N232EA	(N990C)	N72990	SE-DSG	AP-BFG	OB-1634
261	B4-203	Presidential Air	F-GDVA	N233EA	N14975				
262	B4-203	Philippine Airlines	F-WZMH	N971C	N13971	RP-C3008			
263		not built							
265	B4-203	Thai Airways Intl	F-WZMO	HS-TGY	HS-THY				
266		not built							
268	B4-203	Pakistan Intl Airlines	F-WZMV	9V-STG	AP-BCJ				
269	B4-203	Pakistan Intl Airlines	F-WZMB	9V-STH	LX-LGP	ZS-SDI	EI-CBW	AP-BEL	
271	B4-203	Presidential Air	F-GDVB	N234EA	N14976				
272		not built							
274	B4-203	Presidential Air	F-GDVC	N235EA	N14977				
275	B4-220	not built							
277	F4-203	Korean Air	F-WZME	HL7278					
279		not built							
280	B4-220	not built							
282	B4-203	Air Afrique	F-WZML	(G-BIMI)	F-WZXP	TU-TAT			
284	B4-620	Saudia	F-WZLS	HZ-AJA					
286	B4-220	not built							
287	B4-203	not built							
289	B4-203	Hull 753 Corp	F-WZMM	N972C	N13972	N972C	stored Apr93 Mojave, CA		
290		not built							
292	F4-203	Korean Air	F-WZMS	HL7279					
294	B4-620	Saudia	F-WZYA	HZ-AJB					
296	B4-203	not built	(TS-IMB)						
298		not built							
299	B4-203	Finnair	F-WZMX	(LX-LGP)	OH-LAA				
301	B4-620	Saudia	F-WZYB	HZ-AJC					
302	B4-203	Finnair	F-WZMY	OH-LAB					
304	B4-203	Philippine Airlines	F-WZMD	N208PA	F-OHPC				
305	B4-203	Philippine Airlines	F-WZMV	(G-BIMJ)	N209PA	F-OHPD			
307	B4-620	Saudia	F-WZYC	HZ-AJD					
308	B4-203	not built	(9V-STI)						
310	B4-203	not built	(9V-STJ)						
312	B4-620	Saudia	F-WZYD	HZ-AJE					
314	B4-203	not built							
315	B4-203	not built							
317	B4-620	Saudia	F-WZYE	HZ-AJF					
319	B4-203	not built							
321	B4-620	Saudia	F-WZYF	HZ-AJG					
322		not built							
323	B4-203	not built							
324	B4-203	not built							
325	B4-203	not built							
327	C4-620	(Kuwait Airways)	F-WZYG	9K-AHF	dest 15Feb91 Baghdad, Iraq, during Gulf War				
328	B4-620	not built							
330	B4-620	not built							
332	C4-620	(Kuwait Airways)	F-WZYH	9K-AHG	dest 15Feb91 Baghdad, Iraq, during Gulf War				
334		not built							
336	B4-620	Saudia	F-WZYI	HZ-AJH					
337	B4-620	not built							
341	B4-620	Saudia	F-WZYJ	HZ-AJI					
344	C4-620	Kuwait Airways	F-WZYK	9K-AHI					
348	B4-620	Saudia	F-WZYL	HZ-AJJ					
351	B4-620	Saudia	F-WZYB	HZ-AJK					
354	B4-620	Abu Dhabi Private Flt	F-WZYA	(A6-XAI)	(F-ODRM)	A6-SHZ			
358	B4-622	Korean Air	F-WZYC	HL7287					
361	B4-622	Korean Air	F-WWAE	HL7280					
365	B4-622	Korean Air	F-WWAF	HL7281					
366	B4-620	not built	(HZ-AJL)						
368	B4-601	Thai Airways Intl	F-WWAG	HS-TAA					
371	B4-601	Thai Airways Intl	F-WWAH	HS-TAB					
374	C4-620	Abu Dhabi Private Flt	F-WWAJ	F-ODRM	A6-PFD				
377	B4-601	Thai Airways Intl	F-WWAI	HS-TAC					
380	B4-603	Lufthansa	F-WWAA	D-AIAH					
381		not built							
382		not built							
383		not built							
384	B4-601	Thai Airways Intl	F-WWAK	HS-TAD					
388	B4-622	Korean Air	F-WWAB	HL7290					
391	B4-603	Lufthansa	F-WWAL	D-AIAI					
393		not built							
395	B4-601	Thai Airways Intl	F-WWAM	HS-TAE					
398	B4-601	Thai Airways Intl	F-WWAN	HS-TAF					
401	B4-603	Lufthansa	F-WWAO	D-AIAK					
402		not built							
403		not built							
405	B4-603	Lufthansa	F-WWAP	D-AIAL					
408	B4-603	Lufthansa	F-WWAQ	D-AIAM					
411	B4-603	Lufthansa	F-WWAR	D-AIAN					

AIRBUS INDUSTRIE A300

C/n	Series	Last known Operator/Owner	Previous Identities/fate (where known)		
414	B4-603	Lufthansa	F-WWAS	D-AIAP	
417	B4-622	Korean Air	F-WWAT	(HS-TAG)	HL7291
420	B4-605R	American Airlines	F-WWAU	N14053	
423	B4-605R	American Airlines	F-WWAV	N91050	
459	B4-605R	American Airlines	F-WWAX	N50051	
460	B4-605R	American Airlines	F-WWAY	N80052	
461	B4-605R	American Airlines	F-WWAZ	N70054	
462	B4-605R	American Airlines	F-WWAC	N7055A	
463	B4-605R	American Airlines	F-WWAD	N14056	
464	B4-605R	Thai Airways Intl	F-WWAL	HS-TAG	
465	B4-605R	American Airlines	F-WWAM	N80057	
466	B4-605R	American Airlines	F-WWAE	N80058	
469	B4-605R	American Airlines	F-WWAF	N19059	
470	B4-605R	American Airlines	F-WWAA	N11060	
471	B4-605R	American Airlines	F-WWAH	N14061	
474	B4-605R	American Airlines	F-WWAK	N7062A	
477	B4-622R	Korean Air	F-WWAJ	HL7288	
479	B4-622R	Korean Air	F-WWAN	HL7289	
505	B4-505R	Emirates	F-WWAO	A6-EKC	
506	B4-605R	American Airlines	F-WWAP	N41063	
507	B4-605R	American Airlines	F-WWAQ	N40064	
508	B4-605R	American Airlines	F-WWAR	N14065	
509	B4-605R	American Airlines	F-WWAS	N18066	
510	B4-605R	American Airlines	F-WWAU	N8067A	
511	B4-605R	American Airlines	F-WWAV	N14068	
512	B4-605R	American Airlines	F-WWAC	N33069	
513	B4-605R	American Airlines	F-WWAX	N90070	
514	B4-605R	American Airlines	F-WWAY	N25071	
515	B4-605R	American Airlines	F-WWAZ	N70072	
516	B4-605R	American Airlines	F-WWAA	N70073	
517	B4-605R	American Airlines	F-WWAD	N70074	
518	B4-605R	Thai Airways Intl	F-WWAE	HS-TAH	
521	B4-605R	China Eastern A/L	F-WWAF	B-2306	
525	B4-605R	China Eastern A/L	F-WWAJ	B-2307	
529	B4-622R	China Airlines	F-WWAK	(B-1814)	B-1800
530	B4-622R	Aerocancun	F-WWAL	F-ODSX	
532	B4-605R	China Eastern A/L	F-WWAH	B-2308	
533	B4-622R	China Airlines	F-WWAM	B-1802	
536	B4-622R	China Airlines	F-WWAB	(B-1818)	B-1804
540	B4-605R	Monarch Airlines	F-WWAT	G-MONR	VH-YMJ G-MONR
543	B4-622R	Korean Air	F-WWAO	HL7292	
546	B4-603	Lufthansa	F-WWAP	D-AIAR	
553	B4-603R	Lufthansa	F-WWAX	D-AIAS	
554	B4-622R	Korean Air	F-WWAU	HL7293	
555	B4-622R	Air Liberte	F-WWAV	(F-GHEJ)	F-GHEF
556	B4-605R	Monarch Airlines	F-WWAY	G-MONS	VH-YMK G-MONS
557	B4-622R	Egyptair	F-WWAQ	SU-GAR	
558	B4-605R	Emirates	F-WWAR	A6-EKD	
559	B4-622R	Air Liberte	F-WWAS	F-GHEG	
560	B4-622R	Korean Air	F-WWAZ	HL7294	
561	B4-622R	Egyptair	F-WWAN	SU-GAS	
563	B4-605R	Emirates	F-WWAA	A6-EKE	
566	B4-622R	Thai Airways Intl	F-WWAB	HS-TAK	
569	B4-622R	Thai Airways Intl	F-WWAD	HS-TAL	
572	B4-622R	Egyptair	F-WWAE	SU-GAT	
575	B4-622R	Egyptair	F-WWAF	SU-GAU	
577	B4-622R	Thai Airways Intl	F-WWAG	HS-TAM	
578	B4-622R	China Airlines	F-WWAH	B-1814	
579	B4-622R	Egyptair	F-WWAJ	SU-GAV	
580	B4-622R	(China Airlines)	F-WWAK	B-1816	w/o 26Apr94 Nagoya, Japan
581	B4-622R	Egyptair	F-WWAL	SU-GAW	
582	B4-622R	Korean Air	F-WWAM	HL7295	
583	B4-622R	(Korean Air)	F-WWAO	HL7296	w/o 10Aug94 Cheju Island, S Korea
584	B4-605R	China Northwest A/L	F-WWAU	VH-YMA	N165PL B-2309
601	B4-622R	Egyptair	F-WWAP	SU-GAX	
602	B4-622R	Japan Air System	F-WWAT	JA8375	
603	B4-605R	China Northwest A/L	F-WWAV	VH-YMB	N166PL B-2310
604	B4-605R	Monarch Airlines	F-WWAX	(G-MONT)	G-MAJS
605	B4-605R	Monarch Airlines	F-WWAY	(G-MONU)	G-OJMR
606	B4-605R	American Airlines	F-WWAA	N3075A	
607	B4-622R	Egyptair	F-WWAB	SU-GAY	
608	B4-605R	Emirates	F-WWAD	A6-EKF	
609	B4-622R	Korean Air	F-WWAE	HL7297	
610	B4-605R	American Airlines	F-WWAF	N7076A	
611	B4-622R	Ansett Worldwide	F-WWAG	PK-GAK	
612	B4-605R	American Airlines	F-WWAH	N14077	
613	B4-622R	Garuda Indonesia	F-WWAN	PK-GAL	
614	B4-622R	Korean Air	F-WWAZ	HL7298	
615	B4-605R	American Airlines	F-WWAO	N34078	
616	B4-622R	Egyptair	F-WWAJ	SU-GAZ	
617	B4-622R	Japan Air System	F-WWAK	JA8376	

AIRBUS INDUSTRIE A300

C/n	Series	Last known Operator/Owner	Previous Identities/fate (where known)		
618	B4-603	Lufthansa	F-WWAM	D-AIAT	
619	B4-605R	American Airlines	F-WWAU	N70079	
621	B4-622R	Japan Air System	F-WWAA	JA8377	
623	B4-603	Lufthansa	F-WWAT	D-AIAU	
625	B4-622R	Garuda Indonesia	F-WWAQ	PK-GAM	
626	B4-605R	American Airlines	F-WWAR	N77080	
627	B4-622R	Korean Air	F-WWAD	HL7239	
628	B4-622R	Thai Airways Intl	F-WWAE	HS-TAN	
629	B4-622R	Thai Airways Intl	F-WWAF	HS-TAO	
630	B4-622R	Garuda Indonesia	F-WWAL	PK-GAN	
631	B4-622R	Korean Air	F-WWAB	HL7240	
632	B4-605R	Olympic Airways	F-WWAG	SX-BEK	
633	B4-622R	Garuda Indonesia	F-WWAH	PK-GAO	
635	B4-622R	Thai Airways Intl	F-WWAP	HS-TAP	
638	B4-622R	Japan Air System	F-WWAX	JA8558	
639	B4-605R	American Airlines	F-WWAV	N59081	
641	B4-605R	Japan Air System	F-WWAM	JA8559	
643	B4-605R	American Airlines	F-WWAN	N7082A	
645	B4-605R	American Airlines	F-WWAO	N7083A	
657	B4-622R	Garuda Indonesia	F-WWAJ	PK-GAP	
659	B4-622R	Garuda Indonesia	F-WWAK	PK-GAQ	
662	B4-622R	Korean Air	F-WWAT	HL7241	
664	B4-622R	Garuda Indonesia	F-WWAU	PK-GAR	
666	B4-622R	China Airlines	F-WWAY	B-1806	
668	B4-622R	Garuda Indonesia	F-WWAZ	PK-GAS	
670	B4-622R	Japan Air System	F-WWAD	JA8561	
673	B4-605R	Kuwait Airways	F-WWAQ	9K-AMA	
675	B4-605R	American Airlines	F-WWAE	N80084	
677	B4-622R	Garuda Indonesia	F-WWAF	PK-GAT	
679	B4-622R	Japan Air System	F-WWAL	JA8562	
681	B4-622R	Thai Airways Intl	F-WWAB	HS-TAR	
683	B4-622R	Japan Air System	F-WWAJ	JA8563	
685	B4-622R	Korean Air	F-WWAG	HL7242	
688	B4-622R	China Northern A/L	F-WWAH	B-2311	
690	B4-622R	China Northern A/L	F-WWAP	B-2312	
692	B4-622R	Korean Air	F-WWAR	HL7243	
694	B4-605R	Kuwait Airways	F-WWAV	9K-AMB	
696	B4-605R	Olympic Airways	F-WWAK	SX-BEL	
699	B4-605R	Kuwait Airways	F-WWAM	9K-AMC	
701	B4-605R	Emirates	F-WWAN	A6-EKM	
703	B4-622R	Japan Air System	F-WWAO	JA8564	
705	B4-622R	Thai Airways Intl	F-WWAT	HS-TAS	
707	B4-605R	China Eastern Airlines	F-WWAU	B-2318	
709	B4-605R	China Eastern Airlines	F-WWAD	N190PL	B-2320
711	B4-622R	Japan Air System	F-WWAE	JA8565	
713	B4-605R	China Eastern Airlines	F-WWAF	N191PL	B-2321
715	B4-605R	China Eastern Airlines	F-WWAX	N192PL	B-2322
717	B4-622R	Korean Air	F-WWAY	HL7299	
719	B4-605R	Kuwait Airways	F-WWAB	9K-AMD	
721	B4-605R	Kuwait Airways	F-WWAG	9K-AME	
722	B4-622R	Korean Air	F-WWAH	HL7244	
723	B4-605R	Iran Air	F-WWAL	EP-IBA	
724	B4-622R	Japan Air System	F-WWAQ	JA8527	
725	B4-622R	China Northwest A/L	F-WWAR	B-2324	
726	F4-605R	Federal Express	F-WWAP	N650FE	
727	B4-605R	Iran Air	F-WWAZ	EP-IBB	
728	F4-605R	Federal Express	F-WWAJ	N651FE	
729	B4-622R	Japan Air System	F-WWAM	JA8529	
730	B4-622R	Japan Air System	F-WWAV	JA8566	
731	B4-622R	Korean Air	F-WWAK	HL7245	
732	B4-605R	China Eastern Airlines	F-WWAT	B-2319	
733	B4-622R	China Northern A/L	F-WWAU	B-2315	
734	B4-622R	China Northern A/L	F-WWAE	B-2316	
735	F4-605R	Federal Express	F-WWAN	N652FE	
736	F4-605R	Federal Express	F-WWAD	N653FE	
737	B4-622R	Japan Air System	F-WWAF	JA8573	
738	F4-605R	Federal Express	F-WWAX	N654FE	
739	B4-622R	China Northern A/L	F-WWAB	B-2323	
740	B4-622R	Japan Air System	F-WWAG	JA8574	
741	B4-605R	China Northwest A/L	F-WWAY	B-2317	
742	F4-605R	Federal Express	F-WWAJ	N655FE	
743	B4-622R	China Airlines	F-WWAH	N88881	
744	B4-605R	Air Afrique	F-WWAK	TU-TAH	
745	F4-605R	Federal Express	F-WWAP	N656FE	
746	B4-605R	China Eastern Airlines	F-WWAA	B-2325	
747	B4-605R	Emirates	F-WWAT	A6-EKO	
748	F4-605R	Federal Express	F-WWAM	N657FE	
749	B4-605R	Air Afrique	F-WWAN	TU-TAI	
750	B4-622R	China Northern A/L	F-WWAU	B-2327	
752	F4-605R	Federal Express	F-WWAE	N658FE	
753	B4-622R	Japan Air System	F-WWAD	JA8657	

AIRBUS INDUSTRIE A300

C/n	Series	Last known Operator/Owner	Previous Identities/fate (where known)	
754	B4-605R	China Eastern Airlines	F-WWAY	B-2326
755	C4-605R	Airbus Industrie	F-WWAX	stored Toulouse, France
756	B4-655R	Korean Air	F-WWAB	HL7580
757	F4-605R	Federal Express	F-WWAF	N659FE
758	C4-605R	Airbus Industrie	F-WWAR	stored Toulouse, France
759	F4-605R	Federal Express	F-WWAG	N660FE
760	F4-605R	Federal Express	F-WWAL	N661FE
761	F4-605R	Federal Express	F-	N662FE
762	B4-622R	Korean Air	F-WWAZ	HL7581
763	B4-605R	China Northwest A/L	F-WWAH	B-2330
764	B4-605R	Lufthansa	F-WWAJ	D-AIAW
766	F4-605R	Federal Express	F-WWAO	N663FE
767	B4-622R		F-	
768	F4-605R	Federal Express	F-WWAA	N664FE
769	F4-605R	Federal Express	F-WWAM	N665FE
770	B4-622R	Japan Air System	F-WWA.	JA8659
771	F4-605R	Federal Express	F-	N
772	F4-605R	Federal Express	F-	N
773	B4-605R		F-	
774	F4-605R	Federal Express	F-	N
775	B4-622R		F-	
777	F4-605R		F-	
778	F4-605R		F-	
779	F4-605R		F-	
780	F4-605R		F-	
781	F4-605R		F-	
782	B4-6		F-	
783	F4-605R		F-	
784	F4-605R		F-	

AIRBUS INDUSTRIE A310

C/n	Series	Last known Operator/Owner	Previous Identities/fate (where known)
162	221	Air Liberté	F-WZLH prototype; ff 03Apr82 HB-IPE F-GPDJ
172	203	Kibris THY	F-WZLI (HB-IPF) F-GEMF TC-JYK
191	203F	Federal Express	F-WZLJ D-AICA N401FE
201	203F	Federal Express	F-WZLK D-AICB N402FE
217	221	ILFC	F-WZLL HB-IPC F-GOCJ
224	221F	Federal Express	F-WZEA HB-IPA N446FE
230	203F	Federal Express	F-WZEB D-AICC N403FE
233	203F	Federal Express	F-WZEC D-AICD N404FE
237	203F	Federal Express	F-WZED D-AICF N405FE
241	221F	Federal Express	F-WZEE PH-AGA N424FE
245	203	KLM	F-WZEG PH-AGB
248	203	Middle East Airlines	F-WZEF PH-AGC N428FE PH-AGC
251	221F	Federal Express	F-WZEH HB-IPB N447FE
254	203F	Federal Express	F-WZEI D-AICH N407FE
257	203F	Federal Express	F-WZEJ D-AICK TC-JFO D-AICK N408FE
260	221F	Federal Express	F-WZEK HB-IPD N448FE
264	203	Federal Express	F-WZEL PH-AGD N425FE
267	222	Oasis International	F-WZEM 9K-AHA YI-AOC 9K-AHA A7-ABA F-WGYM F-OHPE stored Oct95 Bremen-Lemwerder, Germany
270	222	Nigeria Airways	F-WZEN 5N-AUE stored Bordeaux, France
273	203F	Federal Express	F-WZEO D-AICL N409FE
276	222	Qatar Airways	F-WZEP 9K-AHB YI-AOB 9K-AHB F-WGYO F-WAYB A7-ABB F-WGYN A7-ABB
278	222	Yemenia	F-WZER 9K-AHC YI-AOE 9K-AHC F-WGYP TC-GAC F-WGYP F-OHPP stored 1995 Bremen-Lemwerder, Germany
281	203F	Federal Express	F-WZET PH-MCA N423FE
283	203	Middle East Airlines	F-WZEA PH-AGE
285	222	Nigeria Airways	F-WZEB 5N-AUF stored Brussels, Belgium
288	222F	Federal Express	F-WZEC N801PA N416FE
291	203	Air Algerie	F-WZED 7T-VJC
293	203	Air Algerie	F-WZEE 7T-VJD
295	203	Royal Jordanian	F-WZEF G-BKWT 5A-DLA 7T-VJE
297	203	Middle East Airlines	F-WZEH PH-AGF
300	203	Cyprus Airways	F-WZEG 5B-DAQ
303	222	Sabena	F-WZEI OO-SCA
306	203	Royal Jordanian	F-WZEK G-BKWU 5A-DLB 7T-VJF
309	203	Cyprus Airways	F-WZEM 5B-DAR
311	222	China Northwest A/L	F-WZEJ B-2301
313	222	Sabena	F-WZEP OO-SCB
316	203	Air France	F-GEMA
318	222	Yemenia	F-WZEL 9K-AHD YI-AOA 9K-AHD F-WGYQ F-OHPQ stored Oct95 Brussels, Belgium
320	222	China Northwest A/L	F-WZER B-2302
326	203	Air France	F-GEMB
329	222	Nigeria Airways	F-WZEA 5N-AUG
331	222	Airbus Industrie	F-WZEO 9K-AHE YI-AOD 9K-AHE F-WGYT OO-SCI F-WGYR
333	222F	Federal Express	F-WZEG N802PA N417FE
335	203	Air France	F-GEMC
338	203	Turk Hava Yollari	F-WZET TC-JCL
339	222F	Federal Express	F-WZEF 9K-AHH N805PA N420FE
340	222	Nigeria Airways	F-WZEH 5N-AUH
342	222F	Federal Express	F-WZEI 9K-AHJ N806PA N421FE
343	222F	Federal Express	F-WZEK N803PA N418FE
345	222F	Federal Express	F-WZEL N804PA N804DL N804PA N419FE
346	222F	Federal Express	F-WZEM 9K-AHK N807PA N422FE
347	222	Singapore Airlines	F-WZEO 9V-STI
349	203C	Federal Express	F-WZEP PH-MCB N415FE
350	222	Singapore Airlines	F-WZLH 9V-STJ
352	203	Cyprus Airways	F-WZEO 5B-DAS
353	203	KLM	F-WZLJ PH-AGG
355	203	Air France	F-GEMD
356	203F	Federal Express	F-WZLK D-AICM TC-JKF D-AICM N410FE
357	222	Singapore Airlines	F-WZLL 9V-STK
359	203F	Federal Express	F-WZLS D-AICN N411FE
360	203F	Federal Express	F-WZED D-AICP N412FE
362	203	KLM	F-WZEF PH-AGH
363	222	Singapore Airlines	F-WZEI 9V-STL
364	203	KLM	F-WZEM PH-AGI
367	222	Singapore Airlines	F-WZEP 9V-STM
369	203	Air France	F-GEME
370	203	Turk Hava Yollari	F-WZLH (G-BLPS) TC-JCR
372	222	Singapore Airlines	F-WZEN 9V-STN
373	222	not built	
375	203	Turk Hava Yollari	F-WWBA TC-JCM
376	203	not built	
378	324	Air Niugini	F-WWCA P2-ANA LZ-JXA P2-ANA
379	203	Turk Hava Yollari	F-WWBB TC-JCN
385	221	not built	
386	203	Turk Hava Yollari	F-WWBC TC-JCO
387	221	not built	(OE-LAA)

AIRBUS INDUSTRIE A310

C/n	Series	Last known Operator/Owner	Previous Identities/fate (where known)					
389	203	Turk Hava Yollari	F-WWBG	TC-JCS				
390	203	Turk Hava Yollari	F-WWBH	TC-JCU				
392	304	Air India	F-WWCB	(VT-EJJ)	VT-EJL			
394	203	KLM	F-WWBD	PH-AGK				
396	221	not built	(OE-LAI)					
397	203F	Federal Express	F-WWBE	D-AICR	N413FE			
399	322	Swissair	F-WWCC	HB-IPF				
400	203F	Federal Express	F-WWBF	D-AICS	N414FE			
404	322	Swissair	F-WWCD	HB-IPG				
406	304	Air India	F-WWCG	VT-EJG				
407	304	Air India	F-WWCH	VT-EJH				
409	322	Swissair	F-WWCE	HB-IPH				
410	322	Swissair	F-WWCF	HB-IPI				
412	322	Swissair	F-WWCI	HB-IPK				
413	304	Air India	F-WWCJ	VT-EJI				
415	204	Thai Airways Intl	F-WWBI	HS-TIA				
416	304	Kenya Airways	F-WWCK	5Y-BEL				
418	304	Sudan Airways	F-WWCL	C-FSWD	(F-OGQN)	F-GHUC		
419	222	China Northwest A/L	F-WWBJ	B-2303	LZ-JXB	B-2303		
421	304	French AF	F-WWCN	JY-CAD	F-ODVD	F-RADA		
422	304	French AF	F-WWCO	(JY-CAE)	F-ODVE	F-RADB		
424	204	Thai Airways Intl	F-WWCM	HS-TIC				
425	CC150	Canadian Armed Forces	F-WWCP	C-FWDX	VH-YMI	C-FWDX	Canada 15003	
426	304	Kenya Airways	F-WWCQ	5Y-BEN				
427	204	Hapag-Lloyd	F-WWBK	D-AHLW				
428	304	Air India	F-WWCR	VT-EJJ				
429	304	Air India	F-WWCS	VT-EJK				
430	204	Hapag-Lloyd	F-WWBL	D-AHLV				
431	304	Brunei Govt	F-WWCT	V8-HM1	V8-DPD			
432	304	Emirates	F-WWCU	A6-EKA				
433	324	Singapore Airlines	F-WWCX	(PH-MCC)	9V-STO			
434	304	Lufthansa	F-WWCC	D-AIDA				
435	304	Air Afrique	F-WWCD	B-2304	TU-TAU			
436	304	Emirates	F-WWCV	A6-EKB				
437	322	Sabena	F-WWCY	OO-SCC				
438	304	(Thai Airways Intl)	F-WWCE	C-FGWD	HS-TID	w/o 31Jul92 Kathmandu, Nepal		
439	324	Air Club International	F-WWCI	N811PA	C-GCIL			
440	304	Air Afrique	F-WWCF	B-2305	TU-TAR	stored Nov95 Bristol-Filton, UK		
441	CC150	Canadian Armed Forces	F-WWCQ	C-FHWD	HS-TIF	Canada 15005		
442	324	Aerolineas Argentinas	F-WWCZ	N812PA	F-OGYP	stored Nov95 Toulouse, France		
443	324	Singapore Airlines	F-WWCS	9V-STP				
444	CC150	Canadian Armed Forces	F-WWCR	C-FNWD	(F-OGQO)	F-GHUD	Canada 15004	
445	304	Royal Jordanian	F-ODVF					
446	CC150	Canadian Armed Forces	F-WWCM	C-GBWD	Canada 15001			
447	304	Middle East Airlines	F-WWCN	C-GCWD	A6-KUA	D-APOL	F-OHLH	
448	304	Eurowings	F-WWCO	C-GDWD	A6-KUB	D-APOM		
449	324	Air Club International	F-WWCG	N813PA	C-GCIO			
450	324	(TAROM)	F-WWCH	N814PA	YR-LCC	w/o 31Mar95 Bucharest-Otopeni, Romania		
451	324	Air Club International	F-WWCY	N815PA	C-GCIV			
452	324	Airbus Industrie	F-WWCJ	N816PA				
453	324	Aerolineas Argentinas	F-WWCK	N817PA	F-OGYQ			
454	203	Air France	F-GEMG					
455	324	Air Club International	F-WWCU	N818PA	C-GCIT			
456	324	Aerolineas Argentinas	F-WWCV	N819PA	F-OGYR			
457	324	Diamond Sakha Airlines	F-WWCD	N820PA	F-OGYM			
458	324	Diamond Sakha Airlines	F-WWCF	N821PA	F-WGYN	F-OGYN		
467	324	Aerolineas Argentinas	F-WWCG	N822PA	F-OGYS			
468	204	Hapag-Lloyd	F-WWBM	D-AHLZ				
472	304	Royal Nepal Airlines	F-WWCB	C-GIWD	A6-KUC	D-APON		
473	304	Alyemda	F-WWCC	F-ODSV				
475	304	Lloyd Aereo Boliviano	F-WWCL	C-GJWD	A6-KUE	D-APOO	D-APOQ	CP-2273
476	304	Turk Hava Yollari	F-WWCT	TC-JCV				
478	304	Turk Hava Yollari	F-WWCX	TC-JCY				
480	304	Turk Hava Yollari	F-WWCZ	TC-JCZ				
481	304	Middle East Arilines	F-WWCQ	C-GKWD	A6-KUD	D-APOP	F-OHLI	
482	CC150	Canadian Armed Forces	F-WWCR	C-GLWD	Canada 15002			
483	304	Air Portugal	F-WWCS	CS-TEH				
484	304	Lufthansa	F-WWCI	D-AIDB				
485	304	Lufthansa	F-WWCJ	D-AIDC				
486	204	Cyprus Airways	F-WWBN	5B-DAX				
487	204	Hapag-Lloyd	F-WWBO	D-AHLX				
488	304	Lufthansa	F-WWCE	D-AIDD				
489	324	Austrian Airlines	F-WWCK	OE-LAA				
490	304	Royal Jordanian	F-ODVG					
491	304	Royal Jordanian	F-ODVH					
492	324	Austrian Airlines	F-WWCP	OE-LAB				
493	324	Singapore Airlines	F-WWCN	9V-STQ				
494	304	Air Portugal	F-WWCM	CS-TEJ				
495	304	Air Portugal	F-WWCO	CS-TEI				
496	304	Turk Hava Yollari	F-WWCV	TC-JDA				
497	304	Turk Hava Yollari	F-WWCH	TC-JDB				

AIRBUS INDUSTRIE A310

C/n	Series	Last known Operator/Owner	Previous Identities/fate (where known)					
498	304	Luftwaffe	F-WWCU	(DDR-SZA)	DDR-ABA	D-AOAA	Germany 10+21	
499	304	Luftwaffe	F-WWCT	(DDR-SZB)	DDR-ABB	D-AOAB	Germany 10+22	
500	324	Singapore Airlines	F-WWCX	9V-STR				
501	324	Singapore Airlines	F-WWCB	9V-STS				
502	304	Air France	F-WWCD	(C-FZWD)	F-GEMN			
503	304	Luftwaffe	F-WWCL	(DDR-SZC)	DDR-ABC	D-AOAC	Germany 10+23	
504	304	Air France	F-WWCF	(C-GPWD)	F-GEMO			
519	304	Kenya Airways	F-WWCG	5Y-BFT				
520	304	Hapag-Lloyd	F-WWCI	D-AHLA				
522	304	Lufthansa	F-WWCJ	D-AIDE				
523	304	Lufthansa	F-WWCK	D-AIDI				
524	304	Lufthansa	F-WWCA	D-AIDF				
526	304	Lufthansa	F-WWCC	D-AIDK				
527	304	Lufthansa	F-WWCD	D-AIDH				
528	304	Hapag-Lloyd	F-WWCE	D-AHLB				
531	304	Royal Jordanian	F-ODVI					
534	324	Singapore Airlines	F-WWCM	9V-STT				
535	304	Air Liberté	F-WWCN	F-GHEJ				
537	304	Turk Hava Yollari	F-WWCO	TC-JDC				
538	304	Air India	F-WWCP	VT-EQS				
539	324	Air India	F-WWCQ	N823PA	V2-LEC			
541	304	Air Portugal	F-WWCR	CS-TEW				
542	324	Air India	F-WWCS	N824PA	V2-LED			
544	304	Air India	F-WWCL	VT-EQT				
545	304	Emirates	F-WWCY	(F-GHGM)	A6-EKG			
547	304	Lufthansa	F-WWCU	D-AIDL				
548	324	Singapore Airlines	F-WWCV	9V-STU				
549	324	Air Niugini	F-WWCX	P2-ANG				
550	304	Air France	F-GEMP					
551	304	Air France	F-GEMQ					
552	304	Sudan Airways	F-WWCZ	F-GKTD				
562	304	Lloyd Aereo Boliviano	F-WWCA	F-GKTE	(CP-2338)	CP-2232		
564	304	CSA Czech Airlines	F-WWCB	OK-WAA				
565	304	Air Portugal	F-WWCC	CS-TEX				
567	304	CSA Czech Airlines	F-WWDC	OK-WAB				
568	324	Austrian Airlines	F-WWCE	OE-LAC				
570	324	Singapore Airlines	F-WWCF	9V-STV				
571	304	Air Afrique	F-GHYM	F-WWYM	TU-TAC			
573	304	Emirates	F-WWCG	CS-TEY	LZ-JXC	S7-RGA	A6-EKN	
574	324	Uzbekistan Airways	F-WWCI	(N825PA)	HC-BRA	F-OGQY		
576	324	Uzbekistan Airways	F-WWCJ	(N826PA)	HC-BRB	F-WWCJ	F-OGQZ	
585	308	Pakistan Intl Airlines	F-WWCH	AP-BDZ				
586	304	Turk Hava Yollari	F-WWCK	TC-JDD				
587	308	Pakistan Intl Airlines	F-WWCT	AP-BEB				
588	308	Emirates	F-WWCM	(I-TEAB)	A6-EKI			
589	324	Singapore Airlines	F-WWCW	F-WWCO	9V-STW			
590	308	Pakistan Intl Airlines	F-WWCX	AP-BEC				
591	324	Royal Thai Air Force	F-WWCH	HS-TYQ/44-444				
592	307	Aeroflot	F-WWCN	F-OGQQ				
593	307	Aeroflot	F-WWCP	F-OGQR				
594	324	Air Ambar	F-WWCQ	VR-BMU	HI-659	HI-659CA		
595	304	Lufthansa	F-WWCR	D-AIDM				
596	308	(Aeroflot)	F-WWCS	F-OGQS	w/o 22Mar94 nr Mezhdurechensk, Siberia, Russia			
597	308	Emirates	F-WWCU	A6-EKJ				
598	304	SAETA	F-WWCV	HC-BRP				
599	304	Lufthansa	F-WWCZ	D-AIDN				
600	308	Emirates	F-WWCB	A6-EKH				
620	308	Hapag-Lloyd	F-WWCC	D-AHLC				
622	308	Aeroflot	F-WWCD	F-OGQT				
624	325	Austrian Airlines	F-WWCE	OE-LAD				
634	324	Singapore Airlines	F-WWCF	9V-STY				
636	325	Tarom	F-WWCG	YR-LCA				
638	324	Oasis International	F-WWCK	EC-117	EC-FNI	VR-BOU	EC-640	EC-FXB
640	325	Swissair	F-WWCL	HB-IPL				
642	325	Swissair	F-WWCX	HB-IPM				
644	325	Tarom	F-WWCO	YR-LCB				
646	308	Aeroflot	F-WWCT	F-OGQU				
647	308	Kuwait Airways	F-WWCQ	9K-ALA				
648	308	Kuwait Govt	F-WWCR	A6-EKK	F-WWCR	9K-ALD		
649	308	Kuwait Airways	F-WWCV	9K-ALB				
650	325	Delta Air Lines	F-WWCI	N835AB				
651	304	Air Afrique	F-WWCC	TU-TAD				
652	304	Air Afrique	F-WWCH	TU-TAE				
653	308	Pakistan Intl A/L	F-WWCZ	AP-BEG				
654	324	Singapore Airlines	F-WWCJ	9V-STZ				
656	304	Pakistan Intl A/L	F-WWCB	AP-BEQ				
658	308	Emirates	F-WWCY	A6-EKK				
660	324	Air Jamaica	F-WWCF	N836AB				
661	304	SAETA	F-WWCE	HC-BSF				
663	308	Kuwait Airways	F-WWCK	9K-ALC				
665	324	Singapore Airlines	F-WWCL	9V-STA				

AIRBUS INDUSTRIE A310

C/n	Series	Last known Operator/Owner	Previous Identities/fate (where known)			
667	308	Emirates	F-WWCZ	A6-EKL		
669	324	Singapore Airlines	F-WWCC	9V-STB		
671	304	Air Afrique	F-WWCM	TU-TAF		
672	325	Swissair	F-WWCD	HB-IPN		
674	324	Delta Air Lines	F-WWCH	N837AB		
676	324	Air Jamaica	F-WWCP	(N836AB)	(N837AB)	N838AB
678	324	Air Jamaica	F-WWCU	N839AD		
680	324	Singapore Airlines	F-WWCT	9V-STC		
682	324	Air Jamaica	F-WWCN	N840AB		
684	324	Singapore Airlines	F-WWCJ	9V-STD		
686	324	Air Jamaica	F-WWCX	N841AB		
687	324	Airbus Industrie	F-WWCE	N842AB		
689	324	Delta Air Lines	F-WWCG	N843AB	stored Dec95 Toulouse, France	
691	308	Pakistan Intl A/L	F-WWCD	AP-BEU		
693	324	Singapore Airlines	F-WWCI	9V-STE		
695	304	Emirates	F-WWCO	A6-EKP		
697	324	Singapore Airlines	F-WWCK	9V-STF		
698	325					
700	325					
702						
704						
706						
708						
710						
712						
714						
716						
718						
720						

AIRBUS INDUSTRIE A319

C/n	Series	Last known Operator/Owner	Previous Identities/fate (where known)		
546	112	Airbus Industrie	F-WWDB	prototype; ff 25Aug95	
572	114	Airbus Industrie	F-WWAS		
578	111	Swissair	D-AVYA	F-WWTA	HB-IPX
588	111	Swissair	F-	HB-IPY	
598	114				
600	114				
609	114	Lufthansa	D-AILA*		
610	114	Lufthansa	D-AILB*		
616	114	Lufthansa	D-AILC*		
623	114	Lufthansa	D-AILD*		
627	114	Lufthansa	D-AILE*		
634	114	Lufthansa	D-AILF*		

AIRBUS INDUSTRIE A320

C/n	Series	Last known Operator/Owner	Previous Identities/fate (where known)					
0001	231	Airbus Industrie	F-WWAI	prototype;	ff 22Feb87		F-WWFT	
0002	211	Air France	F-WWDA	F-GFKQ				
0003	111	Air Inter	F-WWDB	F-GGEG				
0004	111	Air Inter	F-WWDC	F-GGEF				
0005	111	Air France	F-WWDI	F-GFKA				
0006	111	British Airways	F-WWDD	(G-BRSA)	G-BUSB			
0007	111	Air France	F-WWDJ	F-GFKB				
0008	111	British Airways	F-WWDE	(G-BRSB)	G-BUSC			
0009	111	(Air France)	F-WWDK	F-GFKC	w/o 26Jun88 Mulhouse/Habsheim, France			
0010	111	Air Inter	F-WWDL	F-GGEA				
0011	111	British Airways	F-WWDF	G-BUSD				
0012	111	Air Inter	F-WWDM	F-GGEB				
0013	111	Air Inter	F-WWDN	F-GGEC				
0014	111	Air France	F-WWDO	F-GFKD				
0015	111	(Air Inter)	F-WWDP	F-GGED	w/o 20Jan92 Mt Sainte Odile, nr Strasbourg, France			
0016	111	Air Inter	F-WWDQ	F-GGEE				
0017	111	British Airways	F-WWDG	G-BUSE				
0018	111	British Airways	F-WWDH	G-BUSF				
0019	111	Air France	F-GFKE					
0020	111	Air France	F-GFKF					
0021	111	Air France	F-GFKG					
0022	211	Ansett Australia	F-WWDR	VH-HYA				
0023	211	Ansett Australia	F-WWDS	VH-HYB				
0024	211	Ansett Australia	F-WWDT	VH-HYC				
0025	211	Ansett Australia	F-WWDU	VH-HYD				
0026	211	Ansett Australia	F-WWDV	VH-HYE				
0027	211	Ansett Australia	F-WWDD	VH-HYF				
0028	231	Cyprus Airways	F-WWDE	5B-DAT	YU-AOB	5B-DAT		
0029	211	Ansett Australia	F-WWDF	VH-HYG				
0030	211	Ansett Australia	F-WWDI	VH-HYH				
0031	211	Northwest Airlines	F-WWDJ	N301US				
0032	211	Northwest Airlines	F-WWDK	N302US				
0033	211	Air Inter	(F-GGEF)	F-GHQA				
0034	211	Northwest Airlines	F-WWDL	N303US				
0035	231	Cyprus Airways	F-WWDX	5B-DAU				
0036	211	Air Inter	(F-GGEG)	F-GHQB				
0037	231	Cyprus Airways	F-WWDN	5B-DAV				
0038	231	Cyprus Airways	F-WWDZ	5B-DAW				
0039	211	British Airways	F-WWDM	G-BUSG				
0040	211	Northwest Airlines	F-WWDD	N304US				
0041	211	Northwest Airlines	F-WWDS	N305US				
0042	211	British Airways	F-WWDT	G-BUSH				
0043	231	Adria Airways	F-WWDO	YU-AOA	SL-AAA	S5-AAA	SX-BAS	S5-AAA
0044	211	Air Inter	(F-GGEH)	F-GHQC				
0045	231	Indian Airlines	F-WWDY	VT-EPB				
0046	231	Indian Airlines	F-WWDG	VT-EPC				
0047	231	Indian Airlines	F-WWDP	VT-EPD				
0048	231	Indian Airlines	F-WWDU	VT-EPE				
0049	231	Indian Airlines	F-WWIA	VT-EPF				
0050	231	Indian Airlines	F-WWDR	VT-EPG				
0051	231	Indian Airlines	F-WWIB	VT-EPH				
0052	231	America West Airlines	F-WWDQ	N901BN	N620AW			
0053	231	America West Airlines	F-WWDV	N902BN	N621AW			
0054	231	America West Airlines	F-WWIH	N903BN	N622AW			
0055	231	America West Airlines	F-WWIM	N904BN	N624AW			
0056	231	Indian Airlines	F-WWIC	VT-EPI				
0057	231	Indian Airlines	F-WWIF	VT-EPJ				
0058	231	Indian Airlines	F-WWID	VT-EPK				
0059	211	Air Canada	F-WWDI	(VH-HYI)	C-FDQQ			
0060	211	Northwest Airlines	F-WWIE	N306US				
0061	211	Air France	F-GFKH					
0062	211	Air France	F-GFKI					
0063	211	Air France	F-GFKJ					
0064	231	America West Airlines	F-WWIK	N905BN	N625AW			
0065	231	America West Airlines	F-WWIL	N906BN	N626AW			
0066	231	America West Airlines	F-WWIG	(N907BN)	N907GP	N627AW		
0067	231	America West Airlines	F-WWIN	(N908BN)	N908GP	N628AW		
0068	211	Air Canada	F-WWDO	(VH-HYJ)	C-FDQV			
0069	211	Lufthansa	F-WWII	D-AIPA				
0070	211	Lufthansa	F-WWIJ	D-AIPB				
0071	211	Lufthansa	F-WWIO	D-AIPC				
0072	211	Lufthansa	F-WWIP	D-AIPD				
0073	211	Air Canada	F-WWDC	(VH-HYK)	C-FDRH			
0074	231	Indian Airlines	F-WWIQ	VT-EPL				
0075	231	Indian Airlines	F-WWIR	VT-EPM				
0076	231	America West Airlines	F-WWIS	(N909BN)	(N909GP)	N910GP	N629AW	
0077	231	America West Airlines	F-WWIT	(N910BN)	N911GP	N631AW		
0078	211	Lufthansa	F-WWIU	D-AIPE				
0079	231	(Indian Airlines)	F-WWIV	VT-EPN	w/o 14Feb90 Bangalore, India			
0080	231	Indian Airlines	F-WWIX	VT-EPO				

AIRBUS INDUSTRIE A320

C/n	Series	Last known Operator/Owner	Previous Identities/fate (where known)					
0081	231	America West Airlines	F-WWIY	(N912BN)	N912GP	N632AW		
0082	231	America West Airlines	F-WWIZ	(N913BN)	N913GP	N633AW		
0083	211	Lufthansa	F-WWDE	D-AIPF				
0084	211	Air Canada	F-WWDP	C-FDRK				
0085	211	Air Inter	F-WWDF	F-GJVZ				
0086	211	Lufthansa	F-WWDJ	D-AIPH				
0087	211	Royal Jordanian	F-WWDM	F-OGYA				
0088	211	Royal Jordanian	F-WWDN	F-OGYB				
0089	221	Indian Airlines	F-WWDT	VT-EPP				
0090	231	Indian Airlines	F-WWDX	VT-EPQ				
0091	231	America West Airlines	F-WWDH	(N914BN)	N914GP	N634AW		
0092	231	America West Airlines	F-WWDK	(N915BN)	N915GP	N635AW		
0093	211	Lufthansa	F-WWDQ	D-AIPK				
0094	211	Lufthansa	F-WWDR	D-AIPL				
0095	231	Indian Airlines	F-WWDS	VT-EPR				
0096	231	Indian Airlines	F-WWDU	VT-EPS				
0097	231	Indian Airlines	F-WWDV	VT-EPT				
0098	231	America West Airlines	F-WWDY	(N916BN)	N916GP	N636AW		
0099	231	America West Airlines	F-WWDL	(N917BN)	N917GP	N637AW		
0100	211	Air France	F-GFKK					
0101	211	Air France	F-GFKL					
0102	211	Air France	F-GFKM					
0103	211	British Airways	F-WWDB	G-BUSI				
0104	211	Lufthansa	F-WWIG	D-AIPM				
0105	211	(Lufthansa)	F-WWDG	D-AIPN	dbf 14Sep93 Warsaw-Okecie, Poland			
0106	211	Northwest Airlines	F-WWIA	N307US				
0107	211	Northwest Airlines	F-WWIB	N308US				
0108	211	Air Inter	F-GHQD					
0109	211	British Airways	F-WWIC	G-BUSJ				
0110	211	Lufthansa	F-WWID	D-AIPP				
0111	211	Lufthansa	F-WWIE	D-AIPR				
0112	211	Air Malta	F-WWIF	9H-ABP				
0113	231	Adria Airways	F-WWIH	YU-AOD	SL-AAB	S5-AAB	SX-BAT	S5-AAB
0114	231	Adria Airways	F-WWII	YU-AOE	SL-AAC	S5-AAC	SX-BAU	S5-AAC
0115	211	Air Inter	F-GHQE					
0116	211	Lufthansa	F-WWIK	D-AIPS				
0117	211	Lufthansa	F-WWIL	D-AIPT				
0118	211	Northwest Airlines	F-WWIM	N309US				
0119	211	Tunis Air	F-WWIJ	TS-IMB				
0120	211	British Airways	F-WWIN	G-BUSK				
0121	211	Northwest Airlines	F-WWIO	N310NW				
0122	211	Air Canada	F-WWIP	C-FDRP				
0123	211	Tunis Air	F-WWIR	F-OGYC	TS-IME			
0124	211	Tunis Air	F-WWIS	TS-IMC				
0125	211	Northwest Airlines	F-WWIT	N311US				
0126	211	Air Canada	F-WWIU	C-FDSN				
0127	211	Air Canada	F-WWIV	C-FDST				
0128	211	Vietnam Airlines	F-GFKN					
0129	211	Air France	F-GFKO					
0130	211	Air Inter	F-GHQF					
0131	212	Air Charter	F-WWIX	N481GX	F-GLGM			
0132	212	Air Charter	F-WWIY	N482GX	F-GLGN			
0133	211	Air France	F-GFKP					
0134	211	Iberia	F-WWIZ	EC-575	EC-FAS			
0135	211	Lufthansa	F-WWDB	D-AIPU				
0136	211	Iberia	F-WWDC	EC-576	EC-FBQ			
0137	211	Lufthansa	F-WWDD	D-AIPW				
0138	211	All Nippon Airways	F-WWDE	JA8381				
0139	211	All Nippon Airways	F-WWDF	JA8382				
0140	211	Ansett Australia	F-WWDG	VH-HYI				
0141	211	Air Canada	F-WWDH	C-FDSU				
0142	211	Ansett Australia	F-WWDI	VH-HYJ				
0143	211	Iberia	F-WWDJ	EC-577	EC-FBS			
0144	211	Air Inter	F-WWDK	F-GJVA				
0145	211	Air Inter	F-WWDL	F-GJVB				
0146	211	Iberia	F-WWDM	EC-578	EC-FBR			
0147	211	Lufthansa	F-WWDN	D-AIPX				
0148	211	All Nippon Airways	F-WWDO	JA8383				
0149	211	Air Canada	F-WWDP	C-FFWI				
0150	211	Air Canada	F-WWDQ	C-FFWJ				
0151	211	All Nippon Airways	F-WWDR	JA8384				
0152	211	Northwest Airlines	F-WWDT	N312US				
0153	211	Northwest Airlines	F-WWDX	N313US				
0154	211	Air Canada	F-WWDY	C-FFWM				
0155	211	Air Inter	F-GHQG					
0156	211	Air Inter	F-GHQH					
0157	211	Ansett Australia	F-WWIB	VH-HYK				
0158	211	Iberia	F-WWIC	EC-579	EC-FCB			
0159	211	Air Canada	F-WWIG	C-FFWN				
0160	211	Northwest Airlines	F-WWDZ	N314US				
0161	211	Lufthansa	F-WWIA	D-AIPY				

AIRBUS INDUSTRIE A320

C/n	Series	Last known Operator/Owner	Previous Identities/fate (where known)					
0162	211	Lufthansa	F-WWDS	D-AIPZ				
0163	231	Premiair	F-WWDU	OY-CND				
0164	231	Premiair	F-WWIE	OY-CNE				
0165	231	Egyptair	F-WWDV	SU-GBA				
0166	231	Egyptair	F-WWID	SU-GBB				
0167	211	All Nippon Airways	F-WWIE	JA8385				
0168	231	Premiair	F-WWIF	OY-CNF				
0169	231	Premiair	F-WWIH	OY-CNG				
0170	211	All Nippon Airways	F-WWII	JA8386				
0171	211	Northwest Airlines	F-WWIJ	N315US				
0172	211	Lufthansa	F-WWIK	D-AIQA				
0173	211	Iberia	F-WWIL	EC-580	EC-FDB			
0174	211	Canadian Airlines Intl	F-WWIM	C-GPWG				
0175	211	Canadian Airlines Intl	F-WWIN	C-FPWE				
0176	211	Iberia	F-WWIO	EC-581	EC-FDA			
0177	211	Iberia	F-WWIP	EC-582	EC-FEO			
0178	231	Egyptair	F-WWIQ	SU-GBC				
0179	231	Premiair	F-WWIS	OY-CNH				
0180	231	Cyprus Airways	F-WWIT	5B-DBA				
0181	212	Kuwait Airways	F-WWIU	F-OGYD	9K-AKA			
0182	212	Kuwait Airways	F-WWIV	F-WWDB	F-OGYE	9K-AKB		
0183	211	Air Canada	F-WWIX	C-FTJO				
0184	211	Air Inter	F-GHQI					
0185	211	Air Portugal	F-WWDB	CS-TNA				
0186	211	Air France	F-GFKR					
0187	211	Air France	F-GFKS					
0188	211	Air France	F-GFKT					
0189	212	Leisure International	F-WWDC	N483GX	G-BWCP	C-GRYY		
0190	212	Leisure International	F-WWDD	N484GX	G-BWKN	G-UKLJ		
0191	231	Air Portugal	F-WWDH	CS-TNB				
0192	211	Northwest Airlines	F-WWIY	N316US				
0193	231	Premiair	F-WWIX	OY-CNI				
0194	231	Egyptair	F-WWZI	F-WWIZ	SU-GBD			
0195	212	Kuwait Airways	F-WWDP	F-OGYF	9K-AKC			
0196	211	All Nippon Airways	F-WWDE	JA8387				
0197	211	Northwest Airlines	F-WWDS	F-WWDF	N317US			
0198	231	Egyptair	F-WWDG	SU-GBE				
0199	211	Iberia	F-WWDI	EC-583	EC-FGU			
0200	211	Lufthansa	F-WWDJ	D-AIQB				
0201	211	Lufthansa	F-WWDL	D-AIQC				
0202	211	Lufthansa	F-WWDM	D-AIQD				
0203	212	Airtours International	F-WWDN	ZS-NZP	F-GLGG	G-		
0204	211	Air Inter	F-GJVC					
0205	211	Tunis Air	F-WWDO	TS-IMD				
0206	211	Northwest Airlines	F-WWDK	N318US				
0207	211	Iberia	F-WWDQ	EC-584	EC-FGV			
0208	211	Northwest Airlines	F-WWDT	N319US				
0209	211	Lufthansa	F-WWDY	D-AIQE				
0210	211	Canadian A/L Intl	F-WWIC	C-GQCA				
0211	211	Air Inter	F-GJVD					
0212	211	All Nippon Airways	F-WWIG	JA8388				
0213	211	Northwest Airlines	F-WWIB	N320US				
0214	211	Air Inter	F-GHQJ					
0215	211	Air Inter	F-GJVE					
0216	211	Lufthansa	F-WWDR	D-AIQF				
0217	211	Lufthansa	F-WWDS	D-AIQH				
0218	211	Lufthansa	F-WWDX	D-AIQK				
0219	211	Air Nippon	F-WWDZ	JA8389				
0220	212	Airtours International	F-WWIJ	ZS-NZR	F-GLGH	G-		
0221	212	Airtours International	F-WWIK	ZS-NZS	F-GLGI	G-		
0222	212	Airtours International	F-WWIL	ZS-NZT	F-GLGJ	G-		
0223	211	Iberia	F-WWIA	EC-585	EC-FGH			
0224	211	Iberia	F-WWIM	EC-586	EC-FGR			
0225	231	Oman Air	F-WWIO	N225RX	SX-BSH	N225RX	A40-MB	stored Dec94 Cambridge, UK
0226	211	Air France	F-GFKU					
0227	211	Air France	F-GFKV					
0228	211	Air Charter	F-GFKX					
0229	211	Ansett Australia	F-WWIN	VH-HYL				
0230	231	Oman Air	F-WWDI	N230RX	SX-BSJ	N230RX	A40-MA	
0231	211	Canadian Airlines Intl	F-WWDV	C-FPWD				
0232	211	Canadian Airlines Intl	F-WWIY	C-FDCA				
0233	211	Air Canada	F-WWIQ	C-FTJP				
0234	211	Air Portugal	F-WWDF	N493GX	CS-TNC			
0235	211	Air Portugal	F-WWDM	N494GX	CS-TND			
0236	211	Air Inter	F-GHQK					
0237	211	Air Inter	F-GHQM					
0238	231	Vietnam Airlines	F-WWDC	N238RX	TC-GAA	N238RX	S7-RGX	
0239	211	Air Inter	F-GHQL					
0240	211	Iberia	F-WWIP	EC-587	EC-FIA			
0241	211	Iberia	F-WWDD	EC-588	EC-FIC			
0242	211	Air Canada	F-WWDJ	C-FTJQ				

AIRBUS INDUSTRIE A320

C/n	Series	Last known Operator/Owner	Previous Identities/fate (where known)							
0243	231	South African Airways	F-WWDL	ZS-SHA						
0244	211	Air Inter	F-GJVF							
0245	211	Air Nippon	F-WWDE	JA8390						
0246	211	Iberia	F-WWII	EC-589	EC-FKH					
0247	231	Canair Cargo	F-WWDK	N247RX	EI-TLH	G-OALA	C-			
0248	211	Air Canada	F-WWDT	C-FTJR						
0249	231	South African Airways	F-WWDO	ZS-SHB						
0250	231	South African Airways	F-WWBB	ZS-SHC						
0251	231	South African Airways	F-WWBC	ZS-SHD						
0252	231	Mexicana	F-WWBD	XA-RZU	F-OHME					
0253	211	Air Canada	F-WWBE	C-FTJS						
0254	211	Air Canada	F-WWBF	C-FGYL						
0255	211	Air Canada	F-WWBG	C-FGYS						
0256	231	Eurocypria	F-WWBH	5B-DBB						
0257	231	Translift Airways	F-WWBI	LZ-ABA	N257RX	EI-TLJ				
0258	212	Sudan Airways	F-WWBJ	(F-GHQN)	F-GMAI	F-OKAI				
0259	231	Mexicana	F-WWBK	XA-RYQ	F-OHMF					
0260	231	Mexicana	F-WWBL	XA-RYS	F-OHMG					
0261	231	Mexicana	F-WWBM	XA-RYT	F-OHMH					
0262	211	Northwest Airlines	F-WWDI	N321US						
0263	211	Northwest Airlines	F-WWDQ	N322US						
0264	211	Iberia	F-WWBN	EC-880	EC-FKD					
0265	211	Air Canada	F-WWDR	C-FKCK						
0266	211	Iberia	F-WWBO	EC-881	EC-FLP					
0267	211	Lufthansa	F-WWDY	D-AIQL						
0268	211	Lufthansa	F-WWIB	D-AIQM						
0269	211	Lufthansa	F-WWIC	D-AIQN						
0270	211	Air Inter	F-GJVG							
0271	231	Balkan Bulgarian	F-WWBQ	LZ-ABB						
0272	211	Northwest Airlines	F-WWBP	N323US						
0273	211	Northwest Airlines	F-WWDS	N324US						
0274	211	Iberia	F-WWBR	EC-882	EC-FLQ					
0275	231	Mexicana	F-WWIG	XA-RJW	F-OHMI					
0276	231	Mexicana	F-WWIM	XA-RJX	F-OHMJ					
0277	211	Air Canada	F-WWDX	C-FKCO						
0278	211	Air Inter	F-GHQO							
0279	211	Canada 3000 Airlines	F-WWDU	C-FLSF	G-MONY	C-GVNY	G-MONY	C-GVNY	G-MONY	C-GVNY
0280	231	Translift Airways	F-WWDV	N280RX	N638AW	N280RX	TC-GAB	G-BVZU		
0281	211	Northwest Airlines	F-WWBS	N325US						
0282	211	Northwest Airlines	F-WWIA	N326US						
0283	211	Canadian A/L Intl	F-WWBT	C-FLSI						
0284	211	Canadian A/L Intl	F-WWBU	C-FLSS						
0285	211	Vietnam Airlines	F-GFKY							
0286	211	Vietnam Airlines	F-GFKZ							
0287	211	Air France	F-GKXA							
0288	211	Onur Air	F-WWBV	TC-ONA						
0289	211	Onur Air	F-WWBX	9H-ABX	TC-ONC					
0290	211	Air Canada	F-WWBY	C-FKCR						
0291	231	Air 2000	F-WWBZ	G-OOAA						
0292	231	Air 2000	F-WWDN	G-OOAB						
0293	211	Air Malta	F-WWDZ	9H-ABQ						
0294	212	Airtours International	F-WWID	G-HAGT	G-HBAP					
0295	231	Eurocypria	F-WWIE	5B-DBC						
0296	231	Mexicana	F-WWIH	XA-RJY	F-OHMK					
0297	211	Northwest Airlines	F-WWIO	N327NW						
0298	211	Northwest Airlines	F-WWIP	N328NW						
0299	212	Airtours International	F-WWIQ	G-SCSR	G-JDFW					
0300	211	Air Nippon	F-WWDD	JA8391						
0301	212	Airtours International	F-WWIX	G-KMAM	G-JANM					
0302	211	Canadian A/L Intl	F-WWIY	C-FMEQ						
0303	211	Iberia	F-WWDT	EC-883	EC-FML					
0304	231	Midway Airlines	F-WWIF	N304RX	N303ML					
0305	211	Canadian A/L Intl	F-WWDE	C-FMES						
0306	211	Northwest Airlines	F-WWDG	N329NW						
0307	211	Northwest Airlines	F-WWDJ	N330NW						
0308	231	Balkan Bulgarian	F-WWDL	LZ-ABC						
0309	211	Canadian A/L Intl	F-WWIJ	C-FLSU						
0310	211	Air Canada	F-WWIK	C-FKPS						
0311	211	Air Canada	F-WWIL	C-FKPO						
0312	211	Iberia	F-WWIS	EC-884	EC-FMN					
0313	211	Gulf Air	F-WWIZ	A40-EA						
0314	231	Balkan Bulgarian	F-WWDO	LZ-ABD						
0315	231	Midway Airlines	F-WWBB	N315RX	N301ML					
0316	231	Eurocypria	F-WWBC	5B-DBD						
0317	231	Midway Airlines	F-WWBD	N317RX	N300ML					
0318	211	Northwest Airlines	F-WWBF	N331NW						
0319	211	Northwest Airlines	F-WWBG	N332NW						
0320	231	Mexicana	F-WWBI	XA-RJZ	F-OHML					
0321	231	Mexicana	F-WWBK	XA-RKA	F-OHMM					
0322	231	Onur Air	F-WWBL	SU-RAA						
0323	211	Iberia	F-WWBM	EC-885	EC-FNR					

AIRBUS INDUSTRIE A320

C/n	Series	Last known Operator/Owner	Previous Identities/fate (where known)						
0324	211	Air Canada	F-WWDC	C-FKPT					
0325	212	Gulf Air	F-WWDI	A40-EB					
0326	231	Shorouk Air	F-WWDK	SU-RAB					
0327	231	Air 2000	F-WWDQ	G-OOAC					
0328	211	All Nippon Airways	F-WWDR	JA8392					
0329	211	Northwest Airlines	F-WWDY	N333NW					
0330	211	Air Canada	F-WWIB	C-FKOJ					
0331	211	Onur Air	F-WWII	TC-ONB					
0332	231	Trans Asia Airways	F-WWIC	B-22301					
0333	211	Air Canada	F-WWBJ	C-FKAJ					
0334	231	South African Airways	F-WWBN	ZS-SHE					
0335	231	South African Airways	F-WWBO	ZS-SHF					
0336	231	Air 2000	F-WWIG	G-OOAD					
0337	211	Air Inter	F-GHQP						
0338	231	Midway Airlines	F-WWIM	N338RX	N302ML				
0339	211	Northwest Airlines	F-WWBP	N334NW					
0340	211	Northwest Airlines	F-WWBQ	N335NW					
0341	211	Air Canada	F-WWBR	C-FPDN					
0342	211	Air Canada	F-WWDB	C-FMJK					
0343	211	Leisure International	F-WWDH	N485GX	G-BWKO	G-UKLL*			
0344	231	Transasia Airways	F-WWDS	SU-RAG	F-WGYU	B-22308			
0345	212	Gulf Air	F-WWDU	A40-EC					
0346	211	Lufthansa	F-WWDX	D-AIQP					
0347	231	Transasia Airways	F-WWBS	TC-SAL	F-WWBS	F-WQAX	B-22306		
0348	211	Airtours International	F-WWBT	F-GLGE	G-TPTT				
0349	211	Airtours International	F-WWBU	G-OEXC	G-DACR				
0350	211	Air Canada	F-WWDF	C-FMST					
0351	231	Egyptair	F-WWDM	SU-GBF					
0352	211	Air Inter	F-GHQQ						
0353	231	Mexicana	F-WWDV	XA-RKB	F-OHMN				
0354	231	Caledonian Airways	F-WWDZ	N301SA	F-WQAY	G-BVYA			
0355	211	Northwest Airlines	F-WWIE	N336NW					
0356	211	Iberia	F-WWIH	EC-886	EC-FQY				
0357	231	Caledonian Airways	F-WWBH	N302SA	F-WQAZ	G-BVYB			
0358	211	Northwest Airlines	F-WWIO	N337NW					
0359	211	Air Canada	F-WWIT	C-FMSV					
0360	211	Northwest Airlines	F-WWBY	N338NW					
0361	231	Onur Air	F-WWDN	N431LF	SX-BAX	N431LF	TC-ONG		
0362	231	Airtours Intl A/W	F-WWIN	G-IEAF	G-YJBM				
0363	231	Airtours Intl A/W	F-WWBX	G-IEAG	G-SUEE				
0365	211	All Nippon Airways	F-WWBZ	JA8393					
0366	231	Egyptair	F-WWDD	SU-GBG					
0367	211	Northwest Airlines	F-WWDG	N339NW					
0368	231	Mexicana	F-WWIF	(XA-SGA)	F-OHMA				
0369	231	Trans Asia Airways	F-WWIL	B-22302					
0370	211	Tunis Air	F-WWIP	TS-IMF					
0371	211	Onur Air	F-WWIQ	N531LF	TC-OND				
0372	211	Northwest Airlines	F-WWIX	N340NW					
0373	231	Midway Airlines	F-WWDE	TC-SAN	F-WWBJ	F-WWDE	F-WQBD	N304ML	
0374	231	Air Lanka	F-WWDJ	4R-ABA					
0375	212	Gulf Air	F-WWDT	A40-ED					
0376	231	China Airlines	F-WWIK	(XA-SGB)	F-OHMB	3B-RGY			
0377	211	Air Inter	F-GHQR						
0378	211	Air Canada	F-WWIY	C-FMSX					
0379	211	Skyservice	F-WWDY	G-MPCD	C-FTDU	G-MPCD	C-FTDU	G-MPCD	C-FTDU
0380	211	Northwest Airlines	F-WWIS	N341NW					
0381	211	Northwest Airlines	F-WWIJ	N342NW					
0382	211	Lufthansa	F-WWIZ	D-AIQR					
0383	211	All Nippon Airways	F-WWBF	JA8394					
0384	211	Air Canada	F-WWBG	C-FMSY					
0386	231	China Airlines	F-WWBI	(XA-SGC)	F-OHMC	3B-RGZ			
0387	211	Northwest Airlines	F-WWBV	N343NW					
0388	211	Northwest Airlines	F-WWDC	N344NW					
0389	211	Skyservice	F-WWDI	G-OZBB	C-FTDW	G-OZBB	C-FTDW	G-OZBB	C-FTDW
0390	211	Tunis Air	F-WWDL	TS-IMG					
0391	212	Monarch Airlines	F-WWDO	G-MONW					
0392	212	Monarch Airlines	F-WWDR	G-MONX					
0393	231	Dragonair	F-WWIR	VR-HYO					
0394	231	Dragonair	F-WWBB	VR-HYP					
0395	211	Air Portugal	F-WWBJ	CS-TNE					
0396	231	Indian Airlines	F-WWBK	VT-ESA					
0397	211	Canada 3000 Airlines	F-WWBM	(C-FNVT)	N541LF	C-GVXA			
0398	231	Indian Airlines	F-WWDQ	VT-ESB					
0399	211	Northwest Airlines	F-WWIG	N345NW					
0400	211	Northwest Airlines	F-WWIT	N346NW					
0401	211	Lufthansa	F-WWBD	D-AIQS					
0402	212	Tunis Air	F-WWBN	TS-IMH					
0403	211	Canadian A/L Intl	F-WWBO	C-FNVU					
0404	211	Canadian A/L Intl	F-WWDF	C-FNVV					
0405	231	Transmeridian	F-WWDK	N441LF	HC-BTV	N141LF	EI-TLI		
0406	231	Air Lanka	F-WWDB	4R-ABB					

AIRBUS INDUSTRIE A320

C/n	Series	Last known Operator/Owner	Previous Identities/fate (where known)					
0407	211	Air Portugal	F-WWDH	CS-TNF				
0408	211	Northwest Airlines	F-WWDN	N347NW				
0409	211	Canada 3000 Airlines	F-WWDU	C-GVXB				
0410	211	Northwest Airlines	F-WWDV	N348NW				
0411	231	Caledonian Airways	F-WWDX	N303SA	F-WQBA	G-BVYC		
0413	211	All Nippon Airways	F-WWIM	JA8395				
0414	231	Dragonair	F-WWIU	VR-HYR				
0415	231	Dragonair	F-WWBL	VR-HYV				
0416	231	Indian Airlines	F-WWBP	VT-ESC				
0417	211	Northwest Airlines	F-WWBR	N349NW				
0418	211	Northwest Airlines	F-WWDG	N350NA				
0419	212	Gulf Air	F-WWDP	A40-EE				
0420	211	Air Inter	F-WWIE	N486GX	(PH-GCX)	F-GJVX		
0421	212	Gulf Air	F-WWIO	A40-EF				
0422	212	Monarch Airlines	F-WWIP	(G-MALE)	G-OZBA			
0423	231	Indian Airlines	F-WWIT	VT-ESD				
0424	231	Airtours International	F-WWIV	F-WQBB	G-CRPH			
0425	232	SAETA/LAPSA	F-WWIX	N340LA	HC-BUH			
0426	211	Air Canada	F-WWBU	C-FNNA				
0427	212	Canada 3000 Airlines	F-WWIH	C-GVXC				
0428	231	Canair Cargo	F-WWIL	N391LF	EI-TLG	C-GMPG		
0429	231	Transmeridian	F-WWIZ	N429RX	EI-TLE			
0430	231	Dragonair	F-WWHB	F-WWBH	VR-HYS			
0431	231	Indian Airlines	F-WWBQ	VT-ESE				
0432	231	Indian Airlines	F-WWBS	VT-ESF				
0433	231	Mexicana	F-WWDC	F-OHMD				
0435	232	United Airlines	F-WWDD	N401UA				
0436	231	Air Inter	F-WWDE	(PH-GCL)	F-GJVY			
0437	231	Skyservice	F-WWDM	N437RX	G-BVJV	C-FWOQ		
0438	212	Gulf Air	F-WWDT	A40-EG				
0439	232	United Airlines	F-WWIJ	N402UA				
0440	231	South African Airways	F-WWIQ	ZS-SHG				
0441	231	Transasia Airways	F-WWIS	F-WQBC	N441KA	B-22307		
0442	232	United Airlines	F-WWIY	N403UA				
0443	231	Dragonair	F-WWBV	VR-HYT				
0444	231	Onur Air	F-WWBY	N444RX	TC-ONF			
0445	232	Gulf Air	F-WWBZ	A40-EH				
0446	212	Monarch Airlines	F-WWDJ	G-MONZ				
0447	231	Dragonair	F-WWDO	VR-HYU				
0448	232	America West Airlines	F-WWDR	N931LF				
0449	231	Virgin Atlantic A/W	F-WWIG	N449RX	SX-BSV	N449RX	EI-VIR	G-OUZO
0450	232	United Airlines	F-WWII	N404UA				
0451	231	Indian Airlines	F-WWIN	VT-ESG				
0452	232	United Airlines	F-WWBF	N405UA				
0453	232	America West Airlines	F-WWBG	N921LF	TC-ONE(1)	N961LF	N641AW*	
0454	232	United Airlines	F-WWBJ	N406UA				
0455	232	America West Airlines	F-WWBK	N638AW				
0456	232	United Airlines	F-WWDB	N407UA				
0457	232	United Airlines	F-WWDG	N408UA				
0459	212	Gulf Air	F-WWDK	A40-EI				
0460	232	LACSA	F-WWDN	N951LF				
0461	232	LACSA	F-WWDP	N941LF				
0462	232	United Airlines	F-WWDQ	N409UA				
0463	232	United Airlines	F-WWDV	N410UA				
0464	232	United Airlines	F-WWDX	N411UA				
0465	232	United Airlines	F-WWIM	N412UA				
0466	212	Gulf Air	F-WWBB	A40-EJ				
0467	231	Skyservice	F-WWBC	G-BVJW	C-FWOR			
0469	231	Indian Airlines	F-WWBD	VT-ESH				
0470	232	United Airlines	F-WWBM	N413UA				
0471	232	America West Airlines	F-WWIR	N639AW				
0472	232	United Airlines	F-WWIU	N414UA				
0475	232	United Airlines	F-WWBP	N415UA				
0476	231	Transmeridian	F-WWBR	EI-TLF				
0478	231	Transasia Airways	F-WWBX	N478RX	B-22305			
0479	232	United Airlines	F-WWDH	N416UA				
0480	231	British Mediterranean Airways	F-WWDU	N480RX	G-MEDA	N480RX		
0481	212	Gulf Air	F-WWIE	A40-EK				
0482	211	All Nippon Airways	F-WWIO	JA8396				
0483	232	United Airlines	F-WWIT	N417UA				
0485	232	United Airlines	F-WWIZ	N418UA				
0486	231	Indian Airlines	F-WWBH	VT-ESI				
0487	232	United Airlines	F-WWDJ	N419UA				
0489	232	United Airlines	F-WWDM	N420UA				
0490	231	Indian Airlines	F-WWDT	VT-ESJ				
0491	211	Air Inter	F-WWBS	N131LF	F-GJVW			
0492	231	Indian Airlines	F-WWBU	VT-ESK				
0496	232	Skyservice	F-WWBV	C-GTDC				
0497	212	Gulf Air	F-WWDF	A40-EL				
0499	231	Indian Airlines	F-WWDO	VT-ESL				

AIRBUS INDUSTRIE A320

C/n	Series	Last known Operator/Owner	Previous Identities/fate (where known)		
0500	232	United Airlines	F-WWDZ	N421UA	
0501	211	All Nippon Airways	F-WWIN	JA8609	
0503	232	United Airlines	F-WWIV	N422UA	
0504	232	United Airlines	F-WWBO	N423UA	
0506	232	United Airlines	F-WWBQ	N424UA	
0507	211	All Nippon Airways	F-WWBT	JA8654	
0508	232	United Airlines	F-WWBY	N425UA	
0510	232	United Airlines	F-WWBZ	N426UA	
0511	211	Tunis Air	F-WWDC	TS-IMI	
0512	232	United Airlines	F-WWDD	N427UA	
0523	232	United Airlines	F-WWDE	N428UA	
0525	211	Air Inter	F-GJVV	N451LF	F-GJVV
0527	232	LAPSA/SAETA	F-WWDI	HC-BUI	
0528	212	Onur Air	F-WWDL	TC-ONE(2)	
0530	232	LAPSA/SAETA	F-WWDP	HC-BUM	
0531	211	All Nippon Airways	F-WWDY	JA8304	
0533	214	Swissair	F-WWIF	HB-IJA	
0534	211	All Nippon Airways	F-WWBC	JA8313	
0536	212	Gulf Air	F-WWBN	A40-EM	
0537	212	Gulf Air	F-WWBX	A40-EN	
0539	232	United Airlines	F-WWIX	N429UA	
0540	212	Sichuan Airlines	F-WWDK	B-2340	
0542	212	Airbus Industrie	F-WWIH	stored Nov95 Toulouse, France	
0543	212	Airbus Industrie	F-WWIY	stored Nov95 Toulouse, France	
0545	214	Swissair	F-WWII	HB-IJB	
0547	214	Ansett Australia	F-WWIU	VH-HYO	
0548	214	Swissair	F-WWIJ	HB-IJC	
0549	211	All Nippon Airways	F-WWIT	JA8300	
0551	232	Sichuan Airlines	F-WWBI	B-2341	
0553	214	Swissair	F-WWIE	HB-IJD	
0554	211	All Nippon Airways	F-WWIG	JA8400	
0556	232	Sichuan Airlines	F-WWIL	B-2342	
0558	233	LACSA	F-WWDF	N981LR	
0559	214	Swissair	F-WWIP	HB-IJE	
0561	233	LACSA	F-WWDM	N991LR	
0562	214	Swissair	F-WWDQ	HB-IJF	
0565	232	Aero Lloyd	F-WWDR	D-ALAA	
0566	214	Swissair	F-WWIN	HB-IJG	
0568	232	United Airlines	F-WWDC	N430UA	
0569	212	Royal Jordanian	F-WWDG	(JY-CAS)	F-OGYC
0571	232	United Airlines	F-WWDH	N431UA	
0572	232	United Airlines	F-WW	N432UA	
0573	232	Air Macau	F-WWDJ	CS-MAD	
0574	214	Swissair	F-WWDN	HB-IJH	
0575	232	Aero Lloyd	F-WWDO	D-ALAB	
0577	214	Swissair	F-WWDT	HB-	
0579	211	Canada 3000	F-WWDU	C-	
0580	232	Aero Lloyd	F-WWDV	D-ALAC	
0582	211				
0584	232		F-WWDZ		
0585	214				
0589	232				
0594	232				
0596	214				
0601	232				

AIRBUS INDUSTRIE A320

C/n	Series	Last known Operator/Owner	Previous Identities/fate (where known)

AIRBUS INDUSTRIE A321

C/n	Series	Last known Operator/Owner	Previous Identities/fate (where known)			
0364	131	Airbus Industrie	F-WWIA	prototype;	ff 11Mar93	
0385	111	Airbus Industrie	F-WWIB			
0412	131	Lufthansa	F-WWIE	D-AVZA	D-AIRH	
0434	111	Alitalia	F-WWID	D-AVZB	I-BIXU	
0458	131	Lufthansa	F-WWIQ	D-AIRA		
0468	131	Lufthansa	F-WWIS	D-AIRB		
0473	131	Lufthansa	D-AVZC	D-AIRC		
0474	131	Lufthansa	D-AVZD	D-AIRD		
0477	112	Alitalia	D-AVZE	I-BIXA		
0484	131	Lufthansa	D-AVZF	D-AIRE		
0488	112	Alitalia	D-AVZG	I-BIXE		
0493	131	Lufthansa	D-AVZH	D-AIRF		
0494	112	Alitalia	D-AVZI	I-BIXI		
0495	112	Alitalia	D-AVZJ	I-BIXO		
0498	111	Air Inter	D-AVZK	F-GMZA		
0502	131	Lufthansa	D-AVZL	D-AIRK		
0505	131	Lufthansa	D-AVZM	D-AIRL		
0509	111	Air Inter	D-AVZN	F-GMZB		
0513	112	Alitalia	D-AVZO	I-BIXL		
0514	112	Alitalia	D-AVZP	I-BIXM		
0515	112	Alitalia	D-AVZQ	I-BIXF		
0516	112	Alitalia	D-AVZR	I-BIXG		
0517	111	Swissair	D-AVZS	HB-IOA	D-AVZS	HB-IOA
0518	131	Lufthansa	D-AVZT	D-AIRM		
0519	111	Swissair	D-AVZU	HB-IOB		
0520	111	Swissair	D-AIZV	HB-IOC		
0521	111	Air Inter	D-AVZW	F-GMZC		
0522	111	Swissair	D-AVZX	HB-IOD		
0524	112	Alitalia	D-AVZY	I-BIXB		
0526	112	Alitalia	D-AVZZ	I-BIXC		
0529	111	Air Inter	D-AVZA	F-GMZD		
0532	112	Alitalia	D-AVZB	I-BIXD		
0535	111	Swissair	D-AVZC	HB-IOE		
0538	131	Transasia Airways	D-AVZD	F-WGYZ	B-22601	
0541	111	Swissair	D-AVZE	HB-IOF		
0544	111	Air Inter	D-AVZF	F-GMZE		
0550	131	Air Macau	D-AVZG	CS-MAA		
0552	111	Austrian Airlines	D-AVZH	OE-LBA		
0555	131	Transasia Airways	D-AVZI	F-WGYZ	B-22602	
0557	131	Air Macau	D-AVZJ	CS-MAB		
0560	131	Lufthansa	D-AVZK	D-AIRN		
0563	131	Lufthansa	D-AVZN	D-AIRO		
0564	131	Lufthansa	D-AVZL	D-AIRP		
0567	131	Lufthansa	D-AVZM	D-AIRR		
0570	111	Austrian Airlines	D-AVZQ	OE-LBB		
0576	112	Alitalia	D-AVZR	I-BIXN		
0581	111	Austrian Airlines	D-AVZS	OE-LBC		
0583	112	Alitalia	D-AVZT	I-BIXP		
0586	112	Alitalia	D-	(I-BIX.)		
0591	131	Onur Air	D-	TC-		
0593	112	Alitalia	D-	(I-BIX.)		
0595	131	Lufthansa	D-	D-AIRS		
0597	131					
0599	112	Alitalia	D-	(I-BIX.)		
0603	131					
0633	231					

AIRBUS INDUSTRIE A321

C/n	Series	Last known Operator/Owner	Previous Identities/fate (where known)

AIRBUS INDUSTRIE A330

C/n	Series	Last known Operator/Owner	Previous Identities/fate (where known)			
012	341	Cathay Pacific A/W	F-WWKA	prototype;	ff 02Nov92	VR-HL.
017	301	Airbus Industrie	F-WWKB			
030	301	Air Inter	F-WWKD	F-GMDA		
037	301	Air Inter	F-WWKE	F-GMDB		
042	321	(Airbus Industrie)	F-WWKH	(HS-TEA)	w/o 30Jun94 Toulouse, France	
045	301	Air Inter	F-GMDC			
050	321	Thai Airways Intl	F-WWKI	HS-TEA		
054	301	Aer Lingus	F-WWKJ	EI-SHN		
055	301	Aer Lingus	F-WWKP	EI-DUB		
059	301	Air Inter	F-GMDD			
060	321	Thai Airways Intl	F-WWKQ	HS-TEB		
062	321	Thai Airways Intl	F-WWKR	HS-TEC		
064	321	Thai Airways Intl	F-WWKS	HS-TED		
065	321	Thai Airways Intl	F-WWKT	HS-TEE		
066	322	Thai Airways Intl	F-WWKJ	HS-TEF		
067	322	Malaysia Airlines	F-WWKX	9M-MKA		
068	322	Malaysia Airlines	F-WWKL	9M-MKB		
069	322	Malaysia Airlines	F-WWKM	9M-MKC		
070	301	Aer Lingus	F-WWKV	(EI-NYC)	EI-CRK	
071	342	Cathay Pacific A/W	F-WWKU	VR-HLA		
072	322	LTU	F-WWKY	D-AERG		
073	322	Malaysia Airlines	F-WWKN	9M-MKD		
077	322	Malaysia Airlines	F-WWKO	9M-MKE		
082	322	LTU	F-WWKD	D-AERF		
083	342	Cathay Pacific A/W	F-WWKE	VR-HLB		
086	301	Aer Lingus	F-GMDE	EI-JFK		
087	322	LTU	F-WWKF	D-AERH		
095	322	LTU	F-WWKH	D-AERJ		
096	322	Malaysia Airlines	F-WWKP	9M-MKZ		
098	341	Dragonair	F-WWKG	VR-HYA		
099	342	Cathay Pacific A/W	F-WWKQ	VR-HLC		
100	322	Malaysia Airlines	F-WWKZ	9M-MKF		
102	342	Cathay Pacific A/W	F-WWKR	VR-HLD		
106	342	Dragonair	F-WWKI	VR-HYB		
107	322	Malaysia Airlines	F-WWKV	9M-MKG		
109	342	Cathay Pacific A/W	F-WWKD	VR-HLE		
110	322	Malaysia Airlines	F-WWKE	9M-MKH		
111	342	Dragonair	F-WWKL	VR-HYC		
112	321	Thai Airways Intl	F-WWKM	HS-TEG		
113	342	Cathay Pacific A/W	F-WWKS	VR-HLF		
116	322	Malaysia Airlines	F-WWKT	9M-MKI		
118	342	Cathay Pacific A/W	F-WWKF	VR-HLG		
119	322	Malaysia Airlines	F-WWKJ	9M-MKJ		
120	322	LTU	F-WWKN	D-AERK		
121	342	Cathay Pacific A/W	F-WWKK	VR-HLH		
122	322	Thai Airways Intl	F-WWKG	HS-TEH		
127	322	LTU	F-WWKO	D-AERQ		
132	341	Garuda Indonesia	F-WWKQ	PK-		
138	321					

AIRBUS INDUSTRIE A330

C/n	Series	Last known Operator/Owner	Previous Identities/fate (where known)

AIRBUS INDUSTRIE A340

C/n	Series	Last known Operator/Owner	Previous Identities/fate (where known)			
001	311	Airbus Industrie	F-WWAI	A340-300 prototype; ff 25Oct91		
002	311	Airbus Industrie	F-WWAS	stored Dec94 Toulouse, France		
003	311	Airbus Industrie	F-WWDA	flight test a/c		
004	211	Airbus Industrie	F-WWBA	A340-200 prototype; ff 01Apr92		
005	311	Air France	F-WWCA	F-GLZA		
006	211	Lufthansa	F-WWBE	D-AIBF		
007	311	Air France	F-GLZB			
008	211	Lufthansa	F-WWJA	D-AIBA		
009	211	Brunei Government	F-WWJB	D-AIBB	V8-BKH	
010	211	(Air France)	F-WWJC	OO-SLF	F-GNIA	dbf 20Jan94 Paris-Charles de Gaulle, France
011	211	Lufthansa	F-WWJD	D-AIBC		
013	311	Virgin Atlantic A/W	F-WWJE	G-VBUS		
014	211	Air France	F-WWJF	OO-SLG	F-GNIB	
015	311	Virgin Atlantic A/W	F-WWJG	G-VAEL		
016	311	Virgin Atlantic A/W	F-WWJH	G-VSKY		
018	211	Lufthansa	F-WWJI	D-AIBD		
019	211	Lufthansa	F-WWJJ	D-AIBE		
020	311	Lufthansa	F-WWJK	D-AIGA		
021	211	Lufthansa	F-WWJL	D-AIBH		
022	211	Air France	F-WWJM	F-GNIC	stored Feb96 Chateauroux, France	
023	311	THY-Turkish Airlines	F-WWJN	TC-JDJ		
024	311	Lufthansa	F-WWJO	D-AIGB		
025	311	THY-Turkish Airlines	F-WWJP	TC-JDK		
026	211	State of Qatar	F-WWJQ	A7-HHK		
027	311	Lufthansa	F-WWJR	D-AIGC		
028	311	Lufthansa	F-WWJS	D-AIGD		
029	311	Air France	F-GLZC			
031	211	Air France Asie	F-GLZD			
032	311	Air Lanka	F-WWJT	(D-AIGF)	4R-ADA	
033	311	Air Lanka	F-WWJU	(D-AIGH)	4R-ADB	
034	311	Air Lanka	F-WWJY	(D-AIGI)	4R-ADC	
035	311	Lufthansa	F-WWJV	D-AIGF		
036	312	Gulf Air	F-WWJX	(D-AIGK)	A4O-LA	
038	211	Air France Asie	F-GLZE			
034	312	Gulf Air	F-WWJZ	A4O-LB		
040	312	Gulf Air	F-WWJA	A4O-LC		
041	312	Air Portugal	F-WWJB	CS-TOA		
043	211	Air France	F-GLZF			
044	312	Air Portugal	F-WWJN	CS-TOB		
046	212	Brunei Government	F-WWJC	(A9C-HH)	V8-PJB	
047	311	Air France	F-GNID			
048	312	Air Mauritius	F-WWJD	3B-NAT		
049	311	Air France	F-GLZG			
051	311	Air France	F-GNIE			
052	311	Lufthansa	F-WWJQ	D-AIGH		
053	311	Lufthansa	F-WWJJ	D-AIGI		
056	311	Lufthansa	F-WWJK	D-AIGK		
057	311	THY-Turkish Airlines	F-WWJF	TC-JDL		
058	311	Virgin Atlantic A/W	F-WWJE	G-VFLY		
061	212	Egypt Government	F-WWII	SU-GGG		
063	211	Cathay Pacific A/W	F-WWJM	VR-HMR		
074	211	Cathay Pacific A/W	F-WWJL	VR-HMS		
075	212	Austrian Airlines	F-WWJR	OE-LAG		
076	312	Air Mauritius	F-WWJG	3B-NAU		
078	311	Air France	F-GLZH			
079	312	Air Portugal	F-WWJS	CS-TOC		
080	211	Cathay Pacific A/W	F-WWJC	VR-HMT		
081	211	Austrian Airlines	F-WWJO	OE-LAH		
084	311	Air France	F-GLZI			
085	211	Cathay Pacific A/W	F-WWJP	VR-HMU		
088	313	Air Canada	F-WWJV	C-FTNQ		
089	313	Kuwait Airways	F-WWJA	F-WWJX	9K-ANA	
090	313	Kuwait Airways	F-WWJZ	9K-ANB		
091	312	Air Portugal	F-WWJA	CS-TOD		
093	313	Air Canada	F-WWJD	C-FTNP		
094	312	Air Mauritius	F-WWJF	3B-NAV		
097	312	Gulf Air	F-WWJT	A4O-LD		
101	313	Kuwait Airways	F-WWJE	9K-ANC		
103	312	Egyptair	F-WWJG	A4O-LE		
104	314	Kuwait Airways	F-WWJJ	9K-AND		
105		not built				
108		not built				
114	311	Virgin Atlantic A/W	(F-GLZJ)	F-WWJI	G-	
115	311	THY Turkish Airlines	F-WWJN	TC-JDM		
117	313X	Singapore Airlines	F-WWJH	9V-SJF		
123	313	Singapore Airlines	F-WWKJ	9V-		
124		not built				
125	313	Iberia	F-WWJB	EC-154		
126	313	Singapore Airlines	F-WWJL	9V-		
128	313	Singapore Airlines	F-WWJZ	9V-		

AIRBUS INDUSTRIE A340

C/n	Series	Last known Operator/Owner	Previous Identities/fate (where known)	
129	313	China Eastern A/L	F-WWJQ	B-
130		not built		
131	313	China Eastern A/L	F-WWJO	B-2381
133	312	Gulf Air	F-WWJP	stored Feb96 Toulouse, France
134	313	Iberia	F-WWJR	EC-155
135	311	Lufthansa	F-WWJS	D-AIGL
136	313	Cathay Pacific	F-WWJV	VR-H
137	313	Cathay Pacific	F-WWJX	VR-HXB
139	313	Singapore Airlines	F-WWJA	9V-
140	341			
145	313	Iberia	F-	EC-156
146	313	Iberia	F-	EC-157

ANTONOV An-72

S/n	Series	Last known Owner/Operator	Identities/fate (where known)		
			CCCP-19773		
			CCCP-19774	protoytpe; ff 22Dec77	
			CCCP-19775		
			CCCP-19793		
			CCCP-19795		
		Antonov Design Bureau	CCCP-71052		
			CCCP-72000		
			CCCP-72002		
		Southern Eng. Factory	CCCP-72003	UR-72003	
		Southern Eng. Factory	CCCP-72004	UR-72004	
		Aeroflot Russian Int A/L	RA-72005		
			CCCP-72010		
			CCCP-72019		
		Aeroflot Russian Int A/L	RA-72024		
			CCCP-72042		
			CCCP-72598		
		Kazakhstan Airlines	CCCP-72904	UN-72904	
		Aeroflot Russian Int A/L	CCCP-72905	RA-72905	
			CCCP-72906		
		Soviet AF	CCCP-72907	72907	
		Soviet AF	CCCP-72908	RA-72908	
			CCCP-72909		
			CCCP-72910		
		Soviet AF	RA-72911		
			RA-72914		
			CCCP-72915		
		Soviet AF	CCCP-72916/02		
		Aeroflot Russian Int A/L	RA-72917		
			CCCP-72918		
			CCCP-72919		
			CCCP-72920		
			CCCP-72921		
			CCCP-72922	RA-72922	
		Aeroflot Russian Int A/L	CCCP-72924	RA-72924	
		Aeroflot Russian Int A/L	CCCP-72925	RA-72925	
		Soviet AF	CCCP-72926	RA-72926	
			CCCP-72927		
			CCCP-72928		
			CCCP-72929		
		Soviet AF	CCCP-72930	RA-72930	
			CCCP-72931		
			ER-72933		
		Moldovan Government	CCCP-72935	ER-72935	
			CCCP-72938		
			RA-72939		
		Aeroflot Russian Int A/L	RA-72940		
			CCCP-72942		
			CCCP-72943		
			CCCP-72944		
			CCCP-72946		
		Soviet AF	'CCCP-72948'	948	
36572093819		Soviet AF	'CCCP-72949'	949	
		Soviet AF	'CCCP-72950'	950	
		Soviet AF	RA-72952		
			RA-72955		
			CCCP-72958		
		Air Ukraine	CCCP-72959	UR-72959	
36572093865		(Fed Frontier Guards)	CCCP-72960	RA-72960	dbr 23Oct94 Vorkuta, Russia
		Russian Min of Interior	CCCP-72961	RA-72961	
		Voyennaya Transportna Aviatsia	CCCP-72962	RA-72962	
			CCCP-72963		
		Aeroflot Russian Int A/L	RA-72964		
			CCCP-72965	RA-72965	
		Antonov Design Bureau	CCCP-72966	72966	UR-72966
			CCCP-72967		
			CCCP-72970		
			CCCP-72972		
			RA-72973		
			CCCP-72974		
36572094888		Renan Air	ER-72975		
		Soviet AF	'CCCP-72976'	976 black	
36572094889		Natair	CCCP-72977	HK-3808X	ER-72977
36572096914		Aviaobshchemash	CCCP-72982	RA-72982	
			CCCP-83966(2)		
			ER-ACA		
		Peruvian AF	OB-1485		
		Peruvian AF	OB-1486/369		
		Aero Tumi	OB-1487	RA-72983?	

ANTONOV An-72

S/n	Series	Last known Owner/Operator	Identities/fate (where known)
		Soviet AF	01 red
		Soviet AF	01 black
		Soviet AF	02 blue
	P	Soviet Navy	02 red
		Soviet AF	03 red
		Soviet AF	03 blue
		Soviet AF	03 black
		Soviet AF	04 blue
36576096906?	P	Soviet AF	06 yellow
36576096915	P	Ukraine AF	07 red
		Soviet AF	09 blue
	P	Ukraine AF	11 red
	P	Soviet Navy	22 blue
	P	Soviet Navy	24 blue
	P	Soviet AF	58 blue
	P	Soviet AF	59 blue
	P	Soviet AF	60 blue

ANTONOV An-74

S/n	Series	Last known Owner/Operator	Identities/fate (where known)		
0202		Aeroflot	CCCP-58642	wfs Kiev-Gostomel, Ukraine; regn later carried on An-26	
		Aeroflot Russian Int A/L	CCCP-74000	RA-74000	
			CCCP-74001		
			CCCP-74002		
		Vitair	CCCP-74003	RA-74003	UR-74003
36547094890		Juz Mashavia	UR-74004	RA-74004	
		Nadym Airlines	CCCP-74005	RA-74005	
		Aeroflot Russian Int A/L	CCCP-74006	RA-74006	
36547095903		Business Airlines	CCCP-74007	HK-3809X	RA-74007
36547095900	T-100	Vitair	CCCP-74008	RA-74008	
		Valeologia	CCCP-74009	MOLDOVA-74009	RA-74009
	T	Antonov Design Bureau	CCCP-74010	UR-74010	
		Aeroflot Russian Int A/L	CCCP-74024	RA-74024	
36547095905		Aviacor	CCCP-74025	RA-74025	
36547096919		Romoco Cargo	CCCP-74026	HK-3810X	UR-74026
		Antonov Design Bureau	UR-74027		
			UR-74028		
		Tsentro Spac Gkus Rosii	RA-74029		
		Aeroflot Russian Int A/L	RA-74030		
		Aero Eko	UR-74031		
		200	UR-74032		
		Artos	RA-74033		
		M.Tjse/S.Rossii	RA-74034		
		Antonov Design Bureau	UR-74037		
36547097936	TK-200	Antonov Design Bureau	UR-74038		
36547097...		Aviaenergo	RA-74040		
36547096924		Aviacor	RA-74041	damaged 16Jun95 Keperveem, Russia (status?)	
	200	Vit Air	UR-74043		
			UN-74044		
		Shonkar	RA-74046		
36547098943		Aeroflot Russian Int A/L	RA-74047		
36547097941		Bashkortostan	RA-74048		
			UR-74053		
	TK-200	Antonov Design Bureau	UR-74055		
		Antonov Design Bureau	CCCP-780151	AEW&C version	
		Antonov Design Bureau	CCCP-780334		
		Natair	ER-AGN		
36547097932		Enimex	(military?)	ES-NOE	
		Soviet AF	01 red		
		Soviet AF	11 red		
36547098970		Antonov Design Bureau	(unmarked)		

ANTONOV An-124 Ruslan

S/n	Series	Last known Owner/Operator	Identities/fate (where known)		
195305010 01?		Antonov Design Bureau	CCCP-680125	prototype	
19530501002?		Antonov Design Bureau	CCCP-680210	2nd prototype	
			CCCP-82001		
19530501003?		(Aeroflot)	CCCP-82002	w/o 13Oct92 nr Ulyanovsk, Russia	
		Transcharter	CCCP-82003	RA-82003	
			CCCP-82004		
9773054516003		Russian AF	CCCP-82005	RA-82005	08 red
19530501004		Aviaobshchemash	CCCP-82006	RA-82006	
19530501005	100	Antonov Design Bureau	CCCP-82007	UR-82007	
19530501006	100	Air Foyle/Antonov	CCCP-82008	UR-82008	
19530501007	100	Air Foyle/Antonov	CCCP-82009	UR-82009	
9773053616017		Voyennaya Transportna Aviatsia	CCCP-82010	RA-82010	
9773054616023		Voyennaya Transportna Aviatsia	CCCP-82011	RA-82011	
		Aviaobshchemash	CCCP-82012	RA-82012	
		Voyennaya Transportna Aviatsia	CCCP-82013	RA-82013	
9773054732039		Voyennaya Transportna Aviatsia	CCCP-82014		
19530502001		Antonov Airlines	CCCP-82020	RA-82020	
19530502002?		Antonov Airlines	CCCP-82021	RA-82021	
19530502003		Voyennaya Transportna Aviatsia	CCCP-82022	RA-82022	
195305020.4?		Voyennaya Transportna Aviatsia	CCCP-82023	RA-82023	
19530502035			CCCP-82024	RA-82024	
19530502106	100	Air Foyle/Antonov	CCCP-82025	RA-82025	
19530502..7?		Soviet AF	(82026)	10 black	
19530502288	100	Air Foyle/Antonov	CCCP-82027	UR-82027	
19530502..9?		Voyennaya Transportna Aviatsia	CCCP-82028	RA-82028	
19530502630	100	Air Foyle/Antonov	CCCP-82029	UR-82029	
9773054732045		Voyennaya Transportna Aviatsia	CCCP-82030	RA-82030	
9773051832049		Voyennaya Transportna Aviatsia	CCCP-82031		
		Voyennaya Transportna Aviatsia	CCCP-82032		
977305..32161		Transaero	CCCP-82033	21 black	RA-82033
9773051932162		Voyennaya Transportna Aviatsia	CCCP-82034	RA-82034	
		Voyennaya Transportna Aviatsia	CCCP-82035	RA-82035	
	100	Transaero	CCCP-82036	RA-82036	
9773052955071		Voyennaya Transportna Aviatsia	CCCP-82037	RA-82037	
9773054955077		Soviet AF	CCCP-82038	09 black/RA-82038	
			CCCP-82039	RA-82039	
			CCCP-82040		
		Voyennaya Transportna Aviatsia	CCCP-82041	RA-82041	
9773054055093	100	Heavylift/Volga Dnepr	CCCP-82042	RA-82042	
9773054155101	100	Heavylift/Volga Dnepr	CCCP-82043	RA-82043	
9773054155109	100	Heavylift/Volga Dnepr	CCCP-82044	RA-82044	
9773052255113	100	Heavylift/Volga Dnepr	CCCP-82045	RA-82045	
19530502761	100	Air Foyle/Air Ukraine	CCCP-82066	UR-82066	
9773052255117	100	Heavylift/Volga Dnepr	CCCP-82067	RA-82067	RA-82046
9773053259121	100	Heavylift/Volga Dnepr	CCCP-82068	RA-82047	
	100	Orel Avia	CCCP-82069	RA-82069	
	100	Aviastar	RA-82070		
	100	(Aviastar)	RA-82071	w/o 16Nov93 Joupar Mts, nr Kerman, Iran	
	100	Rossia Aviation	RA-82072		
9773054359139	100	Rossia Aviation	RA-82073		
9773051459142	100	Atlant	RA-82074		
9773053459147	100	Polet AviaKompania	RA-82075		
9773054459151	100	Polet AviaKompania	RA-82077		
	100	Polet AviaKompania	RA-82078		
	M	Polet AviaKompania	RA-82079		
	100	Antonov Airtrack	UR-UAP		
		Soviet AF	08 black	(possibly CCCP-82039 or CCCP-82040 !)	

ANTONOV An-124 Ruslan

S/n	Series	Last known Owner/Operator	Identities/fate (where known)

ANTONOV An-225 Mirya

S/n	Series	Last known Owner/Operator	Identities/fate (where known)			
		Antonov Design Bureau	CCCP-480182	CCCP-82060	UR-82060	shuttle transporter

A second An-225 is being built

BOEING 707/720

C/n	Series	Line No	Last known Operator/Owner	Previous Identities/fate (where known)
17158	367-80	N/a	Smithsonian Institute	N70700 Prototype, ff 15Jul54; wfu 1969; stored Davis-Monthan AFB, AZ later preserved Museum of Flight, Seattle, WA

17159 to 17183 model 464-201-6; built as B-52C with serials 54-2664 to 54-2688
17184 to 17233 model 464-201-7; built as B-52D-BO with serials 55-0068 to 55-0117
17234 to 17262 model 717-146; built as KC-135A and modified as follows:

C/n	Series	Line No	Last known Operator/Owner	Previous Identities/fate (where known)
17234	EC-135K	T0001	USAF/89thAW	55-3118/OK
17235	NKC-135A	T0002	USAF/55thWg	55-3119/OF stored Davis-Monthan AFB, AZ 06Jul93
17236	NKC-135A	T0003	USAF/4950thTW	55-3120 stored Davis-Monthan AFB, AZ 15Dec93
17237	RC-135T	T0004	(USAF/6thSW)	55-3121 w/o 26Feb85 nr Valdez, AK
17238	NKC-135A	T0005	USAF/4950thTW	55-3122 stored Davis-Monthan AFB, AZ 19Oct93
17239	NKC-135A	T0006	USAF Museum	55-3123 Preserved Wright Field, Wright-Patterson AFB, OH 04May88
17240	GNKC-135A	T0007	USAF/82ndTW	55-3124 Preserved Sheppard AFB, TX 07Mar91
17241	EC-135Y	T0008	USAF/CENTCOM	55-3125 [Op by 19thARW]
17242	KC-135A	T0009	(USAF/1stCW)	55-3126 stored Davis-Monthan AFB, AZ 31Jul75; later b/u
17243	NKC-135A	T0010	USAF/4950thTW	55-3127 stored Davis-Monthan AFB, AZ 31Aug92
17244	NKC-135A	T0011	USAF/412thTW	55-3128
17245	EC-135P	T0012	USAF/6thACCS/1stTFW	55-3129/FF stored Davis-Monthan AFB, AZ 31Jan92
17246	KC-135A	T0013	USAF/7thARS/7thBW	55-3130 Preserved March AFB, CA 15Dec92
17247	NKC-135A	T0014	USAF/4950thTW	55-3131 stored Davis-Monthan AFB, AZ 10Oct92
17248	NKC-135A	T0015	USAF/412thTW	55-3132
17249	KC-135A	T0016	(USAF/509thBW)	55-3133 w/o 24Sep68 Wake Island
17250	NKC-135A	T0017	USN/FIWC	55-3134 553134
17251	NKC-135E	T0018	USAF/412thTW	55-3135
17252	KC-135A	T0019	USAF/917thARS/96thWg	55-3136/DY stored Davis-Monthan AFB, AZ 28Apr93
17253	KC-135A	T0020	USAF/906thARS/43rdARW	55-3137 stored Davis-Monthan AFB, AZ 14Jul93
17254	KC-135A	T0021	(USAF/93rdBW)	55-3138 w/o 02Oct68 U-Tapao, Thailand
17255	KC-135A	T0022	USAF/93rdARS/398thOG	55-3139 Preserved Castle AFB, CA 03Apr93
17256	KC-135A	T0023	(USAF/93rdBW)	55-3140 dbr 19Apr67 Wake Island
17257	KC-135E	T0024	USAF/116thARS/WA ANG	55-3141
17258	KC-135A	T0025	USAF/55thARS/97thAMW	55-3142 stored Davis-Monthan AFB, AZ 12Jul94
17259	KC-135E	T0026	USAF/197thARS/AZ ANG	55-3143
17260	KC-135A	T0027	(USAF/93rdBW)	55-3144 w/o 05Aug62 Hansom AFB, MA
17261	KC-135E	T0028	USAF/314thARS/AFRes	55-3145
17262	KC-135E	T0029	USAF/141stARS/NJ ANG	55-3146

17263 to 17313 model 464-201-7; built as B-52D-BO with serials 56-0580 to 56-0630
17314 to 17339 model 464-259-7; built as B-52E-BO with serials 56-0631 to 56-0656
17340 to 17407 model 717-146; built as KC-135A and modified as follows:

C/n	Series	Line No	Last known Operator/Owner	Previous Identities/fate (where known)
17340	KC-135A	T0030	USAF/906thARS/43rdARW	56-3591 stored Davis-Monthan AFB, AZ 28Jul93
17341	KC-135A	T0031	(USAF/42ndBW)	56-3592 w/o 04Oct89 nr Loring AFB, ME
17342	KC-135E	T0032	USAF/141stARS/NJ ANG	56-3593
17343	KC-135A	T0033	USAF/93rdARS/398thOG	56-3594 stored Davis-Monthan AFB, AZ 17Sep92
17344	KC-135A	T0034	USAF/8thAF Museum	56-3595/LA Preserved Barksdale AFB, LA .93
17345	NKC-135A	T0035	USN/FTRG	56-3596 563596 stored Waco, TX Sep94 later Davis-Monthan AFB, AZ Jun95
17346	KC-135A	T0036	(USAF/93rdBW)	56-3597 w/o 27Feb63 Eielson AFB, AK
17347	KC-135A	T0037	(USAF/42ndBW)	56-3598 w/o 25Mar58 Loring AFB, ME
17348	KC-135A	T0038	(USAF/4050thARW)	56-3599 w/o 27Jun58 Westover AFB, MA
17349	KC-135A	T0039	USAF/398thOG	56-3600 stored Davis-Monthan AFB, AZ 13Apr93
17350	KC-135A	T0040	USAF/398thOG	56-3601 stored Davis-Monthan AFB, AZ 21Jul93
17351	KC-135A	T0041	(USAF/42ndBW)	56-3602 w/o 25Mar69 Loring AFB, ME
17352	KC-135A	T0042	USAF/97thARS/97thWg	56-3603 stored Davis-Monthan AFB, AZ 21Jul92
17353	KC-135E	T0043	USAF/117thARS/KS ANG	56-3604
17354	KC-135A	T0044	(USAF/42ndBW)	56-3605 w/o 18Nov60 Loring AFB, ME
17355	KC-135E	T0045	USAF/132ndARS/ME ANG	56-3606
17356	KC-135E	T0046	USAF/151stARS/TN ANG	56-3607
17357	KC-135A	T0047	USAF/93rdARS/398thOG	56-3608 stored Davis-Monthan AFB, AZ 23Jul92
17358	KC-135E	T0048	USAF/151stARS/TN ANG	56-3609
17359	KC-135A	T0049	USAF/7thARS/19thARW	56-3610 stored Davis-Monthan AFB, AZ 04Nov92
17360	KC-135E	T0050	USAF/146thARS/PA ANG	56-3611
17361	KC-135E	T0051	USAF/146thARS/PA ANG	56-3612
17362	KC-135A	T0052	(USAF/92ndSAW)	56-3613 w/o Shadow Mountain, WA 19Jan67
17363	KC-135A	T0053	USAF/46thARS/305thARW	56-3614 stored Davis-Monthan AFB, AZ 07Jun93
17364	KC-135A	T0054	USAF/71stARS/2ndWg	56-3615 stored Davis-Monthan AFB, AZ 30Jul92
17365	KC-135A	T0055	(USAF/917thARS/96thWg)	56-3616 Wfs & stored Patuxent River NAS, MD 03Jan93; later dbr
17366	KC-135A	T0056	(USAF/93rdARS/7thBW)	56-3617 Wfs & stored Patuxent River NAS, MD 03Mar93; later dbr
17367	KC-135A	T0057	(USAF/42ndBW)	56-3618 w/o 09May62 Loring AFB, AZ
17368	KC-135A	T0058	USAF/305thARW	56-3619 stored Davis-Monthan AFB, AZ 07Oct92
17369	KC-135A	T0059	USAF/906thARS/43rdARW	56-3620 stored Davis-Monthan AFB, AZ 06Mar94
17370	KC-135A	T0060	USAF/55thARS/97thAMW	56-3621 stored Davis-Monthan AFB, AZ 23Jun94
17371	KC-135E	T0061	USAF/132ndARS/ME ANG	56-3622
17372	KC-135E	T0062	USAF/336thARS/AFRes	56-3623
17373	KC-135A	T0063	USAF/55thARS/97thAMW	56-3624 stored Davis-Monthan AFB, AZ 07Jul94
17374	KC-135A	T0064	USAF/917thARS/96thWg	56-3625/DY stored Davis-Monthan AFB, AZ 05May93
17375	KC-135E	T0065	USAF/117thARS/KS ANG	56-3626
17376	KC-135A	T0066	USAF/71stARS/2ndWg	56-3627 stored Davis-Monthan AFB, AZ 21Oct92
17377	KC-135A	T0067	(USAF/6thBW)	56-3628 w/o 03Feb60 Walker AFB, NM
17378	KC-135A	T0068	(USAF/93rdBW)	56-3629 w/o 19Dec69 nr Ching Chuan Kang AB, RoC

BOEING 707/720

C/n	Series	Line No	Last known Operator/Owner	Previous Identities/fate (where known)
17379	KC-135E	T0069	USAF/146thARS/PA ANG	56-3630
17380	KC-135E	T0070	USAF/117thARS/KS ANG	56-3631
17381	KC-135A	T0071	(USAF/71stARS/2ndWg)	56-3632 Wfs & stored Patuxent River NAS, MD 16Feb93; later dbr
17382	KC-135A	T0072	USAF/920thARS/305thARW	56-3633 stored Davis-Monthan AFB, AZ 20Aug92
17383	KC-135A	T0073	USAF/920thARS/305thARW	56-3634 stored Davis-Monthan AFB, AZ 22Sep92
17384	KC-135A	T0074	USAF/917thARS/96thWg	56-3635 stored Davis-Monthan AFB, AZ 25Aug92
17385	KC-135A	T0075	USAF/71stARS/2ndWg	56-3636 stored Davis-Monthan AFB, AZ 28Jul92
17386	KC-135A	T0076	USAF/46thARS/305thARW	56-3637 stored Davis-Monthan AFB, AZ 06Aug92
17387	KC-135E	T0077	USAF/197thARS/AZ ANG	56-3638
17388	KC-135A	T0078	USAF/917thARS/96thWg	56-3639/DY Preserved Dyess AFB, TX 01Jul92
17389	KC-135E	T0079	USAF/132ndARS/ME ANG	56-3640
17390	KC-135E	T0080	USAF/117thARS/KS ANG	56-3641
17391	KC-135A	T0081	USAF/906thARS/43rdARW	56-3642 stored Davis-Monthan AFB, AZ 11Aug93
17392	KC-135E	T0082	USAF/151stARS/TN ANG	56-3643
17393	KC-135A	T0083	USAF/46thARS/305thARW	56-3644 stored Davis-Monthan AFB, AZ 16Jul92
17394	KC-135E	T0084	USAF/314thARS/AFRes	56-3645
17395	KC-135A	T0085	USAF/917thARS/96thWg	56-3646 stored Davis-Monthan AFB, AZ 11Aug92
17396	KC-135A	T0086	USAF/93rdARS/398thOG	56-3647 stored Davis-Monthan AFB, AZ 10Sep92
17397	KC-135E	T0087	USAF/146thARS/PA ANG	56-3648
17398	KC-135A	T0088	USAF/93rdARS/97thAMW	56-3649 stored Davis-Monthan AFB, AZ 16Jun93
17399	KC-135E	T0089	USAF/116thARS/WA ANG	56-3650
17400	KC-135A	T0090	USAF/906thARS/43rdARW	56-3651 stored Davis-Monthan AFB, AZ 01Sep92
17401	KC-135A	T0091	USAF/906thARS/43rdARW	56-3652/DY stored Davis-Monthan AFB, AZ 09Aug93
17402	KC-135A	T0092	USAF/7thARS/19thARW	56-3653 stored Davis-Monthan AFB, AZ 07Jul92
17403	KC-135E	T0093	USAF/132ndARS/ME ANG	56-3654
17404	KC-135A	T0094	(USAF/93rdBW)	56-3655 w/o Mount Lassen, CA 30Jul68
17405	KC-135A	T0095	(USAF/7thARS/19thARW)	56-3656 Wfs & stored Patuxent River NAS, MD 09Aug93; later dbr
17406	KC-135A	T0096	(USAF/1stBW)	56-3657 dbf 25Jan62 Altus AFB, OK
17407	KC-135E	T0097	USAF/117thARS/KS ANG	56-3658

17408 to 17423 model 464-259-7; built as B-52E-BO with serials 57-0014 to 57-0029
17424 to 17467 model 464-250; built as B-52F-BO with serials 57-0030 to 57-0073
17468 to 17488, no details known; possibly a cancelled B-52 order
17489 to 17585 model 717-148; built as KC-135A and modified as follows:

C/n	Series	Line No	Last known Operator/Owner	Previous Identities/fate (where known)
17489	KC-135R	T0098	USAF/153rdARS/MS ANG	57-1418
17490	KC-135R	T0099	USAF/319thARW	57-1419
17491	KC-135A	T0100	USAF/93rdARS/19thARW	57-1420 stored Davis-Monthan AFB, AZ 15Sep92
17492	KC-135E	T0101	USAF/116thARS/WA ANG	57-1421
17493	KC-135E	T0102	USAF/63rdARS/AFRes	57-1422
17494	KC-135E	T0103	USAF/147thARS/PA ANG	57-1423
17495	KC-135A	T0104	(USAF/461stBW)	57-1424 w/o 17May66 Amarillo AFB, TX
17496	KC-135E	T0105	USAF/151stARS/TN ANG	57-1425
17497	KC-135E	T0106	USAF/197thARS/AZ ANG	57-1426
17498	KC-135R	T0107	USAF/145thARS/OH ANG	57-1427
17499	KC-135E	T0108	USAF/196thARS/CA ANG	57-1428
17500	KC-135E	T0109	USAF/117thARS/KS ANG	57-1429
17501	KC-135R	T0110	USAF/92ndARW	57-1430
17502	KC-135E	T0111	USAF/141stARS/NJ ANG	57-1431
17503	KC-135R	T0112	USAF/106thARS/AL ANG	57-1432
17504	KC-135E	T0113	USAF/197thARS/AZ ANG	57-1433
17505	KC-135E	T0114	USAF/116thARS/WA ANG	57-1434
17506	KC-135R	T0115	USAF/55thARS/97thAMW	57-1435
17507	KC-135E	T0116	USAF/196thARS/CA ANG	57-1436
17508	KC-135R	T0117	USAF/319thARW	57-1437
17509	KC-135E	T0118	USAF/63rdARS/AFRes	57-1438
17510	KC-135R	T0119	USAF/351stARS/100thARW	57-1439/D
17511	KC-135R	T0120	USAF/319thARW	57-1440
17512	KC-135E	T0121	USAF/108thARS/IL ANG	57-1441
17513	KC-135A	T0122	(USAF/70thBW)	57-1442 w/o 18Jan65 McConnell AFB, KS
17514	KC-135E	T0123	USAF/132ndARS/ME ANG	57-1443
17515	KC-135A	T0124	(USAF/484thBW)	57-1444 w/o 18May66 Kadena AB, Okinawa, Japan
17516	KC-135E	T0125	USAF/141stARS/NJ ANG	57-1445
17517	KC-135A	T0126	(USAF/6thBW)	57-1446 dbf 22Jun59 Walker AFB, NM
17518	KC-135E	T0127	USAF/147thARS/PA ANG	57-1447
17519	KC-135E	T0128	USAF/132ndARS/ME ANG	57-1448
17520	KC-135A	T0129	(USAF/6thBW)	57-1449 dbf 03Feb60 Walker AFB, NM
17521	KC-135E	T0130	USAF/132ndARS/ME ANG	57-1450
17522	KC-135E	T0131	USAF/116thARS/WA ANG	57-1451
17523	KC-135E	T0132	USAF/197thARS/AZ ANG	57-1452
17524	KC-135R	T0133	USAF/106thARS/AL ANG	57-1453
17525	KC-135R	T0134	USAF/91stARS/43rdARG	57-1454
17526	KC-135E	T0135	USAF/151stARS/TN ANG	57-1455
17527	KC-135R	T0136	USAF/351stARS/100thARW	57-1456/D
17528	KC-135A	T0137	(USAF/6thBW)	57-1457 dbf 03Feb60 Walker AFB, NM
17529	KC-135E	T0138	USAF/108thARS/IL ANG	57-1458
17530	KC-135E	T0139	USAF/196thARS/CA ANG	57-1459
17531	KC-135E	T0140	USAF/117thARS/KS ANG	57-1460
17532	KC-135R	T0141	USAF/173rdARS/NE ANG	57-1461
17533	KC-135R	T0142	USAF/166thARS/OH ANG	57-1462
17534	KC-135E	T0143	USAF/117thARS/KS ANG	57-1463

BOEING 707/720

C/n	Series	Line No	Last known Operator/Owner	Previous Identities/fate (where known)
17535	KC-135E	T0144	USAF/141stARS/NJ ANG	57-1464
17536	KC-135E	T0145	USAF/168thARS/AK ANG	57-1465
17537	KC-135A	T0146	(USAF/7thBW)	57-1466 w/o 08Mar60 Carswell AFB, TX
17538	KC-135A	T0147	USAF/920thARS/305thARW	57-1467 stored Davis-Monthan AFB, AZ 27Aug92
17539	KC-135E	T0148	USAF/336thARS/AFRes	57-1468
17540	KC-135R	T0149	USAF/166thARS/OH ANG	57-1469
17541	KC-135R	T0150	(USAF/126thARS/WI ANG)	57-1470 dbf 10Dec93 Milwaukee-Mitchell Field, WI
17542	KC-135E	T0151	USAF/132ndARS/ME ANG	57-1471
17543	KC-135R	T0152	USAF/72ndARS/AFRes	57-1472
17544	KC-135R	T0153	USAF/909thARS/18thWg	57-1473/ZZ
17545	KC-135R	T0154	USAF/92ndARW	57-1474
17546	KC-135E	T0155	USAF/197thARS/AZ ANG	57-1475
17547	KC-135A	T0156	USAF/920thARS/305thARW	57-1476 stored Davis-Monthan AFB, AZ 13Aug92
17548	KC-135A	T0157	USAF/93rdARS/398thOG	57-1477 stored Davis-Monthan AFB, AZ 18Aug92
17549	KC-135E	T0158	USAF/151stARS/TN ANG	57-1478
17550	KC-135E	T0159	USAF/336thARS/AFRes	57-1479
17551	KC-135E	T0160	USAF/108thARS/IL ANG	57-1480
17552	KC-135E	T0161	(USAF/168thARS/AK ANG)	57-1481 dbf 21Sep89 Eielson AFB, AZ
17553	KC-135E	T0162	USAF/117thARS/KS ANG	57-1482
17554	KC-135R	T0163	USAF/22ndARW	57-1483
17555	KC-135E	T0164	USAF/197thARS/AZ ANG	57-1484
17556	KC-135E	T0165	USAF/151stARS/TN ANG	57-1485
17557	KC-135R	T0166	USAF/351stARS/100thARW	57-1486/D
17558	KC-135R	T0167	USAF/434thARW/AFRes	57-1487
17559	KC-135R	T0168	USAF/55thARS/97thAMW	57-1488
17560	KC-135A	T0169	(USAF/197thARS/AZ ANG)	57-1489 w/o 13Mar82 nr Luke AFB, AZ
17561	KC-135A	T0170	USAF/93rdARS/398thOG	57-1490 stored Davis-Monthan AFB, AZ 29Sep92
17562	KC-135E	T0171	USAF/132ndARS/ME ANG	57-1491
17563	KC-135E	T0172	USAF/151stARS/TN ANG	57-1492
17564	KC-135R	T0173	USAF/91stARS/43rdARG	57-1493
17565	KC-135E	T0174	USAF/108thARS/IL ANG	57-1494
17566	KC-135E	T0175	USAF/197thARS/AZ ANG	57-1495
17567	KC-135E	T0176	USAF/197thARS/AZ ANG	57-1496
17568	KC-135E	T0177	USAF/191stARS/UT ANG	57-1497
17569	KC-135A	T0178	(USAF/409thARW)	57-1498 w/o 21Jun63 Westover AFB, MA
17570	KC-135R	T0179	USAF/351stARS/100thARW	57-1499/D
17571	KC-135A	T0180	(USAF/384thBW)	57-1500 w/o 05Mar74 McConnell AFB, KS
17572	KC-135E	T0181	USAF/116thARS/WA ANG	57-1501
17573	KC-135R	T0182	USAF/319thARW	57-1502
17574	KC-135E	T0183	USAF/151stARS/TN ANG	57-1503
17575	KC-135E	T0184	USAF/63rdARS/AFRes	57-1504
17576	KC-135E	T0185	USAF/132ndARS/ME ANG	57-1505
17577	KC-135R	T0186	USAF/351stARS/100thARW	57-1506/D
17578	KC-135E	T0187	USAF/141stARS/NJ ANG	57-1507
17579	KC-135R	T0188	USAF/203rdARS/HI ANG	57-1508
17580	KC-135E	T0189	USAF/147thARS/PA ANG	57-1509
17581	KC-135E	T0190	USAF/191stARS/UT ANG	57-1510
17582	KC-135E	T0191	USAF/314thARS/AFRes	57-1511
17583	KC-135E	T0192	USAF/336thARS/AFRes	57-1512
17584	KC-135A	T0193	(USAF/4228thSW)	57-1513 w/o 15Oct59 nr Letchworth AFB, KS
17585	KC-135R	T0194	USAF/126thARS/WI ANG	57-1514
17586	707-121B	1	(Pan American World A/W)	N708PA w/o 17Sep65 Chances Mountain, Antigua, Leeward Islands
17587	707-121B	2	(Corporate Air)	N707PA TC-JBA (HP-870) "D-ABCE" N707PA stored Miami FL 17Nov80; b/u May88
17588	707-121	3	(Pan American World A/W)	N709PA w/o 08Dec63 Elkton, MD
17589	707-121B	4	(E-Systems Inc)	N710PA TC-JBB HP-760 HP-792 HP-793 (N4594A) stored Taipei, RoC Jun79, b/u Aug84
17590	707-121B	5	(E-Systems Inc)	N711PA TC-JBC N711 HP-807 N4593U stored Taipei, RoC Sep78; b/u Apr84
17591	707-121B	6	(E-Systems Inc)	N712PA TC-JBD HP-756 HP-794 (N4591Y) stored Taipei, RoC Nov78; b/u Apr84
17592	707-321	13	(Aeroamerica)	N714PA 9M-AQD N714PA N714FC N714 N714PT N714FC stored Boeing Field, WA Oct79; b/u 11Aug81
17593	707-321	20	(Tempair International)	N715PA TC-JAH G-41-174 (HS-BBA) 9G-ACB C9-ARF stored Brussels, Belgium 18Sep76; b/u Jul80
17594	707-321	58	(British Midland Airways)	N716PA (9M-...) N716PA TC-JAN N716PA YU-AGH N716PA N716HH stored Stansted, UK .76; b/u 29Sep77
17595	707-321	61	(ATASCO)	N717PA stored Wichita, KS 01Sep70; later Marana, AZ then Tel Aviv, Israel
17596	707-321	62	(Israel Defence Force/AF)	N718PA 4X-BYZ 240/4X-JYZ stored Tel Aviv, Israel; later b/u
17597	707-321	68	(Intercontl Commercial A/L)	N719PA G-AYBJ N431MA stored Sharjah, UAE Sep80; later b/u
17598	707-321	70	(Jet Power)	N720PA G-AYVG N3791G stored Miami, FL 30Sep81; b/u 13Oct83
17599	707-321	71	(KIVU Cargo/Inter Fret)	N721PA G-AYSL N80703 stored Lasham, UK 10Oct79; b/u Nov82
17600	707-321	75	(Dan-Air London)	N722PA G-AZTG stored Lasham, UK 14Nov78; b/u Apr82
17601	707-321	76	Turkish Authorities	N723PA YU-AGA N723PA N711UT 9Q-CRY TC-JCF stored Ankarra Turkey 25Jan80

BOEING 707/720

C/n	Series	Line No	Last known Operator/Owner	Previous Identities/fate (where known)
17602	707-321F	83	Air Charter Service	N724PA (G-AZOI) N724PA G-BAEL N2276X HK-2477X N2276X 9Q-CZK 9Q-CGO 9Q-CJW stored Kisangani, Zaire Jan92
17603	707-321	84	(General Air Service)	N725PA TC-JAJ G-41-274 G-BCRS (HS-BBB) 9G-ACD N725CA stored Miami, FL May80; b/u Jan84
17604	707-321	91	(Air Manila Intl)	N726PA RP-C7074 stored Manila, Philippines .82; b/u 26Dec85
17605	707-321	98	(Aerotal-Colombia)	N727PA G-AZWA N70798 CX-BML N70798 HK-2410X HK-2410 dbf 20Dec80 Bogota-El Dorado, Colombia
17606	707-321	107	Mariano Cua	N728PA N11RV N99WT (N728PA) RP-C911 Preserved Manila, Philippines 15Oct82 as "Club 707" nightclub
17607	707-321	121	(Jet Power)	N729PA TC-JAM N729JP N731JP N731 N731BA N731JP N427MA stored Miami, FL; b/u 11Jul83
17608	707-321	122	General Electric Corp	N730PA G-AYXR N37681 N707GE stored Mojave, CA, Apr93
17609	707-124	25	(Continental Air Lines)	N70773 w/o 01Jul65 Kansas City, MO
17610	707-124	37	(Pledger Thomas)	N70774 4X-BYA 009/4X-JYA N196CA HI-384 HI-384HA (N) dbr 12Dec81 Miami FL; b/u Dec87
17611	707-124	49	(Continental Air Lines)	N70775 w/o 22May62 nr Centerville, IA
17612	707-124	56	(Israel Defence Force/AF)	N70785 4X-BYD 008/4X-JYD 4X-BYD 001/4X-JYE stored Tel Aviv, Israel Nov95
17613	707-328	65	(Air France)	F-BHSA w/o 27Jul61 Hamburg, FRG
17614	707-328	81	(Air France)	F-BHSB stored Paris-Orly, France; b/u Jan76
17615	707-328	82	Israel Defence Force/AF	N74615 F-BHSC 4X-BYV 115/4X-JYV [ELINT conversion]
17616	707-328	93	(Air France)	F-BHSD stored Paris-Orly, France; b/u Mar76
17617	707-328	110	Israel Defence Force/AF	F-BHSE 4X-BYW 116/4X-JYW stored Tel Aviv, Israel as GIA
17618	707-328	111	Air France	F-BHSF Preserved Merville, France May77 as apprentice trainer
17619	707-328	126	(Israel Defence Force/AF)	N5093K F-BHSG CN-RMD 4X-BYN 119/4X-JYN stored Tel Aviv, Israel 91; b/u Nov93
17620	707-328	138	(Air France)	F-BHSH dbr Ajaccio, Corsica 07Sep76 by bomb
17621	707-328	139	(Air France)	F-BHSI stored Paris-Orly, France Jun76; b/u Sep77
17622	707-328	151	(Air France)	F-BHSJ stored Paris-Orly, France Apr76; b/u Sep77
17623	707-329	78	(SABENA)	OO-SJA Nose preserved Brussels, Belgium 15Apr82
17624	707-329	92	(SABENA)	OO-SJB w/o 15Feb61 Brussels, Belgium
17625	707-329	99	Israel Defence Force/AF	OO-SJC 4X-BYT 137/4X-JYT 140/4X-JYT 4X-BYT 140/4X-JYT [Tanker conversion]
17626	707-329	118	(Sobelair)	OO-SJD stored Belgium, Brussels 15Jan81; later b/u
17627	707-329	133	(SABENA)	OO-SJE dbf 15Feb78 Tenerife, Canary Islands
17628	707-123B	7	(Cyprus Airways)	N7501A 5B-DAM dbr Bahrain, UAE 19Aug79; b/u 79/80
17629	707-123	8	(American Airlines)	N7502A w/o 28Jan61 Montauk, NY
17630	707-123B	9	(American Airlines)	N7503A Wfs 10Sep77; b/u Oct77
17631	707-123B	10	Boeing MAC/USAF	N7504A 5B-DAL EL-AJW N2235W stored Davis-Monthan AFB, AZ 01May90
17632	707-123B	11	(Cyprus Airways)	N7505A G-BFMI 5B-DAK G-BFMI 5B-DAK stored Larnaca, Cyprus 31Oct83; later b/u
17633	707-123B	12	(American Airlines)	N7506A w/o 01Mar62 Jamaica Bay, NY
17634	707-123B	14	Coastal Corp	N7507A N707AR N960CC stored Miami, FL by Mar95
17635	707-123B	15	Boeing MAC/USAF	N7508A 5B-DAP EL-AJV stored Davis-Monthan AFB, AZ 31Aug90
17636	707-123B	16	Boeing MAC/USAF	N7509A stored Davis-Monthan AFB, AZ 02May83
17637	707-123F	17	(Aerocondor de Colombia)	N7510A D-ALAM N8418A N7510A HK-1818X HK-1818 stored Bogota, Colombia Apr80; later b/u
17638	707-123F	26	(Aerocondor de Colombia)	N7511A D-ALAL N8420A N7511A HK-1802X HK-1802 stored Barranquilla, Colombia Apr80; later b/u
17639	707-123B	30	Boeing MAC/USAF	N7512A N701PC stored Davis-Monthan AFB, AZ 04Aug87
17640	707-123B	31	Boeing MAC/USAF	N7513A 9G-ACN G-TJAB G-BHOX N62TA stored Davis-Monthan AFB AZ 02May83
17641	707-123	36	(American Airlines)	N7514A w/o 15Aug59 Calverton, NY
17642	707-123B	41	(Boeing Equipment Holding)	N7515A stored Kingman, AZ; b/u May85
17643	707-123B	42	(Aerocondor de Colombia)	N7516A HK-1942X HK-1942 stored Barranquilla, Colombia Apr80; later b/u
17644	707-123B	50	(ESS Jay AR Inc)	N7517A HZ-DAT N2143H stored San Antonio, TX Oct91; b/u May93
17645	707-123B	51	(Boeing MAC/USAF)	N7518A N702PC stored Davis-Monthan AFB, AZ 09Jun87; later b/u
17646	707-123B	52	Boeing MAC/USAF	N7519A PH-TVA N519GA (N29959) N519GA stored Davis-Monthan AFB AZ 08Apr83
17647	707-123B	53	(Excelair)	N7520A C-GQBG N777NW 5A-DHO N3951A stored Brussels, Belgium, b/u 31Aug84
17648	707-123B	63	(MRH Leasing Co)	N7521A N752TA stored Marana, AZ Apr82; later b/u
17649	707-123B	66	(Tiger Air)	N7522A N751TA stored Luton, UK b/u Jan82; fuselage used as cabin trainer by Monarch Airlines
17650	707-123B	67	(Quebecair)	N7523A C-GQBH dbr 19Feb79 St Lucia, Windward Islands
17651	707-123B	72	Boeing MAC/USAF	N7524A ST-AHG 9G-ACO G-TJAC G-BHOY N61TA stored Davis-Monthan AFB 05Oct83
17652	707-123B	77	Boeing MAC/USAF	N7525A N5038 stored Davis-Monthan AFB, AZ 22Jul83
17653	707-123		(American Airlines)	(N7526A) Allocated but later canx; not built
17654	707-123		(American Airlines)	(N7527A) Allocated but later canx; not built
17655	707-123		(American Airlines)	(N7528A) Allocated but later canx; not built
17656	707-123		(American Airlines)	(N7529A) Allocated but later canx; not built

BOEING 707/720

C/n	Series	Line No	Last known Operator/Owner	Previous Identities/fate (where known)
17657	707-123		(American Airlines)	(N7530A) Allocated but later canx; not built
17658	707-131F	18	(Omega Air)	N731TW F-BUZJ 9Q-CBD 9Q-CKP stored Shannon, Eire 04Aug84; b/u Nov86
17659	707-131	19	(Trans European Airways)	N732TW OO-TEC stored Brussels, Belgium 23Apr82; dbf Jun84
17660	707-131	21	(Ramacor AG)	N733TW stored Tel Aviv, Israel 06Nov71; b/u Jun77
17661	707-131	22	Rodman Aviation	N734TW PI-C7071 N61699 N16648 4X-AGT 4X-BYI .../4X-JYI N198CA stored Mojave, CA Oct81
17662	707-131	23	(Aeroamerica)	N735TW (N61699) N735T stored Boeing Field, WA 15Nov79; b/u Jun81
17663	707-131	24	(Rodman Aviation)	N736TW HS-VGC N194CA stored Mojave, CA May79; later b/u
17664	707-131	27	(Israel Aircraft Industries)	N737TW I-SAVA stored Tel Aviv, Israel Feb75; b/u May77
17665	707-131	28	(Trans European Airways)	N738TW 4X-ACU OO-TED stored Brussels, Belgium 14Sep85; b/u Sep87
17666	707-131	32	(Ramacor AG)	N739TW HS-VGA 4X-ACN OO-TEE B/u Tel Aviv, Israel Oct76
17667	707-131	34	Israel Defence Force/AF	N740TW (4X-JAD) 4X-BYD 008/4X-JYD 4X-BYD 008/4X-JYD Preserved Hatzerim AFB, Israel Jun83
17668	707-131	38	(Federal Aviation Admin)	N741TW PI-C7072 N16649 4X-AGU 4X-BYH 004/4X-JYH 4X-BYH 004/4X-JYH N195CA stored Atlantic City, NJ; b/u early82
17669	707-131	43	(Trans World Airlines)	N742TW dbr 06Nov67 Covington, KY
17670	707-131	46	(Trans World Airlines)	N743TW dbf 22Apr70 Indianapolis, IN
17671	707-131	48	(Lloyd Aereo Boliviano)	N744TW HB-IEG N730JP HK-1773 N730JP w/o 13Oct76 Santa Cruz, Bolivia
17672	707-131	55	(Charlotte Aircraft Corp)	N745TW N197CA stored Tel Aviv, Israel 28Nov71; b/u .72
17673	707-331	69	(Trans World Airlines)	N761TW dbr Las Vegas, NV 08May72 by bomb
17674	707-331	73	(British Midland Airways)	(N762TW) N701PA stored East Midlands Airport, UK; b/u Jun76
17675	707-331	74	(Caledonian Airlines)	(N763TW) N762TW (YN-BWL) N762TW stored Dar-es-Salaam, Tanzania Jul81; later b/u
17676	707-331	79	(Avn Traders Eng'g Ltd)	(N764TW) N763TW N763AB stored Stansted, UK 18Dec80; b/u Jul81
17677	707-331	80	(Monarch Aviation)	(N765TW) N702PA N702TA N702 N702PT stored Stansted, UK Feb76; b/u Mar80
17678	707-331	86	(Allen Aircraft Corp)	(N766TW) N764TW stored Kansas City, MO 19Dec78; b/u Jun80
17679	707-331	88	(Allen Aircraft Corp)	(N767TW) N765TW (N765AB) N765TW stored Kansas City, MO 07Mar79; b/u Jun80
17680	707-331	89	(Air Manila Intl)	(N768TW) N703PA N703 PI-C7073 S2-ABM RP-C7073 stored Manila, Philippines by Feb81; b/u 84
17681	707-331	103	(Allen Aircraft Corp)	(N769TW) N766TW stored Kansas City, MO 30Apr79; b/u Aug80
17682	707-331	104	(Avn Traders Eng'g Ltd)	(N770TW) N767TW N7667AB N767AB stored Stansted, UK 17Dec80; b/u May81
17683	707-331	116	(Aerotron Radio)	(N771TW) N704PA XV-NJD N9230Z stored Long Beach, CA 23Dec75; b/u Jun77
17684	707-331	117	(Allen Aircraft Corp)	(N772TW) N768TW stored Kansas City, MO 12Apr79; b/u May82
17685	707-331	123	(Trans World Airlines)	(N773TW) N769TW w/o 23Nov64 Rome-Fiumicino, Italy
17686	707-331	124	(Malaysian DCA)	(N774TW) N705PA OO-SJP 9Q-CMA N705PA Preserved Kelana Jaya Park, Kuala Lumpur, Malaysia Oct79; later b/u
17687	707-331	125	(Allen Aircraft Corp)	(N775TW) N770TW stored Kansas City, MO 31Oct78; b/u Jun80
17688	707-331	135	(Allen Aircraft Corp)	(N776TW) N771TW stored Kansas City, MO 30Apr79; b/u Jun80
17689	707-331F	136	(Jet Power)	(N778TW) N706PA N706TA N425MA stored Miami, FL Nov80; b/u Oct83
17690	707-331	137	(Allen Aircraft Corp)	(N779TW) N772TW (N772AB) N772TW stored Kansas City, MO 12Apr79; b/u Jun81
17691	707-227	45	(Braniff Airways)	(N707R) N7071 w/o 19Oct59 Arlington, WA
17692	707-227F	87	(Monarch Aviation)	(N707V) N7072 9Y-TDO (N64757) 9Y-TDO N811UT N3842X stored Miami, FL Aug83; b/u Jan84
17693	707-227	96	(ATASCO)	(N707W) N7073 9Y-TDR stored Tel Aviv, Israel 04Jun76; b/u 77
17694	707-227	97	(Sonico Corp)	(N707Y) N7074 9Y-TDP N64740 B/u Moses Lake, WA Feb81
17695	707-227	102	(British West Indian A/W)	(N707Z) N7075 9Y-TDQ stored Port-of-Spain, Trinidad 17Mar75; b/u 77
17696	707-138B	29	HRH Prince Bandar	N31239 VH-EBA CF-PWV C-FPWV (N112TA) N138TA N220AM N138MJ HZ-123 "17696" HZ-123 [Op by RSAF/1Sqdn]
17697	707-138B	39	Comtran International	VH-EBB N790SA D-ADAP N790SA TC-JBP TC-JBN N790SA N790FA (N90MJ) N790FA N138SR
17698	707-138B	44	(Canadian Pacific Airlines)	VH-EBC N791SA w/o 07Feb68 Vancouver, BC
17699	707-138B	54	(Sunnyside Holdings)	VH-EBD G-AVZZ N500JJ stored Paris-le Bourget, France 13Jun80; b/u Jul83
17700	707-138B	59	(Boeing MAC/USAF)	VH-EBE N793SA CF-PWW N793SA VP-BDE N793NA stored Davis-Monthan AFB AZ 24Apr83; b/u 03Apr93

BOEING 707/720

C/n	Series	Line No	Last known Operator/Owner	Previous Identities/fate (where known)
17701	707-138B	60	(FBA Inc)	VH-EBF N792SA D-ADAQ N792SA TC-JBP N792SA N792FA stored Marana, AZ; later b/u
17702	707-138B	64	New First City Houston Trust	VH-EBG G-AWDG N600JJ N707KS N707SK stored
17703	707-436	35	(Boeing Corp)	N31241 G-APFB stored Kingman, AZ 05Nov76; b/u Sep79
17704	707-436	101	(Boeing Corp)	N5088K G-APFC Tested to destruction Wichita, KS Jun75
17705	707-436	112	(Silver Jet Leasing)	N5091K G-APFD N888NW stored Fort Lauderdale, FL; b/u Jul86
17706	707-436	113	(BOAC)	N5092K G-APFE w/o 05Mar66 Mount Fuji, Japan
17707	707-436	127	(Boeing Corp)	G-APFF stored Boeing Field, WA; b/u May81
17708	707-436	128	(Avn Traders Eng'g Ltd)	N5094K G-APFG stored Stansted, UK 03Nov80; b/u Mar89
17709	707-436	144	(Boeing Corp)	G-APFH stored Wichita 11May75; b/u 77
17710	707-436	145	(Boeing Corp)	G-APFI stored Kingman, AZ 12Nov76; b/u Sep79
17711	707-436	163	Cosford Aerospace Museum	G-APFJ Preserved Cosford, UK 12Jun81
17712	707-436	164	(British Airways)	G-APFK w/o 17Mar77 Prestwick, UK
17713	707-436	169	Government of Uganda	G-APFL 9Q-CRW 5X-CAU (G-APFL) (N9149M) 5X-CAU stored Entebbe, Uganda Jan83
17714	707-436	170	(Boeing Corp)	G-APFM stored Kingman AZ 12Nov76; b/u Sep79
17715	707-436	171	(Boeing Corp)	G-APFN stored Kingman AZ 09Apr76; b/u Sep79
17716	707-436	175	(Boeing Corp)	G-APFO stored Kingman AZ 31Mar81; b/u Feb85
17717	707-436	176	(Franklin Institute)	G-APFP Preserved Philadelphia, PA 27May75; b/u Oct88
17718	707-430	90	(Pearl Air)	N31240 D-ABOB (N9986F) 9Q-CRT dbr Sana'a, Yemen Arab Republic 08Aug77; repaired
17719	707-430	106	(United African Airlines)	D-ABOC N64739 EI-BFN (N90498) 5A-CVA stored Tripoli, Libya Jun79; later b/u
17720	707-430	115	Lufthansa	D-ABOD "26000" D-ABOD Preserved Hamburg, Germany 30Nov75 as apprentice trainer
17721	707-430	162	(Liberia Overseas Airways)	D-ABOF 9G-ACK (G-BGFA) 3C-ABT N90498 EL-AJC stored Bournemouth-Hurn UK 14Jul81; b/u Aug83
17722	707-437	94	(Air India)	N5089K VT-DJI dbr 23Jan71 Bombay, India
17723	707-437	100	(Air India)	VT-DJJ dbr 22Jun82 Bombay, India
17724	707-437	105	(Air India)	VT-DJK stored Bombay, India 05Apr80; b/u 80/81
17725 to 17745 model 717-148; built as KC-135A and modified as follows:				
17725	KC-135E	T0195	USAF/55thWg	57-2589/OF [Has ability to be air-refuelled]
17726	KC-135A	T0196	USAF/93rdARS/340thARW	57-2590 stored Davis-Monthan AFB, AZ 03Sep92
17727	KC-135A	T0197	USAF/46thARS/305thARW	57-2591 stored Davis-Monthan AFB, AZ 19Apr93; for conversion to KC-135R for Turk Hava Kuvvetleri
17728	KC-135A	T0198	USAF/906thARS/43rdARW	57-2592 stored Davis-Monthan AFB, AZ 23Jun93; for conversion to KC-135R for Turk Hava Kuvvetleri
17729	KC-135R	T0199	USAF/166thARS/OH ANG	57-2593
17730	KC-135E	T0200	USAF/108thARS/IL ANG	57-2594
17731	KC-135E	T0201	USAF/147thARS/PA ANG	57-2595
17732	KC-135A	T0202	USAF/906thARS/43rdARW	57-2596 stored Davis-Monthan AFB, AZ 21Apr93
17733	KC-135R	T0203	USAF/153rdARS/MS ANG	57-2597
17734	KC-135E	T0204	USAF/336thARS/AFRes	57-2598
17735	KC-135R	T0205	USAF/AMC	57-2599
17736	KC-135E	T0206	USAF/116thARS/WA ANG	57-2600
17737	KC-135E	T0207	USAF/151stARS/TN ANG	57-2601
17738	KC-135E	T0208	USAF/150thARS/NJ ANG	57-2602
17739	KC-135E	T0209	USAF/336thARS/AFRes	57-2603
17740	KC-135E	T0210	USAF/146thARS/PA ANG	57-2604
17741	KC-135R	T0211	USAF/22ndARW	57-2605
17742	KC-135E	T0212	USAF/150thARS/NJ ANG	57-2606
17743	KC-135E	T0213	USAF/147thARS/PA ANG	57-2607
17744	KC-135E	T0214	USAF/147thARS/PA ANG	57-2608
17745	KC-135A	T0215	USAF/917thARS/96thWg	57-2609/DY stored Davis-Monthan AFB, AZ 20Jan93
17746 to 17875 model 717-148; built as KC-135A and modified as follows:				
17746	KC-135R	T0216	USAF/55thARS/97thAMW	58-0001
17747	KC-135A	T0217	(USAF/4130thSW)	58-0002 dbr 31Mar59 Killeen, TX
17748	KC-135E	T0218	USAF/108thARS/IL ANG	58-0003
17749	KC-135R	T0219	USAF/153rdARS/MS ANG	58-0004
17750	KC-135E	T0220	USAF/117thARS/KS ANG	58-0005
17751	KC-135E	T0221	USAF/191stARS/UT ANG	58-0006
17752	EC-135P	T0222	(USAF/6thACCS/1stTFW)	58-0007 dbf 02Jan80 Langley AFB, VA
17753	KC-135E	T0223	USAF/196thARS/CA ANG	58-0008
17754	KC-135R	T0224	USAF/126thARS/WI ANG	58-0009
17755	KC-135R	T0225	USAF/153rdARS/MS ANG	58-0010
17756	KC-135R(RT)	T0226	USAF/19thARW	58-0011 [Has ability to be air-refuelled]
17757	KC-135E	T0227	USAF/191stARS/UT ANG	58-0012
17758	KC-135E	T0228	USAF/63rdARS/AFRes	58-0013
17759	KC-135E	T0229	USAF/108thARS/IL ANG	58-0014
17760	KC-135R	T0230	USAF/74thARS/AFRes	58-0015
17761	KC-135R	T0231	USAF/22ndARW	58-0016
17762	KC-135E	T0232	USAF/146thARS/PA ANG	58-0017
17763	KC-135R(RT)	T0233	USAF/22ndARW	58-0018 [Has ability to be air-refuelled]
17764	EC-135P	T0234	USAF/6thACCS/1stFW	58-0019 stored Davis-Monthan AFB, AZ 12Feb92
17765	KC-135E	T0235	USAF/116thARS/WA ANG	58-0020
17766	KC-135R	T0236	USAF/126thARS/WI ANG	58-0021
17767	EC-135P	T0237	USAF/6thACCS/1stFW	58-0022/FF stored Davis-Monthan AFB, AZ 05Mar92
17768	KC-135R	T0238	USAF/136thARS/NY ANG	58-0023
17769	KC-135E	T0239	USAF/146thARS/PA ANG	58-0024
17770	KC-135A	T0240	USAF/93rdARS/398thOG	58-0025 stored Davis-Monthan AFB, AZ 04Aug93

BOEING 707/720

C/n	Series	Line No	Last known Operator/Owner	Previous Identities/fate (where known)	
17771	KC-135A	T0241	(USAF/22ndBW)	58-0026	w/o 17Jan68 Minot AFB, ND
17772	KC-135R	T0242	USAF/92ndARS/92ndARW	58-0027	
17773	KC-135A	T0243	USAF/46thARS/305thARW	58-0028	stored Davis-Monthan AFB, AZ 07Apr93
17774	KC-135A	T0244	USAF/7thARS/19thARW	58-0029	stored Davis-Monthan AFB, AZ 02Dec92
17775	KC-135R	T0245	USAF/106thARS/AL ANG	58-0030	
17776	KC-135A	T0246	(USAF/108thARS//IL ANG)	58-0031	w/o 19Mar82 nr Wonder Lake, IL
17777	KC-135E	T0247	USAF/150thARS/NJ ANG	58-0032	
17778	KC-135A	T0248	USAF/7thARS/19thARW	58-0033	stored Davis-Monthan AFB, AZ 09Jul92
17779	KC-135R	T0249	USAF/55thARS/97thAMW	58-0034	
17780	KC-135R	T0250	USAF/22ndARW	58-0035	
17781	KC-135R	T0251	USAF/22ndARW	58-0036	
17782	KC-135E	T0252	USAF/147thARS/PA ANG	58-0037	
17783	KC-135R	T0253	USAF/92ndARW	58-0038	
17784	KC-135Q	T0254	(USAF/306thBW)	58-0039	w/o 03Jun71 Torrejon AB, Spain
17785	KC-135E	T0255	USAF/150thARS/NJ ANG	58-0040	
17786	KC-135E	T0256	USAF/63rdARS/AFRes	58-0041	
17787	KC-135T	T0257	USAF/319thARW	58-0042	
17788	KC-135E	T0258	USAF/191stARS/UT ANG	58-0043	
17789	KC-135E	T0259	USAF/141stARS/NJ ANG	58-0044	
17790	KC-135T	T0260	USAF/92ndARW	58-0045	
17791	KC-135T	T0261	USAF/92ndARW	58-0046	
17792	KC-135T	T0262	USAF/319thARW	58-0047	
17793	KC-135A	T0263	(USAF/7thARS/7thBW)	58-0048	w/o 13Mar72 Carswell AFB, TX
17794	KC-135T	T0264	USAF/92ndARW	58-0049	
17795	KC-135T	T0265	USFA/92ndARW	58-0050	
17796	KC-135R	T0266	USAF/91stARS/43rdARG	58-0051	
17797	KC-135E	T0267	USAF/336thARS/AFRes	58-0052	
17798	KC-135E	T0268	USAF/314thARS/AFRes	58-0053	
17799	KC-135T	T0269	USAF/92ndARW	58-0054	
17800	KC-135T	T0270	USAF/92ndARW	58-0055	
17801	KC-135R	T0271	USAF/153rdARS/MS ANG	58-0056	
17802	KC-135E	T0272	USAF/108thARS/IL ANG	58-0057	
17803	KC-135E	T0273	USAF/314thARS/AFRes	58-0058	
17804	KC-135R	T0274	USAF/153rdARS/MS ANG	58-0059	
17805	KC-135T	T0275	USAF/92ndARW	58-0060	
17806	KC-135T	T0276	USAF/319thARW	58-0061	
17807	KC-135T	T0277	USAF/92ndARW	58-0062	
17808	KC-135R	T0278	USAF/42ndARS	58-0063	
17809	KC-135E	T0279	USAF/314thARS/AFRes	58-0064	
17810	KC-135T	T0280	USAF/319thARW	58-0065	
17811	KC-135R	T0281	USAF/465thARS/AFRes	58-0066	
17812	KC-135E	T0282	USAF/108thARS/IL ANG	58-0067	
17813	KC-135E	T0283	USAF/108thARS/IL ANG	58-0068	
17814	KC-135T	T0284	USAF/92ndARW	58-0069	
17815	GKC-135A	T0285	USAF/82ndTW	58-0070	Preserved Sheppard AFB, TX 15Oct92
17816	KC-135T	T0286	USAF/22ndARW	58-0071	
17817	KC-135T	T0287	USAF/92ndARW	58-0072	
17818	KC-135R	T0288	USAF/106thARS/AL ANG	58-0073	
17819	KC-135T	T0289	USAF/92ndARW	58-0074	
17820	KC-135R	T0290	USAF/72ndARS/AFRes	58-0075	
17821	KC-135R	T0291	USAF/74thARS/AFRes	58-0076	
17822	KC-135T	T0292	USAF/92ndARW	58-0077	
17823	KC-135E	T0293	USAF/150thARS/NJ ANG	58-0078	
17824	KC-135R	T0294	USAF/465thARS/AFRes	58-0079	
17825	KC-135E	T0295	USAF/191stARS/UT ANG	58-0080	
17826	KC-135A	T0296	USAF/71stARS/2ndWg	58-0081	stored Davis-Monthan AFB, AZ 16Oct92
17827	KC-135E	T0297	USAF/116thARS/WA ANG	58-0082	
17828	KC-135R	T0298	USAF/166thARS/OH ANG	58-0083	
17829	KC-135T	T0299	USAF/92ndARW	58-0084	
17830	KC-135E	T0300	USAF/336thARS/AFRes	58-0085	
17831	KC-135T	T0301	USAF/92ndARW	58-0086	
17832	KC-135E	T0302	USAF/150thARS/NJ ANG	58-0087	
17833	KC-135T	T0303	USAF/22ndARW	58-0088	
17834	KC-135T	T0304	USAF/22ndARW	58-0089	
17835	KC-135E	T0305	USAF/314thARS/AFRes	58-0090	
17836	KC-135A	T0306	USAF/519thARS/380thARW	58-0091	stored Davis-Monthan AFB, AZ 18Aug93
17837	KC-135R	T0307	USAF/133rdARS/NH ANG	58-0092	
17838	KC-135R	T0308	USAF/319thARW	58-0093	
17839	KC-135T	T0309	USAF/92ndARW	58-0094	
17840	KC-135T	T0310	USAF/22ndARW	58-0095	
17841	KC-135E	T0311	USAF/314thARS/AFRes	58-0096	
17842	KC-135A	T0312	USAF/7thARS/19thARW	58-0097	stored Davis-Monthan AFB, AZ 08Sep92
17843	KC-135R	T0313	USAF/133rdARS/NH ANG	58-0098	
17844	KC-135T	T0314	USAF/22ndARW	58-0099	
17845	KC-135R	T0315	USAF/91stARS/43rdARG	58-0100	
17846	KC-135A	T0316	(USAF/93rdBW)	58-0101	w/o 28Apr77 Beale AFB, CA
17847	KC-135R	T0317	USAF/74thARS/AFRes	58-0102	
17848	KC-135T	T0318	USAF/AMC	58-0103	
17849	KC-135R	T0319	USAF/136thARS/NY ANG	58-0104	
17850	KC-135A	T0320	USAF/906thARS/43rdARW	58-0105	stored Davis-Monthan AFB, AZ 23Aug93
17851	KC-135R	T0321	USAF/22ndARW	58-0106	

BOEING 707/720

C/n	Series	Line No	Last known Operator/Owner	Previous Identities/fate (where known)
17852	KC-135E	T0322	USAF/191stARS/UT ANG	58-0107
17853	KC-135E	T0323	USAF/314thARS/AFRes	58-0108
17854	KC-135R	T0324	USAF/153rdARS/MS ANG	58-0109
17855	KC-135A	T0325	USAF/305thARW	58-0110 stored Davis-Monthan AFB, AZ 27Sep93
17856	KC-135E	T0326	USAF/141stARS/NJ ANG	58-0111
17857	KC-135T	T0327	USAF/92ndARW	58-0112
17858	KC-135R	T0328	USAF/19thARW	58-0113
17859	KC-135R	T0329	USAF/92ndARW	58-0114
17860	KC-135E	T0330	USAF/150thARS/NJ ANG	58-0115
17861	KC-135E	T0331	USAF/197thARS/AZ ANG	58-0116
17862	KC-135T	T0332	USAF/92ndARW	58-0117
17863	KC-135R	T0333	USAF/22ndARW	58-0118
17864	KC-135R	T0334	USAF/319thARW	58-0119
17865	KC-135R	T0335	USAF/55thARS/97thAMW	58-0120
17866	KC-135R	T0336	USAF/92ndARW	58-0121
17867	KC-135R	T0337	USAF/168thARS/AK ANG	58-0122
17868	KC-135R	T0338	USAF/19thARW	58-0123
17869	KC-135R(RT)	T0339	USAF/22ndARW	58-0124 [Has ability to be air-refuelled]
17870	KC-135T	T0340	USAF/92ndARW	58-0125
17871	KC-135R(RT)	T0341	USAF/22ndARW	58-0126 [Has ability to be air-refuelled]
17872	KC-135A	T0342	(USAF/93rdBW)	58-0127 w/o 19Sep79 Castle AFB, CA
17873	KC-135R	T0343	USAF/22ndARW	58-0128
17874	KC-135T	T0344	USAF/AMC	58-0129
17875	KC-135R	T0345	USAF/126thARS/WI ANG	58-0130
17876 to 17902 model 717-148; allocated as KC-135A:				
17876	KC-135A		(USAF)	(58-0131) Allocated but later canx, not built
17877	KC-135A		(USAF)	(58-0132) Allocated but later canx, not built
17878	KC-135A		(USAF)	(58-0133) Allocated but later canx, not built
17879	KC-135A		(USAF)	(58-0134) Allocated but later canx, not built
17880	KC-135A		(USAF)	(58-0135) Allocated but later canx, not built
17881	KC-135A		(USAF)	(58-0136) Allocated but later canx, not built
17882	KC-135A		(USAF)	(58-0137) Allocated but later canx, not built
17883	KC-135A		(USAF)	(58-0138) Allocated but later canx, not built
17884	KC-135A		(USAF)	(58-0139) Allocated but later canx, not built
17885	KC-135A		(USAF)	(58-0140) Allocated but later canx, not built
17886	KC-135A		(USAF)	(58-0141) Allocated but later canx, not built
17887	KC-135A		(USAF)	(58-0142) Allocated but later canx, not built
17888	KC-135A		(USAF)	(58-0143) Allocated but later canx, not built
17889	KC-135A		(USAF)	(58-0144) Allocated but later canx, not built
17890	KC-135A		(USAF)	(58-0145) Allocated but later canx, not built
17891	KC-135A		(USAF)	(58-0146) Allocated but later canx, not built
17892	KC-135A		(USAF)	(58-0147) Allocated but later canx, not built
17893	KC-135A		(USAF)	(58-0148) Allocated but later canx, not built
17894	KC-135A		(USAF)	(58-0149) Allocated but later canx, not built
17895	KC-135A		(USAF)	(58-0150) Allocated but later canx, not built
17896	KC-135A		(USAF)	(58-0151) Allocated but later canx, not built
17897	KC-135A		(USAF)	(58-0152) Allocated but later canx, not built
17898	KC-135A		(USAF)	(58-0153) Allocated but later canx, not built
17899	KC-135A		(USAF)	(58-0154) Allocated but later canx, not built
17900	KC-135A		(USAF)	(58-0155) Allocated but later canx, not built
17901	KC-135A		(USAF)	(58-0156) Allocated but later canx, not built
17902	KC-135A		(USAF)	(58-0157) Allocated but later canx, not built
17903	707-139B	108	(Boeing MAC/USAF)	(CU-...) N74613 N778PA N74613 N778PA TC-JBE N778PA N778 N778PA S2-AAL 9G-ACJ G-TJAA N778PA stored Davis-Monthan AFB, AZ Apr86; later b/u
17904	707-139	119	(Pan American World A/W)	(CU-...) N74614 N779PA dbr 07Apr64 New York-JFK, NY
17905	707-441	114	(BCF Aviation)	N5090K PP-VJA N59RD (9Q-...) stored Houston, TX Jan86; b/u Jul90
17906	707-441	129	(VARIG)	PP-VJB w/o 27Nov62 nr Lima, Peru
17907	720-022	85	(Aeroamerica)	N7201U stored Luton, UK 19Nov79; b/u 13Jul82
17908	720-022	95	(Aviation Sales Co)	N7202U stored Minneapolis/St Paul, MN 73; b/u Dec76
17909	720-022	109	(Aviation Sales Co)	N7203U stored Denver, CO 73; b/u Dec76
17910	720-022	130	(Aviation Sales Co)	N7204U stored Minneapolis/St Paul, MN 73; b/u Dec76
17911	720-022	131	(Aviation Sales Co)	N7205U stored Denver, CO 73; b/u Dec76
17912	720-022	132	(Aviation Sales Co)	N7206U stored Minneapolis/St Paul, MN 73; b/u Dec76
17913	720-022	141	(Marshall M.Landy)	N7207U stored Miami, FL 09Jul79; b/u Jun83
17914	720-022	142	(Aviation Sales Co)	N7208U stored Denver, CO 73; b/u Dec76
17915	720-022	146	(Aeromar Airlines)	N7209U N720CC HI-372 stored Miami, FL Mar84; b/u 30Jun87
17916	720-022	147	(Aviation Sales Co)	N7210U stored Denver, CO 73; b/u Dec76
17917	720-022	148	Belize Airways	N7211U VP-HCP stored Miami, FL Feb80; b/u Feb83
17918	707-328	152	(Air France)	N5095K F-BHSK stored Paris-Orly, France Jan77; b/u Sep77
17919	707-328	153	Air France	F-BHSL Preserved Vilgenis, France Apr77 as apprentice trainer
17920	707-328	159	(Air France)	F-BHSM w/o 03Jun62 Paris-Orly, France
17921	707-328	160	(Charlotte Aircraft Corp)	F-BHSN OO-SBR N90287 stored Stansted, UK Feb82; later b/u
17922	707-328	161	Israel Defence Force/AF	F-BHSO TU-TBY F-BHSO 4X-BYX 117/4X-JYX
17923	707-328	167	(Charlotte Aircraft Corp)	F-BHSP Wfs & stored, b/u Maxton, NC Mar78

BOEING 707/720

C/n	Series	Line No	Last known Operator/Owner	Previous Identities/fate (where known)
17924	707-328	168	(Air France)	F-BHSQ TU-TDC F-BHSQ stored Paris-Orly, France Feb77; b/u Apr77
17925 to 17927 model 707-153B; built as VC-137A and modified as follows:				
17925	C-137B	33	USAF/1stALS/89thAW	58-6970 stored Andrews AFB, MD Jun93
17926	C-137B	40	USAF/89thAW	58-6971 stored Andrews AFB, MD Jan96
17927	C-137B	47	USAF/89thAW	58-6972 stored Andrews AFB, MD Jan96
17928	707-344	134	(Columbia Pictures)	ZS-CKC ZS-SAA CC-CGM ZS-SAA CC-CGM HP-855 N90651 Destroyed in film work
17929	707-344	154	Hang Khong Vietnam	ZS-CKD ZS-SAB EI-BFU VN-A304 stored Ho Chi Minh City, Vietnam Mar80
17930	707-344	155	(Air Region)	ZS-CKE ZS-SAC LX-LGW OO-SBW 9Q-CZF stored Kisangani, Zaire 84; later b/u
17931 to 18011 model 717-148; built as KC-135A and modified as follows:				
17931	KC-135A	T0346	(USAF/93rdBW)	59-1443 dbr 27Aug85 Beale AFB, CA
17932	KC-135R	T0347	USAF/145thARS/OH ANG	59-1444
17933	KC-135E	T0348	USAF/166thARS/WA ANG	59-1445
17934	KC-135R	T0349	USAF/153rdARS/MS ANG	59-1446
17935	KC-135E	T0350	USAF/63rdARS/AFRes	59-1447
17936	KC-135E	T0351	USAF/196thARS/CA ANG	59-1448
17937	KC-135A	T0352	USAF/305thARW	59-1449 stored Davis-Monthan AFB, AZ 27Aug93
17938	KC-135E	T0353	USAF/196thARS/CA ANG	59-1450
17939	KC-135E	T0354	USAF/63rdARS/AFRes	59-1451
17940	KC-135E	T0355	USAF/116thARS/WA ANG	59-1452
17941	KC-135R	T0356	USAF/166thARS/OH ANG	59-1453
17942	KC-135A	T0357	USAF/906thARS/43rdARW	59-1454 stored Davis-Monthan AFB, AZ 01Sep93
17943	KC-135R	T0358	USAF/153rdARS/MS ANG	59-1455
17944	KC-135E	T0359	USAF/150thARS/NJ ANG	59-1456
17945	KC-135E	T0360	USAF/147thARS/PA ANG	59-1457
17946	KC-135R	T0361	USAF/166thARS/OH ANG	59-1458
17947	KC-135R	T0362	USAF/55thARS/97thAMW	59-1459
17948	KC-135T	T0363	USAF/92ndARW	59-1460
17949	KC-135R	T0364	USAF/168thARS/AK ANG	59-1461
17950	KC-135T	T0365	USAF/22ndARW	59-1462
17951	KC-135R	T0366	USAF/173rdARS/NE ANG	59-1463
17952	KC-135T	T0367	USAF/92ndARW	59-1464
17953	KC-135R	T0368	(USAF/55thSRW)	59-1465 w/o 17Jul67 Offutt AFB, NE
17954	KC-135R	T0369	USAF/319thARW	59-1466
17955	KC-135T	T0370	USAF/92ndARW	59-1467
17956	KC-135T	T0371	USAF/92ndARW	59-1468
17957	KC-135R	T0372	USAF/92ndARW	59-1469
17958	KC-135T	T0373	USAF/92ndARW	59-1470
17959	KC-135T	T0374	USAF/92ndARW	59-1471
17960	KC-135R	T0375	USAF/203rdARS/HI ANG	59-1472
17961	KC-135E	T0376	USAF/191stARS/UT ANG	59-1473
17962	KC-135T	T0377	USAF/92ndARW	59-1474
17963	KC-135R	T0378	USAF/91stARS/43rdARG	59-1475
17964	KC-135R	T0379	USAF/55thARS/97thAMW	59-1476
17965	KC-135E	T0380	USAF/63rdARS/AFRes	59-1477
17966	KC-135R	T0381	USAF/153rdARS/MS ANG	59-1478
17967	KC-135E	T0382	USAF/146thARS/PA ANG	59-1479
17968	KC-135T	T0383	USAF/AMC	59-1480
17969	KC-135A	T0384	NASA/Johnson Space Center	59-1481 N98 53-1481 NASA930 / N930NA
17970	KC-135R	T0385	USAF/351stARS/100thARW	59-1482/D
17971	KC-135R	T0386	USAF/166thARS/OH ANG	59-1483
17972	KC-135E	T0387	USAF/147thARS/PA ANG	59-1484
17973	KC-135E	T0388	USAF/150thARS/NJ ANG	59-1485
17974	KC-135R	T0389	USAF/22ndARW	59-1486
17975	KC-135E	T0390	USAF/108thARS/IL ANG	59-1487
17976	KC-135R	T0391	USAF/909thARS/18thWg	59-1488/ZZ
17977	KC-135E	T0392	USAF/191stARS/UT ANG	59-1489
17978	KC-135T	T0393	USAF/AMC	59-1490
17979	RC-135S	T0394	(USAF/6thSW)	59-1491 w/o 13Jan69 Shemya AFB, AK
17980	KC-135R	T0395	USAF/92ndARW	59-1492
17981	KC-135E	T0396	USAF/132ndARS/ME ANG	59-1493
17982	KC-135E	T0397	(USAF/133rdARS/NH ANG)	59-1494 dbf 11Jan90 Pease AFB, NH
17983	KC-135R	T0398	USAF/173rdARS/NE ANG	59-1495
17984	KC-135E	T0399	USAF/146thARS/PA ANG	59-1496
17985	KC-135E	T0400	USAF/150thARS/NJ ANG	59-1497
17986	KC-135R	T0401	USAF/366thWg	59-1498/MO
17987	KC-135E	T0402	USAF/196thARS/CA ANG	59-1499
17988	KC-135R	T0403	USAF/19thARW	59-1500
17989	KC-135R	T0404	USAF/22ndARW	59-1501
17990	KC-135R	T0405	USAF/19thARW	59-1502
17991	KC-135E	T0406	USAF/141stARS/NJ ANG	59-1503
17992	KC-135T	T0407	USAF/22ndARW	59-1504
17993	KC-135E	T0408	USAF/196thARS/CA ANG	59-1505
17994	KC-135E	T0409	USAF/147thARS/PA ANG	59-1506
17995	KC-135R	T0410	USAF/22ndARW	59-1507
17996	KC-135R	T0411	USAF/92ndARW	59-1508
17997	KC-135E	T0412	USAF/196thARS/CA ANG	59-1509
17998	KC-135T	T0413	USAF/22ndARW	59-1510

BOEING 707/720

C/n	Series	Line No	Last known Operator/Owner	Previous Identities/fate (where known)
17999	KC-135R	T0414	USAF/19thARW	59-1511
18000	KC-135T	T0415	USAF/92ndARW	59-1512
18001	KC-135T	T0416	USAF/92ndARW	59-1513
18002	KC-135E(RT)	T0417	USAF/55thWg	59-1514/OF [Has ability to be air-refuelled]
18003	KC-135R	T0418	USAF/22ndARW	59-1515
18004	KC-135E	T0419	USAF/196thARS/CA ANG	59-1516
18005	KC-135R	T0420	USAF/909thARS/18thWg	59-1517/ZZ
18006	EC-135K	T0421	USAF/89thAW	59-1518 N96 59-1518
18007	KC-135E	T0422	USAF/146thARS/PA ANG	59-1519
18008	KC-135T	T0423	USAF/AMC	59-1520
18009	KC-135R	T0424	USAF/168thARS/AK ANG	59-1521
18010	KC-135R	T0425	USAF/136thARS/NY ANG	59-1522
18011	KC-135T	T0426	USAF/92ndARW	59-1523
18012	707-124	57	Ben Gurion A/P Authority	N74612 (4X-ACN) (4X-JAA) 4X-BYA 006/4X-JYA 4X-BYA 006/4X-JYA 4X-BYA stored Tel Aviv, Israel Sep83; derelict Sep89
18013	720-023B	120	(Israel Aircraft Industries)	N7527A G-BCBB 60-SAU G-BCBB C9-ARG G-BCBB 4R-ACS G-BCBB 4X-BMB stored Tel Aviv, Israel 02Nov84; b/u Nov85
18014	720-023B	143	(Boeing MAC/USAF)	N7528A G-BCBA P2-ANG G-BCBA P2-ANG G-BCBA 4X-BMA N341A stored Davis-Monthan AFB, AZ 28Jan86; b/u Jun91
18015	720-023B	149	(Somali Airlines)	N7529A 60-SAW stored Mogadishu, Somalia by Aug83; later b/u
18016	720-023B	150	(Boeing MAC/USAF)	N7530A A6-HHR N7530A A6-HHR 70-ACP N720AC stored Davis-Monthan AFB, AZ 18Oct85; later b/u
18017	720-023B	156	(Middle East Airlines)	N7531A OD-AFP dbr Beirut, Lebanon 13Jun82 by shelling
18018	720-023B	157	(Middle East Airlines)	N7532A OD-AFR dbr Beirut, Lebanon 21Aug81 by bomb
18019	720-023B	158	(Ten Miles High Club)	N7533A OD-AFS N7533A N18KM stored Long Beach, CA Jul86; later b/u
18020	720-023B	165	(Middle East Airlines)	N7534A OD-AFT w/o 01Jan76 nr Al Qaysumah, Saudi Arabia
18021	720-023B	173	Pratt & Whitney Canada	N7535A OD-AGB C-FWXI stored Mojave, CA Jan96
18022	720-023B	174	Boeing MAC/USAF	N7536A N1R (N81R) N1R stored Davis-Monthan AFB, AZ 22Apr83
18023	720-023B	166	(Med-Air)	N7537A N587A HK-1973 stored Miami, FL 18Apr80; b/u Mar81
18024	720-023B	177	Pratt & Whitney Canada	N7538A OD-AFQ C-FETB [engine development aircraft]
18025	720-023B	180	(Middle East Airlines)	N7539A OD-AFZ stored Beirut, Lebanon; b/u Sep94
18026	720-023B	181	(Middle East Airlines)	N7540A OD-AFW dbr Beirut, Lebanon 16Jun82 by shelling
18027	720-023B	189	Pratt & Whitney Canada	N7541A OD-AFM C-FWXL stored Mojave, CA Jan96; later b/u
18028	720-023B	193	(Aerocondor de Colombia)	N7542A HK-1974 stored Barranquilla, Colombia Apr80; later b/u
18029	720-023B	194	(Middle East Airlines)	N7543A OD-AFU dbr Beirut, Lebanon 16Jun82 by shelling
18030	720-023B	195	Omega Air	N7544A OD-AFN EL-AKD stored Shannon, Eire 08May91; dbf Jan96 by Air Rianta Fire Service
18031	720-023B	198	(Somali Airlines)	N7545A 60-SAX stored Mogadishu, Somalia by Aug83; later b/u
18032	720-023B	199	(Alyemda Yemen Airlines)	N7546A 70-ABQ stored Aden, South Yemen by 16Nov85; later b/u
18033	720-023B	206	(Boeing MAC/USAF)	N7547A N780PA N780EC HC-BDP/FAE8033 N720BG stored Davis-Monthan AFB, AZ 15Ovt85; later b/u
18034	720-023B	207	(Middle East Airlines)	N7548A OD-AFL dbr Beirut, Lebanon 21Aug85 after shelling
18035	720-023B	214	(Middle East Airlines)	N7549A OD-AFO dbr Beirut, Lebanon Jun83 by shelling
18036	720-023B	215	(Comtran International)	N7550A N781PA HC-AZP/FAE8036 stored Marana, AZ 28Jul86; b/u May88
18037	720-023B	220	(Boeing MAC/USAF)	N7551A N782PA HC-AZQ/FAE8037 N782PA stored Davis-Monthan AFB, AZ 01Oct84; later b/u
18038 to 18040 model 717-148; allocated as VC-137A:				
18038	VC-137A		(USAF)	Allocated but later canx, not built
18039	VC-137A		(USAF)	Allocated but later canx, not built
18040	VC-137A		(USAF)	Allocated but later canx, not built
18041	720-048	172	(Aeroamerica)	EI-ALA N7083 EI-ALA LN-TUU EI-ALA N734T N1776Q stored Boeing Field, WA 17Jul78; b/u 83
18042	720-048	182	(Aeroamerica)	EI-ALB N7081 N303AS stored Boeing Field, WA Jul76; b/u 10Sep80
18043	720-048	188	Fontshi Aviation Service	EI-ALC LN-TUV EI-ALC OO-TEB N8790R 9Q-CFT stored Mbuji-Maji, Zaire
18044	720-022	178	(United States Global)	N7212U HP-685 N7212U N37777 "N011JS" N28JS N37777 w/o 22Apr76 Barranquilla, Colombia
18045	720-022	179	(Belize Airways)	N7213U VP-HCO stored Miami, FL 11Dec79; b/u Jan83
18046	720-022	183	(Belize Airways)	N7214U VP-HCM stored Miami, FL 10Jan80; b/u Mar83
18047	720-022	184	(Aviation Sales Co)	N7215U stored Denver, CO 72; b/u Dec76
18048	720-022	185	(Hong Kong Government)	N7216U Impounded Hong Kong Dec79; b/u 81
18049	720-022	186	(Hispanolia Airways)	N7217U N304S N421MA HI-401 stored Puerto Plata, Dominican Republic Aug85; later b/u
18050	720-022	191	(Onyx Aviation)	N7218U stored Miami, FL Apr77; b/u Dec83
18051	707-123B		(American Airlines)	Allocated but later canx, not built
18052	707-123B		(American Airlines)	Allocated but later canx, not built
18053	707-123B		(American Airlines)	Allocated but later canx, not built

BOEING 707/720

C/n	Series	Line No	Last known Operator/Owner	Previous Identities/fate (where known)
18054	707-123B	140	Omega Air	N7526A G-BGCT 5B-DAO YN-CCN stored Shannon, Eire 12Jun91
18055	707-437	200	(Air India)	VT-DMN w/o 23Jan66 Mont Blanc, France
18056	707-430F	192	(Israel Aircraft Industries)	D-ABOG N9985F (G-BGFB) 3C-ABH stored Tel Aviv, Israel Mar84; dbf 06Mar89
18057	720-030B	190	(Aviation Sales Co)	D-ABOH N783PA HK-677 stored St Petersburg, FL; b/u 22May80
18058	720-030B	202	(Lufthansa)	D-ABOK w/o 04Dec61 Eberstein, FRG
18059	720-030B	203	(Boeing MAC/USAF)	D-ABOL N784PA HK-676 N3831X stored Davis-Monthan AFB, AZ 18Aug83; b/u mid-93
18060	720-030B	210	(Aerotal Colombia)	D-ABOM N785PA YA-HBA N3746E HK-2558X HK-2558 stored Miami, FL 11Jul83; b/u 84
18061	720-047B	197	(AVIANCA)	N93141 HK-723 dbr Mexico City, Mexico 20Sep76; b/u Mar78
18062	720-047B	204	(Pakistan Intl Airlines)	N93142 AP-AXQ stored Karachi, Pakistan; b/u 74
18063	720-047B	213	AAR Allen Aircraft Corp	N93143 9H-AAK N110DS stored Marana, AZ Apr88; later Davis-Monthan, AZ 10Aug89
18064	720-027	187	(Airline Training Institute)	N7076 N736T stored Boeing Field, WA Apr80; b/u 83
18065	720-027	196	(Lisa Eisenberg)	N7077 N734T "26000" N734T stored Boeing Field, WA May81; later b/u
18066	720-027	208	(NASA)	N7078 N113 N23 N2697V N833NA dbr 01Dec84 Edwards AFB, CA
18067	707-138B	201	Euro Air Financing	N93134 VH-EBH 9Y-TDC VR-CAN stored Marana, AZ 79
18068	707-138B	227	(Boeing MAC/USAF)	VH-EBI N105BN OE-IRA OE-URA SU-FAB N245AC N458AC stored Davis-Monthan AFB, AZ 30Jun86; later b/u
18069	707-138B	228	Misr Air Cargo	N93135 VH-EBJ N106BN OE-INA OE-UNA SU-FAA stored Cairo, Egypt 86
18070	707-458	205	(El Al Israel Airlines)	4X-ATA stored Tel Aviv, Israel; b/u Jul84
18071	707-458	216	Boeing Operations Intl	4X-ATB N32824 4X-ATB N130KR Preserved Berlin-Tegel, FRG 21Nov86
18072	720-022	252	S A de Carga Expressa	N7219U (N7219) N7219U HI-415 XA-SDL
18073	720-022	253	George T. Baker Avn School	N7220U OO-VGM (TF-VVC) OO-VGM Preserved Miami, FL 12Dec80
18074	720-022	259	(Belize Airways)	N7221U VP-HCN stored Miami, FL 13Jun79; b/u Mar83
18075	720-022	260	(Eagle Air)	N7222U TF-VVB stored Keflavik, Iceland late75; later b/u
18076	720-022	261	(Belize Airways)	N7223U VP-HCQ stored Miami, FL Feb80; b/u Apr83
18077	720-022	265	(Boeing MAC/USAF)	N7224U stored Davis-Monthan, AFB, AZ 20Nov86; later b/u
18078	720-022	267	(Air Charter Service)	N7225U 9Q-CTM stored Kinshasa, Zaire; b/u 91
18079	720-022	278	(Aviation Sales Co)	N7226U stored Minneapolis-St Paul, MN 72; b/u Dec76
18080	720-022	284	(Caledonian Airlines)	N7227U (HP-679) N7227U N62215 stored Miami, FL; b/u 88
18081	720-022	297	CAAC	N7228U stored Beijing, PRC Dec84
18082	720-022F	298	Government of India	N7229U TF-VVA (TF-VLB) N417MA N419MA stored Madras, India 78
18083	707-321	209	(Jet Power)	N757PA G-AYVE (N757PA) N423MA B/u Miami, FL Jul83
18084	707-321	212	Government of Benin	N758PA G-AYRZ VP-BDG C6-BDG N433MA N707HD TY-AAM TY-BBW stored Ostend, Belgium 21May89
18085	707-321	217	(D.McEvaddy)	N759PA G-AYAG G-41-372 VP-BDF (C6-BDG) (N435MA) VP-BDF stored Dublin, Eire Sug75; b/u Jun84
18086	720-59B	245	(Leaseway Intl)	HK-724 N4451B stored Miami, FL Jul83; later b/u
18087	720-59B	249	(AVIANCA)	HK-725 dbr 27Jan80 Quito, Ecuador
18088 to 18143 model 717-148; built as KC-135A and modified as follows:				
18088	KC-135R	T0429	USAF/909thARS/18thWg	60-0313/ZZ
18089	KC-135R	T0428	USAF/74thARS/AFRes	60-0314
18090	KC-135R	T0435	USAF/126thARS/WI ANG	60-0315
18091	KC-135E	T0430	USAF/116thARS/WA ANG	60-0316
18092	KC-135A	T0431	(USAF/379thBW)	60-0317 w/o 11Oct88 Wurtsmith AFB, MI
18093	KC-135R	T0432	USAF/203rdARS/HI ANG	60-0318
18094	KC-135R	T0433	USAF/19thARW	60-0319
18095	KC-135R	T0434	USAF/319thARW	60-0320
18096	KC-135R	T0441	USAF/319thARW	60-0321
18097	KC-135R	T0436	USAF/72ndARS/AFRes	60-0322
18098	KC-135R	T0437	USAF/203rdARS/HI ANG	60-0323
18099	KC-135R	T0438	USAF/319thARW	60-0324
18100	KC-135A	T0439	USAF/93rdARS/398thOG	60-0325 stored Davis-Monthan AFB, AZ 22Sep93
18101	KC-135A	T0440	USAF/917thARS/96thWg	60-0326/DY stored Davis-Monthan AFB, AZ 02Sep93
18102	KC-135E	T0447	USAF/191stARS/UT ANG	60-0327
18103	KC-135R	T0442	USAF/92ndARW	60-0328
18104	KC-135R	T0443	USAF/203rdARS/HI ANG	60-0329
18105	KC-135A	T0444	(USAF/340thARW)	60-0330 w/o 13Feb87 Altus AFB, OK
18106	KC-135R	T0445	USAF/55thARS/97thAMW	60-0331
18107	KC-135R	T0446	USAF/319thARW	60-0332
18108	KC-135R	T0427	USAF/55thARS/97thAMW	60-0333
18109	KC-135R	T0448	USAF/168thARS/AK ANG	60-0334
18110	KC-135T	T0449	USAF/22ndARW	60-0335
18111	KC-135T	T0450	USAF/92ndARW	60-0336
18112	KC-135T	T0451	USAF/92ndARW	60-0337
18113	KC-135Q	T0452	(USAF/380thBW)	60-0338 dbf 08Feb80 Plattsburg AFB, NY
18114	KC-135T	T0453	USAF/22ndARW	60-0339

BOEING 707/720

C/n	Series	Line No	Last known Operator/Owner	Previous Identities/fate (where known)
18115	KC-135A	T0454	(USAF/462ndSAW)	60-0340 w/o 08Jul64 Death Valley, CA
18116	KC-135R	T0455	USAF/145thARS/OH ANG	60-0341
18117	KC-135T	T0456	USAF/92ndARW	60-0342
18118	KC-135T	T0457	USAF/319thARW	60-0343
18119	KC-135T	T0458	USAF/22ndARW	60-0344
18120	KC-135T	T0459	USAF/92ndARW	60-0345
18121	KC-135T	T0460	USAF/92ndARW	60-0346
18122	KC-135R	T0461	USAF/166thARS/OH ANG	60-0347
18123	KC-135R	T0462	USAF/91stARS/43rdARG	60-0348
18124	KC-135R	T0463	USAF/916thARW	60-0349
18125	KC-135R	T0464	USAF/91stARS/43rdARG	60-0350
18126	KC-135R	T0465	USAF/91stARS/43rdARG	60-0351
18127	KC-135A	T0466	(USAF/28thBW)	60-0352 w/o 10Sep62 Mount Kit Carson, WA
18128	KC-135R	T0467	USAF/319thARW	60-0353
18129	KC-135A	T0468	(USAF/380thBW)	60-0354 w/o 07Dec75 Eielson AFB, AK
18130	KC-135R	T0469	USAF/91stARS/43rdARG	60-0355
18131	KC-135R(RT)	T0470	USAF/22ndARW	60-0356 [Has ability to be air-refuelled]
18132	KC-135R(RT)	T0471	USAF/22ndARW	60-0357 [Has ability to be air-refuelled]
18133	KC-135R	T0472	USAF/136thARS/NY ANG	60-0358
18134	KC-135R	T0473	USAF/74thARS/AFRes	60-0359
18135	KC-135R	T0474	USAF/909thARS/18thWg	60-0360/ZZ
18136	KC-135A	T0475	(USAF/92ndARW)	60-0361 w/o 13Mar87 Fairchild AFB, WA
18137	KC-135R(RT)	T0476	USAF/22ndARW	60-0362 [Has ability to be air-refuelled]
18138	KC-135R	T0477	USAF/72ndARS/AFRes	60-0363
18139	KC-135R(RT)	T0478	USAF/74thARS/AFRes	60-0364 [Has ability to be air-refuelled]
18140	KC-135R	T0484	USAF/22ndARS/366thWg	60-0365/MO
18141	KC-135R	T0480	USAF/19thARW	60-0366
18142	KC-135R	T0481	USAF/...thARS/OH ANG	60-0367
18143	KC-135A	T0482	(USAF/410thBW)	60-0368 w/o 06Feb76 Torrejon AB, Spain

18144 to 18153 model 717-157; built as C-135A and modified as follows:

C/n	Series	Line No	Last known Operator/Owner	Previous Identities/fate (where known)
18144	GNC-135A	C3001	(USAF/Chanute TTC)	60-0369 Preserved Chanute AFB, IL 09Jun76; b/u Oct91
18145	NC-135A	C3002	(USAF/4949thTW)	60-0370 stored Davis-Monthan AFB, AZ 30Jun77; later b/u
18146	NC-135A	C3003	USAF/Rescue Museum	60-0371 Preserved Kirtland AFB, NM
18147	C-135E	C3004	USAF/412thTW	60-0372
18148	C-135A	C3005	(USAF/1611thATW)	60-0373 w/o 25Jun65 El Toro MCAS, CA
18149	EC-135E	C3006	USAF/412thTW	60-0374
18150	C-135E	C3007	USAF/412thTW	60-0375
18151	C-135E	C3008	USAF/89thAW	60-0376
18152	C-135A	C3009	USAF/412thTW	60-0377
18153	C-135A	C3010	USAF/55thWg	60-0378/OF stored Tinker AFB, OK 23Jul93
18154	720-027	226	(Aeroamerica)	N7078 N730T stored Boeing Field, WA Mar82; b/u 88
18155	720-025	225	(Trans European Airways)	N8701E OO-TEA stored Shannon, Eire 17Apr77; b/u 14Apr80
18156	720-025	232	(American Trans Air)	N8702E N10VG N8702E stored Miami, FL Jan75; b/u Oct77
18157	720-025	233	(Al Muraibad Leasing)	N8703E OY-DSK N3124Z stored Luton, UK 27May82; b/u May85
18158	720-025	234	(Boeing Flight Test Center)	N8704E LN-TUW N8704E N3183B N40102 stored Kingman, AZ Aug77; b/u 80
18159	720-025	235	Continental Aviation	N8705E OY-DSL N7229L VT-ERS stored Nagpur, India mid-91
18160	720-025	236	Korean Air	N8706E HL7402 stored Seoul, South Korea Jul76
18161	720-025	239	(Conair)	N8707E OY-DSM stored Copenhagen, Denmark 26Apr81; b/u Jul84
18162	720-025	240	New ACS	N8708E D-ACIP VP-YNL Z-YNL 9Q-CTD stored Kinshasa, Zaire Nov95
18163	720-025	241	(Eagle Air)	N8709E D-ACIQ N15VG TF-VVE TF-VLA stored Keflavik, Iceland May77; b/u summer 78
18164	720-025	242	(Boeing Corp)	N8710E HL7403 stored Kingman, AZ Nov77; b/u 80
18165	720-068B	250	(Sonico)	(ET-AAG) N93136 HZ-ACA N2628Y stored Van Nuys, CA 28Oct79; b/u Moses Lake, WA Oct82
18166	720-068B	251	(Overseas Intl Distributors)	(ET-AAH) HZ-ACB stored Van Nuys, CA 18Sep79; b/u 19Jun83
18167	720-047B	221	(AAR Allen Aircraft Corp)	N93144 9H-AAL N210DS stored Marana, AZ Nov87; b/u Jul88

18168 to 18232 model 717-148; built as KC-135A and modified as follows:

C/n	Series	Line No	Last known Operator/Owner	Previous Identities/fate (where known)
18168	EC-135L	T0483	USAF/4thACCS/28thWg	61-0261 stored Davis-Monthan AFB, AZ 29May92
18169	EC-135A	T0484	SD Air & Space Museum	61-0262 Preserved Ellsworth AFB, SD 20Mar92
18170	EC-135L	T0485	USAF/70thARS/305thARW	61-0263 stored Davis-Monthan AFB, AZ 05May92
18171	KC-135R	T0486	USAF/145thARS/OH ANG	61-0264
18172	KC-135A	T0487	(USAF/42ndBW)	61-0265 w/o 04Jan65 Loring AFB, ME
18173	KC-135R	T0488	USAF/173rdARS/NE ANG	61-0266
18174	KC-135R	T0489	USAF/319thARW	61-0267
18175	KC-135E	T0490	USAF/314thARS/AFRes	61-0268
18176	EC-135L	T0491	Grissom Heritage Museum	61-0269 Preserved Grissom AFB, IN 29Jun92
18177	KC-135E	T0492	USAF/63rdARS/AFRes	61-0270 [Possibly to 77thARS/916thARW]
18178	KC-135E	T0493	USAF/63rdARS/AFRes	61-0271
18179	KC-135R	T0494	USAF/72ndARS/AFRes	61-0272
18180	KC-135A	T0495	(USAF/340thBW)	61-0273 w/o 17Jan66 Palomares, Spain
18181	EC-135P	T0496	USAF/6thACCS/1stFW	61-0274/FF stored Davis-Monthan AFB, AZ 27Feb92
18182	KC-135R	T0497	USAF/22ndARW	61-0275
18183	KC-135R	T0498	USAF/173rdARS/NE ANG	61-0276

BOEING 707/720

C/n	Series	Line No	Last known Operator/Owner	Previous Identities/fate (where known)
18184	KC-135R	T0499	USAF/22ndARS/366thWg	61-0277/MO
18185	EC-135A	T0500	USAF/4thACCS/28thWg	61-0278 stored Davis-Monthan AFB, AZ 18Sep92
18186	EC-135L	T0501	USAF/70thARS/305thARW	61-0279 stored Davis-Monthan AFB, AZ 22May92
18187	KC-135E	T0502	USAF/336thARS/AFRes	61-0280 [KC-135E Relay Aircraft]
18188	KC-135E(RT)	T0503	USAF/197thARS/AZ ANG	61-0281 [Has ability to be air-refuelled]
18189	GEC-135H	T0504	USAF/82ndTW	61-0282 Preserved Sheppard AFB, TX 15Nov91
18190	EC-135L	T0505	USAF/70thARS/305thARW	61-0283 stored Davis-Monthan AFB, AZ 06May92
18191	KC-135R	T0506	USAF/92ndARW	61-0284
18192	EC-135H	T0507	USAF/6thACCS/1stFW	61-0285 stored Davis-Monthan AFB, AZ 09Mar92
18193	GEC-135H	T0508	USAF/82ndTW	61-0286 Preserved Sheppard AFB, TX 24Jan92
18194	EC-135A	T0509	Offutt AFB Museum	61-0287 Preserved Offutt AFB, NE 10Feb92
18195	KC-135R(RT)	T0510	USAF/909thARS/18thWg	61-0288/ZZ [Has ability to be air-refuelled]
18196	EC-135A	T0511	USAF/4thACCS/28thWg	61-0289 stored Davis-Monthan AFB, AZ 08Jun92
18197	KC-135R	T0512	USAF/203rdARS/HI ANG	61-0290
18198	EC-135H	T0513	(USAF/10thACCS)	61-0291 stored Davis-Monthan AFB, AZ 28May91; later b/u
18199	KC-135R	T0514	USAF/22ndARW	61-0292
18200	KC-135R(RT)	T0515	USAF/22ndARW	61-0293 [Has ability to be air-refuelled]
18201	KC-135R	T0516	USAF/92ndARW	61-0294
18202	KC-135R	T0517	USAF/55thARS/97thAMW	61-0295
18203	KC-135A	T0518	(USAF/410thBW)	61-0296 w/o 26Sep76 Alpena ANGB, MI
18204	EC-135A	T0519	USAF/4thACCS/28thWg	61-0297 stored Davis-Monthan AFB, AZ 02Jun92
18205	KC-135R	T0520	USAF/126thARS/WI ANG	61-0298
18206	KC-135R	T0521	USAF/92ndARW	61-0299
18207	KC-135R	T0522	USAF/19thARW	61-0300
18208	KC-135A	T0523	(USAF/99thBW)	61-0301 w/o 22Oct68 Ching Chuan Kang AB, RoC
18209	KC-135R(RT)	T0524	USAF/92ndARW	61-0302 [Has ability to be air-refuelled]
18210	KC-135E	T0525	USAF/336thARS/AFRes	61-0303 [KC-135E Relay Aircraft]
18211	KC-135R	T0526	USAF/909thARS/18thWg	61-0304/ZZ
18212	KC-135R	T0527	USAF/22ndARW	61-0305
18213	KC-135R	T0528	USAF/91stARS/43rdARG	61-0306
18214	KC-135R	T0529	USAF/74thARS/AFRes	61-0307
18215	KC-135R	T0530	USAF/55thARS/97thAMW	61-0308
18216	KC-135R	T0531	USAF/126thARS/WI ANG	61-0309
18217	KC-135R	T0532	USAF/133rdARS/NH ANG	61-0310
18218	KC-135R	T0533	USAF/22ndARW	61-0311
18219	KC-135R	T0534	USAF/92ndARW	61-0312
18220	KC-135R	T0535	USAF/92ndARW	61-0313
18221	KC-135R	T0536	USAF/909thARS/18thWg	61-0314/ZZ
18222	KC-135R	T0537	USAF/909thARS/18thWg	61-0315/ZZ
18223	KC-135A	T0538	(USAF/71stARS/2ndBW)	61-0316 dbf 19Mar85 Cairo, Egypt
18224	KC-135R	T0539	USAF/319thARW	61-0317
18225	KC-135R	T0540	USAF/319thARW	61-0318
18226	KC-135A	T0541	(USAF/19thBW)	61-0319 w/o 28Aug63 Atlantic Ocean
18227	KC-135R	T0542	USAF/92ndARW	61-0320
18228	KC-135R	T0543	USAF/92ndARW	61-0321 [KC-135R Relay aircraft]
18229	KC-135A	T0544	(USAF/19thBW)	61-0322 w/o 28Aug63 Atlantic Ocean
18230	KC-135R	T0545	USAF/22ndARW	61-0323
18231	KC-135R	T0546	USAF/465thARS/AFRes	61-0324
18232	KC-135A	T0547	USAF/906thARS/43rdARG	61-0325 stored Davis-Monthan AFB, AZ 29Sep93
18233 to 18237 model 717-157; built as C-135A and modified as follows:				
18233	EC-135E	C3011	USAF/412thTW	61-0326
18234	EC-135Y	C3012	USAF/CENTCOM	61-0327 [Op by 19thARW]
18235	EC-135N	C3013	(USAF/4950thTW)	61-0328 w/o 06May81 nr Walkersville, MD
18236	EC-135E	C3014	USAF/412thTW	61-0329
18237	EC-135E	C3015	USAF/412thTW	61-0330
18238 to 18239 model 717-158; built as C-135B:				
18238	C-135B	C3016	(USAF/4950thTW)	61-0331 w/o 13Jun71 Pacific Ocean
18239	C-135B	C3017	(USAF/1501stATW)	61-0332 w/o 11May64 Clark AB, Philippines
18240	720-025	246	Aerotours Dominicano	N8711E D-ACIR N8711E stored Santo Domingo, Dominican Republic Feb85
18241	720-025	247	Danmarks Flygvemuseum	N8712E OY-DSP Preserved Billund, Denmark 86
18242	720-025	248	Air Zimbabwe	N8713E D-ACIS VP-YNM stored Harare, Zimbabwe May83
18243	720-025	254	(Conair)	N8714E OY-DSR dbr Copenhagen, Denmark 13Sep74; b/u Jul75
18244	720-025	255	(Air Charter Service)	N8715E D-ACIT VP-YNN Z-YNN stored Harare, Zimbabwe Jun82; b/u Nov88
18245	707-328	264	(Air France)	N93138 F-BHSR TU-TDB F-BHSR stored Paris-Orly, France Mar76; b/u Apr77
18246	707-328	269	ex-Israel Defence Force/AF	F-BHSS 4X-BYK 118/4X-JYK stored Elifelet, Israel 95 for use as restuarant
18247	707-328	274	(Air France)	F-BHST w/o 22Jun62 nr Pointe-a-Pitre, Guadeloupe
18248	720-030B	258	Museo del Los Linos	D-ABON N786PA HK-749 Preserved Bogota, Colombia Dec80
18249	720-030B	262	(Lufthansa)	D-ABOP w/o 15Jul64 nr Ansbach, FRG
18250	720-030B	263	Pakistan Intl Airlines)	N93137 D-ABOQ N787PA JY-ADS AP-AZP Preserved Karachi, Pakistan Apr81
18251	720-030B	273	(Boeing MAC/USAF)	D-ABOR N788PA JY-ADT 9L-LAZ N720BC stored Davis-Monthan AFB, AZ 15Oct85; later b/u
18292, 18333 model 717-158; built as C-135B and modified as follows:				
18292	RC-135S	C3018	USAF/38thRS/55thWg	61-2662/OF
18333	RC-135S	C3019	USAF/38thRS/55thWg	61-2663/OF

BOEING 707/720

C/n	Series	Line No	Last known Operator/Owner	Previous Identities/fate (where known)
18334	707-138B	229	Government of Morocco	VH-EBK 9Y-TDB VH-EBK 9Y-TDB N58937 CNA-NS [Op by Force Aerienne Royale Morocaine]
18335	707-321B	268	(Boeing MAC/USAF)	N760PA RP-C7076 N4605D stored Davis-Monthan AFB, AZ Aug85; later b/u
18336	707-321B	270	Boeing MAC/USAF	N761PA RP-C7075 N944JW stored Davis-Monthan AFB, AZ 07May86
18337	707-321B	276	(Aviation Systems Intl)	N762PA HL7430 N762TB stored Miami, FL 14Feb80 then Marana, AZ Jun80; later b/u
18338	707-321B	287	(Omega Air)	N763PA N763W N111MF N98WS HZ-TAS stored Stansted, UK then Manston, UK Jan89; b/u May94
18339	707-321B	292	(Boeing MAC/USAF)	N764PA N764SE OE-IEB N897WA stored Davis-Monthan AFB, AZ 27Sep89; later b/u

18340 to 18350 model 717-158; built as C-135B and modified as follows:

C/n	Series	Line No	Last known Operator/Owner	Previous Identities/fate (where known)
18340	RC-135S	C3020	(USAF/6thSW)	61-2664 w/o 15Mar80 Shemya AFB, AK
18341	WC-135B	C3021	USAF/55thWg	61-2665/OF
18342	WC-135B	C3022	USAF/E-Systems Inc	61-2666
18343	TC-135B	C3023	USAF/55thWg	61-2667/OF
18344	C-135C	C3024	USAF/CINCPAC	61-2668 [Op by 15thABW]
18345	C-135C	C3025	USAF/412thTW	61-2669
18346	WC-135B	C3026	USAF/55thWg	61-2670/OF [For conversion to OC-135B]
18347	C-135C	C3027	USAF/1stAS/89thAW	61-2671 Preserved Tinker AFB, OK Oct91
18348	OC-135B	C3028	USAF/55thWg	61-2672
18349	WC-135B	C3029	USAF/55thWRS	61-2673 stored Davis-Monthan AFB, AZ 28Sep93
18350	OC-135B	C3030	USAF/55thWg	61-2674
18351	720-051B	211	Republic of China Air Force	N721US 18351 Preserved RoCAF Museum, Kangshan, RoC
18352	720-051B	218	(Olympic Airways)	N722US SX-DBG stored Athens, Greece Jun81; later b/u
18353	720-051B	219	(Olympic Airways)	N723US SX-DBH stored Athens, Greece Jun81; later b/u
18354	720-051B	224	(Northwest Airlines)	N724US w/o 12Feb63 nr Miami, FL
18355	720-051B	231	(Omega Air)	N725US SX-DBI stored Athens, Greece Jun81 then Shannon, Eire 13Dec84; later b/u
18356	720-051B	238	(Olympic Airways)	N726US SX-DBL stored Athens, Greece Jun81; later b/u
18357	707-458	272	(Wolf Aviation)	4X-ATC 9Q-CPM 9Q-CWR dbr Isiro, Zaire Jul84; b/u Kinshasa, Zaire
18358	707-463		(Ghana Airways)	Allocated but later canx, not built
18359	707-463		(Ghana Airways)	Allocated but later canx, not built
18372	707-465	271	(Boeing Corp)	G-ARWD VR-BBW G-ARWD stored Kingman, AZ 15May81; later b/u
18373	707-465	302	(BOAC)	G-ARWE VR-BBZ G-ARWE w/o 08Apr68 London-Heathrow,UK
18374	707-329	283	Israel Defence Force/AF	OO-SJF OE-LBA OO-SJF 4X-BYL 128/4X-JYL [ELINT configuration]
18375	707-328	293	(Gateway Aircraft Leasing)	(OO-SJG) F-BHSU CN-RMA F-BHSU N707RZ stored Miami, FL 04Jan80; then Fort Lauderdale, FL; b/u Jan/Apr85
18376	720-062	279	(Aviation Sales Co)	N720V N301AS stored Miami, FL 05Dec75; b/u 27Jan84
18377	720-062	285	(Aeroamerica)	N720W N302AS stored Berlin-Templehof, FRG Sep76, b/u Nov78
18378	720-040B	257	(Air Malta)	AP-AMG 9H-AAM stored Luqa, Malta mid-84, used for fire practice
18379	720-040B	321	(Pakistan Intl Airlines)	AP-AMH w/o 20May65 nr Cairo, Egypt
18380	720-040B	324	(Boeing MAC/USAF)	AP-AMJ 9H-AAN N5487N stored Davis-Monthan AFB, AZ 05Oct84; later b/u
18381	720-051B	222	(Boeing MAC/USAF)	N791TW N730US G-AZFB N2464C stored Davis-Monthan AFB, AZ 13Jun83; later b/u
18382	720-051B	223	(Boeing MAC/USAF)	N792TW N731US G-AZKM N2464K stored Davis-Monthan AFB, AZ 22Jun83; b/u Jun91
18383	720-051B	230	(Boeing MAC/USAF)	N793TW N732US G-AZNX N24666 stored Davis-Monthan AFB, AZ 21Jun83; later b/u
18384	720-051B	237	(Allied Signal/Garrett)	N795TW N733US (OY-APP) OY-APZ OO-TYA OY-APZ N720GT stored Phoenix, AZ by Aug89
18385	707-131B	277	(Boeing MAC/USAF)	N746TW stored Davis-Monthan AFB, AZ 28Apr82; later b/u
18386	707-131B	280	(Boeing MAC/USAF)	N747TW stored Davis-Monthan AFB, AZ 13Aug82; later b/u
18387	707-131B	286	(Boeing MAC/USAF)	N748TW stored Davis-Monthan AFB, AZ 07Jul82; later b/u
18388	707-131B	291	(Boeing MAC/USAF)	N749TW stored Davis-Monthan AFB, AZ 01Feb83; later b/u
18389	707-131B	294	(Boeing MAC/USAF)	N750TW stored Davis-Monthan AFB, AZ 22Apr82; later b/u
18390	707-131B	296	(Pima Air & Space Museum)	N751TW Preserved Pima County , AZ Feb83; b/u 95
18391	707-131B	299	Boeing MAC/USAF	N752TW stored Davis-Monthan AFB, AZ 28Apr82
18392	707-131B	301	(Boeing MAC/USAF)	N754TW stored Davis-Monthan AFB, AZ 22Apr82; later b/u
18393	707-131B	306	(Boeing MAC/USAF)	N755TW stored Davis-Monthan AFB, AZ 29Dec82; later b/u
18394	707-131B	308	(Boeing MAC/USAF)	N756TW stored Davis-Monthan AFB, AZ 21Apr82; later b/u
18395	707-131B	309	(Trans World Airlines)	N757TW dbr 16Jan74 Los Angeles, CA
18396	707-131B	311	Boeing MAC/USAF	N758TW stored Davis-Monthan AFB, AZ 21Apr82
18397	707-131B	312	(Boeing MAC/USAF)	N759TW stored Davis-Monthan AFB, AZ 06Jul82; later b/u
18398	707-131B		(Trans World Airlines)	(N760TW) Allocated but later canx, not built
18399	707-131B		(Trans World Airlines)	(N780TW) Allocated but later canx, not built
18400	707-131B	313	(Boeing MAC/USAF)	N781TW stored Davis-Monthan AFB, AZ 12Aug82; b/u Feb92
18401	707-131B	315	(Boeing MAC/USAF)	N782TW stored Davis-Monthan AFB, AZ 13Aug82; later b/u
18402	707-131B	316	(Boeing MAC/USAF)	N783TW stored Davis-Monthan AFB, AZ 06Jul82; later b/u
18403	707-131B	317	Boeing MAC/USAF	N784TW stored Davis-Monthan AFB, AZ 23Apr82
18404	707-131B	318	(Boeing MAC/USAF)	N785TW stored Davis-Monthan AFB, AZ 22Dec82; later b/u
18405	707-331B	305	Boeing MAC/USAF	N773TW stored Davis-Monthan AFB, AZ 13Oct83
18406	707-331B	320	Boeing MAC/USAF	N774TW stored Davis-Monthan AFB, AZ 20Dec83
18407	707-331B	323	Boeing MAC/USAF	N775TW stored Davis-Monthan AFB, AZ 09May84

BOEING 707/720

C/n	Series	Line No	Last known Operator/Owner	Previous Identities/fate (where known)
18408	707-331B	326	Boeing MAC/USAF	N776TW (N8739) N28714 stored Davis-Monthan AFB, AZ 16Dec83
18409	707-331B	331	Boeing MAC/USAF	N778TW stored Davis-Monthan AFB, AZ 03Apr84
18410	707-331B		(Trans World Airlines)	(N779TW) Allocated but later canx, not built
18411	707-436	266	(Coastal Airways)	G-ARRA N4465D dbf 13/14Oct83 Perpignan, France
18412	707-436	330	(Boeing Corp)	G-ARRB stored Kingman, AZ 31Jan76; b/u Sep79
18413	707-436	334	(New ACS)	G-ARRC N4465C 9Q-CTK B/u Kinshasa, Zaire Mar/Apr95
18414	707-437	275	(Air India)	VT-DNY stored Bombay, India 29Jul80; b/u 81
18415	707-437	282	(Air India)	VT-DNZ stored Bombay, India 80; b/u 84
18416	720-024B	288	(Allen Aircraft Corp)	N57201 stored Miami, FL; b/u Mar76
18417	720-024B	295	AAR-Allen Aircraft Corp	N57202 ET-AFK N550DS stored Marana, AZ Oct88; later Davis-Monthan AFB, AZ 09Aug89
18418	720-024B	300	(Boeing MAC/USAF)	N57203 ET-AFA N769BE stored Davis-Monthan AFB, AZ 21Nov85; b/u Oct90
18419	720-024B	304	(Boeing MAC/USAF)	N57204 ET-AFB N770BE stored Davis-Monthan AFB, AZ 20Nov85; later b/u
18420	720-051B	243	(Olympic Airways)	N727US SX-DBL stored Athens, Greece Jun81; later b/u
18421	720-051B	244	Boeing MAC/USAF	N728US (OY-APN) OY-APY G-BHGE OY-APY TF-AYC stored Davis-Monthan AFB, AZ 01Jul87
18422	720-051B	256	(Boeing MAC/USAF)	N729US (OY-APO) OY-APW TF-AYB stored Davis-Monthan AFB, AZ 22May87; later b/u
18423	720-027	289	(Eastern Orient Airlines)	N7079 N731T N321E stored Bournemouth-Hurn, UK Apr80; b/u Mar82
18424	720-058B	281	(Boeing MAC/USAF)	4X-ABA N8498S stored Davis-Monthan AFB, AZ 27Aug84; later b/u
18425	720-058B	290	(Boeing MAC/USAF)	4X-ABB N8498T stored Davis-Monthan AFB, AZ 21Jul83; later b/u
18451	720-047B	307	JAR Aircraft Services	N93145 HZ-NAA HZ-KA1 N2143J N720JR
18452	720-047B	310	(Blue Metals)	N93146 N92GS stored Miami, FL Mar90; later b/u
18453	720-047B	314	Sheikh Kamal Adham	N93147 HZ-KA4
18454	720-060B	319	(Ethiopian Airlines)	ET-AAG dbr 09Jan68 Beirut, Lebanon
18455	720-060B	322	AAR-Allen Aircraft Corp	ET-AAH N330DS stored Marana, AZ Dec87; later Davis-Monthan AFB, AZ 08Aug89
18456	707-328B	325	(Trans European A/w/Tratco)	F-BHSV 4X-ATE stored Luxembourg-Findel 06Nov83, later Brussels, Belgium; then b/u
18457	707-328B	327	(Cargolux/Tratco)	F-BHSX TU-TXA F-BHSX TU-TXB F-BHSX "HB-IDD" F-BHSX stored Paris-Orly, France Apr82; b/u Luxembourg-Findel May83
18458	707-328B	329	(Cargolux/Tratco)	F-BHSY TU-TXF F-BHSY TU-TXJ F-BHSY stored Paris-Orly, France Mar82; b/u Luxembourg-Findel Jul83
18459	707-328B	335	(Air France)	F-BHSZ w/o 04Dec69 nr Caracas, Venezuela
18460	707-328B	328	Israel Defence Force/AF	OO-SJG 4X-BYM 137/4X-JYM [ELINT/SIGINT configuration]
18461 model 707-353B; built as VC-137C and modified as follows:				
18461	C-137C	303	USAF/1stALS/89thAW	62-6000
18462	707-330B	333	(LAN-Chile)	D-ABOS D-ABOV CC-CCG stored Santiago, Chile; b/u 31May86
18463	707-330B	363	(Lufthansa)	D-ABOT w/o 20Dec73 New Delhi, India
18465 to 18479 model 717-158; built as C-135B and modified as follows:				
18465	C-135B	C3031	USAF/15thABW	62-4125
18466	C-135B	C3032	USAF/141stARS/NJ ANG	62-4126
18467	C-135C	C3033	USAF/CINCPAC	62-4127 [Op by 65thALS/15thABW]
18468	RC-135X	C3034	USAF/55thWg	62-4128/OF stored Greenville, TX 22Feb93
18469	TC-135W	C3035	USAF/55thWg	62-4129/OF
18470	C-135B	C3036	USAF/55thWg	62-4130/OF
18471	RC-135W	C3037	USAF/55thWg	62-4131/OF
18472	RC-135W	C3038	USAF/55thWg	62-4132/OF
18473	TC-135S	C3039	USAF/55thWg	62-4133/OF
18474	RC-135W	C3040	USAF/55thWg	62-4134/OF
18475	RC-135W	C3041	USAF/55thWg	62-4135/OF
18476	C-135B	C3042	(USAF/1611thATW)	62-4136 w/o 23Oct62 NAS Leeward Point, Cuba
18477	RC-135E	C3043	(USAF/6thSW)	62-4137 w/o 05Jun69 Bering Sea
18478	RC-135W	C3044	USAF/55thWg	62-4138/OF
18479	RC-135W	C3045	USAF/55thWg	62-4139/OF
18480 to 18563 model 717-148; built as KC-135A and modified as follows:				
18480	KC-135A	T0548	USAF/906thARS/43rdARW	62-3497 stored Davis-Monthan AFB, AZ 16Jul93
18481	KC-135R	T0549	USAF/92ndARW	62-3498
18482	KC-135R	T0550	USAF/55thARS/97thAMW	62-3499
18483	KC-135R	T0551	USAF/126thARS/WI ANG	62-3500
18484	KC-135A	T0552	USAF/7thARS/19thARW	62-3501 stored Davis-Monthan AFB, AZ 07Jul93
18485	KC-135R	T0553	USAF/92ndARW	62-3502
18486	KC-135R	T0554	USAF/909thARS/18thWg	62-3503/ZZ
18487	KC-135R	T0555	USAF/319thARW	62-3504
18488	KC-135R	T0556	USAF/319thARW	62-3505
18489	KC-135R	T0557	USAF/133rdARS/NH ANG	62-3506
18490	KC-135R	T0558	USAF/55thARS/97thAMW	62-3507
18491	KC-135R	T0559	USAF/19thARW	62-3508
18492	KC-135R	T0560	USAF/916thARW/AFRes	62-3509
18493	KC-135R	T0561	USAF/74thARS/AFRes	62-3510
18494	KC-135R	T0562	USAF/145thARS/OH ANG	62-3511
18495	KC-135R	T0563	Turk Hava Kuvvetleri	62-3512 23512
18496	KC-135R	T0564	USAF/22ndARS/366thWg	62-3513/MO

BOEING 707/720

C/n	Series	Line No	Last known Operator/Owner	Previous Identities/fate (where known)
18497	KC-135R	T0565	USAF/203rdARS/HI ANG	62-3514
18498	KC-135R	T0566	USAF/133rdARS/NH ANG	62-3515
18499	KC-135R	T0567	Armee de l'Air/ERV.93	62-3516
18500	KC-135R	T0568	USAF/22ndARW	62-3517
18501	KC-135R	T0569	USAF/72ndARS/AFRes	62-3518
18502	KC-135R	T0570	USAF/319thARW	62-3519
18503	KC-135R	T0571	USAF/909thARS/18thWg	62-3520/ZZ
18504	KC-135R	T0572	USAF/74thARS/AFRes	62-3521
18505	KC-135A	T0573	(USAF/41stARS/416thBW)	62-3522 dbf 04Mar77 Griffiss AFB, NY
18506	KC-135R	T0574	USAF/22ndARW	62-3523
18507	KC-135R	T0575	USAF/106thARS/AL ANG	62-3524
18508	KC-135A	T0576	USAF/906thARS/43rdARW	62-3525 stored Davis-Monthan AFB, AZ 24Aug93
18509	KC-135R	T0577	USAF/55thARS/97thAMW	62-3526
18510	KC-135E	T0578	USAF/150thARS/NJ ANG	62-3527
18511	KC-135R	T0579	USAF/55thARS/97thAMW	62-3528
18512	KC-135R	T0580	USAF/92ndARW	62-3529
18513	KC-135R	T0581	USAF/72ndARS/AFRes	62-3530
18514	KC-135R	T0582	USAF/166thARS/OH ANG	62-3531
18515	KC-135A	T0583	USAF/917thARS/96thWg	62-3532 stored Davis-Monthan AFB, AZ 05Aug93
18516	KC-135R	T0584	USAF/91stARS/43rdARG	62-3533
18517	KC-135R	T0585	USAF/19thARW	62-3534
18518	KC-135A	T0586	(Boeing-Wichita)	62-3535 Cyclic Test Airframe, Wichita, KS
18519	EC-135K	T0587	(USAF/8thTDCS)	62-3536 w/o 14Sep77 nr Kirtland AFB, NM
18520	KC-135R	T0588	USAF/99thARS/19thARW	62-3537
18521	KC-135R	T0589	USAF/92ndARW	62-3538
18522	KC-135A	T0590	USAF/917thARS	62-3539/DY stored Davis-Monthan AFB, AZ 01Apr94
18523	KC-135R	T0591	USAF/92ndARW	62-3540
18524	KC-135R	T0592	USAF/351stARS/100thARW	62-3541/D
18525	KC-135R	T0593	USAF/92ndARW	62-3542
18526	KC-135R	T0594	USAF/72ndARS/AFRes	62-3543
18527	KC-135R	T0595	USAF/19thARW	62-3544
18528	KC-135R	T0596	USAF/19thARW	62-3545
18529	KC-135R	T0597	USAF/92ndARW	62-3546
18530	KC-135R	T0598	USAF/133rdARS/NH ANG	62-3547
18531	KC-135R	T0599	USAF/55thARS/97thAMW	62-3548
18532	KC-135R	T0600	USAF/91stARS/43rdARG	62-3549
18533	KC-135R	T0601	USAF/55thARS/97thAMW	62-3550
18534	KC-135R	T0602	USAF/55thARS/97thAMW	62-3551
18535	KC-135R	T0603	USAF/19thARW	62-3552
18536	KC-135R	T0604	USAF/22ndARW	62-3553
18537	KC-135R	T0605	USAF/19thARW	62-3554
18538	KC-135A	T0606	USAF/46thARS/305thARW	62-3555 stored Davis-Monthan AFB, AZ 20Sep93
18539	KC-135R	T0607	USAF/319thARW	62-3556
18540	KC-135R	T0608	USAF/319thARW	62-3557
18541	KC-135R	T0609	USAF/22ndARW	62-3558
18542	KC-135R	T0610	USAF/92ndARW	62-3559
18543	KC-135A	T0611	USAF/55thARS/97thAMW	62-3560 stored Davis-Monthan AFB, AZ 16Jun94
18544	KC-135R	T0612	USAF/351stARS/100thARW	62-3561/D
18545	KC-135R	T0613	USAF/319thARW	62-3562
18546	KC-135A	T0614	USAF/917thARS	62-3563 stored Davis-Monthan AFB, AZ 18Mar94
18547	KC-135R	T0615	USAF/55thARS/97thAMW	62-3564
18548	KC-135R	T0616	USAF/55thARS/97thAMW	62-3565
18549	KC-135E	T0617	USAF/168thARS/AK ANG	62-3566
18550	KC-135A	T0618	USAF/46thARS/305thARW	62-3567 stored Davis-Monthan AFB, AZ 13Sep93
18551	KC-135R	T0619	Turk Hava Kuvvetleri	62-3568 23568
18552	KC-135R	T0620	USAF/19thARW	62-3569
18553	EC-135G	T0621	USAF/4thACCS/28thWg	62-3570 stored Davis-Monthan AFB, AZ 22Jun92
18554	KC-135R	T0622	USAF/168thARS/AK ANG	62-3571
18555	KC-135R	T0623	USAF/22ndARS/366thWg	62-3572/MO
18556	KC-135R	T0624	USAF/55thARS/97thAMW	62-3573
18557	KC-135A	T0625	USAF/46thARS/305thARW	62-3574 stored Davis-Monthan AFB, AZ 12Jul93
18558	KC-135R	T0626	USAF/91stARS/43rdARG	62-3575
18559	KC-135R	T0627	USAF/133rdARS/NH ANG	62-3576
18560	KC-135R	T0628	USAF/AMC	62-3577
18561	KC-135R	T0629	USAF/92ndARW	62-3578
18562	KC-135A	T0630	USAF/4thACCS/28thWg	62-3579 stored Davis-Monthan AFB, AZ 16Jun92
18563	KC-135R	T0631	USAF/55thARS/97thAMW	62-3580
18564 to 18568 model 717-166; built as KC-135B and modified as follows:				
18564	EC-135C	C2101	USAF/7thACCS/55thWg	62-3581/OF
18565	EC-135C	C2102	USAF/7thACCS/55thWg	62-3582/OF
18566	EC-135C	C2103	USAF/1stACCS/55thRW	62-3583/OF stored Davis-Monthan AFB, AZ 26May92
18567	EC-135J	C2104	(USAF/9thACCS/15thWg)	62-3584 dbr 29May92 Pope AFB, NC
18568	EC-135C	C2105	USAF/7thACCS/55thWg	62-3585/OF
18579	707-321C	332	(IAS Cargo AIrlines)	N765PA G-BEBP w/o 14May77 Lusaka, Zambia
18580	707-321C	336	(Uganda Airlines)	N766PA 5X-UAL dbr 01Apr79 Entebbe, Uganda
18581	720-027	347	(Aeroamerica)	N7080 N733T stored Boeing Field, WA Nov79; b/u Jun81
18582	707-373C	344	(Saudia)	N373WA HZ-ACE dbr Jeddah, Saudi Arabia Nov79
18583	707-373C	346	NASCO	N374WA HZ-ACF D2-TAG D2-TOG stored Manston, UK 17Jul91
18584	707-351B	342	(LAN-Chile)	N351US VR-HGH CC-CCX w/o 03Aug78 Buenos-Aires, Argentina

BOEING 707/720

C/n	Series	Line No	Last known Operator/Owner	Previous Identities/fate (where known)
18585	707-351B	343	(Midair)	N352US VR-HGI G-BFBZ stored Lasham, UK 19Jan83; b/u Jun/Jul86
18586	707-351B	345	Al Wisar Trading	N353US VR-HGO VR-CAO N651TF N351SR EL-SKD G-BSZA VR-BMV VR-BOR HZ-SAK1 stored Manston, UK 22Aug95
18587	720-024B	340	(Allen Aircraft Corp)	N52705 stored, b/u Mar76
18588	720-047B	337	(Kenya Airways)	N93148 5Y-BBX stored Nairobi, Kenya early 89; b/u 28Aug92
18589	720-047B	338	(Pakistan Intl Airlines)	N93149 AP-BAF stored Karachi, Pakistan; b/u 81
18590	720-047B	339	(Pakistan Intl Airlines)	N93150 AP-AXK dbr 08Jan81 Quetta, Pakistan
18591	707-321C	341	(T/A Rioplatense)	N767PA G-BEAF LV-MSG stored Buenos-Aires, Argentina Nov84; b/u Dec90
18592	707-321C		(Pan American World A/W)	Allocated but later canx, not built
18593 to 18662 model 717-148; built as KC-135A and modified as follows:				
18593	KC-135R	T0632	USAF/319thARW	63-7976
18594	KC-135R	T0633	USAF/319thARW	63-7977
18595	KC-135R	T0634	USAF/55thARS/97thAMW	63-7978
18596	KC-135R	T0635	USAF/55thARS/97thAMW	63-7979
18597	KC-135R	T0636	USAF/909thARS/18thWg	63-7980/ZZ
18598	KC-135R	T0637	USAF/136thARS/NY ANG	63-7981
18599	KC-135R	T0638	USAF/91stARS/43rdARG	63-7982
18600	KC-135A	T0639	(USAF/305thARW)	63-7983 w/o 17Jun86 Howard AFB, CZ
18601	KC-135R	T0640	USAF/106thARS/AL ANG	63-7984
18602	KC-135R	T0641	USAF/465thARS/AFRes	63-7985
18603	KC-135A	T0642	USAF/43rdARW	63-7986 stored Davis-Monthan AFB, AZ 15Sep93
18604	KC-135R	T0643	USAF/909thARS/18thWg	63-7987/ZZ
18605	KC-135R	T0644	USAF/92ndARW	63-7988
18606	KC-135A	T0645	(USAF/301stARW)	63-7989 dbr 08Mar73 Lockbourne AFB, OH
18607	KC-135A	T0646	(USAF/410thBW)	63-7990 w/o Dyess AFB, TX 31Jan89
18608	KC-135R	T0647	USAF/173rdARS/NE ANG	63-7991
18609	KC-135R	T0648	USAF/166thARS/OH ANG	63-7992
18610	KC-135R	T0649	USAF/166thARS/OH ANG	63-7993
18611	EC-135G	T0650	USAF/4thACCS/28thWg	63-7994 stored Davis-Monthan AFB, AZ 11Sep92
18612	KC-135R	T0651	USAF/19thARW	63-7995
18613	KC-135R	T0652	USAF/72ndARS/AFRes	63-7996
18614	KC-135R	T0653	USAF/19thARW	63-7997
18615	KC-135A	T0654	NASA/Johnson Space Center	63-7998 NASA931/N931NA
18616	KC-135R	T0655	USAF/319thARW	63-7999
18617	KC-135R	T0656	USAF/22ndARW	63-8000
18618	EC-135G	T0657	USAF/4thACCS/28thWg	63-8001 stored Davis-Monthan AFB, AZ 18May92
18619	KC-135R	T0658	USAF/19thARW	63-8002
18620	KC-135R	T0659	USAF/22ndARW	63-8003
18621	KC-135R	T0660	USAF/22ndARS/366thWg	63-8004/MO
18622	KC-135A	T0661	USAF/55thARW/97thAMW	63-8005 Preserved Grand Forks AFB, ND
18623	KC-135R	T0662	USAF/19thARW	63-8006
18624	KC-135R	T0663	USAF/106thARS/AL ANG	63-8007
18625	KC-135R	T0664	USAF/AMC	63-8008
18626	KC-135A	T0665	USAF/46thARS/305thARW	63-8009 stored Davis-Monthan AFB, AZ 26Jul93
18627	KC-135A	T0666	USAF/46thARS/305thARW	63-8010 Preserved Scott AFB, IL Sep93
18628	KC-135R	T0667	USAF/319thARW	63-8011
18629	KC-135R	T0668	USAF/319thARW	63-8012
18630	KC-135R	T0669	USAF/166thARS/OH ANG	63-8013
18631	KC-135R	T0670	USAF/319thARW	63-8014
18632	KC-135R	T0671	USAF/168thARS/AK ANG	63-8015
18633	KC-135A	T0672	USAF/55thARS/97thAMW	63-8016 stored Davis-Monthan AFB, AZ 12May94
18634	KC-135R	T0673	USAF/92ndARW	63-8017
18635	KC-135R	T0674	USAF/173rdARS/NE ANG	63-8018
18636	KC-135R	T0675	USAF/22ndARW	63-8019
18637	KC-135R	T0676	USAF/55thARS/97thAMW	63-8020
18638	KC-135R	T0677	USAF/319thARW	63-8021
18639	KC-135R	T0678	USAF/22ndARW	63-8022
18640	KC-135R	T0679	USAF/351stARS/100thARW	63-8023/D
18641	KC-135R	T0680	USAF/465thARS/AFRes	63-8024
18642	KC-135R	T0681	USAF/909thARS/18thWg	63-8025/ZZ
18643	KC-135R	T0682	USAF/319thARW	63-8026
18644	KC-135R	T0683	USAF/92ndARW	63-8027
18645	KC-135R	T0684	USAF/168thARS/AK ANG	63-8028
18646	KC-135R	T0685	USAF/126thARS/WI ANG	63-8029
18647	KC-135R	T0686	USAF/203rdARS/HI ANG	63-8030
18648	KC-135R	T0687	USAF/22ndARW	63-8031
18649	KC-135R	T0688	USAF/72ndARS/AFRes	63-8032
18650	KC-135R	T0689	Armee de l'Air/ERV.93	63-8033
18651	KC-135R	T0690	USAF/319thARW	63-8034
18652	KC-135R	T0691	USAF/106thARS/AL ANG	63-8035
18653	KC-135R	T0692	USAF/136thARS/NY ANG	63-8036
18654	KC-135R	T0693	USAF/92ndARW	63-8037
18655	KC-135R	T0694	USAF/133rdARS/NH ANG	63-8038
18656	KC-135R	T0695	USAF/465thARS/AFRes	63-8039
18657	KC-135R	T0696	USAF/319thARW	63-8040
18658	KC-135R	T0697	USAF/72ndARS/AFRes	63-8041
18659	KC-135A	T0698	(USAF/6thSW)	63-8042 w/o 03Jun65 Walker AFB, NM

BOEING 707/720

C/n	Series	Line No	Last known Operator/Owner	Previous Identities/fate (where known)
18660	KC-135R	T0699	USAF/166thARS/OH ANG	63-8043
18661	KC-135R	T0700	USAF/319thARW	63-8044
18662	KC-135R	T0701	USAF/319thARW	63-8045
18663 to 18669 model 717-166; built as KC-135B and modified as follows:				
18663	EC-135C	C2106	USAF/55thWg	63-8046/OF
18664	EC-135C	C2107	USAF/2ndACCS/55thWg	63-8047/OF stored Davis-Monthan AFB, AZ 12Oct93
18665	EC-135C	C2108	USAF/55thWg	63-8048/OF
18666	EC-135C	C2109	USAF/2ndACCS/55thWg	63-8049/OF Preserved Offutt AFB, NE 29Jan92
18667	EC-135C	C2110	USAF/55thWg	63-8050/OF
18668	EC-135C	C2111	USAF/4thACCS/28thWg	63-8051 stored Davis-Monthan AFB, AZ 10Jul92
18669	EC-135C	C2112	USAF/55thWg	63-8052/OF
18670 to 18673 model 739-700; built as RC-135A and modified as follows:				
18670	KC-135D	C2201	USAF/168thARS/AK ANG	63-8058
18671	KC-135D	C2202	USAF/197thARS/AZ ANG	63-8059
18672	KC-135D	C2203	USAF/168thARS/AK ANG	63-8060
18673	KC-135D	C2204	USAF/196thARS/CA ANG	63-8061
18674 to 18678 model 739-700; allocated as RC-135A:				
18674	RC-135A		(USAF)	(63-8062) Allocated but later canx, not built
18675	RC-135A		(USAF)	(63-8063) Allocated but later canx, not built
18676	RC-135A		(USAF)	(63-8064) Allocated but later canx, not built
18677	RC-135A		(USAF)	(63-8065) Allocated but later canx, not built
18678	RC-135A		(USAF)	(63-8066) Allocated but later canx, not built
18679 to 18684 model 717-165; built as C-135F and modified as follows:				
18679	C-135FR	C2001	Armee de l'Air/ERV.93	63-8470 38470/CA 38470/93-CA
18680	C-135FR	C2002	Armee de l'Air/ERV.93	63-8471 38471/CB 38471/93-CB
18681	C-135FR	C2003	Armee de l'Air/ERV.93	63-8472 38473/CC 38472/93-CC
18682	C-135F	C2004	(Armee de l'Air/ERV.93)	63-8473 38473/CD w/o 01Jul72 nr Mururoa Atoll
18683	C-135FR	C2005	Armee de l'Air/ERV.93	63-8474 38474/CE 38474/93-CE
18684	C-135FR	C2006	Armee de l'Air/ERV.93	63-8475 38475/CF 38475/93-CF
18685	707-328B	359	(Tratco)	F-BLCA (3X-GCC) F-BLCA stored Luxembourg-Findel Apr83; b/u Jul83
18686	707-328B	360	(Boeing MAC/USAF)	F-BLCB TU-TXI F-BLCB TU-TXM F-BLCB 5R-MFK F-BLLB 5A-DLT SU-DAJ N83658 stored Davis-Monthan AFB, AZ 22May87; later b/u
18687	720-051B	351	(Olympic Airways)	N734US SX-DBM stored Athens, Greece Jun81; later b/u
18688	720-051B	361	Boeing MAC/USAF	N735US SX-DBN YN-BYI G-BRDR N8215Q stored Davis-Monthan AFB AZ 14Nov89
18689	707-323C	354	Transway Air International	N7555A G-WIND J6-SLF N728U N-902RQ EL-JNS
18690	707-323C	356	Boeing MAC/USAF	N7556A G-SAIL (N7556A) stored Davis-Monthan AFB, AZ 21Apr86
18691	707-323C	357	Boeing MAC/USAF	N7557A 5X-UWM G-BFEO stored Davis-Monthan AFB, AZ 08Apr86
18692	707-323C	358	(Lloyd Aereo Boliviano)	N7558A N309EL CP-1365 dbf Dothan, AL 31Aug91
18693	707-351B	348	(Midair)	N354US VR-HGN G-BFBS stored Lasham, UK 17Jan83; b/u late 86
18694	707-441	353	(Blue Airlines)	PP-VJJ N58RD 9Q-CMD stored Goma, Zaire May93; later b/u
18695 to 18700 model 717-165; built as C-135F and modified as follows:				
18695	C-135FR	C2007	Armee de l'Air/ERV.93	63-12735 12735/CG 12735/93-CG
18696	C-135FR	C2008	Armee de l'Air/ERV.93	63-12736 12736/CH 12736/93-CH
18697	C-135FR	C2009	Armee de l'Air/ERV.93	63-12737 12737/CI 12737/93-CI
18698	C-135FR	C2010	Armee de l'Air/ERV.93	63-12738 12738/CJ 12738/93-CJ
18699	C-135FR	C2011	Armee de l'Air/ERV.93	63-12739 12739/CK 12739/93-CK
18700	C-135FR	C2012	Armee de l'Air/ERV.93	63-12740 12740/CL 12740/93-CL
18701 to 18705 model 717-166; built as KC-135B and modified as follows:				
18701	EC-135C	C2113	USAF/7thACCS/55thWg	63-8053/OF
18702	EC-135C	C2114	USAF/7thACCS/55thWg	63-8054/OF
18703	EC-135J	C2115	USAF/2ndACCS	63-8055/OF stored Davis-Monthan AFB, AZ 04Oct93
18704	EC-135J	C2116	USAF/9thACCS	63-8056 stored Davis-Monthan AFB, AZ 23Mar92
18705	EC-135J	C2117	Pima Air & Space Museum	63-8057 stored Davis-Monthan AFB, AZ 31Mar92; preserved Pima County, AZ
18706 model 739-353B; built as RC-135B and modified as follows:				
18706	RC-135V	C2301	USAF/55thWg	63-9792/OF
18707	707-373C	349	(TAMPA-Colombia)	N375WA G-AYSI (N3751Y) HK-2401X w/o 14Dec83 Medellin, Colombia
18708	707-337B	375	Boeing MAC/USAF	VT-DPM TF-IUE N8880A stored Davis-Monthan AFB, AZ 10Oct89
18709	707-373C	350	SAETA	N789TW HK-2606X HK-2606 (HC-BLY) HP-1027 HC-BLY stored Quito, Ecuador May93
18710	707-351B	352	(AAR-Allen Aircraft Corp)	N355US B-1828 G-BCLZ B-1828 B/u Taipei, RoC Feb85
18711	707-331C-H	370	Phoenix Air	N786TW N700FW CC-CER N700FW CC-CER N700FW PP-PHB
18712	707-331C-H	373	(Trans World Airlines)	N787TW w/o 26Jul69 Pomona, NJ
18713 model 707-331C-H, modified as follows:				
18713	TC-18E	378	USAF/552ndACW	N788TW (N7888) N788TW N131EA 84-1398
18714	707-321C-H	362	TAMPA-Colombia	N790PA HK-1718 HK-1718X HK-1718 TF-AEA N228VV HK-3333X (N228VV) HK-3333X
18715	707-321C-H	364	(Golden Star Air Cargo)	N791PA TC-JCC N791PA ST-ALX w/o 23Mar92 Mount Hymittus, Greece

BOEING 707/720

C/n	Series	Line No	Last known Operator/Owner	Previous Identities/fate (where known)
18716	707-321C-H	365	Atlantic Air Leasing	N792PA JY-AED JY-CAB 4YB-CAB J6-SLR TF-AYE CX-BPQ HI-596CA N66651 HR-AMX N66651
18717	707-321C-H	366	TAMPA-Colombia	N793PA G-BGIS G-TRAD HK-3232X
18718	707-321C-H	368	(Trans Air Services)	N794PA N794 N794EP N794PA N794RN G-BFZF (G-CHGN) G-BNGH 5N-MAS dbr 31Mar92 Istres, France
18719 to 18736 model 717-148; built as KC-135A and modified as follows:				
18719	KC-135R	T0702	USAF/319thARW	63-8871
18720	KC-135R	T0703	USAF/136thARS/NY ANG	63-8872
18721	KC-135R	T0704	USAF/319thARW	63-8873
18722	KC-135R	T0705	USAF/909thARS/18thWg	63-8874/ZZ
18723	KC-135R	T0706	USAF/22ndARS/366thWg	63-8875/MO
18724	KC-135R	T0707	USAF/168thARS/AK ANG	63-8876
18725	KC-135R	T0708	USAF/351stARS/100thARW	63-8877/D
18726	KC-135R	T0709	USAF/55thARS/97thAMW	63-8878
18727	KC-135R	T0710	USAF/92ndARW	63-8879
18728	KC-135R	T0711	USAF/465thARS/AFRes	63-8880
18729	KC-135R	T0712	USAF/319thARW	63-8881 [KC-135R Relay aircraft]
18730	KC-135R	T0713	(USAF/379thBW)	63-8882 w/o 26Feb65 into Atlantic Ocean
18731	KC-135R	T0714	USAF/319thARW	63-8883
18732	KC-135R	T0715	USAF/22ndARW	63-8884
18733	KC-135R	T0716	USAF/319thARW	63-8885
18734	KC-135R	T0717	USAF/909thARS/18thWg	63-8886/ZZ
18735	KC-135R	T0718	USAF/22ndARW	63-8887
18736	KC-135R	T0719	USAF/55thARS/97thAMW	63-8888
18737	707-348C-H	377	(Alyemda Yemen Airlines)	EI-AMW LX-LGV EI-AMW 7O-ACJ dbr 26Jan82 Damascus, Syria; later b/u
18738	707-373C-H	355	(Trans World Airlines)	N790TW w/o 30Nov70 Tel Aviv, Israel
18739	707-138B	385	(Omega Air)	VH-EBL N107BN PK-MBA N46D stored Shannon, Eire 16Jan89; b/u Jun93
18740	707-138B	388	Aviation Methods	VH-EBM N108BN (HZ-KA1) N108BN N707XX
18745	720-040B	380	(ATASCO Leasing)	N68646 AP-ATQ stored Karachi, Pakistan Nov85; b/u Apr86
18746	707-351C-H	367	(EAS Cargo)	N356US CF-PWJ C-FPWJ (OO-BAI) OO-ABA C-GRYO OO-ABA 5A-DIZ 5Y-AXC N8163G TF-ANC 9G-RCA 9G-RBO dbr 29Apr92 Ilorin, Nigeria
18747	707-351C-H	369	Seagreen Air Transport	N357US VR-HHB 5X-UAC N21AZ CC-CDN N21AZ Z-WST N21AZ
18748	707-351C-H	379	Angola Air Charter	N358US VR-HHD VR-CAR 3X-GAZ N18AZ CC-CCE N18AZ CC-CCE N18AZ D2-TOR
18749	720-047B	374	Karachi Planetarium	N93151 AP-AXM Preserved Karachi, Pakistan Nov85
18756	707-331C-H	383	(Boeing MAC/USAF)	N791TW N5791 N791TW stored Davis-Monthan AFB, AZ 01Oct84; later b/u
18757	707-331C-H	387	EdA/Grupo 45	N792TW T.17-2/45-11
18758	707-131B	391	Boeing MAC/USAF	N795TW stored Davis-Monthan AFB, AZ 09Feb83
18759	707-131B	392	(Boeing MAC/USAF)	N796TW stored Davis-Monthan AFB, AZ 07Jul82; later b/u
18760	707-131B	393	(Trans World Airlines)	N797TW dbr 30Nov80 San Francisco, CA
18761	707-131B	395	(Boeing MAC/USAF)	N798TW stored Davis-Monthan AFB, AZ 13Sep82; b/u mid-93
18762	707-131B	396	(Boeing MAC/USAF)	N799TW stored Davis-Monthan AFB, AZ 08Feb83; later b/u
18763	720-024B	382	(Allen Aircraft Corp)	N57206 stored; b/u 22Mar76
18764	707-331BA	399	Boeing MAC/USAF	N779TW stored Davis-Monthan AFB, AZ 14Dec83
18765	707-321C-H	371	(Jamahiriya Air Transport)	N795PA N795RN G-BEZT SU-BAG (5X-UAL) SU-BAG Libyan Arab AF 5A-DHL stored Tripoli, Libya 06Dec82; later b/u
18766	707-321C-H	372	VASP	N796PA HK-1849 N865BX (HR-ANU) HR-AMZ
18767	707-321C-H	376	(Alia-Royal Jordanian A/L)	N797PA JY-AEE w/o 03Aug75 nr Agadir, Morocco
18768 to 18780 model 717-148; built as KC-135A and modified as follows:				
18768	KC-135R	T0720	USAF/22ndARW	64-14828
18769	KC-135R	T0721	USAF/55thARS/97thAMW	64-14829
18770	KC-135R	T0722	USAF/319thARW	64-14830
18771	KC-135R	T0723	USAF/92ndARW	64-14831
18772	KC-135R	T0724	USAF/203rdARS/HI ANG	64-14832
18773	KC-135R	T0725	USAF/22ndARW	64-14833
18774	KC-135R	T0726	USAF/74thARS/AFRes	64-14834
18775	KC-135R	T0727	USAF/22ndARW	64-14835
18776	KC-135R	T0728	USAF/319thARW	64-14836
18777	KC-135R	T0729	USAF/319thARW	64-14837
18778	KC-135R	T0730	USAF/22ndARW	64-14838
18779	KC-135R	T0731	USAF/136thARS/NY ANG	64-14839
18780	KC-135R	T0732	USAF/166thARS/OH ANG	64-14840
18781 to 18789 model 739-445B; built as RC-135B and modified as follows:				
18781	RC-135V	C2302	USAF/55thWg	64-14841/OF
18782	RC-135V	C2303	USAF/55thWg	64-14842/OF
18783	RC-135V	C2304	USAF/55thWg	64-14843/OF
18784	RC-135V	C2305	USAF/55thWg	64-14844/OF
18785	RC-135V	C2306	USAF/55thWg	64-14845/OF
18786	RC-135V	C2307	USAF/55thWg	64-14846/OF
18787	RC-135U	C2308	USAF/55thWg	64-14847/OF
18788	RC-135V	C2309	USAF/55thWg	64-14848/OF
18789	RC-135U	C2310	USAF/55thWg	64-14849/OF
18790	707-321C-H	394	(Pan American World A/W)	N798PA w/o 12Jun68 Calcutta, India

BOEING 707/720

C/n	Series	Line No	Last known Operator/Owner	Previous Identities/fate (where known)
18792	720-051B	381	(Boeing MAC/USAF)	N736US (OY-APU) G-BBZG OY-APU TF-AYA (N92038) stored Davis-Monthan AFB, AZ 05May87; later b/u
18793	720-051B	384	Boeing Equipment Holding	N737US OY-APV N737US N771BE stored Everett-Paine Field, WA 91; b/u 22Feb92
18808	707-338C-H	404	TAMPA-Colombia	VH-EBN 9V-BFW N707GB HK-3030X N707GB HK-3030X stored Medellin, Colombia Oct94
18809	707-338C-H	407	DAS Air Cargo	VH-EBO 9V-BFN (A6-GZA) N4225J 5N-ARQ
18810	707-338C-H	438	Farner Air Service	VH-EBP N14791 SU-BBA stored Cairo, Egypt Mar82; preserved as 'The Plane Restuarant'
18818	720-047B	390	(Pakistan Intl Airlines)	N93152 AP-AXL stored Lahore, Pakistan; b/u Jul86
18819	707-330B	398	African Airlines Intl	D-ABOX VP-WKR Z-WKR 5Y-AXM
18820	720-047B	401	(Aer Lingus)	N93153 TF-VLC stored Stansted, UK Dec79; b/u Jun80
18824	707-321C-H	397	(Pan American World A/W)	N799PA w/o 26Dec68 Elmendorf AFB, AK
18825	707-321C-H	386	(DAS Air Cargo)	(N798PA) N17321 B-1832 N987AA 5X-DAR dbr 25Nov92 Kano, Nigeria
18826	707-321C-H	389	(Pacific Western Airlines)	(N799PA) N17322 CF-PWZ w/o 02Jan73 Telford Lake, Canada
18827	720-047B	410	(Eagle Air)	N3154 TF-VLB stored Shannon, Eire 01Dec82; b/u Aug83
18828	720-047B	423	(Middle East Airlines)	N3155 OD-AGG dbf Beirut, Lebanon 01Aug82 by shelling
18829	720-047B	427	Boeing MAC/USAF	N3156 9H-AAO CX-BQG stored Davis-Monthan AFB, AZ 31Aug90
18830	720-047B	429	Middle East Airlines	N3157 OD-AGF stored Beirut, Lebanon by May94
18831	720-059B	414	(Boeing MAC/USAF)	HK-726 N4450Z stored Davis-Monthan AFB, AZ 02Oct84; b/u Mar91
18832	707-321BA-H	403	Boeing MAC/USAF	N401PA (OO-TYB) N401PA N401 EI-BKQ VN-81416 VN-B1416 5X-JCR stored Davis-Monthan AFB, AZ 22Dec89
18833	707-321BA-H	405	Boeing MAC/USAF	N402PA (N402PD) N402PA stored Davis-Monthan AFB, AZ 08May86
18834	707-321BA-H	406	Boeing MAC/USAF	N403PA TC-JBS N5519V stored Davis-Monthan AFB, AZ 20Dec85 [Official arrival date reversed with c/n 18836]
18835	707-321BA-H	408	USAF/AFSC	N404PA (N404PB) N404PA "N2138T" N404PA
18836	707-321BA-H	409	Boeing MAC/USAF	N405PA TC-JBT N5519U stored Davis-Monthan AFB, AZ 28Jan86 [Official arrival date reversed with c/n 18834]
18837	707-321BA-H	411	Boeing MAC/USAF	N406PA F-OGIV F-BSGT XT-ABZ (XT-BBH) stored Davis-Monthan AFB, AZ 09Oct90
18838	707-321BA-H	412	(Pan American World A/W)	N407PA dbr 17Dec73 Rome-Fiumicino, Italy
18839	707-321BA-H	417	Omega Air	N408PA N4408F N470PC N454PC C5-GOC HR-AMV OM-UFB EL-AKL stored Jan96 Shannon, Eire
18840	707-321BA-H	418	Boeing MAC/USAF	N409PA F-OGIW N707GE stored Davis-Monthan AFB, AZ 24Apr84
18841	707-321BA-H	419	Lineas Aereas Paraguayas	N410PA ZP-CCE stored Ascunsion, Paraguay by Apr92
18842	707-321BA-H	421	(Boeing MAC/USAF)	N412PA TC-JBU (N5517U) N5517Z stored Davis-Monthan AFB, AZ 25Jun86; later b/u
18873	707-337B-H	402	Boeing MAC/USAF	N68655 VT-DSI EL-AJS (EI-BVD) EL-AJS N8870A stored Davis-Monthan AFB, AZ 14Sep89
18880	707-348C-H	413	Jamahiriya Libyan Arab A/L	EI-ANO N318F EI-ANO N318F EI-ANO 5A-DIX (SU-BLJ) 5A-DIX stored Cairo, Egypt92
18881	707-328C-H	436	(Angola Air Charter)	F-BLCC TF-VLR 5A-DIK 5Y-BFC D2-TOV w/o 21Jul88 nr Lagos, Nigeria
18882	707-123B	420	Boeing MAC/USAF	N7550A stored Davis-Monthan AFB, AZ 28Sep81
18883	707-123B	422	(Boeing MAC/USAF)	N7551A stored Davis-Monthan AFB, AZ 14Apr83; later b/u
18884	707-123B	426	(Boeing MAC/USAF)	N7552A stored Davis-Monthan AFB, AZ 28Feb83; later b/u
18885	707-123B	432	(Boeing MAC/USAF)	N7553A stored Davis-Monthan AFB, AZ 25Sep81; later b/u
18886	707-324C-H	430	TAMPA-Colombia	N17323 G-AZJM N17323 HK-2600X HK-2600 (N734Q) HK-3355X
18887	707-324C-H	431	(China Airlines)	N17324 B-1834 w/o 11Sep79 nr Taipei, RoC
18888	707-351C-H	425	(Jamahiriya Libyan Arab A/L)	N359US VR-HHE 5A-DJT dbf 07Dec91 Tripoli, Libya
18889	707-351C-H	428	Jamahiriya Libyan Arab A/L	N360US VR-HHJ 5A-DJU stored Tripoli, Libya Dec91
18890	707-329C-H	416	(SABENA)	OO-SJH dbr 11May80 Douala, Cameroons
18891	707-344BA	441	Omega Air	ZS-DYL ZS-SAD VP-WKW 3B-NAE (N7000Y) EL-AJT stored Miami, FL later Manston, UK early 93
18913	707-331BA	400	Boeing MAC/USAF	N760TW stored Davis-Monthan AFB, AZ 20Dec83
18914	707-331BA	415	Boeing MAC/USAF	N780TW stored Davis-Monthan AFB, AZ 17May84
18915	707-331BA	424	Boeing MAC/USAF	N793TW stored Davis-Monthan AFB, AZ 24May84
18916	707-331BA	455	Boeing MAC/USAF	N8705T stored Davis-Monthan AFB, AZ 15Dec83
18917	707-331BA	460	(Trans World Airlines)	N8715T dbr 13Sep70 el Khana, Jordan
18918	707-331BA	462	Boeing MAC/USAF	N8725T stored Davis-Monthan AFB, AZ 21Dec83
18921	707-351C-H	440	Aeronaves del Peru	N361US (VR-HGP) VR-HGR S2-ACF N8090P OB-1401 stored Lima, Peru Aug94
18922	707-351C-H	444	TransBrasil	N362US (VR-HGQ) VR-HGP N82TF 5N-ASY 5N-JIL HR-AME EL-AKF
18923	707-330BA-H	435	Air Zimbabwe	D-ABUB VP-WKS Z-WKS
18924	707-336C-H	448	(RN Cargo)	N2978G G-ASZF 5N-ARO dbf 25Sep83 Accra, Ghana
18925	707-336C-H	452	Brasair Air Cargo	G-ASZG LX-FCV XT-ABX 18925 EL-AKI PP-BRB
18926	707-330BA-H	446	Fuerza Aerea de Chile/10GT	D-ABUC CC-CEA 903
18927	707-330BA-H	454	African Airlines Intl	D-ABUD VP-WKV Z-WKV 5Y-AXI
18928	707-330BA-H	457	Lowa Inc	D-ABUF N5381X N88ZL [Op by Jet Aviation]
18929	707-330BA-H	461	Air Zimbabwe	D-ABUG VP-WKT Z-WKT stored Harare, Zimbabwe 10Nov88
18930	707-330BA-H	464	Air Zimbabwe	D-ABUH VP-WKU Z-WKU

BOEING 707/720

C/n	Series	Line No	Last known Operator/Owner	Previous Identities/fate (where known)
18931	707-330BA-H	482	(Trans Arabian Air Tpt)	D-ABUK A6-UAE ST-NSR stored Khartoum, Sudan; b/u Mar95
18932	707-330C-H	477	(AeroBrasil)	D-ABUE PT-TCO dbr 11Apr87 Manaus, Brazil
18937	707-330C-H	451	AECA	D-ABUA VR-HTC VH-HTC LZ-PVA HC-BTB stored Marana, AZ by Apr95
18938	707-323C-H	434	(Trans Mediterranean A/W)	N7559A OD-AGN dbr Beirut, Lebanon 16Jun82 by shelling
18939	707-323C-H	437	Kuwait Airways	N7560A OD-AGD
18940	707-323C-H	439	Merchant Express	N7561A PP-VLP N108BV 5N-MXX
18941	707-328B	471	Musee de l'Air	F-BLCD Preserved Paris-le Bourget, France 13Apr83
18948	707-384C-H	495	Royal Jordanian	SX-DBA JY-AEB JY-AJK
18949	707-384C-H	497	USAF/Omega Air	SX-DBB JY-AEC 66-30052 [under conversion to E-8C]
18950	707-384C-H	504	Fuerza Aerea Venezolanas	SX-DBC 8747 [converted to tanker]
18953	707-338C-H	443	(Boeing MAC/USAF)	VH-EBQ 9M-ASQ 9M-MCQ 60-SBM N342A stored Davis-Monthan AFB, AZ 06Mar86
18954	707-338C-H	458	(Boeing MAC/USAF)	VH-EBR 9M-ATR 9M-MCR 60-SBN G-BMJE N449J stored Davis-Monthan AFB, AZ 25Nov85; b/u Oct93
18955	707-338C-H	467	(Jamahiriya Air Transport)	VH-EBS 9M-ASO 9M-MCS 5A-DJO w/o 14Mar83 Sabha, Libya
18956	707-321BA-H	466	(Air Carrier Supply)	N414PA stored Miami, FL; b/u 04Dec80
18957	707-321BA-H	472	Government of Paraguay	N415PA ZP-CCF FAP-01 [Op by Fuerza Aerea Paraguaya]
18958	707-321BA-H	475	Iran Air	N416PA EP-IRJ stored Teheran, Iran
18959	707-321BA-H	478	(Pan American World A/W)	N417PA w/o 23Jul73 Papeete, Tahiti
18960	707-321BA-H	484	(Israel Aircraft Industries)	N418PA stored Tel Aviv, Israel 01Jan81; b/u Oct86

18961 and 18962 built as 707-382BA-H and modified as follows:

C/n	Series	Line No	Last known Operator/Owner	Previous Identities/fate (where known)
18961	TC-18F	456	USN/SCW-1	CS-TBA N45RT 165342
18962	TC-18F	501	USN/SCW-1	CS-TBB TF-VLV CS-TBB N46RT 165343
18963	720-047B	433	(Middle East Airlines)	N3158 OD-AGE (N4466C) dbr Beirut, Lebanon 27Jun76 by shelling
18964	707-351C-H	453	NASCO	N363US (VR-HGR) VR-HGQ N88TF TF-VLP 5A-DJS 5Y-BFB D2-TOU stored Manston, UK 12Jun91
18975	707-349C-H	445	(TAAG-Angola Airlines)	N322F G-AWTK G-BDCN D2-TAC D2-TOB D2-TOI dbr Feb88 Luanda, Angola
18976	707-349C-H	449	(Trans Arabian Air Tpt)	N323F EI-ASN 9J-ADY ST-ALK dbr 14Jul90 Khartoum, Sudan
18977	720-060B	442	US Department of Defense	ET-ABP N440DS N7381 stored Mojave, CA Jan94
18978	707-331BA	465	(Trans World Airlines)	N18701 w/o 22Dec75 Milan-Malpensa, Italy
18979	707-331BA	468	(Boeing MAC/USAF)	N18702 stored Davis-Monthan AFB, AZ 16Feb84; later b/u
18980	707-331BA	469	Boeing MAC/USAF	N18703 stored Davis-Monthan AFB, AZ 12Nov83
18981	707-331BA	476	Boeing MAC/USAF	N18704 stored Davis-Monthan AFB, AZ 21Dec83
18982	707-331BA	483	Boeing MAC/USAF	N18706 stored Davis-Monthan AFB, AZ 12Nov83
18983	707-331BA	485	Boeing MAC/USAF	N18707 stored Davis-Monthan AFB, AZ 14Feb84
18984	707-331BA	487	Boeing MAC/USAF	N18708 stored Davis-Monthan AFB, AZ 14Dec83
18985	707-331BA	496	Boeing MAC/USAF	N18709 4X-ATD N707HP stored Davis-Monthan AFB, AZ 27Aug89
18986	707-131B	479	(Boeing MAC/USAF)	N6720 stored Davis-Monthan AFB, AZ 21Dec82; later b/u
18987	707-131B	486	(Boeing MAC/USAF)	N6721 stored Davis-Monthan AFB, AZ 21Dec82; later b/u
18988	707-131B	489	(Boeing MAC/USAF)	N6722 stored Davis-Monthan AFB, AZ 19May82; later b/u
18989	707-131B	492	(Boeing MAC/USAF)	N6723 stored Davis-Monthan AFB, AZ 12Aug82; later b/u
18991	707-373C	450	(Pakistan Intl Airlines)	N376WA AP-AWU 65-18991 AP-AWU stored Karachi, Pakistan by Dec93; later b/u
19000	707-385C-H	447	Fuerza Aerea de Chile/10GT	N68657 CC-CEB 905 257/4X-JYI (905) 01 [Phalcon AEW conversion]
19001	707-348C-H	488	Jamahiriya Libyan Arab A/L	EI-ANV 9G-ACR EI-ANV 5A-DIY (SU-BLI) 5A-DIY stored Cairo Egypt 92
19002	720-024B	473	(Allen Aircraft Corp)	N17207 B/u 24Mar76
19003	720-024B	474	(Allen Aircraft Corp)	N17208 B/u 01Apr76
19004	707-358BA	459	(Boeing MAC/USAF)	4X-ATR N317F 4X-ATR N53302 TF-AYG N53302 stored Davis-Monthan AFB, AZ 27Sep89; later b/u
19034	707-351C-H	463	Boeing MAC/USAF	N364US (VR-HGS) VR-HGU RP-C1886 stored Davis-Monthan AFB, AZ 19Dec85
19104	707-327C-H	498	Trans Mediterranean A/W	N7095 OD-AGX
19105	707-327C-H	499	Kuwait Airways	N7096 OD-AGY
19106	707-327C-H	502	(VARIG)	N7097 PP-VLJ w/o 09Jun73 Rio de Janeiro, Brazil
19107	707-327C-H	507	(Trans Mediterranean A/W)	N7098 PH-TRV N7098 OD-AFX w/o 23Jul79 Beirut, Lebanon
19108	707-327C-H	511	(Trans Mediterranean A/W)	N7099 OD-AFY dbr 26Jul93 Amsterdam-Schipol, Netherlands
19133	707-344B	538	Boeing MAC/USAF	ZS-EKV ZS-SAE LX-LGU 3B-NAF N237G TF-IUC 5Y-AXS TF-IUG 5Y-LKL N6598W stored Davis-Monthan AFB, AZ 02Oct90
19160	720-047B	470	(Middle East Airlines)	N3159 OD-AGQ dbr Beirut, Lebanon 21Aug85 by shelling
19161	720-047B	481	(Middle East Airlines)	N3160 OD-AGR dbr Beirut, Lebanon 16Jun82 by shelling
19162	707-329C-H	480	(Katale Aero Transport)	OO-SJJ 9Q-CVG dbr 01Mar90 Goma, Zaire
19163	707-351C-H	494	Boeing MAC/USAF	N365US SX-DBP N65010 stored Davis-Monthan AFB, AZ 29Aug90
19164	707-351C-H	505	EdA/Grupo 45	N366US SX-DBO T.17-4/45-13 [SIGINT configuration]
19168	707-351C-H	508	(GAS Air Cargo)	N367US S2-ABN 5N-AYJ w/o 14Dec88 Kom Omran, Egypt
19177	707-324C-H	513	Yugoslav Federal Air Force	N17325 PP-VLN N110BV 5X-UCM 73601 Impounded Zagreb 31Aug91; stored Nis, Serbia
19178	707-324C-H	517	(AAR-Allen Aircraft Corp)	N17326 B-1830 stored Taipei, RoC; b/u Jun85

BOEING 707/720

C/n	Series	Line No	Last known Operator/Owner	Previous Identities/fate (where known)
19179	707-373C-H	500	Skydec Cargo	N372WA CS-TBJ 9Q-CSB Impounded Luanda, Angola
19185	707-123B	490	(Boeing MAC/USAF)	N7554A stored Davis-Monthan AFB, AZ 20Aug85; later b/u
19186	707-123B	491	(Boeing MAC/USAF)	N7570A stored Davis-Monthan AFB, AZ 20Aug85; later b/u
19187	707-123B	493	(Boeing MAC/USAF)	N7571A stored Davis-Monthan AFB, AZ 28Sep81
19188	707-123B	506	(Boeing MAC/USAF)	N7572A stored Davis-Monthan AFB, AZ 28Feb83; b/u Feb92
19207	720-047B	512	(Boeing MAC/USAF)	N3161 stored Van Nuys, CA 11Sep79 then Davis-Monthan AFB, AZ 17Mar83; later b/u
19208	720-047B	514	Boeing MAC/USAF	N3162 stored Van Nuys, CA 25Jan80 then Davis-Monthan AFB, AZ 06Apr83
19209	707-351C-H	510	(Buffalo Airways)	N368US 9Y-TED N29796 N144SP w/o 13Apr87 Kansas City, MO
19210	707-351C-H	515	Jet Aviation Components	N369US YU-AGI N152LM CX-BPZ N152LM HR-ANG HP-1235CTH N777FB stored Miami, FL
19211	707-329C-H	518	(SABENA)	OO-SJK w/o 13Jul68 Lagos, Nigeria
19212	707-331C-H	588	(G-Jet/Jetlease)	N5771T EI-BER LX-FCV CX-BJV LX-BJV 5A-DKA 9G-ACY 9G-MAN N227VV N730FW N851MA N730FW stored Miami, FL 03SeP93; b/u Nov/Dec95
19213	707-331C-H	613	(Trans Mediterranean A/W)	N5772T OD-AGT dbr 23Oct81 Tokyo, Japan; later b/u
19214	707-331C-H	626	Kuwait Airways	N5773T OD-AGS
19215	707-131B	530	(Boeing MAC/USAF)	N6724 stored Davis-Monthan AFB, AZ 01Feb83; later b/u
19216	707-131B	558	(Boeing MAC/USAF)	N6726 stored Davis-Monthan AFB, AZ 19May82; later b/u
19217	707-131B	564	(Boeing MAC/USAF)	N6727 stored Davis-Monthan AFB, AZ 13Sep82; later b/u
19218	707-131B	567	Boeing MAC/USAF	N6728 stored Davis-Monthan AFB, AZ 13Sep82
19219	707-131B	569	(Boeing MAC/USAF)	N6729 stored Davis-Monthan AFB, AZ 28Apr82; later b/u
19220	707-131B	573	(Boeing MAC/USAF)	N6763T stored Davis-Monthan AFB, AZ 23Apr82; later b/u
19221	707-131B	577	(Boeing MAC/USAF)	N6764T stored Davis-Monthan AFB, AZ 07Jul82; later b/u
19222	707-131B	583	(Boeing MAC/USAF)	N6771T stored Davis-Monthan AFB, AZ 12Aug82; later b/u
19223	707-131B	598	Boeing MAC/USAF	N6789T stored Davis-Monthan AFB, AZ 12May82
19224	707-331BA-H	559	Boeing MAC/USAF	N18710 stored Davis-Monthan AFB, AZ 05Apr84
19225	707-331BA-H	568	Boeing MAC/USAF	N18711 stored Davis-Monthan AFB, AZ 05Jun84
19226	707-331BA-H	585	Boeing MAC/USAF	N18712 stored Davis-Monthan AFB, AZ 30Apr84
19227	707-331BA-H	607	Boeing MAC/USAF	N18713 stored Davis-Monthan AFB, AZ 06Apr84
19235	707-323C-H	519	(VARIG)	N7562A PP-VLU w/o 30Jan79 nr Tokyo, Japan
19236	707-323C-H	521	(USAF)	N7563A (81-0897) stored Greenville-Majors, TX; b/u Apr-Aug82
19237	707-323C-H	523	(Boeing MAC/USAF)	N7564A stored Davis-Monthan AFB, AZ 07Jun84; b/u Feb92
19238	707-387B-H	528	LADE	LV-ISA T-96 LV-ISA T-96 LV-ISA T-96 LV-ISA dbr 31Jan93 Recife, Brazil
19239	707-387B-H	542	PLUNA	LV-ISB CX-BNU PP-LBN CX-BNU
19240	707-387B-H	543	(Aerolineas Argentinas)	LV-ISC CX-BOH LV-ISC stored Buenos-Aires, Argentina Feb93; later b/u
19241	707-387B-H	555	FA Argentina/5Esc	LV-ISD T-95 LV-ISD T-95 LV-ISD T-95 LV-ISD T-95
19247	707-337B-H	520	Boeing MAC/USAF	VT-DVA EL-AJR N8840A stored Davis-Monthan AFB, AZ 13Sep89
19248	707-337B-H	549	Indian Air Force/12Sqdn	VT-DVB K-2900
19263	707-351C-H	516	Florida West Airlines	N370US (VR-HHK) N370US 9J-AEB EI-ASM 9J-AEB N720FW stored Miami, FL by Apr95
19264	707-321BA-H	527	Lineas Aereas Paraguayas	N419PA ZP-CCG stored Ascunsion, Paraguay by Apr92
19265	707-321BA-H	529	AECA	N420PA HC-BCT/FAE19255 stored Guaryaquil, Ecuador Sep93
19266	707-321BA-H	531	Boeing MAC/USAF	N421PA HK-2070X HK-2070 9Q-CBL stored Davis-Monthan AFB, AZ 02Oct90
19267	707-321C-H	541	Iran Air	N445PA EP-IRK stored Teheran, Iran
19268	707-321C-H	544	(Pan American World A/W)	N446PA w/o 22Apr74 nr Singaraja, Bali, Indonesia
19269	707-321C-H	570	Trans Mediterranean A/W	N447PA OD-AGO
19270	707-321C-H	572	Air Atlantic Cargo	N448PA N448M (G-BGIR) N448M TF-VLL G-BMAZ N863BX N705FW 5N-EEO
19271	707-321C-H	574	Intl Air Leases	N449PA (N448WA) G-BEVN (N449PA) N707HT TC-JCF N707HT stored Miami, FL Jan96
19272	707-321C-H	578	(Air Afrique)	N450PA YR-ABM w/o 15Jan93 Abidjan-Port Bouet, Ivory Coast
19273	707-321C-H	580	AECA	N451PA N451RN HC-BGP/FAE19273
19274	707-321C-H	594	Trans Mediterranean A/W	N452PA OD-AGP
19275	707-321BA-H	590	(Intl Air Leases)	N422PA stored Miami, FL 03Aug83; b/u Sep84
19276	707-321BA-H	592	(AVIANCA)	N423PA HK-2016 w/o 25Jan90 Long Island, NY
19277	707-321BA-H	603	(Ecuatoriana)	N424PA HC-BFC/FAE19277 4X-ATF stored Tel Aviv, Israel Apr93; b/u late 94
19278	707-321BA-H	605	(Avn Traders Eng'g Ltd)	N425PA stored Stansted, UK Jan82; b/u Jun82
19284	707-340C-H	509	JAT-Jugoslav Airlines	AP-AUO AP-AUN YU-AGE stored Zagreb, Croatia, possibly to Yugoslav AF
19285	707-340C-H	524	JAT-Jugoslav Airlines	AP-AUO YU-AGG stored Zagreb, Croatia, possibly to Yugoslav AF
19286	707-340C-H	625	(Pakistan Intl Airlines)	AP-AUP YU-AGF AP-AXA stored Karachi, Pakistan by Dec93; later b/u
19291	707-328B	536	Israel Defence Force/AF	F-BLCE TU-TXL F-BLCE TU-TXN F-BLCE 3X-GCC (F-BLCE) OO-TYC N2090B 4X-BYC 258/4X-JYC [ELINT conversion]
19292	707-328B	560	Rwandair	F-BLCF 9XR-JA 9XR-VO
19293	707-338C-H	546	USAF/Northrop-Grumman	VH-EBT G-BFLE N861BX (N2178F reserved)

BOEING 707/720

C/n	Series	Line No	Last known Operator/Owner	Previous Identities/fate (where known)
19294	707-338C-H	550	USAF/Omega Air	VH-EBU P2-ANH VH-EBU P2-ANH N707MB 9Q-CDA N707HW OB-T-1264 N707HW B-2426 N707HW G-EOCO stored Davis-Monthan AFB, AZ Sep92
19295	707-338C-H	617	USAF/Northrop-Grumman	VH-EBV 9J-AEL ST-ALP N4115J Regn canx Oct95
19296	707-338C-H	630	USAF/Northrop-Grumman	VH-EBW G-BDEA EL-AKH "PT-TCT" EL-AKH N6546L Regn canx Oct95
19297	707-338C-H	636	(T/A Rioplatense)	VH-EBX G-BCAL LV-MZE stored Miami, FL Nov88; later derelict
19315	707-330B-H	545	Boeing MAC/USAF	D-ABUL 6O-SBS EL-AJU stored Davis-Monthan AFB, AZ 30Oct90
19316	707-330B-H	547	(Somali Airlines)	D-ABUM 6O-SBT dbr 17May89 Nairobi, Kenya
19317	707-330C-H	557	AeroBrasil	D-ABUI PT-TCM
19320	707-341C-H	522	(VARIG)	PP-VJR dbf 07Sep68 Rio de Janeiro-Galeao, Brazil
19321	707-341C-H	532	Azerbaijan Airlines	PP-VJS (FAB2405) PP-VJS N107BV 4K-AZ3
19322	707-341C-H	561	(VARIG)	PP-VJT dbr 11Jun81 Manaus, Brazil
19323	707-123B	526	(Boeing MAC/USAF)	N7573A stored Davis-Monthan AFB, AZ 20Aug85; later b/u
19324	707-123B	533	(Boeing MAC/USAF)	N7574A stored Davis-Monthan AFB, AZ 20Mar83; later b/u
19325	707-123B	535	Boeing MAC/USAF	N7575A stored Davis-Monthan AFB, AZ 25Sep81
19326	707-123B	539	Boeing MAC/USAF	N7576A stored Davis-Monthan AFB, AZ 22Sep81
19327	707-123B	562	Boeing MAC/USAF	N7577A stored Davis-Monthan AFB, AZ 28Sep81
19328	707-123B	565	Boeing MAC/USAF	N7578A stored Davis-Monthan AFB, AZ 23Sep81
19329	707-123B	571	Boeing MAC/USAF	N7579A stored Davis-Monthan AFB, AZ 29Sep81
19330	707-123B	575	Boeing MAC/USAF	N7580A stored Davis-Monthan AFB, AZ 22Sep81
19331	707-123B	579	Boeing MAC/USAF	N7581A stored Davis-Monthan AFB, AZ 24Sep81
19332	707-123B	586	Boeing MAC/USAF	N7582A stored Davis-Monthan AFB, AZ 24Sep81
19333	707-123B	589	Boeing MAC/USAF	N7583A stored Davis-Monthan AFB, AZ 08Apr83
19334	707-123B	591	Boeing MAC/USAF	N7584A stored Davis-Monthan AFB, AZ 28Sep81
19335	707-123B	593	New ACS	N7585A N703PC EL-AKA YN-CDE C5-GOB HR-AMG OM-WFA 9Q-CJT
19336	707-123B	595	(Boeing MAC/USAF)	N7586A stored Davis-Monthan AFB, AZ 29Apr83; b/u Sep90
19337	707-123B	600	(Boeing MAC/USAF)	N7587A stored Davis-Monthan AFB, AZ 29Jan81; later b/u
19338	707-123B	602	Boeing MAC/USAF	N7588A stored Davis-Monthan AFB, AZ 29Apr83
19339	707-123B	604	(Boeing MAC/USAF)	N7589A stored Davis-Monthan AFB, AZ 20Aug85; later b/u
19340	707-123B	622	(Boeing MAC/USAF)	N7590A stored Davis-Monthan AFB, AZ 28Sep91; later b/u
19341	707-123B	682	(Boeing MAC/USAF)	N7591A stored Davis-Monthan AFB, AZ 29Sep91; later b/u
19342	707-123B	787	Boeing MAC/USAF	N7592A stored Davis-Monthan AFB, AZ 28Sep91
19343	707-123B	794	(Boeing MAC/USAF)	N7593A stored Davis-Monthan AFB, AZ 28Sep91; later b/u
19344	707-123B	801	Boeing MAC/USAF	N7594A stored Davis-Monthan AFB, AZ 23Sep91
19345	707-123B		(American Airlines)	(N7595A) Allocated but later canx, not built
19346	707-123B		(American Airlines)	(N7596A) Allocated but later canx, not built
19347	707-123B		(American Airlines)	(N7597A) Allocated but later canx, not built
19348	707-123B		(American Airlines)	(N7598A) Allocated but later canx, not built
19349	707-123B		(American Airlines)	(N7599A) Allocated but later canx, not built
19350	707-324C-H	537	Ariana Cargo	N17327 PP-VLO (N112BV) G-HEVY N17327 G-HEVY EL-LAT
19351	707-324C-H	552	(Boeing MAC/USAF)	N17328 9V-BEW TF-VLJ (F-BMKO) TF-VLJ N419B stored Davis-Monthan AFB, AZ Jun87; later b/u
19352	707-324C-H	576	TAMPA-Colombia	N17329 9V-BEX N707JJ B-2423 N707PM HK-3604X
19353	707-324C-H	587	Amed Air	N47330 9V-BEY N707SH B-2422 N707HG N750FW JY-AFL 5N-ONE
19354	707-349C-H	503	(TransBrasil)	N324F EI-ASO VH-EBZ EI-ASO G-BAWP EI-ASO 9J-AEC EI-ASO 9J-AEC EI-ASO S2-ACB EI-ASO N324F PT-TCS w/o 21Mar89 Sao Paulo-Guarulhos, Brazil
19355	707-349C-H	553	TAAG-Angola Airlines	N325F G-AWWD N325F G-AWWD D2-TAD D2-TOC D2-TOJ stored Luanda, Angola 94
19361	707-321BA-H	618	Legion Express	N426PA HK-2015 N707LE stored Opa Locka, FL Nov94, later Miami, FL
19362	707-321BA-H	620	(Avn Traders Eng'g Ltd)	N427PA stored Stansted, UK 21May80; b/u Oct81
19363	707-321BA-H	623	(Korean Air Lines)	N428PA HL7429 w/o 20Apr78 Ken Murmansk, USSR
19364	707-321BA-H	628	(Avn Traders Eng'g Ltd)	N433PA stored Stansted, UK 26Apr80; b/u Mar82
19365	707-321BA-H	631	(Avn Traders Eng'g Ltd)	N434PA stored Stansted, UK 20Jul81; later b/u
19366	707-321BA-H	633	African Express Airways	N435PA HL7435 5Y-AXW stored Nairobi, Kenya Dec92
19367	707-321C-H	637	Trans Arabian Air Transport	N457PA G-BPAT 9J-AEQ ST-ALM VR-HKL ST-AMF
19368	707-321C-H	640	(Pan American World A/W)	N458PA w/o 03Nov73 Boston-Logan, MA
19369	707-321C-H	648	GM Airlines	N459PA HL7431 9G-ACZ 5Y-AXG 9G-ADL 9G-ADM
19370	707-321C-H	651	(Pan Aviation)	N460PA F-BYCN N720GS stored Miami, FL Mar90; b/u May93
19371	707-321C-H	653	(Pan American World A/W)	N461PA w/o 25Jul71 Manila, Philippines
19372	707-321C-H	655	Alpine Air	N462PA HL7427 TF-IUE 5N-AWO 9G-ESI 9G-EBK stored Southend, UK Sep94
19373	707-321C-H	656	Millon AIr	N463PA F-BYCO N722GS
19374	707-321BA-H	658	Fuerza Aerea de Chile/10GT	N453PA CC-CEK 904 CC-CYO 901
19375	707-321C-H	662	Omega Air	N473PA N473RN HK-2473X HK-2473 OB-R-1243 N864BX 5N-TAS 9Q-CSW EL-AKJ (PP-BRR) EL-AKJ stored Shannon, Eire 24Nov95
19376	707-321BA-H	661	(Pan American World A/W)	N454PA w/o 30Jan74 Pago Pago, American Samoa
19377	707-321C-H	666	(Sudan Air Cargo)	N474PA F-BYCP (EL-AIY) EL-AJA N5366Y N721GS ST-SAC w/o 03Dec90 nr Nairobi, Kenya
19378	707-321BA-H	672	Jamahiriya Libyan Arab A/L	N455PA OO-PS1 OO-PSA OO-PSI 5A-DJM (SU-BLK) 5A-DJM stored Cairo, Egypt 92
19379	707-321C-H	677	Tarom	N475PA YR-ABN believed dbr 17Aug95 N'Djamena, Chad

BOEING 707/720

C/n	Series	Line No	Last known Operator/Owner	Previous Identities/fate (where known)
19380 to 19384 built as 707-323C-H and modified as follows:				
19380	C-18A	525	USAF/412ndTW	N7565A 81-0898
19381	EC-18D	610	USAF/412ndTW	N7566A 81-0895
19382	EC-18B	627	USAF/412ndTW	N7567A 81-0892
19383	707-323C-H	641	Boeing MAC/USAF	N7568A stored Davis-Monthan AFB, AZ 06Jun84
19384	EC-18D	647	USAF/412ndTW	N7569A 81-0893
19410	707-348C-H	599	(Sudan Airways)	EI-APG N8789R EI-APG CF-TAI EI-APG ST-AIM Ditched 10Sep82 in River Nile, nr Khartoum, Sudan
19411	707-351C-H	540	DAS Air Cargo	N371US YU-AGJ N740FW N851MA N740FW 5X-JET
19412	707-351C-H	563	Trans Arabian Air Transport	N372US (VR-HHL) N372US 9Y-TEE 8P-CAC N707DY ST-
19413	720-047B-H	581	(Boeing MAC/USAF)	N3163 stored Davis-Monthan AFB, AZ 05Apr83; later b/u
19414	720-047B-H	597	(Boeing MAC/USAF)	N3164 stored Davis-Monthan AFB, AZ 21Apr83; later b/u
19415	707-399C-H	601	Azerbaijan Airlines	N319F G-AVKA N319F G-AVKA CS-TBH N106BV 4K-AZ4
19416	707-365C-H	556	(AeroBrasil)	G-ATZC N737AL PH-TRW G-ATZC C-GFLG PT-TCP w/o 26Nov92 Manaus, Brazil
19417 built as 707-355C-H and modified as follows:				
19417	EC-137D	582	USAF/SOCOM	N525EJ G-AYEX N525EJ N707HL 67-19417 [Op by 2ndSOF/19thARW]
19433	707-385C-H	534	(Ethiopian AIrlines)	N8400 PP-VLI N109BV ET-AJZ dbr Asmara, Ethiopia 25Mar91 by shelling
19434	707-351C-H	566	Aeronaves del Peru	N373US C-GTAI S2-ACA N8090Q OB-1400 stored Lima, Peru Aug94
19435	707-331C-H	629	Aerovenca	N5774T CC-CAF CX-BPL YV-671C
19436	707-131B	606	(Boeing MAC/USAF)	N6790T stored Davis-Monthan AFB, AZ 31Mar83; later b/u
19438	720-047B-H	615	(Boeing MAC/USAF)	N3165 stored Davis-Monthan AFB, AZ 12May82; later b/u
19439	720-047B-H	621	(Western Air Lines)	N3166 w/o 31Mar71 Ontario, CA
19440	707-327C-H	554	(Trans Mediterranean A/W)	N7100 OD-AGW dbr Beirut, Lebanon 05Jul81 by bomb
19441	707-373C-H	548	(Biman Bangladesh)	N371WA AP-AWV S2-ABQ dbr Singapore 04Apr80; b/u Apr81
19442	707-373C-H	609	USAF/Omega Air	N370WA OO-SBU N760FW stored Davis-Monthan AFB, AZ May92
19443	707-351C-H	611	Fuerza Aerea de Chile/10GT	N374US CC-CCK 902
19498	707-336C-H	645	Seagreen Air Transport	G-ATWV 9G-ACX N14AZ
19502	707-358B	551	Boeing MAC/USAF	4X-ATS N898WA stored Davis-Monthan AFB, AZ 30Aug89
19515	707-323C-H	608	Middle East Airlines	N7595A OD-AHD
19516	707-323C-H	612	Middle East Airlines	N7596A OD-AHE
19517	707-323C-H	614	Seagreen Air Transport	N7597A PT-TCL 4X-AOY 7P-LAN N29AZ CC-CDI N29AZ
19518 built as 707-323C-H and modified as follows:				
19518	EC-18B	616	USAF/412thTW	N7598A 81-0891
19519	707-323C-H	619	ex-Zaire Express	N7599A PT-TCK N5065T 3D-ASB 9G-OLU 3D-ASB 9Q-CKB stored Ostend, Belgium Nov95
19521	707-328C-H	584	Avistar Airlines	F-BLCG SU-DAB ST-AKR SU-DAB XT-BBF HB-IEI (5Y-ANA) 5B-DAZ
19522	707-328C-H	596	South African AF/60Sqdn	F-BLCH (ZS-LSK) 1415 AF-615 [Tanker conversion]
19523	720-047B-H	624	(Boeing MAC/USAF)	N3167 5V-TAD N3833L stored Davis-Monthan AFB, AZ 20Jun83; b/u Jun91
19529	707-327C-H	632	Asnet Inc	N7102 9M-AQB 9V-BFC N707AD PT-TCJ N707AD
19530	707-327C-H	635	JARO International	N7103 9V-BDC N707ME B-2424 N707ME CC-CYA YR-JCA
19531	707-327C-H	646	Ethiopian Airlines	N7104 OD-AGZ ET-AIV
19566 built as 707-331C-H and modified as follows:				
19566	TC-18E	717	USAF/552ndACW	N15710 (N5710) N132EA 84-1399
19567	707-331C-H	720	(Boeing MAC/USAF)	N15711 stored Davis-Monthan AFB, AZ 03Oct84; b/u Feb92
19568	707-131B	669	(Boeing MAC/USAF)	N16738 stored Davis-Monthan AFB, AZ 10Feb83; later b/u
19569	707-131B	680	(Boeing MAC/USAF)	N16739 stored Davis-Monthan AFB, AZ 10Feb83; later b/u
19570	707-331BA-H	674	IAL Air Services	N28724 OK-XFJ LZ-PVB N7232X stored Tucson, AZ Nov93
19571	707-331BA-H	685	(Avn Technical Support)	N28726 stored Waco, TX 18Apr83; b/u Apr84
19572	707-331BA-H	687	(Independent Air)	N28727 N7230T N7231T w/o 08Feb89 Pico Alto mountains, Azores
19573	707-331BA-H	704	(Avn Technical Support)	N28728 stored Waco, TX 21Apr83; b/u Apr84
19574 to 19589 built as 707-323C-H and modified as follows:				
19574	E-8A	710	USAF/4500thJSTARSS(P)	N8411 (N707NR) N8411 (N780JS) N8411 86-0417
19575	KC-137E	714	FA Peruana/Grupo 8	N8412 HK-2842 HP-1028 (ZS-LSI) HP-1028 FAP-319 FAP-319/OB-1371
19576	707-323C-H	719	Pakistan Intl Airlines	N8413 AP-BBK
19577	707-323C-H	722	Shabair	N8414 ZS-LSJ 9Q-CSZ
19578	707-323C-H		(American Airlines)	(N8416) (N8424) Allocated but later canx, not built
19579	707-323C-H		(American Airlines)	(N8417) (N8425) Allocated but later canx, not built
19580	707-323C-H		(American Airlines)	(N8418) (N8426) Allocated but later canx, not built
19581	EC-18D	638	USAF/412thTW	N8401 81-0896
19582	707-323C-H	639	Millon Air	N8402 EL-GNU N751MA
19583	EC-18D	650	USAF/412thTW	N8403 81-0894
19584	707-323C-H	663	(Azerbaijan Airlines)	N8404 (N872BX) N8404 LZ-FEB 4K-401 w/o 30Nov95 nr Baku, Azerbaijan
19585	707-323C-H	668	ex-Buffalo Airways	N8405 (N873BX) N8405 P4- stored Smyrna, TN, regn canx Dec95
19586	707-323C-H	670	Lloyd Aereo Boliviano	N8406 CP-1698

BOEING 707/720

C/n	Series	Line No	Last known Operator/Owner	Previous Identities/fate (where known)
19587	707-323C-H	686	SABENA World Airlines	N8408 N705PC F-GHFT 9G-ADS [Op by Occidental A/L]
19588	707-323C-H	692	(Middle East Airlines)	N8409 OD-AHB dbr Beirut, Lebanon 08Jan87 by shelling
19589	707-323C-H	701	Middle East Airlines	N8410 OD-AHC
19590	707-365C-H	654	Royal Jordanian	G-ATZD VR-BCP (OD-APA) VR-BCP G-ATZD 5A-DJV SU-DAI 5N-AOO OO-CDE JY-AJM
19621 to 19630 built as 707-338C-H and modified as follows:				
19621	E-8C	652	USAF/4500thJSTARSS(P)	VH-EAA OO-YCK P2-ANB TF-AEB (SU-DAF) 5Y-AXA N733Q N526SJ 90-0175/N526SJ 90-0175
19622	E-8C	660	USAF/605thTS	VH-EAB OO-YCL P2-ANA TF-AEC SU-DAE ST-ALL 5B-DAY N4131G 92-3289/JS [will go to 4500thJSTARSS(P) later in 1996]
19623	707-338C-H	671	Royal Australian AF/33Sqdn	VH-EAC G-BDKE VH-EAC C-GRYN A20-623
19624	707-338C-H	689	Royal Australian AF/33Sqdn	VH-EAD A20-624
19625	707-338C-H	693	ADC Airlines	VH-EAE G-BFLD N862BX 5N-BBD
19626	E-8A	703	USAF/93rdASCW	VH-EAF HL7432 N770JS 86-0416/JS
19627	707-338C-H	707	Royal Australian AF/33Sqdn	VH-EAG A20-627
19628	707-338C-H	716	Oil Production Maintenance	VH-EAH HL7433 TF-IUD 5A- [Present status unknown, poss 5A-DTF noted Sep95]
19629	707-338C-H	737	Royal Australian AF/33Sqdn	VH-EAI G-BDLM C-GGAB A20-629
19630	707-338C-H	746	(Uganda Airlines)	VH-EAJ G-BDSJ 5X-UBC w/o 17Oct88 Rome-Leonardi da Vinci, Italy
19631	707-351C-H	634	ALG Group	N375US 9Y-TEJ N2215Y 5N-OCL (N2215Y) stored Smyrna, TN Sep95
19632	707-351C-H	649	Trans Arabian Air Transport	N376US 9Y-TEK 8P-CAD N707KV ST-ANP
19633	707-351C-H	690	Government of Botswana	N377US 5Y-BBJ stored Nairobi, Kenya 01Mar91; used as police ground trainer
19634	707-351C-H	695	African Airlines	N378US 5Y-BBI
19635	707-351C-H	706	Pakistan Air Force/12Sqdn	N379US AP-BAA 68-19635
19636	707-351C-H	732	(Pakistan Intl Airlines)	N380US AP-AZW stored Karachi, Pakistan by Dec93; b/u
19664	707-355C-H	643	Okada Air	N526EJ PH-TRF N526EJ G-AXRS 5N-AOQ TF-VLX 5N-AOQ
19693	707-321BA-H	673	Boeing MAC/USAF	N491PA CC-CEJ N1181Z stored Davis-Monthan AFB, AZ 20Feb86
19694	707-321BA-H	678	(Aircraft Parts Co)	N492PA stored New York-JFK, NY Nov84, later b/u
19695	707-321BA-H	684	Jet Cargo	N493PA N498GA N808ZS
19696	707-321BA-H	688	(Pan American World A/W)	N494PA w/o 12Dec68 off Caracas, Venezuela
19697	707-321BA-H	694	Boeing MAC/USAF	N495PA N495 N495PA stored Davis-Monthan AFB, AZ 27Feb84
19698	707-321BA-H	697	Boeing MAC/USAF	N496PA stored Davis-Monthan AFB, AZ 07Mar85
19699	707-321BA-H	699	Boeing MAC/USAF	N497PA stored Davis-Monthan AFB, AZ 20Mar84
19705	707-344C-H	675	(South African Airways)	ZS-EUW w/o 20Apr68 Windhoek, SW Africa
19706	707-344C-H	691	South African AF/60Sqdn	ZS-EUX ZS-SAF LX-LGT OO-SJR LX-LGT JY-AFR LX-LGT (ZS-SIO) ZS-LSL 3D-ASC 1423 AF-623 [VIP a/c]
19715	707-373C-H	642	(Korean Air Lines)	N369WA AP-AWE N369WA HL7412 w/o 02Aug76 nr Teheran, Iran
19716	707-373C-H	644	FAC/Esc Presidencial	N368WA AP-AWD N368WA HL7425 1201
19723	707-328C-H	665	South African AF/60Sqdn	F-BLCI (ZS-LSJ) 1417 AF-617 [Tanker conversion]
19724	707-328C-H	667	(Air France)	F-BLCJ w/o 05Mar68 Pointe-a-Pitre, Guadaloupe
19736	707-360C-H	696	(Ethiopian Airlines)	ET-ACD w/o 19Nov77 Rome-Fiumicino, Italy
19737	707-312B-H	713	(Tradewinds Airlines)	9V-BBA 4R-ALB stored Shannon, Eire 16Jul80; b/u Mar82
19738	707-312B-H	725	(GPA Group/Air Tara)	9M-AOT 9V-BFB 4R-ALA stored Shannon, Eire 08Aug81; b/u Aug83
19739	707-312B-H	765	Republique Togolaise	9V-BBB N600CS 5V-TAG [Op by Force Aerienne Togolaise]
19740 built as 707-382B-H and modified as follows:				
19740	707T/T	676	AMI/8°Gruppo/14°Stormo	CS-TBC MM62148/14-01
19741	707-359B-H	681	(AVIANCA)	HK-1402 stored Miami, FL .92; b/u 23Jun93
19760	707-384C-H	715	Fuerza Aerea Venezolana	SX-DBD 6944 [Converted to tanker]
19767	707-399C-H	659	Dominicana	G-AVTW CS-TBI HI-442 HI-442CT stored Santo Domingo, Dominican Republic
19773	707-351C-H	705	Omega Air	N382US CN-RMB stored Shannon, Eire 31Jan96
19774	707-351C-H	708	Omega Air	N383US CN-RMC
19775	707-351C-H	729	Egyptair	N384US SU-BAO SU-EAA stored Cairo, Egypt
19776	707-351C-H	732	Brasair Air Cargo	N385US S2-ACA N8091J PP-BRI
19777	707-351C-H	740	(Midair)	N386US 70-ABY stored Aden,South Yemen Jun84; later b/u
19789	707-311C-H	698	Lonsdale Jet III	CF-FAN C-FFAN 9K-ACX N524SJ (F-GIVJ) N524SJ N715FW stored Miami, FL Jul95
19809	707-368C-H	657	(Royal Australian AF)	HZ-ACC N1486B (A20-809) stored Richmond AFB, NSW 16Mar88; b/u for spares
19810	707-368C-H	664	(Boeing MAC/USAF)	HZ-ACD N1673B stored Davis-Monthan AFB, AZ 25Jun87; b/u Melbourne, FL
19820	707-379C-H	709	Ethiopian Airlines	N761U ET-ACQ dbr 25Jul90 Addas Ababa, Ethiopia
19821	707-379C-H	718	DAS Air Cargo	N762U G-AWHU 9Q-CKI VN-83415 G-AWHU 5X-JEF ST-GLD 9G-OLF 9G-ONE 9G-WON 5X-JEF
19822	707-379C-H	726	(VARIG)	N763U PP-VJK w/o 03Jan87 Bingerville, Ivory Coast
19840 to 19842 built as 707-345C-H and modified as follows:				
19840	C-137E	679	FA Brasileira 2/2GTT	N7321S PP-VJY 2401
19841	707-345C-H	683	(VARIG)	N7322S PP-VJZ w/o 11Jul73 Sceaux-le-Chatreaux, France
19842	KC-137E	712	FA Brasileira 2/2GTT	N7323S PP-VJX 2402

BOEING 707/720

C/n	Series	Line No	Last known Operator/Owner	Previous Identities/fate (where known)
19843	707-336C-H	735	Memphis Air	G-AVPB (9G-ACZ) G-AVPB SU-DAC
19844	707-366C-H	744	Express City	SU-AOU (9Q-CKK) 9Q-CJW 9Q-CRA 9Q-CKG
19845	707-366C-H	809	(Egyptair)	SU-AOW w/o 05Dec72 Beni Sueif, Egypt
19866	707-340C-H	738	Pakistan Air Force/12Sqdn	AP-AVL YU-AGD AP-AWY 68-19866
19869	707-324C-H	700	Angola Air Charter	N47331 PP-VLM N112HM S7-2HM TC-GHA S7-2HM TC-GHA N707EL D2-TOK
19870 built as 707-324C-H and modified as follows:				
19870	KC-137E	702	FA Brasileira 2/2GTT	N47332 PP-VLK 2404 stored Rio de Janeiro, Brazil Sep94
19871	707-324C-H	711	Angola Air Charter	(N47333) N67333 PP-VLL N114HM S7-4HM TC-GHB S7-4HM D2-TON
19872	707-351B-H	742	(Kenya Airways)	(N386US) N381US 5Y-BBK w/o 11Jul89 Addis Ababa, Ethiopia
19916	707-328C-H	762	ZAS Airlines of Egypt	F-BLCK SU-DAA Ceased ops 04Apr95
19917	707-328C-H	763	South African AF/60Sqdn	F-BLCL (ZS-LSJ) 1419 AF-619 [ELINT conversion]
19961	707-387C-H	754	(Aerolineas Argentinas)	LV-JGR dbr 27Jan80 Buenos-Aires-Ezeiza, Argentina
19962	707-387C-H	755	FAA/Verificacion Radio Ayudos	LV-JGP TC-93 VR-21
19963	707-347C-H	723	Angola Air Charter Cargo	N1501W (D2-TAM) D2-TOL
19964	707-347C-H	733	Occidental Airlines	N1502W TF-VLG N1502W EI-BLC N707PD B-2425 N707PD TT-WAB TT-EAP HR-AMA 9J-AFT ZS-NLJ EL-AKU
19965	707-347C-H	734	(TAAG-Angola Airlines)	N1503W (D2-TAL) D2-TOM dbf 10Oct88 Luanda, Angola
19966	707-347C-H	743	Middle East Airlines	N1504W OD-AGU
19967	707-347C-H	745	Middle East Airlines	N1505W OD-AGV
19969	707-382B-H	751	Republique du Zaire	CS-TBD 9Q-MNS 9T-MSS [Op by Force Aerienne Zairoise, stored Lisbon, Portugal May95]
19986	707-328C-H	730	Omega Air	N527EJ F-BJCM EL-AIY N-723GS N723GS N707MB stored Shannon, Eire 08Jul95; canx Feb96
19988	707-337C-H	736	Indian Air Force/12Sqdn	VT-DXT K-2899
19996 built as 707-329C-H and modified as follows:				
19996	707-TCA	748	NATO/AEWF	OO-SJL N3238N OO-SJL LX-N19996
19997	707-307C-H	747	German Air Force/FBS	10+01
19998	707-307C-H	750	German Air Force/FBS	10+02
19999	707-307C-H	756	German Air Force/FBS	10+03
20000	707-307C-H	759	German Air Force/FBS	10+04
20008 built as 707-320C-H and modified as follows:				
20008	KC-137E	739	FA Brasileira 2/2GTT	N707N PP-VJH 2403
20016	707-321C-H	752	USAF/Omega Air	N870PA 9K-ACS N146SP N527SJ N770FW stored Davis-Monthan AFB, AZ 13May92
20017	707-321C-H	753	Florida West Airlines	N871PA JY-AES N710FW N202DJ N710FW N517MA*
20018	707-321C-H	761	Boeing MAC/USAF	N872PA 9K-ACU S2-ACK PT-TCR stored Davis-Monthan AFB, AZ 27Jul87
20019	707-321BA-H	767	Boeing MAC/USAF	N880PA stored Davis-Monthan AFB, AZ 07Mar85
20020	707-321BA-H	768	Boeing MAC/USAF	N881PA stored Davis-Monthan AFB, AZ 27Feb84
20021	707-321BA-H	769	LAN-Chile	N882PA CC-CEI stored Santiago, Chile 23Jun90
20022	707-321BA-H	774	JARO International	N883PA N730Q CC-CYB YR-JCB
20023	707-321BA-H	775	(Pan American World A/W)	N884PA stored Stansted, UK 23Nov82; later b/u
20024	707-321BA-H	776	Boeing MAC/USAF	N885PA stored Davis-Monthan AFB, AZ 13Apr84
20025	707-321BA-H	780	Kalair USA Corp	N886PA N728Q N707KS
20026	707-321BA-H	781	Boeing MAC/USAF	N887PA N160GL stored Davis-Monthan AFB, AZ Sep85
20027	707-321BA-H	782	(Boeing MAC/USAF)	N890PA 9Y-TEX N2213E stored Davis-Monthan AFB, AZ 18Oct85; later b/u
20028	707-321BA-H	783	(Omega Air)	N891PA 9Y-TEZ N3127K VR-CBN N320MJ w/o 20Sep90 Marana, AZ
20029	707-321BA-H	790	Omega Air	N892PA N729Q EL-
20030	707-321BA-H	791	CAAC	N893PA stored Tianjin, PRC as ground trainer 15Oct82
20031	707-321BA-H	792	(Jetran International)	N894PA N731Q stored Philadelphia, PA; b/u Oct88
20032	707-321BA-H	793	Wilmington Trust Co	N895PA N895SY stored San Antonio, TX Sep88
20033	707-321BA-H	797	AECA	N896PA HC-BHY/FAE20033 stored Quito, Ecuador Sep93
20034	707-321BA-H	798	LADECO	N897PA N732Q
20035	707-384C-H	770	Boeing MAC/USAF	SX-DBE N6504K EL-AKB stored Davis-Monthan AFB, AZ 24Oct90
20036	707-384C-H	778	Boeing MAC/USAF	SX-DBF N7158T stored Davis-Monthan AFB, AZ 24Jul90
20043 built as 707-396C-H and modified as follows:				
20043	C-137C	786	USAF/89thAW	(CF-QBG) N1786B CF-ZYP C-FZYP OE-IDA 85-6973
20056	707-131B	771	(Boeing MAC/USAF)	N86740 stored Davis-Monthan AFB, AZ 19May82; later b/u
20057	707-131B	777	(Boeing MAC/USAF)	N86741 stored Davis-Monthan AFB, AZ 12May82; later b/u
20058	707-331BA-H	766	Boeing MAC/USAF	N8729 stored Davis-Monthan AFB, AZ 16Feb84
20059	707-331BA-H	772	Boeing MAC/USAF	N8730 stored Davis-Monthan AFB, AZ 04Apr84
20060	707-331BA-H	773	EdA/Grupo 45	N8731 N708A N275B T.17-1/45-10
20061	707-331BA-H	784	Boeing MAC/USAF	N8732 stored Davis-Monthan AFB, AZ 15Dec83
20062	707-331BA-H	785	Boeing MAC/USAF	N8733 stored Davis-Monthan AFB, AZ 23May86
20063	707-331BA-H	789	(Trans World Airlines)	N8734 w/o 08Sep74 off Corfu, Greece
20064	707-331BA-H	799	Boeing MAC/USAF	N8735 stored Davis-Monthan AFB, AZ 19Jun84
20065	707-331BA-H	802	Boeing MAC/USAF	N8736 stored Davis-Monthan AFB, AZ 19Nov85
20066	707-331BA-H	810	Boeing MAC/USAF	N8737 stored Davis-Monthan AFB, AZ 18Oct85
20067	707-331BA-H	812	Boeing MAC/USAF	N8738 stored Davis-Monthan AFB, AZ 06Jul84
20068	707-331C-H	814	(Trans World Airlines)	N15712 w/o 14Sep72 into San Francisco Bay, CA
20069	707-331C-H	815	Skyjet Brazil	N15713 (N164GL) N15713 N345FA CC-CUE N234FA TC-GHA N234FA (LZ-...) N234FA PP-AJP
20076	707-372C-H	721	FA Argentinas/5Esc	N738AL LV-LGO TC-94 TC-93 LV-LGO TC-93

BOEING 707/720

C/n	Series	Line No	Last known Operator/Owner	Previous Identities/fate (where known)
20077	707-372C-H	728	FA Argentinas/5Esc	N739AL LV-LGP TC-92 LV-LGP TC-92 LV-LGP TC-92
20084	707-369C-H	758	Millon Air	9K-ACJ N525SJ (F-GKCT) N525SJ N851JB
20085	707-369C-H	760	Air Atlantic Cargo	9K-ACK N147SP N720FW N528SJ (F-GKCS) N528SJ N725FW
20086	707-369C-H	764	(Sudan Airways)	9K-ACL ST-AIX stored Khartoum, Sudan, later b/u
20087	707-323C-H	724	World Jet Aircraft	N8415 SU-FAC stored Cairo, Egypt
20088	707-323C-H	727	AeroBrasil Cargo	N8416 N8416A N8416 PT-TCN
20089	707-323C-H	741	Boeing MAC/USAF	N8417 G-AYZZ N8417 G-AYZZ N8417 N8417A N8417 N162GL N8417 stored Davis-Monthan AFB, AZ 21Nov85
20097	707-358B-H	779	Boeing MAC/USAF	4X-ATT (N21037) 4X-ATT TF-AYF (N21037) stored Davis-Monthan AFB, AZ 12Sep89
20110	707-344C-H	800	Israel Defence Force/AF	(ZS-FKT) ZS-SAG VP-WGA ZS-SAG 4X-BYQ 4X-JYQ 4X-BYQ 242/4X-JYQ
20122	707-358B-H	807	Espace Aviation	4X-ATU 4X-ATX 9Q-CVG
20123	707-330C-H	788	AZZA Transport Co	D-ABUJ A6-DPA ST-AKW
20124	707-330C-H	806	Challenge Air Cargo	D-ABUO N707HE
20136	707-382B-H	803	TAAG-Angola Airlines	CS-TBE D2-TOP
20170	707-323B-H	795	Middle East Airlines	N8431 OD-AHF
20171	707-323B-H	796	(Skyworld Airlines)	N8432 N910PC stored Waco, TX; b/u Sep86
20172	707-323B-H	804	Saleem Zaidi	N8433 N161GL N711PC HR-AMP N711PC C5-
20173	707-323B-H	805	(Global Intl Airlines)	N8434 dbr 04Dec82 Brasilia, Brazil
20174	707-323B-H	808	(Aviation Consultants)	N8435 N145SP 4X-ATG N145SP stored San Antonio, TX Feb92; b/u El Paso, TX
20175	707-323B-H	811	Omega Air	N8436 N709PC stored Shannon, Eire 18Jan94
20176	707-323B-H	817	Saleem Zaidi	N8437 N712PC HR-AMQ N712PC C5-
20177	707-323B-H	818	Omega Air	N8438 N706PC EL-AKC C5-GOA HR-AMW EL-AKK
20178	707-323B-H	820	(Jetlease Inc)	N8439 N457PC stored Miami, FL 90; b/u 11Nov93
20179	707-323B-H	821	Boeing MAC/USAF	N8440 (N163GL) N8440 S7-LAS 5Y-BFF N7158Z stored Davis-Monthan AFB, AZ 25Jul90
20198 to 20200 built as 707-329C-H and modified as follows:				
20198	707-TCA	813	NATO/AEWF	OO-SJM PH-TVK OO-SJM LX-N20198
20199	707-TCA	816	NATO/AEWF	OO-SJN N3238S OO-SJN LX-N20199
20200	707-329C-H	828	SCIBE Airlift	OO-SJO 9Q-CBS 9Q-CBW
20224	707-3B4C-H	749	(Middle East Airlines)	OD-AFB dbr Beirut, Lebanon 12Jun82 by shelling
20225	707-3B4C-H	757	(Middle East Airlines)	OD-AFC dbr Beirut, Lebanon 28Dec68 by shelling
20230	707-344C-H	819	Israel Defence Force/AF	(ZS-FKG) ZS-SAH 4X-BYS 4X-JYS 4X-BYS 246/4X-JYS stored Tel Aviv, Israel by Nov95
20259	707-3B4C-H	822	Middle East Airlines	OD-AFD
20260	707-3B4C-H	823	Middle East Airlines	OD-AFE
20261	707-309C-H	827	Jet Cargo	B-1824 N707ZS EL-ZGS
20262	707-309C-H	830	(China Airlines)	B-1826 w/o 27Feb80 Manila, Philippines
20275	707-340C-H	844	(Pakistan Intl Airlines)	AP-AWB G-AZPW AP-AWZ w/o 26Nov79 nr Jeddah, Saudi Arabia
20283	707-344C-H	831	South African AF/60Sqdn	ZS-SAI LX-LGS JY-AFD LX-LGS (ZS-SIN) ZS-LSF EL-TBA 1421 AF-621
20287	707-386C-H	832	Iran Air	EP-IRL stored Teheran, Iran
20288	707-386C-H	839	Iran Air	EP-IRM stored Teheran, Iran
20297 and 20298 built as 707-382B-H and modified as follows:				
20297	C-137C	836	USAF/89thAW	CS-TBF N105BV 85-6974
20298	707T/T	840	AMI/8°Gruppo/14°Stormo	CS-TBG MM62149/14-02
20301	707-358C-H	835	Servico Aereo Ejecutive	4X-ATY N707WJ OB-1592
20315 to 20319 built as 707-347C-H and modified as follows:				
20315	707-347C-H	824	Atlantic Air Leasing	N1506W 13701 N803CK HR-AMN N108RA
20316	707-347C-H	825	AeroBrasil Cargo	N1507W 13702 HR-AMF PT-TCU*
20317	CC-137	826	Canadian Forces/437Sqdn	N1508W 13703
20318	CC-137	829	Canadian Forces/437Sqdn	N1509W 13704
20319	CC-137	833	Canadian Forces/437Sqdn	N1510W 13705
20340	707-359B-H	842	(Enterprise Air)	HK-1410 (N22055) stored Bogota, Colombia 91; b/u Jul94
20341	707-366C-H	834	Express Cargo	SU-APD 9Q-CJM
20342	707-366C-H	837	(Egyptair)	N4094 SU-APE w/o 17Oct82 Geneva, Switzerland
20374	707-336C-H	838	Alyemda Yemen Airlines	G-AXGW 7O-ACO
20375	707-336C-H	841	Chapman Freeman Aircharting	G-AXGX A7-AAC "VR-VZA" VR-BZA stored Southend, UK 09Feb95
20395	707-330C-H	848	Lufthansa	D-ABUY w/o 26Jul79 Sierra das Macacos, Brazil
20428	707-331C-H	845	Israel Defence Force/AF	N1793T 4X-BYY 250/4X-JYY
20429	707-331C-H	846	Israel Defence Force/AF	N794TW 4X-BYB 255/4X-JYB [ELINT conversion]
20439	707-320B-H		(Unknown Customer)	Allocated but later canx, not built
20456	707-336C-H	851	(Boeing MAC/USAF)	G-AXXY 4X-BMC (VR-HKC) 4X-BMC N343A PT-TCQ stored Davis-Monthan AFB, AZ 06Aug87; b/u 03Apr93
20457	707-336C-H	853	(Government of Benin)	G-AXXZ 9G-ADB TY-BBR TY-BBM TY-BBR dbr 13Jun85 Sebha, Libya
20474	707-3F9C-H	843	Nigeria Airways	5N-ABJ stored Shannon, Eire .91
20477	707-303C-H		(Unknown Customer)	Allocated but later canx, not built
20478	707-303C-H		(Unknown Customer)	Allocated but later canx, not built
20479	707-303C-H		(Unknown Customer)	Allocated but later canx, not built
20487	707-340C-H	847	(Pakistan Intl Airlines)	AP-AVZ w/o 15Dec71 Urumchi, Sinkiang Province, PRC
20488	707-340C-H	849	Pakistan Intl Airlines	AP-AWA G-AZRO AP-AXG
20494	707-3D3C-H	850	(Alia-Royal Jordanian A/L)	JY-ADO w/o 22Jan73 Kano, Nigeria

BOEING 707/720

C/n	Series	Line No	Last known Operator/Owner	Previous Identities/fate (where known)
20495	707-3D3C-H	852	USAF/Omega Air	JY-ADP 71-1841 stored Davis-Monthan AFB, AZ 15Jul92 for J-STARS
20514 and 20515 built as 707-3F5C-H and modified as follows:				
20514	707T/T	857	AMI/8°Gruppo/14°Stormo	CS-DGI 8801 CS-TBT MM62150/14-03
20515	707T/T	859	AMI/8°Gruppo/14°Stormo	CS-DGJ 8802 CS-TBU MM62151/14-04
20516	707-3F5C-H		(Force Aerea Portuguesa)	Allocated but later canx, not built
20517	707-336C-H	854	Simba Air Cargo	G-AYLT 9Q-CLY SU-DAD "VH-AKK" VR-HKK 9G-TWO (9G-TOO) 9G-TWO 5Y-SIM
20518 and 20519 built as EC-137D and modified as follows:				
20518	EC-137D	856	USAF/Boeing	71-1407
	E-3B	898	USAF/552ndACW	71-1407/OK
20519	EC-137D	858	USAF/Boeing	71-1408
	E-3B	920	USAF/552ndACW	71-1408/OK
20522	707-3B5C-H	855	(Korean Air)	HL7406 w/o 29Nov87 Andaman Sea, off Thailand
20546	707-369C-H	860	Air Afrique	9K-ACM N523SJ (F-GKCI) N523SJ 5X-JON
20547	707-369C-H	861	(Alyemda Yemen Airlines)	9K-ACN 70-ACS dbr 26Nov91 Amman, Jordan
20629	707-3H7C-H	863	Israel Defence Force/AF	TJ-CAA 4X-BYU 248/4X-JYU 4X-BYU
20630 built as 707-353C-H and modified as follows:				
20630	C-137C	862	USAF/89thAW	N8459 72-7000
20669	707-3F9C-H	864	(Nigeria Airways)	5N-ABK w/o 20Dec94 Hadejo, Nigeria
20714	707-3J6B-H	869	China Southwest Airlines	2402 B-2402 dbr 02Oct90 Canton, PRC
20715	707-3J6B-H	870	Government of Angola	2404 B-2404 D2-TPR [Op by Force Aerea Populaire de Angola]
20716	707-3J6B-H	880	Israel Defence Force/AF	2406 B-2406 4X-BYN 2../4X-JYN IAF001
20717	707-3J6B-H	882	Quiet Skies Inc	2408 B-2408 N717QS stored
20718	707-3J6C-H	872	China Southwest Airlines	2410 B-2410
20719	707-3J6C-H	873	Quiet Skies Inc	2412 B-2412 N719QS
20720	707-3J6C-H	874	Royal Jordanian	2414 B-2414 (N-) JY-AJN
20721	707-3J6C-H	875	Israel Defence Force/AF	2416 B-2416 4X-BYH 264/4X-JYH
20722	707-3J6C-H	877	Triangle Airlines	2418 B-2418 B-606L 5X-TRA
20723	707-3J6C-H	879	Royal Jordanian	2420 B-2420 (N) JY-AJO
20741	707-386C-H	866	Iran Air	N1785B EP-IRN stored Teheran, Iran
20760	707-366C-H	865	Egyptair	SU-AVX
20761	707-366C-H	867	Express Cargo	N1785B SU-AVY 9Q-CKK
20762	707-366C-H	868	Omega Air	SU-AVZ stored Davis-Monthan AFB, AZ 15Sep95
20763	707-366C-H	871	(Egyptair)	SU-AXA w/o 25Dec76 Bangkok, Thailand
20803	707-3K1C-H	878	Air Afrique	YR-ABA
20804	707-3K1C-H	883	Aero Asia	YR-ABB
20805	707-3K1C-H	884	Air Afrique	YR-ABC
20830	707-3J9C-H	876	Islamic Republic of Iran AF	N1709B 5-241 5-8301
20831	707-3J9C-H	881	Islamic Republic of Iran AF	5-242 5-8302
20832	707-3J9C-H	886	Islamic Republic of Iran AF	5-243 5-8303
20833	707-3J9C-H	890	Islamic Republic of Iran AF	5-244 5-8304
20834	707-3J9C-H	894	Iran Air	5-245 5-8305 EP-NHW
20835	707-3J9C-H	895	Islamic Republic of Iran AF	5-246 5-8306
20889	707-370C-H	889	Iraqi Airways	YI-AGE stored Amman, Jordan
20890	707-370C-H	891	Islamic Republic of Iran AF	YI-AGF JY-CAC 4YB-CAC YI-AGF 1002
20891	707-370C-H	892	Iraqi Airways	YI-AGG stored Amman, Jordan
20897	707-3J8C-H	885	Sudan Airways	ST-AFA
20898	707-3J8C-H	887	Sudan Airways	ST-AFB
20919	707-366C-H	888	Govt of Arab Republic of Egypt	SU-AXJ [Op by Arab Republic of Egypt Air Force]
20920	707-366C-H	893	Egyptair Cargo	SU-AXK stored Cairo, Egypt, b/u 18Oct93
21046 and 21047 built as E-3A and modified as follows:				
21046	E-3C	901	Boeing Corp	73-1674
21047	E-3B	902	USAF/552ndACW	75-0556/OK
21049	707-3L6B-H	896	TBN Aircraft Corp	N62393 9M-TDM (A6-HHP) A6-HPZ P4-TBN
21070	707-387C-H	897	FA Argentinas/5Esc	T-01 TC-91
21081	707-368C-H	903	Saudi Royal Flight	HZ-HM1 HZ-HM2 [Op by RSAF/1Sqdn]
21092	707-3M1C-H	899	TNI-AU/SkU 17	PK-PJQ A-7002 PK-PJQ A-7002 PK-GAU A-7002
21096	707-3L6C-H	900	JARO International	N48055 9M-TMS G-CDHW A6-HRM P4-MDJ
21103	707-368C-H	905	(RAAF/33Sqdn)	HZ-ACG N1987B (MM.....) A20-103 w/o 29Oct91 Bridgewater, Australia
21104	707-368C-H	906	AZZA Transport Co	HZ-ACH (HZ-HM5) ST-DRS
21123	707-3J9C-H	908	Saha Airline	(5-247) 5-8307 EP-NHA 5-8307 EP-SHF
21124	707-3J9C-H	910	Islamic Republic of Iran AF	(5-248) 5-8308
21125	707-3J9C-H	912	Islamic Republic of Iran AF	(5-249) 5-8309 EP-SHG 5-8309
21126	707-3J9C-H	914	Islamic Republic of Iran AF	(5-250) 5-8310
21127	707-3J9C-H	915	Islamic Republic of Iran AF	(5-251) 5-8311 EP-SHJ 5-8311
21128	707-3J9C-H	917	Islamic Republic of Iran AF	(5-252) 5-8312 EP-SHE 5-8312
21129	707-3J9C-H	918	Islamic Republic of Iran AF	(5-253) 5-8313
21185 built as E-3A and modified as follows:				
21185	E-3B	904	USAF/552ndACW	73-1675/OK
21207 to 21209 built as E-3A and modified as follows:				
21207	E-3B	907	USAF/552ndACW	75-0557/OK
21208	E-3B	909	USAF/552ndACW	75-0558/OK
21209	E-3B	913	USAF/552ndACW	75-0559/OK
21228	707-3L5C-H	911	Government of Libya	5A-DAK [Op by Al Quwwat al Jawwiya al Jamahiriyah al Arabiya al Libyya]
21250 built as E-3A and modified as follows:				
21250	E-3B	916	USAF/909thARS/18thWg	75-0560/ZZ
21261	707-368C-H	919	Royal Australian AF/33Sqdn	HZ-ACI N7486B (MM.....) A20-261

BOEING 707/720

C/n	Series	Line No	Last known Operator/Owner	Previous Identities/fate (where known)
21334	707-3P1C-H	923	State of Qatar	A7-AAA
21367	707-368C-H	922	EdA/Grupo 45	HZ-ACJ N7667B T.17-3/45-12
21368	707-368C-H	925	Saudi Royal Flight	HZ-ACK HZ-HM3 [Op by RSAF/1Sqdn]
21396	707-368C-H	928	Government of Iran	EP-HIM 1001 EP-NHY
21428	707-3F9C-H	929	Nigeria Airways	5N-ANO stored Dublin, Eire 18Jun89
21434 to 21437 built as E-3A and modified as follows:				
21434	E-3B	921	USAF/552ndACW	76-1704/OK
21435	E-3B	924	USAF/552ndACW	76-1705/OK
21436	E-3B	926	USAF/552ndACW	76-1706/OK
21437	E-3B	927	USAF/552ndACW	76-1707/OK
21475	707-3J9C-H	936	Islamic Republic of Iran AF	5-8314
21551 to 21556 built as E-3A and modified as follows:				
21551	E-3B	930	USAF/552ndACW	77-0351/AK
21552	E-3B	931	USAF/552ndACW	77-0352/OK
21553	E-3B	932	USAF/552ndACW	77-0353/AK
21554	E-3B	933	(USAF/3rdWg)	77-0354/AK w/o 22Sep95 Elmendorf AFB, AK
21555	E-3B	934	USAF/552ndACW	77-0355/OK
21556	E-3B	935	USAF/552ndACW	77-0356/OK
21651	707-3K1C-H	938	(Tarom)	YR-ABD dbr 10Jan91 Bucharest, Romania
21752 to 21757 built as E-3A and modified as follows:				
21752	E-3B	937	USAF/552ndACW	78-0576/OK
21753	E-3B	939	USAF/552ndACW	78-0577/OK
21754	E-3B	940	USAF/552ndACW	78-0578/OK
21755	E-3B	942	USAF/552ndACW	79-0001/OK
21756	E-3C	943	USAF/552ndACW	79-0002/OK
21757	E-3B	944	USAF/552ndACW	79-0003/OK
21956	707-3W6C-H	941	Government of Morocco	N707QT CNA-NR [Op by Force Aerienne Royale Marocaine]
22829 to 22837 built as E-3A and modified as follows:				
22829	E-3C	946	USAF/552ndACW	80-0137/OK
22830	E-3C	948	USAF/552ndACW	80-0138/OK
22831	E-3C	950	USAF/552ndACW	80-0139/OK
22832	E-3C	951	USAF/552ndACW	81-0004/OK
22833	E-3C	952	USAF/552ndACW	81-0005/OK
22834	E-3C	958	USAF/552ndACW	82-0006/OK
22835	E-3C	960	USAF/552ndACW	82-0007/OK
22836	E-3C	962	USAF/18thWg	82-0008/ZZ
22837	E-3C	965	USAF/552ndACW	82-0009/OK
22838	E-3A	947	NATO/AEWF	79-0443 LX-N90443
22839	E-3A	949	NATO/AEWF	79-0444 LX-N90444
22840	E-3A	953	NATO/AEWF	79-0445 LX-N90445
22841	E-3A	954	NATO/AEWF	79-0446 LX-N90446
22842	E-3A	955	NATO/AEWF	79-0447 LX-N90447
22843	E-3A	956	NATO/AEWF	79-0448 LX-N90448
22844	E-3A	957	NATO/AEWF	79-0449 LX-N90449
22845	E-3A	959	NATO/AEWF	79-0450 LX-N90450
22846	E-3A	961	NATO/AEWF	79-0451 LX-N90451
22847	E-3A	963	NATO/AEWF	79-0452 LX-N90452
22848	E-3A	964	NATO/AEWF	79-0453 LX-N90453
22849	E-3A	966	NATO/AEWF	79-0454 LX-N90454
22850	E-3A	967	NATO/AEWF	79-0455 LX-N90455
22851	E-3A	968	NATO/AEWF	79-0456 LX-N90456
22852	E-3A	969	NATO/AEWF	79-0457 LX-N90457
22853	E-3A	970	NATO/AEWF	79-0458 LX-N90458
22854	E-3A	971	NATO/AEWF	79-0459 LX-N90459
22855	E-3A	945	NATO/AEWF	79-0442 LX-N90442
22893	E-3A		(Royal Saudi AF)	Allocated but later canx, not built
22894	E-3A		(Royal Saudi AF)	Allocated but later canx, not built
22895	E-3A		(Royal Saudi AF)	Allocated but later canx, not built
22896	E-3A		(Royal Saudi AF)	Allocated but later canx, not built
22897	E-3A		(Royal Saudi AF)	Allocated but later canx, not built
22898	KE-3A		(Royal Saudi AF)	Allocated but later canx, not built
22899	KE-3A		(Royal Saudi AF)	Allocated but later canx, not built
22900	KE-3A		(Royal Saudi AF)	Allocated but later canx, not built
22901	KE-3A		(Royal Saudi AF)	Allocated but later canx, not built
22902	KE-3A		(Royal Saudi AF)	Allocated but later canx, not built
23417	E-3A	972	Royal Saudi AF/18Sqdn	82-0068 1801
23418	E-3A	973	Royal Saudi AF/18Sqdn	82-0067 1802
23419	E-3A	974	Royal Saudi AF/18Sqdn	82-0068 1803
23420	E-3A	976	Royal Saudi AF/18Sqdn	82-0069 1804
23421	E-3A	980	Royal Saudi AF/18Sqdn	82-0070 1805
23422	KE-3A	975	Royal Saudi AF/18Sqdn	82-0071 1811
23423	KE-3A	977	Royal Saudi AF/18Sqdn	82-0072 1812
23424	KE-3A	978	Royal Saudi AF/18Sqdn	82-0073 1813
23425	KE-3A	979	Royal Saudi AF/18Sqdn	82-0074 1814
23426	KE-3A	981	Royal Saudi AF/18Sqdn	82-0075 1815
23427	KE-3A	982	Royal Saudi AF/18Sqdn	82-0076 1816
23428	KE-3A	984	Royal Saudi AF/18Sqdn	83-0510 1817
23429	KE-3A	985	Royal Saudi AF/18Sqdn	83-0511 1818
23430	E-6A	983	USN/SCW-1	162782 [As Mercury]
23889	E-6A	986	USN/SCW-1	162783 [As Mercury]

C/n	Series	Line No	Last known Operator/Owner	Previous Identities/fate (where known)	
23890	E-6A	987	USN/SCW-1	162784	[As Mercury]
23891	E-6A	988	USN/Boeing	163918	[As Mercury]
23892	E-6A	989	USN/SCW-1	163919	[As Mercury]
23893	E-6A	990	USN/SCW-1	163920	[As Mercury]
23894	E-6A	991	USN/SCW-1	164386	[As Mercury]
24109	E-3D	993	Royal Air Force/8Sqdn	ZH101/01	[As Sentry AEW.1]
24110	E-3D	996	Royal Air Force/8Sqdn	ZH102/02	[As Sentry AEW.1]
24111	E-3D	1004	Royal Air Force/8Sqdn	ZH103/03	[As Sentry AEW.1]
24112	E-3D	1007	Royal Air Force/8Sqdn	ZH104/04	[As Sentry AEW.1]
24113	E-3D	1010	Royal Air Force/8Sqdn	ZH105/05	[As Sentry AEW.1]
24114	E-3D	1011	Royal Air Force/8Sqdn	ZH106/06	[As Sentry AEW.1]
24115	E-3F	1000	Armee de l'Air/EDA.36	201/36-CA	[c/s F-ZBCA]
24116	E-3F	1003	Armee de l'Air/EDA.36	202/36-CB	[c/s F-ZBCB]
24117	E-3F	1006	Armee de l'Air/EDA.36	203/36-CC	[c/s F-ZBCC]
24499	E-3D	1012	Royal Air Force/8Sqdn	ZH107/07	[As Sentry AEW.1]
24500	E-6A	992	USN/SCW-1	164387	[As Mercury]
24501	E-6A	994	USN/SCW-1	164388	[As Mercury]
24502	E-6A	995	USN/SCW-1	164404	[As Mercury]
24503 built as YE-8B and modified as follows:					
24503	707-320C-H	1001	E-Systems Inc	88-0322	N707UM
24504	E-6A	997	USN/SCW-1	164405	[As Mercury]
24505	E-6B	998	NATC/Chrysler Technologies	164406	[As Mercury]
24506	E-6A	999	USN/SCW-1	164407	[As Mercury]
24507	E-6A	1002	USN/SCW-1	164408	[As Mercury]
24508	E-6A	1005	USN/SCW-1	164409	[As Mercury]
24509	E-6A	1008	USN/SCW-1	164410	[As Mercury]
24510	E-3F	1009	Armee de l'Air/EDA.36	204/36-CD	[c/s F-ZBCD]

Production Complete

BOEING 727

C/n	Series	Line No	Last known Operator/Owner	Previous Identities/fate (where known)
18252	25	8	(Aeroexo)	N8101N HK-2717X HK-2717 N8101N XB-GBP XA-GBP stored Monterrey, Mexico Jan94; b/u Aug94 (also reported as Oct95)
18253	25	11	(Charlotte Aircraft Corp)	N8102N EL-GOL N727RL stored Maxton, NC Jul88; b/u Feb89
18254	25	13	Kabo Air	N8103N 5N-AWV
18255	25F	14	Seagreen Air Transport	N8104N N8104E N8104N (N101MU) N8104N
18256	25	16	(New World Aviation)	N8105N 5N-AWX (N8105N) stored Opa Locka, FL Mar89; b/u 05Feb90
18257	25	17	(Tracor Flight Systems Inc)	N8106N N901TS stored Mojave, CA by Oct93; later b/u; canx Jan96
18258	25	20	Kabo Air	N8107N 5N-AWY
18259	25	25	(Aviation Sales Co)	N8108N stored Marana, AZ Mar82; later b/u
18260	25	29	(Aviation Sales Co)	N8109N stored Marana, AZ 18Sep81; b/u Macon, GA Oct85
18261	25	30	(Charlotte Aircraft Corp)	N8110N stored Charlotte, NC Jul81; later b/u
18262	25	41	(Aviation Sales Co)	N8111N stored Marana, AZ Nov82; later b/u
18263	25	45	(Aviation Sales Co)	N8112N stored Marana, AZ 18Sep81; b/u Macon, GA May82
18264	25	53	(Aviation Sales Co)	N8113N stored Marana, AZ 18Sep81; later b/u
18265	25	54	(Aviation Sales Co)	N8114N stored Marana, AZ 18Sep81; b/u Macon, GA Jun82
18266	25	61	(Aviation Sales Co)	N8115N HK-2744X N8115N stored Marana, AZ Jun82; later b/u
18267	25	62	Shuttle Inc	N8116N N902TS stored Oklahoma City, OK Apr92
18268	25	71	(Trump Shuttle)	N8117N B/u Ardmore, OK 24Oct89; never entered service
18269	25	74	(AeroPeru)	N8118N OB-R-1081 stored Lima, Peru 16Sep83; later b/u
18270	25F	79	L/A Suramericanas	N8119N VH-LAP N8119N YV-728C YV-448C YV-480C N5111Y HK-3841X
18271	25F	82	Federal Express	N8120N N502FE
18272	25	89	(Tracor Flight Systems Inc)	N8121N N903TS stored Mojave CA by Oct93; later b/u; canx Jan96
18273	25F	91	Federal Express	N8122N N503FE
18274	25F	96	Federal Express	N8123N N504FE
18275	25F	101	DHL Airways	N8124N N283DH N708DH
18276	25F	103	Federal Express	N8125N N505FE
18277	25F	107	Federal Express	N8126N N506FE
18278	25F	113	Federal Express	N8127N N507FE
18279	25F	121	Federal Express	N8128N N508FE
18280	25F	129	Federal Express	N8129N N509FE
18281	25	143	Metroparque	N8130N HK-2541 Preserved Olaya-Herrera AP, Colombia Aug93
18282	25F	149	Federal Express	N8131N HK-2705X HK-2705 N4556W N8131N N510FE
18283	25F	155	Federal Express	N8132N N511FE
18284	25	161	(AeroNica)	N8133N YN-BXW dbf 10Nov91 Managua, Nicaragua
18285	25F	172	Patriot Airlines	N8134N N152FE
18286	25F	182	Morningstar Air Express	N8135N N153FE C-FBWX
18287	25F	190	Federal Express	N8136N HK-2604X HK-2604 N47538 N8136N N154FE
18288	25F	192	Federal Express	N8137N N155FE
18289	25F	194	Federal Express	N8138N N156FE
18290	25	201	(Aviation Sales Co)	N8139N stored Marana, AZ 18Sep81; later b/u
18291	25	204	Westrafa Airlift	N8140N N904TS 9Q-CWT
18293	22	1	Museum of Flight Foundation	N7001U Preserved Seattle, WA Sep90
18294	22	3	City & County of San Francisco	N7002U Preserved San Francisco, CA 21Dec90
18295	22	4	(Piedmont Aviation)	N7003U N68650 w/o 19Jul67 Henderson, NC
18296	22	5	National Air & Space Museum	N7004U stored Davis-Monthan AFB, AZ Dec91
18297	22	6	(Aero Controls)	N68644 N7005U stored Shelton, WA Feb93, later b/u
18298	22	7	(Aero Controls)	N7006U stored Shelton, WA; b/u 28Feb92
18299	22	9	(Aero Controls)	N7007U stored Shelton, WA 01Feb93, later b/u
18300	22	10	(Aero Controls)	N7008U stored Shelton, WA 02Nov92; later b/u
18301	22	12	(Aero Controls)	N7009U stored Shelton, WA 23Nov93, later b/u
18302	22	19	(Aero Controls)	N7010U stored Shelton, WA; b/u 17Jun92
18303	22	22	(Aero Controls)	N7011U stored Shelton, WA 28Apr92, later b/u
18304	22	23	(Aero Controls)	N7012U stored Shelton, WA; b/u 28Feb92
18305	22	27	(Aero Controls)	N7013U stored Shelton, WA 02Nov92, later b/u
18306	22	34	(Aero Controls)	N7014U stored Shelton, WA Sep92, later b/u
18307	22	38	San Jose State University	N7015U Preserved San Jose, CA Feb92
18308	22	40	(Aero Controls)	N7016U stored Shelton, WA Jan93
18309	22	47	Chicago Museum of Science & Ind	N7017U stored 14Nov91; preserved
18310	22	48	(Aero Controls)	N7018U stored Shelton, WA; b/u 28Feb92
18311	22	55	(Aero Controls)	N7019U stored Denver, CO Jul91; later b/u
18312	22	60	University of Purdue	N7020U Preserved Lafayette, LA 13Jan92
18313	22	66	(Aero Controls)	N7021U stored Shelton, WA; b/u 28Feb92
18314	22	73	(The Memphis Group)	N7022U N157FE stored Dothan, AL; b/u Jan92
18315	22	77	(Aero Controls)	N7023U (N158FE) N7023U stored Dothan, AL; b/u Apr92
18316	22	80	(The Memphis Group)	N7024U (N159FE) N7024U stored Dothan, AL; b/u Greenwood, MS Aug91
18317	22	88	(The Memphis Group)	N7025U (N160FE) N7025U stored Greenwood, MS; b/u Feb92
18318	22	95	(The Memphis Group)	N7026U (N162FE) N7026U stored Greenwood, MS; b/u Aug91
18319	22	110	(The Memphis Group)	N7027U (N163FE) N7027U stored Greenwood, MS; b/u Sep91

BOEING 727

C/n	Series	Line No	Last known Operator/Owner	Previous Identities/fate (where known)
18320	22	119	(The Memphis Group)	N7028U N28KA stored Greenwood, MS Oct93; later b/u
18321	22F	122	DHL Airways	N7029U HL7336 HK-2833X HK-2833 N8700R N707DH
18322	22	130	(United Airlines)	N7030U w/o 11Nov65 Salt Lake City, UT
18323	22	136	HD Aviation Services	N7031U HL7337 N1187Z CC-CIW N863SY VR-BMC
18324	22	139	(The Memphis Group)	N7032U N841N N103MU N39KA stored Greenwood, MS Oct93; later b/u
18325	22	141	AVENSA	N7033U YV-82C XA-LEX YV-839C
18326	22	142	TAESA	N7034U YV-80C XA-RLM XA-JJA stored 09Apr95
18327	22	144	Servivensa	N7035U YV-81C YV-763C
18328	22	146	(United Airlines)	N7036U w/o 16Aug65 Lake Michigan, IL
18329	22	154	Polaris Aircraft Leasing	N7037U N40481 stored Mojave, CA 11Jul91
18330	22	156	Aerospace Intl Group	N7038U N40482 5N-ORI 5N-TRT
18331	22	158	Polaris Aircraft Leasing	N7039U N40483 (N483AS) N40483 stored Mojave, CA 15Jul91
18332	22	164	Shabair	N7040U N40485 9Q-CSF
18360	30	24	Federal Aviation Admin	N68649 D-ABIB N68649 N77 N97 N46 stored Atlantic City, NJ Aug94
18361	30	28	New ACS	D-ABIC N16765 N18477 9Q-CRG
18362 built as 727-30 and modified as follows:				
18362	C-22A	33	USAF/310thAS	D-ABID N90558 N78 84-0193 stored Davis-Monthan AFB, AZ 01Nov91
18363	30	35	Islamic Republic of Iran	D-ABIF N16768 EP-SHP EP-PLN
18364	30	37	Nationsbank of Tennessee	D-ABIG N16766 N18748 stored Sherman, TX 06Mar93
18365	30	52	Comtran International	D-ABIH N16767 HZ-TA1 G-BMZU N96B N727MJ*
18366	30	98	Sheikh El Khereiji	D-ABIK N9233Z N44R (N44Q) VR-BGW N727NJ [Op by Sigair Ltd]
18367	30	109	SCIBE Airlift	D-ABIL (N2703J) N727UD N2703J N727UD 9Q-CBG
18368	30	117	MME Farm Maintenance	D-ABIM N9234Z N72700 N728JE N841MM VR-CMM
18369	30	125	Shabair	D-ABIN A40-CF 9Q-CSG
18370	30	134	Aviation Consultants	D-ABIP N26565 VR-BHN Z-WYY N25AZ
18371	30	145	Aimes Company	D-ABIQ N727CH VR-BHP VR-UHM VS-UHM N727CH V8-UHM V8-BG1 V8-BG2 9M-SAS 5B-DBE
18426	23	15	ex-Phoenix Airways	N1970 ZS-NMX Ceased ops 05Nov95, stored Johannesburg, South Africa
18427	23	18	First Security Bank of Utah	N1971 stored Maxton, NC 05Oct92
18428	23	21	Group Air Management	N1972
18429	23F	26	Pacific International Airlines	N1973 (N934FT) N1973 (N528FE) N1973 N517FE HP-1229PFC
18430	23	31	Imperial Air	N1974
18431	23F	32	Emery Worldwide A/L	N1975
18432	23	43	Imperial Air	N1976
18433	23	44	First Security Bank of Utah	N1977 stored Maxton, NC 04Mar93
18434	23F	50	(Caldwell Aircraft Trading)	N1978 stored Maxton, NC 21Feb92; b/u 28Feb92
18435	23F	51	Pacific International Corp	N1979 (N944FT) N1979 (N512FE) N1979 N518FE N518PM HP-
18436	23	58	TAESA	N1980 XA-SXZ
18437	23	59	Aerosur	N1981 stored Maxton, NC 16Apr93, later Miami, FL
18438	23F	65	Emery Worldwide A/L	N1982
18439	23F	67	Emery Worldwide A/L	N1983
18440	23	69	Air Baltic	N1984 YL-BAF stored Riga, Latvia Dec95
18441	23	97	First Security Bank of Utah	N1985 stored Maxton, NC 29Oct92
18442	23	105	Middle East Leasing Corp	N1986 stored Miami, FL 30May94, later Smyrna, TN
18443	23	111	First Security Bank of Utah	N1987 (OK-UGA) N1987 (ZS-NVH) N1987 stored Bucharest, Romania
18444	23	114	Phoenix Airlines	N1988 OK-UGZ N1988
18445	23	115	Aerovias DAP	N1989 CC-CLZ
18446	23F	123	Emery Worldwide A/L	N1990 stored Dayton, OH 02Aug93
18447	23	127	Zimbabwe Express A/L	N1991 ZS-NMY
18448	23	131	AMR Info Service Training	N1992 Preserved Chicago-Midway, IL 31Aug91
18449	23	132	AvAtlantic	N1993 stored Fort Lauderdale, FL
18450	23	140	Aerolineas Internacionales	N1994 XA-SNW
18464	22	2	(Boeing Commercial Airplane Co)	N72700 N1784B N72700 Prototype, stored Everett, WA Feb76; b/u 05Apr78
18569	31	36	(Trans World Airlines)	N850TW stored Kansas City, MO 30Jul91, Dallas-Love Field, TX 26Nov91; later b/u
18570	31	39	US Jet Services	N851TW stored Kansas City, MO 15Jul90 as ground trainer
18571	31	42	(Trans World Airlines)	N852TW dbr 27Aug88 Chicago-O'Hare, IL
18572	31	46	Aeroexo	N853TW XA-RWG
18573	31	49	Trans World Airlines	N854TW stored Kansas City, MO 06Jan92
18574	31	56	Trans World Airlines	N855TW stored Kansas City, MO Dec93
18575	31	57	Trans World Airlines	N856TW stored Kansas City, MO 23Jan92
18576	31	63	Trans World Airlines	N857TW stored Kansas City, MO Dec93
18577	31	64	(Charlotte Aircraft Corp)	N858TW stored Kansas City. MO, b/u 31Oct86
18578	31	68	(The Memphis Group)	N859TW stored Kansas City, MO; b/u Greenwood, MS May90
18741	76	72	(Aero Controls)	VH-TJA N91891 N40AF N18480 stored Mojave, CA 19Jul91, later b/u
18742	76	81	(Quassar)	VH-TJB YN-BWX PT-TCF HK-3442X PT-TCF TC-ATU N66510 HH-PRI TG-ANP HP-1179TLN XA-SHT stored Opa Locka, FL by Oct94; b/u Sep95

BOEING 727

C/n	Series	Line No	Last known Operator/Owner	Previous Identities/fate (where known)
18743	77	78	Quassar	VH-RME XA-MEG PT-TCE N8140V TC-AJT N143CA HK-3588X HK-3651X HH-JEC XA-SDH XA-SIR stored Opa Locka, FL by Oct94
18744	77	86	(Corsair)	VH-RMF PT-TCD N8140P TC-AJS N134CA (OB-) N134CA stored Lima, Peru; b/u Feb95
18750	31	70	(The Memphis Group)	N849TW stored Montgomery, AL; b/u Sep89
18751	31	75	Trans World Airlines	N848TW stored Kansas City, MO 30Dec93
18752	31	76	TAESA	N847TW N727PJ XA-SQO
18753	31	83	SAETA	N846TW HC-BPL stored Guayaquil, Ecuador
18754	31	84	(US Jet Services)	N845TW stored Kansas City, MO 30Mar89; b/u Chicago-O'Hare, IL
18755	31	87	Trans World Airlines	N844TW stored Kansas City, MO 30Dec93
18791	22	165	(Aero Controls)	N7003U N40484 stored Mojave, CA 15Jul91; later b/u
18794	78F	99	Evergreen Intl Airlines	9Y-TCO N305BN PT-TYR N728EV stored Marana, AZ
18795	78	104	Lloyd Aereo Boliviano	9Y-TCP N306BN CP-1223
18796	78	108	(Aeronautical Support Intl Sales)	9Y-TCQ N307BN CC-CFG (N4367J) stored Davis-Monthan AFB, AZ; b/u 08Oct92, fuselage in Dross Metals scrapyard
18797	51	90	Wentworth Technical School	(N401US) N461US N973PS XA-MEN N973PS N461US Preserved Minneapolis, MN Dec91 later Hanscomb Field, ME
18798	51	93	European Airlines	(N402US) N462US N974PS N462US OK-TGX stored Bournmeouth, UK 27Sep95
18799	51	102	(Intl Airline Support Group)	(N403US) N463US N976PS N463US stored Sherman, TX May91, later b/u
18800	51	116	TAESA	(N404US) N464US N977PS XA-MEP N977PS YV-79C XA-TAE XA-ASS XA-PAL XA-ASS
18801	51	120	Transafrik	(N405US) N465US N978PS N465US 5N-MAM S9-TBA
18802	51	128	(Aircraft Support Group)	(N406US) N466US N837N G-BMYT (N101MU) N802SC TC-AJZ (G-BMYT) stored Istanbul, Turkey 05Sep89 as TC-AJZ; b/u Jan92
18803	51	137	(The Memphis Group)	(N407US) N467US N838N N29KA stored Greenwood, MS Oct93, later b/u
18804	51F	162	Amerijet International	(N408US) N468US N5607 (N157FN) N5607 stored Fort Lauderdale, FL May95
18805	51	179	(Transafrik)	(N409US) N469US N5608 N151FN N287AT (S9-) stored Oklahoma City, OK Apr93; b/u May94
18806	51	188	(PMS Repair Station)	(N410US) N470US N5609 stored Miami, FL 05Aug91; later b/u
18807	51	193	(Intl Airline Support Group)	(N411US) N471US (N604NA) N471US stored Minneapolis, MN; b/u Sherman, TX Jan92
18811 to 18817 built as 727-35 and modified as follows:				
18811	C-22B	85	USAF/201stALS/MD ANG	N4610 (N159FN) N4610 83-4610
18812	35	92	(The Memphis Group)	N4611 N158FN N290AT stored Greenwood, MS 17Feb90; later b/u
18813	C-22B	94	USAF/201stALS/MD ANG	N4612 83-4612
18814	35F	100	(Flight International)	N4613 N149FN HK-3229X N149FN scrapped for spares; canx Jul95
18815	35	106	Bradley Air Services	N4614 N154FN C-GOFA stored Ottawa, Canada Mar93
18816	C-22B	112	USAF/201stALS/MD ANG	N4615 (N155FN) N4615 83-4615
18817	C-22B	118	USAF/201stALS/MD ANG	N4616 83-4616
18821	81	124	(Alaska Airlines)	JA8301 N124 XA-SEB N124AS dbr 05Apr76 Ketchikan, AK
18822	81	126	(All Nippon Airlines)	JA8302 w/o 04Feb66 in Tokyo Bay, Japan
18823	81	135	(SAHSA)	JA8303 D-AHLL HR-SHE stored Fort Lauderdale, FL Nov90; b/u Jan91
18843	76F	170	Emery Worldwide A/L	VH-TJC AN-BSQ YN-BSQ N4602D N721JE
18844	77	171	Corsair	VH-RMD PT-TCC N133CA (OB-) N133CA stored Lima, Peru; b/u Feb95
18845	35	175	Faucett	N4617 HK-3203X HK-3203 N4617 OB-1465 stored Lima, Peru
18846	35	183	Intl Pacific Trading	N4618 N153FN HK-3212X N153FN OB-1543 N153FN stored Opa Locka, FL 05Aug94, regn cx Jul95
18847	35F	187	American Intl Airways	N4619 N937FT (N513FE) N937FT N728CK
18848	22	177	Polaris Aircraft Leasing	N7041U N40486 stored Mojave, CA 11Jul91
18849	22F	178	United Nations/WFP	N7042U N40487 N727CD HR-AMG
18850	95	180	(The Memphis Group)	N7043U N1631 N836N N36KA stored Greenwood, MS; b/u Mobile, AL 05Nov92
18851	22	181	AVENSA	N7044U YV-89C
18852	22	186	Polaris Aircraft Leasing	N7045U N40488 (N488AS) N40488 stored Mojave, CA 11Jul91
18853	22	189	AVENSA	N7046U C-GVCH YV-87C XA-BTO (YV-837C) stored Caracas, Venezuela
18854	22	191	Polaris Aircraft Leasing	N7047U N40489 stored Mojave, CA 22Jul91
18855	22	195	Servivensa	N7048U YV-88C YV-765C
18856	22	199	LACSA	N7049U N31KA YV-90C N300AA TI-LRC w/o 23May88 San Jose, Costa Rica
18857	22	200	(The Memphis Group)	N7050U N30KA stored Greenwood, MS Oct93; later b/u
18858	22	207	(The Memphis Group)	N7051U N1632 N834N HK-3168X N834N N101MU N37KA stored Greenwood, MS Oct93; later b/u
18859	22	208	(The Memphis Group)	N7052U N27KA stored Greenwood, MS Oct93; later b/u

BOEING 727

C/n	Series	Line No	Last known Operator/Owner	Previous Identities/fate (where known)
18860	22	210	Polaris Aircraft Leasing	N7053U N40490 stored Mojave, CA 12Jul91
18861	22	212	Aero Controls	N7054U (N164FE) N7054U stored Shelton, WA Mar92
18862	22	216	Aero Controls	N7055U (N165FE) N7055U stored Shelton, WA 14Feb92
18863	22F	227	Federal Express	N7056U N166FE
18864	22F	231	Federal Express	N7057U N167FE
18865	22F	232	Federal Express	N7058U N168FE
18866	22F	241	Federal Express	N7059U N169FE
18867	22F	247	Morningstar Air Express	N7060U N180FE C-GBWS
18868	22F	248	Federal Express	N7061U N181FE
18869	22	253	(Aero Controls)	N7062U stored Shelton, WA; b/u 17Jan92
18870	22F	258	Federal Express	N7063U N184FE
18871	22F	259	Federal Express	N7064U N185FE
18872	22F	261	Federal Express	N7065U N186FE
18874	46	166	Air Taxi International	JA8307 HL7308 HK-2420X N11412 stored Bogota, Colombia by Oct94, later Shelton, WA Jul95
18875	46	202	(SAM-Colombia)	JA8308 HL7307 HK-2421X dbr 04Aug93 Bogota, Colombia
18876	46	217	(SAM-Colombia)	JA8309 HL7309 HK-2422X w/o 19May93 nr Medellin, Colombia
18877	46	226	New ACS	JA8310 G-BAFZ HK-3201X G-BAFZ HK-3270X G-BAFZ EI-BUP N7046A (EL-...) HK-3458X EL-AKE 9Q-CAR 9Q-CRA stored Kinshasa, Zaire by Nov95; cancelled
18878	46F	236	Amerijet International	JA8311 G-BAJW 9N-ABW G-BAJW N190AJ
18879	46	254	Aerorepublica	JA8312 G-BAEF 9N-ABV G-BAEF HK-3384X G-BAEF HK-3599X G-BAEF HR-ALZ HK-3840X
18892	44F	148	Emery Worldwide A/L	ZS-DYM ZS-SBA N92GS EL-AIY N92GS N94GS
18893	44F	157	(Transafrik)	ZS-DYN ZS-SBB N727GS N93GS TF-VLS N188CL S9-TAN dbr 29Apr94 M'Banza-Congo, Angola
18894	44	168	Fuerza Aerea Panama	ZS-DYO ZS-SBC N727CR (FAP-400) HP-500A
18895	44	173	(Aeron Aviation Corp)	ZS-DYP ZS-SBD EL-AIZ N95GS HK-3133X stored San Jose, Costa Rica Jun91; later b/u
18896	44F	184	Air East Africa	ZS-DYR ZS-SBE HK-2957X HK-2957 N5458E N723JE
18897	51C	211	Purolator Courier	N2977G N7270C N303BN N15512 OB-R-1115 N721EV OB-R-1115 C-GKFC [Op by Kelowna Flightcraft]
18898	51C	244	United Parcel Service	N490US N434EX N902UP [RR Tay engines]
18899	51C	256	Emery Worldwide A/L	N491US N414EX
18900	23	151	Air Baltic	N1995 YL-BAE stored Riga. Latvia Dec95
18901	23	153	(American Airlines)	N1996 w/o 08Nov65 Covington, KY
18902	31	138	Trans World Airlines	N831TW stored Kansas City, MS 09Jan92
18903	31F	147	Emery Worldwide A/L	N833TW N210NE [Op by Ryan Intl]
18904	31	152	Trans World Airlines	N839TW stored Kansas City, MO 30Dec93
18905	31F	160	Emery Worldwide A/L	N840TW (N210NE) N220NE [Op by Ryan Intl]
18906	31F	176	Burlington Air Express	N841TW N240NE
18907	31F	224	Front Page Tours	N842TW N230NE stored Grayson, TX Mar96
18908	14	133	Forcea Aerea Mexicana	N970PS XA-SER TP-10503/XA-FAY
18909	14F	150	Forcea Aerea Mexicana	N971PS XA-SEU TP-10504/XA-FAZ
18910	14	159	Thief River Falls Technical School	N972PS XA-IUP N972PS Preserved 13Jun92 for ground instruction
18911	14F	167	TAESA Cargo/Aero Flash	N973PS XA-SEA TP-10505/XA-FAA XA-RRA
18912	14	169	Forcea Aerea Mexicana	N974PS XA-SEK N974PS XA-SEP TP-10501/XA-FAD
18919	81	163	Blue Airlines	JA8305 D-AHLM HR-SHF D-AHLM 9Q-CDM
18920	81	174	Air Panama Internacional	JA8306 HP-619 HP-619API stored Panama City
18933	30	185	Imperial Palace Air	D-ABIR (N4646S) N727CH VR-BHK N129JK N727BE
18934	30	222	Republique du Zaire	D-ABIS N62119 JY-HMH JY-AHS VR-CHS 9Q-CDZ
18935	30	234	DOJ-US Marshals Service	D-ABIT N90557 N833N VR-CBA N18G N113
18936	30	249	Hemsley Spear Co	D-ABIV N16764 N33UT N5073L N18HH
18942	51	198	Aero Continente	N472US N3605 N160FN N289AT OB-1588
18943	51	203	Aero Continente	N473US N3606 N156FN N288AT OB-1601
18944	51	209	Alexandria Technical College	N474US Preserved 28May92 for ground instruction
18945	51C	263	United Parcel Service	N492US N415EX N903UP [RR Tay engines]
18946	51C	274	United Parcel Service	N493US N418EX N904UP [RR Tay engines]
18947	51C	286	United Parcel Service	N494US N419EX N905UP [RR Tay engines]
18951	81	237	Metro Tech Vo Tech District 22	JA8316 HP-620 N500JJ N55AJ HP-620 D-AJAA OO-JAA D-AJAA G-BMUE N55AJ TC-AJU G-BMUE N3211M stored 05Sep90 for ground instruction
18952	81F	306	Burlington Air Express	JA8317 D-AHLN N110NE stored Grayson, TX Jun95
18965	25F	205	Aero Inversiones	N8141N HP-1261PVI
18966	25	214	(Rosemont Leasing)	N8142N N905TS stored Ardmore, OK 02Apr92, later Dallas-Love Field, TX May93; canx Feb96
18967	25	220	Trans Service Airlift	N8143N N906TS 9Q-CAV
18968	25F	223	Itapemirim T/A	N8144N PP-CJL PP-ITA
18969	25	225	TAP Colombia	N8145N PP-CJK HK-3798X
18970	25	229	Bakrie Aviation	N8146N C-GQBE N682FM N680FM N680AM (PK-) N680AM PK-VBA
18971	25F	230	Express One Intl	N8147N N280NE
18972	25F	242	Burlington Air Express	N8148N N290NE stored Grayson, TX Jun95
18973	25	245	(Corsair Inc)	N8149N N907TS stored, b/u Mar96 Oklahoma, OK
18974	25F	252	Express One Intl	N8150N N300NE
18990	14	238	Government of Burkina Faso	N975PS D-AHLP (N975PS) N2741A N21UC XT-BBE
18992	21	207	(Aero Controls)	N314PA N314AS stored Shelton, WA Jun93, b/u Jul95
18993	21F	215	Aerosucre	N315PA HK-1717

BOEING 727

C/n	Series	Line No	Last known Operator/Owner	Previous Identities/fate (where known)
18994	21	219	(Aerotal-Colombia)	N316PA N316AS HK-2559 dbr 01Aug82 Santa Maria, Colombia
18995	21	221	(Pan American World A/W)	N317PA w/o 15Nov66 Doberitz, East Berlin
18996	21	233	(Aerotal-Colombia)	N318PA N318AS HK-2560X dbr 28Nov82 Santa Maria, Colombia
18997	21	235	Air Taxi Intl	N319PA N721PC N319PA N721PC HK-3396X N91392 stored Shelton, WA Jul95
18998	21	239	Continental Avn Services	N320PA N320AS N1CC N727S N300DK N109HT N7271P N111JL*
18999	21	240	(AVIANCA)	N321PA HK-1716 w/o 17Mar88 Zulia, Colombia
19005	21F	257	Angola Air Charter	N323PA HK-2845 N358QS D2-TJB
19006	21	262	Salem Bin Zaid Ahmed Al Hassan	N324PA N324AS N2CC HZ-TFA HZ-OCV
19007	21F	269	Emery Worldwide A/L	N325PA HK-2846X N359QS stored Mojave, CA 14May92
19008	30QC	364	United Parcel Service	D-ABIW N310BN N918UP [RR Tay engines]
19009	30QC	374	VARIG	D-ABIX N705EV PP-VLV
19010	30QC	382	DHL Airways	D-ABIZ CX-BKB N4585L N724JE N750EV N703DH
19011	30QC	387	DHL Airways	D-ABIA EP-AMU D-ABIA OO-TJN 4X-AGJ OO-ATJ N727JE N701DH
19012	30QC	391	United Parcel Service	D-ABIE N311BN N919UP [RR Tay engines]
19035	21	272	(AVIANCA)	N326PA HK-1803 w/o 27Nov89 Soacha, Colombia
19036	21	278	(Pan American World A/W)	N327PA dbr San Jose, Costa Rica 03Sep80; b/u by Aviation Sales Co
19037	21	284	SAM-Colombia	N328PA HK-1804 stored Bogota, Colombia by Oct94
19038	21F	285	Emery Worldwide A/L	N329PA N329QS
19079	22F	268	Federal Express	N7066U N187FE
19080	22F	270	Federal Express	N7067U N147FE
19081	22F	275	Federal Express	N7068U N188FE
19082	22F	279	Federal Express	N7069U N189FE
19083	22F	281	Federal Express	N7070U N190FE
19084	22F	337	Federal Express	N7071U N191FE
19085	22F	349	Morningstar Air Express	N7072U N192FE C-FBWY
19086	22F	353	Federal Express	N7073U N148FE
19087	22F	359	Federal Express	N7074U N149FE
19088	22F	365	MIBA	N7075U PT-TCH N743EV (VR-B) 9Q-CPJ
19089	22QC	250	Emery Worldwide A/L	N7401U N426EX
19090	22QC	277	US Postal Service	N7402U N427EX [Op by Emery Worldwide A/L]
19091	22QC	280	United Parcel Service	N7403U N490W N928UP [RR Tay engines]
19092	22QC	291	United Parcel Service	N7404U N495WC N929UP
19093	22QC	293	Reeve Aleutian Airways	N7405U N498WC N831RV
19094	22QC	295	United Parcel Service	N7406U HK-2475 N422EX N945UP OY-UPT [RR Tay engines, op by Star Air]
19095	22QC	302	(Emery Worldwide A/L)	N7407U N435EX dbf 03May91 Windsor Locks/Bradley, CT
19096	22QC	305	United Parcel Service	N7408U N497WC N930UP [RR Tay engines]
19097	22QC	307	Emery Worldwide A/L	N7409U N428EX
19098	22QC	318	Reeve Aleutian Airways	N7410U N496WC N832RV
19099	22QC	322	US Postal Service	N7411U HK-2474 N421EX [Op by Emery Worldwide A/L]
19100	22QC	324	US Postal Service	N7412U N429EX [Op by Emery Worldwide A/L]
19101	22QC	333	United Parcel Service	N7413U N430EX N942UP
19102	22QC	336	United Parcel Service	N7414U HK-2476 N420EX N943UP OY-UPJ [RR Tay engines, op by Star Air]
19103	22QC	341	United Parcel Service	N7415U N431EX N944UP OY-UPD [RR Tay engines, op by Star Air]
19109	27QC	271	Federal Express	N7270 PT-TYU N724EV N145FE
19110	27QC	283	Federal Express	N7271 PT-TYQ N730EV HP-1063 N730EV N146FE
19111	27QC	297	(TransBrasil)	N7272 PT-TYS w/o 12Apr80 nr Florianopolis, Brazil
19112	27QC	299	Evergreen Intl Airlines	N7273 PT-TYT N725EV stored Marana, AZ Apr92
19113	27QC	310	Evergreen Intl Airlines	N7274 PT-TYP N731EV 9N-ABY N731EV stored Marana, AZ Jan91
19114	27QC	312	United Parcel Service	N7275 N908UP [RR Tay engines]
19115	27QC	328	United Parcel Service	N7276 OB-R-1115 N7276 N909UP
19116	27QC	330	Evergreen Intl Airlines	N7277 PT-TYO N729EV stored Marana, AZ Jun92
19117	27QC	376	United Parcel Service	N7278 N910UP [RR Tay engines]
19118	27QC	379	United Parcel Service	N7279 N907UP [RR Tay engines]
19119	27QC	393	United Parcel Service	N7280 N911UP [RR Tay engines]
19120	27QC	396	Bradley Air Services	N7281 3X-GCA 3X-GCH 5N-AWH C-GFRB
19121	51	264	Clay Lacy Aviation	N475US TP-02/XC-UJB N299LA
19122	51	319	(Air Taxi Intl)	N476US N105RK N727TA HK-3151 HK-3151X HK-3803X N11415 stored Bogota Colombia by Oct94, later Shelton, WA Sep95; later b/u
19123	51	334	Fuerza Aerea Mexicana	N477US TP-01/XC-UJA TP-05/XC-UJA
19124	51	347	Dallah-Albaraka	N478US (N5604) N604NA HZ-DG1
19125	51	361	(Intl Airline Support Group)	N479US stored Minneapolis, MN Oct91; b/u Sherman, TX Oct93
19126	51	363	(Intl Airline Support Group)	N480US stored Minneapolis, MN Jan92; b/u Sherman, TX Oct93
19127	59F	243	Aerosucre	HK-727
19128	23	196	(Aircraft Leasing)	N1997 stored Mojave, CA 95; later b/u; cancelled Jan96
19129	23	197	Cape Atlantic Air	N1998 ZS-NMZ
19130	23	213	Cape Atlantic Air	N1901 ZS-NSA
19131	23F	218	XPS Air Parcels	N1902 (N938FT) N1902 (N514FE) N1902 N512FE ZS-NPX
19132	23F	228	Aerosur	N1903 CP-2274

BOEING 727

C/n	Series	Line No	Last known Operator/Owner	Previous Identities/fate (where known)
19134	21C	289	Burlington Air Express	N339PA N1186Z N874BX* [Op by Amerijet International]
19135	21C	301	United Parcel Service	N340PA J2-KAD N47142 N724PL N934UP [RR Tay engines]
19136	21C	314	Federal Express	N341PA PT-TCA PT-TCG N727GB N727BB N722EV N143FE
19137	21C	316	Federal Express	N342PA PT-TCB N2969V N727LJ N723EV N144FE
19138	89	246	SCIBE Airlift	JA8314 D-AHLR 9Q-CBT
19139	89	255	Viscount Air Service	JA8315 D-AHLS VR-CRB VR-CDB N511DB stored Tucson, AZ Jan96
19140	22	369	Evergreen Intl Airlines	N7076U PT-TCI N742EV stored Marana, AZ Mar92
19141	22F	370	Federal Express	N7077U N150FE
19142	22F	440	Federal Express	N7078U N193FE
19143	22F	446	Federal Express	N7079U N194FE
19144	22F	450	Federal Express	N7080U N195FE
19145	22F	451	Federal Express	N7081U N196FE
19146	22	452	(Aero Controls)	N7082U (N197FE) N7082U stored Shelton, WA Mar92; b/u Dec91
19147	22F	472	Federal Express	N7083U N151FE
19148	22	473	Tracinda Investment Corp	N7084U N341TC
19149	22	481	Relianace Insurance Corp	N7085U N400RG
19150	22	485	AeroPeru	N7086U N283AT (N238TZ) N238AT OB-1546 stored Lima, Peru Apr94
19151	22	504	AeroPeru	N7087U N284AT (N284TZ) N284AT OB-1547 stored Lima, Peru Apr94
19152	22	507	AeroPeru	N7088U N285AT (N285TZ) N285AT OB-1548
19153	22	508	Dinar Lineas Aereas	N7089U N286AT OB-1570
19154	22F	512	Federal Express	N7090U N198FE
19155	22		(United Airlines)	(N7091U) Allocated but order later canx, not built
19156	22		(United Airlines)	(N7092U) Allocated but order later canx, not built
19157	22		(United Airlines)	(N7093U) Allocated but order later canx, not built
19158	22		(United Airlines)	(N7094U) Allocated but order later canx, not built
19159	22		(United Airlines)	(N7095U) Allocated but order later canx, not built
19165	35	292	ACES-Colombia	N4620 YV-91C XA-RAN YV-838C HK-3933X
19166	35F	303	DHL Worldwide Couriers	N4621 N150FN (N517FE) N150FN OO-DHP [Op by European Air Transport]
19167	35F	325	DHL Worldwide Couriers	N4622 N152FN (N518FE) N152FN OO-DHQ [Op by European Air Transport]
19169	90C	320	Bradley Air Services	N797AS C-FRST
19170	90C	332	Omni Air Express	N798AS N270AX
19171	86	276	(Iran Air)	EP-IRA dbr 07Jan83 Teheran, Iran
19172	86	323	(Iran Air)	EP-IRB dbr 27Jul78 Teheran, Iran
19173	92C	308	Allcanada Express	N5055 N18476 C-GKFV
19174	92C	326	(Air Micronesia)	N5092 CF-PXB C-FPXB N18479 dbr 21Nov80 Yap, Caroline Islands
19175	92C	339	(Civil Air Transport)	N5093 B-1018 w/o 16Feb68 nr Taipei, RoC
19176	61	290	DOJ-US Marshals Service	N127 N27 N2777 N530KF
19180	23F	251	Angola Air Charter	N1905 N935FT (N515FE) N935FT 9Q-CSY D2-TJC
19181	23F	265	Aerolineas Internacionales	N1906 XA-SKC
19182	23F	266	Transafrik	N1907 N933FT (N516FE) N933FT HR-AMI
19183	23F	267	American Intl Airways	N1908 N725CK*
19184	23F	282	(Emery Worldwide A/L)	N1909 stored Maxton, NC Apr92, later Dayton, OH 02Aug93 then b/u
19189	22		(United Airlines)	Allocated but order later canx, not built
19190	22		(United Airlines)	Allocated but order later canx, not built
19191	22QC	386	DHL Airways	N7416U C-GAGX N725PL (N236DH) N725PL N705DH
19192	22QC	388	DHL Airways	N7417U C-GAGY N726PL (N237DH) N726PL N706DH
19193	22QC	392	Federal Express	N7418U N102FE
19194	22QC	394	Federal Express	N7419U N105FE
19195	22QC	406	American Intl Airways	N7420U C-GAGZ N727PL N727CK
19196	22QC	407	United Parcel Service	N7421U 901 CC-CLB N941UP
19197	22QC	410	Federal Express	N7422U N101FE
19198	22QC	413	Federal Express	N7423U N104FE
19199	22QC	414	Federal Express	N7424U N103FE
19200	22QC	416	(United Airlines)	N7425U dbr 21Jun68 Chicago-O'Hare, IL
19201	22QC	421	Federal Express	N7426U N106FE
19202	22QC	424	Federal Express	N7427U N107FE
19203	22QC	434	Ting Tai (Hong) Intl	N7428U N753AL N753AS
19204	22QC	436	Kelowna Flightcraft Charter	N7429U N108FE C-GKFZ
19205	22QC	438	Allcanada Express	N7430U N109FE C-GKFP [Op by Kelowna Flightcraft Charter]
19206	51C	294	Eemry Worlwide Airlines	N495US N413EX
19228	31	351	AVIACSA	N889TW XA-RYI
19229	31QC	390	United Parcel Service	N890TW N923UP OY-UPM [Op by Star Air]
19230	31QC	402	United Parcel Service	N891TW N925UP
19231	31QC	404	United Parcel Service	N892TW N922UP
19232	31QC	425	United Parcel Service	N893TW N927UP OY-UPS [RR Tay engines, op by Star Air]
19233	31QC	458	United Parcel Service	N894TW N926UP OY-UPA N926UP
19234	31QC	463	United Parcel Service	N895TW N924UP

BOEING 727

C/n	Series	Line No	Last known Operator/Owner	Previous Identities/fate (where known)
19242	11F	260	Aerocar Colombia	CF-FUN N4509 CF-FUN N302BN CF-FUN PP-CJI HK-3770X stored Bogota Colombia by Oct94
19243	162	273	(Avengair Inc)	(N7271P) N7282 PT-TYN N113CA N65910 (OB-) N65910 stored Lima, Peru Mar93; b/u Feb95
19244	62QC	338	United Parcel Service	(N2727) N7284 N912UP
19245	62QC	342	United Parcel Service	(N3727) N7286 N913UP
19246	62QC	423	United Parcel Service	(N4727) N7287 N914UP
19249	95	304	(The Memphis Group)	N1633 G-BFGM HK-2960X HK-2960 4X-BAE N727ZV EI-BUI N727ZV stored Greenwood, MS Oct93; later b/u
19250	95	313	(Aerocar Corp)	N1634 PP-VLT stored Rio de Janeiro-Galeao, Brazil 29May92, later Miami, FL Oct91; b/u Nov92
19251	95	315	LADECO	N1635 G-BFGN N29895 VR-BHO CC-CHC
19252	95	327	Khalid bin Alwaleed Foundn	N1636 (N835N) N1636 C2-RN5 N740EV HZ-WBT
19253	77	296	Occidental Petroleum	VH-RMR N110AC N111EK VR-CKL N111EK N340DR N440DR N448DR N720DC
19254	76	298	Occidental Petroleum	VH-TJD (N8043B) VH-TJD N8043B N10XY N682G
19255	64	331	(Mexicana)	XA-SEJ w/o 21Sep69 Lake Texcoco, Mexico
19256	64	355	(Mexicana)	XA-SEL w/o 04Jun69 nr Monterey, Mexico
19257	21F	385	Emery Worldwide A/L	N355PA N355QS
19258	21F	397	Emery Worldwide A/L	N356PA N356QS
19259	21F	408	Emery Worldwide A/L	N357PA N357QS
19260	21	412	Funair Corp	N358PA N727SG N727LA
19261	21	422	Guess ? Inc	N359PA N727DG N727RF N260GS
19262	21RE	426	Jim Bath & Associates	N360PA N727WE (N191FS) N199AM VR-BNA [Op by Skyways Aircraft Leasing]
19279	46	288	(Dan-Air London)	JA8318 G-BDAN w/o 25Apr80 Los Rodeos, Tenerife, Spain
19280	46	373	ACES-Colombia	JA8319 HP-661 HK-3246X stored Miami, FL
19281	46	378	Aerorepublica-Colombia	JA8320 G-BCDA HK-3612X N281ZV HK-3814X
19282	46	495	IDG (Cayman)	JA8325 D-AHLQ N4245S VR-CBE VR-CLM VR-CMN
19283	46F	502	TMW Corporation	JA8326 N745EV stored Marana, AZ Jan91
19287	51C	303	US Postal Service	N496US N416EX [Op by Emery Worldwide A/L]
19288	51C	389	Emery Worldwide A/L	N497US N435EX
19289	51C	403	Emery Worldwide A/L	N498US N436EX
19290	51C	417	Emery Worldwide A/L	N499US N417EX
19298	25QC	335	Federal Express	N8151G N116FE
19299	25QC	344	Federal Express	N8152G N117FE
19300	25QC	346	Federal Express	N8153G N118FE
19301	25QC	352	Federal Express	N8154G N119FE
19302	25QC	354	United Parcel Service	N8155G TG-ALA N937UP
19303	59	357	Aerolineas Americanas	HK-1337 [for SATENA]
19304	193	287	(Alaska Airlines)	N2969G w/o 04Sep71 nr Juneau, AK
19305	193	300	(AeroPeru)	N2979G PP-CJH OB-R-1256 OB-1256 stored Lima, Peru Apr94
19310	30QC	395	United Parcel Service	D-ABII N701EV PP-SRY N701EV N917UP
19311	30QC	399	(Evergreen Intl Airlines)	D-ABIO N703EV PP-SRZ N703EV T3-ATB N4936S N726EV stored Marana, AZ; b/u Mar94
19312	30QC	409	(AeroPeru)	D-ABIU OB-R-1141 OB-1141 stored Lima, Peru; b/u Jun94
19313	30QC	411	Itapemirin T/A	D-ABIY SE-DDD N727M N727MJ PP-ITP
19314	30QC	437	United Parcel Service	D-ABIJ EP-AMW EP-AMV D-AFGK CX-BNT N423EX N906UP
19318	44	348	Mike Davis Oil Co	ZS-EKW ZS-SBF N2689E N727MB N727EC N44MD
19319	44F	441	Digex Aero Carga	ZS-EKX ZS-SBG N26877 9Q-CBS N750UA (C-) N750UA PT-TDG PT-MDG
19356	25QC	356	Federal Express	N8156G N120FE
19357	25QC	360	United Parcel Service	N8157G N121FE N948UP
19358	25QC	367	Kelowna Flightcraft Charter	N8158G N122FE C-GKFB
19359	25QC	368	Kelowna Flightcraft Charter	N8159G N123FE C-GKFN
19360	25QC	371	Federal Express	N8160G N124FE
19385	23	311	Bahamasair	N1910 [Op by AvAtlantic]
19386	23	321	(Emery Worldwide A/L)	N1928 stored Maxton, NC Jan92 then Daytom, OH; later b/u
19387	23F	329	Northern Air Cargo	N1929 N930FT (N519FE) N930FT stored Grayson, TX Jun95
19388	23F	340	North Eastern Airlines	N1930 N939FT (N520FE) N939FT N513FE HC-BRF 5N-SMA
19389	23F	343	DHL Airways	N1931 (N940FT) N1931 (N512FE) N1931 N514FE N717DH
19390	23F	350	Transafrik	N1932 N931FT (N522FE) N931FT S9-TAO
19391	191	309	Champion AIr	N7270F N297BN N502RA N502MG
19392	191	317	Cook Aircraft Leasing	N7271F N298BN N503RA N503MG
19393	191F	401	General Avn Technologies	N7272F N299BN PT-TYJ N8140G TC-AJR N135CA PT-SAW TG-LKA HH-JJD N135CA HP-1187LTN N135CA HC-BSP YV-813C N135CA stored Opa Locka, FL Dec95 as YV-813C
19394	191	418	Dart Container Corp	N7273F N300BN N3946A N727X
19395	191	431	American Intl Airways	N7274F N301BN N504RA N504MG
19396	89		(Japan Domestic Airlines)	Allocated but later canx, not built
19397	89		(Japan Domestic Airlines)	Allocated but later canx, not built
19398	14	345	(Mexicana)	N976PS XA-SEN dbr 19Oct73 Meatzalan, Mexico
19399	109	380	Republic of China Air Force	B-1818 2721

BOEING 727

C/n	Series	Line No	Last known Operator/Owner	Previous Identities/fate (where known)
19400	29	400	(AeroPeru)	OO-STA PP-CJJ OB-R-1277 OB-1277 stored Lima, Peru Apr94, b/u mid 95
19401	29F	419	DHL Airways	OO-STC D-AHLO N577JB N711GN (N727AW) N711GN N712DH
19402	29QC	415	Force Aerienne Belge/21Sm	OO-STB CB-01 OO-STB CB-01
19403	29QC	435	Force Aerienne Belge/21Sm	OO-STD CB-02
19404	82	384	Transafrik	CS-TBK (N8183E) C-GWGP S9-NAZ
19405	82F	398	Burlington Air Express	CS-TBL (N81826) C-GWGT N375NE stored Grayson, TX Jun95
19406	82	430	Triax Airlines	CS-TBM (N81827) C-GWGV 5N-TKE
19427	64	375	TAESA	XA-SEM TP-10502/XA-FAC XA-RRB
19428	23F	358	Amerijet International	N1933 N941FT (N523FE) N941FT N515FE N992AJ
19429	23	362	Aerosur	N1934 CP-2277
19430	23F	366	Aerosucre	N1935 N934FT (N524FE) N934FT HK-3667X
19431	23F	372	Sonangol Jet Management	N1955 N942FT (N525FE) N942FT N516FE D2-ESU
19432	23	381	TAESA	N1956 XA-SYA
19444	295	445	Polaris Aircraft Leasing	N1639 N701US stored Amarillo, TX Mar92
19445	295	455	Polaris Aircraft Leasing	N1640 N702US stored Amarillo, TX Mar92
19446	295	471	Polaris Aircraft Leasing	N1641 N703US stored Amarillo, TX Mar92
19447	295	477	Polaris Aircraft Leasing	N1642 N705US stored Amarillo, TX Mar92
19448	295	496	Polaris Aircraft Leasing	N1643 N707US stored Amarillo, TX Mar92
19449	295	500	Polaris Aircraft Leasing	N1644 N708US stored Amarillo, TX Mar92
19450	235	464	(GE Capital Corp)	N4730 stored Oklahoma City Dec91; b/u Amarillo, TX 93
19451	235	483	(GE Capital Corp)	N4731 stored Oklahoma City Dec91; b/u Amarillo, TX 93
19452	235	492	(Nortek Repair Center)	N4732 stored Oklahoma City Aug93; b/u Amarillo, TX 94
19453	235	506	(GE Capital Corp)	N4733 stored Oklahoma City Dec91; b/u Amarillo, TX 93
19454	235	509	(GE Capital Corp)	N4734 stored Oklahoma City Dec91; b/u Amarillo, TX 93
19455	235	513	(American Intl Airways)	N4735 stored Oklahoma City Aug93; b/u Amarillo, TX 94
19456	235	515	(Nortek Repair Center)	N4736 stored Oklahoma City May93; b/u Amarillo, TX 94
19457	235	518	(Pan American World A/W)	N4737 w/o 09Jul82 New Orleans, LA
19458	235	525	(GE Capital Corp)	N4738 stored Atlanta, GA 03May93; b/u Amarillo, TX Sep94
19459	235	530	First Security Bank of Utah	N4739 stored Miami, FL Dec91
19460	235	531	Azerbaijan Airlines	N4740 4K-4201 N4740 4K-AZ1
19461	235	538	Azerbaijan Airlines	N4741 4K-AZ2
19462	235	539	(Aeroexo)	N4742 XA-SFF stored Monterrey, Mexico early 94; b/u Feb95
19463	235	552	First Security Bank of Utah	N4743 stored Miami, FL Dec91
19464	235	553	(Pan American World A/W)	N4744 w/o 08May78 Pensacola, FL
19465	235	554	(GE Capital Corp)	N4745 stored Oklahoma City Dec91; b/u Amarillo, TX 93
19466	235	561	First Security Bank of Utah	N4746 stored Miami, FL Dec91
19467	235	566	(GE Capital Corp)	N4747 stored Oklahoma City Dec91; b/u Amarillo, TX 93
19468	235	567	(GE Capital Corp)	N4748 stored Oklahoma City Dec91; b/u Amarillo, TX 93
19469	235	568	(Aircorp)	N4749 stored Miami, FL 02Jul92 later Tucson, AZ; b/u
19470	235	569	(Aircorp)	N4750 stored Miami, FL 02Jul92 later Tucson, AZ; b/u
19471	235	590	(First Security Bank of UT)	N4751 stored Miami, FL Dec91; b/u 15Nov92
19472	235	591	First Security Bank of Utah	N4752 stored Miami, FL Dec91
19473	235	606	(First Security Bank of UT)	N4753 stored Miami, FL Dec91; b/u 18Nov92
19474	235	607	Aeroexo	N4754 XA-SFG
19475	223F	511	US Postal Service	N6800 [Op by Express One Intl]
19476	223	523	(American Airlines)	N6801 stored Amarillo, TX Feb94; b/u Apr94
19477	223	533	(American Airlines)	N6802 stored Amarillo, TX Feb94; b/u Apr94
19478	223	535	(American Airlines)	N6803 stored Amarillo, TX Dec93; b/u Jan94
19479	223	544	Champion Air	N6804 N705CA
19480	223F	545	Hunting Cargo Airlines	N6805 EI-HCC
19481	223F	548	American Intl Airways	N6806 N719CK*
19482	223	557	American Intl Airways	N6807 N729CK
19483	223F	558	American Intl Airways	N6808 N744CK*
19484	223F	560	Kitty Hawk Cargo	N6809
19485	223F	571	American Intl Airways	N6810 N722CK
19486	223F	578	American Intl Airways	N6811 N743CK*
19487	223F	579	Express One Intl	N6812 N720CK*
19488	223	588	American Airlines	N6813
19489	223F	593	DHL Worldwide Couriers	N6814 (N317NE) N6814 OO-DHT [Op by European Air Transport]
19490	223F	602	Express One Intl	N6815 stored Brussels, Belgium Jun95
19491	223F	611	Express One Intl	N6816
19492	223F	652	Hunting Cargo Airlines	N6817 EI-HCB N6817 EI-HCB
19493	223	657	American Airlines	N6818
19494	223	661	American Airlines	N6819
19495	223F	664	US Postal Service	N6820 N314NE [Op by Emery Worldwide A/L]
19496	223	669	Champion Air	N6821 N706CA
19497	27QC	429	Air Nacota	N7288 PT-TYH N7288 PT-SAV XA-SGY XA-SPK D2-FAT
19499	27	444	(Americana de Aviacion)	N7289 PT-TYK HK-3483X HK-3843X N7289 OB-1512 (N7289) OB-1512 stored Lima, Peru Aug94, b/u Feb95
19500	27	448	Allcanada Express	N7290 PT-TYM N727EV C-FACX [Op by Kelowna Flighcraft Charter]
19501	27	453	(Corsair Inc)	N7291 PT-TYL N129CA N65894 (OB-) N65894 stored Lima, Peru May93; b/u Feb95
19503	108C	420	United Parcel Service	TF-FIE TF-FLH N727TG N936UP

BOEING 727

C/n	Series	Line No	Last known Operator/Owner	Previous Identities/fate (where known)
19504	173C	427	Burlington Air Express	N690WA N875BX* [Op by Amerijet International]
19505	173C	432	(Dominicana)	N691WA HI-312 HI-312CT stored Santo Domingo, Dominican Republic, later Miami, FL; b/u Aug94
19506	173C	447	United Parcel Service	N692WA OB-R-1135 N692WA PJ-BOA TG-AYA N938UP
19507	173C	449	Itapemirin T/A	N693WA (N693) N693WA PP-VLW PP-ITM
19508	173C	457	VARIG	N694WA PP-VLS
19509	173C	459	Federal Express	N695WA TZ-ADR N199FE Regn canx Oct95
19510	224	577	(Nationsbank of Tennessee)	N88701 stored Sherman, TX 20Sep93 later Greenwood, MS; b/u 01May94
19511	224	581	(Continental Airlines)	N88702 stored Mojave, CA Jul92; b/u Jan93
19512	224	582	Nationsbank of Tennessee	N88703 stored Sherman, TX Sep93 later Kingman, AZ
19513	224	595	(Polaris Aircraft Leasing)	N88704 stored Tucson, AZ May94; b/u Jun94
19514	224	597	(TAN/SAHSA)	N88705 w/o 21Oct89 Tegucigalpa, Honduras
19520	109	466	Republic of China Air Force	B-1820 2722
19524	24C	428	L/A Suramericanas	N2471 N5475 N1781B HK-1271 stored Bogota, Colombia by Oct94
19525	24C	439	(AVIANCA)	N2472 N5472 N1781B HK-1272 w/o 30Sep75 Baranquilla, Colombia
19526	24C	442	L/A Suramericanas	N2473 N5473 N1781B N8320 HK-1273 stored Bogota, Colombia by Oct94
19527	24C	460	Federal Express	N2474 N5474 N1781B N1355B CC-CAN N114FE
19528	24C	465	TAESA	N2475 XA-BBI
19532	27QC	469	United Parcel Service	N7295 CC-CGD N939UP
19533	27QC	475	United Parcel Service	N7296 N915UP
19534	27	454	ACES-Colombia	N7293 N293AS N765AS N100MU N803SC XA-TYT YV-821C HK-3845X
19535	27	456	Airfreight Services	N7294 N60FM
19536	284	433	Olympic Airways	N7270L N3182B SX-CBF stored Athens, Greece Jan92
19537	222	563	(United Airlines)	N7620U stored Las Vegas, NV Sep93 later Ardmore, OK; later b/u. Sale reported Apr95
19538	222	580	United Airlines	N7621U stored Ardmore, OK Jun94
19539	222	583	(United Airlines)	N7622U stored Las Vegas, NV Sep93 later Ardmore, OK; b/u Aug94
19540	222	584	(United Airlines)	N7623U stored Las Vegas, NV Nov93 later Ardmore, OK; later b/u
19541	222	585	(United Airlines)	N7624U stored Ardmore, OK Jun94; later b/u. Sale reported Apr95
19542	222	586	(United Airlines)	N7625U stored Las Vegas, NV Oct92 later Ardmore, OK; b/u Aug94
19543	228	541	Institute Aeronautique Amaury de la Grange	F-BOJA Preserved Merville, France 02Jun91
19544	228F	562	DHL Airways	F-BOJB N606AR N720DH
19545	228F	564	DHL Airways	F-BOJC N605AR N721DH
19546	228	572	(Air France)	F-BOJD stored Paris-Orly, France Jan91; later b/u
19557	81	405	Islamic Republic of Iran	JA8321 N329K EP-MRP 1002 EP-GDS
19558	231	528	Air Transport Office	N12301 9Q-CSH
19559	231	550	(National A/c Resale Assoc)	N12302 stored Kansas City 03Apr94; b/u Springfield, MO by Worldwide Aviation
19560	231	565	(Aviation Systems Intl)	N12303 stored Kansas City, MO 03Apr94; b/u Opa Locka, FL
19561	231	574	Pegasus Capital Corp	N12304 YV-909C stored Tucson, AZ Jan96
19562	231	576	Prestige Airways	N12305
19563	231	587	(Trans World Airlines)	N12306 stored Kansas City, MO 05Apr94; b/u San Antonio, TX Jun94
19564	231	601	(Aviation Systems Intl)	N12307 stored Kansas City, MO 05Apr94; b/u Fort Lauderdale, FL Apr94
19565	231	603	C & S Acquisitions	N12308 stored Kansas City, MO 11Jan96, Smyrna, TN 01Feb96
19595	95F	467	SATENA	N1637 PP-VLQ HK-3771X FAC 1146
19596	95	479	SAETA	N1638 PP-VLR HC-BJL
19597	82C	524	Emery Worldwide Airlines	CS-TBN N4546U N528PC
19618	155C	461	DHL AIrways	N530EJ CS-TBV N3254D N720JE N715DH
19619	155C	470	Ariana Afghan Airlines	N531EJ YA-FAW G-BIUR YA-FAW TF-FLJ G-BIUR YA-FAW TF-FLJ YA-FAW
19620	193	377	Government of Tatarstan	N898PC XY-ADR G-BEGZ VR-CBG HZ-AMH VR-CBV VR-CWC "VR-TBV" VR-CBV VR-CWC
19662	59	484	(Banla Intl Airlines)	HK-1400X HK-1400 stored Bogota, Colombia Oct92; later b/u
19663	59	491	(SAM-Colombia)	HK-1401X HK-1401 stored Bogota, Colombia; b/u 07May92
19665	172QC	476	Emery Worldwide Airlines	N725AL CS-TBQ N45498 (N444CM) N527PC
19666	172QC	480	VARIG	N726AL PP-VLE
19683	214	488	Air Charter	N528PS F-BPJU stored Paris-Orly, France Feb91
19684	214	503	Tulsa Co Area Vo-Tech School	N529PS F-BPJV N218TT Preserved Tulsa, OK 24Dec92
19685	214	556	(Tracor Flight Systems)	N530PS N530EA N908TS stored Mojave, CA Nov93; b/u; canx Jan96
19686	214	570	(US Air Shuttle)	N531PS N531EA N909TS stored Miami, FL 30Nov93; b/u Apr94
19687	214	573	New ACS	N532PS N532EA N910TS 5H-ARS
19688	214	589	(Pacific Southwest Airlines)	N533PS w/o San Diego, CA 25Sep78
19689	214	610	(Tracor Flight Systems)	N534PS N534EA N911TS stored Mojave, CA Nov93; b/u; canx Jan96
19690	113C	540	(Ariana Afhan Airlines)	YA-FAR w/o 05Jan69 Fernhurst, UK
19691	134	487	TAME	SE-DDA RP-C1240 HC-BLE/FAE19691

BOEING 727

C/n	Series	Line No	Last known Operator/Owner	Previous Identities/fate (where known)
19692	134	498	TAME	SE-DDB RP-C1241 HC-BLF/FAE19692
19700	223	673	American Airlines	N6822
19701	223	677	American Airlines	N6823
19702	223F	680	US Postal Service	N6824 N313NE [Op by Express One Intl]
19703	223F	684	US Postal Service	N6825 N311NE [Op by Express One Intl]
19704	223F	689	Express One Intl	N6826 stored Brussels, Belgium Jun95
19717	25QC	468	United Parcel Service	N8161G N125FE N949UP
19718	25QC	474	United Parcel Service	N8162G N126FE N950UP
19719	25QC	478	Federal Express	N8163G N127FE
19720	25QC	482	Federal Express	N8164G N128FE
19721	25QC	488	United Parcel Service	N8165G N130FE N946UP
19722	25QC	493	United Parcel Service	N8166G N131FE N947UP
19728	90QC	536	(Alaska Airlines)	N766AS dbf 09Jun87 Anchorage, AK
19788	142C		(Nordair)	Allocated but later canx, not built
19793	30QC	519	DHL Airways	D-ABBI CX-BKA N4555W N725JE N748EV N702DH
19797	224	598	(Continental Airlines)	N88706 stored Tucson, AZ; b/u Jul94
19798	224	608	(Continental Airlines)	N88707 N88777 w/o 07Aug75 Denver, CO
19799	224	612	(Continental Airlines)	N88708 stored Mojave, CA 08Oct92; b/u Kingman, AZ 94
19800	224	616	(Nationsbank of Tennessee)	N88709 stored Houston-Intl, TX Sep93; b/u Greenwood, TX 01May94
19801	224	617	(Continental Airlines)	N88710 stored Tucson, AZ; b/u Jul94
19802	224	621	Nationsbank of Tennessee	N88711 stored Mojave, CA Jan93; later Kingman, AZ
19803	224	623	(Continental Airlines)	N88712 stored Mojave, CA; b/u Kingman, AZ 93
19804	224	624	(Continental Airlines)	N88713 stored Tucson, AZ; b/u Jul94
19805	22QC	543	Kelowna Flightcraft Charter	N7431U N111FE C-GKFW
19806	22QC	547	Kelowna Flightcraft Charter	N7432U N110FE C-GKFA
19807	172QC	575	Kelowna Flightcraft Charter	N727AL N722JE C-GKFT
19808	172QC	615	United Parcel Service	N732AL N309BN N916UP [RR Tay engines]
19811	116	520	LADECO	CC-CAG stored Santiago de Chile by Dec95
19812	116	532	(LAN-Chile)	CC-CAQ w/o 28Apr69 nr Colina, Chile
19813	116C	594	Angola Air Charter	CC-CFD N70708 (9N-ABA) 9N-ABN N77AZ D2-TJA
19814	116C	600	Federal Express	CC-CFE N115FE
19815	114	443	AVENSA	N977PS XA-TUY HK-2637 HP-1001 HP-500 HP-500A FAP-500 N726JE YV-90C XA-NAD YV-840C
19816	86	505	Iran Air	EP-IRC
19817	86	537	(Iran Air)	EP-IRD w/o 21Jan80 Lashgarak, Iran
19818	21C	462	Republic of China Air Force	N388PA XV-NJB B-188 2724
19819	21C	516	(Air Vietnam)	N389PA XV-NJC w/o 15Sep74 Phan Rang AFB, South Vietnam
19826	185C	546	United Parcel Service	N12826 TF-FIA TF-FLG N940UP [RR Tay engines]
19827	185C	527	United Parcel Service	N12827 N308BN PT-TYI N744EV N954UP
19828	231	609	Capitol Air Express	N52309
19829	231	629	Trans World Airlines	N52310
19830	231	633	Trans World Airlines	N52311
19831	231	636	Trans World Airlines	N52312
19832	231	642	Trans World Airlines	N52313
19833	35	486	Capricorn Systems	N1957 D2-FLZ
19834	35F	489	DHL Worldwide Couriers	N1958 N932FT (N526FE) N932FT OO-DHR [Op by European Air Transport]
19835	35	501	Clay Lacy Aviation	N1959 N727HC N900CH N727HC
19836	35F	494	Transafrik	N1962 N936FT (N527FE) N936FT OB-1533 HR-AMR stored Opa Locka, FL Aug95
19837	35	499	(American Airlines)	N1963 w/o 26Apr67 St Thomas, Virgin Islands
19838	123	551	Global Ltda	N1964 HK-3973X
19839	123	542	Capricorn Systems	N1965 D2-FLY
19846	63UDF	555	Boeing Corp	OB-R-902 N37270 [Unducted Fan testbed, stored Mojave, CA Oct89]
19850	25QC	497	United Parcel Service	N8167G N132FE N951UP
19851	25QC	510	Federal Express	N8168G N133FE
19852	25QC	517	Federal Express	N8169G N134FE
19853	25QC	522	Federal Express	N8170G N135FE
19854	25QC	628	Federal Aviation Admin	N8171G N40
19855	25QC	632	Federal Express	N8172G N136FE
19856	25QC	635	United Parcel Service	N8173G (N137FE) N8173G N932UP [RR Tay engines]
19857	25QC	641	United Parcel Service	N8174G (N138FE) N8174G N933UP
19858	25QC	645	United Parcel Service	N8175G N931UP
19859	171C	559	Echo Bay Mines	N1727T C-FPXD
19860	171C	599	Lloyd Aereo Boliviano	N1728T CP-1070
19861	228F	682	DHL Airways	F-BOJE N722DH
19862	228F	685	DHL Airways	F-BOJF N603AR N724DH
19863	228	691	Istanbul Airlines	F-BPJG (N874UM) TC-AFC
19864	228	696	Istanbul Airlines	F-BPJH TC-AFB
19865	228	703	(AAR Financial Services)	F-BPJI N601AR stored Oklahoma City, OK Jan93; later b/u
19867	151C	514	Emery Worldwide A/L	N488US N432EX
19868	151C	529	Emery Worldwide A/L	N489US N433EX
19873	180C	604	United Parcel Service	N9516T N920UP [RR Tay engines]
19874	180C	534	United Parcel Service	N9515T N921UP
19890	22QC	630	Federal Express	N7433U N112FE
19891	22QC	631	(United Airlines)	N7434U w/o 18Jan69 off Los Angeles, CA
19892	22QC	640	RNZAF/40Sqdn	N7435U NZ7271

BOEING 727

C/n	Series	Line No	Last known Operator/Owner	Previous Identities/fate (where known)
19893	22QC	643	(Royal New Zealand AF)	N7436U NZ7273 B/u Christchurch, NZ May81
19894	22QC	647	Federal Express	N7437U N113FE
19895	22QC	658	RNZAF/40Sqdn	N7438U NZ7272
19899	222	614	(Aero Controls)	N7626U stored Shelton, WA Nov92; later b/u
19900	222	618	(United Airlines)	N7627U stored Las Vegas, NV Mar93; b/u Ardmore, OK Jun94
19901	222	620	(Aero Controls)	N7628U stored Las Vegas, NV; b/u Shelton, WA Nov92
19902	222	622	(Aero Controls)	N7629U stored Shelton, WA Apr94; later b/u
19903	222	627	(United Airlines)	N7630U stored Las Vegas, NV 04Oct92; later b/u
19904	222	637	(Aero Controls)	N7631U stored Las Vegas Mar93 later Shelton, WA & b/u
19905	222	639	(Aero Controls)	N7632U stored Shelton, WA 25Apr94, later b/u
19906	222	644	(Continental Air Transport)	N7633U stored Tucson, AZ; b/u May93
19907	222	651	(Aero Controls)	N7634U stored Shelton, WA 21Jun94; b/u Jul95
19908	222F	653	Emery Worldwide A/L	N7635U
19909	222	656	(Omni Air Express)	N7636U stored Las Vegas 04Oct92; b/u Tulsa, OK Aug94
19910	222	659	(Aero Controls)	N7637U stored Las Vegas, NV 14Jul94, later Shelton, WA; b/u Jul95
19911	222F	668	Emery Worldwide A/L	N7638U
19912	222F	670	Emery Worldwide A/L	N7639U [Op by Ryan Intl A/L]
19913	222F	672	Emery Worldwide A/L	N7640U
19914	222	676	(Aero Controls)	N7641U stored Las Vegas, NV Jun94, later Shelton, WA; b/u Jul95
19915	222	681	Emery Worldwide A/L	N7642U [Op by Ryan Intl A/L]
19968	82C	660	DHL AIrways	CS-TBO N251DH N709DH
19970	251	648	AeroTour Dominicana	N251US HI-656CA
19971	251	655	Intl Aero Components	N252US stored Tucson, AZ 19Aug95
19972	251	662	Okada Air	N253US 5N-EDE
19973	251	665	Erocar	N254US N386PA YV-466C HK-3871X stored Bogota, Colombia Apr95
19974	251	667	Northwest Airlines	N255US
19975	251	674	C&S Acquisition Corp	N256US stored Smyrna, TN May94
19976	251	683	(Sandhill Corp)	N257US N388PA stored Tucson, AZ Sep91, later b/u
19977	251	690	Kiwi International Airlines	N258US N258KP*
19978	251	692	Kiwi International Airlines	N259US
19979	251	697	LASER	N260US YV-910C
19980	251	706	First Security Bank of Utah	N261US stored Marana, AZ 07Oct93
19981	251	736	(Aviation Systems Intl)	N262US stored Fort Lauderdale, FL Dec92; b/u Mar93
19982	251F	737	Aircorp Inc/Express One	N263US
19983	251	741	Kiwi International Airlines	N264US
19984	251	744	(Intl Airline Support Group)	N265US stored Sherman, TX 25Jun93; b/u Oct93
19985	251	745	Falcon Air	N266US
19987	29C	634	Sheikh Hassan Enany	OO-STE N696WA N444SA HZ-HE4
19991	291	521	Arriva Air International	N7276F N406BN HI-630CA N406BN
19992	291	526	(Zuliana de Aviacion)	N7277F N407BN N377PA YV-465C stored Miami, FL 01Dec93; later b/u
19993	291	549	(IAL Aircraft Leasing)	N7278F N408BN TC-AJY N408BN stored Opa Locka, FL; b/u Nov93
19994	291	654	(Aerocar Aviation Corp)	N7279F N1748B N1648 N715US stored Amarillo, TX Jul90; b/u Sep94
19995	291	666	(Aerocar Aviation Corp)	N7275F N1785B N1649 N717US stored Amarillo, TX Jul90; b/u Sep94
20003	284	671	Olympic Airways	SX-CBA stored Athens, Greece Mar94
20004	284	678	Olympic Airways	SX-CBB stored Athens, Greece Mar94
20005	284	687	Olympic Airways	SX-CBC
20006	284	688	Olympic Airways	SX-CBD
20037	222F	701	Emery Worldwide A/L	N7643U
20038	222F	716	Emery Worldwide A/L	N7644U
20039	222F	720	Emery Worldwide A/L	N7645U
20040	222F	729	Omni Air Express	N7646U N90AX
20041	222F	732	Omni Air Express	N7647U N180AX
20042	134C	626	Emery Worldwide A/L	SE-DDC N424EX
20044	23	592	Security Pacific Eqt Lsg	N1969
20045	23RE	596	Westfield Aviation	N2913 (N2550) N2913 N727WF
20046	23	605	The Trump Organisation	N2914 (N925DS) N927DS N725DT VR-BSA VR-BDJ [Op by DJ Aerospace] [RR Tay engines]
20047	231	675	Trans World Airlines	N94314
20048	231	679	Trans World Airlines	N64315
20049	231	693	ADC Airlines	N44316 5N-BBG
20050	231	694	ADC Airlines	N74317 5N-BBH
20051	231	708	Paradise Airways	N74318
20052	231	709	Trans World Airlines	N64319
20053	231	713	Trans World Airlines	N64320
20054	231	718	First Security Bank of Utah	N64321 stored Marana, AZ 20Dec94
20055	231	719	Trans World Airlines	N64322
20075	228	704	(AAR Financial Services)	F-BPJJ N602AR stored Oklahoma City, OK Sep93; later b/u
20078	46F	686	Itapemirin T/A	JA8327 N746EV PP-ITL
20079	46		(Japan Air Lines)	(JA8328) Allocated but later canx, not built
20098	231	731	Capitol Air Express	N64323 N590CA
20099	231	734	(Intl Airline Support Group)	N64324 stored Marana, AZ 29May92; b/u Sherman, TX
20111	109C	695	Republic of China Air Force	B-1822 2723

BOEING 727

C/n	Series	Line No	Last known Operator/Owner	Previous Identities/fate (where known)
20112	31F	700	DHL Worldwide Couriers	N7890 N250NE OO-DHO [Op by European Air Transport]
20113	31F	711	DHL Worldwide Couriers	N97891 N260NE OO-DHN [Op by European Air Transport]
20114	31F	712	DHL Worldwide Couriers	N7892 OO-DHM [Op by European Air Transport]
20115	31	735	Northwest Delaware Corp	N7893 N505T N505C N500LS
20139	295	613	(Greyhound Financial Corp)	N1645 N709US stored Amarillo, TX Jan90; b/u Sep94
20140	295	638	(Aerocar Aviation Corp)	N1646 N713US stored Amarillo, TX Jan90; b/u Sep94
20141	295	649	(Greyhound Financial Corp)	N1647 N716US stored Amarillo, TX Jan90; b/u Sep94
20143	1A7C	619	United Parcel Service	N8789R N2915 N935UP
20144	225	742	(Amerijet International)	N8825E stored Mojave, CA Dec91; canx Feb96 as scrapped
20145	225	749	(Tracor Flight Systems)	N8826E stored Mojave, CA Dec91; canx Feb96 as scrapped
20146	225	751	(Amerijet International)	N8827E stored Mojave, CA Dec91; canx Feb96 as scrapped
20147	225	767	Kabo Air	N8828E 5N-SSS
20148	225	769	(Ram Aircraft Sales)	N8829E stored Mojave, CA Dec91; Canx Feb96 as scrapped
20149	225	770	Orient Express Air	N8830E N917TS stored Tucson, AZ Oct95
20150	225	771	(Aeroexo)	N8831E XA-RXI stored Cancun, Mexico 05Jan95; b/u Feb95
20151	225	773	Aeroexo	N8832E XA-RZI
20152	225F	775	Kelowna Flightcraft Charter	N8833E C-GACU
20153	225F	779	International Air Leases	N8834E stored Miami, FL May95
20154	225	780	Aeroexo	N8835E XA-RXJ
20161	214	714	(Dallas Aerospace)	N535PS N858N N718US (N60279) stored Dallas, TX; b/u Jul91
20162	214	715	Interair Leases	N536PS N7279F N499BN N409BN XA-SJM N409BN stored Tucson, AZ Jun94, later Miami, FL
20163	214	723	(Solair Inc)	N537PS N855N N719US (N60282) stored Amarillo, TX; b/u Dec91 by IRMCA
20164	214	724	(Solair Inc)	N538PS N856N N720US (N60362) stored Amarillo, TX; b/u Dec91 by IRMCA
20165	214	725	(Solair Inc)	N539PS N857N N721US (N60446) stored Amarillo, TX; b/u Dec91 by IRMCA
20166	214	727	(Solair Inc)	N540PS N860N N722US (N60471) stored Amarillo, TX; b/u Dec91 by IRMCA
20167	214	728	(Solair Inc)	N541PS N861N N723US (N60507) stored Amarillo, TX; b/u Dec91 by IRMCA
20168	214	740	(Solair Inc)	N542PS N895N N728US (N60690) stored Amarillo, TX; b/u Dec91 by IRMCA
20169	214	743	Aerosur	N545PS N376PA LV-WDS stored Buenos Aires, Argentina Apr94
20180	223F	698	Kitty Hawk Cargo	N6827
20181	223	699	Aerolineas Argentinas	N6828 XA-SPU
20182	223	702	(American Airlines)	N6829 stored Amarillo, TX Jan94; b/u Apr94
20183	223F	705	Hunting Cargo Airlines	N6830 EI-HCI
20184	223F	707	Burlington Air Express	N6831 N742CK* [Op by American Intl Airways]
20185	223F	710	Hunting Cargo Airlines	N6832 EI-HCD
20186	223F	721	Burlington Air Express	N6833 [Op by Kitty Hawk Cargo]
20187	223F	722	American Intl Airways	N6834 N714CK*
20188	223	730	American Airlines	N6835
20189	223F	733	DHL Worldwide Couriers	N6836 OO-DHS [Op by European Air Transport]
20190	223F	738	US Postal Service	N6837 N315NE [Op by Express One Intl]
20191	223	739	American Intl Airways	N6838 N723CK
20192	223F	752	DHL Worldwide Couriers	N6839
20193	223F	755	US Postal Service	N6841 N312NE [Op by Express One Intl]
20201	284	765	Olympic Airways	SX-CBE stored Athens, Greece Mar94
20202	228	774	Air France	F-BPJK stored Paris-Orly, France Jan91, later Annecy, France
20203	228	776	AAR Aircraft Turbine Center	F-BPJL (N) stored Oklahoma City, OK Apr92
20204	228F	778	DHL Airways	F-BPJM N727DH
20217	116	625	Aero Controls	(CC-) N1780B N304BN N1780B XA-SEW HK-2605X N7829A stored Shelton, WA Aug93
20228	76	766	HS Aviation	VH-TJE N8043E (HZ-GP2) HZ-GRP N727RE VR-CCB VR-CHS JY-HS1
20232	231	785	Trans World Airlines	N54325
20233	231	786	Trans World Airlines	N54326
20234	231	790	Trans World Airlines	N54327
20240	2A7	717	(Trans Caribbean Airways)	N8790R w/o 28Dec70 Charlotte Amalie, St Thomas, Virgin Islands
20241	2A7F	726	US Postal Service	N8791R N6842 N310NE [Op by Express One Intl]
20243	224	646	(Continental Airlines)	N1781B N88714 stored Tucson, AZ; b/u Jun94
20244	224	650	(Libyan Arab Airlines)	N1782B 5A-DAH Shot down 21Feb73 over Sinai Desert
20245	224	663	Jamahiriya Libyan Arab A/L	N1783B 5A-DAI
20248	295	761	(Zuliana de Aviacion)	N1650 N371PA YV-463C stored Miami, FL Sep93; later b/u
20249	295	763	First Security Bank of Utah	N11651 N372PA stored Miami, FL Dec91, later Tucson, AZ
20250	254	781	US Air Shuttle	(N7270Q) N547PS N547EA N913TS
20251	254	782	US Air Shuttle	(N7271Q) N548PS N548EA N914TS
20252	254	783	US Air Shuttle	(N7272Q) N549PS N549EA N915TS
20263	247	750	Haiti Trans Air	N2801W OB-R-1301 OB-1301
20264	247	756	Allegro Air	N2802W N324AS XA-SYI
20265	247	758	(Toros Air)	N2803W TC-AJV dbr 25Aug89 Ankarra, Turkey
20266	247	760	(Faucett)	N2804W OB-R-1303 OB-1303 Ditched 11Sep90 in Atlantic Ocean

BOEING 727

C/n	Series	Line No	Last known Operator/Owner	Previous Identities/fate (where known)
20267	247	762	(International Air Leases)	N2805W N325AS HI-606CA N325AS HI-637CA (N325AS) stored Miami, FL 06Oct93; b/u 94
20268	247	764	Allegro Air	N2806W N326AS (HC-BRG) N326AS XA-SXO
20278	77C	768	Premier Airlines	VH-RMS C2-RN7 VH-TBS
20279	1A0	748	Lloyd Aereo Boliviano	CP-861
20285	281	868	Nortek Repair Center	JA8335 N870N N743US stored Marana, AZ 10Apr95
20286	281	875	(Nortek Repair Center)	N1780B JA8336 N864N N744US stored Amarillo, TX later Marana, AZ; b/u
20289	251	746	Kiwi International Airlines	N267US
20290	251	747	Hellenic Air	N268US stored Smyrna, TN by Oct94
20291	251	753	Intl Aero Components	N269US stored Marana, AZ Jul93 later Tucson, AZ
20292	251	754	Intl Aero Components	N270US stored Tucson, AZ Aug93
20293	251	757	Capitol Air Express	N271US N389PA stored Smyrna, TN May94
20294	251	759	UltrAir	N272US stored Smyrna, TN by Oct94
20295	251	772	(Intl Aero Components)	N273US stored Tucson, AZ 09Apr94; b/u Sep95
20296	251	777	(Northwest Airlines)	N274US w/o 01Dec74 Bear Mountain, Stony Point, NY
20302	2B7	789	(IAL Aircraft Holdings)	N750VJ N404BN N207US N379PA HI-612CA (N379PA) stored Tucson, AZ Sep92; b/u 10Sep93
20303	2B7	793	Islena Colombia	N751VJ N405BN N208US N384PA YV-462C HK-3872X
20304	2B6	808	Royal Air Maroc	CN-CCF stored Casablanca, Morroco May93, used as ground trainer
20306	231	791	(Trans World Airlines)	N54328 w/o 01Dec74 Weather Point, Upperville, VA
20307	231	792	Trans World Airlines	N54329
20308	231	795	Trans World Airlines	N54330
20309	231	796	Trans World Airlines	N54331
20310	231	802	Trans World Airlines	N54332
20311	247		(Western Air Lines)	(N2807W) Allocated but later canx, not built
20312	247		(Western Air Lines)	(N2808W) Allocated but later canx, not built
20313	247		(Western Air Lines)	(N2809W) Allocated but later canx, not built
20314	247		(Western Air Lines)	(N2810W) Allocated but later canx, not built
20327	17	797	Amway Corp	CF-CPN N115TA N4002M N529AC
20328	17	806	TAME	CF-CPK N116TA XA-GUU HC-BIC G-BKCG HC-BIC HC-BLV/FAE20328
20343	113C	784	Ariana Afghan Airlines	YA-FAU
20366	214	828	(Solair Inc)	N546PS N859N N729US (N60747) stored Amarillo, TX; b/u Dec91 by IRMCA
20367	214	832	(Solair Inc)	N544PS N896N N730US (N60819) stored Amarillo, TX; b/u Dec91 by IRMCA
20370	77C	821	Emery Worlwide Airlines	VH-RMT C2-RN4 N555BN N526PC
20371	76	822	Skyline International	VH-TJF VR-BAT (N727KA) N888VT VR-BRR VR-CAM
20379	225	818	(The AGES Group)	N8836E stored Mojave, CA 04Dec91; later b/u
20380	225	820	(Amerijet International)	N8837E stored Mojave, CA 04Dec91; canx Feb96 as scrapped
20381	225F	823	Bradley Air Services	N8838E EI-BVO N8838E C-FIFA
20382	225F	825	DHL Worldwide Couriers	N8839E EI-HCA [Op by Hunting Cargo Airlines]
20383	225F	831	Joda Partnership	N8840E (XA-) N8840E stored Tucson, AZ
20384	224	794	(Continental Airlines)	N88715 stored Tucson, AZ; b/u Jul94
20385	224	800	Nationsbank of Tennessee	N32716 stored Sherman, TX Sep93, later Kingman, AZ
20386	224	801	(Nationsbank of Tennessee)	N32717 stored Mojave, CA Oct91; b/u Jan93
20387	224	804	(Continental Airlines)	N32718 stored Tucson, AZ; b/u Jul94
20388	224	805	Kiwi International Airlines	N32719
20392	227	811	Zuliana de Aviacion	N401BN N205US N378PA YV-464C stored Miami, FL Sep93
20393	227	813	C & S Acquisition Corp	N402BN N206US N385PA stored Smyrna, TN Mar94
20394	227	816	Servivensa	N403BN YV-76C YV-608C
20409	228F	845	DHL Airways	F-BPJN N604AR N726DH
20410	228	846	AAR Aircraft Turbine Corp	F-BPJO (N) stored Oklahoma City, OK Apr92
20411	228	847	Puntavia	F-BPJP J2-KBH
20415	225	833	US Air Shuttle	N8841E N922TS N8841E N922TS
20416	225	834	(Amerijet International)	N8842E stored Mojave, CA 04Dec91; canx Feb96 as scrapped
20418	1C3	812	ACES-Colombia	PP-CJE HK-3739X
20419	1C3	815	(New ACS)	PP-CJF 5N-DDD reportedly dismantled for spares 1992
20420	1C3	819	ACES-Colombia	PP-CJG HK-3745X HK-3745
20421	1F8	826	(Royal Nepal Airlines)	PP-CJH N1781B 9N-ABD stored Hamburg, Germany 93; b/u 07Nov93
20422	41	803	Aerorepublica	PP-VLA PP-VLF HK-3870X
20423	41F	810	VARIG	PP-VLB PP-VLG
20424	41	817	Gomair	PP-VLC PP-VLH 9Q-CAU 9Q-CDJ
20425	41F	824	VARIG	PP-VLD
20426	1J1	829	Dominicana	PP-VLE N1781B HI-212 HI-212CT stored Santo Domingo, Dominican Republic
20430	230	830	Air Alfa	N1785B D-ABCI N876UM TC-ALF TC-JUC TC-IHO TC-ALK
20431	230	851	Air Alfa	D-ABDI N878UM TC-ALB TC-JUH TC-IKO TC-ALM
20432	264	827	Triax Airlines	N1780B XA-TAA HK-3421X 5N-TTK
20433	264	838	(Aeron Equities Corp)	XA-TAB TC-JFB HK-3606X N433ZV stored Miami, FL; b/u 25Mar94
20434	264	842	Jet Air Trading	XA-TAC TC-JFA HK-3605X (N434ZV) stored Mobile, AL Apr94; cancelled Jan96
20435	281	787	MIAT-Mongolian Airlines	JA8328 HL7348 MT-1054
20436	281	788	(All Nippon Airways)	JA8329 w/o 31Jul71 nr Shizukuishi, Japan

BOEING 727

C/n	Series	Line No	Last known Operator/Owner	Previous Identities/fate (where known)
20437	254	798	US Air Shuttle	N384PS N548EA N916TS
20438	254	799	US Air Shuttle	N536PS N536EA N912TS
20441	225	835	US Air Shuttle	N8843E N923TS N8843E N923TS
20442	225	836	Kabo Air	N8844E 5N-KBY
20443	225	837	(Eastern Air Lines)	N8845E w/o 24Jun75 New York-JFK, NY
20444	225	839	Kabo Air	N8846E 5N-KBX
20445	225	840	US Air Shuttle	N8847E N918TS
20446	225	841	(The AGES Group)	N8848E stored Mojave, CA Dec91; b/u 95
20447	225	843	US Air Shuttle	N8849E N919TS
20448	225	844	Orient Express Air	N8850E N920TS HS-PTB stored Tucson, AZ
20460	231	859	Trans World Airlines	N54333
20461	231	860	Trans World Airlines	N54334
20462	231	862	Trans World Airlines	N54335
20463	224	807	Kabo Air	TC-JBA N1781B N32721 5N-TTT
20464	224	809	(Continental Airlines)	TC-JBB N1781B N32722 stored Tucson, AZ; b/u Jul94
20465	224	814	Aero Inversions	TC-JBC N1781B N1355B N32723 HP-
20466	281F	865	Hunting Cargo Airlines	JA8332 HL7355 N527MD N903PG EI-LCH
20467	281	866	(Ram Air Sales)	JA8333 N869N N740US stored Marana, AZ, b/u Oct95
20468	281	849	Pacfic Aviation Holding	N1781B JA8330 HL7349 N528MD N904PG stored Long Beach CA Nov93, then Tucson AZ
20469	281	852	(Korean Air)	N1781B JA8331 HL7350 dbr 13Jun91 Seoul-Taego, South Korea
20470	228	853	Mahfooz Aviation	F-BPJQ J2-KBG C5-DSZ
20471	2B6	848	Royal Air Maroc	CN-CCG stored Casablanca, Morocco Sep93
20472	2D6	850	Air Algerie	7T-VEA
20473	2D6	855	Air Algerie	7T-VEB
20475	44C	854	Bradley Air Services	ZS-SBH N26879 C-GVFA [Op by First Air]
20476	44C	857	Ting Tai (Hong) Intl	ZS-SBI N2688Z (C-G) N2688Z stored Phoenix, AZ Jan89, later Atlanta, GA
20489	82	856	F.A.L. Aviation Inc	CS-TBP N46793 N727KS N727FH VR-C
20490	231	863	Trans World Airlines	N54336
20491	231	864	Trans World Airlines	N54337
20509	281	867	(Nortek Repair Center)	JA8334 N867N N741US stored Amarillo, TX later Marana, AZ; b/u
20510	281	876	(Total Aerospace Services)	(JA8335) JA8337 N863N N745US stored Marana, AZ Apr95, b/u Oct95
20511	281		(All Nippon Airways)	Allocated but later canx, not built
20512	17	858	Baker Corp	CF-CUR N99548 CP-1339 N99548 N767RV N311AG
20513	17	861	Jetlease Finance Corp	CF-CUS N117TA XA-GUV N117TA XA-GUV HC-BIB N327JL stored Miami, FL Dec95 as HC-BIB
20524	264		(Mexicana)	(XA-TAY) Allocated but later canx, not built
20525	230	870	ATASCO Leasing	N1779B D-ABFI N877UM XA-RJV N877UM XA-SJK N877UM OB-1512 N877UM stored Kingsman, AZ 27Jan96
20526	230	871	Air Slovakia	D-ABGI N879UM (TC-ALD) N879UM OM-CHD
20533	1H2RE	869	USAL Ltd	N320HG N228G HZ-122 VR-BKC
20538	228	872	(Air Charter)	F-BPJR stored Paris-Orly, France 28Feb91; later b/u
20539	228	873	AAR Aircraft Turbine Center	N1790B F-BPJS N stored Oklahoma City, OK Oct92
20540	228	874	AAR Aircraft Turbine Center	N1781B N1788B F-BPJT N3209Y stored Oklahoma City, OK
20545	2H3	877	Nortek Repair Center	TS-JHN (N190CB) TS-JHN
20548	277A	907	ACES-Colombia	VH-RMU N274WC (N274BN) N274WC HK-3977X
20549	277F	989	Express One Intl	VH-RMV N275WC (N275BN) N275WC YU-AKR N275WC stored Grayson, TX Jun95
20550	277A	1030	Royal Airlines	VH-RMW N276WC (N276BN) N276WC G-BPNS C-GRYZ
20551	277F	1054	Ansett Air Freight	VH-RMX
20552	276A	906	Aviacsa	N1779B VH-TBG XA-SJU
20553	276A	991	(The Memphis Group)	N1787B VH-TBH stored Greenwood, MS Jun91; later b/u
20554	276A	1027	(The Memphis Group)	VH-TBI N3459D stored Greenwood, MS May92; later b/u
20555	276A	1056	Aeroexo	VH-TBJ XA-SDR
20560	230	887	TAME	D-ABHI HC-BRI/FAE20560
20568	281	878	(Intl Aircraft Parts)	N1788B JA8338 N862N N746US stored Amarillo, TX later Marana, AZ; b/u
20569	281	879	(Nortek Repair Center)	JA8339 N866N N747US stored Amarillo, TX, later Marana, AZ; b/u
20570	281	880	(Nortek Repair Center)	JA8340 N865N N748US stored Amarillo, TX, later Marana, AZ; b/u
20571	281F	884	Skypak Intl Couriers	JA8341 HL7367 N530MD N905PG EI-SKY [Op by Hunting Cargo Airlines]
20572	281A	881	MIAT-Mongolian Airlines	JA8342 N1790B JA8343 HL7351 MT-1036
20573	281A	888	MIAT-Mongolian Airlines	JA8343 JA8344 HL7352 MT-1037
20579	247A	886	Delta Air Lines	N2807W
20580	247A	889	TCA-Tropical Airlines	N2808W EI-BRA EI-BRD N502AV XA-TCW N502AV PP-AIU N502AV N580CR PP-TLM N580CR
20581	247A	890	Delta Air Lines	N2809W
20592	256A	882	(Iberia)	N1791B EC-CAI b/u late 1995 Madrid, Spain
20593	256A	883	(Iberia)	EC-CAJ LV-VFJ EC-328 EC-CAJ b/u late 1995 Madrid, Spain
20594	256A	885	VIASA	EC-CAK YV-126C
20595	256A	905	Iberia	N1788B N1787B EC-CBA
20596	256A	908	VIASA	N1788B N1786B EC-CBB YV-125C

BOEING 727

C/n	Series	Line No	Last known Operator/Owner	Previous Identities/fate (where known)
20597	256A	909	VIASA	N1788B EC-CBC YV-127C
20598	256A	910	Iberia	N1788B EC-CBD EC-GCI
20599	256A	911	VIASA	N1788B EC-CBE YV-129C
20600	256A	912	Iberia	N1789B EC-CBF
20601	256A	913	Iberia	N1790B EC-CBG F-GOBR*
20602	256A	914	Iberia	EC-CBH EC-GCJ
20603	256A	915	Iberia	N1788B EC-CBI EC-GCK
20604	256A	916	Iberia	EC-CBJ EC-GCL
20605	256A	921	VIASA	EC-CBK YV-128C
20606	256A	937	Iberia	N1788B EC-CBL LV-VFL EC-326 EC-CBL EC-GCM
20607	256A	943	Iberia	N1788B EC-CBM LV-VFM EC-327 EC-CBM
20608	227A	891	American Airlines	N1780B N410BN N716AA
20609	227A	892	Europe Aero Service	N411BN F-GCGQ stored May95
20610	227A	893	American Airlines	N412BN N717AA
20611	227A	894	American Airlines	N413BN N718AA
20612	227A	928	American Airlines	N414BN N719AA
20613	227A	929	American Airlines	N415BN N720AA
20614	225A	897	Finova Capital Corp	N8851E N351PA YV-856C N351PA stored Tucson, AZ Jan94
20615	225A	898	Aeroexo	N8852E (N401PA) N8852E XA-SXE
20616	225A	899	Kiwi International Airlines	N8853E N352PA
20617	225A	900	Florida West Airlines	N8855E (N403PA) N8855E stored Mojave, CA Jul92 then Miami, FL Mar94
20618	225A	901	Florida West Airlines	N8856E (N405PA) N8856E stored Miami, FL
20619	225A	902	Aeroexo	N8857E (N406PA) N8857E XA-SXC
20620	225A	903	ACES-Colombia	N8858E (N407PA) N8858E HK-3998X
20621	225A	904	Aeron Aviation Resources	N8859E (N408PA) N8859E stored Mojave, CA Jul92
20622	225A	933	Kiwi International Airlines	N8860E N353PA
20623	225A	939	Carnival Airlines	N8861E
20624	225A	940	Kiwi International Airlines	N8862E N354PA
20625	225A	941	AvAtlantic	N8863E N355PA
20626	225A	946	Kiwi Intl Airlines	N8864E N356PA
20627	225A	947	Kiwi Intl Airlines	N8865E N357PA N361KP
20628	225A	948	Miami Heat	N8866E [Op by Carnival A/L]
20634	232A	917	Continental Airlines	(N461DA) N452DA (N501PE) N511PE N17779*
20635	232A	918	Continental Airlines	(N462DA) N453DA (N502PE) N512PE N13780 N77780
20636	232A	919	Continental Airlines	(N463DA) N454DA (N503PE) N513PE N15781
20637	232A	920	Aeron Aviation	(N464DA) N455DA (N504PE) N514PE N68782 stored Marana, AZ Apr95
20638	232A	926	Continental Airlines	(N465DA) N456DA (N505PE) N515PE N27783
20639	232A	927	Continental Airlines	(N466DA) N457DA (N506PE) N516PE N16784
20640	232A	935	Continental Airlines	(N467DA) N458DA (N507PE) N517PE N33785
20641	232A	936	Orca Bay Aviation	(N468DA) N459DA (N508PE) N518PE N18786 stored Marana, AZ Apr95
20642	232A	944	Continental Airlines	(N469DA) N460DA (N509PE) N519PE N14788
20643	232A	951	(Santa Barbara Aerospace)	(N470DA) N461DA (N510PE) N520PE N17789 stored Marana, AZ 20Apr95; b/u Aug95
20644	232A	959	Continental Micronesia	(N471DA) N462DA (N511PE) N521PE N15790
20645	232A	961	Pacific Aircorp 791 Inc	(N472DA) N463DA (N512PE) N522PE N10791 stored Oct95
20646	232A	967	Continental Airlines	(N473DA) N464DA (N513PE) N523PE N59792
20647	232A	968	Continental Airlines	(N474DA) N465DA (N514PE) N524PE N45793
20648	247A	895	Delta Air Lines	N2810W
20649	247A	896	Delta Air Lines	N2811W
20655	224A	930	Kabo Air	N32724 5N-LLL
20656	224A	934	Continental Airlines	N32725 stored Tucson, AZ May95
20657	224A	938	Kabo Air	N66726 5N-MMM
20658	224A	970	Nationsbank of Tennessee	N24728 stored Kingman, AZ 22Mar94
20659	224A	978	Kabo Air	(N24729) N25729 5N-QQQ
20660	224A	979	Capital Cargo Airlines	(N24730) N29730 stored Mojave, CA 16Jul92 later Kingman, AZ
20661	224F	985	Amerijet International	N66731 N895AJ
20662	224A	1064	Sportsflight Airways	N66732
20663	224A	1072	Champion Air	N66733 N707CA*
20664	224A	1073	Continental Airlines	N66734
20665	224A	1079	Continental Airlines	N69735
20666	224A	1149	Continental Airlines	N69736
20667	224A	1151	Continental Airlines	N93738
20668	224F	1153	Custom Air Transport	N69739 stored Miami, FL
20669	224F	1154	Unical Aviation Inc	N69740 stored Kingman, AZ 18May94
20673	230A	922	Comair	D-ABKI 5N-NEC ZS-NVR
20674	230A	923	Sunbird Airways	D-ABLI N358PA
20675	230A	924	Kiwi Intl A irlines	(D-ABYL) D-ABMI N727VA G-BPNY N357KP
20676	230A	925	Wilmington Trust Co	(D-ABYM) D-ABNI "N358PA" N360PA stored Hagerstown, MD Oct94
20677	230A	932	Okada Air	(D-ABYN) D-ABPI 5N-GBA
20678	214A	931	Harco Air	N550PS N373PA LV-WFC N373PA 5N-PAX
20679	214A	942	Harco Air	N551PA (V4-CGC) N374PA 5N-PAL
20705	2B6A	945	Fly Linhas Aereas	CN-CCH N609AG PP-LBF
20706	2J7A	949	Laker Airways	N552PS N552NA OY-SBA N552NA

BOEING 727

C/n	Series	Line No	Last known Operator/Owner	Previous Identities/fate (where known)
20707	2J7A	953	Laker Airways	N553PS N553NA OY-SBB N553NA
20709	264A	950	DHL Airways	XA-CUB N624DH [for conversion to 727-264F]
20710	264A	975	Royal Airlines	XA-CUE N788BR EI-BRF N728ZV G-BMLP C-GRYO
20724	281A	954	AVENSA	JA8345 N711BE YV-92C
20725	281F	958	TNT Express Worldwide	JA8346 HL7366 N526MD N902PG EI-TNT
20726	281A	962	(Dominicana)	JA8347 N504AV HI-616CA HI-617CA dbf 05Sep93 Santa Domingo, Dominican Republic; b/u Apr94
20727	281A	966	AVENSA	JA8348 N775BE YV-96C
20728	281A	969	AeroPeru	JA8349 HL7353 N531MD N906PG OB-1573
20729	227A	955	American Airlines	N416BN N721AA
20730	227A	956	American Airlines	N417BN N722AA
20731	227A	957	American Airlines	N418BN N723AA
20732	227A	963	American Airlines	N419BN N725AA
20733	227A	964	American Airlines	N420BN N726AA
20734	227A	965	American Airlines	N421BN N727AA
20735	227A	973	American Airlines	N422BN N728AA
20736	227A	974	American Airlines	N423BN N729AA
20737	227A	976	American Airlines	N424BN N730AA
20738	227A	977	American Airlines	N425BN N731AA
20739	2H3RE	952	AVIANCA	TS-JHO N189CB PH-AHB N739BN PH-AHB G-BOKV N501DC OY-SCA N726VA HK-3480X
20743	232A	971	Delta Air Lines	N466DA
20744	232A	972	Delta Air Lines	N467DA
20745	232A	980	Delta Air Lines	N468DA
20746	232A	981	Delta Air Lines	N469DA
20747	232A	987	Delta Air Lines	N470DA
20748	232A	988	Delta Air Lines	N471DA
20749	232A	990	Delta Air Lines	N472DA
20750	232A	992	(Delta Air Lines)	N473DA w/o 31Aug88 Dallas-Fort Worth, TX
20751	232A	1000	Delta Air Lines	N474DA
20752	232A	1001	Delta Air Lines	N475DA
20753	232A	1012	Delta Air Lines	N476DA N1785B N476DA
20754	232A	1013	Delta Air Lines	N477DA
20755	232A	1014	Delta Air Lines	N478DA
20756	232A	1028	Delta Air Lines	N479DA
20757	230A	1002	Sun Air	D-ABQI 5N-CMB ZS-NWA
20764	2J4RE	960	Sterling European Airways	N1779B OY-SAU N727BE OY-SAU N221FE OY-SAU CS-TKB OY-SAU
20765	2J4RE	984	Sun Country Airlines	OY-SAS N728BE OY-SAS N728BE N222FE OY-SAS N727VA OY-SAS N727VA OY-SAS CS-TKA N288SC
20766	2J4A	993	Royal Airlines	OY-SAT N729BE OY-SAT (N223FE) OY-SAT C-GRYP
20772	227A	982	Continental Airlines	N426BN N551PE N99763
20773	227A	983	Air Nacoia	N427BN N552PE D2-FAS
20774	227A	997	Aerocar Aviation Corp	N428BN N553PE stored Atlanta, GA 16Sep93, later Marana, AZ
20775	227A	998	Shabair	N429BN N554PE 9Q-CWA
20780	264F	986	DHL Worldwide Couriers	XA-CUN N625DH [Op by Continental Micronesia]
20787	264A	999	GECAS	XA-DAT stored 01Oct95
20788	230A	1011	TAME	D-ABRI HC-BSC D-ABRI/FAE788 HC-BSC/FAE20788
20789	230A	1015	GMH Group	D-ABSI N359PA stored Lasham, UK
20790	230A	1021	Olympic Airways	D-ABTI N1787B D-ABTI N852SY SX-CBH
20791	230A	1022	Government of Greece	D-ABVI N854SY SX-CBI [Op by Olympic Airways]
20792	230A	1023	Holiday Air	D-ABWI N851SY TC-TUR TC-RAC
20811	256A	1003	Iberia	EC-CFA
20812	256A	1004	Iberia	EC-CFB
20813	256A	1005	Iberia	EC-CFC
20814	256A	1006	Iberia	EC-CFD
20815	256A	1007	Iberia	EC-CFE
20816	256A	1008	Iberia	EC-CFF
20817	256A	1009	Iberia	EC-CFG
20818	256A	1010	Iberia	EC-CFH
20819	256A	1018	Iberia	EC-CFI
20820	256A	1019	(Iberia)	EC-CFJ dbr 07Dec83 Madrid, Spain
20821	256A	1035	Iberia	EC-CFK
20822	2H3A	996	Belair Ile de France	TS-JHP N191CB PH-AHD F-GGGR
20823	225A	994	Sunbird Airlines	N8867E
20824	225A	995	Sunbird Airlines	N8869E
20837	227A	1016	Aerocar Aviation Corp	N430BN N555PE stored Atlanta, GA 30Oct93 later Marana, AZ
20838	227F	1017	Amerijet International	N431BN N556PE N196AJ
20839	227A	1031	Continental AIrlines	N432BN N557PE N88770
20840	227A	1036	Sun Pacific Intl	N433BN N558PE N79771
20843	231A	1063	Trans World Airlines	N54338
20844	231A	1065	Trans World Airlines	N64339
20845	231A	1066	Trans World Airlines	N54340
20846	231A		(Trans World Airlines)	(N54341) Allocated but later canx, not built
20847	231A		(Trans World Airlines)	(N54342) Allocated but later canx, not built
20848	231A		(Trans World Airlines)	(N24343) Allocated but later canx, not built
20849	231A		(Trans World Airlines)	(N54344) Allocated but later canx, not built
20850	231A		(Trans World Airlines)	(N54345) Allocated but later canx, not built

BOEING 727

C/n	Series	Line No	Last known Operator/Owner	Previous Identities/fate (where known)
20851	231A		(Trans World Airlines)	(N64346) Allocated but later canx, not built
20852	231A		(Trans World Airlines)	(N64347) Allocated but later canx, not built
20853	231A		(Trans World Airlines)	(N54348) Allocated but later canx, not built
20854	231A		(Trans World Airlines)	(N54349) Allocated but later canx, not built
20855	231A		(Trans World Airlines)	(N54350) Allocated but later canx, not built
20856	231A		(Trans World Airlines)	(N54351) Allocated but later canx, not built
20857	231A		(Trans World Airlines)	(N54352) Allocated but later canx, not built
20858	231A		(Trans World Airlines)	(N54353) Allocated but later canx, not built
20859	231A		(Trans World Airlines)	(N54354) Allocated but later canx, not built
20860	232A	1038	Delta Air Lines	N480DA
20861	232A	1041	Delta Air Lines	N481DA
20862	232A	1042	Delta Air Lines	N482DA
20863	232A	1053	Delta Air Lines	N483DA
20864	232A	1060	Delta Air Lines	N484DA
20865	232A	1062	Delta Air Lines	N485DA
20866	232F	1067	Federal Express	N486DA CS-TCH N497FE
20867	232F	1068	Federal Express	N487DA CS-TCI N498FE
20868	247A	1024	Delta Air Lines	N2812W
20869	247A	1025	Delta Air Lines	N2813W
20870	247A	1032	Delta Air Lines	N2814W
20871	247A	1039	Delta Air Lines	N2815W
20872	247A	1040	Delta Air Lines	N2816W
20873	247A	1043	Delta Air Lines	N2817W
20874	247A	1057	IAL Inc	N2818W PP-AIV stored Miami, FL 02Dec95
20875	214A	1020	Jetlease Finance Corp	N554PS N375PA N227JL stored Miami, FL
20876	214A	1026	Mexicana	JA8350 N772BE YV-93C XA-MXH
20877	214A	1029	AVENSA	JA8351 N773BE YV-94C
20878	214A	1034	AVENSA	JA8352 N774BE YV-95C stored Caracas, Venezuela by Nov94
20879	2J7A	1033	Capital Cargo	N128NA
20880	2J7A	1037	AeroPeru	N129NA
20885	2D3A	1055	AVENSA	JY-ADR YV-97C
20886	2D3A	1061	(Alia-RoyalJordanian A/L)	JY-ADU w/o 14May79 Doha, Qatar
20894	264A	1047	DHL Worldwide Couriers	XA-DUI N9184X
20895	264F	1049	DHL Worldwide Couriers	XA-DUJ N623DH [Op by Continental Micronesia]
20896	264F	1051	DHL Worldwide Couriers	XA-DUK N622DH [Op by Continental Micronesia]
20899	230A	1046	Wilmington Trust Co	D-ABKA N390PA stored Hagerstown, MD Feb92
20900	230A	1050	Wilmington Trust Co	D-ABKB N391PA stored Hagerstown, MD Feb92
20901	230A	1058	Wilmington Trust Co	D-ABKC N392PA stored Hagerstown, MD Feb92
20902	230A	1059	Wilmington Trust Co	D-ABKD N393PA stored Hagerstown, MD Feb92
20903	230A	1089	Americana de Aviacion	N8293V D-ABKE N87790 D-ABKE (N394PA) D-ABKE N87790 OB-1560
20904	230A	1090	Tur European Airlines	D-ABKF TC-RUT
20905	230F	1091	Istanbul Airlines	D-ABKG N860SY YV-855C N866SY TC-AFV
20906	230A	1092	Okada Air	D-ABKH (N395PA) D-ABKH 5N-MML
20918	230A	1093	Olympic Airways	D-ABKJ N397PA SX-CBG
20930	2H9A	1044	(Talia Airways)	YU-AKA TC-AKD w/o 27Feb88 Kyrenian Mountains, Cyprus
20931	2H9A	1045	JAT-Yugoslav Airlines	YU-AKB stored Zagreb, Croatia Oct92
20932	233F	1069	Federal Express	C-GAAA N221FE
20933	233F	1071	Federal Express	C-GAAB N222FE
20934	233F	1074	Federal Express	C-GAAC N220FE
20935	233F	1076	Federal Express	C-GAAD 6Y-JMP C-GAAD N223FE
20936	233F	1078	Federal Express	C-GAAE 6Y-JMH C-GAAE N254FE
20937	233F	1103	Amerijet International	C-GAAF N7152J C-GAAD N495AJ
20938	233F	1105	Bradley Air Services	C-GAAG N727GC C-GAAG
20939	233F	1112	Federal Express	C-GAAH N257FE
20940	233F	1120	Federal Express	C-GAAI N258FE
20941	233F	1128	First Air Cargo	C-GAAJ N727LS C-FUFA [Op by Bradley Air Services]
20942	233F	1130	Amerijet International	C-GAAK N727JH N994AJ
20945	286A	1048	Iran Air	EP-IRP
20946	286A	1052	Iran Air	EP-IRR
20947	286A	1070	Iran Air	EP-IRS
20948	2H3A	1084	Tunis Air	TS-JHQ
20950	276A	1081	Sabre Airways	VH-TBK G-BNNI
20951	276A	1101	Pacific International A/L	VH-TBL TF-FLK YU-AKO TF-AIA N908PG stored Jan96
20955	2D3A	1075	Air Algerie	7T-VEH
20972	282A	1096	(TAP-Air Portugal)	CS-TBR w/o 19Nov77 Funchal, Madeira
20973	282A	1099	SAETA	CS-TBS HC-BRG
20974	256A	1077	Iberia	EC-CID
20975	256A	1080	Iberia	EC-CIE
20978	277F	1083	Federal Express	VH-RMY 6Y-JML VH-RMY N240FE
20979	277F	1098	Federal Express	VH-RMZ N241FE
20980	2F2A	1085	KTHY-Cyprus Turkish A/L	TC-JBF
20981	2F2A	1086	KTHY-Cyprus Turkish A/L	TC-JBG
20982	2F2A	1087	(THY- Turkish Airlines)	TC-JBH w/o 19Sep76 Mt Karapte, Turkey
20983	2F2A	1088	KTHY-Cyprus Turkish A/L	TC-JBJ
20984	223A	1121	American Airlines	N843AA stored Amarillo, TX 26Feb96
20985	223A	1123	American Airlines	N844AA stored Amarillo, TX 20Nov95
20986	223A	1125	American Airlines	N845AA stored Amarillo, TX 29Nov95

BOEING 727

C/n	Series	Line No	Last known Operator/Owner	Previous Identities/fate (where known)
20987	223A	1126	American Airlines	N846AA stored Amarillo, TX 03Nov95
20988	223A	1141	American Airlines	N847AA stored Amarillo, TX 31Dec95
20989	223A	1144	American Airlines	N848AA
20990	223A	1184	American Airlines	N849AA stored Amarillo, TX 31Dec95
20991	223A	1185	American Airlines	N850AA stored Amarillo, TX 31Dec95
20992	223F	1187	DHL Worldwide Couriers	N851AA OO-DHU [Op by European Air Transport]
20993	223F	1189	DHL Worldwide Couriers	N852AA OO-DHW N852AA OO-DHW [Op by European Air Transport]
20994	223F	1190	DHL Worldwide Couriers	N853AA OO-DHX [Op by European Air Transport]
20995	223F	1192	Kitty Hawk Aircargo	N854AA
20996	223F	1193	Kitty Hawk Aircargo	N855AA
20997	223A	1195	American Intl Airways	N856AA
21010	2L4A	1100	Pinecroft Inc	N111AK VS-1HB VS-HB1 V8-HB1 VR-CCA
21018	232F	1095	Federal Express	N488DA CS-TCJ N499FE
21019	232A	1097	Delta Air Lines	N489DA
21020	232A	1102	Delta Air Lines	N490DA
21021	2D3A	1082	Sabre Airways	JY-ADV HI-452 N500AV PH-AHZ G-BPND N500AV OK-EGK G-BPND
21036	2J1A	1129	Dominicana	HI-242 HI-242CT
21037	2H9A	1094	JAT-Jugoslav Airlines	YU-AKE
21038	2H9A	1118	JAT-Jugoslav Airlines	YU-AKF
21039	2H9A	1119	JAT-Jugoslav Airlines	YU-AKG
21040	2L8A	1142	Aviogenex	YU-AKD 14302 74302 YU-AKD OY-SBJ YU-AKD
21041	227A	1104	US Air Shuttle	N434BN N559PE (N15772) N559PE N924TS
21042	227A	1106	Continental Airlines	N435BN N560PE N10756
21043	227A	1113	Bank of New York	N436BN N561PE N16758 stored 30Jun95
21044	227A	1132	First Security Bank of Utah	N437BN N562PE N13759 stored 02Apr95
21045	227A	1133	Continental Airlines	N438BN N563PE N17773
21050	2L5A	1108	(Jamahiriya Libyan Arab A/L)	5A-DIA w/o 22Dec92 15kms from Tripoli, Libya
21051	2L5A	1109	Jamahiriya Libyan Arab A/L	5A-DIB
21052	2L5A	1110	Jamahiriya Libyan Arab A/L	5A-DIC
21053	2D6A	1111	Air Algerie	7T-VEI
21055	217A	1117	Royal Airlines	C-GCPA G-BKAG (C-GRYC) G-BKAG C-GRMU C-GRYC
21056	217A	1122	Royal Airlines	C-GCPB G-BKNG G-NROA C-GRYR
21057	247A	1135	Delta Air Lines	N2819W
21058	247A	1136	Delta Air Lines	N2820W
21059	247A	1137	Delta Air Lines	N2821W
21060	232A	1115	Delta Air Lines	N491DA
21061	232A	1116	Delta Air Lines	N492DA
21062	232A	1127	Delta Air Lines	N493DA
21068	2B6A	1107	Paradise Airways	CC-CCW N610AG
21071	264A	1143	Special Freighter	XA-FID OB-1537 N171G
21072	264A	1145	Faucett	XA-FIE OB-1541
21074	232A	1138	Delta Air Lines	N494DA
21075	232A	1139	Delta Air Lines	N495DA
21076	232A	1140	Delta Air Lines	N496DA
21077	232A	1147	Delta Air Lines	N497DA
21078	286A	1114	Iran Air	EP-IRT
21079	286A	1131	Iran Air	EP-IRU
21080	2L8A	1146	Aviogenex	YU-AKH 14301 74301 YU-AKH OY-SBP YU-AKH
21082	2K3A	1124	Lloyd Aereo Boliviano	N48054 CP-1276
21083	2K3A		(Unknown Customer)	Allocated but later canx, not built
21084	223F	1199	DHL Worldwide Couriers	N857AA OO-DHV N857AA OO-DHV [Op by European Air Transport]
21085	223A	1200	American Intl Airways	N858AA stored Tulsa, OK 31Dec94 later Miami, FL
21086	223A	1248	American Airlines	N859AA
21087	223A	1250	American Airlines	N860AA
21088	223A	1255	American Airlines	N861AA
21089	223A	1263	American Airlines	N862AA
21090	223A	1267	American Airlines	N863AA
21091	2M1A	1134	Government of Senegal	PK-PJP N40104 6V-AEF
21100	233F	1148	Amerijet International	C-GAAL N727SN N395AJ
21101	233F	1150	Federal Express	C-GAAM N218FE
21102	233F	1152	Federal Express	C-GAAN N21FE N219FE
21105	2J0A	1158	Air Jamaica	6Y-JIP 6Y-JMA VR-CMA 6Y-JMM
21106	2J0A	1160	Air Jamaica	6Y-JIQ 6Y-JMB VR-CMB 6Y-JMN
21107	2J0A	1172	Air Jamaica	6Y-JIR 6Y-JMC VR-CMC 6Y-JMO
21108	2J0A	1174	Air Jamaica	6Y-JIS 6Y-JMD VR-CMD 6Y-JMP
21113	230A	1176	Inter Air	D-ABKK N853SY TC-AFD TC-TCA ZS-NOU
21114	230A	1178	Inter Air	D-ABKL N850SY TC-AFE TC-TCB ZS-NOV
21118	227A	1167	Continental Airlines	N439BN N564PE N14760
21119	227A	1175	Continental Airlines	N440BN N565PE N16761
21142	232A	1155	Delta Air Lines	N498DA
21143	232A	1156	Delta Air Lines	N499DA
21144	232A	1157	Delta Air Lines	N400DA
21145	232A	1159	Delta Air Lines	N401DA
21146	232A	1161	Delta Air Lines	N402DA
21147	232A	1162	Delta Air Lines	N403DA
21148	232A	1163	Delta Air Lines	N404DA
21149	232A	1164	Delta Air Lines	N405DA

BOEING 727

C/n	Series	Line No	Last known Operator/Owner	Previous Identities/fate (where known)
21150	232A	1165	Delta Air Lines	N406DA
21151	232A	1166	Delta Air Lines	N407DA
21152	232A	1182	Delta Air Lines	N408DA
21153	232A	1183	Delta Air Lines	N409DA
21154	251A	1168	Northwest Airlines	N275US
21155	251A	1169	Northwest Airlines	N276US
21156	251F	1170	Amerijet International	N277US
21157	251F	1173	Kitty Hawk Aircargo	N278US
21158	251F	1177	Kitty Hawk Aircargo	N279US
21159	251A	1179	PLM International	N280US stored 11Dec95
21160	251A	1180	PLM International	N281US stored 11Dec95
21161	251A	1181	PLM International	N282US stored 11Oct95
21171	276A	1232	Aviacsa	VH-TBM XA-SLG
21178	277F	1237	Federal Express	VH-RMK N242FE
21179	2H3A	1171	Tunis Air	TS-JHR
21197	270A	1186	Iraqi Airways	YI-AGK Current status unknown, stored Jan91
21198	270A	1191	Iraqi Airways	YI-AGL stored Amman, Jordan Feb91
21199	270A	1203	(Iraqi Airways)	YI-AGM w/o 04Jun90 Istanbul, Turkey
21200	2M7A	1206	Northwest Airlines	N721RW
21201	2M7A	1220	Northwest Airlines	N722RW
21202	2M7A	1221	Sportsflight Airways	N723RW stored Tucson, AZ 28Aug95
21203	294A	1188	Syrianair	YK-AGA
21204	294A	1194	Syrianair	YK-AGB
21205	294A	1198	Syrianair	YK-AGC
21210	2D6A	1204	Air Algerie	7T-VEM
21222	232A	1205	Delta Air Lines	N410DA
21223	232A	1207	Delta Air Lines	N411DA
21229	2L5A	1213	Jamahiriya Libyan Arab A/L	5A-DID
21230	2L5A	1215	Jamahiriya Libyan Arab A/L	5A-DIE
21232	232A	1208	Delta Air Lines	N412DA
21233	232A	1211	Delta Air Lines	N413DA
21234	2H3A	1209	Tunis Air	TS-JHS
21235	2H3A	1210	Tunis Air	TS-JHT
21242	227A	1196	Continental Airlines	N441BN N566PE N15774
21243	227F	1197	Amerijet International	N442BN N567PE (N17775) N567PE N794AJ
21244	227A	1201	US Air Shuttle	N443BN N568PE (N17776) N568PE N925TS
21245	227A	1202	Hunting Cargo Airlines	N444BN N569PE N16762
21246	227A	1216	Orient Express	N445BN N570PE (N16778) N570PE HS-PTA
21247	227A	1217	Continental Airlines	N446BN N73751
21248	227A	1218	Continental Airlines	N447BN N76752
21249	227A	1219	Continental Airlines	N448BN N76753
21256	232A	1212	Delta Air Lines	N414DA
21257	232A	1214	Delta Air Lines	N415DA
21258	232A	1223	Delta Air Lines	N416DA
21259	232A	1224	Delta Air Lines	N417DA
21260	2F2A	1222	Top Air	TC-JBM
21264	243A	1225	Continental Airlines	N1787B I-DIRA N571PE (N18401) N571PE
21265	243F	1226	American Intl Airways	I-DIRE I-DIRI N572PE N17402
21266	243A	1227	Viscount Air Services	N40115 I-DIRO N40115 N573PE (N17403) N573PE N521DB
21267	243A	1228	ACES-Colombia	I-DIRU N574PE (N59404) N574PE HK-4010X
21268	243A	1229	Shawmut Bank, Connecticut	I-DIRB N575PE (N14405) N575PE stored Mojave, CA Oct91
21269	243F	1230	TNT Express Worldwide	N41033 I-DIRC N576PE N17406 EI-EWW [Op by Hunting Cargo Airlines]
21270	243A	1231	Continental Airlines	N1236E I-DIRJ N577PE N17407
21271	247A	1242	Delta Air Lines	N418DA
21272	247A	1243	Delta Air Lines	N419DA
21273	247A	1244	Delta Air Lines	N420DA
21274	247A	1245	Delta Air Lines	N421DA
21284	2D6A	1233	Air Algerie	7T-VEP
21288	225F	1234	Federal Express	N8870Z N464FE
21289	225F	1235	Federal Express	N8871Z N465FE
21290	225F	1238	DHL Airways	N8872Z N742DH
21291	225A	1239	Delta Air Lines	N8873Z
21292	225F	1240	Federal Express	N8874Z N466FE
21293	225A	1241	Delta Air Lines	N8875Z
21297	2B6A	1236	Royal Air Maroc	N1246E CN-RMO
21298	2B6A	1246	Royal Air Maroc	CN-RMP
21299	2B6A	1247	Royal Air Maroc	CN-RMQ
21303	232A	1262	Delta Air Lines	(N422DA) N501DA
21304	232A	1264	Delta Air Lines	(N423DA) N502DA
21305	232A	1268	Delta Air Lines	(N424DA) N503DA
21306	232A	1270	Delta Air Lines	(N425DA) N504DA
21307	232A	1272	Delta Air Lines	(N426DA) N505DA
21308	232A	1292	Delta Air Lines	(N427DA) N506DA
21309	232A	1294	Delta Air Lines	(N428DA) N507DA
21310	232A	1298	Delta Air Lines	(N429DA) N508DA
21311	232A	1300	Delta Air Lines	(N430DA) N509DA
21312	232A	1330	Delta Air Lines	(N431DA) N510DA

BOEING 727

C/n	Series	Line No	Last known Operator/Owner	Previous Identities/fate (where known)
21313	232A	1347	Delta Air Lines	(N432DA) N511DA
21314	232A	1358	Delta Air Lines	(N433DA) N512DA
21315	232A	1360	Delta Air Lines	(N434DA) N513DA
21318	2H3A	1252	Tunis Air	TS-JHU
21319	2H3A	1269	(Tunis Air)	TS-JHV stored Tunis, Tunisia; later b/u
21320	2H3A	1271	Tunis Air	TS-JHW
21322	251A	1265	Northwest Airlines	N283US
21323	251A	1284	Kiwi Intl Airlines	N284US
21324	251A	1286	Northwest Airlines	N285US
21325	251A	1288	Northwest Airlines	N286US
21327	247F	1249	Federal Express	N2822W N233FE
21328	247A	1251	Delta Air Lines	N2823W N234FE* [For FedEX Apr96]
21329	247A	1254	Delta Air Lines	N2824W N235FE* [For FedEX Apr96]
21330	247A	1260	Federal Express	N2825W N236FE
21331	247A	1266	Delta Air Lines	N2826W N237FE* [For FedEX Apr96]
21332	2L5A	1257	Jamahiriya Libyan Arab A/L	5A-DIF
21333	2L5A	1259	Jamahiriya Libyan Arab A/L	5A-DIG
21341	2A1F	1253	United Parcel Service	PP-SNE N213UP
21342	2A1F	1256	United Parcel Service	PP-SNF N214UP
21343	2A1A	1320	ACES-Colombia	(PP-SNG) HK-2151X
21344	2A1A	1322	SAM-Colombia	(PP-SNH) HK-2152X
21345	2A1A	1673	Sun Country Airlines	(PP-SNK) PP-SNG N327AS N287SC
21346	2A1A	1675	Mexicana	(PP-SNL) N8285V PP-SNH XA-MXF XA-MXI
21347	212A	1282	(VASP)	(9V-SXA) 9V-SGA PP-SRK w/o 08Jun82 nr Fortaleza, Brazil
21348	212A	1287	Sterling One	(9V-SXB) 9V-SGB PP-SMK N26729 N293AS [Op by AvAtlantic]
21349	212A	1289	Royal Airlines	(9V-SXC) 9V-SGC G-BHVT TI-LRR G-BHVT TI-LRR G-BHVT C-FRYS
21363	227A	1258	Continental Airlines	N449BN N79754
21364	227A	1261	Continental Airlines	N450BN N322AS N86426
21365	227A	1273	Continental Airlines	N451BN N323AS N89427
21366	227A	1274	Continental Airlines	N452BN N70755
21369	223A	1275	American Airlines	N864AA
21370	223A	1276	American Airlines	N865AA
21371	223A	1277	American Airlines	N866AA
21372	223A	1278	American Airlines	N867AA
21373	223A	1279	American Airlines	N868AA
21374	223A	1280	American Airlines	N869AA
21375	251A	1290	Northwest Airlines	N287US
21376	251A	1293	Northwest Airlines	N288US
21377	251A	1295	Northwest Airlines	N289US
21378	251A	1297	Northwest Airlines	N290US
21379	251A	1299	Northwest Airlines	N291US stored Smyrna, TN May94
21382	223A	1304	American Airlines	N870AA
21383	223A	1324	American Airlines	N871AA
21384	223A	1328	American Airlines	N872AA
21385	223A	1331	American Airlines	N873AA
21386	223A	1333	American Airlines	N874AA
21387	223A	1335	American Airlines	N875AA
21388	223A	1345	American Airlines	N876AA
21389	223A	1349	American Airlines	N877AA
21390	223A	1361	American Airlines	N878AA
21391	223A	1367	American Airlines	N879AA
21392	247F	1305	United Parcel Force	N2827W N212UP
21393	247A	1307	American Trans Air	N2828W N749US
21394	227F	1281	Federal Express	N453BN N477FE
21395	227F	1283	Federal Express	N454BN N478FE
21398	222A	1296	United Airlines	N7251U
21399	222A	1303	United Airlines	N7252U
21400	222A	1309	United Airlines	N7253U
21401	222A	1311	United Airlines	N7254U
21402	222A	1313	United Airlines	N7255U
21403	222A	1315	United Airlines	N7256U
21404	222A	1321	United Airlines	N7257U
21405	222A	1323	United Airlines	N7258U
21406	222A	1325	United Airlines	N7259U
21407	222A	1332	United Airlines	N7260U
21408	222A	1334	United Airlines	N7261U
21409	222A	1336	United Airlines	N7262U
21410	222A	1344	United Airlines	N7263U
21411	222A	1346	United Airlines	N7264U
21412	222A	1348	United Airlines	N7265U
21413	222A	1351	United Airlines	N7266U
21414	222A	1354	United Airlines	N7267U
21415	222A	1356	United Airlines	N7268U
21416	222A	1366	United Airlines	N7269U
21417	222A	1368	United Airlines	N7270U
21418	222A	1370	United Airlines	N7271U
21419	222A	1375	United Airlines	N7272U

BOEING 727

C/n	Series	Line No	Last known Operator/Owner	Previous Identities/fate (where known)
21420	222A	1377	United Airlines	N7273U
21421	222A	1383	United Airlines	N7274U
21422	222A	1385	United Airlines	N7275U
21423	222A	1387	United Airlines	N7276U
21424	222A	1393	United Airlines	N7277U
21425	222A	1395	United Airlines	N7278U
21426	2F9A	1285	Continental Micronesia	5N-ANP N528D N298AS N83428
21427	2F9A	1291	Continental Micronesia	5N-ANQ N528E N299AS N75429*
21430	232A	1374	Delta Air Lines	N514DA
21431	232A	1376	Delta Air Lines	N515DA
21432	232A	1381	Delta Air Lines	N516DA
21433	232A	1384	Delta Air Lines	N517DA
21438	2J4RE	1301	Sun Country Airlines	OY-SBC G-BHNF N284SC
21442	230A	1326	Istanbul Airlines	D-ABKM TC-AFP
21449	225F	1306	Federal Express	N8876Z N467FE
21450	225A	1308	Northwest Airlines	N8877Z
21451	225A	1310	Northwest Airlines	N8878Z
21452	225F	1312	Federal Express	N8879Z N468FE
21453	225A	1314	Kiwi Intl Airlines	N8880Z N380KP*
21455	281A	1316	Korean Air	JA8353 HL7354
21456	281A	1318	Korean Air	JA8354 HL7356
21457	2M7A	1302	Servivensa	N724RW LV-MCD N724RW YV-77C N79751 XA-MXE YV-768C
21458	212A	1327	ACES-Colombia	(9V-SXD) 9V-SGD N292AS HK-4047
21459	212A	1329	Continental Micronesia	(9V-SXE) 9V-SGE N296AS (N86425) N296AS N86422*
21460	212A	1340	ARAVCO	(9V-SXF) 9V-SGF HZ-DA5 VR-CBQ [Op by Precision Air]
21461	227F	1337	Federal Express	N455BN N479FE
21462	227F	1342	Federal Express	N456BN N480FE
21463	227F	1353	Federal Express	N457BN N481FE
21464	227F	1355	Federal Express	N458BN N482FE
21465	227F	1363	Federal Express	N459BN N483FE
21466	227F	1372	Federal Express	N460BN N484FE
21469	232A	1398	Delta Air Lines	N518DA
21470	232A	1400	Delta Air Lines	N519DA
21471	232A	1411	Delta Air Lines	N520DA
21472	232A	1413	Delta Air Lines	N521DA
21474	281A	1378	Korean Air	JA8355 HL7357
21479	276A	1357	Aviacsa	VH-TBN XA-SJE
21480	277F	1352	Federal Express	VH-RML N243FE
21481	247A	1338	Delta Air Lines	N2829W
21482	247A	1341	GECAS	N2830W stored Dec95
21483	247A	1350	Delta Air Lines	N831WA
21484	247A	1362	Delta Air Lines	N282WA
21485	247A	1364	Delta Air Lines	N283WA
21488	227F	1388	Federal Express	N461BN N485FE
21489	227F	1390	Federal Express	N462BN N486FE
21490	227F	1396	Federal Express	N463BN N487FE
21491	227F	1402	Federal Express	N464BN N488FE
21492	227F	1440	Federal Express	N465BN N489FE
21493	227F	1442	Federal Express	N466BN N490FE
21494	2K3A	1373	Lloyd Aereo Boliviano	CP-1366
21495	2K3A	1403	Lloyd Aereo Boliviano	CP-1367
21502	2M7A	1339	Northwest Airlines	N725RW
21503	251A	1317	Northwest Airlines	N292US
21504	251A	1319	Northwest Airlines	N293US
21505	251A	1391	Northwest Airlines	N294US
21506	251A	1392	Northwest Airlines	N295US
21510	290A	1359	American Trans Air	N290AS N774AT
21511	290A	1439	American Trans Air	N291AS N775AT
21512	214A	1343	US Air	N555PS N750US
21513	214A	1365	US Air	N556PS N751US
21519	223A	1459	American Airlines	N880AA
21520	223A	1461	American Airlines	N881AA
21521	223A	1463	American Airlines	N882AA
21522	223A	1465	American Airlines	N883AA
21523	223A	1467	American Airlines	N884AA
21524	223A	1473	American Airlines	N885AA
21525	223A	1475	American Airlines	N886AA
21526	223A	1476	American Airlines	N887AA
21527	223A	1477	American Airlines	N889AA
21529	227F	1444	Federal Express	N467BN N491FE
21530	227F	1446	Federal Express	N468BN N492FE
21531	227F	1450	Federal Express	N469BN N493FE
21532	227F	1453	Federal Express	N470BN N492FE
21539	2L5A	1371	Jamahiriya Libyan Arab A/L	5A-DIH
21540	2L5A	1386	Jamahiriya Libyan Arab A/L	5A-DII
21557	222A	1397	United Airlines	N7279U
21558	222A	1399	United Airlines	N7280U
21559	222A	1401	United Airlines	N7281U

BOEING 727

C/n	Series	Line No	Last known Operator/Owner	Previous Identities/fate (where known)
21560	222A	1405	United Airlines	N7282U
21561	222A	1408	United Airlines	N7283U
21562	222A	1410	United Airlines	N7284U
21563	222A	1418	United Airlines	N7285U
21564	222A	1420	United Airlines	N7286U
21565	222A	1424	United Airlines	N7287U
21566	222A	1428	United Airlines	N7288U
21567	222A	1430	United Airlines	N7279U
21568	222A	1432	United Airlines	N7290U
21569	222A	1441	United Airlines	N7291U
21570	222A	1443	United Airlines	N7292U
21571	222A	1445	United Airlines	N7293U
21572	222A	1447	United Airlines	N7294U
21573	222A	1449	United Airlines	N7295U
21574	222A	1451	United Airlines	N7296U stored Oakland, CA 24Jun92
21577	264A	1379	Mexicana	XA-HOH
21578	225A	1409	Kiwi Intl Airlines	N8881Z N381KP*
21579	225A	1412	Kiwi Intl Airlines	N8882Z N382KP*
21580	225A	1435	Kiwi Intl Airlines	N8883Z N383KP*
21581	225F	1437	Federal Express	N8884Z (TF-RMR) N8884Z N469FE
21582	232A	1422	Delta Air Lines	N522DA
21583	232A	1423	Delta Air Lines	N523DA
21584	232A	1478	Delta Air Lines	N524DA
21585	232A	1479	Delta Air Lines	N525DA
21586	232A	1488	Delta Air Lines	N526DA
21587	232A	1492	Delta Air Lines	N527DA
21595	2P1A	1406	State of Qatar	A7-AAB
21600	2A1A	1679	Mexicana	(PP-SNM) PP-SNI XA-MXG XA-MXJ
21601	2A1A	1694	Sun Country Airlines	(PP-SNN) PP-SNJ N328AS N286SC
21603	2F2A	1389	(THY-Turkish Airlines)	TC-JBR w/o 16Jan83 Ankarra, Turkey
21608	2Q8A	1426	American Trans Air	N791L N297AS N776AT
21609	256A	1369	Iberia	EC-DCC
21610	256A	1380	Iberia	EC-DCD
21611	256A	1382	Iberia	EC-DCE
21617	264A	1416	Mexicana	XA-HON
21618	230A	1404	Istanbul Airlines	D-ABKN TC-AFT
21619	230A	1407	Istanbul Airlines	D-ABKP TC-AFN
21620	230A	1419	Istanbul Airlines	D-ABKQ TC-AFO
21621	230A	1425	Istanbul Airlines	D-ABKR TC-AFR
21622	230A	1431	TAME	D-ABKS HC-BSU/FAE21622
21623	230A	1433	Air Terrex	D-ABKT OK-JGY
21624	233F	1468	Federal Express	C-GAAO N262FE
21625	233F	1470	Federal Express	C-GAAP N263FE
21626	233F	1472	Federal Express	C-GAAQ N264FE
21628	231A	1454	Trans World Airlines	N54341
21629	231A	1456	Trans World Airlines	N54342
21630	231A	1458	Trans World Airlines	N24343
21631	231A	1460	Trans World Airlines	N54344
21632	231A	1462	Trans World Airlines	N54345
21633	231A	1464	Trans World Airlines	N64346
21634	231A	1466	Trans World Airlines	N64347
21636	2R1A	1414	Government of Cameroons	TJ-AAM
21637	264A	1429	Mexicana	XA-HOV
21638	264A	1457	Mexicana	XA-HOX
21646	276A	1434	Aviacsa	VH-TBO XA-SMB
21647	277F	1436	Federal Express	VH-RMM N244FE
21655	2M7A	1452		N726RW TN-AEB N5772T TN-AEB VR-CDL
21656	2M7A	1455	Northwest Airlines	N727RW
21661	243A	1394	Continental Airlines	I-DIRD N578PE (N10408) N578PE N17480*
21662	243A	1421	Continental Airlines	I-DIRF N579PE N10409*
21663	243A	1438	Continental Airlines	I-DIRG N580PE N17410
21664	243A	1448	Top Air	I-DIRL (N581PE) TC-JCK
21669	227F	1484	Federal Express	N471BN N495FE
21670	227F	1486	Federal Express	N472BN N496FE
21671	233FRE	1523	Federal Express	C-GAAR N265FE
21672	233FRE	1538	Federal Express	C-GAAS N266FE
21673	233F	1541	Federal Express	C-GAAT N267FE
21674	233F	1543	Federal Express	C-GAAU N268FE
21675	233F	1555	Federal Express	C-GAAV N269FE
21676	2J4RE	1417	Sun Country Airlines	OY-SBD G-BHNE N285SC
21688	287A	1415	Aerolineas Argentinas	LV-MIM
21689	287A	1427	Aerolineas Argentinas	LV-MIN
21690	287A	1469	Aerolineas Argentinas	LV-MIO
21691	214A	1480	American Trans Air	N557PS N752US
21692	214A	1482	American Trans Air	N558PS N753US
21695	277A	1481	EastWest Airlines	VH-RMN
21696	276A	1483	Aeroexo	VH-TBP XA-SLM
21697	247F	1471	United Parcel Service	N284WA N210UP
21698	247F	1474	United Parcel Service	N286WA N209UP
21699	247F	1485	United Parcel Service	N287WA N207US

BOEING 727

C/n	Series	Line No	Last known Operator/Owner	Previous Identities/fate (where known)					
21700	247F	1489	United Parcel Service	N288WA	N211UP				
21701	247F	1493	United Parcel Service	N289WA	N208UP				
21702	232A	1522	Delta Air Lines	N528DA					
21703	232A	1550	Delta Air Lines	N529DA					
21741	2M7A	1491	Northwest Airlines	N728RW					
21742	2M7A	1514	Northwest Airlines	N729RW					
21777	256A	1487	(Iberia)	EC-DDU	w/o 19Feb85 nr Bolivar, Spain				
21778	256A	1490	Iberia	EC-DDV					
21779	256A	1498	Iberia	EC-DDX					
21780	256A	1499	Iberia	EC-DDY					
21781	256A	1501	Iberia	EC-DDZ					
21788	251A	1495	Northwest Airlines	N296US					
21789	251A	1496	Northwest Airlines	N297US					
21813	232A	1552	(Delta Air Lines)	N530DA	dbf 14Oct89 Salt Lake City, UT				
21814	232A	1556	Delta Air Lines	N531DA					
21823	2M7A	1591	Aerolineas Argentinas	N730RW	LV-ODY				
21824	2M7A	1595	Government of Bahrain	(N731RW)	N740RW	A9C-BA			
21826	2Q8A	1509	Delta Air Lines	N831L					
21836	264A	1497	Mexicana	XA-IEU					
21837	264A	1545	Mexicana	(XA-IEV)	XA-MEB				
21838	264A	1547	Mexicana	(XA-IEW)	XA-MEC				
21842	2N8A	1512	Yemenia	4W-ACJ	70-ADA				
21844	2N8A	1518	Yemenia	4W-ACF	70-ACV				
21845	2N8A	1529	Yemenia	4W-ACG	70-ACW				
21846	2N8A	1549	Yemenia	4W-ACH	70-ACX				
21847	2N8A	1557	Yemenia	4W-ACI	70-ACY				
21849	2D4FRE	1527	Federal Express	N720ZK	N361PA	N287FE			
21850	2D4F	1536	Federal Express	N721ZK	N362PA	N288FE			
21851	2K5A	1551	Venus Airways	D-AHLT	ET-AJU	N851AL	SX-BFN		
21852	2K5F	1553	Omni Air Express	D-AHLU	A6-EMC	N909PG			
21853	2K5A	1640	Saudi Oger	N8290V	D-AHLV	LX-MJM	N8290V	LX-MMM	HZ-HR1
21854	225A	1532	Miami Air International	N8885Z	(N27417)	N8885Z	N889MA*		
21855	225A	1535	Miami Air International	N8886Z	(N17418)	N8886Z	N886MA		
21856	225F	1537	IAL Aircraft Holdings	N8887Z	stored Opa Locka, FL May95, later Miami, FL				
21857	225A	1539	Miami Air Intl	N8888Z	(N887MA)	N8888Z	N887MA		
21858	225A	1542	Intrepid Aviation Partners	N8889Z	stored Las Vegas, NV Jun94				
21859	225A	1544	Delta Air Lines	N8890Z					
21860	225A	1546	Delta Air Lines	N8891Z					
21861	225F	1554	Ryan Intl Airlines	N8892Z					
21892	222A	1500	United Airlines	N7297U					
21893	222A	1503	United Airlines	N7298U					
21894	222A	1505	United Airlines	N7299U					
21895	222A	1507	United Airlines	N7441U					
21896	222A	1511	United Airlines	N7442U					
21897	222A	1513	United Airlines	N7443U					
21898	222A	1515	United Airlines	N7444U					
21899	222A	1517	United Airlines	N7445U					
21900	222A	1519	United Airlines	N7446U					
21901	222A	1521	United Airlines	N7447U					
21902	222A	1524	United Airlines	N7448U					
21903	222A	1526	United Airlines	N7449U					
21904	222A	1528	United Airlines	N7450U					
21905	222A	1530	United Airlines	N7451U					
21906	222A	1548	United Airlines	N7452U					
21907	222A	1558	United Airlines	N7453U					
21908	222A	1560	United Airlines	N7454U					
21909	222A	1562	United Airlines	N7455U					
21910	222A	1570	United Airlines	N7456U					
21911	222A	1572	United Airlines	N7457U					
21912	222A	1575	United Airlines	N7458U					
21913	222A	1593	United Airlines	N7459U					
21914	222A	1597	United Airlines	N7460U					
21915	222A	1609	United Airlines	N7461U					
21916	222A	1611	United Airlines	N7462U					
21917	222A	1616	United Airlines	N7463U					
21918	222A	1625	United Airlines	N7464U					
21919	222A	1632	United Airlines	N7465U					
21920	222A	1634	United Airlines	N7466U					
21921	222A	1639	United Airlines	N7467U					
21930	2Q9F	1508	DHL Airways	N1273E	N200AV	N740DH			
21931	2Q9F	1531	DHL Airways	N202AV	N741DH				
21945	212A	1502	Transmile Air Service	9V-SGG	TI-LRQ	N200LR	OY-SCC		
21946	C-22C	1504	USAF/201stALS/MD ANG	9V-SGH	9V-WGA	N48054	83-4618	N8596C	83-4618
21947	212A	1506	Continental AIrlines	9V-SGI	N309AS	N86425*			
21948	212RE	1510	Triangle Aircraft Services	9V-SGJ	N310AS	VR-COJ	N31TR		
21949	282A	1494	Sun Country Airlines	CS-TBW	N281SC	Regn canx Sep95			
21950	282A	1579	Carnival Airlines	N57008	CS-TBX	N609KW			
21951	2M7A	1680	Qatar Airways	N741RW	A6-HRR	A6-EMA	A7-ABC		
21952	2M7A	1693	Northwest Airlines	N742RW					
21953	2B7A	1516	American Trans Air	N760AL	N775US	N770AT			

BOEING 727

C/n	Series	Line No	Last known Operator/Owner	Previous Identities/fate (where known)
21954	2B7A	1525	American Trans Air	N762AL N760US N760AT
21958	214A	1533	American Trans Air	N559PS N754US
21967	231A	1563	Trans World Airlines	N54348
21968	231A	1565	Trans World Airlines	N54349
21969	231A	1567	Trans World Airlines	N54350
21971	2Q6F	1540	Pacific Air Corp 1279 Inc	(N1289E) N1279E stored Miami, FL
21972	2Q6A	1637	American Trans Air	(N1290E) N1280E N782AT
21978	260A	1520	Venus Airways	ET-AHL N978AL SX-BFM
21979	260A	1534	Wilmington Trust	ET-AHM (N289SC) ET-AHM N979AL stored Shannon, Eire 03Aug92; later Miami, FL
21983	231A	1569	Trans World Airlines	N54351
21984	231A	1574	Trans World Airlines	N54352
21985	231A	1576	Trans World Airlines	N54353
21986	231A	1580	Trans World Airlines	N54354
21987	231A	1582	Trans World Airlines	N84355
21988	231A	1586	Miami Air Intl	N84356 TC-AFG F-WKPZ (F-GKPZ) N808MA
21989	231A	1590	Trans World Airlines	N84357
21996	227A	1571	American Trans Air	N473BN N782AL N768US N768AT
21997	227A	1573	ACES-Colombia	N474BN N306AS HK-3738X
21998	227A	1577	American Trans Air	N475BN N783AL N769US N769AT
21999	227A	1581	American Trans Air	N476BN N780AL N766US N766AT
22000	227A	1583	American Trans Air	N477BN N307AS
22001	227A	1585	American Trans Air	N478BN N781AL N767US N767AT
22002	227A	1627	Roadway Global Air	N479BN N308AS [Op by Express One Intl] stored Grayson, TX Jun95
22003	227A	1629	American Trans Air	N480BN N271AF N288AS N772AT
22004	227A	1631	American Trans Air	N481BN N272AF N289AS N773AT
22005	227A	1651	American Trans Air	N482BN N273AF N304AS N778AT
22006	223A	1636	American Airlines	N890AA
22007	223A	1643	American Airlines	N891AA
22008	223A	1646	American Airlines	N892AA
22009	223A	1649	American Airlines	N893AA
22010	223A	1650	American Airlines	N894AA
22011	223A	1653	American Airlines	N895AA
22012	223A	1655	American Airlines	N896AA
22013	223A	1659	American Airlines	N897AA
22014	223A	1663	American Airlines	N898AA
22015	223A	1666	American Airlines	N899AA
22016	277F	1566	Federal Express	VH-RMO N245FE
22017	276A	1564	Aviacsa	VH-TBQ XA-SIJ
22019	2S7A	1584	Northwest Airlines	(N711RC) N715RC
22020	2S7A	1592	Northwest Airlines	N712RC
22021	2S7A	1617	Northwest Airlines	(N713RC) N716RC
22035	233FRE	1578	Federal Express	C-GAAW N270FE
22036	233F	1596	Federal Express	N57002 C-GAAX 6Y-JMG C-GAAX N271FE
22037	233F	1600	Federal Express	C-GAAY N272FE
22038	233F	1612	Federal Express	N57000 C-GAAZ N273FE
22039	233F	1614	Federal Express	N57002 C-GYNA N274FE
22040	233F	1626	Federal Express	N57008 C-GYNB N275FE
22041	233F	1628	Federal Express	C-GYNC N276FE
22042	233F	1630	Federal Express	C-GYND N277FE
22043	294A	1559	US Air Shuttle	YV-74C N921TS
22044	294A	1561	Qatar Airways	YV-75C N221AL A7-ABE
22045	232A	1602	Delta Air Lines	N532DA
22046	232A	1604	Delta Air Lines	N533DA
22047	232A	1606	Delta Air Lines	N534DA
22048	232A	1608	Delta Air Lines	N535DA
22049	232A	1610	Delta Air Lines	N536DA
22052	243A	1568	Wilmington Trust Co	I-DIRM N581PE N12411 Wfs 28Jul95, stored Las Vegas, NV Nov95
22053	243A	1620	Wilmington Trust Co	I-DIRN N582PE N59412 Wfs 02Aug95, stored Las Vegas, NV Nov95
22068	277F	1660	Federal Express	VH-RMP N246FE
22069	276A	1661	Aeroexo	VH-TBR XA-SIE
22073	232A	1624	Delta Air Lines	N537DA
22076	232A	1656	Delta Air Lines	N1786B N538DA
22078	2T3A	1644	TAME	(N710EV) N1239E HC-BHM/FAE-22078
22079	2J4A	1588	Lloyd Aero Boliviano	OY-SBE PP-AIW
22080	2J4F	1598	DHL Worldwide Couriers	N7287V OY-SBF N729DH VH-DHE [Op by Premier Airlines]
22081	228A	1594	Iran Asseman Airlines	N8288V F-GCDA (F-OMOJ) LX-IRA
22082	228A	1603	Iran Asseman Airlines	F-GCDB (F-OMOK) LX-IRB
22083	228A	1605	Air Gabon	F-GCDC F-OHOA
22084	228A	1638	Iran Asseman Airlines	N5711E F-GCDD (F-OMOL) LX-IRC
22085	228A	1665	Iran Asseman Airlines	F-GCDE (F-OMOM) LX-IRD
22091	227A	1706	American Trans Air	N483BN N274AF N305AS N779AT
22092	227A	1718	Sun Country Airlines	N484BN N275AF
22093	227A		(Braniff International)	(N485BN) Allocated but later canx, not built
22094	227A		(Braniff International)	(N486BN) Allocated but later canx, not built
22095	227A		(Braniff International)	(N487BN) Allocated but later canx, not built

BOEING 727

C/n	Series	Line No	Last known Operator/Owner	Previous Identities/fate (where known)
22096	227A		(Braniff International)	(N488BN) Allocated but later canx, not built
22097	227A		(Braniff International)	(N489BN) Allocated but later canx, not built
22098	227A		(Braniff International)	(N490BN) Allocated but later canx, not built
22099	227A		(Braniff International)	(N491BN) Allocated but later canx, not built
22100	227A		(Braniff International)	(N492BN) Allocated but later canx, not built
22101	227A		(Braniff International)	(N493BN) Allocated but later canx, not built
22102	227A		(Braniff International)	(N494BN) Allocated but later canx, not built
22103	227A		(Braniff International)	(N495BN) Allocated but later canx, not built
22104	227A		(Braniff International)	(N496BN) Allocated but later canx, not built
22108	247A	1587	Delta Air Lines	N290WA
22109	247A	1589	Delta Air Lines	N291WA
22110	247A	1613	Delta Air Lines	N292WA
22111	247A	1615	Delta Air Lines	N293WA
22112	247A	1618	Delta Air Lines	N294WA
22146	290A	1621	CIT Leasing Corp	N294AS XA-SPH N294AS stored 13Oct95
22147	290A	1623	AvAtlantic	N295AS
22152	251A	1599	Northwest Airlines	N298US
22153	251A	1601	Northwest Airlines	N299US
22154	251A	1645	Northwest Airlines	N201US
22155	251A	1648	Northwest Airlines	N202US
22156	264A	1607	Mexicana	XA-MED
22157	264A	1619	Mexicana	XA-MEE
22158	264A	1642	Mexicana	N1786B XA-MEF
22162	2B7A	1717	American Trans Air	N770AL N762US N762AT
22163	2B7A	1735	Sterling European Airways	N771AL OY-SBN
22164	2B7A	1743	AeroPeru	N772AL OY-SBH N907PG OB-1590
22165	243A	1635	'Government of Togo'	I-DIRP N583PE N17413 5V-SBB
22166	243A	1725	Pacific Avn Holdings Co	I-DIRQ N584PE N58414 Wfs 06Sep95, stored Las Vegas, NV Nov95
22167	243A	1752	Continental Airlines	N8280V I-DIRR N585PE N34415
22168	243A	1770	Continental Airlines	I-DIRS N586PE N14416
22240	256A		(Iberia)	Allocated but later canx, not built
22241	256A		(Iberia)	Allocated but later canx, not built
22242	256A		(Iberia)	Allocated but later canx, not built
22243	256A		(Iberia)	Allocated but later canx, not built
22244	256A		(Iberia)	Allocated but later canx, not built
22250	224A	1684	Continental Airlines	N69741
22251	224A	1687	Continental Airlines	N69742
22252	224A	1697	Continental Airlines	N79743
22253	224A	1702	Continental Airlines	N79744
22261	270A	1647	Iraqi Airways	N8284V YI-AGQ stored Tunis, Tunisia Feb91 later Amman, Jordan
22262	270A	1686	Iraqi Airways	N8286V YI-AGR stored Tunis, Tunisia Feb91 later Amman, Jordan
22263	270A	1809	Iraqi Airways	N1780B YI-AGS stored Tunis, Tunisia Feb91 later Amman, Jordan
22268	2D3A	1641	Servivensa	N8284V JY-AFT YV-762C
22269	2D3A	1701	Royal Jordanian	JY-AFU
22270	2D3A	1709	Royal Jordanian	N57001 JY-AFV
22271	2D3A	1713	(Alia-Royal Jordanian A/L)	N8286V JY-AFW Dbr 12Jun85 Beirut, Lebanon following hijack
22287	228A	1710	KTHY-Cyprus Turkish A/L	F-GCBF TC-JEC
22288	228A	1712	Ariana Afghan Airlines	N8288V F-GCDG YA-FAZ
22289	228A	1719	Ariana Afghan Airlines	F-GCDH YA-FAY
22290	228A	1724	Ariana Afghan Airlines	F-GCDI YA-FAX
22295	208A	1622	American Trans Air	TF-FLI N329AS N780AT
22344	2S7A	1654	Northwest Airlines	(N714RC) N718RC
22345	233F	1699	Federal Express	(C-GYNE) (C-GABE) C-GYNE N278FE
22346	233F	1704	Federal Express	(C-GYNF) (C-GABF) C-GYNF N279FE
22347	233F	1708	Federal Express	(C-GYNG) (C-GABG) C-GYNG 6Y-JMQ C-GYNG N280FE
22348	233F	1714	Federal Express	(C-GYNH) (C-GABH) C-GYNH N281FE
22349	233F	1722	Federal Express	(C-GYNI) (C-GABI) N8278V C-GYNI N282FE
22350	233F	1745	Federal Express	(C-GYNJ) (C-GABJ) C-GYNJ N283FE
22351	200A		(Unknown Customer)	Allocated but later canx, not built
22359	269A	1652	Government of Kuwait	N8291V 9K-AFA [Op by Kuwait Air Force]
22360	269A	1670	Syrianair	9K-AFB YK-AGD
22361	269A	1716	Syrianair	9K-AFC YK-AGE
22362	2U5A	1657	Al Anwa Establishment	JY-HNH V8-HM1 V8-UB1 V8-HM1 V8-HM2 V8-BG1 HZ-AB3
22372	2D6A	1662	Air Algerie	7T-VET
22373	2D6A	1664	Air Algerie	7T-VEU
22374	2D6A	1711	Air Algerie	N8292V 7T-VEV
22375	2D6A	1723	Air Algerie	N8295V 7T-VEW
22377	2B6A	1633	Royal Air Maroc	CN-RMR
22385	232A	1667	Delta Air Lines	N539DA
22386	232A	1669	Delta Air Lines	N540DA
22387	232A	1672	Delta Air Lines	N541DA
22391	232A	1705	Delta Air Lines	N542DA
22392	232A	1707	Delta Air Lines	N543DA
22393	2H9A	1681	JAT-Jugoslav Airlines	YU-AKI

BOEING 727

C/n	Series	Line No	Last known Operator/Owner	Previous Identities/fate (where known)			
22394	2H9A	1691	JAT-Jugoslav Airlines	N8281V	YU-AKJ		
22409	264A	1676	Mexicana	XA-MEH			
22410	264A	1678	Mexicana	XA-MEI			
22411	264A	1696	Mexicana	XA-MEJ			
22412	264A	1720	Mexicana	XA-MEK			
22413	264A	1728	Mexicana	XA-MEL			
22414	264A	1748	Mexicana	XA-MEM			
22417	227A		(Braniff International)	(N497BN)	Allocated but later canx, not built		
22418	227A		(Braniff International)	(N498BN)	Allocated but later canx, not built		
22419	227A		(Braniff International)	(N499BN)	Allocated but later canx, not built		
22420	227A		(Braniff International)	Allocated but later canx, not built			
22421	227A		(Braniff International)	Allocated but later canx, not built			
22422	227A		(Braniff International)	Allocated but later canx, not built			
22423	227A		(Braniff International)	Allocated but later canx, not built			
22424	2Q4A	1683	GECAS	(PT-TCE)	XA-MEQ	XA-SIV	stored 01Oct95
22425	2Q4A	1698	Mexicana	(PT-TCF)	XA-MER		
22430	282A	1715	Carnival Airlines	N8285V	CS-TBY	6O-SCG	N6167D
22432	225A	1658	Northwest Airlines	N801EA			
22433	225A	1668	Northwest Airlines	N802EA			
22434	225A	1671	Miami Air International	N803EA	N803MA		
22435	225A	1674	Miami Air International	N804EA	N804MA		
22436	225F	1677	Senator Bob Dole	N805EA	[Op by AvAtlantic]		
22437	225A	1682	Miami Air International	N806EA	N806MA		
22438	225F	1685	Aeropostale	N807EA	F-GKDY		
22439	225F	1689	Tayfun Air	N808EA	C-GCWW	N808EA	TC-DEL
22440	225A	1692	Allegro AIrlines	N809EA	XA-TCX		
22441	225F	1695	Aeropostale	N810EA	HI-629CA	N810EA	F-GKDZ
22448	224A	1740	Continental Airlines	N79745			
22449	224A	1756	Continental Airlines	N79746			
22450	224A	1760	Continental Airlines	N79748			
22451	224A	1767	Continental Airlines	N79749			
22452	224A	1772	Continental Airlines	N79750			
22459	223A	1742	American Airlines	N701AA			
22460	223A	1746	American Airlines	N702AA			
22461	223A	1750	American Airlines	N703AA			
22462	223A	1751	American Airlines	N705AA			
22463	223A	1755	American Airlines	N706AA			
22464	223A	1758	American Airlines	N707AA	stored Amarillo, TX 30Dec95		
22465	223A	1761	American Airlines	N708AA			
22466	223A	1763	American Airlines	N709AA			
22467	223A	1765	American Airlines	N710AA			
22468	223A	1766	American Airlines	N712AA	stored Amarillo, TX 18Sep95		
22469	223A	1769	American Airlines	N713AA	stored Amarillo, TX 28Aug95		
22470	223A	1771	American Airlines	N715AA	stored Amarillo, TX 27Sep95		
22474	259A	1688	AvAtlantic	(HK-2474)	N203AV		
22475	259A	1690	Sun Country Airlines	(HK-2475)	N204AV	N289SC	
22476	259A	1747	Itapemirim T/A	(HK-2476)	N205AV	PP-ITV	
22490	2S7A	1721	Northwest Airlines	N719RC			
22491	2S7A	1726	Northwest Airlines	N720RC			
22492	2S7A	1729	Northwest Airlines	N721RC			
22493	232A	1741	Delta Air Lines	N544DA			
22494	232A	1749	Delta Air Lines	N545DA			
22532	247A	1730	Delta Air Lines	N295WA			
22533	247A	1736	Delta Air Lines	N296WA			
22534	247A	1738	Delta Air Lines	N297WA			
22535	221A	1764	Express One Intl	N363PA	stored Grayson, TX Jun95		
22536	221RE	1774	Carnival Airlines	N364PA	OY-SCB	N727VA	
22537	221RE	1779	Carnival Airlines	N365PA	N728VA		
22538	221A	1782	Express One Intl	N366PA			
22539	221F	1794	Express One Intl	N367PA	stored Grayson, TX Jun95		
22540	221F	1796	Express One Intl	N368PA			
22541	221A	1797	Nomads Inc	N369PA	N727M		
22542	221A	1799	Express One Intl	N370PA	stored Grayson, TX Jun95		
22543	251A	1700	Northwest Airlines	N203US			
22544	251A	1703	Northwest Airlines	N204US			
22548	225F	1734	Federal Express	N811EA	N461FE		
22549	225F	1737	Itapemirim T/A	N812EA	PP-ITR		
22550	225F	1739	Federal Express	N813EA	N462FE		
22551	225F	1744	Federal Express	N814EA	N463FE		
22552	225A	1773	Northwest Airlines	N815EA			
22553	225A	1775	Northwest Airlines	N816EA			
22554	225A	1781	Northwest Airlines	N817EA			
22555	225A	1783	Northwest Airlines	N818EA			
22556	225A	1793	(Eastern Air Lines)	N819EA	w/o 01Jan85 Mt Illiamani, Bolivia		
22557	225A	1795	Northwest Airlines	N820EA			
22558	225A	1798	Sun Country Airlines	N821EA	N282SC		
22559	225A	1800	Sun Country Airlines	N822EA	N283SC		
22560	225A		(Eastern Air Lines)	(N823EA)	Allocated but later canx, not built		
22561	225A		(Eastern Air Lines)	(N824EA)	Allocated but later canx, not built		
22562	225A		(Eastern Air Lines)	(N8893Z)	Allocated but later canx, not built		

BOEING 727

C/n	Series	Line No	Last known Operator/Owner	Previous Identities/fate (where known)
22563	225A		(Eastern Air Lines)	(N8894Z) Allocated but later canx, not built
22574	2J4A	1733	Royal Airlines	OY-SBG C-GRYQ
22603	287A	1732	Aerolineas Argentinas	LV-OLN
22604	287A	1777	VIASA	LV-OLO YV-132C
22605	287A	1787	Aerolineas Argentinas	N1782B LV-OLP
22606	287A	1812	Aerolineas Argentinas	LV-OLR
22608	2X3A	1727	Constellation Intl Airways	F-GCMV F-WQCK OO-LLS
22609	2X3A	1731	Constellation Intl Airways	F-GCMX OO-CAH
22621	233F	1791	Federal Express	N5573E C-GYNK N284FE
22622	233F	1792	Federal Express	C-GYNL N285FE
22623	233F	1803	Federal Express	C-GYNM N286FE
22641	277A	1753	Ansett Airlines	N8278V VH-ANA
22642	277A	1759	Ansett Airlines	N57002 VH-ANB
22643	277A	1762	Ansett Airlines	VH-ANE
22644	277A	1768	Ansett Airlines	VH-ANF
22661	264A	1757	Mexicana	XA-MXA
22662	264A	1776	AeroMexico	XA-MXB
22663	264A	1778	Mexicana	XA-MXC
22664	264A	1780	Mexicana	N1779B XA-MXD
22665	2H9A	1786	Tunis Air	N1780B YU-AKK TS-JEA stored Tunis, Tunisia Nov92
22666	2H9A	1790	Tunis Air	YU-AKL TS-JEB stored Tunis, Tunisia Nov92
22676	264A	1754	Mexicana	XA-MEZ
22677	232A	1785	Delta Air Lines	N546DA
22687	2X8A	1784	Wistair International	(N111MF) N4532N N721MF
22702	243A	1814	Aviogenex	I-DIRT YU-AKM HK-3618X YU-AKM
22759	260A	1789	Wilmington Trust	ET-AHK HK-3834X N980AL stored Miami, FL Oct94
22763	269A	1788	Syrianair	9K-AFD YK-AGF
22765	2D6A	1801	Air Algerie	7T-VEX
22770	2K3A	1807	Sterling European Airways	CP-1741 N776AL OY-SBO
22825	2N6A	1805	Federal Govt of Nigeria	5N-AGY 5N-FGN stored Lagos, Nigeria by Apr95
22924	2S2FRE	1818	Federal Express	N201FE
22925	2S2F	1819	Federal Express	N203FE
22926	2S2F	1820	Federal Express	N204FE
22927	2S2FRE	1821	Federal Express	N205FE
22928	2S2FRE	1822	Federal Express	N206FE
22929	2S2FRE	1823	Federal Express	N207FE
22930	2S2FRE	1824	Federal Express	N208FE
22931	2S2FRE	1825	Federal Express	N209FE
22932	2S2FRE	1826	Federal Express	N210FE
22933	2S2F	1827	Federal Express	N211FE
22934	2S2FRE	1828	Federal Express	N212FE
22935	2S2F	1829	Federal Express	N213FE
22936	2S2FRE	1830	Federal Express	N215FE
22937	2S2FRE	1831	Federal Express	N216FE
22938	2S2F	1832	Federal Express	N217FE
22968	2Y4A	1815	Rafic B.Hariri	HZ-RH3 HZ-HR3 [Op by Saudi Oger Ltd]
22982	264A	1802	Qatar Airways	(XA-) N4554N A6-HHM A6-EMB A7-ABD
22983	264A	1806	American Trans Air	(XA-) N4555E N773AL N763US N763AT
22984	264A	1813	American Trans Air	(XA-) N774AL N764US N764AT
22992	2F2F	1804	THY-Turkish Airlines	TC-JCA
22993	2F2A	1808	THY-Turkish Airlines	TC-JCB [For conversion to 727-2F2F]
22998	2F2F	1810	THY-Turkish Airlines	TC-JCD
22999	2F2A	1811	Top Air	TC-JCE
23014	264A	1816	American Trans Air	(XA-) N775AL N765US N765AT
23015	264A		(Mexicana)	Allocated but later canx, not built
23052	270A	1817	Pacific Aviation Holding	N779AL OY-SBI N

Production complete

BOEING 737

C/n	Series	Line No	Last known Operator/Owner	Previous Identities/fate (where known)
19013	130	2	(Rovair Enterprises Inc)	N2282C D-ABEA N701AW ZK-NEA N701PJ stored Christchurch, NZ 02Feb90 then Marana, AZ 29Mar91; b/u late 95
19014	130	3	Far Eastern Air Transport	N2286C D-ABEB B-2621 Used as crew trainer
19015	130	4	(Rovair Enterprises Inc)	N2289C D-ABEC N702AW ZK-NEB N702PJ stored Christchurch, NZ 13Dec89 then Marana, AZ 19Apr91; b/u late 95
19016	130	5	Spectrum Aerospace Inc	D-ABED YV-406C N703AW ZK-NEC N703PJ stored Christchurch, NZ 17Dec89 then Marana, AZ 30Apr91
19017	130	7	Far Eastern Air Transport	D-ABEF B-2623 stored Taipei-Sung Shan, RoC Oct94
19018	130	9	Continental Airlines	D-ABEG N401PE N16201
19019	130	10	Continental Airlines	D-ABEH N402PE N33202
19020	130	11	Continental Airlines	D-ABEI N403PE N16203*
19021	130	15	Continental Airlines	D-ABEK N404PE N77204
19022	130	17	(Wilmington Trust Co)	D-ABEL N405PE N20205 stored Mojave, CA; b/u Jan93
19023	130	23	Continental Airlines	D-ABEM N406PE N14206
19024	130	26	Continental Airlines	D-ABEN N407PE N59207
19025	130	32	Continental Airlines	D-ABEO N408PE (N14208) N408PE stored Mojave, CA Jan93
19026	130	35	Continental Airlines	D-ABEP N409PE N14209
19027	130	52	SARO	D-ABEQ N410PE (N33210) N410PE XA-RSY
19028	130	98	Continental Airlines	D-ABER N411PE N14211
19029	130	108	Continental Airlines	D-ABES N412PE N14212
19030	130	113	Continental Airlines	D-ABET N413PE N24213
19031	130	118	Continental Airlines	D-ABEU N414PE N44214
19032	130	119	Continental Airlines	D-ABEV N415PE N77215
19033	130	120	SARO	D-ABEW N416PE (N14216) N416PE XA-RSZ
19039	222	6	United Airlines	N9001U
19040	222	8	United Airlines	N9002U
19041	222	12	United Airlines	N9003U
19042	222	14	United Airlines	N9004U
19043	222	18	(United Airlines)	N9005U dbr 19Jul70 Philadelphia, PA
19044	222	19	United Airlines	N9006U
19045	222	21	United Airlines	N9007U
19046	222	22	United Airlines	N9008U
19047	222	24	United Airlines	N9009U
19048	222	25	United Airlines	N9010U
19049	222	27	United Airlines	N9011U
19050	222	28	United Airlines	N9012U
19051	222	30	United Airlines	N9013U
19052	222	31	(Intl Airline Support Group)	N9014U stored Las Vegas, NV 13Jan92; b/u Tucson, AZ Oct93
19053	222	34	(Intl Airline Support Group)	N9015U stored Las Vegas, NV 14Sep92; later b/u
19054	222	36	United Airlines	N9016U
19055	222	37	United Airlines	N9017U
19056	222	42	United Airlines	N9018U
19057	222	48	United Airlines	N9019U
19058	222	49	(Intl Airline Support Group)	N9020U N68AF stored Marana, AZ Jun90; later b/u
19059	222	50	Aerocontinente	N9021U N69AF OB-1561 XA-SYX OB-1637
19060	222	55	United Airlines	N9022U
19061	222	58	United Airlines	N9023U
19062	222	59	United Airlines	N9024U
19063	222	62	United Airlines	N9025U
19064	222	63	Air Liberte	N9026U F-GCLL
19065	222	65	United Airlines	N9027U
19066	222	69	Air Liberte	N9028U F-GCSL
19067	222	71	Air Charter	N9029U F-GCJL [Op by Air Liberte]
19068	222	74	(Intl Airline Support Group)	N9030U stored Las Vegas, NV 11Sep92; later b/u
19069	222	75	(United Airlines)	N9031U w/o 08Dec72 Chicago-Midway, IL
19070	222	76	United Airlines	N9032U
19071	222	85	(Intl Airline Support Group)	N9033U stored Tucson, AZ Nov92; b/u Oct93
19072	222	86	(Faucett)	N9034U N73714 N459AC (N662AA) N459AC OB-1451 w/o 29Feb96 near Arequipa, Peru
19073	222	90	(Piedmont Aviation)	N9035U N752N dbr 25Oct86 Charlotte, NC
19074	222	95	AirTran Airways	N9036U G-AZNZ N144AW N468AT*
19075	222	97	Aero Zambia	N9037U N7383F 9J-AFU
19076	222	99	United Airlines	N9038U
19077	222	103	United Airlines	N9039U
19078	222	106	United Airlines	N9040U
19306	293	13	(Phoenix Aviation Dept)	N831PC N461GB (N461AC) N461GB (N8647A) N461GB stored Phoenix, AZ 02Oct91, used as fire trainer
19307	293	20	(Angeles Airmotive)	N832PC N462GB N462AC (N648AA) N462AC stored Kingman, AZ; b/u Oct94
19308	293	40	(Aircorp II)	N833PC N463GB (N463AC) N463GB (N649AA) N463GB stored Phoenix, AZ later b/u
19309	293	47	Express City	N834AC N464GB N464AC (N650AA) N464AC (9Q-...) N464AC N777EC*
19407	205		(Braathens-SAFE)	Allocated but later canx, not built
19408	205	110	Americana de Aviacion	LN-SUS SE-DKG TC-JUP SE-DKG TC-JUP PK-IJA N408CE OB-
19409	205	128	Magnicharters	LN-SUP SE-DLP XA-SYT
19418	201	29	US Air	N734N N200AU stored Marana, AZ Apr95

BOEING 737

C/n	Series	Line No	Last known Operator/Owner	Previous Identities/fate (where known)
19419	201	41	(Aero Controls)	N735N N202AU stored Sherman, TX Feb94; b/u Shelton, WA Sep94
19420	201	43	US Air	N736N N203AU
19421	201	53	Frontier Airlines	N737N N205AU
19422	201	61	Carnival AIrlines	N738N N206AU
19423	201	67	Frontier Airlines	N740N N207AU
19424	248	147	Corporativo Derex	(EI-APP) EI-ASA 9J-ADZ EI-ASA F-GHML OO-PHE N2117X TC-VAA TC-ALC stored Stansted, UK 08Sep94
19425	248	153	(Faucett)	(EI-APS) EI-ASB SU-AYX EI-ASB PP-SRX EI-ASB OB-R-1314 OB-1314 dbr 03Apr89 Iquitos, Peru
19426	202C	73		N2711R C-GQBC N801AL 9J-
19437	130	1	NASA/Langley Research Center	N73700 (N715NA) NASA515/N515NA Prototype
19547	222	107	Vanguard Airlines	N9041U N749N N208AU
19548	222	114	Vanguard Airlines	N9042U N751N N209US
19549	222	115	(IAL Aircraft Leasing)	N9043U N64AF OO-PHF N64AF 5N-DIO N64AF stored Miami, FL Nov93; b/u Apr94
19550	222	116	(Intl Airline Support Group)	N9044U stored Las Vegas, NV; b/u Tucson, AZ Oct93
19551	222	117	United Airlines	N9045U
19552	222	121	(Aloha Airlines)	N9046U N61AF N73714 (N194AW) N73714 stored Honolulu, HI 20Apr94; b/u Kingman, AZ Dec94
19553	222	122	Air Philippines	N9047U N63AF VT-ERN N63AF TF-ABH RDPL-34126 N63AF 9M-PMR RP-C1938
19554	222	123	Faucett	N9048U N67AF OO-PHG N67AF 5N-MCI N67AF OB-1635
19555	222	129	(US Air)	N9049U N210US dbr 22Jul90 Kinston, NC
19556	222	130	(Air Florida)	N9050U N62AF w/o 13Jan82 into Potomac River, Washington, DC
19591	215C		(Lake Central Airlines)	Allocated but later canx, not built
19592	215C		(Lake Central Airlines)	Allocated but later canx, not built
19593	215C		(Lake Central Airlines)	Allocated but later canx, not built
19594	210C	102	Jetall	N4907 C-GQBD (I-) C-GQBD N728JE TF-ABJ N728JE C-GJLN
19598	247	33	Viscount Air Services	N4501W (N457AC) N4501W (N643AA) N4501W
19599	247	39	(Polaris Aircraft Leasing)	N4502W stored Dallas-Love Field, TX Feb90; b/u Mojave, CA
19600	247	44	Piedmont Avn Services	N4503W N307VA N487GS*
19601	247	45	Airfast Indonesia	N4504W N4504 N4504W N466AC (N644AA) N466AC PK-OCF
19602	247	46	(Braniff Airways)	N4505W stored Orlando, FL Nov89; b/u Mojave, CA Aug93
19603	247	51	Vanguard Airlines	N4506W N758N N204AU
19604	247	56	(Polaris Aircraft Leasing)	N4507W stored Orlando, FL 06Nov89; b/u Mojave, CA Feb94
19605	247	57	Westinghouse Electric Corp	N4508W N165W*
19606	247	64	Viscount Air Service	N4509W (CC-CLE) N4509W (N92JF) N4509W N305VA
19607	247	70	Air South	N4510W
19608	247	73	(Soundair Inc)	N4511W stored Shannon, Eire 12Dec91; b/u Aug93
19609	247	81	(Viscount Air Service)	N4512W CC-CLF N4512W N306VA B/u Tucson Jan96
19610	247	83	Faucett	N4513W OB-R-1317 OB-1317
19611	247	92	Sakhalin AIrlines	N4514W (OB-R-) N4514W N470TA RA-73003
19612	247	93	Air South	N4515W
19613	247	104	Viscount Air Service	N4516W N308VA
19614	247	105	Viscount Air Service	N4517W N473AC (N645AA) N473AC N309VA
19615	247	125	Aero Continente	N4518W OB-1620
19616	247	126	Dinar Lineas Aereas	N4519W CC-CRI N4519W OB-1619
19617	247	132	Viscount Air Service	N4520W N304VA
19679	159	89	(GATX Aircraft Corp)	HK-1403 (D-ABWA) N1780B N73715 N472GB (N1640A) N472GB stored Las Vegas, NV 11Apr88; b/u Mojave, CA Feb94
19680	159	94	(AAR Financial Services)	HK-1404 (D-ABWB) N1781B N73717 N471GB (N641AA) N471GB stored Las Vegas, NV 17May88; b/u Oct90
19681	214	68	Angola Air Charter	N378PS N7380F D2-TBI
19682	214	78	(Aero Controls)	N379PS N7387F N10328 (N333RN) N10328 stored Shelton, WA 28Nov94; b/u 25Jul95
19707	244	82	VARSA	(ZS-EUY) ZS-SBL N754UA (N654A) N754UA XA-SFR
19708	244	86	TACA International Airlines	(ZS-EUZ) ZS-SBM 3D-ADA N136AW N236TA
19709	204	38	(Blue Sky Avn Sve & T'ding)	G-AVRL N311XV N197AW stored Mojave, CA 03Sep91; b/u Jan94
19710	204	54	(Pacific Aero Support)	G-AVRM N312XV N198AW dbr Tucson, AZ Dec89 and stored; later b/u
19711	204	155	Air South	G-AVRN PH-TVG G-AVRN N172PL N313VA
19712	204	162	Aero Continente	G-AVRO B-2605 G-AVRO B-2605 G-AVRO N313XV N199AW OB-1493
19713	293	80	(Angeles Airmotive)	(N835PC) N465GB N465AC (N651AA) N465AC stored Kingman, AZ; b/u Sep92
19714	293	88	Americana de Aviacion	(N836PC) N467GB (N652AA) N467GB OB-1572
19742	275	96	(Air Lanka)	CF-PWD C-FPWD EI-BJE 4R-ULH stored Colombo, Sri Lanka; b/u Oct93
19743	275C	139	Westjet	CF-PWE C-FPWE EI-BJP N331XV C-GNWD N331XV C-GWJK
19758	222	16	Continental Airlines	N737Q N1359B ZK-NAM (N7388F) N7302F N12335
19759	205		(Braathens-SAFE)	Allocated but later canx, not built
19768	112	184	COPA	N17117 9M-AOU 9V-BFD N46AF HP-873 HP-873CMP
19769	112	194	Faucett	9V-BBC N40AF OB-R-1288 OB-1288

BOEING 737

C/n	Series	Line No	Last known Operator/Owner	Previous Identities/fate (where known)
19770	112	203	Presidential Air	9M-AOV 9V-BFE N42AF N709AW ZK-NED N73GQ N709SP N333RN*
19771	112	212	America West Airlines	9V-BBE N47AF YV-405C HP-1038 N708AW N708SP N708AW
19772	112	217	UTAPEF	9M-AOW 9V-BFF N48AF TP-04/XB-LCR TP-03/XC-UJL XB-IBV
19794	130	127	SARO	D-ABEY N417PE (N17217) N417PE XA-RSW
19795	130		(Lufthansa)	(D-ABEZ) Allocated but later canx, not built
19796	130		(Lufthansa)	(D-ABEJ) Allocated but later canx, not built
19847	242C	84	TAT European Airlines	N6241 CF-NAB C-FNAB (F-GFVK) F-GGPA
19848	242C	157	Air Afrique	(CF-NAD) CF-NAH C-FNAH (F-GFVR) (F-GGPB) F-GFVK TU-TAV
19849	242C		(Nordair)	(CF-NAF) Allocated but later canx, not built
19884	217	79	Continental Airlines	CF-CPB C-FCPB N431PE N12230
19885	217	91	Continental Airlines	CF-CPC C-FCPC N432PE N12231
19886	217	101	Continental Airlines	CF-CPD C-FCPD N433PE N16232
19887	217	109	Continental Airlines	CF-CPE C-FCPE N434PE N14233
19888	217	112	Continental Airlines	CF-CPU C-FCPU N435PE N13234
19889	217		(CP Air)	Allocated but later canx, not built
19920	214	100	Continental Airlines	N380PS N7388F N14239
19921	214	111	(GPA Group)	N381PS CF-PWM C-FPWM C6-BES C-FPWM N382PA HR-SHG stored Miami, FL; b/u Jun91
19929	219	60	(AGES Aircraft Intl)	ZK-NAC N321XV stored Las Vegas, NV Mar90; b/u Mojave, CA Aug92
19930	219	66	(Charlotte Aircraft Corp)	ZK-NAD N322XV stored Las Vegas, NV Mar90; b/u Maxton, NC Mar91
19931	219	77	Airmark Aviation	ZK-NAE N453AC (N655AA) N453AC stored Phoenix, AZ Aug91 later Alburqueque, NM May95
19932	222	133	United Airlines	N9051U
19933	222	135	United Airlines	N9052U
19934	222	137	United Airlines	N9053U
19935	222	138	United Airlines	N9054U
19936	222	146	Far Eastern Air Transport	N9055U (B-2701) B-2601
19937	222	148	Continental Airlines	N9056U N7389F N10236
19938	222	150	(Intl Airline Support Group)	N9057U stored Tucson, AZ 06Sep92 later b/u
19939	222	151	(Far Eastern Air Transport)	N9058U (B-2703) B-2603 w/o 22Aug81 nr Miao-Li, RoC
19940	222	171	TACA International Airlines	N9059U PH-TVI (N842L) PH-TVI N135AW N135TA
19941	222	174	United Airlines	N9060U
19942	222	175	United Airlines	N9061U
19943	222	179	United Airlines	N9062U
19944	222	183	United Airlines	N9063U
19945	222	185	Aero Chile	N9064U CF-NAI N9064U N7390F N14237 (N628GA) (N737KD) N14237 CC-
19946	222	186	United Airlines	N9065U CF-NAP N9065U
19947	222	187	United Airlines	N9066U EI-ASK N9066U EI-ASK N9066U
19948	222	191	United Airlines	N9067U
19949	222	197	(United Airlines)	N9068U stored, b/u Apr94
19950	222	198	United Airlines	N9069U
19951	222	200	United Airlines	N9070U
19952	222	201	United Airlines	N9071U
19953	222	202	United Airlines	N9072U
19954	222	206	US Air	N9073U N759N N216US stored Marana, AZ Apr95
19955	222	210	Vanguard Airlines	N9074U PH-TVH (N41AF) N841L PH-TVH N841L PH-TVH N603DJ
19956	222	211	United Airlines	N9075U
19989	296		(Quebecair)	(CF-QBK) Allocated but later canx, not built
19990	296		(Quebecair)	(CF-QBN) Allocated but later canx, not built
20070	2C0	124	Continental Airlines	(N7371F) N570GB N7378F N14241
20071	2C0	131	Continental Airlines	(N7372F) N571GB N7379F N10242
20072	2C0	136	Continental Airlines	(N7373F) N572GB N7372F N73243
20073	2C0	142	Continental Airlines	(N7374F) N573GB N7370F N11244
20074	2C0	170	Continental Airlines	(N7375F) N574GB N7371F N14245
20090	299		(Caledonian Airways)	Allocated but later canx, not built
20091	299		(Caledonian Airways)	Allocated but later canx, not built
20092	2A1	161	VASP	PP-SMA
20093	2A1F	169	VASP	PP-SMB
20094	2A1	182	VASP	PP-SMC
20095	2A1	188	US Air	PP-SMD N25SW N767N N215US stored Marana, AZ Apr95
20096	2A1	190	(VASP)	PP-SME dbr 28Jan86 Sao Paulo, Brazil
20125	247	134	Viscount Air Service	N4521W N221AU N303VA
20126	247	140	Viscount Air Service	N4522W N4522 N4522W N470AC (N646AA) N470AC N302VA
20127	247	144	Government of Mexico	N4523W TP-03/XC-UJI B-12001 XC-UJI [Op by Fuerza Aerea Mexicana]
20128	247	145	Magnicharters	N4524W N73718 C6-BEI OO-PLH N501AV HR-SHU N501AV OB-1536 N501AV XA-STB
20129	247	154	Continental Airlines	N4525W N7384F N14246
20130	247	156	Grand Air	N4526W B-2617 RP-C8886
20131	247	165	(Western Air Lines)	N4527W w/o 31Mar75 Caspar, WY
20132	247	167	Far Eastern Air Transport	N4528W B-2607

BOEING 737

C/n	Series	Line No	Last known Operator/Owner	Previous Identities/fate (where known)
20133	247	176	(Aero Controls)	N4529W N7363F N14247 stored Shelton, WA Jul93; b/u Aug93
20134	247	177	Far Eastern Air Transport	N4530W B-2613
20138	210C	173	TAT European Airlines	N4906 F-GGFI wfs Paris-Orly, France 16Jan96
20142	275	253	(Pacific Western Airlines)	CF-PWC C-FPWC w/o 11Feb78 Cranbrook, Canada
20155	214	180	VASP	N382PS PP-SMQ
20156	214	181	Casino Express	N983PS ZK-NAK N323XV TF-ISA N323XV N457TM [Op by TEM Enterprises]
20157	214	189	VASP	N984PS PP-SMR
20158	214	192	AirTran Airways	N985PS ZK-NAL N4264Y N460AC (N656AA) N460AC T3-VAL N460AC N460AT
20159	214	193	VASP	N986PS PP-SMS
20160	214	195	VASP	N987PS PP-SMT
20194	2A6	196	America West Airlines	N520L VR-BEH N8527S N3333M N145AW
20195	2A6	205	LADECO	N1288 N146AW ZK-NEE 4R-ULL N909LH CC-CYR
20196	217	143	Air Service Nantes	CF-CPV C-FCPV N197JQ F-WGTP F-GGTP
20197	217	149	SARO	CF-CPZ C-FCPZ (SE-DLR) TC-JUT N3160M XA-SOM stored Blenheim, NJ
20205	2A9C	242	Pacific East Air Cargo	CF-TAO C-FTAO N383PA F-GFYL
20206	2A9C	249	Jetall	CF-TAN C-FTAN N803AL C-FJLT
20209	297	152	(Aloha Airlines)	N73711 dbr 28Apr88 Honolulu, HI
20210	297	163	(AAR Allen Aircraft Corp)	N73712 stored Honolulu, HI; b/u Jul88
20211	201	141	Bahamasair	N741N N211US C6-BFJ
20212	201	159	Frontier Airlines	N743N N212US
20213	201	160	Museum of Flight Foundation	N744N N213US stored Amarillo, TX, later Boeing Field, WA Sep95
20214	201	172	Frontier Airlines	N745N N214AU
20215	201	207	Frontier Airlines	N746N N217US
20216	201	213	US Air	N747N N218US stored Marana, AZ
20218	248QC	199	TAT European Airlines	EI-ASC PP-SNY EI-ASC EC-DZB EI-ASC F-GGFJ
20219	248QC	208	LAN-Chile	EI-ASD CC-CEI
20220	248QC	215	Transmile Air Service	EI-ASE 9M-PMP
20221	248	227	Kibris-THY	EI-ASF CF-ASF EI-ASF C6-BFB EI-ASF OO-PHC N6658Y TC-VAB TC-ALT
20222	248	240	(Aer Lingus)	EI-ASG SU-AYT EI-ASG N7360F EI-ASG HR-SHD EI-ASG stored Dublin, Eire Oct91; b/u Jan95
20223	248	252	National Airlines	EI-ASH CF-TAR EI-ASH C-GTAR EI-ASH C-GTAR EI-ASH N7361F EI-ASH N80AF EI-ASH C-GTAR EI-ASH HR-TNS EI-ASH CC-CSL
20226	281	168	(China Airlines)	JA8401 N1451Z B-1870 w/o 16Apr76 off Makung, RoC
20227	281	178	(Aviation Systems Intl)	JA8402 N1444Z B-1872 N503AV YU-ANX N503AV stored Tucson, AZ Feb91 later b/u
20229	244	214	South African Airways	(ZS-FKH) ZS-SBN
20231	2B2	204	Air Madagascar	5R-MFA
20236	204	166	Apple Vacations	G-AWSY N173PL N312VA [Op by Viscount Air Service]
20242	297	222	(AAR Allen Aircraft Corp)	N73713 stored Honolulu, HI; b/u Jul88
20253	230QC	223	COPA	D-ABBE N301XV HP-1134 HP-1134CMP
20254	230QC	230	Transmile Air Service	D-ABCE N302XV F-GFVJ 9M-MPQ
20255	230QC	234	Airfast Indonesia	D-ABDE N303XV N800WA PK-OCI
20256	230QC	238	Aeropostale	D-ABFE N304XV F-GFVI
20257	230QC	274	Air Atlanta Iceland	D-ABGE TF-ABX
20258	230QC	276	Air Atlanta Iceland	D-ABHE TF-ABF
20276	281	231	TEAM Aer Lingus	JA8403 9Q-CNL EI-BCR stored Dublin, Eire Jun94
20277	281	235	Aero Continente	JA8405 N1450Z B-1874 N505AV YU-ANY N505AV OB-1511
20280	2B1	224	Lineas Aereas Mocambique	CR-BAA C9-BAA
20281	2B1	228	(Lineas Aereas Mocambique)	CR-BAB C9-BAB dbr 28Mar83 Quelimore, Mozambique
20282	204C	245	TAT European Airlines	G-AXNA PH-TVF G-AXNA F-GGPC
20299	2A3	158	SAHSA	N1787B N1797B CX-BHM HR-TNR HR-SHO
20300	2E1	164	Orient Express Air	N1788B N1733B CF-EPO C-FEPO N197AL HS-
20329	244	250	Comair	ZS-SBO
20330	244	257	LAPA	ZS-SBP (LV-) ZS-SBP LV-WBO
20331	244	260	Comair	ZS-SBR (LV-) ZS-SBR
20334	293	232	(Air California)	N468AC dbr 17Feb81 Orange County, CA
20335	293	237	Airfast Indonesia	N469AC (N653A) N469AC PK-OCG
20336	2H4	239	Casino Express	(N470AC) N22SW EI-BFC (N332XV) EI-BFC EC-DZH EI-BFC N709ML N456TM [Op by TEM Enterprises]
20344	219	229	Continental Airlines	(N73714) ZK-NAJ N7310F N10248
20345	2H4	233	(Marketair Corp)	(N73715) N21SW N73717 (C-GNDS) N73717 stored Mojave, CA 88; b/u 27Dec91
20346	2H4C	258	VASP	(N73717) N23SW PP-SMW
20361	291	209	Continental Airlines	N7373F N10251
20362	291	216	Continental Airlines	N7374F N17252
20363	291	218	Pacific Transair	N7375F (N44253) N7375F RDPL-34125 N7375F VH-
20364	291	219	Ryan Intl Airlines	N7376F (N802AL) N7376F (N190AW) N7376F N730TJ
20365	291	220	Pacific Transair	N7377F N16254 N737RD VH-
20368	214	264	(Aviation Systems Intl)	N988PS N7386F (N10240) N7386F stored Fort Lauderdale, FL; b/u 29Oct93
20369	2H4	267	(Nationsbank of Tennessee)	N989PS N20SW N7381F (N10249) N7381F stored Mojave, CA Jan93; later b/u
20389	204C	251	TAT European Airlines	G-AXNB F-GGPB

BOEING 737

C/n	Series	Line No	Last known Operator/Owner	Previous Identities/fate (where known)
20396	2E1	221	(Polaris Aircraft Leasing)	N1785B CF-EPL C-FEPL stored Vancouver, BC Sep92; b/u Tucson, AZ 95
20397	2E1	226	(Polaris Aircraft Leasing)	N1786B CF-EPR C-FEPR stored Vancouver, BC Sep92; b/u Tucson, AZ 95
20403	287	236	Aerolineas Argentinas	LV-JMW
20404	287	243	Aerolineas Argentinas	LV-JMX
20405	287	248	Aerolineas Argentinas	LV-JMY
20406	287	261	Aerolineas Argentinas	LV-JMZ
20407	287	263	Aerolineas Argentinas	LV-JND
20408	287	265	(Aerolineas Argentinas)	LV-JNE dbr 20Nov92 Buenos Aires-San Luis, Argentina
20412	205	225	Vanguard Airlines	N1787B LN-SUG SE-DKH TC-JUR PK-IJC N412CE
20413	281	241	Arkia Israeli Airlines	JA8406 (EI-BEE) C6-BEC EI-BEE 4X-BAF
20414	281	244	US Air	JA8407 N776N N219US
20417	204	255	National Airlines	G-AXNC TF-ABD CC-CSD
20440	210C	256	Eurolair	N4902W (N155PA) N4902W N200NE F-GJDL
20449	281	259	(General Electric Cap Corp)	JA8408 EI-BEF OB-R-1263 EI-BEF N142AW N722S stored Amarillo, TX 07Dec93; later b/u
20450	281	262	Sempati Air Transport	JA8409 PK-JHA
20451	281	266	Sempati Air Transport	JA8410 PK-JHD
20452	281	270	Sempati Air Transport	JA8411 PK-JHE
20453	2H5	246	Eastwind Airlines	N1790 N1790B LN-MTC N753N N220US
20454	2H5	247	Eastwind Airlines	N1791 N1791B LN-MTD N754N N221US
20455	242C	254	GECAS	CF-NAQ C-FNAQ EI-BOC C-FNAQ stored 31Dec95
20458	205C	278	Transmile Air Service	LN-SUA TF-VLT TF-ABT 9M-PMM
20480	2A8	269	(Indian Airlines)	VT-EAG stored Delhi, India May93, b/u May95
20481	2A8	271	(Indian Airlines)	VT-EAH w/o 19Oct88 Ahmadabad, India
20482	2A8	272	(Indian Airlines)	VT-EAI stored Delhi, India May93, later b/u
20483	2A8	273	Indian Air Force	VT-EAJ K-
20484	2A8	275	Indian Air Force	VT-EAK K-
20485	2A8	277	(Indian Airlines)	VT-EAL dbr 17Dec78 Hyderabad,India
20486	2A8	279	(Indian Airlines)	VT-EAM w/o 31May73 Vassant Vihar, India
20492	212	281	Aero Santa	9V-BCR N7382F (N14250) N7382F EI-BXV VT-EQG HR-SHJ OB-1476
20496	242C	268	GECAS	N1788B CF-NAP C-FNAP stored 31Dec95
20497	242C		(Nordair)	Allocated but later canx, not built
20498	286	283	Iran Air	EP-IRF
20499	286	284	(Iran Air)	EP-IRG dbr 15Oct86 Shiraz, Iran
20500	286	286	Iran Air	EP-IRH
20506	281	280	Sempati Air Transport	JA8412 PK-JHC
20507	281	282	Sempati Air Transport	JA8413 PK-JHG
20508	281	287	(Sempati Air Transport)	JA8414 PK-JHF dbr Yogyakarta, Indonesia 16Jan95; b/u Aug95
20521	212	288	Carnival Airlines	9M-AQC (CF-NAD) CF-NAW C-FNAW EI-BNS N130AW C-GXPW TC-ATE C-GXPW TF-ISB N161FN
20523	287	285	Aerolineas Argentinas	LV-PRQ LV-JTD
20536	281C	289	Lineas Aereas Mocambique	CR-BAC C9-BAC
20537	287	291	Aerolineas Argentinas	LV-JTO
20544	2D6	290	Air Toulouse International	7T-VEC TZ-ADL G-BMMZ F-GLXH
20561	281	292	Air Nippon	N1788B JA8415
20562	281	293	Air Nippon	JA8416
20563	281	296	Air Nippon	JA8417
20564	281		(All Nippon Airways)	(JA8418) Allocated but later canx, not built
20565	281		(All Nippon Airways)	(JA8419) Allocated but later canx, not built
20566	281		(All Nippon Airways)	(JA8420) Allocated but later canx, not built
20567	281		(All Nippon Airways)	(JA8421) Allocated but later canx, not built
20574	268C	294	Saudia	HZ-AGA
20575	268C	295	Saudia	HZ-AGB
20576	268	297	Saudia	HZ-AGC
20577	268	298	Saudia	HZ-AGD
20578	268	299	Saudia	HZ-AGE
20582	2H6	302	AVIATECA	9M-AQL 9M-MBA V2-LDT HR-SHP TG-AOA N126GU
20583	2H6	303	AVIATECA	9M-AQM 9M-MBB N121GU TG-ALA N121GU
20584	2H6	305	(SAHSA)	9M-AQN 9M-MBC N401SH dbr 18Jul93 Managua, Nicaragua
20585	2H6	306	(Malaysian Airlines System)	9M-AQO 9M-MBD w/o 04Dec77 Kampong Ladong, Malaysia
20586	2H6	307	AVIATECA	9M-AQP 9M-MBE N122GU TG-ALA N122GU
20587	2H6	308	AVIATECA	9M-AQQ 9M-MBF N123GU TG-AYA N123GU
20588	275	300	WestJet Airlines	CF-PWP C-FPWP N381PA C-FPWP N861SY HP-1216CMP N861SY XA-SJI N861SY C-FVHC N861SY C-GWJE
20589	2A1	301	VASP	PP-SMF
20590	2H7C	304	Cameroon Airlines	TJ-CBA
20591	2H7C	309	Cameroon Airlines	TJ-CBB
20631	2H6	310	Bouraq Indonesia Airlines	9M-ARG 9M-MBG PK-IJD
20632	204	316	National Airlines	G-BADP CC-CSH
20633	204	318	National Airlines	G-BADR CC-CSI
20650	2D6C	311	Air Algerie	7T-VED
20670	275	315	WestJet Airlines	CF-PWW C-FPWW N380PA C-FPWW N862SY HP-1218CMP N862SY C-FVHG N862SY C-GWJG
20671	2F9	312	Nigeria Airways	5N-ANC stored Dublin, Eire Apr92
20672	2F9	313	Nigeria Airways	5N-AND
20680	2B2	314	Air Madagascar	5R-MFB

BOEING 737

C/n	Series	Line No	Last known Operator/Owner	Previous Identities/fate (where known)
20681	2E1F	319	Canair Cargo	CF-EPP C-FEPP N211PL C-GDCC
20685 to 20703 model 737-253, built as T-43A and modified as follows:				
20685	CT-43A	317	USAF/558thTFS/12thTFW	71-1403
20686	CT-43A	326	USAF/558thTFS/12thTFW	71-1404
20687	CT-43A	329	USAF/558thTFS/12thTFW	71-1405
20688	CT-43A	330	USAF/558thTFS/12thTFW	71-1406
20689	CT-43A	334	Dept of the Air Force/ E.G. & G. Inc	72-0282 (N) 72-0282 N5175U
20690	CT-43A	336	USAF/58thALS/86thWg	72-0283
20691	CT-43A	337	Dept of the Air Force/ E.G. & G. Inc	72-0284 N5294E
20692	CT-43A	339	Dept of the Air Force/ E.G. & G. Inc	72-0285 (N) 72-0285 N5176Y
20693	CT-43A	340	Dept of the Air Force/ E.G. & G. Inc	72-0286 N99890 N57JE 72-0286 (N) 72-0286 N5177C
20694	CT-43A	343	Dept of the Air Force/ E.G. & G. Inc	72-0287 N5294M
20695	CT-43A	345	USAF/200thALS/CO ANG	72-0288
20696	CT-43A	347	(USAF/76thAS)	73-1149 w/o 03Apr96 nr Duborovnic, Croatia
20697	T-43A	349	USAF/558thTFS/12thTFW	73-1150/RA
20698	CT-43A	350	USAF/558thTFS/12thTFW	73-1151
20699	CT-43A	355	USAF/558thTFS/12thTFW	73-1152
20700	CT-43A	357	USAF/558thTFS/12thTFW	73-1153
20701	CT-43A	359	USAF/200thALS/CO ANG	73-1154
20702	T-43A	362	USAF/558thTFS/12thTFW	73-1155/RA
20703	CT-43A	363	USAF/558thTFS/12thTFW	73-1156
20711	205	320	Magnicharters	LN-SUD N197SS SE-DLD XA-SWL
20740	286C	321	Iran Air	EP-IRI
20758	2D6C	322	(Air Algerie)	7T-VEE w/o 21Dec94 Coventry, UK
20759	2D6	332	Air Algerie	7T-VEF
20768	287	331	Aerolineas Argentinas	LV-LEB
20769	287		(Aerolineas Argentinas)	(LV-LEE) Allocated but later canx, not built
20776	2E1F	328	Canair Cargo	CF-EPU C-FEPU N212PL C-GCDG
20777	2A1	324	VASP	PP-SMG
20778	2A1	325	VASP	PP-SMH
20779	2A1	327	VASP	N1782B PP-SMP
20785	275	335	Dept of the Air Force	C-FPWB N4529W (N386PA) N4529W
20786	2B1	323	(Lineas Aereas Mocambique)	N1788B CR-BAD C9-BAD dbr 09Feb89 Lichinga, Mozambique
20793	298C	333	(Air Zaire)	9Q-CNI dbr by Nov95 (details?)
20794	298C	346	Alaska Airlines	9Q-CNJ N87WA 4X-AOX N87WA N745AS
20795	298C	348	Air Zaire	9Q-CNK
20796	298C		(Air Zaire)	(9Q-CNL) Allocated but later canx, not built
20797	298C		(Air Zaire)	(9Q-CNM) Allocated but later canx, not built
20806	204	338	COPA	G-BAZG HP-1195CMP
20807	204	341	Sabre Airways	G-BAZH G-SBEB
20808	204	342	S/A Mexicanas	G-BAZI G-BOSA XA-STE stored Luxembourg-Findel, Luxembourg 19Nov95
20836	2K2C	354	Aeropostale	PH-TVC LV-MDB PH-TVC F-GGZA PH-TVC F-GIXA
20882	268	356	Saudia	HZ-AGF
20883	268	366	Saudia	HZ-AGG
20884	2D6	361	Air Algerie	7T-VEG
20892	270C	368	Iraqi Airways	YI-AGH
20893	270C	371	Iraqi Airways	YI-AGI J2-KAF YI-AGI
20907	229	351	SABENA World Airlines	OO-SDA LX-LGN OO-SDA
20908	229	352	AVENSA	OO-SDB (OO-TEZ) OO-SDB G-BTEC OO-SDB YV-79C
20909	229	353	AVENSA	OO-SDC G-BTED OO-SDC YV-74C
20910	229	358	SABENA World Airlines	OO-SDD EC-EEG
20911	229	360	SABENA World Airlines	OO-SDE C-GNDX OO-SDE C-GNDX OO-SDE
20912	229	365	SABENA World Airlines	OO-SDF
20913	2M6	399	LADECO	(OO-SDG) VR-UEB 4R-ALD VR-UEB VS-UEB V8-UEB CC-CJZ V8-UEB ZK-NAZ LV-VGF CC-CYW
20914	229	396	(Gulf Air)	OO-SDH w/o 04Apr78 Gosselies,Belgium
20915	229	401	Sobelair	OO-SDJ
20916	229	403	SABENA World Airlines	OO-SDK
20917	210C	344	TACA International Airlines	N1786B N4905W
20922	275	370	America West Airlines	C-GAPW N127AW C-GAPW
20925	2H4	373	Southwest Airlines	N24SW
20926	2H6	372	Bouraq Indonesia Airlines	9M-ASR 9M-MBH PK-IJE
20943	2K2C	405	Aeropostale	PH-TVD G-BKBT PH-TVD G-BKBT PH-TVD VT-EKC F-GGVP
20944	2K2C	408	Aeropostale	PH-TVE VT-EKD PH-TVE F-GGVQ
20956	2A9	386	Aero Santa	C-GTAQ C6-BEK C-GTAQ N131AW C-GVRD YU-ANZ C-GVRD HR-SHH YU-ANZ HR-SHI VT-EWA OB-1544
20957	2K6	377	(SAHSA)	HR-SHA EI-CBL dbr 17Nov91 San Jose, Costa Rica
20958	275	391	America West Airlines	C-GBPW N128AW C-GBPW N128AW C-GBPW
20959	275	395	America West Airlines	C-GCPW N126AW C-GCPW
20960	2A8	374	Indian Airlines	VT-ECP
20961	2A8	375	(Indian Airlines)	VT-ECQ w/o 26Apr93 Aurangabad, India
20962	2A8	380	(Indian Airlines)	VT-ECR w/o 26Apr79 Madras, India
20963	2A8	383	(Indian Airlines)	VT-ECS dbr 02Dec95 New Delhi, India

BOEING 737

C/n	Series	Line No	Last known Operator/Owner	Previous Identities/fate (where known)
20964	287	379	(Aerolineas Argentinas)	LV-LIU w/o 27Sep88 Ushuaia, Argentina
20965	287	381	Aerolineas Argentinas	LV-LIV
20966	287	387	Aerolineas Argentinas	LV-LIW
20967	2A1	364	VASP	N1799B PP-SMU
20968	2A1	367	VASP	PP-SMV
20969	2A1	369	(VASP)	PP-SMX dbr 03Apr78 Sao Paulo, Brazil
20970	2A1	376	(VASP)	PP-SMY dbr 24May83 Brasilia, Brazil
20971	2A1	382	VASP	PP-SMZ
20976	2E1	388	AirTran Airways	C-GEPA N461AC N461AT
21000	241	378	VARIG	PP-VME
21001	241	384	VARIG	PP-VMF
21002	241	385	VARIG	PP-VMG
21003	241	389	VARIG	PP-VMH
21004	241	390	VARIG	PP-VMI
21005	241	394	VARIG	PP-VMJ
21006	241	398	(VARIG)	N87569 PP-VMK w/o 03Sep89 Amazon jungle, Brazil
21007	241	400	VARIG	PP-VML
21008	241	402	VARIG	PP-VMM
21009	241	417	VARIG	PP-VMN
21011	248C	411	Air Canada Connector	EI-ASL F-GKTK C-FNVT [Op by NWT Air]
21012	2C3	392	VARIG	PP-CJN
21013	2C3	393	VARIG	PP-CJO
21014	2C3	397	VARIG	PP-CJP
21015	2C3	404	VARIG	PP-CJR
21016	2C3	406	VARIG	PP-CJS
21017	2C3	410	VARIG	PP-CJT
21063	2D6	407	Air Algerie	7T-VEJ
21064	2D6	409	Air Algerie	7T-VEK
21065	2D6	416	Air Algerie	7T-VEL
21066	210C	413	Air Canada Connector	N4951W (N661AA) N4951W C-GNWI [Op by NWT Air]
21067	210C	414	Air Canada Connector	N4952W (N662AA) N4952W C-GNWM [Op by NWT Air]
21069	291	415	Continental AIrlines	N7385F N15255
21073	2L7C	419	VASP	C2-RN3 PP-SPF
21094	2A1	412	VASP	PP-SNA
21095	2A1	432	VASP	PP-SNB
21109	2H6	436	TACA International Airlines	9M-MBI N124GU
21112	2E1	424	LADECO	C-GEPB N4039W C-GEPB N70720 C-GEPB (EI-BEA)
				EI-BDY CN-RML EI-BDY C-GNDD EI-BDY G-BNYT
				EI-BDY CC-CYT
21115	275	425	Canadian Airlines Intl	C-GEPW N129AW C-GEPW
21116	275C	427	GECAS	C-GDPW stored 20Jan96
21117	2H4	423	Southwest Airlines	N26SW
21130	219	426	LAPSA-Air Paraguay	ZK-NAP HC-BTI ZP-CAB
21131	219	428	LADECO	ZK-NAQ EI-BCC (PH-TVM) EI-BCC N7362F OO-TEJ
				G-BGNW CC-CYC
21135	229	418	SABENA World Airlines	OO-SDG
21136	229	420	SABENA World Airlines	OO-SDL
21137	229	421	SABENA World Airlines	OO-SDM
21138	2M6	422	Air New Zealand	(OO-SDQ) VR-UEC VS-UEC V8-UEC 9M-MBQ ZK-NAL
				stored Christchurch, NZ, Jan94
21139	229	437	SABENA World Airlines	OO-SDP
21163	2A8F	434	Blue Dart Avn/FedEx	VT-EDR
21164	2A8F	435	Blue Dart Avn/FedEx	VT-EDS K- VT-EDS
21165	2N3	441	Forca Aerea Brasileira/GTE	VC96-2115
21166	2N3	445	Forca Aerea Brasileira/GTE	VC96-2116
21167	2N1	442	FA Venezolanas/41Esc	0001
21168	2N1		(Fuerza Aerea Venezolanas)	(0002) Allocated but later canx, not built
21169	2J8C	429	Sudan Airways	ST-AFK
21170	2J8C	430	Sudan Airways	ST-AFL
21172	2M2C	439	(TAAG-Angola Airlines)	(CR-LOR) D2-TAA dbf 05Nov80 Benguela, Angola
21173	2M2C	447	TAAG-Angola Airlines	(CR-LOS) D2-TAB D2-TBC
21176	229	431	SABENA World Airlines	N8277V OO-SDN 9M-MBP OO-SDN
21177	229	433	SABENA World Airlines	OO-SDO
21183	270C	446	(Iraqi Airways)	YI-AGJ w/o 25Dec86 Arar, Saudi Arabia
21184	205	440	LADECO	LN-SUI N197QQ TF-AIC TF-ABF N197QQ (V4-THB)
				N197QQ CC-CYS
21186	242	438	Air South	C-GNDL N73AF C-GNDL N132AW C-GNDL N159PL
21187	2A1C	443	(VASP)	PP-SNC dbr 22Feb83 Manaus, Brazil
21188	2A1C	444	(VASP)	PP-SND w/o 22Jun92 nr Cruzeiro do Sul, Brazil
21191	266	450	(Egyptair)	SU-AYH dbr 24Nov85 Luqa, Malta
21192	266	451	Air Philippines	SU-AYI 4R-ULO N192GP TF-ABG
21193	266	453	Kenya Airways	SU-AYJ PH-TVN SU-BBX 5Y-BHV
21194	266	455	AMC Aviation	SU-AYK
21195	266	457	Egyptair	SU-AYL
21196	266	465	Kenya Airways	SU-AYM PH-TVO SU-BBW 5Y-BHW
21206	269	448	Aero Santa	9K-ACV VR-BOX PP-SNP PT-WBB EI-CHB OB-1538
21211	2D6	454	Air Algerie	7T-VEN
21212	2D6	459	Air Algerie	7T-VEO
21214	2B6	449	Royal Air Maroc	CN-RMI
21215	2B6	452	Royal Air Maroc	CN-RMJ
21216	2B6	456	Royal Air Maroc	CN-RMK

BOEING 737

C/n	Series	Line No	Last known Operator/Owner	Previous Identities/fate (where known)
21219	205	460	LADECO	LN-SUH N7031A CC-CYD
21224	284	463	Olympic Airways	SX-BCA
21225	284	464	Olympic Airways	SX-BCB
21226	2N7	458	Air Sinai	SU-AYN SU-GAN
21227	266	466	Egyptair	SU-AYO
21231	2M6	462	LADECO	OO-TEH C6-BDZ OO-TEH C-GBQS OO-TEH C-GBQS OO-TEH (N384PA) OO-TEH C-GQBS OO-TEH 9M-MBN CC-CYN
21236	2M9	461	VASP	(9J-AEA) 9J-AEG PP-SPJ
21262	2H4	470	Southwest Airlines	N27SW
21275	268	467	Saudia	HZ-AGH
21276	268	468	Saudia	HZ-AGI
21277	268	469	Saudia	HZ-AGJ
21278	2L9	479	AirTran Airways	N1787B OY-APG 4R-ALC F-GCGR D2-TBT F-GCGR D2-TBT EI-BMY G-BKRO 4R-ALC C6-BFC XA-TCP N358AS N464AT
21279	2L9	480	AirTran Airways	N1787B OY-APH EI-BII F-GCGS D2-TBU F-GCGS D2-TBU C6-BEQ N737Q N466AT
21280	268	471	Saudia	HZ-AGK
21281	268	472	Saudia	HZ-AGL
21282	268	476	Saudia	N40120 HZ-AGM
21283	268	477	Saudia	N1243E HZ-AGN
21285	2D6	473	Air Algerie	7T-VEQ
21286	2D6	482	Air Algerie	7T-VER
21287	2D6C	486	Air Algerie	7T-VES
21294	275C	481	Canadian Airlines Intl	C-GFPW
21295	2H7C	484	(Cameroon Airlines)	TJ-CBD dbf 30Aug84 Douala, Cameroons
21296	2N8	478	Yemenia	N1238E 4W-ABZ 70-ACU
21301	284	474	Olympic Airways	SX-BCC
21302	284	475	Olympic Airways	N40112 SX-BCD
21317	286	483	Islamic Republic of Iran	EP-AGA
21335	204	487	easyJet	G-BECG [Op by GB Leisure]
21336	204	489	easyJet	G-BECH [Op by GB Leisure]
21337	2H4	490	Southwest Airlines	(N28SW) N20SW
21338	2H4	494	Southwest Airlines	(N29SW) N23SW
21339	2H4	495	Southwest Airlines	(N30SW) N28SW
21340	2H4	499	Southwest Airlines	(N31SW) N29SW
21355	2P6	493	Air Trans Airways	A40-BC (N458TM) EI-CJW
21356	2P6	496	Air South	A40-BD EI-CKL
21357	2P6	497	LAPA	A40-BE LV-WFX
21358	2P6	498	Aerolineas Argentinas	A40-BF LV-WGX
21359	2P6	500	COPA	A40-BG G-BGFS A40-BG OO-ABB OO-TYB A40-BG HR-SHQ HP-1255CMP
21360	268	485	Saudia	HZ-AGO
21361	268	488	Saudia	HZ-AGP
21362	268	511	Saudia	HZ-AGQ
21397	2K2	507	Bouraq Indonesia Airlines	PH-TVP G-BLEA PH-TVP C-GRCP PH-TVP PK-IJH
21440	2P5	502	Lao Aviation	HS-TBA RDPL-34133
21443	2C9	501	Transaero	N8277V LX-LGH RA-73000 EI-CLN
21444	2C9	516	Transaero	LX-LGI RA-73001 EI-CLO
21445	205	506	LADECO	LN-SUM N7031F CC-CYK
21447	2H4	508	Southwest Airlines	N50SW
21448	2H4	509	Southwest Airlines	N51SW
21467	2Q2C	515	Air Gabon	TR-LXL
21476	2Q3	519	VASP	JA8443 PP-SPI
21477	2Q3	545	(Southwest Air Lines)	JA8444 dbf 26Aug82 Ishigaki, Japan
21478	2Q3	591	Japan Trans Ocean Airlines	JA8445
21496	2A8	503	Indian Airlines	VT-EFK
21497	2A8	504	(Indian Airlines)	VT-EFL K-2371 VT-EFL K-2371 VT-EFL w/o 16Aug91 Imphal, India
21498	2A8	505	Indian Airlines	VT-EFM K-2370 VT-EFM K-2370 VT-EFM
21499	2N9C	513	Republique du Niger	(5U-MAF) 5U-BAG [Op by Escadrille Nationale du Niger]
21500	2B4	491	Viscount Air Service	N70721 N195AW N311VA
21501	2B4	492	Viscount Air Service	N70722 N196AW N310VA
21508	291	518	United Airlines	N7391F N977UA
21509	291	521	United Airlines	N7392F N978UA
21518	2Q8	522	LAPSA-Air Paraguay	N977MP B-2611 C-GNDS VR-CNN ZP-CAC
21528	2L9	517	AirTran Airways	OY-API G-BICV C6-BEX XA-TCQ N359AS
21533	2H4	524	Southwest Airlines	N52SW
21534	2H4	526	Southwest Airlines	N53SW
21535	2H4	543	Southwest Airlines	N54SW
21538	2Q5C	520	Air Afrique	EL-AIL (N2655Y) TN-AEE F-GFVR TN-AEE
21544	291	523	United Airlines	N7393F N979UA
21545	291	525	United Airlines	N7394F N980UA
21546	291	527	United Airlines	N7395F N981UA
21593	2H4	544	Southwest Airlines	N55SW
21596	229	529	SABENA World Airlines	OO-SBQ
21597	2A1	510	United Airlines	(PP-SNI) N7340F N974UA
21598	2A1	512	United Airlines	(PP-SNJ) N7341F N975UA
21599	2A1	514	Corsair	(PP-SNK) N1274E YS-08C N171AW F-GHXK
21612	2P6	528	Air South	A40-BH EI-CKK

BOEING 737

C/n	Series	Line No	Last known Operator/Owner	Previous Identities/fate (where known)
21613	2P6	530	AirTran Airways	(A6-HHK) A6-AAA N1PC N469AT*
21616	2L7	533	VASP	C2-RN6 (UR-) PP-SPG
21639	275	539	Canadian Airlines Intl	C-GGPW
21640	291	536	United Airlines	N7396F N982UA
21641	291	537	United Airlines	N7397F N983UA
21642	291	540	United Airlines	N7398F N984UA
21645	219	535	COPA	ZK-NAR N237TA HP-1297CMP
21653	268	531	Saudia	HZ-AGR
21654	268	532	Saudia	HZ-AGS
21665	201	534	US Air	N761N N223US
21666	201	547	US Air	N762N N224US
21667	201	548	US Air	N763N N225US
21677	2P6	538	Air South	A40-BI EI-CKW
21685	2L9	549	Air Ukraine	OY-APJ 9M-MBZ OY-APJ G-BKAP OY-APJ PP-SNO PT-WBA EI-CGZ UR-BFA
21686	2L9	550	Comair	OY-APK 9M-MBY OY-APK PP-SNK OY-APK PP-SNK PT-WBC EI-CHC TF-ABU ZS-NLN
21687	2Q8	554	Far Eastern Air Transport	N821L B-2615
21693	204	541	COPA	G-BFVA HP-1163CMP
21694	204	542	Sabre Airways	G-BFVB C-GNDW G-BFVB G-SBEA
21710	2R8C	546	Air Tanzania	N57001 5H-ATC
21711	2R8C	573	Air Tanzania	(5H-MRF) 5H-MRK
21712	275	556	Canadian Airlines Intl	C-GIPW
21713	275	598	Canadian Airlines Intl	C-GJPW
21714	248	565	East-West Airlines	EI-BEB VT-EWH EI-BEB VT-EWH
21715	248	579	East-West Airlines	EI-BEC TF-VLM EI-BEC VT-EWI EI-BEC VT-EWI
21716	217	560	Canadian Airlines Intl	N1262E C-GCPM
21717	217	581	Canadian Airlines Intl	C-GCPN
21718	217	584	Canadian Airlines Intl	C-GCPO
21719	2Q9	551	Aloha Airlines	OO-TEK C-GNDG OO-TEK C-GQDT C-GQBT OO-TEK C-GQBT OO-TEK N385PA OO-TEK C-GQBT OO-TEK C-GQBT OO-TEK N728AL N804AL
21720	2Q9	552	Aloha Airlines	N73AF N458AC (N6757A) N458AC N809AL
21721	2H4	553	Southwest Airlines	N56SW
21722	2H4	568	Southwest Airlines	N57SW
21723	2M2	567	TAAG-Angola Airlines	N1269E D2-TAH D2-TBD
21728	242C	580	Canadian Airlines Intl	C-GNDC
21729	205	572	Carnival Airlines	LN-SUK N73TH
21732	2H6	559	Bouraq Indonesia Airlines	9M-MBJ PK-IJF
21733	2P6	564	Air South	A40-BJ EI-CLK
21734	2P6	566	(Gulf Air)	A40-BK w/o 23Sep83 nr Abu Dhabi, UAE
21735	2Q8	582	Malev	OO-TEM N133AW EI-BTR HA-LEA
21736	2M8	557	Air Toulouse International	OO-TEL 4X-ABL OO-TEL PH-RAL OO-TEL TC-ATU OO-TEL G-BTEB G-IBTX F-GLXG
21738	229C	576	SABENA World Airlines	OO-SDR
21739	297	561	Aloha Airlines	N70723
21740	297	562	ELTA Electronics	N70724 4X-AOT stored Tel Aviv, Israel 15Sep95
21747	291	555	United Airlines	N7342F N985UA
21748	291	558	United Airlines	N7343F N986UA
21749	291	569	United Airlines	N7344F N987UA
21750	291	574	United Airlines	N7345F N988UA
21751	291	575	United Airlines	N7346F N989UA
21763	2R4C	571	(Sahara India Airlines)	7O-ACI N1269E LN-NPB (N4278L) N801WA N401MG (B-) N401MG VT-SIA w/o 08Mar94 Delhi, India
21765	205	595	Apple Vacations	LN-SUB N73FS [Op by Carnival Airlines]
21766	281	583	Air Nippon	JA8452
21767	281	585	Air Nippon	JA8453
21768	281	586	Air Nippon	JA8454
21769	281	587	Air Nippon	JA8455
21770	281	588	All Nippon Airways	JA8456
21771	281	594	All Nippon Airways	JA8457
21774	2S3	563	Delta Air Lines	N1787B G-BMHG (EI-BPY) OO-TYD EI-BPY N367DL
21775	2S3	570	Air Afrique	G-BMOR EI-BPR (G-BNZU) G-BMOR F-GHXL
21776	2S3	577	Delta Air Lines	G-BMEC EI-BPW N368DL N369DL
21790	236	599	British Airways Regional	N1275E N1285E G-BGDA
21791	236	626	British Airways	N8289V G-BGDB
21792	236	628	LAN-Chile	G-BGDC CC-CHR
21793	236	635	Comair	G-BGDD PH-TSE G-BGDD ZS-NNG
21794	236	643	British Airways	G-BGDE
21795	236	645	British Airways Regional	G-BGDF
21796	236	648	British Airways Regional	G-BGDG
21797	236	653	Comair	G-BGDH PH-TSD ZS-NNH
21798	236	658	British Airways Regional	G-BGDI
21799	236	660	British Airways Regional	G-BGDJ
21800	236	661	British Airways Regional	N5700N G-BGDK
21801	236	669	British Airways	G-BGDL
21802	236	670	LAN-Chile	G-BGDN CC-CHS
21803	236	677	British Airways	G-BGDO
21804	236	686	British Airways	N8280V G-BGDP
21805	236	697	British Airways	N1786B G-BGDR
21806	236	699	GB Airways	G-BGDS

BOEING 737

C/n	Series	Line No	Last known Operator/Owner	Previous Identities/fate (where known)					
21807	236	710	British Airways Regional	G-BGDT					
21808	236	712	GB Airways	G-BGDU					
21809	2M6C	637	Aloha Airlines	VR-UED	VS-UEB	V8-UEB	N805AL		
21810	2P5	604	(Thai Airways)	HS-TBB	w/o 15Apr85 nr Phuket, Thailand				
21811	2H4	609	Southwest Airlines	N59SW					
21812	2H4	611	Southwest Airlines	N60SW					
21815	201	589	US Air	N768N	N226US				
21816	201	592	US Air	N769N	N227AU				
21817	201	602	US Air	N772N	N228US				
21818	201	606	US Air	N773N	N229US				
21819	275	627	Canadian Airlines Intl	C-GKPW					
21820	210	578	Mandala Airlines	N491WC	4X-BAA	G-BKNH	PK-RIJ		
21821	210C	590	Alaska Airlines	N492WC	N743AS				
21822	210C	605	Alaska Airlines	N493WC	N744AS				
21839	229	593	Air One	OO-SBS	LX-OOO	OO-SBS	LX-OOO	OO-SBS	I-JETA
21840	229	617	Sobelair	OO-SBT					
21926	2S2C	597	ARAMCO	N201FE	N720A				
21927	2S2C	600	Aloha Airlines	N203FE	CC-CHU	N806AL			
21928	2S2C	603	ARAMCO	N204FE	N715A				
21929	2S2C	608	ARAMCO	N205FE	N716A				
21955	2M8	659	America West Airlines	OO-TEN	G-BHCL	OO-TEN	(4X-ABK)	OO-TEN	N141AW
21957	2S9	618	Gatari Hutama Airservices	N57008	VR-BEG	VR-BKO	N80CC	PK-HHS	
21959	2Q8	610	Alaska Airlines	N206FE	N741AS				
21960	2Q8	642	LADECO	G-BGTY	EI-BTW	G-IBTW	CC-CLD		
21970	2H4	613	Southwest Airlines	N61SW					
21973	2H3	607	Tunis Air	TS-IOC					
21974	2H3C	615	Tunis Air	TS-IOD					
21975	2Q9	612	US Air	N774N	N230AU				
21976	2Q9	625	US Air	N775N	N231US				
21980	291	596	United Airlines	N7374F	N990UA				
21981	291	601	United Airlines	N7348F	N991UA				
21990	200C		(Unknown Customer)	Allocated but later canx, not built					
22018	2Q8	651	US Air	N778N	N232US				
22022	205	616	Cayman Airways	LN-SUT	ZK-NAQ	N8032M	VR-CAL		
22023	2T5	636	Ryanair	G-BGTW	PH-TVX	OE-ILE	PH-TVX	EI-CKS	
22024	2T5	641	Canadian Airlines Intl	G-BGTV	EI-BPV	C-FHCP			
22025	2K2	647	Ryanair	PH-TVR	(D-AJAA)	PH-TVR	C-FICP	PH-TVR	EI-CKR
22026	236	644	British Airways	G-BGJE					
22027	236	654	British Airways	G-BGJF					
22028	236	656	Transaero	G-BGJG	(RA-71430)	G-BGJG	YL-BAA		
22029	236	662	British Airways	G-BGJH					
22030	236	693	British Airways	G-BGJI					
22031	236	722	British Airways	N8293V	G-BGJJ				
22032	236	742	Riga Airlines	G-BGJK	(YL-BAB)	G-BGJK	YL-BAB		
22033	236	743	(British Airways)	G-BGJL	dbf 22Aug85 Manchester, UK				
22034	236	751	Transaero	G-BGJM	(YL-LAC)	G-BGJM	LY-GBA	G-BGJM	YL-LAC
				G-BGJM	YL-BAC				
22050	268	622	Saudi Royal Flight	HZ-AGT	HZ-HM4	[Op by RSAF/1Sqdn]			
22051	297	634	Aloha Airlines	N725AL					
22054	2T4	624	Southwest Airlines	(N45AF)	N53AF	G-BJXL	N53AF	G-BJXL	C-GNDG
				G-BJXL	C-GNDG	G-BJXL	N702ML		
22055	2T4	633	AirTran Airways	(N46AF)	N54AF	G-BJXM	N54AF	G-BJXM	N54AF
				(N703ML)	N54AF	N705ML	XA-SLC	N467AT	
22056	2T2C	655	Canadian North	C-GDPA	(C-GWPW)	C-GDPA			
22057	204	621	Ryanair	(G-BGRU)	N8278V	G-BGYJ	EI-CJH		
22058	204	629	Ryanair	(G-BGRV)	G-BGYK	PP-SRW	G-BGYK	EI-CJG	
22059	204	631	(COPA)	(G-BGRW)	N8985V	G-BGYL	HP-1205CMP	w/o 06Jun92 Darien	
				Pass, nr Tucuti, Panama					
22060	2H4	638	Southwest Airlines	N62SW					
22061	2H4	639	Southwest Airlines	N63SW					
22062	2H4	640	Southwest Airlines	N64SW					
22070	2L9	614	VASP	OY-APL	(D-ADDA)	(D-AOUP)	OY-APL	C-GQBQ	C2-RN8
				PP-SPH					
22071	2L9	620	LACSA	OY-APN	SU-BCJ	(EI-BMB)	G-BJSO	(EI-BOG)	EI-BOJ
				G-BJSO	G-GPAB	EI-BOJ	VR-HKP	N281LF	
22072	2L9	623	Canadian Airlines Intl	OY-APO	C-GQBA	C2-RN9	C-FACP		
22074	242	619	AVIATECA	C-GNDM	VR-CYB	F-OHKA	N127GU		
22075	242	630	TACA International Airlines	N8536Z	C-GNDR	N238TA			
22086	275	667	Canadian Airlines Intl	C-GLPW					
22087	275	673	Canadian Airlines Intl	N8282V	C-GMPW				
22088	219	676	COPA	ZK-NAS	N318CM	HP-1288CMP			
22089	291	632	United Airlines	N7349F	N992UA				
22090	2M8	664	Malev	OO-TEO	4X-ABM	OO-TEO	TC-AJK	OO-TEO	HA-LEB
22113	230	649	Lufthansa	N5573K	D-ABFB				
22114	230	657	Lufthansa	N1782B	D-ABFA				
22115	230	694	Lufthansa	D-ABFC					
22116	230	701	Croatia Airlines	D-ABFD	RC-CTB	9A-CTB			
22117	230	703	Modiluft	D-ABFF	VT-MGD				
22118	230	704	Croatia Airlines	D-ABFH	RC-CTC	9A-CTC			
22119	230	714	Croatia Airlines	N8298V	D-ABFK	RC-CTA	9A-CTA		
22120	230	715	Modiluft	N8296V	D-ABFL	VT-MGA			

BOEING 737

C/n	Series	Line No	Last known Operator/Owner	Previous Identities/fate (where known)
22121	230	720	Modiluft	D-ABFM VT-MGB
22122	230	721	Modiluft	D-ABFN VT-MGC
22123	230	726	Lufthansa	D-ABFP
22124	230	727	Lufthansa	D-ABFR
22125	230	734	Bouraq Indonesia Airlines	D-ABFS PK-IJI D-ABFS PK-IJI
22126	230	735	Lufthansa	(D-ABFT) D-ABFU
22127	230	745	Lufthansa	(D-ABFU) N5573K D-ABFW
22128	230	752	Lufthansa	(D-ABFW) D-ABFX
22129	230	754	Merpati Nusantara Airlines	(D-ABFX) D-ABFY PK-MBC
22130	230	762	Bouraq Indonesia Airlines	(D-ABFY) D-ABFZ PK-IJJ D-ABFZ PK-IJJ
22131	230	764	Sempati Air	(D-ABFZ) D-ABHA (B-) D-ABHA PK-JHH
22132	230	769	Sempati Air	(D-ABHA) N8298V D-ABHB (B-) D-ABHB PK-JHI
22133	230	772	Lufthansa	(D-ABHB) D-ABHC (B-) D-ABHC
22134	230	777	Lufthansa	(D-ABHC) (D-ABHD) D-ABHF
22135	230	781	Lufthansa	(D-ABHD) (D-ABHF) D-ABHH
22136	230	783	Mandala Airlines	(D-ABHF) (D-ABHH) D-ABHK (B-) D-ABHK TF-ABY D-ABHK PK-RIM
22137	230	788	Mandala Airlines	(D-ABHH) (D-ABHK) N8297V D-ABHL TF-ABV D-ABHL PK-RIL
22138	230	790	Lufthansa	(D-ABHK) (D-ABHL) N1800B D-ABHM
22139	230	791	Lufthansa	(D-ABHL) (D-ABHM) D-ABHN
22140	230	793	Croatia Airlines	(D-ABHM) (D-ABHN) D-ABHP 9A-CTD
22141	230	795	Merpati Nusantara Airlines	(D-ABHN) (D-ABHP) D-ABHR PK-MBD
22142	230	797	Merpati Nusantara Airlines	(D-ABHP) (D-ABHR) D-ABHS PK-MBE D-ABHS PK-MBE
22143	230	838	Bouraq Indonesia Airlines	(D-ABHR) (D-ABHS) D-ABHU PK-IJK
22144	230		(Lufthansa)	(D-ABHS) (D-ABHT) Allocated but later canx, not built
22148	2S5C	663	Aloha Airlines	C-GENL N802AL
22159	275	684	Canadian Airlines Intl	C-GNPW
22160	275	688	Canadian Airlines Intl	N8288V C-GOPW
22161	2U4	652	Sahara India Airlines	G-BOSL G-ILFC (G-BPNY) G-WGEL VT-SIB
22255	217	666	Canadian Airlines Intl	C-GCPP
22256	217	672	Canadian Airlines Intl	C-GCPQ
22257	217	756	Canadian Airlines Intl	(C-GCPR) C-GCPS
22258	217	770	Canadian Airlines Intl	(C-GCPS) C-GCPT
22259	217	771	Canadian Airlines Intl	C-GCPU
22260	217	784	Canadian Airlines Intl	C-GCPV
22264	275	753	Canadian Airlines Intl	C-GPPW
22265	275	755	(CP Air)	N56807 C-GQPW dbf 22Mar84 Calgary, Canada
22266	275	765	Canadian Airlines Intl	C-GRPW
22267	2P5	685	(Thai Airways)	N57008 HS-TBC w/o 31Aug87 off Phuket, Thailand
22273	201	680	US Air	N779N N233US
22274	201	682	US Air	N780N N234US
22275	201	687	US Air	N781N N235US
22276	296	665	Canadian Airlines Intl	(C-GBQU) C-GQBB N8280V N387PA C-GQBB
22277	296	675	TACA International Airlines	(C-GQBV) N57001 C-GQBJ G-BJZV C-GQBJ N388PA C-GQBJ LN-BRL N232TA
22278	2S3	646	LAPA	G-BJFH EI-BXY TF-ABN AP-BEP (RP-C1383) AP-BEP LV-PHT LV-WJS
22279	2S3	650	East-West Airlines	G-BMSM EI-BRB N368DE VT-EWJ
22280	2A8	671	Indian Airlines	VT-EGD
22281	2A8	679	Indian Airlines	N8291V VT-EGE
22282	2A8	681	Indian Airlines	N8292V VT-EGF
22283	2A8	689	Indian Airlines	N8290V VT-EGG
22284	2A8	739	Indian Airlines	VT-EGH
22285	2A8	798	Indian Airlines	VT-EGI
22286	2A8	799	Indian Airlines	VT-EGJ
22296	2K2	668	Ryanair	PH-TVS EC-DVN PH-TVS LV-RAO PH-TVS LV-RBH PH-TVS PP-SRV PH-TVS EI-CKP
22300	284	674	Olympic Airways	SX-BCE
22301	284	683	Olympic Airways	SX-BCF
22338	284	691	Olympic Airways	N8292V SX-BCG
22339	284	692	Olympic Airways	SX-BCH
22340	2K6	678	Southwest Airlines	(HR-) CC-CIM N148AW N129SW
22341	217	786	Canadian Airlines Intl	C-GCPX
22342	217	810	Canadian Airlines Intl	C-GCPY
22343	284	695	Olympic Airways	SX-BCI
22352	201	728	US Air	N782N N236US
22353	201	731	US Air	N783N N237US
22354	201	736	US Air	N784N N239US
22355	201	741	US Air	N785N N240AU
22356	2H4	719	Southwest Airlines	(N65SW) N67SW
22357	2H4	725	Southwest Airlines	(N67SW) N68SW
22358	2H4	732	Southwest Airlines	(N68SW) N71SW
22364	204	696	Air New Zealand	G-BHWE ZK-NAB
22365	204	700	Air New Zealand	N57001 G-BHWF ZK-NAI
22367	2Q3	706	Japan Trans Ocean Airlines	JA8467
22368	2T4	707	LAPA	N52AF (EI-BOM) N52AF EI-BOM N52AF G-GPAA EI-BOM LV-WNA
22369	2T4	708	LAPA	N56AF (EI-BON) N56AF EC-DUL EI-BON LV-WNB
22370	2T4	716	TAESA	N57AF N139AW XA-SIW
22371	2T4	717	TAESA	N58AF N140AW XA-SIX

BOEING 737

C/n	Series	Line No	Last known Operator/Owner	Previous Identities/fate (where known)					
22383	291	713	United Airlines	N7350F	N993UA				
22384	291	718	United Airlines	N7351F	N994UA				
22395	2T5	729	NICA	G-BHVG	C-GEPM	9M-MBO	H4-SAL	N501NG	
22396	2T5	730	East-West Airlines	G-BHVH	(EI-B)	C-GVRE	A40-BM	VT-EWF	
22397	2T5	737	LAN-Chile	N5701E	G-BHVI	CC-CJW			
22398	296	733	US Air	(C-GQBE)	N789N	N238US			
22399	291	723	United Airlines	N7352F	N995UA				
22400	284	766	Olympic Airways	SX-BCK					
22401	284	780	Olympic Airways	SX-BCL					
22402	230	744	LACSA	D-ABFT	CS-TEV	N261LR			
22406	2L9	690	Air Toulouse International	N8295V	OY-APP	G-BNGK	F-GEXI		
22407	2L9	698	LAN-Chile	OY-APR	TS-IEB	OY-APR	EC-DXV	CC-CEE	
22408	2L9	705	LACSA	N8291V	OY-APS	Z-NAL	VR-HYL	N251LF	
22415	2K9	702	Damania Airways	G-DFUB	CS-TET	C-GQCA	CS-TET	VT-DPA	
22416	2K9	709	Damania Airways	N1786B	G-BMON	C-GPWC	G-BMON	C-GPWC	G-BMON
				C-GPWC	CS-TEU	C-GPWC	CS-TEU	VT-PDB	
22426	297	738	Aloha Airlines	N726AL	(N7660A)	N726AL			
22431	2V6	803	Petrolair Systems	N57008	HB-IEH				
22443	201	782	US Air	N786N	N241US				
22444	201	800	US Air	N787N	N242US				
22445	201	837	US Air	N788N	N243US				
22453	2Q8	748	Lithuanian Airlines	OO-RVM	TF-VLK	OO-RVM	G-BKMS	N143AW	G-BKMS
				VR-HYZ	(F-GHXH)	TC-JUS	HA-LEH	(LY-ABL)	LY-GPA
22456	291	740	United Airlines	N7353F	N996UA				
22457	291	757	United Airlines	N7354F	N997UA				
22458	2M8		(Trans European Airways)	Allocated but later canx, not built					
22473	2A8C	747	Indian Airlines	VT-EGM					
22504	2K9	804	VARIG	N4529W	PP-VNF				
22505	2K9	815	VARIG	(N4530W)	N1786B	N1800B	"VP-VNG"	PP-VNG	
22516	296	759	Canadian Airlines Intl	C-GQBH	G-BJZW	C-GQBH	N389PA	C-GQBH	
22529	2T4	750	Sierra Pacific Airlines	N51AF	EI-BRN	N703ML	N703S		
22531	2V5	724	Mandala Airlines	C6-BEH	N167PL	PK-RIK			
22575	2U9	749	America West Airlines	5W-PAL	N149AW	ZK-POL	5W-PAL	N149AW	ZK-NEF
				N149AW					
22576	2U4	761	East-West Airlines	G-OSLA	N134AW	EI-BTZ	G-IBTZ	VT-EWC	
22577	290C	760	Alaska Airlines	N730AS					
22578	290C	767	Alaska Airlines	N740AS					
22580	244	787	South African Airways	ZS-SIA	PP-SNW	ZS-SIA			
22581	244	796	South African Airways	ZS-SIB	D6-CAJ	ZS-SIB			
22582	244	805	South African Airways	ZS-SIC					
22583	244F	809	South African Airways	ZS-SID					
22584	244	821	South African Airways	ZS-SIE					
22585	244	828	South African Airways	ZS-SIF					
22586	244	829	South African Airways	ZS-SIG					
22587	244	835	South African Airways	ZS-SIH					
22588	244	836	South African Airways	ZS-SII					
22589	244	843	South African Airways	N8285V	ZS-SIJ	CC-CHK	ZS-SIJ		
22590	244	854	South African Airways	ZS-SIK					
22591	244	859	South African Airways	ZS-SIL					
22596	2K5	763	Bouraq Indonesia	N8279V	D-AHLD	N2941W	D-AHLD	YU-AOF	
22597	2K5	773	Air France	D-AHLE	EC-DTR	F-GFLV			
22598	2K5	792	Air France	N5573B	D-AHLF	EC-DUB	F-GFLX		
22599	2K5	814	Aigle Azur	D-AHLG	CS-TMD	D-AHLG	F-GMJD		
22600	2K5	816	Sheikh M.Edress	D-AHLH	CS-TME	D-AHLH	HZ-MIS		
22601	2K5	833	Sheikh M.Edress	N1800B	D-AHLI	YU-AOG	HZ-SIR		
22602	2A1	711	(LAN-Chile)	N8286V	CC-CHJ	dbr 05Aug87 Kalama, Chile			
22607	2V2	775	(TAME)	N8283V	HC-BIG	w/o 11Jul83 nr Cuenca, Ecuador			
22618	275C	813	Canada North	C-GSPW					
22619	275C		(Pacific Western Airlines)	(C-GTPW)	Allocated but later canx, not built				
22620	2H6	822	COPA	9M-MBK	HP-1245	HP-1245CMP			
22624	2H3	758	Tunis Air	TS-IOE					
22625	2H3	776	Tunis Air	TS-IOF					
22626	2M2	802	(TAAG-Angola Airlines)	D2-TBV	dbf 09Feb84 Huambo, Angola				
22627	2R6C	779	Air Guinee	3X-GCB					
22628	2W8	820	Ruler of Sharjah	N180RN	A6-ESH				
22629	297	842	Aloha Airlines	N728AL					
22630	297	860	America West Airlines	N729AL	N147AW				
22631	297	894	AirTran Airways	N730AL	N462AT				
22632	2T5	847	LADECO	G-BJBJ	CN-RMX	CN-RMH	CC-CYP		
22633	2S3	746	East-West Airlines	(G-BMMP)	G-DDDV	A40-BL	VT-EWD		
22634	230	840	Croatia Airlines	(D-ABHT)	D-ABHW	9A-CTE			
22635	230	774	(Condor Flug)	(D-ABHU)	N8279V	D-ABHD	w/o 02Jan88 nr Izmir, Turkey		
22636	230	808	First Security Bank of Utah	(D-ABHW)	D-ABHT	CS-TER	N271LR		
22637	230	848	Air Portugal	D-ABHX	CS-TES				
22638	204	858	Air New Zealand	N1780B	G-BJCT	EC-DXK	G-BJCT	ZK-NAA	
22639	204	863	Ryanair	G-BJCU	EC-DVE	G-BJCU	EI-CJE		
22640	204	867	Ryanair	G-BJCV	C-GXCP	G-BJCV	C-GCAU	G-BJCV	CS-TMA
				G-BJCV	EI-CJC				
22645	277	768	America West Airlines	VH-CZM	N178AW				
22646	277	778	America West Airlines	VH-CZN	N179AW				
22647	277	785	America West Airlines	VH-CZO	N180AW				

BOEING 737

C/n	Series	Line No	Last known Operator/Owner	Previous Identities/fate (where known)					
22648	277	789	America West Airlines	N56807	VH-CZP	N181AW			
22649	277	801	America West Airlines	VH-CZQ	N182AW				
22650	277	806	America West Airlines	VH-CZR	N183AW				
22651	277	819	America West Airlines	VH-CZS	N184AW				
22652	277	831	America West Airlines	VH-CZT	N185AW				
22653	277	832	America West Airlines	N8293V	VH-CZU	N186AW			
22654	277	862	America West Airlines	VH-CZV	N187AW				
22655	277	872	America West Airlines	VH-CZW	N188AW				
22656	277	876	America West Airlines	VH-CZX	N189AW				
22657	219	846	Air Afrique	(ZK-NAT)	N6066Z	N851L	G-BJXJ	F-GLXF	
22658	217	861	Canadian Airlines Intl	C-GCPZ					
22659	217	874	Canadian Airlines Intl	C-GFCP					
22660	2S3	849	COPA	(G-BMSR)	N5573L	G-BRJP	VR-HYK	HP-1234CMP	
22667	2P5	794	Shaheen Air International	N5573X	HS-TBD	AP-BEV			
22673	2H4	826	Southwest Airlines	N73SW					
22674	2H4	827	Southwest Airlines	N74SW					
22675	2H4	839	Southwest Airlines	N80SW					
22679	2X2	807	ARAMCO	DQ-FDM	N719A				
22680	200		(Unknown Customer)	Allocated but later canx, not built					
22697	2T4	817	Southwest Airlines	(N80AF)	N81AF	N721ML	N721WN		
22698	2T4	823	Southwest Airlines	(N81AF)	N82AF	N722ML	N722WN		
22699	2T4	855	Southwest Airlines	(N82AF)	N83AF	N130SW			
22700	2T4	885	Air Algerie	(N83AF)	N84AF	N4563H	7T-VEZ		
22701	2T4	886	Lithuanian Airlines	(N84AF)	N85AF	N4569N	LY-BSD		
22703	2E3	811	East-West Airlines	CC-BIN	EI-BRZ	EC-DYZ	G-BNZT	G-IBTY	VT-EWB
22726	2X4		(Supair)	(D-ADDB)	Allocated but later canx, not built				
22727	2X4		(Supair)	(D-ADDC)	Allocated but later canx, not built				
22728	217	911	Canadian Airlines Intl	N178EE	C-GJCP				
22729	217	915	Canadian Airlines Intl	C-GKCP					
22730	2H4	841	Southwest Airlines	N81SW					
22731	2H4	864	Southwest Airlines	N82SW					
22732	2H4	877	Southwest Airlines	N83SW					
22733	2L9	812	Aero Costa Rica	OY-MBZ	VR-HYN	N170PL			
22734	2L9	818	Les Ailes d'Haiti	OY-MBW	VR-HYM	N171PL			
22735	2L9	825	Mandala Airlines	OY-MBV	N164PL	B-2529	N164PL	PK-RIR	
22736	2Q3	896	Japan Trans Ocean Airlines	JA8475					
22737	2A3	830	PLUNA	CX-BON	PH-TSI	CX-BON	PH-TSI	G-BNIA	PH-TSI
				CX-BON	PH-TSI	CX-BON	PH-TSI	CX-BON	
22738	2A3	834	PLUNA	CX-BOO	PH-TSA	CX-BOO	PH-TSA	G-BONM	PH-TSA
				CX-BOO					
22739	2A3	844	PLUNA	N8295V	CX-BOP	PH-TSB	CX-BOP		
22741	291	871	United Airlines	N7355F	N998UA				
22742	291	875	(United Airlines)	N7356F	N999UA	w/o 03Mar91 nr Colorado Springs, CO			
22743	291	909	LAN-Chile	N7357F	(N34256)	N7357F	EI-BXW	CC-CEA	
22744	291	923	LAN-Chile	N7358F	(N34257)	N7358F	EI-BWY	VT-EQH	9J-AFM
				N7358F	CC-CDE				
22751	201	857	US Air	(N791N)	N798N	N245US			
22752	201	845	US Air	(N792N)	N791N	N244US			
22753	201	865	US Air	(N793N)	N792N	N246US			
22754	201	870	US Air	(N794N)	N793N	N247US			
22755	201	873	US Air	(N795N)	N794N	N248US			
22756	201	879	US Air	(N796N)	N795N	N249US			
22757	201	883	US Air	(N797N)	N796N	N251US			
22758	201	889	US Air	(N798N)	N797N	N252AU			
22760	2Q8	852	Air Liberte	N861L	F-GEXJ				
22761	2T7	850	Canadian Airlines Intl	G-DWHH	C-FPWD	G-DWHH	C-FPWD	G-DWHH	C-FPWD
				G-DWHH	C-FCPM				
22762	2T7	856	Canadian Airlines Intl	G-DGDP	C-FPWE	G-DGDP	C-FPWE	G-DGDP	C-FPWE
				G-DGDP	C-FCPN				
22766	2D6	853	Air Algerie	7T-VEY					
22767	2B6	851	Royal Air Maroc	CN-RML					
22771	2F9	866	Nigeria Airways	5N-ANW					
22772	2F9	884	(Nigeria Airways)	5N-ANX	dbr Port Harcourt, Nigeria 02Oct89; b/u Apr93				
22773	2F9	893	Nigeria Airways	5N-ANY					
22774	2F9	895	Nigeria Airways	5N-ANZ					
22775	2M2	869	(TAAG-Angola Airlines)	D2-TBN	w/o 08Nov83 Lubango, Angola				
22776	2M2	891	TAAG-Angola Airlines	N1782B	D2-TBO				
22777	2X9	868	SkU 5/TNI-AU	N1779B	AI-7301				
22778	2X9	947	SkU 5/TNI-AU	N8288V	AI-7302				
22779	2X9	985	SkU 5/TNI-AU	N1786B	AI-7303				
22792	2E3	887	America West Airlines	CC-CIY	N138AW				
22793	2T2	892	Lithunian Airlines	(C-GDPG)	N1779B	(C-GDPG)	N4571M	LY-BSG	
22795	201	912	US Air	N799N	N253AU				
22796	201	914	US Air	N802N	N254AU				
22797	201	916	US Air	N803N	N255AU				
22798	201	924	US Air	N804N	N256AU				
22799	201	932	US Air	N805N	N257AU				
22800	2T4	897	Air Algerie	(N86AF)	N4556L	7T-VJA			
22801	2T4	900	Air Algerie	(N87AF)	N4558L	7T-VJB			
22802	2T4	901	Air Ukraine International	(N88AF)	N6009F	B-2501	B-610L	UR-GAD	
22803	2T4	906	Malev	(N89AF)	N6018N	B-2502	B-614L	HA-LEI	

BOEING 737

C/n	Series	Line No	Last known Operator/Owner	Previous Identities/fate (where known)					
22804	2T4	908	Malev	(N90AF)	N6038E	B-2503	B-615L	HA-LEM	
22806	201	938	US Air	N806N	N259AU				
22807	275	834	Canadian Airlines Intl	C-GTPW					
22824	242		(Nordair)	Allocated but later canx, not built					
22826	2H4	878	Southwest Airlines	N85SW					
22827	2H4	882	Southwest Airlines	N86SW					
22828	244	881	South African Airlines	ZS-SIM					
22856	258	910	Arkia-Israeli AIrlines	4X-ABN	CC-CJK	4X-ABN			
22857	258	919	Arkia-Israeli AIrlines	4X-ABO	CC-CJM	4X-ABO			
22859	2J8	890	Delta Air Lines	ST-AIB	N4562N	N235WA			
22860	2A8	899	Indian Airlines	VT-EHE					
22861	2A8	902	Indian Airlines	VT-EHF					
22862	2A8	903	Indian Airlines	VT-EHG					
22863	2A8	907	Indian Airlines	VT-EHH					
22864	217	945	Canadian Airlines Intl	C-GMCP					
22865	217	960	Canadian Airlines Intl	C-GQCP					
22866	201	940	US Air	N807N	N260AU				
22867	201	961	US Air	N809N	N261AU				
22868	201	963	US Air	N810N	N262AU				
22869	201	964	US Air	N811N	N263AU				
22873	275	898	Canadian Airlines Intl	C-GUPW					
22874	275	904	Canadian Airlines Intl	C-GVPW					
22875	2E7	917	Ryanair	N4570B	4X-BAB	G-BMDF	(PK-RI.)	G-BMDF	EI-CJI
22876	2E7	922	Mandala Airlines	N4571A	4X-BAC	G-BLDE	4X-BAC	G-BLDE	PK-RII
22877	242C	880	Canadian Airlines Intl	C-GNDU					
22878	2B7	921	US Air	N310AU	N266AU				
22879	2B7	926	US Air	N311AU	N267AU				
22880	2B7	927	US Air	N312AU	N268AU				
22881	2B7	931	US Air	N313AU	N269AU				
22882	2B7	934	US Air	N314AU	N270AU				
22883	2B7	935	US Air	N315AU	N271AU				
22884	2B7	956	US Air	N316AU	N272AU				
22885	2B7	966	US Air	N317AU	N273AU				
22886	2B7	974	US Air	N318AU	N274AU	N274US			
22887	2B7	976	US Air	N319AU	N275AU				
22888	2B7	979	US Air	N320AU	N276AU				
22889	2B7	983	US Air	N321AU	N277AU				
22890	2B7	986	US Air	N322AU	N278AU				
22891	2B7	988	US Air	N323AU	N279AU				
22892	2B7	990	US Air	N324AU	N280AU				
22903	2H4	905	Southwest Airlines	N87SW					
22904	2H4	913	Southwest Airlines	N89SW					
22905	2H4	918	Southwest Airlines	N90SW					
22906	2K2	888	Ryanair	PH-TVU	C-FCAV	PH-TVU	G-BPLA	PH-TVU	EI-CKQ
22940	3H4	1037	Southwest Airlines	N300SW					
22941	3H4	1048	Southwest Airlines	N301SW					
22942	3H4	1052	Southwest Airlines	N302SW					
22943	3H4	1101	Southwest Airlines	N303SW					
22944	3H4	1138	Southwest Airlines	N304SW					
22945	3H4	1139	Southwest Airlines	N305SW					
22946	3H4	1148	Southwest Airlines	N306SW					
22947	3H4	1156	Southwest Airlines	N307SW					
22948	3H4	1160	Southwest Airlines	N309SW					
22949	3H4	1161	Southwest Airlines	N310SW					
22950	3B7	1001	US Air	N73700	N350AU	N371US			
22951	3B7	1007	Western Pacific Airlines	N351AU	N372US	N951WP	[Colorado Springs c/s]		
22952	3B7	1015	US Air	N352AU	N373US				
22953	3B7	1022	US Air	N353AU	N374US				
22954	3B7	1030	US Air	N354AU	N375US				
22955	3B7	1043	US Air	N355AU	N376US				
22956	3B7	1057	US Air	N356AU	N383US				
22957	3B7	1127	US Air	N357AU	N384US				
22958	3B7	1137	US Air	N358AU	N385US				
22959	3B7	1140	US Air	N359AU	N387US				
22961	201	984	US Air	N813N	N264AU				
22962	201	987	US Air	N814N	N265AU				
22963	2H4	929	Southwest Airlines	N91SW					
22964	2H4	933	Southwest Airlines	N92SW					
22965	2H4	942	Southwest Airlines	N93SW					
22966	204	946	Ryanair	(G-BKGU)	G-BKHE	EI-CJD			
22967	204	953	Ryanair	(G-BKGV)	G-BKHF	G-BTZF	EI-CJF		
22979	2T5	950	Malev	G-BKHO	HA-LEC				
22985	2F9	920	(Nigeria Airways)	5N-AUA	dbf 13Nov95 Kaduna, Nigeria				
22986	2F9	925	Nigeria Airways	5N-AUB					
22987	2F9		(Nigeria Airways)	(5N-AUC)	Allocated but later canx, not built				
22988	2F9		(Nigeria Airways)	(5N-AUD)	Allocated but later canx, not built				
22994	219C	928	Air New Zealand	ZK-NQC					
23000	228	930	Air France	N1787B	F-GBYA				
23001	228	936	Air France	F-GBYB					
23002	228	937	Air France	F-GBYC					
23003	228	939	Air France	F-GBYD					

BOEING 737

C/n	Series	Line No	Last known Operator/Owner	Previous Identities/fate (where known)					
23004	228	941	Air France	F-GBYE					
23005	228	943	Air France	F-GBYF					
23006	228	944	Air France	F-GBYG					
23007	228	948	Air France	F-GBYH					
23008	228	952	Air France	F-GBYI					
23009	228	958	Air France	F-GBYJ					
23010	228	959	Air France	F-GBYK					
23011	228	971	Air France	F-GBYL					
23023	291	957	Mandala Airlines	N7359F	(N67258)	N7359F	EI-BWZ	VT-EQI	CS-TMB
				EI-BWZ	TF-ABI	PK-RIQ			
23024	291	965	LAN-Chile	N7399F	EI-BWC	VT-EQJ	CS-TMC	EI-BWC	CS-TIS
				CC-CDG					
23036	2A8	977	Indian Air Force/12Sqdn	VT-EHW	K-2412				
23037	2A8	982	Indian Air Force/12Sqdn	VT-EHX	K-2413				
23038	2Y5	949	Air New Zealand	9H-ABA	ZK-NAF				
23039	2Y5	954	Air New Zealand	9H-ABB	ZK-NAH				
23040	2Y5	955	Pacific Airlines	9H-ABC	ZK-NAD	5B-DBF	[Op by TEA Cyprus]		
23041	282	962	Damania Airways	CS-TEK	VT-PDD				
23042	282	967	Damania Airways	CS-TEL	VT-PDC				
23043	282	972	Air Portugal	CS-TEM					
23044	282	973	Air Portugal	CS-TEN					
23045	282	978	Air Portugal	CS-TEO					
23046	282	981	Air Portugal	CS-TEP					
23047	282		(Air Portugal)	(CS-TEQ)	Allocated but later canx, not built				
23049	2B6C	951	Royal Air Maroc	CN-RMM					
23050	2B6C	975	Royal Air Maroc	CN-RMN					
23051	282C	1002	Air Portugal	CS-TEQ					
23053	2H4	968	Southwest Airlines	N94SW					
23054	2H4	969	Southwest Airlines	N95SW					
23055	2H4	970	Southwest Airlines	N96SW					
23059	2Z6	980	Royal Thai AF/Royal Flight	N45733	22-222				
23060	3T5	1069	Southwest Airlines	G-BLKB	N753MA	N668SW			
23061	3T5	1080	Southwest Airlines	G-BLKC	N744MA	N694SW			
23062	3T5	1083	Southwest Airlines	G-BLKD	N733MA	N692SW			
23063	3T5	1092	Southwest Airlines	G-BLKE	N752MA	N667SW			
23064	3T5	1527	Southwest Airlines	G-BNRT	EC-213	EC-ELV	G-BNRT	N748MA	N696SW
23065	2J6C	989	GPA Group	B-2504	(EI-BXM)	N675MA	stored Oklahoma City, OK		
				29Mar96					
23066	2J6C	992	Xiamen Airlines	B-2505	(EI-BX.)	N676MA	(B-2505)	N676MA	B-2505
23073	232	991	Delta Air Lines	N301DL					
23074	232	993	Delta Air Lines	N302DL					
23075	232	994	Delta Air Lines	N303DL					
23076	232	995	Delta Air Lines	N304DL					
23077	232	996	Delta Air Lines	N305DL					
23078	232	1000	Delta Air Lines	N306DL					
23079	232	1003	Delta Air Lines	N307DL					
23080	232	1004	Delta Air Lines	N308DL					
23081	232	1005	Delta Air Lines	N309DL					
23082	232	1006	Delta Air Lines	N310DA					
23083	232	1008	Delta Air Lines	N311DL					
23084	232	1009	Delta Air Lines	N312DL					
23085	232	1011	Delta Air Lines	N313DL					
23086	232	1012	Delta Air Lines	N314DA					
23087	232	1013	Delta Air Lines	N315DL					
23088	232	1018	Delta Air Lines	N316DL					
23089	232	1019	Delta Air Lines	N317DL					
23090	232	1020	Delta Air Lines	N318DL					
23091	232	1021	Delta Air Lines	N319DL					
23092	232	1023	Delta Air Lines	N320DL					
23093	232	1024	Delta Air Lines	N321DL					
23094	232	1026	Delta Air Lines	N322DL					
23095	232	1027	Delta Air Lines	N323DL					
23096	232	1028	Delta Air Lines	N324DL					
23097	232	1029	Delta Air Lines	N325DL					
23098	232	1031	Delta Air Lines	N326DL					
23099	232	1035	Delta Air Lines	N327DL					
23100	232	1038	Delta Air Lines	N328DL					
23101	232	1041	Delta Air Lines	N329DL					
23102	232	1045	Delta Air Lines	N330DL					
23103	232	1051	Delta Air Lines	N331DL					
23104	232	1062	Delta Air Lines	N332DL					
23105	232	1068	Delta Air Lines	N334DL					
23108	2H4	1014	Southwest Airlines	N102SW					
23109	2H4	1016	Southwest Airlines	N103SW					
23110	2H4	1017	Southwest Airlines	N104SW					
23113	2P5	1010	Thai International	HS-TBE	AP-BEW	HS-TBE			
23114	2B7	997	US Air	N325AU	N281AU				
23115	2B7	998	US Air	N326AU	N282AU				
23116	2B7	999	US Air	N327AU	N283AU				
23117	2Q3	1033	Japan Trans Ocean Airlines	JA8492					
23121	2X6C	1025	(Markair)	(N122NA)	N670MA	w/o 02Jun90 Unalakleet, AK			

BOEING 737

C/n	Series	Line No	Last known Operator/Owner	Previous Identities/fate (where known)					
23122	2X6C	1036	Aloha Airlines	(N133NA)	N671MA	(N170AW)	N671	N671MA	N671AW
				N671MA	TF-ABE	N816AL			
23123	2X6C	1042	Alaska Airlines	(N144NA)	N672MA	N746AS			
23124	2X6C	1046	Transmile	(N155MA)	N673MA				
23129	2R4C	1034	Alyemda-Air Yemen	70-ACQ					
23130	2R4C	1040	Alyemda-Air Yemen	70-ACR					
23131	2B7	1039	US Air	N328AU	N284AU				
23132	2B7	1044	US Air	N329AU	N285AU				
23133	2B7	1049	US Air	N330AU	N286AU				
23134	2B7	1050	US Air	N331AU	N287AU				
23135	2B7	1054	US Air	N332AU	N288AU				
23136	290C	1032	Alaska Airlines	N742AS					
23148	2Q8	1059	LADECO	N137AW	CC-CYV				
23152	3Z8	1073	Republic of Korea Air Force	85101					
23153	230	1076	Lufthansa	D-ABMA					
23154	230	1078	Lufthansa	D-ABMB					
23155	230	1079	Lufthansa	D-ABMC					
23156	230	1082	Lufthansa	D-ABMD					
23157	230	1085	Lufthansa	D-ABME					
23158	230	1089	Lufthansa	D-ABMF					
23159	236	1047	British Airways Regional	G-BKYA					
23160	236	1053	British Airways	G-BKYB					
23161	236	1055	British Airways	G-BKYC					
23162	236	1056	Cayman Airways	G-BKYD	VR-CEF	VR-CKX			
23163	236	1058	British Airways Regional	G-BKYE					
23164	236	1060	British Airways Regional	G-BKYF					
23165	236	1064	British Airways	G-BKYG					
23166	236	1067	British Airways Regional	G-BKYH					
23167	236	1074	British Airways	G-BKYI					
23168	236	1077	British Airways Regional	G-BKYJ					
23169	236	1081	British Airways Regional	G-BKYK					
23170	236	1086	British Airways Regional	G-BKYL					
23171	236	1088	British Airways Regional	G-BKYM					
23172	236	1091	British Airways Regional	G-BKYN					
23173	317	1098	Western Pacific Airlines	C-FCPG	PP-SNQ	PT-WBD	EI-CHQ	N946WP	
23174	317	1104	Southwest Airlines	C-FCPI	PP-SNR	N500MH	N775MA	N693SW	
23175	317	1110	Southwest Airlines	C-FCPJ	PP-SNS	PT-WBE	EI-CHU	N686SW	
23176	317	1213	Southwest Airlines	C-FCPK	PP-SNT	PT-WBF	EI-CHD	N698SW	
23177	317	1216	Frontier Airlines	C-FCPL	PP-SNU	PT-WBG	(EI-CGX)	EI-CHH	
23181	347	1087	Delta Air Lines	N3301					
23182	347	1106	Delta Air Lines	N302WA					
23183	347	1108	Delta Air Lines	N303WA					
23184	247	1061	Delta Air Lines	N236WA					
23185	247	1065	Delta Air Lines	N237WA					
23186	247	1066	Delta Air Lines	N238WA					
23187	247	1070	Delta Air Lines	N239WA					
23188	247	1071	Ukraine Intl Airlines	N240WA	B-2509	UR-GAC			
23189	247	1072	(Xiamen Airlines)	N241WA	B-2510	w/o 02Oct90 Canton, PRC			
23218	3G7	1076	America West Airlines	N150AW					
23219	3G7	1090	America West Airlines	N151AW					
23220	2M2	1084	TAAG-Angola Airlines	D2-TBP					
23225	236	1102	British Airways Regional	G-BKYO					
23226	236	1105	British Airways Regional	G-BKYP					
23228	301	1103	US Air	N301P	N300AU				
23229	301	1112	Western Pacific Airlines	N303P	N301AU	N950WP*	[Stardust Casino c/s]		
23230	301	1115	Western Pacific Airlines	N304P	N302AU	N949WP	[Simpson's c/s]		
23231	301	1164	US Air	N313P	N334US				
23232	301	1169	US Air	N314P	N335US				
23233	301	1200	US Air	N315P	N336US				
23234	301	1208	US Air	N316P	N337US				
23235	301	1214	US Air	N317P	N338US				
23236	301	1219	US Air	N319P	N339US				
23237	301	1222	US Air	N320P	N340US				
23238	301		(Piedmont Aviation)	Allocated but later canx, not built					
23239	301		(Piedmont Aviation)	Allocated but later canx, not built					
23240	301		(Piedmont Aviation)	Allocated but later canx, not built					
23241	301		(Piedmont Aviation)	Allocated but later canx, not built					
23242	301		(Piedmont Aviation)	Allocated but later canx, not built					
23249	2H4	1095	Southwest Airlines	N105SW					
23251	3A4	1063	Southwest Airlines	N307AC	N673AA				
23252	3A4	1094	Southwest Airlines	N308AC	N674AA	SU-BLN	N776MA	N674AA	
23253	3A4	1096	Southwest Airlines	N309AC	N675AA	TF-AIC	N675AA		
23254	3Q8	1107	Southwest Airlines	G-SCUH	N780MA	N688SW			
23255	3Q8	1125	Southwest Airlines	N841L	N399P	N327US	N662SW		
23256	3Q8	1128	Southwest Airlines	N871L	G-PROC	N397P	N329US	N663SW	
23257	301	1124	Frontier Airlines	N305P	(N310US)	N578US			
23258	301	1126	America West Airlines	N306P	(N328US)	N579US	N326AW*		
23259	301	1132	Western Pacific Airlines	N307P	(N330US)	N581US	N948WP		
23260	301	1146	America West Airlines	N309P	(N331US)	N582US	N325AW	N582US	N325AW
23261	301	1157	America West Airlines	N312P	(N332US)	N583US	N324AW	N583US	N324AW
23272	2T4	1093	Great Wall Airlines	B-2506					

BOEING 737

C/n	Series	Line No	Last known Operator/Owner	Previous Identities/fate (where known)
23273	2T4	1097	Great Wall Airlines	N5375S B-2507
23274	2T4	1099	Great Wall Airlines	N6067U B-2508
23283	275	1109	Canadian Airlines Intl	C-GWPW
23284	275		(CP Air)	Allocated but later canx, not built
23285	275		(CP Air)	Allocated but later canx, not built
23288	3A4	1100	Southwest Airlines	N301AC N676AA N742MA N676SW
23289	3A4	1182	Southwest Airlines	N303AC N677AA N735MA N677AA
23290	3A4	1205	Southwest Airlines	N304AC N678AA
23291	3A4	1211	Southwest Airlines	N306AA N679AA
23292	2X6C	1113	Aloha Airlines	N674MA N817AL
23294	340	1114	Pakistan Intl Airlines	AP-BCA
23295	340	1116	Pakistan Intl Airlines	AP-BCB
23296	340	1121	Pakistan Intl Airlines	AP-BCC
23297	340	1122	Pakistan Intl Airlines	AP-BCD
23298	340	1123	Pakistan Intl Airlines	AP-BCE
23299	340	1235	Pakistan Intl Airlines	AP-BCF
23302	3J6	1224	Air China	N1792B B-2531
23303	3J6	1237	Air China	N5573B B-2532
23310	3B7	1145	(US Air)	N360AU N388US w/o 01Feb91 Los Angeles, CA
23311	3B7	1149	US Air	N361AU N389US
23312	3B7	1162	US Air	N362AU N390US
23313	3B7	1177	US Air	N363AU N391US
23314	3B7	1179	US Air	N364AU N392US
23315	3B7	1210	US Air	N365AU N393US
23316	3B7	1212	US Air	N366AU N394US
23317	3B7	1221	US Air	N367AU N395US
23318	3B7	1234	US Air	N368AU N396US
23319	3B7	1250	US Air	N369AU N397US
23320	2H6	1120	Bouraq Indonesia Airlines	9M-MBL PK-IJG
23329	3H9	1134	JAT-Jugoslav Airlines	YU-AND
23330	3H9	1136	JAT-Jugoslav Airlines	YU-ANF
23331	3L9	1111	Western Pacific Airlines	OY-MMK EC-129 EC-EHA EC-783 EC-FKS N960WP [Western Pacific c/s]
23332	3L9	1118	Western Pacific Airlines	OY-MML EC-356 EC-EST EC-784 EC-FKC N961WP [Thrifty Car Rentals c/s]
23333	3H4	1183	Southwest Airlines	N311SW
23334	3H4	1185	Southwest Airlines	N312SW
23335	3H4	1201	Southwest Airlines	N313SW
23336	3H4	1229	Southwest Airlines	N314SW
23337	3H4	1231	Southwest Airlines	N315SW
23338	3H4	1232	Southwest Airlines	N316SW
23339	3H4	1255	Southwest Airlines	N318SW
23340	3H4	1348	Southwest Airlines	N319SW
23341	3H4	1350	Southwest Airlines	N320SW
23342	3H4	1351	Southwest Airlines	N321SW
23343	3H4	1377	Southwest Airlines	N322SW
23344	3H4	1378	Southwest Airlines	N323SW
23345	347	1170	Delta Air Lines	N304WA
23346	347	1172	Delta Air Lines	N305WA
23347	347	1173	Delta Air Lines	N306WA
23349	228	1135	Air France	F-GBYM
23351	2M2	1117	TAAG-Angola Airlines	D2-TBX
23352	3T0	1119	Continental Airlines	N16301
23353	3T0	1129	Continental Airlines	N59302
23354	3T0	1130	Continental Airlines	N77303
23355	3T0	1131	Continental Airlines	N61304
23356	3T0	1133	Continental Airlines	N63305
23357	3T0	1141	Continental Airlines	N17306
23358	3T0	1142	Continental Airlines	N14307
23359	3T0	1144	Continental Airlines	N14308
23360	3T0	1147	Continental Airlines	N17309
23361	3T0	1150	Continental Airlines	N16310
23362	3T0	1152	Continental Airlines	N69311
23363	3T0	1153	Continental Airlines	N60312
23364	3T0	1158	Continental Airlines	N12313
23365	3T0	1159	Continental Airlines	N71314
23366	3T0	1174	Continental Airlines	N34315
23367	3T0	1180	Continental Airlines	N17316
23368	3T0	1181	Continental Airlines	N17317
23369	3T0	1188	Continental Airlines	N12318
23370	3T0	1190	Continental Airlines	N12319
23371	3T0	1191	Continental Airlines	N14320
23372	3T0	1192	Continental Airlines	N17321
23373	3T0	1202	Continental Airlines	N12322
23374	3T0	1204	Continental Airlines	N10323
23375	3T0	1207	Continental Airlines	N14324
23376	3B7	1308	Western Pacific Airlines	N370AU N501AU N947WP [Broadmoor c/s]
23377	3B7	1320	America West Airlines	N371AU N502AU N328AW*
23378	3B7	1339	Western Pacific Airlines	N372AU N503AU N952WP [Colorado Tech c/s]
23379	3B7	1362	US Air	N373AU N504AU
23380	3B7	1366	US Air	N374AU N505AU

BOEING 737

C/n	Series	Line No	Last known Operator/Owner	Previous Identities/fate (where known)
23381	3B7	1394	US Air	N375AU N506AU
23382	3B7	1410	US Air	N376AU N507AU
23383	3B7	1425	US Air	N377AU N508AU
23384	3B7	1427	Western Pacific Airlines	N378AU N509AU N953WP*
23385	3B7	1440	US Air	N379AU N510AU
23386	2K9	1143	(Cameroon Airlines)	TJ-CBE w/o 03Dec95 nr Doula, Cameroons
23387	3Q8	1163	Southwest Airlines	(N781L) N152AW VR-CCW N734MA N689SW
23388	3Q8	1187	Southwest Airlines	N891L OO-ILG EC-EDM N317AW SE-DLG N103GU TG-AMA N103GU N687SW
23396	3W0	1166	Yunnan Provincial Aviation	N5573K B-2517
23397	3W0	1193	Yunnan Provincial Aviation	N1791B B-2518
23401	3Q8	1209	Southwest Airlines	OO-ILF G-BOWR N685SW
23404	2K9	1176	Malev	N700ML TC-JUU VR-BMX TC-JUU VR-BMX HA-LEK
23405	2K9	1178	ARAMCO	N701ML N714A
23406	3Q8	1215	Southwest Airlines	N153AW N732S N755MA N672SW
23411	3K2	1195	TAESA	PH-HVF CS-TIR PH-HVF XA-STM PH-HVF XA-STM
23412	3K2	1198	TAESA	PH-HVG XA-SLK PH-HVG XA-STN PH-HVG XA-STN
23414	3H4	1384	Southwest Airlines	N324SW
23415	3H9	1171	Bosphorus Airways	YU-ANH PP-SNY YU-ANH TC-CYO stored Dublin, Eire 29May93
23416	3H9	1175	JAT-Jugoslav Airlines	YU-ANI
23440	347	1218	Delta Air Lines	N307WA
23441	347	1220	Delta Air Lines	N308WA
23442	347	1239	Delta Air Lines	N309WA
23443	2T4	1151	Aloha Airlines	N1785B B-2511 N807AL
23444	2T4	1154	Xiamen Airlines	N1790B B-2512
23445	2T4	1155	Alaska Airlines	N1791B B-2514 N808AL
23446	2T4	1165	Xiamen Airlines	N1792B B-2515
23447	2T4	1167	Xiamen Airlines	N5573B B-2516
23448	3Z0	1168	China Southwest Airlines	N5573P B-2519
23449	3Z0	1184	China Southwest Airlines	N1789B B-2520
23450	3Z0	1196	China Southwest Airlines	N1790B B-2521
23451	3Z0	1240	China Southwest Airlines	N5573K B-2522
23455	3T0	1228	Continental Airlines	N14325
23456	3T0	1230	Continental Airlines	N17326
23457	3T0	1238	Continental Airlines	N12327
23458	3T0	1244	Continental Airlines	N17328
23459	3T0	1247	Continental Airlines	N17329
23460	3T0	1253	Continental Airlines	N70330
23462	317		(CP Air)	(C-FCPM) Allocated but later canx, not built
23463	317		(CP Air)	(C-FCPN) Allocated but later canx, not built
23464	205	1223	Japan Trans Ocean Airlines	LN-SUA PP-SPA LN-SUA JA8528
23465	205	1226	BP Exploration	LN-SUU PP-SPB LN-SUU N736BP [Op by Alaska Airlines]
23466	205	1236	ARCO	LN-SUZ PP-SPC LN-SUZ N733AR [Op by Alaska Airlines]
23467	205	1245	Japan Trans Ocean Airlines	LN-SUQ N890FS JA8577
23468	205	1262	HRH Talal bin Abdul Aziz	LN-SUJ N891FS HZ-TBA
23469	205	1266	Japan Trans Ocean Airlines	LN-SUV JA8366
23470	219	1186	Air New Zealand	ZK-NAT
23471	219	1189	Air New Zealand	ZK-NAU
23472	219	1194	Air New Zealand	ZK-NAV
23473	219	1197	Air New Zealand	ZK-NAW
23474	219	1199	Air New Zealand	ZK-NAX
23475	219	1203	Air New Zealand	ZK-NAY
23477	376	1225	Qantas Airways	N3281U VH-TAF
23478	376	1251	Qantas Airways	VH-TAG
23479	376	1259	Qantas Airways	VH-TAH
23481	2Q3	1241	Japan Trans Ocean Airlines	JA8250
23483	376	1264	Qantas Airways	VH-TAI
23484	376	1270	Qantas Airways	VH-TAJ
23485	376	1277	Qantas Airways	VH-TAK
23486	376	1286	Qantas Airways	VH-TAU
23487	376	1306	Qantas Airways	VH-TAV
23488	376	1352	Qantas Airways	VH-TAW
23489	376	1356	Qantas Airways	VH-TAX
23490	376	1390	Qantas Airways	VH-TAY
23491	376	1391	Qantas Airways	VH-TAZ
23495	3Y0	1206	Southwest Airlines	G-DHSW C-FPWD G-DHSW C-FPWD G-DHSW C-FPWD G-DHSW EC-635 EC-FVT N664WN
23496	3Y0	1217	Southwest Airlines	N67AB N682SW
23497	3Y0	1227	Southwest Airlines	G-MONF C-FPWE G-MONF C-FPWE G-MONF C-FPWE G-MONF N665WN
23498	3Y0	1233	Monarch Airlines	G-MONG C-GPWG G-MONG C-GPWG G-MONG [For easyJet Jun96]
23499	3Y0QC	1242	Vanguard Airlines	PT-TEA N303AL
23500	3Y0QC	1243	Vanguard Airlines	PT-TEB N304AL
23503	228	1256	Air France	F-GBYN
23504	228	1267	Air France	F-GBYO
23505	3A4	1318	Southwest Airlines	N310AC N680AA

BOEING 737

C/n	Series	Line No	Last known Operator/Owner	Previous Identities/fate (where known)					
23506	3Q8	1249	Southwest Airlines	N781L	G-PROK	EC-117	EC-EGQ	N318AW	(N381LF)
				N881LF	N730S	N730MA	N695SW		
23507	3Q8	1252	America West Airlines	N751L	N348AU	N398US	N327AW*		
23510	301	1248	US Air	N321P	N341US				
23511	301	1268	US Air	N322P	N342US				
23512	301	1291	US Air	N323P	N343US	N558AU			
23513	301	1327	US Air	N324P	N344US	N559AU			
23514	301	1331	US Air	N325P	N345US	N560AU			
23515	301	1355	US Air	N326P	N346US				
23516	247	1257	Delta Air Lines	N242WA					
23517	247	1261	Delta Air Lines	N243WA					
23518	247	1265	Delta Air Lines	N244WA					
23519	247	1299	Delta Air Lines	N245WA					
23520	247	1329	Delta Air Lines	N246WA	N373DL				
23521	247	1342	Delta Air Lines	N247WA	N374DL				
23522	330QC	1246	Lufthansa	N1786B	D-ABXA				
23523	330QC	1271	Lufthansa	D-ABXB					
23524	330QC	1272	Lufthansa	D-ABXC					
23525	330	1278	Lufthansa	D-ABXD					
23526	330	1282	Lufthansa	D-ABXE					
23527	330	1285	Lufthansa	D-ABXF					
23528	330	1290	Lufthansa	D-ABXH					
23529	330	1293	Lufthansa	D-ABXI					
23530	330	1297	Lufthansa	D-ABXK					
23531	330	1307	Lufthansa	D-ABXL					
23535	3Q8	1301	GECAS	EC-EAK	N102GU	stored Sep95			
23536	3Q8		(ILFC)	Allocated but later canx, not built					
23537	306	1275	KLM-Royal Dutch Airlines	PH-BDA					
23538	306	1288	KLM-Royal Dutch Airlines	PH-BDB					
23539	306	1295	KLM-Royal Dutch Airlines	PH-BDC					
23540	306	1303	KLM-Royal Dutch Airlines	PH-BDD					
23541	306	1309	KLM-Royal Dutch Airlines	PH-BDE					
23542	306	1317	KLM-Royal Dutch Airlines	PH-BDG					
23543	306	1325	KLM-Royal Dutch Airlines	PH-BDH					
23544	306	1335	KLM-Royal Dutch Airlines	PH-BDI					
23545	306	1343	KLM-Royal Dutch Airlines	PH-BDK					
23546	306	1349	KLM-Royal Dutch Airlines	PH-BDL					
23550	301	1367	US Air	N327P	N347US	N562AU			
23551	301	1380	US Air	N328P	N348US	N563AU			
23552	301	1382	US Air	N334P	N349US				
23553	301	1406	US Air	N335P	N350US				
23554	301	1408	US Air	N336P	N351US				
23555	301	1428	US Air	N337P	N352US				
23556	301	1435	US Air	N340P	N353US				
23557	301	1437	US Air	N341P	N354US				
23558	301	1449	US Air	N342P	N355US				
23559	301	1451	US Air	N348P	N356US				
23560	301	1463	US Air	N349P	N357US	N573US			
23561	301		(Piedmont Aviation)	(N350P)	Allocated but later canx, not built				
23562	301		(Piedmont Aviation)	(N352P)	Allocated but later canx, not built				
23563	301		(Piedmont Aviation)	(N353P)	Allocated but later canx, not built				
23564	301		(Piedmont Aviation)	(N354P)	Allocated but later canx, not built				
23565	301		(Piedmont Aviation)	(N355P)	Allocated but later canx, not built				
23569	3T0	1258	Continental Airlines	N13331					
23570	3T0	1263	Continental Airlines	N47332					
23571	3T0	1276	Continental Airlines	N69333					
23572	3T0	1296	Continental Airlines	N14334					
23573	3T0	1298	Continental Airlines	N14335					
23574	3T0	1328	Continental Airlines	N14336					
23575	3T0	1333	Continental Airlines	N14337					
23576	3T0	1338	Continental Airlines	N59338					
23577	3T0	1340	Continental Airlines	N16339					
23578	3T0	1358	Continental Airlines	N39340					
23579	3T0	1368	Continental Airlines	N14341					
23580	3T0	1373	Continental Airlines	N14342					
23581	3T0	1376	Continental Airlines	N39343					
23582	3T0	1383	Continental Airlines	N17344					
23583	3T0	1385	Continental Airlines	N17345					
23584	3T0	1396	Continental Airlines	N14346					
23585	3T0	1404	Continental Airlines	N14347					
23586	3T0	1411	Continental Airlines	N69348					
23587	3T0	1413	Continental Airlines	N12349					
23588	3T0	1448	Continental Airlines	N18350					
23589	3T0	1466	Continental Airlines	N69351					
23590	3T0	1468	Continental Airlines	N70352					
23591	3T0	1472	Continental Airlines	N70353					
23592	3T0	1476	Continental Airlines	N76354					
23593	3T0	1478	Continental Airlines	N76355					
23594	3B7	1442	US Air	N380AU	N511AU				
23595	3B7	1450	US Air	N381AU	N512AU				
23596	347	1269	Delta Air Lines	N2310					

BOEING 737

C/n	Series	Line No	Last known Operator/Owner	Previous Identities/fate (where known)					
23597	347	1287	Delta Air Lines	N311WA					
23598	347	1289	Delta Air Lines	N312WA					
23599	347	1324	Delta Air Lines	N313WA					
23601	3Z9	1254	Lauda Air	(OE-FGW)	OE-ILF				
23602	247	1347	Delta Air Lines	N248WA	N375DL				
23603	247	1361	Delta Air Lines	N249WA	N376DL				
23604	247	1369	Delta Air Lines	(N254WA)	N377DL				
23605	247	1371	Delta Air Lines	(N255WA)	N378DL				
23606	247	1379	Delta Air Lines	(N256WA)	N379DL				
23607	247	1387	Delta Air Lines	(N257WA)	N380DL				
23608	247	1399	Delta Air Lines	(N258WA)	N381DL				
23609	247	1403	Delta Air Lines	(N259WA)	N382DL				
23625	33A	1283	America West Airlines	(N3281V)	N164AW				
23626	33A	1284	America West Airlines	(N3281W)	N165AW				
23627	33A	1302	America West Airlines	(N3281Y)	N166AW				
23628	33A	1304	America West Airlines	(N3282G)	N167AW				
23629	33A	1311	America West Airlines	(N3282N)	N168AW				
23630	33A	1312	America West Airlines	(N3282P)	N169AW				
23631	33A	1337	America West Airlines	(N3282R)	N172AW				
23632	33A	1344	America West Airlines	(N3282V)	N173AW				
23633	33A	1421	America West Airlines	(N3282W)	N174AW				
23634	33A	1423	America West Airlines	(N3282X)	N175AW				
23635	33A	1436	Air France	N3282Y	N6069P	G-OUTA	F-GFUA		
23636	33A	1438	America West Airlines	N3283G	N1789B	EC-135	EC-EHJ	N509DC	(G-TEAD)
				N509DC					
23642	322	1300	United Airlines	N301UA					
23643	322	1315	United Airlines	N302UA					
23644	322	1322	United Airlines	N303UA					
23646	301		(Piedmont Aviation)	(N350P)	Allocated but later canx, not built				
23647	301		(Piedmont Aviation)	(N352P)	Allocated but later canx, not built				
23648	301		(Piedmont Aviation)	(N353P)	Allocated but later canx, not built				
23649	301		(Piedmont Aviation)	(N354P)	Allocated but later canx, not built				
23650	301		(Piedmont Aviation)	(N355P)	Allocated but later canx, not built				
23653	377	1260	Ansett Australia	VH-CZA					
23654	377	1273	Ansett Australia	N5573B	VH-CZB				
23655	377	1274	Ansett Australia	VH-CZC					
23656	377	1279	Ansett Australia	VH-CZD					
23657	377	1280	Ansett Australia	VH-CZE					
23658	377	1281	Ansett Australia	VH-CZF					
23659	377	1292	Ansett Australia	VH-CZG					
23660	377	1294	Ansett Australia	VH-CZH					
23661	377	1314	Ansett Australia	VH-CZI					
23662	377	1316	Ansett Australia	VH-CZJ					
23663	377	1323	Ansett Australia	VH-CZK					
23664	377	1326	Ansett Australia	VH-CZL					
23665	322	1330	United Airlines	N304UA					
23666	322	1332	United Airlines	N305UA					
23667	322	1334	United Airlines	N306UA					
23668	322	1346	United Airlines	N307UA					
23669	322	1354	United Airlines	N308UA					
23670	322	1364	United Airlines	N309UA					
23671	322	1370	United Airlines	N310UA					
23672	322	1470	United Airlines	N311UA					
23673	322	1479	United Airlines	N312UA					
23674	322	1481	United Airlines	N313UA					
23675	322	1483	United Airlines	N314UA					
23677	2N0	1313	Air Zimbabwe	Z-WPA					
23678	2N0	1405	Air Zimbabwe	Z-WPB					
23679	2N0	1415	Air Zimbabwe	Z-WPC					
23680	3Y0		(GPA Group)	Allocated but later canx, not built					
23681	3Y0		(GPA Group)	Allocated but later canx, not built					
23682	3Y0		(GPA Group)	Allocated but later canx, not built					
23683	3Y0		(GPA Group)	Allocated but later canx, not built					
23684	3Y0	1353	America West Airlines	EI-BTF	F-GLTF	EC-255	EC-FQB	N323AW	
23685	3Y0QC	1357	Aeropostale	G-MONH	F-GIXJ				
23689	3H4	1398	Southwest Airlines	N325SW					
23690	3H4	1400	Southwest Airlines	N326SW					
23691	3H4	1407	Southwest Airlines	N327SW					
23692	3H4	1521	Southwest Airlines	N328SW					
23693	3H4	1525	Southwest Airlines	N329SW					
23694	3H4	1529	Southwest Airlines	N330SW					
23695	3H4	1536	Southwest Airlines	N331SW					
23696	3H4	1545	Southwest Airlines	N332SW					
23697	3H4	1547	Southwest Airlines	N333SW					
23699	3B7	1452	(US Air)	N382AU	N513AU	w/o 08Sep94 nr Pittsburg, PA			
23700	3B7	1461	US Air	N383AU	N514AU				
23701	3B7	1464	US Air	N384AU	N515AU				
23702	3B7	1475	US Air	N385AU	N516AU				
23703	3B7	1480	US Air	N386AU	N517AU				
23704	3B7	1488	US Air	N387AU	N518AU				
23705	3B7	1497	US Air	N388AU	N519AU				

BOEING 737

C/n	Series	Line No	Last known Operator/Owner	Previous Identities/fate (where known)
23706	3B7	1499	US Air	N389AU N520AU
23707	375	1388	Air Europa	(C-GYPW) EC-ECS EC-782 EC-FKI
23708	375	1395	Orbi Georgian Airlines	(C-GZPW) PT-TEC 4L-AAA
23712	3S3	1336	America West Airlines	G-BMTE EC-EBZ G-BMTE EC-355 EC-EBZ N313AW
23713	3S3	1341	America West Airlines	G-BMTF EC-ECA G-BMTF EC-429 EC-ECA G-BMTF N316AW
23714	3H9	1305	Bosphorus Airlines	YU-ANJ TC-MIO stored Dublin, Eire
23715	3H9	1310	JAT-Jugoslav Airlines	YU-ANK
23716	3H9	1321	Tunis Air	YU-ANL TS-IEC stored Tunis, Tunisia Nov92
23717	3L9	1365	Germania Flug	OY-MMM G-EURR D-AGEH
23718	3L9	1402	Air Holland Regional	OY-MMN G-BOZA PH-OZA G-BOZA PH-OZA
23733	3S3	1345	America West Airlines	G-BMTG N314AW
23734	3S3	1359	America West Airlines	G-BMTH N315AW
23738	3K2	1360	Transavia Airlines	PH-HVJ
23739	301	1469	US Air	N350P N358US N574US
23740	301	1477	US Air	N352P N359US N575US
23741	301	1498	US Air	N353P N360US N576US
23742	301	1502	US Air	N354P N361US N577US
23743	301	1510	US Air	N355P (N362US) N584US
23747	3Y0	1363	America West Airlines	EC-EBX EI-BZS SE-DLN PP-SOA PT-WBH EI-CHA EC-377 EC-FRZ XA-SIY EC-667 EC-FYE EI-CKV
23748	3Y0	1381	Western Pacific Airlines	EC-EBY EI-BZT SE-DLO PP-SOB SE-DLO PP-SOB (OO-IIE) EI-BZT EC-356 EC-FRP XA-SIZ SE-DLO N962WP [Winter Wonder Plane c/s]
23749	3Y0	1389	Air Europa	EC-ECR EC-781 EC-FKJ
23750	3Y0	1431	Air Europa	PT-TED EC-135 EC-GEQ
23752	3A4	1484	Southwest Airlines	(N311AC) (N681AA) N32836 N747BH EC-167 EC-EHX EC-591 EC-FFB N736S N758MA N669SW
23753	3A4		(American Airlines)	(N312AC) (N682AA) Allocated but later canx, not built
23754	3A4		(American Airlines)	(N313AC) (N683AA) Allocated but later canx, not built
23755	3A4		(American Airlines)	(N314AC) (N684AA) Allocated but later canx, not built
23766	3Q8QC	1375	Air Belgium	N1716B G-BNCT N315SC EC-153 EC-EHM N188LF N101GU VH-NJE OO-ILK
23768	3Q8		(ILFC)	Allocated but later canx, not built
23771	329	1430	SABENA World Airlines	OO-SDV
23772	329	1432	SABENA World Airlines	OO-SDW
23773	329	1441	SABENA World Airlines	OO-SDX
23774	329	1443	SABENA World Airlines	OO-SDY
23775	329	1412	Sobelair	OO-SBZ
23776	3G7	1417	America West Airlines	N154AW
23777	3G7	1419	America West Airlines	N155AW
23778	3G7	1455	America West Airlines	N156AW
23779	3G7	1457	America West Airlines	N157AW
23780	3G7	1459	America West Airlines	N158AW
23781	3G7	1494	Southwest Airlines	N159AW TC-JTB N784MA N691WN
23782	3G7	1496	America West Airlines	N160AW
23783	3G7	1531	Southwest Airlines	N161AW SE-DPN TC-JTC N785MA N690SW
23784	3G7	1533	Southwest Airlines	N162AW SE-DPO N779MA N670SW
23785	3G7	1535	Southwest Airlines	N163AW N778MA N671SW
23786	3K2	1386	PLUNA	PH-HVK SU-BLC PH-HVK SU-BLR PH-HVK XA-SIH PH-HVK XA-SVQ PH-HVK CX-
23787	3S3	1374	Western Pacific	EC-ECM G-BNXP EC-155 EC-ECM G-BNXP EC-276 EC-ECM G-BNXP OO-CYE CC-CYE N375TA
23788	3S3QC	1393	Aeropostale	EC-ECQ G-BOYN EC-277 EC-ECQ G-BOYN G-NAFH N851LF 5W-FAX N271LF F-GIXH
23789	25A	1392	LACSA	N723ML N222AW N239TA
23790	25A	1422	Air Namibia	N724ML V5-ANA
23791	25A	1486	Aloha Airlines	N725ML N685MA N819AL*
23792	228	1397	Air France	F-GBYP
23793	228	1426	Air France	F-GBYQ
23794	27A	1424	Far East Air Transport	B-2625
23795	209	1319	(China Airlines)	B-180 w/o 26Oct89 Hualien, RoC
23796	209	1420	China Airlines	B-182
23797	3K9	1416	VARIG	PP-VNU
23798	3K9	1429	VARIG	PP-VNV
23800	39A	1409	Aviation Inc	VR-CBZ VR-CCD N117DF N253DV
23808	375	1434	Air Europa	(C-) PT-TEE EC-136 EC-GEU
23809	348QC	1458	Aeropostale	N1786B EI-BUD EC-279 EC-FQP EI-BUD F-OGSY F-GIXI
23810	348QC	1474	Aeropostale	EI-BUE EC-375 EC-FSC EI-BUE F-OCHS F-GIXL
23811	3S3QC	1445	Lufthansa Cargo Airlines	G-BNPA C-FGHQ G-BNPA G-DIAR N841LF D-ABWS
23812	3Y0	1511	TransBrasil	PT-TEI
23826	317	1372	Southwest Airlines	EI-BTM PP-SNV PT-WBI EI-CHE EC-376 EC-FSA EI-CHE N699SW
23827	33A	1444	Air Portugal	LN-NOR G-BNXW LN-NOR G-BNXW LN-NOR G-BNXW CS-TKD (LN-NOR) CS-TKD 9H-ACT CS-TIN
23828	33A	1446	VARIG	PP-VNT
23829	33A	1460	VARIG	PP-VNX
23830	33A	1462	Air Portugal	N5573K LN-NOS G-BRXJ LN-NOS CS-TKC (LN-NOS) CS-TKC 9H-ACS CS-TIO
23831	33A	1471	Ansett Australia	G-OBMA VH-CZV

BOEING 737

C/n	Series	Line No	Last known Operator/Owner	Previous Identities/fate (where known)
23832	33A	1473	Ansett Australia	G-OBMB VH-CZW
23833	330	1439	Germania Flug	D-ABWA
23834	330	1454	Condor Flug	D-ABWB
23835	330QC	1465	Lufthansa Cargo Airlines	D-ABWC
23836	330QC	1508	Lufthansa Cargo Airlines	D-ABWD
23837	330QC	1514	Lufthansa Cargo Airlines	D-ABWE
23838	3T0	1505	Southwest Airlines	N75356 N319AW N764MA N697SW
23839	3T0	1507	Government of PRC	N19357 B-4008
23840	2T0	1516	Government of PRC	N27358 B-4009
23841	3T0	1518	Continental Airlines	N18359 N301AL N19357
23847	2Y5	1414	Air Malta	9H-ABE
23848	2Y5	1418	Air Malta	9H-ABF
23849	2H6	1453	(AVIATECA)	9M-MBM N125GU w/o 09Aug95 nr San Salvador, Salvador
23856	3B7	1501	US Air	N390AU N521AU
23857	3B7	1503	US Air	N391AU N522AU
23858	3B7	1509	US Air	N392AU N523AU
23859	3B7	1551	US Air	N393AU N524AU
23860	3B7	1560	US Air	N394AU N525AU
23861	3B7	1584	US Air	N395AU N526AU
23862	3B7	1586	US Air	N396AU N527AU
23865	4Y0	1582	Modiluft	G-UKLA 9M-MLC G-UKLA VT-MGE
23866	4Y0	1589	China Xinhua Airlines	TC-ADA VT-EWL EI-CMO
23867	4Y0	1603	(British Midland)	G-OBME w/o 08Jan89 Kegworth, UK
23868	4Y0	1616	British Midland	G-OBMF
23869	4Y0	1639	Asiana Airlines	HL7251
23870	4Y0	1647	British Midland	N1791B (TC-...) G-OBMG
23871	330	1433	Lufthansa	D-ABXM
23872	330	1447	Lufthansa	D-ABXN
23873	330	1489	Lufthansa	D-ABXO
23874	330	1495	Lufthansa	D-ABXP
23875	330	1500	Lufthansa	D-ABXR
23876	401	1528	US Air	(N404P) N406US
23877	401	1543	US Air	(N405P) N407US
23878	401	1561	US Air	(N406P) N408US
23879	401	1573	US Air	(N407P) N409US
23880	401	1596	US Air	(N408P) N411US
23881	401	1610	US Air	(N409P) N412US
23882	401	1621	US Air	(N410P) N413US
23883	401	1631	US Air	(N412P) N415US
23884	401	1643	(US Air)	(N414P) N416US dbr 20Sep89 New York-La Guardia, NY
23885	401	1512	US Air	(N403P) N405US
23886	401	1487	US Air	(N402P) N73700 N404US
23912	2K3	1401	Aviogenex	YU-ANP
23913	209	1579	China Airlines	(B-184) B-1876
23914	260	1456	(Ethiopian Airlines)	ET-AJA w/o 15Sep88 nr Bahar Dar, Ethiopia
23915	260	1583	Ethiopian Airlines	ET-AJB
23921	3Y0	1513	Air Holland Charter	EI-BTT F-GLTT 5B-CIO PH-OZB
23922	3Y0	1538	Air Atlanta Icelandic	EC-151 EC-EHZ EI-BZO PP-VOM (PH-...) N922AB TF-ABK
23923	3Y0	1540	Monarch Airlines	EC-152 EC-EIA EI-BZP (LN-AEQ) EI-BZP (N117AW) G-TEAB EI-CEE EI-BZP EC-898 EC-FJZ G-BWJA
23924	3Y0	1542	Eurobelgian Airlines	G-BNGL XA-SEM OO-LTV
23925	3Y0	1544	Eurobelgian Airlines	G-BNGM XA-SEO OO-LTY
23926	3Y0	1562	TAT European Airlines	PT-TEJ F-G
23927	3Y0	1580	TAT European Airlines	PT-TEK F-GLLE
23930	301	1539	US Air	N357P N585US
23931	301	1552	US Air	N358P N586US
23932	301	1554	US Air	N359P N587US
23933	301	1559	US Air	(N360P) N588US
23934	301	1563	US Air	(N361P) N589US
23935	301	1569	US Air	(N362P) N590US
23936	301	1575	US Air	(N364P) N591US
23937	301	1587	US Air	(N365P) N592US
23938	3H4	1549	Southwest Airlines	N334SW
23939	3H4	1553	Southwest Airlines	N335SW
23940	3H4	1557	Southwest Airlines	N336SW
23941	3T0	1520	Southwest Airlines	N76360 EC-138 EC-EID N684WN
23942	3T0	1522	Continental Airlines	N76361 G-BOLM N320AW N17356
23943	3T0	1558	Continental Airlines	N76362 N302AL N14358
23944	3T0		(Continental Airlines)	(N76363) Allocated but later canx, not built
23945	3T0		(Continental Airlines)	(N77364) Allocated but later canx, not built
23946	3T0		(Continental Airlines)	(N78365) Allocated but later canx, not built
23947	322	1485	United Airlines	N315UA
23948	322	1491	United Airlines	N316UA
23949	322	1493	United Airlines	N317UA
23950	322	1504	United Airlines	N318UA
23951	322	1532	United Airlines	N319UA
23952	322	1534	United Airlines	N320UA
23953	322	1546	United Airlines	N321UA
23954	322	1548	United Airlines	N322UA
23955	322	1550	United Airlines	N323UA

BOEING 737

C/n	Series	Line No	Last known Operator/Owner	Previous Identities/fate (where known)
23956	322	1564	United Airlines	N324UA
23957	322	1566	United Airlines	N325UA
23958	322	1568	United Airlines	N326UA
23959	3H4	1567	Southwest Airlines	N337SW
23960	3H4	1571	Southwest Airlines	N338SW
23970	35B	1467	Germania Flug	D-AGEA
23971	35B	1482	Germania Flug	D-AGEB
23972	35B	1537	Germania Flug	D-AGEC
23976	4Y0	1651	Asiana Airlines	HL7252
23977	4Y0	1655	Asiana Airlines	HL7253
23978	4Y0	1659	Asiana Airlines	HL7254
23979	4Y0	1661	Eurobelgian Airlines	EC-239 EC-EMI EI-CEV XA-SCA OO-SBN
23980	4Y0	1667	Asiana Airlines	HL7255
23981	4Y0	1678	Pegasus Airlines	EC-251 EC-EMY EI-CEW SU-BLL F-GNFS EI-CEW TC-AFZ
23984	401	1674	US Air	N417US
23985	401	1676	US Air	N418US
23986	401	1684	US Air	N419US
23987	401	1698	US Air	N420US
23988	401	1714	US Air	N421US
23989	401	1716	US Air	N422US
23990	401	1732	US Air	N423US
23991	401	1746	US Air	N424US
23992	401	1764	US Air	N425US
24008	3G7	1576	Southwest Airlines	N301AW N683SW
24009	3G7	1578	America West Airlines	N302AW
24010	3G7	1606	America West Airlines	N303AW
24011	3G7	1608	America West Airlines	N304AW
24012	3G7	1612	America West Airlines	N305AW
24020	3M8	1614	TEA Italy	(OO-BTA) OO-LTA I-TEAA
24021	3M8QC	1630	Singapore Airlines	(OO-BTB) (F-ODSU) OO-LTB (F-GKTE) OO-LTB N40495 9V-SQZ
24022	3M8	1662	TEA Italy	(OO-BTC) OO-LTC I-TEAE
24023	3M8	1675	TEA Basel	(OO-BTD) (OO-LTD) HB-IIA
24024	3M8	1689	TEA Basel	(OO-BTE) (OO-LTE) HB-IIB
24025	33A	1556	Air France	F-GFUB G-MONU F-GHVO
24026	33A	1595	Air France	F-GFUC G-MONT F-GHVM
24027	33A	1597	Air France	F-GFUD
24028	33AQC	1599	Aeropostale	G-MONP F-GIXK
24029	33A	1601	Ansett Australia	G-MONN VH-CZX
24030	33A	1654	TAESA	G-OBMC XA-SGJ VH-CZS*
24031	2Y5	1523	Aloha Airlines	9H-ABG N810AL
24059	3S3	1517	Philippine Airlines	G-BNPB C-FGHT G-BNPB EC-711 EC-FGG RP-C4006
24060	3S3	1519	Philippine Airlines	G-BNPC N312AW RP-C4005
24068	3Q8	1506	Nordic East International	G-BNNJ G-OCHA SE-DTP
24069	4Q8	1635	GB Airways	G-BNNK
24070	4Q8	1665	GB Airways	G-BNNL
24081	3Z9	1515	Lauda Airways	OE-ILG
24090	3H4	1591	Southwest Airlines	N339SW
24091	3H4	1593	Southwest Airlines	N341SW
24092	33A	1669	British Midland	G-OBMD
24093	33A	1727	VARIG	G-PATE PP-VOR
24094	33A	1729	Air Caledonie International	F-ODGX
24095	33A	1737	Govt of Mexico/Estado Mayor Presidencial	N731XL TP-02/XC-UJB
24096	33A	1739	Jet Airways	PP-SNW G-BUSL VT-JAC
24097	33A	1741	Jet Airways	(PP-SNX) PP-SNZ G-BUSM VT-JAD
24098	33A	1763	TAESA	G-IEAA XA-SLY PH-HVI XA-SLY PH-HVI XA-SLY PH-HVI XA-SLY
24099	33A		(Nordstress)	Allocated but later canx, not built
24100	33A		(Nordstress)	Allocated but later canx, not built
24103	2Q3	1565	Japan Trans Ocean Airlines	(JA8419) JA8282
24123	46B	1663	British Midland	N1790B G-BOPJ G-OBMN
24124	46B	1679	AMC Aviation	G-BOPK N689MA EC-655 EC-FYG SU-SAA
24125	4K5	1689	Hapag Lloyd	D-AHLJ
24126	4K5	1697	Hapag Lloyd	D-AHLK
24127	4K5	1707	Hapag Lloyd	D-AHLL
24128	4K5	1715	Hapag Lloyd	D-AHLO
24129	4K5	1783	Hapag Lloyd	D-AHLP
24130	4K5	1827	Hapag Lloyd	D-AHLQ
24131	3Q8	1541	SATA Air Acores	EC-159 EC-EII EC-592 EC-FFC OO-LTX CS-TGP
24132	3Q8QC	1555	Aeropostale	EC-160 EC-EIR EC-593 EC-FET N241LF F-
24133	3H4	1682	Southwest Airlines	N342SW
24139	2K3	1530	Aviogenex	YU-ANU
24140	3H9	1524	JAT-Jugoslav Airlines	YU-ANV
24141	3H9	1526	JAT-Jugoslav Airlines	YU-ANW TS-IED stored Tunis, Tunisia Nov92
24147	322	1570	United Airlines	N327UA
24148	322	1572	United Airlines	N328UA
24149	322	1574	United Airlines	N329UA
24151	3H4	1686	Southwest Airlines	N343SW
24152	3H4	1688	Southwest Airlines	N344SW

BOEING 737

C/n	Series	Line No	Last known Operator/Owner	Previous Identities/fate (where known)					
24153	3H4	1690	Southwest Airlines	N346SW					
24163	4S3	1700	British Airways	G-BPKA	9M-MJJ	G-BPKA	G-BVNM		
24164	4S3	1702	British Airways	G-BPKB	9M-MLA	G-BPKB	G-BVNN		
24165	4S3	1720	Jet Airways	G-BPKC	N690MA				
24166	4S3	1722	Jet Airways	G-BPKD	N691MA				
24167	4S3	1736	British Airways	G-BPKE	9M-MLB	G-BPKE	G-BVNO		
24178	5H4	1718	Southwest Airlines	N73700	N501SW				
24179	5H4	1744	Southwest Airlines	N502SW					
24180	5H4	1766	Southwest Airlines	N503SW					
24181	5H4	1804	Southwest Airlines	N504SW					
24182	5H4	1826	Southwest Airlines	N505SW					
24183	5H4	1852	Southwest Airlines	N506SW					
24184	5H4	1864	Southwest Airlines	N507SW					
24185	5H4	1932	Southwest Airlines	N508SW					
24186	5H4	1934	Southwest Airlines	N509SW					
24187	5H4	1940	Southwest Airlines	N510SW					
24188	5H4	2029	Southwest Airlines	N511SW					
24189	5H4	2056	Southwest Airlines	N512SW					
24190	5H4	2058	Southwest Airlines	N513SW					
24191	322	1588	United Airlines	N330UA					
24192	322	1590	United Airlines	N331UA					
24193	322	1592	United Airlines	N332UA					
24197	209	1581	China Airlines	(B-186)	B-1878				
24203	382		(Air Portugal)	(CS-TIA)	Allocated but later canx, not built				
24204	382		(Air Portugal)	(CS-TIB)	Allocated but later canx, not built				
24205	382		(Air Portugal)	(CS-TIC)	Allocated but later canx, not built				
24206	382		(Air Portugal)	(CS-TID)	Allocated but later canx, not built				
24207	382		(Air Portugal)	(CS-TIE)	Allocated but later canx, not built				
24208	3Q4	1490	TransBrasil	PT-TEF					
24209	3Q4	1492	TransBrasil	PT-TEG					
24210	3Q4	1577	TransBrasil	PT-TEH					
24211	3K9	1623	VIVA Air	EC-188	EC-ELY				
24212	382	1633	Western Pacific Airlines	CS-TIF	N945WP				
24213	382	1794	Air Portugal	CS-TIG					
24214	382	1796	Air Portugal	CS-TIH					
24219	3L9	1600	Transavia A/L / Air One	N1786B	OY-MMO	G-BOZB	OY-MMO	PH-TSW	
24220	3L9	1602	Germania Flug	N1786B	OY-MMP	(G-BOZC)	OY-MMP	G-CMMP	OY-MMP
				D-AGEI	OY-MMP	D-AGEI			
24221	3L9	1604	Germania Flug	N1786B	OY-MMR	(G-BOZD)	OY-MMR	G-CMMR	OY-MMR
				D-AGEJ					
24228	322	1594	United Airlines	N333UA					
24229	322	1605	United Airlines	N334UA					
24230	322	1607	United Airlines	N335UA					
24231	42C	1871	Air UK Leisure	G-UKLC					
24232	42C	2060	Air UK Leisure	G-UKLD					
24234	4Q8	1627	Carnival Airlines	OO-ILH	N521LF	N403KW			
24236	25C	1585	Xiamen Airlines	B-2524					
24237	35B	1624	Germania Flug	(D-AGED)	N5573B	G-EURP	D-AGEG		
24238	35B	1626	Germania Flug	D-AGEE					
24240	322	1609	United Airlines	N336UA					
24241	322	1611	United Airlines	N337UA					
24242	322	1613	United Airlines	N338UA					
24243	322	1615	United Airlines	N339UA					
24244	322	1617	United Airlines	N340UA					
24245	322	1619	United Airlines	N341UA					
24246	322	1632	United Airlines	N342UA					
24247	322	1634	United Airlines	N343UA					
24248	322	1636	United Airlines	N344UA					
24249	322	1638	United Airlines	N345UA					
24250	322	1644	United Airlines	N346UA					
24251	322	1646	United Airlines	N347UA					
24252	322	1648	United Airlines	N348UA					
24253	322	1650	United Airlines	N349UA					
24255	3Y0	1625	TEA Basel	G-MONL	XA-RJP	OO-IID	EI-CFQ	HB-IID	
24256	3Y0	1629	Air Europa	G-MONM	EC-542	EC-FVJ	EC-204		
24261	306	1640	KLM-Royal Dutch Airlines	PH-BDN					
24262	306	1642	KLM-Royal Dutch Airlines	PH-BDO					
24269	35B	1628	Germania Flug	(D-AGEF)	D-AGED				
24270	405	1726	Braathens-SAFE	LN-BRA					
24271	405	1738	Braathens-SAFE	LN-BRB					
24272	505	1923	Braathens-SAFE	LN-BRG					
24273	505	2018	Braathens-SAFE	(LN-BRJ)	D-ACBC	LN-BRJ			
24274	505	2035	Braathens-SAFE	LN-BRK					
24275	341	1637	VARIG	PP-VOD					
24276	341	1645	VARIG	PP-VOE					
24277	341	1658	VARIG	PP-VOF					
24278	341	1660	VARIG	PP-VOG					
24279	341	1673	VARIG	PP-VOH					
24280	330	1656	Lufthansa	D-ABXS					
24281	330	1664	Lufthansa	D-ABXT					
24282	330	1671	Lufthansa	D-ABXU					

BOEING 737

C/n	Series	Line No	Last known Operator/Owner	Previous Identities/fate (where known)					
24283	330QC	1677	Lufthansa	D-ABWF					
24284	330QC	1685	Lufthansa	D-ABWH					
24295	376	1649	Qantas Airways	VH-TJA					
24296	376	1653	Qantas Airways	VH-TJB					
24297	376	1740	Qantas Airways	VH-TJC					
24298	376	1761	Qantas Airways	VH-TJD					
24299	3Q8	1598	VIVA Air	EC-189	EC-ELJ	EC-594	EC-FER		
24300	3Q8	1666	British Midland	G-KKUH	SE-DLA	G-OBML			
24301	322	1652	United Airlines	N350UA					
24302	377	1618	Ansett Australia	VH-CZM	N113AW	VH-CZM			
24303	377	1620	Ansett Australia	VH-CZN					
24304	377	1622	Ansett Australia	VH-CZO	N114AW	VH-CZO			
24305	377	1641	Ansett Australia	VH-CZP	N115AW	VH-CZP			
24314	4Y0	1680	Asiana Airlines	HL7256					
24319	322	1668	United Airlines	N351UA					
24320	322	1670	United Airlines	N352UA					
24321	322	1672	United Airlines	N353UA					
24326	3K2	1683	Transavia Airlines	PH-HVM					
24327	3K2	1712	Transavia Airlines	PH-HVN					
24328	3K2	1856	Transavia Airlines	PH-HVT					
24329	3K2	1858	Transavia Airlines	PH-HVV					
24332	4Q8	1866	Hainan Airlines	G-BPNZ	N191LF	B-2960			
24344	4Y0	1723	Modiluft	G-UKLB	C-FVNC	C-GTAJ	G-UKLB	9M-MJL	G-UKLB
				9M-MLI	G-UKLB	VT-MGF	G-UKLB	VT-MGF	
24345	4Y0	1731	Jet Airways	EC-308	EC-EPN	EI-CEU	SU-BLM	EI-CEU	F-WQAE
				EI-CEU	VT-JAG				
24352	408	1705	Icelandair	TF-FIA					
24353	408	1721	Icelandair	TF-FIB					
24355	329	1709	SABENA World Airlines	(OO-SQA)	OO-SYA				
24356	329	1711	SABENA World Airlines	(OO-SQB)	OO-SYB				
24360	322	1692	United Airlines	N354UA					
24361	322	1694	United Airlines	N355UA					
24362	322	1696	United Airlines	N356UA					
24364	382QC	1657	Aeropostale	CS-TIA	F-OGSX	F-GIXG			
24365	382	1695	Air Portugal	CS-TIB					
24366	382	1699	Air Portugal	CS-TIC					
24374	3H4	1708	Southwest Airlines	N347SW					
24375	3H4	1710	Southwest Airlines	N348SW					
24376	3M8	1717	Air Europa	(OO-LTF)	OO-LTD	(F-GKTF)	OO-LTD	N681MA	EC-
24377	3M8	1719	TAESA	(OO-LTG)	OO-LTE	(PH-NMB)	OO-LTE	D-AASL	XA-SNC
24378	322	1704	United Airlines	N357UA					
24379	322	1724	Shuttle by United	N358UA					
24387	3B3QC	1693	Aeropostale	F-GFUE					
24388	3B3QC	1725	Aeropostale	F-GFUF					
24403	3Q8	1706	Garuda Indonesia	PK-GWA					
24404	306	1681	KLM-Royal Dutch Airlines	PH-BDP					
24408	3H4	1734	Southwest Airlines	N349SW					
24409	3H4	1748	Southwest Airlines	N350SW					
24410	3B7	1703	US Air	(N527AU)	N528AU				
24411	3B7	1713	US Air	(N528AU)	N529AU				
24412	3B7	1735	US Air	(N529AU)	N530AU				
24413	3M8	1884	TEA Europe Airlines	(OO-LTH)	F-GKTA				
24414	3M8	1895	TEA Europe Airlines	(OO-LTI)	F-GKTB				
24430	476	1820	Qantas Airways	VH-TJE					
24431	476	1863	Qantas Airways	VH-TJF					
24432	476	1879	Qantas Airways	VH-TJG	9M-MLE	VH-TJG			
24433	476	1881	Qantas Airways	VH-TJH					
24434	476	1912	Qantas Airways	VH-TJI	9M-MLD	VH-TJI			
24435	476	1959	Qantas Airways	VH-TJJ					
24436	476	1998	Qantas Airways	VH-TJK					
24437	476	2162	Qantas Airways	VH-TJL					
24438	476	2171	Qantas Airways	VH-TJM					
24439	476	2265	Qantas Airways	VH-TJN					
24440	476	2324	Qantas Airways	VH-TJO					
24441	476	2363	Qantas Airways	VH-TJP					
24442	476	2371	Qantas Airways	VH-TJQ					
24443	476	2398	Qantas Airways	VH-TJR					
24444	476	2454	Qantas Airways	VH-TJS					
24445	476	2539	Qantas Airways	VH-TJT					
24446	476	2569	Qantas Airways	VH-TJU					
24449	382	1857	Air Portugal	CS-TID					
24450	382	1873	Air Portugal	CS-TIE					
24452	322	1728	United Airlines	N359UA					
24453	322	1730	United Airlines	N360UA					
24454	322	1750	United Airlines	N361UA					
24455	322	1752	United Airlines	N362UA					
24460	33A	1831	British Midland	G-OBMH					
24461	33A	1833	British Midland	(G-OBMI)	G-OBMJ				
24462	3Y0	1691	Air Europa	N5573K	EC-244	EC-ENS	EI-BZQ	(N116AW)	EI-BZQ
				G-TEAA	EC-897	EC-FJR			

BOEING 737

C/n	Series	Line No	Last known Operator/Owner	Previous Identities/fate (where known)					
24463	3Y0	1701	AVENSA	N1779B	EC-245	EC-ENT	EI-BZR	YV-99C	EI-BZR
				YV-99C					
24464	3Y0	1753	Philippine Airlines	EI-BZE					
24465	3Y0	1755	Philippine Airlines	EI-BZF					
24466	3Y0	1771	(Philippine Airlines)	EI-BZG	dbr Manila, Philippines 11May90 by bomb				
24467	4Y0	1733	TransBrasil	PT-TEL					
24468	4Y0	1747	Modiluft	G-UKLE	VT-MGG				
24469	4Y0	1749	Asiana Airlines	HL7257					
24470	3Q8	1765	Garuda Indonesia	PK-GWD					
24474	448	1742	Aer Lingus	EI-BXA					
24478	3B7	1743	US Air	(N530AU)	N531AU				
24479	3B7	1745	US Air	(N531AU)	N532AU				
24480	3Z6	1773	(Royal Thai AF/Royal Flight)	33-333/HS-TGQ		w/o 30Mar93 nr Bangkok, Thailand			
24492	3Q8	1808	Garuda Indonesia	PK-GWE					
24493	4Y0	1751	Asiana Airlines	HL7258					
24494	4Y0	1757	Asiana Airlines	HL7259					
24511	4Y0	1759	TransBrasil	PT-TEM					
24512	4Y0	1777	Istanbul Airlines	(PT-TEN)	VR-CAL	TC-AGA			
24513	4Y0	1779	TransBrasil	PT-TEN					
24514	406	1768	KLM-Royal Dutch Airlines	PH-BDR					
24515	3B7	1767	US Air	(N532AU)	N533AU				
24516	3B7	1769	US Air	(N533AU)	N534AU				
24519	4Y0	1781	Istanbul Airlines	VR-CAB	TC-ALA				
24520	4Y0	1803	Asiana Airlines	HL7260					
24521	448	1778	Aer Lingus	EI-BXB					
24529	406	1770	KLM-Royal Dutch Airlines	PH-BDS					
24530	406	1772	KLM-Royal Dutch Airlines	PH-BDT					
24532	322	1754	United Airlines	N363UA					
24533	322	1756	United Airlines	N364UA					
24534	322	1758	United Airlines	N365UA					
24535	322	1760	Shuttle by United	N366UA					
24536	322	1762	United Airlines	N367UA					
24537	322	1774	United Airlines	N368UA					
24538	322	1776	United Airlines	N369UA					
24539	322	1778	United Airlines	N370UA					
24540	322	1780	United Airlines	N371UA					
24545	4Y0	1805	Futura International	C-FVND	EC-401	EC-ETB			
24546	3Y0	1811	Philippine Airlines	EI-BZH					
24547	3Y0	1813	Philippine Airlines	EI-BZI					
24548	4B7	1789	US Air	N426US					
24549	4B7	1791	US Air	N427US					
24550	4B7	1793	US Air	N428US					
24551	4B7	1795	US Air	N429US					
24552	4B7	1797	US Air	N430US					
24553	4B7	1799	US Air	N431US					
24554	4B7	1817	US Air	N432US					
24555	4B7	1819	US Air	N433US					
24556	4B7	1821	US Air	N434US					
24557	4B7	1835	US Air	N435US					
24558	4B7	1845	US Air	N436US					
24559	4B7	1847	US Air	N437US					
24560	4B7	1849	US Air	N438US					
24561	330	1785	Lufthansa	D-ABXW					
24562	330	1787	Lufthansa	D-ABXX					
24563	330	1801	Lufthansa	D-ABXY					
24564	330	1807	Lufthansa	D-ABXZ					
24565	330	1818	Lufthansa	D-ABEA					
24569	3L9	1775	Deutsche-BA	OY-MMD	EC-996	EC-FMS	OY-MMO	D-ADBE	
24570	3L9	1800	Silkair	OY-MME	9V-TRC				
24571	3L9	1815	Deutsche-BA	OY-MMF	D-ABDF				
24572	3H4	1790	Southwest Airlines	N351SW					
24573	46B	1844	Sobelair	G-BROC	OO-SBJ				
24633	3G7	1809	America West Airlines	N306AW					
24634	3G7	1823	America West Airlines	N307AW					
24637	322	1782	United Airlines	N372UA					
24638	322	1784	United Airlines	N373UA					
24639	322	1786	United Airlines	N374UA					
24640	322	1798	Shuttle by United	N375UA					
24641	322	1802	United Airlines	N376UA					
24642	322	1806	United Airlines	N377UA					
24643	405	1860	Braathens-SAFE	LN-BRE					
24644	405	1938	Braathens-SAFE	LN-BRI	9M-MLL	LN-BRI			
24645	505	1917	Braathens-SAFE	LN-BRM					
24646	505	2138	Braathens-SAFE	LN-BRN					
24647	505	2143	Braathens-SAFE	LN-BRO					
24648	505	2213	Braathens-SAFE	LN-BRR					
24649	505	2225	Braathens-SAFE	LN-BRS					
24650	505	1792	Braathens-SAFE	N5573K	LN-BRC				
24651	505	1842	Braathens-SAFE	LN-BRD					
24652	505	1917	Braathens-SAFE	LN-BRF	D-ACBA	LN-BRF			
24653	322	1810	United Airlines	N378UA					

BOEING 737

C/n	Series	Line No	Last known Operator/Owner	Previous Identities/fate (where known)
24654	322	1812	United Airlines	N379UA
24655	322	1814	United Airlines	N380UA
24656	322	1822	Shuttle by United	N381UA
24657	322	1830	United Airlines	N382UA
24658	322	1832	United Airlines	N383UA
24659	322	1836	United Airlines	N384UA
24660	322	1838	Shuttle by United	N385UA
24661	322	1840	United Airlines	N386UA
24662	322	1862	United Airlines	N387UA
24663	322	1875	United Airlines	N388UA
24664	322	1877	United Airlines	N389UA
24665	322	1889	Shuttle by United	N390UA
24666	322	1891	United Airlines	N391UA
24667	322	1893	United Airlines	N392UA
24668	322	1905	United Airlines	N393UA
24669	322	1907	Shuttle by United	N394UA
24670	322	1909	United Airlines	N395UA
24671	322	1913	United Airlines	N396UA
24672	322	1915	United Airlines	N397UA
24673	322	1920	United Airlines	N398UA
24674	322	1928	United Airlines	N399UA
24676	3Y0	1829	Sun Express Air	(PT-TEO) TC-SUN
24677	3Y0	1837	Philippine Airlines	EI-BZJ
24678	3Y0	1853	Philippine Airlines	EI-BZK
24679	3Y0	1897	Silkair	9V-TRA
24680	3Y0	1927	Philippine Airlines	EI-BZL
24681	3Y0	1929	Philippine Airlines	EI-BZM
24682	4Y0	1824	Jet Airways	(C-FVNF) 9M-MJK EC-737 EC-FZX VT-JAH EC-FZX VT-JAH
24683	4Y0	1901	Istanbul Airlines	HR-SHL PP-SOH 9M-MJR TC-AYA
24684	4Y0	1841	Pegasus Airlines	TC-AFK
24685	4Y0	1859	Futura International	EC-402 EC-EVE
24686	4Y0	1861	Air Europa	(G-OOAA) 9M-MJH EC-772 EC-FZZ
24687	4Y0	1865	Air Berlin	TC-ATA N25AB D-ABAC
24688	4Y0	1876	Futura International	(G-OOAB) 9M-MJI EC-738 EC-FZT
24689	4Y0	1883	Futura International	EC-403 EC-EXY
24690	4Y0	1885	TransBrasil	TC-AFL EC-603 EC-FBP PT-TDA
24691	4Y0	1904	Istanbul Airlines	HR-SHK PP-SOI 9M-MJS TC-AZA
24692	4Y0	1963	TransBrasil	(HR-SHM) N6069D EI-CBT PT-TEO
24693	4Y0	1972	Czech Airlines	9M-MJM OK-WGG
24694	59D	1834	British Midland	(SE-DLA) SE-DNA G-BVKA
24695	59D	1872	British Midland	(SE-DLB) SE-DNB G-BVKC
24696	5Y0	1960	China Southern Airlines	B-2541
24698	3Q8	1846	Garuda Indonesia	PK-GWF
24699	3Q8	1886	Garuda Indonesia	PK-GWG
24700	3Q8	1924	Garuda Indonesia	PK-GWH
24701	3Q8	1957	Garuda Indonesia	PK-GWI
24702	3Q8	1994	Garuda Indonesia	PK-GWJ
24703	4Q8	1828	Braathens-SAFE	9M-MJA LN-BUB
24704	4Q8	1855	Carnival Airlines	9M-MJB N405KW
24705	4Q8	1971	Sahara Indian Airlines	9M-MJC TC-AFY N621LF VT-SID N621LF VT-SID
24706	4Q8	1996	Air Europa	9M-MJD EC-644 EC-FXP
24707	4Q8	2057	Air Europa	9M-MJE EC-645 EC-FXQ
24708	4Q8	2076	Sahara Indian Airlines	9M-MJF OO-LTT N631LF VT-SIC
24709	4Q8	2115	Carnival Airlines	9M-MJG N406KW
24710	3G7	1825	America West Airlines	N308AW
24711	3G7	1843	America West Airlines	N309AW
24712	3G7	1869	America West Airlines	N311AW
24717	322	1930	United Airlines	N202UA
24718	322	1937	United Airlines	N203UA
24719	322		(United Airlines)	Allocated but later canx, not built
24720	322		(United Airlines)	Allocated but later canx, not built
24721	322		(United Airlines)	Allocated but later canx, not built
24722	322		(United Airlines)	Allocated but later canx, not built
24723	322		(United Airlines)	Allocated but later canx, not built
24724	322		(United Airlines)	Allocated but later canx, not built
24725	322		(United Airlines)	Allocated but later canx, not built
24726	322		(United Airlines)	Allocated but later canx, not built
24732	322		(United Airlines)	Allocated but later canx, not built
24750	4B3	1916	Corsair	F-GFUG
24751	4B3	2107	Corsair	F-GFUH
24754	53A	1868	British Midland	SE-DNC G-OBMZ
24769	4K5	1839	Air Berlin	N11AB D-ABAB
24770	3Y0	1941	Philippines Airlines	EI-BZN
24773	448	1850	Aer Lingus	EI-BXC
24776	5K5	1848	Hapag Lloyd	(D-AHLA) D-AHLE
24778	5L9	1816	Asiana Airlines	(OY-MMW) OY-MAA HL7230
24781	4B7	1874	US Air	N439US
24785	53A	1882	Uganda Airlines	N35135 F-GGML 5X-USM
24786	53A	1898	Asiana Airlines	HL7261
24787	53A	1900	Asiana Airlines	HL7262

BOEING 737

C/n	Series	Line No	Last known Operator/Owner	Previous Identities/fate (where known)					
24788	53A	1921	Corsair	F-GHXM					
24789	33AQC	1953	Aeropostale	(F-GFUI)	F-OGSD	F-GIXB			
24790	33A	1955	Jet Airways	N1782B	PP-SOC	N223AW	(PT-TEP)	N223AW	VT-JAA
24791	33A	1984	Jet Airways	PP-SOD	N222AW	VT-JAB			
24795	4S3	1870	Maersk Air	G-BRKF	G-IEAE	N686MA	TF-FIE		
24796	4S3	1887	GB Airways	G-BRKG	G-TREN				
24804	408	1851	Icelandair	TF-FIC					
24805	5L9	1878	(Asiana Airlines)	(OY-MMY)	OY-MAB	HL7229	OY-MAB	HL7229	
				w/o 26Jul92 Kwangju, Republic of Korea					
24807	4B6	1880	Royal Air Maroc	CN-RMF					
24808	4B6	1888	Royal Air Maroc	CN-RMG					
24811	4B7	1890	US Air	N440US					
24812	4B7	1892	US Air	N441US					
24813	42C	2062	Air UK Leisure	G-UKLF					
24814	42C	2270	Air UK Leisure	G-UKLG					
24815	530	1933	Lufthansa	N3521N	D-ABIA				
24816	530	1958	Lufthansa	D-ABIB					
24817	530	1967	Lufthansa	D-ABIC					
24818	530	1974	Lufthansa	D-ABID					
24819	530	1979	Lufthansa	D-ABIE					
24820	530	1985	Lufthansa	D-ABIF					
24821	530	1993	Lufthansa	D-ABIH					
24822	530	1997	Lufthansa	D-ABII					
24823	530	2000	Lufthansa	D-ABIK					
24824	530	2006	Lufthansa	D-ABIL					
24825	53C	1894	Air France	F-GHOL	[Op by Air Liberte]				
24826	53C	2041	Air France	F-GHUL	[Op by Air Liberte]				
24827	53C	2243	Air France	F-GINL	[Op by Air Liberte]				
24828	505	1925	Braathens-SAFE	LN-BRH	D-ACBB	LN-BRH			
24829	4Q8		(ILFC)	Allocated but later canx, not built					
24830	4D7	1899	Thai International	HS-TDA					
24831	4D7	1922	Thai International	HS-TDB					
24834	3S1	1896	TACA International Airlines	N371TA					
24841	4B7	1906	US Air	N442US					
24842	4B7	1908	US Air	N443US					
24856	3S1	1911	TACA International Airlines	N372TA					
24857	406	1902	KLM-Royal Dutch Airlines	PH-BDU					
24858	406	1903	KLM-Royal Dutch Airlines	PH-BDW					
24859	5L9	1919	Maersk Air	(OY-MMZ)	OY-MAC				
24862	4B7	1910	US Air	N444US					
24863	4B7	1914	US Air	N445US					
24864	3K9	1918	VARIG	PP-VNY					
24866	448	1867	Aer Lingus	EI-BXD					
24869	3K9	1926	VARIG	PP-VNZ					
24873	4B7	1931	US Air	N446US					
24874	4B7	1936	US Air	N447US					
24877	53A	1943	Air Austral	F-GHXN	F-ODZJ				
24878	548	1939	Aer Lingus	EI-BXE	EI-CDA				
24881	53A	1945	Balkan Bulgarian	LZ-BOA					
24888	3H4	1942	Southwest Airlines	N352SW					
24889	3H4	1947	Southwest Airlines	N353SW					
24892	4B7	1944	US Air	N448US					
24893	4B7	1946	US Air	N449US					
24897	5Y0	2003	China Southern Airlines	B-2542					
24898	5Y0	2079	China Southern Airlines	B-2543					
24899	5Y0	2093	China Southern Airlines	B-2544					
24900	5Y0	2095	China Southern Airlines	B-2545					
24901	4K5	1854	Hapag Lloyd	D-AHLR					
24902	3Y0	1973	Silkair	9V-TRB					
24903	4Y0	1978	Czech Airlines	9M-MJN	OK-WGF				
24904	4Y0	1988	THY-Turkish Airlines	TC-JDE					
24905	4Y0	2001	Transavia Airlines	EI-CBP	CS-TKE	PH-TSU			
24906	4Y0	2009	Air Europa	9M-MJO	EC-850	9M-MJO	EC-850	EC-GAZ	
24907	3Y0	2013	Ukraine International Airlines	EI-CBQ	UR-GAE				
24908	3Y0	2015	Sun Express Air	TC-SUP					
24909	3Y0	2021	Malev	HA-LED					
24910	3Y0	2030	Sun Express Air	TC-SUR					
24911	4Y0	2033	Nordic East International	(TC-ADA)	PP-SOJ	PT-WBJ	OY-MBK	EI-CIX	SE-DTB
24912	4Y0	2064	Air Europa	N1786B	9M-MJQ	EC-851	9M-MJQ	EC-851	EC-GBN
24913	3Y0	2052	(China Southern Airlines)	B-2523	w/o 24Nov92 nr Guilin, PRC				
24914	3Y0	2054	Malev	HA-LEF					
24915	4Y0	2055	Royal Air Cambodge	9M-MJP	OO-VDO	9M-MJT			
24916	3Y0	2066	Malev	HA-LEG					
24917	4Y0	2071	THY-Turkish Airlines	TC-JDF					
24918	3Y0	2087	China Southern A/L	B-2525					
24919	548	1970	Aer Lingus	EI-BXF	EI-CDB				
24921	53A	1962	Balkan Bulgarian	LZ-BOB					
24922	53A	1964	Rio Sul	CN-RMU	PT-SLW				
24926	5K5	1966	Hapag Lloyd	(D-AHLB)	D-AHLD				
24927	5K5	1968	Hapag Lloyd	(D-AHLC)	D-AHLF				
24928	5L9	1961	Maersk Air	(OY-MMO)	OY-MAD				

BOEING 737

C/n	Series	Line No	Last known Operator/Owner	Previous Identities/fate (where known)					
24933	4B7	1954	US Air	N775AU					
24934	4B7	1956	US Air	N776AU					
24935	341	1935	VARIG	PP-VON					
24936	341	1951	VARIG	PP-VOO					
24937	330	2011	Lufthansa	D-ABIM					
24938	330	2023	Lufthansa	D-ABIN					
24939	330	2031	Lufthansa	D-ABIO					
24940	330	2034	Lufthansa	D-ABIP					
24941	330	2042	Lufthansa	D-ABIR					
24942	330	2048	Lufthansa	D-ABIS					
24943	330	2049	Lufthansa	D-ABIT					
24944	330	2051	Lufthansa	D-ABIU					
24945	330	2063	Lufthansa	D-ABIW					
24946	330	2070	Lufthansa	N1786B	D-ABIX				
24959	406	1949	KLM-Royal Dutch Airlines	PH-BDY					
24961	3Q8	2133	VARIG	PP-VOW					
24962	3Q8	2139	VARIG	PP-VOX					
24963	3Q8	2193	British Midland	G-OBMP					
24968	548	1975	Aer Lingus	EI-BXG	EI-CDC				
24970	53A	1977	Theberton Inc	N1789B	N778YY	VR-BOC			
24979	4B7	1980	US Air	N777AU					
24980	4B7	1982	US Air	N778AU					
24986	3Q8	2192	Wuhan Airlines	CS-TII	N551LF	B-2918			
24987	3Q8	2268	Wuhan Airlines	CS-TIJ	N561LF	B-2919			
24988	3Q8	2466	China Southwest Airlines	(CS-TIM)	N841LF	B-2902			
24989	548	1989	Aer Lingus	EI-BXH	EI-CDD				
24996	4B7	1986	US Air	N779AU					
24997	4B7	1990	US Air	N780AU					
25001	522	1948	United Airlines	N901UA					
25002	522	1950	United Airlines	N902UA					
25003	522	1952	United Airlines	N903UA					
25004	522	1965	United Airlines	N904UA					
25005	522	1976	United Airlines	N905UA					
25006	522	1981	United Airlines	N906UA					
25007	522	1983	United Airlines	N907UA					
25008	522	1987	United Airlines	N908UA					
25009	522	1999	United Airlines	N909UA					
25010	33A	2008	Eurobelgian Airlines	PP-SOE	N226AW	VH-OAM	OO-LTW		
25011	33A	2012	Star Europe	PP-SOF	N227AW	OO-LTO	VH-OAN	OO-LTO	F-GRSA
25015	3M8	1991	TEA-Italy	OO-LTF	I-TEAI				
25016	3M8	2004	Mitsui & Co	OO-LTG	(HB-IIC)	OO-LTG	OO-XTG	OO-LTG	HB-IIC
				stored					
25017	3M8	2005	Silkair	(OO-LTH)	N35030	N760BE	9V-TRD		
25020	4B7	1992	US Air	N781AU					
25021	4B7	1995	US Air	N782AU					
25022	4B7	2010	US Air	N783AU					
25023	4B7	2020	US Air	N784AU					
25024	4B7	2026	US Air	N785AU					
25025	4B7		(US Air)	(N786AU)	Allocated but later canx, not built				
25026	4B7		(US Air)	(N787AU)	Allocated but later canx, not built				
25027	4B7		(US Air)	(N788AU)	Allocated but later canx, not built				
25028	4B7		(US Air)	(N789AU)	Allocated but later canx, not built				
25029	4B7		(US Air)	(N790AU)	Allocated but later canx, not built				
25030	4B7		(US Air)	(N791AU)	Allocated but later canx, not built				
25031	4B7		(US Air)	(N792AU)	Allocated but later canx, not built				
25032	33A	2014	Eurobelgian Airlines	PP-SOG	N228AW	OO-LTP			
25033	33A	2025	Maersk Air	G-MONV	OY-				
25037	5K5	2022	Hapag Lloyd	D-AHLI					
25038	59D	1969	British Midland	(SE-DNC)	SE-DND	G-BVZF			
25039	3M8	2007	Eurobelgian Airlines	OO-LTJ					
25040	3M8	2017	Birgenair	OO-LTK	PH-YAA	VR-CRC	TC-BIR		
25041	3M8	2024	Eurobelgian Airlines	OO-LTL					
25048	341	2085	VARIG	PP-VOS					
25049	341	2091	VARIG	PP-VOT					
25050	341	2125	VARIG	PP-VOU					
25051	341	2127	VARIG	PP-VOV					
25052	448	2036	Aer Lingus	EI-BXI					
25056	33A	2045	Air Malawi	7Q-YKP					
25057	33A	2046	TransBrasil	PP-SOK	PT-TEQ				
25062	5K5	2044	Hapag Lloyd	D-AHLN					
25063	408	2032	Icelandair	TF-FID					
25065	59D	2028	British Midland	(SE-DND)	SE-DNE	G-OBMX			
25066	5L9	2038	Maersk Air	OY-MAE					
25069	35B	2053	Germania Flug	N1786E	D-AGEF				
25070	3M8	2037	Eurobelgian Airlines	OO-LTM					
25071	3M8	2039	Air Europa	OO-LTN	N682MA	EC-			
25078	3J6	2002	Air China	B-2535					
25079	3J6	2016	Tian-Jin Airlines	B-2536					
25080	3J6	2254	China Southwest Airlines	B-2580					
25081	3J6	2263	Air China	B-2581					
25084	566	2019	Egyptair	SU-GBH					

BOEING 737

C/n	Series	Line No	Last known Operator/Owner	Previous Identities/fate (where known)					
25089	3Z0	2027	China Southwest Airlines	B-2537					
25090	3W0	2040	Yunnan Airlines	B-2538					
25095	4Q8	2266	Alaska Airlines	N754AS					
25096	4Q8	2278	Alaska Airlines	N755AS					
25097	4Q8	2299	Alaska Airlines	N756AS					
25098	4Q8	2320	Alaska Airlines	N760AS					
25099	4Q8	2334	Alaska Airlines	N762AS					
25100	4Q8	2346	Alaska Airlines	N763AS					
25101	4Q8	2348	Alaska Airlines	N764AS					
25102	4Q8	2350	Alaska Airlines	N765AS					
25103	4Q8	2452	Alaska Airlines	N769AS					
25104	4Q8	2476	Alaska Airlines	N771AS					
25105	4Q8	2505	Alaska Airlines	N772AS					
25106	4Q8	2518	Alaska Airlines	N773AS					
25107	4Q8	2526	Alaska Airlines	N774AS					
25108	4Q8	2551	Alaska Airlines	N775AS					
25109	4Q8	2561	Alaska Airlines	N776AS					
25110	4Q8	2586	Alaska Airlines	N778AS					
25111	4Q8	2605	Alaska Airlines	N779AS					
25112	4Q8	2638	Alaska Airlines	N780AS					
25113	4Q8	2656	Alaska Airlines	N782AS					
25114	4Q8	2666	Alaska Airlines	N783AS					
25115	548	2050	Aer Lingus	(EI-BXJ)	N1789B	EI-CDE	PT-SLM	EI-CDE	
25116	4S3	2061	Futura International	(G-BSRA)	N4249R	9M-MLF	OO-LTR	EC-997	EC-GFE
25118	33A	2065	Air France	(F-GBYR)	F-GFUJ				
25119	33A	2069	TransBrasil	PP-SOL	PT-TER				
25124	38BQC	2047	Aeropostale	(TC-...)	N1792B	N4320B	F-OGSS	F-GIXC	
25125	3L9	2059	Deutsche-BA	OY-MMW	PP-SOR	OY-MMW	D-ADBG		
25134	4S3	2083	GB Airways	(G-BSRB)	N1799B	9M-MLH	G-BUHL		
25138	33A	2153	Air France	F-OGRT	F-GHVN				
25147	4Z9	2043	Lauda Air	OE-LNH					
25148	330	2077	Lufthansa	D-ABEB					
25149	330	2081	Lufthansa	D-ABEC					
25150	3L9	2074	Maersk Air	N1786B	OY-MMY	PP-SOT	OY-MMY		
25153	5H4	2078	Southwest Airlines	N514SW					
25154	5H4	2080	Southwest Airlines	N515SW					
25159	36C	2068	VIVA Air	EC-703	EC-FFN				
25160	5Q8	2114	British Midland	SE-DNF	G-BVZG				
25161	382	2226	Air Portugal	CS-TIK					
25162	382	2241	Air Portugal	CS-TIL					
25163	4Q8	2264	Qantas Airways	H4-SOL	VH-TJV				
25164	4Q8	2447	British Airways	G-BUHJ					
25165	548	2463	Rio-Sul/Nordeste	EI-CDT	PT-MNC				
25166	5Q8	2129	British Midland	SE-DNG	G-BVZH				
25167	5Q8	2173	British Midland	SE-DNH	G-BVZI				
25168	4Q8	2210	British Airways	G-BSNV					
25169	4Q8	2237	British Airways	G-BSNW					
25172	3Y0	2089	China Southern Airlines	B-2526					
25173	3Y0	2097	Zhuhai Airlines	B-2527					
25174	3Y0	2168	China Southern Airlines	B-2528					
25175	5Y0	2150	China Southern Airlines	B-2546					
25176	5Y0	2155	China Southern Airlines	B-2547					
25177	4Y0	2176	British Midland	G-OBMM					
25178	4Y0	2199	Air Berlin	N601TR	D-ABAD				
25179	3Y0	2205	Air One	N3521N	XA-RJR	EI-CLZ			
25180	4Y0	2201	Futura International	EC-936	EC-FLD				
25181	4Y0	2203	THY-Turkish Airlines	TC-JDG					
25182	5Y0	2211	China Southern Airlines	B-2548					
25183	5Y0	2218	China Southern Airlines	B-2549					
25184	4Y0	2227	THY-Turkish Airlines	TC-JDH					
25185	5Y0	2220	TAESA	XA-RJS					
25186	5Y0	2236	Rio-Sul/Nordeste	XA-RKP	PT-SLU				
25187	3Y0	2248	Air One	XA-SAB	EI-CLW				
25188	5Y0	2238	China Southern Airlines	B-2550					
25189	5Y0	2240	Rio-Sul	XA-RKQ	PT-SLV				
25190	4Y0	2256	Sun Express Air	(PT-TE.)	EC-991	EC-FMJ	OY-MBL	TC-SUT	
25191	5Y0	2260	China Southern Airlines	XA-SAS	N191G	B-			
25192	5Y0	2262	TAESA	XA-SAC					
25206	528	2099	Air France	F-GJNA					
25210	3K9	2090	VARIG	PP-VOY					
25215	330	2082	Lufthansa	D-ABED					
25216	330	2084	Lufthansa	D-ABEE					
25217	330	2094	Lufthansa	D-ABEF					
25218	529	2111	SABENA World Airlines	OO-SYE					
25219	3H4	2092	Southwest Airlines	N354SW					
25226	429	2104	SABENA World Airlines	OO-SYC					
25227	528	2108	Air France	F-GJNB					
25228	528	2170	Air France	F-GJNC					
25229	528	2180	Air France	F-GJND					
25230	528	2191	Air France	F-GJNE					
25231	528	2208	Air France	F-GJNF					

BOEING 737

C/n	Series	Line No	Last known Operator/Owner	Previous Identities/fate (where known)		
25232	528	2231	Air France	F-GJNG		
25233	528	2251	Air France	F-GJNH		
25234	528	2411	Air France	F-GJNI		
25235	528	2428	Air France	F-GJNJ		
25236	528	2443	Air France	F-GJNK		
25237	528	2464	Air France	(F-GJNL)	F-GJNM	
25239	3K9	2100	VARIG	PP-VOZ		
25242	330	2102	Lufthansa	D-ABEH		
25243	530	2086	Lufthansa	D-ABIY		
25244	530	2098	Lufthansa	D-ABIZ		
25247	429	2106	SABENA World Airlines	OO-SYD		
25248	429	2120	SABENA World Airlines	OO-SYF		
25249	529	2145	SABENA World Airlines	OO-SYG		
25250	3H4	2103	Southwest Airlines	N355SW		
25251	3H4	2105	Southwest Airlines	N356SW		
25254	522	2073	United Airlines	N910UA		
25255	522	2075	United Airlines	N911UA		
25256	36E	2123	VIVA Air	EC-704	EC-FHR	
25261	4Y0	2258	THY-Turkish Airlines	N600SK	TC-JDT	
25262	46B	2088	Air Belgium	OO-ILJ		
25263	36E	2187	VIVA Air	EC-705	EC-FLF	
25264	36E	2194	VIVA Air	EC-706	EC-FLG	
25265	3B7		(US Air)	(N303AU)	Allocated but later canx, not built	
25267	436	2131	British Airways	G-DOCA		
25270	530	2116	Lufthansa	D-ABJA		
25271	530	2117	Lufthansa	D-ABJB		
25272	530	2118	Lufthansa	D-ABJC		
25282	3B7		(US Air)	(N304AU)	Allocated but later canx, not built	
25288	5Y0	2286	THY-Turkish Airlines	(EI-CFT)	TC-JDU	
25289	5Y0	2288	THY-Turkish Airlines	(EI-CFU)	N6069D	TC-JDV
25290	522	2096	United Airlines	N912UA		
25291	522	2101	United Airlines	N913UA		
25303	405	2137	Braathens-SAFE	LN-BRP	9M-MLK	LN-BRP
25304	436	2144	British Airways	G-DOCB		
25305	436	2147	British Airways	G-DOCC		
25307	566	2135	Egyptair	SU-GBI		
25309	530	2122	Lufthansa	D-ABJD		
25310	530	2126	Lufthansa	D-ABJE		
25311	530	2128	Lufthansa	D-ABJF		
25313	484	2109	Olympic Airways	SX-BKA		
25314	484	2124	Olympic Airways	SX-BKB		
25317	5B6	2157	Royal Air Maroc	CN-RMV		
25318	5H4	2121	Southwest Airlines	N519SW		
25319	5H4	2134	Southwest Airlines	N520SW		
25320	5H4	2136	Southwest Airlines	N521SW		
25321	4D7	2113	Thai International	HS-TDC		
25326	3B7		(US Air)	(N305AU)	Allocated but later canx, not built	
25327	3B7		(US Air)	(N306AU)	Allocated but later canx, not built	
25328	3B7		(US Air)	(N307AU)	Allocated but later canx, not built	
25329	3B7		(US Air)	(N308AU)	Allocated but later canx, not built	
25330	3B7		(US Air)	(N309AU)	Allocated but later canx, not built	
25348	405	2148	Braathens-SAFE	LN-BRQ	(9M-ML.)	LN-BRQ
25349	436	2156	British Airways	G-DOCD		
25350	436	2167	British Airways	G-DOCE		
25352	566	2169	Egyptair	SU-GBJ		
25355	406	2132	KLM-Royal Dutch Airlines	PH-BDZ		
25357	530	2141	Lufthansa	D-ABJH		
25358	530	2151	Lufthansa	D-ABJI		
25359	330	2158	Lufthansa	(D-ABJK)	D-ABEI	[Originally ordered as 737-530]
25360	3L9	2140	Maersk Air	(OY-MMZ)	PP-SOU	OY-MMZ
25361	484	2130	Olympic Airways	SX-BKC		
25362	484	2142	Olympic Airways	SX-BKD		
25364	5B6	2166	Royal Air Maroc	CN-RMW		
25371	4Q8	2195	Carnival Airlines	VR-CAA	N404KW	
25372	4Q8	2280	THY-Turkish Airlines	TC-JDI		
25373	3Q8	2290	LADECO	CC-CYJ		
25374	4Q8	2562	THY-Turkish Airlines	TC-JEG		
25375	4Q8	2598	THY-Turkish Airlines	TC-JEJ		
25376	4Q8	2689	THY-Turkish Airlines	TC-JEN		
25377	4Q8	2717	THY-Turkish Airlines	TC-JEO		
25378	4Q8	2732	THY-Turkish Airlines	TC-JEP		
25381	522	2110	United Airlines	N914UA		
25382	522	2119	United Airlines	N915UA		
25383	522	2146	United Airlines	N916UA		
25384	522	2149	United Airlines	N917UA		
25385	522	2152	United Airlines	N918UA		
25386	522	2154	United Airlines	N919UA		
25387	522	2179	United Airlines	N920UA		
25388	522	2181	United Airlines	N921UA		
25400	3G7	2112	America West Airlines	N322AW		
25401	33AQC	2067	Falcon Aviation	N1786B	SE-DPA	

BOEING 737

C/n	Series	Line No	Last known Operator/Owner	Previous Identities/fate (where known)		
25402	33AQC	2153	Falcon Aviation	N33AW	SE-DPB	
25407	436	2178	British Airways	G-DOCF		
25408	436	2183	British Airways	G-DOCG		
25412	406	2161	KLM-Royal Dutch Airlines	PH-BTA		
25414	330	2164	Lufthansa	(D-ABJL)	D-ABEK	[Originally ordered as 737-530]
25415	330	2175	Lufthansa	(D-ABJM)	D-ABEL	[Originally ordered as 737-530]
25416	330	2182	Lufthansa	(D-ABJN)	D-ABEM	[Originally ordered as 737-530]
25417	484	2160	Olympic Airways	SX-BKE		
25418	529	2163	SABENA World Airlines	OO-SYH		
25419	529	2165	SABENA World Airlines	OO-SYI		
25420	3K2		(Transavia Airlines)	(PH-HVW)	Allocated but later canx, not built	
25423	406	2184	KLM-Royal Dutch Airlines	PH-BTB		
25424	406	2200	KLM-Royal Dutch Airlines	PH-BTC		
25425	53A	2159	Balkan Bulgarian	LZ-BOC		
25426	33AQC	2172	Falcon Aviation	N34AW	SE-DPC	
25428	436	2185	British Airways	G-DOCH		
25429	4C9	2215	Sobelair	LX-LGF		
25430	484	2174	Olympic Airways	SX-BKF		
25431	3K2		(Transavia Airlines)	(PH-HVX)	Allocated but later canx, not built	
25453	4M8		(TEA)	Allocated but later canx, not built		
25502	33A	2310	Xiamen Airlines	B-4018		
25503	33A	2313	Xiamen Airlines	B-4019		
25504	33A	2341	Government of Pakistan	AP-BEH		
25505	33A	2342	Hainan Airlines	N402AW	B-2579	
25506	33A	2360	Air China/Inner Mongolia	N403AW	B-2905	
25507	33A	2373	Air China/Inner Mongolia	N404AW	B-2906	
25508	33A	2414	Air China/Inner Mongolia	N1790B	N405AW	B-2907
25509	33A		(Ansett Worldwide)	Allocated but later canx, not built		
25510	33A		(Ansett Worldwide)	Allocated but later canx, not built		
25511	33A	2599	Air China/Inner Mongolia	B-2947		
25512	33A		(Ansett Worldwide)	Allocated but later canx, not built		
25513	33A		(Ansett Worldwide)	Allocated but later canx, not built		
25514	33A		(Ansett Worldwide)	Allocated but later canx, not built		
25594	4S3	2223	Istanbul Airlines	(G-....)	9M-MLJ	TC-AVA
25595	4S3	2233	Istanbul Airlines	(G-....)	9M-MLG	TC-APA
25596	4S3	2255	British Midland	G-OBMK		
25603	33A	2333	Hainan Airlines	N1784B	N401AW	B-2578
25604	3Y0	2405	China Southern Airlines	(7Q-YKR)	N1784B	N999CZ
25613	5Y5	2446	Air Malta	9H-ABR		
25614	5Y5	2467	Air Malta	9H-ABS		
25615	5Y5	2478	Air Malta	9H-ABT		
25663	497	2382	GECAS	N401AL	stored Everett, WA 15Jan96	
25664	497	2393	GECAS	N402AL	stored Everett, WA 10Jan96	
25665	497		(Aloha Airlines)	(N403AL)	Allocated but later canx, not built	
25666	497		(Aloha Airlines)	(N404AL)	Allocated but later canx, not built	
25667	3G7		(America West Airlines)	Allocated but later canx, not built		
25713	4U3	2531	Garuda Indonesia	PK-GWK		
25714	4U3	2535	Garuda Indonesia	N6067B	PK-GWL	
25715	4U3	2537	Garuda Indonesia	PK-GWM		
25716	4U3	2540	Garuda Indonesia	PK-GWN		
25717	4U3	2546	Garuda Indonesia	PK-GWO		
25718	4U3	2548	Garuda Indonesia	PK-GWP		
25719	4U3	2549	Garuda Indonesia	PK-GWQ		
25729	429	2217	Sobelair	OO-SBM		
25736	448	2269	Apple Vacations	EI-BXK	[Op by Ryan International]	
25737	548	2232	Aer Lingus	EI-CDF		
25738	548	2261	Apple Vacations	EI-CDG	[Op by Ryan International]	
25739	548	2271	Aer Lingus	EI-CDH		
25740	4Q8	2461	THY-Turkish Airlines	TC-JED		
25743	33A	2206	Cronus Airlines	N3519L	EC-970	EC-FMP SX-BBU
25744	33AQC	2198	Aeropostale	N3213T	F-GIXD	
25764	48E	2314	Asiana Airlines	HL7227		
25765	48E	2335	Asiana Airlines	HL7228		
25766	48E	2543	Asiana Airlines	HL7231		
25767	58E	2614	Asiana Airlines	HL7232		
25768	58E	2724	Asiana Airlines	HL7233		
25769	58E	2737	Asiana Airlines	HL7250		
25771	48E		Asiana Airlines	HL7510		
25772	48E		Asiana Airlines	HL7508		
25787	3K9	2302	Shenzen Airlines	(PP-...)	N41069	B-2932
25788	3K9	2331	Shenzen Airlines	(PP-...)	N4113D	B-2933
25789	505	2229	Braathens-SAFE	LN-BRT		
25790	505	2245	Braathens-SAFE	LN-BRU		
25791	505	2351	Braathens-SAFE	LN-BRV		
25792	505	2353	Xiamen Airlines	LN-BRW	B-2591	
25794	505		Braathens-SAFE	LN-BUA		
25796	430		(Lufthansa)	(D-ABKM)	Allocated but later canx, not built	
25797	505	2434	Braathens-SAFE	LN-BRX		
25800	430		(Lufthansa)	(D-ABKP)	Allocated but later canx, not built	
25839	436	2188	British Airways	G-DOCI		
25840	436	2197	British Airways	G-DOCJ		

BOEING 737

C/n	Series	Line No	Last known Operator/Owner	Previous Identities/fate (where known)				
25841	436	2222	British Airways	G-DOCK				
25842	436	2228	British Airways	G-DOCL				
25843	436	2244	British Airways	G-DOCM				
25844	436	2514	Eurobelgian Airlines	(G-DOCY)	G-BVBY	TC-ALS	G-BVBY	OO-LTQ
25848	436	2379	British Airways	G-DOCN				
25849	436	2381	British Airways	G-DOCO				
25850	436	2386	British Airways	G-DOCP				
25851	436	2387	British Airways	G-DOCR				
25852	436	2390	British Airways	G-DOCS				
25853	436	2409	British Airways	G-DOCT				
25854	436	2417	British Airways	G-DOCU				
25855	436	2420	British Airways	G-DOCV				
25856	436	2422	British Airways	G-DOCW				
25857	436	2451	British Airways	G-DOCX				
25858	436	2522	British Airways	(G-DOCZ)	G-BVBZ	EC-457	EC-FXJ	G-DOCZ
25859	436	2532	British Airways	(G-GBTA)	G-BVHA	G-GBTA		
25860	436	2545	Eurobelgian Airlines	(G-GBTB)	G-BVHB	OO-LTS	G-BVHB	OO-LTS
25891	3J6	2385	Air China	B-2584				
25892	3J6	2396	Air China	B-2587				
25893	3J6	2489	Air China	B-2588				
25895	31B	2499	China Southern Airlines	B-2582				
25896	3Z0	2558	China Southwest Airlines	B-2599				
25897	31B	2554	China Southern Airlines	B-2583				
25902	5T0	2736	Continental Airlines	N17356				
25903	5T0	2743	Continental Airlines	N19357				
25904	5T0	2772	Continental Airlines	N14358				
25905	5T0		Continental Airlines	N12359				
25906	5T0		Continental Airlines	N39360				
25971	505		Braathens-SAFE	LN-BRV				
25972	505		Braathens-SAFE	LN-BRW				
25994	332	2439	Turkmenistan Airlines	N301DE	EZ-A002			
25995	332	2455	Turkmenistan Airlines	N302DE	EZ-A003			
25996	332	2488	Government of Philippines	N303DE	RP-C2000	RP-C4007		
25997	332	2506	China Xinhua Airlines	N304DE	B-2942			
25998	332	2510	China Xinhua Airlines	N305DE	B-2943			
25999	332		(Delta Air Lines)	(N306DE)	Allocated but later canx, not built			
26000	332		(Delta Air Lines)	(N307DE)	Allocated but later canx, not built			
26001	332		(Delta Air Lines)	(N308DE)	Allocated but later canx, not built			
26002	332		(Delta Air Lines)	(N309DE)	Allocated but later canx, not built			
26003	332		(Delta Air Lines)	(N310DE)	Allocated but later canx, not built			
26004	332		(Delta Air Lines)	(N311DE)	Allocated but later canx, not built			
26051	566	2282	Egyptair	SU-GBL				
26052	566	2276	Egyptair	SU-GBK				
26065	4Y0	2284	THY-Turkish Airlines	(EI-CFS)	TC-JDY			
26066	4Y0	2301	THY-Turkish Airlines	TC-JDZ				
26067	5Y0	2304	Air Pacific	DQ-FJB				
26068	5Y0	2306	Yunnan Airlines	B-2539				
26069	4Y0	2352	Malev	N1787B	N3509J	UR-GAA	HA-LEN	
26070	3Y0	2349	China National Aviation Corp	B-2534				
26071	4Y0	2361	Malev	N1784B	N35108	UR-GAB	HA-LEO	
26072	3Y0	2369	China Southwest Airlines	B-2595				
26073	4Y0	2375	THY-Turkish Airlines	TC-JER				
26074	4Y0	2376	(THY-Turkish Airlines)	TC-JES	w/o 29Dec94 Van, Turkey			
26075	5Y0	2374	Rio Sul	PT-SLN				
26076	4Y0		(GPA Group)	Allocated but later canx, not built				
26077	4Y0	2425	THY-Turkish Airlines	TC-JET				
26078	4Y0	2431	THY-Turkish Airlines	TC-JEU				
26081	4Y0	2442	Pegasus Airlines	D-ABAF	TC-AFU			
26082	3Y0	2456	China Southern Airlines	B-2909				
26083	3Y0	2459	China Southern Airlines	B-2910				
26084	3Y0	2460	China Southern Airlines	B-2911				
26085	4Y0	2468	THY-Turkish Airlines	TC-JEV				
26086	4Y0	2475	THY-Turkish Airlines	TC-JEY				
26088	4Y0	2487	THY-Turkish Airlines	TC-JEZ				
26097	5Y0	2534	Rio Sul	PT-SLP				
26100	5Y0	2538	Xiamen Airlines	N35108	B-2912			
26101	5Y0	2544	China Southern Airlines	B-2913				
26104	5Y0	2552	Rio Sul	PP-SLS				
26105	5Y0	2553	Rio Sul	(B-....)	PP-SLT			
26279	4Q8	2221	Carnival Airlines	TC-AFM				
26280	4Q8	2239	British Midland	G-OBMO				
26281	4Q8	2380	Fly Cruise	N401KW	[Op by Carnival Airlines]			
26282	3Q8	2355	Polynesian Airlines	5W-ILF				
26283	3Q8	2383	TACA International Airlines	N373TA				
26284	3Q8	2418	China National Aviation Corp	(G-BUHI)	N571LF	B-2901		
26285	4Q8	2416	Carnival Airlines	N402KW				
26286	3Q8	2424	TACA International Airlines	N374TA				
26287	548	2427	Aer Lingus	EI-CDS				
26288	3Q8	2480	China Southwest Airlines	(B-2903)	N471LF	B-2904		
26289	4Q8	2486	British Airways	G-BUHK				
26290	4Q8	2482	THY-Turkish Airlines	TC-JEE				

BOEING 737

C/n	Series	Line No	Last known Operator/Owner	Previous Identities/fate (where known)			
26291	4Q8	2513	THY-Turkish Airlines	TC-JEF			
26292	3Q8	2519	China Southwest Airlines	(B-2904)	B-2903		
26293	3Q8	2541	Air Europa	(CC-CYK)	N351LF	EC-520	EC-FUT
26294	3Q8	2550	Wuhan Airlines	N261LF	B-2928		
26295	3Q8	2557	Hainan Airlines	B-2937			
26296	3Q8	2581	Hainan Airlines	B-2938			
26297	505	2578	Xiamen Airlines	LN-BUA	B-2529		
26298	4Q8	2564	THY-Turkish Airlines	TC-JEI			
26299	4Q8	2602	THY-Turkish Airlines	TC-JEK			
26300	4Q8	2604	THY-Turkish Airlines	TC-JEL			
26301	3Q8	2623	Air Europa	(N841LF)	EC-547	EC-FYF	
26302	4Q8	2620	THY-Turkish Airlines	TC-JEM			
26303	3Q8	2635	Malev	HA-LEJ			
26304	505	2649	Braathens-SAFE	LN-BUC			
26305	3Q8	2651	Air Madagascar	5R-MFH			
26306	4Q8	2653	Carnival Airlines	TC-AFA			
26307	3Q8	2664	TEA Basel	(HB-IIE)	N721LF	HB-IIE	
26308	4Q8	2665	Asiana Airlines	HL7235			
26309	3Q8	2674	Continental Airlines	N73380			
26310	3Q8	2680	Continental Airlines	N14381			
26311	3Q8	2681	Continental Airlines	N19382			
26312	3Q8	2693	Continental Airlines	N14383			
26313	3Q8	2704	Continental Airlines	N14384			
26314	3Q8	2707	Continental Airlines	N73385			
26315	36E	2706	VIVA Air	EC-796	EC-GAP		
26316	4K5	2711	Hapag Lloyd	D-AHLG			
26317	36E	2719	VIVA Air	EC-797	EC-GBU		
26318	3Q8	2731	Air One	PH-TSX			
26319	524	2748	Continental Airlines	N19634			
26320	4Q8	2563	THY-Turkish Airlines	TC-JEH			
26321	3Q8	2764	Continental Airlines	N17386			
26322	36E	2769	VIVA Air	EC-798			
26323	5Q8	2770	Estonian Air	ES-ABD			
26324	5Q8	2735	Estonian Air	ES-ABC			
26325	3Q8	2772	Hainan Airlines	B-2963			
26339	524	2771	Continental Airlines	N33635			
26340	524		Continental Airlines	N19636			
26419	59D	2186	British Midland	SE-DNI	G-OBMY		
26421	59D	2279	British Midland	SE-DNK	G-BVKD		
26422	59D	2412	British Midland	SE-DNL	G-BVZE		
26428	330	2196	Lufthansa	D-ABEN			
26429	330	2207	Lufthansa	D-ABEO			
26430	330	2216	Lufthansa	D-ABEP			
26431	330	2242	Lufthansa	D-ABER			
26432	330	2247	Lufthansa	D-ABES			
26437	4C9	2249	Luxair	LX-LGG			
26438	5C9	2413	Luxair	LX-LGO			
26439	5C9	2444	Luxair	LX-LGP			
26440	3L9	2234	Deutsche BA	OY-MAK	D-ADBB		
26441	3L9	2251	Deutsche BA	OY-MAL	D-ADBA		
26442	3L9	2277	Deutsche BA	OY-MAM	D-ADBC		
26443	4H6	2272	Malaysia Airlines	9M-MMA			
26444	4H6	2308	Malaysia Airlines	9M-MMB			
26445	5H6	2327	Malaysia Airlines	9M-MFA			
26446	5H6	2358	Malaysia Airlines	9M-MFB			
26447	4H6	2479	Malaysia Airlines	(9M-MMQ)	9M-MMU		
26448	5H6	2484	Malaysia Airlines	9M-MFC			
26449	4H6	2491	Malaysia Airlines	(9M-MFD)	9M-MMV	[Originally ordered as 737-5H6]	
26450	5H6	2503	Malaysia Airlines	(9M-MFE)	9M-MFD		
26451	4H6	2496	Malaysia Airlines	(9M-MFF)	9M-MMW	[Originally ordered as 737-5H6]	
26452	4H6	2501	Royal Air Cambodge	9M-MMX			
26453	4H6	2332	Malaysia Airlines	9M-MMC			
26454	5H6	2511	Malaysia Airlines	9M-MFE			
26455	4H6	2507	Myanma Airways Intl	9M-MMY			
26456	5H6	2527	Malaysia Airlines	9M-MFF			
26457	4H6	2521	Malaysia Airlines	9M-MMZ			
26458	4H6	2525	Malaysia Airlines	(9M-MNA)	9M-MQA		
26459	4H6	2530	Malaysia Airlines	(9M-MNB)	9M-MQB		
26460	4H6	2533	Malaysia Airlines	(9M-MNC)	9M-MQC		
26461	4H6	2536	Malaysia Airlines	(9M-MND)	9M-MQD		
26462	4H6	2542	Malaysia Airlines	9M-MQE			
26463	4H6	2560	Malaysia Airlines	9M-MQF			
26464	4H6	2340	Malaysia Airlines	9M-MMD			
26465	4H6	2362	Malaysia Airlines	9M-MME			
26466	4H6	2372	Malaysia Airlines	9M-MMF			
26467	4H6	2378	Malaysia Airlines	9M-MMG			
26468	4H6	2445	Malaysia Airlines	(9M-MMO)	9M-MMR		
26525	5B6	2209	Royal Air Maroc	CN-RMY			
26526	4B6	2219	Royal Air Maroc	CN-RMX			
26527	5B6	2472	Royal Air Maroc	CN-RNB			
26529	4B6	2584	Royal Air Maroc	CN-RNC			

BOEING 737

C/n	Series	Line No	Last known Operator/Owner	Previous Identities/fate (where known)
26530	4B6	2588	Royal Air Maroc	CN-RND
26531	4B6	2453	Royal Air Maroc	CN-RNA
26537	529	2296	SABENA World Airlines	OO-SYJ
26538	529	2298	SABENA World Airlines	OO-SYK
26539	55S	2300	Czech Airlines	(OO-SYL) N1790B OK-XGA [Originally ordered as 737-529]
26540	55S	2317	Czech Airlines	(OO-SYM) OK-XGB [Originally ordered as 737-529]
26541	55S	2319	Czech Airlines	(OO-SYN) OK-XGC [Originally ordered as 737-529]
26542	55S	2337	Czech Airlines	(OO-SYO) OK-XGD [Originally ordered as 737-529]
26543	55S	2339	Czech Airlines	(OO-SYP) OK-XGE [Originally ordered as 737-529]
26564	5H4	2202	Southwest Airlines	N522SW
26565	5H4	2204	Southwest Airlines	N523SW
26566	5H4	2224	Southwest Airlines	N524SW
26567	5H4	2283	Southwest Airlines	N525SW
26568	5H4	2285	Southwest Airlines	N526SW
26569	5H4	2287	Southwest Airlines	N527SW
26570	5H4	2292	Southwest Airlines	N528SW
26571	3H4	2307	Southwest Airlines	N360SW
26572	3H4	2309	Southwest Airlines	N361SW
26573	3H4	2322	Southwest Airlines	N362SW
26574	3H4	2429	Southwest Airlines	N363SW
26575	3H4	2430	Southwest Airlines	N364SW
26576	3H4	2433	Southwest Airlines	N365SW
26577	3H4	2469	Southwest Airlines	N366SW
26578	3H4	2470	Southwest Airlines	N367SW
26579	3H4	2473	Southwest Airlines	N368SW
26580	3H4	2477	Southwest Airlines	N369SW
26581	3H4	2509	Southwest Airlines	N373SW
26582	3H4	2515	Southwest Airlines	N374SW
26583	3H4	2520	Southwest Airlines	N375SW
26584	3H4	2570	Southwest Airlines	N376SW
26585	3H4	2579	Southwest Airlines	N378SW
26586	3H4	2580	Southwest Airlines	N379SW
26587	3H4	2610	Southwest Airlines	N380SW
26588	3H4	2611	Southwest Airlines	N382SW
26589	3H4	2612	Southwest Airlines	N383SW
26590	3H4	2613	Southwest Airlines	N384SW
26591	3H4	2628	Southwest Airlines	N388SW
26592	3H4	2629	Southwest Airlines	N389SW
26593	3H4	2642	Southwest Airlines	N390SW
26594	3H4	2294	Southwest Airlines	N357SW
26595	3H4	2295	Southwest Airlines	N358SW
26596	3H4	2297	Southwest Airlines	N359SW
26597	3H4	2497	Southwest Airlines	N370SW
26598	3H4	2500	Southwest Airlines	N371SW
26599	3H4	2504	Southwest Airlines	N372SW
26600	3H4	2617	Southwest Airlines	N385SW
26601	3H4	2626	Southwest Airlines	N386SW
26602	3H4	2627	Southwest Airlines	N387SW
26603	4Q3	2618	Japan Trans Ocean Airlines	JA8523
26604	4Q3	2684	Japan Trans Ocean Airlines	JA8524
26605	4Q3	2752	Japan Trans Ocean Airlines	JA8525
26611	4D7	2318	Thai International	HS-TDD
26612	4D7	2330	Thai International	HS-TDE
26613	4D7	2338	Thai International	HS-TDF
26614	4D7	2481	Thai International	HS-TDG
26639	5H3	2253	Tunis Air	TS-IOG
26640	5H3	2474	Tunis Air	TS-IOH
26642	522	2189	United Airlines	N922UA
26643	522	2190	United Airlines	N923UA
26645	522	2212	United Airlines	N924UA
26646	522	2214	United Airlines	N925UA
26648	522	2230	United Airlines	N926UA
26649	522	2246	United Airlines	N927UA
26651	522	2257	United Airlines	N928UA
26652	522	2259	United Airlines	N929UA
26655	522	2274	United Airlines	N930UA
26656	522	2289	United Airlines	N931UA
26658	522	2291	United Airlines	N932UA
26659	522	2293	United Airlines	N933UA
26662	522	2312	United Airlines	N934UA
26663	522	2315	United Airlines	N935UA
26667	522	2325	United Airlines	N936UA
26668	522	2329	United Airlines	N937UA
26671	522	2336	United Airlines	N938UA
26672	522	2343	United Airlines	N939UA
26675	522	2345	United Airlines	N940UA
26676	522	2364	United Airlines	N941UA
26679	522	2365	United Airlines	N942UA
26680	522	2366	United Airlines	N943UA
26683	522	2368	United Airlines	N944UA

BOEING 737

C/n	Series	Line No	Last known Operator/Owner	Previous Identities/fate (where known)			
26684	522	2388	United Airlines	N945UA			
26687	522	2402	United Airlines	N946UA			
26688	522	2404	United Airlines	N947UA			
26691	522	2408	United Airlines	N948UA			
26692	522	2421	United Airlines	N949UA			
26695	522	2423	United Airlines	N950UA			
26696	522	2440	United Airlines	N951UA			
26699	522	2485	United Airlines	N952UA			
26700	522	2490	United Airlines	N953UA			
26703	522	2498	United Airlines	N955UA			
26704	522	2508	United Airlines	N956UA			
26707	522	2512	United Airlines	N957UA			
26708	522		(United Airlines)	(N958UA)	Allocated but later canx, not built		
26711	522		(United Airlines)	(N959UA)	Allocated but later canx, not built		
26712	522		(United Airlines)	(N960UA)	Allocated but later canx, not built		
26714	522		(United Airlines)	(N961UA)	Allocated but later canx, not built		
26739	522	2494	United Airlines	N954UA			
26850	3B3QC	2235	Aeropostale	N854WT	F-GIXE		
26851	3B3QC	2267	Aeropostale	N4361V	F-GIXF		
26852	341	2273	VARIG	PP-VPA			
26853	341	2275	Yunnan Airlines	(PP-VPB)	B-2594		
26854	341	2303	China Xinhua Airlines	(PP-VPC)	(F-OGRT)	B-2908	
26855	341	2305	Govt of Turkmenistan	PP-VPD	EKA001	EZ-A001	[Op by Turkmenistan Airlines]
26856	341	2321	VARIG	(PP-VPE)	PP-VPB		
26857	341	2326	VARIG	(PP-VPF)	PP-VPC		
26858	341		(VARIG)	Allocated but later canx, not built			
26859	341		(VARIG)	Allocated but later canx, not built			
26860	341		(VARIG)	Allocated but later canx, not built			
26960	4L7	2483	Air Nauru	C2-RN10			
26961	4L7	2517	Qantas Airways	C2-RN11	VH-TJW		
27000	430	2311	Lufthansa	D-ABKA			
27001	430	2316	Lufthansa	D-ABKB			
27002	430	2323	Lufthansa	D-ABKC			
27003	430	2328	Lufthansa	D-ABKD			
27004	430	2344	Lufthansa	(D-ABKE)	(D-ABKK)	D-ABKF	
27005	430	2359	Lufthansa	(D-ABKF)	D-ABKK		
27007	430	2367	Sun Express Air	(D-ABKH)	D-ABKL	TC-SUS	
27045	3J6	2384	Air China	B-2585			
27046	3Z0	2252	China Southwest Airlines	B-2530			
27047	3Z0	2327	China Southwest Airlines	B-2586			
27061	3L9	2347	Deutsche BA	OY-MAN	D-ADBD		
27074	4K5	2281	Hapag Lloyd	(D-AHLG)	D-AHLS		
27075	4M8		(TEA)	Allocated but later canx, not built			
27081	490	2354	Alaska Airlines	N767AS			
27082	490	2356	Alaska Airlines	N768AS			
27083	4H6	2403	Malaysia Airlines	9M-MMK			
27084	4H6	2391	Myanma Airways Intl	9M-MMH			
27085	4H6	2407	Malaysia Airlines	9M-MML			
27086	4H6	2426	Jet Airways	(9M-MMM)	9M-MMO	VT-JAE	
27087	4H6	2441	Malaysia Airlines	(9M-MMN)	9M-MMQ		
27094	4Z9	2432	Lauda Air	OE-LNI			
27096	4H6	2395	Malaysia Airlines	9M-MMI			
27097	4H6	2399	Malaysia Airlines	9M-MMJ			
27102	4K5	2394	Hapag-Lloyd	D-AHLM			
27125	3H6QC	2415	Malaysia Airlines	(9M-MFZ)	9M-MZA		
27126	3Z0	2370	China Southwest Airlines	B-2590			
27127	3W0	2377	Yunnan Airlines	B-2589			
27128	3J6	2493	Air China	B-2598			
27129	3J6		(Air China)	Allocated but later canx, not built			
27130	55D	2448	LOT-Polish Airlines	SP-LKE			
27131	45D	2458	LOT-Polish Airlines	SP-LLA			
27138	3Z0	2436	China Southwest Airlines	B-2533			
27139	3W0	2400	(Yunnan Airlines)	B-2540	dbr 20Jul94 Kunmig, PRC		
27143	42J	2457	THY-Turkish Airlines	TC-JEA			
27149	484	2471	Olympic Airways	SX-BKG			
27151	31B	2437	China Southern Airlines	B-2596			
27153	505	2516	Xiamen Airlines	LN-BRZ	9M-MMM	B-2592	
27155	505	2449	Xiamen Airlines	LN-BRY	B-2593		
27156	45D	2492	LOT-Polish Airlines	SP-LLB			
27157	45D	2502	LOT-Polish Airlines	SP-LLC			
27166	4H6	2410	Malaysia Airlines	9M-MMM			
27167	4H6	2419	Malaysia Airlines	9M-MMN			
27168	4H6	2435	Jet Airways	9M-MMP	VT-JAF		
27169	4H6	2450	Malaysia Airlines	9M-MMS			
27170	4H6	2462	Malaysia Airlines	9M-MMT			
27171	46J	2465	Air Berlin	D-ABAE			
27176	3Z0	2495	China Southwest Airlines	B-2597			
27179	38J	2524	Tarom	N5573K	YR-BGA		
27180	38J	2529	Tarom	YR-BGB			
27181	38J	2662	Tarom	YR-BGC			
27182	38J	2663	Tarom	YR-BGD			

BOEING 737

C/n	Series	Line No	Last known Operator/Owner	Previous Identities/fate (where known)		
27187	497		(Aloha Airlines)	(N403AL)	Allocated but later canx, not built	
27188	497		(Aloha Airlines)	(N404AL)	Allocated but later canx, not built	
27190	4H6	2568	Malaysia Airlines	9M-MQG		
27191	4H6	2676	Malaysia Airlines	9M-MQL		
27213	46J	2585	Air Berlin	D-ABAG		
27231	430		(Lufthansa)	(D-ABKN)	Allocated but later canx, not built	
27232	406	2591	KLM-Royal Dutch Airlines	PH-BTF		
27233	406	2601	KLM-Royal Dutch Airlines	PH-BTG		
27256	45D	2589	LOT-Polish Airlines	SP-LLD		
27257	5H3	2583	Tunis Air	TS-IOI		
27267	33A	2600	Ansett Australia	VH-CZU		
27268	59D	2592	British Midland	SE-DNM	G-BVKB	
27271	3Q8	2523	China Southern Airlines	B-2920		
27272	31B	2555	China Southern Airlines	B-2922		
27273	31L	2556	China Xinjiang Airlines	B-2930		
27274	39K	2559	China National Aviation Corp	B-2934		
27275	31B	2565	China Southern Airlines	B-2923		
27276	31L	2567	China Xinjiang Airlines	B-2931		
27283	37K	2547	Shenzen Airlines	B-2935		
27284	33A	2606	TAESA	CS-TKF	XA-SWO	
27285	33A	2608	Air Pacific	CS-TKG	N102AN	DQ-FJD
27286	3Q8	2528	China Southern Airlines	B-2921		
27287	31B	2575	China Southern Airlines	B-2924		
27288	31B	2577	China Southern Airlines	B-2925		
27289	31B	2593	China Southern Airlines	B-2926		
27290	31B	2595	China Southern Airlines	B-2927		
27304	528	2572	Air France	F-GJNN		
27305	528	2574	Air France	F-GJNO		
27306	4H6	2685	Malaysia Airlines	9M-MQM		
27314	524	2566	Continental Airlines	(N26600)	N14601	
27315	524	2571	Continental Airlines	(N14601)	N69602	
27316	524	2573	Continental Airlines	(N69602)	N69603	
27317	524	2576	Continental Airlines	(N69603)	N14604	
27318	524	2582	Continental Airlines	(N14604)	N14605	
27319	524	2590	Continental Airlines	(N14605)	N58606	
27320	524	2596	Continental Airlines	(N58606)	N16607	
27321	524	2597	Continental Airlines	(N16607)	N33608	
27322	524	2607	Continental Airlines	(N33608)	N14609	
27323	524	2616	Continental Airlines	(N14609)	N27610	
27324	524	2621	Continental Airlines	(N27610)	N18611	
27325	524	2630	Continental Airlines	(N18611)	N11612	
27326	524	2633	Continental Airlines	(N11612)	N14613	
27327	524	2634	Continental Airlines	(N14613)	N17614	
27328	524	2640	Continental Airlines	(N17614)	N37615	
27329	524	2641	Continental Airlines	(N37615)	N52616	
27330	524	2648	Continental Airlines	(N52616)	N16617	
27331	524	2652	Continental Airlines	(N16617)	N16618	
27332	524	2659	Continental Airlines	(N16618)	N17619	
27333	524	2660	Continental Airlines	(N17619)	N17908	N17620
27334	524	2661	Continental Airlines	(N17620)	N19621	
27335	37K	2609	Zhongyuan Airlines	B-2936		
27336	3L9	2587	Deutsche BA	OY-MAO	D-ADBH	
27337	3L9	2594	Deutsche BA	OY-MAP	D-ADBI	
27343	31B	2619	China Southern Airlines	B-2929		
27344	31B	2622	China Southern Airlines	B-2941		
27345	31L	2625	Shenzen Airlines	B-2939		
27346	31L	2636	Shenzen Airlines	B-2940		
27347	3H6QC	2615	Malaysia Airlines	9M-MZB		
27352	4H6	2624	Malaysia Airlines	9M-MQH		
27353	4H6	2632	Malaysia Airlines	9M-MQI		
27354	5H6	2637	Malaysia Airlines	9M-MFG		
27355	5H6	2646	Malaysia Airlines	9M-MFH		
27356	5H6	2654	Malaysia Airlines	9M-MFI		
27361	3J6	2631	Air China	B-2948		
27362	37K	2639	China Xinhua Airlines	B-2945		
27368	55D	2603	LOT-Polish Airlines	SP-LKF		
27372	3J6	2650	Air China	B-2949		
27373	3Z0	2658	China National Aviation Corp	B-2951		
27374	3Z0	2647	China National Aviation Corp	B-2950		
27375	37K	2655	Zhongyuan Airlines	B-2946		
27378	3H4	2643	Southwest Airlines	N391SW		
27379	3H4	2644	Southwest Airlines	N392SW		
27380	3H4	2645	Southwest Airlines	N393SW		
27381	54K	2708	Air Nippon	N35198	JA8404	
27383	4H6	2657	Malaysia Airlines	9M-MQJ		
27384	4H6	2673	Malaysia Airlines	9M-MQK		
27395	38J	2671	Tarom	YR-BGE		
27416	55D	2389	LOT-Polish Airlines	SP-LKA		
27417	55D	2392	LOT-Polish Airlines	SP-LKB		
27418	55D	2397	LOT-Polish Airlines	SP-LKC		
27419	55D	2401	LOT-Polish Airlines	SP-LKD		

BOEING 737

C/n	Series	Line No	Last known Operator/Owner	Previous Identities/fate (where known)	
27420	306	2406	KLM-Royal Dutch Airlines	PH-BTD	
27421	306	2438	KLM-Royal Dutch Airlines	PH-BTE	
27424	528	2720	Luxair	(F-GJNP)	LX-LGR
27425	528	2730	Luxair	(F-GNJQ)	LX-LGS
27426	528	2739	Fuerza Aerea Peruana	(F-GJNR)	PRP-001
27430	54K	2723	Air Nippon	JA8419	
27431	54K	2751	Air Nippon	JA8500	
27432	54K	2783	Air Nippon	JA8504	
27433	54K		Air Nippon	JA8195	
27452	33A	2679	Air Austral	F-ODZY	
27453	33A	2687	Yunnan Airlines	B-2955	
27454	33A	2703	Ansett Australia	VH-CZT	
27455	33A	2709	Eurobelgian Airlines	OO-LTU	
27456	33A	2749	Continental Heights Resort	9M-LKY	9M-CHG
27457	33A	2756	Silkair	9V-TRE	
27462	33A	2765	Yunnan Airlines	B-2966	
27518	3J6	2768	Air China	B-2954	
27519	31B	2678	China Southern Airlines	B-2952	
27520	31B	2775	China Southern Airlines	B-2959	
27521	3Z0	2738	China National Avn Corp	B-2957	
27522	3W0	2727	Yunnan Airlines	B-2958	
27523	3J6	2710	Air China	B-2953	
27526	524	2669	Continental Airlines	N18622	
27527	524	2672	Continental Airlines	N19623	
27528	524	2675	Continental Airlines	N13624	
27529	524	2683	Continental Airlines	N46625	
27530	524	2686	Continental Airlines	N32626	
27531	524	2700	Continental Airlines	N17627	
27532	524	2712	Continental Airlines	N14628	
27533	524	2725	Continental Airlines	N14629	
27534	524	2726	Continental Airlines	N59630	
27535	524	2728	Continental Airlines	N62631	
27540	524		Continental Airlines	N33637	
27627	505		Braathens-SAFE	LN-BUE	
27628	4Q8		Alaska Airlines	N785AS	
27635	3K2	2721	Transavia Airlines	PH-TSZ	
27678	4B6	2733	Royal Air Maroc	(CN-RNE)	CN-RNF
27679	5B6	2734	Royal Air Maroc	(CN-RNF)	CN-RNG
27689	3H4	2667	Southwest Airlines	N395SW	
27690	3H4	2668	Southwest Airlines	N396SW	
27691	3H4	2695	Southwest Airlines	N397SW	
27692	3H4	2696	Southwest Airlines	N398SW	
27693	3H4	2697	Southwest Airlines	N399WN	
27694	3H4	2699	Southwest Airlines	N600WN	
27695	3H4	2702	Southwest Airlines	N601WN	
27696	3H4	2745	Southwest Airlines	N610WN	
27697	3H4	2750	Southwest Airlines	N611SW	
27698	3H4	2757	Southwest Airlines	N615SW	
27699	3H4	2758	Southwest Airlines	N616SW	
27700	3H4	2759	Southwest Airlines	N1786B	N617SW
27701	3H4	2787	Southwest Airlines	N625SW	
27702	3H4	2789	Southwest Airlines	N626SW	
27703	3H4		Southwest Airlines	N628SW	
27704	3H4		Southwest Airlines	N629SW	
27705	3H4		Southwest Airlines	N630SW	
27706	3H4		Southwest Airlines	N631SW	
27707	3H4		Southwest Airlines	N632SW	
27708	3H4		Southwest Airlines	N635SW	
27709	3H4		Southwest Airlines	N636SW	
27710	3H4		Southwest Airlines	N637SW	
27711	3H4		Southwest Airlines	N638SW	
27712	3H4		Southwest Airlines	N639SW	
27713	3H4		Southwest Airlines	N640SW	
27714	3H4		Southwest Airlines	N641SW	
27715	3H4		Southwest Airlines	N642WN	
27826	46J	2694	Air Berlin	D-ABAH	
27830	4K5	2670	Hapag-Lloyd	D-AHLT	
27831	4K5	2677	Hapag-Lloyd	D-AHLU	
27833	3L9	2688	Maersk Air	OY-MAR	
27834	3L9	2692	Maersk Air	OY-MAS	
27900	524		Continental Airlines	N16632	
27901	524		Continental Airlines	N24633	
27903	330	2682	Lufthansa	D-ABET	
27904	330	2691	Lufthansa	D-ABEU	
27905	330	2705	Lufthansa	D-ABEW	
27906	4Z6	2698	Royal Thai AF/Royal Flight	55-555/HS-RTA	
27907	33A	2690	Yunnan Airlines	B-2956	
27912	5H3	2701	Tunis Air	TS-IOJ	
27914	45D	2724	LOT-Polish Airlines	SP-LLE	
27916	446	2718	Japan Air Lines	JA8991	
27917	446	2729	Japan Air Lines	N1792B	JA8992

BOEING 737

C/n	Series	Line No	Last known Operator/Owner	Previous Identities/fate (where known)
27924	3L9	2760	Maersk Air	OY-MAT
27925	3L9	2763	Maersk Air	OY-MAU
27926	3H4	2740	Southwest Airlines	N606SW
27927	3H4	2741	Southwest Airlines	N607SW
27928	3H4	2742	Southwest Airlines	N608SW
27929	3H4	2744	Southwest Airlines	N609SW
27930	3H4	2753	Southwest Airlines	N612SW
27931	3H4	2754	Southwest Airlines	N613SW
27932	3H4	2779	Southwest Airlines	N622SW
27933	3H4	2780	Southwest Airlines	N623SW
27934	3H4	2781	Southwest Airlines	N624SW
27935	3H4	2790	Southwest Airlines	N627SW
27936	3H4		Southwest Airlines	N633SW
27937	3H4		Southwest Airlines	N634SW
27953	3H4	2713	Southwest Airlines	N602SW
27954	3H4	2714	Southwest Airlines	N603SW
27955	3H4	2715	Southwest Airlines	N604SW
27956	3H4	2716	Southwest Airlines	N605SW
27966	54K		All Nippon	JA8196
28033	3H4	2755	Southwest Airlines	N614SW
28034	3H4	2761	Southwest Airlines	(N618SW) N618WN
28035	3H4	2762	Southwest Airlines	N619SW
28036	3H4	2766	Southwest Airlines	N620SW
28037	3H4	2767	Southwest Airlines	N621SW
28038	46J		Air Berlin	D-ABAI
28081	34N	2746	North China Administration	B-4020
28082	34N	2747	North China Administration	B-4021
28083	5L9	2784	Maersk Air	OY-APA
28084	5L9	2788	Maersk Air	OY-APB
28085	3K2	2722	Transavia Airlines	PH-TSY
28128	5L9		Maersk Air	OY-
28129	5L9		Maersk Air	OY-
28130	5L9		Maersk Air	OY-
28131	5L9		Maersk Air	OY-
28150	476	2773	Qantas Airways	VH-TJX
28151	476	2785	Qantas Airways	VH-TJY
28156	35N	2774	Shandong Airlines	B-2961
28157	35N	2778	Shandong Airlines	B-2962
28158	35N		Shandong Airlines	B-2968
28198	48E	2791	Asiana Airlines	HL7509
28199	4Q8		Alaska Airlines	N784AS
28271	46J		Air Berlin	D-ABAK
28334	46J		Air Berlin	D-ABAL

BOEING 737

C/n	Series	Line No	Last known Operator/Owner	Previous Identities/fate (where known)

BOEING 747

C/n	Series	Line No	Last known Operator/Owner	Previous Identities/fate (where known)
19637	121/SCD	4	Evergreen Intl Airlines	N731PA (9Q-ARW) N731PA N474EV
19638	121/SCD	3	Tower Air	N732PA N475EV N615FF
19639	121/SCD	2	Wilmington Trust Co	N747PA N747QC N747PA stored Portland, OR Aug93 later Norton AFB, CA
19640	121	6	Polaris A/c Leasing/GECAS	N733PA 5N-THG stored Norton AFB, CA Dec93
19641	121/SCD	7	United Parcel Service	N734PA N491GX N691UP
19642	121/SCD	10	Polar Air Cargo	N735PA VR-HKB N735PA N735SJ N830FT
19643	121	11	(Pan American World A/W)	N736PA dbf 27Mar77 Los Rodeos, Tenerife, Canary Islands when struck by 747-206B PH-BUF c/n 20400
19644	121	13	Polaris A/c Leasing/GECAS	N737PA 5N-HHS stored Norton AFB, CA Dec93
19645	121	14	(Pan American World A/W)	N738PA dbr 04Aug83 Karachi, Pakistan
19646	121/SCD	15	(Pan American World A/W)	N739PA w/o 21Dec88 Lockerbie, UK after bomb explosion
19647	121/SCD	16	Tower Air	N740PA N493GX N613FF
19648	121/SCD	17	Polar Air Cargo	N741PA N494GX (N741PA) N741SJ N831FT
19649	121	18	(Wilmington Trust Co)	N742PA stored New York-JFK, NY 04Dec91; b/u Ardmore, OK 92
19650	121/SCD	24	Tower Air	N743PA N490GX N617FF
19651	121	25	General Electric Corp	N744PA N747GE [Engine test-bed]
19652	121/SCD	26	(Evergreen Intl Airlines)	N748PA stored Marana, AZ 04Dec91; b/u Aug93
19653	121	30	(Dallas Aerospace)	N749PA stored Marana, AZ 04Dec91; b/u Jun92
19654	121	32	(Dallas Aerospace)	N750PA stored New York-JFK, NY 04Dec91; b/u Marana, AZ Jun92
19655	121/SCD	33	(Evergreen Intl Airlines)	N751PA (N306TW) N751PA N476EV stored Marana, AZ, later b/u
19656	121	34	(Pan American World A/W)	N752PA dbr 06Sep70 Cairo, Egypt following hijack
19657	121/SCD	37	Evergreen Intl Airlines	N753PA N473EV
19658	121	47	Wilmington Trust Co	N754PA LX-FCV F-GIMJ stored Aug95, to be b/u
19659	121	49	Tower Air	N755PA N604FF
19660	121	50	Corsair	N756PA LX-GCV F-GKLJ
19661	121/SCD	70	United Parcel Service	N771PA N819FT (N621FE) N628FE N681UP
19667	131/SCD	5	Islamic Iranian Air Force	N93101 5-280 5-8101 EP-NHJ EP-NHV 5-8101
19668	131/SCD	8	Islamic Iranian Air Force	N93102 5-282 5-8106 EP-NHD 5-8106
19669	131/SCD	9	Islamic Iranian Air Force	N93103 5-287 5-8108 EP-NHK 5-8108
		[NOTE:	The Iranian civil registrations	of the above two 747s have also been reported as reversed]
19670	131	20	Trans World Airlines	N93104
19671	131	21	Trans World Airlines	N93105 stored Kansas City, MO Sep94
19672	131	28	Tower Air	N93106 N608FF
19673	131	35	Trans World Airlines	N93107
19674	131	38	Trans World Airlines	N93108
19675	131	43	Trans World Airlines	N93109
19676	131	63	Trans World Airlines	(N3201) (N93110) N53110
19677	131/SCD	73	(Imperial Iranian Air Force)	(N3202) (N93111) N53111 5-283 5-8104 w/o 09May76 nr Madrid, Spain
19678	131/SCD	78	Islamic Iranian Air Force	(N3203) (N93112) N53112 5-281 5-8102 EP-NHT 5-8102
19725	146/SCD	31	American Intl Airways	JA8101 N701CK
19726	146	51	Okada Air	JA8102 5N-EDO
19727	146/SCD	54	American Intl Airways	JA8103 N703CK
19729	143	36	Tower Air	I-DEMA N355AS N603PE N17010 N621FF
19730	143	56	Continental Airlines	N1796B I-DEME N356AS N606PE N17011 stored Marana, AZ Mar95
19731	243B	120	(AAR Engine Group)	I-DEMO N357AS N604PE N78020 stored Norton AFB, CA May93 later Las Vegas, NV Mar95; b/u Nov95
19732	243B	134	Virgin Atlantic Airways	I-DEMU N358AS (N611PE) N358AS B-2440 N747BL G-VGIN
19733	124/SCD	42	Polar Air Cargo	N26861 5-289 5-8110 N26861 N750WA N809FT N750WA HK-2900 N822FT (N620FE) N630FE N630SJ N855FT
19734	124	58	Tower Air	N26862 5-290 (5-8111) N747AV HK-2000X HK-2000 N747BA N602FF
19735	124/SCD	64	El Al Israel Airlines	N26863 5-291 5-8112 N8289V 4X-AXZ HK-2400X 4X-AXZ
19744	148	84	Global A/c Lsg (Ireland)	EI-ASI HS-VGB EI-ASI stored Dublin, Eire 23Nov94, Marana, AZ 08Jun95
19745	148	108	Global A/c Lsg (Ireland)	EI-ASJ HS-VGF EI-ASJ G-BDPZ EI-ASJ "G-BZBO" EI-ASJ stored Marana, AZ 09Oct95
19746	130	12	Tower Air	N1800B D-ABYA N610BN D-ABYA N610BN N480GX N780T N603FF
19747	130	29	(Lufthansa)	D-ABYB w/o 20Nov74 Nairobi, Kenya
19748	130	44	Aer Lingus	D-ABYC EI-BED stored Dublin, Eire 05Oct94, later Marana, AZ 08Feb95
19749	128	19	(AAR Aviation Trading)	F-BPVA N611AR stored Oklahoma City, OK 10Dec93; b/u Jan94
19750	128	22	Air France	F-BPVB
19751	128/SCD	39	Atlas Air	F-BPVC N3203Y
19752	128	53	(Tower Air)	F-BPVD N612AR stored Oklahoma City, OK 03Jan94; b/u Feb94
19753	122/SCD	52	Polar Air Cargo	N4703U N853FT
19754	122/SCD	60	Polar Air Cargo	N4704U N854FT
19755	122/SCD	61	Polar Air Cargo	N4710U N850FT
19756	122/SCD	66	Polar Air Cargo	N4711U N851FT

BOEING 747

C/n	Series	Line No	Last known Operator/Owner	Previous Identities/fate (where known)
19757	122/SCD	67	Polar Air Cargo	N4712U N852FT
19761	136	23	British Airways	N1799B G-AWNA
19762	136	41	British Airways	N1798B G-AWNB
19763	136	48	British Airways	G-AWNC
19764	136	107	(British Airways)	G-AWND dbr Kuwait City, Kuwait 27Feb91 by shelling
19765	136	109	British Airways	G-AWNE
19766	136	111	British Airways	G-AWNF
19778	151	27	Northwest Airlines	N601US stored Mojave, CA
19779	151	40	(Charlotte Aircraft Corp)	N602US N602PR stored Maxton, NC, later b/u
19780	151	45	Northwest Airlines	N603US stored Mojave, CA
19781	151	55	(AGES Aviation)	N604US stored Mojave, CA Jan94; later b/u
19782	151	62	(The Memphis Group)	N605US stored Mojave, CA Jan93; b/u Greenwood, MS
19783	151	71	(Charlotte Aircraft Corp)	N606US N606PB stored Mojave, CA May93; b/u Maxton, NC Jan95
19784	151	74	(The Memphis Group)	N607US stored Greenwood, MS; b/u 31Aug94
19785	151	75	Northwest Airlines	N608US stored Mojave, CA
19786	151	83	(TRACOR)	N609US stored Mojave, CA; b/u 95
19787	151	93	(The Memphis Group)	N610US stored Marana, CA Oct93, b/u Greenwood, MS 18Oct94
19790	273C		(World Airways)	Allocated but later canx, not built
19791	273C		(World Airways)	Allocated but later canx, not built
19792	273C		(World Airways)	Allocated but later canx, not built
19823	246B	116	Japan Air Lines	JA8104
19824	246B	122	Japan Air Lines	JA8105
19825	246B	137	Japan Air Lines	JA8106
19875	122	89	United Airlines	N4713U N4724U
19876	122	97	United Airlines	N4714U
19877	122	99	United Airlines	N4716U stored Las Vegas, NV Feb96
19878	122	101	United Airlines	N4717U
19879	122	139	United Airlines	N4718U
19880	122	145	United Airlines	N4719U
19881	122	148	United Airlines	N4720U
19882	122	175	United Airlines	N4723U
19883	122	193	United Airlines	N4727U "N8027U" N4727U
19896	132/SCD	72	Evergreen Intl Airlines	N9896 LV-LRG N9896 N40108 B-1868 N902PA N481EV
19897	132/SCD	82	Air Hong Kong	N9897 N803FT N623FE VR-HKN
19898	132/SCD	94	Evergreen Intl Airlines	N9898 B-1860 EI-BOS N725PA N479EV
19918	135	68	(The Memphis Group)	N77772 N620US stored Marana, AZ Jun93; b/u Greenwood, MS
19919	135	81	(The Memphis Group)	N77773 N621US stored Marana, AZ Oct93; b/u Greenwood, MS
19922	206B	96	(General Aviation Services)	PH-BUA N531AW stored Las Vegas, NV Oct92; b/u 21Feb96
19923	206B	118	(General Avn Technologies)	PH-BUB N532AW stored Mojave, CA 15Oct91; b/u Jul94
19924	206B	138	(Wilmington Trust Co)	PH-BUC N533AW stored Mojave, CA 15Jan92; b/u San Antonio, TX May94
19925	122	205	United Airlines	N4728U
19926	122	206	United Airlines	N4729U
19927	122	207	United Airlines	N4732U
19928	122	208	United Airlines	N4735U
19957	156	76	Trans World Airlines	EC-BRO N133TW
19958	156	91	Trans World Airlines	EC-BRP N134TW
19959	237B	124	(Air India)	VT-EBD w/o 01Jan78 off Bombay, India
19960	237B	130	Air India	VT-EBE
20007	190		(Alaska Airlines)	Allocated but later canx, not built
20009	238B	147	AAR Aviation Trading	VH-EBA 4R-ULF VH-EBA N614AR stored Norton AFB, CA 29Mar93, later Marana, AZ
20010	238B/SCD	149	American Intl Airways	VH-EBB 4R-ULG VH-EBB N706CK
20011	238B	162	Tower Air	VH-EBC (N372EA) VH-EBC N747BM N607PE N747BM N607PE (N50022) N607PE
20012	238B	171	AGES Aviation	VH-EBD N371EA VH-EBD N747BN N608PE (N10023) N608PE stored Norton AFB, CA Nov92
20013	133	104	(AAR Engine Sales & Leasing)	CF-TOA C-FTOA EI-BOU N749R EI-BPH N890FT (N629F) N890FT (N620FE) N890FT stored New York-JFK, NY Jun93, then Marana, AZ; b/u Sep95
20014	133	121	Air Atlanta Icelandic	CF-TOB C-FTOB EC-DXE EI-BRR C-FTOB N621FE C-FTOB TF-ABR N874UM (C-GLUS) N874UM TF-ABR
20015	133	144	Air Canada	CF-TOC C-FTOC
20080	131/SCD	80	Saha Airline	(N7401Q) N93113 5-282 5-8103 EP-NHS EP-SHC
20081	131/SCD	85	Saha Airline	(N7402Q) N93114 5-284 5-8105 EP-NHR EP-SHD
20082	131/SCD	151	Islamic Iranian Air Force	(N7403Q) N93118 5-286 5-8107 EP-NHP
20083	131	153	Trans World Airlines	(N7404Q) N93119 5-288 (5-8109) N93119
20100	123/SCD	46	United Parcel Service	N9661 N800FT N903PA N800FT N9661 N674UP
20101	123/SCD	57	United Parcel Service	N9662 N801FT N662AA N801FT N9676 N676UP
20102	123	59	United Airlines	N9663 N14943 LX-KCV N153UA
20103	123	65	United Airlines	N9664 N14930 N9664 LX-NCV N154UA
20104	123	69	United Airlines	N9665 HI-472 N9665 N155UA
20105	123	77	United Airlines	N9666 N14936 LX-LCV N156UA
20106	123	79	United Airlines	N9667 N14937 LX-MCV N157UA
20107	123	86	NASA [coded 905]	N9668 N905NA [Shuttle Transporter]
20108	123	87	Virgin Atlantic Airways	N9669 N14939 LX-NCV N14939 G-HIHO VH-EEI EI-CAI G-VMIA

BOEING 747

C/n	Series	Line No	Last known Operator/Owner	Previous Identities/fate (where known)
20109	123/SCD	90	Polar Air Cargo	N9670 N858FT
20116	257B	112	Trans World Airlines	HB-IGA LX-SAL N303TW TF-ABK N303TW
20117	257B	126	(Trans World Airlines)	HB-IGB OH-KSA SU-GAK N304TW TF-ABL N304TW stored Ardmore, OK; b/u Sep94 by IBA Group
20118	257B		(Swissair)	(HB-IGC) Allocated but later canx, not built
20119	257B		(Swissair)	(HB-IGD) Allocated but later canx, not built
20120	283B	114	(Aircraft Instrument & Radio)	SE-DDL LN-AET F-GHBM N221MP stored Paris-Orly, France 22Apr92 later Topeka, AZ; b/u San Antonio, TX Jul94
20121	283B	167	Virgin Atlantic Airways	(OY-KFA) OY-KHA LN-AEO G-BMGS G-VOYG
20135	258B	140	El Al Israel Airlines	4X-AXA
20137	256B	173	Iberia	EC-BRQ F-GHPC EC-287 EC-BRQ EC-765 EC-GAG
20207	127/SCD	100	(Tower Air)	(N501BN) N601BN N601FF stored New York-JFK, NY Mar92; b/u Dec93
20208	1D1	123	Air Atlanta Icelandic	N602BN N810U (CF-FUN) CF-DJC C-FDJC N502SR TF-ABO
20235	121	1	Museum of Flight Foundation	N7470 N1352B N7470 prototype, ff 09Feb69 [Leased back to Boeing for 777 flight tests]
20237	244B	154	South African Airways	N1795B ZS-SAL
20238	244B	158	South African Airways	ZS-SAM 3B-NAI PP-VNW ZS-SAM
20239	244B	160	South African Airways	ZS-SAN
20246	132/SCD	155	Polar Air Cargo	N9899 N804FT (N627FE) N624FE VR-HKM N624PL N857FT
20247	132/SCD	159	American Intl Airways	N9900 N805FT (N628FE) N625FE N625PL
20269	136	150	British Airways	G-AWNG
20270	136	169	British Airways	G-AWNH
20271	136	172	(Tower Air)	G-AWNI (N125TW) N17125 N605FF dbr New York-JFK, NY 20Dec95
20272	136	183	British Airways	G-AWNJ
20273	136	184	Tower Air	G-AWNK (N126TW) N17126 N606FF
20274	258B	164	El Al Israel Airlines	4X-AXB
20284	136	187	British Airways	G-AWNL
20305	1D1	146	Air Atlanta Icelandic	N26864 CF-FUN C-FFUN (VR-B..) N875UM TF-ABS
20320	131/SCD	98	Evergreen Intl Airlines	N93115 N472EV
20321	131	102	Trans World Airlines	N53116
20322	131	113	Arab Leasing Intl Finance	N93117 stored Norton AFB, CA 30Nov92
20323	123/SCD	115	United Parcel Service	N9671 N802FT N9671 N671UP
20324	123/SCD	119	United Parcel Service	N9672 N672UP
20325	123/SCD	125	United Parcel Service	N9673 N673UP
20326	123/SCD	133	Polar Air Cargo	N9674 (N674PA) N9674 N859FT
20332	146/SCD	161	American Intl Airways	JA8107 N702CK
20333	246B	166	Japan Air Lines	JA8108
20337	147		(Western Air Lines)	Allocated but later canx, not built
20338	147		(Western Air Lines)	Allocated but later canx, not built
20339	147		(Western Air Lines)	Allocated but later canx, not built
20347	121/SCD	103	Polar Air Cargo	N652PA N652SJ N832FT
20348	121/SCD	106	United Parcel Service	N653PA N480EV N690UP
20349	121/SCD	110	United Parcel Service	N654PA N817FT (N624FE) N626FE N682UP
20350	121/SCD	117	Wilmington Trust Co	N655PA N492GX stored Mojave, CA 04Dec91, later Waco, TX
20351	121	127	(Evergreen Intl Airlines)	N656PA N483EV stored Marana, AZ; b/u Sep92
20352	121	129	(Evergreen Intl Airlines)	N657PA N484EV stored Marana, AZ; b/u Sep92
20353	121/SCD	131	United Parcel Service	N658PA N818FT (N625FE) N818FT N627FE N683UP
20354	121	142	Tower Air	N659PA N609FF
20355	128	105	C.Walton Ltd	F-BPVE Preserved Bruntingthorpe, UK 23Sep94
20356	251B	88	Northwest Airlines	N611US
20357	251B	135	Northwest Airlines	N612US
20358	251B	141	Northwest Airlines	N613US
20359	251B	163	Northwest Airlines	N614US
20360	251B	165	Northwest Airlines	N615US
20372	230B	132	GATX Capital Corp	D-ABYD HL7440 N488GX stored Mojave, CA 23Apr91
20373	230B	168	Korean Air	N1794B D-ABYE HL7441
20376	128	174	AVIANCA	F-BPVF TF-ABW
20377	128	176	Corsair	F-BPVG
20378	128	177	Air France	F-BPVH stored Paris-le Bourget, France Dec95
20390	123/SCD	136	United Parcel Service	N9675 OD-AGM N9675 N675UP
20391	123/SCD	143	United Parcel Service	N9676 OD-AGC N901PA N820FT (N626FE) N629FE N677UP
20398	206B	152	Trans World Airlines	PH-BUD N534AW N306TW
20399	206B	156	Corsair	PH-BUE HS-VGG PH-BUE F-GLNA
20400	206B	157	(KLM-Royal Dutch Airlines)	PH-BUF dbf 27Mar77 Los Rodeos, Tenerife, Canary Islands when struck 747-121 N736PA c/n 19643
20401	129/SCD	92	(SABENA World Airlines)	OO-SGA stored Brussels, Belgium 26Mar93; b/u 10Oct94
20402	129/SCD	95	Arab Leasing Intl Finance	OO-SGB C-GNXH (XA-...) C-GNXH N822AL stored Mojave, CA Jan94
20427	206B	170	Corsair	PH-BUG F-GPJM
20459	237B	185	Air India	VT-EBN
20493	230B	128	GATX Capital Corp	D-ABYF HL7447 N487GX C-FNXA N487GX stored Mojave, CA Apr93, later Everett, WA
20501	282B	178	Tower Air	CS-TJA N301TW N610FF stored New York-JFK, NY by Nov95
20502	282B	189	Tower Air	CS-TJB N302TW N611FF

BOEING 747

C/n	Series	Line No	Last known Operator/Owner	Previous Identities/fate (where known)
20503	246B	180	(Japan Air Lines)	JA8109 dbr Benghazi, Libya 24Jul73 following hijack
20504	246B	181	Japan Air Lines	JA8110
20505	246B	182	Japan Air Lines	JA8111
20520	243B	190	Continental Micronesia	I-DEMB N45224 N359AS N605PE N33021
20527	230B	179	Continental Micronesia	D-ABYG N611BN G-BJXN (C-....) G-BJXN N78019
20528	146A	191	American Intl Airways	JA8112 N704CK
20529	246B	192	Japan Air Lines	JA8113
20530	246B	196	Japan Air Lines	N1800B JA8114
20531	146A	197	Japan Air Lines	JA8115
20532	146A	199	Japan Air Lines	JA8116
20534	238B	195	Tower Air	VH-EBE N609PE N10024 N614FF
20535	238B	217	Continental Airlines	VH-EBF N610PE N17025 stored Marana, AZ Apr95
20541	128	200	Air France	(F-BPVI) N28903 F-BPVJ
20542	128	201	(Air France)	(F-BPVJ) N28888 dbf 12Jun75 Bombay, India
20543	128	203	AAR Aircraft Turbine Center	(F-BPVK) N28899 F-BPVK TF-ABQ (N615AR) stored Ardmore, OK 18Jul94; later Marana, AZ
20556	244B	194	South African Airways	ZS-SAO
20557	244B	198	South African Airways	ZS-SAP
20558	237B	188	(Air India)	VT-EBO dbr 07Apr90 New Delhi, India
20559	230B	186	(Korean Air Lines)	HL7442 Shot down 01Sep83 nr Hokkaido, Japan
20651	273C	209	Evergreen Intl Airlines	N747WA N535PA N747WA N747WR N471EV
20652	273C	211	Korean Air	N748WA HL7471
20653	273C	237	Evergreen Intl Airlines	N749WA (N630FE) N749WA N470EV
20682 to 20684, built as E-4A and modified as follows:				
20682	E-4B	202	USAF/1stACCS/55thWg	73-1676
20683	E-4B	204	USAF/1stACCS/55thWg	73-1677
20684	E-4B	232	USAF/1stACCS/55thWg	74-0787
20704	258B	212	El Al Israel Airlines	N1799B 4X-AXC
20708	136	210	British Airways	G-AWNM
20712	212B/SCD	218	Saudia	9V-SIA N747TA N747FT N728PA N485EV
20713	212B/SCD	219	Evergreen Intl Airlines	9V-SIB N748TA N748FT N729PA N482EV
20742	284B	216	Trans World Airlines	SX-OAA N305TW
20767	133	214	Air Canada	CF-TOD C-FTOD
20770	2B5B	213	Korean Air	N1798B HL7410 N747BA HL7463
20771	2B5B	215	Korean Air	N1796B HL7411 N747BC HL7464
20781	SR-46	221	NASA [coded 911]	N1795B JA8117 N747BL N911NA
20782	SR-46	229	(Boeing Equipment Holding)	JA8118 N747BN [Used for accelerated structure fatigue testing from Jul88]
20783	SR-46	230	(Japan Air Lines)	JA8119 w/o 12Aug85 into Mt Ogwa, Japan
20784	SR-46/SCD	231	United Parcel Service	JA8120 N477EV N688UP
20798	128	224	Air France	N88931 F-BPVL
20799	128	227	Air France	(F-BPVM) N63305 F-BPVM
20800	128	228	FAA Training School	(F-BPVN) N28366 F-BPVN N610AR Preserved Oklahoma City, OK Nov93
20801	217B	225	Pakistan Intl Airlines	N1794B C-FCRA AP-BCN
20802	217B	226	Pakistan Intl Airlines	C-FCRB AP-BCM
20809	136	220	British Airways	G-AWNN
20810	136	222	British Airways	G-AWNO
20825	284B	223	Olympic Airways	SX-OAB
20826	245F	242	Atlas Air	N701SW N811FT (N631FE) N640FE
20827	245F	266	Atlas Air	N702SW N812FT (N632FE) N641FE
20828	245F		(Seaboard World Airlines)	(N703SW) Allocated but later canx, not built
20829	198		(Air Zaire)	(9Q-CKF) Allocated but later canx, not built
20841	238B	233	El Al Israel Airlines	VH-EBG 4X-AXQ VH-EBG 4X-AXQ
20842	238B	238	Virgin Atlantic Airways	VH-EBH G-VJFK
20881	133	236	Air Canada	CF-TOE C-FTOE
20887	228F	245	Atlas Air	(F-BPVO) N18815 F-BPVO LX-DCV
20888	212B/SCD	240	Southern Air Transport	9V-SQC N749TA N749FT N730PA N202PH N745SJ
20921	238B	241	Virgin Atlantic Airways	VH-EBI G-VLAX
20923	SR-46/SCD	234	United Parcel Service	JA8121 N680UP
20924	246B	235	Air Atlantic Icelandic	JA8122 [Rebuilt at Anchorage, AK 75/76 with new fuselage] N550SW TF-ABI
20927	217B	244	Pakistan Intl Airlines	C-FCRD N620BN C-FCRD AP-BCO
20928	282B	239	Pakistan Intl Airlines	CS-TJC AP-AYV
20929	217B	247	Pakistan Intl Airlines	C-FCRE AP-BCL
20949 built as E-4B:				
20949	E-4B	257	USAF/1stACCS/55thWg	75-0125
20952	136	246	British Airways	G-AWNP
20953	136	248	British Airways	G-BBPU
20954	128	252	Air France	F-BPVP
20977	233M	250	Air Canada	(C-FTOF) C-GAGA N8297V C-GAGA
20998	SP-86	275	Iran Air	EP-IAA
20999	SP-86	278	Iran Air	EP-IAB
21022	SP-21	265	(United Airlines)	N747SP N530PA N140UA Regn canx Sep95; b/u Ardmore, OK Feb96
21023	SP-21	268	United Airlines	N247SP N531PA N141UA stored Ardmore, OK; regn canx Jan96
21024	SP-21	270	(United Airlines)	N342SP N532PA N142UA Regn canx Dec95; b/u Ardmore, OK Feb96
21025	SP-21	273	(Aviation Sales Co)	N533PA N41035 N533PA N143UA stored Las Vegas, NV Nov94; b/u Ardmore, OK Aug95

BOEING 747

C/n	Series	Line No	Last known Operator/Owner	Previous Identities/fate (where known)
21026	SP-21	286	United Airlines	N534PA N144UA stored Las Vegas, NV Mar94; b/u Ardmore, OK 29Mar96
21027	SP-21		(Pan American World A/W)	(N535PA) Allocated but later canx, not built
21028	SP-21		(Pan American World A/W)	(N536PA) Allocated but later canx, not built
21029	146A	259	Japan Asia Airlines	JA8128
21030	246B	251	Japan Air Lines	(JA8124) JA8125
21031	246B	255	Japan Air Lines	JA8127
21032	SR-46	249	(American Intl Airways)	(JA8125) JA8124 N705CK stored Detroit-Willow Run, MI Mar94; later b/u
21033	SR-46/SCD	254	United Parcel Service	JA8126 N478EV N689UP
21034	246F	243	Japan Air Lines	JA8123
21035	282B	256	Pakistan Intl Airlines	CS-TJD AP-AYW
21048	212B/SCD	253	Atlas Air	9V-SQD N747BC N726PA (N505MC) N808MC
21054	238B	260	United Airlines	VH-EBJ N158UA
21093	SP-86	307	Iran Air	EP-IAC
21097	2B4M	262	Middle East Airlines	OD-AGH N202AE G-BLVE N202AE
21098	2B4M	263	Philippine Airlines	OD-AGI N203AE G-BLVF N203AE
21099	2B4M	264	Philippine Airlines	OD-AGJ N204AE
21110	206M/EUD	271	KLM-Royal Dutch Airlines	PH-BUH
21111	206M/EUD	276	KLM-Royal Dutch Airlines	N8297V PH-BUI
21120	251F	258	Northwest Airlines	N616US
21121	251F	261	Northwest Airlines	N617US
21122	251F	269	Northwest Airlines	N618US
21132	SP-44	280	Alliance Airlines	ZS-SPA LX-LTM ZS-SPA 3B-NAJ ZS-SPA
21133	SP-44	282	South African Airways	ZS-SPB 7Q-YKL ZS-SPB LX-LGX ZS-SPB N747KS*
21134	SP-44	288	Air Namibia	N8297V ZS-SPC 3B-NAG ZS-SPC
21140	238B	267	United Airlines	VH-EBK N159UA
21141	128	279	ALG Aircraft Management Inc	(F-BPVQ) N40116 F-BPVQ N174GM 5N-GAB N174GM stored Miami, FL 15May95 later Marana, AZ
21162	212B	283	Tower Air	9V-SQE N747BH N727PA (VH-...) N727PA C-FNXP N514DC C-GCIH N511P N620FF*
21174	SP-94	284	Syrianair	YK-AHA
21175	SP-94	290	Syrianair	YK-AHB
21180	270C	287	Iraqi Airways	YI-AGN stored Teheran, Iran Feb91
21181	270C	289	Iraqi Airways	YI-AGO stored Tunis, Tunisia Feb91
21182	237B	277	Air India	VT-EDU
21189	287B	274	Virgin Atlantic Airways	N1791B LV-LZD N354AS G-VIRG
21190	258C	272	El Al Israel Airlines	4X-AXD
21213	136	281	British Airways	G-BDPV
21217	286M	291	Iran Air	EP-IAG
21218	286M	300	Iran Air	EP-IAH (A6-GZB) EP-IAH
21220	230M	294	Atlas Air	N1786B D-ABYJ N512MC
21221	230M	299	Atlas Air	D-ABYK N509MC
21237	238B	285	United Airlines	VH-EBL N160UA
21238	236B	292	British Airways	N1790B G-BDXA
21239	236B	302	British Airways	N8280V G-BDXB
21240	236B	305	British Airways	G-BDXC
21241	236B	317	British Airways	N8285V G-BDXD
21251	2D3M	296	Atlas Air	N1239E JY-AFA F-GFUK N506DC F-GFUK N505MC
21252	2D3M	297	Atlas Air	JY-AFB G-HUGE N512DC LX-ZCV N506MC
21253	SP-44	293	Corsair	ZS-SPD CN-RMS LX-ACO
21254	SP-44	298	South African Airways	ZS-SPE 3B-NAR ZS-SPE V5-SPE ZS-SPE
21255	228F	295	Air France	N1783B F-BPVR
21263	SP-44	301	Air Namibia	ZS-SPF (LX-LTM) ZS-SPF 3B-NAO ZS-SPF LX-LGY ZS-SPF V5-SPF
21300	SP-09	304	China Airlines	B-1862
21316	212B	309	Tower Air	9V-SQF N747BJ N724PA (VH-...) N724PA C-FXCE N504DC TF-ABZ N504DC N619FF*
21321	251F	308	Northwest Airlines	N619US
21326	228M	303	Air France	F-BPVS
21350	236B	321	British Airways	G-BDXE
21351	236B	323	British Airways	G-BDXF
21352	238B	310	United Airlines	N8295V VH-EBM N161UA
21353	238B	316	United Airlines	VH-EBN N163UA
21354	238M	314	Air Canada	VH-ECA C-GAGC
21380	230M	320	Atlas Air	D-ABYL N507MC
21381	283M	311	(AVIANCA)	LN-RNA HK-2910X HK-2910 w/o 27Nov83 nr Madrid, Spain
21429	228M	313	Air France	F-BPVT
21439	212B	312	Tower Air	9V-SQG N747BK N723PA N6186
21441	SP-21	306	United Airlines	N536PA N145UA stored Las Vegas, NV Nov94
21446	237B	318	Air India	VT-EFJ
21454	209M	322	China Airlines	B-1864
21468	2Q2M	324	Air Gabon	N1248E TR-LXK F-ODJG
21473	237B	330	(Air India)	VT-EFO w/o 23Jun85 off Irish coast
21486	2J9F	315	Saha Airline	5-8113 EP-NHN 5-8113 EP-SHB
21487	2J9F	319	Iran Air	5-8114 EP-ICA 5-8114 EP-ICA
21507	2J9F	340	Saha Airline	N8277V 5-8115 EP-ICB 5-8115 EP-SHA
21514	2J9F	343	Iran Air	N8293V 5-8116 EP-ICC
21515	2B3F	337	Air France Cargo Asie	(F-GATN) N1780B F-GPAN
21516	211B	326	Philippine Airlines	N1785B C-GXRA G-GLYN N207AE
21517	211B	368	Philippine Airlines	C-GXRD (G-BMXK) G-NIGB N208AE G-NIGB N208AE

BOEING 747

C/n	Series	Line No	Last known Operator/Owner	Previous Identities/fate (where known)
21536	236B	328	British Airways	G-BDXG
21537	228M	333	Air France	(F-BPVU) N1252E F-BPVU
21541	269M	332	American Intl Airways	9K-ADA N707CK
21542	269M	335	American Intl Airways	9K-ADB N709CK
21543	269M	359	American Intl Airways	9K-ADC N708CK
21547	SP-21	325	United Airlines	N537PA N146UA stored Las Vegas, NV May94
21548	SP-21	331	United Airlines	N538PA N147UA stored Las Vegas, NV Nov94
21549	206M/EUD	336	KLM-Royal Dutch Airlines	PH-BUK
21550	206M/EUD	344	KLM-Royal Dutch Airlines	PH-BUL
21575	283M	358	US Jet	(SE-DEF) SE-DFZ N9727N (EI-BWF) SE-DFZ LX-OCV EI-BWF
21576	228F	334	Air France	F-BPVV
21588	230M	342	Lufthansa	D-ABYM stored Marana, AZ 01Nov93
21589	230B	345	Alitalia	D-ABYN I-DEMY
21590	230B	348	Lufthansa	N8291V D-ABYP
21591	230B	350	Lufthansa	D-ABYQ
21592	230F	347	Lufthansa	D-ABYO
21594	258C	327	El Al Israel Airlines	4X-AXF
21602	2B5F		(Korean Air Lines)	Allocated but later canx, not built
21604	SR-81	346	Qatar Airways	N8286V JA8133 N747BK A7-ABK
21605	SR-81	351	Qatar Airways	JA8134 N747BL A7-ABL
21606	SR-81	360	All Nippon Airways	JA8135
21607	200F		(Unknown Customer)	Allocated but later canx, not built
21614	2B2M	353	Air Madagascar	5R-MFT
21615	2B6M	338	Royal Air Maroc	CN-RME
21627	233M	355	Air Canada	C-GAGB
21635	236B	365	British Airways	G-BDXH
21643	230M	352	Lufthansa	D-ABYR
21644	230M	356	Atlas Air	D-ABYS N508MC
21648	SP-21	367	Sheikh Kalifa bin Hamad Al Thani	N539PA N148UA VR-BAT
21649	SP-21	373	Amadeo Corp/Govt of Brunei	N540PA N149UA V8-JBB N149UA V8-JBB
21650	2R7F	354	Atlas Air	LX-DCV EI-BTQ N809FT (N633FE) N809FT N639FE
21652	SP-68	329	Saudi Royal Flight	N1780B HZ-HM1 HZ-HM1B [Op by RSAF/1Sqdn]
21657	238B	339	United Airlines	VH-EBO N164UA
21658	238B	341	United Airlines	VH-EBP N165UA
21659	206M/EUD	369	KLM-Royal Dutch Airlines	N1792B PH-BUM
21660	206M/EUD	389	KLM-Royal Dutch Airlines	PH-BUN
21668	2J9F	400	Northwest Airlines	5-8117 N1288E N630US
21678	246B	361	Japan Asia Airways	JA8129
21679	246B	376	Japan Air Lines	JA8130
21680	246B	380	Japan Air Lines	JA8131
21681	246F	382	Japan Air Lines	N1782B JA8132
21682	227B	375	Northwest Airlines	N602BN N602PE N635US
21683	212B	387	Olympic Airways	9V-SQH SX-OAC
21684	212B	391	Olympic Airways	9V-SQI SX-OAD
21704	251B	357	Northwest Airlines	N622US
21705	251B	374	Northwest Airlines	N623US
21706	251B	377	Northwest Airlines	N624US
21707	251B	378	Northwest Airlines	N625US
21708	251B	379	Northwest Airlines	N626US
21709	251B	412	Northwest Airlines	N627US
21724	200F		Unknown customer	Allocated but later canx, not built
21725	287B	349	Aerolineas Argentinas	N1789B LV-MLO
21726	287B	403	Aerolineas Argentinas	LV-MLP
21727	287B	404	Aerolineas Argentinas	LV-MLR
21730	259M	372	Tower Air	HK-2300 HK-2980X EI-CEO
21731	228M	364	Air France	F-BPVX
21737	258F	362	(El Al Israel Airlines)	4X-AXG w/o 04Oct92 Bijlmermeer, Netherlands
21743	221F	384	Japan Air Lines	N904PA JA8165
21744	221F	392	Japan Air Lines	N905PA JA8160
21745	228M	370	Air France	F-BPVY
21746	267B	385	Cathay Pacific Airways	VR-HKG
21758	SP-86	371	Iran Air	N1800B EP-IAD
21759	186B	381	Iran Air	N5573P EP-IAM
21760	186B		(Iran Air)	(EP-IAN) Allocated but later canx, not built
21761	186B		(Iran Air)	(EP-IAP) Allocated but later canx, not built
21762	186B		(Iran Air)	(EP-IAR) Allocated but later canx, not built
21764	245F	394	Atlas Air	N703SW N813FT (N634FE) N636FE
21772	2B5B	363	Korean Air	HL7443
21773	2B5B	366	(Korean Air Lines)	HL7445 dbf 19Nov80 Seoul, RoK
21782	2D7B	402	Thai International	HS-TGA (for Atlas Air late.96)
21783	2D7B	417	Thai International	HS-TGB (for Atlas Air late.96)
21784	2D7B	424	Thai International	HS-TGC (for Atlas Air late.96)
21785	SP-27	405	Government of Oman	N603BN N351AS A40-SO
21786	SP-27	413	Qatar Airways	N604BN LV-OHV 3B-NAQ A7-ABM
21787	228F	398	AIr France	F-BPVZ
21825	240M	383	Pakistan Intl Airlines	AP-BAK
21827	249F	406	Southern Air Transport	N806FT (N636FE) N631FE N742SJ
21828	249F	408	(Flying Tiger Line)	N807FT w/o 19Feb89 Puchong, Malaysia
21829	237B	390	Air India	VT-EFU

BOEING 747

C/n	Series	Line No	Last known Operator/Owner	Previous Identities/fate (where known)					
21830	236B	430	British Airways	G-BDXI					
21831	236B	440	British Airways	N1792B	G-BDXJ				
21832	2F6B	421	Philippine Airlines	(N1288E)	N741PR				
21833	2F6B	423	Philippine Airlines	(N1289E)	N742PR				
21834	2F6B	425	Philippine Airlines	(N1290E)	N743PR				
21835	2B3F	388	Air France	F-GBOX					
21841	245F	396	Atlas Air	N704SW	N814FT	(N635FE)	N638FE		
21843	209B	386	China Airlines	B-1866					
21848	206M/EUD	397	KLM-Royal Dutch Airlines	PH-BUO					
21922	SR-81	393	All Nippon Airways	JA8136					
21923	SR-81	395	All Nippon Airways	JA8137					
21924	SR-81	420	All Nippon Airways	JA8138					
21925	SR-81	422	All Nippon Airways	JA8139					
21932	SP-J6	433	Air China	B-2442					
21933	SP-J6	455	Air China	B-2444	B-2438				
21934	SP-J6	467	Air China	(B-2446)	N1304E	B-2452			
21935	212B	399	Olympic Airways	9V-SQJ	SX-OAE				
21936	212B	401	Air India	9V-SQK	VT-ENQ				
21937	212B	419	Tower Air	9V-SQL	G-VRGN	N618FF			
21938	212B	436	Korean Air	9V-SQM	HL7453				
21939	212B	449	Tower Air	9V-SQN	G-TKYO	N616FF			
21940	212B/SCD	457	Japan Air Lines	9V-SQO	JA8193				
21941	212B	470	Singapore Intl Airlines	9V-SQP	RP-C5475	9V-SQP			
21942	212B/SCD	471	Singapore Intl Airlines	9V-SQQ					
21943	212B	475	Philippine Airlines	9V-SQR	RP-C5476				
21944	212B	510	Singapore Intl Airlines	9V-SQS					
21961	SP-31	415	Government of Dubai	N58201	A6-SMR	[Op by Dubai Air Wing]			
21962	SP-31	439		N57202	N601AA	UN-001	P4-AFE		
21963	SP-31	441	Govt of United Arab Emirates	N57203	N602AA	A6-SMM	[Op by Dubai Air Wing]		
21964	271C	416	Cargolux Airlines Intl	N741TV	LX-ACV				
21965	271C	438	Cargolux Airlines Intl	N742TV	LX-ECV				
21966	267B	446	Cathay Pacific Airways	VR-HIA					
21977	238M	409	Qantas Airways	VH-ECB					
21982	228M	428	Air France	F-GCBA					
21991	227B	437	Northwest Airlines	N605BN	N8284V	(7T-V..)	N8284V	N633US	
21992	SP-27	447	Government of Oman	N606BN	N529PA	N606BN	N529PA	N150UA	A40-SP
21993	237B	414	Air India	VT-EGA					
21994	237B	431	Air India	VT-EGB					
21995	237B	434	Air India	VT-EGC					
22063	246F	432	Southern Air Transport	JA8144	N741SJ				
22064	246B	407	Japan Air Lines	JA8140					
22065	246B	411	Japan Air Lines	JA8141					
22066	146B	426	Japan Air Lines	JA8142					
22067	146B	427	Japan Air Lines	JA8143					
22077	240M	429	Pakistan Intl Airlines	AP-BAT					
22105	2L5M	435	VARIG	5A-DIJ	PP-VNA	VR-H..*	[For Air Hong Kong]		
22106	2L5M	443	VARIG	5A-DIK	PP-VNB	VR-HME*	[For Air Hong Kong]		
22107	2L5M	469	VARIG	(5A-DIL)	N1290E	PP-VNC	VR-H..*	[For Air Hong Kong]	
22145	238B	410	Qantas Airways	VH-EBQ					
22149	267B	466	Cathay Pacific Airways	VR-HIB					
22150	245F	476	El Al Israel Airlines	(N705SW)	N815FT	(N640FE)	N634FE	9V-SQT	4X-AXL
22151	245F	478	El Al Israel Airlines	(N706SW)	N816FT	(N641FE)	N635FE	9V-SQU	4X-AXK
22169	2S4F	472	Korean Air	TU-TAP	LX-TAP	HL7474			
22170	244M	486	South African Airways	ZS-SAA	ZS-SAR	3B-NAS	ZS-SAR		
22171	244M	488	(South African Airways)	(ZS-SAB)	ZS-SAS	w/o 28Nov87 off Mauritius			
22234	227B	465	Northwest Airlines	(N607BN)	N1607B	N8285V	(7T-V..)	N8285V	N634US
22235	227B		(Braniff International)	(N609BN)	Allocated but later canx, not built				
22236	227B		(Braniff International)	(N612BN)	Allocated but later canx, not built				
22237	249F	460	Air Hong Kong	(N809FT)	N810FT	(N639FE)	N633FE	VR-HKO	
22238	256B	450	Iberia	EC-DIA					
22239	256B	451	Iberia	EC-DIB					
22245	249F	458	Korean Air	N808FT	(N638FE)	N632FE	9V-SQV	HL7401	
22246	2U3B	452	Garuda Indonesia	(PK-GBA)	PK-GSA				
22247	2U3B	459	Garuda Indonesia	(PK-GBB)	PK-GSB				
22248	2U3B	461	Garuda Indonesia	(PK-GBC)	PK-GSC				
22249	2U3B	468	Garuda Indonesia	(PK-GBD)	PK-GSD				
22254	258B/SCD	418	El Al Israel Airlines	4X-AXH					
22272	228M	463	SABENA World Airlines	(F-GCBB)	N1289E	F-GCBB			
22291	SR-81	453	All Nippon Airways	JA8145					
22292	SR-81	456	All Nippon Airways	JA8146					
22293	SR-81	477	All Nippon Airways	N5973L	JA8147				
22294	SR-81	481	All Nippon Airways	JA8148					
22297	287B	487	Aerolineas Argentinas	LV-OEP					
22298	SP-09	445	Mandarin Airlines	B-1861	B-1880				
22299	209F	462	China Airlines	(B-1865)	B-1885	B-1894			
22302	SP-27	473	Air China	(N608BN)	N1608B	N1301E	B-2454		
22303	236B	495	British Airways	G-BDXK					
22304	236B/SCD	502	Malaysia Airlines	(G-BDXL)	9M-MHI				
22305	236B	506	British Airways	(G-BDXM)	N8280V	G-BDXL			
22306	236F	480	Cathay Pacific Airways	(G-BDXK)	G-KILO	VR-HVY			
22337	2D7B	479	Thai International	HS-TGF		(for Atlas Air late.96)			

BOEING 747

C/n	Series	Line No	Last known Operator/Owner	Previous Identities/fate (where known)				
22363	230M	490	Lufthansa Cargo Airlines	D-ABYT				
22366	270C	565	Iraqi Airways	YI-AGP				
22376	206M/EUD	474	KLM-Royal Dutch Airlines	(PH-BUP)	N1295E	N57004	N1295E	PH-BUP
22378	2H7M	508	Cameron Airlines	TJ-CAB				
22379	206M/EUD	491	KLM-Royal Dutch Airlines	(PH-BUR)	N1298E	PH-BUR		
22380	206M/EUD	539	KLM-Royal Dutch Airlines	(N1301E)	N1309E	(PH-BUT)	N1309E	PH-BUT
22381	283M	500	Philippine Airlines	(OY-KHB)	N4501Q	EI-BTS	N4501Q	EI-BTS
22382	2F6B	498	Philippine Airlines	N744PR				
22388	251F	444	Northwest Airlines	N629US				
22389	251F	442	Northwest Airlines	N628US				
22390	2R7F	482	(China Airlines)	LX-ECV	B-198	w/o 29Dec91 Wanli Village, RoC		
22403	271C	524	Cargolux Airlines Intl	N743TV	LX-BCV			
22404	271C		(Transamerica Airlines)	(N744TV)	Allocated but later canx, not built			
22405	271C		(Transamerica Airlines)	(N745TV)	Allocated but later canx, not built			
22427	228M	485	(Air France)	F-GCBC	dbr 02Dec85 Rio de Janeiro-Galeao, Brazil			
22428	228M	503	Air France	(F-GCBD)	N1305E	F-GCBD		
22429	267B	493	Cathay Pacific Airways	VR-HIC				
22442	236B/SCD	526	MASKargo	G-BDXN	9M-MHJ			
22446	209B	519	China Airlines	B-1886				
22447	209B	556	China Airlines	B-1888	Badly damaged Manila, Philippines 12Dec95			
22454	256M	509	Iberia	EC-DLC				
22455	256M	515	Iberia	EC-DLD				
22471	2D7B	504	Thai International	HS-TGG		(for Atlas Air late.96)		
22472	2D7B	597	Thai International	(HS-TGD)	N6066U	HS-TGS	(for Atlas Air late.96)	
22477	246F	494	Southern Air Transport	JA8151	N740SJ			
22478	246B	489	Japan Air Lines	JA8149				
22479	246B	496	Japan Air Lines	N1783B	JA8150			
22480	2B5F	448	Korean Air	HL7451				
22481	2B5F	454	Korean Air	N5573F	HL7452			
22482	2B5B/SCD	484	Korean Air	HL7454				
22483	SP-B5	501	Korean Air	HL7456				
22484	SP-B5	507	Korean Air	HL7457				
22485	2B5B/SCD	513	Korean Air	HL7458				
22486	2B5F	520	Korean Air	N8281V	HL7459			
22487	3B5	605	Korean Air	(HL7466)	N6069D	HL7468		
22488	2B5F		(Korean Air Lines)	Allocated but later canx, not built				
22489	3B5	611	Korean Air	(HL7467)	N6009F	HL7469		
22495	SP-38	505	Australia Asia Airlines	VH-EAA				
22496	283M	540	Philippine Airlines	(LN-RNB)	N4502R	EI-BZA		
22497	257B		(Swissair)	Allocated but later canx, not built				
22498	168B	512	Saudia	N8281V	HZ-AIA			
22499	168B	517	Saudia	HZ-AIB				
22500	168B	522	Saudia	HZ-AIC				
22501	168B	525	Saudia	HZ-AID				
22502	168B	530	Saudia	N1782B	N8284V	HZ-AIE		
22503	SP-68	529	Saudia	HZ-AIF				
22506	243M	492	Alitalia	I-DEMC				
22507	243M	497	Atlas Air	I-DEMD	N516MC			
22508	243M	499	Alitalia	I-DEMF				
22509	243M		(Alitalia)	Allocated but later canx, not built				
22510	243B	533	Alitalia	I-DEMG				
22511	243B	536	Alitalia	I-DEML				
22512	243B/SCD	542	Atlas Air	I-DEMN				
22513	243B	546	Alitalia	I-DEMP				
22514	2B3M/EUD	518	Air France	F-BTDG				
22515	2B3M/EUD	521	Air France	F-BTDH				
22530	267B	531	Cathay Pacific Airways	VR-HID				
22545	243F	545	Alitalia	I-DEMR				
22546	209B		(China Airlines)	Allocated but later canx, not built				
22547	SP-09	534	Mandarin Airlines	(B-1882)	N1785B	N4508H		
22579	2D3B	514	All Nippon Airways	JY-AFS	G-CITB	JA8192	G-CITB	JA8192
22592	287B	532	Aerolineas Argentinas	LV-OOZ				
22593	287B	552	Aerolineas Argentinas	LV-OPA				
22594	SR-81	511	All Nippon Airways	JA8152				
22595	SR-81	516	All Nippon Airways	JA8153				
22614	238B	464	Qantas Airways	N1782B	N8296V	VH-EBR		
22615	238M	483	Qantas Airways	VH-ECC				
22616	238B	543	Qantas Airways	N1785B	N6005C	N5700T	VH-EBS	
22617	238B		(Qantas Airways)	(VH-EBT)	Allocated but later canx, not built			
22668	230F	538	Lufthansa	N1785B	D-ABYU			
22669	230M	549	Lufthansa Cargo Airlines	D-ABYW				
22670	230M	550	Lufthansa	D-ABYX				
22671	230M	574	Lufthansa Cargo Airlines	D-ABYY				
22672	SP-38	537	Australia Asia Airlines	N1791B	VH-EAB			
22678	228F	535	Air France	(F-GCBE)	N4508E	F-GCBE		
22704	357M	570	Swissair	N6005C	N8277V	HB-IGC		
22705	357M	576	Swissair	N1784B	HB-IGD			
22706	357		(Swissair)	(HB-IGE)	Allocated but later canx, not built			
22707	357		(Swissair)	(HB-IGF)	Allocated but later canx, not built			
22708	357		(Swissair)	(HB-IGG)	Allocated but later canx, not built			
22709	SR-81	541	All Nippon Airways	N5573B	JA8156			

BOEING 747

C/n	Series	Line No	Last known Operator/Owner	Previous Identities/fate (where known)
22710	SR-81	544	All Nippon Airways	JA8157
22711	SR-81/SCD	559	All Nippon Airways	JA8158
22712	SR-81	572	All Nippon Airways	JA8159
22722	219B	523	Air New Zealand	ZK-NZV
22723	219B	527	Air New Zealand	ZK-NZW
22724	219B	528	Air New Zealand	ZK-NZX 9M-MHG ZK-NZX
22725	219B	563	Air Pacific	N6005C ZK-NZY
22740	269M	553	Kuwait Airways	9K-ADD
22745	246B	547	Japan Air Lines	JA8154
22746	246B	548	Japan Asia Airways	JA8155
22747	168B	551	Saudia	HZ-AIG
22748	168B	555	Saudia	HZ-AIH
22749	168B	557	Saudia	HZ-AII
22750	SP-68	560	Saudi Royal Flight	N6046P HZ-AIJ [Op by RSAF/1Sqdn]
22764	256B	554	Iberia	N8296V EC-DNP
22768	2U3B	561	Garuda Indonesia	PK-GSE
22769	2U3B	562	Garuda Indonesia	PK-GSF
22791	219B	568	Air New Zealand	N6108N ZK-NZZ 9M-MHH ZK-NZZ
22794	228M	558	Air France	(F-GCBF) N4506H F-GCBF
22805	SP-09	564	China Airlines	N4522V
22858	SP-70	567	Iraqi Airways	YI-ALM stored Tozeui, Tunisia Jan91
22870	3B3	573	(UTA)	(F-GDUT) N6067B N8278V F-GDUA dbf 16Mar85 Paris-Charles de Gaulle, France
22871	3B3		(UTA)	(F-GDUB) Allocated but later canx, not built
22872	267B	566	Cathay Pacific Airways	VR-HIE
22939	228F	569	Air France	(F-GCBG) N4544F F-GCBG
22969	243B	575	Alitalia	N8289V I-DEMS
22970	344	577	South African Airways	N8279V ZS-SAT
22971	344	578	South African Airways	N8296V ZS-SAU
22989	246F	571	Japan Air Lines	(JA8160) N211JL
22990	246B	579	Japan Air Lines	N6046B JA8161
22991	246B	581	Japan Air Lines	N5573K JA8162
22995	357	585	Swissair	HB-IGE N221GE HB-IGE
22996	357	586	Swissair	HB-IGF N221GF HB-IGF
22997	357		(Swissair)	(HB-IGG) Allocated but later canx, not built
23025	206M		(KLM-Royal Dutch Airlines)	(PH-BUU) Allocated but later canx, not built
23026	312	580	Ansett Australia	(9V-SQT) N6006C N8279V 9V-SKA VH-INH
23027	312	583	South African Airlines	(9V-SQU) (9V-SKB) N116KB ZS-SAJ
23028	312	584	Ansett Australia	(9V-SQV) (9V-SKC) N117KC VH-INK
23029	312	590	Ansett Australia	(9V-SQW) (9V-SKD) N118KD 9V-SKD VH-INJ
23030	312	593	Corsair	(9V-SQX) (9V-SKE) N119KE F-GSUN
23031	312	598	South African Airlines	(9V-SQY) (9V-SKF) N120KF ZS-SAC
23032	312	603	Ansett Australia	(9V-SQZ) (9V-SKG) N121KG
23033	312	609	Singapore Intl Airlines	(9V-SQA) (9V-SKH) N122KH
23048	267B	582	Cathay Pacific Airways	N6066U VR-HIF
23056	306M	587	KLM-Royal Dutch Airlines	(PH-BUU) N4548M PH-BUU
23067	346	588	Japan Air Lines	(JA8163) N212JL
23068	346	589	Japan Air Lines	(JA8164) N213JL
23070	3G1	592	Saudi Royal Flight	N1784B HZ-HMIA [Op by RSAF/1Sqdn]
23071	2J6M	591	Air China	N1781B B-2446
23111	251B	594	Northwest Airlines	N631US
23112	251B	595	Northwest Airlines	N632US
23120	267B/SCD	596	Cathay Pacific Airways	N5573B VR-HIH
23137	306M	600	KLM-Royal Dutch Airlines	(PH-BUV) N4551N PH-BUV
23138	281F	604	Nippon Cargo AIrlines	N6066Z JA8167
23139	281F	608	Nippon Cargo AIrlines	N6046P JA8168
23149	346	599	Japan Air Lines	N5573B JA8163
23150	146B	601	Japan Air Lines	N1781B JA8164
23151	346	607	Japan Air Lines	N1786B JA8166
23210	3B5		(Korean Air)	Allocated but later canx, not built
23211	3B5		(Korean Air)	Allocated but later canx, not built
23221	367	615	Cathay Pacific Airways	(VR-HIJ) N6018N VR-HII
23222	338	602	Qantas Airways	N1784B VH-EBT
23223	338	606	Qantas Airways	N5573P VH-EBU
23224	338	610	Qantas Airways	N6005C VH-EBV
23243	312	612	Singapore Intl Airlines	(9V-SKJ) N123KJ
23244	312	621	Singapore Intl Airlines	(9V-SKK) N124KK
23245	312	626	Singapore Intl Airlines	(9V-SKL) N125KL F-GSKY* [for Corsair]
23246	312		(Singapore Intl Airlines)	Allocated but later canx, not built
23247	312		(Singapore Intl Airlines)	Allocated but later canx, not built
23248	312		(Singapore Intl Airlines)	Allocated but later canx, not built
23262	368	616	Saudia	N6005C HZ-AIK
23263	368	619	Saudia	N6009F HZ-AIL
23264	368	620	Saudia	N6046P HZ-AIM
23265	368	622	Saudia	N6046P HZ-AIN
23266	368	624	Saudia	N6005C HZ-AIO
23267	368	630	Saudia	N6055X HZ-AIP
23268	368	631	Saudia	N6005C HZ-AIQ
23269	368	643	Saudia	N6038E HZ-AIR
23270	368	645	Saudia	N6046P HZ-AIS
23271	368	652	Saudia	N6038N HZ-AIT

BOEING 747

C/n	Series	Line No	Last known Operator/Owner	Previous Identities/fate (where known)			
23286	230M	614	Lufthansa Cargo Airlines	N6055X	D-ABYZ	I-DEMX	D-ABYZ
23287	230M	617	Lufthansa	N6038E	D-ABZA		
23300	243B	613	Atlas Air	N6009F	I-DEMT	N517MC	
23301	243B	618	Alitalia	N6018N	I-DEMV		
23348	230F	625	Atlas Air	N6005F	D-ABZB	N747MC	
23350	281F	623	Nippon Cargo AIrlines	N6018N	JA8172		
23389	246B	635	Japan Air Lines	N6018N	JA8169		
23390	346SR	636	Japan Air Lines	N6009F	JA8170		
23391	246F	654	Japan Air Lines	N6038E	JA8171		
23392	367	634	Cathay Pacific Airways	N6005C	VR-HIJ		
23393	230M	633	Lufthansa Cargo Airlines	N6046P	D-ABZC		
23394	341	627	VARIG	N6005C	PP-VNH		
23395	341	629	VARIG	N6009F	PP-VNI		
23407	230B	639	Lufthansa	N6005C	D-ABZD		
23408	338	638	Qantas Airways	N6055X	VH-EBW		
23409	312M	637	Singapore Intl Airlines	N6065Y	9V-SKM		
23410	312M	653	Singapore Intl Airlines	N6055X	9V-SKN		
23413	3B3M	632	Air France	(F-GDUE)	N6009F	F-GETA	
23439	329M	646	SABENA World Airlines	N6005C	OO-SGC		
23461	2J6M	628	Air China	N60668	B-2448		
23476	243M	647	Atlas Air	I-DEMW	N518MC		
23480	3B3M	641	Air France	N6108N	F-GETB		
23482	346	640	Japan Air Lines	N6009F	JA8173		
23501	281B	648	All Nippon Airways	N6055X	JA8174		
23502	281B	649	All Nippon Airways	N60659	JA8175		
23508	306M	657	KLM-Royal Dutch Airlines	N6055X	PH-BUW		
23509	230M	663	Lufthansa	N6038E	D-ABZE		
23534	367	659	Cathay Pacific Airways	N6038E	VR-HIK		
23547	251B	642	Northwest Airlines	N636US			
23548	251B	644	Northwest Airlines	N637US			
23549	251B	651	Northwest Airlines	N638US			
23600	3H6M	650	Malaysia Airlines	9M-MHK			
23610	SP-Z5	676	Government of Abu Dhabi	N60697	N60659	A6-ZSN	
23611	228M	656	Air France Asie Cargo	N6046P	F-GCBH		
23621	230F	660	Lufthansa Cargo Airlines	N6046P	D-ABZF		
23622	230B	665	Lufthansa	N6046P	D-ABZH		
23637	346SR	655	Japan Air Lines	N60668	JA8176		
23638	346	658	Japan Air Lines	N6009F	JA8177		
23639	346	664	Japan Air Lines	N6009F	JA8178		
23640	346	668	Japan Air Lines	N6009F	JA8179		
23641	246F	684	Japan Air Lines	JA8180			
23652	21AC	669	Martinair Holland	N6038E	PH-MCE		
23676	228M	661	Air France	N6009F	F-GCBI		
23688	338	662	Qantas Airways	N6005C	VH-EBX		
23698	281B	667	All Nippon Airways	N6055C	JA8181		
23709	367	671	Cathay Pacific Airways	N6018N	VR-HOL		
23711	236B	672	British Airways	N6055X	G-BDXM		
23719	451	696	Northwest Airlines	(N301US)	N401PW	N661US	
23720	451	708	Northwest Airlines	(N302US)	N662US		
23721	3D7	681	Thai International	N6046P	HS-TGD		
23722	3D7	688	Thai International	N60668	HS-TGE		
23735	236M	674	British Airways	N6046P	G-BDXN		
23736	222B	673	United Airlines	N151UA			
23737	222B	675	United Airlines	N152UA			
23746	2J6B	670	Air China	N6018N	B-2450		
23751	357M	686	Swissair	N6055X	HB-IGG		
23769	312M	666	Singapore Intl Airlines	N6005C	9V-SKP		
23799	236B	677	British Airways	N6055X	G-BDXO		
23813	281B	683	All Nippon Airways	N60659	JA8182		
23814	467	705	Cathay Pacific Airways	N1788B	VR-HOO		
23815	467	728	Cathay Pacific Airways	VR-HOP			
23816	430	723	Lufthansa	N6055X	D-ABVA		
23817	430	700	Lufthansa	N5573S	D-ABVB		
23818	451	715	Northwest Airlines	(N303US)	N663US		
23819	451	721	Northwest Airlines	(N304US)	N664US		
23820	451	726	Northwest Airlines	(N305US)	N665US		
23821	451	742	Northwest Airlines	(N306US)	N666US		
23823	338	678	Qantas Airways	N6005C	VH-EBY		
23824 and 23825, model 747-2G4B built as VC-25A:							
23824	VC-25A	679	USAF/89thAW	N1788B	N6005C	(86-8800)	82-8000
23825	VC-25A	685	USAF/89thAW	N60659	(86-8900)	92-9000	
23864	267F	687	Cathay Pacific Airways	N6005C	VR-HVZ		
23887	251F	680	Northwest Airlines	N639US			
23888	251F	682	Northwest Airlines	N640US			
23908	436	727	British Airways	N60655	G-BNLA		
23909	436	730	British Airways	G-BNLB			
23910	436	734	British Airways	G-BNLC			
23911	436	744	British Airways	N6018N	G-BNLD		
23919	281F	689	Nippon Cargo Airlines	N6009F	JA8188		
23920	367	690	Cathay Pacific Airways	N6038E	VR-HOM		
23967	346SR	692	Japan Air Lines	N6005C	JA8183		

BOEING 747

C/n	Series	Line No	Last known Operator/Owner	Previous Identities/fate (where known)		
23968	346SR	693	Japan Air Lines	N6055X	JA8184	
23969	346	691	Japan Air Lines	N6005C	JA8185	
23982	406M	735	KLM-Asia	N6038E	PH-BFC	
23999	406	725	KLM-Royal Dutch Airlines	N6018N	PH-BFA	
24000	406	732	KLM-Royal Dutch Airlines	PH-BFB		
24001	406M	737	KLM-Asia	PH-BFD		
24018	346SR	694	Japan Air Lines	N6018N	JA8186	
24019	346SR	695	Japan Air Lines	N6038E	JA8187	
24047	436	753	British Airways	G-BNLE		
24048	436	773	British Airways	G-BNLF		
24049	436	774	British Airways	G-BNLG		
24050	436	779	British Airways	G-BNLH		
24051	436	784	British Airways	G-BNLI		
24052	436	789	British Airways	N6066B	G-BNLJ	
24053	436	790	British Airways	N6009F	G-BNLK	
24054	436	794	British Airways	G-BNLL		
24055	436	795	British Airways	N6009F	G-BNLM	
24056	436	802	British Airways	G-BNLN		
24057	436	817	British Airways	G-BNLO		
24058	436	828	British Airways	G-BNLP		
24061	412	717	Singapore Intl Airlines	N5573B	9V-SMA	
24062	412	722	Singapore Intl Airlines	N6005C	9V-SMB	
24063	412	736	Air China	9V-SMC	3B-SMC	
24064	412	755	Singapore Intl Airlines	9V-SMD		
24065	412	761	Singapore Intl Airlines	9V-SME		
24066	412	791	Singapore Intl Airlines	N6066B	9V-SMF	
24067	228M	698	Air France	N6018N	F-GCBJ	
24071	256B	699	Iberia	N6005C	EC-136	EC-EEK
24088	236M	697	British Airways	N6009F	G-BDXP	
24106	341	701	VARIG	N6046P	PP-VOA	
24107	341	702	VARIG	N6018N	PP-VOB	
24108	341	703	VARIG	N6005C	PP-VOC	
24134	21AC	712	Martinair Holland	N6009F	PH-MCF	
24138	230F	706	Lufthansa Cargo Airlines	N6005C	D-ABZI	
24154	4B3	741	Air France	F-GEXA		
24155	4B3M	864	Air France	F-GEXB		
24156	346	716	Japan Asia Airways	N6046P	JA8189	
24158	228F	714	Air France	N6055X	F-GCBK	
24159	337M	711	Air India	N6018N	VT-EPW	
24160	337M	719	Air India	N6046P	VT-EPX	
24161	366M	704	Egyptair	N6038E	SU-GAL	
24162	366M	707	Egyptair	N6018N	SU-GAM	
24177	212F	710	Singapore Intl Airlines	N6046P	9V-SKQ	
24194	3B5M	713	Korean Air	N6038E	HL7470	
24195	2B5F	718	Korean Air	N6038E	HL7475	
24196	2B5F	720	Korean Air	N6038E	HL7476	
24198	4B5	729	Korean Air	N6038E	HL7477	
24199	4B5	739	Korean Air	HL7478		
24200	4B5	748	Korean Air	HL7479		
24201	406M	763	KLM-Royal Dutch Airlines	N6046P	PH-BFE	
24202	406M	770	KLM-Royal Dutch Airlines	N6046P	PH-BFF	
24215	367	709	Cathay Pacific Airways	N6038E	VR-HON	
24222	451	799	Northwest Airlines	(N307US)	N667US	
24223	451	800	Northwest Airlines	(N308US)	N668US	
24224	451	803	Northwest Airlines	(N309US)	N669US	
24225	451	804	Northwest Airlines	(N311US)	N670US	
24226	412	809	Singapore Intl Airlines	N6005C	9V-SMG	
24227	412	831	Singapore Intl Airlines	N6009F	9V-SMH	
24285	430M	747	Lufthansa	D-ABTA		
24286	430M	749	Lufthansa	D-ABTB		
24287	430M	754	Lufthansa	D-ABTC		
24288	430	757	Lufthansa	D-ABVC		
24308	209F	752	China Airlines	B-160		
24309	409	766	China Airlines	B-161		
24310	409	778	China Airlines	B-162		
24311	409	869	China Airlines	B-163		
24312	409	954	China Airlines	B-164		
24313	409	977	(China Airlines)	B-165	dbr Hong Kong 04Nov93; instructional airframe at Xiamen, PRC	
24315	4H6M	738	Malaysia Airlines	9M-MHL		
24322	422	733	United Airlines	N171UA		
24346	4J6M	743	Air China	B-2456		
24347	4J6M	775	Air China	B-2458		
24348	4J6M	792	Air China	B-2460		
24354	438	731	Qantas Airways	N6046P	VH-OJA	
24359	268F	724	Saudia	N6018N	HZ-AIU	
24363	422	740	United Airlines	N172UA		
24373	438	746	Qantas Airways	VH-OJB		
24380	422	759	United Airlines	N173UA		
24381	422	762	United Airlines	N174UA		
24382	422	806	United Airlines	N175UA		

BOEING 747

C/n	Series	Line No	Last known Operator/Owner	Previous Identities/fate (where known)
24383	422	811	United Airlines	N176UA
24384	422	819	United Airlines	N177UA
24385	422	820	United Airlines	N178UA
24386	419	756	Air New Zealand	(ZK-NZE) ZK-NBS
24399	281B	750	All Nippon Airways	JA8190
24405	4H6M	745	Malaysia Airlines	9M-MHM
24406	438	751	Qantas Airways	VH-OJC
24423	446	758	Japan Air Lines	JA8071
24424	446	760	Japan Air Lines	JA8072
24425	446	767	Japan Air Lines	JA8073
24426	446	768	Japan Air Lines	JA8074
24427	446	780	Japan Air Lines	JA8075
24447	436	829	British Airways	N6005C G-BNLR
24458	4D7	769	Thai International	HS-TGH
24459	4D7	777	Thai International	HS-TGJ
24481	438	764	Qantas Airways	VH-OJD
24482	438	765	Qantas Airways	VH-OJE
24483	438	781	Qantas Airways	VH-OJF
24517	406	782	KLM-Royal Dutch Airlines	PH-BFG
24518	406	783	KLM-Royal Dutch Airlines	N60668 PH-BFH
24568	267F	776	Cathay Pacific Airways	VR-HVX
24576	281F	818	Nippon Cargo Airlines	JA8191
24619	4B5M	793	Korean Air	N6009F HL7480
24620	4B5M		(Korean Air)	(HL7482) Allocated but later canx, not built
24621	4B5	830	Korean Air	HL7481
24629	436	841	British Airways	G-BNLS
24630	436	842	British Airways	G-BNLT
24631	467	771	Cathay Pacific Airways	VR-HOR
24715	430M	785	Lufthansa	D-ABTD
24730	47C	816	Government of Japan	N6055X JA8091 20-1101 [Op by JASDF/701stH'tai]
24731	47C	839	Government of Japan	N6038E JA8092 20-1102 [Op by JASDF/701stH'tai]
24735	228F	772	Air France	F-GCBL
24740	430	786	Lufthansa	N60668 D-ABVD
24741	430	787	Lufthansa	D-ABVE
24761	430	796	Lufthansa	N6018N D-ABVF
24777	446	797	Japan Air Lines	N6046P JA8076
24779	438	801	Qantas Airways	N6009F VH-OJG
24784	446	798	Japan Air Lines	JA8077
24801	481	805	All Nippon Airways	JA8094
24806	438	807	Qantas Airways	VH-OJH
24833	481	812	All Nippon Airways	JA8095
24836	4H6	808	Malaysia Airlines	N6009F 9M-MHN
24837	329M	810	SABENA World Airlines	OO-SGD
24850	467	788	Cathay Pacific Airways	N6009F VR-HOS
24851	467	813	Cathay Pacific Airways	VR-HOT
24855	419	815	Air New Zealand	N6018N ZK-NBT
24870	446	821	Japan Air Lines	N60697 JA8078
24879	228F	822	Air France	F-GCBM
24883	475	823	Canadian Airlines Intl	N6018N C-GMWW
24885	446	824	Japan Air Lines	N6005C JA8079
24886	446	825	Japan Air Lines	JA8080
24887	438	826	Qantas Airways	N6009F VH-OJI
24895	475	837	Canadian Airlines Intl	C-FCRA
24896	475	855	Air New Zealand	(C-FBCA) N6009F PP-VPI N891LF (ZK-ILF) ZK-SUH
24920	481	832	All Nippon Airways	JA8096
24925	467	834	Cathay Pacific Airways	VR-HOU
24955	467	877	Cathay Pacific Airways	N6018N VR-HOX
24956	441	917	Garuda Indonesia	PP-VPG N791LF PK-GSI
24957	441	971	Air New Zealand	PP-VPH N821LF ZK-SUI
24958	4Q8	1028	Virgin Atlantic Airways	G-VFAB
24960	2J6F	814	Air China	B-2462
24966	430M	846	Lufthansa	N6046P D-ABTE
24967	430M	848	Lufthansa	D-ABTF
24969	428	836	Air France	F-GITA
24974	438	835	Qantas Airways	VH-OJJ
24975	412	838	Singapore Intl Airlines	(9V-SMI) (9V-SMJ) 9V-SMI
24976	444	827	South African Airways	N6009F ZS-SAV
24990	428	843	Air France	N6009F F-GITB
24993	4D7	833	Thai International	HS-TGK
24998	433	840	Air Canada	N6018N C-GAGL
25045	430	845	Lufthansa	N6018N D-ABVH
25046	430	847	Lufthansa	N6009F D-ABVK
25047	430M	856	Lufthansa	D-ABTH
25064	446	851	Japan Air Lines	JA8081
25067	438	857	Qantas Airways	VH-OJK
25068	412	852	Singapore Intl Airlines	(9V-SMJ) (9V-SMK) N6005C 9V-SMJ
25074	433	862	Air Canada	C-GAGM
25075	433	868	Air Canada	N6009F C-GAGN
25082	467	849	Cathay Pacific Airways	VR-HOV
25086	406	850	KLM-Royal Dutch Airlines	PH-BFI
25087	406	854	KLM-Royal Dutch Airlines	PH-BFK

BOEING 747

C/n	Series	Line No	Last known Operator/Owner	Previous Identities/fate (where known)				
25126	4H6	858	Malaysia Airlines	9M-MHO				
25127	412	859	Singapore Intl Airlines	(9V-SMK)	(9V-SML)	9V-SMK		
25128	412	860	Singapore Intl Airlines	(9V-SML)	(9V-SMM)	9V-SML		
25135	481	863	All Nippon Airways	JA8097				
25151	438	865	Qantas Airways	VH-OJL				
25152	444	861	South African Airways	N60668	ZS-SAW			
25158	422	866	United Airlines	N179UA				
25171	281F	886	Nippon Cargo Airlines	JA8194				
25205	4B5	853	Korean Air	HL7482				
25207	481	870	All Nippon Airways	JA8098				
25211	467	873	Cathay Pacific Airways	VR-HOW				
25212	446	871	Japan Air Lines	JA8082				
25213	446D	844	Japan Air Lines	N60668	JA8083			
25214	446D	879	Japan Air Lines	JA8084				
25224	422	867	United Airlines	N180UA				
25238	428M	872	Air France	F-GISA				
25245	438	875	Qantas Airways	VH-OJM				
25260	446	876	Japan Air Lines	JA8085				
25266	228F	878	Martinair Holland	F-GCBN	PH-MCN			
25275	4B5	874	Korean Air	HL7483				
25278	422	881	United Airlines	N6005C	N181UA			
25279	422	882	United Airlines	N182UA				
25292	481D	891	All Nippon Airways	JA8099				
25302	428M	884	Air France	F-GISB				
25308	446	885	Japan Air Lines	JA8086				
25315	438	883	Qantas Airways	N6009F	VH-OJN			
25344	428	889	Air France	F-GITC				
25351	467	887	Cathay Pacific Airways	VR-HOY				
25356	406	888	KLM-Royal Dutch Airlines	PH-BFL				
25366	4D7	890	Thai International	HS-TGL				
25379	422	911	United Airlines	N183UA				
25380	422	913	United Airlines	N184UA				
25395	422	919	United Airlines	N185UA				
25405	48E	880	Asiana Airlines	HL7413				
25406	436	895	British Airways	G-BNLU				
25413	406M	938	KLM-Royal Dutch Airlines	PH-BFO				
25422	475	912	Canadian Airlines Intl	C-FBCA				
25427	436	900	British Airways	G-BNLV				
25432	436	903	British Airways	G-BNLW				
25433	436		(British Airways)	(G-BNLX)	Allocated but later canx, not built			
25434	436	1058	British Airways	(G-BNLY)	G-CIVF			
25435	436	908	British Airways	(G-BNLZ)	G-BNLX			
25452	48E	892	Asiana Airlines	HL7414				
25544	438	894	Qantas Airways	N6055X	N6005C	VH-OJO		
25545	438	916	Qantas Airways	VH-OJP				
25546	438	924	Qantas Airways	N6046P	N6005C	VH-OJQ		
25547	438	936	Qantas Airways	N6018N	VH-OJR			
25599	428M	899	Air France	F-GISC				
25600	428	901	Air France	F-GITD				
25601	428	906	Air France	F-GITE				
25602	428	909	Air France	F-GITF				
25605	419	933	Air New Zealand	ZK-NBU				
25628	428M	934	Air France	F-GISD				
25629	428	956	Royal Air Maroc	(F-GITG)	F-OGTG	CN-RGA	F-OGTG	CN-RGA
25630	428M	960	Air France	F-GISE				
25631	428		Air France	F-GITH				
25632	428F	968	Cargolux Airlines Intl	(F-GIUA)	N6005C	LX-ICV		
25639	481D	914	All Nippon Airways	JA8955				
25640	481D	920	All Nippon Airways	JA8956				
25641	481	928	All Nippon Airways	N6009F	JA8958			
25642	481D	927	All Nippon Airways	JA8957				
25643	481D	972	All Nippon Airways	JA8960				
25644	481D	975	All Nippon Airways	JA8961				
25645	481	979	All Nippon Airways	JA8962				
25646	481D	952	All Nippon Airways	JA8959				
25647	481D	991	All Nippon Airways	N6055X	JA8963			
25672	406		(KLM-Royal Dutch Airlines)	(PH-BFN)	Allocated but later canx, not built			
25673	406M		(KLM-Royal Dutch Airlines)	(PH-BFM)	Allocated but later canx, not built			
25699	4H6	965	Malaysia Airlines	9M-MPB				
25700	4H6	974	Malaysia Airlines	9M-MPC				
25701	4H6	997	Malaysia Airlines	9M-MPD				
25702	4H6	999	Malaysia Airlines	9M-MPE				
25703	4H6	1025	Malaysia Airlines	9M-MPG				
25704	4U3	1011	Garuda Indonesia	PK-GSG				
25705	4U3	1029	Garuda Indonesia	N6038E	PK-GSH			
25777	48E	946	Asiana Airlines	HL7415				
25778	48E	983	Asiana Airlines	HL7416				
25779	48E	1006	Asiana Airlines	HL7417				
25780	48E	1035	Asiana Airlines	N6018N	HL7418			
25781	48EF	1044	Asiana Airlines	HL7419				
25783	48EF	1064	Asiana Airlines	HL7420				

BOEING 747

C/n	Series	Line No	Last known Operator/Owner	Previous Identities/fate (where known)		
25784	48E	1086	Asiana Airlines	HL7421		
25811	436	1018	British Airways	(G-BNLY)	G-CIVB	
25812	436	1022	British Airways	(G-BNLZ)	G-CIVC	
25813	436	1059	British Airways	N6009F	G-CIVG	
25814	436		(British Airways)	Allocated but later canx, not built		
25815	436		(British Airways)	Allocated but later canx, not built		
25866	4R7F	1002	Cargolux Airlines Intl	N1785B	LX-FCV	
25867	4R7F	1008	Cargolux Airlines Intl	LX-GCV		
25869	467	993	Cathay Pacific Airways	VR-HUF		
25870	467	1007	Cathay Pacific Airways	VR-HUG		
25871	467	925	Cathay Pacific Airways	VR-HOZ		
25872	467	930	Cathay Pacific Airways	VR-HUA		
25873	467	937	Cathay Pacific Airways	N60665	VR-HUB	
25874	467	949	Cathay Pacific Airways	VR-HUD		
25879	4J6	904	Air China	B-2464		
25880	4J6	926	Air China	B-2466		
25881	4J6	957	Air China	B-2443		
25882	4J6	1021	Air China	B-2445		
25883	4J6	1054	Air China	B-2447		
26055	458	1027	El Al Israel Airlines	4X-ELA		
26056	458	1032	El Al Israel Airlines	N60697	4X-ELB	
26059	45E		(EVA Airways)	(B-16403)	Allocated but later canx, not built	
26060	45E		(EVA Airways)	(B-16405)	Allocated but later canx, not built	
26062	45EM	1016	EVA Airways	B-16465		
26255	4Q8	1081	Virgin Atlantic Airways	G-VBIG		
26326	4Q8	1043	Virgin Atlantic Airways	G-VHOT		
26341	446	902	Japan Air Lines	JA8088		
26342	446	905	Japan Air Lines	JA8089		
26343	446	918	Japan Air Lines	JA8901		
26344	446	929	Japan Air Lines	N6018N	JA8902	
26345	446D	935	Japan Air Lines	JA8903		
26346	446	897	Japan Air Lines	JA8087		
26347	446D	907	Japan Air Lines	JA8090		
26348	446D	941	Japan Air Lines	JA8904		
26349	446D	948	Japan Air Lines	JA8905		
26350	446	961	Japan Air Lines	JA8906		
26351	446D	963	Japan Air Lines	JA8907		
26352	446D	978	Japan Air Lines	JA8908		
26353	446	980	Japan Air Lines	JA8909		
26354	446	1024	Japan Air Lines	JA8910		
26355	446	1026	Japan Air Lines	JA8911		
26356	446D		(Japan Air Lines)	(JA8913)	Allocated but later canx, not built	
26357	446		(Japan Air Lines)	(JA8914)	Allocated but later canx, not built	
26372	406	896	KLM-Royal Dutch Airlines	PH-BFN		
26373	406M	969	KLM-Royal Dutch Airlines	PH-BFM		
26374	406	992	KLM-Royal Dutch Airlines	PH-BFP		
26390	406F		(KLM-Royal Dutch Airlines)	(PH-CKA)	(PH-BFS)	Allocated but later canx, not built
26391	406F		(KLM-Royal Dutch Airlines)	(PH-BFT)	Allocated but later canx, not built	
26392	4B5	893	Korean Air	HL7484		
26393	4B5	958	Korean Air	HL7487		
26394	4B5	986	Korean Air	HL7488		
26395	4B5	922	Korean Air	HL7485		
26396	4B5	951	Korean Air	HL7486		
26397	4B5	1055	Korean Air	HL7492		
26398	4B5	1057	Korean Air	HL7493		
26400	4B5	1083	Korean Air	HL7496		
26401	4B5F	1087	Korean Air	HL7497		
26402	4B5	1092	Korean Air	HL7498		
26425	430	898	Lufthansa	N60659	D-ABVL	
26426	430	910	Government of Brunei	(D-ABVM)	N6009F	V8-AL1
26427	430	915	Lufthansa	D-ABVN		
26473	451	985	United Airlines	(N671US)	N60659	N105UA
26474	451	988	United Airlines	(N672US)	N60688	N106UA
26547	412	921	Singapore Intl Airlines	N6038E	9V-SMM	
26548	412	923	Singapore Intl Airlines	9V-SMN		
26549	412	1030	Singapore Intl Airlines	N6108N	9V-SMZ	
26550	412	1040	Singapore Intl Airlines	9V-SPA		
26551	412	1045	Singapore Intl Airlines	9V-SPB		
26552	412	1056	Singapore Intl Airlines	9V-SPD		
26553	412F	1069	Singapore Intl Airlines	9V-SFD		
26554	412	1070	Singapore Intl Airlines	9V-SPE		
26555	412	1075	Singapore Intl Airlines	9V-SPH		
26560	412F	1052	Singapore Intl Airlines	9V-SFC		
26561	412F	1042	Singapore Intl Airlines	9V-SFB		
26562	412	1074	Singapore Intl Airlines	9V-SPG		
26563	412F	1036	Singapore Intl Airlines	N60659	9V-SFA	
26609	4D7	1001	Thai International	HS-TGO		
26610	4D7	1047	Thai International	HS-TGP		
26615	4D7	950	Thai International	HS-TGN		
26637	444	943	South African Airways	ZS-SAX		
26638	444	995	South African Airways	ZS-SAY		

BOEING 747

C/n	Series	Line No	Last known Operator/Owner	Previous Identities/fate (where known)
26875	422	931	United Airlines	N186UA
26876	422	939	United Airlines	N187UA
26877	422	944	United Airlines	N188UA
26878	422	966	United Airlines	N189UA
26879	422	973	United Airlines	N190UA
26880	422	984	United Airlines	N191UA
26882	422	989	United Airlines	N192UA
26883	422		United Airlines	N193UA
27042	4H6	932	Malaysia Airlines	(9M-MHP) 9M-MPA
27043	4H6	1017	Malaysia Airlines	9M-MPF
27044	4H6	1041	Malaysia Airlines	N60468 9M-MPH
27062	45E	942	EVA Airways	B-16401
27063	45E	947	EVA Airways	B-16402
27066	412	940	Singapore Intl Airlines	9V-SMO
27067	412	953	Singapore Intl Airlines	9V-SMP
27068	412	1000	Singapore Intl Airlines	9V-SMU
27069	412	1010	Singapore Intl Airlines	9V-SMV
27070	412	1049	Singapore Intl Airlines	9V-SPC
27071	412	1072	Singapore Intl Airlines	9V-SPF
27072	4B5	1013	Korean Air	HL7489
27078	437	987	Air India	VT-ESM
27090	436	959	British Airways	G-BNLY
27091	436	964	British Asia Airways	G-BNLZ
27092	436	967	British Asia Airways	G-CIVA
27093	4D7	945	Thai International	HS-TGM
27099	446	1031	Japan Air Lines	JA8912 [originally ordered as -446D]
27117	467	970	Cathay Pacific Airways	N60697 VR-HUE
27132	412	955	Singapore Intl Airlines	9V-SMQ
27133	412	962	Singapore Intl Airlines	9V-SMR
27134	412	981	Singapore Intl Airlines	9V-SMS
27137	412	990	Singapore Intl Airlines	N60697 9V-SMT
27141	45E	976	EVA Airways	(N747BJ) (B-16403) N403EV
27142	45E	982	EVA Airways	(N747BL) (B-16405) N405EV
27154	45EM	994	EVA Airways	B-16461
27163	481D	996	All Nippon Airways	N1785B N5573S JA8964
27164	437	1003	Air India	VT-ESN
27165	437	1009	Air India	VT-ESO
27173	45EM	998	EVA Airways	B-16462
27174	45EM	1004	EVA Airways	B-16463
27175	467F	1020	Cathay Pacific Airways	N6056X VR-HUH
27177	4B5	1019	Korean Air	HL7490
27178	412	1015	Singapore Intl Airlines	N6018N 9V-SMW
27196	4F6		(Philippine Airlines)	(RP-C) Allocated but later canx, not built
27197	4F6		(Philippine Airlines)	(RP-C) Allocated but later canx, not built
27202	406M	1014	KLM-Royal Dutch Airlines	PH-BFR
27214	437	1034	Air India	VT-ESP
27217	412	1023	Singapore Intl Airlines	9V-SMY
27230	467	1033	Cathay Pacific Airways	VR-HUI
27261	4F6	1005	Philippine Airlines	(RP-C5751) N751PR
27262	4F6	1012	Philippine Airlines	(RP-C5752) N752PR
27338	469	1046	Kuwait Airways	9K-ADE
27341	4B5	1037	Korean Air	HL7491
27349	436	1048	British Airways	G-CIVD
27350	436	1050	British Airways	G-CIVE
27436	481D	1060	All Nippon Airways	JA8965
27442	481D	1066	All Nippon Airways	N6018N JA8966
27503	467F	1065	Cathay Pacific Airways	VR-HUK
27595	467	1061	Cathay Pacific Airways	VR-HUJ
27662	4B5	1067	Korean Air	HL7494
27663	469	1068	Philippine Airlines	(9K-ADF) N6009F N754PR
27723	4D7	1071	Thai International	HS-TGR
27827	4F6	1038	Canadian Airlines Intl	(JA8913) N6055X C-FGHZ [originally built as 747-446D]
27828	4F6	1039	Philippine Airlines	(JA8914) N6038E (N774BE) N753PR [originally built as 747-446D]
27898	45EM	1051	EVA Airways	N406EV
27899	45EM	1053	EVA Airways	N6018N N407EV
27915	458	1062	El Al Israel Airlines	N6009F 4X-ELC
27965	409	1063	Mandarin Airlines	B-16801
28086	430	1080	Lufthansa	D-ABVO
28092	45EM	1076	EVA Airways	N408EV
28093	45EM	1077	EVA Airways	N409EV
28094	437	1089	Air India	VT-EVA
28096	4B5	1073	Korean Air	HL7495
28195	406	1090	KLM-Royal Dutch Airlines	PH-BFS
28196	406M		KLM-Royal Dutch Airlines	PH-BFT

BOEING 747

C/n	Series	Line No	Last known Operator/Owner	Previous Identities/fate (where known)

BOEING 757

C/n	Series	Line No	Last known Operator/Owner	Previous Identities/fate (where known)
22172	236	9	British Airways	(N757B) G-BIKA
22173	236	10	British Airways	G-BIKB
22174	236	11	British Airways	G-BIKC
22175	236	13	British Airways	G-BIKD
22176	236	14	Air Europa	(G-BIKF) N5700B G-BKRM EC-117 EC-EGI G-BKRM
				EC-321 G-BKRM C-GANX N501MH EC-451 EC-FTL
22177	236	16	British Airways	(G-BIKG) G-BIKF
22178	236	23	British Airways	(G-BIKH) G-BIKG
22179	236	24	British Airways	(G-BIKI) G-BIKH
22180	236	25	British Airways	(G-BIKJ) G-BIKI
22181	236	29	British Airways	(G-BIKK) G-BIKJ
22182	236	30	British Airways	(G-BIKL) G-BIKK
22183	236	32	British Airways	(G-BIKM) G-BIKL
22184	236	33	British Airways	(G-BIKN) N8293V G-BIKM
22185	236	34	Air Europa	(G-BIKO) (G-BNEP) N8294V G-BPGW EC-265 EC-EOK
				G-BPGW YV-78C N270AE EC-843 EC-GCA
22186	236	50	British Airways	(G-BIKP) G-BIKN
22187	236	52	British Airways	(G-BIKR) G-BIKO
22188	236	54	British Airways	(G-BIKS) G-BIKP
22189	236	58	British Airways	(G-BIKT) G-BIKR
22190	236	63	British Airways	(G-BIKU) G-BIKS
22191	225	2	NASA/Langley Research Center [coded 557]	N501EA N557NA
22192	225	3	US Air	N502EA N600AU
22193	225	4	US Air	N503EA N601AU
22194	225	5	Airtours International	N504EA G-JALC
22195	225	6	Airtours International	N505EA G-PIDS
22196	225	7	US Air	N506EA N602AU
22197	225	8	Airtours International	N507EA N701MG G-RJGR
22198	225	12	US Air	N508EA N603AU
22199	225	17	US Air	N509EA N604AU
22200	225	20	Airtours International	N510EA G-MCEA
22201	225	21	US Air	N511EA N605AU
22202	225	22	US Air	N512EA N606AU
22203	225	26	US Air	N513EA N607AU
22204	225	27	US Air	N514EA N608AU
22205	225	28	US Air	N515EA N609AU
22206	225	31	(Birgenair)	N516EA C-GNXN N7079S TC-GEN 8P-GUL TC-GEN
				w/o 06Feb96 nr Puerto Plata, Dominican Republic
22207	225	35	America West Airlines	N517EA N913AW
22208	225	38	America West Airlines	N518EA N914AW
22209	225	40	America West Airlines	N519EA TC-GUL N747BJ N915AW
22210	225	42	US Air	N520EA N618AU
22211	225	74	Air 2000	N521EA G-OOOV
22212	200	1	Boeing Equipment Holding Co	(N757BC) N757A prototype; ff 18Feb82Canx Feb91
22611	225	75	Air 2000	N522EA G-OOOW
22612	225	114	Air 2000	N523EA G-OOOM
22688	225	115	LTU Sud	N524EA D-AMUU EC-896 EC-FIY D-AMUU
22689	225	117	LTU Sud	N525EA EC-390 EC-ETZ D-AMUK
22690	225	151	Fuerza Aerea Mexicana	(N526EA) TP-01/XC-CBD TP-01/XC-UJM
22691	225	155	America West Airlines	(N527EA) N907AW (XA-SED) XA-TCD N907AW
22780	2T7ER	15	Dinar	G-MONB
22781	2T7ER	18	Monarch Airlines	G-MONC EC-211 G-MONC D-ABNY G-MONC
22782	2Q4		(TransBrasil)	Allocated but later canx, not built
22783	2Q4		(TransBrasil)	Allocated but later canx, not built
22784	2Q4		(TransBrasil)	Allocated but later canx, not built
22808	232	37	Delta Air Lines	N601DL
22809	232	39	Delta Air Lines	N602DL
22810	232	41	Delta Air Lines	N603DL
22811	232	43	Delta Air Lines	N604DL
22812	232	46	Delta Air Lines	N605DL
22813	232	49	Delta Air Lines	N606DL
22814	232	61	Delta Air Lines	N607DL
22815	232	64	Delta Air Lines	N608DA
22816	232	65	Delta Air Lines	N609DL
22817	232	66	Delta Air Lines	N610DL
22818	232	71	Delta Air Lines	N611DL
22819	232	73	Delta Air Lines	N612DL
22820	232	84	Delta Air Lines	N613DL
22821	232	85	Delta Air Lines	N614DL
22822	232	87	Delta Air Lines	N615DL
22823	232	91	Delta Air Lines	N616DL
22907	232	92	Delta Air Lines	N617DL
22908	232	95	Delta Air Lines	N618DL
22909	232	101	Delta Air Lines	N619DL
22910	232	111	Delta Air Lines	N620DL
22911	232	112	Delta Air Lines	N621DL
22912	232	113	Delta Air Lines	N622DL
22913	232	118	Delta Air Lines	N623DL
22914	232	120	Delta Air Lines	N624DL

BOEING 757

C/n	Series	Line No	Last known Operator/Owner	Previous Identities/fate (where known)					
22915	232	126	Delta Air Lines	N625DL					
22916	232	128	Delta Air Lines	N626DL					
22917	232	129	Delta Air Lines	N627DL					
22918	232	133	Delta Air Lines	N628DL					
22919	232	134	Delta Air Lines	N629DL					
22920	232	135	Delta Air Lines	N630DL					
22960	2T7	19	Monarch Airlines	G-MOND	D-ABNZ	G-MOND			
22976	2T4		(Air Florida)	Allocated but later canx, not built					
22977	2T4		(Air Florida)	Allocated but later canx, not built					
22978	2T4		(Air Florida)	Allocated but later canx, not built					
23118	2G5	36	LTE International Airlines	D-AMUR	EC-EFX				
23119	2G5	51	LTE International Airlines	D-AMUS	EC-116	EC-EGH			
23125	212ER	44	American Trans Air	9V-SGK	N751AT				
23126	212ER	45	American Trans Air	9V-SGL	N750AT				
23127	212ER	47	American Trans Air	9V-SGM	N757AT				
23128	212ER	48	American Trans Air	9V-SGN	N752AT				
23190	251	53	Northwest Airlines	N501US					
23191	251	55	Northwest Airlines	N502US					
23192	251	59	Northwest Airlines	N503US					
23193	251	60	Northwest Airlines	N504US					
23194	251	62	Northwest Airlines	N505US					
23195	251	67	Northwest Airlines	N506US					
23196	251	68	Northwest Airlines	N507US					
23197	251	69	Northwest Airlines	N508US					
23198	251	70	Northwest Airlines	N509US					
23199	251	72	Northwest Airlines	N511US					
23200	251	82	Northwest Airlines	N512US					
23201	251	83	Northwest Airlines	N513US					
23202	251	86	Northwest Airlines	N514US					
23203	251	88	Northwest Airlines	N515US					
23204	251	104	Northwest Airlines	N516US					
23205	251	105	Northwest Airlines	N517US					
23206	251	107	Northwest Airlines	N518US					
23207	251	108	Northwest Airlines	N519US					
23208	251	109	Northwest Airlines	N520US					
23209	251	110	Northwest Airlines	N521US					
23227	236	57	Air Europa	(G-CJIG)	(G-BNHG)	G-BLVH	YV-77C	N271AE	EC-847
				EC-GCB					
23293	2T7ER	56	Renaissance Cruise	G-MONE	[Op by Carnival A/L]				
23321	2S7	76	America West Airlines	N601RC	N901AW				
23322	2S7	79	America West Airlines	N602RC	N902AW				
23323	2S7	80	America West Airlines	N603RC	N903AW				
23324	200		(Unknown Customer)	Allocated but later canx, not built					
23325	200		(Unknown Customer)	Allocated but later canx, not built					
23398	236	77	British Airways	G-BIKT					
23399	236	78	British Airways	G-BIKU					
23400	236	81	British Airways	G-BIKV					
23452	2M6	94	Royal Brunei Airlines	N6666U	V8-RBA				
23453	2M6	100	Royal Brunei Airlines	V8-RBB					
23454	2M6	102	Govt of Kazakhstan	N6067U	V8-RBC	V8-HB1	V8-RBC	(UN-002)	VR-CRK
23492	236	89	British Airways	G-BIKW					
23532	236	90	British Airways	G-BIKX					
23533	236	98	British Airways	G-BIKZ					
23495	236	93	British Airways	G-BIKY					
23566	2S7	96	America West Airlines	N604RC	N904AW				
23567	2S7	97	America West Airlines	N605RC	N905AW				
23568	2S7	99	America West Airlines	N606RC	N906AW				
23612	232	138	Delta Air Lines	N631DL					
23613	232	154	Delta Air Lines	N632DL					
23614	232	157	Delta Air Lines	N633DL					
23615	232	158	Delta Air Lines	N634DL					
23616	251	119	Northwest Airlines	N522US					
23617	251	121	Northwest Airlines	N523US					
23618	251	122	Northwest Airlines	N524US					
23619	251	124	Northwest Airlines	N525US					
23620	251	131	Northwest Airlines	N526US					
23651	2G5	116	LTE International Airlines	D-AMUT	EC-256	EC-ENQ			
23686	2B6	103	Royal Air Maroc	N32831	CN-RMT				
23687	2B6	106	Royal Air Maroc	CN-RMZ					
23710	236	123	British Airways	G-BMRA					
23723	24APF	139	United Parcel Service	N401UP					
23724	24APF	141	United Parcel Service	N402UP					
23725	24APF	143	United Parcel Service	N403UP					
23726	24APF	147	United Parcel Service	N404UP					
23727	24APF	149	United Parcel Service	N405UP					
23728	24APF	176	United Parcel Service	N406UP					
23729	24APF	181	United Parcel Service	N407UP					
23730	24APF	184	United Parcel Service	N408UP					
23731	24APF	186	United Parcel Service	N409UP					
23732	24APF	189	United Parcel Service	N410UP					
23760	232	171	Delta Air Lines	N637DL					

BOEING 757

C/n	Series	Line No	Last known Operator/Owner	Previous Identities/fate (where known)					
23761	232	177	Delta Air Lines	N638DL					
23762	232	159	Delta Air Lines	N635DL					
23763	232	164	Delta Air Lines	N636DL					
23767	28A	127	Air 2000	G-000A	C-F00A	G-000A	C-F00A	G-000A	C-FOAA
				G-000A					
23770	2T7ER	125	Monarch Airlines	G-DAJB					
23822	28A	130	Canada 3000 Airlines	G-000B	C-F00B	G-000B	C-F00B	G-000B	C-F00B
				G-000B	C-F00B	G-000B	C-F00B	G-000B	C-F00B
23842	251	136	Northwest Airlines	N527US					
23843	251	137	Northwest Airlines	N528US					
23844	251	140	Northwest Airlines	N529US					
23845	251	188	Northwest Airlines	N530US					
23846	251	190	Northwest Airlines	N531US					
23850	2F8	142	Royal Nepal Airlines	9N-ACA					
23851	24APF	191	United Parcel Service	N411UP					
23852	24APF	193	United Parcel Service	N412UP					
23853	24APF	195	United Parcel Service	N413UP					
23854	24APF	197	United Parcel Service	N414UP					
23855	24APF	199	United Parcel Service	N415UP					
23863	2F8C	182	Royal Nepal Airlines	N5573K	9N-ACB				
23895	2T7	132	Britannia Airways	G-DRJC	G-BYAM				
23903	24APF	318	United Parcel Service	N416UP					
23904	24APF	322	United Parcel Service	N417UP					
23905	24APF	326	United Parcel Service	N418UP					
23906	24APF	330	United Parcel Service	N419UP					
23907	24APF	334	United Parcel Service	N420UP					
23917	258	152	El Al Israel Airlines	4X-EBL					
23918	258	156	El Al Israel Airlines	4X-EBM					
23928	2G5	146	LTU	D-AMUV					
23929	2G5	153	LTU-Sud	D-AMUW					
23975	236	145	British Airways	G-BMRB					
23983	2G5	161	LTU-Sud	D-AMUX					
23993	232	198	Delta Air Lines	N639DL					
23994	232	201	Delta Air Lines	N640DL					
23995	232	202	Delta Air Lines	N641DL					
23996	232	205	Delta Air Lines	N642DL					
23997	232	206	Delta Air Lines	N643DL					
23998	232	207	Delta Air Lines	N644DL					
24014	21B	144	China Southern AIrlines	N1792B	B-2801				
24015	21B	148	China Southern AIrlines	N5573B	B-2802				
24016	21B	150	China Southern AIrlines	N5573K	B-2803				
24017	28A	162	Canada 3000 Airlines	G-000C	C-FX0C	G-000C	C-FX0C	G-000C	C-FX0C
24072	236	160	British Airways	G-BMRC	(N)	G-BMRC			
24073	236	166	British Airways	G-BMRD	(N)	G-BMRD			
24074	236	168	British Airways	G-BMRE	(N)	G-BMRE			
24101	236	175	British Airways	G-BMRF					
24102	236	179	British Airways	G-BMRG					
24104	2T7ER	170	Monarch Airlines	G-MONJ					
24105	2T7ER	172	Monarch Airlines	G-MONK					
24118	236	163	China Southern AIrlines	G-BNSD	EC-204	EC-EMA	G-BNSD	PH-TKY	N769BE
24119	236	167	China Southern AIrlines	EC-157	EC-EHY	G-BPSN	EC-350	EC-EHY	G-BPSN
				PH-TKZ	N770BE				
24120	236ER	174	British Airways	G-BOHC	EC-202	EC-ELA	G-BOHC	EC-516	EC-ELA
				G-BOHC	G-BPEF				
24121	236	183	Istanbul Airways	G-BNSE	EC-544	EC-EXH	G-BNSE	G-BPEH	TC-AHA
24122	236	187	Air Europa	G-BNSF	EC-203	EC-ELS	G-BNSF	(D-AOEB)	G-BNSF
				EC-744	EC-FFK				
24135	27B	165	Air Holland Charter	PH-AHE	OY-SHE	PH-AHE	OY-SHE	PH-AHE	
24136	27B	169	Britannia Airways	PH-AHF	OY-SHF	G-0AHF			
24137	27B	178	Air Europe (Italy)	PH-AHI	OY-SHI	PH-AHI	(G-BSUB)	G-0AHI	PH-AHI
24176	2G5	173	LTU-Sud	D-AMUY					
24216	232	216	Delta Air Lines	N645DL					
24217	232	217	Delta Air Lines	N646DL					
24218	232	222	Delta Air Lines	N647DL					
24233	2G7	244	America West Airlines	N908AW					
24235	28A	180	Air 2000	G-000D	(C-FX0D)	G-000D	C-FX0D	G-000D	C-FX0D
				(G-000D)	C-FX0D	G-000D			
24254	258	185	El Al Israel Airlines	4X-EBR					
24260	28A	204	Guyana Airways	C-FNBC	C-GNXC	C-GTSV	N757GA		
24263	251	192	Northwest Airlines	N532US					
24264	251	194	Northwest Airlines	N533US					
24265	251	196	Northwest Airlines	N534US					
24266	236	210	British Airways	G-BMRH					
24267	236	211	British Airways	G-BMRI					
24268	236	214	British Airways	G-BMRJ					
24289	23A	209	Air 2000	EC-247	EC-EMV	N510SK	G-000I		
24290	23A	212	Air 2000	EC-248	EC-EMU	N510FP	G-000J		
24291	23A	215	America West Airlines	PH-AHK	(G-BSUA)	G-0AHK	N250LA	N916AW	
24292	23A	219	Canada 3000 Airlines	G-000G	C-F00G	G-000G	C-F00G	G-000G	C-F00G
24293	23A	220	Canada 3000 Airlines	G-000H	N989AN	C-F00H			
24294	23A		(Ansett Worldwide Leasing)	Allocated but later canx, not built					

BOEING 757

C/n	Series	Line No	Last known Operator/Owner	Previous Identities/fate (where known)					
24330	21B	200	China Southern Airlines	B-2804					
24331	21B	203	China Southern Airlines	B-2805					
24367	28A	208	Transaero	C-GAWB	C-GNXI	C-GTSK	N240LA	N381LF	EI-CLM
24368	28AER	213	Monarch Airlines	G-MCKE					
24369	28A	226	Canada 3000 Airlines	C-FOOE					
24370	236ER	218	British Airways	G-BPEA					
24371	236ER	225	British Airways	G-BPEB					
24372	232	223	Delta Air Lines	N648DL					
24389	232	229	Delta Air Lines	N649DL					
24390	232	230	Delta Air Lines	N650DL					
24391	232	238	Delta Air Lines	N651DL					
24392	232	239	Delta Air Lines	N652DL					
24393	232	261	Delta Air Lines	N653DL					
24394	232	264	Delta Air Lines	N654DL					
24395	232	265	Delta Air Lines	N655DL					
24396	232	266	Delta Air Lines	N656DL					
24397	236	221	Air 2000	G-BRJD	EC-349	EC-ESC	G-BRJD	G-OOOS	
24398	236	224	British Airways	G-BRJE	EC-278	EC-EOL	G-BRJE	EC-597	EC-EOL
				N602DF	G-CPEL				
24401	21B	232	China Southern Airlines	N6067B	B-2806				
24402	21B	233	China Southern Airlines	N6069D	B-2807				
24419	232	286	Delta Air Lines	N657DL					
24420	232	287	Delta Air Lines	N658DL					
24421	232	293	Delta Air Lines	N659DL					
24422	232	294	Delta Air Lines	N660DL					
24451	2G5	227	LTU-Sud	D-AMUM					
24456	23APF	237	Challenge Air Cargo	N571CA					
24471	26D	231	Shanghai Airlines	N1792B	B-2808				
24472	26D	235	Shanghai Airlines	N5573B	B-2809				
24473	26D	301	Shanghai Airlines	B-2810					
24486	223	234	American Airlines	N610AA					
24487	223	236	American Airlines	N611AM					
24488	223	240	American Airlines	N612AA					
24489	223	242	American Airlines	N613AA					
24490	223	243	American Airlines	N614AA					
24491	223	245	American Airlines	N615AM					
24497	2G5	228	LTU-Sud	D-AMUZ					
24522	2G7	252	America West Airlines	N909AW					
24523	2G7	256	America West Airlines	N910AW					
24524	223	248	American Airlines	N616AA					
24525	223	253	American Airlines	N617AM					
24526	223	260	American Airlines	N618AA					
24527	23A	249	Petrolair Services	(VR-BLC)	HB-IHU	HB-IEE			
24528	23A	250	Sunways Airlines	OO-ILI	SE-DSM				
24543	28A	268	Air Transat	C-GTDL	N911AW	N871LF	C-GNXU	C-GTSN	
24544	28A	280	Canada 3000 Airlines	C-FXOF					
24566	23A	255	TAESA	5Y-BGI	XA-RLM				
24567	23A	257	North American Airlines	N1791B	N757NA				
24577	223	269	American Airlines	N619AA					
24578	223	276	American Airlines	N620AA					
24579	223	283	American Airlines	N621AM					
24580	223	289	American Airlines	N622AA					
24581	223	296	American Airlines	N623AA					
24582	223	297	American Airlines	N624AA					
24583	223	303	American Airlines	N625AA					
24584	223	304	American Airlines	N626AA					
24585	223	308	American Airlines	N627AA					
24586	223	309	American Airlines	N628AA					
24587	223	315	American Airlines	N629AA					
24588	223	316	American Airlines	N630AA					
24589	223	317	American Airlines	N631AA					
24590	223	321	American Airlines	N632AA					
24591	223	324	American Airlines	N633AA					
24592	223	327	American Airlines	N634AA					
24593	223	328	American Airlines	N635AA					
24594	223	336	American Airlines	N636AM					
24595	223	337	American Airlines	N637AM					
24596	223	344	American Airlines	N638AA					
24597	223	345	American Airlines	N639AA					
24598	223	350	American Airlines	N640A					
24599	223	351	American Airlines	N641AA					
24600	223	357	American Airlines	N642AA					
24601	223	360	American Airlines	N643AA					
24602	223	365	American Airlines	N644AA					
24603	223	370	American Airlines	(N645AM)	N645AA				
24604	223	375	American Airlines	N646AA					
24605	223	378	American Airlines	(N647AA)	N647AM				
24606	223	379	American Airlines	N648AA					
24607	223	383	American Airlines	N649AA					
24608	223	384	American Airlines	N650AA					
24609	223	390	(American Airlines)	N651AA	w/o 20Dec95 Mount San Jose, Colombia				

BOEING 757

C/n	Series	Line No	Last known Operator/Owner	Previous Identities/fate (where known)
24610	223	391	American Airlines	N652AA
24611	223	397	American Airlines	N653A
24612	223	398	American Airlines	N654A
24613	223	402	American Airlines	N655AA
24614	223	404	American Airlines	N656AA
24615	223	409	American Airlines	N657AM
24616	223	410	American Airlines	N658AA
24617	23A	417	American Airlines	N659AA
24622	222	241	United Airlines	N501UA
24623	222	246	United Airlines	N502UA
24624	222	247	United Airlines	N503UA
24625	222	251	United Airlines	N504UA
24626	222	254	United Airlines	N505UA
24627	222	263	United Airlines	N506UA
24635	23APF	258	Gulf Air	(PT-TDA) N3502P 9J-AFO VH-AWE
24636	23A	259	Airtours International	G-IEAB G-LCRC
24714	21B	262	China Southern Airlines	B-2811
24737	230	267	Condor Flug	D-ABNA
24738	230	274	Condor Flug	D-ABNB
24739	208	273	Icelandair	TF-FIH
24743	222	270	United Airlines	N507UA
24744	222	277	United Airlines	N508UA
24747	230	275	Condor Flug	D-ABNC
24748	230	285	Condor Flug	D-ABND
24749	230	295	Condor Flug	N35153 D-ABNE
24758	21B	282	(China Southern Airlines)	B-2812 dbr 02Oct90 Canton, PRC
24760	208	281	Icelandair	TF-FII
24763	222	284	United Airlines	N509UA
24771	236	272	Istanbul Airways	G-BRJG PH-AHN P4-AAA G-IEAD TF-FIK G-SRJG TC-AJA
24772	236	271	Air Transat	G-BRJF EC-432 EC-EVD G-BRJF (I-BRJF) G-BRJF I-BRJF C-GNXB C-GTSJ
24774	21B	288	China Southern Airlines	B-2815
24780	222	290	United Airlines	N510UA
24792	236	279	Venus Airlines	G-BRJI EC-446 EC-EVC EC-786 EC-FMQ G-BRJI SX-BBZ G-BRJI SX-BBZ
24793	236	292	Air 2000	G-BRJJ EC-490 G-BRJJ G-OOOT
24794	236	278	Air Europa	G-BRJH EC-669 EC-FEF
24799	222	291	United Airlines	N511UA
24809	222	298	United Airlines	N512UA
24810	222	299	United Airlines	N513UA
24838	2J4	302	Condor Flug	PH-AHL D-ABNX
24839	222	305	United Airlines	N514UA
24840	222	306	United Airlines	N515UA
24845	260PF	300	Ethiopian Airlines	N3519L ET-AJS
24860	222	307	United Airlines	N516UA
24861	222	310	United Airlines	N517UA
24868	23APF	314	Challenge Air Cargo	(PT-TDB) N572CA
24871	222	311	United Airlines	N518UA
24872	222	312	United Airlines	N519UA
24882	236ER	323	British Airways	G-BPEC
24884	258ER	325	El Al Israel Airlines	4X-EBS
24890	222	313	United Airlines	N520UA
24891	222	319	United Airlines	N521UA
24923	23A	332	Freeport McMoran Inc	(5Y-BHF) N5573B N680EM N680FM
24924	23A	333	Canada 3000 Airlines	(5Y-BHG) C-FXOK
24931	222	320	United Airlines	N522UA
24932	222	329	United Airlines	N523UA
24964	2Q8	424	American Trans Air	N754AT
24965	2Q8	438	American Trans Air	N755AT
24971	23APF	340	Challenge Air Cargo	N5002K G-OBOZ N573CA
24972	232	335	Delta Air Lines	N661DN
24977	222	331	United Airlines	N524UA
24978	222	338	United Airlines	N525UA
24991	232	342	Delta Air Lines	N662DN
24992	232	343	Delta Air Lines	N663DN
24994	222	339	United Airlines	N526UA
24995	222	341	United Airlines	N527UA
25012	232	347	Delta Air Lines	N664DN
25013	232	349	Delta Air Lines	N665DN
25014	260	348	Ethiopian Airlines	ET-AJX
25018	222	346	United Airlines	N528UA
25019	222	352	United Airlines	N529UA
25034	232	354	Delta Air Lines	N666DN
25035	232	355	Delta Air Lines	N667DN
25036	258ER	356	El Al Israel Airlines	4X-EBT
25042	222	361	United Airlines	N531UA
25043	222	353	United Airlines	N530UA
25044	2Q8	369	LADECO	CC-CYG
25053	236	358	Air Europa	(G-BSNA) EC-667 EC-FEE

BOEING 757

C/n	Series	Line No	Last known Operator/Owner	Previous Identities/fate (where known)					
25054	236	362	Transwede	(G-BSNB)	(EC-668)	N5002K	N3502P	XA-MMX	EI-CMA
				N100FS	SE-DUK				
25059	236	363	British Airways	G-BPED					
25060	236ER	364	British Airways	G-BPEE					
25072	222	366	United Airlines	N532UA					
25073	222	367	United Airlines	N533UA					
25083	21B	359	China Southern Airlines	B-2816					
25085	208	368	Icelandair	TF-FIJ	G-BTEJ	TF-FIJ			
25129	222	372	United Airlines	N534UA					
25130	222	373	United Airlines	N535UA					
25131	2Q8	458	LADECO	CC-CYH					
25133	236	374	UNI Airways	(G-BSNC)	N1786B	I-AEJA	(OO-TBI)	I-AEJA	OO-TBI
				N127MA	B-17501				
25140	230	382	Condor Flug	D-ABNF					
25141	232	376	Delta Air Lines	N668DN					
25142	232	377	Delta Air Lines	N669DN					
25155	2J4	371	Vulcan Northwest	OY-SHA	XA-SPG	N115FS	N757AS		
25156	222	380	United Airlines	N536UA					
25157	222	381	United Airlines	N537UA					
25220	2J4	387	Diamond Aviation Intl	N35108	OY-SHB	VR-CAU			
25222	222	385	United Airlines	N538UA					
25223	222	386	United Airlines	N539UA					
25240	2Y0	388	Kiwi International	G-OOOU					
25252	222	393	United Airlines	N540UA					
25253	222	394	United Airlines	N541UA					
25258	21B	389	China Southern Airlines	B-2817					
25259	21B	392	China Southern Airlines	B-2818					
25268	2Y0	400	Venus Airways	XA-TAE	N400KL	EI-CLP			
25276	222	396	United Airlines	N542UA					
25277	222	434	United Airlines	N553UA					
25281	24APF	395	United Parcel Service	N421UP					
25294	223	418	American Airlines	N660AM					
25295	223	423	American Airlines	N661AA					
25296	223	425	American Airlines	N662AA					
25297	223	432	American Airlines	N663AM					
25298	223	433	American Airlines	N664AA					
25299	223	436	American Airlines	N665AA					
25300	223	451	American Airlines	N666A					
25301	223	459	American Airlines	N7667A					
25322	222	405	United Airlines	N544UA					
25323	222	406	United Airlines	N545UA					
25324	24APF	399	United Parcel Service	N422UP					
25325	24APF	403	United Parcel Service	N423UP					
25331	232	415	Delta Air Lines	N670DN					
25332	232	416	Delta Air Lines	N671DN					
25333	223	460	American Airlines	N668AA					
25334	223	463	American Airlines	N669AA					
25335	223	468	American Airlines	N670AA					
25336	223	473	American Airlines	N671AA					
25337	223	474	American Airlines	N672AA					
25338	223	483	American Airlines	N681AA					
25339	223	484	American Airlines	N682AA					
25340	223	491	American Airlines	N683A					
25341	223	504	American Airlines	N684AA					
25342	223	507	American Airlines	N685AA					
25343	223	509	American Airlines	N686AA					
25345	23A	412	Government of Turkmenistan	N35153	N58AW	EZ-A010			
25353	260	408	Ethiopian Airlines	ET-AKC					
25367	222	413	United Airlines	N546UA					
25368	222	414	United Airlines	N547UA					
25369	24APF	407	United Parcel Service	N424UP					
25370	24APF	411	United Parcel Service	N425UP					
25396	222	420	United Airlines	N548UA					
25397	222	421	United Airlines	N549UA					
25398	222	426	United Airlines	N550UA					
25399	222	427	United Airlines	N551UA					
25436	230	419	Condor Flug	D-ABNH					
25437	230	422	Condor Flug	D-ABNI					
25438	230	428	Condor Flug	D-ABNK					
25439	230	437	Condor Flug	D-ABNL					
25440	230	433	Condor Flug	D-ABNM					
25441	230	446	Condor Flug	D-ABNN					
25457	24APF	477	United Parcel Service	N426UP					
25458	24APF	481	United Parcel Service	N427UP					
25459	24APF	485	United Parcel Service	N428UP					
25460	24APF	489	United Parcel Service	N429UP					
25461	24APF	493	United Parcel Service	N430UP					
25462	24APF	569	United Parcel Service	N431UP					
25463	24APF	573	United Parcel Service	N432UP					
25464	24APF	577	United Parcel Service	N433UP					
25465	24APF	579	United Parcel Service	N434UP					

BOEING 757

C/n	Series	Line No	Last known Operator/Owner	Previous Identities/fate (where known)					
25466	24APF	581	United Parcel Service	N435UP					
25467	24APF	625	United Parcel Service	N436UP					
25468	24APF	628	United Parcel Service	N437UP					
25469	24APF	631	United Parcel Service	N438UP					
25470	24APF	634	United Parcel Service	N439UP					
25471	24APF	636	United Parcel Service	N440UP					
25472	24APF	659	United Parcel Service	N450UP					
25473	24APF	679	United Parcel Service	N452UP					
25474	24APF	683	United Parcel Service	N453UP					
25475	24APF	687	United Parcel Service	N454UP					
25476	24APF	691	United Parcel Service	N455UP					
25487	23A	470	Government of Argentina	T-01	[Op by Fuerza Aerea Argentina]				
25488	23A	471	Air Transat	N1792B	C-GTSE				
25489	23A	505	AeroPeru	N52AW	XA-SKR	XA-SME	N52AW		
25490	23A	510	AeroPeru	N53AW	XA-SKQ	XA-SMD	N53AW		
25491	23A	511	Air Transat	C-GTSF					
25492	23A		(Ansett Worldwide)	Allocated but later canx, not built					
25493	23A	523	American Trans Air	N59AW	N512AT				
25494	23A	611	AVIANCA	N987AN					
25495	23A	599	Saudi Royal Flight	N1786B	N1789B	N275AW	HZ-HMED	[Op by RSAF/1Sqdn]	
25592	236	453	Sunways Airlines	G-BUDX	(N592KA)	SE-DSK			
25593	236	466	Sunways Airlines	G-BUDZ	C-FNXY	G-BUDZ	N593KA	SE-DSL	
25597	236	441	Air Europa	(G-)	EC-597	EC-FLY	D-AMUL	EC-897	EC-GBX
25598	236	445	China Southern Airlines	(G-)	N5573P	XA-SAD	N5573P	B-2835	
25620	236	449	Airtours International	G-IEAC	G-CSVS				
25621	2Q8	457	Canada 3000 Airlines	C-FXOO					
25622	2Q8	530	Air Seychelles	S7-AAX					
25623	28A	528	Britannia Airways	G-BYAJ					
25624	28A	541	AeroMexico	N801AM	XA-SIK	N801AM			
25625	28A		ILFC	TF-					
25626	28A	549	Britannia Airways	G-BYAL					
25681	2G7		(America West Airlines)	Allocated but later canx, not built					
25682	2G7		(America West Airlines)	Allocated but later canx, not built					
25695	223	536	American Airlines	N687AA					
25696	223	566	American Airlines	N690AA					
25697	223	568	American Airlines	N691AA					
25698	222	401	United Airlines	N543UA					
25730	223	548	American Airlines	N688AA					
25731	223	562	American Airlines	N689AA					
25806	236	601	British Airways	G-BPEI					
25807	236	610	British Airways	G-BPEJ					
25808	236	665	British Airways	G-BPEK					
25884	21B	461	China Southern Airlines	B-2822					
25885	2Z0	476	China Southwest Airlines	B-2820					
25886	2Z0	480	China Southwest Airlines	B-2821					
25887	2Z0	554	China Southwest Airlines	B-2832					
25888	21B	575	China Southern Airlines	B-2823					
25889	21B	583	China Southern Airlines	B-2824					
25890	21B	585	China Southern Airlines	B-2825					
25898	25C	475	Xiamen Airlines	B-2819					
25899	25C	565	Xiamen Airlines	B-2828					
25900	25C	574	Xiamen Airlines	B-2829					
25901	230	464	Condor Flug	D-ABNO					
25977	232	429	Delta Air Lines	N672DL					
25978	232	430	Delta Air Lines	N673DL					
25979	232	439	Delta Air Lines	N674DL					
25980	232	448	Delta Air Lines	N675DL					
25981	232	455	Delta Air Lines	N676DL					
25982	232	456	Delta Air Lines	N677DL					
25983	232	465	Delta Air Lines	N678DL					
26053	258	529	El Al Israel Airlines	4X-EBU					
26054	258	547	El Al Israel Airlines	4X-EBV					
26057	260	444	Ethiopian Airlines	ET-AKE					
26058	260	496	Ethiopian Airlines	ET-AKF					
26151	2Y0	472	Venus Airlines	XA-SCB	XA-KWK	SX-BBY			
26152	2Y0	478	AVIANCA	EI-CEY					
26153	2Y0	482	China Southwest Airlines	(MT-1044)	B-2831				
26154	2Y0	486	AVIANCA	EI-CEZ					
26155	2Y0	495	China Southwest Airlines	B-2826					
26156	2Y0	503	China Southwest Airlines	B-2827					
26158	2Y0	526	Air 2000	G-OOOX					
26160	2Y0	555	Transaero	(B-2830)	N1786B	N3519M	EI-CJX		
26161	2Y0	557	Transaero	N3521N	EI-CJY				
26239	256	553	Iberia	EC-420	EC-FTR				
26240	256	561	Iberia	EC-421	EC-FUA	EC-616	EC-FXU		
26241	256	572	Iberia	EC-422	EC-FUB	EC-618	EC-FXV		
26242	256	593	Iberia	N35030	EC-608	EC-FYJ			
26243	256	603	Iberia	EC-609	EC-FYK				
26244	256	616	Iberia	EC-610	EC-FYL				
26245	256	617	Iberia	EC-611	EC-FYM				
26246	256	620	Iberia	EC-612	EC-FYN				

BOEING 757

C/n	Series	Line No	Last known Operator/Owner	Previous Identities/fate (where known)		
26266	28A	514	Freedom Air	G-BYAF		
26267	28A	538	Britannia Airways	G-BYAK		
26268	2Q8	590	AeroMexico	(N803AM)	XA-SMJ	N803AM
26269	2Q8	612	Baikal Airlines	N321LF		
26270	2Q8	558	AeroMexico	(N802AM)	XA-SJD	N802AM
26271	2Q8	592	AeroMexico	(N804AM)	XA-SMK	N804AM
26272	2Q8	594	AeroMexico	(N805AM)	XA-SML	N805AM
26273	2Q8	597	AeroMexico	(N806AM)	XA-SMM	N806AM
26274	2Q8	676	Transaero	N161LF	EI-CLU	
26275	2Q8	672	Transaero	N151LF	EI-CLV	
26276	28A	704	Icelandair	TF-FIK		
26277	28A	658	North American Airlines	N750NA		
26278	2G5	671	LTU	D-AMUQ		
26332	2Q8	688	LAPA	LV-WMH		
26433	230	521	Condor Flug	D-ABNP		
26434	230	532	Condor Flug	D-ABNR		
26435	230	537	Condor Flug	D-ABNS		
26436	230	587	Condor Flug	N1790B	N3502P	D-ABNT
26482	251	693	Northwest Airlines	N535US		
26483	251	695	Northwest Airlines	N536US		
26484	251	697	Northwest Airlines	N537US		
26485	251	699	Northwest Airlines	N538US		
26486	251	700	Northwest Airlines	N539US		
26487	251	701	Northwest Airlines	N540US		
26488	251	703	Northwest Airlines	N541US		
26489	251	705	Northwest Airlines	N542US		
26490	251	709	Northwest Airlines	N543US		
26491	251		Northwest Airlines	N544US		
26492	251		Northwest Airlines	N545US		
26493	251		Northwest Airlines	N546US		
26494	251		Northwest Airlines	N547US		
26495	251		Northwest Airlines	N548US		
26496	251		Northwest Airlines	N549US		
26633	2K2	519	Transavia Airlines	PH-TKA		
26634	2K2	545	Transavia Airlines	PH-TKB		
26635	2K2	608	Transavia Airlines	PH-TKC		
26641	222	431	United Airlines	N552UA		
26644	222	435	United Airlines	N554UA		
26647	222	442	United Airlines	N555UA		
26650	222	447	United Airlines	N556UA		
26653	222	454	United Airlines	N557UA		
26654	222	462	United Airlines	N558UA		
26657	222	467	United Airlines	N559UA		
26660	222	469	United Airlines	N560UA		
26661	222	479	United Airlines	N561UA		
26664	222	487	United Airlines	N562UA		
26665	222	488	United Airlines	N563UA		
26666	222	490	United Airlines	N564UA		
26669	222	492	United Airlines	N565UA		
26670	222	494	United Airlines	N566UA		
26673	222	497	United Airlines	N567UA		
26674	222	498	United Airlines	N568UA		
26677	222	499	United Airlines	N569UA		
26678	222	501	United Airlines	N570UA		
26681	222	506	United Airlines	N571UA		
26682	222	508	United Airlines	N572UA		
26685	222	512	United Airlines	N573UA		
26686	222	513	United Airlines	N574UA		
26689	222	515	United Airlines	N575UA		
26690	222	524	United Airlines	N576UA		
26693	222	527	United Airlines	N577UA		
26694	222	531	United Airlines	N578UA		
26697	222	539	United Airlines	N579UA		
26698	222	542	United Airlines	N580UA		
26701	222	543	United Airlines	N581UA		
26702	222	550	United Airlines	N582UA		
26705	222	556	United Airlines	N583UA		
26706	222	559	United Airlines	N584UA		
26709	222	563	United Airlines	N585UA		
26710	222	567	United Airlines	N586UA		
26713	222	570	United Airlines	N587UA		
26717	222	571	United Airlines	N588UA		
26721	222		(United Airlines)	(N589UA)	Allocated but later canx, not built	
26722	222		(United Airlines)	(N590UA)	Allocated but later canx, not built	
26955	232	500	Delta Air Lines	N679DA		
26956	232	502	Delta Air Lines	N680DA		
26957	232	516	Delta Air Lines	N681DA		
26958	232	518	Delta Air Lines	N682DA		
26962	204	440	Britannia Airways	G-BYAC		
26963	204	450	Britannia Airways	G-BYAD		
26964	204	452	Britannia Airways	G-BYAE		

BOEING 757

C/n	Series	Line No	Last known Operator/Owner	Previous Identities/fate (where known)		
26965	204	517	Britannia Airways	G-BYAG		
26966	204	520	Britannia Airways	G-BYAH		
26967	204	522	Britannia Airways	G-BYAI		
26972	223	578	American Airlines	N692AA		
26973	223	580	American Airlines	N693AA		
26974	223	582	American Airlines	N694AN		
26975	223	621	American Airlines	N695AN		
26976	223	627	American Airlines	N696AN		
26977	223	633	American Airlines	N697AN		
26980	223	635	American Airlines	N698AN		
27051	223	660	American Airlines	N699AN		
27052	223	661	American Airlines	N601AN		
27053	223	664	American Airlines	N602AN		
27054	223	670	American Airlines	N603AA		
27055	223	677	American Airlines	N604AA		
27056	223	680	American Airlines	N605AA		
27057	223		American Airlines	N606AA		
27058	223		American Airlines	N607AM		
27103	232	533	Delta Air Lines	N683DA		
27104	232	535	Delta Air Lines	N684DA		
27118	2G5		(LTU-Sud)	(D-)	Allocated but later canx, not built	
27119	2G5		(LTU-Sud)	(D-)	Allocated but later canx, not built	
27120	2G5		(LTU-Sud)	(D-)	Allocated but later canx, not built	
27121	2G5		(LTU-Sud)	(D-)	Allocated but later canx, not built	
27122	2B7	525	US Air	N610AU		
27123	2B7	534	US Air	N611AU		
27124	2B7	540	US Air	N612AU		
27144	2B7	544	US Air	N613AU		
27145	2B7	546	US Air	N614AU		
27146	2B7	551	US Air	N615AU		
27147	2B7	552	US Air	N616AU		
27148	2B7	564	US Air	N617AU		
27152	26D	560	Shanghai Airlines	B-2833		
27172	232		(Delta Airlines)	(N687DA)	Allocated but later canx, not built	
27183	26D	576	Shanghai Airlines	B-2834		
27198	2B7	584	US Air	N619AU		
27199	2B7	586	US Air	N620AU		
27200	2B7	589	US Air	N621AU		
27201	2B7	605	US Air	N622AU		
27203	29J	588	Far Eastern Air Transport	(SU-RAC)	N1792B	B-27005
27204	29J	591	Far Eastern Air Transport	(SU-RAD)	B-27007	
27207	232		(Delta Airlines)	(N686DA)	Allocated but later canx, not built	
27208	204	606	Britannia Airways	G-BYAT		
27215	29JPF		(Shorouk Air)	(SU-RAE)	Allocated but later canx, not built	
27216	29JPF		(Shorouk Air)	(SU-RAF)	Allocated but later canx, not built	
27219	204	596	Britannia Airways	G-BYAN		
27220	204	618	Britannia Airways	G-BYAU		
27234	204	663	Britannia Airways	G-BYAW		
27235	204	598	Britannia Airways	G-BYAO		
27236	204	600	Britannia Airways	G-BYAP		
27237	204	602	Britannia Airways	G-BYAR		
27238	204	604	Britannia Airways	G-BYAS		
27244	2B7	607	US Air	N623AU		
27245	2B7	630	US Air	N624AU		
27246	2B7	643	US Air	(N625AU)	N625VJ	
27258	2Z0	595	China Southwest Airlines	B-2836		
27259	2Z0	609	China Southwest Airlines	B-2837		
27260	2Z0	613	China Southwest Airlines	B-2838		
27269	2Z0	615	China Southwest Airlines	B-2839		
27270	2Z0	622	China Southwest Airlines	B-2840		
27281	26D		(Shanghai Airlines)	(B-2843)	Allocated but later canx, not built	
27282	2Z0		(China Southwest Airlines)	(B-2841)	Allocated but later canx, not built	
27291	224	614	Continental Airlines	(N21100)	N58101	
27292	224	619	Continental Airlines	(N58101)	N13102	
27293	224	623	Continental Airlines	(N14102)	N33103	
27294	224	629	Continental Airlines	(N33103)	N17104	
27295	224	632	Continental Airlines	(N17104)	N17105	
27296	224	637	Continental Airlines	(N17105)	N14106	
27297	224	641	Continental Airlines	(N14106)	N14107	
27298	224	645	Continental Airlines	(N14107)	N21108	
27299	224	648	Continental Airlines	(N21108)	N12109	
27300	224	650	Continental Airlines	(N12109)	N13110	
27301	224	652	Continental Airlines	(N13110)	N57111	
27302	224	653	Continental Airlines	(N57111)	N18112	
27303	2B7	647	US Air	N626AU		
27342	26D	626	Shanghai Airlines	B-2842		
27351	2Q8	639	American Trans Air	N756AT		
27367	2Z0	624	China Southwest Airlines	B-2841		
27386	24APF	638	United Parcel Service	N441UP		
27387	24APF	640	United Parcel Service	N442UP		
27388	24APF	642	United Parcel Service	N443UP		

BOEING 757

C/n	Series	Line No	Last known Operator/Owner	Previous Identities/fate (where known)
27389	24APF	644	United Parcel Service	N444UP
27390	24APF	646	United Parcel Service	N445UP
27446	223		American Airlines	N608AA
27447	223		American Airlines	N609AA
27511	2Z0	669	China Southwest Airlines	B-2844
27512	2Z0	674	China National Aviation Co	B-2845
27513	25C	685	Xiamen Airlines	B-2848
27517	25C	698	Xiamen Airlines	B-2849
27555	224	668	Continental Airlines	N13113
27556	224	682	Continental Airlines	N12114
27557	224	686	Continental Airlines	N14115
27558	224	702	Continental Airlines	N12116
27559	224		Continental Airlines	N19117
27560	224		Continental Airlines	N19118
27561	224		Continental Airlines	N18119
27562	224		Continental Airlines	N14120
27563	224		Continental Airlines	N14121
27564	224		Continental Airlines	N17122
27565	224		Continental Airlines	N26123
27566	224		Continental Airlines	N29124
27567	224		Continental Airlines	N12125
27588	232	667	Delta Airlines	N685DA
27589	232	689	Delta Airlines	N686DA
27598	23N	692	American Trans Air	N515AT
27599	2Q8	696	Cabo Verde	D4-CBG
27681	26D	684	Shanghai Airlines	B-2843
27735	24APF	649	United Parcel Service	N446UP
27736	24APF	651	United Parcel Service	N447UP
27737	24APF	654	United Parcel Service	N448UP
27738	24APF	656	United Parcel Service	N449UP
27739	24APF	675	United Parcel Service	N451UP
27805	2B7	655	US Air	N627AU
27806	2B7	657	US Air	N628AU
27807	2B7	662	US Air	N629AU
27808	2B7	666	US Air	N630AU
27809	2B7	673	US Air	N631AU
27810	2B7	678	US Air	N632AU
27811	2B7	681	US Air	N633AU
27812	2G5		LTU	D-AMUH
27971	23N	690	American Trans Air	N514AT
27972	23N	694	American Trans Air	N516AT
27973	23N		American Trans Air	N517AT
27974	23N		American Trans Air	N518AT
28112	2G5	708	LTU Sud	D-AMUI
28142	222		United Air Lines	N591UA
28143	222		United Air Lines	N592UA
28144	222		United Air Lines	N593UA
28145	222		United Air Lines	N594UA
28336	22K		Turkmenistan Airlines	EZ-A011
28337	22K		Turkmenistan Airlines	EZ-A012
28338	23P		Uzbekistan Airways	UK-75700

BOEING 757

C/n	Series	Line No	Last known Operator/Owner	Previous Identities/fate (where known)

BOEING 767

C/n	Series	Line No	Last known Operator/Owner	Previous Identities/fate (where known)
21862	222	2	United Airlines	N601UA
21863	222ER	3	United Airlines	N602UA
21864	222	4	United Airlines	N603UA
21865	222	5	United Airlines	N604UA
21866	222ER	7	United Airlines	N605UA
21867	222ER	9	United Airlines	N606UA
21868	222ER	10	United Airlines	N607UA
21869	222ER	11	United Airlines	N608UA
21870	222ER	13	United Airlines	N609UA
21871	222ER	15	United Airlines	N610UA
21872	222ER	20	United Airlines	N611UA
21873	222ER	41	United Airlines	N612UA
21874	222ER	42	United Airlines	N613UA
21875	222	43	United Airlines	N614UA
21876	222	45	United Airlines	N615UA
21877	222	46	United Airlines	N617UA
21878	222	48	United Airlines	N618UA
21879	222	49	United Airlines	N619UA
21880	222	50	United Airlines	N620UA
21881	222		(United Airlines)	(N621UA) Allocated but later canx, not built
21882	222		(United Airlines)	(N622UA) Allocated but later canx, not built
21883	222		(United Airlines)	(N623UA) Allocated but later canx, not built
21884	222		(United Airlines)	(N624UA) Allocated but later canx, not built
21885	222		(United Airlines)	(N625UA) Allocated but later canx, not built
21886	222		(United Airlines)	(N626UA) Allocated but later canx, not built
21887	222		(United Airlines)	(N627UA) Allocated but later canx, not built
21888	222		(United Airlines)	(N628UA) Allocated but later canx, not built
21889	222		(United Airlines)	(N629UA) Allocated but later canx, not built
21890	222		(United Airlines)	(N630UA) Allocated but later canx, not built
21891	222		(United Airlines)	(N631UA) Allocated but later canx, not built
22213	232	6	Delta Air Lines	N101DA
22214	232	12	Delta Air Lines	N102DA
22215	232	17	Delta Air Lines	N103DA
22216	232	26	Delta Air Lines	N104DA
22217	232	27	Delta Air Lines	N105DA
22218	232	31	Delta Air Lines	N106DA
22219	232	37	Delta Air Lines	N107DL
22220	232	38	Delta Air Lines	N108DL
22221	232	53	Delta Air Lines	N109DL
22222	232	56	Delta Air Lines	N110DL
22223	232	74	Delta Air Lines	N111DN
22224	232	76	Delta Air Lines	N112DL
22225	232	77	Delta Air Lines	N113DA
22226	232	78	Delta Air Lines	N114DL
22227	232	83	Delta Air Lines	N115DA
22228	232		(Delta Air Lines)	(N116DL) Allocated but later canx, not built
22229	232		(Delta Air Lines)	(N117DL) Allocated but later canx, not built
22230	232		(Delta Air Lines)	(N118DL) Allocated but later canx, not built
22231	232		(Delta Air Lines)	(N119DL) Allocated but later canx, not built
22232	232		(Delta Air Lines)	(N120DL) Allocated but later canx, not built
22233	200	1	Boeing Corp	N767BA prototype; ff 26Sep81Airborne Surveillance Testbed
22307	223	8	American Airlines	N301AA
22308	223	19	American Airlines	N302AA
22309	223	23	American Airlines	N303AA
22310	223	25	American Airlines	N304AA
22311	223	34	American Airlines	N305AA
22312	223	44	American Airlines	N306AA
22313	223	72	American Airlines	N307AA
22314	223	73	American Airlines	N308AA
22315	223ER	94	American Airlines	N312AA
22316	223ER	95	American Airlines	N313AA
22317	223ER	109	American Airlines	N315AA
22318	223ER	111	American Airlines	N316AA
22319	223ER	112	American Airlines	N317AA
22320	223ER	128	American Airlines	N319AA
22321	223ER	130	American Airlines	N320AA
22322	223ER	139	American Airlines	N321AA
22323	223ER	140	American Airlines	N322AA
22324	223ER	146	American Airlines	N323AA
22325	223ER	147	American Airlines	N324AA
22326	223ER	157	American Airlines	N325AA
22327	223ER	159	American Airlines	N327AA
22328	223ER	160	American Airlines	N328AA
22329	223ER	164	American Airlines	N329AA
22330	223ER	166	American Airlines	N330AA
22331	223ER	168	American Airlines	N332AA
22332	223ER	169	American Airlines	N334AA
22333	223ER	194	American Airlines	N335AA
22334	223ER	195	American Airlines	N336AA

BOEING 767

C/n	Series	Line No	Last known Operator/Owner	Previous Identities/fate (where known)
22335	223ER	196	American Airlines	N338AA
22336	223ER	198	American Airlines	N339AA
22517	233ER	16	Air Canada	C-GAUB
22518	233	22	Air Canada	C-GAUE
22519	233	40	Air Canada	C-GAUH
22520	233	47	Air Canada	C-GAUN
22521	233	66	Air Canada	N1791B C-GAUP
22522	233	75	Air Canada	N60659 C-GAUS
22523	233	87	Air Canada	N1784B C-GAUU
22524	233	88	Air Canada	N6038E C-GAUW
22525	233ER	91	Air Canada	N6055X C-GAUY
22526	233ER	92	Air Canada	C-GAVA
22527	233ER	102	Air Canada	N1783B C-GAVC
22528	233ER	105	Air Canada	N6066U C-GAVF
22564	231ER	14	Trans World Airlines	N601TW
22565	231ER	21	Trans World Airlines	N602TW
22566	231ER	29	Trans World Airlines	N603TW
22567	231ER	30	Trans World Airlines	N604TW
22568	231ER	33	Trans World Airlines	N605TW
22569	231ER	39	Trans World Airlines	N606TW
22570	231ER	63	Trans World Airlines	N607TW
22571	231ER	64	Trans World Airlines	N608TW
22572	231ER	65	Trans World Airlines	N609TW
22573	231ER	70	Trans World Airlines	N610TW
22681	209ER	18	Air Canada	B-1836 ZK-NBF (C-FUCN) C-FVNM
22682	209ER	60	Air Canada	N1781B B-1838 ZK-NBH N682SH C-FUCL
22683	275	36	Air Canada	C-GPWA
22684	275	52	Air Canada	N1791B C-GPWB
22685	275		(Pacific Western Airlines)	(C-GPWC) Allocated but later canx, not built
22686	275		(Pacific Western Airlines)	(C-GPWD) Allocated but later canx, not built
22692	277	24	Ansett Australia	N8278V VH-RMD
22693	277	28	Ansett Australia	N8292V VH-RME
22694	277	32	Ansett Australia	N8287V VH-RMF
22695	277	35	Ansett Australia	N8289V VH-RMG
22696	277	100	Ansett Australia	N1791B VH-RMH
22713	222		(United Airlines)	(N632UA) Allocated but later canx, not built
22714	222		(United Airlines)	(N633UA) Allocated but later canx, not built
22715	222		(United Airlines)	(N634UA) Allocated but later canx, not built
22716	222		(United Airlines)	(N635UA) Allocated but later canx, not built
22717	222		(United Airlines)	(N636UA) Allocated but later canx, not built
22718	222		(United Airlines)	(N637UA) Allocated but later canx, not built
22719	222		(United Airlines)	(N638UA) Allocated but later canx, not built
22720	222		(United Airlines)	(N639UA) Allocated but later canx, not built
22721	222		(United Airlines)	(N640UA) Allocated but later canx, not built
22785	281	51	All Nippon Airways	N1784B JA8479
22786	281	54	All Nippon Airways	N6018N JA8480
22787	281	58	All Nippon Airways	N60668 JA8481
22788	281	61	All Nippon Airways	N1784B JA8482
22789	281	67	All Nippon Airways	N1792N JA8483
22790	281	69	All Nippon Airways	N5573B JA8484
22921	2Q4	55	TransBrasil	N6038E N8277V N4574M PT-TAA
22922	2Q4	57	TransBrasil	N6067B N45742 PT-TAB
22923	2Q4	59	TransBrasil	N6018N N8286V N4575L PT-TAC
22972	258	62	El Al Israel Airlines	N6066Z 4X-EAA
22973	258	68	El Al Israel Airlines	N6018N 4X-EAB
22974	258ER	86	El Al Israel Airlines	N6018N 4X-EAC
22975	258ER	89	El Al Israel Airlines	N6046P 4X-EAD
22980	204	71	Ansett Australia	N8289V N5573K G-BKPW VH-RML
22981	204	79	Ansett Australia	N1785B G-BKVZ VH-RMK
23016	281	80	All Nippon Airways	N1788B JA8485
23017	281	82	All Nippon Airways	N1789B N56807 JA8486
23018	281	84	All Nippon Airways	N1781B JA8487
23019	281	85	All Nippon Airways	N1791B JA8488
23020	281	96	All Nippon Airways	N1784B JA8489
23021	281	103	All Nippon Airways	N1785B JA8490
23022	281	104	All Nippon Airways	N1792B JA8491
23034	2X6		(Alaska Intl Airlines)	Allocated but later canx, not built
23035	2X6		(Alaska Intl Airlines)	Allocated but later canx, not built
23057	205	81	Trans World Airlines	N57008 LN-SUV N767BE PP-VNL N90549 G-BNAX N650TW
23058	205	101	Trans World Airlines	N6018N LN-SUW N768BE PP-VNM N768BE ZK-NBD DQ-FJA N651TW
23072	204	107	Air New Zealand	N6067E G-BLKV ZK-NBI
23106	260ER	90	Ethiopian Airlines	N1792B ET-AIE
23107	260ER	93	Ethiopian Airlines	N6065Y ET-AIF
23140	281	106	All Nippon Airways	N6067B JA8238
23141	281	108	All Nippon Airways	N5573K JA8239
23142	281	110	All Nippon Airways	N6038E JA8240
23143	281	114	All Nippon Airways	N6018N JA8241
23144	281	115	All Nippon Airways	N6038E JA8242
23145	281	116	All Nippon Airways	N6005C JA8243

BOEING 767

C/n	Series	Line No	Last known Operator/Owner	Previous Identities/fate (where known)					
23146	281	121	All Nippon Airways	N6055X	JA8244				
23147	281	123	All Nippon Airways	N6005C	JA8245				
23178	266ER	97	Egyptair	N1785B	SU-GAH				
23179	266ER	98	Egyptair	N1788B	SU-GAI				
23180	266ER	99	Egyptair	N1789B	SU-GAJ				
23212	264	117	Japan Air Lines	N6046P	JA8231				
23213	264	118	Japan Air Lines	N6038E	JA8232				
23214	264	122	Japan Air Lines	N6038E	JA8233				
23215	364	132	Japan Air Lines	N767S	JA8236				
23216	364	148	Japan Air Lines	N6005C	JA8234				
23217	364	150	Japan Air Lines	N60659	JA8235				
23250	204	113	Air New Zealand	N6066U	G-BLKW	ZK-NBJ			
23275	332	136	Delta Air Lines	N116DL					
23276	332	151	Delta Air Lines	N117DL					
23277	332	152	Delta Air Lines	N118DL					
23278	332	153	Delta Air Lines	N119DL					
23279	332	154	Delta Air Lines	N120DL					
23280	269ER	131	ALAS Nacionales	N6038E	9K-AIA	5W-TEA	9K-AIA	TC-ASK	HI-660CA
23281	269ER	135	(Kuwait Airways)	N60659	9K-AIB	dbr Feb91 Baghdad, Iraq			
23282	269ER	138	(Kuwait Airways)	N60668	9K-AIC	dbr Feb91 Baghdad, Iraq			
23304	238ER	119	Qantas Airways	N6055X	VH-EAJ				
23305	238ER	120	Qantas Airways	N6009F	VH-EAK				
23306	238ER	125	Qantas Airways	N6009F	VH-EAL				
23307	2J6ER	126	Air China	(VH-EAM)	N6065Y	B-2551			
23308	2J6ER	127	Air China	(VH-EAN)	N60659	B-2552			
23309	238ER	129	Qantas Airways	(VH-EAO)	N6018N	VH-EAM			
23326	219ER	124	Air New Zealand	N6018N	ZK-NBA				
23327	219ER	134	Air New Zealand	N6055X	ZK-NBB				
23328	219ER	149	Air New Zealand	N6009F	ZK-NBC				
23402	238ER	133	Qantas Airways	N6018N	VH-EAN				
23403	238ER	137	Qantas Airways	N6046P	VH-EAO				
23431	281	143	All Nippon Airways	N6009F	JA8251				
23432	281	145	All Nippon Airways	N6005C	JA8252				
23433	281	167	All Nippon Airways	N6038E	JA8254				
23434	281	171	All Nippon Airways	N6046P	JA8255				
23435	332	162	Delta Air Lines	N121DE					
23436	332	163	Delta Air Lines	N122DL					
23437	332	188	Delta Air Lines	N123DN					
23438	332	189	Delta Air Lines	N124DE					
23494	2S1	141	(TACA Intl Airlines)	N767TA	dbr 05Apr93 Guatemala City, Guatemala				
23623	216ER	142	TACA Intl Airlines	(N4528Y)	N4529T	CC-CJU	N762TA		
23624	216ER	144	TransBrasil	(N4529T)	N4528Y	CC-CJV	PT-TAH		
23645	346	174	Japan Trans Ocean Airlines	N6038E	JA8253				
23744	2J6ER	155	Air China	N60659	B-2553				
23745	2J6ER	156	Air China	N6009F	B-2554				
23756	381	176	All Nippon Airways	N6005C	JA8256				
23757	381	177	All Nippon Airways	N6038E	JA8257				
23758	381	179	All Nippon Airways	N6055X	JA8258				
23759	381	185	All Nippon Airways	N6038E	JA8259				
23764	3P6ER	158	TransBrasil	N767GE	N6009F	A40-GF	PT-TAL		
23765	3Z9ER	165	Lauda Air	N767PW	(OE-LAA)	N6009F	OE-LAU		
23801	241ER	170	VARIG	N6009F	PP-VNO				
23802	241ER	172	VARIG	N6018N	PP-VNP				
23803	241ER	161	VARIG	N60668	PP-VNN				
23804	241ER	178	VARIG	N6009F	PP-VNQ				
23805	241ER	180	VARIG	N6005C	PP-VNR				
23806	241ER	181	VARIG	N6018N	PP-VNS				
23807	204	184	Britannia Airways	N6005C	G-BNCW				
23896	238ER	183	Qantas Airways	N6009F	VH-EAQ				
23897	201ER	173	US Air	N603P	N645US				
23898	201ER	175	US Air	N604P	N646US				
23899	201ER	182	US Air	N607P	N647US				
23900	201ER	190	US Air	N608P	N648US				
23901	201ER	197	US Air	N614P	N649US				
23902	201ER	217	US Air	N617P	N650US				
23916	260ER	187	Ethiopian Airlines	N6009F	ET-AIZ				
23961	346	192	Japan Air Lines	N6005C	JA8265				
23962	346	193	Japan Trans Ocean Airlines	N6038E	JA8267				
23963	346	224	Japan Air Lines	N6055X	JA8268				
23964	346	225	Japan Air Lines	N6046P	JA8269				
23965	346	186	Japan Air Lines	N6018N	JA8264				
23966	346	191	Japan Air Lines	N6018N	JA8266				
23973	23BER	208	Air Mauritius	N6046P	3B-NAK				
23974	23BER	214	Air Mauritius	N6018N	3B-NAL				
24002	381	199	All Nippon Airways	N60668	JA8271				
24003	381	212	All Nippon Airways	N6038E	JA8272				
24004	381	218	All Nippon Airways	N6055X	JA8273				
24005	381	222	All Nippon Airways	N6046P	JA8274				
24006	381	223	All Nippon Airways	N6018N	JA8275				
24007	2J6ER	204	Air China	N60668	B-2555				
24013	204ER	210	Britannia Airways	N6009F	G-BNYS				

BOEING 767

C/n	Series	Line No	Last known Operator/Owner	Previous Identities/fate (where known)				
24032	323ER	202	American Airlines	N351AA				
24033	323ER	205	American Airlines	N352AA				
24034	323ER	206	American Airlines	N353AA				
24035	323ER	211	American Airlines	N354AA				
24036	323ER	221	American Airlines	N355AA				
24037	323ER	226	American Airlines	N39356				
24038	323ER	227	American Airlines	N357AA				
24039	323ER	228	American Airlines	N358AA				
24040	323ER	230	American Airlines	N359AA				
24041	323ER	232	American Airlines	N360AA				
24042	323ER	235	American Airlines	N361AA				
24043	323ER	237	American Airlines	N362AA				
24044	323ER	238	American Airlines	N363AA				
24045	323ER	240	American Airlines	N39364				
24046	323ER	241	American Airlines	N39365				
24075	332	200	Delta Air Lines	N125DL				
24076	332	201	Delta Air Lines	N126DL				
24077	332	203	Delta Air Lines	N127DL				
24078	332	207	Delta Air Lines	N128DL				
24079	332	209	Delta Air Lines	N129DL				
24080	332	216	Delta Air Lines	N130DL				
24082	375ER	213	Canadian Airlines Intl	N6055X	C-FCAB			
24083	375ER	215	Canadian Airlines Intl	N6046P	C-FCAE			
24084	375ER	219	Canadian Airlines Intl	N6038E	C-FCAF			
24085	375ER	220	Canadian Airlines Intl	N6009F	C-FCAG			
24086	375ER	248	Canadian Airlines Intl	N6055X	C-FCAJ			
24087	375ER	249	Canadian Airlines Intl	N6038E	C-FCAU			
24089	29BER		(Government of Brunei)	Allocated but later canx, not built				
24142	233ER	229	Air Canada	N6009F	C-GDSP			
24143	233ER	233	Air Canada	N6005C	C-GDSS			
24144	233ER	234	Air Canada	N6018N	C-GDSU			
24145	233ER	236	Air Canada	N6005C	C-GDSY			
24146	338ER	231	Qantas Airways	N6055X	VH-OGA			
24150	219ER	239	TransBrasil	N6038E	ZK-NBE	PT-TAG		
24157	2J6ER	253	Air China	N6018N	B-2556			
24239	204ER	243	Britannia Airways	N6009F	G-BOPB			
24257	3G5ER	251	LTU-Sud	N6046P	D-AMUR			
24258	3G5ER	255	LTU-Sud	D-AMUS				
24259	3G5ER	268	LTU-Sud	D-AMUN				
24306	375ER	258	Canadian Airlines Intl	C-FPCA				
24307	375ER	259	Canadian Airlines Intl	C-FTCA				
24316	338ER	242	Qantas Airways	N6005C	VH-OGB			
24317	338ER	246	Qantas Airways	N6005C	VH-OGC			
24318	383ER	257	Scandinavian A/L System	N6046P	SE-DKO	LN-RCH		
24323	233ER	250	Air Canada	N6009F	C-FBEF			
24324	233ER	252	Air Canada	N6009F	C-FBEG			
24325	233ER	254	Air Canada	N6038E	C-FBEM			
24333	336ER	265	British Airways	N6009F	G-BNWA			
24334	336ER	281	British Airways	N6046P	G-BNWB			
24335	336ER	284	British Airways	G-BNWC				
24336	336ER	286	British Airways	N6018N	G-BNWD			
24337	336ER	288	British Airways	G-BNWE				
24338	336ER	293	British Airways	N1788B	G-BNWF			
24339	336ER	298	British Airways	G-BNWG				
24340	336ER	335	British Airways	N6005C	G-BNWH			
24341	336ER	341	British Airways	G-BNWI				
24342	336ER	363	British Airways	G-BNWJ				
24343	336ER	364	British Airways	G-BNWK				
24349	3P6ER	244	TransBrasil	(A40-GE)	N6108N	A40-GG	PT-TAM	
24350	381	245	All Nippon Airways	N1789B	JA8285			
24351	381	271	All Nippon Airways	JA8287				
24357	383ER	262	AVIANCA	LN-RCB	I-AEJC	LN-RCB	N984AN	
24358	383ER	263	Scandinavian A/L System	OY-KDH	I-AEJB	OY-KDH	(SE-DOF)	OY-KDH
24400	381ER	269	All Nippon Airways	JA8286				
24407	338ER	247	Qantas Airways	N6009F	VH-OGD			
24415	381	276	All Nippon Airways	JA8288				
24416	381	280	All Nippon Airways	JA8289				
24417	381	290	All Nippon Airways	JA8290				
24428	31AER	279	Martinair Holland	PH-MCG				
24429	31AER	294	Martinair Holland	PH-MCH				
24448	2Q8ER	272	Air Seychelles	(S7-1HM)	S7-AAS			
24457	204ER	256	Air Europa	G-BPFV	EC-			
24475	383ER	273	Scandinavian A/L System	OY-KDI	SE-DOA	(N763BT)	SE-DOA	LN-RCG
24476	383ER	274	Scandinavian A/L System	OY-KDK	SE-DOB	LN-RCI		
24477	383ER	337	Scandinavian A/L System	(SE-DKR)	OY-KDL			
24484	3P6ER	260	Gulf Air	A40-GH				
24485	3P6ER	264	Gulf Air	A40-GI				
24495	3P6ER	267	Gulf Air	A40-GJ				
24496	3P6ER	270	Gulf Air	A40-GK				
24498	346	277	Japan Air Lines	N6055X	JA8299			
24531	338ER	278	Qantas Airways	VH-OGE				

BOEING 767

C/n	Series	Line No	Last known Operator/Owner	Previous Identities/fate (where known)
24541	366ER	275	Egyptair	SU-GAO
24542	366ER	282	Egyptair	SU-GAP
24574	375ER	302	Canadian Airlines Intl	C-FXCA
24575	375ER	311	Canadian Airlines Intl	C-FOCA
24618	259ER	292	AVIANCA	N985AN
24628	3Z9ER	283	(Lauda Air)	OE-LAV w/o 26May91 nr Suphan Bari, Thailand
24632	381	285	All Nippon Airways	JA8362
24713	2N0ER	287	Air Zimbabwe	Z-WPE
24716	284ER	297	LAN-Chile	(SX-ERA) N6046P CC-CEX XA-RVZ CC-CDH
24727	283ER	301	TransBrasil	N6018N SE-DKP PT-TAI
24728	283ER	305	TransBrasil	LN-RCC (N762BT) LN-RCC PT-TAJ
24729	383ER	358	Scandinavian A/L System	(LN-RCD) SE-DKU LN-RCK
24733	25DER	261	LOT-Polish Airlines	N6046P SP-LOA
24734	25DER	266	LOT-Polish Airlines	SP-LOB
24736	204ER	296	Britannia Airways	G-BRIF (PH-AHM) G-BRIF
24742	284ER	303	Vietnam Airlines	(SX-ERB) N6046P V8-RBD VH-RMA [Op by Ansett Australia]
24745	3Q8ER	355	Air France	F-GHGF
24746	3Q8ER	378	Air France	F-GHGG
24752	341ER	289	VARIG	PP-VOI
24753	341ER	291	VARIG	PP-VOJ
24755	381	295	All Nippon Airways	JA8291
24756	381	300	All Nippon Airways	JA8363
24757	204ER	299	Britannia Airways	G-BRIG
24759	332ER	304	Delta Air Lines	N171DN
24762	284ER	307	LAN-Chile	(SX-ERC) CC-CEY XA-RVY CC-CDJ
24764	2B7ER	306	US Air	N651US
24765	2B7ER	308	British Airways	N652US
24766	3D6ER	310	Air Algerie	7T-VJG
24767	3D6ER	323	Air Algerie	7T-VJH
24768	3D6ER	332	Air Algerie	N6009F 7T-VJI
24775	332ER	312	Delta Air Lines	N172DN
24782	346	327	Japan Air Lines	JA8364
24783	346	329	Japan Air Lines	JA8365
24797	38EER	328	Asiana Airlines	HL7263
24798	38EER	331	Asiana Airlines	HL7264
24800	332ER	313	Delta Air Lines	N173DN
24802	332ER	317	Delta Air Lines	N174DN
24803	332ER	318	Delta Air Lines	N175DN
24832	27EER	316	Balkan Bulgarian Airlines	F-GHGD
24835	259ER	321	AVIANCA	N986AN
24843	341ER	314	VARIG	PP-VOK
24844	341ER	324	VARIG	PP-VOL
24846	383ER	309	Scandinavian A/L System	N60697 SE-DKR LN-RCE
24847	383ER	315	Scandinavian A/L System	LN-RCD
24848	383ER	325	Scandinavian A/L System	SE-DKS OY-KDN
24849	383ER	330	Scandinavian A/L System	SE-DKT OY-KDO
24852	332	320	Delta Air Lines	N131DN
24853	338ER	319	Qantas Airways	VH-OGF
24854	27EER	326	Balkan Bulgarian Airlines	N6018N F-GHGE
24865	35DER	322	Air New Zealand	SP-LPA
24867	2N0ER	333	Air Zimbabwe	Z-WPF
24875	219ER	371	Air New Zealand	ZK-NCE
24876	219ER	413	Air New Zealand	ZK-NCF
24880	381	336	All Nippon Airways	JA8368
24894	2B7ER	338	US Air	N653US
24929	338ER	343	Qantas Airways	VH-OGG
24930	338ER	344	Qantas Airways	VH-OGH
24947	3Y0ER	351	LAN-Chile	N60659 CC-CDL PT-TAD CC-CEY
24948	3Y0ER	380	TransBrasil	(CC-) N6005C PT-TAE
24949	3Y0ER		(GPA Group)	Allocated but later canx, not built
24950	3Y0ER		(GPA Group)	Allocated but later canx, not built
24951	3Y0ER		(GPA Group)	Allocated but later canx, not built
24952	3Y0ER	354	Trans World Airlines	EI-CAL XA-RWW EI-CAL
24953	3Y0ER	405	Trans World Airlines	(EI-CAM) XA-RWX EI-CAM
24954	3Y0ER		(GPA Group)	Allocated but later canx, not built
24973	216ER	347	Ansett Australia	CC-CEF N483GX VH-RMM
24981	332	345	Delta Air Lines	N132DN
24982	332	348	Delta Air Lines	N133DN
24983	3P6ER	334	Gulf Air	N6046P A4O-GL
24984	3P6ER	339	Gulf Air	A4O-GM
24985	3P6ER	340	Gulf Air	A4O-GN
24999	3Y0ER	354	Spanair	EC-547 EC-FCU
25000	3Y0ER	386	Spanair	EC-548 EC-FHA
25055	381	352	All Nippon Airways	JA8360
25058	204ER	362	Britannia Airways	N60659 G-BYAA PH-AHM G-BYAA
25061	332ER	341	Delta Air Lines	N176DN
25076	3T7ER	366	EVA Airways	B-16601 N601EV
25077	37EER	385	Air France	F-GHGH
25088	383ER	359	Scandinavian A/L System	OY-KDM
25091	322ER	360	United Airlines	N641UA

BOEING 767

C/n	Series	Line No	Last known Operator/Owner	Previous Identities/fate (where known)
25092	322ER	367	United Airlines	N642UA
25093	322ER	368	United Airlines	N643UA
25094	322ER	369	United Airlines	N644UA
25117	3T7ER	370	EVA Airways	B-16602 N602EV
25120	375ER	361	Canadian Airlines Intl	C-GLCA
25121	375ER	372	China Southern Airlines	C-GSCA B-2564
25122	332ER	346	Delta Air Lines	N177DN
25123	332	353	Delta Air Lines	N134DL
25132	38EER	417	Asiana Airlines	HL7268
25136	381ER	379	All Nippon Airways	JA8356
25137	330ER	377	Trans World Airlines	D-ABUX N691LF
25139	204ER	373	Britannia Airways	G-BYAB PH-AHN G-BYAB
25143	332ER	349	Delta Air Lines	N178DN
25144	332ER	350	Delta Air Lines	N179DN
25145	332	356	Delta Air Lines	N135DL
25146	332	374	Delta Air Lines	N136DL
25170	31BER	542	China Southern Airlines	B-2566
25193	323ER	388	American Airlines	N366AA
25194	323ER	394	American Airlines	N39367
25195	323ER	404	American Airlines	N368AA
25196	323ER	422	American Airlines	N369AA
25197	323ER	425	American Airlines	N370AA
25198	323ER	431	American Airlines	N371AA
25199	323ER	433	American Airlines	N372AA
25200	323ER	435	American Airlines	N373AA
25201	323ER	437	American Airlines	N374AA
25202	323ER	441	American Airlines	N7375A
25203	336ER	365	British Airways	G-BNWL
25204	336ER	376	British Airways	G-BNWM
25208	330ER	381	Air Europe Italy	D-ABUY EI-CIY
25209	330ER	382	Trans World Airlines	D-ABUZ N634TW
25221	3S1ER	384	EVA Airways	(YS-) B-16688
25225	2B7ER	375	British Airways	N654US
25241	3P6ER	389	Gulf Air	A40-GO
25246	338ER	387	Qantas Airways	VH-OGI
25257	2B7ER	383	British Airways	N655US
25269	3P6ER	390	Gulf Air	A40-GP
25273	31AER	393	Lauda Air	N6046P PH-MCK OE-LAT I-LAUD PH-MCK OE-LAT PH-MCK
25274	338ER	396	Qantas Airways	VH-OGJ
25280	322ER	391	United Airlines	N645UA
25283	322ER	420	United Airlines	N646UA
25284	322ER	424	United Airlines	N647UA
25285	322ER	443	United Airlines	N648UA
25286	322ER	444	United Airlines	N649UA
25287	322ER	449	United Airlines	N650UA
25293	381	401	All Nippon Airways	JA8357
25306	332	392	Delta Air Lines	N137DL
25312	31AER	400	Martinair Holland	PH-MCI
25316	338ER	397	Qantas Airways	N6018N VH-OGK
25346	33AER	403	Royal Brunei Airlines	V8-RBE
25347	38EER	399	Asiana Airlines	HL7266
25354	3P6ER	406	Gulf Air	A40-GR
25363	338ER	402	Qantas Airways	N6018N VH-OGL
25365	383ER	395	Scandinavian A/L System	SE-DKX LN-RCL
25389	322ER	452	United Airlines	N651UA
25390	322ER	457	United Airlines	N652UA
25391	322ER	460	United Airlines	N653UA
25392	322ER	462	United Airlines	N654UA
25393	322ER	468	United Airlines	N655UA
25394	322ER	472	United Airlines	N656UA
25403	33AER	409	LAN-Chile	CC-CEU
25404	38EER	411	Asiana Airlines	HL7267
25409	332	410	Delta Air Lines	N138DL
25410	2B1ER		(GPA Group)	Allocated but later canx, not built
25411	3Y0ER	408	Air Europe Italy	(EI-CEA) PT-TAF XA-SKY EI-CLR
25421	2B1ER	407	TransBrasil	(EI-CAG) EI-CEM PT-TAK
25442	336ER	418	British Airways	G-BNWO
25443	336ER	419	British Airways	G-BNWP
25444	336ER	398	British Airways	G-BNWN
25445	323ER	422	American Airlines	N376AN
25446	323ER	453	American Airlines	N377AN
25447	323ER	469	American Airlines	N378AN
25448	323ER	481	American Airlines	N379AA
25449	323ER	489	American Airlines	N380AN
25450	323ER	495	American Airlines	N381AN
25451	323ER	498	American Airlines	N382AN
25530	33AER	414	Royal Brunei Airlines	V8-RBF
25531	33AER	423	LTU-Sud	D-AMUP
25532	33AER	442	Vietnam Airlines	N6055X V8-RBG
25533	33AER	454	Royal Brunei Airlines	N6009F N67AW V8-RBJ

BOEING 767

C/n	Series	Line No	Last known Operator/Owner	Previous Identities/fate (where known)			
25534	33AER	477	Royal Brunei Airlines	N6055X	V8-RBH		
25535	33AER	491	Vietnam Airlines	N6018N	N768TA	VH-NOE	
25536	33AER	504	Royal Brunei Airlines	N6018N	N96AC	V8-RBK	
25537	27GER	517	Government of Brunei	V8-MJB	[Op by Royal Brunei Airlines]		
25568	375ER		(Canadian Airlines Intl)	Allocated but later canx, not built			
25569	375ER		(Canadian Airlines Intl)	Allocated but later canx, not built			
25575	338ER	451	Qantas Airways	VH-OGM			
25576	338ER	549	Qantas Airways	VH-OGN			
25577	338ER	550	Qantas Airways	VH-OGO			
25583	333ER	508	Air Canada	C-FMWP			
25584	333ER	596	Air Canada	C-FMWQ			
25585	333ER	597	Air Canada	C-FMWU			
25586	333ER	599	Air Canada	C-FMWV			
25587	333ER	604	Air Canada	C-FMWY			
25588	333ER	606	Air Canada	C-FMXC			
25616	381ER	432	All Nippon Airways	JA8358			
25617	281	439	All Nippon Airways	JA8359			
25618	381	458	All Nippon Airways	JA8322			
25654	381ER	463	All Nippon Airways	JA8323			
25655	381	465	All Nippon Airways	JA8324			
25656	381	510	All Nippon Airways	JA8567			
25657	381	515	All Nippon Airways	JA8568			
25658	381	519	All Nippon Airways	JA8578			
25659	381	520	All Nippon Airways	JA8579			
25660	381	539	All Nippon Airways	JA8670			
25661	381	543	All Nippon Airways	JA8674			
25662	381	551	All Nippon Airways	JA8677			
25732	336ER	421	British Airways	G-BNWR			
25757	38E	523	Asiana Airlines	HL7247			
25758	38E	582	Asiana Airlines	HL7248			
25761	28EF	616	Asiana Airlines	HL7507			
25826	336ER	473	British Airways	N6018N	G-BNWS		
25828	336ER	476	British Airways	G-BNWT			
25829	336ER	483	British Airways	G-BNWU			
25831	336ER	526	British Airways	G-BNWW			
25832	336ER	529	British Airways	G-BNWX			
25834	336ER	608	British Airways	G-BNWY			
25864	375ER	426	China Southern Airlines	C-FXCA	HA-LHC	B-2562	
25865	375ER	430	China Southern Airlines	(C-GCAW)	N6063S	EI-CFR	B-2561
25868	375ER		(Canadian Airlines Intl)	Allocated but later canx, not built			
25875	3J6	429	Air China	B-2557			
25876	3J6	478	Air China	B-2558			
25877	3J6	530	Air China	B-2559			
25878	3J6	569	Air China	B-2560			
25984	332	427	Delta Air Lines	N139DL			
25985	332ER	428	Delta Air Lines	N180DN			
25986	332ER	446	Delta Air Lines	N181DN			
25987	332ER	461	Delta Air Lines	N182DN			
25988	332	499	Delta Air Lines	N140LL			
25989	332	506	Delta Air Lines	N1402A			
25992	332		(Delta Air Lines)	(N143DA)	Allocated but later canx, not built		
25993	332		(Delta Air Lines)	(N144DA)	Allocated but later canx, not built		
26063	35EER	434	EVA Airways	B-16603			
26064	35EER	438	EVA Airways	B-16605			
26200	3Y0ER	450	AeroMexico	XA-RKI			
26204	3Y0ER	464	AeroMexico	XA-RKJ			
26205	3Y0ER	474	Aeroflot Russian Intl A/L	N6046P	EI-CKD		
26206	3Y0ER	487	Asiana Airlines	HL7269			
26207	3Y0ER	503	Asiana Airlines	HL7286			
26208	3Y0ER	505	Aeroflot Russian Intl A/L	N6009F	EI-CKE		
26209	3Y0ER		(GPA Group)	Allocated but later canx, not built			
26210	3Y0ER		(GPA Group)	Allocated but later canx, not built			
26233	3P6ER	501	Gulf Air	A40-GU			
26234	3P6ER	538	Gulf Air	A40-GY			
26235	3P6ER	502	Gulf Air	A40-GV			
26236	3P6ER	436	Gulf Air	A40-GS			
26237	3P6ER	544	Gulf Air	A40-GZ			
26238	3P6ER	440	Gulf Air	A40-GT			
26256	39HER	484	Leisure International A/W	G-UKLH			
26257	39HER	488	Leisure International A/W	G-UKLI			
26259	31BER	534	China Southern Airlines	B-2565			
26260	3X2ER	552	Air Pacific	DQ-FJC			
26261	352ER	575	LAN-Chile	(N807AM)	N181LF	CC-CDM	
26262	352ER	583	Air Europe Italy	(N808AM)	N171LF	EI-CLS	
26263	306ER	592	KLM-Royal Dutch Airlines	PH-BZC			
26264	319ER	555	Air New Zealand	ZK-NCH			
26265	3Q8ER	570	Asiana Airlines	HL7249			
26387	35HER	445	Air Europe Italy	(I-AEJD)	S7-AAQ	EI-CJA	
26388	35HER	456	Air Europe Italy	(I-AEJE)	S7-AAV	EI-CJB	
26389	35HER	459	China Southern Airlines	N60659	N800CZ		
26417	3Z9ER	448	Lauda Air	OE-LAW			

BOEING 767

C/n	Series	Line No	Last known Operator/Owner	Previous Identities/fate (where known)
26469	31AER	415	Martinair Holland	PH-MCL
26470	31AER	416	Martinair Holland	PH-MCM
26471	2B1ER	511	South African Airways	(C9-) ZS-SRA
26544	383ER	412	Scandinavian A/L System	N6055X SE-DOC
26608	3S1ER	559	TACA International	N769TA
26847	2B7ER	486	British Airways	N656US
26912	319ER	509	Air New Zealand	ZK-NCG
26913	319ER	558	Air New Zealand	N6009F ZK-NCI
26915	319ER	574	Air New Zealand	N6018N ZK-NCJ
26983	330ER	471	Condor Flug	(D-ABUA) D-ABUD
26984	330ER	518	Condor Flug	(D-ABUB) N1788B D-ABUE
26985	330ER	537	Condor Flug	D-ABUF
26986	330ER	553	Condor Flug	N6046P D-ABUH
26987	330ER	466	Condor Flug	D-ABUB
26988	330ER	562	Condor Flug	D-ABUI
26989	330ER		(Condor Flug)	(D-ABUK) Allocated but later canx, not built
26990	330ER		(Condor Flug)	(D-ABUL) Allocated but later canx, not built
26991	330ER	455	Condor Flug	D-ABUA
26992	330ER	470	Condor Flug	(D-ABUB) D-ABUC
26995	323ER	500	American Airlines	N383AN
26996	323ER	512	American Airlines	N384AA
27048	27GER	475	Malev	N6009F HA-LHA
27049	27GER	482	Malev	N60668 HA-LHB
27050	381	516	All Nippon Airways	JA8569
27059	323ER	536	American Airlines	N385AM
27060	323ER	540	American Airlines	N386AA
27079	366ER		(Egyptair)	Allocated but later canx, not built
27080	366ER		(Egyptair)	Allocated but later canx, not built
27095	3Z9ER	467	Lauda Air	OE-LAX
27110	332ER	492	Delta Air Lines	N183DN
27111	332ER	496	Delta Air Lines	N184DN
27112	322ER	479	United Airlines	N657UA
27113	322ER	480	United Airlines	N658UA
27114	322ER	485	United Airlines	N659UA
27115	322ER	494	United Airlines	N660UA
27135	328ER	493	Air France	F-GHGI
27136	328ER	497	Air France	F-GHGJ
27140	336ER	490	British Airways	G-BNWV
27158	322ER	507	United Airlines	N661UA
27159	322ER	513	United Airlines	N662UA
27160	322ER	514	United Airlines	N663UA
27161	322ER		(United Airlines)	(N664UA) Allocated but later canx, not built
27162	322ER		(United Airlines)	(N665UA) Allocated but later canx, not built
27184	323ER	541	American Airlines	N387AM
27186	322ER		(United Airlines)	(N666UA) Allocated but later canx, not built
27189	33AER	521	Royal Brunei Airlines	N1794B V8-RBL
27192	25E	524	EVA Airways	(B-16606) B-16621
27193	25E	527	EVA Airways	(B-16607) B-16622
27194	25E	532	EVA Airways	(B-16608) B-16623
27195	25E	535	EVA Airways	(B-16609) B-16625
27205	3K1ER	528	Airtours International	N6038E G-SJMC
27206	3K1ER	533	Airtours International	G-DAJC
27209	322ER		(United Airlines)	(N667UA) Allocated but later canx, not built
27210	322ER		(United Airlines)	(N668UA) Allocated but later canx, not built
27211	322ER		(United Airlines)	(N669UA) Allocated but later canx, not built
27212	328ER	531	Sobelair	F-GHGK OO-STF
27239	34AFER	580	United Parcel Service	N301UP
27240	34AFER	590	United Parcel Service	N302UP
27241	34AFER	594	United Parcel Service	N303UP
27242	34AFER	598	United Parcel Service	N304UP
27243	34AFER	600	United Parcel Service	N305UP
27254	3P6ER	522	Gulf Air	A40-GW
27255	3P6ER	525	Gulf Air	A40-GX
27309	36D	546	Shanghai Airlines	B-2563
27310	33AER	545	Sobelair	OO-SBY
27311	346	547	Japan Air Lines	JA8397
27312	346	548	Japan Air Lines	JA8398
27313	346	554	Japan Air Lines	JA8399
27339	381ER	556	Air Nippon	JA8664
27376	33AER	560	Alitalia	N1794B N276AW VH-ITA G-OITA
27377	33AER	561	Alitalia	N6009F N361AW VH-ITB G-OITB
27385	27CER	557	Boeing Military Airplane Co	N60697 N767JA [AWACS conversion]
27391	27CER	588	Boeing Military Airplane Co	N60659 N767JB [AWACS conversion]
27392	324ER	568	Vietnam Airlines	(N48901) N1785B EI-CMD S7-RGV
27393	324ER	571	Vietnam Airlines	(N58902) N1794B EI-CME S7-RGW
27394	324ER	572	Asiana Airlines	(N68903) N5573S HL7505
27427	328ER	579	Boeing Corp	(F-GHGL) N6065S N60659 stored Everett, WA by Oct95
27428	328ER	586	Royal Brunei Airlines	(F-GHGO) N60668 V8-RBM
27429	328ER		Air France	F-GIYQ
27444	381	567	All Nippon Airways	JA8669
27445	381	573	All Nippon Airways	JA8342

BOEING 767

C/n	Series	Line No	Last known Operator/Owner	Previous Identities/fate (where known)		
27448	323ER	563	American Airlines	N388AA		
27449	323ER	564	American Airlines	N389AA		
27450	323ER	565	American Airlines	N390AA		
27451	323ER	566	American Airlines	N391AA		
27468	33AER	584	Alitalia	(VH-ITH)	G-OITC	
27568	324ER	593	Vietnam Airlines	N47904	EI-CMH	S7-RGU
27569	324ER	601	Ansett Australia	(N84905)	N6055X	VH-BZF
27582	332ER	617	Delta Air Lines	N187DN		
27583	332ER	631	Delta Air Lines	N188DN		
27597	316ER	602	LAN-Chile	CC-CDP		
27610	306ER	605	KLM-Royal Dutch Airlines	PH-BZD	[8000th Boeing commercial jet delivery]	
27611	306ER	633	KLM-Royal Dutch Airlines	PH-BZH		
27612	306ER		KLM-Royal Dutch Airlines	PH-BZJ		
27614	306ER		KLM-Royal Dutch Airlines	PH-BZK		
27619	31AER	595	Martinair Holland	PH-MCV		
27658	346	581	Japan Air Lines	JA8975		
27683	36D		Shanghai Airlines	B-2567		
27902	35DER	577	LOT-Polish Airlines	SP-LPB		
27908	33AER	578	Alitalia	N6055X	G-OITF	
27909	33AER	591	Lauda Air	OE-LAS		
27918	33AER	603	Alitalia	G-OITG		
27957	306ER	587	KLM-Royal Dutch Airlines	PH-BZA		
27958	306ER	589	KLM-Royal Dutch Airlines	PH-BZB		
27959	306ER	609	KLM-Royal Dutch Airlines	PH-BZF		
27960	306ER	625	KLM-Royal Dutch Airlines	PH-BZG		
27961	332ER	576	Delta Air Lines	N185DN		
27962	332ER	585	Delta Air Lines	N186DN		
27993	3Q8ER	619	Air Europe Italy	EI-CMQ		
28016	27CER	618	Boeing Military Airplane Co	N767JC	[AWACS conversion]	
28039	304ER		Britannia Airways	G-OBYA		
28040	304ER	613	Britannia Airways	G-OBYB		
28041	304ER	614	Britannia Airways	G-OBYC		
28042	304ER		Britannia Airways	G-OBYD		
28098	306ER	605	KLM-Royal Dutch Airlines	PH-BZE		
28111	3G5ER	612	LTU	D-AMUJ		
28370	33PER		Uzbekistan Airways	UK-76701		
28392	33PER		Uzbekistan Airways	UK-76702		

C/n	Series	Line No	Last known Operator/Owner	Previous Identities/fate (where known)

BOEING 777

C/n	Series	Line No	Last known Operator/Owner	Previous Identities/fate (where known)		
26916	222	7	United Airlines	N777UA		
26917	222	8	United Airlines	(N77776)	N766UA	
26918	222	9	United Airlines	N767UA		
26919	222	11	United Airlines	N768UA		
26921	222	12	United Airlines	N769UA		
26925	222	13	United Airlines	N770UA		
26926	222		United Airlines	(N775UA)		
26927	222	27	United Airlines	N776UA		
26928	222		United Airlines	(N777UA)	N781UA	
26929	222	4	United Airlines	(N77774)	N7774	N773UA
26930	222	5	United Airlines	(N77775)	N772UA	
26931	222		United Airlines	N778UA		
26932	222	3	United Airlines	(N77773)	N7773	N771UA
26933	222		United Airlines	N779UA		
26934	222		United Airlines	N780UA		
26935	222		United Airlines	N782UA		
26936	222	2	United Airlines	(N77772)	N7772	N774UA
26937	222		United Airlines	N783UA		
26938	222		United Airlines	N784UA		
26939	222		United Airlines	N785UA		
26940	222		United Airlines	N786UA		
26941	222		United Airlines	N787UA		
26942	222		United Airlines	N788UA		
26943	222		United Airlines	N789UA		
26944	222		United Airlines	N790UA		
26945	222		United Airlines	N791UA		
26946	222		United Airlines	N792UA		
26947	222	22	United Airlines	(N793UA)	N775UA	
26948	222		United Airlines	N794UA		
26950	222		United Airlines	N795UA		
26951	222		United Airlines	N796UA		
26952	222		United Airlines	N797UA		
26953	222		United Airlines	N798UA		
26954	222		United Airlines	N799UA		
27027	281	16	All Nippon Airlines	N5016R	JA8197	
27028	281	21	All Nippon Airlines	JA8198		
27029	281	29	All Nippon Airlines	JA8199		
27030	281	37	All Nippon Airlines	JA8967		
27031	281	38	All Nippon Airlines	JA8968		
27032	281		All Nippon Airlines	JA8969		
27105	236	6	British Airways	N77779	G-ZZZA	
27106	236	10	British Airways	N77771	G-ZZZB	
27107	236	15	British Airways	N5014K	G-ZZZC	
27108	236	17	British Airways	G-ZZZD		
27109	236	19	British Airways	G-ZZZE		
27116	200	1	Boeing Aircraft Co	(N77771)	N7771	prototype; ff 12Jun94
27247	200		(Emirates)	Allocated but later canx, not built		
27248	200		(Emirates)	Allocated but later canx, not built		
27249	200		(Emirates)	Allocated but later canx, not built		
27250	200		(Emirates)	Allocated but later canx, not built		
27251	200		(Emirates)	Allocated but later canx, not built		
27252	200		(Emirates)	Allocated but later canx, not built		
27253	200		(Emirates)	Allocated but later canx, not built		
27263	267	28	Cathay Pacific Airways	VR-HNC		
27264	267	31	Cathay Pacific Airways	VR-HND		
27265	267	14	Cathay Pacific Airways	N77772	VR-HNA	
27266	267	18	Cathay Pacific Airways	N77773	VR-HNB	
27357	21B	20	China Southern Airlines	B-2051		
27358	21B	24	China Southern Airlines	N5017V	B-2052	
27364	246	23	Japan Air Lines	JA8981		
27365	246	26	Japan Air Lines	JA8982		
27366	246		Japan Air Lines	JA8983		
27636	289		Japan Air System	JA8977		
27637	289		Japan Air System	JA8978		
27638	289		Japan Air System	JA8979		
27726	2D7	25	Thai International	HS-TJA		
27727	2D7	32	Thai International	HS-TJB		
27728	2D7		Thai International	HS-TJC		
27729	2D7		Thai International	HS-TJD		
27843	236		British Airways	(G-ZZZF)	G-VIIA	
27844	236		British Airways	(G-ZZZG)	G-VIIB	
27845	236		British Airways	(G-ZZZH)	G-VIIC	
27846	236		British Airways	(G-ZZZI)	G-VIID	
27847	236		British Airways	(G-ZZZJ)	G-VIIE	
27848	236		British Airways	(G-ZZZK)	G-VIIF	
27849	236		British Airways	(G-ZZZL)	G-VIIG	
27850	236		British Airways	(G-ZZZM)	G-VIIH	
27851	236		British Airways	(G-ZZZN)	G-VIIJ	
27853	236		British Airways	(G-ZZZP)	G-RAES	

BOEING 777

C/n	Series	Line No	Last known Operator/Owner	Previous Identities/fate (where known)

BRITISH AEROSPACE 146

C/n	Series	Last known Operator/Owner	Previous Identities/fate (where known)
E1001	100	British Aerospace	G-BIAD prototype; ff 03Sep81 G-SSSH last flt 07Aug86; cvtd to Srs.300 as E3001
E3001	300	British Aerospace	G-5-300 G-LUXE Srs.300 prototype; cvtd fm E1001
E1002	100	Australian Air Express	(G-BIAE) G-SSHH G-OPSA G-5-146 N5828B G-SSHH N101RW G-5-005 N801RW G-BPNP N720BA G-BPNP G-BSTA (OE-BRL) ZS-NCA G-6-002 G-BSTA VH-NJV
E1003	100	United Express	(G-BIAF) G-SSCH G-5-14 G-SSCH G-5-14 N246SS N631AW*
E1004	100	Pel-Air Aviation	(G-BIAG) (G-SSCH) G-OBAF ZD695 G-5-04 G-BRJS (N346SS) G-5-537 G-OJET VH-
E1005	100	Qantas/Airlink	(G-BIAJ) G-SCHH ZK-SHH G-SCHH ZD696 G-5-02 G-SCHH VH-NJY
E1006	100	Malmo Aviation	(G-ODAN) G-BKMN SE-DRH
E1007	100	Pan-Air	G-BKHT EC-969 EC-GEO
E2008	200	(British Aerospace)	G-WISC G-5-146 G-WAUS (G-OHAP) G-BMYE reduced to spares May95 Bristol-Filton, UK
E1009	100	Qantas/Airlink	TZ-ADT G-BRUC G-6-009 VH-NJZ
E1010	100	Jersey European A/W	PT-LEP G-BKXZ PT-LEP G-5-512 (N102RW) N802RW C-GNVX G-UKPC G-JEAO
E1011	100	Air UK	PT-LEQ G-5-513 (N103RW) N803RW C-GNVY G-UKJF
E2012	200	Air Atlantic	N601AW C-FHAV
E1013	100	Qantas/Airlink	N146AP G-6-013 VH-NJC
E2014	200	Air Atlantic	N602AW C-FHAX
E1015	100	Pan-Air	G-5-01 N461AP XA-RST N568BA EC-971 EC-GEP
E2016	200	Air Atlantic	N605AW C-FHAZ
E1017	100	Tristar Airlines	G-5-02 G-BLRA N462AP CP-2249 N462AP
E2018	200	Jersey European A/W	N603AW G-OSKI G-BSRU G-HWPB G-JEAR
E1019	100	China Northwest A/L	G-5-019 G-5-523 G-5-019 G-XIAN B-2701
E2020	200	Jersey European A/W	N604AW C-FEXN G-OSUN G-BSRV G-OLHB G-JEAS
E1021	100	Royal Air Force 32Sqn	G-5-02 G-5-507 ZE700
E2022	200	USAir	N346PS N163US stored Apr91 Mojave, CA
E2023	200	USAir	N347PS N165US stored Apr91 Mojave, CA
E2024	200	Debonair	N348PS N166US
E2025	200	USAir	N349PS N167US stored Apr91 Mojave, CA
E1026	100	China Northwest A/L	G-5-02 B-2702
E2027	200	(Pacific Southwest A/L)	N350PS w/o 07Dec87 Paso Robles, CA
E2028	200	Debonair	N351PS N171US
E1029	100	Royal Air Force 32Sqn	G-5-03 ZE701
E2030	200	World Airways	N352PS N172US G-WLCY
E2031	200	USAir	N353PS N173US stored May91 Mojave, CA
E1032	100	China Northwest A/L	G-5-03 B-2703
E2033	200	United Express	N606AW
E2034	200	USAir	N354PS N174US stored May91 Mojave, CA
E1035	100	Carib Express	G-5-035 B-2704 B-584L G-BVUW J8-VBC
E2036	200	Business Air	N355PS N175US HB-IXB G-GNTZ
E2037	200	Ansett Australia	VH-JJP
E2038	200	Ansett Australia	VH-JJQ
E2039	200	USAir	N356PS N177US stored May91 Mojave, CA
E2040	200	USAir	N357PS N178US stored May91 Mojave, CA
E2041	200	USAir	N358PS N179US stored May91 Mojave, CA
E2042	200	USAir	N359PS G-BMFM N359PS N181US stored May91 Mojave, CA
E2043	200	USAir	N360PS N183US stored May91 Mojave, CA
E2044	200	USAir	N361PS N184US stored May91 Mojave, CA
E2045	200	USAir	N362PS N185US stored May91 Mojave, CA
E2046	200	USAir	N363PS N187US stored May91 Mojave, CA
E2047	200	Flightline	N364PS N188US G-OZRH
E2048	200	USAir	N365PS N189US stored May91 Mojave, CA
E2049	200	United Express	N608AW G-5-002 N608AW
E2050	200	Pelita Air Service	G-5-004 G-5-517 PK-PJP
E2051	200	Malmo Aviation	G-5-003 N141AC G-5-003 N141AC N694AA SE-DRE
E2052	200	United Express	N607AW G-5-001 N607AW
E2053	200	Malmo Aviation	G-5-053 N142AC G-5-053 N142AC N695AA SE-DRC
E2054	200	Malmo Aviation	G-5-054 N144AC G-5-054 N144AC N696AA SE-DRG
E2055	200	Malmo Aviation	G-5-055 N145AC G-5-055 N145AC N697A CP-2254 SE-DRF
E2056	200QT	TNT/Air Foyle	G-5-056 N146FT N146QT G-5-056 G-TNTA
E2057	200	Malmo Aviation	N146AC G-5-057 N146AC N698AA SE-DRB
E2058	200	Malmo Aviation	N148AC G-5-058 G-ECAL G-5-058 N148AC N699AA SE-DRI
E2059	200	LAN-Chile	G-5-059 N401XV G-5-059 N401XV CC-CEJ
E2060	200	Hamburg Airlines	N402XV G-5-060 N402XV XA-RMO N352BA CP-2260 (N352BA) D-AZUR
E2061	200	(LAN-Chile)	N403XV G-OHAP G-5-061 N403XV CC-CET w/o 20Feb91 Puerto Williams, Navarino Is, S Chile
E2062	200	Atlantic Southeast	G-5-062 (G-BNDR) N406XV G-5-062 N880DV N810AS*
E1063	100	United Express	N463AP G-5-063 N463AP N70NA N463AP N632AW*
E2064	200	LAN-Chile	N404XV G-5-064 N404XV CC-CEN
E2065	200	Air Zimbabwe	G-5-065 Z-WPD
E2066	200	Hamburg Airlines	N405XV G-5-066 N405XV C-FHNX N405XV XA-RTI N356BA C-FHNX N356BA D-ALOA
E2067	200QT	TNT/Air Foyle	G-5-067 G-TNTB
E1068	100	British Aerospace	G-5-068 B-2705 B-585L G-BVUX J8-VBA G-BVUX

BRITISH AEROSPACE 146

C/n	Series	Last known Operator/Owner	Previous Identities/fate (where known)						
E2069	200	Delta Air Transport	G-5-069	G-BNKJ	G-5-069	N407XV	G-BNKJ	(OO-DJY)	OO-DJC
			G-UKLN	OO-DJC					
E2070	200	United Express	G-5-070	G-BNKK	N609AW				
E1071	100	Carib Express	G-5-071	B-2706	G-BVUY	J8-VBB			
E2072	200	CityJet	G-5-072	G-BNJI	N366PS	N190US	HB-IXC	G-BNJI	EI-CTY
E2073	200	CityJet	G-5-073	N367PS	N191US	HB-IXD	G-BVFV	EI-JET	
E2074	200	Atlantic Southeast	G-5-074	(G-BNND)	N368PS	N192US	N146SB	G-BNND	HS-TBQ
			G-BNND	N881DV	N812AS				
E2075	200	Atlantic Airways	G-5-075	N369PS	N193US	OY-CRG			
E1076	100	Air China	G-5-076	B-2707					
E2077	200	Delta Air Transport	N408XV	G-5-077	N408XV	G-BRNG	(OO-DJZ)	OO-DJD	G-UKRH
			OO-DTD						
E2078	200QT	TNT/Mistral Air	G-BNPJ	G-5-078	I-TNTC				
E2079	200	Manx Airlines	G-5-079	G-CNMF	G-5-079	G-CNMF	G-MIMA		
E2080	200	Atlantic Southeast	G-5-080	N290UE	N814AS				
E1081	100	Air China	G-5-081	B-2708					
E2082	200	United Express	N610AW	G-5-082	N610AW				
E1083	100	Air China	G-5-083	B-2709					
E2084	200	Atlantic Southeast	G-5-084	N291UE	N815AS				
E1085	100	Air China	G-5-085	B-2710					
E2086	200QT	TNT/Eurowings	G-5-086	G-BNUA	G-5-086	SE-DEI	D-ADEI		
E2087	200	Atlantic Southeast	G-5-087	N292UE	N816AS				
E2088	200	Manx Airlines	G-5-088	G-CSHR	G-MANS				
E2089	200QT	TNT/Pan Air	G-BNYC	(F-GTNT)	G-TNTH	EC-281	EC-EPA		
E2090	200	Air Canada	G-5-090	C-FBAB					
E1091	100	Abu Dhabi Private Flight		G-5-091	G-BOMA	A6-SHK			
E2092	200	Air Canada	G-5-092	C-FBAE					
E2093	200	Ansett Australia	G-5-093	VH-JJS					
E2094	200	Malmo Aviation	G-5-094	G-CSJH	SE-DRD				
E1095	100	Druk Air	G-5-095	G-BOEA	A5-RGD				
E2096	200	Air Canada	G-5-096	C-FBAF					
E2097	200	United Express	G-5-097	N293UE	N461EA	N293UE			
E2098	200	Ansett Australia	G-5-098	VH-JJT					
E2099	200	Jersey European A/W	G-5-099	G-OLCA	G-JEAJ				
E2100	200QT	TNT/Eurowings	G-5-100	G-BOHK	G-TNTJ	D-ANTJ			
E1101	100	Air Botswana	G-5-101	A2-ABD					
E2102	200QT	TNT/Pan Air	G-BOKZ	G-5-102	EC-198	EC-ELT			
E2103	200	Jersey European A/W	G-5-103	G-OLCB	G-JEAK				
E1104	100	British Aerospace	G-5-104	HS-TBO	G-BTXO	CP-2247	G-BTXO	stored Cambridge, UK	
E2105	200QT	TNT/Pan-Air	G-5-105	G-BOMI	HA-TAB	G-TNTP	EC-719	EC-FZE	
E2106	200	Air Canada	G-5-106	C-GRNZ					
E2107	200	United Express	G-5-107	N294UE	N462EA	N294UE			
E2108	200	British Aerospace	G-5-108	N295UE	stored				
E2109	200QT	Pacific East Asia Cargo	G-BOMJ	SE-DHM	G-TNTD	RP-C481			
E2110	200	Ansett Australia	G-5-110	VH-JJW					
E2111	200	Air Canada	G-5-111	G-11-111	C-FBAO				
E2112	200QT	Pacific East Asia Cargo	G-BOMK	(EC-231)	G-5-112	F-GTNU	RP-C482		
E2113	200QT	Ansett Air Freight	G-BOXD	VH-JJY					
E2114	200QT	Ansett Air Freight	G-BOXE	VH-JJZ					
E2115	200	Malmo Aviation	G-11-115	G-5-115	C-GRNY	G-BRXT	SE-DRA		
E2116	200	Ansett Australia	G-5-116	ZK-NZA	VH-JJU				
E2117	200QT	TNT/Pan-Air	G-BPBS	F-GTNT	EC-615	EC-FVY			
E3118	300	Hamburg Airlines	G-OAJF	G-6-118	HB-IXZ				
E2119	200QC	Ansett New Zealand	G-BPBT	ZK-NZC					
E3120	300	United Express	G-BOWW	G-5-0120	N146UK	N611AW			
E2121	200	Air Canada	G-11-121	C-FBAV					
E3122	300	United Express	N612AW	G-5-122	N612AW				
E3123	300	Air UK	G-5-123	G-UKHP					
E1124	100	Royal Air Force 32Sqn	G-5-124	ZE702	G-6-124	ZE702			
E3125	300	Air UK	G-5-125	G-UKSC					
E3126	300	Palmair Flightline	G-BPNT						
E2127	200	Ansett Australia	G-11-127	G-5-127	ZK-NZB	VH-JJX			
E3128	300	Jersey European A/W	G-11-128	HS-TBK	G-BTJT	G-JEAM			
E3129	300	Jersey European A/W	G-5-129	HS-TBM	G-BTXN	G-JEAL			
E2130	200	Air Canada	G-5-130	C-GRNX					
E3131	300	Aer Lingus Commuter	G-11-131	G-BRAB	HS-TBL	G-BRAB	EI-CLG		
E3132	300	United Express	N614AW	G-5-132	N614AW				
E2133	200	Air Canada	G-5-133	(G-BPUV)	C-GRNV	G-5-133	C-GRNV		
E3134	300	Ansett New Zealand	G-11-134	G-5-134	ZK-NZF				
E3135	300	Ansett New Zealand	G-5-135	ZK-NZG					
E2136	200	Tristar Airlines	G-5-136	N882DV	(N719TA)	N136TR			
E3137	300	Ansett New Zealand	G-11-137	G-5-137	ZK-NZH				
E2138	200	Tristar Airlines	G-5-138	N883DV	(N729TA)	N138TR			
E2139	200	Air Nova	G-5-139	C-GRNU					
E2140	200	Air Nova	G-11-140	C-GRNT					
E3141	300	United Express	G-5-141	N615AW					
E3142	300	Air UK	G-UKAC						
E3143	300	Ansett New Zealand	G-5-143	ZK-NZI					
E1144	100	National Air Charter	G-BRLM	G-11-144	G-6-144	(PK-DTA)	G-BSLP	PK-DTA	N3206T

BRITISH AEROSPACE 146

C/n	Series	Last known Operator/Owner	Previous Identities/fate (where known)						
E3145	300	United Express	G-5-145	N616AW					
E3146	300	Aer Lingus Commuter	G-6-146	G-BOJJ	I-ATSC	G-BOJJ	EI-CLH		
E3147	300	Ansett New Zealand	G-5-147	G-11-147	G-6-147	ZK-NZJ			
E2148	200QC	Titan Airways	G-PRIN	G-6-148	G-BTIA	ZS-NCB	G-BTIA	G-ZAPK	
E3149	300	British World Airlines	G-11-149	HS-TBN	G-BTZN	N146PZ	G-BTZN		
E3150	300QT	TNT/Air Foyle	G-BRGK	SE-DIM	G-TJPM				
E3151	300QT	TNT/Air Foyle	G-BRGM	SE-DIT	G-TNTR				
E1152	100	Qantas/Airlink	G-6-152	G-BRLN	(PK-DTC)	G-BRLN	VH-NJR		
E3153	300QT	TNT/Air Foyle	G-BRPW	G-TNTE					
E3154	300QT	TNT/Pan Air	G-6-154	G-BRXI	G-TNTF	EC-712	EC-FFY		
E3155	300	Aer Lingus Commuter	G-6-155	(G-BSLS)	G-BTNU	EI-CLG	EI-CLJ		
E2156	200	Tristar Airlines	G-11-156	N884DV	(N749TA)	N156TR			
E3157	300	Air UK	G-6-157	G-UKID					
E3158	300	Air UK	G-6-158	G-BSMR	G-6-158	G-UKRC			
E3159	300	Aer Lingus Commuter	G-5-159	G-6-159	I-ATSD	G-BVSA	EI-CLI		
E1160	100	National Jet Systems	G-6-160	A2-ABF	G-BVLJ	EI-CJP	G-BVLJ	VH-JSF	VH-NJD
E3161	300	Makung Airlines	G-6-161	G-BSOC	B-1775				
E3162	300	Air UK	G-6-162	G-UKAG					
E3163	300	Eurowings	G-6-163	N885DV	G-6-163	G-BTJG	EC-876	EC-FIU	G-BTJG
			G-3-163	G-BTJG	HB-IXY	G-BTJG	D-AEWA		
E2164	200	Delta Air Transport	G-6-164	OO-DJE					
E3165	300	Air UK	G-6-165	(N886DV)	G-BSNR	G-6-165	G-BSNR	G-6-165	EC-807
			EC-FGT	G-BSNR					
E3166	300QT	TNT/Air Foyle	G-6-166	G-BSLZ	G-TNTM	RP-C480	G-TNTM		
E2167	200	Delta Air Transport	G-6-167	OO-DJF					
E3168	300QT	TNT/Air Foyle	G-BSGI	(RP-C479)	G-BSGI	G-TNTL	RP-C479	G-TNTL	
E3169	300	Air UK	G-6-169	(N887DV)	G-BSNS	G-6-169	EC-839	EC-FHU	G-BSNS
E2170	200	Qantas/Airlink	G-BSOH	(PK-DTD)	G-BSOH	I-FLRX	G-BSOH	VH-NJG	
E3171	300	Ansett Australia	G-6-171	VH-EWI	G-6-171	VH-EWI			
E2172	200	Delta Air Transport	G-6-172	(G-BSSG)	OO-DJH				
E3173	300	Ansett New Zealand	G-6-173	VH-EWJ	ZK-NZM				
E3174	300	Makung Airlines	G-6-174	G-BSXZ	B-1776				
E3175	300	Ansett New Zealand	G-6-175	VH-EWK	ZK-NZL				
E2176	200QC	Air Jet	G-PRCS	VH-NJQ	G-BWLG	F-GMMP			
E3177	300	Ansett Australia	G-6-177	VH-EWL					
E2178	200	Qantas/Airlink	G-6-178	G-BTCP	I-FLRW	G-BTCP	VH-NJH		
E3179	300	Ansett Australia	G-6-179	VH-EWM					
E2180	200	Delta Air Transport	G-6-180	(G-BSZZ)	OO-DJG				
E3181	300	Thai Airways Intl	G-6-181	G-BSYR	G-6-181	HS-TBL	stored Bangkok, Thailand		
E3182	300QT	TNT/Air Foyle	G-BSUY	G-TNTG					
E3183	300	Eurowings	G-6-183	G-BSYS	G-BUHB				
E2184	200	Qantas/Airlink	G-6-184	G-BTKC	I-FLRV	G-BTKC	VH-NJJ		
E3185	300	Thai Airways Intl	G-6-185	HS-TBK	stored U Tapao, Thailand				
E3186	300QT	TNT/Air Foyle	G-6-186	G-BSXL	G-TNTK				
E3187	300	Hamburg Airlines	G-6-187	G-BSYT	EC-899	EC-FKF	G-BSYT	D-AHOI	
E2188	200QC	Air Jet	G-BTDO	F-GLNI					
E3189	300	Thai Airways Intl	G-6-189	HS-TBO	stored U Tapao, Thailand				
E3190	300	Ansett New Zealand	G-6-190	VH-EWN	ZK-NZK				
E3191	300	Thai Airways Intl	G-6-191	HS-TBJ	stored U Tapao, Thailand				
E2192	200	Delta Air Transport	G-6-192	OO-NJE					
E3193	300	Air UK	G-6-193	G-BTMI	G-BUHC				
E3194	300QT	Australia Air Express	G-BTHT	G-6-194	N599MP	G-BTHT	VH-NJM		
E3195	300	Ansett Australia	G-6-195	VH-EWR					
E2196	200	Delta Air Transport	G-6-196	OO-DJJ					
E3197	300	Ansett Australia	G-6-197	VH-EWS					
E3198	300QT	Australia Air Express	G-BTLD	VH-NJF					
E1199	100	Druk Air	G-RJET	N170RJ	G-RJET	A5-RGE			
E2200	200	Eurowings	G-6-200	G-BTVT	(I-FLRZ)	G-BTVT	D-ACFA		
E2201	200	Eurowings	G-6-201	D-AJET					
E3202	300	Makung Airlines	G-6-202	G-BTUY	B-1781				
E3203	300	Air UK	G-6-203	G-BTTP					
E2204	200	Meridiana	G-6-204	G-OSAS	I-FLRA	I-FLRU			
E3205	300	Makung Airlines	G-6-205	G-BTVO	B-1777				
E3206	300	Thai Airways Intl	G-6-206	HS-TBM	stored Bangkok, Thailand				
E3207	300	China Northwest A/L	G-6-207	G-BUHV	B-2711				
E2208	200	British Aerospace	G-ISEE						
E3209	300	Makung Airlines	G-6-209	G-BVCE	B-1778				
E2210	200	Meridiana	G-6-210	G-BVMP	I-FLRE				
E2211	200	Air Jet	G-6-220	G-BVCD	F-GOMA	G-6-211	F-GOMA		
E3212	300	China Northwest A/L	G-6-212	B-2712					
E3213	300	Qantas/Airlink	G-6-213	G-BVPE	VH-NJL				
E3214	300	China Northwest A/L	G-6-214	B-2715					
E3215	300	(China Northwest A/L)	G-6-215	B-2716	w/o 23Jul93 Yingchuan, China				
E3216	300	China Northwest A/L	G-6-216	B-2717					
E3217	300	Qantas/Airlink	G-6-217	G-BUHW	VH-NJN				
E3218	300	China Northwest A/L	G-6-218	B-2719					
E3219	300	China Northwest A/L	G-6-219	B-2720					
E2220	200	Meridiana	G-6-220	G-BVMT	I-FLRI				
E3221	RJ-100A	SAM	G-OIII	N504MM					
E3222	300	China Northwest A/L	G-6-222	B-2718					
E1223	RJ-70	Business Express	G-6-223	N832BE	YL-BAK				

BRITISH AEROSPACE 146

C/n	Series	Last known Operator/Owner	Previous Identities/fate (where known)				
E1224	RJ-70	Business Express	G-6-224	N833BE	YL-BAL		
E1225	RJ-70	Air Baltic	G-6-225	N834BE	YL-BAN	N834BE	YL-BAN
E2226	RJ-85	Crossair	G-CROS	HB-IXF			
E1227	200	Meridiana	G-6-227	G-BVMS	I-FLRO		
E1228	RJ-70A	National Jet Systems	G-6-228	G-OLXX	VH-NJT		
E1229	RJ-70	THY Turkish Airlines	G-BUFI	TC-			
E1230	RJ-70	THY Turkish Airlines	G-	TC-			
E2231	RJ-85	Crossair	G-6-231	HB-IXG			
E3232	RJ-100	THY Turkish Airlines	G-6-232	TC-THA			
E2233	RJ-85	Crossair	G-6-233	HB-IXH			
E3234	RJ-100	THY Turkish Airlines	G-6-234	TC-THB			
E2235	RJ-85	Crossair	G-XAIR	HB-IXK			
E3236	RJ-100	THY Turkish Airlines	G-6-236	TC-THC			
E3237	RJ-100	THY Turkish Airlines	G-6-237	TC-THD			
E3238	RJ-100	THY Turkish Airlines	G-6-238	TC-THE			
E2239	RJ-85	Pelita Air Service	G-BVAE	G-6-239	PK-PJJ		
E3240	RJ-100	THY Turkish Airlines	G-6-240	TC-THF			
E3241	RJ-100	THY Turkish Airlines	G-6-241	TC-THG			
E3242	RJ-100	SAM Colombia	G-6-242	N505MM			
E3243	RJ-100	THY Turkish Airlines	G-6-243	TC-THH			
E3244	RJ-100	SAM Colombia	G-6-244	N506MM			
E3245	RJ-100	SAM Colombia	G-6-245	N507MM			
E2246	RJ-85	Lufthansa CityLine	G-6-246	D-AVRO			
E3247	RJ-100	SAM Colombia	G-6-247	N508MM			
E3248	RJ-100	SAM Colombia	G-6-248	N509MM			
E1249	RJ-70	THY Turkish Airlines	G-	TC-			
E3250	RJ-100	SAM Colombia	G-6-250	N510MM			
E2251	RJ-85	Lufthansa CityLine	G-6-251	D-AVRC			
E1252	RJ-70	THY Turkish Airlines	G-	TC-			
E2253	RJ-85	Lufthansa CityLine	G-6-253	(G-BVWD)	D-AVRB		
E1254	RJ-70	Air Malta	G-BVRJ	9H-ACM			
E3255	RJ-100	SAM Colombia	G-6-255	N511AM			
E2256	RJ-85	Lufthansa CityLine	G-6-256	D-AVRA			
E2257	RJ-85	Lufthansa CityLine	G-6-257	D-AVRD			
E1258	RJ-70	Air Malta	G-6-258	9H-ACN			
E3259	RJ-100	Crossair	G-6-259	G-BVYS	HB-IXT		
E1260	RJ-70	Air Malta	G-6-260	9H-ACO			
E2261	RJ-85	Lufthansa CityLine	G-6-261	D-AVRE			
E3262	RJ-100	Crossair	G-6-262	HB-IXX			
E3263	RJ-100	SAM Colombia	G-6-263	N512MM			
E3264	RJ-100	THY Turkish Airlines	G-6-264	TC-THM			
E3265	RJ-100	THY Turkish Airlines	G-6-265	TC-THO			
E2266	RJ-85	Lufthansa CityLine	G-6-266	D-AVRG			
E1267	RJ-70	Air Malta	G-6-267	9H-ACP			
E2268	RJ-85	Lufthansa CityLine	G-6-258	G-OCLH	D-AVRH		
E2269	RJ-85	Lufthansa CityLine	G-JAYV	D-AVRF			
E2270	RJ-85	Lufthansa CityLine	G-6-270	G-CLHX	D-AVRI		
E2271	RJ-85	Delta Air Transport	G-6-271	OO-DJK			
E3272	RJ-100	Crossair	G-6-272	HB-IXW			
E2273	RJ-85	Delta Air Transport	G-6-273	OO-DJL			
E3274	RJ-100	Crossair	G-6-274	HB-IXV			
E2275	RJ-85	Delta Air Transport	G-6-275	OO-DJN			
E3276	RJ-100	Crossair	G-6-276	HB-IXU			
E2277	RJ-85	Lufthansa CityLine	G-6-277	G-BWKY	D-AVRJ		
E2278	RJ-85	Lufthansa CityLine	G-6-278	D-AVRK			
E2279	RJ-85	Delta Air Transport	G-6-279	OO-DJO			
E3280	RJ-100	Crossair	G-6-280	HB-IXS			
E3281	RJ-100	Crossair	G-	HB-IXR			
E3282	RJ-100	Crossair	G-	HB-IXQ			
E 283							
E 284							
E2285	RJ-85	Lufthansa CityLine	G-6-285	D-AVRL			
E 286							
E 287							
E 288							
E 289							
E 290							
E 291							
E 292							
E 293							
E 294							
E 295							
E 296							
E 297							
E 298							
E 299							
E 300							

Two of the five Series 300s listed as stored at U Tapao/Bangkok are now in service with Thai International again, but their identities have not yet been confirmed

BRITISH AIRCRAFT CORPORATION/AEROSPATIALE CONCORDE

C/n	Series	Last known Operator/Owner	Previous Identities/fate (where known)			
001		Museé de l'Air	F-WTSS	prototype; ff 02Mar69		preserved Paris-Le Bourget, France
13520/002		Science Museum	G-BSST	preserved Fleet Air Arm Museum, Yeovilton, UK		
13522/01		Duxford Avn Museum	G-AXDN	preserved Duxford, UK		
02		Aerospatiale	F-WTSA	preserved Paris-Orly, France		
201	100	Aerospatiale	F-WTSB	wfs Toulouse, France		
13523/202	100	British Aerospace	G-BBDG	wfs 24Dec81 Filton, UK		
203	100	Air France	F-WTSC	F-BTSC		
204	102	British Airways	G-BOAC	G-N81AC/N81AC	G-BOAC	
205	101	Air France	F-BVFA	N94FA F-BVFA		
206	102	British Airways	G-BOAA	G-N94AA/N94AA	G-BOAA	
207	101	Air France	F-BVFB	N94FB F-BVFB		
208	102	British Airways	G-BOAB	G-N94AB/N94AB	G-BOAB	
209	101	Air France	F-BVFC	N94FC F-BVFC		
210	102	British Airways	G-BOAD	G-N94AD/N94AD	G-BOAD	
211	101	(Air France)	F-BVFD	N94FD F-BVFD	scrapped 1994 Paris-Charles de Gaulle, France	
212	102	British Airways	G-BOAE	G-N94AE/N94AE	G-BOAE	
213	101	Air France	F-WJAM	F-BTSD N94SD	F-BTSD	
214	102	British Airways	G-BFKW	G-BOAG		
215	101	Air France	F-WJAN	F-BVFF		
216	102	British Airways	G-BFKX	G-N94AF/N94AF	G-BOAF	

Production complete

BRITISH AIRCRAFT CORPORATION BAC 1-11

C/n	Series	Last known Operator/Owner	Previous Identities/fate (where known)
004	200AB	(British Aircraft Corp)	G-ASHG w/o 22Oct63 Chicklade, UK
005	201AC	(Calcutta A/C Leasing)	G-ASJA G-52-1 N734EB XB-MUO TP-0201 XB-MUO VR-CAQ N3756F N97KR N88NB b/u for spares Jul89
006	201AC	(British Aircraft Corp)	G-ASJB dbr 18Mar64 Wisley, UK
007	201AC	(British Air Ferries)	G-ASJC N101EX EI-BWI (G-ASJC) b/u Jan94 Southend, UK
008	201AC	Defence Research Agency	G-ASJD XX105
009	201AC	(Guinness Peat Group)	G-ASJE (N29967) N102EX EI-BWJ b/u for spares Mar91 Orlando-MCO, FL
010	201AC	(Florida Express)	G-ASJF N103EX scr for spares Jan86
011	201AC	Balkh Airlines	G-ASJG N104EX EI-BWK G-DBAF EL-ALD
012	201AC	(British World)	G-ASJH N105EX EI-BWL G-OCNW dest in film crash scene Aug95 St Leonards, UK
013	201AC	Shabair	G-ASJI N106EX EI-BWM 9Q-CSJ
014	201AC	(British United A/W)	G-ASJJ w/o 14Jan69 Milan-Linate, Italy
015	203AE	Nationwide Advertising Services	N1541 G-ASUF N1541 N111QA N541BN N5LG N5LC N8LG N523AC N583CC
016	203AE	(Ocean Air)	N1542 b/u Aug87 Miami, FL
017	203AE	Ludlow Industries	N1543 VR-BAC N1543 stored Orlando-MCO, FL
018	203AE	CRL Inc	N1544 stored Hondo, TX
019	203AE	CRL Inc	N1545 stored Hondo, TX
020	203AE	(Guinness Peat Group)	N1546 EI-BWN b/u for spares Jan91 Orlando-MCO, FL
021	202AD	not built	
022	202AD	not built	
023	202AD	not built	
024	202AD	not built	
025	202AD	not built	
026	202AD	not built	
027	202AD	not built	
028	202AD	not built	
029	204AF	(ALG Inc)	N2111J b/u Feb92 Southend, UK
030	204AF	(Kabo Air)	N1112J b/u for spares Mar91
031	204AF	Kabo Air	N1113J 5N-KBS
032	204AF	Kabo Air	N1114J 5N-KBV
033	301AG	LADECO	(9K-ACI) G-ATPJ CC-CYF wfu Dec92
034	301AG	Okada Air	(9K-ACJ) G-ATPK VP-BCP G-ATPK 5N-OMO
035	301AG	LADECO	(9K-ACK) G-ATPL CC-CYI wfu Jan91
036	206AH	not built	
037	206AH	not built	
038	206AH	not built	
039	207AJ	LADECO	VP-YXA G-ATTP 9J-RCH 7Q-YKE 9J-RCH G-ATTP CC-CYM wfu Apr94
040	207AJ	LADECO	VP-YXB 9J-RCI G-ATVH 9J-RCI G-ATVH CC-CYL wfu Dec94
041	203AE	ADC Airlines	N1547 (G-BLVO) N1547 EI-BWO 5N-BAA
042	203AE	CRL Inc	N1548 stored Hondo, TX
043	203AE	ADC Airlines	N1549 (G-BLVP) N1549 EI-BWP 5N-AYY stored 15Oct94 Southend, UK
044	203AE	(Allegheny Airlines)	N1550 dbr 09Jul78 Rochester, NY
045	203AE	Antonio A/p Fire Dept	N1551 N1134J stored San Antonio, TX
046	203AE	CRL Inc	N1552 N1135J stored Hondo, TX
047	202AD	not built	
048	202AD	not built	
049	208AL	Hold-Trade Air Svces	EI-ANE 5N-HTC stored 29Jan93 Southend, UK
050	208AL	Hold-Trade Air Svces	EI-ANF AN-BBS EI-ANF 5N-HTD
051	208AL	(Hold-Trade Air Svces)	EI-ANG 5N-HTA w/o 29Aug92 Kaduna, Nigeria
052	208AL	Hold-Trade Air Svces	EI-ANH 5N-HTB
053	475EZ	Brooklands Museum	G-ASYD development a/c, originally types 400AM, 500EN, 475EZ and 670 preserved fm 14Jul94 Weybridge, UK
054	410AQ	Yukaipa Management	G-ASYE (N4111X) N3939V N77CS N77QS HZ-AMK N77QS N8007U N17VK N17MK
055	401AK	(Aviation Resources)	N5015 N111NA N1JR N56B b/u for spares Aug91
056	401AK	Calcutta A/C Leasing	N5016 N120TA N12CZ N172FE N491ST
057	401AK	Shabair	N5017 N277NS VR-CBI N170FE EI-BWQ 9Q-CUG 9Q-CEH
058	401AK	(National A/C Leasing)	N5018 N711ST (N97GA) N711ST w/o 09Feb75 Lake Tahoe, CA; nose section used in rebuild of c/n 117
059	2400	(Dee Howard Co)	N5019 N112NA N5019 N100CC N700JA N650DH Rolls Royce Tay development a/c; b/u Mar95 San Antonio, TX
060	401AK	Saudi Arabian Govt	N5020 N111NA N102GP HZ-GRP HZ-GP2 HZ-NB3 HZ-MAA HZ-AMB2
061	401AK	Detroit Red Wings	N5021 N69HM N5021 N40AS N171FE EI-BWR N682RW
062	401AK	Okada Air	N5022 VP-BDN C6-BDN N5022 N800MC 5N-AYU
063	401AK	Intl Air Tours	N5023 VP-BDP C6-BDP N217CA (G-BSXJ) N217CA 5N-
064	401AK	Commercial Bank of Saudi Arabia	N5024 HZ-NB2
065	401AK	Citra Aviation	N5025 N111NA N5025 N76GW N825AC N825AQ N117MR PK-PJF
066	401AK	Maersk Air	N5026 G-AZMI G-16-19 G-BBME
067	401AK	Calumet Inc	N5027 HZ-GRP N909CH N102ME N109TH N765B
068	401AK	I-X Jet Centre	N5028 N3E N5028 N200CC N18HH N18HD N111LP
069	401AK	Sheikh Salem bin Laden	N5029 3D-LLG VR-CAM HZ-AMB VR-CCS

BRITISH AIRCRAFT CORPORATION BAC 1-11

C/n	Series	Last known Operator/Owner	Previous Identities/fate (where known)
070	203AE	(Braniff Intl Airways)	N1553 w/o 06Aug66 Falls City, NB
071	203AE	CRL Inc	N1554 N1136J stored Hondo, TX
072	401AK	SS Aviation	N5030 N310EL N119GA
073	401AK	Lukenbill Enterprises	N5031 N111FL N5LC N401SK
074	401AK	Okada Air	N5032 G-ATVU N5032 AN-BHN N5032 VP-BDI G-BBMF 5N-EHI
075	401AK	(Florida Express)	N5033 N55JT N5033 A6-SHJ N179FE scr for spares early 1987
076	2400	(Dee Howard Co)	N5034 VR-BHS N333GB b/u 1995 San Antonio, TX
077	401AK	Tarom	N5035 YR-BCG stored Bucharest, Romania
078	401AK	Huizenga Holdings Inc	N5036 N111NS N9WP N800MC N9WP N800PW HZ-TA1 N62WH
079	401AK	Round Ball One Corp	N5037 N800DM N880DP
080	401AK	Sheikh Salem bin Laden	N5038 N10HM N22RB N90TF HZ-MFA HZ-BL1 stored 12Apr95 Southend, UK
081	401AK	Gazelle	N5039 HZ-RH1 HZ-HR1 VR-CTM VR-CCG
082	204AF	(Kabo Air)	N1115J 5N-KGB 5N-KBG w/o 15Sep91 Port Harcourt, Nigeria
083	212AR	Pionus Corp of Delaware	N502T VR-CBZ N70611 N490ST
084	211AH	Alendros de la Cruz	D-ABHH N504T VR-CBX A6-RAK S9-TAE XA-ADC
085	201AC	SA Rutas Oriente	G-ASTJ N107EX EI-BWS XA-RTN stored Monterrey, Mexico
086	401AK		N5040 N111NA N500CS N950CC HR-AMO
087	401AK	Westinghouse Electric Corp	N5041 G-AXCP N173FE N162W
088	401AK	Jarallah Corp	N5042 N112NA N5042 HZ-NIR HZ-MAJ
089	401AK	Tikal Jets	N5043 VP-BDJ C6-BDJ N218CA (G-BSXK) N97JF TG-TJF
090	401AK	Westinghouse Electric Corp	N5044 G-AXCK N164W
091	402AP	Defence Research Agency	PI-C1121 (D-AFWC) XX919
092	402AP	(Philippine Airlines)	PI-C1131 w/o 12Sep69 Manila, Philippines
093	407AW	(Kabo Air)	YS-17C (G-BSXU) 5N-KBR reduced to spares Aug93
094	402AP	(Okada Air)	PI-C1141 G-16-1 G-AVEJ PI-C1141 (D-AFWB) CF-QBR C-FQBR 5N-AOW dbr 26Jun91 nr Sokoto, Nigeria
BAC.095	200AT	(British Aircraft Corp)	(G-ASVT) planned rebuild of c/n 006; not proceeded with
BAC.096	215AU	Hellenic Air	N11181 N1130J (SX-BAR) stored Athens, Greece
BAC.097	215AU	ALG Inc	N11182 N1131J stored Orlando-MCO, FL
BAC.098	204AF	(Mohawk Airlines)	N1116J w/o 23Jun67 Blossburg, PA
BAC.099	204AF	ALG Inc	N1117J stored Orlando, FL
BAC.100	204AF	Kabo Air	N1118J 5N-SKS 5N-KBT
BAC.101	204AF	(Comtran International)	N1119J b/u Mar91 Bournemouth, UK
BAC.102	204AF	Kabo Air	N1120J 5N-KBD
BAC.103	204AF	(Kabo Air)	N1122J b/u for spares Jun91
BAC.104	204AF	Kabo Air	N1123J 5N-KBC
BAC.105	215AU	Kabo Air	N11183 N1132J 5N-KBM
BAC.106	407AW	Kabo Air	YS-18C (G-BSXV) 5N-KBW
BAC.107	320L-AZ	Okada Air	G-AVBW G-BKAU 5N-AOZ
BAC.108	F 409AY	Nationwide Air Charter	TI-1056C YS-01C G-BGTU ZS-NNM
BAC.109	320L-AZ	Okada Air	G-AVBX G-BKAV 5N-AOP
BAC.110	304AX	Okada Air	G-ATPH CF-QBN C-FQBN G-YMRU G-BPNX 5N-MZE
BAC.111	412EB	Yuman Group Intl	AN-BBI N221CN N767RV N90AM HZ-JAM N71MA N111AC
BAC.112	304AX	Okada Air	G-ATPI CF-QBO C-FQBO G-WLAD 5N-OVE
BAC.113	320L-AZ	(AEA Technology)	G-AVBY G-BKAW 5N-AOK fuselage used for non-destructive testing research
BAC.114	408EF	Maersk Air	G-AVGP (HI-148) G-AVGP
BAC.115	408EF	Maersk Air	G-AWEJ G-BBMG
BAC.116	413FA	(Air Pacific)	G-AWGG D-ALLI DQ-FCR sold as spares Sep81
BAC.117	420EL	(TABAC Inc)	LV-JGX LV-PKB LV-JGX N128TA N128GA rebuilt using nose section fm c/n 058 after earlier w/o 27Jan78 Buenos Aires, Argentina; b/u for spares Sep89
BAC.118	423ET	Ford Motor Co	G-16-2 VC92-2111 G-BEJM
BAC.119	422EQ	Montex Drilling	PP-SRT N18814 N114M
BAC.120	419EP	Amway Corp	N270E N44R N524AC
BAC.121	432FD	Okada Air	G-16-5 VP-BCY G-AXOX A40-BX G-AXOX 5N-AXT
BAC.122	420EL	(Okada Air)	LV-IZR G-AVTF LV-PID LV-IZR (N3126H) C-GQBP 5N-AOM b/u for spares Los Angeles, CA
BAC.123	420EL	Okada Air	LV-IZS LV-PIF LV-IZS (N3126Q) C-GQBV 5N-AOS
BAC.124	217EA	Okada Air	A12-124 G-EXPM 5N-TOM 5N-NRC
BAC.125	217EA	Okada Air	A12-125 G-KROO 5N-SDP
BAC.126	422EQ	Aravco	PP-SRU N18813 N80GM N809M N341TC N111GS A6-KTH A6-RKT VR-CCJ N51387
BAC.127	414EG	ADC Airlines	G-16-3 D-ANDY w/o 19Jul70 Gerona, Italy; remains rebuilt on One-Eleven production line (G-AZDG) G-AZED (N174FE) G-AZED N174FE EI-BWT 5N-BAB
BAC.128	408EF	Okada Air	G-AWKJ G-BIII RP-C1 G-NIII 5N-AYV G-NIII 5N-AYV
BAC.129	416EK	(Okada Air)	G-AVOE G-SURE G-AVOE N390BA 5N-AYS reduced to spares Oct92
BAC.130	424EU	(Tarom)	G-16-4 YR-BCA w/o 07Dec70 Constanta, Romania
BAC.131	416EK	Okada Air	G-AVOF G-BMAN G-16-32 G-BMAN G-AVOF N392BA 5N-AYT
BAC.132	416EK	Maersk Air	G-AWBL
BAC.133	320L-AZ	(Okada Air)	G-AVYZ G-BKAX 5N-AOT dbr 07Sep89 Port Harcourt, Nigeria
BAC.134	204AF	(ALG Inc)	N1124J G-AWDF N1124J b/u for spares Jan91 Waco, TX

BRITISH AIRCRAFT CORPORATION BAC 1-11

C/n	Series	Last known Operator/Owner	Previous Identities/fate (where known)
BAC.135	204AF	(Southern A/C Sales)	N1125J HZ-MO1 N4550T b/u for spares Oct90
BAC.136	510ED	European Aircharter	G-AVMH
BAC.137	510ED	European Aircharter	G-AVMI
BAC.138	510ED	(European Aviation)	G-AVMJ dismantled Jun95 Filton, UK; fuselage stored Bournemouth, UK
BAC.139	510ED	European Aircharter	G-AVMK
BAC.140	510ED	European Aircharter	G-AVML
BAC.141	510ED	European Aviation	G-AVMM stored Jan95 Bournemouth, UK
BAC.142	510ED	Air Belfast	G-AVMN
BAC.143	510ED	Cosford Aerospace Museum	G-AVMO preserved RAF Cosford, UK
BAC.144	510ED	European Aircharter	G-AVMP
BAC.145	510ED	European Aviation	G-AVMR stored Jan95 Bournemouth, UK
BAC.146	510ED	European Aircharter	G-AVMS
BAC.147	510ED	AB Shannon	G-AVMT
BAC.148	510ED	Duxford Aviation Soc	G-AVMU preserved Duxford, UK
BAC.149	510ED	European Aviation	G-AVMV stored Aug92 Bournemouth, UK
BAC.150	510ED	Air Bristol	G-AVMW
BAC.151	510ED	European Aviation	G-AVMX 5N-USE G-AVMX stored 16May95 Bournemouth, UK
BAC.152	510ED	European Aircharter	G-AVMY
BAC.153	510ED	European Aviation	G-AVMZ 5N-OSA G-AVMZ stored 15Feb95 Bournemouth, UK
BAC.154	423ET	Kabo Air	VC92-2110 G-BEJW 5N-KKK
BAC.155	420EL	(Austral Lineas Aereas)	LV-JGY LV-PKA LV-JGY w/o 21Nov77 San Carlos de Bariloche, Argentina
BAC.156	424EU	(Tarom)	YR-BCB b/u 1988
BAC.157	432FD	Okada Air	VP-BCZ G-AXMU PI-C1151 G-16-14 G-AXMU A40-BU G-AXMU 5N-AXQ
BAC.158	414EG	Sheikh Abdul Aziz al Ibrahim	(D-ANDI) D-AISY HZ-MF1 HZ-AMH HZ-AB1 HZ-KB1
BAC.159	424EU	GAS Air	YR-BCD 5N-AXV
BAC.160	414EG	Kabo Air	D-ANNO G-BFMC 5N-GGG
BAC.161	402AP	Tarom	PI-C1151 EC-BQF G-AYHM (D-AFWA) YR-BCH stored Bucharest, Romania
BAC.162	409AY	Okada Air	G-16-6 G-AXBB YR-BCP G-AXBB TI-1055C G-AXBB A40-BB G-AXBB 5N-AYR
BAC.163	414EG	BAC 1-11 Corp	D-AILY N123H
BAC.164		not built	
BAC.165	424EU	Liniile Aerienne Romane	YR-BCE stored Bucharest, Romania
BAC.166	416EK	Okada Air	(YR-BCC) G-AWXJ HB-ITK G-AWXJ 9V-BEF PK-PJC G-16-24 G-CBIA 5N-AYW
BAC.167	424EU	GAS Air	YR-BCC 5N-AVX
BAC.168	424EU	Okada Air	YR-BCF 5N-OKA
BAC.169		not built	
BAC.170		not built	
BAC.171		not built	
BAC.172		not built	
BAC.173		not built	
BAC.174	501EX	Maersk Air	G-AWYR EI-CID G-AWYR
BAC.175	501EX	Maersk Air	G-AWYS
BAC.176	501EX	Express City	G-AWYT EI-CIE G-AWYT 9Q-CKY
BAC.177	501EX	Express City	G-AWYU EI-CIC G-AWYR 9Q-CKI
BAC.178	501EX	Maersk Air	G-AWYV
BAC.179	204AF	(Kabo Air)	N1126J 5N-KBA w/o 23Aug92 Sokoto, Nigeria
BAC.180	204AF	Kabo Air	N1127J 5N-KBO
BAC.181	204AF	(Comtran International)	N1128J b/u Mar91 Bournemouth, UK
BAC.182	204AF	(ALG Inc)	N1129J reduced to spares 1990
BAC.183	212AR	Ashmawi Aviation	N503T VR-CBY HZ-AMH VR-CBY VR-CMI (HZ-ND1) VR-CMI
BAC.184	509EW	Oriental Airlines	G-AWWX (G-OBWG) 5N-
BAC.185	509EW	(Austral Lineas Aereas)	G-AWWY LV-PSW LV-JNU G-AWWY LV-LHT b/u Oct94 San Fernando, Argentina
BAC.186	509EW	Nationwide Air Charter	G-AWWZ G-BSYN EI-CCW (G-AWWZ) ZS-NMS
BAC.187	515FB	(Austral Lineas Aereas)	D-ALAT G-AZPY D-AMAS LV-PEW LV-MZM b/u Oct93 Moran, Argentina
BAC.188	517FE	Thameside Airspares	VP-BCN G-AZEB VP-LAP G-AZEB RP-C1186 stored Manila, Philippines; reduced to spares
BAC.189	517FE	Thameside Airspares	VP-BCO G-AZEC VP-LAR G-AZEC RP-C1187 stored Manila, Philippines; reduced to spares
BAC.190	524FF	Thameside Airspares	D-AMIE RP-C1184 stored Manila, Philippines; reduced to spares
BAC.191	501EX	Express City	G-AXJK EI-CIB G-AXJK 9Q-CKP
BAC.192	521FH	(Austral Lineas Aereas)	G-16-7 LV-JNR PP-SDP LV-JNR G-AYXB LV-JNR dbr 04Dec73 Bahia Blanca, Argentina
BAC.193	520FN	European Aircharter	G-16-8 G-AXLL PP-SDT OB-R1137 OB-R-1173 G-AXLL
BAC.194	521FH	(Austral Lineas Aereas)	G-16-9 G-AXPH LV-JNS b/u May93 Quilmes, Argentina
BAC.195	524FF	European Aviation	D-AMUR G-AXSY D-AMUR RP-C1185 VR-BEA for storage Hurn, UK
BAC.196	521FH	(Austral Lineas Aereas)	G-16-10 LV-JNT b/u Jul94 Moran, Argentina
BAC.197	524FF	(Austral Lineas Aereas)	G-16-11 G-AXVO D-AMOR LV-PFR LV-OAX b/u Oct93 Moran, Argentina
BAC.198	517FE	(British World)	G-16-12 VP-BCQ VP-LAN G-BCCV G-BCXR (G-OBWK) b/u Southend, UK
BAC.199	523FJ	Thameside Airspares	G-AXLM PP-SDV G-AXLM G-16-23 4X-BAS RP-C1194 stored Manila, Philippines; reduced to spares

BRITISH AIRCRAFT CORPORATION BAC 1-11

C/n	Series	Last known Operator/Owner	Previous Identities/fate (where known)
BAC.200	518FG	Air Patagonia	G-AXMF PT-TYV (G-AXMF) LV-MEX
BAC.201	518FG	Nationwide Air Charter	G-AXMG 5B-DAF G-AXMG G-FLRU EI-CDO G-AXMG ZS-NMT
BAC.202	518FG	British World	G-AXMH G-BDAS G-OBWB
BAC.203	518FG	British World	G-AXMI G-BDAE G-OBWD
BAC.204	518FG	Thameside Airspares	G-AXMJ G-BCWG RP-C1189 stored Manila, Philippines; reduced to spares
BAC.205	518FG	(British World)	G-AXMK TG-ARA G-AXMK VP-LAK G-AXMK G-BCWA (G-OBWI) b/u Southend, UK
BAC.206	518FG	(Austral Lineas Aereas)	G-AXML AN-BHJ G-AXML PT-TYW TG-AVA LV-MRZ b/u Mar95 Tigre, Argentina
BAC.207	515FB	(Paninternational)	D-ALAR w/o 06Sep71 nr Hamburg, W Germany
BAC.208	515FB	Oriental Airlines	D-ALAS G-AZPE TI-LRK G-BJYL (G-OBWH) 5N-ENO
BAC.209	501EX	Thameside Airspares	G-AXJL RP-C1188 stored Manila, Philippines; reduced to spares
BAC.210	509EW	Oriental Airlines	G-AXYD (G-OBWF) 5N-
BAC.211	523FJ	Oriental Airlines	G-AXLN PP-SDU TG-AYA VR-CAL G-AXLN G-EKPT EI-CCX 5N-EYI
BAC.212	529FR	(Austral Lineas Aereas)	G-16-13 HB-ITL LV-LOX w/o 07May81 Buenos Aires, Argentina
BAC.213	527FK	(Philippine Airlines)	PI-C1161 G-AYOS PI-C1161 RP-C1161 dest by hijackers 23May76 Zamboanga, Philippines
BAC.214	501EX	Oriental Airlines	G-AXJM 7Q-YKI G-AXJM 5N-OAL
BAC.215	527FK	Thameside Airspares	PI-C1171 G-AYKN PI-C1171 G-AYKN PI-C1171 RP-C1171 stored Manila, Philippines; reduced to spares
BAC.216		not built	
BAC.217		not built	
BAC.218		not built	
BAC.219		not built	
BAC.220		not built	
BAC.221		not built	
BAC.222		not built	
BAC.223		not built	
BAC.224		not built	
BAC.225		not built	
BAC.226	527FK	Thameside Airspares	PI-C1181 RP-C1181 VR-BEB for storage Hurn, UK
BAC.227	528FL	(Austral Lineas Aereas)	D-AMUC LV-OAY b/u May94 Tigre, Argentina
BAC.228	520FN	(TransBrasil)	PP-SDQ w/o 02Feb74 Sao Paulo, Brazil
BAC.229	515FB	(Oriental Airlines)	D-ALAQ G-AZPZ D-AMAM G-AZPZ 5N-IMO w/o 18Sep94 Tamanrasset, Algeria
BAC.230	520FN	British World	PP-SDR G-BEKA G-16-22 4X-BAR G-BEKA G-OBWC
BAC.231	516FP	(Philippine Airlines)	PI-C1191 TG-AZA RP-C1193 dbr 21Jul89 Manila, Philippines
BAC.232	518FG	British World	G-AYOR G-BDAT G-OBWA
BAC.233	530FX	European Aircharter	G-AYOP
BAC.234	528FL	JARO International	D-ALFA G-BJRT YR-JBA
BAC.235	524FF	Okada Air	(G-AYSC) D-AMAT 7Q-YKK 5N-USE(2)
BAC.236	520FN	(Tigerair)	G-16-15 PP-SDS (N110TA) dbr 05Jan77 Sao Paulo, Brazil
BAC.237	531FS	Nationwide Air Charter	(G-AYWB) TI-1084C TI-LRF TI-LRL VR-CAB G-AYWB G-DJOS EI-CCU (G-AYWB) ZS-NUG
BAC.238	528FL	JARO International	D-ANUE G-BJRU YR-JBB
BAC.239	476FM	AIM Aviation	G-AYUW G-16-17 OB-R-953 G-AYUW fuselage only at Hurn for water sprinkler trials
BAC.240	530FX	European Aircharter	G-AZMF PT-TYY G-AZMF 7Q-YKJ G-AZMF
BAC.241	476FM	Oriental Airlines	OB-R-1080 G-16-16 G-AZUK OB-R-1080 G-AZUK 5N-
BAC.242	531FS	British World	TI-1095C TI-LRI G-BJYM G-OBWE
BAC.243	481FW	GAS Airlines	7Q-YKF 5N-SKS
BAC.244	531FS	British World	TI-1096C TI-LRJ G-BJMV (G-OBWJ) stored Southend, UK
BAC.245	479FU	GEC Ferranti Defence Systems	(VQ-FBQ) DQ-FBQ 7Q-YKG DQ-FBQ ZE433
BAC.246	527FK	(Philippine Airlines)	RP-C1182 w/o 04Aug84 Tacloban, Philippines
BAC.247	F 485GD	Sultan of Oman's AF	1001 551
BAC.248	527FK	Thameside Airspares	RP-C1183 stored Manila, Philippines; reduced to spares
BAC.249	F 485GD	Sultan of Oman's AF	1002 552
BAC.250	479FU	Empire Test Pilots' School	DQ-FBV ZE432
BAC.251	F 485GD	Sultan of Oman's AF	1003 553
BAC.252	525FT	Tarom	YR-BCI
BAC.253	525FT	Tarom	YR-BCJ TC-ARI YR-BCJ TC-AKB YR-BCJ
BAC.254	525FT	Tarom	YR-BCK TC-JCP YR-BCK
BAC.255	525FT	Tarom	YR-BCL OE-ILC YR-BCL TC-AKA YR-BCL EI-BVG YR-BCL EI-BVG YR-BCL
BAC.256	525FT	Tarom	YR-BCM OE-ILD YR-BCM EI-BVI YR-BCM
BAC.257	537GF	Nationwide Air Charter	5B-DAG ZS-NUH
BAC.258	537GF	Nationwide Air Charter	5B-DAH ZS-NUI
BAC.259	488GH	Alatief Corp	HZ-MAM LX-MAM 5N-UDE G-BWES PK-TAL
BAC.260	492GM	Sheikh Kamal Adham	G-16-25 G-BLHD HZ-KA7
BAC.261	537GF	Nationwide Air Charter	5B-DAJ G-BFWN 5B-DAJ ZS-NUJ
BAC.262	492GM	Indonesia Air Tpt	G-BLDH PK-TRU
BAC.263	539GL	Defence Research Agency	G-BGKE ZH763
BAC.264	539GL	Okada Air	G-BGKF 5N-ORO
BAC.265	539GL	Okada Air	G-BGKG 5N-BIN
BAC.266	525FT	Tarom	YR-BCN YU-AKN YR-BCN YU-ANM YR-BCN EI-BSY YR-BCN
BAC.267	F 487GK	Tarom	YR-BCR G-TOMO YR-BCR stored Bucharest, Romania
BAC.268			airframe shipped to Bucharest for final assembly in Romania as c/n 401

BRITISH AIRCRAFT CORPORATION BAC 1-11

C/n	Series	Last known Operator/Owner	Previous Identities/fate (where known)
BAC.269			airframe shipped to Bucharest for final assembly in Romania as c/n 402
BAC.270			airframe shipped to Bucharest for final assembly in Romania as c/n 403
BAC.271			airframe shipped to Bucharest for final assembly in Romania as c/n 404
BAC.272	525FT	(Tarom)	YR-BCO G-TARO YR-BCO YU-ANN YR-BCO EI-BSZ YR-BCO w/o Dec95 Istanbul, Turkey
BAC.273			airframe shipped to Bucharest for final assembly in Romania as c/n 405
BAC.274			airframe shipped to Bucharest for final assembly in Romania as c/n 406
BAC.275			airframe shipped to Bucharest for final assembly in Romania as c/n 407
BAC.276			airframe shipped to Bucharest for final assembly in Romania as c/n 408
BAC.401	561RC	Aero Asia	YR-BRA YU-ANR YR-BRA AP-BFC
BAC.402	561RC	Tarom	YR-BRB EI-BSS YR-BRB EI-BSS YR-BRB EI-BSS YR-BRB EI-BSS YR-BRB
BAC.403	561RC	Tarom	YR-BRC YU-ANS YR-BRC
BAC.404	561RC	Aero Asia	YR-BRD YU-ANT YR-BRD AP-BFD
BAC.405	561RC	Romavia	YR-BRE
BAC.406	561RC	Aero Asia	YR-BRF G-BNIH EI-CAS YR-BRF AP-BFE
BAC.407	561RC	Aero Asia	YR-BRG EI-BVH YR-BRG AP-BFF
BAC.408	561RC	Aero Asia	YR-BRH
BAC.409	561RC	Aero Asia	YR-BRI
BAC.410	475	Romaero	construction suspended
BAC.411	500	Romaero	construction suspended

F indicates fitted with forward main deck freight floor
C/ns 401 and above assembled in Romania; 11 ordered Feb93 for Kiwi International

CANADAIR RJ100 REGIONAL JET (CL-600-2B19)

C/n	Last known Operator/Owner	Previous Identities/fate (where known)				
7001	(Bombardier)	C-FCRJ	prototype;	ff 10May91		w/o 26Jul93 Iuka, KS; cancelled Feb96
7002	Bombardier	C-FNRJ				
7003	Air Littoral/Air France/ Air Inter	C-GVRJ	F-GNMN			
7004	Lufthansa CityLine	C-GRJJ	(D-ARJA)	D-ACLA		
7005	Lufthansa CityLine	C-GRJN	(D-ARJB)	D-ACLB		
7006	Lufthansa CityLine	C-GRJO	(D-ARJC)	D-ACLC		
7007	Lufthansa CityLine	C-FMKV(2)	(D-ACLG)	D-ACLH		
7008	Xerox Corp	C-FMKV(1)	N5100X			
7009	Lufthansa CityLine	C-FMKW(1)	D-ACLD			
7010	Lufthansa CityLine	C-GRJW	D-ACLE			
7011	Comair	C-FMKZ(1)	N912CA			
7012	Comair	C-FMLA	N914CA			
7013	Comair	C-FMLF	(D-ARJD)	C-FMLQ	N915CA	
7014	Comair	C-FMLI	(D-ARJE)	N916CA		
7015	Lufthansa CityLine	C-FMLQ	(D-ARJF)	D-ACLF		
7016	Lufthansa CityLine	C-FMLS	(D-ACLH)	D-ACLG		
7017	Comair	C-FMLT	N917CA			
7018	Comair	C-FMLU	N918CA			
7019	Lufthansa CityLine	C-FMLV	D-ACLI			
7020	Air Littoral/Air France/ Air Inter	C-FMMB	F-GNME			
7021	Lufthansa CityLine	C-FMML	D-ACLJ			
7022	Comair	C-FMMN	N920CA			
7023	Lufthansa CityLine	C-FMMQ	(D-ARJG)	D-ACLK		
7024	Lufthansa CityLine	C-FMMT	(D-ARJH)	D-ACLL		
7025	Lufthansa CityLine	C-FMMW	(D-ARJI)	D-ACLM		
7026	Comair	C-FMMX	N924CA			
7027	Comair	C-FMMY	N926CA			
7028	Skywest Airlines	C-FMNB	(D-ARJJ)	N403SW		
7029	Skywest Airlines	C-FMND	N405SW			
7030	Skywest Airlines	C-FMNH	N406SW			
7031	Comair	C-FMNQ	N927CA			
7032	Lauda Air	C-FMNW	C-FRKQ	OE-LRA		
7033	Lauda Air	C-FMNX	C-FRSA	OE-LRB		
7034	Skywest Airlines	C-FMNY	(D-ARJK)	N407SW		
7035	Comair	C-FMOI	N929CA			
7036	Lufthansa CityLine	C-FMOL	OE-LRC	D-ACLX(1)		
7037	Comair	C-FMOS	(D-ARJL)	N931CA		
7038	Comair	C-FMOW	(D-ARJM)	N932CA		
7039	Lauda Air	C-FMKV(3)	D-ACLN			
7040	Comair	C-FMKW(2)	N933CA			
7041	Lufthansa CityLine	C-FMKZ(2)	D-ACLO			
7042	Comair	C-FMLB	N934CA			
7043	Comair	C-FMLF	N936CA			
7044	Comair	C-FMLI	N937CA			
7045	Air Canada	C-FMLQ	C-FRIA			
7046	Comair	C-FMLS	N938CA			
7047	Air Canada	C-FMLT	C-FRIB			
7048	Comair	C-FMLU	N940CA			
7049	Air Canada	C-FMLV	C-FRID			
7050	Comair	C-FMMB	N941CA			
7051	Air Canada	C-FMML	C-FRIL			
7052	Lauda Air	C-FMMN	OE-LRD			
7053	Air Littoral/Air France/ Air Inter	C-FMMQ	F-GLIY			
7054	Air Canada	C-FMMT	C-FSJF			
7055	Skywest Airlines	C-FMMW	N408SW			
7056	Skywest Airlines	C-FMMX	N409SW			
7057	Air Littoral/Air France/ Air Inter	C-FMMY	(C-FSJJ)	F-GLIZ		
7058	Air Canada	(C-FSJU)	C-FSJJ			
7059	Lauda Air	OE-LRE				
7060	Air Canada	C-FSJU				
7061	Lauda Air	C-FMNQ	OE-LRF			
7062	Comair	C-FMNW	N943CA			
7063	Lauda Air	C-FMNY	OE-LRG			
7064	Lufthansa CityLine	C-FMNX	(C-FSKE)	D-ACLP		
7065	Air Canada	C-FMOI	C-FSKE			
7066	Skywest Airlines	C-FMOL	N410SW			
7067	Skywest Airlines	C-FMOS	(C-FSKI)	N411SW		
7068	Air Canada	C-FMOW	(C-FSKM)	C-FSKI		
7069	Comair	C-FMKV(4)	N945CA			
7070	Brit'Air	C-FMKW(3)	F-GRJA			
7071	Air Canada	C-FMKZ(3)	C-FSKM			
7072	Comair	C-FMLB	N946CA			
7073	Lufthansa CityLine	C-FMLF	D-ACLQ			
7074	Air Canada	C-FMLI	C-FVKM			
7075	Canadair Challenger	C-FMLQ	N877SE			
7076	Brit'Air	C-FMLS	F-GRJB			

CANADAIR RJ100 REGIONAL JET (CL-600-2B19)

C/n	Last known Operator/Owner	Previous Identities/fate (where known)	
7077	Comair	C-FMLT	N947CA
7078	Air Canada	C-FMLU	C-FVKN
7079	Comair	C-FMLV	N948CA
7080	Comair	C-FMMB	N949CA
7081	Air Littoral	C-	F-GLIJ
7082	Air Canada	C-FVMD	
7083	Air Canada	C-FMNQ	C-FVKR
7084	Air Littoral/Air France/ Air Inter	C-FMMT	F-GLIK
7085	Brit'Air	C-	F-GRJC
7086	Lufthansa CityLine	C-	D-ACLR
7087	Air Canada	C-	C-FWJB
7088	Brit'Air	C-FMLU	F-GRJD
7089	SAEAGA	C-FWRN	9M-EKC
7090	Lufthansa CityLine	C-	D-ACLS
7091	Comair	C-	N951CA
7092	Comair	C-	N952CA
7093	Lufthansa CityLine	C-	D-ACLT
7094	Tyrolean Airways	C-	OE-LCF
7095	Air Canada	C-	C-FWJF
7096	Air Canada	C-	C-FWJI
7097	Air Canada	C-	C-FWJS
7098	Air Canada	C-	C-FWJT
7099			
7100	Comair	C-FXFB	N954CA
7101	Skywest Airlines	C-	N412SW
7102	Skywest Airlines	C-	N413SW
7103	Tyrolean Airways	C-	OE-LCG
7104	Lufthansa CityLine	C-	D-ACLU*
7105	Comair	C-	N956CA
7106			
7107			
7108			
7109			
7110	Tyrolean Airways	C-	OE-LCH*
7111			
7112			
7113	Lufthansa CityLine	C-	D-ACLV*
7114	Lufthansa CityLine	C-	D-ACLW*
7115			
7116			
7117			
7118			
7119	Lufthansa CityLine	C-	D-ACLX(2)*
7120			
7121			
7122			
7123			
7124			
7125			
7126			
7127			
7128			
7129			
7130			
7131			
7132			
7133	Tyrolean Airways	C-	OE-LCK*
7134			
7135			
7136			
7137			
7138			
7139			
7140			
7141			
7142	Tyrolean Airways	C-	OE-LC.
7143			
7144			
7145			
7146			
7147			
7148			
7149			
7150			

CONVAIR 880

C/n	Series	Last known Operator/Owner	Previous Identities/fate (where known)
22-00-1	22-1	(Gulfstream Aerospace)	prototype; ff 27Jan59 N801TW N8489H N871TW N880AJ b/u 1990
22-00-2	22-1	(Trans World Airlines)	N802TW b/u Dec79 Kansas City, MO
22-00-3	22-1	FAA	N803TW N801AJ
22-00-4	F	Profit Express	N8801E AN-BLW N8801E N817AJ wfs 1984 and stored
22-00-5	22-1	(Trans World Airlines)	(N804TW) N8478H N804TW b/u Oct79 Kansas City, MO
22-00-6	22-1	Torco Oil Co	N805TW N802AJ stored Mojave, CA
22-00-7	22-2	(Groth Air)	N8802E N55NW N880SR b/u May83
22-00-8	22-1	Torco Oil Co	(N806TW) N8479H N806TW N803AJ stored Mojave, CA
22-00-9	22-1	(Gulfstream American)	N807TW N8492H AN-BIB N90452 N818AJ AN-BIB b/u Dec81 Miami, FL (still as AN-BIB)
22-00-10	22-1	(Gulfstream Aerospace)	N808TW N804AJ b/u Oct90 Atlantic City, NJ
22-00-11	22-2	(Gulfstream Aerospace)	N8803E N880NW b/u Apr83 Miami, FL
22-00-12	22-1	(Gulfstream Aerospace)	(N809TW) N8480H N809TW N806AJ b/u Laurinburg, NC
22-00-13	22-1	FAA	N810TW N807AJ
22-00-14	22-1	(Trans World Airlines)	N811TW b/u May77 Kansas City, MO
22-00-15	22-1	Torco Oil Co	N812TW N808AJ stored Mojave, CA
22-00-16	22-1	(Delta Air Lines)	N8804E w/o 23May60 Atlanta, GA
22-00-17	22-2	Haiti Air Freight	N8805E HH-SMA der Port-au-Prince, Haiti
22-00-18	22-1	Torco Oil Co	N813TW N8493H stored Mojave, CA
22-00-19	22-1	Torco Oil Co	N814TW N809AJ stored Mojave, CA
22-00-20	22-1	Torco Oil Co	(N815TW) N8481H N815TW N810AJ stored Mojave, CA
22-00-21	22-2	Concordia Corp	N8806E in use as restaurant Lisbon, Portugal
22-00-22	22-1	Torco Oil Co	(N816TW) N8482H N816TW N811AJ stored Mojave, CA
22-00-23	22-1	Aviation Warehouse	(N817TW) N8483H N817TW N812AJ stored Mojave, CA
22-00-24	22-1	Torco Oil Co	N818TW N813AJ stored Mojave, CA
22-00-25	22-1	(Trans World Airlines)	N819TW b/u 1979 Kansas City, MO
22-00-26	22-1	(Trans World Airlines)	N820TW w/o 13Sep65 Kansas City, MO
22-00-27	22-1	(Trans World Airlines)	N821TW w/o 21Nov67 Cincinatti, OH
22-00-28	22-1	(Trans World Airlines)	N822TW b/u Dec79 Kansas City, MO
22-00-29	22-2	(Delta Air Lines)	N8807E w/o 20Dec72 Chicago, IL
22-00-30	22-1	(Trans World Airlines)	N823TW b/u Dec79 Kansas City, MO
22-00-31	22-1	(Trans World Airlines)	N824TW b/u Sep79 Kansas City, MO
22-00-32	22-1	Torco Oil Co	N825TW N814AJ stored Mojave, CA as N375 for film work
22-00-33	22-1	(Trans World Airlines)	N826TW b/u Sep79 Kansas City, MO
22-00-34	22-1	Torco Oil Co	N827TW N8494H stored Mojave, CA
22-00-35	22-1	Torco Oil Co	N828TW N815AJ stored Mojave, CA
22-00-36	F	Torco Oil Co	N8808E AN-BLX N90450 N819AJ stored Mojave, CA
22-00-37M	22M-3	(Cathay Pacific Airways)	(N8487H) YV-C-VIC VR-HFX w/o 05Nov67 Hong Kong
22-00-38	22-2	LM Corp	N8809E N880EP preserved Graceland Museum, Memphis, TN
22-00-39	22-1	(Gulfstream American)	(N829TW) N8495H AN-BIA N90455 N820AJ b/u Jan84 Miami, FL
22-00-40	22-1	Torco Oil Co	N830TW N816AJ stored Mojave, CA
22-00-41	22-2	(Inair Panama)	N8810E HP-821 dbr 29Mar80 Panama City, Panama
22-00-42	22-1	(Trans World Airlines)	(N831TW) N801TW b/u Nov79 Kansas City, MO
22-00-43M	22M-3	(IASCO)	N8485H HB-ICL N94284 VR-HFT N48058 b/u May86 Cincinatti, OH
22-00-44M	22M-4	(Airtrust Singapore)	N8486H B-1008 VR-HGA N48059 b/u 1984 Seletar, Singapore
22-00-45M	22M-3	(Japan Domestic A/L)	N8487H HB-ICM N94285 JA8030 w/o 26Aug66 Tokyo, Japan
22-00-46M	F	(Profit Express)	N8488H JA8026 N5858 N54CP used for fire practice San Juan, PR
22-00-47M	22M-3	(Airtrust Singapore)	N8489H VR-HFS N48060 w/o 21Aug76 Seletar, Singapore
22-00-48M	22M-3	(FAA)	N8490H JA8027 N5863 TF-AVB N5863 N58RD N5863 dbf Oct86 Mojave, CA
22-00-49M	22M-3	(Japan Air Lines)	N8491H JA8028 w/o 25Jun69 Moses Lake, WA
22-00-50	22-2	SERCA	N8811E stored Caracas-Maiquieta, Venezuela
22-00-51	22-2	(Fair Air)	N8812E N880WA b/u Nov85 Miami, FL
22-00-52	22-2	Inair Panama	N8813E HP-876 HP-876P
22-7-1-53	22M-21	(Cathay Pacific A/W)	N8490H YV-C-VIA VR-HFZ w/o 15Jun72 nr Pleiku, S Vietnam
22-7-2-54	22M-21	(Airtrust Singapore)	N8477H VR-HFY N48062 b/u 1984 Seletar, Singapore
22-7-3-55	UC-880	US Navy	N112 N42 N84790 161572
22-7-4-56	22M-21	US Navy	N8488H YV-C-VIB VR-HGC N48063 spares use Patuxent River, MD
22-7-5-57	22M-22	(Air Trine)	JA8021 N5865 N1RN N5865 b/u Oct81 Miami, FL
22-7-6-58	22M-22	Ciskei Intl Airways	JA8022 VR-HGF N88CH stored East London, S Africa
22-7-7-59	22M-22	(Japan Air Lines)	JA8023 w/o 27Feb65 Kyushi, Japan
22-7-8-60	22M-22	(IAL)	JA8024 VR-HGG N880JT b/u Apr85 Miami, FL
22-7-9-61	22M-22	(IAL)	JA8025 N5866 N4339D b/u 1985 Orlando, FL
22-00-62	22-2	Torco Oil Co	N8814E N900NW stored Mojave, CA
22-00-63	22-2	(Groth Air)	N8815E N700NW b/u Oct81 Miami, FL
22-00-64	22-2	(Latin Carga)	N8816E YV-145C w/o 03Nov80 Caracas, Venezuela
22-00-65	22-2	(Monarch Aviation)	N8817E w/o 20Aug77 San Jose, Costa Rica

Production complete

CONVAIR 990

C/n	Series	Last known Operator/Owner	Previous Identities/fate (where known)
30-10-1	30A-5	(NASA)	prototype; ff 24Jan61 (N5601) N5601G NASA711 N711NA w/o 12Apr73 Sunnyvale, CA
30-10-2	30A-5	Gulfstream Aerospace	(N5602) N5602G OB-R-765 N990AB stored Mojave, CA
30-10-3	30A-5	(Garuda Indonesia)	(N5603) N5603G PK-GJA w/o 28May68 Bombay, India
30-10-4	30A-5	(California Airmotive)	(N5604) N5604G PK-GJB N7876 w/o 10Sep73 Guam
30-10-5	30A-6	NASA	(OY-KVA) N8484H OB-OAG-728 OB-R-728 N990AC stored Marana, AZ
30-10-6	30A-6	(MBB)	(LN-LMA) N8485H HB-ICF b/u 1975 Hamburg-Finkenwerder, W Germany
30-10-7	30A-6	Spantax	N8497H HB-ICA EC-CNG stored Apr82 Palma, Spain
30-10-8	30A-6	Spantax	N8498H SE-DAY HB-ICG EC-CNF stored Jan83 Palma, Spain
30-10-9	30A-5	(Ports of Call)	N5605 N8160C b/u Marana, AZ
30-10-10	30A-5	(Lebanese Intl)	N5606 OD-AEX dest by commandos 28Dec68 Beirut, Lebanon
30-10-11	30A-5	(MBB)	N8499H HB-ICB b/u Apr75 Hamburg-Finkenwerder, W Germany
30-10-12	30-1	(Convair)	N94280 airframe not completed
30-10-12(2)	30A-5	Verkehrshaus der Schweiz	HB-ICC preserved Lucerne, Switzerland
30-10-13	30A-8	(Modern Air Tpt)	PP-VJE N987AS N5603 w/o 08Aug70 Acapulco, Mexico
30-10-14	30A-6	Spantax	(OY-KVA) (N8484H) HB-ICE EC-CNJ stored Mar81 Palma, Spain
30-10-15	30A-6	(Swissair)	HB-ICD w/o 21Feb70 nr Zurich, Switzerland
30-10-16	30A-5	(Christ Is The Answer Inc)	N5607 N990E b/u ca 1990 Ft Lauderdale, FL
30-10-17	30A-6	Spantax	(OY-KVA) SE-DAZ HS-TGE SE-DAZ HB-ICH EC-CNH stored Sep83 Palma, Spain
30-10-18	30A-5	Spantax	N5608 OD-AFF N6844 EC-BZP stored Palma, Spain
30-10-19	30A-8	Ports of Call	PP-VJF N5625 N8258C stored 1980 Denver, CO
30-10-20	30A-8	(Ports of Call)	PP-VJG N5623 N8259C b/u Marana, AZ
30-10-21	30A-5	Spantax	N5609 EC-BTE stored Oct81 Palma, Spain
30-10-22	30A-5	Spantax	N5610 EC-BJC stored Oct79 Palma, Spain
30-10-23	30A-5	Spantax	N5611 EC-BJD stored Apr83 Palma, Spain
30-10-24	30A-5	Seagreen Air Tpt	N5612 OB-R-925 N6846 N8357C stored Feb91 Mexico City, Mexico
30-10-25	30A-5	(Spantax)	N5613 OY-ANI N5616 OD-AFH N6845 EC-BZR w/o 03Dec72 Tenerife, Canary Is
30-10-26	30A-5	(Ports of Call)	N5614 OD-AFK N5614 b/u Apr76 Denver, CO
30-10-27	30A-5	(Ports of Call)	N5615 N8356C b/u Marana, AZ
30-10-28	30A-5	(American Airlines)	N5616 dbf 30May63 Newark, NJ
30-10-29	30A-5	NASA	N5617 N713NA N710NA stored 1983 Marana, AZ
30-10-30	30A-5	Museo del Aire	N5618 OD-AFG N6843 EC-BZO preserved Jan88 Madrid-Cuatro Vientos, Spain
30-10-31	30A-5	(Lebanese Intl)	N5619 OD-AEW dest by commandos 28Dec68 Beirut, Lebanon
30-10-32	30A-5	(Spantax)	N5620 EC-BNM w/o 05Jan70 Stockholm-Arlanda, Sweden
30-10-33	30A-5	(Ports of Call)	N5601 OD-AFJ N5601 b/u Mar81 Opa Locka, FL
30-10-34	30A-5	Spantax	N5602 SE-DDK N5606 EC-BQQ stored Jun81 Palma, Spain
30-10-35	30A-5	Spantax	N5603 OD-AFI N2920 EC-BXI stored Jun81 Palma, Spain
30-10-36	30A-5	Spantax	N5604 OY-ANL N5612 EC-BQA stored Palma, Spain
30-10-37	30A-5	(NASA)	PK-GJC N7878 N712NA dbf 17Jul85 March AFB, CA
30-10-38	30A-5		re-allocated as c/n 30-10-12(2)

Production complete

DASSAULT MERCURE

C/n	Series	Last known Operator/Owner	Previous Identities/fate (where known)
01	100	(Avions M Dassault)	F-WTCC prototype; ff 28May71 wfu 1980 and b/u
02	100	(Avions M Dassault)	F-WTMD F-BTMD became c/n 11
1	100	Air Inter	F-WTTA F-BTTA wfs 29Apr95 and stored
2	100	Hermeskeil Museum	F-BTTB preserved Jun95 Speyer, Germany
3	100		F-BTTC wfs 29Apr95 and stored Paris-Orly, France
4	100	Air Inter	F-BTTD wfs 29Apr95
5	100	Air Inter	F-BTTE wfs 29Apr95 and stored Montpellier, France
6	100	Air Inter	F-BTTF wfs 29Apr95
7	100	Air Inter	F-BTTG wfs 29Apr95 and stored Morlaix, France
8	100	Air Inter	F-BTTH wfs 29Apr95 and stored Marseille, France
9	100	Air Inter	F-BTTI wfs 29Apr95
10	100	Air Inter	F-BTTJ wfs 29Apr95
11	100	Air Inter	F-WTMD F-BTMD (F-BTTX) F-WTMD F-BTMD cvtd fm c/n 02 wfs 29Apr95

Production complete

DE HAVILLAND DH.106 COMET

C/n	Series	Last known Operator/Owner	Previous Identities/fate (where known)
06001	1	(Ministry of Supply)	G-5-1 prototype; ff 27Jul49 G-ALVG b/u Jul53 RAE Farnborough, UK
06002	1	(Ministry of Supply)	G-5-2 G-ALZK b/u Jul57 Hatfield, UK
06003	1	(BOAC)	G-ALYP w/o 10Jan54 nr Elba, Italy
06004	1	(BOAC)	G-ALYR w/o 25Jul53 Calcutta, India
06005	1	(Royal A/C Est)	G-ALYS b/u 1955 RAE Farnborough, UK
06006	2X	(Royal Air Force)	G-ALYT 7610M b/u Sep67 RAF Halton, UK
06007	1	(Royal A/C Est)	G-ALYU b/u 1963 Stansted, UK; fuselage to Pengham Moors, UK
06008	1	(BOAC)	G-ALYV w/o 02May53 Calcutta, India
06009	1	(BOAC)	G-ALYW b/u Jun55 (fuselage stored RAF Abingdon, UK, as Nimrod mock-up)
06010	1	(Ministry of Supply)	G-ALYX b/u Jun55 RAE Farnborough, UK (nose section to Lasham, UK)
06011	1	(BOAC)	G-ALYY w/o 08Apr54 N of Stromboli, Italy
06012	1	(BOAC)	G-ALYZ w/o 26Oct52 Rome-Ciampino, Italy
06013	1A	(Royal A/C Est)	CF-CUM G-ANAV b/u 1955 RAE Farnborough, UK (nose section to Science Museum, UK)
06014	1A	(Canadian Pacific)	G-ALZB CF-CUN w/o 03Mar53 Karachi, Pakistan
06015	1A	(UAT)	F-BGSA b/u 1961 Paris-Le Bourget, France
06016	1A	(UAT)	F-BGSB b/u 1961 Paris-Le Bourget, France
06017	1XB	(RCAF)	5301 b/u Oct64 (nose section to Rockcliffe Air Museum, Canada)
06018	1XB	(RC Rose)	RCAF 5302 CF-SVR N373S b/u 1975 Miami, FL
06019	1A	(UAT)	F-BGSC w/o 25Jun53 Dakar, Senegal
06020	1A	(Mosquito A/C Museum)	F-BGNX G-AOJT b/u Oct56 RAE Farnborough, UK (fuselage to London Colney, UK)
06021	1XB	(A&AEE)	F-BGNY G-AOJU XM829 dbf 1970 Stansted, UK
06022	1XB	Cosford Aerospace	F-BGNZ G-5-23 G-APAS XM823 8351M preserved RAF Museum, Cosford, UK
06023	2R	(Strathallan A/C Colln)	G-AMXA XK655 b/u Jul90 Strathallan, UK
06024	C.2	(Royal Air Force)	G-AMXB XK669 b/u Apr67
06025	2R	(Royal Air Force)	G-AMXC XK659 b/u Manchester, UK
06026	2E	(Royal A/C Est)	G-AMXD XN453 b/u
06027	2R	(Royal Air Force)	G-AMXE XK663 dbf 13Sep57 RAF Wyton, UK
06028	C.2	(Royal Air Force)	G-AMXF XK670 7926M dbf 1968 RAF Lyneham, UK
06029	C.2	(Royal Air Force)	G-AMXG XK671 7927M b/u RAF Topcliffe, UK
06030	2R	Imperial War Museum	G-AMXH XK695 preserved Duxford, UK
06031	C.2	(Royal Air Force)	G-AMXI XK696 b/u Nov69
06032	C.2R	(Royal Air Force)	G-AMXJ XK697 b/u Dec87 RAF Wyton, UK
06033	2E	(Royal A/C Est)	G-AMXK XV144 b/u Aug75 RAE Farnborough, UK
06034	C.2	(Royal Air Force)	G-AMXL XK698 8031M b/u Apr73 RAF St Athan, UK
06035	C.2	Royal Air Force	XK699 7971M preserved on gate RAF Lyneham, UK
06036		Ministry of Aviation	used for water tank tests
06037	C.2	(Royal Air Force)	XK715 7905M b/u W Bromwich, UK
06038 to 06044	2	not completed	
06045	C.2	(Royal Air Force)	XK716 7958M b/u 1973 RAF Halton, UK
06046 to 06070	2	not completed	
06100	3B	Royal A/C Est	G-ANLO XP915 used as Nimrod test-rig
06101	3	(De Havilland)	fuselage and wings only b/u 1966 Hatfield, UK
06102 to 06110	3	not completed	
6401	4	(Dan-Air Services)	G-APDA 9M-AOA 9V-BAS G-APDA b/u Sep72 Lasham, UK
6402	4	De Havilland	used for Nimrod testsstored Woodford, UK
6403	4	E Anglian Avn Society	G-APDB 9M-AOB G-APDB preserved Duxford, UK
6404	4	(Dan-Air Services)	G-APDC 9M-AOC 9V-BAT G-APDC b/u Apr75 Lasham, UK
6405	4	(Dan-Air Services)	G-APDD 9M-AOD G-APDD 5Y-AMT G-APDD b/u Mar73 Lasham, UK
6406	4	(Dan-Air Services)	G-APDE 9M-AOE 9V-BAU G-APDE 5Y-ALF G-APDE b/u Apr73 Lasham, UK
6407	4	Royal A/C Est	G-APDF XV814
6408	4	(Dan-Air Services)	(G-APDG) LV-PLM LV-AHN b/u Mar73 Lasham, UK
6409	4	(BOAC)	G-APDH w/o 22Mar64 Singapore
6410	4	(Aerolineas Argentinas)	(G-APDI) LV-PLO LV-AHO w/o 20Feb60 Buenos Aires-Ezeiza, Argentina
6411	4	(Aerolineas Argentinas)	(G-APDJ) LV-PLP LV-AHP w/o 27Aug59 nr Asuncion, Paraguay
6412	4	(Dan-Air Services)	G-APDK 5Y-ALD G-APDK b/u Sep80 Lasham, UK
6413	4	(Dan-Air Services)	G-APDL 5Y-ADD G-APDL w/o 07Oct70 Newcastle, UK
6414	4	Catering Training Unit	G-APDM OD-AEV G-APDM 9V-BBJ G-APDM ground trainer London-Gatwick, UK
6415	4	(Dan-Air Services)	G-APDN w/o 03Jul70 nr Barcelona, Spain
6416	4	(Dan-Air Services)	G-APDO b/u Jun74 Lasham, UK
6417	4	Royal A/C Est	G-APDP 9V-BBH G-APDP XX944 stored Apr75 RAE Farnborough, UK
6418	4	(British Airports Auth)	G-APDR XA-NAZ XA-NAP G-APDR b/u Stansted, UK
6419	4	A&AEE	G-APDS XW626 stored as Nimrod AEW.3 testbed RAE Bedford, UK
6420	4	(British Airports Auth)	G-APDT XA-POW XA-NAB G-APDT used for fire-training London-Heathrow, UK; b/u Aug90
6421	4B	(BEA)	G-APMA b/u Jul72 London-Heathrow, UK
6422	4B	Gatwick Handling	G-APMB crew-trainer London-Gatwick, UK
6423	4B	(Dan-Air Services)	G-APMC b/u Apr75 Lasham, UK

DE HAVILLAND DH.106 COMET

C/n	Series	Last known Operator/Owner	Previous Identities/fate (where known)
6424	4C	Redmond Air	(G-APMD) G-AOVU XA-NAR N888WA stored Jan80 Everett-Paine Field, WA
6425	4C	Redmond Air	(G-APME) G-AOVV XA-NAS N999WA derelict Sep89 Chicago-O'Hare, IL
6426	4B	(Dan-Air Services)	G-APMF b/u Feb76 Lasham, UK
6427	4	(Dan-Air Services)	G-APDG 9K-ACI G-APDG b/u Jun74 Lasham, UK
6428	4	(Commercial Aviation Co)	G-APDI HC-ALT b/u Feb78 Miami, FL
6429	4	(Dan-Air Services)	G-APDJ b/u Jun74 Lasham, UK
6430	4	(Aerolineas Argentinas)	LV-POY LV-AHR w/o 23Nov61 Sao Paulo, Brazil
6431	4	(Dan-Air Services)	VP-KPJ 5X-AAO b/u Feb73 Lasham, UK
6432	4	(Dan-Air Services)	LV-POZ LV-AHS G-AZLW b/u Jan73 Lasham, UK
6433	4	(Dan-Air Services)	VP-KPK 5H-AAF b/u Feb73 Lasham, UK
6434	4	(Dan-Air Services)	LV-PPA LV-AHU G-AZIY b/u Mar77 Lasham, UK
6435	4B	(Dan-Air Services)	G-APMD b/u 1978 Lasham, UK
6436	4B	(Dan-Air Services)	G-APME b/u Jun79 Lasham, UK
6437	4B	(Ministry of Defence)	G-APYC SX-DAK G-APYC b/u 1979 RAF Kemble, UK
6438	4B	Science Museum	G-APYD SX-DAL G-APYD preserved Wroughton, UK
6439	4C	(United Arab Airlines)	SU-ALC w/o 02Jan71 nr Tripoli, Libya
6440	4C	(Dan-Air Services)	G-APZM SX-DAN G-APZM b/u Sep80 Lasham, UK
6441	4C	(United Arab Airlines)	SU-ALD w/o 28Jul63 nr Bombay, India
6442	4B	(Dan-Air Services)	G-APMG b/u Apr78 Lasham, UK
6443	4C	Redmond Air	G-ARBB XA-NAT N777WA derelict Mexico City, Mexico
6444	4C	(United Arab Airlines)	SU-ALE w/o 09Feb70 nr Munich, W Germany
6445	4C	(Middle East Airlines)	(OD-ADK) OD-ADR dest by commandos 28Dec68 Beirut, Lebanon
6446	4C	(Middle East Airlines)	(G-ARJH) OD-ADQ dest by commandos 28Dec68 Beirut, Lebanon
6447	4B	(Dan-Air Services)	G-ARDI SX-DAO G-ARDI b/u Jun72 Southend, UK
6448	4C	(Middle East Airlines)	OD-ADS dest by commandos 28Dec68 Beirut, Lebanon
6449	4B	(BEA)	G-ARCO w/o 12Oct67 nr Rhodes, Greece
6450	4C	(Dan-Air Services)	OD-ADT b/u Jun75 Lasham, UK
6451	4B	(Dan-Air Services)	G-ARCP G-BBUV b/u Oct79 Lasham, UK
6452	4B	(Dan-Air Services)	(G-ARJE) G-ARJK b/u Oct77 Lasham, UK
6453	4B	(Dan-Air Services)	(G-AREI) G-ARGM b/u Sep74 Lasham, UK
6454	4C	(Dan-Air Services)	SU-ALL b/u Oct76 Cairo, Egypt
6455	4B	(Dan-Air Services)	(G-ARJF) G-ARJL b/u Sep74 Lasham, UK
6456	4B	(BEA)	(G-ARJG) G-ARJM w/o 21Dec61 Ankara, Turkey
6457	4C	(Dan-Air Services)	(XA-NAD) G-ASDZ ST-AAW G-ASDZ b/u Oct75 Lasham, UK
6458	4C	Lincolnshire Avn	SU-ALM G-BEEX b/u Aug77 Lasham, UK (nose section to E Kirkby, Heritage Centre, UK)
6459	4B	(Dan-Air Services)	(G-ARJH) G-ARJN b/u Nov78 Lasham, UK
6460	4C	(Dan-Air Services)	G-AROV LV-PTS LV-AIB G-AROV b/u Nov78 Lasham, UK
6461	4C	(Saudi Arabian Govt)	SA-R-7 w/o 20Mar63 nr Cuneo, Italy
6462	4C	(Dan-Air Services)	SU-AMV G-BEEY b/u Sep77 Lasham, UK
6463	4C	(Dan-Air Services)	(XA-NAE) ST-AAX G-BDIF b/u Oct80 Lasham, UK
6464	4C	(United Arab Airlines)	SU-AMW w/o 19Jul62 NE of Bangkok, Thailand
6465	4C	(Dan-Air Services)	9K-ACA G-AYWX b/u Oct79 Lasham, UK
6466	4C	(Dan-Air Services)	SU-ANC G-BEEZ b/u Nov77 Lasham, UK
6467	C.4	(D Arnold)	XR395 G-BDIT b/u Jul84 Blackbushe, UK
6468	C.4	(Royal Air Force)	XR396 G-BDIU 8882M b/u Jul81 Bitteswell, UK (nose section to RAF Kinloss, UK)
6469	C.4	(Dan-Air Services)	XR397 G-BDIV b/u Lasham, UK
6470	C.4	Flugausstellung Leo Jr	XR398 G-BDIW preserved Hermeskeil, W Germany
6471	C.4	Royal Museum of Scotland	XR399 G-BDIX preserved E Fortune, UK
6472	4C	(Dan-Air Services)	VP-KRL 5Y-AAA b/u Feb73 Lasham, UK
6473	4C	A&AEE	XS235
6474	4C	(Dan-Air Services)	9K-ACE G-AYVS b/u Apr78 Lasham, UK
6475	4C	(United Arab Airlines)	SU-ANI w/o 14Jan70 Addis Ababa, Ethiopia
6476	4C	Ministry of Defence	G-5-1 XV147 stored 1973 as HS.801 Nimrod Woodford, UK
6477	4C	A&AEE	XV148 cvtd to HS.801 Nimrod

Production complete

DOUGLAS DC-8

C/n	Series	Line No	Last known Operator/Owner	Previous Identities/fate (where known)
45252	51	1	Agro Air International	N8008D prototype; ff 30May58 CF-CPN N8008D XA-DOE N8008D stored 30May89 Marana, AZ as XA-DOE
45253	33	5	(VARIG)	N800PA PP-PEA w/o 04Mar67 Monrovia, Liberia
45254	33	6	(Charlotte Aircraft Corp)	N801PA N8016 b/u Jan88 Laurinburg, NC; cancelled Jul95
45255	33	7	(TRAFE)	N8068D N802PA N8027 LV-LTP dbf 13Dec92 Buenos Aires-Ezeiza, Argentina
45256	33	40	(Grand Investment)	N803PA N8038A 9G-ACG N8038A LN-PIP b/u Oct84 Copenhagen, Denmark; fuselage still present Aug86
45257	33F	44	Zantop International	N804PA N8240U stored Aug85 Macon, GA
45258	33F	46	(PK Finans Intl)	N805PA N8243U b/u Nov85 Miami, FL
45259	32F	58	Transafrik	N806PA N8245U HP-1048 N8245U S9-NAG stored Sep92 Grayson, TX
45260	33F	66	(Zantop International)	N807PA N8209U N711LF N8209U b/u Mar86 Macon, GA
45261	33F	68	(Conner Airlines)	N808PA N8215U b/u Oct85 Miami, FL
45262	33F	70	(Intl Airline Support)	N809PA N8246U b/u Jan86 Miami, FL
45263	33F	77	(Zantop International)	N810PA N8217U b/u Mar85 Macon, GA
45264	33F	86	(Intl Airline Support)	N811PA N8252U b/u Dec85 Miami, FL
45265	33	91	Flagship Express	N812PA OO-TCP N900CL EC-CUS N900CL stored Jun82 Medford, OR
45266	33	100	(Air Zaire)	N813PA 9Q-CLE b/u Apr87 Kinshasa, Zaire
45267	33F	102	Charlotte Aircraft Corp	N814PA N8148A derelict Laurinburg, NC
45268	33	104	Air Zaire	N815PA 9Q-CLF stored Nov74 Kinshasa, Zaire
45269	33F	109	(LA de Sao Tome)	N816PA N8166A b/u May88 Luanda, Angola
45270	33F	112	(Charlotte Aircraft Corp)	N817PA N8170A dbf 11Dec77 Lake City, FL
45271	33F	114	Intercontinental Airways	N818PA PP-PEF N818PA N8184A stored Oct81 Wilmington, OH
45272	33F	118	(Export Air)	N819PA PP-PDS N59AJ HP-1166TCA OB-1456 dbr 28Mar92 Iquitos, Peru
45273	33	121	(Panair do Brasil)	N820PA PP-PDT w/o 20Aug62 Rio de Janeiro-Galeao, Brazil
45274	31	52	Vuelos Especiales Liberianos	N8274H N1800 N4901C (N901CL) N905CL stored Mar83 Waco,TX
45275	31F	64	(Conner Airlines)	N8275H N8207U N578JC b/u Dec83 Miami, FL
45276	31F	72	Flagship Express	N8276H N1801 N4902C (N902CL) N906CL stored Jun82 Medford, OR
45277	31	94	(Capitol International)	N8277H N1802 (N4903C) w/o 28Apr68 Atlantic City, NJ
45278	21	2	(Boeing)	N8018D N8001U stored Jan78 Kingman, AZ, b/u
45279	21	3	(Plymouth Leasing Corp)	N8028D N8002U b/u May83 Detroit-Willow Run, MI
45280	21	4	Project Orbis	N8038D N8003U N220RB stored May94 Beijing, China
45281	21	8	(Boeing)	N8004U stored 04Jan78 Kingman, AZ, b/u
45282	21	10	(Boeing)	N8005U stored 11Jan78 Kingman, AZ, b/u
45283	21	11	(Boeing)	N8006U stored 21Aug78 Kingman, AZ, b/u Apr80
45284	51	12	United Airlines	N8007U stored 26May81 San Francisco, CA
45285	51	13	Faucett	N8008U OB-R-1296 OB-1296 stored Jan89 Lima, Peru
45286	51	15	TPI International Airways	N8009U stored since 1983
45287	51	16	(United Airlines)	N8010U b/u Jul81 San Francisco, CA
45288	51	17	TPI International Airways	N8011U stored since 1981
45289	21F	20	(Allied A/C Sales)	N8012U N579JC b/u Marana, AZ
45290	11	22	(United Airlines)	N8013U w/o 16Dec60 Brooklyn, NY
45291	21	30	(Zantop International)	N8018U b/u Oct79 Detroit-Willow Run, MI
45292	21	43	(Boeing)	N8023U b/u 1980 Kingman, AZ
45293	21	47	(Concord International)	N8024U b/u Nov82 Miami, FL
45294	21	51	Plymouth Leasing Corp	N8025U stored Mar78 Medford, OR
45295	21F	63	(Jet Way)	N8026U b/u Nov83 Detroit-Willow Run, MI
45296	21F	65	(Southern Air Transport)	N8027U XA-LSA N4929U b/u Feb86 Miami, FL
45297	21	67	(Overseas National A/W)	N8028U b/u 1980 Cairo, Egypt
45298	21F	85	(Tropical A/C Leasing)	N8029U HP-826 b/u Aug85 Miami, FL
45299	21F	92	(Air Traffic Service)	N8031U b/u Oct81 Detroit-Willow Run, MI
45300	21	101	(Jamahiriya Air Transport)	N8033U TL-AHI 5A-DGK b/u; front fuselage section on roof at Frankfurt, Germany
45301	52	128	(Evergreen Intl Airlines)	N8034U ZK-NZG N800EV b/u Feb84 Marana, AZ; canx Aug94
45302	52	133	TPI International Airways	N8035U stored since 1983
45303	52	141	Evergreen Intl Airlines	N8036U ZK-NZF N99862 (5B-CAC) N99862 N804EV derelict Sep88 Marana, AZ
45304	21F	125	(Connie Kalitta)	N8037U b/u Aug89 Detroit-Willow Run, MI
45305	21	129	(Plymouth Leasing Corp)	N8038U b/u Dec79 Detroit-Willow Run, MI
45306	21	140	National Airlines	N8039U stored since 1984
45307	12	146	(United Airlines)	N8040U w/o 11Jul61 Denver, CO
45376	33	48	(Overseas National Airways)	PH-DCA OO-AMI PH-DCA N904CL b/u May81 Ft Lauderdale, FL
45377	33F	53	Conner Airlines	PH-DCB YV-C-VIE YV-127C N53CA stored Miami, FL
45378	33	59	(FBA Corp)	PH-DCC PI-C827 RP-C827 N833FA b/u Jun83 Opa Locka, FL
45379	33	75	(Transmeridian Air Cargo)	PH-DCD 5Y-ASA G-BETJ b/u Jul85 Stansted, UK
45380	33	87	(Response Air)	PH-DCE PI-C829 RP-C829 N833DA b/u 1984 Marana, AZ
45381	33	96	(Zantop International)	PH-DCF YV-C-VIF YV-128C N71UA b/u Jul78 Detroit-Willow Run, MI
45382	33	106	(United African Airlines)	PH-DCG OO-CMB N903CL 5A-DGN b/u Oct81 Luxembourg-Findel, Luxembourg
45383	53	120	(KLM)	N9603Z PH-DCH dbf 29Jun68 Amsterdam-Schiphol, Netherlands
45384	33F	50	APISA Air Cargo	OY-KTA HS-TGT N718UA OB-T-1316 OB-1316
45385	33F	55	(Zantop International)	LN-MOA HS-TGS N716UA b/u Jan85 Detroit-Willow Run, MI

DOUGLAS DC-8

C/n	Series	Line No	Last known Operator/Owner	Previous Identities/fate (where known)
45386	33F	62	(Aeronaves del Peru)	SE-DBA HS-TGO N715UA w/o 11Sep80 nr Iquitos, Peru
45387	33F	76	(Aeromar Airlines)	OY-KTB N8258U C-GSWQ HI-413 b/u Mar87 Miami, FL
45388	33F	90	(Aviation Technology & Resources)	LN-MOT N8266U C-GSWX w/o 03Apr86 Abbotsford, Canada
45389	33F	98	(United Air Leasing Corp)	SE-DBB HS-TGR N45914 N713UA b/u Jan85 Detroit-Willow Run, MI
45390	33F	108	(CAM Air Intl)	SE-DBC HS-TGP N717UA b/u Aug84 Miami, FL
45391	21	38	(Barron Thomas Aviation)	N6571C b/u Jul84 Islip, NY
45392	21	45	Pegasus International	N6572C stored Jun81
45393	21	116	(Rosenbalm Aviation)	N6573C b/u Oct76 Detroit-Willow Run, MI
45394	21		not built	(N6574C)
45395	21		not built	(N6575C)
45396	21		not built	(N6576C)
45408	51	14	(FB Ayer)	N801E b/u 29Jul81
45409	51	19	(Delta Air Lines)	N802E w/o 30Mar67 New Orleans, LA
45410	51	21	Midas Air	N803E HI-452 HI-452CA YV-810C YV-505C
45411	51	23	(Barocas A/C Parts)	N804E b/u Sep88 Marana, AZ
45412	51	24	(FBA Corp)	N805E EC-DKH N805E b/u Mar85 Paris-Charles de Gaulle, France; fuselage at Paris-Le Bourget, France
45413	51	25	(Navaero Aviation Corp)	N806E b/u Aug86 Marana, AZ
45414	21		not built	
45415	21		not built	
45416	33F	54	LAC Colombia	HB-IDA D-ADIM HS-TGW N45908 N712UA HI-435 HK-3178X stored Jan92
45417	53	69	(Excelair)	HB-IDB LX-IDB 5A-DGL 5A-DJD N3951B b/u Aug84 Brussels, Belgium
45418	32	78	Japan Air Lines	JA8001 used since Jun74 as crew trainer Tokyo-Haneda, Japan
45419	32F	81	(Agro Air Associates)	JA8002 N420AJ wfu 19Jun91; b/u
45420	53F	93	Faucett	JA8003 JA8008 OB-R-1223 stored Sep90 Lima, Peru
45421	32F	113	(Transafrik)	JA8005 N421AJ 5N-AYZ S9-NAB wfu 28Sep89; b/u Sep89 Johannesburg-Jan Smuts, S Africa
45422	21	34	(American Jet Inds)	N8601 EC-BXR N48CA b/u 1977 Van Nuys, CA
45423	21	36	(Zaire Intl Cargo)	N8602 EC-CAD N8602 b/u 28Mar76 Marana, AZ
45424	21	37	(Conner Airlines)	N8603 EC-CDB N8603 b/u Jan84 Miami, FL
45425	21	41	American Jet Industries	N8604 derelict May87 Mojave, CA
45426	21	49	(American Jet Industries)	N8605 EC-BZQ N8605 b/u Oct78 Smyrna, TN
45427	21	56	(Eastern Air Lines)	N8606 EC-CAM N8606 b/u 1978 Marana, AZ
45428	21	61	(Eastern Air Lines)	N8607 w/o 25Feb64 Lake Pontchartrain, New Orleans, LA
45429	21	82	(Omega Air)	N8608 EC-CDA N8608 A6-SHA TC-JBV b/u Dec84 Maastricht-Beek, Netherlands
45430	21	99	(American Jet Industries)	N8609 b/u 1977 Van Nuys, CA
45431	21	103	(Trans Union Leasing Corp)	N8610 b/u Mar78 Miami, FL
45432	21	105	(Aeronaves de Mexico)	N8611 XA-XAX w/o 19Jan61 New York-Idlewild, NY
45433	21F	110	Aircraft Support Group	N8612 N821F S9-NAN N821F stored Jul92 Grayson, TX still marked as S9-NAN
45434	21	148	(Overseas Natl Airways)	N8613 used as restaurant Newmarket, OH
45435	33F	149	Aircraft Support Group	N8614 N820F TI-VEL S9-NAS N1976P stored Jul92 Grayson, TX still marked as S9-NAS
45436	21	150	(American Jet Industries)	N8615 b/u Aug81 Miami, FL
45437	21F	152	(Intl Airline Support Grp)	N8617 N819F b/u Jan86 Miami, FL
45438	21		not built	(N8618)
45439	21		not built	(N8619)
45442	43	9	(Aeronaves del Peru)	N6577C CF-TJA 6Y-JME OB-R-1205 b/u Jan86 Lima, Peru
45443	43	18	(Transvalair)	N6578C CF-TJB b/u Dec77 Sion, Switzerland
45444	43	31	(International Air Leases)	CF-TJC N72488 b/u Mar81 Miami, FL
45445	43	42	(FB Ayer)	CF-TJD 4R-ACT TF-ECV N9047F b/u Mar81 Opa Locka, FL
45526	33	89	(Thai A/W Intl)	HB-IDC D-ADIR HS-TGU w/o 10May73 Kathmandu, Nepal
45565	43	111	(FAA)	CF-TJE dest under test Jun78
45566	43	117	(Cargolux)	CF-TJF b/u Oct77 Luxembourg-Findel, Luxembourg
45567	33	71	(Trabajos Aereos y Enlaces)	N9601Z F-BJLA EC-CDC b/u Palma, Spain
45568	53	83	Zurich Airport Authority	F-BJLB EC-CMT F-BJLB TU-TCP used since Sep85 for training Zurich, Switzerland
45569	33	80	(Trabajos Aereos y Enlaces)	F-BIUY TU-TCE F-BIUY EC-CCN b/u Jul84 Palma, Spain
45570	53	134	L'Armee de l'Air	F-BIUZ 45570/F-ZARK 45570/F-RAFE
45571			not built	
45572			not built	
45588	21	26	(Boeing)	N8014U stored Jan78 Kingman, AZ, b/u
45589	21	27	Gulfstream American	N8015U derelict Sep88 Mojave, CA
45590	21	28	(Boeing)	N8016U stored Jan78 Kingman, AZ, b/u
45591	21F	29	(Tropical A/C Leasing)	N8017U b/u 1983 Miami, FL
45592	21	32	(Boeing)	N8019U stored Jan78 Kingman, AZ, b/u
45593	21	33	(Plymouth Leasing Corp)	N8020U b/u 1981 Medford, OR
45594	21F	35	(General Air Services)	N8021U N580JC stored Jan82 Miami, FL, b/u
45595	21F	39	(Jet Traders Investment)	N8022U b/u 1984 Ft Lauderdale, FL
45596	21F	88	(Zantop International)	N8030U b/u Jul79 Detroit-Willow Run, MI
45597	21F	97	(United Air Carriers)	N8032U b/u Feb79 Cairo, Egypt
45598	43F	57	(Aeronaves del Peru)	I-DIWA N64799 OB-R-1143 w/o 01Aug80 nr Mexico City, Mexico
45599	43	73	(IAS Cargo Airlines)	I-DIWE 9J-ABR b/u Aug76 Luton, UK
45600	43F	79	(Aeronaves del Peru)	I-DIWI N64804 N8418 OB-R-1214 b/u Dec88 Lima, Peru
45601	43	107	(ARCA Colombia)	I-DIWO N453FA b/u Tulsa, OK

DOUGLAS DC-8

C/n	Series	Line No	Last known Operator/Owner	Previous Identities/fate (where known)
45602	32	60	Overseas National A/W	N801US N7181C OH-SOB N1776R derelict Mar81 Jeddah, Saudi Arabia
45603	32F	74	(Interamericana de Avn)	N802US N7182C N995WL YV-392C b/u Jan90 Caracas, Venezuela
45604	53	84	(FBA Corp)	N803US F-BLLC TU-TBX F-BLLC 4R-ACQ N53KM b/u Oct84 Miami, FL
45605	32	95	(Overseas National A/W)	N804US N7183C b/u 01Dec75
45606	32F	115	Andes Airlines	N805US N7184C OH-SOA N831F HC-BEI stored 01Jun85 Guayaquil, Ecuador
45607	53	154	African Air Charter	N9607Z PI-C801 PH-DCR PI-C804 RP-C804 9Q-CQM stored Aug88
45608	53	155	(Navaero Aviation Corp)	N9608Z PH-DCP PI-C801 RP-C801 b/u Apr87 Manila, Philippines
45609	43	119	(International Air Leases)	CF-TJG N70051 N8434B N70051 b/u
45610	54F	122	Transair Cargo Zaire	CF-TJH N10DC N4561B N803CK 9Q-CLV
45611	43	127	(Cubana)	CF-TJI CU-T1201 w/o 07Oct76 in sea nr Barbados
45612	43	135	Capitol Intl Airlines	CF-TJJ CU-T1210 C-FTJJ OB-R-1142 6Y-JMF C-FTJJ N8021V stored 1981 Smyrna, TN
45613	53	123	(Aeronaves del Peru)	PH-DCI YV-131C b/u 1985 Opa Locka, FL
45614	53	126	International Air Leases	N9605Z PH-DCK YV-132C stored Mar84 Miami, FL
45615	53	131	(KLM)	PH-DCL w/o 30May61 en route Lisbon-Azores
45616	53	147	(International Air Leases)	PH-DCM YV-C-VIG YV-129C b/u May85 Opa Locka, FL
45617	52	136	(Aviaco)	EC-ARA w/o 06Jul72 off Las Palmas, Canary Is, Spain
45618	52	138	(Onyx Aviation)	EC-ARB N60AJ C-GNDE (N892AF) N4489M used for spares 1992 Miami, FL; cancelled May95
45619	52	142	(Intl Airline Support Grp)	EC-ARC OB-R-931 EC-ARC N57AJ C-GNDF N3751X N893AF C-GNDF N893AF b/u 15Jul90 Miami, FL
45620	43	124	(ARCA Colombia)	CF-CPF C-FCPF stored Nov81 Miami, FL and b/u
45621	43	132	(Miami Aviation Corp)	CF-CPH C-FCPH b/u Jan83 Opa Locka, FL
45622	43	137	Opa Locka Fire Dept	CF-CPI C-FCPI
45623	43	130	(Concord Intl Airlines)	N9604Z CF-CPG C-FCPG b/u May81 Opa Locka, FL
45624	43	139	ARCA Colombia	I-DIWU N353FA used for spares
45625	43	144	(Alitalia)	I-DIWB w/o 05May72 Mt Lunga, Palermo, Italy
45626	33F	143	(Canus Investments)	JA8006 N124AJ b/u Aug85 Miami, FL
45627	33	145	Air Afrique	F-BJUV TU-TCD stored Oct79 Dakar, Senegal
45628	51	151	(AirXport)	(N806US) N8780R SE-DCR N8780R OH-KDM b/u May86 Brussels, Belgium
45629	53	158	Aviation Facilities	(N807US) PH-DCN OB-R-962 PH-DCN OB-R-1116 (5Y-QSR) 5Y-BAS S7-SIA 9Q-CBF stored Dec85 Brussels, Belgium
45630	43	159	(Alitalia)	(N808US) I-DIWF w/o 02Aug68 nr Milan-Malpensa, Italy
45631	43	160	(Alitalia)	(N809US) I-DIWD w/o 07Jul62 Bombay, India
45632	53	164	ARCA Colombia	(N810US) PH-DCO PK-GEC PH-DCO N121GA HK-3746X N121GA HK-3746X
45633	51	162	(Aeronaves de Mexico)	XA-NUS w/o 24Dec66 Lake Texcoco, Mexico
45634	51	161	(Braniff Airways)	N774C N811BN b/u Jan83 Miami, FL
45635	51F	163	ARCA Colombia	N875C N812BN HK-2587X stored Sep88 Miami, FL
45636	43	153	ARCA Colombia	I-DIWP HK-1854 stored Bogota, Colombia
45637	54F	157	Fine Air	I-DIWR N53AF N54FA wfs May95 Miami, FL
45638	43	156	(Cubana)	CF-TJK CU-T1200 dbr 18Mar78 nr Havana, Cuba; scrapped 1978
45639			not built	
45640	54F	175	Zuliana de Aviacion	N9609Z CF-TJL C-FTJL LX-GCV TF-GCV HI-459 HC-BLM HC-BMC YV-460C stored Jan96 Miami, FL
45641	51	165	Aeromexico	N276C XA-DOD stored 15Aug87 Mexico City, Mexico
45642	51	172	(Sonico Inc)	N877C N813BN b/u Dec82
45643	51	173	(Capitol Air)	N278C 6Y-JGF OB-R-1125 N921CL used since Jul83 for fire practice Smyrna, TN
45644	51	174	(Sonico Inc)	N779C N814BN b/u
45645	51	166	(Maldives Intl Airways)	N807E RP-C840 b/u Jun84 Manila, Philippines
45646	51	167	(Mark A Cohen)	N808E RP-C837 N808E b/u Mexico City, Mexico
45647	53	168	(Airborne Express)	JA8007 N903R b/u Apr86 Wilmington, OH; cancelled Jul94
45648	51	169	Capitol Air	N8781R SE-DCT N8781R 6Y-JGE OB-R-1124 6Y-JGE N918CL stored Jul84 Smyrna, TN
45649	51	170	American Intl Airways	N809E 8Q-CA003 8Q-PNB N805CK
45650	51	177	(FB Ayer)	N810E b/u Sep76 Tulsa, OK
45651	54F	198	Andes Airlines	JA8010 HK-2667 HC-BPV
45652	51	176	(Aeronaves de Mexico)	XA-PEI w/o 13Aug66 nr Acapulco, Mexico
45653	54F	178	(Air Canada)	N9612Z CF-TJM w/o 19May67 nr Ottawa, Canada
45654	54F	179	(Trans Canada Airlines)	CF-TJN w/o 29Nov63 St Therese de Blainville, Canada
45655	54F	180	(Royal Canadian Mounted Police)	CF-TJO C-FTJO used for training Montreal-Dorval, Canada; b/u 29Nov93
45656	53	191	(Swissair)	HB-IDD dest by terrorists 13Sep70 Dawson Field, Jordan
45657	52	188	(Aviaco)	EC-AUM used as bar Candas, Spain
45658	52	181	Jetstar	EC-ATP Spanish AF T.15-2/401-07 N7034E C-FHAB VR-BIA stored May95 Lasham, UK
45659	52	171	(Faucett)	EC-ASN 5A-DJP LX-III OB-R-1259 b/u Feb91 Lima, Peru
45660	43	184	Summit Philippines	I-DIWG N253FA HP-807 N253FA RP-C349 stored Oct83 Manila, Philippines
45661	43	183	ARCA Colombia	CF-CPJ C-FCPJ stored 09Dec81 Miami, FL
45662	53	186	G & B Aviation	JA8009 F-GDPM N245HG stored Oct89 Opa Locka, FL
45663	54F	189	Agro Air International	N108RD YV-445C stored Dec93 Caracas, Venezuela
45664	53	206	(Minerve)	JA8011 F-BYFM used for spares Jul88 Nimes, France

DOUGLAS DC-8

C/n	Series	Line No	Last known Operator/Owner	Previous Identities/fate (where known)
45665	43	194	(ARCA Colombia)	I-DIWS HK-1855X b/u Jun89 Miami, FL
45666	43	202	(ARCA Colombia)	I-DIWT N53FA b/u
45667	54F	185	Fine Air	N8782R (D-ACCA) G-BDHA HI-426 HI-426CT HI-426CA N426FB
45668	54F	187	Tptes Aereos Bolivianos	N4904C N8740 N4904C EC-CQM HC-BLU N355Q N356WS CP-2217
45669	54F	182	Fine Air	N8008F TU-TCG N1041W N141RD N57FB
45670	53	190	(Minerve)	TU-TCA used for spares Nimes-Garons, France, b/u Apr85
45671	53	196	(Air Afrique)	TU-TCB F-BJCB TU-TCB b/u Nov85 Luxembourg-Findel, Luxembourg; fuselage used as restaurant Purmerend, Netherlands
45672	51	192	Batch Air	N811E TI-LRP N3128H stored Marana, AZ
45673	51	193	(FB Ayer)	N812E b/u 07Apr76
45674	54F	201	(Arrow Air)	N109RD b/u Aug84 Miami, FL
45675	54F	200	Zantop International Airlines	N8041U (N41UA) N8041U
45676	54F	197	Zantop International Airlines	N8042U N42UA N8042U
45677	54F	199	(Millon Air)	N8043U N43UA w/o 28Apr95 Guatemala City, Guatemala; cancelled Sep95
45678	55F	218	Fine Air	JA8014 HP-950 N55FB
45679	54F	203	American International Airways	CF-TJP C-FTJP N4768G N802CK
45680	53	213	(Japan Air Lines)	JA8012 w/o 14Jun72 New Delhi-Palam, India
45681	53	214	(Japan Air Lines)	JA8013 dbr 29Mar72 Bombay-Juha, India
45682	54F	220	(Aeral)	I-DIWL N153AF I-ALEC b/u Apr85 Rome-Fiumicino, Italy
45683	55F	208	Liberia World Airways	PH-DCS RP-C843 9Q-CKI EL-AJO
45684	54F	195	Fine Air	N8783R (D-ACCB) G-BDDE HI-427 YV-447C N427FB
45685	51F	204	Aero Transportes Colombiana	XA-PIK C-FFRZ HI-588CT HI-588CA HK-3816X
45686	54F	210	Zuliana de Aviacion	CF-TJQ C-FTJQ N4769F 9Q-CDM 9Q-CSJ EL-AJQ YV-499C
45687	51	211	Agro Air International	N814E XA-AMP N814E stored Marana, AZ as XA-AMP
45688	51	205	(Intercontinental A/L)	N813E RP-C830 5N-AVY b/u Aug84 Stansted, UK
45689	51F	212	American International Airways	N815E 8Q-CA005 N804CK
45690	51	219	(DMI of Tucson)	N816E RP-C831 b/u Mar86 Marana, AZ
45691	55F	209	(National Airlines)	PH-DCT N29953 b/u 1984
45692	55F	207	MK Air Cargo	N801SW 45692/F-RAFB 5V-TAF 9G-MKC
45693	52	221	(Beek Airport Authorities)	N8060U TC-JBZ b/u May85 Maastricht-Beek, Netherlands
45694	52	224	(Omega Air)	N8061U TC-JBY b/u Dec84 Maastricht-Beek, Netherlands
45750	52	217	(Evergreen International)	N9683Z ZK-NZA PH-ADA ZK-NZA N801EV b/u Marana, AZ
45751	52	231	(Air New Zealand)	ZK-NZB w/o 04Jul66 Auckland, New Zealand
45752	52	233	FB Air	ZK-NZC N42920 C-FCRN N42920 OB-1421 N42920 stored Dec94 Opa Locka, FL
45753	55F	223	MK Airlines	SE-DBD N721UA EC-DIH N721UA N916R TF-FLB 5N-AWE 5N-OCM 5N-MKE 9G-MKE
45754	55F	225	(AECA)	N3325T F-BOLI N29922 HC-BKN w/o 18Sep84 Quito, Ecuador
45755	43	222	Summit Philippines	I-DIWM N153FA RP-C348 stored Dec83 Manila, Philippines
45756	52	230	(Intercontinental A/L)	N8065U 5N-AVS b/u Stansted, UK
45757	52	226	(Faucett)	N8062U OB-R-1270 b/u Nov85 Lima, Peru
45758	52	227	(Intercontinental A/L)	N8063U 5N-AVR b/u May88 Stansted, UK
45759	52	228	(Faucett)	N8064U OB-R-1287 OB-1287 b/u Aug94 Lima, Peru
45760	51	216	Charlotte Aerospace	N8779R 6Y-JGD OB-R-1123 6Y-JGD OB-R-1181 6Y-JGD stored Jun81 Laurinburg, NC
45761	43	237	(Canadian Pacific)	CF-CPK w/o 04Mar66 Tokyo-Haneda, Japan
45762	55F	232	American International Airways	PI-C802 PH-DCW N4809E C-FCWW N6161M
45763	55F	241	Aeronaves del Peru	JA8015 N100JJ OB-T-1244 OB-1244 stored Sep92 Opa Locka, FL
45764	55F	251	TMC Airlines	JA8016 N907R ST-AJD N907R N812TC stored Apr94 Macon, GA
45765	55F	265	LAC Colombia	N2310B PK-GJD PH-DCY PK-GJD PK-GEA N225VV HI-573CA N573FB HK-3753X dam 15Oct92 Medellin, Colombia, stored Jul93
45766	55	272	Omega Air	(PK-GJC) PH-DCV PK-GJN PK-GEB N226VV b/u 15Aug87
45767	55F	250	American International Airways	LN-MOH N722UA N902R N807CK
45768	54F	240	LAC Colombia	YV-C-VID OB-R-1083 N5768X G-BTAC HK-2632X
45769	54F	215	(Trans Caribbean Airways)	N8784R dbf 24Oct65 Miami, FL; remains to Charlotte A/C Corp
45800	54F	234	Fine Air	N8044U N44UA
45801	54F	235	Emery Worldwide Airlines	N8045U N45UA N991CF
45802	54F	247	African International Airways	N8046U N46UA 3D-AFR
45803	55F	229	American International Airways	N8785R TL-AAK N6842 F-BOLK N29549 N809CK
45804	55F	254	MK Airlines	OY-KTC PH-DCZ HP-927 N855BC C-GMXP CX-BLN N855BC 9G-MKA
45805	55F	244	Affretair	N4905C TR-LVK Z-WSB Badly damaged 28Jan96 Harare; possible insurance w/o
45806	51	245	(DMI of Tucson)	N819E HP-768 RP-C832 b/u Mar86 Marana, AZ
45807	51	239	(Connie Kalitta)	N817E RP-C345 N817E wfs and used for spares Detroit-Willow Run, MI
45808	51	243	(Connie Kalitta)	N818E 8Q-CA004 8Q-PNC N806CK b/u Jun90 Detroit-Willow Run, MI
45809	53F	264	ARCA Colombia	CF-CPM C-FCPM HK-3125X stored Jan96 Miami, FL
45810	71F	252	Fast Air Carrier	N8070U CC-CYQ
45811	71F	262	Burlington Air Express	N8071U N821BX
45812	71F	277	Emery Worldwide Airlines	N8072U EI-TLD N500MH
45813	71F	284	Burlington Air Express	N8073U N822BX

DOUGLAS DC-8

C/n	Series	Line No	Last known Operator/Owner	Previous Identities/fate (where known)
45814	52	258	American International Airways	EC-BAV N45814 EC-BAV Spain T.15-1/401-01 Spain T15-1/401-30 N810CK stored Nov89 Opa Locka, FL
45815	51	249	(Navaero Aviation Corp)	N820E b/u 01Aug86 Marana, AZ
45816	55F	236	American International Airways	N804SW YV-C-VIM N804SW G-BIAS N804SW N801CK
45817	55F	248	American International Airways	N805SW N805U HB-IDU N9110V N911R TF-AED HP-1088 5N-ATS N808CK
45818	55F	242	(Garuda Indonesia)	N802SW TF-LLK N802SW PH-MBH w/o 04Dec74 nr Colombo, Sri Lanka
45819	55F	238	L'Armee de l'Air	F-BNLD TU-TXG F-BNLD 45819/F-RAFC TU-TXK F-BNLD 45819/F-RAFC
45820	55F	246	MK Airlines	F-BLKX 45820/F-RAFA (C-GRWW) C-FIWW 9G-MKF
45821	55F	255	Affretair	N803SW TR-LQR A40-PA TR-LQR VP-WMJ Z-WMJ
45822	62	270	(Scandinavian A/L System)	N1501U LN-MOO w/o 13Jan69 Santa Monica Bay, nr Los Angeles, CA
45823	62	279	(Scandinavian A/L System)	N1502U SE-DBE dbf 19Apr70 Rome-Fiumicino, Italy
45824	55F	267	G & B Aviation	N851F PH-MAS N5824A PH-MAS EC-DBE N5824A stored May95 Miami, FL
45848	61	285	Airborne Express	N8778 JA8050 N844AX
45849	71F	289	TAMPA Colombia	N8074U HK-3786X
45850	52	257	Los Angeles Museum of Science & Industry	N8066U preserved Los Angeles Coliseum, CA
45851	52	260	Faucett	N8067U OB-R-1267 OB-1267 stored Dec93 Lima, Peru
45852	52	263	Faucett	N8068U OB-R-1269 derelict Feb91 Lima, Peru
45853	52	266	Faucett	N8069U OB-R-1268 OB-1268 derelict Feb91 Lima, Peru
45854	55	278	African International Airways	JA8017 N910R 5N-AUS N81906 C-FFDK N81906 OO-PHA N819SL 3D-AIA wfs 28Feb95 Luxembourg-Findel, Luxembourg
45855	51F	281	Agro Air Associates	XA-SIB (C-FFQI) N507DC stored Jan96 Miami, FL
45856	55F	269	American International Airways	N852F PH-MAU EC-DEM C-FDWW N6161C
45857	55F	271	Air Afrique	TU-TCC stored Sep83
45858	55F	274	Liberia World Airways	N1509U CF-CPT N789FT CF-CPT G-BSKY HC-BJT 3D-ADV 5N-ATY
45859	55F	253	(Arax Airlines)	PH-DCU N29954 5N-ARH w/o 31Mar88 Cairo, Egypt
45860	54F	256	(MK Air Cargo)	CF-TJR C-FTJR N4769G C-GQBG N8888B HC-BQH 9G-MKB w/o 15Feb92 Kano, Nigeria
45861	54F	261	Aeronaves del Peru	CF-TJS C-FTJS N47691 YV-128C OB-R-1300 OB-1300
45862	55F	259	Ibero Americana de Carga	N4906C (F-BOLN) F-BUOR 9Q-CVH HK-3984X
45877	51	273	(Intl Aircraft Enterprises)	N821E b/u Marana, AZ
45878	51	280	Zuliana de Aviacion	N8954U XA-SIA N810GB YV-461C stored Jan96 Opa Locka, FL
45879	54F	268	(LAC Colombia)	YV-C-VIC OB-R-1084 N5879X G-BFHW HK-2380 w/o 18Sep84 Barranquilla, Colombia
45880	54F	275	(United Airlines)	N8047U w/o 18Dec77 nr Salt Lake City, UT
45881	EC-24A	276	US Navy/Chrysler	N8048U 163050
45882	55F	282	(LAC Colombia)	JA8018 OB-R-1200 N7015Q HR-AMU HK-3979X w/o 02Feb96 Asunion, Colombia
45883	55F	308	TMC Airlines	N806SW (YU-AGB) N806SW TU-TCH N52958 N811TC stored Apr94 Macon, GA
45884	54F	340	Emery Worldwide	N8050U N50UA N992CF
45885	54F	342	Buffalo Airways	N8051U EC-DYA N7046G N925BV
45886	54F	283	African International Airways	N8049U N49UA N8049U 3D-AFX
45887	61	287	American International Airways	N8777 JA8049 N26UA N817CK
45888	61	290	Fine Air	N8776 JA8060 N755UA EC-DYY N30UA semi-derelict May92 Dallas-Love Field, TX
45889	61	291	(Japan Air Lines)	N8775 JA8061 w/o 09Feb82 Tokyo-Haneda, Japan
45890	61F	301	American International Airways	CF-TJT C-FTJT N20UA N812CK
45891	61F	305	Airborne Express	CF-TJU C-FTJU N21UA N849AX
45892	61	306	American International Airways	CF-TJV C-FTJV N22UA N816CK
45893	61F	310	American International Airways	CF-TJW C-FTJW N23UA N813CK
45894	61	297	Airborne Express	N8774 6Y-JGG N915CL N850AX
45895	62F	299	International Air Leases	N1803 EC-288 EC-EQI N1803
45896	62F	303	IAL Aircraft Holding	N1804
45897	71CF	313	United Parcel Service	N8786R EC-CCF EI-BPF N797UP
45898	71CF	320	United Parcel Service	N8787R EC-CCG EI-BPG N8787R N798UP
45899	62	304	Rich International Airways	N1805
45900	71CF	316	United Parcel Service	N8962T N803U N8962T TF-BCV N8962T N861FT N700UP
45901	63F	293	Emery Worldwide Airlines	N1504U PH-DEB N929R
45902	71CF	294	United Parcel Service	N8961T 9V-BEH N8961T (C-FNAA) C-GNDA N810EV N702UP
45903	63F	286	Emery Worldwide Airlines	N1503U PH-DEA N908CL N950R
45904	62CF	309	John Hancock Leasing Corp	N1807 stored Tucson, AZ
45905	62AF	298	Arrow Air	SE-DBF N810BN EC-214 EC-ELM N810BN
45906	62	300	Airborne Express	OY-KTD SE-DDU N762UA N805AX
45907	71F	288	United Parcel Service	N822E N707UP
45908	61	296	Airborne Express	N45090 N912CL N912R N954R EC-EAM N841AX
45909	62F	307	Arrow Air	N1505U I-DIWN N802BN XA-AMT N802BN N802BN
45910	62	311	Trans Continental Airlines	I-DIWV N39307 N803MG N181SK
45911	62F	318	Air Transport International	N1806 N806BN N1806 XA-AMS N1806 N31CX
45912	61F	315	Buffalo Airways	N8771 6Y-JGH N914CL TF-VLW C-GMXD (N848AX) 5N-HAS N914BV

DOUGLAS DC-8

C/n	Series	Line No	Last known Operator/Owner	Previous Identities/fate (where known)
45913	61	325	G & B Aviation	N8770 N869F EC-CZE N814GB stored 03Sep91 Miami, FL
45914	71	292	United Parcel Service	N823E N709UP
45915	71	295	United Parcel Service	N824E N715UP
45916	55	302	(AirXport)	JA8019 N915R b/u May86 Brussels, Belgium
45917	62	332	Airborne Express	F-BNLE N4761G N803AX
45918	62F	353	Air Transport International	F-BOLF N728PL
45919	62	312	(Swissair)	HB-IDE dbf 07Oct79 Athens, Greece
45920	62	319	Buffalo Airways	HB-IDF N923CL C-GMXY N924BV
45921	62AF	322	Cargosur	SE-DBG N756UA N729PL EC-230 EC-EMX
45922	62CF	335	Arrow Air	OY-KTE HS-TGQ R Thai AF 60112 N799AL
45923	63F	383	(Burlington Air Express)	LN-MOU HS-TGX OY-SBK N794AL w/o 15Feb92 Toledo Express A/P, OH; cancelled Mar93
45924	63F	392	Aer Turas	SE-DBH HS-TGZ OY-SBM SE-DBH (N791AL) N353AS EI-CGO
45925	62	333	Cargo Lion	HB-IDG N922CL C-GMXR CX-BQN-F CX-BQN N922BV LX-TLB
45926	63F	323	American International Airways	CF-CPO C-FCPO N781AL
45927	63F	327	Airborne Express	N19B CF-CPP F-BOLJ CF-CPP C-FCPP N783AL N819AX
45928	63	334	Airborne Express	CF-CPQ N625FT CF-CPQ C-FCPQ N780AL N817AX
45929	63F	367	(Air Transport International)	N19B CF-CPS N624FT CF-CPS C-FCPS N782AL w/o 16Feb95 Kansas City, MO
45930	63	378	(Iberia)	EC-BMX dbr 03Mar78 Santiago de Compostela, Spain
45931	63	391	Rich International	EC-BMY N4935C
45932	54F	328	American International Airways	ZK-NZD N806CK(2)
45933	53	384	(Air Canada)	CF-TIH C-FTIH b/u Jul82 Montreal-Dorval, Canada
45934	53	390	(Air Canada)	CF-TII C-FTII b/u Jul82 Montreal-Dorval, Canada
45935	51	330	Fine Air	XA-SID C-FFSB N508DC (N51FB) stored May93 Miami, FL
45936	73CF	344	United Parcel Service	N8631 TF-FLB N8631 N836UP
45937	53	324	(Philippine Airlines)	PI-C803 RP-C803 dbr 18Apr77 Tokyo-Haneda, Japan
45938	71CF	331	United Parcel Service	N8960T N804U N8960T N860FT N701UP
45939	71CF	351	United Parcel Service	N801U N867F N867FT N703UP
45940	61	314	Airborne Express	N8075U N851AX
45941	71F	317	Emery Worldwide Airlines	N8076U PP-SOQ PT-WBK C-FQPM N8076U
45942	61F	349	Fine Air	N8773 JA8058 N27UA stored Feb89 Waco, TX
45943	61	359	Nationair	N8772 JA8059 N4578C C-GMXB stored Nov93 Smyrna, TN
45944	71F	326	United Parcel Service	N825E N744UP
45945	71F	337	Cargosur	N8077U F-GNFM EC-529 EC-FVA
45946	71F	339	Burlington Air Express	N8078U N824BX
45947	71F	341	Emery Worldwide Airlines	N8079U
45948	71CF	321	United Parcel Service	N8955U N862FT N748UP
45949	71CF	329	United Parcel Service	N8956U HS-TGF N8956U N863FT N705UP
45950	71CF	354	United Parcel Service	N802U N868F N868FT N750UP
45951	61CF	414	(Trans International Airlines)	N4863T w/o 08Sep70 New York-Kennedy, NY
45952	71CF	338	United Parcel Service	N8788R HS-TGG N864FT N752UP
45953	62F	348	Digex Aero Cargo	JA8031 N807AX OB-R-1323 OB-1323 N66656 PP-DGX
45954	62	362	Airborne Express	JA8032 TF-BBA 5N-AON N808AX
45955	62F	365	Air Transport International	JA8033 N163CA XA-AMR N163CA N21CX
45956	62AF	376	Emery Worldwide Airlines	JA8034 N162CA N162QS N752UA N814ZA N994CF
45957	62		not built	
45958	62		not built	
45959	62		not built	
45960	62CF	347	Cargo Lion	I-DIWC F-GDJM LX-TLA
45961	62CF	361	America International Airways	N8964U I-DIWQ N3931A C-FHAA N3931A N818CK* stored Jan96 Phoenix, AZ as "N3931"
45962	53	402	(Air Canada)	CF-TIJ dbf 21Jun73 Toronto-Malton, Canada
45963	61F	355	American International Airways	CF-TJX 6Y-JGC CF-TJX C-FTJX N24UA stored Macon, GA
45964	61F	364	Air Transport International	CF-TJY C-FTJY TF-ISB N47UA N861PL
45965	55F	346	MK Airlines	EC-BMV N801FB 5N-ATZ 9G-MKD
45966	73CF	393	United Parcel Service	N8632 N773FT N866UP
45967	73CF	385	United Parcel Service	N4907C N907CL N867UP
45968	73CF	389	United Parcel Service	N4908C (N908CL) HB-IDS N871TV N868UP
45969	63CF	396	Arrow Air	N6161A N661AV
45970	71F	343	Fast Air Carrier	N8080U CC-CAX
45971	71F	356	Burlington Air Express	N8081U SE-DLM N827BX
45972	61	357	(United Airlines)	N8082U w/o 28Dec78 nr Portland, OR
45973	71F	358	United Parcel Service	N8083U EI-TLA N8083U N783UP
45974	71F	368	Emery Worldwide Airlines	N8084U PP-SOO PT-WBL C-FQPL N8084U
45975	71F	369	Emery Worldwide Airlines	N8085U Z-WZL N8085U
45976	71F	372	Fast Air Carrier	N8086U PP-SOP PT-WBM EI-CGY PT-WBM CC-CAR
45977	71F	373	Emery Worldwide Airlines	N8087U N871SJ N8087U
45978	71F	381	Burlington Air Express	N8088U N825BX
45979	73AF	363	United Parcel Service	N826E N779UP
45980	61F	374	Buffalo Airways	CF-TJZ C-FTJZ TF-ISA N48UA N161DB
45981	61F	352	Buffalo Airways	N45191 N911CL F-GDPS C-GMXL N849AX N52845 N915BV
45982	61	345	(Nationair)	N8769 JA8057 N4582N C-GMXQ w/o 11Jul91 Jeddah, Saudi Arabia
45983	71F	350	Emery Worldwide Airlines	N8768 JA8068 N8177U
45984	62CF	370	Peruvian AF	HB-IDH FAP 371/OB-1373

DOUGLAS DC-8

C/n	Series	Line No	Last known Operator/Owner	Previous Identities/fate (where known)
45985	52	336	Lineas Aereas del Caribe	ZK-NZE N4292P C-FNZE N223FB OB-1438 HK-3842X
45986	62F	379	American International Airways	I-DIWJ N3931G N801MG*
45987	62	366	Airborne Express	F-BOLG OH-LFZ N804AX
45988	63CF	416	Arrow Air	EC-BMZ N941JW N441J
45989	63CF	371	Saudia	N779FT LX-ACV EI-BNA
45990	73CF	375	DHL Airways	N780FT TF-CCV N816EV N816UP
45991	73CF	380	Lufthansa Cargo Airlines	N781FT D-ADUI
45992	61AF	360	Aeronaves del Peru	N8767 JA8067 OB-R-1222 OB-1222 HP-1169TLN OB-1222
45993	71F	382	Burlington Air Express	N8089U (EI-TLB) N828BX
45994	71F	387	Burlington Air Express	N8090U EI-BZU SE-DLH EI-BZU N501SR N829BX
45995	71F	388	Emery Worldwide Airlines	N8091U EI-TLC N8091U
45996	71F	397	Fast Air Carrier	N8092U CC-CDS
45997	71F	398	Fast Air Carrier	N8093U CC-CDU
45998	71	399	Burlington Air Express	N8094U N826BX
45999	63F	377	Air Transport International	PH-DEC TF-FLU N820TC N863E N787AL N788AL
46000	63F	386	Emery Worldwide Airlines	PH-DED N904R N964R
46001	73CF	395	United Parcel Service	N863F N799FT HB-IDM N872TV EI-BTG N706FT N404FE N810UP
46002	73CF	394	DHL Airways	N782FT LX-BCV TF-BCV (LX-TAM) LX-BCV N815EV N815UP
46003	73CF	401	Lufthansa Cargo Airlines	N783FT D-ADUA
46004	73AF	403	United Parcel Service	N784FT N804UP
46005	63AF	412	(Flying Tiger Line)	N785FT w/o 27Jul70 Okinawa-Naha, Japan
46006	73AF	413	United Parcel Service	N786FT N806UP
46007	73AF	422	United Parcel Service	N787FT N807UP
46008	73AF	423	United Parcel Service	N788FT N808UP
46009	54F	404	Zantop International Airlines	N8052U ST-AJR N5094Q N8052U
46010	54F	406	(United Airlines)	N8053U w/o 11Jan83 Detroit, MI
46011	54F	408	Fine Air	N8054U EC-DYB N7046H N56FA*
46012	54F	410	African International Airways	N8055U EL-AJK 5N-AWZ 3D-ADV(2)
46013	72CF	427	L'Armee de l'Air	OH-LFR OH-LFT 46013/F-RAFG
46014	71	400	United Parcel Service	N1300L N713UP
46015	61	405	Airborne Express	N8766 N766RD EC-DZC N766RD N842AX
46016	61	409	Airborne Express	N8765 EC-DVC TF-IUF TC-MAB N852AX
46017	61	418	Airborne Express	N8764 N64RD N843AX
46018	71F	420	United Parcel Service	N1301L N718UP
46019	73F	411	United Parcel Service	PH-DEE TF-VLY N819UP
46020	63CF	415	(Loftleidir)	N8633 TF-FLA w/o 15Nov78 Colombo, Sri Lanka
46021	63CF	424	(Seaboard World)	N8634 dbf 16Oct69 Stockton, CA
46022	62AF	417	Evergreen Intl Airlines	JA8036 N771CA N36UA N817EV
46023	62AF	407	Cargosur	JA8035 N731PL EC-217 EC-EMD
46024	62AF	428	Emery Worldwide	JA8037 N753UA N815ZA N995CF
46025			not built	
46026	62	452	(Alitalia)	I-DIWZ w/o 15Sep70 New York-Kennedy, NY, b/u 1972
46027	62F	437	Air Transport International	I-DIWY OB-R-1248 OB-1248 N51CX
46028	62AF	461	Emery Worldwide Airlines	F-BOLH TF-BBD N812ZA N993CF
46029	71F	425	United Parcel Service	N1302L N729UP
46030	71F	426	United Parcel Service	N1303L N730UP
46031	61	435	Airborne Express	JA8038 N28UA N847AX
46032	61	436	Airborne Express	JA8039 EC-DZA N51UA C-GEMV N51UA N848AX
46033	73AF	431	DHL Airlines	CF-TIK C-FTIK N801DH
46034	63AF	434	Burlington Air Express	CF-TIL C-FTIL N868BX
46035	63AF	438	Burlington Air Express	CF-TIM C-FTIM N869BX
46036	63AF	445	Burlington Air Express	CF-TIN C-FTIN N870BX
46037	61	419	Airborne Express	N8763 EC-DVB ZP-CCR N853AX
46038	61	429	Haiti Trans Air	N8762 F-GETM C-FCMV N811GB OB-1407 OB-1452 wfs Apr95 Miami, FL
46039	71F	448	Emery Worldwide Airlines	N8095U N870SJ N801GP
46040	71F	449	Southern Air Transport	N8096U N872SJ
46041	63F	439	Airborne Express	OY-KTF N792AL HK-3490X N792AL N814AX
46042	63	421	Arrow Air	YV-C-VIA YV-125C 8P-PLC TF-FLE N7043U N345JW
46043	72CF	443	L'Armee de l'Air	OH-LFS OH-LFV 46043/F-RAFD
46044	73AF	432	Lufthansa Cargo Airlines	N790FT D-ADUE
46045	73CF	441	Emery Worldwide Airlines	N791FT
46046	73CF	444	Emery Worldwide Airlines	N792FT
46047	73CF	447	Lufthansa Cargo Airlines	N793FT D-ADUO
46048	71F	450	United Parcel Service	N1304L N708UP
46049	63CF	479	Burlington Air Express	N8639 TF-FLC N778FT TF-FLC N867BX
46050	63CF	430	(Overseas National Airways)	N8635 w/o 04Mar77 Niamey, Niger
46051	73CF	440	United Parcel Service	N8636 N836EV N811EV N851UP
46052	73CF	442	United Parcel Service	N8637 YV-C-VIN YV-130C N2919N N31EK N852UP
46053	73CF	446	Gabon Government	N8638 TR-LTZ stored May95 Le Bourget, France
46054	63F	453	Emery Worldwide Airlines	LN-MOY HS-TGY OY-SBL N796AL
46055	71F	492	United Parcel Service	N1306L N755UP
46056	71F	495	United Parcel Service	N1307L N706UP
46057	62	474	(Japan Air Lines)	JA8040 w/o 28Nov72 Moscow-Sheremetyevo, USSR
46058	63PF	433	(Arrow Air)	N8759 F-BOLM N920CL N950JW w/o 12Dec85 Gander, Canada
46059	73CF	456	United Parcel Service	N4864T N703FT (N402FE) N703FT N813UP
46060	63CF	472	(Capitol Intl Airways)	N4909C w/o 27Nov70 Anchorage, AK
46061	63CF	480	Airborne Express	N6162A N952R N826AX

DOUGLAS DC-8

C/n	Series	Line No	Last known Operator/Owner	Previous Identities/fate (where known)
46062	73CF	486	Emery Worldwide Airlines	N6163A TF-FLF N6163A N2674U
46063	73F	457	Southern Air Transport	YV-C-VIB YV-126C N4805J F-GDRM N789AL N875SJ
46064	71F	459	Burlington Air Express	N8097U N823BX
46065	71F	460	Burlington Air Express	N8098U N820BX
46066	71F	462	TAMPA Colombia	N8099U HK-3785X
46067	72	455	Al Nassr Ltd	N8966U VR-BJR
46068	62F	463	Emery Worldwide Airlines	N8967U N816ZA N990CF
46069	62F	465	Canarias Air Cargo	N8968U EC-963 EC-GEE
46070	62H	467	Interair Leases	N8969U PT-AIY N8969U PP-AIY N8969U
46071	62H	469	Australian Consolidated Press	N8970U VR-BMR VR-BLG
46072	71F	477	United Parcel Service	N1305L N772UP
46073	73CF	485	United Parcel Service	N4865T N702FT N402FE N803UP
46074	73PF	468	United Parcel Service	N8760 HB-IDZ N874UP
46075	63F	484	Airborne Express	PH-DEH TF-FLT N512FP N818AX
46076	73AF	451	DHL Airways	CF-TIO C-FTIO N802DH
46077	62	470	Airborne Express	HB-IDI N923R N801AX
46078	62CF	475	Peruvian AF	HB-IDK FAP 370/OB-1372
46079	63	476	Airborne Express	EC-BQS N4934Z N822AX
46080	73F	466	United Parcel Service	PH-DEF TF-VLZ N880UP
46081	72	471	Aramco	N8971U N728A
46082	72	458	NASA	I-DIWK N801BN N717NA
46083	62		not built	
46084	72	473	Saudi Arabian Govt	N8972U 6Y-JII N2547R HZ-MS11 HZ-HM11
46085	62F	481	American International Airways	N8973U N803CK
46086	73CF	478	Emery Worldwide Airlines	N794FT N870TV
46087	63CF	454	Air Transport International	N864F N774FT N906R
46088	63CF	464	Emery Worldwide Airlines	N865F OE-IBO N865F TF-FLC N865F
46089	73CF	501	United Parcel Service	N4866T N707FT N407FE N811UP
46090	73CF	504	United Parcel Service	N4867T N705FT N405FE N814UP
46091	73CF	519	Southern Air Transport	N4868T F-GESM N873SJ
46092	63AF	505	Emery Worldwide Airlines	PH-DEG N926CL N951R
46093	63F	496	Airborne Express	N8758 OY-KTG N790AL N816AX
46094	73CF	482	United Parcel Service	N4910C N910CL N894UP
46095	73PF	497	Emery Worldwide Airlines	N8757 CF-CPL C-FCPL N29180 VR-CKL VR-CKA N809CK N105WP
46096	63PF	499	(UTA)	N8756 F-BOLL TU-TXT F-BOLL w/o 10Mar84 N'Djamena, Tchad
46097	63PF	503	Airborne Express	N8755 OY-KTH LN-MOF N793AL N815AX
46098	62F	516	American International Airways	I-DIWW N39305 N802MG
46099	71	507	Emery Worldwide Airlines	JA8041 N917R F-GMFM EI-BWG 9J-AFL N811AL
46100	73AF	502	United Parcel Service	CF-TIP C-FTIP N802UP
46101	73CF	489	United Parcel Service	N8630 TF-FLE N8630 N801UP
46102	62	512	AeroPeru	LN-MOG OB-R-1260 OB-1260 wfu and engineless Aug90 Lima, Peru
46103	73CF	483	Emery Worldwide Airlines	N795FT
46104	73CF	488	Emery Worldwide Airlines	N796FT
46105	62	494	Canarias Air Cargo	N1808E EC-892 EC-GCY
46106	73CF	490	Lufthansa Cargo Airlines	N8641 F-GATO N919CL N919JW D-ADUC
46107	62	498	(Surinam Airways)	N1809E w/o 06Jun89 nr Paramaribo-Zanderij, Surinam
46108	73CF	522	United Parcel Service	N123AF N798FT N818UP
46109	73CF	493	United Parcel Service	N8642 N772FT N809UP
46110	62F	487	Rich International	N8974U (F-GGLC) HI-576CT N8974U
46111	62H	491	Brisair	N8975U VR-BHM
46112	73CF	520	United Parcel Service	N866F TF-FLF N866F TF-FLF N866F TF-FLF N776FT TF-FLF N776FT N812UP
46113	63AF	521	Airborne Express	(CF-TIT) CF-TIU C-FTIU N818EV N811AX
46114	63	526	(Air Canada)	(CF-TIV) CF-TIW w/o 05Jul70 nr Toronto, Canada
46115	63	530	Airborne Express	(CF-TIW) CF-TIX C-FTIX ZP-CCH N825AX
46116	63	518	Airborne Express	EC-BSD N4574P C-GQBF N821AX
46117	73CF	525	United Parcel Service	N4869T N701FT N401FE N805UP
46118	54F		not built	(N8717U)
46119	54F		not built	(N8724U)
46120	54F		not built	(N8731U)
46121	63F	500	Air Transport International	(PI-C827) PH-DEK TF-FLV EI-CAK N786AL
46122	63	506	Airborne Express	(PI-C829) PH-DEL 5Y-ZEB N823AX
46123	73AF	508	DHL Airways	CF-TIQ C-FTIQ N803DH
46124	73AF	511	DHL Airways	CF-TIR C-FTIR N804DH
46125	73AF	515	DHL Airways	CF-TIS C-FTIS N805DH
46126	63F	524	Airborne Express	(CF-TIU) CF-TIV C-FTIV N819EV N812AX
46127	61	510	(American Intl Airways)	JA8042 N25UA N821TC N25UA N814CK w/o 18Aug93 nr Guantanamo Bay, Cuba; cancelled Sep93
46128	61	514	(Saudia)	JA8043 N913R dbf 15Jan81 Luxembourg-Findel, Luxembourg
46129	62CF	523	Air Transport International	SE-DBI HS-TGZ R Thai AF 60110 HS-TGQ N798AL N41CX
46130	72CF	542	L'Armee de l'Air	N8731U OH-LFY 46130/F-RAFF
46131	62	517	Rich International	LN-MOW N772CA
46132	62F	535	Faucett	I-DIWH OB-R-1249 OB-1249 N42086 OB-1618
46133	73CF	534	Emery Worldwide Airlines	(N6165A) N801WA N961R
46134	62	513	Airborne Express	HB-IDL N924CL N802AX
46135	63CF	531	Air Transport International	TU-TCF N784AL
46136	63	509	Airborne Express	SE-DBK N795AL N813AX
46137	63CF	527	Emery Worldwide Airlines	D-ADIX N65518 N804WA N957R

DOUGLAS DC-8

C/n	Series	Line No	Last known Operator/Owner	Previous Identities/fate (where known)
46138	63CF		not built	(N797FT)
46139	62AF	537	Emery Worldwide Airlines	JA8044 N751UA N813ZA N998CF
46140	73CF	528	United Parcel Service	N124AF N797FT N840UP
46141	63	533	Airborne Express	PH-DEM S7-SIS HB-IBF N824AX
46142	62	546	Airborne Express	I-DIWX OB-R-1210 OB-1210 N61CX
46143	63CF	547	Emery Worldwide Airlines	D-ADIY N65516 N805WA N959R
46144	63CF	532	(Airlift International)	N6164A dbf 23Mar74 Travis AFB, CA
46145	63CF	548	Emery Worldwide Airlines	D-ADIZ N65517 N806WA N921R
46146	63CF	536	(World Airways)	(N6166A) N802WA w/o 08Sep73 nr Cold Bay, AK
46147	63CF	549	American International Airways	9Q-CLH N811CK
46148	62AF	553	(Japan Air Lines)	JA8054 w/o 13Jan77 Anchorage, AK
46149	73CF	538	Air India	(N6167A) N803WA A40-HM A40-HMQ N785AL N874SJ
46150	62AF	539	Arrow Air	LN-MOC HS-TGS R Thai AF 60109 HS-TGQ R Thai AF 60109 N791AL
46151	73CF	540	American International Airways	9Q-CLG N815CK
46152	62H	550	(Japan Air Lines)	JA8051 w/o 27Sep77 Kampang Merba, Malaysia
46153	62AF	551	Air Transport International	JA8052 N735PL
46154	62AF	554	Emery Worldwide Airlines	JA8055 TF-BBC N811ZA N997CF
46155	63	529	Airborne Express	EC-BSE N940JW C-GQBA N820AX
46156			not built	
46157	61	541	Airborne Express	JA8045 N845AX
46158	61	543	Airborne Express	JA8046 N846AX
46159	61F	544	Fine Air	JA8047 N29UA F-GFCN (TC-GUL) N29UA N61FB*
46160	61	545	(Japan Air Lines)	JA8048 w/o 17Sep82 Shanghai, China; remains to Avn Enthusiasts Centre, Shanghai, China
46161	62AF	552	(Air Transport Intl)	JA8053 N730PL w/o 12Mar91 New York-Kennedy, NY
46162	62AF	555	Emery Worldwide Airlines	JA8056 TF-BBB N47978 N810ZA N996CF
46163	63F	556	Emery Worldwide Airlines	SE-DBL N797AL
46164	62		not built	(JA8057)

Production complete

DOUGLAS DC-9

C/n	Series	Line No	Last known Operator/Owner	Previous Identities/fate (where known)
45695	14	1	Intl Airline Support Group	N9DC prototype; ff 25Feb65 N1301T EC-622 EC-FCQ N914LF stored May93 Sherman, TX for spares use
45696	14	2	Midwest Express	N3301L EC-CGY N3301L N700ME
45697	14	3	McDonnell-Douglas	N3302L used for structural tests Long Beach, CA
45698	14	5	Allegro Air	N3303L EC-DIR N931EA XA-SPA
45699	14	8	Allegro Air	N3304L EC-CGZ N932EA YV-830C XA-SNR
45700	14	11	(Delta Air Lines)	N3305L w/o 30May72 Fort Worth, TX
45701	14	12	Intl Airline Support Group	N3306L stored Oct91 Sherman, TX for spares use
45702	14	15	Aerocalifornia	N3307L I-SARJ N15NP N99YA HB-IAA HB-IEF XA- c May95
45703	14	21	Intl Airline Support Group	N3308L YV-C-AVB N3308L stored May93 Sherman, TX for spares use
45704	14	24	Intl Airline Support Group	N3309L stored Sherman, TX for spares use
45705	14	53	Northwest Airlines	N3310L
45706	14	61	Jerrold Perechio	N3311L I-SARV N5NE N13FE
45707	14	70	Northwest Airlines	N3312L
45708	14	77	(Northwest Airlines)	N3313L dbr 03Dec90 Detroit, MI
45709	14	78	Intl Airline Support Group	N3314L stored May93 Sherman, TX for spares use
45710	32	100	Servivensa	N3315L YV-66C N900ML N939ML YV-612C
45711	14	4	Midwest Express	N9684Z CF-TLB N13699 OH-LYC N85AS N500ME
45712	14	6	Intercontinental Colombia	CF-TLC N1792U OH-LYB G-BMAH HK- c Dec95
45713	14	9	TAESA	CF-TLD N13614 OH-LYA G-BMAI XA- c Apr95
45714	14	7	TAESA	N1051T N651TX XA-RXG
45715	14	10	TAESA	N1052T N652TX HK-3830X XA-SSZ XA-SXV
45716	14	13	Intercontinental Colombia	N1053T N653TX HK-3833X
45717	15F	20	Airborne Express	N901H I-TIGE N927AX
45718	15	17	Midwest Express	PH-DNA I-TIGU N928AX N300ME
45719	15	18	TAESA	PH-DNB G-BMAG XA- c Apr95
45720	15	27	UAS Leasing	PH-DNC N31UA stored Jun93 Dallas, TX
45721	15	44	(Intercontinental Colombia)	PH-DND PJ-DNC N48200 XA-GOJ N908DC HK-2864X dbr 26Mar92 Tumaco, Colombia
45722	15	55	Intercontinental Colombia	PH-DNE PJ-DNA N54648 XA-GOK N2896W HK-2865X FAC-1142 HK-2865X
45723	15	63	Intl Airline Support Group	PH-DNF PJ-DNB N48075 YV-65C N48075 wfs 01May93, stored Sherman, TX
45724	15	22	(Itavia)	N902H I-TIGI w/o 27Jun80 Tyrrhenian Sea, Italy
45725	14	19	Midwest Express	CF-TLE N15335 OH-LYD N25AS N600ME
45726	14	36	(Continental Airlines)	CF-TLF N5726 N626TX w/o 15Nov87 Denver-Stapleton, CO
45727	14	43	Midwest Express	CF-TLG N5728 N628TX N400ME
45728	14F	14	Airborne Express	N945L I-TIGA N925AX
45729	14F	16	Northwest Airlines	N946L OH-LYE N930RC
45730	14	37	Estrellas del Aire	N947L OH-LYG N930EA XA-RSQ
45731	15	34	Topeka Management	HB-IFA N8500 N60FM N901B N2H N120NE HB-IFA N120NE
45732	15	41	US Department of Justice	HB-IFB N119 N29 N813TL
45733	31	48	(Aeron Aviation Resources)	N8916E b/u Nov93 Mojave, CA; cancelled Feb95
45734	31	60	(Aeron Aviation Resources)	N8917E b/u Nov93 Mojave, CA; cancelled Feb95
45735	14	25	Aerocaribe	N1054T N654TX HK-3832X HK-3867X XA-SSW
45736	14	45	Aerocalifornia	N1055T N655TX XA-LMM
45737	14	49	(Polaris Aircraft Leasing)	N1056T stored Sep91 Kingman, AZ in Midway c/s, b/u
45738	15	54	Intercontinental Colombia	N1057T G-BMAB HK-3958X
45739	15	56	TAESA	N1058T G-BMAC N29259 G-BMAC XA-SZC
45740	15	62	PharmAir Corp	N1059T N310MJ N711SW N911KM
45741	15	66	(Polaris Aircraft Leasing)	N1060T stored Sep91 Kingman, AZ in Midway c/s, b/u
45742	14	26	(Intercontinental Colombia)	N8901E HK-3839X w/o 11Jan95 over Maria La Baja, Colombia; cancelled 24Apr95
45743	14	29	Aerocalifornia	N8902E XA-CSL
45744	14	31	Northwest Airlines	N8903E
45745	14	32	Intl Airline Support Group	N8904E YV-852C stored Jun95 Sherman, TX
45746	14	38	Northwest Airlines	N8905E
45747	14	40	Northwest Airlines	N8906E
45748	14	47	Northwest Airlines	N8907E
45749	14	50	Northwest Airlines	N8908E
45770	14	57	Northwest Airlines	N8909E
45771	14	58	(Eastern Air Lines)	N8910E w/o 09Feb79 Dade-Collier, FL
45772	15	30	Trans World Airlines	N970Z
45773	15	39	Trans World Airlines	N971Z
45774	32	336	Valujet Airlines	TC-JAB N926VV N937VV
45775	15	71	Seattle Seahawks	N1061T N241TC N9KR N89SM N40SH
45776	15	72	Intercontinental Colombia	N1062T HK-3795X cancelled 12Apr93
45777	15	80	(Trans World Airlines)	N1063T w/o 09Mar67 nr Urbana, OH
45778	15	82	Great American Airways	N1064T
45779	15	92	(Polaris Aircraft Leasing)	N1065T stored Sep91 Kingman, AZ in Midway c/s, b/u
45780	15	93	TAESA	N1066T HK-3710X XA- c Jun95
45781	15	101	Intercontinental Colombia	N1067T HK-3752X
45782	15	114	Great American Airways	N1068T
45783	15	128	Intercontinental Colombia	N1069T HK-3720X
45784	15	140	Target Airways	N1070T
45785	15	64	Aerocalifornia	HB-IFC N1790U XA-SOJ EI-CBB XA-RRY
45786	15	90	Aerocalifornia	HB-IFD N1791U HP-505 N1791U N968E XA-AGS

DOUGLAS DC-9

C/n	Series	Line No	Last known Operator/Owner	Previous Identities/fate (where known)
45787	15	127	Northwest Airlines	HB-IFE N1793U D-AMOR N1793U 5Y-AKX N1793U HL7205 N1793U N9348
45788	32	171	Spirit Airlines	HB-IFF N3505T N12505
45789	32	217	Continental Airlines	HB-IFG N543TX N543NY N17543
45790	32	264	Northwest Airlines	HB-IFH N982US
45791	32	349	Continental Airlines	HB-IFI N532TX N12532
45792	32	372	Continental Airlines	HB-IFK EC-DQP N539TX N539NY N12539
45793	32	381	Continental Airlines	HB-IFL N541TX N541NY (N17541) N58541*
45794	14	52	(West Coast Airlines)	N9101 w/o 01Oct66 Portland, OR
45795	14	65	Midwest Express	N9102 N80ME
45796	14	74	(Texas International)	N9103 w/o 17Mar80 Baton Rouge, LA
45797	15	51	Richard M Scaife	(EC-BAX) N8953U N8860
45798	15	59	Trans World Airlines	(EC-BAY) N490SA
45799	15	69	Trans World Airlines	(EC-BAZ) N491SA
45825	14	67	Northwest Airlines	N8911E
45826	15RC	79	US Dept of Energy	N8901 CF-TON N29AF
45827	32	135	Northwest Airlines	HL7201 N9347 stored Atlanta, GA
45828	15RC	242	Emery Worldwide Airlines	N8918 N9359 N566PC
45829	14	68	Northwest Airlines	N8912E
45830	14	75	Northwest Airlines	N8913E
45831	14	76	Northwest Airlines	N8914E
45832	14	84	Northwest Airlines	N8915E
45833	31	73	(Aeron Aviation Resources)	N8918E stored 1992 Mojave, CA, b/u, cancelled Jan95
45834	31	85	McDonnell Douglas	N8919E cancelled Aug94, used for structural tests
45835	31	95	Northwest Airlines	N8920E
45836	31	96	Northwest Airlines	N8921E
45837	31	103	ASERCA	N8922E YV-720C
45838	31	104	Northwest Airlines	N8923E
45839	31	116	Sun Jet International	N8924E
45840	31	117	Northwest Airlines	N8925E
45841	15	46	Midwest Express	N972Z OH-LYK N2892Q N900ME
45842	14	23	Midwest Express	N8961 N800ME
45843	14	28	Intercontinental de Aviacion	N8962 HK-3891X
45844	14	33	Intl Airline Support Group	N8963 N949L stored 31Mar96 Sherman, TX
45845	32	91	Air Canada	CF-TLH C-FTLH
45846	32	112	USAir	CF-TLI C-FTLI N901AK N705PS N913VJ
45847	32	394	Continental Airlines	HB-IFM N531TX N17531
45863	31	124	Northwest Airlines	N8926E
45864	31	130	Air Train	N8927E
45865	31	137	Northwest Airlines	N8928E
45866	31	138	Northwest Airlines	N8929E
45867	31	283	ASERCA	N8952E YV-705C
45868	31	290	USAir	N8953E N930VJ
45869	31	331	Northwest Airlines	N8960E
45870	31	332	(Eastern Air Lines)	N8961E dbf 18May72 Fort Lauderdale, FL
45871	31	344	ADC Airlines	N8962E N962ML 5N-BBC stored 31Mar96 Sherman, TX
45872	31	345	(ADC Airlines)	N8963E N963ML 5N-BBE dbf 18Aug94 Monrovia-Spriggs Payne, Liberia
45873	31	350	Charlotte Aircraft Corp	N8964E N964ML stored Jun92 Maxton, NC for spares use
45874	31	351	Airborne Express	N8965E N965ML N929AX
45875	31	365	Servivensa	N8968E N967ML YV-815C
45876	31	366	Sun Air	N8969E N968ML stored Nov91 Johannesburg, South Africa
47000	15	83	(Aeropostal)	HZ-AEA YV-C-ANP YV-03C Venezuela YV-03 Venezuela 0003 YV-03C w/o 03Apr93 in Caribbean Sea, North of Margarita Island, Venezuela
47001	15	94	Trans World Airlines	HZ-AEB N969Z YV-18C N969Z
47002	15	105	(Airborne Express)	HZ-AEC YV-C-ANV YV-02C I-TIGB N926AX dbr 06Feb85 Philadelphia, PA
47003	31	86	Airborne Express	VH-CZA N3281G US Navy 162390 N3281G N535MD N946AX
47004	31	81	Airborne Express	VH-CZB N3281K US Navy 162391 N537MD N947AX
47005	31	151	Express One International	VH-CZC N937ML stored Jun95 Sherman, TX
47006	31	99	Aeromexico	N981PS YV-C-LEV YV-51C XA-IOV VR-BMG XA-SDF
47007	31	87	ASERCA	VH-TJJ N938ML YV-714C
47008	31CF	98	Airborne Express	VH-TJK N908AX
47009	31	152	Airborne Express	VH-TJL N938AX
47010	15RC	97	Fortune Aviation	N8902 CF-TOO N50AF I-TIAN
47011	15RC	102	US Dept of Energy	N8903 CF-TOP N60AF N79SL
47012	15RC	115	Kitty Hawk Airways	N8904 CF-TOQ N75AF N562PC
47013	15RC	129	Kitty Hawk Airways	N8905 CF-TOR C-FTOR N73AF N557AS N112PS
47014	15RC	141	Kitty Hawk Airways	N8906 CF-TOS N70AF N561PC
47015	15RC	156	Norman Aviation	N8907 CF-TOT C-FTOT N72AF I-TIAR
47016	15RC	173	USA Jet Airlines	N8909 N9349 YL-BAA N9349 N194US
47017	15RC	186	USA Jet Airlines	N8911 N9352 N195US
47018	15RC	203	Intl Airline Support Group	N8913 N9354 XA-SMI stored Jun95 Sherman, TX
47019	32	113	Air Canada	CF-TLJ C-FTLJ
47020	32	126	USAir	CF-TLK C-FTLK N902AK N706PS N912VJ
47021	32	133	Air Canada	CF-TLL C-FTLL
47022	32	144	Air Canada	CF-TLM C-FTLM
47023	32	158	USAir	CF-TLN C-FTLN N903AK N707PS N916VJ
47024	32	159	Air Canada	CF-TLO C-FTLO

DOUGLAS DC-9

C/n	Series	Line No	Last known Operator/Owner	Previous Identities/fate (where known)
47025	32	106	(AVENSA)	N3316L YV-67C dbf 11Mar83 Barquisimeto, Venezuela
47026	32	119	USAir	N3317L N946VJ
47027	32	132	Trans World Airlines	N3318L N995Z
47028	32	145	Trans World Airlines	N3319L N996Z
47029	32	157	Trans World Airlines	N3320L N997Z
47030	32	174	Trans World Airlines	N3321L N998R
47031	32	187	Northwest Airlines	N3322L YV-68C N3322L
47032	32	204	(Delta Air Lines)	N3323L w/o 27Nov73 Chattanooga, TN
47033	15	147	Trans World Airlines	N973Z
47034	15	162	(Ozark Air Lines)	N974Z w/o 27Dec68 Sioux City, IA
47035	15	178	Trans World Airlines	N975Z
47036	31	375	Servivensa	N8973E N972ML YV-817C
47037	32	121	Sun Air	EC-BIG N8270A ZS-NRD
47038	32	136	Northwest Airlines	I-DIKA N901DC I-DIBR I-DIBA N601NW
47039	32	154	Aerocalifornia	I-DIKE N902DC I-DIBS N4157A XA- c Aug95
47040	32CF	172	Airborne Express	N931F N904AX
47041	32CF	200	US Navy	N932F CF-TMN N932F N59T 163036
47042	31	486	Northwest Airlines	N89S
47043	14	88	Aerocalifornia	N1302T XA-BCS(2)
47044	15MC	165	Evergreen Intl Airlines	N1303T OH-LYH N916F stored Mar92 Marana, AZ
47045	15RC	184	USA Jet Airlines	N1304T OH-LYI N558HA N902CK N198US
47046	32	168	Northwest Airlines	I-DIKI N903DC I-DIBT I-DIBE N602NW
47047	32	183	Zuliana Air	I-DIKO N904DC I-DIBU YV-495C
47048	15	35	Intercontinental Colombia	N8964 TC-JAA XA-DEV YV-C-AVC YV-52C N65358 G-BFIH G-BMAA HK-3827X
47049	14	42	Northwest Airlines	N6140A N948L
47050	31	118	USAir	(N6141A) N970VJ
47051	31	131	USAir	(N6142A) N971VJ
47052	31	142	USAir	(N6143A) N972VJ
47053	31	107	USAir	N970NE N940VJ stored Jul95 Marana, AZ
47054	31	110	USAir	N971NE N941VJ
47055	15RC	194	Kitty Hawk Airways	N1305T N563PC
47056	14	89	(AVENSA)	YV-C-AVM w/o 22Dec74 nr Maturin, Venezuela
47057	31	122	USAir	N972NE N942VJ
47058	31	123	USAir	N973NE N943VJ
47059	15	125	Aerocalifornia	XA-SOA EI-BZX XA-RNQ
47060	14	109	Allegro Air	YV-C-AVR YV-57C N38641 XA-SKA
47061	15RC	207	Evergreen Intl Airlines	N1306T XA-BCS N915F EC-489 EC-EYS N915F stored Mar91 Marana, AZ in Air Sur c/s
47062	15MC	223	Kitty Hawk Airways	N1307T N564PC
47063	15	111	Northwest Airlines	N91S
47064	15	120	Northwest Airlines	N92S
47065	31	269	Airborne Express	VH-CZD N3281R US Navy 162392 N534MD N948AX
47066	31	150	USAir	N974NE N945VJ
47067	31	143	Valujet Airlines	N951N N17560 N960VV
47068	32	160	USAir	CF-TLP C-FTLP N715CL C-FTLP N904AK N708PS N914VJ
47069	32	175	Air Canada	CF-TLQ C-FTLQ
47070	32	176	Air Canada	CF-TLR C-FTLR
47071	32	188	Air Canada	CF-TLS C-FTLS
47072	31CF	270	Airborne Express	VH-TJM N906AX
47073	31	161	Northwest Airlines	N952N
47074	31	376	Airborne Express	N8974E N973ML N937AX stored Las Vegas-McCarran, NV
47075	31	166	(Delta Air Lines)	N975NE w/o 31Jul73 Boston-Logan, MA
47076	32	134	Aviaco	EC-BIH
47077	32	148	(Iberia)	EC-BII w/o 05Mar73 Nantes, France
47078	15	146	Northwest Airlines	N93S
47079	32	163	Austral Lineas Aereas	EC-BIJ LV-WJH
47080	32	164	Aviaco	EC-BIK
47081	14	155	(Texas International)	N9104 dbf 16Nov76 Denver-Stapleton, CO
47082	31	181	Trans World Airlines	N976NE N993Z
47083	31	177	Northwest Airlines	N953N
47084	32	179	Airborne Express	EC-BIL N988AX stored Mar93 Las Vegas-McCarran, NV
47085	15	139	Aerocalifornia	XA-SOB XA-SOY EI-BZY XA-GDL
47086	15RC	219	Emery Worldwide Airlines	N8915 N9356 N568PC
47087	15RC	234	SETRA	N8916 N9358 XC-BCO XA-BDM
47088	32	180	Binter Canarias	EC-BIM
47089	32	189	Valujet Airlines	EC-BIN N8270H EI-CMP N939VV
47090	32	190	Sun Air	EC-BIO N82702 ZS-NRC
47091	32	206	Iberia	EC-BIP
47092	32	222	Aviaco	EC-BIQ dbr 18Feb90 Mahon, Spain and stored Palma, Spain
47093	32	237	Binter Canarias	EC-BIR
47094	32	149	Continental Airlines	HB-IFN SE-DBZ HB-IFN N545TX N545NY N58545
47095	31	191	Trans World Airlines	N977NE N992Z
47096	31	192	Trans World Airlines	N978NE N991Z
47097	32	193	Northwest Airlines	N979NE N994Z
47098	31	108	Servivensa	(N1938R) N938PR N8988E YV-760C
47099	31	197	USAir	(N6144A) N973VJ
47100	15	153	(Aeromexico)	XA-SOC w/o 20Jun73 nr Puerto Vallarta, Mexico
47101	32	195	Northwest Airlines	I-DIKU N905DC I-DIBV I-DIBL N603NW
47102	32	198	Midwest Express	PH-DNG N940ML N302ME

DOUGLAS DC-9

C/n	Series	Line No	Last known Operator/Owner	Previous Identities/fate (where known)
47103	32	205	Northwest Airlines	N3324L YV-70C N3324L
47104	32	220	(Servivensa)	N3325L YV-71C N901ML YV-613C dbr 19Jul93 Ciudad Bolivar, Venezuela, used for spares
47105	32	221	Servivensa	N3326L YV-72C N902ML YV-614C
47106	32	235	Aeromexico	N3327L YV-73C XA-JEC
47107	32	236	Trans World Airlines	N3328L N921L
47108	32	251	Trans World Airlines	N3329L N922L
47109	32	252	Trans World Airlines	N3330L N923L
47110	32	167	Continental Airlines	(HB-IFO) OY-KGU HB-IFO N534TX N14534
47111	32	182	Continental Airlines	(HB-IFP) (LN-RTB) LN-RLS HB-IFP N535TX N17535
47112	32	199	Continental Airlines	(HB-IFR) SE-DBY HB-IFR N537TX N43537
47113	32	213	Spirit Airlines	(HB-IFS) OY-KGW HB-IFS N536TX N12536
47114	41	218	Northwest Airlines	N8960U SE-DBX (HB-IDV) SE-DBX N750NW
47115	41	261	Northwest Airlines	N8961U OY-KGA HB-IDW OY-KGA N751NW
47116	41	308	Northwest Airlines	LN-RLK HB-IDV LN-RLK N752NW
47117	41	319	Northwest Airlines	SE-DBW HB-IDX SE-DBW N753NW
47118	32	196	(Alitalia)	I-DIKB dbf 07Jan80 Rome-Fiumicino, Italy
47119	31	378	Jet Leasing of Boca	N8975E N974ML stored Jan92 Las Vegas-McCarran, NV in Midway c/s
47120	31	209	(OK Aviation)	(N1939R) N939PR N8990E b/u May94 Mojave, CA
47121	31	277	AVENSA	N967PR N8989E YV-82C
47122	15	224	Aerocalifornia	XA-SOD EI-BZZ XA-RKT
47123	15	253	(GPA Group)	XA-SOE EI-CBA stored 1989 Waco, TX, b/u
47124	15	254	(Aeromexico)	XA-SOF dbr 02Sep76 Leon, Mexico
47125	15	388	Aerovias Caribe	XA-SOG HK-3486X XA-SVZ
47126	15	405	Aerocalifornia	XA-SOH EI-BZW XA-LAC
47127	15	417	(Intercontinental Colombia)	XA-SOI HK-3564X dbf 17Mar95 Barranquilla, Colombia
47128	32	210	Alitalia	I-DIKC N516MD I-RIZH I-RIFH
47129	32	225	Alitalia	I-DIKD N906DC I-DIBW I-DIBI
47130	31	211	USAir	(N6145A) N974VJ
47131	32	214	Spirit Airlines	PH-DNH N941ML
47132	32	229	Midwest Express	PH-DNI N944ML N501ME
47133	32	230	Midwest Express	PH-DNK N943ML N401ME
47134	31	215	Trans World Airlines	N980NE N988Z
47135	31	233	Trans World Airlines	N981NE N989Z
47136	31	243	Trans World Airlines	N982NE N990Z
47137	31	258	Trans World Airlines	N983NE N987Z
47138	31	318	Northwest Airlines	(N9105) N9330
47139	31	169	Northwest Airlines	N8930E N915RW
47140	31	212	Sun Jet International	N8931E
47141	31	227	MDFC Equipment Leasing Corp	N8932E
47142	31	232	MDFC Equipment Leasing Corp	N8933E
47143	31	238	MDFC Equipment Leasing Corp	N8934E
47144	31	239	Northwest Airlines	N8935E N916RW
47145	31	247	Northwest Airlines	N8936E N917RW
47146	31	226	USAir	(N6146A) N975VJ stored Jul95 Marana, AZ
47147	32CF	208	Airborne Express	N933F N905AX
47148	32CF	246	Airborne Express	N934F N909AX
47149	31	202	Northwest Airlines	N903H N911RW
47150	31	284	Northwest Airlines	N905H N912RW
47151	15	285	Aeronautic Services	N228Z N112AK VR-CKE VR-CKO
47152	15RC	170	Ross Aviation	N8908 CF-TOU N73AF C-FTOU N65AF C-FTOU N65AF C-FTOU N65AF C-FTOU N65AF N66AF
47153	15RC	185	Emery Worldwide Airlines	N8910 N9350 N567PC
47154	15RC	201	USA Jet Airlines	N8912 N9352 XC-BDM N9353 N901CK N197US
47155	15RC	216	USA Jet Airlines	N8914 N9355 N196US
47156	15RC	228	Roadway Global Air	N8916 N9357 stored 31Mar96 Sherman, TX
47157	31	322	Aeron Aviation Resources	N8959E YV-719C
47158	31	248	Northwest Airlines	N8937E N918RW
47159	31	231	(North Central Airlines)	N954N w/o 20Dec72 Chicago-O'Hare, IL
47160	31	241	Northwest Airlines	N955N
47161	31	249	Northwest Airlines	N8938E 5N-GIN N8938E
47162	31	255	Northwest Airlines	N8939E N919RW
47163	31	256	Northwest Airlines	N8940E N920RW
47164	31	259	Northwest Airlines	N8941F N921RW
47165	31	260	Airborne Express	N8942E N923AX
47166	31	265	Interglobal	N8943E XA-SHW N8943E
47167	31	266	Northwest Airlines	N8944E
47168	32	423	Valujet Airlines	PH-DNS N945ML N966VV*
47169	32	424	Charlotte Aircraft Corp	PH-DNT N948ML stored Jun92 Maxton, NC for spares use
47170	32	425	Valujet Airlines	PH-DNV N946ML N967VV
47171	31	473	Northwest Airlines	N906H N913RW
47172	32	263	Trans World Airlines	N3331L YU-AJX N3331L YU-AJY N26175 N926L
47173	32	273	Trans World Airlines	N3332L N931L
47174	32	286	Trans World Airlines	N3333L N929L
47175	32	298	Northwest Airlines	N3334L PJ-SNE N3991C
47176	32	314	Airborne Express	N3335L N980AX
47177	32	330	Valujet Airlines	N3336L N902VJ
47178	41	323	Northwest Airlines	OY-KGB N754NW
47179	41	335	Northwest Airlines	LN-RLC N755NW
47180	41	354	Northwest Airlines	SE-DBU N756NW

DOUGLAS DC-9

C/n	Series	Line No	Last known Operator/Owner	Previous Identities/fate (where known)
47181	31	267	Northwest Airlines	N8945E
47182	31	271	Northwest Airlines	N8946E N922RW
47183	31	272	Northwest Airlines	N8947E N923RW
47184	31	274	Eastern Air Lines	N8948E dbr 28Dec87 Pensacola, FL; remains at Maxton, NC Jun93
47185	31	275	Northwest Airlines	N8949E N924RW
47186	31	276	Northwest Airlines	N8950E C-FBKT N8950E
47187	31	282	Servicios Aereos Rutas Oriente	N8951E YV-718C
47188	31	291	USAir	N8954E N931VJ
47189	31	303	USAir	N8955E N932VJ
47190	32	240	Midwest Express	PH-DNL N942ML N301ME
47191	33RC	280	Evergreen Intl Airlines	PH-DNM N33UA N933F
47192	33RC	287	(Evergreen Intl Airlines)	N8963U PH-DNN N35UA N931F w/o 18Mar89 Carswell AFB, TX
47193	33RC	311	Ansett Air Freight	PH-DNO N941F VH-IPC
47194	33RC	324	Evergreen Intl Airlines	PH-DNP N944F
47195	32	278	Air Canada	CF-TLT C-FTLT
47196	32	288	(Air Canada)	CF-TLU C-FTLU w/o 02Jun83 Cincinatti, OH
47197	32	289	(Air Canada)	CF-TLV w/o 26Jun78 Toronto-Malton, Canada
47198	32	302	Air Canada	CF-TLW C-FTLW
47199	32	321	Air Canada	CF-TLX C-FTLX
47200	32	338	(Air Canada)	CF-TLY C-FTLY dbf 02Jun82 Montreal-Dorval, Canada
47201	32	459	Airborne Express	PH-DNW N9743Z EC-ECU N939AX
47202	31	400	Valujet Airlines	VH-CZE N931ML
47203	31CF	401	Airborne Express	VH-TJN N907AX
47204	15	245	Northwest Airlines	N94S
47205	15	250	Northwest Airlines	N95S
47206	15	328	Northwest Airlines	N96S
47207	31	293	USAir	N984VJ
47208	31	307	USAir	N985VJ
47209	31	327	USAir	N986VJ
47210	31	341	USAir	N987VJ
47211	31	357	(Allegheny Airlines)	N988VJ w/o 09Sep69 Shelbyville, IN
47212	31	368	USAir	N989VJ stored Jul95 Marana, AZ
47213	32	358	(Turk Hava Yollari)	TC-JAC w/o 21Jan72 nr Adana, Turkey
47214	31	306	Aerocalifornia	N8956E XA-SHV N8956E XA-
47215	31	313	Northwest Airlines	N8957E
47216	31	315	USAir	N8958E N933VJ
47217	31	360	(ADC Airlines)	N8966E N966ML 5N-BBA dbf 26Jul95 Monrovia-Spriggs Payne, Liberia
47218	32	312	Continental Airlines	D-ACEB HB-IFX N538TX N12538
47219	32	325	Continental Airlines	D-ACEC HB-IFY N544TX N18544
47220	32F	296	Evergreen Intl Airlines	I-DIKF N935F
47221	32F	305	US Navy	I-DIKG N938F 163037
47222	32	299	Northwest Airlines	I-DIKJ N43265 I-DIBZ I-DIBP N604NW
47223	32	300	Northwest Airlines	I-DIKL N2786 I-DIBY I-DIBM N605NW
47224	32	316	Alitalia	I-DIKM
47225	32	317	Northwest Airlines	I-DIKN N515MD I-RIZG I-RIFG N606NW
47226	32	333	Valujet Airlines	I-DIKP N946VV
47227	32	334	(Alitalia)	I-DIKQ w/o 23Dec78 nr Palermo, Italy
47228	32	355	Alitalia	I-DIKR
47229	32	356	Alitalia	I-DIKS I-RIKS I-RIFS
47230	32	395	Aerocalifornia	(I-DIKW) I-DIKT I-RIKT N277AW XA-SWG
47231	32	396	Aerorepublica	(I-DIKZ) I-DIKV I-RIKV N285AW HK-3926X
47232	32	428	Northwest Airlines	I-DIKY I-RIZY I-RIFY N607NW
47233	32	429	Northwest Airlines	I-DIBC I-RIBC I-RIFC N608NW
47234	32	435	Northwest Airlines	I-DIBD I-RIBD I-RIFD N609NW
47235	32	436	Alitalia	I-DIBJ I-RIBJ I-RIFJ
47236	32	450	Aerocalifornia	I-DIBQ I-RIBQ N274AW XA-SWH
47237	32	451	Zuliana de Aviacion	I-DIBO I-RIZX YV-496C
47238	32	465	Valujet Airlines	I-DIZA I-RIZA N945VV
47239	32	466	Adria Airways	I-DIZE YU-AHJ SL-ABF S5-ABF
47240	15F	346	(Emery Worldwide Airlines)	N8919 N9351 N565PC w/o 17Feb91 Cleveland-Hopkins, OH
47241	C-9A	281	USAF	67-22583
47242	C-9A	304	USAF	67-22584
47243	32	448	(VIASA)	YV-C-AVD w/o 16Mar69 Maracaibo, Venezuela
47244	31	498	Northwest Airlines	N90S
47245	31	510	(Southern Airways)	N97S w/o 14Nov70 Huntingdon, WV
47246	31	292	Northwest Airlines	(N950L) N9333
47247	31	342	Northwest Airlines	N9334
47248	31	257	Trans World Airlines	N976Z
47249	31	297	Trans World Airlines	N977Z
47250	31	309	Trans World Airlines	N978Z
47251	31	244	Trans World Airlines	N982PS
47252	31	294	Northwest Airlines	N956N
47253	31	295	Northwest Airlines	N957N
47254	31	301	Northwest Airlines	N958N
47255	31	310	Northwest Airlines	N959N
47256	31	326	Northwest Airlines	N960N
47257	32	386	Airborne Express	N1262L N983AX
47258	32	387	Airborne Express	N1263L N984AX
47259	32	409	Bellview Airlines	N1264L 5N-VWE 5N-KAY

DOUGLAS DC-9

C/n	Series	Line No	Last known Operator/Owner	Previous Identities/fate (where known)
47260	32	410	Valujet Airlines	N1265L LV-WAW N530MD N919VV
47261	32	411	Valujet Airlines	N1266L N903VJ
47262	32	412	Valujet Airlines	N1267L LV-WAX N529MD N920VV
47263	31	320	Northwest Airlines	(N9106) N9331
47264	31	329	Northwest Airlines	(N9107) N9332
47265	32	339	Air Canada	CF-TLZ C-FTLZ
47266	32	352	Air Canada	CF-TMA C-FTMA
47267	31	361	(Eastern Air Lines)	N8967E dbr 27Jan73 Akron-Canton, OH
47268	31	370	Spirit Airlines	N8970E N969ML
47269	31	371	Airborne Express	N8971E N970ML N936AX
47270	31	374	Aviation Systems Intl	N8972E N971ML stored Jun91 Mojave, CA
47271	31	389	Air Aruba	N8976E N975ML P4-MDD
47272	31	390	Servivensa	N8977E N976ML YV-816C
47273	32	347	Airborne Express	N3337L N981AX
47274	32	348	Valujet Airlines	N3338L XA-TCT N527MD N922VV*
47275	32	363	Valujet Airlines	N3339L N901VJ
47276	32	373	Bellview Airlines	N3340L 5N-COE N3340L 9G-ADN 5N-BLV
47277	32	379	Valujet Airlines	N5341L N910VJ
47278	32	380	Grand Airways	N5342L
47279	33RC	337	Evergreen Intl Airlines	PH-DNR N945F stored Marana, AZ
47280	31	597	Northwest Airlines	N1334U
47281	32	427	Continental Airlines	HB-IFT N533TX N17533
47282	32	446	Northwest Airlines	HB-IFU N983US
47283	32	397	Aerocalifornia	(I-DIKT) I-DIKW N2786S I-DIBX N2786S XA- c May95
47284	32	413	Valujet Airlines	N1268L XA-SHR N528MD N921VV
47285	32	414	Valujet Airlines	N1269L N911VV
47286	41	359	Northwest Airlines	OY-KGC N758NW
47287	41	364	Northwest Airlines	LN-RLJ N759NW
47288	41	369	Northwest Airlines	SE-DBT N760NW
47289	32	353	Air Canada	CF-TMB C-FTMB
47290	32	367	Air Canada	CF-TMC C-FTMC
47291	33RC	343	Airborne Express	PH-MAN N94454 N933AX
47292	32	383	Air Canada	CF-TMD C-FTMD
47293	32	384	Air Canada	CF-TME C-FTME
47294	32	402	Air Canada	CF-TMF C-FTMF
47295	C-9A	340	USAF	67-22585
47296	C-9A	362	(USAF)	67-22586 w/o 16Sep71 Scott AFB, IL
47297	C-9A	377	USAF	68-8932
47298	C-9A	399	USAF	68-8933
47299	C-9A	421	USAF	68-8934
47300	C-9A	438	USAF	68-8935
47301	21	382	Scandinavian A/L System	N8965U LN-RLL OY-KIA
47302	21	422	Valujet Airlines	OY-KGD N125NK
47303	21	432	Valujet Airlines	SE-DBS OY-KIF N126NK
47304	21	440	(Scandinavian A/L System)	N1794U LN-RLM dbr 30Jan73 Oslo-Fornebu, Norway
47305	21	441	Valujet Airlines	OY-KGE N129NK
47306	21	462	Scandinavian A/L System	SE-DBR OY-KIE
47307	21	463	Valujet Airlines	LN-RLO OY-KIB N128NK
47308	21	474	Scandinavian A/L System	OY-KGF
47309	14	393	(Midwest Express)	YV-C-AAA YV-01C YV-69C N2405T N100ME w/o 06Sep85 Milwaukee, WI
47310	31	449	USAir	N991VJ
47311	32	398	Aerorepublica	(I-DIKV) I-DIKZ I-RIKZ N286AW HK-3928X
47312	32	262	Austral Lineas Aereas	EC-BIS LV-WIS
47313	32	268	Binter Canarias	EC-BIT
47314	32	279	Airborne Express	EC-BIU N989AX
47315	31	433	Northwest Airlines	N1308T
47316	31	439	Northwest Airlines	N1309T
47317	32	385	Airborne Express	N1261L N982AX
47318	32	426	Valujet Airlines	N1270L N913VV
47319	32	434	Grand Airways	N1271L
47320	32	454	Valujet Airlines	N1272L YV-715C N523MD N918VV
47321	32	455	(Valujet Airlines)	N1273L N908VJ dbf 08Jun95 Atlanta; b/u Oct95
47322	32	456	Valujet Airlines	N1274L N909VJ
47323	32	468	Valujet Airlines	N1275L YV-717C N522MD N917VV
47324	32	469	Trans World Airlines	N1276L N924L
47325	31	515	Airborne Express	VH-CZF N3281N US Navy 162393 N540MD N949AX
47326	31	516	Spirit Airlines	VH-TJO N731L N928ML
47327	31	391	Northwest Airlines	N8978E
47328	31	392	Northwest Airlines	N8979E
47329	31	406	Grand Airways	N8980E N977ML
47330	31	407	Servivensa	N8981E YV-770C
47331	31	408	Servivensa	N8982E YV-764C
47332	31	461	USAir	N993VJ
47333	31	481	(Allegheny Airlines)	N994VJ dbr 23Jun76 Philadelphia, PA
47334	31	493	USAir	N995VJ stored Marana, AZ
47335	31	494	USAir	N996VJ stored Sep95 Marana, AZ
47336	31	500	USAir	N997VJ
47337	31	415	Northwest Airlines	N9335
47338	31	416	Northwest Airlines	N9336
47339	32	437	(Alitalia)	I-DIBN I-RIBN dbr 17Dec91 Warsaw-Okecie, Poland

DOUGLAS DC-9

C/n	Series	Line No	Last known Operator/Owner	Previous Identities/fate (where known)					
47340	32	403	Air Canada	CF-TMG	C-FTMG				
47341	32	404	Air Canada	CF-TMH	C-FTMH				
47342	32	418	Air Canada	CF-TMI	C-FTMI				
47343	31	460	Trans World Airlines	N979Z					
47344	31	472	Trans World Airlines	N980Z					
47345	31	485	Trans World Airlines	N981Z					
47346	31	464	Northwest Airlines	N9337					
47347	31	478	Northwest Airlines	N9338					
47348	32	419	Air Canada	CF-TMJ	C-FTMJ				
47349	32	420	Air Canada	CF-TMK	C-FTMK				
47350	32	431	Air Canada	CF-TML	C-FTML				
47351	32	442	USAir	CF-TMM	6Y-JGA	N958VJ	stored Jul95 Marana, AZ		
47352	32	453	USAir	CF-TMN	6Y-JGB	N959VJ	stored Jul95 Marana, AZ		
47353	32	471	Air Canada	CF-TMO	C-FTMO				
47354	32	483	Air Canada	CF-TMP	C-FTMP				
47355	32F	452	Evergreen Intl Airlines	I-DIBK	N932F				
47356	32	470	(Aeromexico)	N1277L	XA-JED	w/o 31Aug86 Cerritos, nr Los Angeles, CA			
47357	32	476	Trans World Airlines	N1278L	N925L				
47358	32	477	ASERCA	N1279L	YV-716C	wfs			
47359	32	495	Valujet Airlines	N1280L	N912VV				
47360	21	475	Scandinavian A/L System	SE-DBP	OY-KID				
47361	21	488	Valujet Airlines	SE-DBO	OY-KIC	SE-DBO	N127NK		
47362	31	492	Northwest Airlines	N907H	N914RW				
47363	33RC	445	Airborne Express	PH-MAO	N502MD	N930AX			
47364	32	484	Airborne Express	EC-BPF	N987AX	stored Mar92 Las Vegas-McCarran, NV			
47365	32	504	Austral Lineas Aereas	EC-BPG	LV-WFT				
47366	C-9A	530	USAF	68-10958					
47367	C-9A	539	USAF	68-10959					
47368	32	505	Austral Lineas Aereas	EC-BPH	LV-WHL				
47369	31	529	Northwest Airlines	N1798U					
47370	31	551	Northwest Airlines	N1799U					
47371	31	506	USAir	N978VJ					
47372	31	513	USAir	N979VJ	stored Oct95 Marana, AZ				
47373	31	522	(USAir)	N964VJ	dbr 18Jan92 Elmira-Corning, NY				
47374	31	523	USAir	N965VJ	stored Oct95 Marana, AZ				
47375	31	531	USAir	N967VJ					
47376	32	517	Northwest Airlines	N394PA	N9346				
47377	32	496	Valujet Airlines	N1281L	N904VJ				
47378	32	508	Valujet Airlines	N1282L	N905VJ				
47379	32	509	Valujet Airlines	N1283L	N906VJ				
47380	32CF	514	Airborne Express	N1284L	N900AX				
47381	32CF	519	Airborne Express	N1285L	N901AX				
47382	31	479	Northwest Airlines	N9339					
47383	32	538	Northwest Airlines	HB-IFV	N984US				
47384	33F	543	Airborne Express	HB-IFW	N931AX				
47385	32	542	Merpati Nusantara	PK-GJE	PK-GNA				
47386	32	550	Merpati Nusantara	PK-GJF	PK-GNB				
47387			not built						
47388			not built						
47389	32	489	Northwest Airlines	N9340					
47390	31	490	Northwest Airlines	N9341					
47391	31	491	Northwest Airlines	N9342					
47392	32	447	Airborne Express	N393PA	YU-AJB	N928AX			
47393	31	608	(Southern Airways)	N1335U	w/o 04Apr77 New Hope, GA				
47394	32	458	Aeromexico	N950PB	YV-19C	XA-JEB			
47395	41	555	Northwest Airlines	OY-KGG	HS-TGM	OY-KGG	HB-IDY	OY-KGG	N762NW
47396	41	557	Northwest Airlines	LN-RLR	HS-TGN	LN-RLD	N763NW		
47397	32	636	Valujet Airlines	TC-JAK	N925VV	N936VV			
47398	32		not built						
47399	31	430	Aerorepublica	N8983E	YV-818C	HK-3905X			
47400	31	443	(Eastern Air Lines)	N8984E	w/o 11Sep74 Douglas, NC				
47401	31	444	Aerorepublica	N8985E	YV-819C	HK-3906X			
47402	31	482	Northwest Airlines	N8986E	5N-INZ	N8986E			
47403	31	507	Airborne Express	N8987E	N924AX				
47404	31	554	Northwest Airlines	N1332U					
47405	31	487	Northwest Airlines	N961N					
47406	31	499	Northwest Airlines	N962N					
47407	33CF	457	(ALM)	(N915U)	N935F	w/o 02May70 nr St Croix, US Virgin Is			
47408	33CF	467	Ansett Air Freight	(N916U)	N936F	YU-AJP	VH-IPF		
47409	33CF	497	Trans World Airlines	(N917U)	N937F				
47410	33RC	480	US Navy	(N918U)	PH-MAR	N909DC	162753		
47411	31	533	Trans World Airlines	N1330U	N983Z				
47412	31	534	Trans World Airlines	N1331U	N984Z				
47413	33RC	521	Airborne Express	SE-DBN	N939F	N935AX			
47414	33F	536	Evergreen Intl Airlines	LN-RLW	N940F				
47415	31	511	Northwest Airlines	N963N					
47416	31	512	Northwest Airlines	N964N					
47417	31	518	Northwest Airlines	N965N					
47418	31F	570	NASA	VH-TJP	N741L	N929ML	N192SA	N650UG	
47419	31	602	Airborne Express	VH-TJQ	N941AX				
47420	31	556	USAir	N966VJ					

DOUGLAS DC-9

C/n	Series	Line No	Last known Operator/Owner	Previous Identities/fate (where known)
47421	31	558	USAir	N969VJ
47422	32	576	Air Canada	CF-TMQ C-FTMQ
47423	32	581	Continental Airlines	CF-TMR C-FTMR N556NY N10556
47424	32	582	Continental Airlines	CF-TMS C-FTMS N557NY N17557
47425	32	589	Northwest Airlines	YU-AHL N926NW
47426	32	572	Airborne Express	N1286L N902AX
47427	32	573	Airborne Express	N1287L N903AX
47428	33RC	669	US Navy	EC-BYK N521MD 164607/RS
47429	31	532	USAir	N968VJ
47430	32	609	Sun Air	5H-MOI 5Y-BBH HB-IKB I-SARW N503MD G-BMAK ZS-NRA
47431	32	520	US Navy	(I-DIZI) I-ATIA N506MD 163511
47432	32	525	Northwest Aircraft Inc	I-DIZI I-RIZB I-RIFB N610NW
47433	32	526	Alitalia	I-DIZU I-RIZU I-RIFU
47434	32	537	Aerorepublica	I-DIZB N871UM I-RIZJ HK-3964X
47435	32	540	Northwest Airlines	I-DIZC I-RIZC I-RIFL N611NA
47436	32	541	Northwest Airlines	(I-DIZF) I-ATIE N873UM I-RIZK I-RIFZ N612NW
47437	32	544	Aerorepublica	(I-DIZG) I-ATIO N872UM I-RIZL HK-3963X
47438	32	545	Northwest Airlines	(I-DIZL) I-ATIU I-RIZP I-RIFP N613NW
47439	31	501	Northwest Airlines	N9343
47440	31	502	Northwest Airlines	N9344
47441	31	503	(Northwest Airlines)	N9345 w/o 06Jun71 Azusa, CA
47442	32	524	Valujet Airlines	N1795U TC-JAG N927VV N938VV
47443	32	577	Valujet Airlines	N1288L N915VV
47444	32	578	Valujet Airlines	N1289L N907VJ
47445	32	585	Valujet Airlines	N1290L N916VV
47446	32	561	Austral Lineas Aereas	EC-BQT LV-WEG
47447	32	563	Austral Lineas Aereas	EC-BQU LV-WEH
47448	C-9A	548	USAF	68-10960
47449	C-9A	552	USAF	68-10961
47450	32	535	Northwest Airlines	N1796U D-ADIT N941N
47451	32	547	Valujet Airlines	N1797U TC-JAF N921VV N932VV
47452	32	660	Aviaco	EC-BYI
47453	32	565	Iberia	EC-BQV
47454	32	567	Austral Lineas Aereas	EC-BQX LV-WGU
47455	32	579	Aviaco	EC-BQY
47456	32	580	Binter Canaries	EC-BQZ
47457	32	620	(Inex Adria)	D-ADIU YU-AJO w/o 30Oct75 Sadlec, nr Prague, Czechoslovakia
47458	32	646	Northwest Airlines	OE-LDF EC-DSV OE-LDF N987US
47459	32	549	Northwest Airlines	D-ADIS N942N
47460	32	627	Jugoslovenski Aerotpt	YU-AHV
47461	32	663	Aviaco	EC-BYJ
47462	33RC	564	Airborne Express	PH-DNY N32UA N934AX
47463	32	649	(Garuda Indonesia)	PK-GJH PK-GND dbr 13Jan80 Banjarmasin, Indonesia
47464	41	575	Airborne Express	SE-DAN N969AX
47465	33CF	584	Airborne Express	HB-IDN N7465B N932AX
47466	32	621	Dallas Mavericks	N1291L N800DM
47467	C-9A	647	USAF	71-0874
47468	32	611	Sun Air	5Y-ALR HB-IKC I-SARZ N504MD G-BMAM ZS-NRB
47469	32	590	Northwest Airlines	YU-AHM N927RC
47470	32	591	Jugoslovenski Aerotpt	YU-AHN
47471	C-9A	650	USAF	71-0875
47472	32	596	Northwest Airlines	YU-AHO N925US
47473	32	598	Northwest Airlines	YU-AHP N926RC
47474	32	600	US Navy	I-ATIX N507MD 163512
47475	C-9A	653	USAF	71-0876
47476	33RC	569	US Navy	PH-DNZ N2679T YV-139C N907DC 162754
47477	32	613	US Navy	I-ATIK N508MD 163513
47478	32	612	Spirit Airlines	5X-UVY 5Y-BBR N942ML
47479	32	605	Northwest Airlines	HB-IFZ N985US
47480	32	607	Northwest Airlines	HB-IDO N988US N986US
47481	32	616	Merpati Nusantara	PK-GJG PK-GNC stored Oct95 Jakarta, Indonesia
47482	32	592	(Jugoslovenski Aerotpt)	YU-AHT w/o 26Jan72 nr Ceska Kamenice, Czechoslovakia
47483			not built	
47484	32	648	British Midland	OE-LDG G-ELDG
47485	32	666	Air Canada	CF-TMX C-FTMX
47486	32	628	Valujet Airlines	N1293L N914VV
47487	31	553	Continental Airlines	N1310T N18563
47488	32	527	Valujet Airlines	TC-JAD N923VV N934VV
47489	32	528	Valujet Airlines	TC-JAE N922VV N933VV
47490	31	560	Continental Airlines	N1311T N14564
47491	31	599	Trans World Airlines	N985Z
47492	41	559	Airborne Express	SE-DAK N979AX
47493	41	562	Airborne Express	OY-KGH SE-DLC N990AX
47494	41	601	Airborne Express	OY-KGI N970AX
47495	C-9A	656	USAF	71-0877
47496	33RC	673	US Navy	EC-BYM N536MD 164606
47497	41	604	Airborne Express	LN-RLB N971AX
47498	41	566	Airborne Express	SE-DAL N965AX
47499	41	568	Airborne Express	SE-DAM N968AX
47500	32	546	(Dominicana)	HI-177 w/o 15Feb70 Santo Domingo-Punta Caucedo, Dominican Rep

DOUGLAS DC-9

C/n	Series	Line No	Last known Operator/Owner	Previous Identities/fate (where known)					
47501	31	571	Aeromexico	VH-CZG	N936ML				
47502	32	574	Alitalia	I-DIZE					
47503	32	587	(Egyptair)	YU-AHR	w/o 19Mar72 nr Aden				
47504	32	651	Aviaco	EC-BYE					
47505	31	586	USAir	N960VJ					
47506	31	588	(USAir)	N961VJ	dbr 21Feb86 Erie, PA				
47507	31	594	USAir	N962VJ					
47508	31	595	USAir	N963VJ					
47509	41	643	Airborne Express	SE-DAO	N967AX				
47510	41	645	Airborne Express	OY-KGK	N966AX				
47511	41	677	Airborne Express	LN-RLU	N973AX				
47512	41	678	Airborne Express	SE-DAP	N974AX				
47513	41	679	Airborne Express	LN-RLX	N977AX				
47514	32	619	Spirit Airlines	PH-MAX	N947ML				
47515			not built						
47516	32	630	Sun Air	N1294L	ZS-NNN				
47517	31	583	Northwest Airlines	N908H					
47518	32	614	Alitalia	I-DIZO	I-RIZQ	I-RIFE			
47519	32	615	Aerorepublica	I-DIZF	I-RIZF	N29LR	HK-3927X		
47520	32	635	Continental Airlines	OE-LDC	N523TX	N523NY	N69523		
47521	32	629	Continental Airlines	OE-LDA	N521TX	N16521			
47522	32	606	Airborne Express	N1336U	EC-BYD	N985AX			
47523	32	593	Valujet Airlines	HB-IDP	G-PKBE	N940VV			
47524	32	632	Continental Airlines	OE-LDB	N522TX	N27522			
47525	32	631	Intl Airline Support Group	N1295L	stored Sep92 Sherman, TX for spares use				
47526	31	603	Spirit Airlines	VH-CZH	N934ML				
47527	31	618	Zuliana de Aviacion	VH-CZI	N930ML	YV-458C			
47528	31	617	Airborne Express	VH-TJR	N943AX				
47529	32	625	Valujet Airlines	N1292L	N923VV				
47530	33CF	624	Macedonian Airlines	YU-AHW	SL-ABG	S5-ABG	Z3-ARA		
47531	32	638	Continental Airlines	OE-LDE	EC-DQQ	N525TX	N525NY	N15525	
47532	32	626	Jugoslovenski Aerotpt	YU-AHU					
47533	32	641	Alitalia	I-ATIW	I-RIZV	I-RIFV			
47534	32	644	Valujet Airlines	TC-JAL	N924VV	N935VV			
47535	32	610	Continental Airlines	HB-IDR	N542TX	N70542			
47536	C-9A	659	USAF	71-0878					
47537	C-9A	662	USAF	71-0879					
47538	C-9A	665	USAF	71-0880					
47539	32	637	Continental Airlines	OE-LDD	N524TX	N14524			
47540	C-9A	668	USAF	71-0881					
47541	C-9A	670	USAF	71-0882					
47542	32	652	Aviaco	EC-BYF					
47543	32	654	Airborne Express	EC-BYG	N986AX	stored Mar93 Las Vegas, NV			
47544	32	676	Alitalia	I-ATIJ	I-RIZR	I-RIFM			
47545	33RC	671	US Navy	EC-BYL	N538MD	164605			
47546	32	655	Air Canada	CF-TMT	C-FTMT				
47547	31	622	Spirit Airlines	VH-CZJ	N932ML				
47548	31	633	Zuliana de Aviacion	VH-CZK	N933ML	YV-459C			
47549	31	639	Aeromexico	VH-CZL	N935ML				
47550	31	623	Airborne Express	VH-TJS	N944AX				
47551	31	634	Airborne Express	VH-TJT	N945AX				
47552	31	640	Airborne Express	VH-TJU	N942AX				
47553	32	642	Aerocalifornia	I-ATIH	I-RIZS	N136AA	XA-		
47554	32	658	Air Canada	CF-TMU	C-FTMU				
47555	32	667	Valujet Airlines	OE-LDH	G-ELDH	N964VV			
47556	32	657	(Aviaco)	EC-BYH	dbr 30Mar92 Grenada, Spain				
47557	32	661	Air Canada	CF-TMV	C-FTMV				
47558			not built						
47559	32	672	British Midland	OE-LDI	G-ELDI				
47560	32	664	Air Canada	CF-TMW	C-FTMW				
47561	32	674	(Garuda Indonesia)	(N982Z)	PK-GJI	PK-GNE	dbr 11Jun84 Djakarta, Indonesia		
47562	32	685	Jugoslovenski Aerotpt	N1345U	YU-AJH				
47563	32	687	Jugoslovenski Aerotpt	N1346U	YU-AJI				
47564	31	681	USAir	N950VJ					
47565	33RC	675	US Navy	EC-BYN	N539MD	164608			
47566	32	691	Northwest Airlines	N949N					
47567	32	688	Jugoslovenski Aerotpt	N1347U	YU-AJJ				
47568	32	689	Jugoslovenski Aerotpt	YU-AJK					
47569	32	683	Merpati Nusantara	PK-GJJ	PK-GNF	stored Oct95 Jakarta, Indonesia			
47570	32	684	Adria Airways	N1343U	YU-AJF	G-BMWD	YU-AJF	G-BMWD	YU-AJF
				SL-ABH	S5-ABH				
47571	32	695	Jugoslovenski Aerotpt	YU-AJL					
47572	32	708	Northwest Airlines	N940N					
47573	32	694	Northwest Airlines	N967N					
47574	31	690	USAir	N952VJ					
47575	32	680	Alitalia	I-ATIY	I-RIZW	I-RIFW			
47576	31	682	USAir	N951VJ					
47577	C-9B	686	US Navy	159113					
47578	C-9B	702	US Navy	159119					
47579	32	693	(Jugoslovenski Aerotpt)	YU-AJN	dbr 23Nov74 Belgrade-Surcin, Yugoslavia				
47580	C-9B	704	US Navy	159116					

DOUGLAS DC-9

C/n	Series	Line No	Last known Operator/Owner	Previous Identities/fate (where known)
47581	C-9B	692	US Navy	159117
47582	32	701	Jugoslovenski Aerotpt	YU-AJM
47583	31	697	USAir	N953VJ
47584	C-9B	696	US Navy	159114
47585	C-9B	698	US Navy	159118
47586	C-9B	707	US Navy	159120
47587	C-9B	700	US Navy	159115
47588	31	699	USAir	N54630 N956VJ
47589	31	711	Trans World Airlines	N986Z
47590	31	703	(USAir)	N954VJ w/o 02Jul94 nr Charlotte; cancelled May95
47591	32	706	Alitalia	I-ATIQ I-RIZT I-RIFT
47592	32	712	Air Canada	CF-TMY C-FTMY
47593	31	705	USAir	N955VJ
47594	32	717	Aeromexico	XA-DEJ
47595	32	709	Italian AF	MM62012/SM-12 MM62012/31-12
47596	41	714	Scandinavian A/L System	SE-DAR
47597	41	713	Scandinavian A/L System	N54631 OY-KGL
47598	32	719	Air Canada	CF-TMZ C-FTMZ
47599	41	716	Scandinavian A/L System	LN-RLA
47600	32	710	Italian AF	N54635 MM62013/SM-13 MM62013/31-13
47601	32	715	Merpati Nusantara	PK-GJK PK-GNG stored Oct95 Jakarta, Indonesia
47602	32	718	Aeromexico	XA-DEK
47603	41	720	Trans World Airlines	JA8423 OH-LNA N935L
47604	41	722	Finnair	JA8424 OH-LNB
47605	41	724	Finnair	JA8425 OH-LNE
47606	41	727	Australian Aircraft Sales	JA8426 OH-LND wfs Oct95 Helsinki, Finland
47607	32	721	Aeromexico	XA-DEL
47608	41	732	Airborne Express	JA8427 N953AX
47609	32	723	Aeromexico	XA-DEM
47610	41	725	Scandinavian A/L System	SE-DAS
47611	32	726	Air Canada	C-FTMM
47612	41	736	Airborne Express	JA8428 N954AX
47613	41	742	Australian Aircraft Sales	JA8429 OH-LNC EC-DQT OH-LNC wfs Nov95 Helsinki, Finland
47614	41	747	Finnair	JA8430 OH-LNF
47615	41	751	Airborne Express	JA8432 N952AX
47616	41	759	Airborne Express	JA8433 N951AX
47617	41	762	Trans World Airlines	JA8434 N933L
47618	41	764	Trans World Airlines	JA8435 N934L
47619	41	768	Airborne Express	N54645 JA8436 N955AX
47620	41	777	Airborne Express	JA8437 N956AX
47621	32	729	(Aeromexico)	XA-DEN w/o 27Jul81 Chihuahua, Mexico
47622	32	753	(Aeromexico)	XA-DEO w/o 08Nov81 nr Zihuatanejo, Mexico
47623	41	728	Scandinavian A/L System	LN-RLS
47624	41	733	Scandinavian A/L System	OY-KGM
47625	41	737	(Scandinavian A/L System)	SE-DAT dbr 23Feb87 Trondheim, Norway
47626	41	738	Scandinavian A/L System	LN-RLT
47627	41	739	Scandinavian A/L System	SE-DAU
47628	41	740	Scandinavian A/L System	OY-KGN
47629	41	744	Scandinavian A/L System	SE-DAW
47630	41	745	Scandinavian A/L System	LN-RLN
47631	41	743	Scandinavian A/L System	SE-DAX
47632	41	748	Scandinavian A/L System	OY-KGO
47633	41	752	Scandinavian A/L System	SE-DBM
47634	41	756	Scandinavian A/L System	LN-RLZ
47635	32	754	Roll Ball One Inc	PK-GNH N880RB
47636	32	758	(Garuda Indonesia)	PK-GNI w/o 30Dec84 Bali-Ngurah Aai, Indonesia
47637	32	731	Aviaco	EC-CGN
47638	32	730	Continental Airlines	N3504T N19504
47639	32F	735	US Navy	6Y-JIJ PJ-SND 6Y-JIJ PJ-SND 6Y-JIJ D-ALLD C-GBWO EC-DTI N4549V 163208/JS
47640	32	734	Aviaco	EC-CGO
47641	32	746	(Alitalia)	I-ATJA w/o 14Nov90 Weiach, nr Zurich, Switzerland
47642	32	749	Aviaco	EC-CGP
47643	32	750	Aviaco	EC-CGQ
47644	32	767	Aviaco	EC-CGR
47645	32	770	(Aviaco)	EC-CGS w/o 07Dec83 Madrid-Barajas, Spain
47646	41	755	Scandinavian A/L System	OY-KGP
47647	32	773	Northwest Airlines	N943N
47648	32	761	Valujet Airlines	PJ-SNA G-PKBM N942VV
47649	32	741	(Inex Adria)	N54638 YU-AJR w/o 10Sep76 nr Zagreb, Yugoslavia
47650	32	771	Aeromexico	XA-DEI
47651	51	780	Northwest Airlines	N13627 OE-LDK N675MC stored Aug93 Marana, AZ
47652	51	798	Northwest Airlines	OE-LDL N676MC
47653	32	760	Zuliana de Aviacion	I-ATJB I-RIZN YV-497C
47654	51	757	Hawaiian Airlines	N54641 HB-ISK N669HA N966HA*
47655	51	763	Meridiana	N54642 HB-ISL LN-RMC OY-CTA I-SMEO
47656	51	783	Meridiana	HB-ISM SU-BKK EC-246 EC-ENZ I-SMEE
47657	51	797	Meridiana	HB-ISN SE-DFN OY-CTB I-SMEJ
47658	51	790	Hawaiian Airlines	HB-ISO SE-DFO OY-CTD N601AP N959HA*
47659	51	807	Northwest Airlines	HB-ISP N670MC stored Oct93 Marana, AZ

DOUGLAS DC-9

C/n	Series	Line No	Last known Operator/Owner	Previous Identities/fate (where known)			
47660	51	810	Northwest Airlines	HB-ISR	N671MC	stored Oct93 Marana, AZ	
47661	51	812	Hawaiian Airlines	N8706Q	HB-ISS	N672MC	N965HA*
47662	51	850	Hawaiian Airlines	HB-IST	N679HA		
47663	51	851	Private Jet Expeditions	HB-ISU	N689HA	N919PJ	
47664	32	775	Northwest Airlines	N945N			
47665	51	796	AVENSA	N923VJ	N404EA	YV-90C	
47666	32	772	Valujet Airlines	PJ-SNB	G-PKBD	N941VV	
47667	32	766	(Aero Trasporti Italiani)	I-ATJC	w/o 13Sep79 nr Cagliari, Sardinia		
47668	VC-9C	765	USAF	73-1681			
47669	32	776	Trans World Airlines	PJ-SNC	N932L		
47670	VC-9C	769	USAF	73-1682			
47671	VC-9C	774	USAF	73-1683			
47672	32	778	Midwest Express	PK-GNJ	D-ALLC	N202ME	
47673	32	779	Midwest Express	PK-GNK	D-ALLA	N203ME	
47674	32	793	Valujet Airlines	TC-JBK	N920VV	N931VV	
47675	32	782	Aviaco	EC-CLD			
47676	51	785	Trans World Airlines	N609HA	N418EA		
47677	51	791	Sun Jet International	N619HA	N419EA	N920PJ	
47678	32	789	(Aviaco)	EC-CLE	w/o 21Mar94 Vigo		
47679	51	797	Servivensa	N629HA	N421EA	YV-766C	
47680	32	781	Midwest Express	PK-GNL	D-ALLB	N204ME	
47681	C-9B	784	US Navy	160048			
47682	51	788	Northwest Airlines	N920VJ	N401EA	stored Jan92 Las Vegas-McCarran, NV	
47683	51	792	AVENSA	N921VJ	N402EA	YV-85C	
47684	C-9B	786	US Marines	160046			
47685	51	794	AVENSA	N922VJ	N403EA	YV-87C	
47686	51	800	Trans World Airlines	N925VJ	N406EA		
47687	C-9B	795	US Navy	160047			
47688	51	799	Trans World Airlines	N924VJ	N405EA		
47689	51	802	Hawaiian Airlines	N639HA	N420EA		
47690	32CF	843	Kuwait AF	160750	KAF 321		
47691	32CF	840	(Kuwait AF)	160749	KAF 320	dest 02Aug90 by Iraqi troops, Kuwait International A/P, Kuwait	
47692	51	803	AVENSA	N926VJ	N407EA	YV-80C	
47693	51	804	Trans World Airlines	N927VJ	N408EA		
47694	51	805	Finnair	OH-LYN			
47695	51	806	Finnair	OH-LYO			
47696	51	808	Finnair	OH-LYP	N9MD	OH-LYP	
47697	51	816	Eurofly	N8709Q	YU-AJT	N54UA	I-FLYZ
47698	C-9B	809	US Navy	160049			
47699	C-9B	801	US Navy	160050			
47700	C-9B	811	US Navy	160051			
47701	32	822	Garuda Indonesia	PK-GNM	stored Oct95 Jakarta, Indonesia		
47702	34CF	817	Iberia	N19B	EC-CTR		
47703	51	841	Aeropostal	YV-22C	stored Sep94 Caracas, Venezuela		
47704	34CF	819	Aviaco	EC-CTS			
47705	51	842	Aeropostal	YV-20C	stored Sep94 Caracas, Venezuela		
47706	34CF	821	Iberia	EC-CTT			
47707	34CF	823	Aviaco	EC-CTU			
47708	51	813	Northwest Airlines	N760NC			
47709	51	814	Northwest Airlines	N761NC			
47710	51	818	Northwest Airlines	N762NC			
47711	34	844	Trans World Airlines	HB-IDT	N936L		
47712	51	815	Aeropostal	N649HA	YV-35C	stored Sep94 Caracas, Venezuela	
47713	51	820	Meridiana	N659HA	HB-IKH	I-SMEA	
47714	51	824	Meridiana	N669HA	HB-IKF	I-SMEI	
47715	51	825	Meridiana	N679HA	HB-IKG	I-SMEU	
47716	51	832	Northwest Airlines	N763NC			
47717	51	833	Northwest Airlines	N764NC			
47718	51	834	Northwest Airlines	N765NC			
47719	51	845	Aeropostal	YV-21C	stored Sep94 Caracas, Venezuela		
47720	32	846	(Aeropostal)	YV-23C	w/o 05Mar91 nr Lake Maracaibo, Venezuela		
47721	32	847	Aeropostal	YV-25C	stored Sep94 Caracas, Venezuela		
47722	32	826	Merpati Nusantara	PK-GNN	stored Oct95 Jakarta, Indonesia		
47723	32	838	Valujet Airlines	TC-JBL	N919VV	N930VV	
47724	51	853	Northwest Airlines	N767NC			
47725	41	831	Scandinavian A/L System	OY-KGR			
47726	51	849	Hawaiian Airlines	OE-LDM	N673MC	N964HA*	
47727	32	848	Aeropostal	YV-24C	stored Sep94 Caracas, Venezuela		
47728	51	858	Trans World Airlines	N991EA	N409EA		
47729	51	854	Northwest Airlines	N768NC			
47730	32	828	Midwest Express Airlines	PK-GNO	N209ME		
47731	51	860	Trans World Airlines	N992EA	N410EA		
47732	51	861	Trans World Airlines	N993EA	N411EA		
47733	51	862	Trans World Airlines	N994EA	N412EA		
47734	32	868	Trans World Airlines	N920L			
47735	51	869	Hawaiian Airlines	OE-LDN	N674MC	(N963HA)	stored Oct93 Honolulu, HI
47736	51	827	Finnair	OH-LYR			
47737	51	829	Finnair	OH-LYS	9Y-TFF	OH-LYS	
47738	51	830	Finnair	OH-LYT			
47739	51	852	Northwest Airlines	N766NC			

DOUGLAS DC-9

C/n	Series	Line No	Last known Operator/Owner	Previous Identities/fate (where known)
47740	32	835	Merpati Nusantara	PK-GNP stored Oct95 Jakarta, Indonesia
47741	32	836	(Garuda Indonesia)	PK-GNQ w/o 04Apr87 Medan, Indonesia
47742	51	857	Hawaiian Airlines	9Y-TFG EI-CBG
47743	51	859	Servivensa	9Y-TFH YV-820C
47744	32	837	Merpati Nusantara	PK-GNR stored Oct95 Jakarta, Indonesia
47745	51	863	Servivensa	N995EA N413EA YV-767C
47746	51	864	Trans World Airlines	N996EA N414EA
47747	41	839	Scandinavian A/L System	SE-DDP
47748	41	855	Scandinavian A/L System	LN-RLH
47749	51	865	Trans World Airlines	N997EA N415EA
47750	41	870	Scandinavian A/L System	SE-DDR
47751	51	866	Trans World Airlines	N998EA N416EA
47752	34CF	872	Aeropostal	9Y-TFI YV-37C stored Sep94 Caracas, Venezuela
47753	51	867	Trans World Airlines	N999EA N417EA
47754	51	856	Eurofly	YU-AJU N56UA I-FLYY
47755	51	878	Ghana Airways	9G-ACM
47756	51	873	Northwest Airlines	OE-LDO N677MC stored Oct93 Marana, AZ
47757	51	877	Northwest Airlines	N769NC
47758	51	880	Northwest Airlines	N770NC
47759	41	871	Airborne Express	JA8439 N957AX
47760	41	874	Japan Air System	JA8440
47761	41	875	Japan Air System	N8710Q JA8441
47762	41	876	Japan Air System	JA8442
47763	51	879	Hawaiian Airlines	N699HA N969HA*
47764	51	882	Hawaiian Airlines	N709HA (N970HA) stored Oct93 Honolulu, HI
47765	32	900	Continental Airlines	N3506T N33506
47766	41	886	Scandinavian A/L System	OY-KGS
47767	41	885	(Japan Air System)	JA8448 w/o 18Apr93 Hanamaki, Japan and burnt out
47768	41	887	Japan Air System	JA8449
47769	51	881	Northwest Airlines	N771NC
47770	51	892	Aeropostal	YV-32C stored Sep94 Caracas, Venezuela
47771	51	883	Finnair	OH-LYU
47772	51	890	Finnair	N8713Q OH-LYV
47773	51	891	Finnair	N8714Q OH-LYW
47774	51	884	Northwest Airlines	N772NC
47775	51	888	Northwest Airlines	N773NC
47776	51	889	Northwest Airlines	N774NC
47777	41	896	Scandinavian A/L System	SE-DDS
47778	41	897	Scandinavian A/L System	LN-RLP
47779	41	898	Scandinavian A/L System	SE-DDT
47780	41	894	Japan Air System	JA8450
47781	41	895	Japan Air System	JA8451
47782	51	893	Aeropostal	N1002N YV-33C stored Sep94 Caracas, Venezuela
47783	51	899	Northwest Airlines	HB-ISV YV-40C N600TR
47784	51	902	Hawaiian Airlines	N13627 HB-ISW YV-41C N603DC N957HA*
47785	51	904	Northwest Airlines	N775NC
47786	51	905	Northwest Airlines	N776NC
47787	51	912	Northwest Airlines	N777NC
47788	32	901	Continental Airlines	N3507T N12507
47789	32	906	Cebu Pacific Air	PK-GNS RP-C c Nov95
47790	32	907	Garuda Indonesia	PK-GNT dbr 21Jun93 Denpassar; preserved Taman Theme Park, Jakarta, Indonesia
47791	32	908	Midwest Express	PK-GNU N206ME
47792	32	910	Cebu Pacific Air	PK-GNV RP-C c Nov95
47793	32	911	Cebu Pacific Air	PK-GNW RP-C1505
47794	32	915	Midwest Express	PK-GNX N207ME
47795	32	916	Cebu Pacific Air	PK-GNY RP-C c Nov95
47796	51	903	Air Tara	9Y-TGC EI-CBH
47797	32	913	Continental Airlines	N3508T N12508
47798	32	914	Continental Airlines	N3509T N27509
47799	32	918	Continental Airlines	N3510T N12510
48100	51	927	Northwest Airlines	N778NC
48101	51	931	Northwest Airlines	N779NC
48102	51	932	Northwest Airlines	N780NC
48103	34	925	Iberia	EC-DGB
48104	34	928	Aviaco	EC-DGC
48105	34	929	Aviaco	EC-DGD
48106	34	933	Aviaco	EC-DGE
48107	51	936	Northwest Airlines	N782NC
48108	51	937	Northwest Airlines	N783NC
48109	51	939	Northwest Airlines	N784NC
48110	51	945	Northwest Airlines	N785NC
48111	32	923	Continental Airlines	N3512T N13512
48112	32	926	Continental Airlines	N3513T N18513
48113	32	930	Continental Airlines	N3514T N12514
48114	31	919	USAir	N934VJ
48115	31	920	USAir	N935VJ
48116	31	921	USAir	N936VJ
48117	31	922	USAir	N937VJ
48118	31	942	USAir	N929VJ
48119	31	943	USAir	N938VJ

DOUGLAS DC-9

C/n	Series	Line No	Last known Operator/Owner	Previous Identities/fate (where known)		
48120	31	949	USAir	N939VJ		
48121	51	935	Northwest Airlines	N781NC		
48122	51	972	Hawaiian Airlines	9Y-TGP	EI-CBI	
48123	34	934	Trans World Airlines	N927L		
48124	34	954	Trans World Airlines	N928L		
48125	32	947	Aeromexico	XA-AMA		
48126	32	951	Aeromexico	XA-AMB		
48127	32	961	Aeromexico	XA-AMC		
48128	32	964	Aeromexico	XA-AMD		
48129	32	968	Aeromexico	XA-AME		
48130	32	976	Aeromexico	XA-AMF		
48131	31	940	USAir	N928VJ		
48132	32	956	Midwest Express	PH-DOA	N943U	N502ME
48133	32	959	Midwest Express	PH-DOB	N944U	N602ME
48134	51	980	Finnair	OH-LYX		
48135	51	987	Finnair	OH-LYY		
48136	51	993	Finnair	OH-LYZ		
48137	C-9B	982	US Navy	N10028	161266	
48138	31	1021	USAir	N918VJ		
48139	31	1024	USAir	N919VJ		
48140	31	1027	USAir	N920VJ		
48141	31	1030	USAir	N921VJ		
48142	31	1033	USAir	N922VJ		
48143	31	1036	USAir	N923VJ		
48144	31	1039	USAir	N924VJ		
48145	31	1042	USAir	N925VJ		
48146	31	1044	USAir	N926VJ		
48147	31	1048	USAir	N976VJ		
48148	51	984	Northwest Airlines	N786NC		
48149	51	990	Northwest Airlines	N787NC		
48150	32	1014	Aeromexico	(XA-AMG)	N1003P	
48151	32	1017	Aeromexico	(XA-AMH)	N1003U	
48152	32		not built	(XA-AMI)		
48153	32		not built			
48154	31	1046	USAir	N927VJ		
48155	31	1050	USAir	N977VJ		
48156	31	1052	USAir	N980VJ		
48157	31	1054	USAir	N981VJ		
48158	31	1056	USAir	N982VJ		
48159	31	1058	USAir	N983VJ		
48160			not built			
48161			not built			
48162			not built			
48163			not built			
48164			not built			
48165	C-9B	1081	US Navy	161529		
48166	C-9B	1084	US Navy	161530		

Production continued with McDonnell-Douglas DC-9-80 Series (see MD-80)

DOUGLAS DC-10

C/n	Series	Line No	Last known Operator/Owner	Previous Identities/fate (where known)
46500	10	1	American Airlines	N10DC prototype; ff 29Aug70 N101AA stored Feb95 Marana, AZ
46501	10	2	Project Orbis International	N101AA N10DC G-BELO N183AT G-GCAL N220AU
46502	10	3	American Airlines	N102AA stored Jun93 Amarillo, TX
46503	10	5	American Airlines	N103AA stored Oct93 Amarillo, TX
46504	10	7	(American Airlines)	N104AA b/u by 05Sep95 Amarillo, TX
46505	10	9	American Airlines	N105AA stored Nov93 Amarillo, TX
46506	10	12	American Airlines	N106AA stored Nov93 Amarillo, TX
46507	10	13	American Airlines	N107AA stored Nov93 Amarillo, TX
46508	10	20	American Airlines	N108AA stored Oct93 Amarillo, TX
46509	10	21	(American Airlines)	N109AA b/u Sep95 Amarillo, TX
46510	10	22	(American Airlines)	N110AA w/o 25May79 Chicago-O'Hare, IL
46511	10	23	(American Airlines)	N111AA b/u by 14Feb95 Amarillo, TX
46512	10	24	American Airlines	N112AA stored Aug93 Amarillo, TX
46513	10	30	American Airlines	N113AA stored Aug93 Amarillo, TX
46514	10	31	American Airlines	N114AA stored Aug93 Amarillo, TX, used for spares
46515	10	37	American Airlines	N115AA stored Feb94 Amarillo, TX
46516	10	48	Hawaiian Airlines	N116AA
46517	10	49	American Airlines	N117AA stored Dec93 Marana, AZ
46518	10	51	American Airlines	N118AA stored Apr94 Amarillo, TX
46519	10	52	Hawaiian Airlines	N119AA
46520	10	54	American Airlines	N120AA stored Apr94 Amarillo, TX
46521	10	55	American Airlines	N121AA stored Apr94 Amarillo, TX
46522	10	56	Hawaiian Airlines	N122AA
46523	10	58	GATX Capital Corp	N123AA stored Jan95 Marana, AZ
46524	10	65	Hughes Aircraft	N124AA stored Jun95 Donaldson Air Park, Marana, AZ
46525	10	72	GATX Capital Corp	N125AA stored Jan95 Marana, AZ
46540	30	268	Canadian Airlines Intl	C-GCPC PP-VMO C-GCPC
46541	30	281	Canadian Airlines Intl	C-GCPD PP-VMP C-GCPD
46542	30	295	Canadian Airlines Intl	C-GCPE
46543	30	341	Canadian Airlines Intl	C-GCPF (N1849U) C-GCPF
46550	30	46	Krasnoyarsk Air	N1339U PH-DTA N525MD
46551	30	60	Northwest Airlines	N1342U PH-DTB N4655Y N229NW
46552	30	71	Northwest Airlines	PH-DTC N4655Z N230NW
46553	30	82	Krasnoyarsk Air	PH-DTD N533MD
46554	30	84	Skyjet	N1349U PH-DTE N130FA SE-DFG LN-ALN YU-AMD N821CC V2-LEA OO-PHN
46555	30	91	American Airlines	PH-DTF YV-133C N143AA
46556	30	146	VIASA	PH-DTG YV-134C
46557	30	197	VIASA	PH-DTH YV-138C
46575	30	57	Concord Asset Management	N1340U HB-IHA HC-BKO stored Sep93
46576	30	73	Continental Airlines	HB-IHB EC-DUG N19072
46577	30	114	Northwest Airlines	(HB-IGI) HB-IHC N220NW
46578	30	131	Northwest Airlines	HB-IHD YU-AMC VR-BMP (ZS-NPZ) N228NW
46579	30	132	Northwest Airlines	(HB-IGL) HB-IHE N221NW
46580	30	183	Northwest Airlines	(HB-IGM) HB-IHF N223NW
46581	30	184	Northwest Airlines	HB-IHG N224NW
46582	30	187	Northwest Airlines	HB-IHH N225NW
46583	30ER	292	Northwest Airlines	N1002X HB-IHL N226NW
46584	30ER	293	Continental Airlines	N1002Y HB-IHM N610PH N15069
46590	30	266	Continental Airlines	G-BFGI N68065
46591	30	287	Continental Airlines	G-BGAT N13066
46595	30	299	Condor	D-ADPO
46596	30	301	Condor	D-ADQO
46600	10	4	United Airlines	N1801U stored Sep94 Las Vegas-McCarran, NV
46601	10	6	United Airlines	N1802U stored Sep94 Las Vegas-McCarran, NV
46602	10	8	United Airlines	N1803U stored Sep94 Las Vegas-McCarran, NV
46603	10	10	United Airlines	N1804U stored Aug95 Ardmore, OK; used for spares
46604	10	11	United Airlines	N1805U stored Aug95 Ardmore, OK; used for spares
46605	10	15	United Airlines	N1806U stored Sep94 Denver, CO
46606	10	17	United Airlines	N1807U stored Sep94 Las Vegas-McCarran, NV
46607	10	25	United Airlines	N1808U stored Sep94 Las Vegas-McCarran, NV
46608	10	26	United Airlines	N1809U stored Sep94 Las Vegas-McCarran, NV
46609	10	27	United Airlines	N1810U stored Sep94 Las Vegas-McCarran, NV
46610	10	32	United Airlines	N1811U
46611	10	35	United Airlines	N1812U
46612	10	39	United Airlines	N1813U
46613	10	42	United Airlines	N1814U
46614	10	45	United Airlines	N1815U
46615	10	76	United Airlines	N1816U
46616	10	86	United Airlines	N1817U
46617	10	89	United Airlines	N1818U stored Sep93 Las Vegas-McCarran, NV
46618	10	118	(United Airlines)	N1819U w/o 19Jul89 Sioux City, IA
46619	10	119	United Airlines	N1820U stored Sep94 Las Vegas-McCarran, NV
46620	10	138	United Airlines	N1821U stored Sep94 Las Vegas-McCarran, NV
46621	10	140	United Airlines	N1822U stored Sep94 Las Vegas-McCarran, NV
46622	10	144	United Airlines	N1823U
46623	10	154	United Airlines	N1824U
46624	10	155	United Airlines	N1825U
46625	10	169	United Airlines	N1826U stored Oct95 Marana, AZ

DOUGLAS DC-10

C/n	Series	Line No	Last known Operator/Owner	Previous Identities/fate (where known)
46626	10	198	United Airlines	N1827U stored Oct95 Marana, AZ
46627	10	205	United Airlines	N1828U
46628	10	207	United Airlines	N1829U stored Jan96 Las Vegas-McCarran, NV
46629	10	208	United Airlines	N1830U
46630	10	209	United Airlines	N1831U
46631	10	210	United Airlines	N1832U
46632	10	296	United Airlines	N1838U
46633	10	297	United Airlines	N1839U
46634	10	298	United Airlines	N1841U
46635	10	307	United Airlines	N1842U
46636	10	309	United Airlines	N1843U
46640	30	240	Wilmington Trust	9M-MAT N962GF
46645	10	283	Sun Country Airlines	N912WA SE-DHX N571SC
46646	10	285	Premiair	N913WA SE-DHS
46660	40	220	Japan Asia Airways	N8705Q JA8532
46661	40	224	Japan Air Lines	N19B N54652 JA8533
46662	40	230	Japan Air Lines	N19B JA8535
46685	30	284	Garuda Indonesia	PK-GIE
46686	30	286	Garuda Indonesia	PK-GIF
46700	10	14	American Airlines	N60NA N145AA stored Aug94 Marana, AZ
46701	10	16	Hawaiian Airlines	N61NA N146AA
46702	10	18	American Airlines	N62NA N147AA
46703	10	19	Hawaiian Airlines	N63NA N148AA
46704	10	29	(Turk Hava Yollari)	N1337U TC-JAV w/o 04Mar74 Senlis, France
46705	10F	33	Federal Express	N1338U TC-JAU N68058
46706	10	38	American Airlines	N64NA N151AA stored May94 Marana, AZ
46707	10	61	Hawaiian Airlines	N65NA N152AA
46708	10	62	Hawaiian Airlines	N66NA N153AA
46709	10	68	Polaris Holding	N67NA N154AA stored Jan96 Greensboro, NC
46710	10	70	American Airlines	N68NA N160AA
46711	30	105	(American Airlines)	N80NA N139AA dbr 14Apr93 Dallas-Fort Worth, TX; canx Jun93
46712	30	106	American Airlines	N81NA CC-CJN N81NA N140AA stored Nov93 Marana, AZ
46713	30	165	American Airlines	N82NA N141AA stored Dec93 Marana, AZ
46714	30	167	American Airlines	N83NA N142AA stored May95 Marana, AZ
46727	10F	83	ARCA Colombia	N1348U G-BBSZ N917CL N917JW EC-EAZ N917JW N40KA N917JW N40KA N104WA
46750	40	28	Northwest Airlines	N141US
46751	40	36	(American Trans Air)	N142US N184AT dbf 10Aug86 Chicago-O'Hare, IL
46752	40	53	Northwest Airlines	N143US N133JC
46753	40	66	Northwest Airlines	N144US N144JC
46754	40	79	Northwest Airlines	N145US
46755	40	97	Northwest Airlines	N146US
46756	40	102	Northwest Airlines	N147US
46757	40	108	Northwest Airlines	N148US
46758	40	111	Northwest Airlines	N149US
46759	40	113	Northwest Airlines	N150US
46760	40	120	Northwest Airlines	N151US
46761	40	124	Northwest Airlines	N152US
46762	40	126	Northwest Airlines	N153US
46763	40	128	Northwest Airlines	N154US
46764	40	130	Northwest Airlines	N155US
46765	40	143	Northwest Airlines	N156US
46766	40	151	Northwest Airlines	N157US
46767	40	161	Northwest Airlines	N158US
46768	40	164	Northwest Airlines	N159US
46769	40	168	Northwest Airlines	N160US
46770	40	175	Northwest Airlines	N161US
46771	40	180	Northwest Airlines	N162US
46800	30CF	96	Federal Express	N101TV N301FE
46801	30CF	103	Federal Express	N102TV N302FE
46802	30CF	110	Federal Express	N103TV N303FE
46825	30CF	81	(Overseas National Airways)	N1031F dbr 02Jan76 Istanbul, Turkey
46826	30CF	109	(Overseas National Airways)	N1032F dbf 12Nov75 New York-Kennedy, NY
46827	30CF		not built	(N1033F)
46835	30CF	277	Federal Express	N106WA N317FE
46836	30CF	280	World Airways	N107WA
46837	30CF	282	Federal Express	N108WA N318FE
46850	30	63	Air Europe Italy	(F-BTDA) N1341U F-BTDB OO-JOT
46851	30	85	AOM French Airlines	N1350U (F-BTDB) F-BTDC HS-TGA F-BTDC F-GTDH
46852	30	93	(UTA)	(F-BTDC) (F-BTDD) N54629 F-BTDF N54629 w/o by bomb explosion 19Sep89 nr Termit, Niger
46853	30	134	AOM French Airlines	(N54639) (F-BTDD) (F-BTDE) N54639 F-BTDE
46854	30	193	AOM French Airlines	(N54649) (F-BTDF) (F-GHOJ) N54649 (F-GRMR) F-GTDF
46855	30		not built	
46856	30		not built	
46857	30		not built	
46865	30		not built	
46866	30		not built	
46867	30		not built	
46868	30	171	Northwest Airlines	LN-RKA HB-IHP N211NW
46869	30	174	AOM French Airlines	(SE-DEA) SE-DFD F-ODLZ

DOUGLAS DC-10

C/n	Series	Line No	Last known Operator/Owner	Previous Identities/fate (where known)
46870	30	217	AOM French Airlines	OY-KDA F-GHOI
46871	30F	219	Federal Express	LN-RKB N311FE
46872	30	233	AOM French Airlines	(SE-DEB) SE-DFE (F-GKMR) F-ODLX
46890	30	77	Air Afrique	(TU-TCG) TU-TAL
46891	30CF	127	World Airways	PH-MBG N105WA UN-10200 RA-10200 N105WA (OO-HVA) N105WA
46892	30	204	AOM French Airlines	(TU-TBD) TU-TAM HS-TGB TU-TAM F-GNEM
46900	10	34	Continental Airlines	N68041
46901	10	40	Continental Airlines	N68042
46902	10	41	Continental Airlines	N68043
46903	10	43	Continental Airlines	N68044
46904	10	44	(Continental Airlines)	N68045 dbr 01Mar78 Los Angeles, CA
46905	10	47	Sun Country Airlines	G-AZZC N902CL N902JW N52UA N102UA N573SC
46906	10	50	Hawaiian Airlines	G-AZZD N916CL N916JW N171AA
46907	10F	78	Federal Express	TC-JAY N68059
46908	10	95	American Airlines	N901WA N166AA
46910	30	182	(Air New Zealand)	ZK-NZP w/o 28Nov79 Mt Erebus, Antarctica
46911	30	189	Continental Airlines	ZK-NZQ N138AA N14074
46912	30	188	Korean Air	HL7316
46913	40	206	Japan Air Charter	N54652 JA8534
46914	30	195	American Airlines	PH-DTK N163AA
46915	30	199	Korean Air	HL7317
46916	30	202	VARIG	PP-VMD
46917	30	211	Condor	D-ADLO
46918	30	223	Garuda Indonesia	PK-GWA PK-GIA
46919	30	226	Garuda Indonesia	PK-GWB PK-GIB
46920	40	212	Japan Air Lines	N8702Q JA8530
46921	30	214	British Airways	N8704Q N54640 G-BEBM
46922	30	221	Iberia	EC-CSJ
46923	40	216	Japan Asia Airways	N8703Q JA8531
46924	30CF	218	(Martinair Holland)	PH-MBN w/o 21Dec92 Faro, Portugal
46925	30	87	(Iberia)	N54627 EC-CBN w/o 17Dec73 Boston, MA
46926	30	99	Iberia	EC-CBO
46927	30	100	Iberia	EC-CBP
46928	10	104	Aero Express	N902WA (5N-OGI) 9Q-CSS stored Sep94 Ostend, Belgium
46929	10	107	(Western Air Lines)	N903WA w/o 31Oct79 Mexico City, Mexico
46930	10	112	American Airlines	N904WA N167AA
46931	30	137	Laker Airways	N54637 AP-AXC C-FCRA XA-AMR N832LA
46932	30	158	Caledonian Airways	9Q-CLT G-NIUK
46933	30	159	LOT-Polish Airlines	PH-DTI N801AL OY-KDB N109WA 9M-MAZ
46934	30	160	Korean Air	(PH-DTK) N19B HL7315
46935	30	172	(Pakistan Intl Airlines)	AP-AXE dbf 03Feb81 Karachi, Pakistan
46936	30	147	Laker Airways	XA-DUG N417DG N831LA G-BWIN
46937	30	152	Laker Airways	XA-DUH N8228P N833LA
46938	10	153	American Airlines	N905WA N168AA
46939	10	203	United Airlines	N906WA N1849U
46940	30	141	Continental Airlines	AP-AXD C-FCRB PP-SOM N234DC N76073
46941	30	176	VARIG	(PP-VMC) PP-VMQ
46942	10	162	American Airlines	N69NA N161AA stored Apr94 Marana, AZ
46943	10	163	American Airlines	N70NA N162AA
46944	30	133	VARIG	PP-VMA
46945	30	156	VARIG	PP-VMB
46946	10	222	Sun Country Airlines	N907WA
46947	10	247	American Airlines	N126AA
46948	10	249	American Airlines	N127AA
46949	30	179	British Airways	N54643 G-BEBL
46950	30	242	American Airlines	ZK-NZT CC-CJT N164AA stored Jan94 Tulsa, OK
46951	30	246	Garuda Indonesia	PK-GID
46952	30	185	African Safari	N54646 (PK-GWA) PH-DTL HS-TGC PH-DTL (YV-139C) PH-DTL
46953	30	225	VIASA	EC-CSK YV-139C
46954	30	227	AOM French Airlines	ZK-NZS (N85NA) CC-CJS SE-DFH (F-GKMS) F-ODLY
46955	30	228	Malaysian Airline System	9M-MAS
46956	KDC-10	235	Royal Netherlands AF	PH-MBP T-235
46957	30	231	Nigeria Airways	(9M-MAT) 5N-ANN
46958	30	232	Dormacken Ltd	(PH-DTM) (RP-C2000) RP-C2003 EI-DLA stored Dec95 Greensboro, NC
46959	30	234	Malaysian Airline System	N8707Q HS-TGD HS-TMC OY-KDC 9M-MAW
46960	30CF	237	(Korean Air Lines)	N1033F HL7339 w/o 23Dec83 Anchorage, AK
46961	30	236	Northwest Airlines	N8708Q HS-TGE HS-TMD LN-RKD 9M-MAX N961GF N232NW*
46962	30CF	238	(Spantax)	N1034F EC-DEG dbf 13Sep82 Malaga, Spain
46963	30	244	AOM French Airlines	F-BTDD
46964	30	239	Garuda Indonesia	PK-GIC
46965	30F	245	Gemini Air Cargo	D-ADMO N600GC
46966	40	262	Japan Air Lines	JA8536
46967	40	265	Japan Asia Airways	JA8537
46968	30	243	(Nigeria Airways)	(5N-ANO) 5N-ANR dbf 10Jan87 Ilorin, Nigeria
46969	30	241	Northwest Airlines	HB-IHI N227NW
46970	10	269	Federal Express	N1002D G-GFAL G-BJZD N581LF N10060
46971	30	258	VIASA	YV-135C PH-AAI YV-135C

DOUGLAS DC-10

C/n	Series	Line No	Last known Operator/Owner	Previous Identities/fate (where known)
46972	30	276	VIASA	YV-136C PH-AAJ YV-136C
46973	10F	272	Federal Express	G-GSKY G-BJZE N591LF N40061
46974	40	274	Japan Air Charter	JA8538
46975	30CF	248	United Airlines	N103WA N1856U
46976	30	254	Aero USA Inc	N8712Q C-GXRB EI-BZD N602DC stored Jul94 Fort Worth-Meacham Field, TX
46977	10	251	Sun Country Airlines	N908WA SE-DHZ N572SC
46978	30	256	Aero USA Inc	C-GXRC OH-LHE N777SJ stored Dec95 Greensboro, NC; canx Sep95
46981	30	259	Air Liberte	YU-AMA F-WNBB F-GNBB F-OKBB F-GPVE
46982	30	290	VIASA	YV-137C PH-AAK YV-137C
46983	10	252	Premiair	N909WA SE-DHY OY-CNY
46984	10	250	American Airlines	N128AA
46985	KDC-10	264	Royal Netherlands AF	PH-MBT T-264
46986	30CF	253	United Airlines	N104WA N1857U
46987	30CF	255	United Airlines	N105WA N1858U
46988	30	278	Jugoslovenski Aerotpt	YU-AMB stored Jul92
46989	10	271	American Airlines	N130AA
46990	30	260	TAESA	9V-SDA C-GFHX F-GGMZ XA-SYE
46991	30	261	Canadian Airlines Intl	9V-SDC C-GCPJ
46992	30CF	257	Federal Express	N1035F EC-DSF N304FE
46993	30	263	Bangladesh Biman	9V-SDB S2-ACO
46994	10	273	American Airlines	N131AA
46995	30	275	Bangladesh Biman	9V-SDD S2-ACP
46996	10	270	American Airlines	N129AA
46997	30	288	AOM French Airlines	TU-TAN F-GTDG
46998	30	267	ChallengAir	HB-IHK PH-MCO N526MD OO-LRM
46999	30F	289F	McDonnell Douglas/Aeroflot	9V-SDE PP-VMZ N518MD N114WA S2-ADA N524MD
47800	10	92	Continental Airlines	N68046
47801	10	98	Continental Airlines	N68047
47802	10	101	Continental Airlines	N68048 stored Jun93 Kingman, AZ
47803	10CF	139	Federal Express	N68049
47804	10CF	142	Federal Express	N68050
47805	10CF	145	Federal Express	N68051
47806	10CF	148	Federal Express	N68052
47807	10CF	173	Federal Express	N68053 (N301FE) N68053
47808	10CF	177	Federal Express	N68054 (N302FE) N68054
47809	10CF	191	Federal Express	N68055 (N303FE) N68055
47810	10CF	194	Federal Express	N68056 (N304FE) N68056
47811	30	302	United Airlines	G-BGXE N1852U
47812	30	303	United Airlines	G-BGXF N1853U
47813	30	312	United Airlines	G-BGXG N1854U
47814	30	315	AOM French Airlines	G-BGXH N5463Y LN-RKC F-GLMX
47815	30	325	AOM French Airlines	G-BGXI N5464M SE-DFF F-GKMY
47816	30	316	British Airways	G-BHDH
47817	30	300	Bangladesh Biman	9V-SDF PP-VMR 9V-SDF S2-ACQ
47818	30	305	Bangladesh Biman	9V-SDG PP-VMS N519MD N115WA S2-ADB
47819	30CF	314	United Airlines	N109WA N1859U
47820	30CF	317	Federal Express	N112WA N319FE
47821	30CF	320	(World Airways)	N113WA w/o 23Jan82 Boston, MA
47822	40	304	Japan Air Charter	JA8539
47823	40	306	Japan Air Lines	JA8540
47824	40	308	Japan Air Lines	JA8541
47825	40	310	Japan Air Lines	JA8542
47826	40	313	Japan Air Lines	JA8543
47827	10	294	American Airlines	N132AA
47828	10	319	American Airlines	N133AA
47829	10	321	American Airlines	N134AA
47830	10	323	American Airlines	N135AA
47831	30	327	British Airways	G-BHDI
47832	10	318	Premiair	N914WA SE-DHU OY-CNU
47833	10	322	Premiair	N915WA SE-DHT OY-CNT
47834	30	324	Iberia	EC-DHZ
47835	30F	326	Federal Express	OO-SLD N320FE
47836	30F	330	Federal Express	OO-SLE N321FE
47837	30	328	United Airlines	N84NA N1855U
47838	30	338	Polaris Aircraft Lsg Corp	RP-C2114
47840	30	337	British Airways	N19B G-BHDJ
47841	30F	329	VARIG	PP-VMT
47842	30F	332	VARIG	PP-VMU
47843	30	335	VARIG	PP-VMV
47844	30	336	PLUNA	PP-VMW
47845	30	356	VARIG	PP-VMX
47846	30	69	(American Airlines)	ZK-NZL N136AA dbr 21May88 Dallas-Ft Worth, TX
47847	30	116	American Airlines	ZK-NZM N137AA
47848	30	136	American Airlines	ZK-NZN N821L N144AA
47849	30	213	AOM French Airlines	ZK-NZR (F-ODOV) F-GDJK F-GNDC
47850	30	331	Continental Airlines	N68060
47851	30	334	Continental Airlines	N12061
47852	40	340	Japan Air Charter	JA8544
47853	40	343	Japan Air Lines	JA8545

DOUGLAS DC-10

C/n	Series	Line No	Last known Operator/Owner	Previous Identities/fate (where known)					
47855	40	349	Japan Air Lines	N13627	JA8546				
47856	40	366	Japan Air Charter	JA8547					
47857	40	367	Japan Air Lines	JA8548					
47861	30	75	Skyjet	I-DYNA	N3878P	XA-RIY	N17804	V2-LEH	
47862	30	88	Continental Airlines	I-DYNE	N390EA	N12064			
47863	30	94	Continental Airlines	I-DYNI	N3878M	N14062			
47864	30	121	Continental Airlines	I-DYNO	N3878F	N14063			
47865	30	135	Air Liberte	I-DYNU	OH-LHD	F-GPVD			
47866	30	149	Continental Airlines	I-DYNB	N391EA	N13067			
47867	30	178	Continental Micronesia	I-DYNC	N392EA	N41068*			
47868	30	200	Canadian Airlines Intl	I-DYND	AP-BBL	C-FCRE	N42783	PP-SON	N42783
				C-FCRE					
47870	30CF	339	Federal Express	(OE-ILD)	N305FE				
47886	30	90	Air Zaire	N54633	9Q-CLI	F-OGQC	9Q-CLI	stored Feb95 Tel Aviv,	
				Israel					
47887	30	125	(Korean Air)	N54634	HS-VGE	HL7328	w/o 27Jul89 nr Tripoli, Libya		
47888	30	291	British Airways	YA-LAS	G-MULL				
47889	30	229	Canadian Airlines Intl	N19B	AP-AYM	C-FCRD	N31208	PP-SOV	N6150Z
				C-FCRD					
47906	30CF	115	DAS Air Cargo	OO-SLA	N116WA	5X-JOE			
47907	30CF	157	NMB Air Operations Corp	OO-SLB	N10MB				
47908	30CF	215	Federal Express	OO-SLC	N322FE				
47921	30	117	Sun Country Airlines	D-ADAO	N601GC				
47922	30	122	Gemini Air Cargo	D-ADBO	(9J-AFN)	D-ADBO	stored May93 Marana, AZ		
47923	30	123	Sun Country Airlines	D-ADCO	N602GC				
47924	30	129	Lufthansa	D-ADDO	stored Apr94 Marana, AZ				
47925	30	166	Lufthansa	D-ADFO	stored Feb94 Tucson, AZ				
47926	30	170	SABENA	D-ADGO	OO-SLG				
47927	30	190	SABENA	D-ADHO	OO-SLH				
47928	30	192	Condor	N54644	D-ADJO				
47929	30	196	Skyjet Brazil	D-ADKO	PP-AJM				
47956	30	181	Finnair	OH-LHA					
47957	30	201	Air Liberte	OH-LHB	F-GPVB				
47965	10	59	United Airlines	(N601DA)	N1833U	stored Dec95 Las Vagas, NV			
47966	10	64	United Airlines	(N602DA)	N1834U				
47967	10	67	United Airlines	(N603DA)	N1835U	stored Dec95 Las Vegas, NV			
47968	10	74	United Airlines	(N604DA)	N1836U				
47969	10	80	United Airlines	(N605DA)	N1837U				
47980	30	150	Iberia	EC-CEZ					
47981	30	186	Iberia	EC-CLB					
47982	30	279	Iberia	EC-DEA					
48200	KC-10A	311	USAF	N110KC	79-0433				
48201	KC-10A	333	USAF	N434KC	79-0434				
48202	KC-10A	359	USAF	79-1710					
48203	KC-10A	360	USAF	79-1711					
48204	KC-10A	361	USAF	79-1712					
48205	KC-10A	363	USAF	79-1713					
48206	KC-10A	373	USAF	79-1946					
48207	KC-10A	375	USAF	79-1947					
48208	KC-10A	376	USAF	79-1948					
48209	KC-10A	377	USAF	79-1949					
48210	KC-10A	378	USAF	79-1950					
48211	KC-10A	380	USAF	79-1951					
48212	KC-10A	382	(USAF)	82-0190	dbf 17Sep87 Barksdale AFB, LA				
48213	KC-10A	383	USAF	82-0191					
48214	KC-10A	384	USAF	82-0192					
48215	KC-10A	385	USAF	82-0193					
48216	KC-10A	386	USAF	83-0075					
48217	KC-10A	387	USAF	83-0076					
48218	KC-10A	388	USAF	83-0077					
48219	KC-10A	389	USAF	83-0078					
48220	KC-10A	390	USAF	83-0079					
48221	KC-10A	391	USAF	83-0080					
48222	KC-10A	392	USAF	83-0081					
48223	KC-10A	393	USAF	83-0082					
48224	KC-10A	394	USAF	84-0185					
48225	KC-10A	395	USAF	84-0186					
48226	KC-10A	396	USAF	84-0187					
48227	KC-10A	397	USAF	84-0188					
48228	KC-10A	398	USAF	84-0189					
48229	KC-10A	399	USAF	84-0190					
48230	KC-10A	400	USAF	84-0191					
48231	KC-10A	401	USAF	84-0192					
48232	KC-10A	402	USAF	85-0027					
48233	KC-10A	403	USAF	85-0028					
48234	KC-10A	404	USAF	85-0029					
48235	KC-10A	405	USAF	85-0030					
48236	KC-10A	406	USAF	85-0031					
48237	KC-10A	407	USAF	85-0032					
48238	KC-10A	408	USAF	85-0033					
48239	KC-10A	410	USAF	85-0034					

DOUGLAS DC-10

C/n	Series	Line No	Last known Operator/Owner	Previous Identities/fate (where known)			
48240	KC-10A	411	USAF	86-0027			
48241	KC-10A	413	USAF	86-0028			
48242	KC-10A	414	USAF	86-0029			
48243	KC-10A	415	USAF	86-0030			
48244	KC-10A	417	USAF	86-0031			
48245	KC-10A	418	USAF	86-0032			
48246	KC-10A	420	USAF	86-0033			
48247	KC-10A	421	USAF	86-0034			
48248	KC-10A	423	USAF	86-0035			
48249	KC-10A	424	USAF	86-0036			
48250	KC-10A	425	USAF	86-0037			
48251	KC-10A	426	USAF	86-0038			
48252	30	342	Condor	D-ADSO			
48253	30		not built				
48254	30		not built				
48255	30AF		not built				
48256	30AF		not built				
48257	30		not built				
48258	15	346	Mexicana	(XA-MEX)	N19B	N1003L	stored Nov94 Marana, AZ
48259	15	357	Mexicana	(XA-MET)	N13627	N10045	stored Sep94 Mexico City, Mexico
48260	10	344	United Airlines	N1844U			
48261	10	347	United Airlines	N1845U	stored Jan96 Las Vegas-McCarran, NV		
48262	10	351	United Airlines	N1846U			
48263	10	353	United Airlines	N1847U			
48264	10CF	379	Federal Express	N1848U	N68057		
48265	30ER	345	Finnair	(OH-LHC)	N345HC		
48266	30	348	Monarch Airlines	N3016Z	G-DMCA		
48267	30ER	434	Thai Airways International	N6203U	HS-TMA	wfs	
48268	30		not built				
48275	15	358	Aeromexico	(XA-AMM)	N10038		
48276	15	362	Aeromexico	(XA-AMN)	N1003N		
48277	30	354	British Airways	G-DCIO			
48282	30	355	VARIG	PP-VMY			
48283	30	350	Malaysian Airlines System	9M-MAV			
48285	30	352	Canadian Airlines Intl	C-GCPG	N1850U	C-GCPG	
48286	30	369	Ghana Airways	9G-ANA			
48287	30AF	409	Federal Express	N306FE			
48288	30	364	Canadian Airlines Intl	C-GCPH	(N1851U)	C-GCPH	
48289	15	365	Sun Country Airlines	(XA-MEU)	N1003W	N152SY	
48290	30ER	435	Thai Airways International	HS-TMB	wfs		
48291	30AF	412	Federal Express	N307FE			
48292	30ER	368	Continental Airlines	N6200N	HB-IHN	N87070	
48293	30ER	371	Continental Airlines	HB-IHO	N83071		
48294	15	372	GATX Capital Corp	N1004A	XA-MEW	N1004A	stored Marana, AZ
48295	15	374	Sun Country Airlines	N1004B	XA-MEX	N151SY	
48296	30	370	Canadian Airlines Intl	C-GCPI			
48297	30AF	416	Federal Express	N308FE			
48298	30AF	419	Federal Express	N309FE			
48299	30AF	422	Federal Express	N310FE			
48300	30AF	433	Federal Express	N312FE			
48301	30	381	Japan Air Lines	JA8549			
48303	KC-10A	427	USAF	87-0117			
48304	KC-10A	428	USAF	87-0118			
48305	KC-10A	429	USAF	87-0119			
48306	KC-10A	430	USAF	87-0120			
48307	KC-10A	431	USAF	87-0121			
48308	KC-10A	432	USAF	87-0122			
48309	KC-10A	439	USAF	87-0123			
48310	KC-10A	441	USAF	87-0124	N6204N	87-0124	
48311	30F	440	Federal Express	N313FE			
48312	30F	442	Federal Express	N314FE			
48313	30F	443	Federal Express	N315FE			
48314	30F	444	Federal Express	N316FE			
48315	30	436	Japan Air System	JA8550			
48316	30	437	Japan Air System	JA8551	HL7329	JA8551	
48317	30	445	Bangladesh Biman	(N317FE)	S2-ACR		
48318	30	446	World Airways	(N318FE)	(5N-AUI)	N3024W	N117WA
48319	30ER	438	Thai Airways International	HS-TMC	wfs		

Production complete

Refer to McDonnell-Douglas for MD-11 production

FOKKER F.28 FELLOWSHIP

C/n	Series	Last known Operator/Owner	Previous Identities/fate (where known)
11001	various	(TAT)	PH-JHG prototype; ff 28Apr71 used for spares Apr88
11002	1000	(Fokker)	PH-WEV second prototype; b/u early 1975
11003	1000	TAT European Airlines	PH-MOL LN-SUM PH-MOL LN-SUM PH-MOL EP-PBF PH-MOL F-GMOL P2-ANL F-GIMG P2-ANL F-GIMH
11004	1000	TAT European Airlines	PH-ZAA D-ABAQ I-TIDU F-GECK
11005		Fokker	static test airframe
11006	1000	Canadian Regional A/L	PH-ZAB D-ABAX I-TIDB C-GTUU
11007		Fokker	static test airframe
11008	1000	Ansett Australia	(PH-ZAC) PH-MAT VH-FKF
11009	1000	Aero Continente	PH-ZAD LN-SUC I-TIAP N37RT OB-1636
11010	1000	Alinord	PH-ZAE LN-SUX I-TIBB stored Jul91 Dinard, France
11011	1000	(Braathens-SAFE Air Transport)	PH-ZAF LN-SUY w/o 23Dec72 Oslo, Norway
11012	1000	Cambodian Govt	PH-ZAG LN-SUN C-GQBR F-GIAH XU-001
11013	1000	TAT European Airlines	PH-ZAH LN-SUO VH-MMJ PH-EXA LN-SUO C-GQBS F-GIAI
11014	1000	(Itavia)	PH-ZAI I-TIDA w/o 09Apr75 Bergamo, Italy
11015	1000	(Itavia)	PH-ZAK I-TIDE w/o 01Jan74 Turin, Italy
11016	1000	Peregrine Air Charter	PH-ZAL N281FH N27W N930TL VR-BNC (also reported as VR-BCN) C-FHFP
11017	1000	Horizon Airlines	PH-ZAM EC-BVA PH-ZAM XY-ADV PH-ZAM PH-EZF PH-ZAM N802PH
11018	1000C	FA Argentina/LADE	PH-ZAN N282FH PH-EXW TC-54 LV-VCS TC-54
11019	1000	Myanma Airways	PH-ZAO EC-BVB PH-ZAO XY-ADU
11020	1000C	FA Argentina/LADE	PH-ZAP N283FH PH-EXX TC-53
11021	1000	Ansett Australia	PH-ZAS VH-FKA
11022	1000	Air Niugini	PH-ZAT VH-FKB P2-ANH
11023	1000	(Iberia)	PH-EXA (PH-ZAV) EC-BVC dbr 28Dec72 Bilbao, Spain
11024	1000C	FA Argentina/LADE	(PH-ZAN) PH-EXC N284FH PH-EXZ TC-55
11025	1000	Ansett Australia	PH-EXF VH-FKC stored 10Mar91 Perth, Australia
11026	1000	Ansett Australia	PH-EXA VH-FKD
11027	1000	Iran Asseman Airlines	PH-ZBG D-AHLA PH-ZBG EP-PAS ZS-KAW F-GBBX
11028	1000	FA Argentina (VIP)	PH-EXA T-01 T-02 T-01 T-04
11029	1000	Canadian Regional A/L	D-ABAN PK-PJU C-FCRW
11030	1000	Pelita/Pertamina	D-ABAM PK-PJS
11031	1000	Horizon Air	(D-ABAS) D-AHLB PH-ZBH F-BUTE VH-FKG N803PH
11032	1000	Canadian Regional A/L	(N285FH) I-VAGA PH-ZAV D-AHLD PH-ZAV LN-SUM OB-R-390 OB-R-1030 TC-JAZ PH-ZAV PK-GVM PH-EXW N282N N461AU C-FAIF C-FCRU
11033	1000	Air Niugini	N285FH C-FTAV P2-ANE
11034	1000	Air Sicilia	D-AHLC PH-ZBI F-BUTI P2-ANZ F-BUTI
11035	1000	Canadian Regional A/L	PH-EXF OB-R-231 PK-GJZ PK-GVA PH-EXN N283N N456US C-FCRM
11036	1000	USAir	PK-GJY PK-GVB PH-EXY N284N N457US stored Apr93 Marana, AZ
11037	1000	Canadian Regional A/L	(I-TIDO) PH-EXE PH-ZBF PK-GJR PK-GVI PH-EZA N293N N458US C-FCRP
11038	1000	Air Niugini	N286FH PH-EXM C-FTAY P2-ANF
11039	1000	(Garuda Indonesia)	PK-GJX PK-GVC w/o 24Sep75 Palembang, Indonesia
11040	1000	Ansett Australia	VH-FKE
11041	1000	Air Niugini	PH-EXF (VH-FKF) C2-RN1 P2-ANU
11042	1000	TNI-AU	(PK-PJX) PK-PJT A2801
11043	1000	Canadian Regional A/L	N287FH PH-EXM PK-GVN PH-EZY N291N N459US C-FCRI
11044	1000	USAir	N288FH PH-EXR PK-GVO PH-EXV N286N N460AU stored Apr93 Marana, AZ
11045	1000	Netherlands Royal Flt	PH-PBX
11046	1000	Aerolineas Argentinas	D-AGAB LV-LRG
11047	1000	Australian DCA	N289FH PH-EXI VH-ATD
11048	1000	FA Argentina	(D-ABAS) PH-EXF N280FH TG-CAO PH-ZBM LV-LZN T-02
11049	1000	(Air Niugini)	(N280FH) PH-EXD PH-EXG 5N-AGN P2-ANB w/o 31May95 Padang, Papua New Guinea
11050	1000	TAT European Airlines	D-AGAC F-GBBS
11051	1000	TAT European Airlines	D-AGAD F-GBBR
11052	1000	TAT European Airlines	PH-ZAW D-AGAE EP-PBA F-GBBT
11053	2000	TAT European Airlines	PH-EXF PH-ZAX 5N-ANB F-GDUS
11054	1000	Horizon Air	PK-GJW PK-GVD PH-EZG N288N N462AU
11055	1000	(Garuda Indonesia)	PK-GJV PK-GVE w/o 11Jul79 Mt Sibayak, N Sumatra, Indonesia
11056	1000	Air Niugini	(VH-FKF) PH-EXB PH-EXH C2-RN2 P2-ANW
11057	1000	(Turk Hava Yollari)	PH-ZBA TC-JAO w/o 26Jan74 Izmir, Turkey
11058	1000	(Turk Hava Yollari)	PH-ZBB TC-JAP w/o 30Jan75 in Sea of Marmara
11059	1000	(Aero Peru)	PH-ZBD OB-R-397 OB-R-1020 w/o 25Oct88 Juliaca, Peru
11060	1000	(Air Ontario)	PH-ZBC TC-JAR F-GEXT C-FONF w/o 10Mar89 Dryden, Canada
11061	1000	Canadian Regional A/L	PK-GJU PK-GVF PH-EXD N280N N463AU C-FCRZ
11062	2000	Ghana Airways	PH-ZBE (9G-ACB) 9G-ABZ
11063	1000	USAir	PH-EXE PK-GJT PK-GVG PH-EZE N290N N464US stored Apr93 Marana, AZ
11064	1000	Canadian Regional A/L	PH-EXD PK-GJS PK-GVH PH-EZH N289N N465AU C-FXTA
11065	1000	Aero Peru	PH-EXN OB-R-398 OB-R-1018 OB-1018 stored Apr93 Lima, Peru
11066	1000	Aero Peru	PH-EXO OB-R-399 OB-R-1019 OB-1019 stored Apr93 Lima, Peru
11067	1000	Scandinavian A/L Sys	PH-EXL SE-DGA
11068	1000	Scandinavian A/L Sys	PH-EXI SE-DGB
11069	1000	Scandinavian A/L Sys	PH-EXK SE-DGC

FOKKER F.28 FELLOWSHIP

C/n	Series	Last known Operator/Owner	Previous Identities/fate (where known)
11070	1000	(Iran Asseman Airlines)	PH-EXP TC-JAS F-GEXU C-FONG P2-ANY F-GIAJ EP-PAV w/o 10Oct94 nr Isfahan, Iran
11071	1000	(Turk Hava Yollari)	PH-EXR TC-JAT w/o 23Dec79 Ankara, Turkey
11072	1000	Lina Congo	PH-EXS TN-ACP
11073	1000	Delta Air Transport	PH-EXT PK-PJV F-GGKC F-ODZB F-GNZB
11074	1000C	FA Argentina/LADE	PH-EXG Argentine AF TC-52 LV-RCS TC-52
11075	1000	Horizon Air	PH-EXV PK-GJQ PK-GVJ PH-EXM N281N N466US
11076	1000C	(FA Argentina/LADE)	PH-EXY TC-51 w/o 16Aug89 Bariloche, Argentina
11077	2000	(Ghana Airways)	PH-EXU 9G-ACA w/o 11Mar81 Accra, Ghana
11078	1000	(Garuda Indonesia)	PH-EXZ PK-GJP PK-GVK w/o 20Mar82 Lampong, Sumatra, Indonesia
11079	1000	Togo Government	PH-EXB PH-ZBK 5V-TAB 5V-MAB 5V-TAI
11080	2000	Air Gabon	(SE-DGD) PH-EXC TR-LST
11081	2000	Air Gabon	(SE-DGE) PH-EXD TR-LSU
11082	1000	Canadian Regional A/L	PH-EXN VH-ATE C-GTAH
11083	1000	Aerolineas Argentinas	PH-EXO LV-LOC
11084	1000	Australian DCA	PH-EXP VH-ATG
11085	1000	Aerolineas Argentinas	PH-EXT LV-LOA HK-3126X LV-LOA
11086	1000	(Aerolineas Argentinas)	PH-EXU LV-LOB w/o 15Nov75 Concordia, Argentina
11087	1000	Canadian Regional A/L	PH-EXV PK-GVL PH-EZF N287N N467US C-FCRK
11088	1000	Royal Malaysian AF	PH-EXI FM2101 M28-01 VIP a/c
11089	1000	Air Niugini	PH-EXL FM2102 M28-02 P2-ANC
11090	2000	(Nigeria Airways)	PH-EXH 5N-ANF w/o 28Nov83 Enugu, Nigeria
11091	2000	TAT European Airlines	PH-EXT 5N-ANH F-GDUT
11092	4000	(Air Mauritanie)	PH-SIX PH-PBG PH-SIX 5T-CLF (OO-DJC) 5T-CLF built as srs 6000 w/o 01Jul94 Tidjikja, Mauritius
11093	4000	Air Mauritanie	PH-ZBL EP-PBB PH-ZBL 5T-CLG built as srs 6000
11094	1000	(Garuda Indonesia)	PH-EXY PK-GVP w/o 06Mar79 Mt Bromo, E Java, Indonesia
11095	1000	USAir	PH-EXO PK-PJW PK-GVT PH-EZK N272N N468US stored Apr93 Marana, AZ
11096	1000	USAir	PH-EXH PK-GVQ PH-EZE N296N N469US
11097	1000	Horizon Airlines	PH-EXS PH-ZBN TU-VAA TU-TIM PH-ZBN N801PH
11098	1000	Canadian Regional A/L	PH-EXI PK-GVR PH-EZL N297N N470US C-FTAS
11099	1000C	Air Ivoire	PH-EXL TU-VAB TU-TIN TU-VAB PH-VAB TU-TIZ
11100	1000	FA del Peru	PH-EXY 390/OB-1396
11101	1000	Horizon Air	PH-EXG PK-GVS PH-EZH N294N N450US
11102	1000C	Iran Asseman Airlines	PH-EXZ TR-LTS F-GEXX EP-PAX
11103	1000	Canadian Regional A/L	PH-EXH PK-GVU PH-EZI N298N N451US C-FJRI
11104	1000	Iranian Govt	PH-EXU TR-LTR F-GIAK EP-PAZ
11105	1000	Canadian Regional A/L	PH-EXV PK-GVV PH-EZJ N271N N452US
11106	1000	Canadian Regional A/L	PH-EXD PK-GVW PH-EZM N273N N453US C-FTAV
11107	1000	Horizon Air	PH-EXE PK-GVX PH-EZN N274N N454US
11108	2000	TAT European Airlines	PH-EXF 5N-ANI F-GDUU
11109	2000	TAT European Airlines	PH-EXG 5N-ANJ F-GDUV
11110	2000	Aviona Leasing/Zimex Avn	PH-EXL PH-ZBO 5N-ANK F-GDUX HB-AAS
11111	4000	Pelita Air Service	PH-EXZ SE-DGD PH-EZA PK-PJL
11112	4000	Scandinavian A/L Sys	PH-EXK SE-DGE
11113	3000R	Merpati Nusantara	PH-EXR PK-GFR
11114	4000	Myanma Airways	PH-EXU XY-ADW
11115	4000	Scandinavian A/L Sys	PH-EXM SE-DGF
11116	4000	Scandinavian A/L Sys	PH-EXV SE-DGG
11117	3000R	Merpati Nusantara	PH-EXW PK-GFQ
11118	4000	Air Niugini	PH-EXN TU-VAH TU-TIJ PH-RRJ P2-AND
11119	3000R	Merpati Nusantara	PH-EXX PK-GFS
11120	4000	Scandinavian A/L Sys	PH-EXY SE-DGH
11121	4000	Air Ivoire	PH-EXO TU-VAN TU-TIK
11122	4000	Scandinavian A/L Sys	PH-EXP SE-DGI
11123	4000	Scandinavian A/L Sys	PH-EXZ SE-DGK
11124	4000	Delta Air Transport	PH-EXY (TU-VAZ) TU-VAJ TU-TIR PH-TIR (PH-TVG) PH-VGR
11125	3000	Ghana AF	PH-EXP PH-ZBP G530
11126	4000	Scandinavian A/L Sys	PH-EXV SE-DGL
11127	4000	(Aerolineas Argentinas)	PH-EXT PH-BBV LV-MZD w/o 05Jan90 Villa Gesell, Argentina
11128	4000	Scandinavian A/L Sys	PH-EXR SE-DGM
11129	3000R	Merpati Nusantara	PH-EXS PK-GFT
11130	4000	Scandinavian A/L Sys	PH-EXU SE-DGN PH-JPV SE-DGN
11131	3000R	(Merpati Nusantara)	PH-EXW PK-GFU w/o 01Jul93 Sorong, Indonesia
11132	3000RC	(Garuda Indonesia)	PH-EXX PK-GFV w/o 02Jun83 Tanjungkarang-Beranti, Sumatra, Indonesia
11133	4000	TAT European Airlines	PH-EXO PH-ZBU G-WWJC F-GDFC
11134	3000RC	Merpati Nusantara	PH-EXZ PK-GFW
11135	4000	TAT European Airlines	PH-EXR PH-ZBT G-JCWW F-GDFD
11136	3000	Royal Swazi National Airways	PH-EXN PH-ZBR 3D-ALN
11137	3000	Tanzanian Government	PH-EXS PH-ZBS 5H-CCM
11138	4000	KLM Cityhopper	PH-EXT PH-CHB
11139	4000	KLM Cityhopper	PH-EXU PH-CHD
11140	4000	KLM Cityhopper	PH-EXN PH-CHF
11141	4000	(NLM)	PH-EXP PH-CHI w/o 06Oct81 Moerdijk, Netherlands
11142	4000	TAT European Airlines	PH-EXY 5N-ANU F-GDUY
11143	3000	Ansett Australia	PH-EXZ OY-BRM VH-EWF VH-FKM
11144	4000	TAT European Airlines	PH-EXS 5N-ANV F-GDUZ
11145	3000RC	Charter Fly	PH-EXV Argentine Navy 0741/5-T-20 LV-RRA
11146	4000	Pelita/Pertamina	PH-EXN PK-PJY

FOKKER F.28 FELLOWSHIP

C/n	Series	Last known Operator/Owner	Previous Identities/fate (where known)
11147	3000	Argentine Navy	PH-EXW 0740/5-T-10
11148	4000	Trigana Air Service	PH-EXT PK-PJW PK-YPJ
11149	4000	USAir	PH-EXP N106UR N489US (F-OHCN) N489US stored Sep95 Las Vegas, NV
11150	3000C	Argentine Navy	PH-EXX Argentine Navy 0742/5-T-21 stored 26Feb91 Chateauroux, France
11151	3000	Ansett Australia	PH-EXU OY-BRN VH-EWG VH-FKP
11152	4000	USAir	PH-EXR N504 N490US
11153	3000	Philippine Government	PH-EXV PH-ZBV RP-C1177 RP-1250 VIP a/c
11154	4000	Merpati Nusantara	PH-EXW (PK-GHA) PK-GKA
11155	4000	Merpati Nusantara	PH-EXX (PK-GHB) PK-GKB
11156	4000	USAir	PH-EXY N505 N491US stored Sep95 Las Vegas, NV
11157	4000	Merpati Nusantara	PH-EXZ PH-ZBW (PK-GHC) PK-GKC
11158	4000	Merpati Nusantara	PH-EXN (PK-GHD) PK-GKD
11159	4000	USAir	PH-EXT PH-ZBX N107UR N492US (F-OHCO) N492US
11160	4000	Merpati Nusantara	PH-EXO (PK-GHE) PK-GKE
11161	4000	USAir	PH-EXS N509 N493US
11162	3000C	FA Colombiana/SATENA	PH-EXU PH-EXY PH-EXT PH-EZL FAC-1141
11163	3000	Delta Air Transport	PH-EXW PH-ZBJ XT-FZP N163PM OO-DJA
11164	4000	Iran Asseman Airlines	PH-EXR PH-ZCA EP-PAT
11165	3000	(FA Colombiana/SATENA)	PH-EXV PH-EXS PH-ZCG FAC-1140 w/o 28Mar85 Florencia, Colombia
11166	4000	Iran Asseman Airlines	PH-EXY PH-ZCB EP-PAU
11167	4000	USAir	PH-EXO PH-ZBZ N510 N494US
11168	4000	USAir	PH-EXP PH-ZCC N512 N495US stored 29Mar96 Oklahoma, OK
11169	4000	Air 21	PH-EXS PH-EXT PH-ZBY N513 N496US
11170	4000	Merpati Nusantara	PH-EXU PK-GKF
11171	4000	Merpati Nusantara	PH-EXR PK-GKG
11172	4000	Bangladesh Biman	PH-EXX S2-ACH
11173	4000	USAir	PH-EXN (VH-EWA) N1346U N108UR N497US
11174	4000	Merpati Nusantara	PH-EXO PK-GKH
11175	4000	Merpati Nusantara	PH-EXT (N521) PK-GKL
11176	4000	KLM Cityhopper	PH-EXU (N522) PH-CHN
11177	4000	Merpati Nusantara	PH-EXR (N523) PH-ZCD PK-GKM
11178	4000	Pelita/Pertamina	PH-EXW PK-PJM
11179	4000	TAT European Airlines	PH-EXX PH-LEX F-GDSK
11180	4000	Bangladesh Biman	PH-EXZ (S2-ACI) S2-ACJ
11181	4000	USAir	PH-EXS (VH-EWB) N109UR N498US
11182	4000	USAir	PH-EXN N110UR N499US stored Marana, AZ
11183	4000	Ansett Australia	PH-EXZ VH-FKI
11184	4000	Delta Air Transport	PH-EXO (N524) PH-ZCE TY-BBN OO-DJB
11185	4000	Air Burkina	PH-EXP (N112UR) (N111UR) PH-ZCF XT-FZP
11186	4000	Ansett Australia	PH-EXS VH-FKJ VH-EWH VH-FKJ
11187	4000	Ghana Airways	PH-EXW 9G-ADA
11188	4000	Merpati Nusantara	PH-EXN PK-GKI
11189	4000	Merpati Nusantara	PH-EXX PK-GKJ
11190	4000	Scandinavian A/L Sys	PH-EXU SE-DGO
11191	4000	Scandinavian A/L Sys	PH-EXZ SE-DGP
11192	4000	Pelita/Pertamina	PH-EXW PK-PJK
11193	4000	Merpati Nusantara	PH-EXR PK-GKK
11194	4000	Libyan Arab Airlines	PH-EXZ 5A-DLW
11195	4000	Ansett Australia	PH-EXO VH-EWA VH-FKK
11196	4000	Merpati Nusantara	PH-EXU PK-GKN
11197	4000	Libyan Arab Airlines	PH-EXS 5A-DLU stored Oct89 Dinard, France
11198	4000	Merpati Nusantara	PH-EXP PK-GKO
11199	4000	Merpati Nusantara	PH-EXN PK-GKP
11200	4000	Libyan Arab Airlines	PH-EXV 5A-DLV
11201	4000	Merpati Nusantara	PH-EXO PK-GKQ
11202	4000	Merpati Nusantara	PH-EXT PK-GKR
11203	4000	Fokker	PH-EXP HL7265 PH-RRC
11204	4000	Scandinavian A/L Sys	PH-EXR SE-DGR
11205	4000	Ansett Australia	PH-EXO VH-EWB VH-FKL
11206	4000	Merpati Nusantara	PH-EXU PK-GKS
11207	4000	Ansett Australia	PH-EXX VH-EWC VH-FKN
11208	4000	Ansett Australia	PH-EXT VH-EWD VH-FKQ
11209	4000	Merpati Nusantara	PH-EXF PK-GKT
11210	4000	Merpati Nusantara	PH-EXO PK-GKU
11211	4000	Merpati Nusantara	PH-EXU PK-GKV
11212	4000	Ansett Australia	PH-EXZ VH-LAR VH-FKO
11213	4000	Merpati Nusantara	PH-EZA PK-GKW
11214	4000	Merpati Nusantara	PH-EZB PK-GKX
11215	4000	Merpati Nusantara	PH-EZC PK-GKY
11216	4000	Merpati Nusantara	PH-EZD PK-GKZ
11217	4000	Merpati Nusantara	PH-EZE PH-EZZ PK-GQA
11218	4000	Merpati Nusantara	PH-EZP PK-GQB
11219	4000	Fokker	PH-EZR HL7270 PH-RRA ZS-NGB PH-RRA stored Nov95 Woensdrecht, Netherlands
11220	4000	TAME	PH-EZS PH-ZCH HC-BMD/FAE220
11221	4000	(Korean Air)	PH-EZT N281MP HL7285 w/o 25Nov89 Seoul-Kimpo, S Korea
11222	4000	USAir	PH-EZU N117UR N475AU
11223	4000	Air Niugini	PH-EZV N2703Y N282MP HL7284 PH-RRB P2-ANI
11224	4000	USAir	PH-EZW N118UR N476US
11225	4000	Scandinavian A/L Sys	PH-EZX SE-DGX

FOKKER F.28 FELLOWSHIP

C/n	Series	Last known Operator/Owner	Previous Identities/fate (where known)				
11226	4000	USAir	PH-EZB	(N283MP)	N119UR	N477AU	
11227	4000	USAir	PH-EZC	N204P	N478US		
11228	4000	USAir	PH-EZO	N205P	N479AU	stored Marana, AZ	
11229	4000	USAir	PH-EZP	N206P	N480AU	N480US	N480AU
11230	4000	USAir	PH-EZZ	N207P	N481US		
11231	4000	USAir	PH-EZD	(N284MP)	N120UR	N482US	stored Sep95 Kingman, AZ
11232	4000	Myanma Airways	PH-EZG	XY-AGA			
11233	4000	USAir	PH-EZI	N208P	N483US		
11234	4000	USAir	PH-EZJ	N209P	N484US		
11235	4000	(USAir)	PH-EZU	N214P	N485US	w/o 22Mar92 New York-La Guardia, NY	
11236	4000	Scandinavian A/L Sys	PH-EZA	SE-DGS			
11237	4000	USAir	PH-EZE	N121UR	N486US		
11238	4000	USAir	PH-EZR	N122UR	N487US	stored Marana, AZ	
11239	4000	Scandinavian A/L Sys	PH-EZL	SE-DGT			
11240	4000	USAir	PH-EZK	N215P	N488US		
11241	4000	Scandinavian A/L Sys	PH-EZT	SE-DGU			
11991	1000	Canadian Regional A/L	I-TIDI	PH-ZAR	C-GTEO		
11992	1000	FA Colombiana	(PH-ZAU)	PH-EXA	PH-EXF	FAC001	
11993	1000	(Nigeria Airways)	(PH-ZAX)	PH-EXE	PH-ZAU	5N-ANA	w/o 01Mar78 Kano, Nigeria
11994	1000	(Nigeria Airways)	PH-EXB	I-VAFE	PH-FPT	w/o 18Sep72 Port Harcourt, Nigeria	

Production complete

FOKKER 70

C/n	Last known Operator/Owner	Previous Identities/fate (where known)		
11243	Fokker	PH-MKC	prototype;	ff 02Apr93
11521	Ford Motors	PH-MKS	N322K	
11528	Mesa Airlines	PH-EZS	PH-JCH	N528YV
11529	Sempati Air Transport	PH-EZL	PK-JGI	
11532	Sempati Air Transport	PH-EZR	PK-JGJ	
11536	Silk Air	PH-EZH	9V-SLK	
11537	Mesa Airlines	PH-EZV	PH-JCT	N537YV
11538	British Midland	PH-EZX	G-BVTE	
11539	British Midland	PH-EZA	PH-EZZ	G-BVTF
11540	Air Littoral	PH-EZS	(F-GLIS)	PH-RRS
11541	Air Littoral	PH-EZN	(F-GLIT)	PH-RRT
11543	Air Littoral	PH-EZM	(F-GLIU)	PH-RRU
11545	Ford Motors	PH-EZH	N324K	
11547	Dutch Royal Flight	PH-KBX		
11549	Tyrolean Airways	PH-EZW	OE-LFG	
11551	British Midland	PH-EZK	G-BVTG	
11553	Pelita Air Service	PH-EZZ	PH-MXN	PK-PFE
11554	Tyrolean Airways	PH-EZN	OE-LFH	
11555	Tyrolean Airways	PH-EZP	OE-LFK	
11556	Air Littoral	PH-RRV	(F-GLIV)	PH-RRV
11557	Kenya Air Force	PH-MXM	KAF908	
11558	Air Littoral	PH-RRW	F-GLIX	PH-RRW
11559	Austrian Airlines	PH-EZV	OE-LFO	
11560	Austrian Airlines	PH-EZW	OE-LFP	
11561	Silk Air	PH-EZR	9V-SLL	
11562	KLM CityHopper	PH-KZB		
11563	Avianova	PH-EZT	I-REJA	
11564	Malev	PH-EZR	HA-LMA	
11565	Malev	PH-EZX	HA-LMB	
11566	KLM CityHopper	PH-KZC		
11567	KLM CityHopper	PH-KZA		
11568	Austrian Airlines	PH-EZC	OE-LFQ	
11569	Malev	PH-EZA	HA-LMC	
11570	Avianova	PH-EZZ	I-REJO	
11571	Avianova	PH-	I-REJB	
11572	Austrian Airlines	PH-EZD	OE-LFR	
11573	Avianova	PH-EZW	I-REJE	
11574	Avianova	PH-EZY	I-REJI	
11575	Avianova	PH-EZB	I-REJU	
11576	Pelita Air Service	PH-	PK-	
11577	British Midland	PH-	G-BVTH*	
11578	British Midland	PH-	G-BWTI*	
11579	Avianova	PH-	I-REJC	
11580	Vietnam Airlines	PH-	VN-A502*	
11581	Avianova	PH-	I-REJD*	
11582	KLM CityHopper	PH-KZD*		
11583	Malev	PH-	HA-	
11584	Sempati Air Transport	PH-	PK-JGK*	
11585	Vietnam Airlines	PH-	VN-A504*	
11586	Sempati Air Transport	PH-	PK-JGL*	
11587	Tyrolean Airways	PH-	OE-	

FOKKER 100

C/n	Last known Operator/Owner	Previous Identities/fate (where known)					
11242	Fokker	PH-MKH	prototype; ff 30Nov86				
11243	Fokker	PH-MKC	second prototype			cvtd to Fokker 70 1993	
11244	Swissair	PH-EZB	HB-IVA	wfs			
11245	Republique du Cote d'Ivoire	PH-EZA	PH-CDI	TU-VAA			
11246	Air UK	PH-EZB	C-FICY	N602RP	G-UKFA		
11247	Air UK	PH-EZC	C-FICW	N602TR	G-UKFB		
11248	Air UK	PH-EZD	PH-INC	C-FICB	F-GIOV	G-UKFJ	
11249	Air UK	PH-EZE	PH-INA	C-FICO	F-GIOX	G-UKFK	
11250	Swissair	PH-EZC	HB-IVB	wfs			
11251	Swissair	PH-EZD	HB-IVC				
11252	Swissair	PH-EZE	HB-IVD				
11253	Swissair	PH-EZF	HB-IVE				
11254	Swissair	PH-EZG	HB-IVF				
11255	Swissair	PH-EZH	HB-IVG				
11256	Swissair	PH-EZI	HB-IVH				
11257	Portugalia	PH-EZA	(N202BN)	PH-LMF	CS-TPA		
11258	Portugalia	PH-EZD	TR-LCR	PH-EZD	CS-TPF		
11259	Air UK	PH-EZJ	C-FICP	G-UKFD			
11260	Air UK	PH-EZK	C-FICQ	G-UKFE			
11261	TAT European Airlines	PH-EZK	F-GIOA				
11262	Portugalia	PH-EZE	CS-TPB				
11263	Air UK	PH-EZF	C-FICL	N602DG	G-UKFC		
11264	Sempati Air Transport	PH-EZL	PK-JGA				
11265	Sempati Air Transport	PH-EZM	PK-JGC				
11266	Sempati Air Transport	PH-EZN	PK-JGD				
11267	Iran Air	PH-EZO	PH-LMH	(EP-IDB)	EP-IDC		
11268	KLM	PH-KLC	F-OGQI	F-GIDT	F-OGQI	F-GIDT	PH-KLC
11269	KLM	PH-KLD	F-GIDQ	PH-KLD			
11270	KLM	PH-KLE	F-GIDP	PH-KLE			
11271	KLM	PH-KLG	F-GIDO	PH-KLG			
11272	KLM	PH-KLH	F-OGQA	F-GIDN	F-OGQA	F-GIDN	PH-KLH
11273	KLM	PH-KLI	F-OGQB	F-GIDM	PH-KLI		
11274	Air UK	(PH-KLK)	PH-EZB	PH-ZCK	G-UKFF		
11275	Air UK	(PH-KLL)	PH-EZV	PH-ZCL	G-UKFG		
11276	USAir	PH-EZF	PH-ZCI	N850US			
11277	Air UK	(PH-KLN)	PH-EZW	PH-ZCM	G-UKFH		
11278	USAir	PH-EZG	N851US				
11279	Air UK	(PH-KLO)	PH-EZX	PH-ZCN	G-UKFI		
11280	USAir	PH-EZH	N852US				
11281	USAir	PH-EZI	N853US				
11282	USAir	PH-EZP	N854US				
11283	USAir	PH-EZR	N855US				
11284	TAM	(PH-EZS)	PH-LMI	PT-MRA			
11285	TAM	PH-EZT	PH-LMK	PT-MRB			
11286	USAir	PH-EZU	N856US				
11287	Portugalia	PH-LML	(EP-IDD)	CS-TPC			
11288	Pelita Air Service	PH-EZN	PH-LMU	PK-PJN			
11289	USAir	PH-EZG	N857US				
11290	Fokker	PH-EZP	PH-TAB	(B-11150)	F-OLGA	PH-TAB	
11291	USAir	PH-EZH	N858US				
11292	Iran Air	PH-EZG	PH-LMG	EP-IDA			
11293	USAir	PH-EZY	N859US				
11294	Iran Air	PH-LMM	(EP-IDE)	EP-IDD			
11295	USAir	PH-EZZ	N860US				
11296	Fokker	PH-TAC	(B-11152)	F-OLGB			
11297	USAir	PH-EZB	N861US				
11298	Iran Air	PH-LMN	(EP-IDF)	(EP-IDE)	EP-IDF		
11299	Iran Air	PH-LMO	(EP-IDC)	EP-IDB			
11300	USAir	PH-EZC	N862US				
11301	Sempati Air Transport	PH-EZY	PH-LMV	PK-JGE			
11302	Iran Air	PH-EZB	PH-LMW	(EP-IDF)	EP-IDG		
11303	USAir	PH-EZD	N863US				
11304	TAM Brasil	PH-EZX	PH-LMX	(EP-IDH)	PT-MRG		
11305	TAM Brasil	PH-EZO	PH-LMY	(EP-IDI)	PT-MRH		
11306	USAir	PH-EZF	N864US				
11307	Deutsche BA	PH-EZX	F-GIOB	D-ADFA			
11308	USAir	PH-EZI	N865US				
11309	Mexicana	PH-EZS	PH-LMZ	EP-IDJ	PH-LMZ	XA-SHI	
11310	USAir	PH-EZJ	N866US				
11311	Deutsche BA	PH-EZE	F-GIOC	D-ADFB			
11312	USAir	PH-EZU	N867US				
11313	USAir	PH-EZR	N868US				
11314	USAir	PH-EZH	N869US				
11315	Deutsche BA	PH-EZF	F-GIOD	D-ADFC			
11316	Air Ivoire	PH-EZW	G-FIOO	PH-RRG	TU-TIV		
11317	Portugalia	PH-LNA	EP-IDK	CS-TPD			
11318	Air Ivoire	PH-EZB	G-FIOR	PH-RRH	TU-TIS		
11319	Mexicana	PH-LNB	(EP-IDL)	PH-LNB	XA-SHJ		
11320	TAM Brasil	PH-LND	PT-MRC				

FOKKER 100

C/n	Last known Operator/Owner	Previous Identities/fate (where known)						
11321	Midway Airlines	PH-EZA	G-FIOS	PH-RRC	SE-DUA	N132ML		
11322	TAM Brasil	PH-LNE	PT-MRD					
11323	Midway Airlines	PH-EZC	(G-FIOT)	PH-EZC	(PH-LNP)	PH-CFA	SE-DUB	N131ML
11324	Transwede	PH-EZG	(G-FIOU)	PH-EZG	(PH-LNR)	PH-CFB	SE-DUC	
11325	Transwede	PH-EZI	(G-FIOV)	PH-EZI	(PH-LNT)	PH-CFC	SE-DUD	
11326	Transwede	PH-EZJ	(G-FIOW)	PH-EZJ	PH-CFD	SE-DUE		
11327	Fokker	PH-EZL	(G-FIOX)	PH-EZL	PH-CFE	F-GJAO	PH-CFE	stored Nov95
		Woensdrecht, Netherlands						
11328	Air Littoral	PH-EZM	(G-FIOY)	PH-EZM	PH-CFF	F-GKLX	PH-CFF	stored Jul95
		Woensdrecht, Netherlands						
11329	Transwede	PH-EZV	(G-FIOZ)	PH-EZV	PH-CFG	SE-DUF		
11330	Midway Airlines	PH-EZB	(G-FIOA)	PH-EZB	PH-CFH	SE-DUG	N133ML	
11331	USAir	PH-EZT	N880US					
11332	Air Littoral	PH-EZH	F-GKLY					
11333	USAir	PH-EZW	N881US					
11334	USAir	PH-EZD	N882US					
11335	Royal Swazi Natl A/W	PH-EZR	3D-ALM					
11336	Sempati Air Transport	PH-LNF	(PK-JGH)	PK-JGG				
11337	USAir	PH-EZO	N883US					
11338	USAir	PH-EZS	N884US					
11339	Sempati Air Transport	(PH-EZU)	PH-LNG	(PK-JGG)	PK-JGH			
11340	American Airlines	PH-EZY	PH-LNI	N1400H				
11341	Transwede	PH-LNH	XA-RKM	PH-LNH	SE-			
11342	Portugalia	PH-LNJ	CS-TPE					
11343	Fokker	PH-LNK	XA-RKN	PH-LNK	stored Dec95 Woensdrecht, Netherlands			
11344	Deutsche BA	PH-EZD	F-GIOE	D-ADFD				
11345	USAir	PH-EZE	N885US					
11346	USAir	PH-EZO	N886US					
11347	Sempati Air Transport	PH-LNL	PK-JGF					
11348	TAM Brasil	PH-LNM	(PK-JGG)	PT-MRE				
11349	USAir	PH-EZB	N887US					
11350	Transwede	PH-LNN	(PK-JGH)	XA-SBH	PH-LNN	SE-DUH		
11351	TAM Brasil	PH-LNO	PT-MRF					
11352	American Airlines	PH-EZZ	N1401G					
11353	American Airlines	PH-EZA	N1402K					
11354	American Airlines	PH-EZC	N1403M					
11355	American Airlines	PH-EZI	N1404D					
11356	American Airlines	PH-EZJ	N1405J					
11357	USAir	PH-EZL	N888AU					
11358	USAir	PH-EZM	N889US					
11359	American Airlines	PH-EZG	N1406A					
11360	American Airlines	PH-EZO	N1407D					
11361	American Airlines	PH-EZS	N1408B					
11362	TAT European Airlines	PH-EZT	F-GMPG					
11363	Deutsche BA	PH-EZV	F-GIOF	D-ADFE				
11364	Corse Mediterranee	PH-EZA	F-GIOG					
11365	USAir	PH-EZC	N890US					
11366	USAir	PH-EZP	N891US					
11367	American Airlines	PH-EZI	N1409B					
11368	American Airlines	PH-EZJ	N1410E					
11369	American Airlines	PH-EZB	N1411G					
11370	American Airlines	PH-EZD	N1412A					
11371	Transwede	PH-JXP	XA-SCD	PH-JXP	SE-DUI			
11372	USAir	PH-EZE	N892US					
11373	USAir	PH-EZL	N893US					
11374	Mexicana	PH-JXX	XA-TCG					
11375	Mexicana	PH-JXR	(F-GKLX)	XA-TCH				
11376	American Airlines	PH-EZO	N1413A					
11377	American Airlines	PH-EZS	N1414D					
11378	Korean Air	PH-KXA	HL7206					
11379	USAir	PH-EZM	N894US					
11380	USAir	PH-EZG	N895US					
11381	Swissair	PH-JXY	HB-IVI	stored Jan96 Geneva, Switzerland				
11382	Mexicana	PH-JXS	XA-SGE					
11383	China Eastern Airlines	(PH-JXU)	PH-JXT	B-2231				
11384	Mexicana	PH-JXU	XA-SGF					
11385	American Airlines	PH-EZY	N1415K					
11386	Swissair	PH-JXK	HB-IVK	stored Jan96 Geneva, Switzerland				
11387	Korean Air	PH-KXB	HL7207					
11388	Korean Air	PH-KXC	HL7208					
11389	China Eastern Airlines	PH-JXV	B-2232					
11390	Mexicana	PH-JXW	XA-SGS					
11391	USAir	PH-EZB	N896US					
11392	USAir	PH-EZD	N897US					
11393	(Palair Macedonian)	PH-KXL	w/o 05Mar93 Aracinovo, nr Skopje, Macedonia					
11394	China Eastern Airlines	PH-KXI	B-2233					
11395	American Airlines	PH-EZC	N1416A					
11396	American Airlines	PH-EZE	N1417D					
11397	American Airlines	PH-EZI	N1418A					
11398	USAir	PH-EZJ	N898US					
11399	USAir	PH-EZL	N899US					

FOKKER 100

C/n	Last known Operator/Owner	Previous Identities/fate (where known)				
11400	Mexicana	PH-KXJ	XA-SGT			
11401	China Eastern Airlines	PH-KXK	B-2234			
11402	American Airlines	PH-EZM	N1419D			
11403	American Airlines	PH-EZO	N1420D			
11404	American Airlines	PH-EZB	N1421K			
11405	American Airlines	PH-EZG	N1422J			
11406	American Airlines	PH-EZP	N1423A			
11407	American Airlines	PH-EZS	N1424M			
11408	American Airlines	PH-EZE	N1425A			
11409	China Eastern Airlines	PH-KXP	B-2235			
11410	Mexicana	PH-KXR	XA-SHG			
11411	American Airlines	PH-EZB	N1426A			
11412	American Airlines	PH-EZC	N1427A			
11413	American Airlines	PH-EZI	N1428D			
11414	American Airlines	PH-EZJ	N1429G			
11415	American Airlines	PH-EZL	N1430D			
11416	American Airlines	PH-EZY	N1431B			
11417	American Airlines	PH-EZZ	N1432A			
11418	American Airlines	PH-EZO	N1433B			
11419	American Airlines	PH-EZM	N1434A			
11420	Mexicana	PH-LXG	XA-SHH			
11421	China Eastern Airlines	PH-LXH	B-2237			
11422	TAM Brasil	PH-LXI	PT-MRM			
11423	China Eastern Airlines	PH-KXZ	B-2238			
11424	TAT European Airlines	PH-LXV	F-GIOH			
11425	American Airlines	PH-EZD	N1435D			
11426	American Airlines	PH-EZE	N1436A			
11427	American Airlines	PH-EZG	N1437B			
11428	American Airlines	PH-EZP	N1438H			
11429	China Eastern Airlines	PH-LXA	B-2239			
11430	China Eastern Airlines	PH-LXB	B-2236			
11431	China Eastern Airlines	PH-LXC	B-2240			
11432	Korean Air	PH-EZJ	HL7209			
11433	TAT European Airlines	PH-NXA	PH-MXA	F-GIOI		
11434	American Airlines	PH-EZA	N1439A			
11435	American Airlines	PH-EZB	N1440A			
11436	American Airlines	PH-EZC	N1441A			
11437	American Airlines	PH-EZI	N1442E			
11438	Korean Air	PH-EZL	HL7210			
11439	Korean Air	PH-EZM	HL7211			
11440	TAM Brasil	PH-LXD	PT-MRK			
11441	TAM Brasil	PH-LXS	PT-MRL			
11442	TAM Brasil	PH-MXK	PT-MRI			
11443	TAM Brasil	PH-MXB	PT-MRN			
11444	Midway Airlines	PH-MXC	N103ML			
11445	Midway Airlines	PH-MXD	N104ML			
11446	American Airlines	PH-EZN	N1443A			
11447	American Airlines	PH-EZO	N1444N			
11448	American Airlines	PH-EZP	N1445B			
11449	American Airlines	PH-EZS	N1446A			
11450	Midway Airlines	PH-MXL	N107ML			
11451	TAM Brasil	PH-EZT	PT-MRJ			
11452	TAM Brasil	PH-EZU	PT-MCN	PH-RRN	PT-WHK	
11453	Merpati Nusantara	PH-MXO	PK-MJA			
11454	TAT European Airlines	PH-EZF	F-GIOJ			
11455	TAT European Airlines	PH-EZG	F-GIOK			
11456	American Airlines	PH-EZA	N1447L			
11457	American Airlines	PH-EZB	N1448A			
11458	American Airlines	PH-EZC	N1449D			
11459	American Airlines	PH-EZD	N1450A			
11460	American Airlines	PH-EZE	N1451N			
11461	TAM Brasil	PH-EZT	PT-MRR			
11462	TAM Brasil	PH-EZX	PT-MRS			
11463	Merpati Nusantara	PH-EZV	PK-MJC			
11464	American Airlines	PH-EZI	N1452B			
11465	American Airlines	PH-EZJ	N1453D			
11466	American Airlines	PH-EZK	N1454D			
11467	American Airlines	PH-EZL	N1455K			
11468	American Airlines	PH-EZM	N1456D			
11469	American Airlines	PH-EZN	N1457B			
11470	TAM Brasil	PH-EZR	PT-MRO			
11471	TAM Brasil	PH-EZO	PH-MXW	PT-MCO	PH-MXW	PT-WHL
11472	TAM Brasil	PH-EZU	PT-MRP			
11473	TAM Brasil	PH-EZV	PT-MRQ			
11474	Merpati Nusantara	PH-EZW	PK-MJD			
11475	Midway Airlines	PH-EZX	N105ML			
11476	Korean Air	PH-EZY	HL7212			
11477	Midway Airlines	PH-EZZ	N106ML			
11478	American Airlines	PH-EZA	N1458H			
11479	American Airlines	PH-EZB	N1459A			
11480	American Airlines	PH-EZC	PH-JCA	N1460A		

FOKKER 100

C/n	Last known Operator/Owner	Previous Identities/fate (where known)		
11481	American Airlines	PH-EZD	PH-JCB	N1461C
11482	American Airlines	PH-EZE	PH-JCC	N1462C
11483	American Airlines	PH-EZF	PH-JCD	N1463A
11484	Midway Airlines	PH-EZA	N108ML	
11485	Midway Airlines	PH-EZB	N109ML	
11486	Midway Airlines	PH-EZC	N110ML	
11487	Air Inter	PH-EZN	F-GPXA	
11488	British Midland	PH-EZD	G-BVJB	
11489	British Midland	PH-EZE	G-BVJA	
11490	American Airlines	PH-EZU	N1464A	
11491	American Airlines	PH-EZV	N1456K	
11492	Air Inter	PH-EZK	F-GPXB	
11493	Air Inter	PH-EZY	F-GPXC	
11494	Air Inter	PH-EZO	F-GPXD	
11495	Air Inter	PH-EZP	F-GPXE	
11496	Formosa Airlines	PH-	B-12292	
11497	British Midland	PH-EZJ	G-BVJC	
11498	American Airlines	PH-EZK	N1466A	
11499	American Airlines	PH-EZL	N1467A	
11500	Formosa Airlines	PH-EZN	PH-JCO	B-12291
11501	American Airlines	PH-EZM	N1468A	
11502	American Airlines	PH-EZN	N1469D	
11503	British Midland	PH-EZO	G-BVJD	
11504	Korean Air	PH-EZP	HL7213	
11505	TAM Brasil	PH-JCJ	PT-MRT	
11506	American Airlines	PH-EZF	N1470K	
11507	American Airlines	PH-EZG	N1471K	
11508	TAM Brasil	PH-	PT-MRX	
11509	Air Littoral	PH-EZF	F-GLIR	
11510	TAM Brasil	PH-	PT-MRY	
11511	TAM Brasil	PH-JCK	PT-MRU	
11512	Merpati Nusantara	PH-EZH	PK-MJE	
11513	Korean Air	PH-EZI	HL7214	
11514	American Airlines	PH-EZZ	N1472B	
11515	American Airlines	PH-EZY	N1473K	
11516	TAM Brasil	PH-JCL	PT-MRV	
11517	Merpati Nusantara	PH-EZX	PH-ONS	PK-MJF
11518	TAM Brasil	PH-JCM	PT-MRW	
11519	Korean Air	PH-EZK	HL7215	
11520	American Airlines	PH-EZV	N1474D	
11522	Korean Air	PH-EZG	HL7216	
11523	Korean Air	PH-EZM	HL7217	
11524	TAM Brasil	PH-	PT-MRZ	
11525	TAM Brasil	PH-	PT-	
11526	TAM Brasil	PH-	PT-	
11527	Merpati Nusantara	PH-EZN	PK-MJG	
11530	TAM Brasil	PH-	PT-	
11531				
15533				
15534				
15535				
15542				
11544				
11546				
11548				
11550				
11552				

HAWKER-SIDDELEY HS.121 TRIDENT

C/n	Series	Last known Operator/Owner	Previous Identities/fate (where known)
2101	1C	(British Airways)	G-ARPA b/u Apr76 Prestwick, UK
2102	1C	(British Airways)	G-ARPB b/u Jan85 Prestwick, UK
2103	1C	(British Airways)	G-ARPC dbf 28Dec75 Heathrow, UK
2104	1C	CAA Fire Service Training School	G-ARPD used for fire-training Teesside, UK
2105	1C	(British Airways)	G-ARPE b/u May76 Prestwick, UK
2106	1C	(British Airways)	G-ARPF b/u May76 Prestwick, UK
2107	1C	(British Airways)	G-ARPG b/u May76 Prestwick, UK
2108	1C	Cosford Aerospace Museum	G-ARPH preserved RAF Cosford, UK
2109	1C	(BEA)	G-ARPI badly dam 03Jul68 London-Heathrow, UK; rebuilt; w/o 18Jun72 Staines, UK
2110	1C	(British Airways)	G-ARPJ b/u May76 Prestwick, UK
2111	1C	Manchester Airport Authority	G-ARPK used for fire-training Manchester, UK
2112	1C	British A/P Authority	G-ARPL used for fire-training Edinburgh, UK
2113	1C	(British Airways)	G-ARPM b/u May76 Prestwick, UK
2114	1E	(British Airways)	9K-ACF G-ASWU 9K-ACF (G-ASWU) 5B-DAD G-ASWU b/u May81 London-Heathrow, UK
2115	1C	British A/P Authority	G-ARPN used for fire-training Aberdeen, UK
2116	1C	CAA Fire Service Training School	G-ARPO used for fire-training Teesside, UK
2117	1C	British A/P Authority	G-ARPP used for fire-training Glasgow, UK
2118	1E	(Kuwait Airways)	(9K-ACG) G-ASWV 9K-ACG w/o 30Jun66 Kuwait City, Kuwait
2119	1C	CAA Fire Service Training School	G-ARPR used for fire-training Teesside, UK
2120	1C	(BEA)	G-ARPS dbf 29Jul69 London-Heathrow, UK
2121	1C	(BEA)	G-ARPT dbr 03Jul68 London-Heathrow, UK; remains sold to Channel Airways; finally b/u Jul72 Southend, UK
2122	1C	(British Airways)	G-ARPU b/u Nov75 London-Heathrow, UK
2123	1C	CAA Fire Service Training School	G-ARPW used for fire-training Teesside, UK
2124	1C	Air Svce Training (Perth)	G-ARPX stored Nov82 Perth, UK
2125	1E	Iraqi Airways	YI-AEA stored Jun77 Baghdad, Iraq
2126	1C	(Hawker Siddeley Avn)	G-ARPY w/o 03Jun66 Felthorpe, UK
2127	1E	Iraqi Airways	YI-AEB stored Apr77 Baghdad, Iraq
2128	1C	RFD	G-ARPZ escape systems test airframe, Dunsfold, UK
2129	1E	Iraqi Airways	YI-AEC stored Jun77 Baghdad, Iraq
2130	1E	Chinese AF	AP-ATK G-ATNA AP-ATK 50056 stored
2131	1E	(Chinese AF)	AP-ATL w/o 13Aug71 Mongolia
2132	1E	Chinese United A/L	AP-ATM 50050 stored
2133	1E	Chinese United A/L	AP-AUG 50152 stored
2134	1E	(Cyprus Airways)	9K-ACH G-AZND 9K-ACH 5B-DAE w/o 22Jul74 Larnaca, Cyprus
2135	1E	Air Ceylon	G-AVYA 4R-ACN used as ground trainer Colombo, Sri Lanka
2136	1E	(British Airways)	G-AVYB b/u May81 London-Heathrow, UK (fuselage to Ewyas Harold, Hereford, UK)
2137	1E	(British Airways)	G-AVYC b/u May81 London-Heathrow, UK
2138	1E	(Northeast Airlines)	G-AVYD w/o 15Sep75 Bilbao, Spain
2139	1E	Science Museum	G-AVYE preserved Wroughton, UK
2140	2E	(British Airways)	G-AVFA b/u Jan84 London-Heathrow, UK
2141	2E	Duxford Avn Society	G-AVFB 5B-DAC G-AVFB preserved Duxford, UK
2142	2E	(British Airways)	G-AVFC b/u Nov81 London-Heathrow, UK
2143	2E	(British Airways)	G-AVFD b/u Apr82 London-Heathrow, UK
2144	2E	Belfast A/P Authority	G-AVFE used for fire-training Belfast, UK
2145	2E	(British Airways)	G-AVFF b/u Jan85 Southend, UK
2146	2E	British Airways	G-AVFG painted in new British A/W colours and used as ground ops training airframe
2147	2E	(British Airways)	G-AVFH b/u May82 London-Heathrow, UK (fwd fuselage to Mosquito Museum, London Colney, UK)
2148	2E	(British Airways)	G-AVFI b/u May82 London-Heathrow, UK
2149	2E	CAA Fire Service Training School	G-AVFJ used for fire-training Teesside, UK
2150	2E	British Airways	G-AVFK with Metropolitan Police Training Centre, Hounslow Heath, UK
2151	2E	(British Airways)	G-AVFL b/u Feb85 Southend, UK
2152	2E	Brunel Tech College	G-AVFM used for ground training Bristol-Lulsgate, UK
2153	2E	(British Airways)	G-AVFN b/u Jan85 Southend, UK
2154	2E	(British Airways)	(G-AVFO) 5B-DAA G-AZXM b/u Feb85 Southend, UK
2155	2E	(Cyprus Airways)	5B-DAB w/o 22Jul74 Larnaca, Cyprus
2156	2E	(British Airways)	G-AVFO b/u Feb85 Southend, UK
2157	2E	CAAC	G-AZFT 240 B-240 B-2201 wfs Nov91
2158	2E	Air China	G-AZFU 242 B-242 B-2202 wfs Nov91 and stored Tianjin, China
2159	2E	(CAAC)	G-AZFV 244 B-244 B-2218 w/o 31Aug88 Hong Kong
2160	2E	CAAC	G-AZFW 246 B-246 B-2219 wfs Nov91 and stored Guangzhou, China
2161	2E	CAAC	G-AZFX 248 B-248 B-2223 wfs Nov91
2162	2E	CAAC	G-AZFY 250 B-250 B-2212 wfs Nov91
2163	2E	CAAC	G-BABP B-252 B-2214 wfs Nov91
2164	2E	CAAC	G-BABR B-254 B-2209 wfs Nov91
2165	2E	(CAAC)	G-BABS B-256 B-261 B-2208 w/o 22Mar90 Guilin, China
2166	2E	CAAC	G-BABT B-258 B-2215 wfs Nov91
2167	2E	(CAAC)	G-BABU B-260 w/o 27Dec83 Fuzhou, China

HAWKER-SIDDELEY HS.121 TRIDENT

C/n	Series	Last known Operator/Owner	Previous Identities/fate (where known)
2168	2E	CAAC	G-BABV B-262 B-2203 wfs Nov91
2169	2E	(CAAC)	G-BAJF B-264 dbr 14Sep83 Giulin, China
2170	2E	(CAAC)	G-BAJG B-266 w/o 26Apr82 Yangsu, China
2171	2E	Chinese AF	G-BAJH B-272 50052
2172	2E	(CAAC)	G-BAJI B-274 w/o 14Mar79 nr Canton, China
2173	2E	CAAC	G-BAJJ B-276 B-2213 wfs Nov91
2174	2E	China United Airlines	G-BAJK B-278 50158 stored
2175	2E	CAAC	G-BBVS B-280 B-2204 wfs Nov91 and stored Tianjin, China
2176	2E	CAAC	G-BBVT B-282 B-2205 wfs Nov91
2177	2E	CAAC	G-BBVU B-284 B-2216 wfs Nov91 and stored Tianjin, China
2178	2E	CAAC	G-BBVV B-286 B-2210 wfs Nov91 and stored Nanjing, China
2179	2E	CAAC	G-BBVW B-288 B-2217 wfs Nov91 and stored Guangzhou, China
2180	2E	CAAC	G-BBVX B-290 B-2211 wfs Nov91 and stored Shanghai, China
2181	2E	Air China	G-BBVY B-292 B-2206 wfs Nov91 and stored Tianjin, China
2182	2E	CAAC	G-BBVZ B-294 B-2207 wfs Nov91 and stored Tianjin, China
2183	2E	CAAC	G-BBWA B-296 B-2220 wfs Nov91
2184	2E	CAAC	G-BBWB B-298 B-2221 wfs Nov91
2185	2E	Chinese AF	G-BBWD B-263
2186	2E	Chinese AF	G-BBWE B-265 50054
2187	2E	Chinese AF	G-BBWF B-267
2188	2E	Chinese AF	G-BBWG B-269
2189	2E	China United Airlines	G-BBWH B-271 50053
2301	3B	(British Airways)	G-AWYZ b/u Jun84 London-Heathrow, UK
2302	3B	(British Airways)	G-AWZA b/u Jan84 London-Heathrow, UK
2303	3B	British Airways	G-AWZB b/u Aug84 London-Heathrow, UK
2304	3B	Air Charter Service	G-AWZC 9Q-CTM believed wfu and b/u
2305	3B	Air Charter Service	G-AWZD 9Q-CTI believed wfu and b/u
2306	3B	(British Airways)	G-AWZE b/u Jun84 London-Heathrow, UK
2307	3B	Air Charter Service	G-AWZF 9Q-CTZ used for spares Apr86
2308	3B	Air Charter Service	G-AWZG 9Q-CTY 9Q-CTD believed wfu and b/u
2309	3B	(British Airways)	G-AWZH b/u Jun86 London-Heathrow, UK
2310	3B	(British Airways)	G-AWZI b/u Jun87 London-Heathrow, UK; fuselage to fire brigade Reigate, UK
2311	3B	British Airways	G-AWZJ with Prestwick Airport Fire Service, UK
2312	3B	British Airways	G-AWZK used in new British Airways colours London-Heathrow, UK as ground trainer
2313	3B	(British Airways)	G-AWZL b/u Jun86 London-Heathrow, UK
2314	3B	Science Museum	G-AWZM preserved Wroughton, UK
2315	3B	Cranfield College Aeronautics	G-AWZN used as ground trainer Cranfield, UK
2316	3B	Mosquito A/c Museum	G-AWZO stored Hatfield, UK
2317	3B	(British Airways)	G-AWZP b/u Jun86 London-Heathrow, UK (nose section to Manchester Museum of Science & Industry, UK)
2318	3B	CAA Fire Service Training School	G-AWZR used for fire-training Teesside, UK
2319	3B	CAA Fire Service Training School	G-AWZS used for fire-training Teesside, UK
2320	3B	(British Airways)	G-AWZT w/o 10Sep76 nr Zagreb, Yugoslavia
2321	3B	British Airways	G-AWZU with Stansted Airport Fire Service, UK
2322	3B	Air Charter Service	G-AWZV 9Q-CTZ believed wfu and b/u
2323	3B	(British Airways)	G-AWZW b/u Jun84 London-Heathrow, UK
2324	3B	British A/P Authority	G-AWZX used for fire service training London-Gatwick, UK
2325	3B	(British Airways)	(G-AWZY) G-AYVF b/u Jun84 London-Heathrow, UK
2326	3B	Birmingham Airport	G-AWZZ used for fire service training Birmingham Intl, Fire Service, UK
2327	3B	China United Airlines	G-BAJL B-268 50057 wfu and stored
2328	3B	China United Airlines	G-BAJM B-270 50058 wfu and stored

Production complete

HAWKER-SIDDLEY HS.801 NIMROD

C/n	Series	Last known Owner/Operator	Identities/fate (where known)
6476	HS.801	Ministry of Defence	G-5-1 XV147 1st prototype ff 23Oct66 wfu; fuselage BAe Warton, UK
6477	HS.801	A&AEE	XV148 2nd prototype ff 23May67 wfu; fatigue test airframe BAe Woodford, UK
8001	MR.2	Royal Air Force	XV226/26 ff 28Jun68
8002	MR.2	Royal Air Force	XV227/27
8003	MR.2	Royal Air Force	XV228/28
8004	MR.2	Royal Air Force	XV229/29
8005	MR.2	Royal Air Force	XV230/30
8006	MR.2	Royal Air Force	XV231/31
8007	MR.2	Royal Air Force	XV232/32
8008	MR.2	Royal Air Force	XV233/33
8009	MR.2	Royal Air Force	XV234/34 stored Sep93 RAF Kinloss, UK
8010	MR.2	Royal Air Force	XV235/35
8011	MR.2	Royal Air Force	XV236/36
8012	MR.2	Royal Air Force	XV237/37
8013	MR.2	Royal Air Force	XV238/38
8014	MR.2	(Royal Air Force)	XV239/39 w/o 02Sep95 Lake Ontario, Canada
8015	MR.2	Royal Air Force	XV240/40
8016	MR.2	Royal Air Force	XV241/41
8017	MR.2	Royal Air Force	XV242/42 stored Sep93 RAF Kinloss, UK
8018	MR.2	Royal Air Force	XV243/43
8019	MR.2	Royal Air Force	XV244/44
8020	MR.2	Royal Air Force	XV245/45
8021	MR.2	Royal Air Force	XV246/46
8022	MR.2	Royal Air Force	XV247/47 stored Sep93 RAF Kinloss, UK
8023	MR.2	Royal Air Force	XV248/48
8024	MR.2	Royal Air Force	XV249/49 stored Sep93 RAF Kinloss, UK; to be converted to R.2 model
8025	MR.2	Royal Air Force	XV250/50
8026	MR.2	Royal Air Force	XV251/51
8027	MR.2	Royal Air Force	XV252/52
8028	MR.2	Royal Air Force	XV253/53 wfu 06Nov91; instructional airframe 9118M RAF Kinloss, UK
8029	MR.2	Royal Air Force	XV254/54
8030	MR.2	Royal Air Force	XV255/55
8031	MR.2	(Royal Air Force)	XV256/56 w/o 17Nov80 Roseisle Forest, nr RAF Kinloss, UK
8032	MR.2	(Royal Air Force)	XV257/57 sold as scrap Mar92 BAe Woodford, UK
8033	MR.2	Royal Air Force	XV258/58
8034	AEW.3	(Royal Air Force)	XV259/59 wfu; sold as scrap 1991 RAF Abingdon, UK
8035	MR.2	Royal Air Force	XV260/60
8036	AEW.3	Royal Air Force	XV261/61 wfu; instructional airframe 8986M RAF Lyneham, UK
8037	AEW.3	(Royal Air Force)	XV262/62 wfu 1988; sold as scrap Jan89 RAF Abingdon, UK
8038	AEW.3	Royal Air Force	XV263/63 wfu; instructional airframe 8967M RAF Finningley, UK
8039	R.1	Royal Air Force	XW664/64
8040	R.1	Royal Air Force	XW665/65
8041	R.1	(Royal Air Force)	XW666/66 w/o 16May95 in Moray Firth, 4m N of RAF Lossiemouth, UK
8042	AEW.3	(Royal Air Force)	XZ280/80 wfu; sold as scrap Apr92 RAF Abingdon, UK
8043	AEW.3	(Royal Air Force)	XZ281/81 wfu; sold as scrap 1991 RAF Abingdon, UK
8044	AEW.3	(Royal Air Force)	XZ282/82 wfu; instructional airframe 9000M; fire dump RAF Kinloss, UK; sold as scrap Sep92
8045	AEW.3	(Royal Air Force)	XZ283/83 wfu; sold as scrap 1991 RAF Abingdon, UK
8046	MR.2	Royal Air Force	XZ284/84
8047	AEW.3	(Royal Air Force)	XZ285/85 wfu; sold as scrap May92 RAF Abingdon, UK
8048	AEW.3	Royal Air Force	XZ286/86 wfu; scrapped Jan89 RAF Abingdon; sections RAF Kinloss, UK
8049	AEW.3	Royal Air Force	XZ287/87 wfu; instructional airframe 9140M; fuselage RAF Stafford, UK

Production complete

ILYUSHIN Il-62

Il-62s use two serial number systems:

1 Five figure serial numbers indicate by the second and third figures the batch number and by the final figure the number of the aircraft (from 1-5) in that batch; the first figure indicates year of construction

2 Seven figure serial numbers indicate by the third and fourth figures the batch number and by the sixth figure the number of the aircraft (from 1-5) in that batch; the second figure indicates year of construction and the first figure the quarter of that year

S/n	Series	Last known Owner/Operator	Identities/fate (where known)				
30001		(Aeroflot)	CCCP-06156	w/o in 1965	prototype		
30002		Aeroflot	CCCP-06153	wfu	prototype		
30003		Aeroflot	CCCP-06176	wfu	prototype		
40004		Aeroflot	CCCP-06170	wfu	prototype (marks later use on a Mi-8)		
40005		Aeroflot	CCCP-06300	wfu; watertank pressurisation testframe	prototype		
50001		Aeroflot	CCCP-86661	c/n plate believed incorrect (should be 50101)	wfu		
50102		Aeroflot	CCCP-86662	wfu			
50103		Aeroflot	CCCP-86663	wfu			
50104		Aeroflot	CCCP-86664	wfu			
50105		Aeroflot	CCCP-86665	wfu			
60201		Aeroflot	CCCP-86666	wfu			
60202		Aeroflot	CCCP-86667	wfu			
60203		Aeroflot	CCCP-86668	wfu			
60204		Aeroflot	CCCP-86669	wfu			
70205		Aeroflot	CCCP-86670	preserved Monino Museum, Moscow, Russia			
70301		(Aeroflot)	CCCP-86671	w/o 13Oct72 Moscow-Sheremetyevo, USSR			
70302		Aeroflot	CCCP-86672	preserved Civil Avn Museum, Ulyanovsk, Russia			
70303		Aeroflot	CCCP-86673(1)	instructional airframe Riga-Spilve, Latvia			
70304		Flight Research Inst	CCCP-86674	RA-86674			
80305		Krasnoyarsk Airlines	CCCP-86675	SU-ARX	CCCP-86675	RA-86675	
80401		Aeroflot	CCCP-86676	dumped by Apr92 Tashkent, Uzbekistan			
80402		(Aeroflot)	CCCP-86677	b/u Jun94 Krasnoyarsk-Yemelianovo, Russia			
80403		Aeroflot	CCCP-86678	wfu Krasnoyarsk-Yemelianovo, Russia			
80404		Aeroflot	CCCP-86679	wfu			
80405		Aeroflot	CCCP-86680	wfu			
90501		Aeroflot	CCCP-86681	SU-ARW	CCCP-86681	wfu	
90502		Aeroflot	CCCP-86682	wfu			
90503		Aeroflot	CCCP-86683	wfu			
90504		Aeroflot	CCCP-86684	2004	CCCP-86684	wfu	
90505		Aeroflot	CCCP-86685	wfu; displayed Ulyanovsk, Russia			
90601		Aeroflot	CCCP-86686	wfu			
90602		CSA	OK-YBA	wfu 04Sep87; intended for restaurant use in 1989 Ceska Skalice, Czechoslovakia			
90603		CSA	OK-YBB	wfu 05Sep83			
90604		Aeroflot	CCCP-86687	wfu			
90605			CCCP-86648				
00605	M	Russian Min of Defence	CCCP-86538	RA-86538			
00701		(CSA)	OK-ZBC	wfu 28Sep84; b/u Sep90 Prague-Ruzyne, Czechoslovakia			
00702		(Interflug)	DM-SEA	w/o 12Aug72 Konigs Wusterhausen, E Germany			
00703		Domodedovo CAPA	CCCP-86649	RA-86649			
00704		(Interflug)	DM-SEB	DDR-SEB	dbf 05Aug90 Rangsdorf, Berlin, Germany		
00705		Aeroflot	CCCP-86650	SU-ARO	CCCP-86650	preserved Museum of Civil Aviation, Ulyanovsk, Russia	
00801		(Egyptair)	CCCP-86651	SU-ARN	w/o 16Jun72 Almaza, Egypt		
00802			CCCP-88652	SU-AVU	CCCP-86652		
00803			CCCP-86653	SU-AWJ	CCCP-86653		
00804			CCCP-86654	SU-AVL	CCCP-86654		
00805		Aeroflot	CCCP-86655	SU-AVW	CCCP-86655	wfu	
10901	M	Domodedovo Airlines	CCCP-86656	RA-86656			
10902		CSA	OK-ABD	wfu 30Aug86; used as restaurant, Lipa, Czech Republic			
10903		Interflug	DM-SEC	DDR-SEC	preserved Grunbergallee Technical School, Berlin-Schonefeld, Germany		
10904		Domodedovo Airlines	CCCP-86657	RA-86657			
10905		Aeroflot	CCCP-86658	wfu			
11001		Aeroflot	CCCP-86689	CU-T994	CCCP-86689	wfu	
11002		Aeroflot	CCCP-86690	wfu			
11003		Aeroflot	CCCP-86691	wfu			
11004		(LOT)	SP-LAA	w/o 14Mar80 nr Warsaw, Poland			
11005		(CAAC)	2022	B-2022	b/u during 1993 Beijing, China		
11101		CAAC	2024	B-2024	preserved Datang San Museum, China		
11102		Far East Avia	CCCP-86692	RA-86692			
11103		Far East Avia	CCCP-86693	RA-86693	wfs May95 Khabarovsk, Russia		
11104		Uzbekistan Airways	CCCP-86694	UK-86694			
21105		Krasnoyarsk Airlines	SP-LAB	CCCP-86706	RA-86706		
21201		(CAAC)	2026	B-2026	b/u during 1994 Beijing, China		
21202		(CAAC)	2028	B-2028	CU-T992	B-2028	b/u during 1994 Beijing, China
21203		(CAAC)	B-2020	b/u during 1993 Beijing, China			
21204		Aeroflot	CCCP-86695	wfu			
21205		Aeroflot	CCCP-86696	wfs by Jun93 Kiev-Zhulyany, Ukraine			

ILYUSHIN Il-62

S/n	Series	Last known Owner/Operator	Identities/fate (where known)			
21301		Aeroflot	CCCP-86697	dumped by Apr92 Tashkent, Uzbekistan		
21302		Tarom	YR-IRA	stored Jun95 Bucharest-Otopeni, Romania		
21303		(Aeroflot)	CCCP-86698	b/u 1993 Moscow-Domodedovo, Russia		
21304		Domodedovo Airlines	CCCP-86699	RA-86699		
21305		Tarom	YR-IRB	stored Jun95 Bucharest-Otopeni, Romania		
31401		Russian Min of Defence	SP-LAC	CCCP-86556	RA-86556	
31402		Interflug	DM-SEF	DDR-SEF	preserved Mar90 Leipzig, Germany	
31403		Interflug	DM-SEG	DDR-SEG	preserved Oct89 Stolln Rhinow, Germany	
31404		Uzbekistan Airways	CCCP-86659	86659	UK-86659	
31405		Interflug	DM-SEH	DDR-SEH	preserved Jan90 Erfurt, Germany	
31501		CSA	OK-DBE	wfs Dec88		
31502		(CSA)	OK-DBF	w/o 20Aug75 Damascus, Syria		
31503		Far East Avia	CCCP-86700	RA-86700		
31504		Aeroflot	CCCP-86701	RA-86701	wfs Moscow-Domodedovo, Russia	
31505		Far East Avia	CCCP-86702	RA-86702		
41601		(Aeroflot)	CCCP-86703	RA-86703	dbr Oct92 Moscow-Domodedovo, Russian	
41602		(CSA)	OK-EBG	scrapped Jun93 Maxton, Laurinburg, NC, USA		
41603		Uzbekistan Airways	CCCP-86704	UK-86704		
41604		Krasnoyarsk Airlines	SP-LAD	CCCP-86707	RA-86707	
41605		Domodedovo Airlines	CCCP-86705	RA-86705		
41701		Aeroflot	CCCP-86605	wfu		
41702		Aeroflot	CCCP-86606	wfu	(marks were used on Kamov Ka-15)	
41703		(Aeroflot)	CCCP-86607	b/u 1992/3 Moscow-Domodedovo, Russia		
41704		Aeroflot	CCCP-86608	wfs		
41705		(Aeroflot)	CCCP-86609	wfs Alma Ata, Kazakhstan; b/u		
41801		Uzbekistan Airways	CCCP-86610	UK-86610		
41802		Krasnoyarsk Airlines	SP-LAE	CCCP-86708	RA-86708	
41803		Domodedovo Airlines	CCCP-86611	RA-86611		
41804			CCCP-86612			
41805		Georgia Air	OK-BYV	OK-FBF		
51901		(Aeroflot)	CCCP-86613	w/o 21Nov92 Yakutsk-Magan, Russia		
51902		Tarom	YR-IRC	stored Jun95 Bucharest-Otopeni, Romania		
51903	M	(Aeroflot)	CCCP-86614	w/o 27May77 Havana, Cuba		
51904			CCCP-86615			
51905			CCCP-86616			
52001			CCCP-86617			
52002	M	Far East Avia	CCCP-86618	RA-86618	c/n also quoted as 3520422	
52003	M	Krasnoyarsk Airlines	CCCP-86619	RA-86619	c/n also quoted as 3520233	
52004	M	Far East Avia	CCCP-86620	RA-86620		
52005	M	Domodedovo Airlines	CCCP-86621	RA-86621	c/n also quoted as 3520556	
52101	M	Domodedovo Airlines	CCCP-86622	RA-86622	c/n also quoted as 4521617	
52102	M	Far East Avia	CCCP-86623	RA-86623		
52103			CCCP-86624			
52104	M	Ulyanovsk Civil Avn Sch	CCCP-86450			
52105		Atlant	CCCP-86451	RA-86451	UR-86451	c/n also quoted as 4521152
62201	M	Far East Avia	CCCP-86452	RA-86452	c/n also quoted as 1622212	
62202	M	Krasnoyarsk Airlines	CCCP-86453	RA-86453	c/n also quoted as 1622323	
62203	M	Far East Avia	CCCP-86454	RA-86454	c/n also quoted as 1622434	
62204	M	Krasnoyarsk Airlines	SP-LAF	CCCP-86709	RA-86709	
62205	M	Domodedovo Airlines	CCCP-86455	RA-86455	c/n also quoted as 2622656	
62301	M	(Aeroflot)	CCCP-86456	dbr 21Nov90 Yakutsk, Russia (30Jun90 also reported)		
62302	M	(Domodedovo Airlines)	CCCP-86457	RA-86457	b/u Domodedovo Aug95 c/n also quoted as 2623828	
62303	M	Ulyanovsk Civil Avn Sch	CCCP-86458	RA-86458	c/n also quoted as 3623834	
62304	M	Krasnoyarsk Airlines	CCCP-86459	RA-86459	c/n also quoted as 3623945	
62305	M	Domodedovo Airlines	CCCP-86460	RA-86460	c/n also quoted as 3623856	
62401	M	Domodedovo Airlines	CCCP-86461	RA-86461	c/n also quoted as 3624711	
62402	M	Domodedovo Airlines	CCCP-86462	RA-86462	c/n also quoted as 3624623	
62403	M	Domodedovo Airlines	CCCP-86463	RA-86463	c/n also quoted as 4624434	
62404		Georgia Air	OK-GBH			
62405	M	Far East Avia	CCCP-86464	RA-86464		
62501	M	Domodedovo Airlines	CCCP-86465	RA-86465	c/n also quoted as 4625315	
72502	M	Domodedovo Airlines	CCCP-86469	RA-86469	c/n also quoted as 1725121	
72503	M	(Aeroflot)	CCCP-86470	w/o 29Sep82 Luxembourg-Findel, Luxembourg		
72504	M	Far East Avia	CCCP-86471	RA-86471		
2725456		Russian Min of Defence	SP-LAG	CCCP-86557	RA-86557	
2726517	M	Domodedovo Airlines	CCCP-86472	RA-86472		
2726628	MK	Russian Min of Defence	CCCP-86495	RA-86495		
3726739	M	Cubana	CU-T1208			
3726841	M	Domodedovo Airlines	CCCP-86473	RA-86473		
3726952	M	Aeroflot Russian Int A/L	CCCP-86474	RA-86474		
3727113	M	Domodedovo Airlines	CCCP-86475	RA-86475		
4727324	M	Domodedovo Airlines	CCCP-86484	RA-86484		
4727435	M	(Aeroflot)	CCCP-86477	b/u Sep94 Moscow-Sheremetyevo, Russia		
4727546	M	Tarom	YR-IRD	SP-LBR	YR-IRD	stored Jun95 Bucharest-Otopeni, Romania
4727657	M	Aeroflot Russian Int A/L	CCCP-86478	RA-86478		
4728118	M	Far East Avia	CCCP-86479	RA-86479		
4728229	M	Far East Avia	CCCP-86476	RA-86476		
1828132	M	Cubana	CU-T1209	wfu Dec93 Havana, Cuba		

ILYUSHIN Il-62

S/n	Series	Last known Owner/Operator	Identities/fate (where known)			
1828243	M	Cubana	CU-T1215			
2828354	M	Domodedovo Airlines	CCCP-86480	RA-86480		
2829415	M	Far East Avia	CCCP-86481	RA-86481		
2829526	M	Domodedovo Airlines	CCCP-86482	RA-86482		
2829637	M	Aeroflot Russian Int A/L	CCCP-86483	RA-86483		
3829748	M	Cubana	CU-T1216			
3829859	M	Aeroflot Russian Int A/L	CCCP-86484	RA-86484		
3830912	M	Aeroflot Russian Int A/L	CCCP-86485	RA-86485		
3830123	M	Far East Avia	CCCP-86486	RA-86486		
3830234	M	Domodedovo Airlines	CCCP-86487	RA-86487		
4830345	M	Aeroflot Russian Int A/L	CCCP-86488	RA-86488		
4830456	M	Aeroflot Russian Int A/L	CCCP-86489	RA-86489		
4831517	M	Aeroflot Russian Int A/L	E German AF 121	DM-SEK	DDR-SEK	D-AOAE
			CCCP-86562	RA-86562		
4831628	M	Tarom	YR-IRE	stored Jun95 Bucharest-Otopeni, Romania		
4831739	M	Domodedovo Airlines	CCCP-86490	SP-LBI	CCCP-86490	RA-86490
1931142	M	Domodedovo Airlines	CCCP-86491	RA-86491		
1931253	M	Aeroflot Russian Int A/L	CCCP-86497	RA-86497		
1932314	M	Domodedovo Airlines	CCCP-86498	RA-86498		
2932526	M	Air Ukraine	SP-LBA	CCCP-86581	UR-86581	
2932637	M	Domodedovo Airlines	CCCP-86499	RA-86499		
2932748	M	CSA	OK-JBI			
2932859	M	Aeroflot	CCCP-86500	stored Inst of Civil Avn, Moscow-Sheremetyevo, Russia		
3933913	M	Air Koryo	885	P-885	(also reported as c/n 3933916)	
3933121	M	Domodedovo Airlines	CCCP-86501	RA-86501		
3933232	M	Cubana	CU-T1217	stored Feb90 Havana, Cuba		
3933345	M	Aeroflot Russian Int A/L	CCCP-86502	RA-86502		
4933456	M	CSA	OK-JBJ	HA-LIA	OK-JBJ	
4934512	M	Far East Avia	CCCP-86503	RA-86503		
4934621	M	Far East Avia	CCCP-86504	RA-86504		
4934734	M	Aeroflot Russian Int A/L	E German AF 122	DM-SEL	DDR-SEL	D-AOAF
			CCCP-86564	RA-86564		
4934847	M	Russian Min of Defence	CCCP-86505	RA-86505		
1034152	M	Air Ukraine	SP-LBB	CCCP-86132	UR-86132	
1035213	M	Aeroflot Russian Int A/L	CCCP-86510	RA-86510		
1035324	M	Aeroflot Russian Int A/L	CCCP-86506	RA-86506		
1035435	M	CSA	OK-KBK			
2035546	M	Moscow Airways	CCCP-86507	RA-86507		
2035657	M	Cubana	CU-T1218			
2036718	M	Ulyanovsk Training Sch	CCCP-86508	RA-86508		
2036829	M	Domodedovo Airlines	CCCP-86509	RA-86509		
3036931	M	Domodedovo Airlines	DM-SEI	DDR-SEI	D-AOAD	CCCP-86563
			RA-86563			
3036142	M	Gosnii GA	CCCP-86511	RA-86511		
3036253	M	Air Ukraine	SP-LBC	CCCP-86582	UR-86582	
3037314	M	Aeroflot Russian Int A/L	CCCP-86512	RA-86512		
4037425	M	CSA	OK-BYW	OK-KBN		
4037536	M	(Aeroflot)	CCCP-86513	w/o 06Jul82 Moscow-Sheremetyevo, USSR		
4037647	M	Aeroflot Russian Int A/L	CCCP-86514	RA-86514		
4037758	M	Ukraine Government	CCCP-86527	86527	UR-86527	
4038111	M	Atlant	CCCP-86528	UR-86528		
4038625	M	Atlant	CCCP-86529	RA-86529	UR-86529	
1138234	M	Air Ukraine	SP-LBD	CCCP-86133	UR-86133	
1138546	M	Air Ukraine	SP-LBE	CCCP-86134	UR-86134	
2138657	M	Moscow Airways	CCCP-86515	RA-86515		
13951.	M	Chosonminhang	889	reportedly w/o 01Jul83 Fouta Djall Mts, Guinea Bissau		
2139524	M	Domodedovo Airlines	CCCP-86516	RA-86516		
3139732	M	Aeroflot Russian Int A/L	CCCP-86517	RA-86517		
3139845	M	Cubana	CU-T1225			
3139956	M	Aeroflot Russian Int A/L	CCCP-86518	RA-86518		
4140212	M	Domodedovo Airlines	CCCP-86519	RA-86519		
4140324	M	Aeroflot Russian Int A/L	CCCP-86492	RA-86492		
4140536	M	Uzbekistan Airways	DDR-SEM	D-AOAG	CCCP-86573	86573
			UK-86573			
4140748	M	Far East Avia	CCCP-86493	RA-86493		
4140952	M	Domodedovo Airlines	CCCP-86494	RA-86494		
1241314	M	Aeroflot Russian Int A/L	CCCP-86520	RA-86520		
1241425	M	Domodedovo Airlines	CCCP-86521	RA-86521		
2241536	M	Aeroflot Russian Int A/L	CCCP-86522	RA-86522		
2241647	M	Aeroflot Russian Int A/L	CCCP-86523	RA-86523		
41.5.		Air Koryo	P-880?			
3242219	M	Cubana	CU-T1226	stored by Jun95 Havana, Cuba		
3242321	M	Aeroflot Russian Int A/L	CCCP-86524	RA-86524		
3242432	M	ALIM Airlines	E German AF 120	DDR-SEN	German AF 11+21	UK-86932
4242543	M	Domodedovo Airlines	CCCP-86530	RA-86530		
4242654	M	Aeroflot Russian Int A/L	CCCP-86531	RA-86531		
4243111	M	Aeroflot Russian Int A/L	CCCP-86532	RA-86532		
1343123	M	Aeroflot Russian Int A/L	CCCP-86533	RA-86533		
1343332	M	Aeroflot Russian Int A/L	CCCP-86534	RA-86534		
2343341	M	Cubana	CU-T1252			
2343554	M	Air Ukraine	SP-LBF	CCCP-86580	UR-86580	

ILYUSHIN Il-62

S/n	Series	Last known Owner/Operator	Identities/fate (where known)			
2344615	M	Russian Min of Defence	CCCP-86539	RA-86539		
3344724	M	NEBO Aircompany	C9-BAE	RA-86931		
3344833	M	Uzbekistan Airways	DDR-SEO	D-AOAH	CCCP-86574	86574
			UK-86574			
3344942	M	(LOT)	SP-LBG	w/o 09May87 Warsaw, Poland		
4344851	M	Domodedovo Airlines	CCCP-86535	RA-86535	(also reported as c/n 2444555)	
3445111	M	Cubana	CU-T1259			
4445827	MK	Uzbekistan Airways	E German AF 176	DDR-SEP	German AF 11+22	UK-86934
4445032	M	Air Moravia	OK-OBL			
4445948	M	Rossia	CCCP-86536	RA-86536		
1545951	M		OK-PBM	RA-		
2546812	M	Aeroflot Russian Int A/L	DDR-SER	D-AOAI	CCCP-86565	RA-86565
2546624	M	Air Koryo	P-618			
3546733	M	Rossia	CCCP-86537	RA-86537		
3546548	M	Rossia/Russian Govt	CCCP-86540	86540	RA-86540	
4546257	M	Uzbekistan Airways	DDR-SET	D-AOAK	CCCP-86576	86576
			UK-86576			
4547315	M	Russian Min of Defence	CCCP-86555	RA-86555		
1647928	M	Uzbekistan Airways	DDR-SES	D-AOAJ	CCCP-86575	86575
			UK-86575			
2647737	M	Orient Avia	OK-BYZ	OK-RBZ	RA-86590	
2647646	M	Rossia	CCCP-86710	RA-86710		
3647853	M	Air Koryo	P-881			
4648414	M	Rossia/Russian Govt	CCCP-86711	86711	RA-86711	
4648525	M	TAAG Angola	D2-TIF			
4648339	M	Rossia/Russian Govt	CCCP-86712	86712	RA-86712	
1748445	M	Air Ukraine	SP-LBH	CCCP-86135	UR-86135	
2748552	M	Uzbekistan Airways	DDR-SEU	D-AOAL	CCCP-86577	86577
			UK-86577			
2749316	M	Rossia	CCCP-86466	RA-86466		
3749224	M	ALIM Airlines	E German AF 108	DDR-SEV	German AF 11+20	UK-86933
3749733	M	Rossia	CCCP-86467	RA-86467		
3749648	M	Cubana	CU-T1280			
4749857	M	Rossia/Russian Govt	CCCP-86468	86468	RA-86468	
4750919	M	TAAG Angola	D2-TIG			
2850324	M	(Interflug)	DDR-SEW	w/o 17Jun89 Berlin-Schonefeld, E Germany		
2850236	M	Air Koryo	P-882			
3850145	M	Georgia Air	OK-BYV(2)			
3850453	M	(Cubana)	CU-T1281	w/o 03Sep89 Havana, Cuba		
4851612	M	Far East Avia	CCCP-86525	RA-86525		
1951525	M	Uzbekistan Airways	DDR-SEY	D-AOAM	CCCP-86578	86578
			UK-86578			
2951636	M	Uzbekistan Govt	DDR-SEZ	D-AOAN	CCCP-86579	86579
			UK-86579			
2951447	M	Domodedovo Airlines	CCCP-86526	RA-86526		
3951359	M	Domodedovo Airlines	CCCP-86541	RA-86541		
3952714	M	Domodedovo Airlines	CCCP-86542	RA-86542		
1052128	M	Aeroflot Russian Int A/L	CCCP-86558	RA-86558	c/n also quoted as 4952928	
2052435	M	Domodedovo Airlines	CCCP-86552	RA-86552		
2052546	M	Cubana	CU-T1282			
3052657	M	Rossia	CCCP-86553	RA-86553		
4053514	M	Rossia	CCCP-86554	86554	RA-86554	
4053823	M	Cubana	CU-T1283			
4053732	M	Cubana	CU-T1284			
2153258	M	Rossia	CCCP-86559	RA-86559		
.53.4.	M	Far East Avia	CCCP-86560	RA-86560		
3154416	M	Domodedovo Airlines	RA-86673(2)			
154.2.	M					
4154535	M	Orient Avia	RA-86126			
4154841	M	Rossia	CCCP-86561	RA-86561		
1254851	M	Domodedovo Airlines	RA-86127			
2255719	M	Far East Avia	RA-86128			
2255525	M	Domodedovo Airlines	RA-86129			
3255333	M	Aral Air	UN-86130			
2255637	M	Far East Avia	RA-86131	s/n possibly 3255647		
3255859	M	Aeroflot Russian Int A/L	RA-86566			
4256314	M	Orient Avia	RA-86567			
4256223	M	Orient Avia	RA-86568			
1356234	M	Uzbekistan Govt	RA-86569	UK-86569		

The following are aircraft for which there are no confirmed serial numbers at the present time:

S/n	Series	Last known Owner/Operator	Identities/fate (where known)
	M		CCCP-86544
	M	Aeroflot Russian Int A/L	RA-86551
5604	M	Orient Avia	RA-86570
5605	M	Aviaenergo	RA-86571
	M	Russian Min of Defence	RA-86572
	M		CCCP-86688

Production complete

ILYUSHIN Il-76

In common with the system favoured by most researchers serial numbers have been listed below in numerical sequence of the last five digits, after arrangement in order of the year of manufacture (signified by the first non-zero digit of a nine and ten digit number). The s/n is believed (but not confirmed) to be the five digit number or the last five digits of a number with more than five digits.

S/n	Series	Last known Owner/Operator	Identities/fate (where known)			
01300101	T	Aeroflot	CCCP-86712	second prototype; regn subsequently worn by Il-62		
01300103		Aeroflot	CCCP-86711	first prototype; instructional airframe Riga, Latvia registration subsequently worn by Il-62		
01030104	T		CCCP-76500	first pre-production a/c; derelict Aug92 Moscow-Zhukovsky, Russia		
033401022	M	Aeroflot Russian Int A/L	CCCP-86600	RA-86600		
043402041	T	Dobrolet Airlines	Soviet AF 21 red	RA-76416		
043402046	T	Dobrolet Airlines	Soviet AF	RA-76417		
053404103	M		CCCP-86812			
053405124	M		CCCP-86823			
063405137	M	Ural Inter Avia	CCCP-86627	RA-86627		
063406146?		"YA-.AA"				
063407170	M	Ural Airlines	CCCP-86747	RA-86747		
063406188	T		CCCP-06188	D-236T propfan testbed		
063407191	M	Erewan Aviation	CCCP-86817	EK86817		
073409237	T	Dobrolet Airlines	CCCP-86640	RA-76418		
073409267	T	Ural Inter Avia	CCCP-86720	RA-86720		
073410284	M	Yerevan Avia/Erewan Avn	CCCP-86724	EK86724		
073410292	TD	Scoda Air	YI-AIK	CCCP-76495	RA-76495	ST-SFT
			RA-76495			
073410293	T	Volare Airtransport	YI-AIL	CCCP-76528	RA-76528	
073410308	LL		YI-AIP	CCCP-76529	RA-76529	D-236T propfan testbed (port inner engine)
073410315		(Iraqi Airways)	YI-AIO	w/o 23Sep80 Baghdad, Iraq		
073410320	MD	Aeroflot Russian Int A/L	CCCP-76497	RA-76497		
073411328	T	Abakan Avia	CCCP-76504	RA-76504		
073411331	T	Abakan Avia	CCCP-76505	RA-76505		
073411334	T	Ural Inter Avia	CCCP-76506	RA-76506		
073411338	T	Tyumen Airlines	CCCP-76507	RA-76507		
083411363	T		CCCP-11363			
083412380	M	Solar Wind	CCCP-86726	RA-86726		
083414432	TD	Inversija	CCCP-76510	RA-76510	YL-LAJ	
083414444	T	Aeroflot	CCCP-76511	wfs by 1992 Kiev-Zhulyany Technical School		
083414447	TD	Tyumen Airlines	CCCP-76512	RA-76512	wfs by May95 Tyumen, Russia, engineless	
083414451	T	Spair	CCCP-76513	RA-76513		
083415453	T	Dacono Air	CCCP-76514	RA-76514		
083415469	M	Libyan Arab	5A-DRR	wfs		
093416506	T	Flight Research Inst	Iraq AF 2803	YI-AKO	CCCP-76490	RA-76490
093417526	T	Krasnoyarsk Airlines	CCCP-76515	RA-76515		
093418539	M		CCCP-86043			
093418543	MD	Atlant	Iraq AF 2068	YI-AKS	CCCP-76759	RA-76759
093418548	T	Vladivostok Air	YI-AKT	RA-76492		
093420594	T	Tyumen Airlines	CCCP-76518	RA-76518		
093420599	T	Aeroflot Russian Int A/L	CCCP-76519	RA-76519		
093420605	T	Baikal Airlines	CCCP-76520	RA-76520		
093421613	M	Syrianair	YK-ATA			
093421619	M	Syrianair	YK-ATB			
093421628	M	Russian AF	CCCP-86891	RA-86891		
093421630	T	Volga-Dnepr	YI-AKP	CCCP-76491	RA-76491	
093421635	M	Iraqi Airways	YI-AKQ			
093421637	T	Aviatrans Cargo Airlines	YI-AKU	CCCP-76754	RA-76754	
0003422661	M		CCCP-86836			
0003423699	T	Magadanaerogruz	CCCP-76521	RA-76521		
0003424707	T	Inversija	CCCP-76522	RA-76522	YL-LAK	
0003424711	M		CCCP-86844			
0003424715	MD	Aeroflot Russian Int A/L	CCCP-86851	RA-86851		
0003425732	T	Tyumen Airlines	CCCP-76523	RA-76523		
0003425744	M	Russian Min of Defence	CCCP-86857	RA-86857		
0003426762	M		CCCP-86845			
0003426765	T	Veteran Airlines	CCCP-86846	RA-86846		
0003427782	M	Aeroflot Russian Int A/L	CCCP-86850	RA-86850		
0003427796	T	Tyumen Airlines/Spair	CCCP-76527	RA-76527		
0003428809	M	Russian Min of Defence	CCCP-86863	RA-86863		
0003428816	M		CCCP-86864			
0003428821	M	Russian Min of Defence	CCCP-86866	RA-86866		
0013428839	TD	Elf Air	YI-AKW	CCCP-76756	RA-76756	
0013428844	MD	Aeroflot Russian Int A/L	CCCP-86869	RA-86869		
0013429853	M	Aeroflot Russian Int A/L	CCCP-86874	RA-86874		
0013431911	M	Syrianair	YK-ATC			
0013431915	M	Syrianair	YK-ATD			
0013431928	T	Aeroflot Russian Int A/L	CCCP-76460	RA-76460	wfs Moscow-Sheremetyevo, Russia	
0013431935	T	Aeroflot	CCCP-76461	RA-76461	wfs Moscow-Sheremetyevo, Russia	
0013432960	T	Krasnoyarsk Airlines	CCCP-76463	76463	RA-76463	
0013432961	TD	Libyan Arab Airlines	5A-DNG	wfs		
0013433984	T	Northern-East Cargo A/L	Iraq AF 4600	YI-ALL	CCCP-76755	RA-76755

ILYUSHIN Il-76

S/n	Series	Last known Owner/Operator	Identities/fate (where known)			
0013433990	M	Sakhaviatrans	YI-AKX	CCCP-76757	RA-76757	
0013433996	T	Inversija	Iraq AF 4660	YI-ALO	CCCP-76788	RA-76788
0013433999	M	Aviatrans Cargo Airlines	Iraq AF 4601	YI-ALP	CCCP-76789	RA-76789
0013434018	MD	Dacono Air	CCCP-86896	RA-86896		
0013436048	MD	Atlant	UR-86903	UR-76382	RA-76382	
0023437076	MD	Atlant	CCCP-86909	RA-86909	RA-76383	
0013437086	TD	Libyan Arab Airlines	5A-DNB	wfs		
0023437093	MD		CCCP-86911			
0023437127	MD	Atlant	CCCP-86918	UR-76318		
0013438129	MD	Atlant	CCCP-86919	UR-76319		
0023439140	TD	Libyan Arab Airlines	5A-DNA	wfs impounded Moscow-Bykovo, Russia		
0023439141	TD	Libyan Arab Airlines	5A-DNT	wfs		
0023440157	TD	Aeroflot Russian Int A/L	CCCP-76467	RA-76467		
0023441174	MD	Airservice/UN	CCCP-86924	UR-86924/UN-185		
0023441186	TD	Korsar Airlines	CCCP-76499	RA-76499		
0023441189	TD	Elf Air	YI-ALQ	CCCP-76823	RA-76823	
0023441195	TD	Aeroflot Russian Int A/L	CCCP-76468	RA-76468		
0023441200	MD	Iraqi Airways	YI-ALR			
0023442210	MD	Hoseba	CCCP-76534	UR-76534		
0023442218	TD	Moscow Airways	CCCP-76498	RA-76498		
0033442225	MD	Air Service/UN	CCCP-76537	UR-76537		
0033442234	MD	Hoseba Sic	CCCP-76539	UR-76539		
0033442238	MD		CCCP-76540	RA-76540		
0033442241	MD	Air Service/UN	CCCP-76541	UR-76541/(UN-186)		
0033442247	TD	Volare Airtransport	YI-ALS	CCCP-78738	RA-78738	
0033443255	MD	Khors Air	UR-76395			
0033443266	MD	Aeroflot Russian Int A/L	CCCP-76545	RA-76545		
0033444286	TD	Aeroflot Russian Int A/L	CCCP-76469	RA-76469		
0033445291	TD	Aeroflot Russian Int A/L	CCCP-76470	RA-76470		
0033445294		Russian Min of Defence	CCCP-76556	RA-76556	Il-78M tanker version	
0033445309	MD	Aeroflot Russian Int A/L	CCCP-76551	RA-76551		
0033446333		Russian AF	CCCP-76558	RA-76558	Il-78 version	
0033446350	TD	Aeroflot Russian Int A/L	CCCP-76472	RA-76472		
0033447372	MD	Air Ukraine Cargo	UR-76563			
0033448393	MD	Iraqi Airways	YI-ALT			
0033448398	MD	Iraqi Airways	YI-ALU			
0033448404	TD	Aeroflot Russian Int A/L	CCCP-76473	RA-76473		
0033448407	TD	Aeroflot Russian Int A/L	CCCP-76474	RA-76474		
0033448409	MD	Iraqi Airways	YI-ALV			
0033448416	MD	Iraqi Airways	YI-ALW			
0033448420	MD	Atlant	CCCP-76568	UR-76568		
0033448427	MD	Atlant	CCCP-76570	UR-76570		
0033448429	MD	Bepbek SP	CCCP-76571	UR-76571		
0043449437	MD	Veteran A/L/Ukraine AF	CCCP-76573	UR-76573		
0043449449	MD	Ukraine AF	CCCP-76576	UR-76576		
0043449455	MD	Iraqi Airways	YI-ALX			
0043449468	MD	Atlant	CCCP-76578	UR-76578		
0043449471	MD	Atlant	CCCP-76579	UR-76568		
0043450476	MD	Bepbek SP	CCCP-76580	UR-76580		
0043450484	MD	Atlant	CCCP-76581	UR-76581		
0043450487	MD	Atlant	CCCP-76582	UR-76582		
0043450491	MD	Atlant	CCCP-76583	UR-76583		
0043451508	MD	Khors Air	CCCP-76586	UR-76586		
0043451517	MD	Khors Air	CCCP-76587	UR-76587		
0043451523	TD	Samara Airlines	CCCP-76475	RA-76475		
0043451528	TD	Aeroflot Russian Int A/L	CCCP-76476	RA-76476		
0043452534	MD	Atlant/United Nations	CCCP-76589	CCCP-76443	RA-76443	UR-76443
0043452544	MD	Atlant	CCCP-76590	UR-76590		
0043452546	MD	Atruvera	CCCP-76591	RA-76591		
0043452549	MD		CCCP-76492	PS90A testbed		
0043453562	MD	Atlant	CCCP-76592	UR-76390		
0043453568	MD	Atlant	CCCP-76594	UR-76391		
0043453571	MD	Atlant	CCCP-76595	UR-76595		
0043453575	TD	Aeroflot Russian Int A/L	CCCP-76477	RA-76477		
0043454602	MD	Atlant	UR-76392			
0043454606	MD	Atlant	CCCP-76601	UR-76601		
0043454611	MD	Azerbaijan Govt	CCCP-76602	76602	4K-78130	
0043454615	MD	Cubana	CU-T1258			
0043454623	MD	Atlant	CCCP-76603	UR-76603		
0043454633	MD	Lana Aircompany	CCCP-76606	UR-76316		
0043455653	MD	Atlant/United Nations	CCCP-7661.?	UR-76393		
0043455665	MD	Atlant	CCCP-76614	UR-76614		
0043455686	MD	Lana Aircompany	CCCP-76619?	UR-76320		
0043456700	TD	Vega Aircompany	CCCP-76493	RA-76493		
0043457702	MD	Atlant	CCCP-76622	UR-76622		
0053457713	MD	Atlant/United Nations	CCCP-?	UR-76321		
0053457720	MD	Atlant	CCCP-7662.?	CCCP-76423	UR-76423	RA-76423
....58725	MD	Indian AF	K2662/B			
0053458733	MD	Atlant	CCCP-76627	UR-76317		
0053458741	MD		CCCP-76628			
0053458749	MD	Atlant/United Nations	CCCP-76630	UR-76630/UN-189		
0053459767	MD	Cubana	CU-T1271			

ILYUSHIN Il-76

S/n	Series	Last known Owner/Operator	Identities/fate (where known)		
0053459770	MD		CCCP-76634		
0053459788	TD	Aeroflot Russian Int A/L	CCCP-76478	RA-76478	
0053460790	TD	Aeroflot Russian Int A/L	CCCP-76479	RA-76479	
005346079.	TD	DRAS	CCCP-76480	RA-76480	
0053460795	TD	Gosnii GA	CCCP-76481	RA-76481	
0053460797	MD	Atlant	CCCP-76637	UR-76637	
0053460805	MD		CCCP-76639	also quoted as s/n 0053462003	
0053460820	MD	Atlant	CCCP-76642	UR-76408	
0053460827	MD	Atlant	CCCP-76644	UR-76433	
0053460832	TD	Aeroflot Russian Int A/L	CCCP-76482	RA-76482	
0053461834	MD		CCCP-76645	also quoted as s/n 0053463981	
0053462865	MD	Aeroflot Russian Int A/L	CCCP-76650	RA-76650	
0053462872	MD	Khors Air	CCCP-76651	UR-76651	
0053462873	MD	Atlant	CCCP-76652	UR-76322	
0053463885	MD	Air Service Ukraine	CCCP-76655	RA-76655	UR-76655
0053463891	MD	ANTAU	CCCP-76656	UR-76656	
0053463902	TD	Aviacon Zito-Trans	CCCP-76659	RA-76659	
0053463910	MD	Ukraine AF	CCCP-76660	UR-76660	
0053464922	MD	Air Service	CCCP-76663	UR-76663	
0053464926	MD	Khors Air	CCCP-76664	UR-76664	
0053464934	MD	Dacono Air	CCCP-76666	RA-76666	
0063465958		BSL Airlines	CCCP-76670	UR-76670	Il-78 version
0063465963	MD	Improtex	CCCP-76671	UR-76671	4K-76671
0063465965	TD	Avia Obshchemash	CCCP-76494	RA-76494	
0063466981	MD	Atruvera	CCCP-76672	RA-76672	
0063466988	MD	Atlant/United Nations	CCCP-76673	UR-76323	
0063466989	MD	Atlant	CCCP-76674	UR-76394	
0063466995	A-50	Russian Min of Defence	CCCP-76453	RA-76453	AWACS a/c
0063467005	MD	Improtex	CCCP-76677	UR-76677	4K-76677
0063467020	MD	BSL Airlines	CCCP-76680	UR-76680	
0063467021	MD	Bepbek SP	CCCP-76681	UR-76681	
0063467027		BSL Airlines	CCCP-76682	UR-76682	Il-78 version
0063468042	TD	Northern-East Cargo A/L	CCCP-76483	RA-76483	
0063469051	MD	Ukraine AF	CCCP-76687	UR-76687	
0063469055	MD	Iraqi Airways	YI-ANA		
0063469062	MD	Air Ukraine	CCCP-76688	UR-76688	
0063469071	MD	Iraqi Airways	YI-ANB		
0063469081	TD	Baikal Airlines	CCCP-76484	RA-76484	
0063470088	TD	Yakutavia	CCCP-76485	76485	RA-76485
0063470096	MD	Atlant	CCCP-76692	RA-76692	UR-76424
0063470102	MD	Iraqi Airways	YI-ANC		
0063470107	MD	Veteran Airlines	CCCP-76694	UR-76694	
0063470113	MD	Atlant	CCCP-76696	UR-76444	RA-76444
0063470118	MD		CCCP-76697		
0063471123	MD	Veteran Airlines	CCCP-76698	UR-76698	water bomber conversion
0063471134	MD	Ukraine AF	CCCP-76700	UR-76700	
0063471155	MD	Iraqi Airways	YI-AND		
0063472158	MD	Air Ukraine	CCCP-76705	UR-76705	
0063472163	MD	ANTAU	CCCP-76706	RA-76706	UR-76706
0063473171	MD	Aeroflot Russian Int A/L	CCCP-76708	76708	RA-76708
0063473183	MD		CCCP-76710		
006347318.	MD		CCCP-76711		
0063473190	MD		CCCP-76712		
0073474203	TD	Volga-Dnepr	CCCP-76758	RA-76758	
0073474208	A-50	Russian Min of Defence	CCCP-76456	AWACS a/c	
0073474224	MD	Iraqi Airways	YI-ANE		
0073475229	MD	Aeroflot Russian Int A/L	CCCP-76720	RA-76720	
0073475236	MD	Iraqi Airways	YI-ANF		
0073475239		BSL Airlines	UR-76721	Il-78 version	
0073475242	MD	Aeroflot Russian Int A/L	CCCP-76722	RA-76722	
0073475268	MD	East Air ?	CCCP-76727	RA-76727	
0073475270	MD	Veteran Airlines	CCCP-76728	UR-76728	
0073476275	MD	Veteran Airlines	CCCP-76729	UR-76729	
0073476277		BSL Airlines	UR-76730	Il-78 tanker version	
0073476281	TD	Yakutavia	CCCP-76486	RA-76486	
0073476288	MD	Iraqi Airways	YI-ANG		
0073476296	MD	Air Service Ukraine	CCCP-76732	UR-76732	
0073476304	MD	Russian Min of Defence	CCCP-76733	RA-76733	
0073476307	MD	Iraqi Airways	YI-ANH		
0073477326	MD	Russian Min of Defence	CCCP-76738	RA-76738	
0073478346		Ukraine AF	UR-76742	76742	Il-78 tanker version
0073478359		BSL Airlines	CCCP-76744	UR-76744	Il-78 tanker version
0073479362	MD	Aeroflot Russian Int A/L	CCCP-76745	RA-76745	
0073479367	TD	Yakutavia	CCCP-76487	RA-76487	
0073479371	TD	Aeroflot Russian Int A/L	CCCP-76488	RA-76488	
0073479392			CCCP-76749	Il-78M tanker version	
0073479400		BSL Airlines	CCCP-76760	UR-76760	Il-78 tanker version
0073479401	MD	Aeroflot Russian Int A/L	CCCP-76761	RA-76761	
0073480413	MD		CCCP-76763	RA-76763	
0073481431	MDK	Aeroflot Russian Int A/L	CCCP-76766	RA-76766	
0083481440	MD	BSL Airlines	CCCP-76775	UR-76415	
0073481442	MD	Iraqi	YI-ANI		

ILYUSHIN Il-76

S/n	Series	Last known Owner/Operator	Identities/fate (where known)			
0073481461	MD	Aeroflot Russian Int A/L	CCCP-76753	RA-76753		
0083482478	MD	BSL Airlines	UR-76414			
0083482486	MD	Russian Min of Defence	CCCP-76776	RA-76776		
0083482502	MD	Air Ukraine	CCCP-76778	UR-76778		
0083483513	MD	Eco Patrol Envir Organis	CCCP-76438	76438	UR-76438	
0083483519	MD	Hoseba Sic	CCCP-78752	UR-78752		
0083484522	MD	Khors Air	CCCP-78753	UR-76398		
0083484527	MD	Eco Patrol Envir Organis	CCCP-78754	CCCP-76437	UR-76437	
0083484531	MD	Khors Air/Air Foyle	CCCP-78755	UR-78755		
0083484536	MD	ANTAU/Air Service	CCCP-78756	UR-78756		
0083484542	MD	Iraqi Airways	YI-ANL	wfs		
0083484551	MD	Air Ukraine	CCCP-78758	UR-78758		
0083485554	TD	Northern-East Cargo A/L	CCCP-76489	RA-76489		
0083485561	TD	Aeroflot Russian Int A/L	CCCP-76750	RA-76750		
0083485566	MD	Khors Air	CCCP-78760	UR-76399		
0083486582	MD		CCCP-78763			
0083486590	MD	Trans Avia Export	CCCP-78765	EW-78765		
0083486595	MD	Russian Min of Defence	CCCP-78766	RA-78766		
0083487603	MD		CCCP-78768	RA-78768		
0083487607	MD	Trans Avia Export	CCCP-78769	EW-78769		
0083487610	TD	Aeroflot Russian Int A/L	CCCP-76751	RA-76751		
0083487617	MDK	Russian Min of Defence	CCCP-78770	RA-78770		
0083488634	A-50	Soviet AF	51 red	AWACS a/c		
0083488643	MD	Air Service	CCCP-78774	UR-78774		
0083489647	MD	Khors Air	CCCP-78775	UR-78775		
0083489652	MD	Aeroflot Russian Int A/L	CCCP-78776	RA-78776		
0083489662	MD	Trans Avia Export	CCCP-78779	EW-78779		
0083489683	MD	Azerbaijan Govt	4K-78129	AHY-78001	AHY-78129	
0083489691	MD	Atlant	CCCP-78785	RA-78785	UR-78785	
0083490698	MD	Trans Avia Export	CCCP-78787	EW-78787		
0083490703	MD	BSL Airlines	CCCP-78778	RA-78778	UR-78778	
0083490706	MD	Aeroflot Russian Int A/L	CCCP-78789	RA-78789		
0093490726	MD	Aeroflot Russian Int A/L	CCCP-78794	RA-78794		
0093491735	MD	Russian AF	CCCP-78796	RA-78796		
0093491754	MD	Trans Avia Export	CCCP-78799	EW-78799		
0093492763	MD	Trans Avia Export	CCCP-78801	EW-78801		
0093492771	MD		CCCP-78802			
0093492783	MD	Aeroflot Russian Int A/L	CCCP-78805	RA-78805		
0093492786			CCCP-78806	Il-78 tanker version		
0093493794	MD	Trans Avia Export	CCCP-78808	EW-78808		
0093494835	TD	(Metro Cargo)	CCCP-76784	LZ-INK	w/o 24May91 nr Bakhtaran, W Iran	
0093495842	MD	Aeroflot Russian Int A/L	CCCP-78815	RA-78815		
0093495846	MD	Soviet AF	CCCP-78816	RA-78816		
0093495851	MD	Russian Min of Defence	CCCP-78817	RA-78817		
0093495854	TD	Northern-East Cargo A/L	CCCP-76787	RA-76787		
0093495858	MD		CCCP-78818	RA-78818		
0093495863	TD	Aeroflot Russian Int A/L	CCCP-76785	RA-76785		
1013495871	MDK	Tubelair	CCCP-78825	RA-78825		
0093495883	MD	Trans Avia Export	CCCP-78819	EW-78819		
0093496903	MD	Spair	CCCP-76790	RA-76790		
0093496907	MD	Atlant	CCCP-78820	UR-78820	RA-78820	
0093496912	MD	Indian AF	K3078/W			
0093496923	TD	Domodedovo Airlines	CCCP-76786	RA-76786		
0093497936	TD	Samara Airlines	CCCP-76791	RA-76791		
0093497942	TD	Krasnoyarsk Airlines	CCCP-76792	RA-76792		
0093498951	TD	Uzbekistan Airways	CCCP-76793	76793	UK-76793	
0093498954	TD	Uzbekistan Airways	CCCP-76794	76794	UK-76794	
0093498962	TD	Aeroflot Russian Int A/L	CCCP-76795	RA-76795		
0093498967	TD	Krasnoyarsk Airlines	CCCP-76752	RA-76752		
0093498971	TD	Uzbekistan Airways	CCCP-76782	UK-76782		
0093498974	TD	Ulyanovsk Higher Civil Aviation School	CCCP-76783	RA-76783	badly damaged 31Oct95 Rostov na Don, Russia	
1023498978	TD	Turkmenistan Airlines	EZ-F421			
0093499982	MD	Ilavia	CCCP-76822	RA-76822		
0093499986	MD	Trans Avia Export	CCCP-78836	EW-78836		
1003499991	MD	Trans Avia Export	CCCP-78826	EW-78826		
1003499997	MD	Trans Avia Export	CCCP-78827	EW-78827		
1003401004	MD	Trans Avia Export	CCCP-78828	EW-78828		
1003401015	TD	Sayakhat	UN-76384			
1003401024	MD	Soviet AF	CCCP-78837	01 red		
1003401025	MD	Aeroflot Russian Int A/L	CCCP-78833	RA-78833		
1003402044	MD	Aeroflot Russian Int A/L	CCCP-78838	RA-78838		
1003402047	MD	Trans Avia Export	CCCP-78839	EW-78839		
1003403052	TD	Yakutavia	CCCP-76797	RA-76797		
1003403056	MD	Russian Min of Defence	CCCP-78840	RA-78840		
1003403058	TD	Uzbekistan Airways	CCCP-76449	76449	UK-76449	also quoted as s/n 1023413058
1003403063	TD	Samara Airlines	CCCP-76798	RA-76798		
1003403069	MD	Russian Min of Defence	CCCP-78842	RA-78842		
1003403075	TD	Domodedovo Airlines	CCCP-76799	RA-76799		
1003403082	MD	Trans Avia Export	CCCP-78843	EW-78843		
1003403104	MD	Air Koryo	P-912			

ILYUSHIN Il-76

S/n	Series	Last known Owner/Operator	Identities/fate (where known)			
1003403105	TD	Uzbekistan Airways	CCCP-76805	76805	UK-76805	
1003403121	TD	Domodedovo Airlines	CCCP-76806	RA-76806		
1003404126	TD	Air Koryo	P-913			
1003404138		Soviet AF	34 blue	Il-78M tanker version		
1003404146	TD	Air Koryo	P-914			
1003405159	MD	Trans Avia Export	CCCP-78848	EW-78848		
1003405164	MD		CCCP-76828			
1003405167	TD	Atlant	CCCP-76425	RA-76425		
1013405176	TD	Tyumen Airlines/UN	CCCP-76807	RA-76807		
1013405177	TD	Baikal Airlines	CCCP-76808	RA-76808		
1013405184	TD	ALLWE	CCCP-76426	RA-76426		
1013405192	MD	Trans Avia Export	CCCP-78849	EW-78849		
1003405196	MD	Russian Min of Defence	CCCP-78850	RA-78850		
1013406204	MD	Veteran Airlines	RA-76388			
1013406206	MD	Aeroflot Russian Int A/L	CCCP-76753	RA-76753		
1013407212	MD	Veteran Airlines	CCCP-78852	RA-78852	RA-76389	
1013407215	TD	BSL Airlines	RA-76413	UR-76413		
1013407220	MD	Russian AF	CCCP-78854	RA-78854		
1013407223	TD	Uzbekistan Airways	CCCP-76811	76811	UK-76811	
1013407230	TD	Domodedovo Airlines	CCCP-76812	RA-76812		
1013408240	TD	Uzbekistan Airways	UK-76351			
1013408244	TD	Zhukovsky Flight Research Institute	CCCP-76835	RA-76835	water bomber conversion	
1013408246	TD	Uzbekistan Airways	CCCP-76813	76813	UK-76813	
1013408252	TD	Aviatrans Cargo Airlines	CCCP-76809	RA-76809		
1013408257	TD	Hungarian-Ukrainian A/L	CCCP-78736	UR-78736	HA-TCB	
1013408264	TD	Exparc Airlines	CCCP-76818	76818	RA-76818	
1013408265	TD	Moscow Airways	RA-76355			
1013408269	TD	Alak Airlines	CCCP-76814	RA-76814		
1013409274	TD	Atlant	CCCP-76819	76819	RA-76819	
1013409282	TD	Kazakhstan Airlines/UN	CCCP-76810	UN-76810		
1013409284	MD	China United Airlines	B-4031			
1013409287	TD	Tashkent A/c Prod Corp	CCCP-76831	UK-76831		
1013408288	MD	China United Airlines	B-4030			
1013409289	MD	China United Airlines	B-4032			
1013409295	TD	Aviatrans Cargo Airlines	CCCP-76820	RA-76820		
1013409297	TD	Mahan Air	SU-OAA	EP-JAY		
1013409303	TD	Atlant	CCCP-78734	UR-78734	HA-TCA	UR-78734
1013409305	TD	Belair	CCCP-76836	76836	EW-76836	damaged 29Dec94
			Sarajevo, Bosnia-Herzegovina			
1013409310	TD	Kyrgyzstan Airlines	CCCP-76815	EX-76815		
1023409316	TD	Belair	CCCP-76837	76837	EW-76837	
1023409319	TD	Sayakhat	CCCP-76834	RA-76834	UN-76834	
1013409321	TD	Mahan Air	SU-OAB	EP-JAZ		
1023410327	TD	Uzbekistan Airways	CCCP-76824	76824	UK-76824	
1023410336	TD	Turkmenistan Airlines	EZ-F425			
1023410339	TD	Uzbekistan Airways	UK-76358			
1023410348	TD	Turkmenistan Airlines	CCCP-76422?	EZ-F422		
1023410355	TD	Atlant	RA-76409			
1023410360	TD	Gulf Avn Tech & Services	CCCP-76832	RA-76832		
1023411368	TD	Gulf Avn Tech & Services	CCCP-76436	76436	RA-76436	
1023411370	TD	Aeroflot Russian Int A/L	CCCP-76838	RA-76838		
1023411375	TD	Aeroflot Russian Int A/L	CCCP-76839	RA-76839		
1023411378	TD	Ural Inter Avia	UK-76352	RA-76352		
1023411384	TD	Trans-Charter Airlines/ Gulf Avn Tech & Services	RA-76411			
1023412389	TD	Uzbekistan Airways	CCCP-76447	76447	UK-76447	
1023412395	TD	Sayakhat	CCCP-76434	UN-76434		
1023412399	TD	Volga-Dnepr/Heavylift Cargo Airlines	CCCP-76401	RA-76401		
1023412411	TD	Sayakhat	UN-76410			
1023412414	TD	Vladivostok Air	CCCP-76403	RA-76403		
1023413428	TD	Kazakhstan Airlines	CCCP-76435	UN-76435		
1023413430	TD	Elf Air	CCCP-76402	RA-76402		
1023413435	TD	Algerian Govt	7T-WIG			
1023413438	TD	Vladivostok Air	CCCP-76400	RA-76400		
1023413443	TD	Uzbekistan Airways	CCCP-76448	76448	UK-76448	
1023413446	TD	Aviatrans Cargo Airlines	CCCP-76420	RA-76420		
1023414450	TD	Sayakhat	CCCP-76442	UN-76442		
1023414454	TD	Uzbekistan Airways	76353	UK-76353		
1023414458	TD	Elf Air	RA-76370			
1023414463	TD	Avial	RA-76406			
1023414470	TD	Algerian Govt	CCCP-76419	RA-76419	UK-76419	7T-WID
1033414474	TD	C-Air	RA-76367			
1033414480	TD	Airstan	RA-76369			
1033414483	TD	Uzbekistan Airways	UK-76359			
1033414485	TD	Kazakhstan Airlines	RA-76371	76371	UN-76371	
1033415497	TD	Yemenia	CCCP-76361	RA-76361	70-ADG	
1033415504	TD	Dacono Air	CCCP-76421	RA-76421		
1033416515	TD	Sayakhat	UN-76385			
1033416520	TD	Kazakhstan Airlines	UN-76374			
1033416525	TD	Tashkent A/c Prod Corp	RA-76844	UK-76844		

ILYUSHIN Il-76

S/n	Series	Last known Owner/Operator	Identities/fate (where known)	
1033416533	TD	M.Tjse.S.Rossii	RA-76362	
1033417540	TD	Tsentro Spas Gkus Rosii	RA-76363	
1033417553	TD	M.Tjse.S.Rossii	RA-76840	
1053417563	MF	Ilyushin OKB	17563	IS-76900
1033417569	TD	Krilo Air	RA-76379	
1033418578	TD	Yemenia	RA-76360	70-ADF
1033418584	TD	Aviaenergo	RA-76843	
1033418592	TD	Turkmenistan Airlines	EZ-F424	
1033418600	TD	Ural Inter Avia	RA-76386	
1033418601	TD	M.Tjse.S.Rossii	CCCP-76841	RA-76841
1033418608	TD	Turkmenistan Airlines	EZ-F423	
1033418609	TD	Turkmenistan Airlines	EZ-F426	
1033418616	TD	Airstan	CCCP-76842	RA-76842
1033418620	TD	Turkmenistan Airlines	EZ-F427	
1043418624	TD	Turkmenistan Airlines	EZ-F428	
1043420696	TD	M.Tjse.S.Rossii	RA-76845	

The following are aircraft for which there are no confirmed serial numbers at the present time:

Series	Last known Owner/Operator	Identities/fate (where known)			
TD		06207	test a/c		
T		CCCP-72502			
T		CCCP-72503			
TD		CCCP-76012			
TD		4K-76130	possibly miss-sighting for 4K-78130 (s/n 0043454611)		
TD	Atlant	UR-76345			
TD	Kazakhstan Airlines	RA-76347			
TD	C-Air Cargo	CCCP-76350	RA-76350		
TD	Aeroflot Russian Int A/L	RA-76354			
		UK-76356			
	Aeroflot Russian Int A/L	RA-76357			
TD	Tashkent A/c Prod Corp	UK-76375			
		UR-76376			
TD	Transaero-Samara A/L	RA-76381			
TD	Veteran Airlines	UR-76389			
MD	Khors Air	UR-76396			
MD	Khors Air	UR-76397			
MD	Khors Air	UR-76398			
TD	Aeroflot Russian Int A/L	RA-76404			
TD	Aeroflot Russian Int A/L	RA-76405			
	BSL Airlines	RA-76412	UR-76412		
TD	Uzbekistan Airways	UK-76419			
TD	Tashkent A/C Prod Corp	UK-76427			
T		CCCP-76428			
	Aeroflot Russian Int A/L	RA-76440			
	Romoco Cargo	CCCP-76441	76441	RA-76441	UR-76441
	Aeroflot Russian Int A/L	CCCP-76445	RA-76445		
	Aeroflot Russian Int A/L	RA-76446			
MD	Russian AF	CCCP-76450	RA-76450	Satellite tracer	
MD		CCCP-76451	RA-76451	Satellite tracer	
A-50	Russian Min of Defence	CCCP-76452	AWACS a/c		
A-50	Russian Min of Defence	CCCP-76454	AWACS a/c		
A-50	Russian Min of Defence	CCCP-76455	AWACS a/c		
TD	Aeroflot Russian Int A/L	CCCP-76457	RA-76457		
T	Baikal Airlines	CCCP-76458	76458	RA-76458	
T	Krasnoyarsk Airlines	CCCP-76459	RA-76459		
T	Baikal Airlines	CCCP-76462	RA-76462		
TD	Krasnoyarsk Airlines	CCCP-76464	RA-76464		
TD	Krasnoyarsk Airlines	CCCP-76465	RA-76465		
TD	(Aeroflot)	CCCP-76466	w/o 20Oct89 Leninakan, USSR		
TD		CCCP-76471	RA-76471	EP-MKA	
TD		CCCP-76496			
T		CCCP-76501	dumped by Aug93 Kirovograd, Russia		
T		CCCP-76502	wfs by Jul93 Omsk, Russia		
T		CCCP-76503	RA-76503		
T	Krasnoyarsk Airlines	CCCP-76508	RA-76508		
T	Ural Inter Avia	CCCP-76509	RA-76509		
T	Krasnoyarsk Airlines	CCCP-76516	RA-76516		
T	Krasnoyarsk Airlines	CCCP-76517	RA-76517		
T	Krasnoyarsk Airlines	CCCP-76524	RA-76524		
T	Baikal Airlines	CCCP-76525	RA-76525		
LL		CCCP-76526	RA-76526	D-236T propfan testbed	
MD	Hoseba	CCCP-76532	UR-76532		
MD	Vilocity	CCCP-76533	RA-76533		
MD	Veteran Airlines	CCCP-76535	UR-76535		
MD		CCCP-76536			

ILYUSHIN Il-76

S/n	Series	Last known Owner/Operator	Identities/fate (where known)		
	MD		CCCP-76538		
	MD		CCCP-76542		
	MD		CCCP-76543		
	MD	Aeroflot Russian Int A/L	CCCP-76544	RA-76544	
	MD		CCCP-76546	RA-76546	
	MD	Aeroflot Russian Int A/L	CCCP-76547	RA-76547	
	MD	Aeroflot Russian Int A/L	CCCP-76548	RA-76548	
	MD	Aeroflot Russian Int A/L	CCCP-76549	RA-76549	
	MD	Russian AF	CCCP-76550	RA-76550	
	MD	Aeroflot Russian Int A/L	CCCP-76552	RA-76552	
	MD		CCCP-76553		
	MD		CCCP-76554		
	MD	Air Ukraine Cargo	CCCP-76555	UR-76555	
	MD	Russian Min of Defence	CCCP-76557	RA-76557	
	MD		CCCP-76559		
	MD		CCCP-76561		
	MD		CCCP-76566		
	MD		CCCP-76567		
	MD	(Aeroflot)	CCCP-76569	w/o 18Oct89 Caspian Sea	
	MD	Russian Min of Defence	CCCP-76572	RA-76572	
	MD		CCCP-76574		
	MD		CCCP-76577	RA-76577	
	MD	Air Service	CCCP-76584	UR-76584	
	MD		CCCP-76585		
	MD	Atruvera	CCCP-76588	RA-76588	
	MD	Russian Min of Defence	RA-76592		
	MD	Spaero Air Company	CCCP-76596	UR-76596	
	MD		CCCP-76598		
	MD	Aeroflot Russian Int A/L	CCCP-76599	RA-76599	
	MD		CCCP-76600		
	MD	Aeroflot Russian Int A/L	CCCP-76604	RA-76604	
	MD	Aeroflot Russian Int A/L	CCCP-76605	RA-76605	
		BSL Airlines	CCCP-76609	UR-76609	Il-78 tanker version
			CCCP-76610	Il-78 tanker version	
	MD		CCCP-76611		
	MD		CCCP-76612		
	MD		CCCP-76613		
	MD	Aeroflot Russian Int A/L	CCCP-76615	RA-76615	
		Russian AF	CCCP-76616	"616" black	Il-78 tanker version
	MD		CCCP-76617		
	MD	Lana Aircompany	CCCP-76618	UR-76618	
	MD	Aeroflot Russian Int A/L	CCCP-76620	RA-76620	
	MD	Flight Research Inst	CCCP-76623	RA-76623	prototype water bomber conversion
	MD	Baikal Airlines	CCCP-76625	RA-76625	
	MD		CCCP-76626		
	MD		CCCP-76631		
			CCCP-76632	RA-76632	Il-78 tanker version
	MD		CCCP-76633		
	MD	Russian AF	RA-76635		
	MD		CCCP-76636	UR-76636	
	MD		CCCP-76638		
	MD	Dobrolet Airlines	CCCP-76640	RA-76640	
	MD	Russian Min of Defence	CCCP-76643	RA-76643	
	MD		CCCP-76647		
	MD		CCCP-76648		
	MD		CCCP-76649		
	MD	Ukraine AF	CCCP-76653	76653	
	MD		CCCP-76654		
	MD		CCCP-76657		
	MD	Air Service	CCCP-76658	UR-76658	
	MD		CCCP-76661		
	MD		CCCP-76665		
	MD		CCCP-76667	UR-76667	
	MD		CCCP-76668		
	MD		CCCP-76669	RA-76669	
	MD	Ukraine AF	76675		
	MD	Veteran Airlines	CCCP-76676	UR-76676	
	MD	Atlant	CCCP-76683	UR-76683	
	MD	Veteran Airlines	UR-76684		
		Ukraine AF	CCCP-76689	76689	Il-78M tanker version
		Busol Airlines	CCCP-76690	UR-76690	Il-78 tanker version
	MD	Aeroflot Russian Int A/L	RA-76693		
	MD		CCCP-76695		
	MD		CCCP-76699		
			CCCP-76701	RA-76701	Il-78M tanker version
	MD		CCCP-76703		
	MD	East Air ?	CCCP-76704	UR-76704	
	MD	Veretan Airlines	CCCP-76707	UR-76707	
	MD		CCCP-76709		
	MD		CCCP-76713		
	MD		CCCP-76715		
	MD	Lana Aircompany	CCCP-76716	UR-76716	

ILYUSHIN Il-76

S/n	Series	Last known Owner/Operator	Identities/fate (where known)		
	MD	Veteran Airlines	CCCP-76717	UR-76717	
	MD		CCCP-76723		
			CCCP-76724		
	MD		CCCP-76725		
	MD	Russian Min of Defence	CCCP-76726		
	MD		RA-76731		
	MD		CCCP-76734		
	MD		CCCP-76735		
	MD		CCCP-76736		
	MD		CCCP-76737		
	MD		CCCP-76739		
		BSL Airlines	CCCP-76740	UR-76740	Il-78 tanker version
	MD		CCCP-76743		
	MD	Aeroflot Russian Int A/L	RA-76746		
	MD	Ukraine AF/Air Ukraine	CCCP-76748	76748	UR-76748
	MD	BSL Airlines	UR-76759		
	MD	Russian Min of Defence	CCCP-76762	RA-76762	
	MD	Aeroflot Russian Int A/L	CCCP-76764	RA-76764	
	MD		CCCP-76765		
	MD	BSL Airlines	CCCP-76767	UR-76767	
	MD		CCCP-76768		
	MDK		CCCP-76769		
	MD		CCCP-76770		
	MD		CCCP-76771		
	MD	Russian Min of Defence	CCCP-76772	RA-76772	
	MD		CCCP-76773		
	MD		CCCP-76774		
	MD		CCCP-76777		
	MD		CCCP-76779		
	T	Aeroflot Russian Int A/L	CCCP-76780	RA-76780	
	TD	Aeroflot Russian Int A/L	CCCP-76781	RA-76781	
	TD	Alak Airlines	CCCP-76796	RA-76796	
	TD		CCCP-76800	RA-76800	
	MD	Russian AF	CCCP-76801	RA-76801	
	MD		CCCP-76802		
	MD	Russian AF	CCCP-76803	RA-76803	
	MD	Soviet AF	CCCP-76804		
			CCCP-76816		
	TD	Aeroflot Russian Int A/L	CCCP-76817	RA-76817	
	TD	Tashkent A/c Prod Corp	CCCP-76821	UK-76821	
	MD	Russian AF	RA-76825		
	MD	Soviet AF	CCCP-76827		
	TD		CCCP-76830		
	TD	Aeroflot Russian Int A/L	CCCP-76833	RA-76833	
			CCCP-76855		
		Aeroflot Russian Int A/L	RA-76872		
	TD	Iron Dragonfly	RA-76896		
	MD		4K-78030		
			4K-78710		
			CCCP-78711		
			CCCP-78730		
	T	Transsuper	CCCP-78731	RA-78731	
	MD	Aeroflot Russian Int A/L	RA-78750		
	MD		CCCP-78751		
	MD	Aeroflot Russian Int A/L	CCCP-78757	RA-78757	
	MD		CCCP-78759		
	MD		CCCP-78761		
	MD	Russian Min of Defence	CCCP-78764	RA-78764	
	MD		CCCP-78767		
	MD	Air Ukraine	CCCP-78772	UR-78772	
	MD		CCCP-78777		
	MD		CCCP-78780		
	MD	(Aeroflot)	CCCP-78781	w/o 27Mar90 Kabul, Afghanistan	
			CCCP-78782	Il-78 tanker version	
	MD	Aeroflot Russian Int A/L	CCCP-78783	RA-78783	
	MD	Aeroflot Russian Int A/L	CCCP-78784	RA-78784	
	MD	Air Service Ukraine	CCCP-78786	UR-78786	
	MD		CCCP-78788		
	MD		CCCP-78791		
	MD		CCCP-78792		
	MD		Belarus AF?	UN-78793	
	MD	Russian Min of Defence	CCCP-78795	RA-78795	
	MD	Aeroflot Russian Int A/L	CCCP-78797	RA-78797	
	MD		CCCP-78798		
	MD		CCCP-78803		
	MD		CCCP-78804		
	MD	Aeroflot Russian Int A/L	CCCP-78807	RA-78807	
	MD	Aeroflot Russian Int A/L	CCCP-78809	RA-78809	
	MD	Russian Min of Defence	CCCP-78811	RA-78811	
			CCCP-78812		
	MD		CCCP-78813		
			CCCP-78814	Il-78 tanker version	

ILYUSHIN Il-76

S/n	Series	Last known Owner/Operator	Identities/fate (where known)	
	MD		CCCP-78824	
	MD	Russian Min of Defence	CCCP-78829	RA-78829
	MD	Russian Min of Defence	CCCP-78831	RA-78831
	MD	Russian Min of Defence	CCCP-78834	RA-78834
	MD	Aeroflot Russian Int A/L	CCCP-78835	RA-78835
	MD	Aeroflot Russian Int A/L	CCCP-78844	RA-78844
	MD	Russian Min of Defence	CCCP-78845	RA-78845
	MD	Aeroflot Russian Int A/L	CCCP-78846	RA-78846
	MD	Aeroflot Russian Int A/L	CCCP-78847	RA-78847
	MD	Aeroflot Russian Int A/L	CCCP-78851	RA-78851
	MD	Russian Min of Defence	CCCP-78878	RA-78878
	M		CCCP-86020	
	M		CCCP-86021	
	M		CCCP-86022	
	M		CCCP-86023	
	M		CCCP-86024	
	M	Aeroflot Russian Int A/L	CCCP-86025	RA-86025
	M	Aeroflot Russian Int A/L	CCCP-86026	RA-86026
	M	Russian Min of Defence	CCCP-86027	RA-86027
	M		CCCP-86028	
	M		CCCP-86029	
	M		CCCP-86030	
	M		CCCP-86031	
	M	Russian Min of Defence	CCCP-86032	RA-86032
	M		CCCP-86033	
	M		CCCP-86034	
	M	Aeroflot Russian Int A/L	CCCP-86035	RA-86035
	M	Russian Min of Defence	CCCP-86037	RA-86037
	M	Russian Min of Defence	CCCP-86038	RA-86038
	M		CCCP-86039	
	M	Russian Min of Defence	CCCP-86040	RA-86040
	M	Aeroflot Russian Int A/L	CCCP-86041	RA-86041
	M	Russian Min of Defence	CCCP-86042	RA-86042
	M		CCCP-86044	
	M		CCCP-86045	
	M		CCCP-86046	
	M	Aeroflot	CCCP-86047	preserved by Aug89 military school adj to Monino Museum
	M		CCCP-86048	
	M	Russian Min of Defence	CCCP-86049	RA-86049
		Russian AF	CCCP-86604	RA-86604
		Soviet AF	CCCP-86624	"624" black
		Soviet AF	CCCP-86625	
		Soviet AF	CCCP-86626	"626"
		Soviet AF	CCCP-86629	"629"
		Soviet AF	RA-86632	"632" black
	M	Soviet AF	CCCP-86635	"635" black
		Soviet AF	CCCP-86637	
			CCCP-86642	
		Soviet AF	CCCP-86644	"644"
			CCCP-86713	
			CCCP-86714	
		Soviet AF	CCCP-86715	RA-86715
		Soviet AF	CCCP-86717	
		Soviet AF	CCCP-86719	"719" black
	TD		CCCP-86721	
	T		CCCP-86722	
		Russian AF	CCCP-86725	"725" black
	M		CCCP-86727	
	M		CCCP-86728	
	M		CCCP-86729	
	M		CCCP-86731	
	M		CCCP-86733	
	M		CCCP-86734	
	M		CCCP-86735	
	M		CCCP-86736	
	M		CCCP-86737	
	M		CCCP-86738	
	M		CCCP-86739	
	M		CCCP-86740	
	M		CCCP-86741	
	M		CCCP-86742	
	M		CCCP-86744	
	M	Soviet AF	CCCP-86745	
	M		CCCP-86746	
	M	Soviet AF	CCCP-86748	
	M		CCCP-86749	
	T		CCCP-86786	engine testbed
	M		CCCP-86806	
	M		CCCP-86807	
	M		CCCP-86808	
	M		CCCP-86809	
	M	Azerbaijan Govt	CCCP-86810	RA-86610

ILYUSHIN Il-76

S/n	Series	Last known Owner/Operator	Identities/fate (where known)	
	M		CCCP-86811	
	M		CCCP-86813	
		Soviet AF	CCCP-86815	
		Soviet AF	CCCP-86819	"819" black
			RA-86820	
	M		CCCP-86822	
	M		CCCP-86824	
	MDK	Russian Min of Defence	CCCP-86825	RA-86825
	M		CCCP-86826	
	M	Russian Min of Defence	CCCP-86827	RA-86827
	M		CCCP-86828	
	M		CCCP-86829	
	M	Russian Min of Defence	CCCP-86830	RA-86830
	M		CCCP-86831	
	M	Aeroflot Russian Int A/L	CCCP-86832	RA-86832
	M	Russian Min of Defence	CCCP-86833	RA-86833
			CCCP-86834	wfs by 1992 Irkutsk Technical School, Russia
	M	Russian Min of Defence	CCCP-86835	RA-86835
	M		CCCP-86837	
	M		CCCP-86838	
	M	Russian Min of Defence	CCCP-86839	RA-86839
	M		CCCP-86840	
	M		CCCP-86841	
	M	Russian Min of Defence	CCCP-86842	RA-86842
	M	Russian Min of Defence	CCCP-86843	RA-86843
	M	Aeroflot Russian Int A/L	RA-86847	
	M		CCCP-86848	
	M		CCCP-86849	
	M		CCCP-86852	
	M	Aeroflot Russian Int A/L	CCCP-86853	RA-86853
	M		CCCP-86855	
	M		CCCP-86856	
	M	Russian Russian Min of Defence	CCCP-86858	RA-86858
	M		CCCP-86859	
	M		CCCP-86860	
	M		CCCP-86861	
	M		CCCP-86862	
	M		CCCP-86865	
	M		CCCP-86867	
	M	Russian Min of Defence	CCCP-86868	RA-86868
	MD		CCCP-86871	
	MD	Russian Min of Defence	CCCP-86872	RA-86872
	M	Russian Min of Defence	CCCP-86873	RA-86873
	M		CCCP-86875	
	MD	Russian Min of Defence	CCCP-86876	RA-86876
	M		CCCP-86877	
	M		CCCP-86880	
	M		CCCP-86881	
	M		CCCP-86882	
	M		CCCP-86883	
	M		CCCP-86884	
	M		CCCP-86885	
	M		CCCP-86886	
	M		CCCP-86887	
	M		CCCP-86888	
	MD		CCCP-86889	wfs, Irkutsk Technical School, Russia
	M		CCCP-86893	
	M	Russian AF	RA-86894	
	M		CCCP-86895	
	MD		CCCP-86897	
	MD	Aeroflot Russian Int A/L	CCCP-86898	RA-86898
	MD		CCCP-86899	
	MD		CCCP-86901	
	MD	Russian Min of Defence	CCCP-86902	RA-86902
	MD		CCCP-86904	
	MD		CCCP-86905	
	MD	Aeroflot Russian Int A/L	CCCP-86906	RA-86906
	MD	Aeroflot Russian Int A/L	CCCP-86907	RA-86907
	MD	Russian Min of Defence	CCCP-86908	RA-86908
	MD	Aeroflot Russian Int A/L	CCCP-86910	RA-86910
	MD		CCCP-86912	
	MD		CCCP-86913	
	MD		CCCP-86914	
	MD		CCCP-86915	
	MD		CCCP-86916	
	MD		CCCP-86917	
	MD		CCCP-86921	UR-86921
	MD	Russian AF	CCCP-86925	RA-86925
	MD		CCCP-86926	
	MD		CCCP-86927	
			UR-98775	
			UR-ALC	

ILYUSHIN Il-76

S/n	Series	Last known Owner/Operator	Identities/fate (where known)	
		Enimex	ES-NIT	
	TD	Turkmenistan Airlines	EZ-F429	
	T	Iraqi Airways	YI-AIM	
		Iraqi Airways	YI-AIN	
	M	Iraqi Airways	YI-AKV	
	MD	Iraqi Airways	YI-ANJ	
	MD	Iraqi Airways	YI-ANK	wfs
	T	Inversija	YL-LAL	
	T	(Libyan Arab Airlines)	5A-DKK	reportedly dbr in 1985 Sheba
	T	Libyan Arab Airlines	5A-DLL	wfs
	M	Libyan Arab Airlines	5A-DMM	wfs
	TD	Libyan Arab Airlines	5A-DNC	wfs
	TD	Libyan Arab Airlines	5A-DND	wfs
	T	Libyan Arab Airlines	5A-DNE	wfs
	TD	(Libyan Arab Airlines)	5A-DNF	w/o 06Mar86 Tripoli, Libya
	TD	Libyan Arab Airlines	5A-DNH	wfs
	T	Libyan Arab Airlines	5A-DNI	wfs
	T	Libyan Arab Airlines	5A-DNJ	wfs
	TD	Libyan Arab Airlines	5A-DNK	wfs
	T	Libyan Arab Airlines	5A-DNL	wfs
	TD	Libyan Arab Airlines	5A-DNO	wfs
	TD	Libyan Arab Airlines	5A-DNP	wfs
	TD	Libyan Arab Airlines	5A-DNQ	wfs
	TD	Libyan Arab Airlines	5A-DNS	wfs
	TD	Libyan Arab Airlines	5A-DNW	wfs
	M	(Libyan Arab Airlines)	5A-DZZ	w/o 15Apr86 Tripoli, Libya
	TD	Yemenia	RA-76380	70-ADH
	MD	Algerian Govt	7T-WIA	
	MD	Algerian Govt	7T-WIB	
	MD	Algerian Govt	7T-WIC	
	TD	Algerian Govt	RA-78...	7T-WIE
	TD	Algerian Govt	7T-WIU	
	MD	Indian AF	K2661/A	
	MD	Indian AF	K2663/C	
	MD	Indian AF	K2664/D	
	MD	Indian AF	K2665/E	
	MD	Indian AF	K2878	
	MD	Indian AF	K2879/H	
	MD	Indian AF	K2901	
	MD	Indian AF	K2902/M	
	MD	Indian AF	K2903	
	MD	Indian AF	K2999/U	
	MD	Indian AF	K3000	
	MD	Indian AF	K3001	
	MD	Indian AF	K3002	
	MD	Indian AF	K3003	
	MD	Indian AF	K3004	
	MD	Indian AF	K3005/E	
	MD	Indian AF	K3012	
	MD	Indian AF	K3013	
	MD	Indian AF	K3014	
	MD	Indian AF	K3015	
	MD	Indian AF	K3077/V	
	A-50	Soviet AF	20 red	AWACS a/c wfs by Aug92 Taganrog Tech Centre, Russia
		Soviet AF	21 black	Il-78 tanker version
		Soviet AF	32 blue	Il-78M tanker version
		Soviet AF	32 red	Il-78 tanker version
		Soviet AF	38 blue	Il-78M tanker version
	A-50	Soviet AF	33 red	AWACS a/c
	A-50	Soviet AF	40 red	AWACS a/c
	A-50	Soviet AF	42 red	AWACS a/c
	A-50	Soviet AF	50 red	AWACS a/c
		Soviet AF	88	
		Soviet AF	92	
		Soviet AF	97	

One Aeroflot or Soviet AF Il-76 w/o 11Dec88 nr Leninakan, one Soviet AF Il-76 w/o 01Feb90 in Lithuania and one Soviet AF Il-76 w/o 09Jul93 Pskov

ILYUSHIN Il-86

The second digit of the final five digits of the serial number indicates the year of construction, and the last three digits are believed to represent the s/n

S/n	Last known Owner/Operator	Identities/fate (where known)		
0101?	Aeroflot	CCCP-86000	prototype; ff 22Dec76	wfs Kiev-Zhulyany, Ukraine
0102?	Ilyushin	CCCP-86001	Static test airframe Voronezh, Russia	
0103?	Gosnii GA	CCCP-86002	RA-86002	
51483201026	CIS AF	01		
51483200001	Aeroflot	CCCP-86003	at Moscow Inst of Civil Aviation, Sheremetyevo, Russia	
51483200002	Vnukovo Airlines	CCCP-86004	RA-86004	
51483200003	Vnukovo Airlines	CCCP-86005	wfs by Jun92 engineless Moscow-Vnukovo, Russia	
51483200004	Vnukovo Airlines	CCCP-86006	RA-86006	
51483200005	Vnukovo Airlines	CCCP-86007	RA-86007	
51483200006	Vnukovo Airlines	CCCP-86008	wfs by Sep94 Moscow-Vnukovo, Russia	
51483200007	Vnukovo Airlines	CCCP-86009	RA-86009	
51483200008	Vnukovo Airlines	CCCP-86010	RA-86010	
51483200009	Vnukovo Airlines	CCCP-86011	86011	RA-86011
51483202010	Uzbekistan Airways	CCCP-86012	86012	UK-86012
51483202011	Vnukovo Airlines	CCCP-86013	RA-86013	
51483202012	Vnukovo Airlines	CCCP-86014	wfs by Sep94 Moscow-Vnukovo, Russia	
51483202013	Aeroflot Russian Int A/L	CCCP-86015	RA-86015	
51483202014	Uzbekistan Airways	CCCP-86016	86016	UK-86016
51483202015	Vnukovo Airlines	CCCP-86017	RA-86017	
51483202016	Vnukovo Airlines	CCCP-86018	RA-86018	
51483202017	China Northern Airlines	CCCP-86050	RA-86050	
51483202018	Ural Airlines	CCCP-86051	RA-86051	
51483202019	Uzbekistan Airways	CCCP-86052	UK-86052	wfs by May95 engineless Tashkent, Uzbekistan
51483203020	Uzbekistan Airways	CCCP-86053	UK-86053	
51483203021	Aeroflot Russian Int A/L	CCCP-86054	RA-86054	
51483203022	Vnukovo Airlines	CCCP-86055	RA-86055	
51483203023	Uzbekistan Airways	CCCP-86056	86056	UK-86056
51483203024	Uzbekistan Airways	CCCP-86057	UK-86057	
51483203025	Aeroflot Russian Int A/L	CCCP-86058	RA-86058	
51483203026	Aeroflot Russian Int A/L	CCCP-86059	RA-86059	
51483203027	St Petersburg Avia Ent	CCCP-86060	RA-86060	
51483203028	St Petersburg Avia Ent	CCCP-86061	RA-86061	
51483203029	Belavia	CCCP-86062	RA-86062	EW-86062
51483203030	China Northern Airlines	CCCP-86063	RA-86063	
51483203031	Uzbekistan Airways	CCCP-86064	UK-86064	
51483203032	Aeroflot Russian Int A/L	CCCP-86065	RA-86065	
51483203033	Aeroflot Russian Int A/L	CCCP-86066	RA-86066	
51483204034	Aeroflot Russian Int A/L	CCCP-86067	RA-86067	
51483204035	Kazakhstan Airlines	CCCP-86068	UN-86068	
51483204036	Kazakhstan Airlines	CCCP-86069	UN-86069	
51483204037	St Petersburg Avia Ent	CCCP-86070	RA-86070	
51483204038	Kazakhstan Airlines	CCCP-86071	UN-86071	
51483204039	Uzbekistan Airways	CCCP-86072	86072	UK-86072
51483204040	St Petersburg Avia Ent	CCCP-86073	RA-86073	
51483205041	Aeroflot Russian Int A/L	CCCP-86074	RA-86074	
51483205042	Russian Min of Defence	CCCP-86146	RA-86146	Satellite tracker
51483205043	Russian Min of Defence	CCCP-86147	RA-86147	Satellite tracker
51483205044	Aeroflot Russian Int A/L	CCCP-86075	RA-86075	
51483205045	Armenian Airlines	CCCP-86076	wfs reportedly used for spares in 1993 Yerevan, Armenia	
51483205046	Russian Min of Defence	CCCP-86148	RA-86148	Satellite tracker
51483205047	Kazakhstan Airlines	CCCP-86077	UN-86077	
51483205048	Russian Min of Defence	CCCP-86149	RA-86149	Satellite tracker
51483205049	Ural Airlines	CCCP-86078	RA-86078	
51483206050	Aeroflot Russian Int A/L	CCCP-86079	RA-86079	
51483206051	Aeroflot Russian Int A/L	CCCP-86080	RA-86080	
51483206052	Vnukovo Airlines	CCCP-86081	RA-86081	
51483206053	Vnukovo Airlines	CCCP-86082	RA-86082	
51483206054	Uzbekistan Airways	CCCP-86083	86083	UK-86083
51483206055	Vnukovo Airlines	CCCP-86084	RA-86084	
51483206056	Vnukovo Airlines	CCCP-86085	RA-86085	
51483206057	Kazakhstan Airlines	CCCP-86086	UN-86086	
51483206058	Aeroflot Russian Int A/L	CCCP-86087	RA-86087	
51483206059	Aeroflot Russian Int A/L	CCCP-86088	RA-86088	
51483207060	Vnukovo Airlines	CCCP-86089	RA-86089	
51483207061	Uzbekistan Airways	CCCP-86090	86090	UK-86090
51483207062	Vnukovo Airlines	CCCP-86091	RA-86091	
51483207063	St Petersburg Avia Ent	CCCP-86092	RA-86092	
51483207064	(Ural Airlines)	CCCP-86093	RA-86093	w/o 30Nov95 Ekaterinburg-Koltsovo A/p,Russia
51483207065	St Petersburg Avia Ent	CCCP-86094	RA-86094	
51483207066	Aeroflot Russian Int A/L	CCCP-86095	RA-86095	
51483207067	Aeroflot Russian Int A/L	CCCP-86096	RA-86096	
51483207068	Vnukovo Airlines	CCCP-86097	RA-86097	
51483207069	Kazakhstan Airlines	CCCP-86101	UN-86101	
51483207070	Siberia Airlines	CCCP-86102	RA-86102	
51483208071	Aeroflot Russian Int A/L	CCCP-86103	RA-86103	
51483208072	Vnukovo Airlines	CCCP-86104	RA-86104	
51483208073	Siberia Airlines	CCCP-86105	RA-86105	
51483208074	St Petersburg Avia Ent	CCCP-86106	RA-86106	

ILYUSHIN Il-86

S/n	Last known Owner/Operator	Identities/fate (where known)		
51483208075	Siberia Airlines	CCCP-86107	RA-86107	
51483208076	Siberia Airlines	CCCP-86108	RA-86108	
51483208077	Siberia Airlines	CCCP-86109	RA-86109	
51483208078	Aeroflot Russian Int A/L	CCCP-86110	RA-86110	
51483208079	Vnukovo Airlines	CCCP-86111	RA-86111	
51483208080	Siberia Airlines	CCCP-86112	RA-86112	
51483209081	Aeroflot Russian Int A/L	CCCP-86113	RA-86113	
51483209082	Ural Airlines	CCCP-86114	RA-86114	
51483209083	Aeroflot Russian Int A/L	CCCP-86115	RA-86115	
51483209084	Kazakhstan Airlines	CCCP-86116	UN-86116	
51483209085	Armenian Airlines	CCCP-86117	EK86117	
51483209086	Armenian Airlines	CCCP-86118	EK86118	
51483209087	(Aeroflot)	CCCP-86119	RA-86119	dbr 08Mar94 New Delhi, India by B737 VT-SIA
51483209088	Siberia Airlines	CCCP-86120	RA-86120	
51483209089	Krasnoyarsk Airlines	CCCP-86121	RA-86121	
51483210090	Krasnoyarsk Airlines	CCCP-86122	RA-86122	
51483210091	Transaero Airlines	CCCP-86123	RA-86123	
51483210092	Aeroflot Russian Int A/L	CCCP-86124	RA-86124	
51483210093	Air Transport School	CCCP-86125	RA-86125	
51483210094	Aeroflot Russian Int A/L	CCCP-86136	RA-86136	
51483210095	Krasnoyarsk Airlines	CCCP-86137	RA-86137	
51483210096	Aeroflot Russian Int A/L	CCCP-86138	RA-86138	
51483210097		CCCP-86139	RA-86139	wfs in 1994 Guangzhou, China
51483210098?	China Xinjiang Airlines	B-2016		
51483210099?	China Xinjiang Airlines	B-2018		
51483210100?	China Xinjiang Airlines	B-2019		
51483211101	AJT Air	CCCP-86145	RA-86145	
51483211102	AJT Air	RA-86140		
5148321.103				

The following are aircraft for which there are no confirmed serial numbers at the present time:

514832.....	CCCP-86098	
514832.....	86142	
514832.....	CCCP-86141	Satellite tracker

Production complete

ILYUSHIN Il-96

The last five digits are believed to represent the s/n.

S/n	Series	Last known Owner/Operator	Identities/fate (where known)		
0101	M	Ilyushin Design Bureau	CCCP-96000	RA-96000	prototype; ff 28Sep88; converted from series 300
30000103		Ilyushin Design Bureau	CCCP-96001	RA-96001	
	300	Ilyushin Design Bureau	CCCP-96002	RA-96002	
74393201002	300	Aeroflot Russian Int A/L	CCCP-96005	96005	RA-96005
74393201003	300	Domodedovo Airlines	CCCP-96006	RA-96006	also quoted as s/n 34893006
74393201004	300	Aeroflot Russian Int A/L	RA-96007		
74393201005	300	Aeroflot Russian Int A/L	RA-96008		
74393201006	300	Domodedovo Airlines	RA-96009		
74393201007	300	Aeroflot Russian Int A/L	RA-96010		
74393201008	300	Aeroflot Russian Int A/L	RA-96011		
74393201009	300	Rossia/Russian Govt	RA-96012		
74393201010	300		RA-96013		
74393201011	300	Rossia/Russian Govt	RA-96014		
74393201012	300		RA-96015		
74393201013	300	Rossia/Russian Govt	RA-96016		

KAWASAKI C-1

Line No	Series	Last known Owner/Operator	Identities/fate (where known)	
8001	C-1A	JASDF	28-1001	
8002	EC-1	JASDF	28-1002	
8003	C-1A	JASDF	38-1003	
8004	C-1A	JASDF	48-1004	
8005	C-1A	JASDF	48-1005	
8006	C-1A	JASDF	58-1006	
8007	C-1A	JASDF	58-1007	
8008	C-1A	JASDF	58-1008	
8009	C-1A	(JASDF)	58-1009	w/o 19Apr83 Suga-Shima Island, Japan
8010	C-1A	(JASDF)	58-1010	dbr 18Feb86 Iruma AB, Japan
8011	C-1A	JASDF	58-1011	
8012	C-1A	JASDF	58-1012	
8013	C-1A	JASDF	58-1013	
8014	C-1A	JASDF	68-1014	
8015	C-1A	(JASDF)	68-1015	w/o 19Apr83 Suga-Shima Island, Japan
8016	C-1A	JASDF	68-1016	
8017	C-1A	JASDF	68-1017	
8018	C-1A	JASDF	68-1018	
8019	C-1A	JASDF	68-1019	
8020	C-1A	JASDF	68-1020	
8021	EC-1	JASDF	78-1021	
8022	C-1A	JASDF	78-1022	
8023	C-1A	JASDF	78-1023	
8024	C-1A	JASDF	78-1024	
8025	C-1A	JASDF	78-1025	
8026	C-1A	JASDF	78-1026	
8027	C-1A	JASDF	88-1027	
8028	C-1A	JASDF	88-1028	
8029	C-1A	JASDF	98-1029	
8030	C-1A	JASDF	08-1030	
8031	C-1A	JASDF	18-1031	

Production complete

LOCKHEED C-5 GALAXY (Model 500)

C/n	Series	Last known Owner/Operator	Identities/fate (where known)	
500-0001	C-5A	(USAF)	66-8303	ff 30Jun68 dbf 17Oct70
500-0002	C-5A	USAF	66-8304	
500-0003	C-5A	USAF	66-8305	
500-0004	C-5A	USAF	66-8306	
500-0005	C-5A	USAF	66-8307	
500-0006	C-5A	USAF	67-0167	
500-0007	C-5A	USAF	67-0168	
500-0008	C-5A	USAF	67-0169	
500-0009	C-5A	USAF	67-0170	
500-0010	C-5A	USAF	67-0171	
500-0011	C-5A	(USAF)	67-0172	w/o 25May70; derelict Palmdale; nose at Travis AFB, CA Nov87
500-0012	C-5A	USAF	67-0173	
500-0013	C-5A	USAF	67-0174	
500-0014	C-5A	USAF	68-0211	
500-0015	C-5A	USAF	68-0212	
500-0016	C-5C	USAF	68-0213	
500-0017	C-5A	USAF	68-0214	
500-0018	C-5A	USAF	68-0215	
500-0019	C-5A	USAF	68-0216	
500-0020	C-5A	USAF	68-0217	
500-0021	C-5A	(USAF)	68-0218	w/o 04Apr75 on landing at Saigon, Thailand.
500-0022	C-5A	USAF	68-0219	
500-0023	C-5A	USAF	68-0220	
500-0024	C-5A	USAF	68-0221	
500-0025	C-5A	USAF	68-0222	
500-0026	C-5A	USAF	68-0223	
500-0027	C-5A	USAF	68-0224	
500-0028	C-5A	USAF	68-0225	
500-0029	C-5A	USAF	68-0226	
500-0030	C-5A	(USAF)	68-0227	w/o 27Sep74
500-0031	C-5A	(USAF)	68-0228	w/o 29Aug90 nr Ramstein, West Germany
500-0032	C-5A	USAF	69-0001	
500-0033	C-5A	USAF	69-0002	
500-0034	C-5A	USAF	69-0003	
500-0035	C-5A	USAF	69-0004	
500-0036	C-5A	USAF	69-0005	
500-0037	C-5A	USAF	69-0006	
500-0038	C-5A	USAF	69-0007	
500-0039	C-5A	USAF	69-0008	
500-0040	C-5A	USAF	69-0009	
500-0041	C-5A	USAF	69-0010	
500-0042	C-5A	USAF	69-0011	
500-0043	C-5A	USAF	69-0012	
500-0044	C-5A	USAF	69-0013	
500-0045	C-5A	USAF	69-0014	
500-0046	C-5A	USAF	69-0015	
500-0047	C-5A	USAF	69-0016	
500-0048	C-5A	USAF	69-0017	
500-0049	C-5A	USAF	69-0018	
500-0050	C-5A	USAF	69-0019	
500-0051	C-5A	USAF	69-0020	
500-0052	C-5A	USAF	69-0021	
500-0053	C-5A	USAF	69-0022	
500-0054	C-5A	USAF	69-0023	
500-0055	C-5A	USAF	69-0024	
500-0056	C-5A	USAF	69-0025	
500-0057	C-5A	USAF	69-0026	
500-0058	C-5A	USAF	69-0027	
500-0059	C-5A	USAF	70-0445	
500-0060	C-5A	USAF	70-0446	
500-0061	C-5A	USAF	70-0447	
500-0062	C-5A	USAF	70-0448	
500-0063	C-5A	USAF	70-0449	
500-0064	C-5A	USAF	70-0450	
500-0065	C-5A	USAF	70-0451	
500-0066	C-5A	USAF	70-0452	
500-0067	C-5A	USAF	70-0453	
500-0068	C-5A	USAF	70-0454	
500-0069	C-5A	USAF	70-0455	
500-0070	C-5A	USAF	70-0456	
500-0071	C-5A	USAF	70-0457	
500-0072	C-5A	USAF	70-0458	
500-0073	C-5A	USAF	70-0459	
500-0074	C-5A	USAF	70-0460	
500-0075	C-5A	USAF	70-0461	
500-0076	C-5A	USAF	70-0462	
500-0077	C-5A	USAF	70-0463	
500-0078	C-5A	USAF	70-0464	
500-0079	C-5A	USAF	70-0465	
500-0080	C-5A	USAF	70-0466	

LOCKHEED C-5 GALAXY (Model 500)

C/n	Series	Last known Owner/Operator	Identities/fate (where known)	
500-0081	C-5A	USAF	70-0467	
500-0082	C-5B	USAF	83-1285	ff 10Sep85
500-0083	C-5B	USAF	84-0059	
500-0084	C-5B	USAF	84-0060	
500-0085	C-5B	USAF	84-0061	
500-0086	C-5B	USAF	84-0062	
500-0087	C-5B	USAF	85-0001	
500-0088	C-5B	USAF	85-0002	
500-0089	C-5B	USAF	85-0003	
500-0090	C-5B	USAF	85-0004	
500-0091	C-5B	USAF	85-0005	
500-0092	C-5B	USAF	85-0006	
500-0093	C-5B	USAF	85-0007	
500-0094	C-5B	USAF	85-0008	
500-0095	C-5B	USAF	85-0009	
500-0096	C-5B	USAF	85-0010	
500-0097	C-5B	USAF	86-0011	
500-0098	C-5B	USAF	86-0012	
500-0099	C-5B	USAF	86-0013	
500-0100	C-5B	USAF	86-0014	
500-0101	C-5B	USAF	86-0015	
500-0102	C-5B	USAF	86-0016	
500-0103	C-5B	USAF	86-0017	
500-0104	C-5B	USAF	86-0018	
500-0105	C-5B	USAF	86-0019	
500-0106	C-5B	USAF	86-0020	
500-0107	C-5B	USAF	86-0021	
500-0108	C-5B	USAF	86-0022	
500-0109	C-5B	USAF	86-0023	
500-0110	C-5B	USAF	86-0024	
500-0111	C-5B	USAF	86-0025	
500-0112	C-5B	USAF	86-0026	
500-0113	C-5B	USAF	87-0027	
500-0114	C-5B	USAF	87-0028	
500-0115	C-5B	USAF	87-0029	
500-0116	C-5B	USAF	87-0030	
500-0117	C-5B	USAF	87-0031	
500-0118	C-5B	USAF	87-0032	
500-0119	C-5B	USAF	87-0033	
500-0120	C-5B	USAF	87-0034	
500-0121	C-5B	USAF	87-0035	
500-0122	C-5B	USAF	87-0036	
500-0123	C-5B	USAF	87-0037	
500-0124	C-5B	USAF	87-0038	
500-0125	C-5B	USAF	87-0039	
500-0126	C-5B	USAF	87-0040	
500-0127	C-5B	USAF	87-0041	
500-0128	C-5B	USAF	87-0042	
500-0129	C-5B	USAF	87-0043	
500-0130	C-5B	USAF	87-0044	
500-0131	C-5B	USAF	87-0045	

Production complete

LOCKHEED C-141 STARLIFTER (Model 300)

C/n	Series	Last known Owner/Operator	Identities/fate (where known)	
6001	NC-141A	USAF	61-2775	ff 17Dec63
6002	NC-141A	USAF	61-2776	
6003	NC-141A	USAF	61-2777	to AMARC Sep94, storage code CR010
6004	C-141B	USAF	61-2778	
6005	NC-141A	USAF	61-2779	preserved Edwards AFB, CA by May95
6006	C-141B	USAF	63-8075	wfu Travis AFB by May93
6007	C-141B	USAF	63-8076	
6008	C-141A	(USAF)	63-8077	w/o 28Aug73
6009	C-141B	USAF	63-8078	wfu in 1993 Altus AFB, OK
6010	C-141B	USAF	63-8079	wfu Charleston AFB by Aug93; preserved by Apr95
6011	C-141B	USAF	63-8080	
6012	C-141B	USAF	63-8081	
6013	C-141B	USAF	63-8082	
6014	C-141B	USAF	63-8083	
6015	C-141B	USAF	63-8084	
6016	C-141B	USAF	63-8085	
6017	C-141B	USAF	63-8086	
6018	C-141B	USAF	63-8087	
6019	C-141B	USAF	63-8088	
6020	C-141B	USAF	63-8089	
6021	C-141B	USAF	63-8090	
6022	C-141B	USAF	64-0609	
6023	C-141B	USAF	64-0610	
6024	C-141B	USAF	64-0611	
6025	C-141B	USAF	64-0612	
6026	C-141B	USAF	64-0613	
6027	C-141B	USAF	64-0614	
6028	C-141B	USAF	64-0615	
6029	C-141B	USAF	64-0616	
6030	C-141B	USAF	64-0617	
6031	C-141B	USAF	64-0618	
6032	C-141B	USAF	64-0619	
6033	C-141B	USAF	64-0620	
6034	C-141B	USAF	64-0621	
6035	C-141B	USAF	64-0622	
6036	C-141B	USAF	64-0623	
6037	C-141B	(USAF)	64-0624	w/o 12Jul84 nr Sigonella, Sicily
6038	C-141B	USAF	64-0625	
6039	C-141B	USAF	64-0626	
6040	C-141B	USAF	64-0627	
6041	C-141B	USAF	64-0628	
6042	C-141B	USAF	64-0629	
6043	C-141B	USAF	64-0630	
6044	C-141B	USAF	64-0631	
6045	C-141B	USAF	64-0632	
6046	C-141B	USAF	64-0633	
6047	C-141B	USAF	64-0634	
6048	C-141B	USAF	64-0635	stored Jan88 Travis AFB, CA
6049	C-141B	USAF	64-0636	to AMARC Jun93, storage code CR004
6050	C-141B	USAF	64-0637	
6051	C-141B	USAF	64-0638	
6052	C-141B	USAF	64-0639	
6053	C-141B	USAF	64-0640	
6054	C-141A	(USAF)	64-0641	w/o 20Mar75
6055	C-141B	USAF	64-0642	
6056	C-141B	USAF	64-0643	
6057	C-141B	USAF	64-0644	
6058	C-141B	USAF	64-0645	
6059	C-141B	USAF	64-0646	
6060	C-141B	(USAF)	64-0647	w/o 18Sep79
6061	C-141B	USAF	64-0648	to AMARC Jul93, storage code CR005
6062	C-141B	USAF	64-0649	
6063	C-141B	USAF	64-0650	
6064	C-141B	USAF	64-0651	
6065	C-141B	(USAF)	64-0652	w/o 31Aug82 Hoopers Bald Mountain, nr Murphy, NC
6066	C-141B	USAF	64-0653	
6067	C-141B	USAF	65-0216	
6068	C-141B	USAF	65-0217	to AMARC
6069	C-141B	USAF	65-0218	
6070	C-141B	USAF	65-0219	
6071	C-141B	USAF	65-0220	
6072	C-141B	USAF	65-0221	
6073	C-141B	USAF	65-0222	
6074	C-141B	USAF	65-0223	
6075	C-141B	USAF	65-0224	
6076	C-141B	USAF	65-0225	
6077	C-141B	USAF	65-0226	
6078	C-141B	USAF	65-0227	
6079	C-141B	USAF	65-0228	wfu in 1993 Altus AFB, OK; instructional airframe Sheppard TTC, TX
6080	C-141B	USAF	65-0229	

LOCKHEED C-141 STARLIFTER (Model 300)

C/n	Series	Last known Owner/Operator	Identities/fate (where known)	
6081	C-141B	USAF	65-0230	
6082	C-141B	USAF	65-0231	
6083	C-141B	USAF	65-0232	
6084	C-141B	USAF	65-0233	to AMARC Jul93, storage code CR009
6085	C-141B	USAF	65-0234	
6086	C-141B	USAF	65-0235	
6087	C-141B	USAF	65-0236	wfu Altus AFB, OK, by Aug93; to Scott AFB, IL by May94
6088	C-141B	USAF	65-0237	
6089	C-141B	USAF	65-0238	
6090	C-141B	USAF	65-0239	
6091	C-141B	USAF	65-0240	
6092	C-141B	USAF	65-0241	
6093	C-141B	USAF	65-0242	
6094	C-141B	USAF	65-0243	
6095	C-141B	USAF	65-0244	
6096	C-141B	USAF	65-0245	
6097	GC-141B	USAF	65-0246	instructional airframe Travis AFB, CA by Mar91
6098	C-141B	USAF	65-0247	
6099	C-141B	USAF	65-0248	
6100	C-141B	USAF	65-0249	
6101	C-141B	USAF	65-0250	
6102	C-141B	USAF	65-0251	
6103	C-141B	USAF	65-0252	
6104	C-141B	(USAF)	65-0253	dbf 07Oct93 Travis AFB, CA
6105	C-141B	USAF	65-0254	
6106	C-141B	(USAF)	65-0255	w/o 30Nov92 over Harlem, MT, mid-air collision with 66-0142
6107	C-141B	USAF	65-0256	
6108	C-141B	USAF	65-0257	
6109	C-141B	USAF	65-0258	
6110	L-300-50A	NASA	N4141A	N714NA
6111	C-141B	USAF	65-0259	
6112	C-141B	USAF	65-0260	
6113	C-141B	USAF	65-0261	
6114	C-141B	USAF	65-0262	to AMARC Jul93, storage code CR007
6115	C-141B	USAF	65-0263	
6116	C-141B	USAF	65-0264	wfu in 1993 Altus AFB, OK
6117	C-141B	USAF	65-0265	
6118	C-141B	USAF	65-0266	
6119	C-141B	USAF	65-0267	
6120	C-141B	USAF	65-0268	
6121	C-141B	USAF	65-0269	
6122	C-141B	USAF	65-0270	
6123	C-141B	USAF	65-0271	
6124	C-141B	USAF	65-0272	
6125	C-141B	USAF	65-0273	
6126	C-141A	(USAF)	65-0274	w/o 19Aug74
6127	C-141B	USAF	65-0275	
6128	C-141B	USAF	65-0276	
6129	C-141B	USAF	65-0277	
6130	C-141B	USAF	65-0278	wfu at Norton AFB, CA by Jan94
6131	C-141B	USAF	65-0279	
6132	C-141B	USAF	65-0280	
6133	C-141A	(USAF)	65-0281	w/o 07Sep66
6134	C-141B	USAF	65-9397	
6135	C-141B	USAF	65-9398	to AMARC May93, storage code CR002
6136	C-141B	USAF	65-9399	stored Travis AFB, CAto AMARC
6137	C-141B	USAF	65-9400	
6138	C-141B	USAF	65-9401	
6139	C-141B	USAF	65-9402	
6140	C-141B	USAF	65-9403	
6141	C-141B	USAF	65-9404	
6142	C-141B	USAF	65-9405	
6143	C-141B	USAF	65-9406	SOC at Norton AFB, CA Oct93
6144	C-141A	(USAF)	65-9407	w/o 23Mar67
6145	C-141B	USAF	65-9408	
6146	C-141B	USAF	65-9409	
6147	C-141B	USAF	65-9410	to AMARC May93, storage code CR003
6148	C-141B	USAF	65-9411	
6149	C-141B	USAF	65-9412	
6150	C-141B	USAF	65-9413	
6151	C-141B	USAF	65-9414	
6152	GC-141B	USAF	66-0126	wfu McGuire AFB by May93; to G.I. Sheppard TTC, TX by Aug94
6153	C-141A	(USAF)	66-0127	w/o 13Apr67
6154	C-141B	USAF	66-0128	
6155	C-141B	USAF	66-0129	
6156	C-141B	USAF	66-0130	
6157	C-141B	USAF	66-0131	
6158	C-141B	USAF	66-0132	
6159	C-141B	USAF	66-0133	
6160	C-141B	USAF	66-0134	
6161	C-141B	USAF	66-0135	

LOCKHEED C-141 STARLIFTER (Model 300)

C/n	Series	Last known Owner/Operator	Identities/fate (where known)	
6162	C-141B	USAF	66-0136	
6163	C-141B	USAF	66-0137	
6164	C-141B	USAF	66-0138	
6165	C-141B	USAF	66-0139	
6166	C-141B	USAF	66-0140	
6167	C-141B	USAF	66-0141	
6168	C-141B	(USAF)	66-0142	w/o 30Nov92 over Harlem, MT, mid-air collision with 65-0255
6169	C-141B	USAF	66-0143	to AMARC May93, storage code CR001
6170	C-141B	USAF	66-0144	
6171	C-141B	USAF	66-0145	
6172	C-141B	USAF	66-0146	
6173	C-141B	USAF	66-0147	
6174	C-141B	USAF	66-0148	
6175	C-141B	USAF	66-0149	
6176	C-141B	(USAF)	66-0150	w/o 20Feb89 3 miles N of Hurlburt Field, FL
6177	C-141B	USAF	66-0151	
6178	C-141B	USAF	66-0152	
6179	C-141B	USAF	66-0153	
6180	C-141B	USAF	66-0154	
6181	C-141B	USAF	66-0155	
6182	C-141B	USAF	66-0156	
6183	C-141B	USAF	66-0157	
6184	C-141B	USAF	66-0158	
6185	C-141B	(USAF)	66-0159	w/o 22Feb89
6186	C-141B	USAF	66-0160	
6187	C-141B	USAF	66-0161	
6188	C-141B	USAF	66-0162	
6189	C-141B	USAF	66-0163	
6190	C-141B	USAF	66-0164	
6191	C-141B	USAF	66-0165	
6192	C-141B	USAF	66-0166	
6193	C-141B	USAF	66-0167	
6194	C-141B	USAF	66-0168	
6195	C-141B	USAF	66-0169	
6196	C-141B	USAF	66-0170	to AMARC Jul93, storage code CR006
6197	C-141B	USAF	66-0171	
6198	C-141B	USAF	66-0172	
6199	C-141B	USAF	66-0173	Badly damaged 23Mar94 Pope AFB, NC, by falling debris (main fuselage) from GD F-16D 88-0171
6200	C-141B	USAF	66-0174	
6201	C-141B	USAF	66-0175	
6202	GC-141B	USAF	66-0176	wfu McChord AFB by Mar93; to G.I. Sheppard TTC, TX by Aug94
6203	C-141B	USAF	66-0177	
6204	C-141B	USAF	66-0178	
6205	C-141B	USAF	66-0179	
6206	C-141B	USAF	66-0180	
6207	C-141B	USAF	66-0181	
6208	C-141B	USAF	66-0182	
6209	C-141B	USAF	66-0183	
6210	C-141B	USAF	66-0184	
6211	C-141B	USAF	66-0185	
6212	C-141B	USAF	66-0186	wfu Altus AFB by May93
6213	C-141B	USAF	66-0187	
6214	C-141B	USAF	66-0188	to AMARC Jul93, storage code CR008
6215	C-141B	USAF	66-0189	wfu in 1993 Altus AFB, OK; to G.I. Sheppard TTC, TX by Aug94
6216	C-141B	USAF	66-0190	
6217	C-141B	USAF	66-0191	
6218	C-141B	USAF	66-0192	
6219	C-141B	USAF	66-0193	
6220	C-141B	USAF	66-0194	
6221	C-141B	USAF	66-0195	
6222	C-141B	USAF	66-0196	
6223	C-141B	USAF	66-0197	
6224	C-141B	USAF	66-0198	
6225	C-141B	USAF	66-0199	
6226	C-141B	USAF	66-0200	
6227	C-141B	USAF	66-0201	
6228	C-141B	USAF	66-0202	
6229	C-141B	USAF	66-0203	
6230	C-141B	USAF	66-0204	
6231	C-141B	USAF	66-0205	
6232	C-141B	USAF	66-0206	
6233	C-141B	USAF	66-0207	
6234	C-141B	USAF	66-0208	
6235	C-141B	USAF	66-0209	
6236	C-141B	USAF	66-7944	
6237	C-141B	USAF	66-7945	stored Travis AFB, CA
6238	C-141B	USAF	66-7946	
6239	C-141B	USAF	66-7947	
6240	C-141B	USAF	66-7948	
6241	C-141B	USAF	66-7949	

LOCKHEED C-141 STARLIFTER (Model 300)

C/n	Series	Last known Owner/Operator	Identities/fate (where known)	
6242	C-141B	USAF	66-7950	
6243	C-141B	USAF	66-7951	
6244	C-141B	USAF	66-7952	
6245	C-141B	USAF	66-7953	
6246	C-141B	USAF	66-7954	
6247	C-141B	USAF	66-7955	
6248	C-141B	USAF	66-7956	
6249	C-141B	USAF	66-7957	
6250	C-141B	USAF	66-7958	
6251	C-141B	USAF	66-7959	
6252	C-141B	USAF	67-0001	
6253	C-141B	USAF	67-0002	
6254	C-141B	USAF	67-0003	
6255	C-141B	USAF	67-0004	
6256	C-141B	USAF	67-0005	
6257	C-141A	(USAF)	67-0006	w/o 28Aug76
6258	C-141B	USAF	67-0007	
6259	C-141A	(USAF)	67-0008	w/o 28Aug76
6260	C-141B	USAF	67-0009	
6261	C-141B	USAF	67-0010	
6262	C-141B	USAF	67-0011	
6263	C-141B	USAF	67-0012	
6264	C-141B	USAF	67-0013	
6265	C-141B	USAF	67-0014	
6266	C-141B	USAF	67-0015	
6267	C-141B	USAF	67-0016	
6268	C-141B	(USAF)	67-0017	dbf 07Mar82 MacEntire ANGB, SC
6269	C-141B	USAF	67-0018	
6270	C-141B	USAF	67-0019	
6271	C-141B	USAF	67-0020	
6272	C-141B	USAF	67-0021	
6273	C-141B	USAF	67-0022	
6274	C-141B	USAF	67-0023	
6275	C-141B	USAF	67-0024	
6276	C-141B	USAF	67-0025	
6277	C-141B	USAF	67-0026	
6278	C-141B	USAF	67-0027	
6279	C-141B	USAF	67-0028	
6280	C-141B	USAF	67-0029	
6281	C-141A	(USAF)	67-0030	w/o 12Nov80 nr Cairo-West, Egypt
6282	C-141B	USAF	67-0031	
6283	C-141B	USAF	67-0164	
6284	C-141B	USAF	67-0165	
6285	C-141B	USAF	67-0166	

Production complete

LOCKHEED L-1011 TRISTAR

C/n	Series	Last known Operator/Owner	Previous Identities/fate (where known)
1001	1	(Aviation Sales Co)	N1011 prototype; ff 16Nov70 b/u Aug86 Ardmore, OK
1002	1	International Air Leases	(N301EA) N31001 N1301L N301EA OB-1344 stored Jan93 Miami, FL
1003	1	Lockheed Marietta	N301EA N302EA N781DL fuselage used for testing Oct95 Marietta, GA
1004	1	Rich International	N303EA
1005	1	Rich International	N304EA TF-ABG N304EA
1006	1	Delta Air Lines	N305EA N782DL
1007	1	(Aviation Sales Co)	N306EA b/u Jan84 Ardmore, OK
1008	1	American Trans Air	N307EA D-AERO N22679 D-AERO N371EA D-AERY N178AT spares use Jun95 Ardmore, OK
1009	1	Delta Air Lines	N308EA N783DL
1010	150	Air Transat	N309EA C-FTNB
1011	1	(Eastern Air Lines)	N310EA w/o 29Dec72 in Everglades, FL
1012	F	Tradewinds Intl Air Cargo	N311EA
1013	1	Air Ops of Europe	N31001 SE-DSE
1014	1	(Trans World Airlines)	N11002 dbf 30Jul92 New York-Kennedy, NY
1015	1	Trans World Airlines	N11003
1016	1	Trans World Airlines	N11004
1017	1	Trans World Airlines	N11005
1018	1	Trans World Airlines	N11006
1019	150	Air Transat	N312EA CF-TNA N312EA C-FTNA N312EA C-FTNA N312EA C-FTNA N312EA C-FTNA N312EA C-FTNA N312EA C-FTNA N312EA C-FTNA N312EA C-FTNA
1020	1	Rich International	N313EA
1021	1	Cathay Pacific Airways	CF-TNB C-FTNB 4R-ULJ VR-HOE
1022	1	Air Atlantic Icelandic	N314EA VR-HOA TF-ABE
1023	150	Air Transat	N315EA CF-TNC N315EA C-FTNC N315EA C-FTNC N315EA C-FTNC N315EA C-FTNC N315EA C-FTNC N315EA C-FTNC N315EA C-FTNC N315EA C-FTNC
1024	1	Cathay Pacific Airways	G-BAAA VR-HHV
1025	1	Air Canada	CF-TND C-FTND 4R-ALG C-FTND A40-TP C-FTND
1026	1	(Trans World Airlines)	N31007 dbf 19Apr74 Boston, MA
1027	1	Cathay Pacific Airways	CF-TNE C-FTNE 4R-ULK VR-HOF stored Nov94 Avalon, Australia
1028	1	Trans World Airlines	N31008
1029	1	(Air Ops of Europe)	N31009 HR-AMC b/u Aug95 Bournemouth, UK
1030	1	Air Ops of Europe	N31010 SE-DPV stored Feb96 Teesside, UK
1031	1	General Avn Services	N31011 stored 29Dec92 Marana, AZ
1032	1	Air India	G-BAAB VR-HHW (SE-) V2-LEM
1033	1	Nordic East Intl	N1181L D-AERA N372EA VR-HMV SE-DTD
1034	1	Norick Repair Center	N41012 stored Dec92 Marana, AZ; used for spares
1035	1	Trans World Airlines	N31013
1036	1	Trans World Airlines	N31014
1037	1	Cathay Pacific Airways	N316EA VR-HOB
1038	1	Delta Air Lines	N317EA N784DA
1039	1	Cathay Pacific Airways	N318EA VR-HOI
1040	1	Rich International	N319EA
1041	50	American Trans Air	N701DA N701TT N195AT
1042	1	Venada Aviation	N320EA VR-HOC N9115G
1043	1	Cathay Pacific Airways	N321EA VR-HOD
1044	1	Air Atlanta Icelandic	N322EA VR-HOJ TF-ABL stored Nov95 Bremen-Lemwerder, Germany
1045	1	Air Atlanta Icelandic	N323EA VR-HOG TF-ABP stored Oct95 Bremen-Lemwerder, Germany
1046	1	GPA Group	N702DA N702TT EI-BTN stored Dec93 Mojave, CA
1047	1	Air Canada	CF-TNF C-FTNF 4R-ALE C-FTNF A40-TR C-FTNF stored 23Nov90 Marana, AZ
1048	150	Air Canada	CF-TNG C-FTNG stored Jan96 Marana, AZ
1049	1	Air Transat	CF-TNH C-FTNH
1050	1	Nordic East Intl	N324EA VR-HOH SE-DTC
1051	1	Cathay Pacific Airways	N325EA VR-HHY
1052	50	American Trans Air	N703DA N185AT
1053	100	Air Lanka	JA8501 4R-ALF 4R-ULC
1054	1	Air Atlantic Icelandic	N326EA VR-HHX TF-ABH
1055	1	Cathay Pacific Airways	N327EA VR-HOK
1056	200	Omani Avn Services	N328EA VR-HHG A40-TV stored Dec94 Cambridge, UK
1057	50	American Trans Air	N704DA N192AT
1058	100	Royal Airlines	N64854 CF-TNI C-FTNI
1059	1	Air Ops of Sweden	N31015 SE-DSB
1060	1	Trans World Airlines	N41016
1061	100	(Air Lanka)	JA8502 4R-ALH 4R-ULD w/o 03May86 Colombo, Sri Lanka
1062	100	Air Lanka	JA8503 4R-ULE
1063	1	Trans World Airlines	N15017
1064	100	Operation Blessing International Relief	N10112 C-GIES N787M stored Sep91 Kingman, AZ
1065	50	Air Ops of Sweden	N31018 SE-DSC
1066	50	Trans World Airlines	N31019
1067	100	Orbital Sciences Corp	N64854 C-FTNJ 4R-TNJ C-FTNJ N140SC
1068	100	GPA Group	JA8505 A40-TS (EI-CBM) EL-AKG 5N-BBB stored Dec94 Abu Dhabi, UAE
1069	100	Royal Airlines	N64854 C-FTNK 4R-TNK C-FTNK
1070	50	Rich International	JA8506 N762BE (N762HA) N762BE

LOCKHEED L-1011 TRISTAR

C/n	Series	Last known Operator/Owner	Previous Identities/fate (where known)
1071	50	American Trans Air	N705DA N193AT
1072	50	Air Ops of Europe	N41020 SE-DPP
1073	100	Air Canada	N64854 C-FTNL 4R-TNL C-FTNL stored Jan96 Marana, AZ
1074	50	American Trans Air	N706DA N186AT
1075	50	Faucett	N31021 OB-1545
1076	50	American Trans Air	N31022 N196AT
1077	50	American Trans Air	N707DA N187AT
1078	50	American Trans Air	N708DA N188AT
1079	100	Worldways Canada	N10114 C-GIFE N125DT
1080	50	FSBU	N31023
1081	50	American Trans Air	N709DA N189AT
1082	50	American Trans Air	JA8507 N763BE N197AT
1083	100	Caledonian Airways	G-BBAE C-FCXB G-BBAE C-FCXB G-BBAE
1084	50	American Trans Air	N710DA N191AT
1085	1	Comerica Bank	N329EA D-AERC N329SN stored Dec92 Mobile, AL
1086	50	American Trans Air	N711DA N190AT
1087	1	Faucett	N330EA OB-1504
1088	1	Delta Air Lines	N712DA
1089	1	Delta Air Lines	N713DA
1090	1	Delta Air Lines	N714DA
1091	50	Air Ops of Sweden	N31024 (N769HA) SE-DPX
1092	1	Delta Air Lines	N715DA
1093	100	Caledonian Airways	G-BBAF
1094	1	Air Transat	G-BBAG VR-HMW C-GTSX
1095	1	Delta Air Lines	N716DA
1096	1	Delta Air Lines	N717DA
1097	1	Delta Air Lines	N718DA
1098	100	Trans World Airlines	N81025 stored Dec94 Marana, AZ
1099	1	Air Transat	JA8508 C-FWCR
1100	1	A L Aircraft 4 Corp	JA8509 N312GB
1101	100	Caledonian Airways	G-BBAH stored 17Jan93 Cambridge, UK
1102	1	Caledonian Airways	G-BBAI C-FCXJ G-BBAI C-FCXJ G-BBAI
1103	50	Air Transat	N62355 JA8510 N764BE N703TT C-GTSZ
1104	100	Trans World Airlines	N81026 stored Dec94 Marana, AZ
1105	50	Rich International	N62357 JA8511 N765BE (N765HA) N765BE
1106	100	Caledonian Airways	G-BBAJ
1107	50	Trans World Airlines	N81027 stored Feb96 Marana, AZ
1108	100	Trans World Airlines	N81028 stored Dec94 Marana, AZ
1109	100	Trans World Airlines	N31029
1110	200	Saudia	N64854 HZ-AHA
1111	100	Trans World Airlines	N31030 stored Dec94 Marana, AZ
1112	50	Rich International	JA8512 N766BE (N766HA) N766BE
1113	50	Rich International	JA8513 N764BE (N764HA) N764BE
1114	1	(LTU)	N10115 D-AERI dbf 27Jun91 Dusseldorf, Germany; b/u by 11Oct91
1115	100	Trans World Airlines	N31031
1116	200	Saudia	HZ-AHB
1117	1	(Boeing Equipment Holding Corp)	JA8514 b/u Oct94 Mojave, CA
1118	100	Cathay Pacific Airways	N64854 VR-HHK
1119	1	(Boeing Equipment Holding Corp)	JA8515 b/u Oct94 Mojave, CA
1120	1	American Trans Air	N10116 D-AERE N179AT stored May95 Amarillo, TX
1121	1	Delta Air Lines	N331EA N785DL
1122	100	Cathay Pacific Airways	VR-HHL stored Oct95 Marana, AZ
1123	1	Delta Air Lines	N332EA N786DL
1124	200	Saudia	(N31032) HZ-AHE
1125	100	American Trans Air	N10117 D-AERU N625SA D-AERU N181AT
1126	1	Delta Air Lines	N333EA N787DL
1127	1	Rich International	JA8516 N305GB
1128	1	(Boeing Equipment Holding Corp)	JA8517 stored Oct93 Marana, AZ; b/u
1129	1	Rich International	JA8518 N302MB
1130	200	Saudia	(N31033) HZ-AHF
1131	200	IAL Aircraft Holding	(A40-TC) G-BDCW A40-TW N307GB stored Mar95 Cambridge, UK
1132	50	British Airways	G-BEAK stored Jun91 Mojave, CA
1133	200	IAL Aircraft Holding	G-BDCX A40-TX N308GB stored Nov95 Cambridge, UK
1134	1	Rich International	JA8519 N300AW
1135	1	Delta Air Lines	N719DA
1136	1	Delta Air Lines	N720DA
1137	200	Saudia	HZ-AHC
1138	200F	Arrow Air	G-BDCY A40-TY N306GB
1139	1	Delta Air Lines	N721DA
1140	200	Gulf Air	G-BDCZ A40-TZ stored Dec94 Cambridge, UK
1141	1	Delta Air Lines	N334EA N788DA
1142	1	Delta Air Lines	N335EA N789DL
1143	1	Delta Air Lines	N336EA N790DL
1144	200	Saudia	N48354 HZ-AHD
1145	50	Air Ops of Europe	G-BEAL SE-DPM
1146	50	British Airways	G-BEAM stored May91 Mojave, CA
1147	1	Delta Air Lines	N722DA
1148	200	Saudia	HZ-AHG

LOCKHEED L-1011 TRISTAR

C/n	Series	Last known Operator/Owner	Previous Identities/fate (where known)
1149	200	Saudia	HZ-AHH
1150	1	Delta Air Lines	N723DA
1151	200	Delta Air Lines	N724DA
1152	1	Avtek	N337EA D-AERP stored Apr95 Tucson, AZ
1153	1	American Trans Air	N338EA D-AERM N183AT
1154	1	(Boeing Equipment Holding Co)	JA8520 (C-FRIX) b/u Aug94 Marana, AZ
1155	1	Intl Air Leases	JA8521
1156	1	A L Aircraft 4 Corp	JA8522 N309GB
1157	KC.1	Royal Air Force	N48354 G-BFCA ZD948
1158	200F	Millon Air	N339EA D-AERN N851MA
1159	K.1	Royal Air Force	G-BFCB ZD949
1160	200	Saudia	HZ-AHI
1161	200	Saudia	HZ-AHJ
1162	1	Delta Air Lines	N725DA
1163	1	(Delta Air Lines)	N726DA w/o 02Aug85 Dallas-Ft Worth, TX
1164	K.1	Royal Air Force	G-BFCC ZD950
1165	K.1	Royal Air Force	G-BFCD ZD951 G-BFCD ZD951
1166	500	Delta Air Lines	N751DA
1167	1	Delta Air Lines	N727DA
1168	KC.1	Royal Air Force	G-BFCE ZD952 G-BFCE ZD952
1169	200	(Saudia)	HZ-AHK dbf 19Aug80 Riyadh, Saudi Arabia
1170	200	Saudia	HZ-AHL
1171	200	Saudia	HZ-AHM
1172	500	Delta Air Lines	N752DA
1173	1	Delta Air Lines	N728DA
1174	K.1	Royal Air Force	G-BFCF ZD953
1175	200	Saudia	HZ-AHN
1176	500	Delta Air Lines	N64911 N4005X N501PA N759DA
1177	K.2	Royal Air Force	N4003G N503PA ZE706
1178	200F	American International	G-BGBB 4R-ULN G-BGBB 4R-ULN G-BGBB 4R-ULN G-BGBB N105CK
1179	500	BWIA International	9Y-TGJ
1180	1	Delta Air Lines	N729DA
1181	500	Delta Air Lines	N504PA N754DL
1182	200	British Airways	G-BGBC stored Jan92 Mojave, CA
1183	500	LTU	D-AERT
1184	500	Delta Air Lines	N505PA N755DL
1185	500	Delta Air Lines	N507PA N756DR
1186	K.2	Royal Air Force	N508PA ZE704
1187	200	Saudia	HZ-AHO
1188	K.2	Royal Air Force	N509PA ZE705
1189	500	Delta Air Lines	N753DA
1190	200	Saudia	HZ-AHP
1191	500	BWIA International	9Y-TGN
1192	200	Saudia	HZ-AHQ
1193	200F	American International	G-BHBL N104CK
1194	500	Delta Air Lines	N4003G N510PA N760DH
1195	500	Jetstream Holding	N511PA D-AERV VR-CFG
1196	500	LTU	D-AERL
1197	500	Delta Air Lines	N512PA N763DL
1198	200F	American International	G-BHBM N102CK
1199	1	Delta Air Lines	N730DA
1200	1	Delta Air Lines	N1731D
1201	200	Intl Air Leases	(A40-TA) N92TA A40-TA
1202	500	Delta Air Lines	C-GAGF N764DA
1203	200	Intl Air Leases	(A40-TB) N92TB A40-TB
1204	200	British Airways	G-BHBN stored Jun91 Mojave, CA
1205	200	British Airways	G-BHBO stored Jun91 Mojave, CA
1206	500	Delta Air Lines	C-GAGG N765DA
1207	500	Delta Air Lines	C-GAGH N766DA
1208	500	Delta Air Lines	N513PA N761DA
1209	500	Delta Air Lines	C-GAGI N767DA
1210	500	Delta Air Lines	N514PA N762DA
1211	200F	American International	G-BHBP 4R-ULM G-BHBP N106CK
1212	200F	American International	G-BHBR N103CK
1213	1	Delta Air Lines	N1732D
1214	200	Saudia	HZ-AHR
1215	100	Air Ops of Sweden	N31032 SE-DSD
1216	500	Delta Air Lines	C-GAGJ N768DL
1217	500	Royal Jordanian A/L	JY-AGA
1218	500	Delta Air Lines	C-GAGK N769DL
1219	500	Air Lanka	JY-AGB
1220	500	Royal Jordanian A/L	JY-AGC
1221	100	Royal Airlines	N31033 TF-ABM N357AT C-GRYU
1222	500	BWIA International	9Y-THA
1223	200	Intl Air Leases	A40-TT
1224	1	Delta Air Lines	N733DS
1225	1	Delta Air Lines	N1734D
1226	1	Delta Air Lines	N735D
1227	250	Delta Air Lines	N736DY

LOCKHEED L-1011 TRISTAR

C/n	Series	Last known Operator/Owner	Previous Identities/fate (where known)					
1228	250	Delta Air Lines	N737D					
1229	500	Royal Jordanian A/L	JY-AGD					
1230	100	American Trans Air	N8034T	N194AT				
1231	100	GECC	N7035T	SE-DPR	stored Feb93 Tucson, AZ			
1232	100	Trans World Airlines	N7036T					
1233	500	BWIA International	(9Y-THB)	N3140D				
1234	250	Delta Air Lines	N1738D					
1235	500	Air Lanka	4R-ULA	G-BLUS	4R-ULA			
1236	500	Air Lanka	4R-ULB	G-BLUT	4R-ULB			
1237	250	Delta Air Lines	N1739D					
1238	500	Royal Jordanian A/L	JY-AGE					
1239	500	BWIA International	CS-TEA					
1240	500	Air India	CS-TEB	V2-LEO				
1241	500	TAAG Angola Airlines	CS-TEC					
1242	500	Air Portugal	CS-TED					
1243	500	Air Portugal	CS-TEE					
1244	250	Delta Air Lines	N740DA					
1245	250	Delta Air Lines	N741DA					
1246	500	Air India	N48354	JY-AGI	CS-TEF	V2-LEJ		
1247	500	Jordanian Royal Flight	N64854	JY-HKJ				
1248	500	Air India	N64959	JY-AGJ	CS-TEG	V2-LEK		
1249	500	Govt of Saudi Arabia	N64996	JY-AGH	VR-CZZ	G-52-19	VR-CZZ	HZ-HM6
1250	500	Govt of Saudi Arabia	(7T-VRA)	N64911	N5129K	HZ-HE5	HZ-HM5	

Production complete

McDONNELL-DOUGLAS MD-11

C/n	Series	Line No	Last known Operator/Owner	Previous Identities/fate (where known)
48401	F	447	Federal Express	N111MD prototype; ff 10Jan90 N601FE N111MD N601FE
48402	F	448	Federal Express	N211MD N602FE
48404		523	VARIG	PP-VPJ
48405		524	VARIG	PP-VPK
48406		547	VARIG	N9166X PP-VPL
48407		456	Korean Air	HL7371
48408	F	457	Korean Air	HL7372
48409	F	490	Korean Air	HL7373
48410		495	Korean Air	HL7374
48411		453	VASP	(G-MDII) N514MD N891DL PP-SPD
48412		454	VASP	(G-OLAN) N892DL PP-SPE
48413		488	VASP	PP-SOW
48414		491	VASP	PP-SOZ
48415		576	EVA Airways	N103EV
48416		466	Thai Airways International	HS-TMD
48417		467	Thai Airways International	HS-TME
48418		501	Thai Airways International	HS-TMF
48419		450	American Airlines	N411MD N1750B
48420		451	American Airlines	N511MD N1751A
48421		452	American Airlines	N510MD N1752K
48426	C	468	Alitalia	N9020Z I-DUPA
48427	C	471	Alitalia	N9020Z I-DUPE
48428	C	474	Alitalia	N9020U I-DUPI
48429	C	500	Alitalia	I-DUPO
48430	C	508	Alitalia	I-DUPU
48431	C	534	Alitalia	I-DUPB
48434		476	VARIG	PP-VOP
48435		478	VARIG	PP-VOQ
48436		483	American Airlines	N1768D
48437		506	World Airways	N272WA
48438			not built	
48439		554	VARIG	N6200N PP-VPM
48440			not built	
48441			not built	
48442			not built	
48443		458	Swissair	HB-IWA
48444		459	Swissair	HB-IWB
48445		460	Swissair	HB-IWC
48446		463	Swissair	HB-IWD
48447		464	Swissair	HB-IWE
48448		465	Swissair	HB-IWF
48449		455	Finnair	OH-LGA
48450		479	Finnair	OH-LGB
48451		505	Thai Airways International	HS-TMG
48452		472	Swissair	HB-IWG
48453		473	Swissair	HB-IWH
48454		477	Swissair	HB-IWI
48455		487	Swissair	HB-IWK
48456		494	Swissair	HB-IWL
48457		498	Swissair	HB-IWM
48458		449	World Airways	N311MD N489GX N280WA
48459	F	470	Federal Express	N603FE
48460	F	497	Federal Express	N604FE
48461	F	475	China Eastern Airlines	B-2170
48462			not built	
48463			not built	
48464			not built	
48465			not built	
48466			not built	
48467			not built	
48468		518	Mandarin Airlines	B-150
48469		519	Mandarin Airlines	B-151
48470		546	Mandarin Airlines	B-152
48471		558	Mandarin Airlines	B-153
48472		480	Delta Air Lines	N801DE
48473		481	Delta Air Lines	N802DE
48474		485	Delta Air Lines	N30075 N803DE
48475		489	Delta Air Lines	N804DE
48476		510	Delta Air Lines	N805DE
48477		511	Delta Air Lines	N806DE
48478		514	Delta Air Lines	N807DE
48479		536	Delta Air Lines	N808DE
48480		538	Delta Air Lines	N809DE
48481		482	American Airlines	(F-GKMR) N1759
48482			not built	(F-GKMQ)
48483			not built	(YU-AMG)
48484		484	LTU	D-AERB
48485		502	LTU	D-AERW
48486		509	LTU	D-AERX

McDONNELL-DOUGLAS MD-11

C/n	Series	Line No	Last known Operator/Owner	Previous Identities/fate (where known)			
48487		469	American Airlines	N1753			
48488			not built				
48489		492	American Airlines	N1754			
48490		499	American Airlines	N1755			
48491		503	American Airlines	N1756			
48492			not built				
48493			not built				
48494	C		not built				
48495		461	China Eastern Airlines	B-2171			
48496		496	China Eastern Airlines	B-2172			
48497		512	China Eastern Airlines	B-2173			
48498		522	China Eastern Airlines	B-2174			
48499		486	Garuda Indonesia	EI-CDI			
48500		493	Garuda Indonesia	EI-CDJ	PK-GIH	EI-CDJ	PK-GIH
48501		513	Garuda Indonesia	EI-CDK			
48502		520	Garuda Indonesia	(EI-CDL)	N9076Y	PK-GIG	
48503		528	Garuda Indonesia	(EI-CDM)	N9020U	PK-GII	
48504		548	Garuda Indonesia	(EI-CDN)	N9020Q	PK-GIJ	
48505		462	American Airlines	N1757A			
48506			not built				
48507			not built				
48508			not built				
48509			not built				
48510			not built				
48511			not built				
48512		529	Finnair	OH-LGC			
48513		564	Finnair	OH-LGD			
48514	F	515	Federal Express	N605FE			
48515			not built				
48516			not built				
48517			not built				
48518		525	Gauda Indonesia	N271WA			
48519		539	Gauda Indonesia	N273WA			
48520		541	China Eastern Airlines	B-2175			
48521	F		not built				
48522	CF		not built				
48523		521	Korean Air	HL7375			
48524			not built				
48525			not built				
48526			not built	(F-GKMP)			
48527		504	American Airlines	N1758B			
48528	F	507	Federal Express	(N1759)	N614FE		
48529			not built				
48530			not built				
48531			not built				
48532		532	Saudi Arabian Govt	N9093P	stored Sep93 Mojave, CA		
48533		544	Saudi Arabian Govt	N9020Z	stored Dec93 Mojave, CA		
48534			not built				
48535			not built				
48536			not built				
48537			not built				
48538		533	LTU	D-AERZ			
48539		571	Swissair	HB-IWN			
48540			Swissair	HB-IWO			
48541			Swissair	HB-IWP			
48542		570	EVA Airways	B-16101			
48543		572	EVA Airways	B-16102			
48544	F	580	EVA Airways	(B-16105)	N105EV		
48545	F	587	EVA Airways	B-16106			
48546	F	589	EVA Airways	(B-16107)	(N107EV)	B-16107	
48547	F	516	Federal Express	N607FE			
48548	F	517	Federal Express	N608FE			
48549	F	545	Federal Express	N609FE			
48550		526	American Airlines	N1760A			
48551		527	American Airlines	N1761R			
48552		530	American Airlines	N1762B			
48553		531	American Airlines	N1763			
48554		535	American Airlines	N1764B			
48555		557	KLM	N6202D	PH-KCA		
48556		561	KLM	PH-KCB			
48557		569	KLM	PH-KCC			
48558		573	KLM	PH-KCD			
48559		575	KLM	N91566	PH-KCE		
48560		578	KLM	PH-KCF			
48561		585	KLM	PH-KCG			
48562		591	KLM	PH-KCH			
48563		593	VASP	PH-KCI	PP-SPM		
48564		612	KLM	PH-KCK			
48565		542	Delta Air Lines	N810DE			
48566		543	Delta Air Lines	N811DE			
48567			not built				

McDONNELL-DOUGLAS MD-11

C/n	Series	Line No	Last known Operator/Owner	Previous Identities/fate (where known)		
48568			Garuda Indonesia			
48569			Garuda Indonesia			
48570			Garuda Indonesia			
48571		552	Japan Air Lines	N91566	JA8580	
48572		556	Japan Air Lines	N90187	JA8581	
48573		559	Japan Air Lines	JA8582		
48574		566	Japan Air Lines	JA8583		
48575		569	Japan Air Lines	JA8584		
48576		574	Japan Air Lines	JA8585		
48577		583	Japan Air Lines	JA8586		
48578		588	Japan Air Lines	JA8587		
48579			Japan Air Lines	JA8588		
48580			not built	(JA8589)		
48581		565	Alitalia	I-DUPC		
48582			not built	(YU-AMH)		
48583			not built			
48584			not built			
48585			not built			
48586			not built			
48587			not built			
48588			not built			
48589			not built			
48590			not built			
48591			not built			
48592			not built			
48593			not built			
48594			not built			
48595			not built			
48596		537	American Airlines	N1765B		
48597		540	American Airlines	N1766A		
48598		550	American Airlines	N1767A		
48599			not built	(N1768D)		
48600		560	Delta Air Lines	N90178	N812DE	stored Yuma, AZ
48601		562	Delta Air Lines	N6202S	N813DE	
48602	F	549	Federal Express	N606FE		
48603	F	551	Federal Express	N610FE		
48604	F	553	Federal Express	N611FE		
48605	F	555	Federal Express	N612FE		
48606	F		Federal Express	(N613FE)		
48607			not built	(YU-AME)		
48608			not built	(YU-AMF)		
48609			not built	(YU-AMG)		
48611			not built	(N1769B)		
48612			not built			
48613			not built			
48614			not built			
48615			not built			
48616	CF	577	Martinair	N90187	PH-MCP	
48617	F	581	Martinair	PH-MCR		
48618	F	584	Martinair	PH-MCS		
48619			McDonnell-Douglas Finance			
48620			McDonnell-Douglas Finance			
48621			not built			
48622	F		Federal Express	(N615FE)		
48623			Delta Air Lines	N814DE		
48624			Delta Air Lines	N815DE		
48625			not built	(F-GKMR)		
48626	F		Federal Express			
48627	F		Federal Express			
48629	F	586	Martinair	PH-MCT		
48630		567	Alitalia	I-DUPD		
48631	CF	579	Malaysian Airline System	N275WA		
48632	CF	582	Malaysian Airline System	N276WA		
48633	F	563	Malaysian Airline System	N274WA		
48742			not built	(F-GKMO)		
48743		590	World Airways	N6203D	N277WA	
48744		592	VASP	PP-SPK		
48745		596	VASP	N90187	PP-SPL	
48746		597		N9020Q		
48747	F	594	Federal Express	N616FE		
48748	F	595	Federal Express	N617FE		
48749	F		Federal Express	N613FE*		
48750	F		Martinair	PH-MCU		
48751			Delta Air Lines	N815DE		
48753			not built			
48754	F		Federal Express	N618FE*		
48755	F		not built			
48756	F		not built			
48757	F		not built			
48758			not built			
48759			not built			

McDONNELL-DOUGLAS MD-11

C/n	Series	Line No	Last known Operator/Owner	Previous Identities/fate (where known)
48760			not built	
48761			not built	
48762			not built	
48763			not built	
48764			not built	
48765			not built	
48766		600		N6203U
48767	F		Federal Express	N615FE*
48768		601		N9134D
48770	F		not built	
48773	F		not built	
48774			Japan Air Lines	JA8589
48775	F		not built	
48776	F		not built	
48777	F		not built	

McDONNELL-DOUGLAS MD-80 Series/MD-90

Development of the Douglas DC-9 beyond the DC-9-51 began with the McDonnell-Douglas DC-9-81, DC-9-82 and DC-9-83, marketed as the MD-81, MD-82 and MD-83. For subsequent models use of the DC-9 prefix was discontinued, and models were known as the MD-87, MD-88 and most recently MD-90, variants of the last being described as MD-90-30 etc. Aircraft assembled by Shanghai Aviation have a second line number-c/n, which is shown alongside the McDonnell-Douglas line number.

C/n	Series	Line No	Last known Operator/Owner	Previous Identities/fate (where known)
48000	81	909	Intl A/L Support Group	(HB-INA) N980DC prototype; ff 18Oct79 N560MD stored May93 Sherman, TX; for spares use still marked N980DC
48001	81	917	(McDonnell-Douglas)	(HB-INB) N1002G dbr 19Jun80 Yuma, AZ
48002	81	938	Swissair	HB-INC
48003	81	944	Swissair	HB-IND
48004	81	950	Swissair	HB-INE
48005	81	957	Swissair	HB-INF
48006	81	966	Scandinavian A/L System	HB-ING OY-KIG
48007	81	971	Scandinavian A/L System	HB-INH OY-KIH
48008	81	981	Scandinavian A/L System	HB-INI OY-KII
48009	81	985	Scandinavian A/L System	HB-INK SE-DMZ
48010	81	992	Scandinavian A/L System	HB-INL SE-DMY
48011	81	994	Swissair	HB-INM
48012	81	997	Swissair	HB-INN
48013	81	1000	Swissair	HB-INO
48014	81	1013	Swissair	HB-INP
48015	81	924	Austrian Airlines	N13627 N1002W OE-LDP
48016	81	941	Austrian Airlines	OE-LDR
48017	81	958	Austrian Airlines	OE-LDS
48018	81	995	Austrian Airlines	OE-LDT
48019	81	1001	Austrian Airlines	OE-LDU
48020	81	1045	Austrian Airlines	OE-LDV
48021	82	1078	Austrian Airlines	OE-LDX
48022	82	1079	Continental Airlines	N1004W PH-MCD OE-LYM PH-MCD N80UA EC-495 EC-EYP N80UA EC-793 EC-FGQ N80UA N14871
48023			not built	
48024	81	948	Austral Lineas Aereas	N10022
48025	81	952	Austral Lineas Aereas	N10027 LV-WFN
48026	81	960	USAir	(N10046) N10028 N826US
48027	81	973	Continental Airlines	N475AC N37882
48028	81	979	USAir	N476AC N950PS N828US
48029	81	953	Japan Air System	JA8458
48030	81	962	Japan Air System	JA8459
48031	81	969	Japan Air System	JA8460
48032	81	978	Japan Air System	JA8461
48033	81	988	Japan Air System	JA8462
48034	81	946	USAir	N924PS N800US
48035	81	955	USAir	N925PS N803US
48036	81	963	USAir	N926PS N802US
48037	81	965	USAir	N927PS N801US
48038	81	1002	USAir	N928PS N806US
48039	81	1003	USAir	N931PS N807US
48040	81	1006	USAir	N932PS N808US
48041	81	1008	USAir	N933PS N809US
48042	81	1009	USAir	N934PS N810US
48043	81	1010	USAir	N935PS N811US
48044	81	967	Continental Airlines	N809HA N14880
48045	81	970	Continental Airlines	N819HA N13881
48046	81	977	Valujet Airlines	YU-AJZ SL-ABE S5-ABE N801VV
48047	82	998	(Inex Adria Airways)	YU-ANA w/o 01Dec81 nr Ajaccio-Campo dell'Oro, Corsica
48048	82	1005	Skybus	YU-ANB PH-MBY YU-ANB SL-ABA S5-ABA SX-BBV N802VV
48049	81	983	USAir	N10029 N827US
48050	81	989	(Austral Lineas Aereas)	N1003G w/o 12Jun88 Posadas, Argentina; cancelled Jul93
48051	81	975	Sun Jet International	N829HA N920PS N829HA N817SJ
48052	81	974	USAir	N928PS N804US
48053	81	986	USAir	N929PS N805US
48054	82	996	Northwest Airlines	(N302RP) N301RC
48055	82	1007	Northwest Airlines	(N303RP) N302RC
48056	82	1012	Continental Airlines	(N304RP) N304RC N10034 N930MC N83870
48057	82	1023	Northwest Airlines	(N305RP) N306RC N10035 N931MC
48058	81	991	Sun Jet International	N839HA N818SJ
48059	81	1047	Austrian Airlines	OE-LDW
48060	82		not built	
48061	82		not built	
48062	82	1015	Continental Airlines	N477AC
48063	82	1020	Continental Airlines	N478AC
48064	82		not built	
48065	82		not built	
48066	82	1019	Continental Airlines	N479AC N813NY N16813
48067	82	1028	Aeromexico	(XA-AMI) N1003X
48068	82	1031	Aeromexico	(XA-AMJ) N1003Y XA-SFK N1003Y
48069	82	1032	Aeromexico	(XA-AMK) N1003Z XA-SFL
48070	81	999	Japan Air System	JA8468

McDONNELL-DOUGLAS MD-80 Series/MD-90

C/n	Series	Line No	Last known Operator/Owner	Previous Identities/fate (where known)					
48071	81	1003	Japan Air System	JA8469					
48072	81	1011	Japan Air System	JA8470					
48073	81	1018	Continental Airlines	N849HA	N16883				
48074	81	1026	Continental Airlines	N859HA	N16884				
48075			not built						
48076			not built						
48077	82		not built						
48078	82		not built						
48079	82	1016	Alaska Airlines	N779JA	N956AS				
48080	82	1022	Alaska Airlines	N778JA	N955AS				
48081	82		not built						
48082	82		not built						
48083	82	1043	Aeromexico	(XA-AML)	N10033				
48084	82		not built						
48085	82		not built						
48086	82	1029	Northwest Airlines	(N306RP)	N307RC				
48087	82	1035	Skybus	(N307RP)	(N308RC)	N19B	YU-ANC	SL-ABB	S5-ABB
				SX-BBW	N803VV				
48088	82	1037	Northwest Airlines	(N309RC)	N1004S	N309RC			
48089	82	1038	Northwest Airlines	(N311RC)	N1004D	N311RC			
48090	82	1040	(Northwest Airlines)	(N312RC)	N1004F	N312RC	w/o 16Aug87 Detroit, MI		
48091	82	1041	Northwest Airlines	(N313RC)	N1004G	N313RC			
48092	81	1034	USAir	N936PS	N812US				
48093	81	1049	USAir	N937PS	N813US				
48094	81	1053	USAir	N938PS	N814US				
48095	82	1055	USAir	N940PS	N815US				
48096	82	1057	USAir	N941PS	N816US				
48097	82	1059	USAir	N942PS	N817US				
48098	82	1060	USAir	N943PS	N818US				
48099	82	1067	USAir	N939PS	N819US				
49100	81	1025	Swissair	HB-INA					
49101	82	1051	Swissair	HB-INB					
49102	82	1076	Continental Airlines	N1004U	N9805F	N13891			
49103	82	1083	Alaska Airlines	(YV-158C)	N1005A	N782JA	N967AS		
49104	82	1085	Alaska Airlines	(YV-159C)	N1005B	N783JA	N966AS		
49105			not built						
49106			not built						
49107			not built						
49108			not built						
49109			not built						
49110	82	1062	Northwest Airlines	N1004L	N314RC				
49111	82	1064	Alaska Airlines	N1004N	N781JA	N951AS			
49112	82	1068	Continental Airlines	N480AC	N814NY	N14814			
49113	82	1069	Continental Airlines	N481AC	N815NY	N16815			
49114	82	1066	Continental Airlines	N10037	N9804F	N14890			
49115	82	1135	Austrian Airlines	OE-LDY					
49116	82	1061	Continental Airlines	N9801F	N16887				
49117	82	1063	Continental Airlines	N9802F	N35888				
49118	82	1065	Continental Airlines	N9803F	N14889				
49119	82	1070	USAir	(N869HA)	N944PS	N820US			
49120	82	1071	Continental Airlines	N932MC	N83872				
49121	82	1072	Continental Airlines	N933MC	N83873				
49122	82	1073	Continental Airlines	N934MC	N92874				
49123	82	1075	ALM	PJ-SEF					
49124	82	1077	ALM	PJ-SEG					
49125	82	1074	Continental Airlines	N935MC	N93875				
49126	82	1080	Alaska Airlines	N482AC	N780JA	N957AS			
49127	82	1082	Continental Airlines	N483AC	N801NY	N10801			
49138	82	1090	USAir	N945PS	N821US				
49139	82	1091	USAir	N946PS	N822US				
49140	82	1092	China Eastern Airlines	(N947PS)	N1004S	B-2101			
49141	82	1093	China Eastern Airlines	(N948PS)	N10046	B-2102			
49142	82	1094	USAir	N1005G	N947PS	N823US			
49143	82	1095	USAir	N1005J	N948PS	N824US			
49144	82	1096	Target Airways	PH-MBZ	EC-994	EC-FMO	N500TR		
49145	82	1097	American Airlines	N203AA					
49149	82	1086	Aeromexico	N1005V	XA-AMO	PP-CJM	N505MD	XA-SFM	N505MD
49150	82	1087	Finnair	(XA-AMP)	OH-LMN				
49151	82	1088	Finnair	(XA-AMQ)	OH-LMO				
49152	82	1089	Finnair	(XA-AMS)	OH-LMP				
49153	82	1101	Trans World Airlines	N902TW					
49154	82	1102	Trans World Airlines	N903TW					
49155	82	1103	American Airlines	N205AA					
49156	82	1104	Trans World Airlines	N904TW					
49157	82	1105	Trans World Airlines	N905TW					
49158	82	1106	American Airlines	N207AA					
49159	82	1107	American Airlines	N208AA					
49160	82	1108	Trans World Airlines	N906TW					
49161	82	1109	American Airlines	N210AA					
49162	82	1110	American Airlines	N214AA					
49163	82	1111	American Airlines	N215AA					

McDONNELL-DOUGLAS MD-80 Series/MD-90

C/n	Series	Line No	Last known Operator/Owner	Previous Identities/fate (where known)	
49164	82	1182	Austrian Airlines	OE-LDZ	
49165	82	1117	Trans World Airlines	N907TW	
49166	82	1098	Trans World Airlines	N901TW	
49167	82	1099	American Airlines	N216AA	
49168	82	1100	American Airlines	N218AA	
49169	82	1118	Trans World Airlines	N908TW	
49170	82	1119	Trans World Airlines	N909TW	
49171	82	1112	American Airlines	N219AA	
49172	82	1113	American Airlines	N221AA	
49173	82	1114	American Airlines	N223AA	
49174	82	1115	American Airlines	N224AA	
49175	82	1116	American Airlines	N225AA	
49176	82	1120	American Airlines	N226AA	
49177	82	1121	American Airlines	N227AA	
49178	82	1122	American Airlines	N228AA	
49179	82	1123	American Airlines	N232AA	
49180	82	1124	American Airlines	N233AA	
49181	82	1125	American Airlines	N234AA	
49182	82	1128	Trans World Airlines	N911TW	
49183	82	1129	Trans World Airlines	N912TW	
49184	82	1131	Trans World Airlines	N913TW	
49185	82	1132	Trans World Airlines	N914TW	
49186	82	1133	Trans World Airlines	N915TW	
49187	82	1134	Trans World Airlines	N916TW	
49188	82	1172	Aeromexico	XA-AMO	N501AM
49189	82	1173	Aeromexico	XA-AMP	
49190	82	1180	Aeromexico	XA-AMQ	
49191	82		not built	(XA-AMR)	
49192	82	1126	Alitalia	I-DAWA	
49193	82	1127	Alitalia	N13627	I-DAWE
49194	82	1130	Alitalia	I-DAWI	
49195	82	1136	Alitalia	I-DAWO	
49196	82	1137	Alitalia	I-DAWU	
49197	82	1138	Alitalia	I-DAWB	
49198	82	1142	Alitalia	I-DAWC	
49199	82	1143	Alitalia	I-DAWD	
49200	82	1147	Alitalia	I-DAWF	
49201	82	1148	Alitalia	I-DAWG	
49202	82	1170	Alitalia	I-DAWH	
49203	82	1174	Alitalia	I-DAWJ	
49204	82	1179	Alitalia	I-DAWL	
49205	82	1184	Alitalia	I-DAWM	
49206	82	1188	Alitalia	I-DAWP	
49207	82	1189	Alitalia	I-DAWQ	
49208	82	1190	Alitalia	I-DAWR	
49209	82	1191	Alitalia	I-DAWS	
49210	82	1192	Alitalia	I-DAWT	
49211	82	1202	Alitalia	I-DAWV	
49212	82	1233	Alitalia	I-DAWW	
49213	82	1243	Alitalia	I-DAWY	
49214	82	1245	Alitalia	I-DAWZ	
49215	82	1253	Alitalia	I-DAVA	
49216	82	1262	Alitalia	I-DAVB	
49217	82	1268	Alitalia	I-DAVC	
49218	82	1274	Alitalia	I-DAVD	
49219	82	1310	Alitalia	I-DAVF	
49220	82	1319	Alitalia	I-DAVG	
49221	82	1330	Alitalia	I-DAVH	
49222	82	1139	Continental Airlines	N802NY	N16802
49229	82	1140	Continental Airlines	N803NY	N69803
49230	82	1141	Trans World Airlines	N950U	
49231	82	1177	Alaska Airlines	N930AS	
49232	82	1178	Alaska Airlines	N931AS	
49233	82	1203	Alaska Airlines	N932AS	
49234	82	1204	Alaska Airlines	N933AS	
49235	83	1234	Alaska Airlines	N934AS	
49236	83	1235	Alaska Airlines	N935AS	
49237	82	1144	USAir	N949PS	N825US
49238	82		not built		
49239	82		not built		
49240	82		not built		
49241	82		not built		
49242	82		not built		
49243	90		McDonnell-Douglas		
49244	90		McDonnell-Douglas		
49245	82	1145	Trans World Airlines	N951U	
49246	82	1146	Continental Airlines	N804NY	N16804
49247	82	1151	Meridiana	HB-IKK	I-SMEL
49248	82	1152	Meridiana	HB-IKL	I-SMEM
49249	82	1149	Continental Airlines	N805NY	N33805
49250	82	1186	Continental Airlines	N812NY	N17812

McDONNELL-DOUGLAS MD-80 Series/MD-90

C/n	Series	Line No	Last known Operator/Owner	Previous Identities/fate (where known)	
49251	82	1154	American Airlines	N236AA	
49252	83	1169	Finnair	N19B	OH-LMS
49253	82	1155	American Airlines	N237AA	
49254	82	1156	American Airlines	N241AA	
49255	82	1157	American Airlines	N242AA	
49256	82	1158	American Airlines	N244AA	
49257	82	1160	American Airlines	N245AA	
49258	82	1161	American Airlines	N246AA	
49259	82	1162	American Airlines	N248AA	
49260	82	1150	Continental Airlines	N806NY	N16806
49261	82	1153	Continental Airlines	N807NY	N16807
49262	82	1159	Continental Airlines	N808NY	N16808
49263	82	1163	Continental Airlines	N809NY	
49264	82	1171	Continental Airlines	N810NY	N14810
49265	82	1185	Continental Airlines	N811NY	N12811
49266	82	1238	Trans World Airlines	N952U	
49267	82	1239	Trans World Airlines	N953U	
49268			not built		
49269	82	1164	American Airlines	N249AA	
49270	82	1165	American Airlines	N251AA	
49271	82	1166	American Airlines	N274AA	
49272	82	1167	American Airlines	N275AA	
49273	82	1168	American Airlines	N276AA	
49274			not built		
49275			not built		
49276	82		not built		
49277	81	1181	Crossair	HB-INR	
49278	82	1183	Austrian Airlines	OE-LMA	
49279	82	1230	Austrian Airlines	OE-LMB	
49280	81	1194	Japan Air System	JA8496	
49281	81	1200	Japan Air System	JA8497	
49282	81	1282	Japan Air System	N62025	JA8498
49283	81	1299	Japan Air System	JA8499	
49284	83	1209	Finnair	OH-LMR	
49285	83		not built		
49286	82	1175	American Airlines	N253AA	
49287	82	1176	American Airlines	N255AA	
49288	82	1187	American Airlines	N258AA	
49289	82	1193	American Airlines	N259AA	
49290	82	1195	American Airlines	N262AA	
49291	82	1210	American Airlines	N266AA	
49292	82	1211	American Airlines	N269AA	
49293	82	1212	American Airlines	N271AA	
49294	82	1213	American Airlines	N278AA	
49295	82	1214	American Airlines	N279AA	
49296	82	1215	American Airlines	N283AA	
49297	82	1216	American Airlines	N285AA	
49298	82	1217	American Airlines	N286AA	
49299	82	1218	American Airlines	N287AA	
49300	82	1219	American Airlines	N288AA	
49301	82	1220	American Airlines	N289AA	
49302	82	1221	American Airlines	N290AA	
49303	82	1222	American Airlines	N291AA	
49304	82	1223	American Airlines	N292AA	
49305	82	1226	American Airlines	N293AA	
49306	82	1227	American Airlines	N294AA	
49307	82	1228	American Airlines	N295AA	
49308	82	1229	American Airlines	N296AA	
49309	82	1246	American Airlines	N297AA	
49310	82	1247	American Airlines	N298AA	
49311	82	1248	American Airlines	N400AA	
49312	82	1249	American Airlines	N70401	
49313	82	1255	American Airlines	N402A	
49314	82	1256	American Airlines	N403A	
49315	82	1257	American Airlines	N70404	
49316	82	1258	American Airlines	N405A	
49317	82	1259	American Airlines	N406A	
49318	82	1265	American Airlines	N407AA	
49319	82	1266	American Airlines	N408AA	
49320	82	1267	American Airlines	N409AA	
49321	82	1273	American Airlines	N410AA	
49322	82	1280	American Airlines	N411AA	
49323	82	1281	American Airlines	N412AA	
49324	82	1289	American Airlines	N413AA	
49325	82	1290	American Airlines	N33414	
49326	82	1295	American Airlines	N415AA	
49327	82	1296	American Airlines	N416AA	
49328	82	1301	American Airlines	N417AA	
49329	82	1302	American Airlines	N418AA	
49331	82	1306	American Airlines	N419AA	
49332	82	1307	American Airlines	N420AA	

McDONNELL-DOUGLAS MD-80 Series/MD-90

C/n	Series	Line No	Last known Operator/Owner	Previous Identities/fate (where known)					
49333	82	1311	American Airlines	N77421					
49334	82	1312	American Airlines	N422AA					
49335	82	1320	American Airlines	N423AA					
49336	82	1321	American Airlines	N424AA					
49337	82	1325	American Airlines	N70425					
49338	82	1327	American Airlines	N426AA					
49339	82	1328	American Airlines	N427AA					
49340	82	1329	American Airlines	N428AA					
49341	82	1336	American Airlines	N429AA					
49342	82	1337	American Airlines	N430AA					
49343	82	1339	American Airlines	N431AA					
49344	83	1370	American Airlines	N562AA					
49345	83	1371	American Airlines	N563AA					
49346	83	1372	American Airlines	N564AA					
49347	83	1373	American Airlines	N565AA					
49348	83	1374	American Airlines	N566AA					
49349	83	1375	American Airlines	N568AA					
49350	82	1376	American Airlines	N432AA					
49351	83	1385	American Airlines	N569AA					
49352	83	1386	American Airlines	N570AA					
49353	83	1387	American Airlines	N571AA					
49355	82	1224	(China Eastern Airlines)	N1005S	B-2103	dbr 26Oct93 Fuzhou, China			
49356	81	1250	Swissair	HB-INS					
49357	81	1251	Swissair	HB-INT					
49358	81	1294	Swissair	HB-INU					
49359	81	1349	Crossair	HB-INV					
49363	83	1275	Alaska Airlines	N936AS					
49364	82	1276	Alaska Airlines	N937AS					
49365	83	1277	Alaska Airlines	N938AS					
49366	82	1196	Trans World Airlines	N917TW					
49367	82	1197	Trans World Airlines	N918TW					
49368	82	1198	Trans World Airlines	N919TW					
49369	82	1199	Trans World Airlines	N920TW					
49370	82	1206	Continental Airlines	(N784JA)	N816NY	N14816			
49371	82	1207	Continental Airlines	(N785JA)	N817NY	N33817			
49372	82	1252	Austrian Airlines	OE-LMC					
49373	82	1201	Korean Air	N1004Y	HL7272				
49374	82	1208	Korean Air	N1005N	HL7273				
49375	82		not built	(N938MC)					
49376	82		not built	(N939MC)					
49377	82		not built	(N940MC)					
49378	82		not built	(N941MC)					
49379	82	1205	Aero Lloyd	YU-ANG	SL-ABC	S5-ABC	D-ALLS		
49380	82	1225	Scandinavian A/L System	N19B	OY-KGT	N845RA	OY-KGT		
49381	81	1231	Scandinavian A/L System	OY-KGZ					
49382	82	1232	Scandinavian A/L System	LN-RLE					
49383	82	1236	Scandinavian A/L System	LN-RLF	VH-LNJ	LN-RLF			
49384	82	1237	Scandinavian A/L System	SE-DFS					
49385	82	1244	Scandinavian A/L System	SE-DFT					
49386	82	1287	Alaska Airlines	N784JA	N953AS				
49387	82	1288	Alaska Airlines	N785JA	N954AS				
49388	87	1326	McDonnell-Douglas	N87MD					
49389	87	1333	Transwede	N287MD	SE-DHG	SX-BAW	SE-DHG		
49390	83	1269	BWIA International	9Y-THN					
49391	83	1270	Continental Airlines	EI-BTA	N16892				
49392	83	1272	Continental Airlines	EI-BTB	N16893				
49393	83	1279	Continental Airlines	EI-BTC	N16894				
49394	83	1285	Continental Airlines	EI-BTD	N16895				
49395	83	1286	Aeropostal	YV-36C	stored Sep94 Caracas, Venezuela				
49396	83	1305	Transwede	SE-DHB	EC-389	EC-FIX	SE-DHB		
49397	83	1331	Valujet Airlines	SE-DHC	N830VV				
49398	83	1332	Swissair	(G-LOGI)	G-PATA	EI-CBE	EC-479	EC-EXX	EI-CBE
				SE-DPS	HB-IUK				
49399	83	1343	AOM French Airlines	N6200N	EI-BTL	(F-GGMA)	EI-BTL	F-GGMA	
49400	83	1356	Trans World Airlines	(G-DAIO)	G-PATB	9Y-THY	EI-CKB	N9407R	
49401	83	1357	Centennial Airlines	N6200N	EC-ECN	EI-CBN	EC-714	EC-FEQ	EI-CBN
				N902PJ	EC-749	EC-FZQ			
49402	83	1261	Aero Lloyd	D-ALLD					
49403	87	1404	Finnair	N19B	OH-LMA				
49404	87	1430	Finnair	OH-LMB					
49405	87	1525	Finnair	OH-LMC					
49406	87		not built	(OH-LMD)					
49407	83		not built	(OH-LME)					
49408	87		not built	(OH-LMF)					
49409	87		not built	(OH-LMG)					
49410	87		not built	(OH-LMH)					
49411	87ER	1412	Austrian Airlines	OE-LMK					
49412	87ER	1424	Austrian Airlines	OE-LML					
49413	87	1681	Austrian Airlines	OE-LMM					
49414	87	1682	Austrian Airlines	OE-LMN					
49415	82	1260/1	China Northern Airlines	B-2106					

McDONNELL-DOUGLAS MD-80 Series/MD-90

C/n	Series	Line No	Last known Operator/Owner	Previous Identities/fate (where known)					
49416	82	1271	Korean Air	HL7275					
49417	82	1278	Korean Air	N6200N	HL7276				
49418	82	1394	Korean Air	HL7282					
49419	82	1403	Korean Air	HL7283					
49420	81	1254	Scandinavian A/L System	OY-KGY					
49421	82	1263	Reno Air	SE-DFU	N841RA				
49422	81	1264	Scandinavian A/L System	(SE-DFW)	SE-DFV	SE-DFR			
49423	82	1283	Scandinavian A/L System	LN-RLG	VH-LNK	LN-RLG	N844RA	LN-RLG	
49424	82	1284	Reno Air	SE-DFX	N840RA				
49425	82	1240	China Northern Airlines	N1005T	B-2104				
49426	82	1399	Trans World Airlines	N786JA	N954U				
49427	82	1401	Trans World Airlines	N787JA	N955U				
49428	82	1241	China Northern Airlines	N1005U	B-2105				
49429	82	1242	USAir	N951PS	N829US				
49430	82	1334	Alitalia	I-DAVI					
49431	82	1377	Alitalia	I-DAVJ					
49432	82	1378	Alitalia	I-DAVK					
49433	82	1428	Alitalia	I-DAVL					
49434	82	1446	Alitalia	I-DAVM					
49435	82	1504	Alitalia	I-DAVN					
49436	81	1303	Scandinavian A/L System	OY-KHC					
49437	82	1345	Scandinavian A/L System	LN-RLR	VH-LNL	LN-RLR			
49438	81	1353	Scandinavian A/L System	SE-DFY					
49439	82	1318	(Continental Airlines)	N6200N	N18835	w/o 02Mar94 New York-La Guardia, NY			
49440	82	1304	Oasis International	YU-ANO	SL-ABD	S5-ABD	D-ALLT		
49441	82	1332	Continental Airlines	N6202D	N35836				
49442	83	1358	Swissair	N6203D	EC-ECO	EI-CBO	TC-TRU	SE-DRU	HB-IUL
49443	82	1291	USAir	N952PS	N830US				
49444	82	1323	Continental Airlines	N9806F	N936MC	N98876			
49448	83	1313	BWIA International	9Y-THQ					
49449	83	1354	Aero Lloyd	D-ALLE					
49450	82	1324	Continental Airlines	N9807F	N937MC				
49451	83	1388	American Airlines	N433AA					
49452	83	1389	American Airlines	N434AA					
49453	83	1390	American Airlines	N435AA					
49454	83	1391	American Airlines	N436AA					
49455	83	1392	American Airlines	N437AA					
49456	83	1393	American Airlines	N438AA					
49457	83	1398	American Airlines	N439AA					
49458	83	1406	American Airlines	N572AA					
49459	82	1407	American Airlines	N440AA					
49460	82	1408	American Airlines	N441AA					
49461	81	1359	Japan Air System	JA8260					
49462	81	1477	Japan Air System	JA8261					
49463	81	1488	Japan Air System	JA8262					
49464	87	1476	Japan Air System	JA8278					
49465	87	1604	Japan Air System	JA8279					
49466	87	1727	Japan Air System	JA8280					
49467	87	1742	Japan Air System	JA8281					
49468	82	1409	American Airlines	N442AA					
49469	82	1410	American Airlines	N443AA					
49470	82	1417	American Airlines	N73444					
49471	82	1418	American Airlines	N445AA					
49472	82	1426	American Airlines	N446AA					
49473	82	1427	American Airlines	N447AA					
49474	82	1431	American Airlines	N448AA					
49475	82	1432	American Airlines	N449AA					
49476	82	1439	American Airlines	N450AA					
49477	82	1441	American Airlines	N451AA					
49478	82	1293	Continental Airlines	N818NY	N14818				
49479	82	1297	Continental Airlines	N819NY					
49480	82	1298	Continental Airlines	N820NY	N15820				
49481	82	1308	Continental Airlines	N72821					
49482	82	1309	Continental Airlines	N72822					
49483	82	1314	Continental Airlines	N6200N	N76823				
49484	82	1315	Continental Airlines	N72824					
49485	82	1316	Continental Airlines	N72825					
49486	82	1317	Continental Airlines	N69826					
49487	82	1335	Continental Airlines	N77827					
49488	82	1350	Continental Airlines	N71828					
49489	82	1351	Continental Airlines	N72829					
49490	82	1352	Continental Airlines	N72830					
49491	82	1360	Continental Airlines	N14831					
49492	82	1361	Continental Airlines	N35832					
49493	82	1364	Continental Airlines	N18833					
49494	82	1368	Continental Airlines	N10834					
49495	83		not built						
49496	82		not built						
49497	82		not built						
49498	82		not built						
49499	82		not built						

McDONNELL-DOUGLAS MD-80 Series/MD-90

C/n	Series	Line No	Last known Operator/Owner	Previous Identities/fate (where known)					
49500	82		not built						
49501	82	1292/2	China Eastern Airlines	B-2107					
49502	82	1300/3	China Eastern Airlines	B-2108					
49503	82	1346/4	China Eastern Airlines	B-2109					
49504	82	1363/5	China Eastern Airlines	B-2120					
49505	82	1381/6	Beiya Airlines	B-2121					
49506	82	1400/7	China Northern Airlines	B-2122					
49507	82	1425/8	China Eastern Airlines	B-2123					
49508	82	1449/9	China Northern Airlines	B-2124					
49509	82	1482/10	China Eastern Airlines	B-2125					
49510	82	1514/11	China Northern Airlines	B-2126					
49511	82	1537/12	China Eastern Airlines	B-2127					
49512	82	1548/13	China Northern Airlines	B-2128					
49513	82	1568/14	China Eastern Airlines	B-2129					
49514	82	1589/15	China Northern Airlines	B-2130					
49515	82	1609/16	China Eastern Airlines	B-2131					
49516	82	1622/17	China Northern Airlines	B-2132					
49517	82	1633/18	China Eastern Airlines	B-2133					
49518	82	1647/19	China Northern Airlines	B-2134					
49519	82	1658/20	China Eastern Airlines	B-2135					
49520	82	1671/21	China Northern Airlines	B-2136					
49521	82	1690/22	China Eastern Airlines	B-2137					
49522	82	1702/23	China Northern Airlines	B-2138					
49523	82	1724/24	China Northern Airlines	B-2139					
49524	82	1746/25	China Northern Airlines	B-2140					
49525	83	1340	Continental Airlines	N938MC					
49526	83	1342	Continental Airlines	N939MC	N14879				
49527	82	1382	Trans World Airlines	N931TW					
49528	82	1383	Trans World Airlines	N9302B					
49529	82	1396	Trans World Airlines	N9303K					
49530	82	1397	Trans World Airlines	N9304C					
49531	82	1362	Meridiana	I-SMET					
49532	88	1338	Delta Air Lines	N901DL					
49533	88	1341	Delta Air Lines	N902DL					
49534	88	1344	Delta Air Lines	N903DL					
49535	88	1347	Delta Air Lines	N904DL					
49536	88	1348	Delta Air Lines	N905DL					
49537	88	1355	Delta Air Lines	N906DL					
49538	88	1365	Delta Air Lines	N907DL					
49539	88	1366	Delta Air Lines	N908DL					
49540	88	1395	Delta Air Lines	N909DL					
49541	88	1416	Delta Air Lines	N910DL					
49542	88	1433	Delta Air Lines	N911DL					
49543	88	1434	Delta Air Lines	N912DL					
49544	88	1443	Delta Air Lines	N913DL					
49545	88	1444	Delta Air Lines	N914DL					
49546	88	1447	Delta Air Lines	N915DL					
49547	82		not built						
49549	82	1544	Alitalia	I-DAVP					
49550	82	1584	Alitalia/Eurofly	I-DAVR					
49551	82	1586	Alitalia	I-DAVS					
49552	82	1597	Alitalia	I-DAVT					
49553	82	1450	American Airlines	N452AA					
49554	81	1379	Scandinavian A/L System	(LN-RLI)	LN-RMA				
49555	82	1402	Scanair	(OY-KHD)	LN-RMD				
49556	83	1415	Scandinavian A/L System	(SE-DFP)	LN-RMF				
49557	83	1436	Scandinavian A/L System	LN-RMB	SE-DPI				
49558	82	1451	American Airlines	N453AA					
49559	82	1460	American Airlines	N454AA					
49560	82	1462	American Airlines	N455AA					
49561	82	1474	American Airlines	N456AA					
49562	82	1475	American Airlines	N457AA					
49563	82	1485	American Airlines	N458AA					
49564	82	1486	American Airlines	N459AA					
49565	82	1496	American Airlines	N460AA					
49566	82	1497	American Airlines	N461AA					
49567	83	1367	Trans World Airlines	YV-38C	YV-937C	N9306T			
49568	83	1380	BWIA International	9Y-THR					
49569	82	1405	Crossair	HB-INW					
49570	81	1440	Swissair	HB-INX					
49571	81	1458	Swissair	HB-INY					
49572	81	1468	Crossair	HB-INZ					
49573	88	1469	Delta Air Lines	N917DL					
49574	83	1413	Spanair	EC-EFU	EC-348	EC-EFU	N574PJ	EC-591	EC-FVR
49575	83	1414	Trans World Airlines	EC-102	EC-EFJ	EI-BWD	9Y-THT	EI-BWD	
49576	83	1422	Air Liberte Tunisie	EC-EFK	EI-BWE	F-GHED			
49577	83	1454	Spanair	EC-147	EC-EHT	EC-463	EC-FSY		
49578	83	1455	Centennial Airlines	SE-DHD	EC-390	EC-FSZ			
49579	83	1465	Spanair	EC-148	EC-EIG				
49580	82	1369	Continental Airlines	N14840					
49581	82	1384	Continental Airlines	N15841					

McDONNELL-DOUGLAS MD-80 Series/MD-90

C/n	Series	Line No	Last known Operator/Owner	Previous Identities/fate (where known)
49582	82	1411	Continental Airlines	N57837
49583	88	1470	Delta Air Lines	N918DL
49584	88	1471	Delta Air Lines	N919DL
49585	87	1457	Scandinavian A/L System	HB-IUA LN-RMX
49586	87	1472	Scandinavian A/L System	HB-IUB LN-RMY
49587	87	1541	Reno Air	HB-IUC N753RA
49588	83		not built	
49589	83		not built	
49590	83		not built	
49591	88	1448	Delta Air Lines	N916DL
49592	82	1505	American Airlines	N462AA
49593	82	1506	American Airlines	N463AA
49594	82	1507	American Airlines	N464AA
49595	82	1509	American Airlines	N465AA
49596	82	1510	American Airlines	N466AA
49597	82	1511	American Airlines	N467AA
49598	82	1513	American Airlines	N468AA
49599	82	1515	American Airlines	N469AA
49600	82	1516	American Airlines	N470AA
49601	82	1518	American Airlines	N471AA
49602	83	1435	Aero Lloyd	D-ALLF
49603	81	1442	Scandinavian A/L System	N19B SE-DIA
49604	82	1456	Reno Air	N6200N OY-KHE N842RA
49605	87	1501	Scandinavian A/L System	N19B SE-DIB
49606	87	1569	Scandinavian A/L System	SE-DIF
49607	87	1512	Scandinavian A/L System	SE-DIC
49608	87	1572	Scandinavian A/L System	SE-DIH
49609	87	1517	Scandinavian A/L System	OY-KHF
49610	87	1705	Scandinavian A/L System	(OY-KHK) LN-RMK
49611	87	1522	Scandinavian A/L System	LN-RMG
49612	87	1827	Scandinavian A/L System	N6203U LN-RMH
49613	81	1519	Scandinavian A/L System	OY-KHG
49614	87	1556	Scandinavian A/L System	OY-KHI
49615	82	1543	Reno Air	SE-DID N843RA
49616	87		not built	
49617	83	1464	AOM French Airlines	F-GGMB
49618	83	1611	AOM French Airlines	F-GGMD
49619	83	1483	Aero Lloyd	EI-BTU N600DF EC-642 EC-FEB EI-BTU N915PJ D-ALLU
49620	83	1484	Aero LLoyd	EI-BTV EC-531 EC-EZU EI-BTV D-ALLV
49621	83	1495	Spanair	EC-149 EC-EJU EC-479 EC-FTS
49622	83	1498	Spanair	EC-179 EC-EJZ EC-382 EC-EJZ EC-206 EC-FNU EC-485 EC-FTT
49623	83	1499	Transwede	SE-DHN
49624	83	1502	Air Liberte Tunisie	EC-178 EC-EKM EC-279 EC-EKM EI-CGI
49625	83	1503	Finnair	OH-LMG
49626	83	1538	Spanair	N2606Z EC-223 EC-EMG EI-CGS EC-805 EC-GBA
49627	83	1580	Spanair	EC-215 EC-EOZ EC-646 EC-FXY
49628	83	1582	Oasis International	EC-260 EC-EOM VR-BMH EC-524 EC-FVB
49629	83	1583	Oasis International	EC-269 EC-EOY VR-BMI EC-525 EC-FVC
49630	83	1591	Spanair	EC-216 EC-EPL EC-638 EC-FXI
49631	83	1596	Eurofly	EC-261 EC-EPM EI-CEK EC-113 EC-FMY EI-CEK
49632	83	1603	BWIA International	9Y-THV
49633	83		not built	
49634	82	1419	Continental Airlines	N34838
49635	82	1420	Continental Airlines	N14839
49636	83		not built	
49637	83		not built	
49638	83		not built	
49639	83		not built	
49640	83		not built	
49641	87	1617	Reno Air	HB-IUD N754RA
49642	83	1421	Oasis International	(EC-EFL) SE-DHF EC-190 EC-EKT XA-TUR EC-257 EC-EMT F-GMCD EI-CGR EC-807 EC-GBY
49643	83	1423	Alaska Airlines	N19B G-BNSA N945AS
49644	88	1473	Delta Air Lines	N920DL
49645	88	1480	Delta Air Lines	N921DL
49646	88	1481	Delta Air Lines	N922DL
49647	82	1520	American Airlines	N472AA
49648	82	1521	American Airlines	N473AA
49649	82	1526	American Airlines	N474
49650	82	1527	American Airlines	N475AA
49651	82	1528	American Airlines	N476AA
49652	82	1529	American Airlines	N477AA
49653	82	1534	American Airlines	N478AA
49654	82	1535	American Airlines	N479AA
49655	82	1536	American Airlines	N480AA
49656	82	1545	American Airlines	N481AA
49657	83	1459	Alaska Airlines	N939AS
49658	83	1461	Alaska Airlines	G-BNSB N946AS
49659	83	1438	Aeropostal	YV-39C stored Sep94 Caracas, Venezuela

McDONNELL-DOUGLAS MD-80 Series/MD-90

C/n	Series	Line No	Last known Operator/Owner	Previous Identities/fate (where known)					
49660	82	1445	Aeromexico	(N59842)	EI-BTX				
49661	82	1452	ALM	(N11843)	(EI-BTY)	EI-BWB	SU-DAK	EC-421	EC-EVY
				PJ-SEH					
49662	83	1429	Air Liberte Tunisie	(N940MC)	N1005W	G-PATC	F-GHEC		
49663	83	1437	Trans World Airlines	(N941MC)	N30008	G-PATD	F-GHEH	G-PATD	EC-438
				EC-EUF	SE-DPH	N9307R			
49664	83		not built						
49665	83		not built						
49666	83		not built						
49667	82	1466	Aeromexico	(N12844)	EI-BTY				
49668	83	1467	Centennial Airlines	(N14845)	EI-BWC	EC-163	EC-EIK	EC-289	EC-EIK
				EI-CGA	F-GMPP	EI-CGA	EC-898	EC-GBV	
49669	82	1493	Meridiana	I-SMEV					
49670	87	1453	Aero Lloyd	D-ALLG					
49671	87	1463	Surinam Airways	D-ALLH	N107PY				
49672	83	1494	Spanair	EC-150	EC-EJQ	EC-487	EC-FTU		
49673	87	1508	Aeromexico	(A3-RTA)	9V-TRY	XA-RUO	(EI-CBU)	XA-RUO	XA-SFO
49674	88		not built						
49675	82	1546	American Airlines	N482AA					
49676	82	1550	American Airlines	N483AA					
49677	82	1551	American Airlines	N484AA					
49678	82	1555	American Airlines	N485AA					
49679	82	1557	American Airlines	N486AA					
49680	82	1558	American Airlines	N487AA					
49681	82	1560	American Airlines	N488AA					
49682	82	1562	American Airlines	N489AA					
49683	82	1563	American Airlines	N490AA					
49684	82	1564	American Airlines	N491AA					
49685			not built						
49686			not built						
49687			not built						
49688			not built						
49689			not built						
49690			not built						
49701	82	1478	Trans World Airlines	(N14846)	N956U				
49702	82	1479	Trans World Airlines	(N14847)	N957U				
49703	82	1489	Trans World Airlines	(N14848)	N958U				
49704	82	1490	Trans World Airlines	(N14849)	N959U				
49705	88	1491	Delta Air Lines	N923DL					
49706	87	1614	Transwede	SE-DHI	SX-BAV	SE-DHI			
49707	83	1487	Air Liberte	F-GFZB					
49708	83	1561	Centennial Airlines	N6203U	XA-TUR(2)	TC-RTU	EC-607	EC-FVV	
49709	83	1542	Spanair	F-GGMC	EC-835	EC-GAT			
49710	83	1547	Centennial Airlines	XA-TOR	HB-IUI	SX-BAQ	EC-159		
49711	88	1492	Delta Air Lines	N924DL					
49712	88	1500	Delta Air Lines	N925DL					
49713	88	1523	Delta Air Lines	N926DL					
49714	88	1524	Delta Air Lines	N927DA					
49715	88	1530	Delta Air Lines	N928DL					
49716	88	1531	Delta Air Lines	N929DL					
49717	88	1532	Delta Air Lines	N930DL					
49718	88	1533	Delta Air Lines	N931DL					
49719	88	1570	Delta Air Lines	N932DL					
49720	88	1571	Delta Air Lines	N933DL					
49721	88	1574	Delta Air Lines	N934DL					
49722	88	1575	Delta Air Lines	N935DL					
49723	88	1576	Delta Air Lines	N936DL					
49724	87	1549	Great American Airways	N801ML	SU-DAP	N1075T			
49725	87	1552	Ford Motor Co	N802ML	VR-BOP				
49726	87	1610	Aeromexico	N803ML					
49727	87	1621	Great American Airways	N804ML	N1074T				
49728	82	1553	Scandinavian A/L System	SE-DIK					
49729	82		not built	(SE-DII)					
49730	82	1565	American Airlines	N492AA					
49731	82	1566	American Airlines	N493AA					
49732	82	1567	American Airlines	N494AA					
49733	82	1607	American Airlines	N495AA					
49734	82	1619	American Airlines	N496AA					
49735	82	1635	American Airlines	N497AA					
49736	82	1640	American Airlines	N498AA					
49737	82	1641	American Airlines	N499AA					
49738	82	1648	American Airlines	N501AA					
49739	82	1649	American Airlines	N33502					
49740	82	1618	Meridiana	I-SMEP					
49741	83	1630	Finnair	OH-LMU					
49742			not built						
49743			not built						
49744			not built						
49745			not built						
49746			not built						
49747			not built						

McDONNELL-DOUGLAS MD-80 Series/MD-90

C/n	Series	Line No	Last known Operator/Owner	Previous Identities/fate (where known)					
49748			not built						
49749			not built						
49750			not built						
49751			not built						
49752			not built						
49753			not built						
49754			not built						
49755			not built						
49756			not built						
49757			not built						
49758			not built						
49759	88	1606	Air Aruba	N156PL	N903ML	P4-MDA	N11FQ		
49760	88	1620	Midwest Express	N157PL	N701ME				
49761	88	1623	Aeromexico	N158PL					
49762	88	1624	Midwest Express	(N159PL)	N601ME				
49763	88	1626	Aeromexico	N160PL					
49764	88	1632	Aeromexico	N161PL					
49765	88	1645	Aeromexico	N162PL					
49766	88	1657	Air Aruba	N163PL	N904ML	P4-MDC	N12FQ		
49767	87	1587	Golden Nugget Aviation	D-ALLI	N721EW				
49768	87	1595	Aero Lloyd	D-ALLJ					
49769	83	1559	Aero Lloyd	D-ALLK					
49770			not built						
49771			not built						
49772			not built						
49773			not built						
49774			not built						
49775			not built						
49776			not built						
49777	87	1634	Great American Airways	N805ML	XA-RJT	N497PJ	N750RA		
49778	87	1646	Ford Motor Co	N806ML	VR-BOO				
49779	87	1670	Reno Air	N807ML	SU-DAO	N807ML	EC-642	EC-FXX	N751RA
49780	87	1674	Reno Air	N808ML	SU-DAQ	N21555	N780EG	N752RA	
49781	82		not built						
49782	82		not built						
49783	82		not built						
49784	83	1627	Austral Lineas Aereas	EI-BZV	N509MD	LV-WGM			
49785	83	1678	Trans World Airlines	HL7271	EI-CIW				
49786	83	1631	BWIA International	9Y-THW					
49787	83	1636	Trans World Airlines	HL7274	N110HM				
49788	83	1637	Reno Air	D-AGWE	YV-43C	N817RA			
49789	83	1642	BWIA International	9Y-THX					
49790	83	1643	Spanair	EC-307	EC-ESJ	EC-742	EC-FZC		
49791	83	1644	Oasis International	F-ODTN	VR-BMJ	EC-546	EC-FVX	EC-166	
49792	83	1655	Sunway Airlines	XA-RPH	EC-733	EC-FEP	XA-RPH	EI-CKM	D-ALLW
				EI-CKM	TC-INC				
49793	83	1656	Reno Air	(F-GGME)	C-GKMV	N511RP	D-AGWF	YV-42C	N793DG
				N872RA					
49794	82	1600	Alitalia	I-DAVU					
49795	82	1639	Alitalia	I-DAVV					
49796	82	1713	Alitalia	I-DAVW					
49797	82	1650	American Airlines	N44503					
49798	82	1651	American Airlines	N70504					
49799	82	1652	American Airlines	N505AA					
49800	82	1660	American Airlines	N7506					
49801	82	1661	American Airlines	N3507A					
49802	82	1662	American Airlines	N7508					
49803	82	1663	American Airlines	N7509					
49804	82	1669	American Airlines	(N62510)	N510AM				
49805	82	1672	American Airlines	N90511					
49806	82	1673	American Airlines	N7512A					
49807	83	1829	Far Eastern Air Transport	N6200N	B-28007				
49808	83	1836	North American Airlines	N3010G	N183NA				
49809	83	1843	Kuwait AF	KAF26					
49810	88	1588	Delta Air Lines	N937DL					
49811	88	1590	Delta Air Lines	N938DL					
49812	88	1593	Delta Air Lines	N939DL					
49813	88	1599	Delta Air Lines	N940DL					
49814	88	1602	Delta Air Lines	N941DL					
49815	88	1605	Delta Air Lines	N942DL					
49816	88	1608	Delta Air Lines	N943DL					
49817	88	1612	Delta Air Lines	N944DL					
49818	88	1613	Delta Air Lines	N945DL					
49819	88	1629	Delta Air Lines	N946DL					
49820	81	1598	Japan Air System	JA8294					
49821	81	1615	Japan Air System	JA8295					
49822	83	1539	Air Liberte	F-GHEB					
49823	83	1540	Air Liberte	G-BPSC	N83MV	F-GHEK			
49824	83	1554	BWIA International	9Y-THU					
49825	83	1577	Alaska Airlines	N940AS					

McDONNELL-DOUGLAS MD-80 Series/MD-90

C/n	Series	Line No	Last known Operator/Owner	Previous Identities/fate (where known)					
49826	83	1578	Aeromexico	N13627	G-BPSD	N82MV	F-GFUU	EC-546	EC-EZR
				N861LF					
49827	87	1654	Iberia	EC-290	EC-EUE				
49828	87	1667	Iberia	EC-291	EC-EUD				
49829	87	1678	Iberia	EC-292	EC-EUC				
49830	87	1684	Iberia	EC-293	EC-EUL				
49831	87	1688	Iberia	EC-294	EC-EVB				
49832	87	1703	Iberia	EC-295	EC-EXF				
49833	87	1706	Iberia	EC-296	EC-EXG				
49834	87	1714	Iberia	EC-297	EC-EXR				
49835	87	1717	Iberia	EC-298	EC-EXM				
49836	87	1721	Iberia	EC-299	EC-EXN				
49837	87	1730	Iberia	EC-300	EC-EXT				
49838	87	1733	Iberia	EC-301	EC-EYB				
49839	87	1739	Iberia	EC-302	EC-EYX				
49840	87	1745	Iberia	EC-303	EC-EYY				
49841	87	1751	Iberia	EC-304	EC-EYZ				
49842	87	1763	Iberia	EC-305	EC-EZA				
49843	87	1771	Iberia	EC-306	EC-EZS				
49844	81	1579	Swissair	HB-ISX					
49845	83	1573	Allegro Air	D-AGWA	N845CP	SU-DAL	XA-SXJ		
49846	83	1581	Aero Lloyd	D-AGWB					
49847	83	1585	Aero Lloyd	N62020	D-AGWC				
49848	83	1592	Allegro Air	D-AGWD	N848CP	SU-DAM	XA-SWW		
49849	82	1772/26	(China Northern Airlines)	B-2141	w/o 14Nov93 Urumqi, China				
49850	82	1798/27	Beiya Airlines	B-2142					
49851	82	1807/28	Beiya Airlines	B-2143					
49852	82	1959/34	China Northern Airlines	B-2144	B-2151				
49853	82T	1981/35	China Northern Airlines	B-2145	prototype MD-82T				
49854	83	1601	Aero Lloyd	D-ALLL					
49855	83	1728	AOM French Airlines	F-GGME					
49856	83	1675	Aero Lloyd	D-ALLM					
49857	83	1687	Aero Lloyd	D-ALLN					
49858			not built						
49859			not built						
49860			not built						
49861			not built						
49862			not built						
49863			not built						
49864			not built						
49865			not built						
49866			not built						
49867			not built						
49868			not built						
49869			not built						
49870			not built						
49871			not built						
49872			not built						
49873			not built						
49874			not built						
49875			not built						
49876			not built						
49877	82	1594	Finnair	OH-LMT					
49878	88	1664	Delta Air Lines	N947DL					
49879	88	1666	Delta Air Lines	N948DL					
49880	88	1676	Delta Air Lines	N949DL					
49881	88	1677	Delta Air Lines	N950DL					
49882	88	1679	Delta Air Lines	N951DL					
49883	88	1683	Delta Air Lines	N952DL					
49884	88	1685	Delta Air Lines	N953DL					
49885	88	1689	Delta Air Lines	N954DL					
49886	88	1691	Delta Air Lines	N955DL					
49887	88	1699	Delta Air Lines	N956DL					
49888	87	1692	Austrian Airlines	OE-LMO					
49889	82	1761	Reno Air	N811ML	N823RA				
49890	82	1686	American Airlines	N513AA					
49891	82	1694	American Airlines	N7514A					
49892	82	1695	American Airlines	N3515					
49893	82	1696	American Airlines	(N91516)	N516AM				
49894	82	1697	American Airlines	N7517A					
49895	82	1698	American Airlines	N7518A					
49896	82	1707	American Airlines	N7519A					
49897	82	1708	American Airlines	N7520A					
49898	82	1709	American Airlines	N7521A					
49899	82	1722	American Airlines	N7522A					
49900	82	1765	Finnair	N6202D	N66480	EC-893	EC-FJQ	OH-LPA	
49901	82	1766	Meridiana	N6202S	I-SMER				
49902	82	1948	Meridiana	I-SMES					
49903	82	1949	Meridiana	N3010C	PH-SEZ				
49904	83	1680	Finnair	OH-LMV					
49905	82	1767	Finnair	OH-LMW					

McDONNELL-DOUGLAS MD-80 Series/MD-90

C/n	Series	Line No	Last known Operator/Owner	Previous Identities/fate (where known)				
49906	82	1786	Finnair	OH-LMX				
49907	81	1734	Japan Air System	JA8296				
49908	81	1749	Japan Air System	JA8297				
49909	81	1625	Scandinavian A/L System	SE-DII				
49910	81	1638	Scandinavian A/L System	OY-KHK				
49911	81	1653	Scandinavian A/L System	OY-KHL				
49912	81	1659	Scandinavian A/L System	LN-RMJ				
49913	81	1665	Scandinavian A/L System	SE-DIL				
49914	81	1693	Scandinavian A/L System	OY-KHM				
49915	82	1723	American Airlines	N59523				
49916	82	1729	American Airlines	N70524				
49917	82	1735	American Airlines	N7525A				
49918	82	1743	American Airlines	N7526A				
49919	82	1744	American Airlines	N7527A				
49920	82	1750	American Airlines	N7528A				
49921	82	1752	American Airlines	N70529				
49922	82	1753	American Airlines	N7530				
49923	82	1758	American Airlines	N7531A				
49924	82	1759	American Airlines	N7532A				
49925	83	1616	Alaska Airlines	N941AS				
49926	88	1715	Aeromexico	XA-AMS				
49927	88	1716	Aeromexico	XA-AMT				
49928	88	1732	Aeromexico	N166PL	XA-AMU			
49929	88	1741	Aeromexico	XA-AMV				
49930	83	1720	Crossair	HB-ISZ				
49931	82	1754	Reno Air	N809ML	N821RA			
49932	82	1756	Reno Air	N810ML	N822RA			
49933	83	1837	Austrian Airlines	OE-LMD				
49934	83	1764	Austral Lineas Aereas	N907MD	LV-WGN			
49935	83	1773	Edelweiss Air	N3004C	G-DCAC	HB-IKM		
49936	83	1778	Sunway Airlines	N3001D	G-HCRP	TC-INB		
49937	83	1784	Eurofly	N30010	G-COES	EI-CMM		
49938	83	1785	Spanair	XA-RTK	VH-LNH	SE-DPU	EC-592	EC-FXA
49939	83	1787	AVIANCA	EI-CBR				
49940	83	1788	Sunway Airlines	N30016	G-TTPT	TC-IND		
49941	83	1793	Airtours International	N3002A	G-JSMC	G-DEVR		
49942	83	1799	AVIANCA	EI-CBS				
49943	83	1887	Sunway Airlines	EI-CBX	TC-INA			
49944	83	1888	AVIANCA	EI-CBY				
49945	83	1889	AVIANCA	N6206F	EI-CBZ			
49946	83	1898	AVIANCA	EI-CCC				
49947	83	1900	AVIANCA	EI-CCE				
49948	83	1905	AVIANCA	EI-CDY				
49949	83	1906	Airtours International	G-RJER				
49950	83	1913	Air Aruba	EI-CEH	P4-MDE			
49951	83	1915	Edelweiss Air	G-GMJM	HB-IKN			
49952	83	1934	Far Eastern Air Transport	N9012J	G-TONW	B-28023		
49953			not built					
49954			not built					
49955			not built					
49956	88	2039	Delta Air Lines	N913DE				
49957	88	2049	Delta Air Lines	N914DE				
49958	88	2054	Delta Air Lines	N917DE				
49959	88	2055	Delta Air Lines	N918DE				
49960	88		not built	(N923DE)				
49961	88		not built	(N924DE)				
49962	88		not built	(N925DE)				
49963	88		not built					
49964	88		not built					
49965	83	2044	Transwede	SE-DLV	OH-LPC*			
49966	83	2047	Finnair	SE-DLX	OH-LPB			
49967	88	2037	Delta Air Lines	N911DE				
49968	83	1668	Air Liberte	N19B	F-GHEI			
49969	82	1719	Alitalia	I-DAVX				
49970	82	1737	Alitalia	I-DAVZ				
49971	82	1755	Alitalia	I-DACM				
49972	82	1757	Alitalia	I-DACN				
49973	82	1762	Alitalia	I-DACP				
49974	82	1774	Alitalia	I-DACQ				
49975	82	1775	Alitalia	I-DACR				
49976	88	1700	Delta Air Lines	N957DL				
49977	88	1701	Delta Air Lines	N958DL				
49978	88	1710	Delta Air Lines	N959DL				
49979	88	1711	Delta Air Lines	N960DL				
49980	88	1712	Delta Air Lines	N961DL				
49981	88	1725	Delta Air Lines	N962DL				
49982	88	1726	Delta Air Lines	N963DL				
49983	88	1747	Delta Air Lines	N964DL				
49984	88	1748	Delta Air Lines	N965DL				
49985	83	1838	Air Liberte	F-GHHO				
49986	83	1842	Air Liberte	F-GHHP				

McDONNELL-DOUGLAS MD-80 Series/MD-90

C/n	Series	Line No	Last known Operator/Owner	Previous Identities/fate (where known)			
49987	82	1760	American Airlines	N7533A			
49988	82	1768	American Airlines	N7534A			
49989	82	1769	American Airlines	N7535A			
49990	82	1770	American Airlines	N7536A			
49991	82	1780	American Airlines	N7537A			
49992	82	1781	American Airlines	N7538A			
49993	82	1782	American Airlines	N7539A			
49994	82	1790	American Airlines	N7540A			
49995	82	1791	American Airlines	N7541A			
49996	82	1792	American Airlines	N7542A			
49997	88	2038	Delta Air Lines	N912DE			
49998	81	1800	Scandinavian A/L System	(SE-DIM)	SE-DIX		
49999	81	1803	Scandinavian A/L System	SE-DIN			
53000	81	1812	Scandinavian A/L System	OY-KHN			
53001	81	1815	Scandinavian A/L System	(SE-DIP)	OY-KHS	LN-RMT	OY-KHS
53002	81	1835	Scandinavian A/L System	LN-RML			
53003	81	1844	(Scandinavian A/L System)	OY-KHO	w/o 27Dec91 nr Stockholm-Arlanda, Sweden		
53004	81	1846	Scandinavian A/L System	SE-DIR			
53005	81	1855	Scandinavian A/L System	LN-RMM			
53006	81	1869	Scandinavian A/L System	SE-DIS			
53007	81	1882	Scandinavian A/L System	OY-KHP			
53008	81	1895	Scanair	SE-DIY			
53009	87	1916	Scandinavian A/L System	SE-DMA			
53010	87	1921	Scandinavian A/L System	N6202D	(OY-KHS)	SE-DIP	
53011	87	1931	Scandinavian A/L System	SE-DIU			
53012	83	1736	Aero Lloyd	D-ALLO			
53013	83	1738	Aero Lloyd	D-ALLP			
53014	83	1740	Aero Lloyd	D-ALLQ			
53015	83	1818	Aero Lloyd	N13627	D-ALLR		
53016	83	1850	Alaska Airlines	(D-ALLS)	N968AS		
53017	82	1797	Reno Air	N812ML	N824RA		
53018	83	1779	Alaska Airlines	N943AS			
53019	83	1783	Alaska Airlines	N944AS			
53020	83	1789	Alaska Airlines	N947AS			
53021	83	1801	Alaska Airlines	N948AS			
53022	83	1809	Alaska Airlines	N949AS			
53023	83	1821	Alaska Airlines	N950AS			
53024	83	1825	Alaska Airlines	N958AS			
53025	82	1802	American Airlines	N7543A			
53026	82	1804	American Airlines	N7544A			
53027	82	1805	American Airlines	N16545			
53028	82	1813	American Airlines	N7546A			
53029	82	1814	American Airlines	N7547A			
53030	82	1816	American Airlines	N7548A			
53031	82	1819	American Airlines	N7549A			
53032	82	1820	American Airlines	N7550			
53033	82	1822	American Airlines	N14551			
53034	82	1826	American Airlines	N552AA			
53035	88		not built				
53036	88		not built				
53037	88		not built				
53038	88		not built				
53039	87	1881	Japan Air System	JA8370			
53040	87	1897	Japan Air System	JA8371			
53041	87	1945	Japan Air System	JA8372			
53042	87	1969	Japan Air System	N90126	JA8373		
53043	81	1982	Japan Air System	JA8374			
53044	83	1776	Reno Air	N905ML	N832RA		
53045	83	1777	Reno Air	N906ML	P4-MDB	N833RA	
53046	83	1794	Reno Air	N907ML	YV-44C	N836RA	
53047	88	2016	Aerolineas Argentinas	LV-VBX			
53048	88	2030	Aerolineas Argentinas	LV-VBY			
53049	88	2031	Aerolineas Argentinas	LV-VBZ			
53050	83	1704	Aeromexico	EC-439	EC-EUZ	N831LF	
53051	83	1718	Aeromexico	EC-440	EC-EVU	N881LF	
53052	83	1731	Alaska Airlines	N942AS			
53053	82	1806	Alitalia	I-DACS			
53054	82	1856	Alitalia	I-DACT			
53055	82	1857	Alitalia	I-DACU			
53056	82	1880	Alitalia	I-DACV			
53057	82	1894	Alitalia	I-DACW			
53058	82	1927	Alitalia	I-DACZ			
53059	82	1942	Alitalia	I-DACY			
53060	82	1944	Alitalia	I-DACX			
53061	82	1957	Alitalia	I-DAND			
53062	82	1960	Alitalia	I-DANF			
53063	83	1851	Alaska Airlines	(D-ALLT)	N969AS		
53064	82	1908	Far Eastern Air Transport	(N812ML)	N6203D	B-28001	
53065	82	1925	Far Eastern Air Transport	(N814ML)	N9012S	B-28003	
53066	82	1938	Far Eastern Air Transport	(N815ML)	B-28005		
53067	82		not built	(N816ML)			

McDONNELL-DOUGLAS MD-80 Series/MD-90

C/n	Series	Line No	Last known Operator/Owner	Previous Identities/fate (where known)			
53068	82		not built	(N817ML)			
53069	82		not built	(N818ML)			
53070	82		not built	(N819ML)			
53071	82		not built	(N820ML)			
53072	82		not built	(N821ML)			
53073	82		not built	(N823ML)			
53074	83	1976	Alaska Airlines	N960AS			
53075	83	1977	Alaska Airlines	N961AS			
53076	83	1988	Alaska Airlines	N962AS			
53077	83	1995	Alaska Airlines	N963AS			
53078	83	1996	Alaska Airlines	N964AS			
53079	83	2004	Alaska Airlines	N965AS			
53080	82		not built				
53081	82		not built				
53082	82		not built				
53083	83	1828	American Airlines	N553AA			
53084	83	1830	American Airlines	N554AA			
53085	83	1839	American Airlines	N555AN			
53086	83	1840	American Airlines	N556AA			
53087	83	1841	American Airlines	N557AN			
53088	83	1852	American Airlines	N558AA			
53089	83	1853	American Airlines	N559AA			
53090	83	1858	American Airlines	N560AA			
53091	83	1863	American Airlines	N561AA			
53092	83	1864	American Airlines	N573AA			
53093	83	2066	Reno Air	N345AW	N873RA		
53094	83		not built				
53095	83		not built				
53096	83		not built				
53097	83		not built				
53098	83		not built				
53099	83		not built				
53100	82		not built	(N824ML)			
53101	82		not built	(N825ML)			
53102	82		not built	(N826ML)			
53103	82		not built	(N827ML)			
53104	82		not built	(N828ML)			
53105	82		not built	(N829ML)			
53106	82		not built	(N830ML)			
53107	82		not built	(N831ML)			
53108	82		not built	(N832ML)			
53109	82		not built	(N833ML)			
53110	82		not built	(N834ML)			
53111	82		not built	(N835ML)			
53112	82		not built	(N836ML)			
53113	82		not built	(N837ML)			
53114	82		not built	(N838ML)			
53115	88	1795	Delta Air Lines	N966DL			
53116	88	1796	Delta Air Lines	N967DL			
53117	83	1951	Aerolineas Argentinas	N6202D	LV-VAG		
53118	82	1954	Far Eastern Air Transport	N6202S	(VH-LNN)	B-28011	
53119	82	1956	Far Eastern Air Transport	N6203D	B-28013		
53120	82	1964	AVIANCA	N6206F	EI-CFZ		
53121	83	1971	Trans World Airlines	N9012J	VH-LNI	N532MD	N9409F
53122	83	1984	AVIANCA	EI-CEP			
53123	83	1987	AVIANCA	EI-CEQ			
53124	83	1991	Reno Air	N9017P	N834RA		
53125	83	1993	AVIANCA	EI-CER			
53126	83	2026	Trans World Airlines	N9406W			
53127	83		not built				
53128	83		not built				
53129	83		not built				
53130	83		not built				
53131	83		not built				
53132	82		not built				
53133	82		not built				
53134	82		not built				
53135	82		not built				
53136	82		not built				
53137	83	1872/29	Trans World Airlines	N9001L	N9401W		
53138	83	1886/30	Trans World Airlines	N9001D	N9402W		
53139	83	1899/31	Trans World Airlines	N9035C	N9403W		
53140	83	1923/32	Trans World Airlines	N9075H	N9404V		
53141	83	1935/33	Trans World Airlines	N9405T			
53142	83		not built				
53143	83		not built				
53144	83		not built				
53145	83		not built				
53146	83		not built				
53147	82	2069	Korean Air	HL7203			
53148	82	2072	Korean Air	HL7204			

McDONNELL-DOUGLAS MD-80 Series/MD-90

C/n	Series	Line No	Last known Operator/Owner	Previous Identities/fate (where known)		
53149	81	1817	Crossair	HB-IUG		
53150	81	1831	Swissair	HB-IUH		
53151	82	1866	American Airlines	N574AA		
53152	82	1875	American Airlines	N575AM		
53153	82	1876	American Airlines	N576AA		
53154	82	1878	American Airlines	N577AA		
53155	82	1883	American Airlines	N578AA		
53156	82	1884	American Airlines	N579AA		
53157	82	1885	American Airlines	N580AA		
53158	82	1891	American Airlines	N581AA		
53159	82	1892	American Airlines	N582AA		
53160	82	1893	American Airlines	N583AA		
53161	88	1808	Delta Air Lines	N968DL		
53162	82	2010	China Northern Airlines	N831US	B-2146	
53163	82	2025	China Northern Airlines	N832AU	B-2147	
53164	82	2041	China Northern Airlines	N833AU	B-2152	
53165	82	2042	Spanair	N834AU	EC-894	EC-GCV
53166	82	2052	Far Eastern Air Transport	N835AU	B-28017	
53167	82	2056	Far Eastern Air Transport	N836AU	B-	
53168	82	2061	Far Eastern Air Transport	N837AU	B-28015	
53169	82	2063	China Northern Airlines	N838AU	B-2148	
53170	82	2065	China Northern Airlines	N839AU	B-2149	
53171	82	2067	China Northern Airlines	N840AU	B-2150	
53172	88	1810	Delta Air Lines	N969DL		
53173	88	1811	Delta Air Lines	N970DL		
53174	88	1854	Aeromexico	N168PL		
53175	88	1868	Aeromexico	N169PL		
53176	82	1972	Eurofly	I-DANG		
53177	82	1973	Eurofly	I-DANH		
53178	82	1994	Alitalia	I-DANL		
53179	82	1997	Alitalia	I-DANM		
53180	82	2002	Alitalia	I-DANP		
53181	82	2005	Alitalia	I-DANQ		
53182	83	2068	Reno Air	N456AW	N875RA	
53183	83	2071	Reno Air	N567AW	N876RA	
53184	83	2088	Reno Air	N878RA		
53185	83	2090	Reno Air	N879RA		
53186	83	2092	Reno Air	N880RA		
53187	83	2118	Trans World Airlines	N9412W		
53188	83	2119	Trans World Airlines	N9413T		
53189	83	2121	Trans World Airlines	N9414W		
53190	83		Ansett Worldwide			
53191	83		Ansett Worldwide			
53192	83		Ansett Worldwide			
53193	88	1890	Aviaco	N19B	EC-751	EC-FGM
53194	88	1911	Aviaco	EC-752	EC-FHG	
53195	88	1929	Aviaco	EC-753	EC-FIG	
53196	88	1930	Aviaco	EC-754	EC-FIH	
53197	88	1940	Aviaco	EC-755	EC-FJE	
53198	83	1847	Transwede	SE-DLS		
53199	83	1968	Transwede	N13627	SE-DLU	
53200	88		not built			
53201	88		not built			
53202			not built			
53203	82	2007	Alitalia	I-DANR		
53204	82	2009	Alitalia	I-DANU		
53205	82	2028	Alitalia	I-DANV		
53206	82	2034	Alitalia	I-DANW		
53207	87	1862	Iberia	EC-633	EC-FEZ	
53208	87	1865	Iberia	EC-634	EC-FEY	
53209	87	1867	Iberia	EC-635	EC-FFA	
53210	87	1871	Iberia	EC-636	EC-FFI	
53211	87	1874	Iberia	EC-637	EC-FFH	
53212	87	1877	Iberia	EC-638	EC-FHD	
53213	87	1879	Iberia	EC-639	EC-FHK	
53214	88	1823	Delta Air Lines	N971DL		
53215	88	1824	Delta Air Lines	N972DL		
53216	82	2048	Alitalia	I-DATA		
53217	82	2053	Alitalia	I-DATE		
53218	82	2060	Alitalia	I-DATI		
53219	82	2062	Alitalia	I-DATO		
53220	82	2073	Alitalia	I-DATU		
53221	82	2079	Alitalia	I-DATB		
53222	82	2080	Alitalia	I-DATC		
53223	82	2081	Alitalia	I-DATD		
53224	82	2084	Alitalia	I-DATF		
53225	82	2086	Alitalia	I-DATG		
53226	82	2087	Alitalia	I-DATH		
53227	82	2103	Alitalia	I-DATJ		
53228	82	2104	Alitalia	I-DATK		
53229	82	2105	Alitalia	I-DATL		

McDONNELL-DOUGLAS MD-80 Series/MD-90

C/n	Series	Line No	Last known Operator/Owner	Previous Identities/fate (where known)	
53230	82	2106	Alitalia	I-DATM	
53231	82	2107	Alitalia	I-DATN	
53232	82	2108	Alitalia	I-DATP	
53233	82	2110	Alitalia	I-DATQ	
53234	82	2111	Alitalia	I-DATR	
53235	82	2113	Alitalia	I-DATS	
53236	82		Alitalia		
53237	82		Alitalia		
53238	82		Alitalia		
53239	82		Alitalia		
53240	82		Alitalia		
53241	88	1832	Delta Air Lines	N973DL	
53242	88	1833	Delta Air Lines	N974DL	
53243	88	1834	Delta Air Lines	N975DL	
53244	82	1901	Finnair	OH-LMY	
53245	83	1978	Finnair	OH-LMH	
53246	82	1918	Finnair	OH-LMZ	
53247	82	1902	American Airlines	N584AA	
53248	82	1903	American Airlines	N585AA	
53249	82	1904	American Airlines	N586AA	
53250	82	1907	American Airlines	N587AA	
53251	83	1909	American Airlines	N588AA	
53252	83	1910	American Airlines	N589AA	
53253	83	1919	American Airlines	N590AA	
53254	83	1920	American Airlines	N591AA	
53255	83	1932	American Airlines	N592AA	
53256	83	1933	American Airlines	N593AA	
53257	88	1845	Delta Air Lines	N976DL	
53258	88	1848	Delta Air Lines	N977DL	
53259	88	1849	Delta Air Lines	N978DL	
53260	88		not built		
53261	88		not built		
53262	88		not built		
53263	88		not built		
53266	88	1859	Delta Air Lines	N979DL	
53267	88	1860	Delta Air Lines	N980DL	
53268	88	1861	Delta Air Lines	N981DL	
53269	83		not built		
53270	83		not built		
53271	83		not built		
53272	83		not built		
53273	88	1870	Delta Air Lines	N982DL	
53274	88	1873	Delta Air Lines	N983DL	
53275	81	1896	Scandinavian A/L System	OY-KHR	
53284	83	1966	American Airlines	N594AA	
53285	83	1989	American Airlines	N595AA	
53286	83	2000	American Airlines	N596AA	
53287	83	2006	American Airlines	N597AA	
53288	83	2011	American Airlines	N598AA	
53289	83	2012	American Airlines	N599AA	
53290	83	2013	American Airlines	N76200	
53291	83	2019	American Airlines	N76201	
53292	83	2020	American Airlines	N76202	
53293	83	2021	American Airlines	N567AM	
53294	82	1917	Scandinavian A/L System	SE-DIZ	
53295	82	1922	Scandinavian A/L System	LN-RMN	
53296	82	1937	Scandinavian A/L System	OY-KHT	
53297	81	2040	Japan Air System	JA8552	
53298	81	2045	Japan Air System	JA8553	
53299	81	2075	Japan Air System	JA8554	
53300	81	2076	Japan Air System	JA8555	
53301	81	2082	Japan Air System	JA8556	
53302	81	2085	Japan Air System	JA8557	
53303	88	1974	Aviaco	EC-945	EC-FLN
53304	88	1975	Aviaco	EC-946	EC-FLK
53305	88	2001	Aviaco	EC-964	EC-FND
53306	88	2014	Aviaco	EC-965	EC-FOF
53307	88	2015	Aviaco	EC-966	EC-FOG
53308	88	2022	Aviaco	EC-987	EC-FOZ
53309	88	2023	Aviaco	EC-988	EC-FPD
53310	88	2024	Aviaco	EC-989	EC-FPJ
53311	88	1912	Delta Air Lines	N984DL	
53312	88	1914	Delta Air Lines	N985DL	
53313	88	1924	Delta Air Lines	N986DL	
53314	81	1946	Scandinavian A/L System	SE-DMB	
53315	81	1947	Scandinavian A/L System	LN-RMO	
53316	90-30		not built		
53336	81	1953	Scandinavian A/L System	OY-KHU	
53337	87	1962	Scandinavian A/L System	LN-RMP	
53338	88	1926	Delta Air Lines	N987DL	
53339	88	1928	Delta Air Lines	N988DL	

McDONNELL-DOUGLAS MD-80 Series/MD-90

C/n	Series	Line No	Last known Operator/Owner	Previous Identities/fate (where known)	
53340	87	1967	Scandinavian A/L System	SE-DMC	LN-RMU
53341	88	1936	Delta Air Lines	N989DL	
53342	88	1939	Delta Air Lines	N990DL	
53343	88	1941	Delta Air Lines	N991DL	
53344	88	1943	Delta Air Lines	N992DL	
53345	88	1950	Delta Air Lines	N993DL	
53346	88	1952	Delta Air Lines	N994DL	
53347	81	1979	Scandinavian A/L System	N90125	SE-DMD
53348	81	1985	Scandinavian A/L System	OY-KHW	
53351	88	2043	Aerolineas Argentinas	LV-VCB	
53352	90-30	2098	Japan Air System	JA8062	stored Jul95 Kingman, AZ
53353	90-30	2120	Japan Air System	JA8063	stored Nov95 Kingman, AZ
53354	90-30		Japan Air System	JA8064	
53355	90-30		Japan Air System	JA8065	
53356	90-30		Japan Air System	JA8066	
53357	90-30		Japan Air System	JA8069	
53358	90-30		Japan Air System	JA8070	
53359	90-30		Japan Air System	JA8004	
53360	90-30		Japan Air System	JA8020	
53361	90-30		Japan Air System	JA8029	
53362	88	1955	Delta Air Lines	N995DL	
53363	88	1958	Delta Air Lines	N996DL	
53364	88	1961	Delta Air Lines	N997DL	
53365	81	1998	Scandinavian A/L System	LN-RMR	
53366	81	1999	Scandinavian A/L System	SE-DME	
53367	90-30		McDonnell Douglas	N901DC	prototype, ff 22Feb93
53368	81	2003	Scandinavian A/L System	LN-RMS	
53369	81		not built	(SE-DMF)	
53370	88	1963	Delta Air Lines	N998DL	
53371	88	1965	Delta Air Lines	N999DN	
53372	88	1970	Delta Air Lines	N900DE	
53374	83		not built		
53375	83		not built		
53377	83	2057	Austrian Airlines	OE-LME	
53378	88	1980	Delta Air Lines	N901DE	
53379	88	1983	Delta Air Lines	N902DE	
53380	88	1986	Delta Air Lines	N903DE	
53381	90-30	2100	Delta Air Lines	N902DC	N901DA
53382	90-30	2094	Delta Air Lines	N902DA	
53383	90-30	2095	Delta Air Lines	N903DA	
53384	90-30	2096	Delta Air Lines	N904DA	
53385	90-30	2097	Delta Air Lines	N905DA	
53386	90-30	2099	Delta Air Lines	N906DA	
53387	90-30	2115	Delta Air Lines	N907DA	
53388	90-30	2117	Delta Air Lines	N908DA	
53389	90-30	2122	Delta Air Lines	N909DA	
53390	90-30		Delta Air Lines	(N910DA)	N910DN
53391	90-30	2126	Delta Air Lines	N911DA	
53392			Delta Air Lines		
53393			Delta Air Lines		
53394			Delta Air Lines		
53395			Delta Air Lines		
53396			Delta Air Lines		
53397			Delta Air Lines		
53398			Delta Air Lines		
53399			Delta Air Lines		
53407	81		not built	(LN-RMT)	
53408	81		not built	(SE-DMG)	
53409	88	1990	Delta Air Lines	N904DE	
53410	88	1992	Delta Air Lines	N905DE	
53411	82		not built	(SE-DMH)	
53412	82		not built	(OY-KHY)	
53413	82		not built	(SE-DMI)	
53414	82		not built	(OY-KHZ)	
53415	88	2034	Delta Air Lines	N906DE	
53416	88	2038	Delta Air Lines	N907DE	
53417	88	2032	Delta Air Lines	N908DE	
53418	88	2033	Delta Air Lines	N909DE	
53419	88	2036	Delta Air Lines	N910DE	
53420	88	2050	Delta Air Lines	N915DE	
53421	88	2051	Delta Air Lines	N916DE	
53422	88	2058	Delta Air Lines	N919DE	
53423	88	2059	Delta Air Lines	N920DE	
53424	88		not built	(N921DE)	
53425	88		not built	(N922DE)	
53426	87		not built		
53427	83		not built		
53432	87		not built		
53433	87		not built		
53434	87		not built		
53435	83		not built		

McDONNELL-DOUGLAS MD-80 Series/MD-90

C/n	Series	Line No	Last known Operator/Owner	Previous Identities/fate (where known)	
53436	83		not built		
53437	83		not built		
53438	83		not built		
53439	83		not built		
53440	83		not built		
53441	83		not built		
53442	83		not built		
53446	88	2046	Aerolineas Argentinas	LV-VGB	
53447	88	2064	Aerolineas Argentinas	LV-VGC	
53448	88	2074	Alaska Airlines	N972AS	
53449	88	2077	Alaska Airlines	N973AS	
53450	88	2078	Alaska Airlines	N974AS	
53451	88	2083	Alaska Airlines	N975AS	
53452	88	2109	Alaska Airlines	N976AS	
53453	88	2112	Alaska Airlines	N977AS	
53457	90-30		not built		
53458	90-30		not built		
53459	90-30		not built		
53460	90-30		not built		
53461	90-30		not built		
53462	90-30		not built		
53463	83	2089	AOM French Airlines	F-GGMF	
53464	83	2091	AOM French Airlines	F-GRMG	
53465	83	2093	AOM French Airlines	F-GRMH	
53466	83	2101	AOM French Airlines	F-GRMC	
53467	82	2102	Korean Air	HL7225	
53468	82	2114	Korean Air	HL7236	
53469	82	2116	Korean Air	HL7237	
53471	83				
53472	83				
53473	83				
53479	82		U-Land Group	N9012S	B-88888
53480	82		U-Land Group	B-88889	
53481	82				
53485	83	2128	Korean Air	HL	
53492	90-30				
53493	90-30				
53494	90-30				
53495	90-30				
53496	90-30				
53497	90-30				
53498	90-30				
53499	90-30				
53500	90-30				
53501	90-30				
53523	90-30				
53524	90-30				
53525	90-30				
53526	90-30				
53527	90-30				
53528	90-30				
53529	90-30				
53530	90-30				
53531	90-30				
53534	90-30				
53535	90-30				
53536	90-30				
53537	90-30				
53538	90-30				
53539	90-30				

McDONNELL-DOUGLAS MD-80 Series/MD-90

C/n	Series	Line No	Last known Operator/Owner	Previous Identities/fate (where known)

McDONNELL-DOUGLAS C-17 GLOBEMASTER III

Production is expected to total 120 aircraft

Line No	Series	Last known Owner/Operator	Identities/fate (where known)	
T1	YC-17A	USAF	87-0025	
P1	C-17A	USAF	88-0265	ff 19May92
P2	C-17A	USAF	88-0266	
P3	C-17A	USAF	89-1189	
P4	C-17A	USAF	89-1190	
P5	C-17A	USAF	89-1191	
P6	C-17A	USAF	89-1192	
P7	C-17A	USAF	90-0532	
P8	C-17A	USAF	90-0533	
P9	C-17A	USAF	90-0534	
P10	C-17A	USAF	90-0535	
P11	C-17A	USAF	92-3291	
P12	C-17A	USAF	92-3292	
P13	C-17A	USAF	92-3293	
P14	C-17A	USAF	92-3294	
P15	C-17A	USAF	93-0599	
P16	C-17A	USAF	93-0600	
P17	C-17A	USAF	93-0601	
P18	C-17A	USAF	93-0602	
P19	C-17A	USAF	93-0603	
P20	C-17A	USAF	93-0604	
P21	C-17A	USAF	94-0065	
P22	C-17A	USAF	94-0066	
P23	C-17A	USAF	94-0067	
P24	C-17A	USAF	94-0068	
P25	C-17A	USAF	94-0069	
P26	C-17A	USAF	94-0070	
P27	C-17A	USAF	9 -	
P28	C-17A	USAF	9 -	
P29	C-17A	USAF	9 -	
P30	C-17A	USAF	9 -	
P31	C-17A	USAF	9 -	
P32	C-17A	USAF	9 -	
P33	C-17A	USAF	9 -	
P34	C-17A	USAF	9 -	
P35	C-17A	USAF	9 -	
P36	C-17A	USAF	9 -	
P37	C-17A	USAF	9 -	
P38	C-17A	USAF	9 -	
P39	C-17A	USAF	9 -	
P40	C-17A	USAF	9 -	
P41	C-17A	USAF	9 -	
P42	C-17A	USAF	9 -	
P43	C-17A	USAF	9 -	
P44	C-17A	USAF	9 -	
P45	C-17A	USAF	9 -	
P46	C-17A	USAF	9 -	
P47	C-17A	USAF	9 -	
P48	C-17A	USAF	9 -	
P49	C-17A	USAF	9 -	
P50	C-17A	USAF	9 -	
P51	C-17A	USAF	9 -	
P52	C-17A	USAF	9 -	
P53	C-17A	USAF	9 -	
P54	C-17A	USAF	9 -	
P55	C-17A	USAF	9 -	
P56	C-17A	USAF	9 -	
P57	C-17A	USAF	9 -	
P58	C-17A	USAF	9 -	
P59	C-17A	USAF	9 -	
P60	C-17A	USAF	9 -	
P61	C-17A	USAF	9 -	
P62	C-17A	USAF	9 -	
P63	C-17A	USAF	9 -	
P64	C-17A	USAF	9 -	
P65	C-17A	USAF	9 -	
P66	C-17A	USAF	9 -	
P67	C-17A	USAF	9 -	
P68	C-17A	USAF	9 -	
P69	C-17A	USAF	9 -	
P70	C-17A	USAF	9 -	
P71	C-17A	USAF	9 -	
P72	C-17A	USAF	9 -	
P73	C-17A	USAF	9 -	
P74	C-17A	USAF	9 -	
P75	C-17A	USAF	9 -	
P76	C-17A	USAF	9 -	
P77	C-17A	USAF	9 -	

McDONNELL-DOUGLAS C-17 GLOBEMASTER III

Line No	Series	Last known Owner/Operator	Identities/fate (where known)
P78	C-17A	USAF	-
P79	C-17A	USAF	-
P80	C-17A	USAF	-
P81	C-17A	USAF	-
P82	C-17A	USAF	-
P83	C-17A	USAF	-
P84	C-17A	USAF	-
P85	C-17A	USAF	-
P86	C-17A	USAF	-
P87	C-17A	USAF	-
P88	C-17A	USAF	-
P89	C-17A	USAF	-
P90	C-17A	USAF	-
P91	C-17A	USAF	-
P92	C-17A	USAF	-
P93	C-17A	USAF	-
P94	C-17A	USAF	-
P95	C-17A	USAF	-
P96	C-17A	USAF	-
P97	C-17A	USAF	-
P98	C-17A	USAF	-
P99	C-17A	USAF	-
P100	C-17A	USAF	-
P101	C-17A	USAF	-
P102	C-17A	USAF	-
P103	C-17A	USAF	-
P104	C-17A	USAF	-
P105	C-17A	USAF	-
P106	C-17A	USAF	-
P107	C-17A	USAF	-
P108	C-17A	USAF	-
P109	C-17A	USAF	-
P110	C-17A	USAF	-
P111	C-17A	USAF	-
P112	C-17A	USAF	-
P113	C-17A	USAF	-
P114	C-17A	USAF	-
P115	C-17A	USAF	-
P116	C-17A	USAF	-
P117	C-17A	USAF	-
P118	C-17A	USAF	-
P119	C-17A	USAF	-
P120	C-17A	USAF	-

Production expected to be complete

SUD AVIATION SE210 CARAVELLE

C/n	Series	Last known Operator/Owner	Previous Identities/fate (where known)
01		(Aeroport de Paris)	F-WHHH F-BHHH b/u Oct86 Paris-Orly, France
02		(Centre d'Instruction Vilgenis)	F-WHHI F-BHHI scr Jan76 Vilgenis, Paris, France (nose section to Museé de l'Air, Paris-Le Bourget, France)
1	III	Centre d'Instruction Vilgenis	F-WHRA F-BHRA stored Feb76 Vilgenis, Paris, France and used for ground instruction
2	III	(Air France)	F-WHRB F-BHRB b/u Jan78 Paris-Orly, France
3	III	Norwegian Air Museum	LN-KLH stored Sep74 Oslo-Gardermoen, Norway
4	III	(Luftfartsverket)	SE-DAA used for fire practice Stockholm-Arlanda, Sweden
5	III	Air Afrique	F-BHRC (6W-SBC) (6V-ACP) 6V-AAR(2) used for ground instruction Mar85 Air Afrique Maintenance School, Dakar, Senegal
6	III	(Scandinavian A/L Sys)	OY-KRA b/u Aug74 Stockholm-Arlanda, Sweden
7	III	(Scandinavian A/L Sys)	LN-KLI b/u Sep74 Stockholm-Arlanda, Sweden
8	III	(Air France)	F-BHRD b/u Sep81 Paris-Orly, France
9	III	(Air France)	F-BHRE b/u Dec80 Paris-Orly, France
10	III	(Central African Republic Govt)	F-WJAP PP-VJC XV-NJA F-BNGE TL-AAI b/u Feb83 Paris-Orly, France
11	III	(Scandinavian A/L Sys)	F-BHOR SE-DAB b/u Sep74 Stockholm-Arlanda, Sweden
12	III	(Air France)	F-BHRF displayed Roanne, France
13	III	(Air France)	F-BHRG b/u Oct78 Paris-Orly, France
14	I	(Scandinavian A/L Sys)	OY-KRB w/o 19Jan60 Ankara-Esenboga, Turkey
15	III	(VARIG)	PP-VJD dbf 27Sep61 Brasilia, Brazil
16	III	Air France	F-BHRH stored Jun81 Pau, France
17	III	(Air France)	F-BHRI b/u Paris-Orly, France; used as nightclub Coulonges sur l'Autize, France
18	III	(Air Algerie)	F-WBNG F-OBNG 7T-VAG stored Jun76 Algiers, Algeria; b/u
19	VI-N	(Europe Aero Service)	F-WJAQ F-BJAQ F-WJAK LV-PRR LV-HGX Argentine AF T-91 N45SB F-GBMI b/u 1983/84 Perpignan, France
20	III	(AVENSA)	F-WJAK F-OBNH PP-VJI YV-C-AVI dbr 20Aug73 Barquisimento, Venezuela
21	III	ATS Airlines	F-WJAK OH-LEA D-ABAF PH-TRM F-WLGA F-BSRR I-GISA 9Q-CPS
22	III	Museé de l'Air	OH-LEB F-BJTR preserved Paris-Le Bourget, France
23	III	(Middle East Airlines)	F-WHRJ F-BHRJ OD-AEM w/o 17Apr64 nr Dhahran, Saudi Arabia
24	III	Luftfartsverket	F-WJAM (LN-KLJ) LN-KLP used for ground instruction Aug74 Malmo-Sturup, Sweden
25	III	(Thai Intl Airways)	SE-DAC HS-TGI w/o 29Jun67 nr Hong Kong
26	III	(Air France)	F-WHRK F-BHRK b/u Dec80 Paris-Orly, France
27	III	(Air France)	OH-LEC F-BJTS b/u Dec80 Paris-Orly, France
28	III	(Air Algerie)	F-WBNI F-OBNI 7T-VAI w/o 23Sep73 Algiers, Algeria
29	III	(Luftfartsverket)	OY-KRC HS-TGH OY-KRC used for fire practice Stockholm-Arlanda, Sweden
30	III	(Scandinavian A/L Sys)	LN-KLR HS-TGL LN-KLR b/u Oct74 Stockholm-Arlanda, Sweden
31	III	(Air France)	F-BHRL dbr 12Mar79 and b/u May79 Frankfurt, W Germany
32	III	(Royal Air Maroc)	F-WJAL CN-CCV w/o 01Apr70 Berrechid, Morocco
33	III	(Transavia)	F-WJAM HB-ICW PH-TRO b/u Mar76 Amsterdam-Schiphol, Netherlands (nose section to Aviodome Museum, Schiphol)
34	III	(Thai Intl Airways)	SE-DAD HS-TGK w/o 09Jul69 Bangkok-Don Muang, Thailand
35	VI-N	SAETA	F-WJAO I-DAXA HC-BAD wfs May77 and stored Quito, Ecuador
36	VI-N	Luchthaven Schiphol	I-DAXE PH-TVW used for evacuation training Amsterdam-Schiphol, Netherlands
37	III	Aeroport International de Lyon-Satolas	F-BHRM preserved Lyon-Satolas, France
38	III	(Aerospatiale)	F-WJAM HB-ICX F-BSRD B-1854 F-WJAL dismantled 1978 Toulouse, France; dest 1980 in structural testing
39	III	(Air France)	F-BHRN b/u Aug78 Paris-Orly, France
40	V-N	(SAETA)	I-DAXI HC-BAE w/o 18Jan86 Santa Elena, Guatemala
41	III	(Air France)	F-BHRO b/u Jan85 Angers-Avrille, France
42	III	Central African Rep Govt	F-WJAM N420GE F-BJAO F-WLKF F-BLKF (TL-KAB) TL-FCA wfs Jul89; stored
43	III	(Transavia)	HB-ICY PH-TRP b/u Dec75 Amsterdam-Schiphol, Netherlands (tail section to Delft, Netherlands)
44	VI-N	(Transavia)	I-DAXO PH-TVV b/u Jun76 Amsterdam-Schiphol, Netherlands
45	III	(Air France)	F-BHRP b/u Jul80 Paris-Orly, France
46	III	(Intercontinental A/W)	F-BHRQ used for spares Feb83 Lagos, Nigeria
47	III	Scandinavian A/L Sys	OY-KRD wfs Aug74 and stored Copenhagen-Kastrup, Denmark
48	III	(Transavia)	HB-ICZ PH-TRR b/u Dec75 Amsterdam-Schiphol, Netherlands
49	III	(Luftfartsverket)	OY-KRE HS-TGG OY-KRE b/u Oct77 Stockholm-Arlanda, Sweden
50	III	(Kabo Air)	F-BHRR 5N-AWK w/o 06Aug86 Calaba, Nigeria
51	III	Air Algerie	F-OBNJ OD-ADZ F-BLCZ 7T-VAE wfs Jun76 and stored Algiers, Algeria
52	III	(Air Inter)	F-BHRZ b/u 13Oct81 Paris-Orly, France
53	III	Air Cambodge	F-BJTA XU-JTB derelict Bangkok, Thailand
54	III	(Altair)	F-BHRS w/o 02Jul83 Milan-Malpensa, Italy
55	III	Inst Aeronautique Amaury de la Grange	F-BHRT used as instructional airframe Merville, France
56	III	(Luftfartsverket)	SE-DAE HS-TGF SE-DAE b/u Oct77 Stockholm-Arlanda, Sweden
57	III	Royal Air Maroc	CN-CCX stored May76 Casablanca-Anfar, Morocco
58	III	(Air France)	F-BHRU b/u Dec80 Paris-Orly, France; nose section to Athis-Mons, nr Paris-Orly, France
59	III	(Air France)	F-BHRV b/u Jan82 Paris-Orly, France

SUD AVIATION SE210 CARAVELLE

C/n	Series	Last known Operator/Owner	Previous Identities/fate (where known)
60	III	(Air France)	F-BHRX b/u Dec80 Paris-Orly, France
61	III	Museé de l'Aeronautique	F-BHRY preserved Nancy-Essey, France
62	VI-R	Ohio History of Flight Museum	F-WJAP (N2001U) F-BJAP F-WJAP PP-CJC N901MW preserved Columbus, OH
63	10A	(Sud Aviation)	F-WJAO b/u 1969 Toulouse, France (nose section to c/n 259)
64	VI-N	Museé de l'Air Brussels	F-WJAK OO-SRA preserved Brussels, Belgium
65	VI-N	(Sobelair)	F-WJAL OO-SRB b/u Jan80 Brussels, Belgium
66	VI-N	(Europe Aero Service)	F-WJAM OO-SRC F-BYCA b/u 1986 Perpignan, France; fuselage remains
67	VI-N	Corse Air Intl	F-WJAK OO-SRE F-BYCD wfs Feb87 and preserved Chateauroux, France
68	III	(Air France)	F-BJTB w/o 12Sep61 Rabat, Morocco
69	VI-N	(Royal Air Maroc)	F-WJAN OO-SRD w/o 22Dec73 nr Tetuan, Morocco
70	VI-N	(Indian Airlines)	F-WJAK F-BJAU OO-SRG VT-ECG b/u 1978 Bombay, India
71	VI-N	Afro Cargo	F-WJAK I-DABA 9Q-CRU stored 1985 Entebbe, Uganda
72	VI-N	(SAETA)	I-DABE used for spares Dec76 Quito, Ecuador
73	VI-N	(Air Algerie)	F-WBNK F-OBNK 7T-VAK w/o 26Jul69 Biskra, Algeria
74	VI-N	(African Air Charter)	I-DABI 9Q-CMD w/o 08Oct85 Mbujimayi, Zaire (remains extant)
75	VI-N	Air Algerie	F-OBNL 7T-VAL stored Jun76 Algiers, Algeria
76	VI-N	(Europe Aero Service)	F-WJAO OO-SRF F-BXOO b/u 1987 Perpignan, France
77	VI-N	Alitalia	I-DABU wfs 26Sep76 Rome-Fiumicino, Italy; used as instructional airframe
78	VI-N	Air Afrique	F-WJAL OO-SRH F-WLGA VT-ECH TU-TXR used for ground instruction Air Afrique Maintenance School, Dakar, Senegal
79	VI-N	(Alitalia)	I-DAXU used as restaurant Valcamonica, Italy
80	VI-N	(Alitalia)	I-DAXT b/u 1983 Venice-Tesseria, Italy
81	VI-N	(Alitalia)	I-DABR used as restaurant Alidelta, Perugio, Italy (painted as I-ALBA)
82	VI-N	(SAETA)	I-DABZ HC-BAI wfs Nov75 and used for spares Quito, Ecuador
83	III	(Air France)	F-BJTC OD-ADY F-BKGZ XW-PNH F-BSGZ dbr 28Aug76 Ho Chi Minh City, Vietnam; fuselage still present 1985
84	III	(Tunis Air)	F-BJTD TS-IKM b/u Aug77 Tunis, Tunisia
85	VI-N	(Soc Aerea Mediterranea)	I-DABT b/u Treviso, Italy
86	VI-R	Pima County Air Museum	N1001U PT-DUW N1001U preserved Jun90 Pima Air Museum, AZ
87	VI-R	Turbo Air Holdings	N1002U PH-TRY N777VV (N240RC) N777VV stored Jun88 Tucson, AZ
88	VI-R	Bradley Air Museum	N1003U OY-SAH N902MW displayed Bradley/Windsor Locks, Hartford, CT
89	VI-R	Airborne Express	N1004U OY-SAL N903MW stored Jul81 Wilmington, OH
90	VI-R	(Sterling Airways)	N1005U OY-SAP PI-C970 RP-C970 b/u Jan77 Copenhagen-Kastrup, Denmark
91	VI-R	Mauritanian Govt	N1006U (OY-SBV) PH-TVZ OY-SBV 5T-CJW 5T-MAL 5T-RIM wfs and used for ground instruction Dakar, Senegal
92	VI-R	(Schiphol Fire Service)	N1007U PH-TRX dbf Dec78 Amsterdam-Schiphol, Netherlands
93	VI-R	(Airborne Express)	N1008U OY-SBW PH-TVT OY-SBW I-STAE N904MW b/u Oct88 Wilmington, OH; cx Dec89
94	VI-R	Minerve	N1009U OY-SBY F-BUZC stored Jan86 Nimes, France
95	VI-R	(Midwest Air Charter)	N1010U OY-SAM N905MW w/o 19Jun80 Atlanta, GA
96	VI-R	(Transavia)	N1011U PH-TRH b/u Jan76 Amsterdam-Schiphol, Netherlands
97	VI-R	(Minerve)	N1012U OO-CVA F-BTON b/u Jun84 Toulouse-Montaudran, France
98	VI-R	(Sterling Airways)	N1013U OY-SAN b/u Oct74 Stockholm-Arlanda, Sweden
99	VI-R	Minerve	N1014U OY-SAK F-GAPA used for spares 1986 Nimes, France
100	VI-R	Tchad Government	N1015U PH-TRS TT-AAD TT-AAM stored N'Djamena, Tchad
101	VI-R	(Europe Aero Service)	N1016U OY-SAO F-BUFF b/u Feb80 Perpignan, France
102	VI-R	MPC Barton Associates	N1017U PH-TRU N555SL (N2296N) N98KT stored Van Nuys, CA
103	VI-R	(Filipinas Orient A/W)	N1018U OY-SAR PI-C969 b/u Oct76 Manila, Philippines
104	VI-R	(Sterling Airways)	N1019U OY-SAJ b/u Aug77 Copenhagen-Kastrup, Denmark (nose section to Egeskov Museum, Denmark)
105	III	ATS Airlines	F-BJTI 9Q-CZZ
106	VI-N	Coastal Airways	I-DABS EL-AIW impounded Jun83 and stored Thessaloniki, Greece
107	VI-R	(TAC Colombia)	F-WJAL EC-ARI b/u Jul77 Madrid-Barajas, Spain
108	VI-R	Far Eastern Air Tpt	F-WJAM EC-ARJ (EI-AVY) B-2501 stored May77 Taipei, Taiwan
109	VI-R	Aerocesar Colombia	EC-ARK HK-1812X HK-1812 stored Bogota, Colombia
110	VI-R	Far Eastern Air Tpt	EC-ARL (EI-ATR) B-2503 stored Jul79 Taipei, Taiwan
111	III	Kabo Air	F-BJTE used for spares Apr82
112	III	Swedish Air Museum	SE-DAF preserved Stockholm-Arlanda, Sweden
113	III	(Air France)	F-BJTF b/u Dec80 Paris-Orly, France
114	VI-R	(Gabon Government)	N1020U OY-SBZ TR-LWD b/u; fuselage at Castrette, Italy
115	III	(Fontshi Aviation Svce)	F-BJTG 9Q-CLP b/u Aug81 Kinshasa, Zaire
116	III	CEV	OH-LED 116/F-ZACE
117	VI-R	Servicios Aereos Nacionales	F-WJAN CS-TCA HC-BAJ wfs Jan86 and stored Guayaquil, Ecuador
118	VI-R	(Panair do Brasil)	F-WJAO PP-PDU auctioned for scrap 28Apr69 Rio de Janeiro, Brazil
119	III	Fontshi Aviation Svce	F-BJTJ HB-ICR F-BJTJ 9Q-CGC b/u Feb92 Kinshasa, Zaire
120	VI-R	(Cruzeiro do Sul)	F-WJAK PP-PDV dbf 23Dec73 Manaus, Brazil
121	III	(China Airlines)	HB-ICS B-1850 b/u 1979 Taipei, Taiwan
122	III	(China Airlines)	HB-ICT B-1852 w/o 20Nov71 Formosa Strait, nr Taiwan
123	III	(Inter Fret Transport Aerien)	HB-ICU OO-SBQ F-BUFH 9Q-CZL b/u 1986
124	III	Aeroport de Nice	F-BJTH F-WJTH preserved without markings Nice-Cote d'Azur, France
125	VI-R	(Servicios Aereos Nacionales)	CS-TCB HC-BAT w/o 29Apr83 Guayaquil, Ecuador
126	VI-R	(Cruzeiro do Sul)	F-WJAN PP-PDX w/o 01Jun73 Sao Luiz, Maranhao, Brazil
127	VI-N	(Aerolineas Argentinas)	LV-PVT LV-HGY w/o 03Jul63 Cordoba/Pajas Blanca, Argentina
128	VI-N	(Indian Airlines)	F-WLKJ VT-DPO w/o 03Jul73 Bombay, India

SUD AVIATION SE210 CARAVELLE

C/n	Series	Last known Operator/Owner	Previous Identities/fate (where known)
129	VI-R	Airborne Express	PP-CJA N907MW stored 1985 Wilmington, OH
130	VI-N	(Indian Airlines)	VT-DPP w/o 15Feb66 Delhi-Palam, India
131	VI-R	Aerotal Colombia	F-WJAO PP-PDZ HK-2212X HK-2212 stored 1985 Bogota, Colombia
132	VI-N	(Alitalia)	I-DABL b/u (fuselage to Livorno, Italy)
133	VI-R	Aerotal Colombia	PP-CJB HK-1709X used for spares Bogota, Colombia
134	VI-N	(Indian Airlines)	F-WLGA VT-DSB w/o 04Sep66 Bombay, India
135	VI-N	Jugoslovenski Aerotpt	F-WJAK YU-AHB wfs May76; preserved National Aviation Museum, Belgrade-Surcin, Yugoslavia
136	VI-R	LA Suramericanas	F-WLKI F-BLKI OE-LCU F-BTDL F-OGJD HK-2597X stored Dec93 Panama City, Panama
137	VI-R	(Servicios Aereos Nacionales)	CS-TCC HC-BFN w/o 12Sep79
138	VI-R	Aerocesar Colombia	N210G EC-AXU HK-1811X HK-1811 stored Bogota, Colombia
139	VI-N	(Corse Air Intl)	YU-AHA F-BYAI b/u Nov80 Paris-Orly, France
140	VI-R	(Aerotal Colombia)	F-WJAQ CC-CCO HK-1778 w/o 20Jul79 Bogota, Colombia
141	III	Musee de l'Air	F-BJTK 141/F-RAFG preserved Paris-Le Bourget, France
142	III	(Amt Feuer Luftverkehr)	F-BJTL w/o in fire exercise 27Sep85 Zurich, Switzerland
143	VI-N	(Alitalia)	F-WJSO F-BJSO I-DABM b/u Venice-Tesseria, Italy
144	III	Air Burundi	F-BJTM 9U-BTA wfs Jan93 Bujumbura, Burundi
145	III	(Air Cambodge)	F-BJTN XU-JTA w/o 22Jan71 Phnom Penh, Kampuchea
146	VI-N	SAETA	I-DABV HC-BDS (N5019K) stored 1986 Quito, Ecuador
147	III	(Swissair)	HB-ICV w/o 04Sep63 Durrenasch, Switzerland
148	III	(Air France Technical School)	F-BJTO b/u Jul81 Paris-Orly, France (nose and tail sections at Vilgenis, Paris, France)
149	VI-N	(Europe Aero Service)	LV-PVU LV-HGZ Argentine AF T-92 N46SB F-GBMJ b/u 1988 Perpignan, France
150	VI-N	SAETA	I-DABW used for spares Quito, Ecuador
151	VI-N	(Jugoslovenski Aerotpt)	YU-AHD w/o 11Sep73 Moganik, Yugoslavia
152	III	CCI Bordeaux	F-BJTP preserved as F-CCIB Bordeaux-Merignac, France
153	VI-N	(Middle East Airlines)	F-WJAL OD-AEE dest by commandos 28Dec68 Beirut, Lebanon
154	III	(Aerotours Dominicana)	CN-CCY SU-BBU EL-AAS HI-499 displayed as restaurant Expo Cuba, Havana, Cuba
155	VI-N	(Pushpaka Aviation)	VT-DPN used for spares Bombay, India
156	VI-R	(SAN Ecuador)	F-WJAN OE-LCE LX-LGG HC-BFM used for spares Quito, Ecuador
157	VI-N	(Middle East Airlines)	OD-AEF dest by commandos 28Dec68 Beirut, Lebanon
158	VI-R	Libyan Arab Airlines	F-WLHY F-BLHY 158/F-RAFA F-BLHY 5A-DAA stored 1976 Tripoli, Libya
159	VI-R	(Iberia)	EC-AVZ b/u Dec73 Madrid-Barajas, Spain
160	VI-R	Aerotal Colombia	CC-CCQ HK-1780 stored 1981 Bogota, Colombia
161	VI-R	Aerotal Colombia	F-WJAL OE-LCA F-BUFC HK-2402X stored 1981 Bogota, Colombia
162	VI-R	Libyan Arab Airlines	OH-LER F-BJTD 5A-DAB stored 1976 Benghazi, Libya
163	VI-R	(Iberia)	EC-ATV w/o 07Jan72 nr San Jose, Ibiza, Spain
164	VI-R	Aerotal Colombia	CC-CCP HK-1779 stored 1981 Bogota, Colombia
165	VI-R	(TAC Colombia)	EC-ATX HK-1810 w/o 21Dec80 nr Rio Hacha, Colombia
166	VI-R	Servicios Aereos Nacionales	OE-LCI LX-LGF HC-BFN stored May83 Quito, Ecuador
167	VI-R	LA Suramericanas	F-WJAQ OE-LCO F-BSEL F-OGJE HK-2598X stored Dec93 Panama City, Panama
168	VI-R	Aerocesar Colombia	PP-CJD HK-2287X stored 1983 Bogota, Colombia
169	10B3	Aero Jet	F-WLKJ F-BLKJ OH-LSG (LN-BSC) I-GISU F-GELQ HB-ICJ
170	III	China Airlines	OY-KRF F-BUOE B-1856 stored Oct79 Taipei, Taiwan
171	VI-R	(Iberia)	EC-BBR dbf 23Sep73 Madrid-Barajas, Spain
172	III	Swedish Air Force	SE-DAG Fv85172
173	VI-R	(Iberia)	EC-AVY b/u Dec73 Madrid-Barajas, Spain
174	VI-N	(Aerospatiale)	OD-AEO F-WJAN b/u Nov78 Toulouse, France
175	VI-N	AOM French Airlines	F-WJAL OO-SRI F-BYCB OO-SRI F-GATZ stored
176	10R	Aero Lloyd	F-WLKS F-BLKS EC-BDC EC-CAE D-ACVK stored Sep91 Bordeaux-Merignac, France
177	III	(Air France)	F-BJTQ b/u Dec80 Paris-Orly, France
178	III	Tunis Air	TS-TAR stored Aug77 Tunis, Tunisia
179	VI-N	(Alitalia)	I-DABF w/o 02Aug69 Marseilles, France
180	VI-N	Okada Air	LV-PBJ LV-III T-93 Arg AF N49SB F-GBMK 5N-AOY stored Perpignan, France
181	10B3	Air Toulouse Intl	F-WJAQ OH-LSA F-BMKS
182	10B3	(SERCA Colombia)	F-WJAL OH-LSB F-GDFY HK-3835X w/o 06May93 Cayenne, Guyana
183	10B3	Waltair	OY-STA YK-AFC F-GDJU 9Q-CPI
184	10B3	(Americana de Aviacion)	YK-AFA TZ-ADS F-GEPC HK-3962X w/o 04Nov95 Todos Santos, Baja California, Mexico
185	10B3	Europe Aero Service	OH-LSC F-BJEN stored Mar95 Perpignan, France
186	10B3	Syrianair	OY-STB YK-AFD stored Dec94
187	10B3	Air Toulouse Intl	OH-LSD I-GISO F-GELP
188	10B3	Americana de Aviacion	OH-LSF I-GISI SE-DEH F-GJDM HK-3914X HK-3947X
189	10B3	Americana de Aviacion	OH-LSE F-BJTU HK-3955X
190	10B3	Syrianair	YK-AFB stored Dec94
191	III	(Jugoslovenski Aerotpt)	OY-KRG PH-TRN YU-AJG w/o 21Nov72 Belgrade, Yugoslavia (fuselage to ground training)
192	VI-N	(Aerotour)	I-DABP F-BYAU w/o 09Dec77 Oujda, Morocco
193	III	CEV	SE-DAH F-BRIM 193/F-ZACF
194	VI-N	(Jugoslovenski Aerotpt)	YU-AHE b/u Belgrade, Yugoslavia
195	III	Royal Air Maroc	CN-CCZ ground trainer Casablanca, Morocco
196	VI-N	(Corse Air Intl)	F-WJAL OO-SRK F-BVPU b/u Jul84 Paris-Orly, France

SUD AVIATION SE210 CARAVELLE

C/n	Series	Last known Operator/Owner	Previous Identities/fate (where known)
197	VI-R	Far East Air Tpt	EC-AYD B-2505 stored Aug79 Taipei, Taiwan
198	VI-R	(Iberia)	EC-AYE b/u May74 Madrid-Barajas, Spain
199	10R	Europe Aero Service	JY-ACS TU-TCN EC-DCN (F-GEQL) F-GFBH stored Perpignan, France
200	10R	(SATA)	F-BNFE JY-ACT HB-ICK w/o 18Dec77 Funchal, Madeira
201	10R	LA Suramericanas	F-BNRA TU-TXQ F-BNRA TU-TXQ 201/F-RAFH HK-3932X
202	10R	(Iberia)	EC-BDD w/o 04Nov67 Fernhurst, Sussex, UK
203	VI-N	(Pushpaka Aviation)	F-WJAL VT-DUH b/u May95 Bombay, India
204	VI-N	Pushpaka Aviation	F-WJAQ VT-DUI stored 1983 Bombay, India
205	VI-N	(Corse Air Intl)	I-DABG F-BYAT b/u 04Feb85 Paris-Orly, France
206	III	Kabo Air	F-BNKA 5N-AWF stored 1989
207	III	Tunis Air	TS-MAC preserved Hotel Diar, Port el Kantaoui, Tunisia
208	III	(Altair)	F-BNKB I-GISE used as restaurant Porto Recanati, Italy
209	III	Westrafa Airlift	LN-KLN F-BRUJ YU-AJE F-BUFM 9XR-CH 9Q-CVO 9Q-CWK
210	III	Swedish Air Force	SE-DAI Fv85210
211	10B3	SEC Colombia	OH-LSH F-GDFZ HK-3836X HK-3836 stored Mar95 Sonora, Mexico
212	10B3	Global Colombia	F-BOEE OY-STC OH-LSK EC-CUM OY-STC (F-GHKO) HK-3858X
213	VI-N	(Pushpaka Aviation)	VT-DVI b/u May95 Bombay, India
214	III	(Air Inter)	D-ABAM F-BNKI dbf 04Jan71 Paris-Orly, France
215	11R	(Aerosucre)	F-WJAL TU-TCO 5N-AWT HK-3325X w/o 29Sep91 Bogota, Colombia
216	VI-N	(Indian Airlines)	VT-DVJ w/o 17Jun75 Bombay, India
217	III	Kabo Air	F-BNKC 5N-AWO stored 1988 Lagos, Nigeria
218	VI-N	Corse Air Intl	YU-AHF F-BVPZ displayed Athis-Mons, nr Paris-Orly, France
219	11R	(Aerosucre)	F-WJAK F-BJAK TU-TCY 5N-AWQ HK-3288X w/o 26Apr89 Barranquilla, Colombia
220	III	Intercontinental A/W	F-BNKD 5N-AVQ stored 1988 Lagos, Nigeria
221	VI-R	Libyan Arab Airlines	5A-DAE stored Apr75 Tripoli, Libya
222	10R	(Istanbul Airlines)	F-BNRB HB-ICQ TC-ASA used for spares Ercan, Cyprus
223	10R	Aerosucre	F-WJAQ EC-BIB HK-2860 stored 1983 Barranquilla, Colombia
224	III	Air Inter	F-BNKE preserved Marseilles-Marignane, France
225	10R	(Aviaco)	EC-BIC w/o 13Aug73 Coruna-Alvedro, Spain
226	VI-R	(Iberia)	EC-BIA dbf 05Nov73 Madrid-Barajas, Spain
227	III	(Air Inter)	F-BNKF b/u Feb83 Paris-Orly, France
228	10R	(Aviaco)	EC-BID w/o 05Mar73 Funchal, Madeira
229	III	ATS Airlines	F-BNKG 9Q-CCP stored Kinshasa, Zaire
230	10R	Aero Lloyd	EC-BIE D-AAST stored Jun91 Bordeaux-Merignac, France
231	VI-N	(Indian Airlines)	F-WLGB VT-DWN w/o 12Oct76 Bombay, India
232	10R	Transapel	EC-BIF D-ABAK HK-3676X HK-3869X stored Aug94 Sombrero Sacatecas, Mexico
233	VI-N	Corse Air Intl	YU-AHG F-BYCY fuselage displayed Epinal, France
234	VI-R	CEV	F-WJAL LX-LGE HB-ICP F-BRGX 234/F-ZACQ
235	10R	(Istanbul Airlines)	F-WJAM D-ABAP TC-ARI used for spares Ercan, Cyprus
236	10R	Europe Aero Service	JY-ADG EC-CPI F-GFBI stored Perpignan, France
237	VI-N	AOM French Airlines	YU-AHK VT-ECI F-BRGU stored
238	10B3	Sterling Airways	F-WLGB OY-STD EC-CMS OY-STD stored Apr91 Copenhagen-Kastrup, Denmark
239	10R	Istanbul Airlines	F-WLGC D-ABAW TC-AKA stored Nov91 Ercan, Cyprus
240	11R	(Armeé de l'Air)	9Q-CLC 240/F-RBPR dbr Jun79 Tahiti, French Polynesia
241	VI-N	Corse Air Intl	7601 Yugoslav AF 74101 Yugoslav AF F-BVSF wfs Oct88 and stored
242	III	Air France	F-BOHA preserved Avignon-Caumont, France, as F-POHA
243	10R	Europe Aero Service	F-WJAM D-ABAV F-GFBA stored Jun89 Perpignan, France
244	III	(Air France)	F-BOHB w/o 11Sep68 nr Antibes, France
245	III	(Air France)	F-BOHC b/u Dec80 Paris-Orly, France
246	III	Tunis Air	TS-ITU stored Jun77 Tunis, Tunisia
247	10R	Pelican Express A/W	F-WJAM D-ANYL EC-CIZ SE-DEB stored May88 Bordeaux, France
248	III	(Air Inter)	F-BNKH b/u May83 Paris-Orly, France
249	10B3	Air Toulouse Intl	F-WJAK OY-STE TL-ABB F-GCJT HB-IKD F-GHMU
250	10R	LA Suramericanas	EC-BRJ HB-ICI TC-ALA HK-3837X
251	11R	Armeé de l'Air	9Q-CLD 251/F-RBPS
252	III	(Air Inter)	F-BNKJ b/u Feb83
253	10R	Istanbul Air Museum	HB-ICN TC-ABA preserved Dec92
254	III	Fontshi Aviation Svce	CN-CCT SU-BBV EL-AAG EL-OSZ 9Q-CFN stored Kinshasa, Zaire
255	10B1R	LA del Norte Colombia	OY-SAY HB-ICO F-GGKD HK-3948X
256	III	Intercontinental A/W	F-BNKK 5N-AVO stored Lagos, Nigeria
257	10B3	Aerosucre	OY-STF RP-C123 EC-DFP OY-STF EC-DFP OY-STF (F-GHKN) HK-3806
258	III	(Air Inter)	F-OCPJ (F-BJGY) F-BSRY w/o 22Mar74 Bastia, Corsica
259	10B3	LA Suramericanas	OY-STG OH-LSI OY-STG F-GATP LN-BSE SE-DHA TC-JUN HK-3756X
260	III	Intercontinental A/W	F-BNKL 5N-AVP stored Lagos, Nigeria
261	11R	(Aerosucre)	EC-BRX HK-2850X w/o 27Nov86 Arauca, Colombia
262	10B3	Aerosucre	OY-STH F-GHKM OY-STH
263	10B1	(Transwede)	F-WJAN OY-SAZ F-WJAN D-ABAF F-OCKH F-WJAK EC-CYI (LN-TEC) SE-DEC w/o 06Jan87 Stockholm-Arlanda, Sweden; remains still present 1989
264	11R	Armeé de l'Air	EC-BRY 264/F-RBPT
265	10B3	(SEC Colombia)	OY-STI F-GHKN HK-3855X w/o 15Mar94 Bogota, Colombia
266	10B3	(Sterling Airways)	OY-STK w/o 15Mar74 Tehran, Iran
267	10B3	(Sterling Airways)	OY-STL w/o 14Mar72 Al Fujayrah, Dubai
268	10B3	Global Colombia	OY-STM F-GHKP HK-3857X
269	12	(Air Inter)	F-WJAN OY-SAC F-BNOH b/u 14Mar91 Paris-Orly, France
270	12	Air Provence Intl	OY-SAA (F-BVTB) OY-SAA F-GCVM

SUD AVIATION SE210 CARAVELLE

C/n	Series	Last known Operator/Owner	Previous Identities/fate (where known)
271	12	(Air Inter)	OY-SAB F-BVPY OY-SAB F-BNOG b/u May93 Paris-Orly, France
272	12	Inst Aeronautique Amaury de la Grange	OY-SAD F-GCVI rear fuselage Sep93 Merville, France
273	12	Air Provence Intl	OY-SAE F-GCVL
274	12	Air Inter	F-WTOA F-BTOA stored Apr91 Marseille, France
275	12	Air Inter	F-WJAL OY-SAF F-GCVJ stored Oct93 Rennes, France
276	12	Air Inter	OY-SAG F-GCVK stored May93 Merville, France
277	12	(Air Inter)	F-BTOB wfs Jun90; b/u Paris-Orly, France
278	12	Air Inter	F-BTOC stored Sep91 Paris-Orly, France
279	12	(Air Inter)	F-BTOD b/u Apr93 Paris-Orly, France
280	12	(Air Inter)	F-BTOE b/u Paris-Orly, France

Production complete

TUPOLEV Tu-104

Most serial numbers are believed to contain the c/n in the last four digits, the first and second of these last four digits representing the batch number and the third and fourth digits the number of the aircraft (from 1-5, with one exception) in that batch

S/n	Series	Last known Owner/Operator	Identities/fate (where known)			
1681301	G	Aeroflot	CCCP-L5411			
1681302?	G	Aeroflot	Soviet AF 05 red	CCCP-L5412	CCCP-42318	wfs 1967 for water tank tests
1681303?	G	Aeroflot	CCCP-L5413			
1681304?	G	(Aeroflot)	CCCP-L5414	w/o 19Feb58 Savosteevka		
1681305?	G	Aeroflot	CCCP-L5415	wfs by Jun93 Kiev Inst of Civil Engineering, Ukraine		
7350204	A	Aeroflot	CCCP-42338			
7350302	A	Aeroflot	CCCP-42341			
8350602	A	Aeroflot	CCCP-42382			
8350603	A	Aeroflot	CCCP-42383			
8350604	A	Aeroflot	CCCP-42384			
8350605	A	Aeroflot	CCCP-42385			
8350701	A	Aeroflot	CCCP-42386			
8350702	A	Aeroflot	CCCP-42387			
8350703?	A	(Aeroflot)	CCCP-42388	dbr 17Sep61 Tashkent, USSR		
8350704	A	Aeroflot	CCCP-42389	Soviet AF 47 red	preserved Kharkov, Russia	
8350705	A	Aeroflot	CCCP-42390	Soviet AF 46 red	preserved Monino Museum, Russia	
9350801	A	CSA	CCCP-42391	OK-NDF	preserved as restaurant Oloumouc, Czechoslovakia	
9350802	A	Aeroflot	CCCP-42392			
9350803	A	Aeroflot	CCCP-42393			
9350804?	A	Aeroflot	CCCP-42394			
9350805	A	Aeroflot	CCCP-42395			
9350901?	A	Aeroflot	CCCP-42396			
9350902	A	Aeroflot	CCCP-42397			
9350903	A	Aeroflot	CCCP-42398			
9350905	A	Aeroflot	CCCP-42456			
76600302			Tu-107 model			
6600501	A	Aeroflot	CCCP-42451	displayed Khabarovsk, Russia		
76600503	A	Vojenske Museum	OK-LDA	preserved Kbely, Czechoslovakia		
76600601	A	(CSA)	OK-LDB	w/o 16Jun63 Bombay, India		
76600602	A	CSA	OK-LDC	preserved Touzim, Brno, Czechoslovakia		
86601202	A	(CSA)	OK-MDE	w/o 29Aug73 Nicosia, Cyprus		
96601803	A	(CSA)	OK-NDD	w/o 01Jun70 Tripoli, Libya		
06601901	A	Aeroflot	CCCP-42459			
06601902	A	Aeroflot	CCCP-42460	preserved Rybinsk, Russia		
06601903	A	Aeroflot	CCCP-42461			
06602001	A	Aeroflot	CCCP-42462			
06602002	A	Aeroflot	CCCP-42463			
020806?	B	Aeroflot	CCCP-42465			
021201?	B	Aeroflot	CCCP-42468			
021202?	B	Aeroflot	CCCP-42469			
021203?	B	Aeroflot	CCCP-42470			
021204	B	(Aeroflot)	CCCP-42471	w/o 28Nov76 Moscow-Sheremetyevo, USSR		
021205?	B	(Aeroflot)	CCCP-42472	dbr 30Aug75 Novosibirsk, USSR		
021301?	B	Aeroflot	CCCP-42473			
021302	B	Aeroflot	CCCP-42474			
021303?	B	Aeroflot	CCCP-42475			
021304?	B	(Aeroflot)	CCCP-42476	w/o 09Jun64 Novosibirsk, USSR		
021305	B	Aeroflot	CCCP-42477			
021401?	B	Aeroflot	CCCP-42478			
021402?	B	Aeroflot	CCCP-42479			
021403	B	Aeroflot	CCCP-42480			
021404?	B	Aeroflot	CCCP-42481			
021405	B	Aeroflot	CCCP-42482			
021501	B	Aeroflot	CCCP-42483			
021502?	B	Aeroflot	CCCP-42484			
021503?	B	Aeroflot	CCCP-42485	present N of Monino to Moscow road, Russia		
021504?	B	(Aeroflot)	CCCP-42486	w/o 13Oct73 Moscow-Domodedovo, USSR		
021505	B	Aeroflot	CCCP-42487			
021601	B	Aeroflot	CCCP-42488			
021602?	B	Aeroflot	CCCP-42489			
021603?	B	(Aeroflot)	CCCP-42490	w/o 10Oct71 Moscow-Vnukovo, USSR		
021604	B	(Aeroflot)	CCCP-42491	w/o 04Jun62 Sofia, Bulgaria		
021605	B	(Aeroflot)	CCCP-42492	w/o 13Jul63 Irkutsk, USSR		
021701	B	Aeroflot	CCCP-42493			
021702	B	Aeroflot	CCCP-42494			
021703	B	(Aeroflot)	CCCP-42495	w/o 25Oct62 Moscow-Sheremetyevo, USSR		
021704?	B	Aeroflot	CCCP-42496			
021705?	B	Aeroflot	CCCP-42497			
021801?	B	Aeroflot	CCCP-42498			
021802?	B	Aeroflot	CCCP-42499			
021803	B	Aeroflot	CCCP-42500			
021804?	B	(Aeroflot)	CCCP-42501	w/o 05Nov74 Chita, USSR		
021805	B	Aeroflot	CCCP-42502			
021901?	B	(Aeroflot)	CCCP-42503	w/o 07Dec73 Moscow-Domodedovo, USSR		
021902	B	(Aeroflot)	CCCP-42504	w/o 02Nov61 Vladivostok, USSR		

TUPOLEV Tu-104

S/n	Series	Last known Owner/Operator	Identities/fate (where known)	
021903	B	Aeroflot	CCCP-42505	
021904?	B	(Aeroflot)	CCCP-42506	w/o 30Sep73 Sverdlovsk, USSR
021905	B	Aeroflot	CCCP-42507	
022001	B	Aeroflot	CCCP-42508	
022002	B	Aeroflot	CCCP-42509	

The following are aircraft for which there are no confirmed serial numbers at the present time:

S/n	Series	Last known Owner/Operator	Identities/fate (where known)	
		Aeroflot	CCCP-L5400	prototype; ff 17Jun55
		Aeroflot	CCCP-L5401	
	G	Aeroflot	CCCP-L5402	
		Aeroflot	CCCP-L5403	
		Aeroflot	CCCP-L5404	
		Aeroflot	CCCP-L5406	
		Aeroflot	CCCP-L5416	
		Aeroflot	CCCP-L5417	
		Aeroflot	CCCP-L5419	
		Aeroflot	CCCP-L5420	
	A	Aeroflot	CCCP-L5421	
		Aeroflot	CCCP-L5422	
		Aeroflot	CCCP-L5423	
		Aeroflot	CCCP-L5425	
		Aeroflot	CCCP-L5427	
		Aeroflot	CCCP-L5428	
		Aeroflot	CCCP-L5429	
	A	Aeroflot	CCCP-L5430	
	A	Aeroflot	CCCP-L5432	
		Aeroflot	CCCP-L5433	
		Aeroflot	CCCP-L5434	
		Aeroflot	CCCP-L5435	
	A	Aeroflot	CCCP-L5436	
		Aeroflot	CCCP-L5437	
	A	Aeroflot	CCCP-L5439	
	A	Aeroflot	CCCP-L5440	
	A	(Aeroflot)	CCCP-L5442	w/o 15Aug58 nr Chita, USSR
	A	Aeroflot	CCCP-L5443	
	A	Aeroflot	CCCP-L5444	
	A	Aeroflot	CCCP-L5445	
	A	Aeroflot	CCCP-L5446	
	A	Aeroflot	CCCP-L5458	
	A	Aeroflot	CCCP-L5413	CCCP-42313
		Aeroflot	CCCP-06195	derelict by Aug92 Moscow-Zhukovsky, Russia
	A	Aeroflot	CCCP-42319	
	A	Aeroflot	CCCP-42322	wfs Aug81, preserved Ulyanovsk, Russia
	A	Aeroflot	CCCP-42325	
	A	Aeroflot	CCCP-42326	dumped by Aug93 Moscow-Zhukovsky, Russia
	A	(Aeroflot)	CCCP-42327	w/o 09Feb76 Irkutsk, USSR
	A	Aeroflot	CCCP-42329	
	A	Aeroflot	CCCP-42330	
	A	Aeroflot	CCCP-42334	
	A	(Aeroflot)	CCCP-42335	w/o 17Jul76 Chita, USSR
	A	Aeroflot	CCCP-42336	
	A	Aeroflot	CCCP-42337	
	A	Aeroflot	CCCP-42340	
	A	Aeroflot	CCCP-L5442	CCCP-42342
	A	Aeroflot	CCCP-42343	
	A	Aeroflot	CCCP-42344	
	A	Aeroflot	CCCP-L5445	CCCP-42345
	A	Aeroflot	CCCP-42346	dumped by Aug92 Moscow-Zhukovsky, Russia
	A	Aeroflot	CCCP-L5447	CCCP-42347
	A	Aeroflot	CCCP-42348	
	A	Aeroflot	CCCP-42350	
	A	Aeroflot	CCCP-42351	
	A	Aeroflot	CCCP-L5453	CCCP-42353
	A	Aeroflot	CCCP-42354	
	A	Aeroflot	CCCP-42355	Tu-16 model
	A	Aeroflot	CCCP-42356	
	A	(Aeroflot)	CCCP-42357	w/o 01Feb61 Vladivostok, USSR
	A	Aeroflot	CCCP-42358	
	A	Aeroflot	CCCP-L5459	CCCP-42359
	A	Aeroflot	CCCP-L5460	CCCP-42360
	A	Aeroflot	CCCP-42361	
	A	(Aeroflot)	CCCP-42362	w/o 17Oct58
	A	(Aeroflot)	CCCP-42366	w/o 02Sep62 nr Khabarovsk, USSR
	A	Aeroflot	CCCP-42367	
	A	Aeroflot	CCCP-42368	
	A	(Aeroflot)	CCCP-42369	w/o 13Jan77 nr Alma-Ata, USSR
	A	(Aeroflot)	CCCP-42370	w/o 30Jun62 Krasnoyarsk, USSR
	A	Aeroflot	CCCP-42371	
	A	Aeroflot	CCCP-42372	

TUPOLEV Tu-104

S/n	Series	Last known Owner/Operator	Identities/fate (where known)	
	A	Aeroflot	CCCP-42373	
	A	Aeroflot	CCCP-42374	
	A	Aeroflot	CCCP-42375	
	A	Aeroflot	CCCP-42377	
	A	Aeroflot	CCCP-42378	
	A	Aeroflot	CCCP-42379	
	A	Aeroflot	CCCP-42380	
	A	Aeroflot	CCCP-42381	
	B	Aeroflot	CCCP-42399	
	B	Aeroflot	CCCP-42400	
	B	Aeroflot	CCCP-42401	
	B	Aeroflot	CCCP-42402	
	B	Aeroflot	CCCP-42403	
	B	Aeroflot	CCCP-42404	
	B	(Aeroflot)	CCCP-42405	w/o 25Jul71 Irkutsk, USSR
	B	Aeroflot	CCCP-42407	
	B	(Aeroflot)	CCCP-42408	w/o 19Mar72 Omsk, USSR
	B	Aeroflot	CCCP-42409	
	B	Aeroflot	CCCP-42410	
	B	Aeroflot	CCCP-42411	
	B	Aeroflot	CCCP-42412	
	B	Aeroflot	CCCP-42413	
	B	Aeroflot	CCCP-42414	
	B	Aeroflot	CCCP-42415	
	B	Aeroflot	CCCP-42416	
	B	Aeroflot	CCCP-42417	
	B	Aeroflot	CCCP-42418	
	B	Aeroflot	CCCP-42419	
	B	Aeroflot	CCCP-42420	
	B	Aeroflot	CCCP-42421	
	B	Aeroflot	CCCP-42422	
	B	Aeroflot	CCCP-42423	
	B	Aeroflot	CCCP-42424	
	B	Aeroflot	CCCP-42425	
	B	Aeroflot	CCCP-42426	
	B	Aeroflot	CCCP-42427	
	B	Aeroflot	CCCP-42428	
	B	Aeroflot	CCCP-42429	
	B	Aeroflot	CCCP-42430	
	B	Aeroflot	CCCP-42431	
	B	Aeroflot	CCCP-42432	
	B	Aeroflot	CCCP-42433	
	B	Aeroflot	CCCP-42434	
	B	Aeroflot	CCCP-42435	
	B	(Aeroflot)	CCCP-42436	w/o 28Apr69 Irkutsk, USSR
	B	Aeroflot	CCCP-42437	
	B	(Aeroflot)	CCCP-42438	w/o 13Mar61 Sverdlovsk, USSR
	B	Aeroflot	CCCP-42439	
	B	Aeroflot	CCCP-42440	
	B	Aeroflot	CCCP-42441	
	B	Aeroflot	CCCP-42442	
	B	Aeroflot	CCCP-42443	
	B	(Aeroflot)	CCCP-42444	w/o 17Mar79 Moscow-Vnukovo, USSR
	B	Aeroflot	CCCP-42445	
	B	Aeroflot	CCCP-42446	
	B	(Aeroflot)	CCCP-42447	w/o 10Jul61 Odessa, USSR
	B	Aeroflot	CCCP-42448	
		Aeroflot	CCCP-42449	
		Aeroflot	CCCP-42450	
	A	(Aeroflot)	CCCP-42452	w/o 21Oct60 Ust-Orda, USSR
	A	Aeroflot	CCCP-42453	
	A	Aeroflot	CCCP-42454	
	A	Aeroflot	CCCP-42455	
		Aeroflot	CCCP-42457	
		Aeroflot	CCCP-42458	
	B	Aeroflot	CCCP-42464	
		Aeroflot	CCCP-42466	
	B	Aeroflot	CCCP-42467	
	B	Aeroflot	CCCP-42468	
	B	Aeroflot	CCCP-42469	
		Aeroflot	CCCP-42470	
	B	Aeroflot	CCCP-42512	

Production complete; all are believed wfs

One Aeroflot Tu-104 w/o 23Apr73 nr Leningrad, one Aeroflot Tu-104 w/o 18May73 nr Chita, east of Lake Baikal and one Tu-104 w/o 07Feb81 20km N of Leningrad

TUPOLEV Tu-124

Serial numbers are believed to contain the c/n in the last four digits, the first and second of these last four digits representing the batch number and the third and fourth digits the number of the aircraft in that batch

S/n	Series	Last known Owner/Operator	Identities/fate (where known)	
350101?		Aeroflot	CCCP-45000	prototype; ff Jun60
350102?		Aeroflot	CCCP-45001	
350103?		Aeroflot	CCCP-45002	possibly static airframe
350201?		Aeroflot	CCCP-45003	possibly static airframe
350202?		(Aeroflot)	CCCP-45004	w/o 23Dec73 nr Lvov, Poland
350203?		Aeroflot	CCCP-45005	
350301?		Aeroflot	CCCP-45006	
350302?		Aeroflot	CCCP-45007	
1350303		Soviet AF	Soviet AF 21	55
350401?		Aeroflot	CCCP-45008	
350402?		Aeroflot	CCCP-45009	
350403?		Aeroflot	CCCP-45010	b/u May90 Pushkin, Russia
350501?		Aeroflot	CCCP-45011	
350502?		(Aeroflot)	CCCP-45012	w/o 02Sep70 over Ukraine
350503?		Aeroflot	CCCP-45013	
350504?		Aeroflot	CCCP-45014	
350505?		Aeroflot	CCCP-45015	
350601?		Aeroflot	CCCP-45016	
2350602		Aeroflot	CCCP-45017	
0610		Soviet AF	22 red	preserved as "CCCP-45017" Ulyanovsk, Russia
2350603?		Aeroflot	CCCP-45018	
2350604?		(Aeroflot)	CCCP-45019	w/o 07Mar68 Volgograd, USSR
2350605?		Aeroflot	CCCP-45020	
2350701?		(Aeroflot)	CCCP-45021	w/o 02Feb63 River Neva, Leningrad, USSR
2350702?		Aeroflot	CCCP-45022	
2350703?		Aeroflot	CCCP-45023	
2350704?		Aeroflot	CCCP-45024	
2350705		Aeroflot	CCCP-45025	preserved Monino Museum, Moscow, Russia
2350801?		Aeroflot	CCCP-45026	
2350802?		Aeroflot	CCCP-45027	
2350803		(Aeroflot)	CCCP-45028	w/o 08Mar65 Kyubishev, USSR
2350804		Aeroflot	CCCP-45029	preserved Grodno, Belarus
2350805?		Aeroflot	CCCP-45030	
2350901?		(Aeroflot)	CCCP-45031	w/o 20Nov73 Kazan, USSR
350902?		Aeroflot	CCCP-45032	
350903?		Aeroflot	CCCP-45033	
350904?		Aeroflot	CCCP-45034	
350905?		Aeroflot	CCCP-45035	
351001?		Aeroflot	CCCP-45036	
351002?		(Aeroflot)	CCCP-45037	w/o 03Jan76 Moscow-Vnukovo, USSR
3351003		(Aeroflot)	CCCP-45038	w/o 29Aug79
3351004?		Aeroflot	CCCP-45039	
3351005?		Aeroflot	CCCP-45040	
3351101?		Aeroflot	CCCP-45041	
3351102?		Aeroflot	CCCP-45042	
3351103?		Aeroflot	CCCP-45043	
3351104?		Aeroflot	CCCP-45044	
3351105?		Aeroflot	CCCP-45045	
3351201?		Aeroflot	CCCP-45046	
3351202?		Aeroflot	CCCP-45047	
3351203?		Aeroflot	CCCP-45048	
351204?		Aeroflot	CCCP-45049	
351205?		Aeroflot	CCCP-45050	
351301		Aeroflot	CCCP-45051	
351302?		Aeroflot	CCCP-45052	preserved Moscow by Jun70; removed by Mar73
351303?		Aeroflot	CCCP-45053	
351304?		Aeroflot	CCCP-45054	
351305?		Aeroflot	CCCP-45055	
351401?		Aeroflot	CCCP-45056	
351402?		Aeroflot	CCCP-45057	
351403?		Aeroflot	CCCP-45058	
351404?		Aeroflot	CCCP-45059	
351405?		Aeroflot	CCCP-45060	
351406?		(Aeroflot)	CCCP-45061	w/o 16Dec73
351407?		(Aeroflot)	CCCP-45062	w/o 09Jul73 Kyubishev, USSR
351408?		Aeroflot	CCCP-45063	
351409?		Aeroflot	CCCP-45064	
351410?		Aeroflot	CCCP-45065	
351501?		Aeroflot	CCCP-45066	
351502?		Aeroflot	CCCP-45067	
4351503	V	Iraqi Airways	OK-TEA	YI-AEY
4351504	V	(CSA)	OK-TEB	w/o 18Aug70 Zürich-Kloten, Switzerland
4351505	V	E German AF	495/DM-VBA	CCCP-?
4351506?		Aeroflot	CCCP-45068	
4351507?		Aeroflot	CCCP-45069	
4351508	V	Interflug	DM-SDA	CCCP-?
4351509?		Aeroflot	CCCP-45070	
4351510		Aeroflot	CCCP-45071	

TUPOLEV Tu-124

S/n	Series	Last known Owner/Operator	Identities/fate (where known)			
4351601		Soviet AF	50			
4351602?		Iraq AF	634			
4351603?		Iraq AF	635			
4351604	V	Aeroflot	CCCP-45072			
351605?	V	Aeroflot	CCCP-45073			
351606?		Aeroflot	CCCP-45074			
5351607	V	Iraqi Airways	OK-UEC	YI-AEL		
5351608?		Aeroflot	CCCP-45075	to prototype Tu-134		
5351609?		Aeroflot	CCCP-45076	to prototype Tu-134		
5351610?	V	Aeroflot	CCCP-45077			
5351701?	V	Aeroflot	CCCP-45078			
5351702?	V	Aeroflot	CCCP-45079			
5351703?		Aeroflot	CCCP-45080			
5351704?		Aeroflot	CCCP-45081			
5351705?		Aeroflot	CCCP-45082	partially derelict by Jun93 Omsk, Russia		
5351706?		(Aeroflot)	CCCP-45083	w/o 29Jan70 nr Murmansk, USSR		
5351707?		Aeroflot	CCCP-45084			
5351708	V	E German AF	DM-SDB	496/DM-VBC	CCCP-?	
5351709?		Chinese AF	50255			
5351710?		Aeroflot	CCCP-45085			
5351801?		(Aeroflot)	CCCP-45086	w/o 10Nov65 Murmansk, USSR		
5351802?		Aeroflot	CCCP-45087			
5351803?		Aeroflot	CCCP-45088			
5351804?	V	Aeroflot	CCCP-45089			
5351805?	V	Aeroflot	CCCP-45090			
5351806	V	Aeroflot	CCCP-45091			
5351807?		Aeroflot	CCCP-45092	preserved Kharkov, Russia		
5351808		Chinese AF	50256	preserved Datang-Shau, China		
6351809?		Aeroflot	CCCP-45093			
351810?		Aeroflot	CCCP-45094			
351901?		Aeroflot	CCCP-45095			
6351902?	K	Indian AF	CCCP-45097?	V642	1642	V642/'VU-AVA'
6351903?	K	(Indian AF)	CCCP-45098?	V643	1643	V643/'VU-AVB'
			w/o 05Nov77 Jorhat, Assam, India			
6351904?	K	Indian AF	CCCP-45099?	V644	1644	V644/'VU-AVC'
6351905?	K	Aeroflot	CCCP-45200	possibly to CCCP-64452		
6351906?		Aeroflot	CCCP-45135			
6351907?		Aeroflot	CCCP-45146			
6351908?		Aeroflot	CCCP-45158			
6351909?		Aeroflot	CCCP-45173			
6351910?		Aeroflot	CCCP-45199			
6352001?		Aeroflot	CCCP-45200?	CCCP-64452		
6352002		Chinese AF	50257	preserved Datang-Shau, China		

The following are aircraft for which there are no confirmed serial numbers at the present time:

Owner/Operator	Identities	Fate
Soviet AF	CCCP-64452	preserved Savelovo (see c/n 6351905 & 6352001)
Aeroflot	CCCP-83961	
Interflug	DM-SDC	
CIS AF	15 blue	
Czech AF	608	

Production complete; all are believed wfs

One Iraqi AF Tu-124 reportedly destroyed at Baghdad in Feb91 during Gulf war

TUPOLEV Tu-134

There appear to be two serial number systems for Tu-134s; in the first, the serial numbers are believed to contain the c/n in the last four digits, the first and second of these last four digits representing the batch number and the third and fourth digits the number of the aircraft in that batch. In the second, beginning with serial number 08056, the last five digits tend to be regarded as those which relate to the c/n.

S/n	Series	Last known Owner/Operator	Identities/fate (where known)
0001?		Aeroflot	CCCP-45075 prototype; ff 1963 preserved Moscow, Russia
0002?		Aeroflot	CCCP-45076 second prototype
0002?		Aeroflot	CCCP-65600 preserved Urgench, USSR
0003		Aeroflot	CCCP-65601 Kiev Inst of Civil Engineering, Ukraine by Jun93
0004		Aeroflot	CCCP-65602 wfu
0005			CCCP-65603 possibly static test airframe
0101		Flt Research Int Gromov/ United Nations	CCCP-65604 RA-65604
0102		Aeroflot	CCCP-65605(1) wfs
0103		Aeroflot	CCCP-65606(1) wfs
0104		Aeroflot	CCCP-65607(1) wfs
0105		Aeroflot	CCCP-65608(1) wfs
6350201		Aeroflot	CCCP-65609(1) wfs
6350202		Aeroflot	CCCP-65610(1) derelict by Sep92 Ulyanovsk, Russia
6350203?		Soviet AF	01 red
7350204		Aeroflot	CCCP-65611(1) wfs
7350205		(Aeroflot)	CCCP-65612(1) used for fire-fighting St Petersburg-Pulkovo, Russia; remains present Apr91
7350301		Aeroflot	CCCP-65613(1) wfs
7350302		Aeroflot	CCCP-65614(1) Minsk-Chizovka Technical School by Sep93
7350303		Aeroflot	CCCP-65615(1) wfs
7350304		Soviet AF	CCCP-65616(1) 77 blue
7350305		Aeroflot	CCCP-65617(1) wfs
8350401		Aeroflot	CCCP-65618(1) preserved in playground by Aug92 Ulyanovsk, Russia
8350402		Aeroflot	CCCP-65619(1) wfs
8350403		Aeroflot	CCCP-65620(1) wfs
8350404		Aeroflot	CCCP-65621(1) wfs
8350405		Balkan Bulgarian A/L	LZ-TUA derelict by May92 Sofia, Bulgaria
8350501		(Balkan Bulgarian A/L)	LZ-TUB w/o 16Mar78 Vratsa, Bulgaria
8350502		(Interflug)	DM-SCA w/o 30Oct72 Dresden, E Germany
8350503		Interflug	DM-SCB DDR-SCB wfu Nov75; preserved as cafe Oct88 Oschersteben, Germany
8350504		Aeroflot	CCCP-65622(1) wfs
8350505		Aeroflot	CCCP-65623(1) wfs
8350601		Aeroflot	CCCP-65624(1) wfs
8350602		LOT	SP-LGA wfs
8350603		(LOT)	SP-LGB w/o 23Jan80 Warsaw-Okecie, Poland
8350604		(Malev)	HA-LBA w/o 19Nov69 Istanbul, Turkey
8350605		(Malev)	HA-LBB HA-LBC w/o 21Sep77 Bucharest, Romania
9350701			YU-AHH CCCP-?
9350702		(Interflug)	DM-SCD w/o 01Sep75 Leipzig, E Germany
9350703		Aeroflot	CCCP-65625 derelict by Aug95 Perm, Russia
9350704		Aeroflot	CCCP-65626(1) wfs
9350705		Soviet AF	YU-AHI 01 red
8350801		(Malev)	HA-LBD w/o 16Sep71 Kiev, USSR
8350802		Malev	HA-LBE preserved Feb90 in museum Budapest, Hungary
9350803		Aeroflot	CCCP-65627 wfu
9350804		LOT	SP-LGC wfs
9350805		LOT	SP-LGD wfs
9350806		LOT	SP-LGE wfs
9350807		Balkan Bulgarian A/L	LZ-TUC wfs Sofia, Bulgaria
9350808		Balkan Bulgarian A/L	LZ-TUD wfs Sofia, Bulgaria
9350809		Aeroflot	CCCP-65628 wfu
9350810		Aeroflot	CCCP-65629 wfu
9350901		Aeroflot	CCCP-65630 wfu
9350902		Aeroflot	CCCP-65631 wfu
9350903		Aeroflot	CCCP-65632 wfu
9350904		(Interflug)	E German AF 183 DM-SCE DDR-SCE b/u Jun86 Berlin-Schonefeld, E Germany
9350905		Interflug	DM-SCF DDR-SCF preserved Leipzig, Germany
9350906		German AF	DM-SCH DDR-SCH German AF 11+13 preserved Finow, Germany as DDR-SCH
9350907		Aeroflot	CCCP-65633 wfu
9350908		Aeroflot	CCCP-65634 preserved Murmansk, Russia
9350909		Aeroflot	CCCP-65635 derelict by Aug93 Kharkov, Russia
9350910		Aeroflot	CCCP-65636 derelict by Sep93 Minsk-Loshitsa, Belarus
9350911		Aeroflot	CCCP-65637 wfu
9350912		Interflug	DM-SCG DDR-SCG wfs, used as anti-terrorist trainer
9350913		Interflug	E German AF 177/DM-VBB DM-SCZ DDR-SCZ preserved 1986 Bernsdorf, E Germany
9350914		Balkan Bulgarian A/L	LZ-TUE wfs Sofia, Bulgaria
9350915		Iraqi Airways	YI-AED possibly w/o 22Jul71 Jeddah, Saudi Arabia
9350916			CCCP-65638
9350917			CCCP-65639
9350918		(Balkan Bulgarian A/L)	LZ-TUF b/u May87 Sofia, Bulgaria

TUPOLEV Tu-134

S/n	Series	Last known Owner/Operator	Identities/fate (where known)
9350919		Aeroflot	CCCP-65640 wfu
9350920		(Aeroflot)	CCCP-65641 b/u by Sep94 Rostov na Don, Russia
0350921			YU-AHS CCCP-?
0350922		Balkan Bulgarian A/L	Bulgarian AF 050(1) LZ-TUO
0350923		Malev	HA-LBF wfs Dec88; preserved by Feb95 Szolnok, Hungary
0350924		Malev	HA-924 HA-LBG wfs Dec88 Budapest, Hungary
0350925		Auto-und Technik-Museum	HA-925 HA-LBH preserved Sinsheim, Germany
0350926		Aeroflot	CCCP-65642 wreck at St Petersburg-Pulkovo, Russia
0350927		Aeroflot	CCCP-65643 cabin trainer Aug91 St Petersburg-Pulkovo, Russia
0350928	A		CCCP-65644
0351001	A		CCCP-65646
0351002	A	Aeroflot Russian Int A/L	CCCP-65647 RA-65647
0351003	A	Aeroflot	CCCP-65648 preserved Ulyanovsk, Russia
0351004	A	(Aeroflot)	CCCP-65649 w/o 31May79 Tyuman, USSR
0351005	A	Aeroflot	CCCP-65645 instructional airframe by Aug93 Riga-Spilve, Latvia
0351006	A-3	Armenian Airlines	CCCP-65650 EK65650
0351007	A-3	Tyumen Airlines	CCCP-65651 RA-65651
0351008	A		CCCP-65652
0351009	A	Novosibirsk Avn Prod Ass	CCCP-65653 RA-65653
0351010	A	Aeroflot	CCCP-65654 wfs, stored by Apr95 Riga-Spilve, Latvia
0351101	A	Aeroflot	CCCP-65655 possibly wfs by Jul93
0351102	A		CCCP-65656
0351103	A	Aeroflot	CCCP-65657 wreck nr a lake Oct94 at Hrazdan, Armenia
351104	A		CCCP-65658
351105	A		CCCP-65659
351106	A		CCCP-65660
351107	A	Tyumen Airlines	CCCP-65661 RA-65661
351108	A	Aeroflot	CCCP-65662 firedump by Apr93 Samara, Russia
351109	A	Aeroflot	CCCP-65663 Minsk-Chizovka Technical School, Belarus by Sep93
1351110	A	Belavia	CCCP-65664 EW-65664
1351201	A	Air Ulyanousk	CCCP-65665
1351202	A-3	Donavia Airlines	CCCP-65666 RA-65666
1351203	A	Imperial Air	YU-AHX OB-1489 wfs
1351204	A	Russian Govt	YU-AHY TC-ALV YU-AHY 93926 RA-93926
1351205	A	(Aviogenex)	YU-AHZ w/o 23May71 nr Rijeka, Yugoslavia
1351206	A-3	Russian Govt	YU-AJA TC-ALU YU-AJA CCCP-93929
1351207	A-3	Tupolev Design Bureau	CCCP-65667 RA-65667
1351208	A	(Aeroflot)	CCCP-65668 w/o 30Jun73 Amman, Jordan
1351209	A	Bulgarian Govt	LZ-TUK wfs, parts missing by Apr95 Sofia, Bulgaria
1351210	A	Belavia	CCCP-65669 RA-65669 EW-65669
1351301	A-3	Malev	HA-LBI
1351302	A	Malev	HA-LBK
1351303	A	Bulgarian AF	LZ-TUP Bulgarian AF 050(2) LZ-TUP LZ D 050
1351304	A	Interflug	DM-SCK DDR-SCK D-AOBB preserved by May95 Hermeskeil, Germany
1351305	A	Interflug	DM-SCL E German AF 182/DM-VBC DM-SCL DDR-SCL on display Biberach, Germany
1351401?	A		CCCP-65670
1351402?	A-3	Bashkirian Airlines	CCCP-65671 RA-65671
1351403?	A		CCCP-65672
1351404?	A		CCCP-65673
1351405	A		CCCP-65674
1351406	A	CSA	OK-AFA wfs Jun88, to CCCP-?
1351407	A	Czech AF	Czech AF 1407 OK-AFD 1407
1351408	A-3	Balkan Bulgarian A/L	OK-BYR LZ-TUV
1351409	A-3	Moscow Airways	OK-BYQ LZ-TUU RA-65939
1351410	A	CSA	OK-AFB wfs May89, used as a cafe nr Slovak AF base, Piestany
1351501?	A	(Aeroflot)	CCCP-65675 w/o 27Feb88 Surgut, USSR
1351502	A	Belavia	CCCP-65676 RA-65676 EW-65676
1351503	A-3	Balkan Bulgarian A/L	OK-BYS LZ-TUZ
2351504	A	(CSA)	OK-CFC b/u Jul92 Prague, Czechoslovakia
2351505	A	(CSA)	OK-CFD w/o 02Jan77 Prague, Czechoslovakia
2351506	A	Energya	CCCP-65726 RA-65726
2351507?	A		CCCP-65727
2351508	A-3	Gagarin Aviation Factory	YU-AJD CCCP-93927 RA-93927
2351509?	A		CCCP-65728
2351510	A	Flt Research Int Gromov	CCCP-65740 RA-65740
2351511?	A-3	Tajik Air	CCCP-65730 EY-65730
2351512?	A-3	Armenian Airlines	CCCP-65731 EK65731
2351513?	A		CCCP-65732
2351514	A	(Aeroflot)	CCCP-65733 b/u by Sep94 Rostov na Don, Russia
2351515?	A		CCCP-65734
2351516?	A	(Aeroflot)	CCCP-65735 mid-air collision with Tu-134 CCCP-65816 11Aug79 over Ukraine
2351517?	A	Air Moldova	CCCP-65736 ER-65736
2351518?	A		CCCP-65737
2351519?	A	Novosibirsk Avn Prod Ass	CCCP-65738 RA-65738
2351520?	A	Russian Govt	CCCP-65739 RA-65739
2351601			CCCP-65729
2351602?	A	Air Moldova	CCCP-65741 ER-65741
2351602	A	CSA	OK-CFE OK-9522 preserved 14Dec90 in Ancona Museum, Italy
2351603	A	CSA	OK-CFF wfs 1991 Prague-Ruzyne, Czechoslovakia

TUPOLEV Tu-134

S/n	Series	Last known Owner/Operator	Identities/fate (where known)
2351604	A	Aeroflot	CCCP-65742 dumped by Aug92 Zhukovsky, Russia
2351605	A	Aeroflot	CCCP-65743 instructional airframe by Aug93 Kiev Inst Civil Engineering, Ukraine
2351606?	A		CCCP-65744
2351607	A	Aeroflot	CCCP-65745 anti-terrorist trainer in East Germany
2351608	A-3	Air Ukraine	CCCP-65746 UR-65746
2351609?	A		CCCP-65747
2351610?	A	Aeroflot	CCCP-65748 wfs by Aug93 Ulyanovsk, Russia
2351701?	A-3		CCCP-65949
2351702	A	Tyumen Airlines	CCCP-65950 RA-65950
2351703	A	(Aeroflot)	CCCP-65951 reportedly w/o 13Jan90 Pervouralsk, USSR
235170.?	A	Aeroflot	CCCP-65952 dumped by Sep92 Kiev-Borispol, Ukraine
235170.?			
2351706	A	(Aeroflot)	CCCP-65953 b/u by Sep94 Rostov na don, Russia
2351707	A-3	Syktyvkar Avia	CCCP-65954 RA-65954
2351708	A-3	Arkhangelsk Airlines	CCCP-65955 RA-65955
2351709	A	Korsar Airlines	CCCP-65956 RA-65956
2351710	A	(CSA)	OK-CFG b/u Jul92 Prague-Ruzyne, Czechoslovakia
2351801	A	CSA	OK-CFH preserved as a bar on outskirts of Brno City
2351802	A	Belavia	CCCP-65957 EW-65957
2351803	A		CCCP-65965
3351804	A	Syktyvkar Avia	CCCP-65958 RA-65958
3351805	A	Adjal Avia	CCCP-65959 4L-65959
3351806	A	Tyumen Airlines	CCCP-65960 RA-65960
3351807	A-3	Bashkirian Airlines	CCCP-65961 RA-65961
3351808	A	LOT	SP-LHA Polish AF 104 SP-LHA Polish AF 104 SP-LHA wfs by Jul95 Warsaw-Okecie, Poland
3351809	A	LOT	SP-LHB Polish AF 103 SP-LHB wfs by Jul95 Warsaw-Okecie, Poland
3351810	A	LOT	SP-LHC wfs by Jul95 Warsaw-Okecie, Poland
3351901			
3351902	A-3	Tupolev Design Bureau	CCCP-65966 RA-65966
3351903	A	Syktyvkar Avia	DM-SCI DDR-SCI D-AOBA CCCP-65611(2) RA-65611
3351904	A	Brandenburg Aero Park	DM-SCM w/o 22Nov77 E Berlin, E Germany; parts preserved Diepensee, Germany
3351905	A-3	St.Petersburg Avia Ent	CCCP-65967 RA-65967
3351906	A-3	Kish Air	LZ-TUM
3351907	A		CCCP-65968
3351908	A	(CSA)	OK-DFI b/u Oct93 Prague, Czechoslovakia
3351909	A-3	Syktyvkar Avia	CCCP-65969 RA-65969
3351910?	A	Nizhny Novgorod Airlines	CCCP-65970 RA-65970
3352001	A-3	Syktyvkar Avia	CCCP-65971 RA-65971
3352002	A-3	Syktyvkar Avia	CCCP-65972 RA-65972
3352003	A	Lithuanian Airlines	CCCP-65973 LY-ABA
3352004	A	Belavia	CCCP-65974 EW-65974
3352005	A	LOT	Polish AF 101(1) SP-LHF wfs by Jul95 Warsaw-Okecie, Poland
3352006?	A-3	Armenian Airlines	CCCP-65975 EK65975
3352007	A-3	Arkhangelsk Airlines	CCCP-65976 RA-65976
3352008	A	LOT	Polish AF 102(1) SP-LHG wfs by Jul95 Warsaw-Okecie, Poland
3352009?	A	Samara Airlines	CCCP-65800 RA-65800
3352010	A	Ulyanovsk Higher Civil Aviation School	CCCP-65801 RA-65801
3352101	A	Tyumen Airlines	CCCP-65802 RA-65802
3352102	A	Harco Air	E German AF 170 DM-SCN DDR-SCN D-AOBC CCCP-65612(2) RA-65612
3352103	A	Belavia	CCCP-65803 EW-65803
3352104?	A	Aeroflot	CCCP-65804 RA-65804 derelict by Apr93 Samara, Russia
3352105	A-3	Syktyvkar Avia	CCCP-65805 RA-65805
3352106	A	Syktyvkar Avia	E German AF 171 DM-SCO DDR-SCO D-AOBD CCCP-65613(2) 65613 RA-65613
352107?	A		CCCP-65806
352108?	A		CCCP-65807
352109	A	Adjal Avia	CCCP-65808 4L-65808
3352110	A	(Transair Georgia)	CCCP-65809 65809 w/o 23Sep93 Sukhumi, Georgia
352201	A-3	Orbi Georgian Airways	CCCP-65810 4L-65810
352202	A-3	Arkhangelsk Airlines	CCCP-65811 RA-65811
352203?	A		CCCP-65812
352204	A-3	Syktyvkar Avia	CCCP-65813 RA-65813
4352205	A-3	Aerotransservice	E German AF 175 DM-SCP DDR-SCP D-AOBE CCCP-65615(2) RA-65615
4352206	A	Komi Avia	DM-SCR E German AF 176 DM-SCR DDR-SCR D-AOBF CCCP-65616(2) RA-65616
4352207	A	Aviaprima	E German AF 178 DM-SCS DDR-SCS D-AOBG CCCP-65614(2) RA-65614
4352208	A-3	Tajik Air	CCCP-65814 EY-65814
4352209	A-3	St.Petersburg Avia Ent	CCCP-65815 RA-65815
4352210	A	(Aeroflot)	CCCP-65816 mid-air collision with Tu-134 CCCP-65735 11Aug79 over Ukraine
4352301	A	Adjal Avia	CCCP-65817 4L-65817
4352302	A		CCCP-65818
4352303	A-3	Hemus Air	LZ-TUL
4352304	A-3	Arkhangelsk Airlines	CCCP-65819 RA-65819

TUPOLEV Tu-134

S/n	Series	Last known Owner/Operator	Identities/fate (where known)				
4352305							
4352306							
4352307	A-3	Arberia Airways	LZ-TUN				
4352308	A	(Balkan Bulgarian A/L)	LZ-TUR	w/o 10Jan84 Sofia, Bulgaria			
08056	A-3	Tajik Air	CCCP-65820	EY-65820			
08060	A	Belavia	CCCP-65821	EW-65821			
4308068	A	(Harka Air)	DM-SCT	DDR-SCT	D-AOBH	CCCP-65617(2)	RA-65617
			dbf 24Jun95 Murtala Muhammed Airport, Lagos, Nigeria				
09070	A	Belair	DM-SCU	DDR-SCU	D-AOBI	CCCP-65605(2)	EW-65605
09071	A	Armenian Airlines	CCCP-65822	EK65822			
0907.?	A	Nizhny Novgorod Airlines	CCCP-65823	RA-65823			
09074	A-3	Kaliningrad Avia Ent	CCCP-65824	HA-LBS	RA-65824		
09078	A-3	Astral	CCCP-65825	RA-65825			
12083	A-3	Air Ukraine	CCCP-65826	UR-65826			
12084	A-3	(Arkhangelsk Airlines)	CCCP-65827	RA-65827	b/u Oct94 Riga-Skulve, Latvia		
12093	A	Aeroflot Russian Int A/L	CCCP-65830	RA-65830			
12095	A	Syktyvkar Avia	DM-SCV	DDR-SCV	D-AOBJ	CCCP-65618(2)	RA-65618
12096	A-3	Malev	HA-926	HA-YSA	HA-LBN		
17102	A-3	Armenian Airlines	CCCP-65831	EK65831			
17103	A-3	Malev	HA-927	HA-YSB	HA-LBO		
17106	A	Belavia	CCCP-65832	65832	EW-65832		
1710.?	A		CCCP-65833				
17109	A-3	Donavia Airlines	CCCP-65834	RA-65834			
17112	A-3	Tajik Air	CCCP-65835	EY-65835			
17113?	A	(Aeroflot)	CCCP-65836	w/o 14Aug82 Sukhumi, Georgia in collision with			
			LET-410 CCCP-67101				
17114	A-3	St.Petersburg Avia Ent	CCCP-65837	RA-65837			
18116	A	Tyumen Airlines	CCCP-65838	RA-65838			
18117?	A	(Aeroflot)	CCCP-65839	dbf 19May79 Ufa, USSR			
18118	A	Syktyvkar Avia	CCCP-65840	RA-65840			
18120	A	Air Ukraine	CCCP-65841	UR-65841			
1812.?	A	Izhevsk Air Enterprise	CCCP-65842	RA-65842			
18123	A-3	Bashkirian Airlines	CCCP-65843	RA-65843			
4323128	A	(CSA Czech Airlines)	OK-EFJ	wfs; scrapped Oct95			
4323130	A	(CSA Czech Airlines)	OK-EFK	wfs; scrapped Oct95			
23131	A	Kaliningrad Avia Ent	CCCP-65845	RA-65845			
2313.?	A-3	Arkhangelsk Airlines	CCCP-65846	RA-65846			
23135	A-3	Orenburg Avia Enterprise	CCCP-65847	RA-65847			
23136	A-3	Armenian Airlines	CCCP-65848	EK65848			
23241	A-3	St.Petersburg Avia Ent	CCCP-65851	RA-65851			
23244	A	Air Ukraine	CCCP-65852	UR-65852			
2324.?	A		CCCP-65853	RA-65853			
23248	A-3	St.Petersburg Avia Ent	CCCP-65854	65854	RA-65854		
23249	A	Russian AF	CCCP-65679	RA-65679			
23252	A-3	Ais Airlines	CCCP-65855	RA-65855			
2325.?		(Aeroflot)	CCCP-65856	w/o 03May85 in collision with Soviet AF AN-26 over Ukraine			
23255	A-3	Orbi Georgian Airways	CCCP-65857	4L-65857			
23264	A-3	Tyumen Airlines	CCCP-65859	RA-65859			
28265	A-3	Orenburg Avia Enterprise	CCCP-65860	RA-65860			
28269	A-3	Belavia	CCCP-65861	RA-65861	EW-65861		
28270	A-3	St.Petersburg Avia Ent	CCCP-65862	RA-65862			
28284	A	Air Ukraine	CCCP-65864	UR-65864			
28286	A-3	Orbi Georgian Airways	CCCP-65865	RA-65865	4L-65865		
28292	A-3	Syktyvkar Avia	CCCP-65866	RA-65866			
28306	A-3	Volga Airlines	CCCP-65869	RA-65869			
28310	A	Kaliningrad Avia Ent	CCCP-65870	RA-65870			
2.311?	A	(Aeroflot)	CCCP-65871	dbr 28Jun81 Borispol, USSR			
29312	A-3	St.Petersburg Avia Ent	CCCP-65872	RA-65872			
2931.?	A-3		CCCP-65873				
29315	A	Aeroflot	CCCP-65874	derelict Sep93 Riga-Spilve, Latvia			
29317	A-3	Tajik Air	CCCP-65875	EY-65875			
31218	A	Aerotransservice	E German AF 179	DM-SCW	DDR-SCW	D-AOBK	
			CCCP-65619(2)	RA-65619			
31220	A-3	Sarco Air Lines	CCCP-65876	EY-65876			
31250	A-3	Adjarian Airlines	CCCP-65877	UR-65877			
31265	A-3	Taifun	CCCP-65879	4L-65879			
35180	A-3	Syktyvkar Avia	E German AF 181/DM-VBD		DDR-SDC	D-AOBN	
			CCCP-65620(2)	RA-65620			
35200	A-3	Voronezh Avia	CCCP-65880	RA-65880			
35220	A-3	Voronezh Avia	CCCP-65881	RA-65881			
35270	A	Estonian Air	CCCP-65882	ES-AAH	Cancelled late 1994		
36150	A	Armenian Airlines	CCCP-65884	EK65884			
36160	A-3	St.Petersburg Avia Ent	CCCP-65885	RA-65885			
36165	A	Adjal Avia	CCCP-65886	4L-65886			
36170?	A	Mineralnye Vody	CCCP-65887	RA-65887			
36175	A-3	Air Ukraine	CCCP-65888	UR-65888			
38020	A-3	Estonian Air	CCCP-65890	ES-AAP			
38030	A-3	Syktyvkar Avia	CCCP-65891	RA-65891			
5338040	A	Harco Air	DM-SDE	DDR-SDE	D-AOBO	CCCP-65608(2)	RA-65608
38050	A	Belavia	CCCP-65892	EW-65892			
40120	A	(Transair Georgia)	CCCP-65893	65893	w/o 21Sep93 by SAM missile Sukhumi, Georgia		

TUPOLEV Tu-134

S/n	Series	Last known Owner/Operator	Identities/fate (where known)				
40130	A-3	St.Petersburg Avia Ent	CCCP-65894	RA-65894			
40140	A-3	Tajik Air	CCCP-65895	EY-65895			
40150	A	Harco Air	E German AF 185	DM-SDF	DDR-SDF	D-AOBP	
			CCCP-65610(2)	RA-65610			
42210	A	Air Moldova	CCCP-65897	ER-65897			
42225	A-3	Tyumen Airlines	CCCP-65899	RA-65899			
42230	A-3		CCCP-65000				
44020	A-3	Izhevsk Air Enterprise	CCCP-65002	RA-65002			
44040	A-3	Tajik Air	CCCP-65003	65003	EY-65003		
44060	A-3	St.Petersburg Avia Ent	CCCP-65004	RA-65004			
44065	A-3	Syktyvkar Avia	CCCP-65005	RA-65005			
44080	A-3	Syktyvkar Avia	CCCP-65006	RA-65006			
46105	A-3	Volga Airlines	CCCP-65008	RA-65008			
46120	A	Tyumen Airlines	CCCP-65009	RA-65009			
46130	A	Kaliningrad Avia Ent	CCCP-65010	RA-65010			
46140	A-3	Kaliningrad Avia Ent	CCCP-65011	RA-65011			
46155	A	Harco Air	DM-SDG	E German AF 186	DDR-SDG	D-AOBQ	
			CCCP-65609(2)	RA-65609			
46175	A	Tyumen Airlines	CCCP-65012	RA-65012			
46200	A	Stigl	CCCP-65014	65014			
46300	A	Syktyvkar Avia	DM-SDH	DDR-SDH	German AF 11+14	D-AOBR	
			CCCP-65606(2)	RA-65606			
6348320	A	Archangelsk Airlines	DM-SCX	DDR-SCX	D-AOBL	CCCP-65621(2)	RA-65621
48360	A-3	Tyumen Airlines	CCCP-65017	RA-65017			
48365	A	Ulyanovsk Higher Civil Aviation School	CCCP-65018	RA-65018			
48370	A-3	(Aviogenex)	YU-AJS	w/o 02Apr77 Libreville, Gabon			
48375	A	Kaliningrad Avia Ent	CCCP-65019	RA-65019			
48380	A-3	St.Petersburg Avia Ent	CCCP-65020	RA-65020			
48390	A	Cheboksary Air Ent	CCCP-65021	RA-65021			
48395	A	Estonian Air	CCCP-65022	ES-AAE			
48400	A	LOT	SP-LHD	wfs by Jul95 Warsaw-Okecie, Poland			
48405	A	LOT	SP-LHE	wfs by Jul95 Warsaw-Okecie, Poland			
48415	A-3	Lithuanian Airlines	CCCP-65023	LY-ABB			
48420	A	Cheboksary Air Ent	CCCP-65024	RA-65024			
48430	A	(Vietnam Airlines)	VN-A108	dbr 17Feb88 Hanoi, Vietnam			
48450	A	Tyumen Airlines	CCCP-65025	RA-65025			
48470	A-3	Bashkirian Airlines	CCCP-65026	RA-65026			
48485	A	(Kaliningrad Avia Ent)	CCCP-65027	RA-65027	dbr 15Sep95 St.Petersburg, Russia		
48490	A-3	Bashkirian Airlines	CCCP-65028	RA-65028			
48500	A-3	Syktyvkar Avia	CCCP-65029	RA-65029			
48540	A-3	Cheboksary Air Ent	CCCP-65033	RA-65033			
6348560	A	Ural Interavia	DM-SDI	DDR-SDI	German AF 11+15	D-AOBS	
			CCCP-65607(2)	RA-65607			
48565	A	Air Transport Europe	CCCP-65034	ES-AAF	OM-GAT		
48590	A	Perm Avia Enterprise	CCCP-65035	RA-65035			
48700	A	Air Moldova	CCCP-65036	ER-65036			
48850	A-3	Kirov Avia Enterprise	CCCP-65037	UR-65037	RA-65037		
48950	A	Tyumen Airlines	CCCP-65038	RA-65038			
49100	A	Bashkirian Airlines	CCCP-65040	LY-ABC	RA-65040		
492.0?	A		CCCP-65041				
49350	A-3	St.Petersburg Avia Ent	CCCP-65042	RA-65042			
49400?	A-3	Nizhny Novgorod Airlines	CCCP-65043	RA-65043			
49450	A-3	Armenian Airlines	CCCP-65044	65044			
49500?	A	Nizhny Novgorod Airlines	CCCP-65045	RA-65045			
49600	A	Gosnii GA	CCCP-65047	RA-65047			
49700	A-3	Perm Avia Enterprise	CCCP-65046	RA-65046			
49750	A-3	Air Ukraine	CCCP-65048	UR-65048			
49752	A	Vietnam Airlines	VN-A106				
49755	A	Belavia	CCCP-65049	EW-65049			
49756	A-3	Air Moldova	CCCP-65050	ER-65050			
49758	A-3	Air Moldova	CCCP-65051	ER-65051			
49760	A-3	Atlant	CCCP-65681	Soviet AF "681" red		RA-65681	
49825	A	Arkhangelsk Airlines	CCCP-65052	RA-65052			
49830	A	Angola Government	D2-ECC				
49838	A	Adjal Avia	CCCP-65053	4L-65053			
49840	A-3	Kaliningrad Avia Ent	CCCP-65054	RA-65054			
49856	A-3	Astral	CCCP-65055	RA-65055			
49858	A-3	Balkan Bulgarian A/L	OK-BYT	LZ-TUG			
49865	A	Voronezh Avia	CCCP-65057	RA-65057			
49870	A	Perm Avia Enterprise	CCCP-65059	RA-65059			
49872	A	Kirov Avia Enterprise	CCCP-65060	RA-65060			
49874	A-3	Taifun	CCCP-65061	4L-65061			
49875	A	Voronezh Avia	CCCP-65062	RA-65062			
49880	A	Tyumen Airlines	CCCP-65063	RA-65063			
49886	A	Perm Avia Enterprise	CCCP-65064	RA-65064			
49890	A-3	Aeroflot Russian Int A/L	CCCP-65065	XU-101	RA-65065		
49900	A	Vietnam Airlines	E German AF 123	DM-SDK	DDR-SDK	VN-A122	
49907	A-3	Aeroflot	CCCP-65068	ES-AAG	RA-65068		
49908	A-3	Syktyvkar Avia	CCCP-65069	RA-65069			
49909	A-3	Aeroflot Russian Int A/L	Polish AF 101(2)	RA-65559			

TUPOLEV Tu-134

S/n	Series	Last known Owner/Operator	Identities/fate (where known)				
49912	A-3	Syktyvkar Avia	CCCP-65070	RA-65070			
7349913	A	CSA	OK-HFL				
49915	A-3	Air Moldova	CCCP-65071	ER-65071			
49972	A-3	Armenian Airlines	CCCP-65072	EK65072			
49980	A	Air Ukraine	CCCP-65073	UR-65073			
49985	A-3	Aeroflot Russian Int A/L	Polish AF 102(2)	SP-LHI	Polish AF 96102	CCCP-65623(2)	RA-65623
49987	A-3	Mineralnye Vody	CCCP-65074	RA-65074			
49998	A-3	Stigl	CCCP-65075	65075			
60001	A-3	Air Ukraine	CCCP-65076	UR-65076			
60028	A-3	Air Ukraine	CCCP-65077	65077	UR-65077		
60035	A-3	Aviogenex	YU-AJV	CCCP-?			
60043	A	Ulyanovsk Higher Civil Aviation School	CCCP-65078	RA-65078			
60054	A	Lithuanian Airlines	CCCP-65079	LY-ABD			
60065	A	Astrakhan Airlines	CCCP-65080	RA-65080	GR-65080	RA-65080	
60076	A	Lithuanian Airlines	CCCP-65081	LY-ABE			
60081	A-3	Belavia	CCCP-65082	EW-65082			
60090	A-3	Arkhangelsk Airlines	CCCP-65083	RA-65083			
60108	A-3	Vietnam Airlines	E German AF 115	DM-SDL	DDR-SDL	VN-A124	
60115	A-3	Arkhangelsk Airlines	CCCP-65084	RA-65084			
60123	A	Belavia	CCCP-65085	EW-65085			
60130	A-3	Volga Airlines	CCCP-65086	RA-65086			
7360142	A	CSA Czech Airlines	OK-HFM				
60155	A	Kaliningrad Avia Ent	CCCP-65087	RA-65087			
60172	A-3	Lithuanian Airlines	CCCP-65088	LY-ABF			
60180	A	Air Ukraine	CCCP-65089	UR-65089			
60185	A-3	Kaliningrad Avia Ent	CCCP-65090	RA-65090			
60195	A-3	Lithuanian Airlines	CCCP-65091	LY-ABG			
60206	A-3	Imperial Air	CCCP-65092	UR-65092	OB-1553	damaged 15Apr95, status?	
60215	A-3	Air Ukraine	CCCP-65093	UR-65093	(OB-1555)	OB-1552	UR-65093
60255	A-3	Moldova Government	CCCP-65094	65094	ER-65094		
60256?	A-1	(Aeroflot)	CCCP-65095	derelict Minsk 2 by Sep93			
60257	A-3	Arkhangelsk Airlines	CCCP-65096	RA-65096			
60258	A-3	Donavia Airlines	CCCP-65100	RA-65100			
60260	A-3	Orenburg Avia Enterprise	CCCP-65101	RA-65101			
60267	A-3	Astral	CCCP-65102	RA-65102			
8360282	A	CSA Czech Airlines	OK-IFN				
60297	A-3	Arkhangelsk Airlines	CCCP-65103	RA-65103			
60301	A-3	Donavia Airlines	CCCP-65104	RA-65104			
60308	A-3	Samara Airlines	CCCP-65105	LY-ABH	RA-65105		
60315	A-3	Pyramid Airlines	CCCP-65106	RA-65106	EW-65106		
60321	A-3	Central District A/L	YU-AJW	CCCP-65550	RA-65550		
60328	A	Air Ukraine	CCCP-65107	UR-65107			
60332	A	Belavia	CCCP-65108	EW-65108			
60342	A-3	Air Ukraine	CCCP-65109	UR-65109			
60343	A-3	Orenburg Avia Enterprise	CCCP-65110	RA-65110			
60346	A-3	Kyrgyzstan Airlines	CCCP-65111	EX-65111			
60350	A	Estonian Air	CCCP-65112	ES-AAI			
60380	A	Aeroflot	CCCP-65113	ES-AAM	RA-65113		
60395	A-3	Air Ukraine	CCCP-65114	UR-65114			
60420	A-3	Arkhangelsk Airlines	CCCP-65116	RA-65116			
60435	A-1	(Vietnam Airlines)	E German AF 116	DM-SDM	DDR-SDM	VN-A126	w/o 12Jan91 Ho Chi Minh City, Vietnam
60450	A-3	Orenburg Avia Enterprise	CCCP-65117	RA-65117			
60462	A-3	Chelyabinsk Air Ent	CCCP-65118	RA-65118			
60475	A-3	Kyrgyzstan Airlines	CCCP-65119	EX-65119			
60495	A-3	Syktyvkar Avia	DM-SCY	DDR-SCY	D-AOBM	CCCP-65622(2)	RA-65622
60505	A-3	Kazakhstan Airlines	CCCP-65121	UN-65121			
60525	A-3	Imperial Air	CCCP-65123	OB-1490	UR-65123		
60540	A	Flt Research Int Gromov/ United Nations	CCCP-65097	RA-65097			
60560	A	Estonian Air	CCCP-65124	ES-AAN			
60575	A-3	Kyrgyzstan Airlines	CCCP-65125	EX-65125			
60612	A-1	Air Vietnam	E German AF 117	DM-SDN	DDR-SDN	VN-A128	
60627	A	Tyumen Airlines	CCCP-65127	ES-AAJ	EY-65127	RA-65127	
60628	A	Lithuanian Airlines	CCCP-65128	LY-ABI			
60635	A-3	Kazakhstan Airlines	CCCP-65130	UN-65130			
60637	A-3	Aviaprima Sochi Airlines	CCCP-65131	RA-65131			
60639	A-3	Clintondale Aviation	CCCP-65132	RA-65132			
60642	A-3	Balkan Bulgarian A/L	Bulgarian	LZ-TUS			
60645	A-3	Pyramid Airlines	CCCP-65133	EW-65133			
60647	A-3	Air Ukraine	CCCP-65134	65134	UR-65134		
60648	A-3	Air Ukraine	CCCP-65135	UR-65135			
60885	A-3	Orenburg Avia Enterprise	CCCP-65136	RA-65136			
60890	A-3	Kirov Avia Enterprise	CCCP-65137	RA-65137			
60907	A	Kazakhstan Airlines	CCCP-65138	UN-65138			
60932	A-3	Air Moldova	CCCP-65140	ER-65140			
60945	A-3	Izhevsk Air Enterprise	CCCP-65141	RA-65141			
60967	A-3	Arkhangelsk Airlines	CCCP-65143	RA-65143			
60977	A	Orient Avia	CCCP-65144	ES-AAK	RA-65144		
60985	A	Belavia	CCCP-65145	65145	EW-65145		

TUPOLEV Tu-134

S/n	Series	Last known Owner/Operator	Identities/fate (where known)				
61000	B-3	Latvijas Aviolinijas	CCCP-65146	YL-LBA			
61012	A-3	Kazakhstan Airlines	CCCP-65147	UN-65147			
61025	A-3	Aerotransservice	CCCP-65148	RA-65148			
61033	A	Belavia	CCCP-65149	EW-65149			
61042	A-3	Orbi Georgian Airways	CCCP-65750	65750	4L-65750		
61055	A	Vietnam Airlines	VN-A104				
61066	A-3	Perm Avia Enterprise	CCCP-65751	RA-65751			
61079	A-3	Air Ukraine	CCCP-65752	UR-65752			
62144	A	Vietnam Airlines	VN-A110				
62154	A	Belavia	CCCP-65754	EW-65754			
62165	A-3	Syktyvkar Avia	CCCP-65755	RA-65755			
62179	A-3	Central District A/L	CCCP-65756	RA-65756			
62187	A		CCCP-65760	RA-65760	w/o 09Sep94 nr Samoilikha, NE of		
			Yegoryevsky, Russia				
62199	A		CCCP-65683	UN-65683			
62205	A	Russian Min of Defence	CCCP-65684	RA-65684		Tu-135 model	
62215	A-3	Air Ukraine	CCCP-65757	UR-65757			
62239	A	Aeroflot	CCCP-65759	ES-AAO	RA-65759		
62244	A-3	Air Ukraine	CCCP-65761	UR-65761			
62259	A-1	Vietnam Airlines	E German AF 118	DM-SDO	DDR-SDO	VN-A130	
62279	A-3	Voronezh Avia	CCCP-65762	RA-65762			
62299	A-3	Tajik Air	CCCP-65763	EY-65763			
62305	A-3	Air Ukraine	CCCP-65764	UR-65764			
62315	A-3	Air Ukraine	CCCP-65765	UR-65765			
62350	A	Estonian Air	CCCP-65768	ES-AAL			
62415	A-3	Aeroflot Russian Int A/L	CCCP-65769	RA-65769			
62430	A-3	Aeroflot Russian Int A/L	CCCP-65770	RA-65770			
62445	A-3	Donavia Airlines	CCCP-65771	RA-65771			
62458	A-3	Vietnam Airlines	VN-A112				
62472	A	Belavia	CCCP-65772	EW-65772			
62495	A-3	Air Ukraine	CCCP-65773	UR-65773			
62519	A-3	Orbi Georgian Airways	CCCP-65774	65774	4L-65774		
62530	A-3	Perm Avia Enterprise	CCCP-65775	RA-65775			
62545	A-3	Kazakhstan Airlines	CCCP-65776	RA-65776	UN-65776		
62552	A-3	Syktyvkar Avia	CCCP-65777	RA-65777			
62590	A-3	Kyrgyzstan Airlines	CCCP-65778	EX-65778			
62602	A-3	Kyrgyzstan Airlines	CCCP-65779	EX-65779			
62622	A-3	Syktyvkar Avia	CCCP-65780	RA-65780			
62645	A-3	Aeroflot Russian Int A/L	CCCP-65781	RA-65781			
62672	A-3	Air Ukraine	CCCP-65782	UR-65782			
62713	A-3	Aeroflot Russian Int A/L	CCCP-65783	RA-65783			
62715	A-3	Aeroflot Russian Int A/L	CCCP-65784	RA-65784			
62750	A-3	Aeroflot Russian Int A/L	CCCP-65785	RA-65785			
62775	A-3	Chelal	CCCP-65786	RA-65786			
62835	A-3	Tajik Air	CCCP-65788	EY-65788			
62850	A-3	Kyrgyzstan Airlines	CCCP-65789	EX-65789			
63100	A-3	Air Ukraine	CCCP-65790	UR-65790			
63110	A-3	Air Moldova	CCCP-65791	ER-65791			
63128	A-3	Syktyvkar Avia	CCCP-65793	RA-65793			
63150	A-3	Donavia Airlines	CCCP-65796	RA-65796			
63165	A	Gagarin Aviation Factory	YU-ANE	CCCP-65564	RA-65564		
63179	A-3	Orbi Georgian Airways	CCCP-65798	65798	4L-65798		
63187	B-3	Latvijas Aviolinijas	CCCP-65799	YL-LBN	spares use by Sep93 Riga-Spilve, Latvia		
63195	A	Volga Airlines	CCCP-65691	RA-65691			
63215	B-3	LAT Charter	CCCP-65692	YL-LBB	stored Jan96 Riga-Spilve, Latvia		
63221	B-3	Latvijas Aviolinijas	CCCP-65693	YL-LBC	stored by Sep93 Riga-Spilve, Latvia;		
			cancelled by Apr94				
63235	B-3	Latvijas Aviolinijas	CCCP-65694	YL-LBD	spares use by May93 Riga-Spilve, Latvia		
63245	A-3	Syktyvkar Avia	CCCP-65977	RA-65977			
63260	A-1	Vietnam Airlines	E German AF 119	DM-SDP	DDR-SDP	VN-A132	
63285	B-3	LAT Charter	CCCP-65695	YL-LBE			
63295	B-3	LAT Charter	CCCP-65696	YL-LBF			
63307	A-3	Aeroflot Russian Int A/L	CCCP-65697	RA-65697			
63333	B-3	Latvijas Aviolinijas	CCCP-65699	YL-LBG	stored by Oct94 Riga-Spilve, Latvia		
63340	B-3	LAT Charter	CCCP-65700	YL-LBH			
63357	A-3	Russian State Transport	CCCP-65978	RA-65978			
63365	B-3	Latavio	CCCP-65701	YL-LBI	stored Jan96 Riga-Spilve, Latvia		
63375	B-3	Azerbaijan Airlines	CCCP-65702	65702	4K-65702		
63383	B-3	(Azerbaijan Airlines)	CCCP-65703	4K-65703	w/o 05Dec95 Baku, Azerbaijan		
63410	B-3	Latavio	CCCP-65704	YL-LBJ	stored Jan96 Riga-Spilve, Latvia		
63415	A-3	Azerbaijan Airlines	CCCP-65705	65705	4K-65705		
63425	B-3	Baltic International	CCCP-65706	YL-LBK	stored Dec95 Riga-Spilve, Latvia		
63435	A	Air Moldova	CCCP-65707	ER-65707			
63447	A-3	Azerbaijan Airlines	CCCP-65708	AL-65708	65708	4K-65708	
63457	A	(Mozambique Government)	Mozambique Govt 63457		C9-CAA	w/o 19Oct86 nr	
			Komatipoort, S Africa				
63484	B-3	Azerbaijan Airlines	CCCP-65709	65709	4K-65709		
63490	B-3	Azerbaijan Airlines	CCCP-65710	AL-65710	4K-65710		
63498	A-3	Azerbaijan Airlines	CCCP-65711	AL-65711	65711	AL-65711	4K-65711
63505	A-3	Russian Min of Defence	CCCP-65987	RA-65987		Tu-135 model	
63515	B-3	Latavio	CCCP-65712	YL-LBL	stored Jan96 Riga-Spilve, Latvia		

TUPOLEV Tu-134

S/n	Series	Last known Owner/Operator	Identities/fate (where known)				
63520	B-3	Azerbaijan Airlines	CCCP-65713	65713	4K-65713		
63527	A	Azerbaijan Airlines	CCCP-65714	65714	4K-65714		
63536	B-3	Baltic International	CCCP-65715	YL-LBM	stored by Apr95 Riga-Spilve, Latvia		
63560	A	Malev	HA-LBP				
63580	A	Malev	HA-LBR				
63595	B-3	Syktyvkar Avia	CCCP-65716	RA-65716			
63637	A	Korsar Airlines	CCCP-65719	RA-65719			
63657	A-3	Aeroflot Russian Int A/L	CCCP-65717	RA-65717			
63668	A-3	Air Ukraine	CCCP-65718	UR-65718			
63684	A-3	Kazakhstan Airlines	CCCP-65900	UN-65900			
63700	A	Stolichny Savings Bank	CCCP-65099	RA-65099			
63720	A	Korsar Airlines	CCCP-65726	RA-65726			
63731	A-3	Syktyvkar Avia	CCCP-65901	RA-65901			
63742	A-3	Syktyvkar Avia	CCCP-65902	RA-65902			
63750	A-3	Volga Airlines	CCCP-65903	RA-65903			
63761	A	Soviet AF	25 red				
63820	B-3	Archangelsk Airlines	CCCP-65720	RA-65720			
63870	A	Flt Research Int Gromov	CCCP-65908	RA-65908			
63892	A-3	Ukraine AF	03 yellow				
63952	A-1	Aeroflot Russian Int A/L	E German AF 184	DDR-SDS	German AF 11+11	9A-ADL	
			German AF 11+11	RA-65566			
63953	A-3	Russian State Transport	CCCP-65904	RA-65904			
63955?	A		CCCP-63955		Tu-135 model		
63965	A-3	Russian State Transport	CCCP-65905	65905	RA-65905		
63967	A-1	Aeroflot Russian Int A/L	E German AF 176	DDR-SDR	German AF 11+10	9A-ADP	
			German AF 11+10	RA-65568			
63970?	A		CCCP-65909				
63971?	A	(Aeroflot)	CCCP-65910	w/o 01Feb85 Minsk			
63972	A-3	Russian State Transport	CCCP-65911	65911	RA-65711		
63985	A-3	Russian State Transport	CCCP-65912	RA-65912			
63986?	A		CCCP-65913				
63989	B-3	Syrianair	YK-AYC				
2763990	B-3	Syrianair	YK-AYD				
63991	A-3CX	Soviet Dept of Agric	CCCP-65917	RA-65917			
63992	B-3	Syrianair	YK-AYA				
63993?	A	Voronezh Avia	CCCP-65918	RA-65918			
63994	B-3	Syrianair	YK-AYB				
63996	A	Alrosa Avia	CCCP-65907	RA-65907			
63997	A-3	Russian State Transport	CCCP-65921	RA-65921			
63998	A	Belair	E German AF 183	DDR-SDT	CCCP-65565	EW-65565	RA-65565
64400	UBL	Soviet AF	27 red				
64740	UBL	Soviet AF	(unmarked)				
64845	UBL	Soviet AF	30 red				
66101	A	Volare Transaero Express	CCCP-65926	RA-65926			
66109	A-3	Russian State Transport	CCCP-65914	TC-GRD	RA-65914		
66120	A-3	Russian State Transport	CCCP-65915	TC-GRE	RA-65915		
66135	A	Aeroflot Russian Int A/L	E German AF 193	DDR-SDU	German AF 11+12	9A-ADR	
			German AF 11+12	RA-65567			
66143	A-3	Irkutsk Aviation Factory	CCCP-65934	RA-65934			
66152	A-3	Atlant-Soyuz	CCCP-65916	RA-65916			
66168	A-3	Russian State Transport	CCCP-65919	RA-65919			
66175	A	Flt Research Int Gromov	CCCP-65906	RA-65906			
66180	A	Avia Obshchemash	CCCP-65935	RA-65935			
66187	B-3	Syrianair	YK-AYE				
66190	B-3	Syrianair	YK-AYF				
66198		Flt Research Int Gromov/ Soviet AF	CCCP-65927	RA-65927			
66207	A-3	Russian State Transport	CCCP-65994	RA-65994			
66212	A-3	Kazakhstan Airways	CCCP-65551	UN-65551			
66220	B-3	Vietnam Airlines	VN-A114				
66230	B-3	Vietnam Airlines	VN-A116				
66250	B-3	Vietnam Airlines	VN-A118				
66270	A-3	Russian State Transport	CCCP-65552	RA-65552			
66300	A-3	Russian State Transport	CCCP-65553	RA-65553			
66320	A-3	Russian State Transport	CCCP-65554	RA-65554			
66350	A-3	Russian State Transport	CCCP-65555	RA-65555			
66360	B-3	Vietnam Airlines	VN-A120				
66372	A-3	Ukraine Govt	CCCP-65556	65556	UR-65556		
66380	A-3	Russian State Transport	CCCP-65557	RA-65557			
66400	A-3	Russian State Transport	CCCP-65995	RA-65995			
66405	A	Russian Govt/Rossia	CCCP-65932	65932	RA-65932		
66440	A-3CX	Voronezh Avia	CCCP-65723	RA-65723			
66445	A-3CX	Voronezh Avia	CCCP-65724	RA-65724			
66472	A-3CX	Central District A/L	CCCP-65725	RA-65725			
66500	A-3CX	Voronezh Avia	CCCP-65930	RA-65930			
66550	A-3	Aeroflot Russian Int A/L	CCCP-64451	XU-102	CCCP-64451	XU-102	RA-64451

TUPOLEV Tu-134

The following are aircraft for which there are no confirmed serial numbers at the present time:

S/n	Series	Last known Owner/Operator	Identities/fate (where known)			
	A	Flt Research Int Gromov	CCCP-64454	RA-64454		
	A	(Transair Georgia)	CCCP-65001	dbr 23Sep93 Sukhumi, Georgia by mortar shell		
	A-3	Cheboksary Air Ent	CCCP-65007	RA-65007		
	A		CCCP-65013			
	A-3	Cheboksary Air Ent	CCCP-65015	RA-65015		
	A-3	Donavia Airlines	CCCP-65016	RA-65016		
	A-3	Stigl	CCCP-65030	65030		
	A	(Aeroflot)	CCCP-65031	w/o 22Mar79 Liepaya, USSR		
	A		CCCP-65032	RA-65032		
	A-3	Aeroflot Russian Int A/L	CCCP-65039	RA-65039		
	A-3	Izhevsk Air Enterprise	CCCP-65056	RA-65056		
	A	(Aeroflot)	CCCP-65058	w/o 27Aug92 nr Ivanovo, Russia		
	A-3	Arkhangelsk Airlines	CCCP-65066	RA-65066		
	A-3	Voronezh Avia	CCCP-65067	RA-65067		
	UBL	Russian Navy	CCCP-65098			
	A-3	Kazakhstan Airlines	CCCP-65115	UN-65115		
	A	(Aeroflot)	CCCP-65120	w/o 02Jul86 Syktyvkar, USSR		
	A-3	Samara Airlines	CCCP-65122	RA-65122		
	A-3	Mineralnye Vody	CCCP-65126	RA-65126		
	A	(Aeroflot)	CCCP-65129	w/o 30Aug83 in mts nr Alma-Ata, USSR		
	A	Mineralnye Vody	CCCP-65139	RA-65139		
	A	(Aeroflot)	CCCP-65142	w/o 22Jun86 Penza, USSR		
	A	Aerotransservice	RA-65156			
	B-3	Flt Research Int Gromov	CCCP-65562	RA-65562	(out of sequence s/n 2350204 quoted)	
	A-3	Russian Govt	YU-A..?	CCCP-65563	RA-65563	(ex.YU-AJV s/n 60035 perhaps)
	A		CCCP-65570	RA-65570		
	A	Aeroflot Russian Int A/L	RA-65585			
	A		CCCP-65594			
	A-3	Tupolev Design Bureau	CCCP-65624(2)	RA-65624		
	A	Aeroflot Russian Int A/L	CCCP-65626(2)	RA-65626		
	A		CCCP-65677			
	A		CCCP-65678			
	A-3	Soviet AF	CCCP-65680	"680" red		
	A	Russian Min of Defence	CCCP-65682	RA-65682		Tu-135 model
	A	Russian Min of Defence	CCCP-65685			
	A	Russian Min of Defence	CCCP-65686			
	A		CCCP-65687			
	A	Russian Min of Defence	CCCP-65689	RA-65689		
	A-3	Russian Min of Defence	CCCP-65690	RA-65690		
	A	(Aeroflot)	CCCP-65698	dbr 06Jan81 Sochi, USSR		
	A-3CX	Voronezh Avia	CCCP-65721	RA-65721		
	A-3CX	Central District A/L	CCCP-65722	RA-65722		
	A-3	Samara Airlines	CCCP-65753	RA-65753		
	A-3	Samara Airlines	CCCP-65758	RA-65758		
	A	(Aeroflot)	CCCP-65766	w/o 20Oct86 Kiubishev, USSR		
	A-3	Kazakhstan Airlines	CCCP-65767	65767	UN-65767	
	A	Kazakhstan Airlines	CCCP-65787	UN-65787	damaged 21Dec93 Alma-Ata, Kazakhstan,status?	
	A-3	Samara Airlines	CCCP-65792	RA-65792		
	A-3	Voronezh Avia	CCCP-65794	RA-65794		
	A	(Aeroflot)	CCCP-65795	w/o 12Dec86 Bohnsdorf, E Germany		
	A-3	Samara Airlines	CCCP-65797	RA-65797		
	A	Astral	CCCP-65828	RA-65828		
	A-3	Nizhny Novgorod Airlines	CCCP-65829	RA-65829		
	A	Mineralnye Vody	CCCP-65844	RA-65844		
	A	Aeroflot	CCCP-65850	derelict by Jun94 Syktyvkar, Russia		
	A	Yug Avia	CCCP-65858	RA-65858		
	A	Donavia Airlines	CCCP-65863	RA-65863		
	A-3	Nizhny Novgorod Airlines	CCCP-65867	RA-65867		
	A	Yug Avia	CCCP-65868	RA-65868		
	A-3	Aeroflot	CCCP-65878	derelict by Apr93 Samara, Russia		
	A-3	Aeroflot	CCCP-65883	preserved Museum of Economic Achievement		
	A	Samara Airlines	CCCP-65889	RA-65889		
	A		CCCP-65896			
	A-3	Arkhangelsk Airlines	CCCP-65898	RA-65898		
	A	Aeroflot	CCCP-65922	wfs by Jun93 Omsk, Russia		
	A		CCCP-65923			
	A	Central District A/L	CCCP-65928	RA-65928		
	A	Voronezh Avia	CCCP-65929	RA-65929		
	A-3		CCCP-65931			
	A	Aeroflot Russian Int A/L	CCCP-65933	RA-65933		
	A		CCCP-65937			
	A-3	Aeroflot Russian Int A/L	RA-65940			
	A-3	Moscow Airways	RA-65941			
	A		CCCP-65962			
	A		CCCP-65963	RA-65963		
	A		CCCP-65964			
	A-3	Russian Min of Defence	CCCP-65979	RA-65979		
	A-3	Russian Min of Defence	CCCP-65980	RA-65980		

TUPOLEV Tu-134

S/n	Series	Last known Owner/Operator	Identities/fate (where known)				
	A-3	Russian Min of Defence	CCCP-65981	RA-65981			
	A-3	Russian Min of Defence	CCCP-65982	RA-65982		Tu-135 model	
	A	Russian Min of Defence	CCCP-65983	RA-65983		Tu-135 model	
	A-3	Soviet AF	CCCP-65984	RA-65984		Tu-135 model	
	A-3	Azerbaijan Govt	CCCP-65985	65985	4K-65985	Tu-135 model	
	A	Russian Min of Defence	CCCP-65986	RA-65986			
	A	Russian Min of Defence	CCCP-65988	RA-65988		Tu-135 model	
	A-3	Russian Min of Defence	CCCP-65989	RA-65989			
	A	Russian Min of Defence	CCCP-65990	RA-65990			
	A	Russian Min of Defence	CCCP-65991	RA-65991			
	A	Russian Min of Defence	CCCP-65992	RA-65992			
	A	Russian Min of Defence	CCCP-65993	Soviet AF "993" black		CCCP-65993	RA-65993
	A-3	Russian Min of Defence	CCCP-65996	RA-65996		Tu-135 model	
	B-3	Balkan Bulgarian A/L	LZ-TUT				
	A	Aero Tumi	OB-1492				
	B-3	Air Koryo	P-813				
	B-3	Air Koryo	P-814				
	A	(Hang Khong Viet Nam)	VN-A102	w/o 09Sep88 Bangkok, Thailand			
	A	Kampuchea Airlines	XU-122				
		Iraqi Airways	YI-AOQ				
	A	Angolan AF	SG-104				
		Soviet AF	02 red				
	A	Soviet AF	05 red				
		Soviet AF	10 red				
	UBL	Soviet AF	11 red				
		Soviet AF	12 red				
		Soviet AF	15 red				
	A	Soviet AF	16 blue				
	UBL	Soviet AF	17 red				
	A	Soviet AF	21	fitted with Tu-22 nose cone			
	UBL	Soviet AF	23 red				
	UBL	Soviet AF	26 red				
	UBL	Soviet AF	31 red				
	A	Soviet AF	40	fitted with Tu-22 nose cone			
	UBL	Soviet AF	48 red				
	A	Soviet AF	51	out of sequence s/n 3350305 quoted			
	A	Soviet AF	74 blue				
	A	Soviet AF	78	out of sequence s/n 3350401 quoted			
	A	Soviet AF	82 red				
	A	Soviet AF	84 red				
	A	Soviet AF	86 red				
	A	Soviet AF	86 blue				
	A	Soviet AF	87	out of sequence s/n 3350403 quoted			
		Soviet AF	101 blue		Tu-135 model		
	A	Soviet AF/Russia	"RA-19"				
		Ukraine AF	01 yellow				
		Ukraine AF	02 yellow				
	UBL	Ukraine AF	42 red				
	A	Ukraine AF	71				

One Aeroflot Tu-134 w/o 27Aug92 Ivanovo, Russia quoted as CCCP-65058 (since seen)

TUPOLEV Tu-144

Line/no	Series	Last known Owner/Operator	Identities/fate (where known)	
044		(Aeroflot)	CCCP-68001	prototype; ff 31Dec68; b/u
01-1		(Aeroflot)	CCCP-77101	broken up
01-2		(Aeroflot)	CCCP-77102	w/o 03Jun73 Paris-Le Bourget, France
01-3			Pressure test static airframe	
01-4			Pressure test static airframe	
02-1		(Aeroflot)	CCCP-77103	broken up
02-2		(Aeroflot)	CCCP-77144	broken up
03-1	D	Aeroflot	CCCP-77105	dumped by Aug92 Zhukovsky, Russia
04-1		Aeroflot	CCCP-77106	preserved Monino Museum, Moscow, Russia
04-2		Aeroflot	CCCP-77108	wfu Novosibirsk, Russia
05-1		(Aeroflot)	CCCP-77107	broken up
05-2		Aeroflot	CCCP-77109	static test airframe; later dumped Voronezh, Russia
06-1		Aeroflot	CCCP-77110	preserved Ulyanovsk, Russia
06-2	D	(Aeroflot)	CCCP-77111	dbr 23May78 Jegoriewskiem, USSR
07-1	D	Aeroflot	CCCP-77112	wfs Zhukovsky, Russia
08-1	D	Aeroflot	CCCP-77113	wfs Zhukovsky, Russia
08-2	D	Aeroflot/NASA	CCCP-77114	RA-77114 [for NASA SST research program]
09-1	D	Aeroflot	CCCP-77115	wfs Zhukovsky, Russia
09-2			CCCP-77116	not completed, fate unknown

Production complete

TUPOLEV Tu-154

The s/n comprises the year of manufacture followed by A, and then a consecutive numerical sequence.

S/n	Series	Last known Owner/Operator	Identities/fate (where known)				
67-KH1		Aeroflot	CCCP-85000	prototype; ff 04Oct68; reportedly wfs Moscow, Russia			
7-01		Aeroflot	CCCP-87001(1)	CCCP-85001	wfs Moscow-Sheremetyevo, Russia		
7-02			CCCP-87002(1)	CCCP-85002			
7-03		Aeroflot	CCCP-87003(1)	CCCP-85003	wfu by Apr93 Sammara-Uchenby Research Inst		
7-04			CCCP-87004(1)	CCCP-85004			
7-05		Aeroflot	CCCP-85005	preserved Moscow, Russia			
7-06		Aeroflot	CCCP-85006	wfs Moscow-Sheremetyevo, Russia			
7-07		Aeroflot	CCCP-85007	RA-85007	wfs by Jul95 Moscow-Vnukovo, Russia		
7-08			CCCP-85008				
7-09		Aeroflot	CCCP-85009	wfs Kiev Institute of Civil Aviation, Ukraine			
71A-010			CCCP-85010	wfs Aeroflot Technical School, Yegorevsk, Russia			
71A-011			CCCP-85011	wfs Aeroflot Technical School, Yegorevsk, Russia			
71A-012		Aeroflot	CCCP-85012	wfs Irkutsk, Russia			
71A-013	B	Ulyanovsk Higher Civil Aviation School	CCCP-85013	RA-85013			
71A-014		Aeroflot	CCCP-85014	wfs Irkutsk, Russia			
71A-015			CCCP-85016				
71A-016	B	Ulyanovsk Higher Civil Aviation School	CCCP-85016	RA-85016			
71A-017			CCCP-85017	tested to destruction OVB Research Institute, Russia			
71A-018	B	Tatarstan Airlines	CCCP-85018	RA-85018			
71A-019	S	Transaero	CCCP-85019	RA-85019	derelict by May95 Khabarovsk, Russia		
71A-020		Aeroflot	CCCP-85020	dbr & wfs Kiev Institute for Engineering, Ukraine			
71A-021	B-1	Kyrgyzstan Airlines	CCCP-85021	EX-85021			
7.A-022			CCCP-85022	tested to destruction OVB Research Institute, Russia			
72A-023		(Aeroflot)	CCCP-85023	w/o 19Feb73 Prague, Czechoslovakia			
72A-024	B	Aeroflot Russian Int A/L	CCCP-85024	RA-85024			
72A-025	B	Ulyanovsk Higher Civil Aviation School	CCCP-85025	RA-85025			
72A-026	B	Balkan Bulgarian	LZ-BTA				
72A-027		(Balkan Bulgarian)	LZ-BTB	w/o 24Mar78 Damascus, Syria			
72A-028	B	Vnukovo Airlines	CCCP-85028	RA-85028	wfs by Jul95 Moscow-Vnukovo		
72A-029		(Aeroflot)	CCCP-85029	dbr 13Jun81 Bratsk, USSR			
72A-030		(Aeroflot)	CCCP-85030	w/o 07May73 Moscow-Vnukovo, USSR			
72A-031		Far East Avia	CCCP-85031	RA-85031			
72A-032	B	Aeroflot	CCCP-85032	preserved by May93 Zhukovsky, Russia; dbf in 1993 (status?)			
72A-033	B	Vnukovo Airlines	CCCP-85033	RA-85033	wfs by Jul95 Moscow-Vnukovo, Russia		
72A-034	B-1	Aeroflot Russian Int A/L	CCCP-85034	RA-85034			
72A-035		Flight Research Inst	CCCP-85035	cvtd to prototype Tu-155; ff as such 15Apr88			
73A-036	B	Balkan Bulgarian	LZ-BTC				
73A-037	S	Far East Avia	CCCP-85037	RA-85037			
73A-038	B-1	Baikal Airlines	CCCP-85038	RA-85038			
73A-039	B	Aeroflot	CCCP-85039	wfs by Sep94 Moscow-Vnukovo, Russia			
73A-040			CCCP-85040				
73A-041	B	Aeroflot Russian Int A/L	CCCP-85041	RA-85041			
73A-042	B-2	Aeroflot Russian Int A/L	CCCP-85042	RA-85042			
73A-043	B	Far East Avia	CCCP-85043	RA-85043			
73A-044	B	Air Moldova	CCCP-85044	ER-85044			
73A-045	B-2	Malev	HA-LCA	wfs, cancelled			
73A-046	B-2	Malev	HA-LCB	wfs by Jan95 for firebrigade, Stuttgart, Germany			
73A-047	B-2	Malev	HA-LCE				
73A-048		(Egypt Air)	SU-AXB	w/o 09Jul74 nr Cairo, Egypt			
73A-049			SU-AXC	CCCP-85049			
73A-050	S	Uzbekistan Airways	SU-AXD	CCCP-85050	UK-85050		
73A-051		Aeroflot Russian Int A/L	SU-AXE	CCCP-85051	LZ-BTL(1)	CCCP-85051	LZ-BTR(1)
			CCCP-85051	HA-LCL	CCCP-85051	RA-85051	
74A-052	B	Russian Min of Defence	SU-AXF	CCCP-85052	RA-85052		
74A-053	A	(Malev)	SU-AXG	CCCP-85053	HA-LCI	w/o 30Sep75 nr Beirut, Lebanon	
74A-054		(Balkan Bulgarian)	SU-AXH	CCCP-85054	HA-LCK	CCCP-85054	LZ-BTM(1)
			CCCP-85054	LZ-BTN(1)	CCCP-85054	w/o 02Dec77 Labrak, Libya	
74A-055			SU-AXI	CCCP-85055			
74A-056		Aeroflot Russian Int A/L	CCCP-85056	RA-85056			
74A-057	B	Vnukovo Airlines	CCCP-85057	RA-85057			
74A-058	B	(Balkan Bulgarian)	LZ-BTD	dbr 05Jun92 Varna, Bulgaria			
74A-059	B	Belavia	CCCP-85059	EW-85059			
74A-060	S	Far East Avia	CCCP-85060	RA-85060			
74A-061	B	Ulyanovsk Higher Civil Aviation School	CCCP-85061	RA-85061			
74A-062	S	Aeroflot Russian Int A/L	CCCP-85062	RA-85062			
74A-063	S	Aeroflot Russian Int A/L	CCCP-85063	RA-85063	wfs by Sep94 Moscow-Sheremetyevo, Russia		
74A-064	A	Omskavia	CCCP-85064	RA-85064			
74A-065	A		CCCP-85065				
74A-066	A	Kazakhstan Airlines	CCCP-85066	UN-85066			
74A-067	A	(Aeroflot)	CCCP-85067	dbr 13Jan89 Monrovia, Liberia			
74A-068	B	Air Ukraine	CCCP-85068	UR-85068			
74A-069	B-1	Far East Avia	CCCP-85069	RA-85069			
74A-070	B	Siberia Airlines	CCCP-85070	RA-85070			

TUPOLEV Tu-154

S/n	Series	Last known Owner/Operator	Identities/fate (where known)		
74A-071	A		CCCP-85071	wfs by Apr93 Moscow-Vnukovo, Russia	
74A-072	A		CCCP-85072		
74A-073	B	Balkan	LZ-BTE		
74A-074	A	Air Ukraine	CCCP-85074	UR-85074	
74A-075	A	AIS Skytriumph	CCCP-85075	RA-85075	
74A-076	B-1	Kazakhstan Airlines	CCCP-85076	UN-85076	
74A-077	B	Balkan	LZ-BTF		
74A-078	B	Ulyanovsk Higher Civil Aviation School	CCCP-85078	RA-85078	
74A-079	A		CCCP-85079		
74A-080	B	Nizhny Novgorod Airlines	CCCP-85080	RA-85080	
74A-081	S	Aeroflot Russian Int A/L	CCCP-85081	RA-85081	
74A-082	A	Aeroflot Russian Int A/L	CCCP-85082	RA-85082	
74A-083	DLya	Flight Research Inst	CCCP-85083	test a/c	
74A-084	S	Vnukovo Airlines	CCCP-85084	RA-85084	
74A-085	A		CCCP-85085		
74A-086	A	Aeroflot	CCCP-85087	derelict Dushanbe, Tajikistan	
74A-087	A		CCCP-85087		
74A-088	A	Aeroflot	CCCP-85088	reportedly wfs, Irkutsk, Russia	
74A-089	B-1	Aeroflot Russian Int A/L	CCCP-85089	RA-85089	
74A-090	B	Air Moldova	CCCP-85090	ER-85090	
74A-091	B	Ulyanovsk Higher Civil Aviation School	CCCP-85091	RA-85091	
7.A-092	B-1		CCCP-85092	85092	RA-85092
75A-093	B	Air Ukraine	CCCP-85093	UR-85093	
75A-094	B	Barnaul State Avn Ent	CCCP-85094	RA-85094	
75A-095	B	Balkan	LZ-BTG		
75A-096	B-1	St.Petersburg Avia Ent	CCCP-85096	RA-85096	
75A-097	B-1	(Aeroflot)	CCCP-85097	w/o 23May91 Leningrad-Pulkovo, USSR	
75A-098	B	Chelal	CCCP-85098	RA-85098	
75A-099	B	Vnukovo Airlines	CCCP-85099	RA-85099	
75A-100	A		CCCP-85100		
75A-101	A	St.Petersburg Avia Ent	CCCP-85101	RA-85101	
75A-102	A	(Aeroflot)	CCCP-85102	w/o 01Jun76 nr Malabo, Equatorial Guinea	
75A-103	A	(Aeroflot)	CCCP-85103	dbr 01Mar80 Orenburg	
75A-104	B	Ural Airlines	CCCP-85104	85104	RA-85104
75A-105	A	(Armenian Airlines)	CCCP-85105	reportedly dbr 05Dec92 Yerevan, Armenia (status?)	
75A-106	B-2	Siberia Airlines	CCCP-85106	RA-85106	
75A-107	B-1	St.Petersburg Avia Ent	CCCP-85107	RA-85107	
75A-108	B-1	Flight Research Inst	CCCP-85108	RA-85108	
75A-109	B-1	Aeroflot Russian Int A/L	CCCP-85109	RA-85109	
75A-110	B-1	Siberia Airlines	CCCP-85110	RA-85110	
75A-111	B-1	Kazakhstan Airlines	CCCP-85111	UN-85111	
75A-112	B-1	Bashkirian Airlines	CCCP-85112	RA-85112	
75A-113	B-1	Kazakhstan Airlines	CCCP-85113	UN-85113	
75A-114	B	Chelal	CCCP-85114	RA-85114	
75A-115	B	Tomsk State Avia Ent	CCCP-85115	RA-85115	
75A-116	B-1	Air Ukraine	CCCP-85116	UR-85116	
75A-117	B-1	Barnaul State Avn Ent	CCCP-85117	RA-85117	
75A-118	B	Air Ukraine	CCCP-85118	UR-85118	
75A-119	B	Flight Research Inst	CCCP-85119	RA-85119	
75A-120	B		CCCP-85120	tested to destruction OVB Research Institute, Russia	
75A-121	B	Aeroflot	CCCP-85121	derelict by Apr93 Alma Ata	
75A-122	B	Aeroflot	CCCP-85122	wfs by Sep93 Minsk-Chizovka Technical School, Belarus	
75A-123	B	Baikal Airlines	CCCP-85123	RA-85123	
75A-124	B-1	Krasnoyarskavia	CCCP-85124	RA-85124	
75A-125	B	Aeroflot	CCCP-85125	derelict by Apr93 Alma Ata, Kazakhstan	
75A-126	B	(Malev)	HA-LCF	dbr 21Nov81 Prague, Czechoslovakia	
75A-127	B-2	Malev	HA-LCG	wfs, cancelled	
75A-128	B-2	Malev	HA-LCH		
75A-129	B	Chosonminhang	551	P-551	
75A-130	B	Far East Avia	CCCP-85130	RA-85130	
75A-131	B	Aeroflot Russian Int A/L	CCCP-85131	RA-85131	
76A-132	B	Air Ukraine	CCCP-85132	UR-85132	
76A-133	B	Latavio	CCCP-85133	YL-LAA	(RA-85133) wfs Riga-Skulte, Latvia
76A-134	B	Aeroflot	CCCP-85134	reportedly wfs by Jul93 Krasnoyarsk, Russia	
76A-135	B	Siberia Airlines	CCCP-85135	RA-85135	
76A-136	B	Aeroflot	CCCP-85136	dumped by Apr93 Novosibirsk, Russia, reported as RA-85136 in Jul92 !	
76A-137	B	Air Ukraine	CCCP-85137	UR-85137	
76A-138	B		CCCP-85138	wfs Baku, Azerbaijan	
76A-139	B-1	St.Petersburg Avia Ent	CCCP-85139	RA-85139	wfs with no marks St.Petersburg, Russia
76A-140	B	Vnukovo Airlines	CCCP-85140	RA-85140	
76A-141	B-1	Ural Airlines	CCCP-85141	RA-85141	
76A-142	B	Ural Airlines	CCCP-85142	RA-85142	
76A-143	B	Air Koryo	552	P-552	
76A-144	B	Balkan	LZ-BTK		
76A-145	B	Baikal Airlines	CCCP-85145	RA-85145	
76A-146	B	Baikal Airlines	CCCP-85146	RA-85146	
76A-147	B-1	Azerbaijan Airways	CCCP-85147	85147	4K-85147
76A-148	B	Air Ukraine	CCCP-85148	UR-85148	

TUPOLEV Tu-154

S/n	Series	Last known Owner/Operator	Identities/fate (where known)		
76A-149	B	Ulyanovsk Avia Ent	CCCP-85149	RA-85149	
76A-150	B	Samara Airlines	CCCP-85150	RA-85150	
76A-151	B-1	Kazakhstan Airlines	CCCP-85151	RA-85151	
76A-152	B	Air Ukraine	CCCP-85152	UR-85152	
76A-153	B-1	St.Petersburg Avia Ent	CCCP-85153	RA-85153	
76A-154	B	Air Ukraine	CCCP-85154	UR-85154	
76A-155	B	Samara Airlines	CCCP-85155	RA-85155	
76A-156	B-1	Vnukovo Airlines	CCCP-85156	RA-85156	
76A-157	B-1	Far East Avia	CCCP-85157	RA-85157	
76A-158	B-1	Azerbaijan Airways	CCCP-85158	85158	4K-85158
76A-159	B	Tarom	YR-TPA	wfs, Otopeni	
76A-160	B	Khakasic Airlines	CCCP-85160	RA-85160	
76A-161	B	Tarom	YR-TPB		
76A-162	B	Armenian Airlines	CCCP-85162	EK85162	
76A-163	B	(Transair Georgia)	CCCP-85163	85163	w/o 22Sep93 Sukhumi, Georgia
76A-164	B	(Far East Avia)	CCCP-85164	RA-85164	w/o 07Dec95 en-route to Khabarovsk
76A-165	B	Krasnoyarskavia	CCCP-85165	RA-85165	
76A-166	B-1	Armenian Airlines	CCCP-85166	EK85166	
76A-167	B	Chitaavia	CCCP-85167	RA-85167	
76A-168	B	Orbi Georgian Airlines	CCCP-85168	85168	4L-85168
76A-169	B	(Aeroflot)	CCCP-85169	w/o 19May78 en-route in Pochinok/Smolensk region, USSR	
76A-170	B-1	Orbi Georgian Airlines	CCCP-85170	4L-85170	
76A-171	B-1	Chelal	CCCP-85171	RA-85171	
76A-172	B	Baikal Airlines	CCCP-85172	RA-85172	
76A-173	B	Kazakhstan Airlines	CCCP-85173	UN-85173	
76A-174	B	Khakasia Airlines	CCCP-85174	RA-85174	
76A-175	B	Tarom	YR-TPC	wfs, Otopeni	
76A-176	B-2	Far East Avia	CCCP-85176	RA-85176	
76A-177	B-1	Azerbaijan Airways	CCCP-85177	85177	4K-85177
76A-178	B	Far East Avia	CCCP-85178	RA-85178	
76A-179	B	Air Ukraine	CCCP-85179	UR-85179	
76A-180	B	Chelal	CCCP-85180	RA-85180	
76A-181	B-1	Krasnoyarskavia	CCCP-85181	RA-85181	
76A-182	B-1	Vnukovo Airlines	CCCP-85182	RA-85182	
76A-183	B-1	Chelal	CCCP-85183	RA-85183	
76A-184	B	Krasnoyarskavia	CCCP-85184	RA-85184	
76A-185	B	Far East Avia	CCCP-85185	RA-85185	
76A-186	B		CCCP-85186		
76A-187	B	Far East Avia	CCCP-85187	RA-85187	
76A-188	B	Orbi Georgian Airlines	CCCP-85188	85188	4L-85188
76A-189	B	Uzbekistan Airways	CCCP-85189	UK-85189	
76A-190	B	Far East Avia	CCCP-85190	RA-85190	
7.A-191	B	Air Koryo	553	P-553	
77A-192	B-1	Azerbaijan Airways	CCCP-85192	85192	4K-85192
77A-193	B	Ural Airlines	CCCP-85193	RA-85193	
77A-194	B-1	Aeroflot Russian Int A/L	CCCP-85194	UN-85194	RA-85194
77A-195	B-2	Khakasia Airlines	CCCP-85195	RA-85195	
77A-196	B-1	Armenian Airlines	CCCP-85196	EK85196	
77A-197	B	Orbi Georgian Airlines	CCCP-85197	4L-85197	
77A-198	B	Orbi Georgian Airlines	CCCP-85198	4L-85198	
77A-199	B-1	Azerbaijan Airways	CCCP-85199	85199	4K-85199
77A-200	B	Armenian Airlines	CCCP-85200	EK85200	
77A-201	B-1	Krasnoyarskavia	CCCP-85201	RA-85201	
77A-202	B	Krasnoyarskavia	CCCP-85202	RA-85202	
77A-203	B	Orbi Georgian Airlines	CCCP-85203	4L-85203	
77A-204	B-2	Baikal Airlines	CCCP-85204	RA-85204	
77A-205	B-1	Far East Avia	CCCP-85205	RA-85205	
77A-206	B	Far East Avia	CCCP-85206	RA-85206	
77A-207	B-1	Far East Avia	CCCP-85207	RA-85207	
77A-208	B	Balkan Bulgarian	LZ-BTL(2)		
77A-209	B	Balkan Bulgarian	LZ-BTM(2)		
77A-210	B	Armenian Airlines	CCCP-85210	EK85210	
77A-211	B-1	Azerbaijan Airways	CCCP-85211	4K-85211	
77A-212	B-1	Perm Avia Enterprise	CCCP-85212	RA-85212	
77A-213	B	Krasnoyarskavia	CCCP-85213	RA-85213	
77A-214	B-1	Azerbaijan Airways	CCCP-85214	4K-85214	
77A-215	B-1	Vnukovo Airlines	CCCP-85215	RA-85215	
77A-216	B	Far East Avia	CCCP-85216	RA-85216	
77A-217	B	Neryungri Sakha Avia	CCCP-85217	RA-85217	
77A-218	B	Air Ukraine	CCCP-85218	UR-85218	
77A-219	B	Ural Airlines	CCCP-85219	RA-85219	
77A-220	B	Far East Avia	CCCP-85220	RA-85220	
77A-221	B-2	Kazakhstan Airlines	CCCP-85221	RA-85221	UN-85221
77A-222	B-1	(Georgian Airlines)	CCCP-85222	w/o 20Jul92 Tblisi, Georgia	
77A-223	B-1	Khakasia Airlines	CCCP-85223	RA-85223	
77A-224	B	Tarom	YR-TPD		
77A-225	B-1	Tarom	YR-TPE		
77A-226	B	Mineralnye Vody CAPO	CCCP-85226	RA-85226	
77A-227	B		CCCP-85227	tested to destruction OVB Research Institute, Russia	
77A-228	B-1	Nizhny Novgorod Airlines	CCCP-85228	RA-85228	
77A-229	B-2	St.Petersburg Avia Ent	CCCP-85229	RA-85229	

TUPOLEV Tu-154

S/n	Series	Last known Owner/Operator	Identities/fate (where known)		
77A-230	B-1	Kazakhstan Airlines	CCCP-85230	UN-85230	
77A-231	B-1	Kazakhstan Airlines	CCCP-85231	UN-85231	
77A-232	B-1	Air Ukraine	CCCP-85232	UR-85232	
77A-233	B-1	Aeroflot Russian Int A/L	CCCP-85233	RA-85233	
77A-234	B-1	(Aeroflot)	CCCP-85234	dbf Jun92 Bratsk, Russia	
77A-235	B-1	Siberia Airlines	CCCP-85235	RA-85235	
77A-236	B-1	St.Petersburg Avia Ent	CCCP-85236	RA-85236	
77A-237	B-1	Aerokuznetsk	CCCP-85237	RA-85237	
77A-238	B-1	St.Petersburg Avia Ent	CCCP-85238	RA-85238	
77A-239	B-1		YR-TPF		
77A-240	B-1	Kazakhstan Airlines	CCCP-85240	UN-85240	
77A-241	B-1	Turkmenistan Airlines	CCCP-85241	EZ-85241	
77A-242	B-1	St.Petersburg Avia Ent	CCCP-85242	RA-85242	
77A-243	B-1	(Aeroflot)	CCCP-85243	dbr 11Nov84 Omsk, USSR	
77A-244	B-1		CCCP-85244	UR-85244	
77A-245	B-1	Uzbekistan Airways	CCCP-85245	UK-85245	
77A-246	B-1	Turkmenistan Airlines	CCCP-85246	EZ-85246	
77A-247	B-1	Tajik Air	CCCP-85247	EY-85247	
77A-248	B-1	Uzbekistan Airways	CCCP-85248	UK-85248	
77A-249	B-1	Uzbekistan Airways	CCCP-85249	85249	UK-85249
77A-250	B-1	Turkmenistan Airlines	CCCP-85250	EZ-85250	
77A-251	B-1	Tajik Air	CCCP-85251	RA-85251	EY-85251
77A-252	B-1	Kyrgyzstan Airlines	CCCP-85252	EX-85252	
77A-253	B-1	Nizhny Novgorod Airlines	CCCP-85253	RA-85253	
77A-254	B-1	(Aeroflot)	CCCP-85254	w/o 18Jan88 Krasnovodsk, USSR	
77A-255	B-1	Tyumen Airlines	CCCP-85255	RA-85255	
78A-256	B-1	Aerokuznetsk	CCCP-85256	RA-85256	
78A-257	B-1	Kyrgyzstan Airlines	CCCP-85257	EX-85257	
78A-258	B-1	Balkan Bulgarian	LZ-BTO		
77A-259	B-2	Kyrgyzstan Airlines	CCCP-85259	EX-85259	
78A-260	B-1	Belavia	CCCP-85260	UN-85260	EW-85260
78A-261	B-1	Siberia Airlines	CCCP-85261	RA-85261	
78A-262	B-1	Tarom	YR-TPG		
78A-263	B-1	Nizhny Novgorod Airlines	CCCP-85263	RA-85263	
78A-264	B-2	Samara Airlines	CCCP-85264	RA-85264	
78A-265	B-1	Bashkirian Airlines	CCCP-85265	RA-85265	
78A-266	B-1	Far East Avia	CCCP-85266	RA-85266	
78A-267	B-1	Samara Airlines	CCCP-85267	RA-85267	
78A-268	B-1	(Aeroflot)	CCCP-85268	w/o 20Nov90 Kutayissi, USSR	
78A-269	B-1		CCCP-85269	UR-85269	dbr 05Sep92 Kiev-Borispol, Ukraine; remains still present Jun93
78A-270	B-1	Balkan Bulgarian	LZ-BTJ		
78A-271	B-1	Kazakhstan Airlines	CCCP-85271	UN-85271	
78A-272	B-1	Uzbekistan Airways	CCCP-85272	UK-85272	
78A-273	B-2	Aeroflot Russian Int A/L	CCCP-85273	RA-85273	
78A-274	B-1	Azerbaijan Airways	CCCP-85274	85274	4K-85274
78A-275	B-1	Bashkirian Airlines	CCCP-85275	RA-85275	
78A-276	B-1	Kazakhstan Airlines	CCCP-85276	UN-85276	
78A-277	B-1	(Tarom)	YR-TPH	w/o 07Aug80 nr Nouadhibou, Mauritania	
78A-278	B-1	Balkan Bulgarian	LZ-BTP		
78A-279	B-1	Armenian Airlines	CCCP-85279	EK85279	
78A-280	B-1	Chitaavia	CCCP-85280	RA-85280	
78A-281	B-1	Tajik Air	CCCP-85281	EY-85281	
78A-282	B-1	(Aeroflot)	CCCP-85282	dbf Jun92 Bratsk, Russia	
78A-283	B-1	Bashkirian Airlines	CCCP-85283	RA-85283	
78A-284	B-1	Perm Avia Enterprise	CCCP-85284	RA-85284	
78A-285	B-1	Air Moldova	CCCP-85285	85285	ER-85285
78A-286	B-1	Uzbekistan Airways	CCCP-85286	UK-85286	
78A-287	B-1	Nizhny Novgorod Airlines	CCCP-85287	RA-85287	
78A-288	B-1	Donavia Airlines	CCCP-85288	UR-85288	RA-85288
78A-289	B-1	Aerokuznetsk	CCCP-85289	RA-85289	
78A-290	B-1	Kazakhstan Airlines	CCCP-85290	UN-85290	
78A-291	B-1	Omsk Avia	CCCP-85291	RA-85291	
78A-292	B-1	Siberia Airlines	CCCP-85292	RA-85292	
78A-293	B-1	St.Petersburg Avia Ent	CCCP-85293	RA-85293	
78A-294	B-1	Kyrgyzstan Airlines	CCCP-85294	85294	EX-85294
78A-295	B-1	Donavia Airlines	CCCP-85295	RA-85295	
78A-296	B-1	(Aeroflot)	CCCP-85296	RA-85296	w/o 25Dec93 Grozny, Chechnya
78A-297	B-1	(Aeroflot)	CCCP-85297	tested to destruction Apr93 with OVB Research Institue, Russia	
78A-298	B-2	St.Petersburg Avia Ent	CCCP-85298	RA-85298	
78A-299	B-2	Vnukovo Airlines	CCCP-85299	RA-85299	
78A-300	B-2	St.Petersburg Avia Ent	CCCP-85300	RA-85300	
78A-301	B-2	Vnukovo Airlines	CCCP-85301	RA-85301	
78A-302	B-2	Arkhangelsk Airlines	CCCP-85302	RA-85302	
78A-303	B-2	Mineralnye Vody CAPO	CCCP-85303	RA-85303	
78A-304	B-2	Vnukovo Airlines	CCCP-85304	RA-85304	
78A-305	B-2	Donavia Airlines	CCCP-85305	RA-85305	
78A-306	B-2	Donavia Airlines	CCCP-85306	RA-85306	
78A-307	B-2	Donavia Airlines	CCCP-85307	RA-85307	
78A-308	B-2	Donavia Airlines	CCCP-85308	RA-85308	
78A-309	B-2	Donavia Airlines	CCCP-85309	RA-85309	

TUPOLEV Tu-154

S/n	Series	Last known Owner/Operator	Identities/fate (where known)		
78A-310	B-2	Ural Airlines	CCCP-85310	RA-85310	noted Aug95 engineless Ekaterinburg, Russia
78A-311	B-2	(Aeroflot)	CCCP-85311	w/o 10Jun85	
78A-312	B-2	Tyumen Airlines	CCCP-85312	RA-85312	
78A-313	B-2	Kyrgyzstan Airlines	CCCP-85313	85313	EX-85313
78A-314	B-2	Tyumen Airlines	CCCP-85314	RA-85314	
78A-315	B-2	Ulyanovsk Higher Civil Aviation School	CCCP-85315	RA-85315	
78A-316	B-2	Air Ukraine	CCCP-85316	UR-85316	
78A-317	M	Tupolev Design Bureau	CCCP-85317	RA-85317	in-flight simulator test a/c
78A-318	B-2	Nizhny Novgorod Airlines	CCCP-85318	RA-85318	
78A-319	B-2	Ural Airlines	CCCP-85319	RA-85319	
78A-320	B-2	Amur Avia	LZ-BTR(2)	RA-85742	
78A-321	B-2	(Aeroflot)	CCCP-85321	dbr 08Aug80 Chita, USSR	
78A-322	B-2	Uzbekistan Airways	CCCP-85322	85322	UK-85322
78A-323	B-2	Neryungri Sakha Avia	CCCP-85323	RA-85323	
78A-324	B-2	Air Moldova	CCCP-85324	RA-85324	ER-85324
78A-325	B-2	Malev	HA-LCM		
78A-326	B-2	Malev	HA-LCN		
7.A-327	B-2	Aeroflot	CCCP-85327	dbr 21May86 Moscow-Sheremetyevo, Russia; to Technical School	
79A-328	B-2	SP Air	CCCP-85328	RA-85328	
79A-329	B-2	Azerbaijan Airways	CCCP-85329	85329	4K-85329
79A-330	B-2	Mineralnye Vody CAPO	CCCP-85330	RA-85330	
78A-331	B-2	Belavia	CCCP-85331	EW-85331	
79A-332	B-2	Air Moldova	CCCP-85332	ER-85332	
79A-333	B-2	Gosnii GA	CCCP-85333	RA-85333	
79A-334	B-2	Aeroflot Russian Int A/L	CCCP-85334	RA-85334	
79A-335	B-2	Tyumen Airlines	CCCP-85335	RA-85335	
79A-336	B-2	Far East Avia	CCCP-85336	RA-85336	
79A-337	B-2	Ural Airlines	CCCP-85337	RA-85337	
79A-338	B-2	(Aeroflot)	CCCP-85338	w/o 23Dec84 Krasnoyarsk, USSR	
79A-339	B-2	Belavia	CCCP-85339	EW-85339	
79A-340	B-2	Mineralnye Vody CAPO	CCCP-85340	RA-85340	
79A-341	B-2	Far East Avia	CCCP-85341	RA-85341	
79A-342	B-2	Tarom	YR-TPI		
79A-343	B-2	St.Petersburg Avia Ent	CCCP-85343	RA-85343	
79A-344	B-2	Uzbekistan Airways	CCCP-85344	UK-85344	
79A-345	B-2	Turkmenistan Airlines	CCCP-85345	85345	EZ-85345
79A-346	B-2	St.Petersburg Avia Ent	CCCP-85346	RA-85346	
79A-347	B-2	Bashkirian Airlines	CCCP-85347	RA-85347	
79A-348	B-2	Yakutavia	CCCP-85348	RA-85348	
79A-349	B-2	Bashkirian Airlines	CCCP-85349	RA-85349	
79A-350	B-2	Air Ukraine	CCCP-85350	UR-85350	
79A-351	B-2	Aerokuznetsk	CCCP-85351	RA-85351	
79A-352	B-2	Belavia	CCCP-85352	EW-85352	
79A-353	B-2	Russian Min of Defence	CCCP-85353	RA-85353	
79A-354	B-2	Yakutavia	CCCP-85354	RA-85354	
79A-355	B-2	(Aeroflot)	CCCP-85355	w/o 07Jun80 Alma-Ata, USSR	
79A-356	B-2	Uzbekistan Airways	CCCP-85356	UK-85356	
79A-357	B-2	Ural Airlines	CCCP-85357	RA-85357	
79A-358	B-2	Omskavia	CCCP-85358	RA-85358	damaged 29Dec93 Omsk, Russia - status?
79A-359	B-2	Orbi Georgian Airlines	CCCP-85359	85359	4L-85359
79A-360	B-2	Russian Min of Defence	CCCP-85360	RA-85360	
79A-361	B-2	Tyumen Airlines	CCCP-85361	RA-85361	
79A-362	B-2	Air Ukraine	CCCP-85362	RA-85362	UR-85362
79A-363	B-2	Aeroflot Russian Int A/L	CCCP-85363	RA-85363	
79A-364	B-2	Azerbaijan Airways	CCCP-85364	4K-85364	
79A-365	B-2	Arkhangelsk Airlines	CCCP-85365	RA-85365	
79A-366	B-2	Tyumen Airlines	CCCP-85366	RA-85366	
79A-367	B-2	Neryungri Sakha Avia	CCCP-85367	RA-85367	
79A-368	B-2	Air Ukraine	CCCP-85368	UR-85368	
79A-369	B-2	Kyrgyzstan Airlines	CCCP-85369	EX-85369	
79A-370	B-2	Uzbekistan Airways	CCCP-85370	85370	UK-85370
79A-371	B-2	Mineralnye Vody CAPO	CCCP-85371	RA-85371	
79A-372	B-2	Belavia	CCCP-85372	EW-85372	
79A-373	B-2	Mineralnye Vody CAPO	CCCP-85373	RA-85373	
79A-374	B-2	Ural Airlines	CCCP-85374	RA-85374	
79A-375	B-2	Ural Airlines	CCCP-85375	RA-85375	
79A-376	B-2	Yakutavia	CCCP-85376	RA-85376	
79A-377	B-2	St.Petersburg Avia Ent	CCCP-85377	RA-85377	
79A-378	B-2	Tyumen Airlines	CCCP-85378	RA-85378	
79A-379	B-2	Air Ukraine/UN	CCCP-85379	UR-85379	
79A-380	B-2	Russian Min of Defence	CCCP-85380	RA-85380	
79A-381	B-2	St.Petersburg Avia Ent	CCCP-85381	RA-85381	
79A-382	B-2	Mineralnye Vody CAPO	CCCP-85382	RA-85382	
79A-383	B-2	Turkmenistan Airlines	CCCP-85383	EZ-85383	
79A-384	B-2	Air Moldova	CCCP-85384	ER-85384	
79A-385	B-2	Tajik Air	CCCP-85385	EY-85385	
79A-386	B-2	Arkhangelsk Airlines	CCCP-85386	RA-85386	
79A-387	B-2	Kazakhstan Airlines	CCCP-85387	UN-85387	
79A-388	B-2	Ulyanovsk Higher Civil Aviation School	CCCP-85388	RA-85388	

TUPOLEV Tu-154

S/n	Series	Last known Owner/Operator	Identities/fate (where known)				
79A-389	B-2	Kemerovo Avia Ent	CCCP-85389	RA-85389			
79A-390	B-2	St.Petersburg Avia Ent	CCCP-85390	RA-85390			
80A-391	B-2	Azerbaijan Airways	CCCP-85391	85391	4K-85391		
80A-392	B-2	Aerokuznetsk	CCCP-85392	RA-85392			
80A-393	B-2	Mineralnye Vody CAPO	CCCP-85393	85393	RA-85393		
80A-394	B-2	Turkmenistan Airlines	CCCP-85394	85394	EZ-85394		
80A-395	B-2	Improtex	CCCP-85395	UR-85395	4K-85395		
80A-396	B-2	Kazakhstan Airlines	CCCP-85396	UN-85396			
80A-397	B-2	Uzbekistan Airways	CCCP-85397	85397	UK-85397		
80A-398	B-2	Uzbekistan Airways	CCCP-85398	85398	UK-85398		
80A-399	B-2	Air Ukraine	CCCP-85399	UR-85399			
80A-400	B-2	Donavia Airlines	CCCP-85400	RA-85400			
80A-401	B-2	Uzbekistan Airways	CCCP-85401	85401	UK-85401		
80A-402	B-2	Barnaul State Avn Ent	CCCP-85402	RA-85402			
80A-403	B-2	Armenian Airlines	CCCP-85403	EK85403			
80A-404	B-2	Bashkirian Airlines	CCCP-85404	RA-85404			
80A-405	B-2	Air Moldova	CCCP-85405	ER-85405			
80A-406	B-2	Tajik Air	CCCP-85406	EY-85406			
80A-407	B-2	Air Ukraine	CCCP-85407	UR-85407			
80A-408	B-2	(Tarom)	YR-TPJ	w/o 09Feb89 Otopeni, Romania			
80A-409	B-2	Donavia Airlines	CCCP-85409	RA-85409	ER-85409	RA-85409	
80A-410	B-2	Turkmenistan Airlines	CCCP-85410	EZ-85410			
80A-411	B-2	Belavia	CCCP-85411	EW-85411			
80A-412	B-2	Tatarstan Airlines	CCCP-85412	RA-85412			
80A-413	B-2	(Aeroflot)	CCCP-85413	w/o 08Mar88 nr Leningrad, USSR			
80A-414	B-2	Donavia Airlines	CCCP-85414	RA-85414			
80A-415	B-2	Tarom	YR-TPK				
80A-416	B-2	Uzbekistan Airways	CCCP-85416	UK-85416			
80A-417	B-2	Krasnoyarskavia	CCCP-85417	RA-85417			
80A-418	B-2	Krasnoyarskavia	CCCP-85418	RA-85418			
80A-419	B-2	Belavia	CCCP-85419	EW-85419			
80A-420	B-2	Slovak AF	OK-BYA	Czech AF 0420	OK-0420	Czech AF 0420	0420
80A-421	B-2	Tomsk State Avia Ent	CCCP-85421	RA-85421			
80A-422	B-2	Balkan Bulgarian	LZ-BTS				
80A-423	B-2	Uzbekistan Airways	CCCP-85423	UK-85423			
80A-424	B-2	Air Ukraine	CCCP-85424	UR-85424			
80A-425	B-2	Donavia Airlines	CCCP-85425	RA-85425			
80A-426	B-2	Russian Min of Defence	CCCP-85426	RA-85426			
80A-427	B-2	Tyumen Airlines	CCCP-85427	RA-85427			
80A-428	B-2	Tarom	YR-TPL				
80A-429	B-2	Baikal Airlines	CCCP-85429	RA-85429			
80A-430	B-2	Orbi Georgian Airlines	CCCP-85430	85430	4L-85430		
80A-431	B-2	Kazakhstan Airlines	CCCP-85431	UN-85431			
80A-432	B-2	Ural Airlines	CCCP-85432	RA-85432			
80A-433	B-2	Uzbekistan Airways	CCCP-85433				
80A-434	B-2	Tyumen Airlines	CCCP-85434	RA-85434			
80A-435	B-2	Donavia Airlines	CCCP-85435	RA-85435			
80A-436	B-2	Donavia Airlines	CCCP-85436	RA-85436			
80A-437	B-2	Donavia Airlines	CCCP-85437	RA-85437			
80A-438	B-2	Uzbekistan Airways	CCCP-85438	85438	UK-85438		
80A-439	B-2	Ural Airlines	CCCP-85439	RA-85439			
80A-440	B-2	Tajik Air	CCCP-85440	EY-85440			
80A-441	B-2	St.Petersburg Avia Ent	CCCP-85441	RA-85441			
80A-442	B-2	Armenian Airlines	CCCP-85442	EK85442			
80A-443	B-2	Far East Avia	CCCP-85443	RA-85443			
80A-444	B-2	Kyrgyzstan Airlines	CCCP-85444	EX-85444			
80A-445	B-2	Air Ukraine	CCCP-85445	UR-85445			
80A-446	B-2	Russian Min of Defence	CCCP-85446	RA-85446			
80A-447	B-2	Cubana	CU-T1222				
80A-448	B-2	Aeroflot Russian Int A/L	CCCP-85448	RA-85448			
80A-449	B-2	Uzbekistan Airways	CCCP-85449	UK-85449			
80A-450	B-2	Tyumen Airlines	CCCP-85450	RA-85450			
80A-451	B-2	Tyumen Airlines	CCCP-85451	RA-85451			
80A-452	B-2	Baikal Airlines	CCCP-85452	RA-85452			
80A-453	B-2	Baikal Airlines	CCCP-85453	RA-85453			
80A-454	B-2	Donavia Airlines	CCCP-85454	RA-85454			
80A-455	B-2	Kazakhstan Airlines	CCCP-85455	UN-85455			
80A-456	B-2	Nizhny Novgorod Airlines	CCCP-85456	RA-85456			
80A-457	B-2	Mineralnye Vody CAPO	CCCP-85457	RA-85457			
80A-458	B-2	Nizhny Novgorod Airlines	CCCP-85458	RA-85458			
80A-459	B-2	Ural Airlines	CCCP-85459	RA-85459			
80A-460	B-2	Air Ukraine	CCCP-85460	UR-85460			
80A-461	B-2	Siberia Airlines	CCCP-85461	RA-85461			
80A-462	B-2	Baikal Airlines	CCCP-85462	RA-85462			
80A-463	B-2	Russian Min of Defence	CCCP-85463	RA-85463			
80A-464	B-2	Kazakhstan Airlines	CCCP-85464	85464	UN-85464		
80A-465	B-2	Belavia	CCCP-85465	85465	EW-85465		
8.A-466	B-2	Tajik Air	CCCP-85466	EY-85466			
81A-467	B-2	Chelal	CCCP-85467	RA-85467			
81A-468	B-2	Arkhangelsk Airlines	CCCP-85468	RA-85468			
81A-469	B-2	Tajik Air	CCCP-85469	EY-85469			

TUPOLEV Tu-154

S/n	Series	Last known Owner/Operator	Identities/fate (where known)		
81A-470	B-2	Ulyanovsk Higher Civil Aviation School	CCCP-85470	RA-85470	
81A-471	B-2	Aerokuznetsk	RA-85471		
81A-472	B-2	Air Moravia	CCCP-85472	RA-85472	
81A-473	B-2	Malev	HA-LCO		
81A-474	B-2	Malev	HA-LCP		
81A-475	B-2	Tajik Air	CCCP-85475	RA-85475	EY-85475
81A-476	B-2	Air Ukraine	CCCP-85476	UR-85476	
81A-477	B-2	Far East Avia	CCCP-85477	RA-85477	
81A-478	B-2	Kazakhstan Airlines	CCCP-85478	UN-85478	
81A-479	B-2	(Aeroflot)	CCCP-85479	w/o 24Sep88 Aleppo, Syria	
81A-480	B-2	(Aeroflot)	CCCP-85480	w/o 16Nov81 Norilsk, USSR	
81A-481	B-2	Tyumen Airlines	CCCP-85481	RA-85481	
81A-482	B-2	Air Ukraine	CCCP-85482	UR-85482	
81A-483	B-2	Balkan Bulgarian	LZ-BTT		
81A-484	B-2	Balkan Bulgarian	LZ-BTU		
81A-485	B-2	Tomsk State Avia Ent	CCCP-85485	RA-85485	
81A-486	B-2	Neryungri Sakha Avia	CCCP-85486	RA-85486	
81A-487	B-2	Tajik Air	CCCP-85487	EY-85487	
81A-488	B-2	Tatarstan Airlines	OK-BYB	OK-LCP	RA-85488
81A-489	B-2	Krasnoyarskavia	CCCP-85489	RA-85489	
81A-490	B-2	Air Ukraine	CCCP-85490	UR-85490	
81A-491	B-2	Kyrgyzstan Airlines	CCCP-85491	EX-85491	
81A-492	B-2	Turkmenistan Airlines	CCCP-85492	85492	EZ-85492
81A-493	B-2	Cubana	CU-T1224		
81A-494	B-2	Mineralnye Vody CAPO	CCCP-85494	RA-85494	
81A-495	B-2	Donavia Airlines	CCCP-85495	RA-85495	
81A-496	B-2	Orbi Georgian Airlines	CCCP-85496	85496	4L-85496
81A-497	B-2	Kyrgyzstan Airlines	CCCP-85497	EX-85497	
81A-498	B-2	Tyumen Airlines	CCCP-85498	RA-85498	
81A-499	B-2	Air Ukraine	CCCP-85499	UR-85499	
81A-500	B-2	Samara Airlines	CCCP-85500	RA-85500	
81A-501	B-2	(Alyemda)	70-ACN	possibly w/o in 1986 Aden or to CCCP-?	
81A-502	B-2	Tyumen Airlines	CCCP-85502	RA-85502	
81A-503	B-2	Baikal Airlines	CCCP-85503	RA-85503	
81A-504	B-2	Kemerovo Avia Ent	CCCP-85504	RA-85504	
81A-505	B-2	Krasnoyarskavia	CCCP-85505	RA-85505	
81A-506	B-2	Chitaavia	CCCP-85506	RA-85506	
81A-507	B-2	Turkmenistan Airlines	CCCP-85507	85507	EZ-85507
81A-508	B-2	Ural Airlines	CCCP-85508	RA-85508	
81A-509	B-2		CCCP-85509	EW-85509	UN-85509
81A-510	B-2	Russian Min of Defence	CCCP-85510	RA-85510	
81A-511	B-2	Tajik Air	CCCP-85511	RA-85511	EY-85511
81A-512	B-2	Baikal Airlines	CCCP-85512	RA-85512	
81A-513	B-2	Air Ukraine	CCCP-85513	UR-85513	
81A-514	B-2	Chelal	CCCP-85514	RA-85514	
81A-515	B-2	Latavio	CCCP-85515	YL-LAB	
81A-516	B-2	Aeroservice Kazakhstan	CCCP-85516	YL-LAC	UN-85516
81A-517	B-2	Tatarstan Airlines	OK-BYC	OK-LCS	RA-85804
81A-518	B-2	Orbi Georgian Airlines	CCCP-85518	85518	4L-85518
81A-519	B-2	Kyrgyzstan Airlines	CCCP-85519	EX-85519	
81A-520	B-2	Yakutavia	CCCP-85520	RA-85520	
8.A-521	B-2	Kazakhstan Airlines	CCCP-85521	UN-85521	
82A-522	B-2	Tyumen Airlines	CCCP-85522	RA-85522	
82A-523	B-2	Moscow Airways	CCCP-85523	RA-85523	
82A-524	B-2	Improtex	CCCP-85524	YL-LAG	4K-85524
82A-525	S	Bashkirian Airlines	CCCP-85525	RA-85525	
82A-526	B-2	Air Ukraine	CCCP-85526	UR-85526	
82A-527	B-2	Donavia Airlines	CCCP-85527	RA-85527	
82A-528	B-2	(Byelorussian Airlines)	CCCP-85528	dbr 13Oct92 Vladivostok, USSR	
82A-529	B-2	Krasnoyarskavia	CCCP-85529	RA-85529	
82A-530	B-2	St.Petersburg Avia Ent	CCCP-85530	HA-LCS	CCCP-85530 RA-85530
82A-531	B-2	Malev	CCCP-85531	HA-LCU	
82A-532	B-2	Turkmenistan Airlines	CCCP-85532	EZ-85532	
82A-533	B-2	(Indian Airlines)	CCCP-85533	85532	dbf 08Jan93 Delhi, India
82A-534	B-2	Russian Min of Defence	CCCP-85534	RA-85534	
82A-535	B-2	Air Ukraine	CCCP-85535	UR-85535	
82A-536	B-2	Armenian Airlines	CCCP-85536	EK85536	
82A-537	B-2	Kazakhstan Airlines	CCCP-85537	85537	UN-85537
82A-538	B-2	Belavia	CCCP-85538	EW-85538	
82A-539	B-2	Aeroservice Kazakhstan	CCCP-85539	YL-LAF	UN-85539
82A-540	B-2	Aeroflot Russian Int A/L	CCCP-85541	RA-85541	
82A-541	B-2	(Cubana)	CU-T1227	w/o 14Sep91 Mexico City, Mexico	
82A-542	B-2	St.Petersburg Avia Ent	CCCP-85542	HA-LCT	CCCP-85542 RA-85542
82A-543	B-2	Malev	HA-LCR		
82A-544	B-2	Malev	CCCP-85544	HA-LCV	
82A-545	B-2	Belavia	CCCP-85545	RA-85545	
82A-546	B-2	Latavio	CCCP-85546	YL-LAE	
82A-547	B-2	Air Georgia	CCCP-85547	GR-85547	4L-85547
82A-548	B-2	Azerbaijan Airways	CCCP-85548	85548	4K-85548
82A-549	B-2	Turkmenistan Airlines	CCCP-85549	85549	EZ-85549

TUPOLEV Tu-154

S/n	Series	Last known Owner/Operator	Identities/fate (where known)				
82A-550	B-2	Tyumen Airlines	CCCP-85550	RA-85550			
82A-551	B-2	Arkhangelsk Airlines	CCCP-85551	85551	RA-85551		
82A-552	B-2	St.Petersburg Avia Ent	CCCP-85552	RA-85552			
82A-553	B-2	St.Petersburg Avia Ent	CCCP-85553	RA-85553			
82A-554	B-2	Russian Min of Defence	CCCP-85554	RA-85554			
82A-555	B-2	Russian Min of Defence	CCCP-85555	RA-85555			
82A-556	B-2	Latavio	CCCP-85556	YL-LAD	Cancelled by Apr94		
82A-557	B-2	Magadan Airlines	CCCP-85557	RA-85557			
82A-558	B-2	Latavio	CCCP-85558	YL-LAH			
82A-559	B-2	Russian Min of Defence	CCCP-85559	RA-85559			
82A-560	B-2	Turkmenistan Airlines	CCCP-85560	EZ-85560			
82A-561	B-2	BSL Airlines	CCCP-85561	85561	UR-85561		
82A-562	B-2	Magadan Airlines	CCCP-85562	RA-85562			
82A-563	B-2	Russian Min of Defence	CCCP-85563	RA-85563			
82A-564	B-2	Aeroflot Russian Int A/L	CCCP-85564	bHMAY85564	CCCP-85564	RA-85564	
82A-565	B-2	Air Moldova	CCCP-85565	RA-85565	CCCP-85565?	ER-85565	
82A-566	B-2	Armenian Airlines	CCCP-85566	EK85566			
82A-567	B-2	Magadan Airlines	CCCP-85567	RA-85567			
82A-568	B-2	Yakutavia	CCCP-85568	RA-85568			
82A-569	B-2	Balkan Bulgarian	LZ-BTV				
83A-570	B-2	Aeroflot Russian Int A/L	CCCP-85570	RA-85570			
83A-571	B-2	Russian Min of Defence	CCCP-85571	RA-85571			
83A-572	B-2	Russian Min of Defence	CCCP-85572	RA-85572			
83A-573	B-2		CCCP-85573				
83A-574	B-2	Russian Min of Defence	CCCP-85574	RA-85574			
83A-575	B-2	Uzbekistan Airways	CCCP-85575	85575	UK-85575		
83A-576	B-2	Cubana	CU-T1253				
83A-577	B-2	Sacha Avia	CCCP-85577	RA-85577			
83A-578	B-2	Uzbekistan Airways	CCCP-85578	85578	UK-85578		
83A-579	B-2	St.Petersburg Avia Ent	CCCP-85579	RA-85579			
83A-580	B-2	Belavia	CCCP-85580	EW-85580			
83A-581	B-2	Belavia	CCCP-85581	EW-85581			
83A-582	B-2	Belavia	CCCP-85582	EW-85582			
83A-583	B-2	Belavia	CCCP-85583	EW-85583			
83A-584?	B-2	Magadan Airline	P-561	RA-85584			
83A-585	B-2	Samara Airlines	CCCP-85585	RA-85585	UR-85585		
83A-586	B-2	Russian Min of Defence	CCCP-85586	RA-85586			
83A-587	B-2	Russian Min of Defence	CCCP-85587	RA-85587			
83A-588	B-2	Magadan Airlines	CCCP-85588	RA-85588			
83A-589	B-2	Kazakhstan Airlines	CCCP-85589	UN-85589			
83A-590	B-2	Kyrgyzstan Airlines	CCCP-85590	EX-85590			
83A-591	B-2	Belavia	CCCP-85591	EW-85591			
83A-592	B-2	Aeroflot Russian Int A/L	CCCP-85592	RA-85592			
83A-593	B-2	Belavia	CCCP-85593	EW-85593			
84A-594	B-2	Russian Min of Defence	CCCP-85594	RA-85594			
84A-595	B-2	Orenburg Avia Enterprise	CCCP-85595	RA-85595			
84A-596	B-2	Magadan Airlines	CCCP-85596	RA-85596			
84A-597	B-2	Yakutavia	CCCP-85597	RA-85597			
84A-598	B-2		CCCP-85598				
84A-599	B-2	Cubana	CU-T1256				
84A-600	B-2	Uzbekistan Govt	CCCP-85600	YA-TAT	CCCP-85600	85600	UK-85600
84A-601	B-2	Czech AF	OK-BYD	0601			
84A-602	B-2	Orenburg Avia Enterprise	CCCP-85602	RA-85602			
85A-603	B-2	Orenburg Avia Enterprise	CCCP-85603	RA-85603			
85A-604	B-2	Orenburg Avia Enterprise	CCCP-85604	RA-85604			
85A-605	B-2	Russian Min of Defence	CCCP-85605	RA-85605			
85A-606	M	Flight Research Inst	CCCP-85606	RA-85606			
85A-607	M	Arax Airlines	CCCP-85607	RA-85607	EK85607	(also s/n 85A-702)	
85A-608	M	(Aeroflot)	CCCP-85608	tested to destruction Apr93 OVB Research Institute, Russia			
85A-609	M	Ulyanovsk Higher Civil Aviation School	CCCP-85609	RA-85609			
85A-705	M	Vnukovo Airlines	CCCP-85610	RA-85610	wfs by Sep94 Moscow-Vnukovo, Russia		
85A-706	M	Balkan Bulgarian	LZ-BTI				
85A-707	M	Balkan Bulgarian	LZ-BTW				
85A-708	M	Syrianair	YK-AIA				
85A-709	M	Syrianair	YK-AIB				
85A-710	M	Syrianair	YK-AIC				
85A-711	M	China United Airlines	B-4001				
85A-712	M	CAAC	B-4002	B-4138			
85A-713	M	China United Airlines	B-4003				
85A-714	M	China United Airlines	B-4004				
85A-715	M	Vnukovo Airlines	CCCP-85611	RA-85611			
85A-716	M	China Northwest Airlines	B-2601				
86A-717	M	China Northwest Airlines	B-2602				
86A-718	M	Xinjiang Airlines	B-2603				
86A-719	M	Omsk Avia	8R-GGA	CU-T1276	RA-85818		
86A-720	M	Cubana	CU-T1264				
86A-721	M	Vnukovo Airlines	CCCP-85612	RA-85612			
86A-722	M	Baikal Airlines	CCCP-85613	RA-85613			
86A-723	M	Russian Min of Defence	CCCP-85614	RA-85614			
86A-724	M	China Northwest Airlines	B-2604				

TUPOLEV Tu-154

S/n	Series	Last known Owner/Operator	Identities/fate (where known)			
86A-725	M	China Northwest Airlines	B-2605			
86A-726	M	Xinjiang Airlines	B-2611			
86A-727	M	Turanair	SP-LCA	4K-727		
86A-728	M	Xinjiang Airlines	B-2606			
86A-729	M	Xinjiang Airlines	B-2607			
86A-730	M	CAAC	B-2612			
86A-731	M	Vnukovo Airlines	CCCP-85615	RA-85615		
86A-732	M	Russian Min of Defence	CCCP-85616	RA-85616		
86A-733	M	Turanair	SP-LCB	4K-733		
86A-734	M	China Northwest Airlines	B-2608			
86A-735	M	Xinjiang Airlines	B-2609			
86A-736	M	Ulyanovsk Higher Civil Aviation School	CCCP-85617	RA-85617	UK-85617?	
86A-737	M	Vnukovo Airlines	CCCP-85618	RA-85618		
86A-738	M	Vnukovo Airlines	CCCP-85619	RA-85619		
86A-739	M	Active Air	CCCP-85620	TC-GRA	RA-85620	TC-ACT
87A-740	M	(China Northwest Airlines)		B-2610	w/o 06Jun94	
87A-741	M	CAAC	B-2614			
87A-742	M	Vnukovo Airlines	CCCP-85621	RA-85621		
87A-743	M	Balkan Bulgarian	LZ-BTQ			
87A-744	M	Balkan Bulgarian	LZ-BTX			
87A-745	M	LOT	SP-LCC			
87A-746	M	Vnukovo Airlines	CCCP-85622	RA-85622		
87A-747	M	(Ariana Afghan)	YA-TAP	dbr 29May92 Kabul, Afghanistan		
87A-748	M	Ariana Afghan	YA-TAR			
87A-749	M	Vnukovo Airlines	CCCP-85623	RA-85623		
87A-750	M	Vnukovo Airlines	CCCP-85624	85624	RA-85624	
87A-751	M	Cubana	CU-T1265			
87A-752	M	Aeroflot Russian Int A/L	CCCP-85625	RA-85625		
87A-753	M	Aeroflot Russian Int A/L	CCCP-85626	RA-85626		
87A-754	M	Balkan Bulgarian	LZ-BTH			
87A-755	M	LOT	SP-LCD			
87A-756	M	Flight Research Inst	CCCP-85627	RA-85627		
87A-757	M	Vnukovo Airlines	CCCP-85628	RA-85628		
87A-758	M	Rossia	CCCP-85629	RA-85629		
87A-759	M	Rossia	CCCP-85630	RA-85630		
87A-760	M	Rossia	CCCP-85631	RA-85631		
87A-761	M	Vnukovo Airlines	CCCP-85632	RA-85632		
87A-762	M	Vnukovo Airlines	CCCP-85633	RA-85633		
87A-763	M	Aeroflot Russian Int A/L	CCCP-85634	RA-85634		
87A-764	M	Vnukovo Airlines	CCCP-85635	RA-85635		
87A-765	M	China United Airlines	(CCCP-85765)	OK-SCA	B-4022	
87A-766	M	Ulyanovsk Higher Civil Aviation School	CCCP-85636	RA-85636		
87A-767	M	Aeroflot Russian Int A/L	CCCP-85637	RA-85637		
87A-768	M	Aeroflot Russian Int A/L	CCCP-85638	RA-85638		
88A-769	M	LOT	SP-LCE			
88A-770	M	China United Airlines	(CCCP-85770)	OK-TCB	B-4023	
88A-771	M	Aeroflot Russian Int A/L	CCCP-85639	RA-85639		
88A-772	M	Aeroflot Russian Int A/L	CCCP-85640	RA-85640		
88A-773	M	Aeroflot Russian Int A/L	CCCP-85641	RA-85641		
88A-774	M	LOT	(CCCP-85774)	SP-LCF		
88A-775	M	Kazakhstan Airlines	(CCCP-85775)	SP-LCG	RA-85823	UN-85775
88A-776	M	LOT	(CCCP-85776)	SP-LCH	wfs by Jul95 Warsaw, Poland	
88A-777	M	Cubana	CU-T1275			
88A-778	M	Aeroflot Russian Int A/L	CCCP-85642	RA-85642		
88A-779	M	Aeroflot Russian Int A/L	CCCP-85643	RA-85643	wfs by Sep94 Moscow-Sheremetyevo, Russia	
88A-780	M	Aeroflot Russian Int A/L	CCCP-85644	MPR-85644	RA-85644	
88A-781	M	Balkan Bulgarian	LZ-BTZ			
88A-782	M	Rossia	CCCP-85645	RA-85645		
88A-783	M	China Southwest Airlines	B-2615			
88A-784	M	Aeroflot Russian Int A/L	CCCP-85646	RA-85646		
88A-785	M	Aeroflot Russian Int A/L	CCCP-85647	RA-85647		
88A-786	M	Aeroflot Russian Int A/L	CCCP-85648	RA-85648		
88A-787	M	Aeroflot Russian Int A/L	CCCP-85649	RA-85649		
88A-788	M	Aeroflot Russian Int A/L	CCCP-85650	RA-85650		
88A-789	M	China United Airlines	(CCCP-85789)	OK-TCC	B-4024	
88A-790	M	China Southwest Airlines	B-2616			
88A-791	M	China Southwest Airlines	B-2617			
88A-792	M	CSA	OK-TCD			
88A-793	M	Rossia	CCCP-85651	85651	RA-85651	
88A-794	M	Baikal Airlines	CCCP-85652	RA-85652		
88A-795	M	Rossia	CCCP-85653	85653	RA-85653	
89A-796	M	Baikal Airlines	CCCP-85654	RA-85654		
89A-797	M	China Southwest Airlines	B-2618			
89A-798	M-LK1	Russian Min of Defence	CCCP-85655	RA-85655	Cosmonaut training a/c	
89A-799	M	German AF	E German AF 114	DDR-SFA	11+01	
89A-800	M	Balkan Bulgarian	LZ-BTY			
89A-801	M	(Baikal Air)	CCCP-85656	RA-85656	w/o 02Jan94 Mamony nr Irkutsk, Russia	
89A-802	M	Baikal Airlines	CCCP-85657	RA-85657		
89A-803	M	Slovak Government	OK-BYO	OM-BYO		

TUPOLEV Tu-154

S/n	Series	Last known Owner/Operator	Identities/fate (where known)			
89A-804	M	CSA	OK-UCE			
89A-805	M	Samara Avia	SP-LCI	RA-85821		
89A-806	M	Samara Avia	SP-LCK	RA-85822		
89A-807	M	CSA	OK-UCF			
89A-808	M	Rossia	CCCP-85658	RA-85658		
89A-809	M	Rossia	CCCP-85659	RA-85659		
89A-810	M	Iran Air Tours	CCCP-85660	RA-85660	EP-ITL	
89A-811	M	Aeroflot Russian Int A/L	CCCP-85661	RA-85661		
89A-812	M	LOT	SP-LCL			
89A-813	M	German AF	E German AF 121	DDR-SFB	11+02	
89A-814	M	China Northwest Airlines	B-2619			
89A-815	M	China Northwest Airlines	B-2620			
89A-816	M	Aeroflot Russian Int A/L	CCCP-85662	RA-85662		
89A-817	M	Aeroflot Russian Int A/L	CCCP-85663	RA-85663		
89A-818	M	(Aeroflot)	CCCP-85664	w/o 18Nov90 nr Velichovky, Czechoslovakia		
89A-819	M	Aeroflot Russian Int A/L	CCCP-85665	RA-85665		
89A-820	M	Rossia	CCCP-85666	85666	RA-85666	
89A-821	M	Aeronica	YN-CBT	derelict by Feb93 Managua, Nicaragua		
89A-822	M	Aeroflot Russian Int A/L	70-ACT	CCCP-85803	RA-85803	
89A-823	M	Xinjiang Airlines	B-2621			
89A-824	M	Aeroflot Russian Int A/L	SP-LCM	RA-85810		
89A-825	M	Magadan Airlines	CCCP-85667	RA-85667		
89A-826	M	Aeroflot Russian Int A/L	CCCP-85668	RA-85668		
89A-827	M	Aeroflot Russian Int A/L	CCCP-85669	RA-85669		
89A-828	M	Aeroflot Russian Int A/L	CCCP-85670	RA-85670		
89A-829	M	Magadan Airlines	CCCP-85671			
90A-830	M	Krasnoyarskavia	CCCP-85672	RA-85672		
90A-831	M	Aeroflot Russian Int A/L	SP-LCN	RA-85811		
90A-832	M	Lao Aviation/UN	LZ-BTN(2)			
90A-833	M	Active Air	CCCP-85673	TC-GRB	RA-85673	TC-ACV
90A-834	M	Kibris THY	CCCP-85674	TC-GRC	RA-85674	TC-ACI
90A-835	M	Rossia	CCCP-85675	85675	RA-85675	
90A-836	M	Khakasia Airlines	CCCP-85676	RA-85676		
90A-837	M	Polish Government	837/01			
90A-838	M	CSA	OK-VCG			
90A-839	M	Magadan Airlines	CCCP-85677	RA-85677		
90A-840	M	Air VIA	LZ-MIG			
90A-841	M	Kish Air	CCCP-85678	RA-85678	EP-LAO	
90A-842	M	Kish Air	CCCP-85679	RA-85679	EP-LAP	
90A-843	M	Magadan Airlines	CCCP-85680	RA-85680		
90A-844	M	Air VIA	LZ-MIK			
90A-845	M	Air VIA/Macedonia Air Services	LZ-MIL			
90A-846	M	Xinjiang Airlines	B-2622			
90A-847	M	China United Airlines	B-4014			
90A-848	M	Khakasia Airlines	CCCP-85681	RA-85681		
90A-849	M	Krasnoyarskavia	CCCP-85682	RA-85682		
90A-850	M	Kish Air	CCCP-85683	RA-85683	EP-LAQ	
90A-851	M	Chitaavia	CCCP-85684	RA-85684		
90A-852	M	Air VIA	LZ-MIR			
90A-853	M	Magadan Airlines	CCCP-85685	RA-85685		
90A-854	M	Rossia	CCCP-85686	85686	RA-85686	
90A-855	M	China Northwest Airlines	B-2623			
90A-856	M	China United Airlines	B-4015			
90A-857	M	Siberia Airlines	CCCP-85687	RA-85687		
90A-858	M	Ensor Air	OK-BYP	OK-VCP		
90A-859	M		CCCP-85688	RA-85688	EP-ITS	RA-85688
90A-860	M	Baikal Airlines	CCCP-85689	EP-ITF	RA-85689	
90A-861	M	Baikal Airlines	CCCP-85690	RA-85690		
90A-862	M	Polish AF	SP-LCO	862/02		
90A-863	M	Avioimpex	LZ-MIS			
90A-864	M	Tajik Air	CCCP-85691	EY-85691		
90A-865	M	Tajik Air	CCCP-85692	RA-85692	EY-85692	
90A-866	M	Sibir Airlines	CCCP-85693	RA-85693	EP-ITG	RA-85693
91A-867	M	Iran Air Tours	CCCP-85694	RA-85694	EP-ITS	
91A-868	M	Baikal Airlines	CCCP-85695	RA-85695		
91A-869	M	Magadan Airlines	CCCP-85696	RA-85696		
91A-870	M	Siberia Airlines	CCCP-85697	RA-85697		
91A-871	M	Azerbaijan Airlines	CCCP-85698	85698	4K-85698	
91A-872	M	China United Airlines	B-4016			
91A-873	M	China United Airlines	B-4017			
91A-874	M	Siberia Airlines	CCCP-85699	RA-85699		
91A-875	M	Air Ukraine	CCCP-85700	85700	UR-85700	
91A-876	M	Air Ukraine	CCCP-85701(2)	85701	UR-85701	
91A-877	M	Krasnoyarskavia	CCCP-85702(2)	RA-85702	EP-ITK	RA-85702
91A-878	M	Belavia	CCCP-85703(2)	EW-85703		
91A-879	M	Air AJT	CCCP-85704(2)	RA-85704		
91A-880	M	Siberia Airlines	CCCP-85705	EP-ITB	RA-85705	
91A-881	M	Belavia	CCCP-85706	EW-85706		
91A-882	M	Air Ukraine	CCCP-85707	UR-85707		
91A-883	M	Krasnoyarskavia	CCCP-85708	85708	EP-ITJ	RA-85708

TUPOLEV Tu-154

S/n	Series	Last known Owner/Operator	Identities/fate (where known)				
91A-884	M	Iran Air Tours	CCCP-85709	RA-85709	EP-ITM		
91A-885	M	Alant	CCCP-85710	UR-85710	CCCP-85710	UR-85710	RA-85710
91A-886	M	Sichuan Airlines	B-2624				
91A-887	M	Uzbekistan Airways	CCCP-85711	UK-85711			
91A-888	M	ALAK Airlines	CCCP-85712	RA-85712			
91A-889	M	Holiday Airlines	CCCP-85713	RA-85713			
91A-890	M	Holiday Airlines	CCCP-85714	RA-85714	TC-RAD		
91A-891	M	Mineralnye Vody CAPO	CCCP-85715	85715	EP-LAI	RA-85715	
91A-892	M	Air Volga	CCCP-85716	RA-85716			
91A-893?	M	Tajik Air	CCCP-85717	EY-85717			
91A-894?	M	Kyrgyzstan Airlines	CCCP-85718	EX-85718			
91A-895	M	Baltic Express Line	CCCP-85740	(ES-AAC)	ES-LAI	YL-LAI	
91A-896	M	ELK Estonian	CCCP-85741	(ES-AAD)	ES-LTR		
91A-897?	M	Sichuan Airlines	B-2625				
91A-898	M	Cairo Charter & Cargo	SU-OAC				
91A-899	M	Cairo Charter & Cargo	SU-OAD				
91A-900?	M	Sichuan Airlines	B-2626				
91A-901	M	Kazakhstan Airlines	CCCP-85719	UN-85719			
91A-902	M	Krasnoyarskavia	CCCP-85720	EP-ITA	RA-85720		
9.A-903	M	(Iran Air Tours)	CCCP-85721	EP-ITD	w/o 08Feb93 nr Tehran, Iran		
92A-904	M	Mineralnye Vody CAPO	CCCP-85722	RA-85722	EP-LAH	RA-85722	
92A-905	M	Samara Airlines	CCCP-85723	RA-85723			
92A-906	M	Belavia	CCCP-85724	EW-85724			
92A-907?	M	Belavia	CCCP-85725	EW-85725			
92A-908	M	Mals Air Company	CCCP-85726	RA-85726	LZ-MNA	RA-85726	
92A-909	M	ELK Estonian	CCCP-85727	ES-LTP			
92A-910	M	Makhachkala Air Ent	CCCP-85728	RA-85728			
92A-911	M	Azerbaijan Airways	CCCP-85729	4K-85729			
92A-912	M	Omsk Avia	CCCP-85730	RA-85730			
92A-913	M	Samara Airlines	CCCP-85731	RA-85731			
92A-914	M	Improtex	CCCP-85732	4K-85732			
92A-915	M	Murmansk State Avn Ent	CCCP-85733	RA-85733			
92A-916	M	Azerbaijan Airlines	85734	4K-85734			
92A-917	M	Air Great Wall	CCCP-85735	B-2627			
92A-918	M	Vnukovo Airlines	85736	RA-85736			
92A-919?	M	Air Great Wall	CCCP-85765	B-2628			
92A-920	M	Avioimpex	CCCP-85737	LZ-MIV	RA-85737	LZ-MIV	
92A-921?	M	Azerbaijan Airways	CCCP-85738	4K-85738			
92A-922	M	Samara Airlines	CCCP-85739	RA-85739			
92A-923?	M	Sichuan Airlines	B-2629				
92A-924	M	Belavia	CCCP-85748	EW-85748			
92A-925	M						
92A-926	M	Vnukovo Airlines	CCCP-85743				
92A-927	M	Kazamat	CCCP-85744	UN-85744			
92A-928	M	Vnukovo Airlines	CCCP-85745	RA-85745			
92A-929	M	Mineralnye Vody CAPO	CCCP-85746	EP-LAD	RA-85746		
92A-930	M	Aerokuznetsk	RA-85747				
92A-931	M	Aerokuznetsk	85749	RA-85749			
92A-932	M						
92A-933	M	Vak-Rosat	CCCP-85750	RA-85750			
92A-934?	M	Surget Avia	RA-85751				
92A-935	M	Amur Avia	RA-85752				
92A-936	M	ARIA	RA-85754				
92A-937?	M	Amur Avia	RA-85753				
92A-938?	M	Murmansk State Avn Ent	RA-85755				
92A-939?	M	Makhachkala Air Ent	RA-85756				
92A-940	M	Aerokuznetsk	RA-85758				
92A-941?	M	Iran Air Tours	RA-85757	EP-ITI			
92A-942	M	Iran Air Tours	RA-85760	EP-ITN			
92A-943?	M	Baikal Airlines	CCCP-85759	RA-85759			
93A-944	M	Kogalymavia	85761	RA-85761			
93A-945	M	Star of Asia	RA-85762				
93A-946	M	Aero Volga	CCCP-85763	RA-85763			
93A-947	M	Uzbekistan Airways	RA-85764	UK-85764			
93A-948?	M	Chitaavia	85766	RA-85766			
93A-949?	M	Touch & Go Airlines	RA-85767				
93A-950	M	China United Airlines	RA-85768	B-4029			
93A-951	M	St.Petersburg Avia Ent	RA-85769				
93A-952	M	St.Petersburg Avia Ent	RA-85770				
93A-953	M	C-Air	RA-85771				
93A-954	M	Sichuan Airlines	RA-85772	B-2630			
93A-955	M	Bashkirian Airlines	RA-85773				
93A-956	M	Bashkirian Airlines	RA-85774				
93A-957	M	Kazakhstan Airlines	RA-85775	UN-85775			
93A-958	M	Uzbekistan Airways	UK-85776				
93A-959	M	Bashkirian Airlines	RA-85777				
93A-960	M	Flight Research Inst	CCCP-85801	RA-85801			
93A-961	M	Chitaavia	85802	RA-85802			
93A-962?	M	Aeroflot Russian Int A/L	RA-85778				
93A-963	M	St.Petersburg Avia Ent	RA-85779				
93A-964?	M	Kazakhstan Airlines	UN-85780				

TUPOLEV Tu-154

S/n	Series	Last known Owner/Operator	Identities/fate (where known)	
93A-965	M	Kazakhstan Airlines	RA-85781	UN-85781
93A-966	M	Samara Airlines	85782	RA-85782
93A-967	M	China United Airlines	RA-85783	B-4028
93A-968	M	Kogalymavia	RA-85784	
93A-969	M	St.Petersburg Avia Ent	RA-85785	
93A-970	M	Samara Airlines	RA-85786	
93A-971	M	Kogalymavia	85787	RA-85787
93A-972	M	Kalingrad Avia Ent	RA-85788	
93A-973	M	Kalingrad Avia Ent	RA-85789	
93A-974	M	Yakutavia	85790	RA-85790
93A-975	M	Yakutavia	RA-85791	
93A-976	M	Samara Airlines	85792	RA-85792
93A-977	M	Yakutavia	85793	RA-85793
93A-978	M	Sacha Avia	RA-85794	
93A-979	M	Tyumenaviatrans	RA-85805	
93A-980?	M	Vak-Rosat	RA-85795	
93A-981	M	Aviaenergo	RA-85797	
93A-982	M	Aviaenergo	RA-85798	
93A-983	M	Murmansk State Avn Ent	RA-85799	
94A-984	M	St.Petersburg Avia Ent	RA-85800	
94A-985	M	Aviaenergo	RA-85809	
94A-986?	M	Tyumenaviatrans	RA-85796	
94A-987	M	Tyumenaviatrans	RA-85806	
94A-988	M	Ural Airlines	RA-85807	
94A-989?	M	Tyumenaviatrans	RA-85808	
94A-990?	M			
94A-991?	M	Tyumenaviatrans	RA-85813	
9.A-992	M			
9.A-993	M			
9.A-994	M	Ural Airlines	RA-85814	
9.A-995	M			
9.A-996	M			
9.A-997	M			
9.A-998	M			
9.A-999	M			
9.A-1000	M			
9.A-1001	M			
9.A-1002	M			
9.A-1003	M			
9.A-1004	M			
9.A-1005	M	Sacha Avia	RA-85812	
9.A-1006	M	Bashkirian Airlines	RA-85816	
9.A-1007	M	Tatarstan Airlines	RA-85817	
9.A-1008	M			
9.A-1009	M			
9.A-1010	M	Belarus Government	EW-85815	
9.A-1011	M			
9.A-1012	M			
9.A-1013	M			
9.A-1014	M			
9.A-1015	M			
9.A-1016	M	Czech Government	OK-BYZ	

The following are aircraft for which there are no confirmed c/ns at the present time:

A-...	M	CAAC	B-2660
A-...	M	Mahan Air	EP-ARG
A-...	M	Mahan Air	EP-GAY
A-...	M	Iran Air Tours	EP-ITC
A-...	M	Iran Air Tours	EP-ITT
A-...	M	Kish Air	EP-LAS
A-...		Air VIA	LZ-MIF
A-...	M	Omsk Avia	RA-85818

One Aeroflot Tu-154 w/o 07Jul80 Alma-Ata and one Aeroflot Tu-154 w/o 15Oct84 Omsk

TUPOLEV Tu-204

S/n	Series	Last known Owner/Operator	Identities/fate (where known)		
1450743164001		Tupolev Design Bureau	CCCP-64001	RA-64001	prototype; ff 02Jan89; to prototype Tu-234 with six metre shorter version
1450743164002		Tupolev Design Bureau	CCCP-64002	RA-64002	
1450743164003		Tupolev Design Bureau	CCCP-64003	RA-64003	
1450743164004		Tupolev Design Bureau	CCCP-64004	RA-64004	
1450743164005			CCCP-64005	tested to destruction Apr93 Novosibirsk, Russia	
1450743164006	220	Tupolev-Bravia	CCCP-64006	RA-64006	RB.211-535E4 engine testbed
1450743164007	C	Aeroflot Russian Int A/L	CCCP-64007	ROSSIA-64007	RA-64007
1450743164008	C	Aeroflot Russian Int A/L /Orel Avia	RA-64008		
1450743164009	C	Aeroflot Russian Int A/L /Orel Avia	RA-64009		
1450743164010	F	Aeroflot Russian Int A/L	RA-64010		
1450743164011		Vnukovo Airlines	RA-64011		
1450743164012		Vnukovo Airlines	RA-64012		
1450743164013		Vnukovo Airlines	RA-64013		
1450743164014		Rossia	RA-64014		
1450743164015		Rossia	RA-64015		
1450743164016			RA-64016		
1450743164017			RA-64017		
1450743164018			RA-64018		
1450743164019			RA-64019		
1450743164020			RA-64020		
1450743164021			RA-64021		
1450743164022			RA-64022		
1450743164023			RA-64023		
1450743164024			RA-64024		
1450743164025			RA-64025		

VFW-FOKKER VFW-614

C/n	Last known Operator/Owner	Previous Identities/fate (where known)
G-001	(VFW-Fokker)	D-BABA w/o 01Feb72 nr Lemwerder, W Germany
G-002	(VFW-Fokker)	D-BABB b/u Jun80 Lemwerder, W Germany
G-003	(VFW-Fokker)	D-BABC b/u Jan81 Lemwerder, W Germany (fuselage used for explosion tests Meppen, W Germany
G-004	(VFW-Fokker)	D-BABD OY-TOR b/u Dec80 (fuselage used for painting tests Lemwerder, W Germany)
G-005	(VFW-Fokker)	D-BABE F-GATG b/u Nov80 Lemwerder, W Germany
G-006	(VFW-Fokker)	D-BABF b/u Aug80 Lemwerder, W Germany
G-007	(VFW-Fokker)	D-BABG b/u May80 Lemwerder, W Germany
G-008	(VFW-Fokker)	D-BABH OY-ASA b/u Feb81 Lemwerder, W Germany (fuselage used for explosion tests Meppen, W Germany)
G-009	(VFW-Fokker)	D-BABI b/u Jul80 Lemwerder, W Germany
G-010	(VFW-Fokker)	D-BABJ b/u Jan81 Lemwerder, W Germany (fuselage used for explosion tests Meppen, W Germany)
G-011	(VFW-Fokker)	D-BABK b/u Apr80 Lemwerder, W Germany
G-012	(VFW-Fokker)	D-BABL b/u Dec80 Lemwerder, W Germany
G-013	VFW-Fokker	D-BABM F-GATH D-BABM stored Lemwerder, W Germany (was mock-up for D-ADAM)
G-014	Luftwaffe	1701
G-015	VFW-Fokker	D-BABN F-GATI stored Lemwerder, W Germany
G-016	(VFW-Fokker)	D-BABO b/u Dec80 Lemwerder, W Germany
G-017	DLR	D-BABP D-ADAM in use as Advanced Technology Testing Aircraft System (ATTAS)
G-018	Luftwaffe	1702
G-019	Luftwaffe	1703
G-020	(VFW-Fokker)	D-BABQ b/u Oct80 when fuselage 60% completed (wings to Luftwaffe for spares)
G-021	(VFW-Fokker)	D-BABR b/u Aug80 when fuselage 45% completed (wings to Luftwaffe for spares)
G-022	(VFW-Fokker)	D-BABS b/u Sep80 when fuselage 15% completed (wings to DLR for spares)
G-023	(VFW-Fokker)	D-BABT b/u Sep80 when fuselage 0% completed (wings and rear fuselage for spares)
G-024 to G-035		parts only under manufacture when production ceased

Production complete

DLR = Deutsche Forschungs- und Versuchenschaft fuer Luft- und Raumfahrt (formerly DFVLR)

VICKERS VC-10

C/n	Series	Last known Operator/Owner	Previous Identities/fate (where known)
801	-		static test fuselage
802	-		static test fuselage
803	1109	(British Caledonian)	G-ARTA OD-AFA G-ARTA w/o 28Jan72 London-Gatwick, UK
804	1101	(Nigeria Airways)	G-ARVA 5N-ABD w/o 20Nov69 nr Lagos, Nigeria
805	1101	(BOAC)	G-ARVB b/u Oct76 London-Heathrow, UK
806	1101/K.2	Royal Air Force	G-ARVC A40-VC ZA144/E
807	1101	(BOAC)	G-ARVE b/u Oct76 London-Heathrow, UK
808	1101	Flugausstellung Leo Jr	G-ARVF preserved Hermeskeil, Germany
809	1101/K.2	Royal Air Force	G-ARVG A40-VG ZA141/B
810	1101	(BOAC)	G-ARVH b/u Oct76 London-Heathrow, UK
811	1101/K.2	Royal Air Force	G-ARVI A40-VI ZA142/C
812	1101	(Royal Air Force)	G-ARVJ ZD493 dbf 18May94 RAF Brize Norton, UK; only nose section remains
813	1101/K.2	Royal Air Force	G-ARVK A40-VK ZA143/D
814	1101/K.2	Royal Air Force	G-ARVL A40-VL ZA140/A
815	1101	Cosford Aerospace Museum	G-ARVM preserved RAF Cosford, UK
816	1101	not built	(G-ARVN)
817	1101	not built	(G-ARVO)
818	1101	not built	(G-ARVP)
819	1103	(Air Malawi)	G-ASIW 7Q-YKH b/u Blantyre, Malawi
820	1103	Brooklands Museum	G-ASIX A40-AB preserved Brooklands, nr Weybridge, UK
821	1103	not built	
822	1103	not built	
823	1102	(Ghana Airways)	9G-ABO b/u 1983 Prestwick, UK
824	1102	(Middle East Airlines)	9G-ABP dest by commandos 28Dec68 Beirut, Lebanon
825	1103	Royal Air Force	(9G-ABQ) G-ATDJ XX914 8777M fuselage at RAF Brize Norton, UK
826	1106/C.1K	Royal Air Force	XR806
827	1106/C.1K	Royal Air Force	XR807
828	1106/C.1K	Royal Air Force	XR808
829	1106/C.1	(Rolls Royce)	XR809 G-AXLR b/u 1982 RAF Kemble, UK
830	1106/C.1K	Royal Air Force	XR810
831	1106/C.1K	Royal Air Force	XV101
832	1106/C.1K	Royal Air Force	XV102
833	1106/C.1K	Royal Air Force	XV103
834	1106/C.1K	Royal Air Force	XV104
835	1106/C.1K	Royal Air Force	XV105
836	1106/C.1K	Royal Air Force	XV106
837	1106/C.1K	Royal Air Force	XV107
838	1106/C.1K	Royal Air Force	XV108
839	1106/C.1K	Royal Air Force	XV109
840	1102	(Ghana Airways)	(9G-ABU) Allocation cancelled, not built
851	1151/K.4	Royal Air Force	G-ASGA ZD230/K
852	1151	(Royal Air Force)	G-ASGB ZD231 b/u Mar87 RAF Abingdon, UK
853	1151	Imperial War Museum	G-ASGC preserved Duxford, UK
854	1151	(Royal Air Force)	G-ASGD ZD232 b/u 1982 RAF Brize Norton, UK
855	1151	(Royal Air Force)	G-ASGE ZD233 b/u 1982 RAF Brize Norton, UK (fuselage to RAF Manston)
856	1151	(Royal Air Force)	G-ASGF ZD234 8700M b/u 1982 RAF Brize Norton, UK (nose section only remains)
857	1151/K.4	Royal Air Force	G-ASGG ZD235/L
858	1151	(Royal Air Force)	G-ASGH ZD236 b/u Apr87 RAF Abingdon, UK
859	1151	(Royal Air Force)	G-ASGI ZD237 b/u Mar87 RAF Abingdon, UK
860	1151	(Royal Air Force)	G-ASGJ ZD238 b/u Apr87 RAF Abingdon, UK
861	1151	(Royal Air Force)	G-ASGK ZD239 b/u Apr87 RAF Abingdon, UK
862	1151/K.4	Royal Air Force	G-ASGL ZD240/M
863	1151/K.4	Royal Air Force	G-ASGM ZD241/N
864	1151	(BOAC)	G-ASGN dest by terrorists 12Sep70 Dawson Field, Jordan
865	1151	(BOAC)	G-ASGO dbf 03Mar74 Amsterdam-Schiphol, Netherlands; part of fuselage preserved Netherlands National Air Museum
866	1151/K.4	Royal Air Force	G-ASGP ZD242/P
867	1151	(Royal Air Force)	G-ASGR ZD243 stored Apr81 RAF Abingdon, UK (fuselage to Filton Aug93)
868	1151	not built	(G-ASGS)
869	1151	not built	(G-ASGT)
870	1151	not built	(G-ASGU)
871	1151	not built	(G-ASGV)
872	1151	not built	(G-ASGW)
873	1151	not built	(G-ASGX)
874	1151	not built	(G-ASGY)
875	1151	not built	(G-ASGZ)
881	1154	(East African Airways)	5X-UVA w/o 18Apr72 Addis Ababa, Ethiopia
882	1154/K.3	Royal Air Force	5H-MMT ZA147/F
883	1154/K.3	Royal Air Force	5Y-ADA ZA148/G
884	1154/K.3	Royal Air Force	5X-UVJ ZA149/H
885	1154/K.3	Royal Air Force	5H-MOG ZA150/J

Production complete

YAKOVLEV Yak-40

The first digit of the serial number identifies the factory at which the aircraft was built, the second digit the year of construction and the third the quarter of that year. Seven figure serial numbers contain the c/n in the last four digits, the third and fourth of these digits representing the batch number and the first and second digits indicating the number of the aircraft in that batch

S/n	Series	Last known Owner/Operator	Identities/fate (where known)	
019			CCCP-19661	at Moscow Park of Economic Achievement, Russia by Jun70; fate?
9....00			CCCP-87672	
9831100			CCCP-87675	at Moscow Inst of Civil Aviation, Sheremetyevo, Russia
9831200			CCCP-87676	at Moscow Inst of Civil Aviation, Sheremetyevo, Russia
9840201			CCCP-87678	derelict by Apr92 Aktyubinsk, Kazakhstan
9840301			CCCP-87679	derelict by Apr93 Aktyubinsk, Kazakhstan
9840401			CCCP-87680	derelict by Apr92 Aktyubinsk, Kazakhstan
9840501			CCCP-87681	derelict by Apr92 Aktyubinsk, Kazakhstan
9..0102			CCCP-87682	wfs by Jul93, Kirovograd, Ukraine
9..0202				
9..0302				
9840402			CCCP-87684	derelict Riga-Spilve, Latvia
9840502			CCCP-87685	wfs, Kiev Inst of Civil Engineering, Kiev, Ukraine
9..0103			CCCP-87686	
9920203		Flight Research Inst	CCCP-87791	RA-87791
9910303			CCCP-87792	
9..0403		(Aeroflot)	CCCP-87689	w/o 12Jun80 nr Dushanbe, USSR
9..0503		(Aeroflot)	CCCP-87690	w/o 03Sep90 in mts, 70km from Leningrad, USSR
9..0104			CCCP-87691	
9..0204			CCCP-87692	
9..0304			CCCP-87693	
9..0404			CCCP-87694	
9..0504			CCCP-87695	
9910105		(Aeroflot)	CCCP-87696	w/o 25Jan87 St.Petersburg-Pulkovo, USSR
9910205		Tajik Air	CCCP-87697	EY-87697
9..0305			CCCP-87698	
9220405			CCCP-87699	derelict by Apr92 Aktyubinsk, Kazakhstan
9..0505			CCCP-87700	
9920106			CCCP-87701	derelict by Apr92 Aktyubinsk, Kazakhstan
9920206			CCCP-87702	derelict by Apr92 Aktyubinsk, Kazakhstan
9920306			CCCP-87703	
9920406			CCCP-87704	derelict by Apr92 Aktyubinsk, Kazakhstan
9920506			CCCP-87705	
9930107			CCCP-87706	
9930207			CCCP-87707	
9930307			CCCP-87708	
9930407			CCCP-87709	
9940507			CCCP-87710	derelict by Apr92 Aktyubinsk, Kazakhstan
9940607			CCCP-87711	
9..0707			CCCP-87712	
9..0807			CCCP-87713	derelict by Apr92 Aktyubinsk, Kazakhstan
9..0907			CCCP-87714	
9..1007			CCCP-87715	
9..0108			CCCP-87716	
9..0208			CCCP-87717	
9330308			CCCP-87718	derelict by Apr92 Aktyubinsk, Kazakhstan
9..0408		(Aeroflot)	CCCP-87719	dbr 28Jul71 Moscow-Bykovo, USSR
9..0508			CCCP-87720	
9..0608			CCCP-87721	
9..0708			CCCP-87722	
9..0808			CCCP-87723	
9..0908			CCCP-87724	
9..1008			CCCP-87725	
9..0109			CCCP-87726	
9..0209			CCCP-87727	
9..0309			CCCP-87728	
9020409	EC		(CCCP-87729)	I-JAKA CCCP-?
9..0509			CCCP-87730	
9..0609			CCCP-87731	dumped by Sep93 Zhukovsky, Russia
9940709			CCCP-87732	
9..0809			CCCP-87733	
9..0909			CCCP-87734	
9..1009			CCCP-87735	
9..0110			CCCP-87736	
9..0210			CCCP-87737	
9010310		(Aeroflot)	CCCP-87738	w/o 30Mar77 nr Zhadanof
9010410			CCCP-87739	derelict by Apr92 Aktyubinsk, Kazakhstan
9..0510			CCCP-87740	
9010610			CCCP-87741	derelict by Apr92 Aktyubinsk, Kazakhstan
9..0710			CCCP-87742	
9010810			CCCP-87743	
9..0910			CCCP-87744	
9011010			CCCP-87745	
9..0111			CCCP-87746	
9..0211			CCCP-87747	

YAKOVLEV Yak-40

S/n	Series	Last known Owner/Operator	Identities/fate (where known)		
9..0311			CCCP-87748		
9020411			CCCP-87749		
9..0511			CCCP-87750		
9..0611			CCCP-87751		
9020711			CCCP-87752	derelict by Apr92 Aktyubinsk, Kazakhstan	
9020811			CCCP-87753	derelict by Apr92 Aktyubinsk, Kazakhstan	
9..0911		Georgian Airlines	CCCP-87754	GR-87754	4L-87754
9021011		Aviastar Factory	CCCP-87755	RA-87755	
9020112		(Aeroflot)	CCCP-87756	w/o 07Dec76 nr Armavir, USSR	
9020212			CCCP-87757	derelict by Apr92 Aktyubinsk, Kazakhstan	
9..0312			CCCP-87758		
9030412			CCCP-87759	derelict by Apr92 Aktyubinsk, Kazakhstan	
9..0512			CCCP-87760		
9030612			CCCP-87761		
9..0712			CCCP-87762		
9030812			CCCP-87763		
9030912			CCCP-87764	derelict by Apr92 Aktyubinsk, Kazakhstan	
9031012			CCCP-87765		
9..0113			CCCP-87766		
9030213			CCCP-87767		
9030313			CCCP-87768		
9030413			CCCP-87769		
9030513			CCCP-87770		
9030613			CCCP-87771		
9..0713		(Aeroflot)	CCCP-87772	w/o 09Sep76 collided with AN-24 CCCP-46518	
9..0813			CCCP-87773		
9030913		Aeroflot	CCCP-87774	preserved by Apr92 nr Aktyubinsk Airport, Kazakhstan	
9031013			CCCP-87775	wfs by Sep93, Minsk-Chizovka Technical School, Belarus	
9..0114			CCCP-87776		
9..0214			CCCP-87777		
9..0314		(Aeroflot)	CCCP-87778	w/o 04May72 nr Bratsk, Russia	
9..0414			CCCP-87779		
9..0514			CCCP-87780		
9..0614			CCCP-87781		
9..0714			CCCP-87782		
9..0814			CCCP-87783		
9..0914			CCCP-87784		
9..1014			CCCP-87785		
9..0115			CCCP-87786		
9..0215			CCCP-87787		
9..0315			CCCP-87788		
9..0415			CCCP-87789		
9..0515		(Aeroflot)	CCCP-87790	w/o 08Aug73 Archangelsk, USSR	
9..0615			CCCP-87793		
9..0715			CCCP-87794		
9..0815			CCCP-87795		
9040915			CCCP-87796		
9..1015					
9..0116			CCCP-87797		
9..0216			CCCP-87798		
9040316		Uzbekistan Airways	CCCP-87799	UK-87799	
9..0416		Aeroflot	CCCP-87590	preserved Aktyubinsk, Kazakhstan	
9..0516			CCCP-87591		
9110616		Kazakhstan Airlines	CCCP-87592	UN-87592	
9..0716			CCCP-87593		
9..0816			CCCP-87594	derelict Kransodar, Russia	
9..0916			CCCP-87595		
9..1016			CCCP-87596		
9110117		Aeroflot	CCCP-87597	CCCP-87490	preserved Monimo Museum, Moscow, Russia
9..0217			CCCP-87598		
9..0317			CCCP-87599		
9120417		(Ariana Afghan)	YA-KAB	dbr 01Aug92 Kabul, Afghanistan	
9120517		(Bakhtar Afghan)	YA-KAD	w/o 25Jan72 Khost, Afghanistan	
9120617		(Ariana Afghan)	YA-KAF	dbr 01Aug92 Kabul, Afghanistan	
9120717		Serbian AF	Yugoslav AF 71501		71501/YU-AKP
9120817		Serbian AF	Yugoslav AF 71502		71502
9..0917			CCCP-87600		
9..1017			CCCP-87601		
9..0118			CCCP-87602		
9..0218		(Aeroflot)	CCCP-87603	w/o 28Feb73 Semipalatinsk, USSR	
9..0318			CCCP-87604		
9..0418			CCCP-87605		
9120518		Vologda State Avn Ent	CCCP-87606	RA-87606	
9..0618			CCCP-87607		
9..0718			CCCP-87608		
9..0918			CCCP-87609		
9..0918			CCCP-87610		
9..1018		Vologda State Avn Ent	CCCP-87611	RA-87611	
9..1118			CCCP-87612		
9..1218			CCCP-87613		
9..1318			CCCP-87614		
9141418	EC	(Avioligure)	I-JAKE	w/o 28May77 Genoa, Italy	

YAKOVLEV Yak-40

S/n	Series	Last known Owner/Operator	Identities/fate (where known)			
9141518	EC	Alinord	I-JAKI			
9131618		Air Ukraine	CCCP-87615	UR-87615		
9..1718			CCCP-87616			
9..1818			CCCP-87617			
9131918		(Aeroflot)	CCCP-87618	w/o 16Jan87 Tashkent, USSR		
9..2018			CCCP-87619(1)	cancelled		
9130119			CCCP-87620			
9130219			CCCP-87621			
9130319			CCCP-87622			
9130419			CCCP-87623			
9140519		Air Ukraine	CCCP-87624	UR-87624		
9140619		Solar Wind	CCCP-87625	RA-87625		
9..0719			CCCP-87626			
9..0819			CCCP-87627			
9..0919			CCCP-87628			
9..1019		(Aeroflot)	CCCP-87629	dbr 21Dec73 Yerevan, USSR		
9141119		(Aeroflot)	CCCP-87630	w/o 14Dec74 Yerevan, USSR		
9141219			CCCP-87631			
9141319			CCCP-87632			
9..1419			CCCP-87633			
9..1519			CCCP-87634			
9141619			CCCP-87635	derelict by Apr93 Aktyubinsk, Kazakhstan		
9141719			CCCP-87636			
9..1819			CCCP-87637			
9141919		(Aeroflot)	CCCP-87638	w/o 16Dec76 nr Zaporozhye		
9142019		Neryungri Sakha Avia	CCCP-87639	RA-87639		
9140120		Solar Wind	CCCP-87640	RA-87640		
9..0220		Air Ukraine	CCCP-87641	UR-87641		
9..0320		Iren	CCCP-87642	UR-87642		
9140420		Azerbaijan Airlines	CCCP-87643	87643	4K-87643	
9140520		Azerbaijan Airlines	CCCP-87644	87644	4K-87644	
9140620		Cheremshanka Airlines	CCCP-87645	RA-87645		
9140720		Cheremshanka Airlines	CCCP-87646	RA-87646		
9140820		Amur Avia	CCCP-87647	RA-87647		
9140920			CCCP-87648			
9141020		Air Ukraine	CCCP-87649	UR-87649		
9..1120			CCCP-87650			
9141220		Solar Wind	CCCP-87651	RA-87651		
9141320		Air Tsolak	CCCP-87652	UN-87652	RA-87652	
9211420	FG	Aeroflot Russian Int A/L	D-COBA	D-BOBA	CCCP-48111	RA-48111
9211520	FG	Flight Research Inst	D-COBB	D-BOBB	CCCP-48112	RA-48112
9..1620		Bugurulan Flying School	CCCP-87653	RA-87653		
9211720		Aktyubinsk Higher Flying School of Civil Aviation	CCCP-87654	UN-87654		
9211820		Orel/Cheremshanka A/L	CCCP-87655	RA-87655		
9211920		Neryungri Sakha Avia	CCCP-87656	RA-87656		
9222020		Serbian AF	Yugoslav AF 71503	71503		
9210121		Center-South Airlines	CCCP-87550	RA-87550		
9210221		Cheremshanka Airlines	CCCP-87551	RA-87551		
9210321		Cheremshanka Airlines	CCCP-87552	RA-87552		
9210421		(Aeroflot)	CCCP-87553	b/u Sep93 Moscow-Bykovo, Russia		
9210521		Tajik Air	CCCP-87554	EY-87554		
9210621			CCCP-87555			
9210721		Cheremshanka Airlines	CCCP-87556	RA-87556		
9210821		Barnaul State Avn Ent	CCCP-87557	RA-87557		
9210921		Barnaul State Avn Ent	CCCP-87558	RA-87558		
9211021		Amur Avia	CCCP-87559	RA-87559		
9211121		Achinsk Enterprise	CCCP-87560	RA-87560		
9..1221		Kyrgyzstan Airlines	CCCP-87561	EX-87561		
9211321		Air Ukraine	CCCP-87562	UR-87562		
9..1.21			CCCP-87563			
9..1.21						
9211621		Uzbekistan Airways	CCCP-87564	UK-87564		
9211721		Chelal	CCCP-87565	RA-87565		
9211821		Air Ukraine	CCCP-87566	UR-87566		
9211921		Aktyubinsk Higher Flying School of Civil Aviation	CCCP-87567	UN-87567		
9212021		Aeroflot Russian Int A/L	CCCP-87568	RA-87568		
9230122	FG	Republic of Angola	D-COBC	D-BOBC	CCCP-87819	D2-EAG
			I-JAKO	D2-EAG		
9220222		Kazakhstan Airlines	CCCP-87569	UN-87569		
9220322			CCCP-87570			
9220422			CCCP-87572			
9220522		Novgorod Avia Enterprise	CCCP-87573	RA-87573		
9220622			CCCP-87574			
9220722		Novgorod Avia Enterprise	CCCP-87575	RA-87575		
9220822			CCCP-87576	RA-87576		
9220922		Belavia	CCCP-87577	EW-87577		
9221022		Aeroflot Russian Int A/L	CCCP-87578	RA-87578		
9221122		(Aeroflot)	CCCP-87579	w/o 23May74 Kiev-Zhulyani, USSR		
9221222		Aeroflot Russian Int A/L	CCCP-87580	RA-87580		
9221322		Volga Airlines	CCCP-87581	RA-87581		

YAKOVLEV Yak-40

S/n	Series	Last known Owner/Operator	Identities/fate (where known)			
9221422		Vologda State Avn Ent	CCCP-87582	RA-87582		
9221522		Tatarstan Airlines	CCCP-87583	RA-87583		
9..1622			CCCP-87584			
9..1722			CCCP-87585			
9221822		Rossia/Russian Govt	CCCP-87586	RA-87586		
9221922			CCCP-87587			
9222022		Tatarstan Airlines	CCCP-87588	RA-87588		
9..0123			CCCP-87589			
9220223		Baikal Airlines	CCCP-87800	RA-87800		
9230323	FG	(General Air)	D-COBD	D-BOBD	w/o 19Dec75 Saarbrucken, W Germany	
9230423		Cheremshanka Airlines	CCCP-87801	RA-87801		
9230523		Barnaul State Avn Ent	CCCP-87802	RA-87802		
9230623	FG	Aeroflot Russian Int A/L	D-COBE	D-BOBE	CCCP-48110	RA-48110
9230723		Czech AF	OK-BYG	0723	preserved Kbely Museum, Czech Republic	
9230823		Slovak AF	OK-BYF	Czech AF 0823	0823	
9..0923		(Aeroflot)	CCCP-87803	w/o 11Oct85 nr Kutayissi, USSR		
9231023		Georgian Airways	CCCP-87804	4L-87804		
9231123		Tatarstan Airlines	CCCP-87805	RA-87805		
9..1223						
9..1323						
9231423		Hemus Air	LZ-DOS			
9231523		Serbian AF	Yugoslav AF 71504	71504		
9231623		Hemus Air	LZ-DOR			
9231723		Int Industrial Bank	CCCP-87807	RA-87807		
9..1823		(Aeroflot)	CCCP-87808	w/o 29Jun83		
9..1923		Central Districts A/L	CCCP-87809	RA-87809		
9..2023		Cheremshanka Airlines	CCCP-87810	RA-87810		
9230124		Baikal Airlines	CCCP-87811	RA-87811		
9230224		LOT	SP-GEA			
9230324			CCCP-87619(2)	stored Tashkent, Uzbekistan		
9230424		Azerbaijan Airlines	CCCP-87812	87812	4K-87812	
9230524		Aerolik	CCCP-87814	RA-87814		
9230624		Buguruslan Flying School	CCCP-87815	RA-87815		
9..0724			CCCP-87816			
9230824		Azerbaijan Airlines	CCCP-87817	87817	4K-87817	
9..0924						
9231024		Iren	CCCP-87818	UR-87818		
9..1124		(Aeroflot)	CCCP-87819(1)	w/o 22Nov72 Krasnoyarsk-Yemelianovo, USSR		
9..1224			CCCP-87820			
9241324		Tatarstan Airlines	CCCP-87821	RA-87821		
9241424		Tatarstan Airlines	CCCP-87822	RA-87822		
9..1524		Buguruslan Flying School	CCCP-87823	RA-87823		
9241624		Aktyubinsk Higher Flying School of Civil Aviation	CCCP-87824	UN-87824		
9241724		(Aeroflot)	CCCP-87825	w/o 28Jan75 Zaporozhye		
9..1824		(Aeroflot)	CCCP-87826	w/o 19Jun87 Berdiansk, USSR		
9241924		Tajik Air	CCCP-87827	EY-87827		
9242024		Impulse Aero	CCCP-87828	RA-87828		
9..0125		Aeroflot Russian Int A/L	CCCP-87829	RA-87829		
9240225		Belavia	CCCP-87658	EW-87658		
9240325		Yak Service	CCCP-87659	RF-87659		
9240425		Air Ukraine	CCCP-87660	UR-87660		
9240525		Aktyubinsk Higher Flying School of Civil Aviation	CCCP-87661	UN-87661		
9240625		Trans-Charter Airlines	CCCP-87662	RA-87662		
9..0725		Cheremshanka Airlines	CCCP-87663	RA-87663		
9..0825			CCCP-87664			
9..0925		Vologda State Avn Ent	CCCP-87665	RA-87665		
9241025		Tajik Air	CCCP-87666	EY-87666		
9..1125						
9..1225						
9..1325		Kazakhstan Airlines	CCCP-87377	UN-87377		
9241425		Uzbekistan Airways	CCCP-87378	UK-87378		
9241525		Cheremshanka Airlines	CCCP-87667	RA-87667		
9241625		Uzbekistan Airways	CCCP-87830	UK-87830		
9241725			CCCP-87831			
9241825		Air Ukraine	CCCP-87832	UR-87832		
9241925			CCCP-87833			
9242025			CCCP-87834			
9240126		Tajik Air	CCCP-87835	EY-87835		
9240226			CCCP-87836			
9240326		Vologda State Avn Ent	CCCP-87837	RA-87837		
9..0426		Central Districts A/L	CCCP-87838	RA-87838		
9240526		Volga Airlines	CCCP-87839	RA-87839		
9240626		Aeroflot Russian Int A/L	CCCP-87840	RA-87840		
9310726		Kyrgyzstan Airlines	CCCP-87250	EX-87250		
9310826		Aeroflot Russian Int A/L	CCCP-87251	RA-87251		
9310926		Barnaul State Avn Ent	CCCP-87253	RA-87253		
9311026		Donavia Airlines	CCCP-87254	RA-87254		
9311126		Novgorod Avia Enterprise	CCCP-87260	RA-87260		
9..1226		Ariana Afghan	CCCP-87255	YA-KAM		
9311326		(Impulse Aero)	CCCP-87256	RA-87256	dbf 17Jul94 Boma, Russia	

YAKOVLEV Yak-40

S/n	Series	Last known Owner/Operator	Identities/fate (where known)			
9311426		Azerbaijan Airlines	CCCP-87257	4K-87257		
9311526		Georgian Airways	CCCP-87258	4L-87258		
9311626			CCCP-87259			
9311726		Baikal Airlines	CCCP-87261	RA-87261		
9321826		Tyumen Avia Trans	CCCP-87262	RA-87262		
9311926		Uzbekistan Airways	CCCP-87263	UK-87263		
9312026		Uzbekistan Airways	CCCP-87264	UK-87264		
9310127		Aktyubinsk Higher Flying School of Civil Aviation	CCCP-87265	UN-87265		
9310227		Air Ukraine	CCCP-87266	UR-87266		
9310327		Aktyubinsk Higher Flying School of Civil Aviation	CCCP-87267	UN-87267		
9310427		Donavia Airlines	CCCP-87268	RA-87268		
9310527		Tajik Air	CCCP-87269	EY-87269		
9310627		Cheremshanka Airlines	CCCP-87270	RA-87270		
9310727		Kazakhstan Airlines	CCCP-87271	UN-87271		
9330827		Aktyubinsk Higher Flying School of Civil Aviation	CCCP-87272	UN-87272		
9310927		Vladivostok Aviation	CCCP-87273	RA-87273		
9311027		Kazakhstan Airlines	CCCP-87274	UN-87274		
9311127		Kazakhstan Airlines	CCCP-87275	UN-87275		
9311227		Air Ukraine	CCCP-87276	UR-87276		
9321327		Vologda State Avn Ent	CCCP-87277	RA-87277		
9311427		Azerbaijan Airlines	CCCP-87278	87278	4K-87278	
9..1527			CCCP-87280			
9311627		Central Districts A/L	CCCP-87281	RA-87281		
9..1727		Kazakhstan Airlines	CCCP-87282	UN-87282		
9321827		Aktyubinsk Higher Flying School of Civil Aviation	CCCP-87283	UN-87283		
9..1927		Vologda State Avn Ent	CCCP-87284	RA-87284		
9..2027			CCCP-87285			
9..0128		Elista Avia Enterprise	CCCP-87286	RA-87286		
9320228		Buguruslan Flying School	CCCP-87287	RA-87287		
9320328		Cheremshanka Airlines	CCCP-87288	RA-87288		
9320428		Uzbekistan Airways	CCCP-87289	UK-87289		
9320528		Novgorod Avia Enterprise	CCCP-87290	RA-87290		
9..0628		(Aeroflot)	CCCP-87291	w/o 19Apr83 Leninakan, USSR		
9320728		Tyumen Avia Trans	CCCP-87292	RA-87292		
9320828		Kyrgyzstan Airlines	CCCP-87293	EX-87293		
9..0928		Baikal Airlines	CCCP-87294	RA-87294		
9321028		UNA/Ironimpex	OK-BYI	UR-88299		
9321128		Tatarstan Airlines	OK-BYH	RA-87977		
9321228		Donavia Airlines	CCCP-87295	RA-87295		
9321328		Uzbekistan Airways	CCCP-87296	UK-87296		
9321428		Barnaul State Avn Ent	CCCP-87297	87297	RA-87297	
9321528		Southern Eng Factory	CCCP-87298	UR-87298		
9..1628		Buguruslan Flying School	CCCP-87299	RA-87299		
9..1728		Cheremshanka Airlines	CCCP-87300	RA-87300		
9..1828		(Aeroflot)	CCCP-87301	w/o 17May86 Hanty-Mansiyesk, USSR		
9..1928		Vladivostok Aviation	CCCP-87303	RA-87303		
9..2028		Central Districts A/L	CCCP-87304	RA-87304		
9320129		Georgian Airways	CCCP-87305	4L-87305		
9320229		Kazakhstan Airlines	CCCP-87306	UN-87306		
9320329		Donavia Airlines	CCCP-87307	RA-87307		
9320429		Columbus Avia	CCCP-87308	UR-87308		
9320529		Uzbekistan Airways	CCCP-87309	UK-87309		
9320629		Vologda State Avn Ent	CCCP-87311	RA-87311		
9320729		Aktyubinsk Higher Flying School of Civil Aviation	CCCP-87312	UN-87312		
9330829		Tajik Air	CCCP-87313	EY-87313		
9..0929			CCCP-87314			
9331029		Petronord Avia	Polish AF 031	SP-PGA	88294	RA-88294
9331129		Polish AF	032			
9331229		Polish AF	034			
9331329		Yak Service	Polish AF 035	RA-88295		
9331429		Ulyanovsk Avia Ent	CCCP-87315	RA-87315		
9..1529			CCCP-87316			
9331629			CCCP-87317	RA-87317		
9..1729			CCCP-87318			
9331829		Tyumen Avia Trans	CCCP-87319	RA-87319		
9331929		Belavia	CCCP-87320	UR-87320	EW-87320	
9332029		Solar Wind	CCCP-87321	RA-87321		
9330130		Georgian Airways	CCCP-87322	4L-87322		
9..0230		(Aeroflot)	CCCP-87323	w/o 15Aug75 Krasnodovsk, USSR		
9..0330		Buguruslan Flying School	CCCP-87324	RA-87324		
9..0430		Vladivostok Aviation	CCCP-87325	RA-87325		
9..0530		Barnaul State Avn Ent	CCCP-87326	RA-87326		
9330630		UNA/Ironimpex	CCCP-87327	UR-87327		
9..0730		(Aeroflot)	CCCP-87328	w/o 06Oct75 nr Kirov, USSR		
9..0830			CCCP-87329	UR-87329		
9320930		Dnepr Air	CCCP-87841	UR-87841		
9321030		Vologda State Avn Ent	CCCP-87842	RA-87842		

YAKOVLEV Yak-40

S/n	Series	Last known Owner/Operator	Identities/fate (where known)		
9331130		Kotlas Avia Enterprise	CCCP-87843	RA-87843	
9341230		Czech Civil Avn Dept	OK-DHA		
9331330		Vologda State Avn Ent	CCCP-87844	RA-87844	
9331430		Central Districts A/L	CCCP-87845	RA-87845	
9331530		Uzbekistan Airways	CCCP-87846	UK-87846	
9331630		Afrik Air Links	CCCP-87847	RA-87847	
9331730		Uzbekistan Airways	CCCP-87848	UK-87848	
9..1830		Central Districts A/L	CCCP-87849	RA-87849	
9..1930			CCCP-87850		
9412030		Aeroflot Russian Int A/L	CCCP-87351	RA-87351	
9330131		Aktyubinsk Higher Flying School of Civil Aviation	CCCP-87352	UN-87352	
9330231		Lukoil	CCCP-87353	RA-87353	
9330331		Kyrgyzstan Airlines	CCCP-87354	EX-87354	derelict by May95 Bishkek, Kyrgyzstan
9340431			CCCP-87355		
9340531		Tajik Air	CCCP-87356	EY-87356	
9340631		Volga Dnepr	CCCP-87357	RA-87357	
9340731		Aeroflot Russian Int A/L	CCCP-87358	RA-87358	
9340831		Banat Air	CCCP-87359	UN-87359	RA-87359 ER-87359
9..0931		(Aeroflot)	CCCP-87360	w/o 14Dec74 Bukhara, USSR	
9341031		Achinsk Avia Enterprise	CCCP-87361	RA-87361	
9341131		Amur Avia	CCCP-87362	RA-87362	
9341231		Aktyubinsk Higher Flying School of Civil Aviation	CCCP-87363	UN-87363	
9341331		Cheremshanka Airlines	CCCP-87364	RA-87364	
9341431		Hemus Air	LZ-DOA		
9341531		Tyumen Avia Trans	CCCP-87365	RA-87365	
9341631		Kyrgyzstan Airlines	CCCP-87366	EX-87366	
9341731		Uzbekistan Airways	CCCP-87367	UK-87367	
9341831		Cheremshanka Airlines	CCCP-87368	RA-87368	
9..1931		(Aeroflot)	CCCP-87369	w/o 09Apr74 Kazan, USSR	
9..2031					
9340132		Georgian Airways	CCCP-87370	4L-87370	
9340232		Central Districts A/L	CCCP-87371	RA-87371	
9340332		Orel Avia	CCCP-87372	RA-87372	
9340432		Hemus Air	LZ-DOB		
9340532		Hemus Air	LZ-DOC		
9340632		Hemus Air	LZ-DOD		
9410732		Bryansk Avia Enterprise	CCCP-87373	RA-87373	
9410832		Georgian Airways	CCCP-87374	4L-87374	
9410932		Tyumen Avia Trans	CCCP-87375	RA-87375	
9411032		Vladivostok Aviation	CCCP-87376	RA-87376	
9..1132		Premium Air Shuttle	CCCP-87380	RA-87380	
9411232			CCCP-87381	RA-87381	
9411332		Aeroflot Russian Int A/L	CCCP-87382	RA-87382	
9411432	K	Tyumen Avia Trans	CCCP-87383	RA-87383	
9..1532			CCCP-87384		
9411632		Kamchatavia	CCCP-87385	wfu, found to be dbr on overhaul Mar93	
9411732		Tuva Airlines	CCCP-87386	RA-87386	
9411832		Turkmenistan Airlines	CCCP-87387	EZ-87387	
9341932		Syrianair	YK-AQA		
9412032		Lithuanian Airlines	CCCP-87388	LY-AAD	
9410133			CCCP-87389		
9..0233		(Aeroflot)	CCCP-87390	w/o 20Mar79 Chardzhow, USSR	
9..0333		(Aeroflot)	CCCP-87391	dbr 15Sep89 Dzhalal-Abad, USSR	
9410433		Kotlas Avia Enterprise	CCCP-87392	RA-87392	
9..0533		Neryungri Sakha Avia	CCCP-87393	RA-87393	
9..0633			CCCP-87394		
9410733		Amur Avia	CCCP-87395	RA-87395	
9410833		Uzbekistan Airways	CCCP-87396	UK-87396	
9..0933		Elista Avia Enterprise	CCCP-87397	RA-87397	
9..1033		(Aeroflot)	CCCP-87398	dbr 02May74 Rostov, USSR	
9411133		Baikal Airlines	CCCP-87399	RA-87399	
9411233		Amur Avia	CCCP-87400	RA-87400	
9411333		Estonian Air	CCCP-87401	ES-AAU	
9411433		Aktyubinsk Higher Flying School of Civil Aviation	CCCP-87402	UN-87402	
9411533		Kazakhstan Airlines	CCCP-87403	UN-87403	
9411633		Tatarstan Airlines	CCCP-87404	RA-87404	
9421733		Aeroflot Russian Int A/L	CCCP-87405	RA-87405	
9421833		Central Districts A/L	CCCP-87406	RA-87406	
9421933			CCCP-87407		
9422033		Kazakhstan Airlines	CCCP-87408	RA-87408	UN-87408
9420134		Turkmenistan Airlines	CCCP-87409	EZ-87409	
9420234		Tyumen Avia Trans	CCCP-87410	RA-87410	
9420334		(Yakutavia)	CCCP-87411	87411	dbr 14Sep92 Neryungry, Russia
9420434		Kyrgyzstan Airlines	CCCP-87412	EX-87412	
9420534		Azerbaijan Airlines	CCCP-87413	87413	4K-87413
9420634		Baikal Airlines	CCCP-87414	RA-87414	
9420734		Azerbaijan Airlines	CCCP-87415	4K-87415	
9420834		Elista Avia Enterprise	CCCP-87416	RA-87416	
9420934		Cheremshanka Airlines	CCCP-87417	RA-87417	

YAKOVLEV Yak-40

S/n	Series	Last known Owner/Operator	Identities/fate (where known)			
9421034		Central Districts A/L	CCCP-87418	RA-87418		
9421134		Belavia	CCCP-87419	EW-87419		
9..1234			CCCP-87420			
9421334		Vietnam Airlines	VN-A441			
9211434		Vietnam Airlines	VN-A442			
9421534		Vietnam Airlines	VN-A443			
9421634		Rossia/Russian Govt	VN-A445	RA-88296		
9421734		UNA/Ironimpex	CCCP-87421	UR-87421		
9421834		Tyumen Avia Trans	CCCP-87422	RA-87422		
9..1934		Neryungri Sakha Avia	CCCP-87423	RA-87423		
9422034		Komi Avia	CCCP-87424	RA-87424		
9..0135		Tuva Airlines	CCCP-87425	RA-87425		
9..0235		Kyrgyzstan Airlines	CCCP-87426	EX-87426		
9420335		Turkmenistan Airlines	CCCP-87427	EZ-87427		
9420435		Komi Avia	CCCP-87428	RA-87428		
9420535		Vologda State Avn Ent	CCCP-87429	RA-87429		
9420635		Uzbekistan Airways	CCCP-87430	UK-87430		
9420735		Neryungri Sakha Avia	CCCP-87431	RA-87431		
9420835		Columbus Avia	CCCP-87432	UR-87432		
9420935		Vologda State Avn Ent	CCCP-87433	RA-87433		
9431035		Tajik Air	CCCP-87434	EY-87434		
9431135		Air Ukraine	CCCP-87435	UR-87435		
9431235		Volga Airlines	CCCP-87436	RA-87436		
9..1335		(Aeroflot)	CCCP-87437	w/o 07Oct78 Sverdlovsk, USSR		
9..1435		Barnaul State Avn Ent	CCCP-87438	RA-87438		
9431535		Komi Avia/United Nations	CCCP-87439	RA-87439		
9431635		Bryansk Avia Enterprise	CCCP-87440	RA-87440		
9..1735			CCCP-87441	wfs by Apr94 Baku-Zabrat, Azerbaijan		
9..1835						
9431935		Kyrgyzstan Airlines	CCCP-87442	EX-87442		
9..2035		Tuva Airlines	CCCP-87443	RA-87443		
9430136		Chelal	CCCP-87444	RA-87444		
9430236		Kyrgyzstan Airlines	CCCP-87445	EX-87445		
9430336		Tajik Air	CCCP-87446	EY-87446		
9430436		Tatarstan Airlines	CCCP-87447	RA-87447		
9430536		Baikal Airlines	CCCP-87448	RA-87448		
9430636		Tyumen Avia Trans	CCCP-87449	RA-87449		
9..0736		Neryungri Sakha Avia	CCCP-87450	RA-87450		
9..0836			CCCP-87451			
9..0936		Amur Avia	CCCP-87452	RA-87452		
9..1036		(Aeroflot)	CCCP-87453	w/o 01Aug90 Stepanakert, Russia		
9..1136		(Aeroflot)	CCCP-87454	w/o 16Nov79 Vologada		
9..1236		(Aeroflot)	CCCP-87455	w/o 18Sep81 Zheleznogorsk		
9..1336		Kotlas Avia Enterprise	CCCP-87456	RA-87456		
9431436		VZLU	OK-EEA	OK-EXB	OK-020	engine testbed
9431536			OK-EEB	CCCP-87211 or 87212 !		
9431636		Uzbekistan Airways	CCCP-87457	UK-87457		
9..1736		(Aeroflot)	CCCP-87458	w/o 22Oct75 nr Novogrod, Russia		
9431836		Georgian Airways	CCCP-87459	4L-87459		
9431936		Barnaul State Avn Ent	CCCP-87460	RA-87460		
9432036		Tajik Air	CCCP-87461	EY-87461		
9430137		Tatarstan Airlines	CCCP-87462	RA-87462		
9..0237		Air Ukraine	CCCP-87463	UR-87463		
9430337		(Volga Airlines)	CCCP-87464	RA-87464	dbr 25Jan95 Rostov, Russia	
9430437		Central Districts A/L	CCCP-87465	RA-87465		
9430537		Georgian Airways	CCCP-87466	87466	4L-87466	
9440637		Center-South Airlines	CCCP-87467	3X-GAW	CCCP-87467	RA-87467
9440737			OK-EEC	CCCP-87211 or 87212 !		
9440837		Aviaexpress	OK-EED	HA-LRA		
9440937		Azerbaijan Airlines	OK-EEF	CCCP-87218	HA-LJC	4K-87218
9441037		Ariana Afghan	OK-EEG	YA-KAE		
9441137		Polish AF	039			
9441237		Polish AF	038			
9..1337		(Cheremshanka Airlines)	CCCP-87468	RA-87468	w/o 26Sep94	
9441437		UNA Southern Ind Air Co	CCCP-87469	UR-87469		
9441537			CCCP-87470			
9441637		Aktyubinsk Higher Flying School of Civil Aviation	CCCP-87471	UN-87471		
9441737		Neryungri Sakha Avia	CCCP-87472	RA-87472		
9441837		Achinsk Avia Enterprise	CCCP-87473	RA-87473		
9441937		Barnaul State Avn Ent	CCCP-87474	RA-87474		
9..2037		(Aeroflot)	CCCP-87475	w/o 15Jul75 Batumi		
9510138		Aeroflot Russian Int A/L	Polish AF 036	SP-PGA	CCCP-88293	RA-88293
9510238		Polish AF	037			
9440338		Slovak Government	OK-BYE	OM-BYE		
9..0438		Tuva Airlines	CCCP-87476	RA-87476		
9..0538		Tuva Airlines	CCCP-87477	RA-87477		
9440638		Azerbaijan Airlines	CCCP-87478	87478	4K-87478	
9510738		Aeroflot Russian Int A/L	CCCP-87334	RA-87334		
9..0838		Solar Wind	CCCP-87480	RA-87480		
9440938		Cheremshanka Airlines	CCCP-87481	RA-87481		
9441038		Neryungri Sakha Avia	CCCP-87482	RA-87482		

YAKOVLEV Yak-40

S/n	Series	Last known Owner/Operator	Identities/fate (where known)			
9441138		Vologda State Avn Ent	CCCP-87483	RA-87483		
9441238		Aeroflot Russian Int A/L	CCCP-87484	RA-87484		
9..1338		(Aeroflot)	CCCP-87485	w/o 31May82 Dnepropretovsk, USSR		
9441438		Tyumen Avia Trans	CCCP-87486	RA-87486		
9441538		Aeroflot Russian Int A/L	CCCP-87487	RA-87487		
9441638		Aktyubinsk Higher Flying School of Civil Aviation	CCCP-87488	UN-87488		
9..1738						
9441838		Air Ukraine	CCCP-87479	UR-87479		
9..1938						
9512038		Kazakhstan Airlines	CCCP-87489	RA-87489	UN-87489	
9510139		Belavia	CCCP-87330	EW-87330		
9510239		Kyrgyzstan Airlines	CCCP-87331	EX-87331		
9..0339		Komi Avia	CCCP-87332	RA-87332		
9510439		Estonian Air	CCCP-87333	ES-AAR		
9510539		Kotlas Avia Enterprise	CCCP-87336	RA-87336		
9510639		Kazakhstan Airlines	CCCP-87337	87337	UN-87337	
9510739		Turkmenistan Airlines	CCCP-87338	EZ-87338		
9510839		Baikal Airlines	CCCP-87339	RA-87339		
9510939		Elista Avia Enterprise	CCCP-87340	RA-87340		
9511039		Aeroflot Russian Int A/L	CCCP-87341	RA-87341		
9511139		Tatarstan Airlines	CCCP-87342	RA-87342		
9511239		Tyumen Avia Trans	CCCP-87343	RA-87343		
9511339		Ulyanovsk Avia Ent	CCCP-87344	RA-87344		
9511439		Air Ukraine	CCCP-87345	UR-87345		
9..1539		(Aeroflot)	CCCP-87346	w/o 29Aug82 nr Zeya, USSR		
9511639		Estonian Air	CCCP-87347	ES-AAT		
9511739		Tyumen Avia Trans	CCCP-87348	RA-87348		
9511839		Uzbekistan Airways	CCCP-87349	UK-87349		
9511939		Volga Airlines	CCCP-87500	RA-87500		
9..2039		Kazakhstan Airlines	CCCP-87501	UN-87501		
9510140		Barnaul State Avn Ent	CCCP-87502	RA-87502		
9520240		Tulpar	CCCP-87503	RA-87503		
9510340		Tajik Air	OK-FEH	CCCP-87217	EY-87217	HA-LJA
			EY-87217			
9510440		Aviaenergo	OK-FEI	CCCP-87216	RA-87216	
9510540		Air Ukraine	OK-FEJ	CCCP-87215	UR-87215	
9510640		Azerbaijan Airlines	CCCP-87504	4K-87504		
9510740		Tatarstan Airlines	CCCP-87505	RA-87505		
9..0840		Buguruslan Flying School	CCCP-87506	RA-87506		
9520940		Lithuanian Airlines	CCCP-87507	LY-AAB		
9521040		Southern Eng Factory	CCCP-87508	UR-87508		
9521140		(Aeroflot)	CCCP-87509	w/o 02Sep89 Manus, USSR		
9521240		Bryansk Avia Enterprise	CCCP-87510	RA-87510		
9521340		Elista Avia Enterprise	CCCP-87511	RA-87511		
9521440		Air Ukraine	CCCP-87512	UR-87512		
9521540		Bryansk Avia Enterprise	CCCP-87513	RA-87513		
9521640		Flight Research Inst	CCCP-87514	RA-87514		
9521740		Uzbekistan Airways	CCCP-87515	UK-87515		
9521840		Tyumen Avia Trans	CCCP-87516	RA-87516		
9521940		Tatarstan Airlines	CCCP-87517	RA-87517		
9..2040		Vladivostok Aviation	CCCP-87518	RA-87518		
9..0141		Tuva Airlines	CCCP-87519	RA-87519		
9520241		Komi Avia	CCCP-87520	RA-87520		
9520341			CCCP-87521			
9510441		Tajik Air	CCCP-87522	EY-87522		
9520541		Vladivostok Aviation	CCCP-87523	RA-87523		
9520641		Baikal Airlines	CCCP-87524	RA-87524		
9520741			CCCP-87525			
9520841		(Aeroflot)	CCCP-87526	w/o 07Nov91 Caucasus Mts, nr Makhackkala, USSR		
9520941		Tyumen Avia Trans	CCCP-87527	RA-87527		
9521041		Dnepr Air	CCCP-87528	UR-87528		
9521141			CCCP-87529			
9521241		Barnaul State Avn Ent	CCCP-87530	RA-87530		
9521341		Turkmenistan Airlines	CCCP-87531	EZ-87531		
9521441		Hemus Air	LZ-DOE			
9521541		Hemus Air	LZ-DOF			
9..1641			CCCP-87532			
9511741		Komi Avia/United Nations	CCCP-87533	RA-87533		
9521841		Central Districts A/L	CCCP-87534	RA-87534		
9521941		Elista Avia Enterprise	CCCP-87535	RA-87535		
9..2041			CCCP-87536			
9530142		Soviet AF	01 red			
9520242		Kazakhstan Airlines	CCCP-87537	UN-87537		
9..0342		Kyrgyzstan Airlines	CCCP-87538	EX-87538		
9530442		Uzbekistan Airways	CCCP-87539	UK-87539	derelict by May95 Tashkent, Uzbekistan	
9530542		Uzbekistan Airways	CCCP-87540	RA-87540	UK-87540	
9530642		Aeroflot Russian Int A/L	CCCP-87541	RA-87541		
9530742		Uzbekistan Airways	CCCP-87542	UK-87542		
9530842			CCCP-87543			
9..0942		(Aeroflot)	CCCP-87544	w/o 02Oct78 Tblisi, Georgia		
9531042		Baikal Airlines	CCCP-87545	RA-87545		

YAKOVLEV Yak-40

S/n	Series	Last known Owner/Operator	Identities/fate (where known)			
9531142		Vladivostok Aviation	CCCP-87546	RA-87546		
9531242		Air Ukraine	CCCP-87547	UR-87547		
9531342		Turkmenistan Airlines	CCCP-87548	EZ-87548		
9531442		(Aeroflot)	CCCP-87549	w/o 24Jan88 Nizhnevartovsk, USSR		
9541542		Air Ukraine	CCCP-87230	87230	UR-87230	
9..1642		(Aeroflot)	CCCP-87231	scrapped 1987		
9531742		Kolpashevo State Avn Ent	CCCP-87232	RA-87232		
9..1842		Kazakhstan Airlines	CCCP-87233	UN-87233		
9..1942		Komi Avia	CCCP-87234	RA-87234		
9532042		Zambian AF	AF605	stored Jan96 Lusaka		
9530143		Harka Air (Nigeria)	CCCP-87235	RA-87235		
9..0243			CCCP-87236	wfu Kazan		
9530343		UNA Southern Ind Air Co	CCCP-87237	87237	CCCP-87237	UR-87237
9530443		Syrianair	YK-AQB			
9..0543		(Syrianair)	YK-AQC	w/o 19Mar76 Beirut, Lebanon		
9530643		Neryungri Sakha Avia	CCCP-87238	RA-87238		
9530743		Tatarstan Airlines	CCCP-87239	RA-87239		
9530843		Tyumen Avia Trans	CCCP-87240	RA-87240		
9530943		Elista Avia Enterprise	CCCP-87241	RA-87241		
9531043		Georgian Airways	CCCP-87242	4L-87242		
9531143		Elista Avia Enterprise	CCCP-87243	RA-87243		
9531243		Lukoil	CCCP-87244	RA-87244	RA-88297	
9531343		Air Ukraine	CCCP-87245	UR-87245		
9541443		Aktyubinsk Higher Flying School of Civil Aviation	CCCP-87246	UN-87246		
9531543		Tatarstan Airlines	CCCP-87247	RA-87247		
9541643		Polish AF	040			
9541743		Aeroflot Russian Int A/L	CCCP-87248	RA-87248		
9541843		Polish Government	Polish AF 041	SP-LEB	041	
9541943		Polish Government	Polish AF 042	SP-LEC	042	
9542043		Polish Government	Polish AF 043	SP-LED	043	
9..0144			CCCP-87249			
9..0244						
9530344		Harka Air	CCCP-87980	LY-AAC		
9540444		Aeroflot Russian Int A/L	CCCP-87981	RA-87981		
9540544			CCCP-87982			
9540644		Aeroflot Russian Int A/L	CCCP-87983	RA-87983		
9540744			CCCP-87984			
9540844		Uzbekistan Airways	CCCP-87985	87985	UK-87985	
9540944		Aeroflot Russian Int A/L	CCCP-87986	RA-87986		
9541044		Malev	HA-YLR			
9541144		Air Ukraine	CCCP-87987	UR-87987		
9..1244			CCCP-87988			
9541344		Uzbekistan Airways	CCCP-87989	87989	UK-87989	
9541444		Kazakhstan Airlines	CCCP-87990	UN-87990		
9541544		Tatarstan Airlines	CCCP-87991	RA-87991		
9541644			CCCP-87992			
9541744		Aeroflot Russian Int A/L	CCCP-87993	RA-87993		
9541844		Komi Avia	CCCP-87994	RA-87994		
9541944		(Tajik Air)	CCCP-87995	87995	w/o 27Aug93 nr Khorog, Tajikistan	
9542044		Uzbekistan Airways	CCCP-87996	UK-87996		
9540145		Tyumen Avia Trans	CCCP-87997	RA-87997		
9540245		Air Ukraine	CCCP-87998	UR-87998		
9540345	K	Aeroflot Russian Int A/L	CCCP-87999	RA-87999		
9540445		Cheremshanka Airlines	CCCP-87940	RA-87940		
9540545		Tyumen Avia Trans	CCCP-87941	RA-87941		
9610645	K	Tyumen Avia Trans	CCCP-87942	RA-87942		
9..0745	K		CCCP-87943			
9..0845		Aeroflot Russian Int A/L	CCCP-87944	RA-87944		
9..0945			CCCP-87945			
9611045	K	Azerbaijan Airlines	CCCP-87946	87946	4K-87946	
9621145		Solar Wind	CCCP-87947	RA-87947		
9..1245						
9621345		Kazakhstan Airlines	CCCP-87491	UN-87491		
9541445		Cubana	CU-T1442			
9..1545			CCCP-87492			
9..1645		Kolpashevo State Avn Ent	CCCP-87493	RA-87493		
9..1745		Kolpashevo State Avn Ent	CCCP-87494	RA-87494		
9..1845		Tuva Airlines	CCCP-87495	RA-87495		
9541945		Volga Airlines	CCCP-87496	RA-87496		
9542045		Buguruslan Flying School	CCCP-87497	RA-87497		
9540146		Kazakhstan Airlines	CCCP-87498	UN-87498		
9610246		Donavia Airlines/Resola	CCCP-87499	RA-87499		
9..0346						
9..0446						
9610546		Southern Eng Factory	CCCP-88151	UR-88151		
9610646		Georgian Airways	CCCP-88152	4L-88152		
9610746		Amur Avia	CCCP-88153	RA-88153		
9..0846			CCCP-88154			
9610946		Komi Avia	CCCP-88155	RA-88155		
9611046		Tatarstan Airlines	CCCP-88156	RA-88156		
9..1146			CCCP-88157			

YAKOVLEV Yak-40

S/n	Series	Last known Owner/Operator	Identities/fate (where known)			
9611246		Georgian Airways	CCCP-88158	4L-88158		
9611346		Orel Avia	CCCP-88159	RA-88159		
9611446			CCCP-88160			
9611546		Belavia	CCCP-88161	EW-88161		
9..1646			CCCP-88162			
9611746		Far East Avia	CCCP-88163	RA-88163		
9..1846			CCCP-88164			
9611946		Tatarstan Airlines	CCCP-88165	RA-88165		
9..2046			CCCP-88166			
9..0147			CCCP-88167			
9620247		(Hemus Air)	LZ-DOK	w/o 02Aug88 Sofia, Bulgaria		
9620347		Balkan	LZ-DOL			
9620447		ADA Air Albania	LZ-DOM			
9620547		Balkan	LZ-DON			
9610647		Komi Avia	CCCP-88168	RA-88168		
9610747		Turkmenistan Airlines	CCCP-88169	EZ-88169		
9620847		Aeroflot Russian Int A/L	CCCP-88170	RA-88170		
9620947		Aeroflot Russian Int A/L	CCCP-88171	RA-88171		
9..1047			CCCP-88172			
9621147		Kazakhstan Airlines	CCCP-88173	UN-88173		
9621247		Azerbaijan Airlines	CCCP-88174	88174	4K-88174	
9..1347			CCCP-88175			
9621447		Tatarstan Airlines	CCCP-88176	RA-88176		
9621547		Bulgarian AF	060			
9..1.47						
9621747			CCCP-88177	RA-88177		
9631847	K	Turkmenistan Airlines	CCCP-88178	EZ-88178		
9621947		Ulyanovsk Avia Ent	CCCP-88179	RA-88179		
9..2047		Far East Avia	CCCP-88180	RA-88180		
9620148	K	(Kazakhstan Airlines)	CCCP-88181	UN-88181	w/o 13Apr95 Jambyl	
9620248		Tatarstan Airlines	CCCP-88182	RA-88182		
9620348		Georgian Airways	CCCP-88183	4L-88183		
9620448		Donavia Airlines	CCCP-88184	RA-88184		
9620548		Uzbekistan Airways	CCCP-88185	UK-88185		
9620648		Tyumentransgaz Avia	CCCP-88186	RA-88186		
9620748		Belavia	CCCP-88187	EW-88187		
9620848		Aeroflot Russian Int A/L	CCCP-88188	RA-88188		
9620948			CCCP-88189			
9..1048			CCCP-88190			
9621148			CCCP-88191			
9..1248			CCCP-88192			
9621348			CCCP-88193	RA-88193		
9621448		Uzbekistan Airways	CCCP-88194	UK-88194		
9..1548			CCCP-88195			
9631648		Tajik Air	CCCP-88196	EY-87196		
9631748		Vietnam Airlines	VN-A446			
9631848		(Vietnam Airlines)	VN-A449	w/o 14Nov92 Song Trung, Vietnam		
9631948			CCCP-88197	UN-88197		
9..2048			CCCP-88198			
9..0149			CCCP-88199	88199		
9630249		Rossia/Russian Govt	CCCP-88200	RA-88200		
9630349	K	Aviaobshchemash	CCCP-88201	RA-88201		
9630449		Air Moldova	CCCP-88202	EW-88202	ER-88202	
9630549		Dnepr Air/UN	CCCP-88203	88203	UR-88203/UN-171	UR-88203
9630649			CCCP-88204			
9630749		Baikal Airlines	CCCP-88205	RA-88205		
9630849		Serbian AF	Yugoslav AF 71505	71505/YU-AKV		
9....49			CCCP-88206			
9..1.49			CCCP-88207	RA-88207		
9..1.49		(Aeroflot)	CCCP-88208	w/o 17Dec76 Ust-Kut		
9631249		Cubana	CU-T1440	"CU-t-1440"		
9....49						
9631449		(Cubana)	CU-T1202	w/o 24Oct90 Punta Jardinero, Cuba		
9..1549	K	Tyumen Avia Trans	CCCP-88209	RA-88209		
9631649		Tyumen Avia Trans	CCCP-88210	RA-88210		
9631749	K	Azerbaijan Airways	CCCP-88211	88211	4K-88211	
9..1849			CCCP-88212			
9631949		Tyumen Avia Trans	CCCP-88213	RA-88213		
9632049		Estonian Air	CCCP-88214	ES-AAS		
9630150	K	Aeroflot Russian Int A/L	CCCP-88215	RA-88215		
9630250	K	Komi Avia	CCCP-88216	RA-88216		
9630350		Uzbekistan Airways	CCCP-88217	88217	UK-88217	
9630450		Donavia Airlines	CCCP-88218	RA-88218		
9..0550	K		CCCP-88219			
9..0650		Orel Avia	CCCP-88220	RA-88220		
9..0750			CCCP-88221			
9..0850			CCCP-88222			
9..0950		(Expresso Aero SA)	CCCP-88223	OB-1559	w/o 25Feb94 Tingo Maria, 140m N of Lima, Peru	
9641050	K	Kazakhstan Airlines	OK-GEK	CCCP-87213	UN-87213	
9641150		Krasnoyarsk Airlines	CCCP-88224	RA-88224		
9641250		Donavia Airlines/Resola	CCCP-88225	RA-88225		

YAKOVLEV Yak-40

S/n	Series	Last known Owner/Operator	Identities/fate (where known)			
9641350		Cheremshanka Airlines	CCCP-88226	RA-88226		
9641450		Cubana	CU-T1203			
9641550		Tyumen Avia Trans	CCCP-88227	RA-88227		
9641650		Cubana	CU-T1204	wfs Santiago de Cuba, Cuba		
9641750		Baikal Airlines	CCCP-88228	RA-88228		
9..1850			CCCP-88229	RA-88229		
9641950		Turkmenistan Airlines	CCCP-88230	EZ-88230		
9..2050		Aeroflot Russian Int A/L	CCCP-88231	RA-88231		
9640151		Aeroflot Russian Int A/L	CCCP-88232	RA-88232		
9..0251			CCCP-88233			
9640351		Chelal	CCCP-88234	RA-88234		
9..0451		(Turkmen Avia)	CCCP-88235	w/o 13May92 Chardzhev, Turkmenistan		
9640551		Aeroflot Russian Int A/L	CCCP-88236	RA-88236		
9640651	K	CSA	OK-GEL			
9640751		Dnepr Air	CCCP-88237	88237	UR-88237/UN-170	UR-88237
9640851	K	Malev	OK-GEM	CCCP-87214	EY-87214	HA-LJB
9640951	REO	Sankuru Air Services	CCCP-88238	RA-88238		
9641051		Flight Research Inst	CCCP-88239	RA-88239		
9641151		Bryansk Avia Enterprise	CCCP-88240	RA-88240		
9641251	K	Tajik Air	OK-GEN	EY-1251		
9641351		Solar Wind	CCCP-88241	RA-88241		
9641451	K	CSA	OK-GEO	stored Minsk-Loshitsa, Belarus		
9641551		Uzbekistan Airways	CCCP-88242	88242	UK-88242	
9641651	K	Chelal	CCCP-88243	RA-88243		
9641751		Tyumen Avia Trans	CCCP-88244	88244	(damaged 17May93 - status?)	
9641851		Lithuanian Airlines	CCCP-88245	LY-AAZ		
9641951		Krasnoyarsk Airlines	CCCP-88246	RA-88246		
9642051		Aeroflot Russian Int A/L	CCCP-88247	RA-88247		
9..0.52			CCCP-88248			
9..0.52		Kazakhstan Airlines	CCCP-88249	UN-88249		
9..0.52			CCCP-88250			
9..0.52						
9710552	K	Volga Airlines	CCCP-88251	RA-88251		
9..0652			CCCP-88252			
9710752		Aerogaviota	CU-T1443			
9..0852			CCCP-88253			
9710952		(Don Avia)	CCCP-88254	RA-88254	dbr 26Oct94 Makhachkala, USSR	
9..1052			CCCP-88255			
9..1152			CCCP-88256			
9711252	K	Tyumen Avia Trans	CCCP-88257	RA-88257		
9711352		Aeroflot Russian Int A/L	CCCP-88258	RA-88258		
9..1452			CCCP-88259			
9..1552			CCCP-88260			
9711652			CCCP-88261	RA-88261		
9..1752			CCCP-88262			
9711852		Krasnoyarsk Airlines	CCCP-88263	RA-88263		
9711952		Solar Wind	CCCP-88264	RA-88264		
9722052		Aeroflot Russian Int A/L	CCCP-88265	RA-88265		
9..0153	K		CCCP-87938	RA-87938		
9710253		Tatarstan Airlines	CCCP-98113	RA-98113		
9..0353			CCCP-98114			
9710453	K	Kazakhstan Airlines	CCCP-88266	UN-88266		
9720553	K	Tajik Air	CCCP-88267	EY-88267		
9..0653			CCCP-88268			
9720753	K	Lithuanian Airlines	CCCP-88269	LY-AAY		
9720853		Donavia Airlines	CCCP-88270	RA-88270		
9720953	K	Kazakhstan Airlines	CCCP-88271	88271	UN-88271	
9..1053			CCCP-88272			
9721153	K	Krasnoyarsk Airlines	CCCP-88273	RA-88273		
9721253		Krasnoyarsk Airlines	CCCP-88274	RA-88274		
9721353		Aeroflot Russian Int A/L	CCCP-88275	RA-88275		
9721453		Bryansk Avia Enterprise	CCCP-88276	RA-88276		
9721553	FG	TAAG Angola	D2-TYA	derelict by Nov89 Luanda, Angola		
9721653	FG	TAAG Angola	D2-TYB	derelict by Nov89 Luanda, Angola		
9721753	FG	(TAAG Angola)	D2-TYC	w/o 08Jun80 Matala, Angola		
9721853	FG	(TAAG Angola)	D2-TYD	w/o 08Jan88 Luanda, Angola		
9721953		Kazakhstan Airlines	CCCP-88277	UN-88277		
9722053	K	Volga Airlines	CCCP-88278	RA-88278		
9720154		Lithuanian Airlines	CCCP-88279	LY-AAA		
9720254		Orel Avia	CCCP-87900	RA-87900		
9720354		Tyumen Avia Trans	CCCP-87901	RA-87901		
9..0.54		(Aeroflot)	CCCP-87902	dbr 16Jan82		
9..0.54			CCCP-87903	RA-87903		
9..0.54						
9..0.54						
9720854	K	Bryansk Avia Enterprise	CCCP-87904	RA-87904		
9720954	K	Aeroflot Russian Int A/L	CCCP-87905	RA-87905		
9731054		Bryansk Avia Enterprise	CCCP-87906	RA-87906		
9..1154						
9731254		Tyumen Avia Trans	CCCP-87907	RA-87907		
9..1354			CCCP-87908	EK87908		
9731454	K	Kazakhstan Airlines	CCCP-87909	UN-87909		

YAKOVLEV Yak-40

S/n	Series	Last known Owner/Operator	Identities/fate (where known)			
9731554		Cubana	CU-T1211			
9731654		Aeroflot	CCCP-87910	RA-87910		
9731754		Cubana	CU-T1212			
9..1854		(Aeroflot)	CCCP-87911	w/o 08Apr78 Aldan, USSR		
9731954		Aero Caribbean	CU-T1213			
9732054	K	Aviaobshchemash	CCCP-87912	RA-87912		
9..0.55			CCCP-87913			
9..0.55		(Aeroflot)	CCCP-87914	dbr 09Sep90 Pavlodar, Russia		
9..0.55			CCCP-87915			
9730555	K	CSA	OK-HEP	stored Minsk-Loshitsa, Belarus		
9..0.55			CCCP-87916			
9..0.55			CCCP-87917			
9730855		Dnepr Air	CCCP-87918	87918	UR-87918	
9..0955		Aeroflot Russian Int A/L	CCCP-87919	RA-87919		
9731055		Kazakhstan Airlines	CCCP-87920	UN-87920		
9..1155	K	Aeroflot Russian Int A/L	CCCP-87921	RA-87921		
9731255		Serbian AF	Yugoslav AF 71506	71506		
9731355	K	Tajik Air	CCCP-87922	EY-87922		
9741455		Uzbekistan Airways	CCCP-87923	UK-87923		
9..1555	K	Aeroflot Russian Int A/L	CCCP-87924	RA-87924		
9731655		Aeroflot Russian Int A/L	CCCP-87925	RA-87925		
9741755	K	Kazakhstan Airlines	CCCP-87926	UN-87296		
9741855	K	Kazakhstan Airlines	CCCP-87927	UN-87927		
9..1955			CCCP-87928			
9..2055			CCCP-87929			
9..0156	K		CCCP-87930			
9..0256			CCCP-87931			
9..0356			CCCP-87932	RA-87932		
9740456	K	Aktyubinsk Higher Flying School of Civil Aviation	CCCP-87933	UN-87933		
9..0556	K		CCCP-87934	w/o 30Nov90 Dixon		
9740656		Kazakhstan Airlines	CCCP-87935	UN-87935		
9..0756		Aeroflot Russian Int A/L	CCCP-87936	RA-87936		
9..0856			CCCP-87937			
9740956	K	Aeroflot Russian Int A/L	CCCP-98109	RA-98109		
9741056	K	CSA	OK-HEQ	stored Minsk-Loshitsa, Belarus		
9741156	K	CSA	OK-HER	stored Minsk-Loshitsa, Belarus		
9..1256						
9741356	K	Partner Aviakompanija	CCCP-21500	RA-21500		
9741456		Rossia/Russian Govt	CCCP-87203	RA-87203		
9..1556		Kazakhstan Airlines	CCCP-87204	RA-87204	UN-87204	
9741656	K	Aeroflot Russian Int A/L	CCCP-98111	RA-98111		
9741756	K	Bykovo Avia	CCCP-21501	RA-21501		
9811856		Kazakhstan Airlines	CCCP-87935	UN-87935		
9811956	K	Aeroflot Russian Int A/L	CCCP-87200	RA-87200		
9..2056		(Aeroflot)	CCCP-87201	w/o 25Aug83 Omsukchan, USSR		
9..0157		Kazakhstan Airlines	CCCP-87202	UN-87202		
9..0257		Neryungri Sakha Avia	CCCP-87205	RA-87205		
9..0357	K	Neryungri Sakha Avia	CCCP-87206	RA-87206		
9..0457			CCCP-87207			
9..0557			CCCP-87208			
9810657		Tatarstan Airlines	CCCP-87209	RA-87209		
9810757		Ulyanovsk Avia Ent	CCCP-87210	RA-87210		
9810857	K	Aeroflot Russian Int A/L	CCCP-87950	RA-87950		
9810957	K	Southern Eng Factory	CCCP-87951	UR-87951		
9821057	K	Aeroflot Russian Int A/L	CCCP-87952	RA-87952		
9811157		SAT Aircompany	CCCP-87953	RA-87953		
9821257	K	Czech Government	OK-BYJ			
9811357	K	Aeroflot Russian Int A/L	CCCP-87954	RA-87954		
9811457	K	Aktyubinsk Higher Flying School of Civil Aviation	CCCP-87955	UN-87955		
9821557		Equatorial Guinea Govt	3C-MNB	3C-CGE	wfs	
9..1657						
9821757		Aeroflot Russian Int A/L	CCCP-87956	RA-87956		
9821857		Aeroflot Russian Int A/L	CCCP-87957	RA-87957		
9..1957			CCCP-87958			
9..2057		Aeroflot Russian Int A/L	CCCP-87959	RA-87959		
9830158		Syrianair	YK-AQD			
9830258		Syrianair	YK-AQE			
9..0358			CCCP-87960			
9820458	K	Motor Sich	CCCP-87961	UR-87961		
9820558			CCCP-87962	RA-87962		
9820658		Tyumen Avia Trans	CCCP-88280	RA-88280		
9830758		Ukraine Govt	CCCP-87964	87964	UR-87964	
9820858		Donavia Airlines	CCCP-87965	RA-87965		
9820958		Volga Airlines	CCCP-87966	RA-87966		
9831058	K	Tajik Air	CCCP-87963	EY-87963		
9831158	K	Tajik Air	CCCP-87967	EY-87967		
9841258		Rossia/Russian Govt	CCCP-87968	87968	RA-87968	
9841358		Rossia	CCCP-87969	RA-87969		
9831458		Rossia	CCCP-87970	RA-87970		
9831558		Rossia/Russian Govt	CCCP-87971	RA-87971	87971	RA-87971

YAKOVLEV Yak-40

S/n	Series	Last known Owner/Operator	Identities/fate (where known)			
9..1658		Rossia	CCCP-87972	87972	RA-87972	
9831758		Aeroflot Russian Int A/L	CCCP-21504	RA-21504		
9..1858						
9831958	K	Aeroflot Russian Int A/L	RA-87221			
9832058	K	Aeroflot Russian Int A/L	CCCP-21503	RA-21503		
9830159	K	Krasnoyarsk Airlines	CCCP-21505	RA-21505		
9840259	K	Aeroflot Russian Int A/L	CCCP-21506	RA-21506		
9840359	K	Central Districts A/L	CCCP-87223	RA-87223		
9840459	K		CCCP-88290	88290	UR-88290	
9..0559						
9840659		Polish AF	044			
9840759		Polish AF	045			
9840859		Madagascar Govt	5R-MUA			
9840959		(Cubana)	CU-T1219	w/o 03Feb80 Baracoa, Cuba		
9841059		Aero Caribbean	CU-T1220			
9841159		Aero Caribbean	CU-T1221			
9841259		Aviacor	CCCP-87224	RA-87224		
9841359		Rybinsk Motors Factory	CCCP-87225	RA-87225		
9841459		Aeroflot Russian Int A/L	CCCP-87226	RA-87226		
9841559	K	Central Districts A/L	CCCP-87227	RA-87227		
9841659		18-UKV	CCCP-87228			
9841759	K		CCCP-87229			
9931859	K	Syrianair	YK-AQF			
9941959	K	Syrianair	YK-AQG			
9932059	K	Pragma	CCCP-87219	RA-87219		
9930160		Korsar Airlines	YK-AQH	RA-88298		
9940260	K	Czech Government	OK-BYK			
9940360	K	Rossia/Kuznetsov Design	N10199	CCCP-88287	RA-88287	
9..0460						
9940560	K	Tatra Air/Slovak Govt	OK-BYL	OM-BYL		
9940660		LA Guinea Equatorial	3C-4GE	wfs		
9..0760						
9920860		Vietnam Airlines	VN-A452			
9920960		Vietnam Airlines	VN-A450			
9011060		Aero Caribbean	CU-T1232			
9011160		Aerogaviota	CU-T1448			
9021260		Aerogaviota	CU-T1450			
9021360		Aerogaviota	CU-T1449			
9021460		Turkmenistan Airlines	Polish AF 046	CCCP-87668	EZ-87668	
9021560		Polish Government	Polish AF 047	SP-LEE	047	
9021660		Polish Government	Polish AF 048	SP-LEA	048	
9021760		Petronord Avia	Polish AF 049	CCCP-87669	EW-87669	RA-87669
9041860		Orel Avia	CCCP-87973	RA-87973		
9041960	K		CCCP-87974			

The following are aircraft for which there are no confirmed serial numbers at the present time:

Series	Owner/Operator	Identity			
	Aeroflot	CCCP-1966	prototype; ff 21Oct66		pres Monino, Russia
	Aeroflot	CCCP-1967	second prototype derelict Aug92 Zhukovsky, Russia		
		CCCP-1968			
		CCCP-19671	marks since used by Kamov Ka-26		
		CCCP-19672			
		CCCP-19673			
		CCCP-19674			
		CCCP-19675			
		CCCP-19676	marks since used by Kamov Ka-26		
		CCCP-19681			
	Aeroflot Russian Int A/L	CCCP-21502	RA-21502		
	Rybinsk Motors Factory	CCCP-87211	RA-87211	ex OK-EEB or OK-EEC	
	Central Districts A/L	CCCP-87212	RA-87212	ex OK-EEB or OK-EEC	
	Tajikstan Airlines	CCCP-87310	EY-87310		
	Amur Avia	CCCP-87350	RA-87350		
	Kyrgyzstan Airlines	CCCP-87379	EX-87379		
		CCCP-87571			
		CCCP-87673			
		CCCP-87687			
		CCCP-87688			
		CCCP-87854			
		CCCP-87883			
		CCCP-87891			
		CCCP-87892			
	(Aeroflot)	CCCP-87893	w/o 18Jul80 Archangelsk, USSR		
K	Solar Wind	CCCP-87949	RA-87949		
		CCCP-88109			
	Aeroflot Russian Int A/L	RA-88285			
	(Aeroflot)	CCCP-88286	w/o 07Dec86 Moscow-Bykovo, Russia		
	Aeroflot Russian Int A/L	RA-88291			
	Aeroflot Russian Int A/L	RA-88300			

YAKOVLEV Yak-40

S/n	Series	Last known Owner/Operator	Identities/fate (where known)	
		Aeroflot Russian Int A/L	RA-98101	
		(Aeroflot)	CCCP-98102	w/o 14Aug82 en-route Kazan-Kyubishev, USSR
	K	Aeroflot Russian Int A/L	CCCP-98106	RA-98106
	K	Aeroflot Russian Int A/L	CCCP-98110	RA-98110
		Cubana	CU-T1207	
		Cubana	CU-T1233	
		Cubana	CU-T1441	
		Amazonicas SA	OB-1568	
		(Amazonicas SA)	OB-1569	w/o 05Nov94 Peru
		Air Laos	RDPL-34001	
		Air Laos	RDPL-34002	
		Vietnam Airlines	VN-A444	
		Madagascar Govt	5R-MUB	
		Pathet Lao Airlines	974	
		Pathet Lao Airlines	976	
		Soviet AF	05 red	
		Polish AF	033	
		Ethiopian AF	1601	
		Zambia AF	AF604	
		Zambia AF	AF606	stored Jan96 Lusaka

One Aeroflot Yak-40 w/o 01Aug90 nr Farradzh, Azerbaijan, one Azerbaijan Airlines Yak-40 w/o 21Nov91 nr Khodzhavend, Nagorno-Karabakh and one Krasnoyarsk Airlines Yak-40 w/o 26Sep94 nr Vanavara, Russia

YAKOVLEV Yak-42

The serial number sequence remains obscure, and it appears that there may be at least two independent sequences. Poduction is therefore listed in registration order, with serial numbers quoted where known.

S/n	Series	Last known Owner/Operator	Identities/fate (where known)		
		Aeroflot	CCCP-1974	prototype; ff 07Mar75	wfu
		Aeroflot	CCCP-1975	second prototype wfu	
		(Aeroflot)	CCCP-1976	CCCP-42303	preserved Kiev Institute of Civil Aviation, Ukraine
		Aeroflot	CCCP-1977	dumped by Sep93 Zhukovsky, Russia	
422075380			CCCP-10985	preserved Smolensk Town	
			CCCP-42300		
			CCCP-42301		
427401004		Aeroflot	CCCP-42302	preserved Monino Museum, Moscow, Russia	
		Aeroflot	CCCP-42303	preserved Kiev, Ukraine	
11820201		Aeroflot	CCCP-42304	preserved Moscow, Russia	
0102			CCCP-42305		
11840202		Flight Research Inst	CCCP-42306		
0203			CCCP-42307		
11040303		Air Ukraine	CCCP-42308	UR-42308	
01005		Aeroflot	CCCP-42309	instructional airframe Samara-Smyshlyaevka, Russia	
11040403		Air Ukraine	CCCP-42310	UR-42310	
103			CCCP-42311	wfu Yegorevsk Technical School	
		Aeroflot	CCCP-42312	instructional airframe Irkutsk, Russia	
11030503		Aeroflot	CCCP-42313	dumped by Jun92 Moscow-Bykovo, Russia	
2204245134		Flight Research Inst	CCCP-42314		
			CCCP-42520		
49136		Aeroflot	CCCP-42523	instructional airframe by Aug93 Riga-Spilve, Latvia	
11030603	D	Bykovo Avia	CCCP-42524	RA-42524	also quoted as s/n 30604
110.0703	E-LL	Yakovlev Design Bureau	CCCP-42525	D236 propfan testbed a/c	
11040803		Kuban Airlines	CCCP-42526		
11040903		Air Ukraine	CCCP-42527	UR-42527	
11041003		Ulyanovsk Civil Avn Sch	CCCP-42528	RA-42528	possibly wfs Jun94 Ulyanovsk, Russia
.8040104		Aeroflot	CCCP-42529	w/o 28Jun82	
4253011120204		Air Ukraine	CCCP-42530	UR-42530	
4253011130304	D	Aeroflot	CCCP-42531	dumped by May94 Moscow-Bykovo, Russia	
			CCCP-42532		
			CCCP-42534		
		Aeroflot	CCCP-42536	derelict 1992 Moscow-Bykovo, Russia	
			CCCP-42537		
11130404		Kuban Airlines	CCCP-42538	RA-42538	
11140504		Ulyanovsk Civil Avn Sch	CCCP-42539	RA-42539	
11140604		Air Alfa	CCCP-42540	UR-42540	
11140704		Kuban Airlines	CCCP-42541	RA-42541	
11140804		Bykovo Avia	CCCP-42542	RA-42542	
11250904		Ulyanovsk Civil Avn Sch	CCCP-42543	RA-42543	
11151004		Avia Express	CCCP-42544	UR-42544	
11040105		Bykovo Avia	CCCP-42549	RA-42549	
11140205	D	Saratov Airlines	CCCP-42550	RA-42550	
11140305	D	Saratov Airlines	CCCP-42551	RA-42551	
4520422202030		Saratov Airlines	CCCP-42316	RA-42316	
4520422202039		Air Ukraine	CCCP-42317	42317	UR-42317
452042..020..		Aeroflot Russian Int A/L	CCCP-42318	UR-42318	RA-42318
4520423402062		Air Ukraine	CCCP-42319	42319	UR-42319
4520421302075		Flight Research Inst	CCCP-42320	RA-42320	
4520423402088	D	Bykovo Avia	CCCP-42321	RA-42321	
4520423402108		Bykovo Avia	CCCP-42322	RA-42322	
4520423402116	D	Voronezh Avia	CCCP-42323	RA-42323	
4520421402125		Bykovo Avia	CCCP-42324	RA-42324	
452042.4021..		Ulyanovsk Avia Ent	CCCP-42325	RA-42325	
4520424402154	D	Macedonian Airlines	CCCP-42326	RA-42326	
4520424402161		Dnepr-Air	CCCP-42327	UR-42327	
4520421505058		Saratov Airlines	CCCP-42328	RA-42328	
4520422505093	D	Saratov Airlines	CCCP-42329	RA-42329	
4520422505122		Ulyanovsk Avia Ent	CCCP-42330	RA-42330	
452042..051..		Kuban Airlines	CCCP-42331	42331	RA-42331
4520421605135	D	Tatarstan Airlines	CCCP-42332	RA-42332	
4520422606156		Tatarstan Airlines	CCCP-42333	RA-42333	
4520422606...		Air Ukraine	CCCP-42334	UR-42334	
4520422606204		Tatarstan Airlines	CCCP-42335	RA-42335	
452042.6062..		Kuban Airlines	CCCP-42336	RA-42336	
4520423606235		Lithuanian Airlines	CCCP-42337	LY-AAM	
4520423606256		Lithuanian Airlines	CCCP-42338	LY-AAN	
4520423606267		Lithuanian Airlines	CCCP-42339	LY-AAO	
4520424606270		Volga Airlines	CCCP-42340	RA-42340	
4520421706292		Bykovo Avia	CCCP-42341	RA-42341	
4520421706302			CCCP-42342	LY-AAP	42342
4520421706305	D	Volga Airlines	CCCP-42343	RA-42343	
4520422708295		Lithuanian Airlines	CCCP-42344	LY-AAQ	
4520422708304		Lithuanian Airlines	CCCP-42345	LY-AAR	
4520423708311		Krasnodar Avia	CCCP-42346	RA-42346	
4520423711322		Tatarstan Airlines	CCCP-42347	RA-42347	

YAKOVLEV Yak-42

S/n	Series	Last known Owner/Operator	Identities/fate (where known)			
4520423711342		Air Ukraine	CCCP-42348	UR-42348		
4520424711372		Kuban Airlines	CCCP-42350	RA-42350		
452042..113..		(Aeroflot)	CCCP-42351	w/o 14Sep90 Sverdlovsk, USSR		
4520421811395	D	Lithuanian Airlines	CCCP-42352	"LT-AAS"	LY-AAS	
4520424711396		Lithuanian Airlines	CCCP-42353	LY-AAT		
4520424711397	D	Lithuanian Airlines	CCCP-42354	LY-AAU		
4520424711399	D	Bhoja Air	CCCP-42355	LY-AAV		
4520422811400		Bykovo Avia	CCCP-42356	RA-42356		
4520422811408		Tatarstan Airlines	CCCP-42357	RA-42357		
4520422811413	D	Air Ukraine	CCCP-42358	UR-42358		
4520423811417	D	Lithuanian Airlines	CCCP-42359	LY-AAW		
4520423811421		Volga Airlines	CCCP-42360	RA-42360		
4520423811427	D	Saratov Airlines	CCCP-42361	RA-42361		
4520424811431	D	Bhoja Airlines	CCCP-42362	LY-AAX		
4520424811438	D	Kuban Airlines	CCCP-42363	RA-42363		
4520424811442		Volga Airlines	CCCP-42364	RA-42364		
4520424811447	D	Saratov Airlines	CCCP-42365	RA-42365		
4520421814047		Air Ukraine	CCCP-42366	UR-42366	also quoted as s/n 4520421914047	
4520424914057	D	Cubana	CU-T1279			
4520424914068	D	Cubana	CU-T1285	wfu Santiago de Cuba, Cuba		
4520424914090	F	Yak Service	CCCP-42644			
4520421914133	D	Kuban Airlines	CCCP-42367	RA-42367		
4520422914166	D	Bykovo Avia	CCCP-42368	RA-42368		
4520422914190	D	Air Ukraine	CCCP-42369	UR-42369		
4520422914203	D	Ulyanovsk Avia Ent	CCCP-42370	RA-42370		
4520422914225	D	Volga Airlines	CCCP-42371	RA-42371		
4520423914266	D	Air Ukraine	CCCP-42372	UR-42372		
4520423914323	D	Trans Congo	CCCP-42373	RA-42373		
4520423914340	D	Tatarstan Airlines	CCCP-42374	RA-42374		
4520424914410	D	Kuban Airlines	CCCP-42375	RA-42375		
4520424914477	D	Dnepr-Air	CCCP-42376	UR-42376		
4520421014479	D	Air Ukraine	CCCP-42377	UR-42377		
4520421014494	D	Palair	CCCP-42378	RA-42378	TC-FAR	RA-42378
4520421014543	D	Voronezh Avia	CCCP-42379	RA-42379		
4520422014549	D	Tatarstan Airlines	CCCP-42380	RA-42380		
4520422014576	D	Air Ukraine	CCCP-42381	UR-42381		
4520422016196	D	Astral	CCCP-42382	RA-42382		
4520422016201	D	Air Ukraine	CCCP-42383	UR-42383		
4520423016230	D	Astral	CCCP-42384	RA-42384		
4520423016238	D	Cubana	CU-T1277			
4520423016269	D	Cubana	CU-T1278			
4520423016309	D	Bykovo Avia	CCCP-42385	RA-42385		
4520424016310	D	Kuban Airlines	CCCP-42386	RA-42386		
4520424016436	D	Chelal	CCCP-42387	RA-42387		
4520424016510	D	Chelal	CCCP-42388	RA-42388		
4520424016542	D	Avioimpex	CCCP-42389	RA-42389		
4520424016557		(Avioimpex)	CCCP-42390	RA-42390	w/o 20Nov93 nr Ohrid, Macedonia	
452042..165..		Aeroflot Russian Int A/L	CCCP-42391	RA-42391		
4520421316562	D	Turkmenistan Airlines	EZ-J672			
4520421116567	D	Chelal	CCCP-42401	RA-42401		
4520421316574	D	Turkmenistan Airlines	EZ-J673			
4520423116579	D	China General	B-2754			
4520422116583	D	Central Districts A/L	CCCP-42402	RA-42402		
4520422116588	D	Moldavian Airlines	CCCP-42403	UR-42403		
4520424216606	D	Yakovlev	RA-42423			
4520422116617	D	Turkmenistan Airlines	CCCP-42404	EZ-42404		
4520423116624	D	Dnepr-Air	CCCP-42405	UR-42405		
4520424116638	D	Volga Airlines	CCCP-42406	RA-42406		
4520422116644	D	(China General)	B-2755	w/o 31Jul92 Nanjing, China		
4520423116650	D	China General	B-2751			
4520424116664	D	China General	B-2752			
4520424116669	D	China General	B-2756			
4520424116677	D	China General	B-2753			
4520424116690	D	Kazakhstan Airlines	CCCP-42407	UN-42407		
4520424116698	D	Chelal	CCCP-42408	RA-42408		
4520421216707	D	Dnepr-Air	CCCP-42409	UR-42409		
4520421319020	D	Turkmenistan Airlines	EZ-J674			
4520421219029	D	Dnepr-Air	CCCP-42410	UR-42410		
4520421219043	D	Vardar Air	CCCP-42411	RA-42411		
4520422219055	D	Chelal	CCCP-42412	RA-42412		
4520422219066	D	Chelal	CCCP-42413	RA-42413		
4520422219073	D	Aerovolga	CCCP-42414	RA-42414		
4520422219089	D	Astrakan Airlines	CCCP-42415	RA-42415		
4520423219102	D	Dnepr-Air	CCCP-42416	UR-42416	EP-CPA	UR-42416
4520423.191..	D	Astral	CCCP-42417	RA-42417		
4520423201016	D	Dnepr-Air	CCCP-42419	UR-42419		
4520421502016	100	Lukoil	RA-42424		prototype Yak-142	
4520423303016	D	Dacono Air	RA-42425	EP-LAH	RA-42425	
4520423304016	D	Top Air	RA-42426	EP-LAM	RA-42426	TC-IYI
4520422305016	D	Aeroflot Russian Int A/L	RA-42427			
4520422306016	D	Skyjet/Moaet Flight	RA-42428			

YAKOVLEV Yak-42

S/n	Series	Last known Owner/Operator	Identities/fate (where known)		
4520423407016	D	Yak Air	RA-42429		
4520423408016	D	Chelal	RA-42430		
4520424410016	D	Albatros Airlines	RA-42432	TC-ALY	
4520421301017	D	Tatarstan Airlines	RA-42433		
4520423302017	D	Kazakhstan Airlines	UN-42557		
4520422303017	D	Kuban Airlines	RA-42421		
4520424304017	D	Orel Avia	RA-42422		
4520424305017	D	Orel Avia	RA-42434		
4520424306017	D	Orel Avia	RA-42435		
4520423307017	D	Kazakhstan Airlines	UN-42558		
4520424309017	D	Kazakhstan Airlines	UN-42447		
4520421401018	D	Dnepr-Air	UR-42449		
4520421402018	D	Dacono Air	RA-42441	EP-LAN?	RA-42441
4520423403018	D	China General	B-2757		
4520423404018	D	China General	B-2758		

The following are aircraft for which there are no confirmed serial numbers at the present time:

Series	Owner/Operator	Identity	Notes
	Kuban Airlines	RA-42436	
D	Kazakhstan Airlines	UN-42446	(possibly s/n 452042.308017)
	Kazakhstan Airlines	UN-42448	(possibly s/n 452042..10017)
D	Caspian Airlines	EP-CPB	
D	Caspian Airlines	EP-CPC	
D	Caspian Airlines	EP-CPE	
	Oriental de Aviacion	YV-598C	

EXPERIMENTAL AND LIMITED PRODUCTION AIRCRAFT

ANTONOV An-70

S/n	Series	Last known Owner/Operator	Identities/fate (where known)		
		(Antonov Design Bureau)	UR-	prototype; ff 16Dec94	w/o 10Feb95 Gostomel, Ukraine

AVRO CANADA C102

C/n	Series	Last known Operator/Owner	Previous Identities/fate (where known)
			CF-EJD-X prototype ff 10Aug49

BOEING C-14

Line No	Series	Last known Operator/Owner	Previous Identities/fate (where known)	
	YC-14A	USAF	72-1873	ff 06Aug76 N8780B preserved Pima County Air Museum, Tucson, AZ
	YC-14A	USAF	72-1874	stored Aug79 AMARC coded CW-001

EMBRAER 145

C/n	Series	Last known Operator/Owner	Previous Identities/fate (where known)		
145801		Embraer	PT-ZJA	prototype; ff 11Aug95	certification planned for late 1996
145802		Embraer	structural test airframe		
145803		Embraer	structural test airframe		
145001		Embraer	PT-ZJB		
145002		Embraer	PT-ZJC		
145003		Embraer	PT-		

McDONNELL-DOUGLAS C-15

Line No	Series	Last known Operator/Owner	Previous Identities/fate (where known)	
	YC-15A	USAF	72-1875	ff 26Aug75 preserved 1981 Pima County Air Museum, Tucson, AZ
	YC-15A	USAF	72-1876	stored Aug79 AMARC coded CX-002

SATIC A300B4

C/n	Series	Last known Operator/Owner	Previous Identities/fate (where known)		
655/001	608ST	Airbus Inter Transport	F-WAST	prototype; ff 13Sep94	F-GSTA
751/002	608ST	Airbus Inter Transport	F-GSTB		
765/003	608ST	Airbus Inter Transport	F-GSTC		
776/004	608ST	Airbus Inter Transport	F-GSTD*		

TUPOLEV Tu-155

S/n	Series	Last known Owner/Operator	Identities/fate (where known)	
72A-035		Aeroflot	CCCP-85035	prototype; cvtd from TU-154; ff 15Apr88

TUPOLEV Tu-234

S/n	Series	Last known Owner/Operator	Identities/fate (where known)	
1450743164001		Tupolev Design Bureau	RA-64001	prototype; ff 95

TUPOLEV Tu-334

S/n	Series	Last known Owner/Operator	Identities/fate (where known)	
01001		Tupolev Design Bureau	RA-94001	prototype; r/o 29Oct93

VEB BB-152

C/n	Series	Last known Operator/Owner	Previous Identities/fate (where known)
1	I		DM-ZYA prototype; ff 04Dec58 w/o 04Mar59; fuselage at Rothenburg, Germany
2			static structural test fuselage
3	II		DM-ZYB b/u after Mar61
4			dynamic structural test fuselage
5	II		DM-ZYC not completed; b/u after Mar61
6	A-1		DM-SCA not completed; b/u after Mar61
7	A-1		DM-SCB not completed; b/u after Mar61
8	A-1		DM-SCC not completed; b/u after Mar61

YAKOVLEV Yak-142

S/n	Series	Last known Owner/Operator	Identities/fate (where known)
4520421502016	100	Lukoil	RA-42424

NOTES

NOTES

Master Index

Civil-registered commercial jet aircraft are arranged in order of country registration prefix, registrations relating to each country being listed in alphabetical or numerical order as appropriate. The short-lived number sequence for Russia is included under CCCP-. For each registration a three-, four-, five- or six- character abbreviation for each type of aircraft is given (see decode below), followed by the c/n (or s/n).

For ease of reference, all aircraft flying with registration prefixes, whether operated in civilian or government roles are included in the civil section of the Master Index. Aircraft flying with purely numerical identities (except the former Soviet Union) or with recognised military alphabetical prefixes or with military call-signs are included in the military section, which is listed by country name.

All civil and military aircraft which are in current use are indicated in bold typeface; reserved marks are given in the normal typeface

Code	Type
A300	Airbus Industrie A300
A310	Airbus Industrie A310
A319	Airbus Industrie A319
A320	Airbus Industrie A320
A321	Airbus Industrie A321
A330	Airbus Industrie A330
A340	Airbus Industrie A340
AN-70	Antonov AN-70
AN-72	Antonov AN-72
AN-74	Antonov AN-74
AN124	Antonov AN-124
AN225	Antonov AN-225
B707	Boeing 707
B720	Boeing 720
B727	Boeing 727
B737	Boeing 737
B747	Boeing 747
B757	Boeing 757
B767	Boeing 767
B777	Boeing 777
BB152	VEB BB-152
C-1	Kawasaki C-1
C-5	Lockheed C-5 Galaxy (Model 500)
C-9	Douglas DC-9
C-10	Douglas DC-10
C-14	Boeing C-14
C-15	McDonnell-Douglas C-15
C-17	McDonnell-Douglas C-17 Globemaster III
C-18	Boeing 707
C-22	Boeing 727
C-25	Boeing 747
C-102	Avro Canada C-102
C-135	Boeing 707
C-137	Boeing 707
C-141	Lockheed C-141 Starlifter (Model 300)
CNCRD	BAC/Aerospatiale Concorde
COMET	De Havilland DH.106 Comet
CRVL	Sud Aviation SE.210 Caravelle
CV880	Convair 880
CV990	Convair 990
DC-8	Douglas DC-8
DC-9	Douglas DC-9
DC-10	Douglas DC-10

Code	Type
E-3	Boeing 707
E-4	Boeing 747
E-6	Boeing 707
E-8	Boeing 707
EMB145	Embraer 145
F-28	Fokker F-28
F-70	Fokker F-70
F-100	Fokker F-100
IL-62	Ilyushin IL-62
IL-76	Ilyushin IL-76
IL-86	Ilyushin IL-86
IL-96	Ilyushin IL-96
KC-10	Douglas DC-10
L1011	Lockheed 1011 Tristar
MD-11	McDonnell Douglas MD-11
MD-81	McDonnell Douglas MD-81
MD-82	McDonnell Douglas MD-82
MD-83	McDonnell Douglas MD-83
MD-87	McDonnell Douglas MD-87
MD-88	McDonnell Douglas MD-88
MD-90	McDonnell Douglas MD-90
MERC	Dassault Mercure
NIMROD	Hawker-Siddley HS.801 Nimrod
RJ100	Canadair RJ100 Regional Jet
SA300	SATIC A300B4
T-43	Boeing 737
TRDNT	Hawker-Siddley HS.121 Trident
TU104	Tupolev TU-104
TU124	Tupolev TU-124
TU134	Tupolev TU-134
TU144	Tupolev TU-144
TU154	Tupolev TU-154
TU155	Tupolev TU-155
TU204	Tupolev TU-204
TU234	Tupolev TU-234
TU334	Tupolev TU-334
VC-10	Vickers VC-10
VFW614	VFW-Fokker VFW-614
YAK40	Yakovlev YAK-40
YAK42	Yakovlev YAK-42
1-11	British Aircraft Corporation BAC 1-11
146	British Aerospace 146
367-80	Boeing 707

Civil Index

B-182	**B737**	**23796**
(B-184)	B737	23913
(B-186)	B737	24197
B-188	B727	19818
B-190	**A300**	**193**
B-192	**A300**	**197**
B-194	**A300**	**221**
B-196	**A300**	**232**
B-198	B747	22390
B-240	TRDNT	2157
B-242	TRDNT	2158
B-244	TRDNT	2159
B-246	TRDNT	2160
B-248	TRDNT	2161
B-250	TRDNT	2162
B-252	TRDNT	2163
B-254	TRDNT	2164
B-256	TRDNT	2165
B-258	TRDNT	2166
B-260	TRDNT	2167
B-261	TRDNT	2165
B-262	TRDNT	2168
B-263	**TRDNT**	**2185**
B-264	TRDNT	2169
B-265	TRDNT	2186
B-266	TRDNT	2170
B-267	**TRDNT**	**2187**
B-268	TRDNT	2327
B-269	**TRDNT**	**2188**
B-270	TRDNT	2328
B-271	TRDNT	2189
B-272	TRDNT	2171
B-274	TRDNT	2172
B-276	TRDNT	2173
B-278	TRDNT	2174
B-280	TRDNT	2175
B-282	TRDNT	2176
B-284	TRDNT	2177
B-286	TRDNT	2178
B-288	TRDNT	2179
B-290	TRDNT	2180
B-292	TRDNT	2181
B-294	TRDNT	2182
B-296	TRDNT	2183
B-298	TRDNT	2184
B-584L	146	E1035
B-585L	146	E1068
B-606L	B707	20722
B-610L	B737	22802
B-614L	B737	22803
B-615L	B737	22804
B-1008	CV880	22-00-44M
B-1018	B727	19175
B-1775	**146**	**E3161**
B-1776	**146**	**E3174**
B-1777	**146**	**E3205**
B-1778	**146**	**E3209**
B-1781	**146**	**E3202**
B-1800	**A300**	**529**
B-1802	**A300**	**533**
B-1804	**A300**	**536**
B-1806	**A300**	**666**
B-1810	**A300**	**179**
B-1812	**A300**	**171**
(B-1814)	A300	529
B-1814	**A300**	**578**
B-1816	A300	580
(B-1818)	A300	536
B-1818	B727	19399
B-1820	B727	19520
B-1822	B727	20111
B-1824	B707	20261
B-1826	B707	20262
B-1828	B707	18710
B-1830	B707	19178
B-1832	B707	18825
B-1834	B707	18887
B-1836	B767	22681
B-1838	B767	22682
B-1850	CRVL	121
B-1852	CRVL	122
B-1854	CRVL	38
B-1856	**CRVL**	**170**
B-1860	B747	19898
B-1861	B747	22298
B-1862	**B747**	**21300**
B-1864	**B747**	**21454**
(B-1865)	B747	22299
B-1866	**B747**	**21843**
B-1868	B747	19896
B-1870	B737	20226
B-1872	B737	20227
B-1874	B737	20277
B-1876	**B737**	**23913**
B-1878	**B737**	**24197**
B-1880	**B747**	**22298**
(B-1882)	B747	22547
B-1885	B747	22299
B-1886	**B747**	**22446**
B-1888	**B747**	**22447**
B-1894	**B747**	**22299**
B-2016	**IL-86**	**51483210098?**
B-2018	**IL-86**	**51483210099?**
B-2019	**IL-86**	**51483210100?**
B-2020	IL-62	21203
B-2022	IL-62	11005
B-2024	**IL-62**	**11101**
B-2026	IL-62	21201
B-2028	IL-62	21202
B-2051	**B777**	**27357**
B-2052	**B777**	**27358**
B-2101	**MD-82**	**49140**
B-2102	**MD-82**	**49141**
B-2103	MD-82	49355
B-2104	**MD-82**	**49425**
B-2105	**MD-82**	**49428**
B-2106	**MD-82**	**49415**
B-2107	**MD-82**	**49501**
B-2108	**MD-82**	**49502**
B-2109	**MD-82**	**49503**
B-2120	**MD-82**	**49504**
B-2121	**MD-82**	**49505**
B-2122	**MD-82**	**49506**
B-2123	**MD-82**	**49507**
B-2124	**MD-82**	**49508**
B-2125	**MD-82**	**49509**
B-2126	**MD-82**	**49510**
B-2127	**MD-82**	**49511**
B-2128	**MD-82**	**49512**
B-2129	**MD-82**	**49513**
B-2130	**MD-82**	**49514**
B-2131	**MD-82**	**49515**
B-2132	**MD-82**	**49516**
B-2133	**MD-82**	**49517**
B-2134	**MD-82**	**49518**
B-2135	**MD-82**	**49519**
B-2136	**MD-82**	**49520**
B-2137	**MD-82**	**49521**
B-2138	**MD-82**	**49522**
B-2139	**MD-82**	**49523**
B-2140	**MD-82**	**49524**
B-2141	MD-82	49849
B-2142	**MD-82**	**49850**
B-2143	**MD-82**	**49851**
B-2144	MD-82	49852
B-2145	**MD-82**	**49853**
B-2146	**MD-82**	**53162**
B-2147	**MD-82**	**53163**
B-2148	**MD-82**	**53169**
B-2149	**MD-82**	**53170**
B-2150	**MD-82**	**53171**
B-2151	**MD-82**	**49852**
B-2152	**MD-82**	**53164**
B-2170	**MD-11**	**48461**
B-2171	**MD-11**	**48495**
B-2172	**MD-11**	**48496**
B-2173	**MD-11**	**48497**
B-2174	**MD-11**	**48498**
B-2175	**MD-11**	**48520**
B-2201	**TRDNT**	**2157**
B-2202	**TRDNT**	**2158**
B-2203	**TRDNT**	**2168**
B-2204	**TRDNT**	**2175**
B-2205	**TRDNT**	**2176**
B-2206	**TRDNT**	**2181**
B-2207	**TRDNT**	**2182**
B-2208	TRDNT	2165
B-2209	**TRDNT**	**2164**
B-2210	**TRDNT**	**2178**
B-2211	**TRDNT**	**2180**
B-2212	**TRDNT**	**2162**
B-2213	**TRDNT**	**2173**
B-2214	**TRDNT**	**2163**
B-2215	**TRDNT**	**2166**
B-2216	**TRDNT**	**2177**
B-2217	**TRDNT**	**2179**
B-2218	TRDNT	2159
B-2219	**TRDNT**	**2160**
B-2220	**TRDNT**	**2183**
B-2221	**TRDNT**	**2184**
B-2223	**TRDNT**	**2161**
B-2231	**F-100**	**11383**
B-2232	**F-100**	**11389**
B-2233	**F-100**	**11394**
B-2234	**F-100**	**11401**
B-2235	**F-100**	**11409**
B-2236	**F-100**	**11430**
B-2237	**F-100**	**11421**
B-2238	**F-100**	**11423**
B-2239	**F-100**	**11429**
B-2240	**F-100**	**11431**
B-2301	**A310**	**311**
B-2302	**A310**	**320**
B-2303	**A310**	**419**
B-2304	A310	435
B-2305	A310	440
B-2306	**A300**	**521**
B-2307	**A300**	**525**
B-2308	**A300**	**532**
B-2309	**A300**	**584**
B-2310	**A300**	**603**
B-2311	**A300**	**688**
B-2312	**A300**	**690**
B-2315	**A300**	**733**
B-2316	**A300**	**734**
B-2317	**A300**	**741**
B-2318	**A300**	**707**
B-2319	**A300**	**732**
B-2320	**A300**	**709**
B-2321	**A300**	**713**
B-2322	**A300**	**715**
B-2323	**A300**	**739**
B-2324	**A300**	**725**
B-2325	**A300**	**746**
B-2326	**A300**	**754**
B-2327	**A300**	**750**
B-2330	**A300**	**763**
B-2340	**A320**	**0540**
B-2341	**A320**	**0551**
B-2342	**A320**	**0556**
B-2381	**A340**	**131**
B-2402	B707	20714
B-2404	B707	20715
B-2406	B707	20716
B-2408	B707	20717
B-2410	**B707**	**20718**
B-2412	B707	20719
B-2414	B707	20720
B-2416	B707	20721
B-2418	B707	20722
B-2420	B707	20723
B-2422	B707	19353
B-2423	B707	19352
B-2424	B707	19530
B-2425	B707	19964
B-2426	B707	19294
B-2438	**B747**	**21933**
B-2440	B747	19732
B-2442	**B747**	**21932**
B-2443	**B747**	**25881**
B-2444	B747	21933
B-2445	**B747**	**25882**
(B-2446)	B747	21934
B-2446	**B747**	**23071**
B-2447	**B747**	**25883**
B-2448	**B747**	**23461**
B-2450	**B747**	**23746**
B-2452	**B747**	**21934**
B-2454	**B747**	**22302**
B-2456	**B747**	**24346**
B-2458	**B747**	**24347**
B-2460	**B747**	**24348**
B-2462	**B747**	**24960**
B-2464	**B747**	**25879**
B-2466	**B747**	**25880**
B-2501	B737	22802
B-2501	**CRVL**	**108**
B-2502	B737	22803
B-2503	B737	22804
B-2503	**CRVL**	**110**
B-2504	B737	23065
B-2505	CRVL	197
B-2505	**B737**	**23066**
B-2506	**B737**	**23272**
B-2507	**B737**	**23273**
B-2508	**B737**	**23274**
B-2509	B737	23188
B-2510	**B737**	**23189**
B-2511	B737	23443
B-2512	**B737**	**23444**
B-2514	B737	23445
B-2515	**B737**	**23446**
B-2516	**B737**	**23447**
B-2517	**B737**	**23396**
B-2518	**B737**	**23397**
B-2519	**B737**	**23448**
B-2520	**B737**	**23449**
B-2521	**B737**	**23450**
B-2522	**B737**	**23451**
B-2523	B737	24913
B-2524	**B737**	**24236**
B-2525	**B737**	**24918**
B-2526	**B737**	**25172**
B-2527	**B737**	**25173**
B-2528	**B737**	**25174**
B-2529	B737	22735
B-2529	**B737**	**26297**
B-2530	**B737**	**27046**
B-2531	**B737**	**23302**
B-2532	**B737**	**23303**
B-2533	**B737**	**27138**
B-2534	**B737**	**26070**
B-2535	**B737**	**25078**
B-2536	**B737**	**25079**
B-2537	**B737**	**25089**
B-2538	**B737**	**25090**
B-2539	**B737**	**26068**
B-2540	B737	27139
B-2541	**B737**	**24696**
B-2542	**B737**	**24897**
B-2543	**B737**	**24898**
B-2544	**B737**	**24899**
B-2545	**B737**	**24900**
B-2546	**B737**	**25175**
B-2547	**B737**	**25176**
B-2548	**B737**	**25182**
B-2549	**B737**	**25183**
B-2550	**B737**	**25188**
B-2551	**B767**	**23307**
B-2552	**B767**	**23308**
B-2553	**B767**	**23744**
B-2554	**B767**	**23745**
B-2555	**B767**	**24007**
B-2556	**B767**	**24157**
B-2557	**B767**	**25875**
B-2558	**B767**	**25876**
B-2559	**B767**	**25877**
B-2560	**B767**	**25878**
B-2561	**B767**	**25865**
B-2562	**B767**	**25864**
B-2563	**B767**	**27309**
B-2564	**B767**	**25121**
B-2565	**B767**	**26259**
B-2566	**B767**	**25170**
B-2567	**B767**	**27683**
B-2578	**B737**	**25603**
B-2579	**B737**	**25505**
B-2580	**B737**	**25080**
B-2581	**B737**	**25081**
B-2582	**B737**	**25895**
B-2583	**B737**	**25897**
B-2584	**B737**	**25891**
B-2585	**B737**	**27045**
B-2586	**B737**	**27047**
B-2587	**B737**	**25892**
B-2588	**B737**	**25893**
B-2589	**B737**	**27127**
B-2590	**B737**	**27126**
B-2591	**B737**	**25792**
B-2592	**B737**	**27153**
B-2593	**B737**	**27155**
B-2594	**B737**	**26853**
B-2595	**B737**	**26072**
B-2596	**B737**	**27151**

B-2597	**B737**	**27176**
B-2598	**B737**	**27128**
B-2599	**B737**	**25896**
B-2601	**B737**	**19936**
B-2601	**TU154**	**716**
B-2602	**TU154**	**717**
B-2603	B737	19939
B-2603	**TU154**	**718**
B-2604	**TU154**	**724**
B-2605	B737	19712
B-2605	**TU154**	**725**
B-2606	**TU154**	**728**
B-2607	B737	20132
B-2607	**TU154**	**729**
B-2608	**TU154**	**734**
B-2609	**TU154**	**735**
B-2610	TU154	740
B-2611	B737	21518
B-2611	**TU154**	**726**
B-2612	**TU154**	**730**
B-2613	**B737**	**20134**
B-2614	**TU154**	**741**
B-2615	**B737**	**21687**
B-2615	**TU154**	**783**
B-2616	**TU154**	**790**
B-2617	B737	20130
B-2617	**TU154**	**791**
B-2618	**TU154**	**797**
B-2619	**TU154**	**814**
B-2620	**TU154**	**815**
B-2621	B737	19014
B-2621	**TU154**	**823**
B-2622	**TU154**	**846**
B-2623	B737	19017
B-2623	**TU154**	**855**
B-2624	**TU154**	**886**
B-2625	**B737**	**23794**
B-2625	**TU154**	**897?**
B-2626	**TU154**	**900?**
B-2627	**TU154**	**917**
B-2628	**TU154**	**919?**
B-2629	**TU154**	**923?**
B-2630	**TU154**	**954**
B-2660	**TU154**	
(B-2701)	B737	19936
B-2701	**146**	**E1019**
B-2702	**146**	**E1026**
(B-2703)	B737	19939
B-2703	**146**	**E1032**
B-2704	146	E1035
B-2705	146	E1068
B-2706	146	E1071
B-2707	**146**	**E1076**
B-2708	**146**	**E1081**
B-2709	**146**	**E1083**
B-2710	**146**	**E1085**
B-2711	**146**	**E3207**
B-2712	**146**	**E3212**
B-2715	**146**	**E3214**
B-2716	146	E3215
B-2717	**146**	**E3216**
B-2718	**146**	**E3222**
B-2719	**146**	**E3218**
B-2720	**146**	**E3219**
B-2751	**YAK42**	**4520423116650**
B-2752	**YAK42**	**4520424116664**
B-2753	**YAK42**	**4520424116677**
B-2754	**YAK42**	**4520423116579**
B-2755	YAK42	4520422116644
B-2756	**YAK42**	**4520424116669**
B-2757	**YAK42**	**4520423403018**
B-2758	**YAK42**	**4520423404018**
B-2801	**B757**	**24014**
B-2802	**B757**	**24015**
B-2803	**B757**	**24016**
B-2804	**B757**	**24330**
B-2805	**B757**	**24331**
B-2806	**B757**	**24401**
B-2807	**B757**	**24402**
B-2808	**B757**	**24471**
B-2809	**B757**	**24472**
B-2810	**B757**	**24473**
B-2811	**B757**	**24714**
B-2812	B757	24758
B-2815	**B757**	**24774**
B-2816	**B757**	**25083**
B-2817	**B757**	**25258**

B-2818	**B757**	**25259**
B-2819	**B757**	**25898**
B-2820	**B757**	**25885**
B-2821	**B757**	**25886**
B-2822	**B757**	**25884**
B-2823	**B757**	**25888**
B-2824	**B757**	**25889**
B-2825	**B757**	**25890**
B-2826	**B757**	**26155**
B-2827	**B757**	**26156**
B-2828	**B757**	**25899**
B-2829	**B757**	**25900**
(B-2830)	B757	26160
B-2831	**B757**	**26153**
B-2832	**B757**	**25887**
B-2833	**B757**	**27152**
B-2834	**B757**	**27183**
B-2835	**B757**	**25598**
B-2836	**B757**	**27258**
B-2837	**B757**	**27259**
B-2838	**B757**	**27260**
B-2839	**B757**	**27269**
B-2840	**B757**	**27270**
(B-2841)	B757	27282
B-2841	**B757**	**27367**
B-2842	**B757**	**27342**
(B-2843)	B757	27281
B-2843	**B757**	**27681**
B-2844	**B757**	**27511**
B-2845	**B757**	**27512**
B-2848	**B757**	**27513**
B-2849	**B757**	**27517**
B-2901	**B737**	**26284**
B-2902	**B737**	**24988**
(B-2903)	B737	26288
B-2903	**B737**	**26292**
(B-2904)	B737	26292
B-2904	**B737**	**26288**
B-2905	**B737**	**25506**
B-2906	**B737**	**25507**
B-2907	**B737**	**25508**
B-2908	**B737**	**26854**
B-2909	**B737**	**26082**
B-2910	**B737**	**26083**
B-2911	**B737**	**26084**
B-2912	**B737**	**26100**
B-2913	**B737**	**26101**
B-2918	**B737**	**24986**
B-2919	**B737**	**24987**
B-2920	**B737**	**27271**
B-2921	**B737**	**27286**
B-2922	**B737**	**27272**
B-2923	**B737**	**27275**
B-2924	**B737**	**27287**
B-2925	**B737**	**27288**
B-2926	**B737**	**27289**
B-2927	**B737**	**27290**
B-2928	**B737**	**26294**
B-2929	**B737**	**27343**
B-2930	**B737**	**27273**
B-2931	**B737**	**27276**
B-2932	**B737**	**25787**
B-2933	**B737**	**25788**
B-2934	**B737**	**27274**
B-2935	**B737**	**27283**
B-2936	**B737**	**27335**
B-2937	**B737**	**26295**
B-2938	**B737**	**26296**
B-2939	**B737**	**27345**
B-2940	**B737**	**27346**
B-2941	**B737**	**27344**
B-2942	**B737**	**25997**
B-2943	**B737**	**25998**
B-2945	**B737**	**27362**
B-2946	**B737**	**27375**
B-2947	**B737**	**25511**
B-2948	**B737**	**27361**
B-2949	**B737**	**27372**
B-2950	**B737**	**27374**
B-2951	**B737**	**27373**
B-2952	**B737**	**27519**
B-2953	**B737**	**27523**
B-2954	**B737**	**27518**
B-2955	**B737**	**27453**
B-2956	**B737**	**27907**
B-2957	**B737**	**27521**
B-2958	**B737**	**27522**

B-2959	**B737**	**27520**
B-2960	**B737**	**24332**
B-2961	**B737**	**28156**
B-2962	**B737**	**28157**
B-2963	**B737**	**26325**
B-2966	**B737**	**27462**
B-2968	**B737**	**28158**
B-4001	**TU154**	**711**
B-4002	TU154	712
B-4003	**TU154**	**713**
B-4004	**TU154**	**714**
B-4008	**B737**	**23839**
B-4009	**B737**	**23840**
B-4014	**TU154**	**847**
B-4015	**TU154**	**856**
B-4016	**TU154**	**872**
B-4017	**TU154**	**873**
B-4018	**B737**	**25502**
B-4019	**B737**	**25503**
B-4020	**B737**	**28081**
B-4021	**B737**	**28082**
B-4022	**TU154**	**765**
B-4023	**TU154**	**770**
B-4024	**TU154**	**789**
B-4028	**TU154**	**967**
B-4029	**TU154**	**950**
B-4030	**IL-76**	**1013408288**
B-4031	**IL-76**	**1013409284**
B-4032	**IL-76**	**1013409289**
B-4138	**TU154**	**712**
(B-11150)	F-100	11290
(B-11152)	F-100	11296
B-12001	B737	20127
B-12291	**F-100**	**11500**
B-12292	**F-100**	**11496**
B-16101	**MD-11**	**48542**
B-16102	**MD-11**	**48543**
(B-16105)	MD-11	48544
B-16106	**MD-11**	**48545**
B-16107	**MD-11**	**48546**
B-16401	**B747**	**27062**
B-16402	**B747**	**27063**
(B-16403)	B747	26059
(B-16403)	B747	27141
(B-16405)	B747	26060
(B-16405)	B747	27142
B-16461	**B747**	**27154**
B-16462	**B747**	**27173**
B-16463	**B747**	**27174**
B-16465	**B747**	**26062**
B-16601	B767	25076
B-16602	B767	25117
B-16603	**B767**	**26063**
B-16605	**B767**	**26064**
(B-16606)	B767	27192
(B-16607)	B767	27193
(B-16608)	B767	27194
(B-16609)	B767	27195
B-16621	**B767**	**27192**
B-16622	**B767**	**27193**
B-16623	**B767**	**27194**
B-16625	**B767**	**27195**
B-16688	**B767**	**25221**
B-16801	**B747**	**27965**
B-17501	**B757**	**25133**
B-22301	**A320**	**0332**
B-22302	**A320**	**0369**
B-22305	**A320**	**0478**
B-22306	**A320**	**0347**
B-22307	**A320**	**0441**
B-22308	**A320**	**0344**
B-22601	**A321**	**0538**
B-22602	**A321**	**0555**
B-27005	**B757**	**27203**
B-27007	**B757**	**27204**
B-28001	**MD-82**	**53064**
B-28003	**MD-82**	**53065**
B-28005	**MD-82**	**53066**
B-28007	**MD-83**	**49807**
B-28011	**MD-82**	**53118**
B-28013	**MD-82**	**53119**
B-28015	**MD-82**	**53168**
B-28017	**MD-82**	**53166**
B-28023	**MD-83**	**49952**
B-88888	**MD-82**	**53479**
B-88889	**MD-82**	**53480**

Canada

C-	**A320**	**0247**
C-	**A320**	**0579**
C-	RJ100	7081
C-	RJ100	7085
C-	RJ100	7086
C-	RJ100	7087
C-	RJ100	7090
C-	RJ100	7091
C-	RJ100	7092
C-	RJ100	7093
C-	RJ100	7094
C-	RJ100	7095
C-	RJ100	7096
C-	RJ100	7097
C-	RJ100	7098
C-	RJ100	7101
C-	RJ100	7102
C-	RJ100	7103
C-	RJ100	7104
C-	RJ100	7105
C-	RJ100	7110
C-	RJ100	7113
C-	RJ100	7114
C-	RJ100	7119
C-	RJ100	7133
C-	RJ100	7142
(C-)	B727	19319
(C-)	B737	23808
(C-)	B747	20527
C-FACP	**B737**	**22072**
C-FACX	**B727**	**19500**
C-FAIF	F-28	11032
C-FBAB	**146**	**E2090**
C-FBAE	**146**	**E2092**
C-FBAF	**146**	**E2096**
C-FBAO	**146**	**E2111**
C-FBAV	**146**	**E2121**
C-FBCA	**B747**	**25422**
(C-FBCA)	B747	24896
C-FBEF	**B767**	**24323**
C-FBEG	**B767**	**24324**
C-FBEM	**B767**	**24325**
C-FBKT	DC-9	47186
C-FBWX	**B727**	**18286**
C-FBWY	**B727**	**19085**
C-FCAB	**B767**	**24082**
C-FCAE	**B767**	**24083**
C-FCAF	**B767**	**24084**
C-FCAG	**B767**	**24085**
C-FCAJ	**B767**	**24086**
C-FCAU	**B767**	**24087**
C-FCAV	B737	22906
C-FCMV	DC-8	46038
C-FCPB	B737	19884
C-FCPC	B737	19885
C-FCPD	B737	19886
C-FCPE	B737	19887
C-FCPF	DC-8	45620
C-FCPG	B737	23173
C-FCPG	DC-8	45623
C-FCPH	DC-8	45621
C-FCPI	B737	23174
C-FCPI	**DC-8**	**45622**
C-FCPJ	B737	23175
C-FCPJ	**DC-8**	**45661**
C-FCPK	B737	23176
C-FCPL	B737	23177
C-FCPL	DC-8	46095
C-FCPM	**B737**	**22761**
C-FCPM	DC-8	45809
(C-FCPM)	B737	23462
C-FCPN	**B737**	**22762**
(C-FCPN)	B737	23463
C-FCPO	DC-8	45926
C-FCPP	DC-8	45927
C-FCPQ	DC-8	45928
C-FCPS	DC-8	45929
C-FCPU	B737	19888
C-FCPV	B737	20196
C-FCPZ	B737	20197
C-FCRA	B747	20801
C-FCRA	**B747**	**24895**
C-FCRA	DC-10	46931
C-FCRB	B747	20802
C-FCRB	DC-10	46940

C-FCRD	B747	20927
C-FCRD	**DC-10**	**47889**
C-FCRE	B747	20929
C-FCRE	**DC-10**	**47868**
C-FCRI	**F-28**	**11043**
C-FCRJ	RJ100	7001
C-FCRK	**F-28**	**11087**
C-FCRM	**F-28**	**11035**
C-FCRN	DC-8	45752
C-FCRP	**F-28**	**11037**
C-FCRU	**F-28**	**11032**
C-FCRW	**F-28**	**11029**
C-FCRZ	**F-28**	**11061**
C-FCWW	DC-8	45762
C-FCXB	L1011	1083
C-FCXJ	L1011	1102
C-FDCA	**A320**	**0232**
C-FDJC	B747	20208
C-FDQQ	**A320**	**0059**
C-FDQV	**A320**	**0068**
C-FDRH	**A320**	**0073**
C-FDRK	**A320**	**0084**
C-FDRP	**A320**	**0122**
C-FDSN	**A320**	**0126**
C-FDST	**A320**	**0127**
C-FDSU	**A320**	**0141**
C-FDWW	DC-8	45856
C-FEPL	B737	20396
C-FEPO	B737	20300
C-FEPP	B737	20681
C-FEPR	B737	20397
C-FEPU	B737	20776
C-FETB	**B720**	**18024**
C-FEXN	146	E2020
C-FFAN	B707	19789
C-FFDK	DC-8	45854
(C-FFQI)	DC-8	45855
C-FFRZ	DC-8	45685
C-FFSB	DC-8	45935
C-FFUN	B747	20305
C-FFWI	**A320**	**0149**
C-FFWJ	**A320**	**0150**
C-FFWM	**A320**	**0154**
C-FFWN	**A320**	**0159**
C-FGHQ	B737	23811
C-FGHT	B737	24059
C-FGHZ	**B747**	**27827**
C-FGWD	A310	438
C-FGYL	**A320**	**0254**
C-FGYS	**A320**	**0255**
C-FHAA	DC-8	45961
C-FHAB	DC-8	45658
C-FHAV	**146**	**E2012**
C-FHAX	**146**	**E2014**
C-FHAZ	**146**	**E2016**
C-FHCP	**B737**	**22024**
C-FHFP	**F-28**	**11016**
C-FHNX	146	E2066
C-FHWD	A310	441
C-FICB	F-100	11248
C-FICL	F-100	11263
C-FICO	F-100	11249
C-FICP	B737	22025
C-FICP	F-100	11259
C-FICQ	F-100	11260
C-FICW	F-100	11247
C-FICY	F-100	11246
C-FIFA	**B727**	**20381**
C-FIWW	DC-8	45820
C-FJLT	**B737**	**20206**
C-FJRI	**F-28**	**11103**
C-FKAJ	**A320**	**0333**
C-FKCK	**A320**	**0265**
C-FKCO	**A320**	**0277**
C-FKCR	**A320**	**0290**
C-FKOJ	**A320**	**0330**
C-FKPO	**A320**	**0311**
C-FKPS	**A320**	**0310**
C-FKPT	**A320**	**0324**
C-FLSF	A320	0279
C-FLSI	**A320**	**0283**
C-FLSS	**A320**	**0284**
C-FLSU	**A320**	**0309**
C-FMEQ	**A320**	**0302**
C-FMES	**A320**	**0305**
C-FMJK	**A320**	**0342**
C-FMKV	RJ100	7007
C-FMKV	RJ100	7008
C-FMKV	RJ100	7039
C-FMKV	RJ100	7069
C-FMKW	RJ100	7009
C-FMKW	RJ100	7040
C-FMKW	RJ100	7070
C-FMKZ	RJ100	7011
C-FMKZ	RJ100	7041
C-FMKZ	RJ100	7071
C-FMLA	RJ100	7012
C-FMLB	RJ100	7042
C-FMLB	RJ100	7072
C-FMLF	RJ100	7013
C-FMLF	RJ100	7043
C-FMLF	RJ100	7073
C-FMLI	RJ100	7014
C-FMLI	RJ100	7044
C-FMLI	RJ100	7074
C-FMLQ	RJ100	7013
C-FMLQ	RJ100	7015
C-FMLQ	RJ100	7045
C-FMLQ	RJ100	7075
C-FMLS	RJ100	7016
C-FMLS	RJ100	7046
C-FMLS	RJ100	7076
C-FMLT	RJ100	7017
C-FMLT	RJ100	7047
C-FMLT	RJ100	7077
C-FMLU	RJ100	7018
C-FMLU	RJ100	7048
C-FMLU	RJ100	7078
C-FMLU	RJ100	7088
C-FMLV	RJ100	7019
C-FMLV	RJ100	7049
C-FMLV	RJ100	7079
C-FMMB	RJ100	7020
C-FMMB	RJ100	7050
C-FMMB	RJ100	7080
C-FMML	RJ100	7021
C-FMML	RJ100	7051
C-FMMN	RJ100	7022
C-FMMN	RJ100	7052
C-FMMQ	RJ100	7023
C-FMMQ	RJ100	7053
C-FMMT	RJ100	7024
C-FMMT	RJ100	7054
C-FMMT	RJ100	7084
C-FMMW	RJ100	7025
C-FMMW	RJ100	7055
C-FMMX	RJ100	7026
C-FMMX	RJ100	7056
C-FMMY	RJ100	7027
C-FMMY	RJ100	7057
C-FMNB	RJ100	7028
C-FMND	RJ100	7029
C-FMNH	RJ100	7030
C-FMNQ	RJ100	7031
C-FMNQ	RJ100	7061
C-FMNQ	RJ100	7083
C-FMNW	RJ100	7032
C-FMNW	RJ100	7062
C-FMNX	RJ100	7033
C-FMNX	RJ100	7064
C-FMNY	RJ100	7034
C-FMNY	RJ100	7063
C-FMOI	RJ100	7035
C-FMOI	RJ100	7065
C-FMOL	RJ100	7036
C-FMOL	RJ100	7066
C-FMOS	RJ100	7037
C-FMOS	RJ100	7067
C-FMOW	RJ100	7038
C-FMOW	RJ100	7068
C-FMST	**A320**	**0350**
C-FMSV	**A320**	**0359**
C-FMSX	**A320**	**0378**
C-FMSY	**A320**	**0384**
C-FMWP	**B767**	**25583**
C-FMWQ	**B767**	**25584**
C-FMWU	**B767**	**25585**
C-FMWV	**B767**	**25586**
C-FMWY	**B767**	**25587**
C-FMXC	**B767**	**25588**
(C-FNAA)	DC-8	45902
C-FNAB	B737	19847
C-FNAH	B737	19848
C-FNAP	**B737**	**20496**
C-FNAQ	**B737**	**20455**
C-FNAW	B737	20521
C-FNBC	B757	24260
C-FNNA	**A320**	**0426**
C-FNRJ	**RJ100**	**7002**
C-FNVT	**B737**	**21011**
(C-FNVT)	A320	0397
C-FNVU	**A320**	**0403**
C-FNVV	**A320**	**0404**
C-FNWD	A310	444
C-FNXA	B747	20493
C-FNXP	B747	21162
C-FNXY	B757	25593
C-FNZE	DC-8	45985
C-FOAA	B757	23767
C-FOCA	**B767**	**24575**
C-FONF	F-28	11060
C-FONG	F-28	11070
C-FOOA	B757	23767
C-FOOB	**B757**	**23822**
C-FOOE	**B757**	**24369**
C-FOOG	**B757**	**24292**
C-FOOH	**B757**	**24293**
C-FPCA	**B767**	**24306**
C-FPDN	**A320**	**0341**
C-FPWB	B737	20785
C-FPWC	B737	20142
C-FPWD	**A320**	**0231**
C-FPWD	B737	19742
C-FPWD	B737	22761
C-FPWD	B737	23495
C-FPWE	**A320**	**0175**
C-FPWE	B737	19743
C-FPWE	B737	22762
C-FPWE	B737	23497
C-FPWJ	B707	18746
C-FPWM	B737	19921
C-FPWP	B737	20588
C-FPWV	B707	17696
C-FPWW	B737	20670
C-FPXB	B727	19174
C-FPXD	**B727**	**19859**
C-FQBN	1-11	BAC.110
C-FQBO	1-11	BAC.112
C-FQBR	1-11	094
C-FQPL	DC-8	45974
C-FQPM	DC-8	45941
C-FRIA	**RJ100**	**7045**
C-FRIB	**RJ100**	**7047**
C-FRID	**RJ100**	**7049**
C-FRIL	**RJ100**	**7051**
(C-FRIX)	L1011	1154
C-FRKQ	RJ100	7032
C-FRSA	RJ100	7033
C-FRST	**B727**	**19169**
C-FRYS	**B727**	**21349**
C-FSJF	**RJ100**	**7054**
C-FSJJ	**RJ100**	**7058**
(C-FSJJ)	RJ100	7057
C-FSJU	**RJ100**	**7060**
(C-FSJU)	RJ100	7058
C-FSKE	**RJ100**	**7065**
(C-FSKE)	RJ100	7064
C-FSKI	**RJ100**	**7068**
(C-FSKI)	RJ100	7067
C-FSKM	**RJ100**	**7071**
(C-FSKM)	RJ100	7068
C-FSWD	A310	418
C-FTAN	B737	20206
C-FTAO	B737	20205
C-FTAS	**F-28**	**11098**
C-FTAV	F-28	11033
C-FTAV	**F-28**	**11106**
C-FTAY	F-28	11038
C-FTCA	**B767**	**24307**
C-FTDU	**A320**	**0379**
C-FTDW	**A320**	**0389**
C-FTIH	DC-8	45933
C-FTII	DC-8	45934
C-FTIK	DC-8	46033
C-FTIL	DC-8	46034
C-FTIM	DC-8	46035
C-FTIN	DC-8	46036
C-FTIO	DC-8	46076
C-FTIP	DC-8	46100
C-FTIQ	DC-8	46123
C-FTIR	DC-8	46124
C-FTIS	DC-8	46125
C-FTIU	DC-8	46113
C-FTIV	DC-8	46126
C-FTIX	DC-8	46115
C-FTJJ	DC-8	45612
C-FTJL	DC-8	45640
C-FTJO	**A320**	**0183**
C-FTJO	DC-8	45655
C-FTJP	**A320**	**0233**
C-FTJP	DC-8	45679
C-FTJQ	**A320**	**0242**
C-FTJQ	DC-8	45686
C-FTJR	**A320**	**0248**
C-FTJR	DC-8	45860
C-FTJS	**A320**	**0253**
C-FTJS	DC-8	45861
C-FTJT	DC-8	45890
C-FTJU	DC-8	45891
C-FTJV	DC-8	45892
C-FTJW	DC-8	45893
C-FTJX	DC-8	45963
C-FTJY	DC-8	45964
C-FTJZ	DC-8	45980
C-FTLH	**DC-9**	**45845**
C-FTLI	DC-9	45846
C-FTLJ	**DC-9**	**47019**
C-FTLK	DC-9	47020
C-FTLL	**DC-9**	**47021**
C-FTLM	**DC-9**	**47022**
C-FTLN	DC-9	47023
C-FTLO	**DC-9**	**47024**
C-FTLP	DC-9	47068
C-FTLQ	**DC-9**	**47069**
C-FTLR	**DC-9**	**47070**
C-FTLS	**DC-9**	**47071**
C-FTLT	**DC-9**	**47195**
C-FTLU	DC-9	47196
C-FTLW	**DC-9**	**47198**
C-FTLX	**DC-9**	**47199**
C-FTLY	DC-9	47200
C-FTLZ	**DC-9**	**47265**
C-FTMA	**DC-9**	**47266**
C-FTMB	**DC-9**	**47289**
C-FTMC	**DC-9**	**47290**
C-FTMD	**DC-9**	**47292**
C-FTME	**DC-9**	**47293**
C-FTMF	**DC-9**	**47294**
C-FTMG	**DC-9**	**47340**
C-FTMH	**DC-9**	**47341**
C-FTMI	**DC-9**	**47342**
C-FTMJ	**DC-9**	**47348**
C-FTMK	**DC-9**	**47349**
C-FTML	**DC-9**	**47350**
C-FTMM	**DC-9**	**47611**
C-FTMO	**DC-9**	**47353**
C-FTMP	**DC-9**	**47354**
C-FTMQ	**DC-9**	**47422**
C-FTMR	DC-9	47423
C-FTMS	DC-9	47424
C-FTMT	**DC-9**	**47546**
C-FTMU	**DC-9**	**47554**
C-FTMV	**DC-9**	**47557**
C-FTMW	**DC-9**	**47560**
C-FTMX	**DC-9**	**47485**
C-FTMY	**DC-9**	**47592**
C-FTMZ	**DC-9**	**47598**
C-FTNA	**L1011**	**1019**
C-FTNB	**L1011**	**1010**
C-FTNB	L1011	1021
C-FTNC	**L1011**	**1023**
C-FTND	**L1011**	**1025**
C-FTNE	L1011	1027
C-FTNF	**L1011**	**1047**
C-FTNG	**L1011**	**1048**
C-FTNH	**L1011**	**1049**
C-FTNI	**L1011**	**1058**
C-FTNJ	L1011	1067
C-FTNK	**L1011**	**1069**
C-FTNL	L1011	1073
C-FTNP	**A340**	**093**
C-FTNQ	**A340**	**088**
C-FTOA	B747	20013
C-FTOB	B747	20014

C-FTOC B747 20015
C-FTOD B747 20767
C-FTOE B747 20881
(C-FTOF) B747 20977
C-FTOR DC-9 47013
C-FTOT DC-9 47015
C-FTOU DC-9 47152
C-FUCL B767 22682
(C-FUCN) B767 22681
C-FUFA B727 20941
C-FVHC B737 20588
C-FVHG B737 20670
C-FVKM RJ100 7074
C-FVKN RJ100 7078
C-FVKR RJ100 7083
C-FVMD RJ100 7082
C-FVNC B737 24344
C-FVND B737 24545
(C-FVNF) B737 24682
C-FVNM B767 22681
C-FWCR L1011 1099
C-FWDX A310 425
C-FWJB RJ100 7087
C-FWJF RJ100 7095
C-FWJI RJ100 7096
C-FWJS RJ100 7097
C-FWJT RJ100 7098
C-FWOQ A320 0437
C-FWOR A320 0467
C-FWRN RJ100 7089
C-FWXI B720 18021
C-FWXL B720 18027
C-FXCA B767 24574
C-FXCA B767 25864
C-FXCE B747 21316
C-FXFB RJ100 7100
C-FXOC B757 24017
C-FXOD B757 24235
C-FXOF B757 24544
C-FXOK B757 24924
C-FXOO B757 25621
C-FXOO B757 26521
C-FXTA F-28 11064
(C-FZWD) A310 502
C-FZYP C-137 20043
(C-G   ) B727 20476
C-GAAA B727 20932
C-GAAB B727 20933
C-GAAC B727 20934
C-GAAD B727 20935
C-GAAD B727 20937
C-GAAE B727 20936
C-GAAF B727 20937
C-GAAG B727 20938
C-GAAH B727 20939
C-GAAI B727 20940
C-GAAJ B727 20941
C-GAAK B727 20942
C-GAAL B727 21100
C-GAAM B727 21101
C-GAAN B727 21102
C-GAAO B727 21624
C-GAAP B727 21625
C-GAAQ B727 21626
C-GAAR B727 21671
C-GAAS B727 21672
C-GAAT B727 21673
C-GAAU B727 21674
C-GAAV B727 21675
C-GAAW B727 22035
C-GAAX B727 22036
C-GAAY B727 22037
C-GAAZ B727 22038
(C-GABE) B727 22345
(C-GABF) B727 22346
(C-GABG) B727 22347
(C-GABH) B727 22348
(C-GABI) B727 22349
(C-GABJ) B727 22350
C-GACU B727 20152
C-GAGA B747 20977
C-GAGB B747 21627
C-GAGC B747 21354
C-GAGF L1011 1202
C-GAGG L1011 1206
C-GAGH L1011 1207
C-GAGI L1011 1209
C-GAGJ L1011 1216
C-GAGK L1011 1218
C-GAGL B747 24998
C-GAGM B747 25074
C-GAGN B747 25075
C-GAGX B727 19191
C-GAGY B727 19192
C-GAGZ B727 19195
C-GANX B757 22176
C-GAPW B737 20922
C-GAUB B767 22517
C-GAUE B767 22518
C-GAUH B767 22519
C-GAUN B767 22520
C-GAUP B767 22521
C-GAUS B767 22522
C-GAUU B767 22523
C-GAUW B767 22524
C-GAUY B767 22525
C-GAVA B767 22526
C-GAVC B767 22527
C-GAVF B767 22528
C-GAWB B757 24367
C-GBPW B737 20958
C-GBQS B737 21231
(C-GBQU) B737 22276
C-GBWD A310 446
C-GBWO DC-9 47639
C-GBWS B727 18867
C-GCAU B737 22640
(C-GCAW) B767 25865
C-GCDG B737 20776
C-GCIH B747 21162
C-GCIL A310 439
C-GCIO A310 449
C-GCIT A310 455
C-GCIV A310 451
C-GCPA B727 21055
C-GCPB B727 21056
C-GCPC DC-10 46540
C-GCPD DC-10 46541
C-GCPE DC-10 46542
C-GCPF DC-10 46543
C-GCPG DC-10 48285
C-GCPH DC-10 48288
C-GCPI DC-10 48296
C-GCPJ DC-10 46991
C-GCPM B737 21716
C-GCPN B737 21717
C-GCPO B737 21718
C-GCPP B737 22255
C-GCPQ B737 22256
(C-GCPR) B737 22257
C-GCPS B737 22257
(C-GCPS) B737 22258
C-GCPT B737 22258
C-GCPU B737 22259
C-GCPV B737 22260
C-GCPW B737 20959
C-GCPX B737 22341
C-GCPY B737 22342
C-GCPZ B737 22658
C-GCWD A310 447
C-GCWW B727 22439
C-GDCC B737 20681
C-GDPA B737 22056
(C-GDPG) B737 22793
C-GDPW B737 21116
C-GDSP B767 24142
C-GDSS B767 24143
C-GDSU B767 24144
C-GDSY B767 24145
C-GDWD A310 448
C-GEMV DC-8 46032
C-GENL B737 22148
C-GEPA B737 20976
C-GEPB B737 21112
C-GEPM B737 22395
C-GEPW B737 21115
C-GFCP B737 22659
C-GFHX DC-10 46990
C-GFLG B707 19416
C-GFPW B737 21294
C-GFRB B727 19120
C-GGAB B707 19629
C-GGPW B737 21639
C-GIES L1011 1064
C-GIFE L1011 1079
C-GIPW B737 21712
C-GIWD A310 472
C-GIZJ A300 138
C-GIZL A300 192
C-GIZN A300 212
C-GJCP B737 22728
C-GJLN B737 19594
C-GJPW B737 21713
C-GJWD A310 475
C-GKCP B737 22729
C-GKFA B727 19806
C-GKFB B727 19358
C-GKFC B727 18897
C-GKFN B727 19359
C-GKFP B727 19205
C-GKFT B727 19807
C-GKFV B727 19173
C-GKFW B727 19805
C-GKFZ B727 19204
C-GKMV MD-83 49793
C-GKPW B737 21819
C-GKWD A310 481
C-GLCA B767 25120
C-GLPW B737 22086
(C-GLUS) B747 20014
C-GLWD A310 482
C-GMCP B737 22864
C-GMPG A320 0428
C-GMPW B737 22087
C-GMWW B747 24883
C-GMXB DC-8 45943
C-GMXD DC-8 45912
C-GMXL DC-8 45981
C-GMXP DC-8 45804
C-GMXQ DC-8 45982
C-GMXR DC-8 45925
C-GMXY DC-8 45920
C-GNDA DC-8 45902
C-GNDC B737 21728
C-GNDD B737 21112
C-GNDE DC-8 45618
C-GNDF DC-8 45619
C-GNDG B737 21719
C-GNDG B737 22054
C-GNDL B737 21186
C-GNDM B737 22074
C-GNDR B737 22075
C-GNDS B737 21518
(C-GNDS) B737 20345
C-GNDU B737 22877
C-GNDW B737 21694
C-GNDX B737 20911
C-GNPW B737 22159
C-GNVX 146 E1010
C-GNVY 146 E1011
C-GNWD B737 19743
C-GNWI B737 21066
C-GNWM B737 21067
C-GNXB B757 24772
C-GNXC B757 24260
C-GNXH B747 20402
C-GNXI B757 24367
C-GNXN B757 22206
C-GNXU B757 24543
C-GOFA B727 18815
C-GOPW B737 22160
C-GPPW B737 22264
C-GPWA B767 22683
C-GPWB B767 22684
C-GPWC B737 22416
(C-GPWC) B767 22685
(C-GPWD) A310 504
(C-GPWD) B767 22686
C-GPWG A320 0174
C-GPWG B737 23498
C-GQBA B737 22072
C-GQBA DC-8 46155
C-GQBB B737 22276
C-GQBC B737 19426
C-GQBD B737 19594
C-GQBE B727 18970
(C-GQBE) B737 22398
C-GQBF DC-8 46116
C-GQBG B707 17647
C-GQBG DC-8 45860
C-GQBH B707 17650
C-GQBH B737 22516
C-GQBJ B737 22277
C-GQBP 1-11 BAC.122
C-GQBQ B737 22070
C-GQBR F-28 11012
C-GQBS B737 21231
C-GQBS F-28 11013
C-GQBT B737 21719
C-GQBV 1-11 BAC.123
(C-GQBV) B737 22277
C-GQCA A320 0210
C-GQCA B737 22415
C-GQCP B737 22865
C-GQDT B737 21719
C-GQPW B737 22265
C-GRCP B737 21397
C-GRJJ RJ100 7004
C-GRJN RJ100 7005
C-GRJO RJ100 7006
C-GRJW RJ100 7010
C-GRMU B727 21055
C-GRNT 146 E2140
C-GRNU 146 E2139
C-GRNV 146 E2133
C-GRNX 146 E2130
C-GRNY 146 E2115
C-GRNZ 146 E2106
C-GRPW B737 22266
(C-GRWW) DC-8 45820
C-GRYC B727 21055
C-GRYN B707 19623
C-GRYO B707 18746
C-GRYO B727 20710
C-GRYP B727 20766
C-GRYQ B727 22574
C-GRYR B727 21056
C-GRYU L1011 1221
C-GRYY A320 0189
C-GRYZ B727 20550
C-GSCA B767 25121
C-GSPW B737 22618
C-GSWQ DC-8 45387
C-GSWX DC-8 45388
C-GTAH F-28 11082
C-GTAI B707 19434
C-GTAJ B737 24344
C-GTAQ B737 20956
C-GTAR B737 20223
C-GTDC A320 0496
C-GTDL B757 24543
C-GTEO F-28 11991
C-GTPW B737 22807
(C-GTPW) B737 22619
C-GTSE B757 25488
C-GTSF B757 25491
C-GTSJ B757 24772
C-GTSK B757 24367
C-GTSN B757 24543
C-GTSV B757 24260
C-GTSX L1011 1094
C-GTSZ L1011 1103
C-GTUU F-28 11006
C-GUPW B737 22873
C-GVCH B727 18853
C-GVFA B727 20475
C-GVNY A320 0279
C-GVPW B737 22874
C-GVRD B737 20956
C-GVRE B737 22396
C-GVRJ RJ100 7003
C-GVXA A320 0397
C-GVXB A320 0409
C-GVXC A320 0427
C-GWGP B727 19404
C-GWGT B727 19405
C-GWGV B727 19406
C-GWJE B737 20588
C-GWJG B737 20670
C-GWJK B737 19743
C-GWPW B737 23283
(C-GWPW) B737 22056
C-GXCP B737 22640
C-GXPW B737 20521

C-GXRA	B747	21516
C-GXRB	DC-10	46976
C-GXRC	DC-10	46978
C-GXRD	B747	21517
C-GYNA	B727	22039
C-GYNB	B727	22040
C-GYNC	B727	22041
C-GYND	B727	22042
C-GYNE	B727	22345
C-GYNF	B727	22346
C-GYNG	B727	22347
C-GYNH	B727	22348
C-GYNI	B727	22349
C-GYNJ	B727	22350
C-GYNK	B727	22621
C-GYNL	B727	22622
C-GYNM	B727	22623
(C-GYPW)	B737	23707
(C-GZPW)	B737	23708

Chile

CC-	**B737**	**19945**
(CC-)	B727	20217
(CC-)	B767	24948
CC-BIN	B737	22703
CC-CAF	B707	19435
CC-CAG	**B727**	**19811**
CC-CAN	B727	19527
CC-CAQ	B727	19812
CC-CAR	**DC-8**	**45976**
CC-CAX	**DC-8**	**45970**
CC-CCE	B707	18748
CC-CCG	B707	18462
CC-CCK	B707	19443
CC-CCO	CRVL	140
CC-CCP	CRVL	164
CC-CCQ	CRVL	160
CC-CCW	B727	21068
CC-CCX	B707	18584
CC-CDE	**B737**	**22744**
CC-CDG	**B737**	**23024**
CC-CDH	**B767**	**24716**
CC-CDI	B707	19517
CC-CDJ	**B767**	**24762**
CC-CDL	B767	24947
CC-CDM	**B767**	**26261**
CC-CDN	B707	18747
CC-CDP	**B767**	**27597**
CC-CDS	**DC-8**	**45996**
CC-CDU	**DC-8**	**45997**
CC-CEA	B707	18926
CC-CEA	**B737**	**22743**
CC-CEB	B707	19000
CC-CEE	**B737**	**22407**
CC-CEF	B767	24973
CC-CEI	B707	20021
CC-CEI	**B737**	**20219**
CC-CEJ	**146**	**E2059**
CC-CEJ	B707	19693
CC-CEK	B707	19374
CC-CEN	**146**	**E2064**
CC-CER	B707	18711
CC-CET	146	E2061
CC-CEU	**B767**	**25403**
CC-CEX	B767	24716
CC-CEY	B767	24762
CC-CEY	**B767**	**24947**
CC-CFD	B727	19813
CC-CFE	B727	19814
CC-CFG	B727	18796
CC-CGD	B727	19532
CC-CGM	B707	17928
CC-CHC	**B727**	**19251**
CC-CHJ	B737	22602
CC-CHK	B737	22589
CC-CHR	**B737**	**21792**
CC-CHS	**B737**	**21802**
CC-CHU	B737	21927
CC-CIM	B737	22340
CC-CIW	B727	18323
CC-CIY	B737	22792
CC-CJK	B737	22856
CC-CJM	B737	22857
CC-CJN	DC-10	46712
CC-CJS	DC-10	46954
CC-CJT	DC-10	46950
CC-CJU	B767	23623
CC-CJV	B767	23624
CC-CJW	**B737**	**22397**
CC-CJZ	B737	20913
CC-CLB	B727	19196
CC-CLD	**B737**	**21960**
(CC-CLE)	B737	19606
CC-CLF	B737	19609
CC-CLZ	**B727**	**18445**
CC-CRI	B737	19616
CC-CSD	**B737**	**20417**
CC-CSH	**B737**	**20632**
CC-CSI	**B737**	**20633**
CC-CSL	**B737**	**20223**
CC-CUE	B707	20069
CC-CYA	B707	19530
CC-CYB	B707	20022
CC-CYC	**B737**	**21131**
CC-CYD	**B737**	**21219**
CC-CYE	B737	23787
CC-CYF	**1-11**	**033**
CC-CYG	**B757**	**25044**
CC-CYH	**B757**	**25131**
CC-CYI	**1-11**	**035**
CC-CYJ	**B737**	**25373**
CC-CYK	**B737**	**21445**
(CC-CYK)	B737	26293
CC-CYL	**1-11**	**040**
CC-CYM	**1-11**	**039**
CC-CYN	**B737**	**21231**
CC-CYO	B707	19374
CC-CYP	**B737**	**22632**
CC-CYQ	**DC-8**	**45810**
CC-CYR	**B737**	**20195**
CC-CYS	**B737**	**21184**
CC-CYT	**B737**	**21112**
CC-CYV	**B737**	**23148**
CC-CYW	**B737**	**20913**

Russia

06207	IL-76	
42317	YAK42	4520422202039
42319	YAK42	4520423402062
42331	YAK42	452042..051..
42342	**YAK42**	**4520421706302**
65003	TU134	44040
65014	**TU134**	**46200**
65030	**TU134**	
65044	**TU134**	**49450**
65075	**TU134**	**49998**
65077	TU134	60028
65094	TU134	60255
65134	TU134	60647
65145	TU134	60985
65556	TU134	66372
65613	TU134	3352106
65702	TU134	63375
65705	TU134	63415
65708	TU134	63447
65709	TU134	63484
65711	TU134	63498
65713	TU134	63520
65714	TU134	63527
65750	TU134	61042
65767	TU134	
65774	TU134	62519
65798	TU134	63179
65809	TU134	3352110
65832	TU134	17106
65854	TU134	23248
65893	TU134	40120
65905	TU134	63965
65911	TU134	63972
65932	TU134	66405
65985	TU134	
72907	**AN-72**	
72966	AN-72	
76353	IL-76	1023414454
76371	IL-76	1033414485
76436	IL-76	1023411368
76438	IL-76	0083483513
76441	IL-76	
76447	IL-76	1023412389
76448	IL-76	1023413443
76449	IL-76	1003403058
76458	IL-76	
76463	IL-76	0013432960
76485	IL-76	0063470088
76602	IL-76	0043454611
76653	**IL-76**	
76675	**IL-76**	
76689	**IL-76**	
76708	IL-76	0063473171
76748	IL-76	
76793	IL-76	0093498951
76794	IL-76	0093498954
76805	IL-76	1003403105
76811	IL-76	1013407223
76813	IL-76	1013408246
76818	IL-76	1013408264
76819	IL-76	1013409274
76824	IL-76	1023410327
76836	IL-76	1013409305
76837	IL-76	1023409316
(82026)	AN124	19530502..7?
85092	TU154	092
85104	TU154	104
85147	TU154	147
85158	TU154	158
85163	TU154	163
85168	TU154	168
85177	TU154	177
85188	TU154	188
85192	TU154	192
85199	TU154	199
85249	TU154	249
85274	TU154	274
85285	TU154	285
85294	TU154	294
85313	TU154	313
85322	TU154	322
85329	TU154	329
85345	TU154	345
85359	TU154	359
85370	TU154	370
85391	TU154	391
85393	TU154	393
85394	TU154	394
85397	TU154	397
85398	TU154	398
85401	TU154	401
85430	TU154	430
85438	TU154	438
85464	TU154	464
85465	TU154	465
85492	TU154	492
85496	TU154	496
85507	TU154	507
85518	TU154	518
85532	TU154	533
85537	TU154	537
85548	TU154	548
85549	TU154	549
85551	TU154	551
85561	TU154	561
85575	TU154	575
85578	TU154	578
85600	TU154	600
85624	TU154	750
85651	TU154	793
85653	TU154	795
85666	TU154	820
85675	TU154	835
85686	TU154	854
85698	TU154	871
85700	TU154	875
85701	TU154	876
85708	TU154	883
85715	TU154	891
85734	TU154	916
85736	TU154	918
85749	TU154	931
85761	TU154	944
85766	TU154	948?
85782	TU154	966
85787	TU154	971
85790	TU154	974
85792	TU154	976

85793 TU154 977
85802 TU154 961
86011 IL-86 51483200009
86012 IL-86 51483202010
86016 IL-86 51483202014
86056 IL-86 51483203023
86072 IL-86 51483204039
86083 IL-86 51483206054
86090 IL-86 51483207061
86142 IL-86 514832.....
86468 IL-62 4749857
86527 IL-62 4037758
86540 IL-62 3546548
86554 IL-62 4053514
86573 IL-62 4140536
86574 IL-62 3344033
86575 IL-62 1647928
86576 IL-62 4546257
86577 IL-62 2748552
86578 IL-62 1951525
86579 IL-62 2951636
86659 IL-62 31404
86711 IL-62 4648414
86712 IL-62 4648339
87230 YAK40 9541542
87237 YAK40 9530343
87278 YAK40 9311427
87297 YAK40 9321428
87337 YAK40 9510639
87411 YAK40 9420334
87413 YAK40 9420534
87466 YAK40 9430537
87478 YAK40 9440638
87643 YAK40 9140420
87644 YAK40 9140520
87812 YAK40 9230424
87817 YAK40 9230824
87918 YAK40 9730855
87946 YAK40 9611045
87964 YAK40 9830758
87968 YAK40 9841258
87971 YAK40 9831558
87972 YAK40 9..1658
87985 YAK40 9540844
87989 YAK40 9541344
87995 YAK40 9541944
88174 YAK40 9621247
88199 YAK40 9..0149
88203 YAK40 9630549
88211 YAK40 9631749
88217 YAK40 9630350
88237 YAK40 9640751
88242 YAK40 9641551
88244 YAK40 9641751
88271 YAK40 9720953
88290 YAK40 9840459
88294 YAK40 9331029
93926 TU134 1351204
96005 IL-96 74393201002300
CCCP-? IL-76 0053457713
CCCP-? TU124 4351505
CCCP-? TU124 4351508
CCCP-? TU124 5351708
CCCP-? TU134 9350701
CCCP-? TU134 0350921
CCCP-? TU134 1351406
CCCP-? TU134 60035
CCCP-? YAK40 9020409
CCCP-L5400 TU104
CCCP-L5401 TU104
CCCP-L5402 TU104
CCCP-L5403 TU104
CCCP-L5404 TU104
CCCP-L5406 TU104
CCCP-L5411 TU104 1681301
CCCP-L5412 TU104 1681302?
CCCP-L5413 TU104 1681303?
CCCP-L5413 TU104
CCCP-L5414 TU104 1681304?
CCCP-L5415 TU104 1681305?
CCCP-L5416 TU104
CCCP-L5417 TU104
CCCP-L5419 TU104
CCCP-L5420 TU104
CCCP-L5421 TU104
CCCP-L5422 TU104
CCCP-L5423 TU104
CCCP-L5425 TU104
CCCP-L5427 TU104
CCCP-L5428 TU104
CCCP-L5429 TU104
CCCP-L5430 TU104
CCCP-L5432 TU104
CCCP-L5433 TU104
CCCP-L5434 TU104
CCCP-L5435 TU104
CCCP-L5436 TU104
CCCP-L5437 TU104
CCCP-L5439 TU104
CCCP-L5440 TU104
CCCP-L5442 TU104
CCCP-L5443 TU104
CCCP-L5444 TU104
CCCP-L5445 TU104
CCCP-L5446 TU104
CCCP-L5447 TU104
CCCP-L5453 TU104
CCCP-L5458 TU104
CCCP-L5459 TU104
CCCP-L5460 TU104
CCCP-1966 YAK40
CCCP-1967 YAK40
CCCP-1968 YAK40
CCCP-1974 YAK42
CCCP-1975 YAK42
CCCP-1976 YAK42
CCCP-1977 YAK42
CCCP-06153 IL-62 30002
CCCP-06156 IL-62 30001
CCCP-06170 IL-62 40004
CCCP-06176 IL-62 30003
CCCP-06188 IL-76 063406188
CCCP-06195 TU104
CCCP-06300 IL-62 40005
CCCP-10985 YAK42 422075380
CCCP-11363 IL-76 083411363
CCCP-19661 YAK40 019
CCCP-19671 YAK40
CCCP-19672 YAK40
CCCP-19673 YAK40
CCCP-19674 YAK40
CCCP-19675 YAK40
CCCP-19676 YAK40
CCCP-19681 YAK40
CCCP-19773 AN-72
CCCP-19774 AN-72
CCCP-19775 AN-72
CCCP-19793 AN-72
CCCP-19795 AN-72
CCCP-21500 YAK40 9741356
CCCP-21501 YAK40 9741756
CCCP-21502 YAK40
CCCP-21503 YAK40 9832058
CCCP-21504 YAK40 9831758
CCCP-21505 YAK40 9830159
CCCP-21506 YAK40 9840259
CCCP-42300 YAK42
CCCP-42301 YAK42
CCCP-42302 YAK42 427401004
CCCP-42303 YAK42
CCCP-42304 YAK42 11820201
CCCP-42305 YAK42 0102
CCCP-42306 YAK42 11840202
CCCP-42307 YAK42 0203
CCCP-42308 YAK42 11040303
CCCP-42309 YAK42 01005
CCCP-42310 YAK42 11040403
CCCP-42311 YAK42 103
CCCP-42312 YAK42
CCCP-42313 TU104
CCCP-42313 YAK42 11030503
CCCP-42314 YAK42 2204245134
CCCP-42316 YAK42 4520422202030
CCCP-42317 YAK42 4520422202039
CCCP-42318 TU104 1681302?
CCCP-42318 YAK42 452042..020..
CCCP-42319 TU104
CCCP-42319 YAK42 4520423402062
CCCP-42320 YAK42 4520421302075
CCCP-42321 YAK42 4520423402088
CCCP-42322 TU104
CCCP-42322 YAK42 4520423402108
CCCP-42323 YAK42 4520423402116
CCCP-42324 YAK42 4520421402125
CCCP-42325 TU104
CCCP-42325 YAK42 452042.4021..
CCCP-42326 TU104
CCCP-42326 YAK42 4520424402154
CCCP-42327 TU104
CCCP-42327 YAK42 4520424402161
CCCP-42328 YAK42 4520421505058
CCCP-42329 TU104
CCCP-42329 YAK42 4520422505093
CCCP-42330 TU104
CCCP-42330 YAK42 4520422505122
CCCP-42331 YAK42 452042..051..
CCCP-42332 YAK42 4520421605135
CCCP-42333 YAK42 4520422606156
CCCP-42334 TU104
CCCP-42334 YAK42 4520422606...
CCCP-42335 TU104
CCCP-42335 YAK42 4520422606204
CCCP-42336 TU104
CCCP-42336 YAK42 452042.6062..
CCCP-42337 TU104
CCCP-42337 YAK42 4520423606235
CCCP-42338 TU104 7350204
CCCP-42338 YAK42 4520423606256
CCCP-42339 YAK42 4520423606267
CCCP-42340 TU104
CCCP-42340 YAK42 4520424606270
CCCP-42341 TU104 7350302
CCCP-42341 YAK42 4520421706292
CCCP-42342 TU104
CCCP-42342 YAK42 4520421706302
CCCP-42343 TU104
CCCP-42343 YAK42 4520421706305
CCCP-42344 TU104
CCCP-42344 YAK42 4520422708295
CCCP-42345 TU104
CCCP-42345 YAK42 4520422708304
CCCP-42346 TU104
CCCP-42346 YAK42 4520423708311
CCCP-42347 TU104
CCCP-42347 YAK42 4520423711322
CCCP-42348 TU104
CCCP-42348 YAK42 4520423711342
CCCP-42350 TU104
CCCP-42350 YAK42 4520424711372
CCCP-42351 TU104
CCCP-42351 YAK42 452042..113..
CCCP-42352 YAK42 4520421811395
CCCP-42353 TU104
CCCP-42353 YAK42 4520424711396
CCCP-42354 TU104
CCCP-42354 YAK42 4520424711397
CCCP-42355 TU104
CCCP-42355 YAK42 4520424711399
CCCP-42356 TU104
CCCP-42356 YAK42 4520422811400
CCCP-42357 TU104
CCCP-42357 YAK42 4520422811408
CCCP-42358 TU104
CCCP-42358 YAK42 4520422811413
CCCP-42359 TU104
CCCP-42359 YAK42 4520423811417
CCCP-42360 TU104
CCCP-42360 YAK42 4520423811421
CCCP-42361 TU104
CCCP-42361 YAK42 4520423811427
CCCP-42362 TU104
CCCP-42362 YAK42 4520424811431
CCCP-42363 YAK42 4520424811438
CCCP-42364 YAK42 4520424811442
CCCP-42365 YAK42 4520424811447
CCCP-42366 TU104
CCCP-42366 YAK42 4520421814047
CCCP-42367 TU104
CCCP-42367 YAK42 4520421914133
CCCP-42368 TU104
CCCP-42368 YAK42 4520422914166
CCCP-42369 TU104
CCCP-42369 YAK42 4520422914190
CCCP-42370 TU104
CCCP-42370 YAK42 4520422914203
CCCP-42371 TU104
CCCP-42371 YAK42 4520422914225
CCCP-42372 TU104

CCCP-42372 YAK42 4520423914266
CCCP-42373 TU104
CCCP-42373 YAK42 4520423914323
CCCP-42374 TU104
CCCP-42374 YAK42 4520423914340
CCCP-42375 TU104
CCCP-42375 YAK42 4520424914410
CCCP-42376 YAK42 4520424914477
CCCP-42377 TU104
CCCP-42377 YAK42 4520421014479
CCCP-42378 TU104
CCCP-42378 YAK42 4520421014494
CCCP-42379 TU104
CCCP-42379 YAK42 4520421014543
CCCP-42380 TU104
CCCP-42380 YAK42 4520422014549
CCCP-42381 TU104
CCCP-42381 YAK42 4520422014576
CCCP-42382 TU104 8350602
CCCP-42382 YAK42 4520422016196
CCCP-42383 TU104 8350603
CCCP-42383 YAK42 4520422016201
CCCP-42384 TU104 8350604
CCCP-42384 YAK42 4520423016230
CCCP-42385 TU104 8350605
CCCP-42385 YAK42 4520423016309
CCCP-42386 TU104 8350701
CCCP-42386 YAK42 4520424016310
CCCP-42387 TU104 8350702
CCCP-42387 YAK42 4520424016436
CCCP-42388 TU104 8350703?
CCCP-42388 YAK42 4520424016510
CCCP-42389 TU104 8350704
CCCP-42389 YAK42 4520424016542
CCCP-42390 TU104 8350705
CCCP-42390 YAK42 4520424016557
CCCP-42391 TU104 9350801
CCCP-42391 YAK42 452042..165..
CCCP-42392 TU104 9350802
CCCP-42393 TU104 9350803
CCCP-42394 TU104 9350804?
CCCP-42395 TU104 9350805
CCCP-42396 TU104 9350901?
CCCP-42397 TU104 9350902
CCCP-42398 TU104 9350903
CCCP-42399 TU104
CCCP-42400 TU104
CCCP-42401 TU104
CCCP-42401 YAK42 4520421116567
CCCP-42402 TU104
CCCP-42402 YAK42 4520422116583
CCCP-42403 TU104
CCCP-42403 YAK42 4520422116588
CCCP-42404 TU104
CCCP-42404 YAK42 4520422116617
CCCP-42405 TU104
CCCP-42405 YAK42 4520423116624
CCCP-42406 YAK42 4520424116638
CCCP-42407 TU104
CCCP-42407 YAK42 4520424116690
CCCP-42408 TU104
CCCP-42408 YAK42 4520424116698
CCCP-42409 TU104
CCCP-42409 YAK42 4520421216707
CCCP-42410 TU104
CCCP-42410 YAK42 4520421219029
CCCP-42411 TU104
CCCP-42411 YAK42 4520421219043
CCCP-42412 TU104
CCCP-42412 YAK42 4520422219055
CCCP-42413 TU104
CCCP-42413 YAK42 4520422219066
CCCP-42414 TU104
CCCP-42414 YAK42 4520422219073
CCCP-42415 TU104
CCCP-42415 YAK42 4520422219089
CCCP-42416 TU104
CCCP-42416 YAK42 4520423219102
CCCP-42417 TU104
CCCP-42417 YAK42 4520423.191..
CCCP-42418 TU104
CCCP-42419 TU104
CCCP-42419 YAK42 4520423201016
CCCP-42420 TU104
CCCP-42421 TU104
CCCP-42422 TU104
CCCP-42423 TU104
CCCP-42424 TU104
CCCP-42425 TU104
CCCP-42426 TU104
CCCP-42427 TU104
CCCP-42428 TU104
CCCP-42429 TU104
CCCP-42430 TU104
CCCP-42431 TU104
CCCP-42432 TU104
CCCP-42433 TU104
CCCP-42434 TU104
CCCP-42435 TU104
CCCP-42436 TU104
CCCP-42437 TU104
CCCP-42438 TU104
CCCP-42439 TU104
CCCP-42440 TU104
CCCP-42441 TU104
CCCP-42442 TU104
CCCP-42443 TU104
CCCP-42444 TU104
CCCP-42445 TU104
CCCP-42446 TU104
CCCP-42447 TU104
CCCP-42448 TU104
CCCP-42449 TU104
CCCP-42450 TU104
CCCP-42451 TU104 6600501
CCCP-42452 TU104
CCCP-42453 TU104
CCCP-42454 TU104
CCCP-42455 TU104
CCCP-42456 TU104 9350905
CCCP-42457 TU104
CCCP-42458 TU104
CCCP-42459 TU104 06601901
CCCP-42460 TU104 06601902
CCCP-42461 TU104 06601903
CCCP-42462 TU104 06602001
CCCP-42463 TU104 06602002
CCCP-42464 TU104
CCCP-42465 TU104 020806?
CCCP-42466 TU104
CCCP-42467 TU104
CCCP-42468 TU104 021201?
CCCP-42468 TU104
CCCP-42469 TU104 021202?
CCCP-42469 TU104
CCCP-42470 TU104 021203?
CCCP-42470 TU104
CCCP-42471 TU104 021204
CCCP-42472 TU104 021205?
CCCP-42473 TU104 021301?
CCCP-42474 TU104 021302
CCCP-42475 TU104 021303?
CCCP-42476 TU104 021304?
CCCP-42477 TU104 021305
CCCP-42478 TU104 021401?
CCCP-42479 TU104 021402?
CCCP-42480 TU104 021403
CCCP-42481 TU104 021404?
CCCP-42482 TU104 021405
CCCP-42483 TU104 021501
CCCP-42484 TU104 021502?
CCCP-42485 TU104 021503?
CCCP-42486 TU104 021504?
CCCP-42487 TU104 021505
CCCP-42488 TU104 021601
CCCP-42489 TU104 021602?
CCCP-42490 TU104 021603?
CCCP-42491 TU104 021604
CCCP-42492 TU104 021605
CCCP-42493 TU104 021701
CCCP-42494 TU104 021702
CCCP-42495 TU104 021703
CCCP-42496 TU104 021704?
CCCP-42497 TU104 021705?
CCCP-42498 TU104 021801?
CCCP-42499 TU104 021802?
CCCP-42500 TU104 021803
CCCP-42501 TU104 021804?
CCCP-42502 TU104 021805
CCCP-42503 TU104 021901?
CCCP-42504 TU104 021902
CCCP-42505 TU104 021903
CCCP-42506 TU104 021904?
CCCP-42507 TU104 021905
CCCP-42508 TU104 022001
CCCP-42509 TU104 022002
CCCP-42512 TU104
CCCP-42520 YAK42
CCCP-42523 YAK42 49136
CCCP-42524 YAK42 11030603
CCCP-42525 YAK42 110.0703
CCCP-42526 YAK42 11040803
CCCP-42527 YAK42 11040903
CCCP-42528 YAK42 11041003
CCCP-42529 YAK42 .8040104
CCCP-42530 YAK42 4253011120204
CCCP-42531 YAK42 4253011130304
CCCP-42532 YAK42
CCCP-42534 YAK42
CCCP-42536 YAK42
CCCP-42537 YAK42
CCCP-42538 YAK42 11130404
CCCP-42539 YAK42 11140504
CCCP-42540 YAK42 11140604
CCCP-42541 YAK42 11140704
CCCP-42542 YAK42 11140804
CCCP-42543 YAK42 11250904
CCCP-42544 YAK42 11151004
CCCP-42549 YAK42 11040105
CCCP-42550 YAK42 11140205
CCCP-42551 YAK42 11140305
CCCP-42644 YAK42 4520424914090
CCCP-45000 TU124 350101?
CCCP-45001 TU124 350102?
CCCP-45002 TU124 350103?
CCCP-45003 TU124 350201?
CCCP-45004 TU124 350202?
CCCP-45005 TU124 350203?
CCCP-45006 TU124 350301?
CCCP-45007 TU124 350302?
CCCP-45008 TU124 350401?
CCCP-45009 TU124 350402?
CCCP-45010 TU124 350403?
CCCP-45011 TU124 350501?
CCCP-45012 TU124 350502?
CCCP-45013 TU124 350503?
CCCP-45014 TU124 350504?
CCCP-45015 TU124 350505?
CCCP-45016 TU124 350601?
CCCP-45017 TU124 2350602
CCCP-45018 TU124 2350603?
CCCP-45019 TU124 2350604?
CCCP-45020 TU124 2350605?
CCCP-45021 TU124 2350701?
CCCP-45022 TU124 2350702?
CCCP-45023 TU124 2350703?
CCCP-45024 TU124 2350704?
CCCP-45025 TU124 2350705
CCCP-45026 TU124 2350801?
CCCP-45027 TU124 2350802?
CCCP-45028 TU124 2350803
CCCP-45029 TU124 2350804
CCCP-45030 TU124 2350805?
CCCP-45031 TU124 2350901?
CCCP-45032 TU124 350902?
CCCP-45033 TU124 350903?
CCCP-45034 TU124 350904?
CCCP-45035 TU124 350905?
CCCP-45036 TU124 351001?
CCCP-45037 TU124 351002?
CCCP-45038 TU124 3351003
CCCP-45039 TU124 3351004?
CCCP-45040 TU124 3351005?
CCCP-45041 TU124 3351101?
CCCP-45042 TU124 3351102?
CCCP-45043 TU124 3351103?
CCCP-45044 TU124 3351104?
CCCP-45045 TU124 3351105?
CCCP-45046 TU124 3351201?
CCCP-45047 TU124 3351202?
CCCP-45048 TU124 3351203?
CCCP-45049 TU124 351204?
CCCP-45050 TU124 351205?
CCCP-45051 TU124 351301
CCCP-45052 TU124 351302?
CCCP-45053 TU124 351303?
CCCP-45054 TU124 351304?
CCCP-45055 TU124 351305?

Registration	Type	c/n
CCCP-45056	TU124	351401?
CCCP-45057	TU124	351402?
CCCP-45058	TU124	351403?
CCCP-45059	TU124	351404?
CCCP-45060	TU124	351405?
CCCP-45061	TU124	351406?
CCCP-45062	TU124	351407?
CCCP-45063	TU124	351408?
CCCP-45064	TU124	351409?
CCCP-45065	TU124	351410?
CCCP-45066	TU124	351501?
CCCP-45067	TU124	351502?
CCCP-45068	TU124	4351506?
CCCP-45069	TU124	4351507?
CCCP-45070	TU124	4351509?
CCCP-45071	TU124	4351510
CCCP-45072	TU124	4351604
CCCP-45073	TU124	351605?
CCCP-45074	TU124	351606?
CCCP-45075	TU124	5351608?
CCCP-45075	**TU134**	**0001?**
CCCP-45076	TU124	5351609?
CCCP-45076	**TU134**	**0002?**
CCCP-45077	TU124	5351610?
CCCP-45078	TU124	5351701?
CCCP-45079	TU124	5351702?
CCCP-45080	TU124	5351703?
CCCP-45081	TU124	5351704?
CCCP-45082	**TU124**	**5351705?**
CCCP-45083	TU124	5351706?
CCCP-45084	TU124	5351707?
CCCP-45085	TU124	5351710?
CCCP-45086	TU124	5351801?
CCCP-45087	TU124	5351802?
CCCP-45088	TU124	5351803?
CCCP-45089	TU124	5351804?
CCCP-45090	TU124	5351805?
CCCP-45091	TU124	5351806
CCCP-45092	**TU124**	**5351807?**
CCCP-45093	TU124	6351809?
CCCP-45094	TU124	351810?
CCCP-45095	TU124	351901?
CCCP-45097?	TU124	6351902?
CCCP-45098?	TU124	6351903?
CCCP-45099?	TU124	6351904?
CCCP-45135	TU124	6351906?
CCCP-45146	TU124	6351907?
CCCP-45158	TU124	6351908?
CCCP-45173	TU124	6351909?
CCCP-45199	TU124	6351910?
CCCP-45200	TU124	6351905?
CCCP-45200?	TU124	6352001?
CCCP-48110	YAK40	9230623
CCCP-48111	YAK40	9211420
CCCP-48112	YAK40	9211520
CCCP-58642	**AN-74**	**0202**
CCCP-63955	**TU134**	**63955?**
CCCP-64001	TU204	1450743164001
CCCP-64002	TU204	1450743164002
CCCP-64003	TU204	1450743164003
CCCP-64004	TU204	1450743164004
CCCP-64005	TU204	1450743164005
CCCP-64006	TU204	1450743164006
CCCP-64007	TU204	1450743164007
CCCP-64451	TU134	66550
CCCP-64452	TU124	6352001?
CCCP-64452	**TU124**	
CCCP-64454	TU134	
CCCP-65000	**TU134**	**42230**
CCCP-65001	TU134	
CCCP-65002	TU134	44020
CCCP-65003	TU134	44040
CCCP-65004	TU134	44060
CCCP-65005	TU134	44065
CCCP-65006	TU134	44080
CCCP-65007	TU134	
CCCP-65008	TU134	46105
CCCP-65009	TU134	46120
CCCP-65010	TU134	46130
CCCP-65011	TU134	46140
CCCP-65012	TU134	46175
CCCP-65013	**TU134**	
CCCP-65014	TU134	46200
CCCP-65015	TU134	
CCCP-65016	TU134	
CCCP-65017	TU134	48360
CCCP-65018	TU134	48365
CCCP-65019	TU134	48375
CCCP-65020	TU134	48380
CCCP-65021	TU134	48390
CCCP-65022	TU134	48395
CCCP-65023	TU134	48415
CCCP-65024	TU134	48420
CCCP-65025	TU134	48450
CCCP-65026	TU134	48470
CCCP-65027	TU134	48485
CCCP-65028	TU134	48490
CCCP-65029	TU134	48500
CCCP-65030	TU134	
CCCP-65031	TU134	
CCCP-65032	TU134	
CCCP-65033	TU134	48540
CCCP-65034	TU134	48565
CCCP-65035	TU134	48590
CCCP-65036	TU134	48700
CCCP-65037	TU134	48850
CCCP-65038	TU134	48950
CCCP-65039	TU134	
CCCP-65040	TU134	49100
CCCP-65041	**TU134**	**492.0?**
CCCP-65042	TU134	49350
CCCP-65043	TU134	49400?
CCCP-65044	TU134	49450
CCCP-65045	TU134	49500?
CCCP-65046	TU134	49700
CCCP-65047	TU134	49600
CCCP-65048	TU134	49750
CCCP-65049	TU134	49755
CCCP-65050	TU134	49756
CCCP-65051	TU134	49758
CCCP-65052	TU134	49825
CCCP-65053	TU134	49838
CCCP-65054	TU134	49840
CCCP-65055	TU134	49856
CCCP-65056	TU134	
CCCP-65057	TU134	49865
CCCP-65058	TU134	
CCCP-65059	TU134	49870
CCCP-65060	TU134	49872
CCCP-65061	TU134	49874
CCCP-65062	TU134	49875
CCCP-65063	TU134	49880
CCCP-65064	TU134	49886
CCCP-65065	TU134	49890
CCCP-65066	TU134	
CCCP-65067	TU134	
CCCP-65068	TU134	49907
CCCP-65069	TU134	49908
CCCP-65070	TU134	49912
CCCP-65071	TU134	49915
CCCP-65072	TU134	49972
CCCP-65073	TU134	49980
CCCP-65074	TU134	49987
CCCP-65075	TU134	49998
CCCP-65076	TU134	60001
CCCP-65077	TU134	60028
CCCP-65078	TU134	60043
CCCP-65079	TU134	60054
CCCP-65080	TU134	60065
CCCP-65081	TU134	60076
CCCP-65082	TU134	60081
CCCP-65083	TU134	60090
CCCP-65084	TU134	60115
CCCP-65085	TU134	60123
CCCP-65086	TU134	60130
CCCP-65087	TU134	60155
CCCP-65088	TU134	60172
CCCP-65089	TU134	60180
CCCP-65090	TU134	60185
CCCP-65091	TU134	60195
CCCP-65092	TU134	60206
CCCP-65093	TU134	60215
CCCP-65094	TU134	60255
CCCP-65095	TU134	60256?
CCCP-65096	TU134	60257
CCCP-65097	TU134	60540
CCCP-65098	**TU134**	
CCCP-65099	TU134	63700
CCCP-65100	TU134	60258
CCCP-65101	TU134	60260
CCCP-65102	TU134	60267
CCCP-65103	TU134	60297
CCCP-65104	TU134	60301
CCCP-65105	TU134	60308
CCCP-65106	TU134	60315
CCCP-65107	TU134	60328
CCCP-65108	TU134	60332
CCCP-65109	TU134	60342
CCCP-65110	TU134	60343
CCCP-65111	TU134	60346
CCCP-65112	TU134	60350
CCCP-65113	TU134	60380
CCCP-65114	TU134	60395
CCCP-65115	TU134	
CCCP-65116	TU134	60420
CCCP-65117	TU134	60450
CCCP-65118	TU134	60462
CCCP-65119	TU134	60475
CCCP-65120	TU134	
CCCP-65121	TU134	60505
CCCP-65122	TU134	
CCCP-65123	TU134	60525
CCCP-65124	TU134	60560
CCCP-65125	TU134	60575
CCCP-65126	TU134	
CCCP-65127	TU134	60627
CCCP-65128	TU134	60628
CCCP-65129	TU134	
CCCP-65130	TU134	60635
CCCP-65131	TU134	60637
CCCP-65132	TU134	60639
CCCP-65133	TU134	60645
CCCP-65134	TU134	60647
CCCP-65135	TU134	60648
CCCP-65136	TU134	60885
CCCP-65137	TU134	60890
CCCP-65138	TU134	60907
CCCP-65139	TU134	
CCCP-65140	TU134	60932
CCCP-65141	TU134	60945
CCCP-65142	TU134	
CCCP-65143	TU134	60967
CCCP-65144	TU134	60977
CCCP-65145	TU134	60985
CCCP-65146	TU134	61000
CCCP-65147	TU134	61012
CCCP-65148	TU134	61025
CCCP-65149	TU134	61033
CCCP-65550	TU134	60321
CCCP-65551	TU134	66212
CCCP-65552	TU134	66270
CCCP-65553	TU134	66300
CCCP-65554	TU134	66320
CCCP-65555	TU134	66350
CCCP-65556	TU134	66372
CCCP-65557	TU134	66380
CCCP-65562	TU134	
CCCP-65563	TU134	
CCCP-65564	TU134	63165
CCCP-65565	TU134	63998
CCCP-65570	TU134	
CCCP-65594	**TU134**	
CCCP-65600	**TU134**	**0002?**
CCCP-65601	**TU134**	**0003**
CCCP-65602	**TU134**	**0004**
CCCP-65603	**TU134**	**0005**
CCCP-65604	TU134	0101
CCCP-65605	TU134	0102
CCCP-65605	TU134	09070
CCCP-65606	TU134	0103
CCCP-65606	TU134	46300
CCCP-65607	TU134	0104
CCCP-65607	TU134	6348560
CCCP-65608	TU134	0105
CCCP-65608	TU134	5338040
CCCP-65609	TU134	6350201
CCCP-65609	TU134	46155
CCCP-65610	TU134	6350202
CCCP-65610	TU134	40150
CCCP-65611	TU134	7350204
CCCP-65611	TU134	3351903
CCCP-65612	TU134	7350205
CCCP-65612	TU134	3352102
CCCP-65613	TU134	7350301
CCCP-65613	TU134	3352106
CCCP-65614	TU134	7350302
CCCP-65614	TU134	4352207
CCCP-65615	TU134	7350303

CCCP-65615 TU134 4352205
CCCP-65616 TU134 7350304
CCCP-65616 TU134 4352206
CCCP-65617 TU134 7350305
CCCP-65617 TU134 4308068
CCCP-65618 TU134 8350401
CCCP-65618 TU134 12095
CCCP-65619 TU134 8350402
CCCP-65619 TU134 31218
CCCP-65620 TU134 8350403
CCCP-65620 TU134 35180
CCCP-65621 TU134 8350404
CCCP-65621 TU134 6348320
CCCP-65622 TU134 8350504
CCCP-65622 TU134 60495
CCCP-65623 TU134 8350505
CCCP-65623 TU134 49985
CCCP-65624 TU134 8350601
CCCP-65624 TU134
CCCP-65625 TU134 9350703
CCCP-65626 TU134 9350704
CCCP-65626 TU134
CCCP-65627 TU134 9350803
CCCP-65628 TU134 9350809
CCCP-65629 TU134 9350810
CCCP-65630 TU134 9350901
CCCP-65631 TU134 9350902
CCCP-65632 TU134 9350903
CCCP-65633 TU134 9350907
CCCP-65634 TU134 9350908
CCCP-65635 TU134 9350909
CCCP-65636 TU134 9350910
CCCP-65637 TU134 9350911
CCCP-65638 TU134 9350916
CCCP-65639 TU134 9350917
CCCP-65640 TU134 9350919
CCCP-65641 TU134 9350920
CCCP-65642 TU134 0350926
CCCP-65643 TU134 0350927
CCCP-65644 TU134 0350928
CCCP-65645 TU134 0351005
CCCP-65646 TU134 0351001
CCCP-65647 TU134 0351002
CCCP-65648 TU134 0351003
CCCP-65649 TU134 0351004
CCCP-65650 TU134 0351006
CCCP-65651 TU134 0351007
CCCP-65652 TU134 0351008
CCCP-65653 TU134 0351009
CCCP-65654 TU134 0351010
CCCP-65655 TU134 0351101
CCCP-65656 TU134 0351102
CCCP-65657 TU134 0351103
CCCP-65658 TU134 351104
CCCP-65659 TU134 351105
CCCP-65660 TU134 351106
CCCP-65661 TU134 351107
CCCP-65662 TU134 351108
CCCP-65663 TU134 351109
CCCP-65664 TU134 1351110
CCCP-65665 TU134 1351201
CCCP-65666 TU134 1351202
CCCP-65667 TU134 1351207
CCCP-65668 TU134 1351208
CCCP-65669 TU134 1351210
CCCP-65670 TU134 1351401?
CCCP-65671 TU134 1351402?
CCCP-65672 TU134 1351403?
CCCP-65673 TU134 1351404?
CCCP-65674 TU134 1351405
CCCP-65675 TU134 1351501?
CCCP-65676 TU134 1351502
CCCP-65677 TU134
CCCP-65678 TU134
CCCP-65679 TU134 23249
CCCP-65680 TU134
CCCP-65681 TU134 49760
CCCP-65682 TU134
CCCP-65683 TU134 62199
CCCP-65684 TU134 62205
CCCP-65685 TU134
CCCP-65686 TU134
CCCP-65687 TU134
CCCP-65689 TU134
CCCP-65690 TU134
CCCP-65691 TU134 63195
CCCP-65692 TU134 63215
CCCP-65693 TU134 63221
CCCP-65694 TU134 63235
CCCP-65695 TU134 63285
CCCP-65696 TU134 63295
CCCP-65697 TU134 63307
CCCP-65698 TU134
CCCP-65699 TU134 63333
CCCP-65700 TU134 63340
CCCP-65701 TU134 63365
CCCP-65702 TU134 63375
CCCP-65703 TU134 63383
CCCP-65704 TU134 63410
CCCP-65705 TU134 63415
CCCP-65706 TU134 63425
CCCP-65707 TU134 63435
CCCP-65708 TU134 63447
CCCP-65709 TU134 63484
CCCP-65710 TU134 63490
CCCP-65711 TU134 63498
CCCP-65712 TU134 63515
CCCP-65713 TU134 63520
CCCP-65714 TU134 63527
CCCP-65715 TU134 63536
CCCP-65716 TU134 63595
CCCP-65717 TU134 63657
CCCP-65718 TU134 63668
CCCP-65719 TU134 63637
CCCP-65720 TU134 63820
CCCP-65721 TU134
CCCP-65722 TU134
CCCP-65723 TU134 66440
CCCP-65724 TU134 66445
CCCP-65725 TU134 66472
CCCP-65726 TU134 2351506
CCCP-65726 TU134 63720
CCCP-65727 TU134 2351507?
CCCP-65728 TU134 2351509?
CCCP-65729 TU134 2351601
CCCP-65730 TU134 2351511?
CCCP-65731 TU134 2351512?
CCCP-65732 TU134 2351513?
CCCP-65733 TU134 2351514
CCCP-65734 TU134 2351515?
CCCP-65735 TU134 2351516?
CCCP-65736 TU134 2351517?
CCCP-65737 TU134 2351518?
CCCP-65738 TU134 2351519?
CCCP-65739 TU134 2351520?
CCCP-65740 TU134 2351510
CCCP-65741 TU134 2351602?
CCCP-65742 TU134 2351604
CCCP-65743 TU134 2351605
CCCP-65744 TU134 2351606?
CCCP-65745 TU134 2351607
CCCP-65746 TU134 2351608
CCCP-65747 TU134 2351609?
CCCP-65748 TU134 2351610?
CCCP-65750 TU134 61042
CCCP-65751 TU134 61066
CCCP-65752 TU134 61079
CCCP-65753 TU134
CCCP-65754 TU134 62154
CCCP-65755 TU134 62165
CCCP-65756 TU134 62179
CCCP-65757 TU134 62215
CCCP-65758 TU134
CCCP-65759 TU134 62239
CCCP-65760 TU134 62187
CCCP-65761 TU134 62244
CCCP-65762 TU134 62279
CCCP-65763 TU134 62299
CCCP-65764 TU134 62305
CCCP-65765 TU134 62315
CCCP-65766 TU134
CCCP-65767 TU134
CCCP-65768 TU134 62350
CCCP-65769 TU134 62415
CCCP-65770 TU134 62430
CCCP-65771 TU134 62445
CCCP-65772 TU134 62472
CCCP-65773 TU134 62495
CCCP-65774 TU134 62519
CCCP-65775 TU134 62530
CCCP-65776 TU134 62545
CCCP-65777 TU134 62552
CCCP-65778 TU134 62590
CCCP-65779 TU134 62602
CCCP-65780 TU134 62622
CCCP-65781 TU134 62645
CCCP-65782 TU134 62672
CCCP-65783 TU134 62713
CCCP-65784 TU134 62715
CCCP-65785 TU134 62750
CCCP-65786 TU134 62775
CCCP-65787 TU134
CCCP-65788 TU134 62835
CCCP-65789 TU134 62850
CCCP-65790 TU134 63100
CCCP-65791 TU134 63110
CCCP-65792 TU134
CCCP-65793 TU134 63128
CCCP-65794 TU134
CCCP-65795 TU134
CCCP-65796 TU134 63150
CCCP-65797 TU134
CCCP-65798 TU134 63179
CCCP-65799 TU134 63187
CCCP-65800 TU134 3352009?
CCCP-65801 TU134 3352010
CCCP-65802 TU134 3352101
CCCP-65803 TU134 3352103
CCCP-65804 TU134 3352104?
CCCP-65805 TU134 3352105
CCCP-65806 TU134 352107?
CCCP-65807 TU134 352108?
CCCP-65808 TU134 352109
CCCP-65809 TU134 3352110
CCCP-65810 TU134 352201
CCCP-65811 TU134 352202
CCCP-65812 TU134 352203?
CCCP-65813 TU134 352204
CCCP-65814 TU134 4352208
CCCP-65815 TU134 4352209
CCCP-65816 TU134 4352210
CCCP-65817 TU134 4352301
CCCP-65818 TU134 4352302
CCCP-65819 TU134 4352304
CCCP-65820 TU134 08056
CCCP-65821 TU134 08060
CCCP-65822 TU134 09071
CCCP-65823 TU134 0907.?
CCCP-65824 TU134 09074
CCCP-65825 TU134 09078
CCCP-65826 TU134 12083
CCCP-65827 TU134 12084
CCCP-65828 TU134
CCCP-65829 TU134
CCCP-65830 TU134 12093
CCCP-65831 TU134 17102
CCCP-65832 TU134 17106
CCCP-65833 TU134 1710.?
CCCP-65834 TU134 17109
CCCP-65835 TU134 17112
CCCP-65836 TU134 17113?
CCCP-65837 TU134 17114
CCCP-65838 TU134 18116
CCCP-65839 TU134 18117?
CCCP-65840 TU134 18118
CCCP-65841 TU134 18120
CCCP-65842 TU134 1812.?
CCCP-65843 TU134 18123
CCCP-65844 TU134
CCCP-65845 TU134 23131
CCCP-65846 TU134 2313.?
CCCP-65847 TU134 23135
CCCP-65848 TU134 23136
CCCP-65850 TU134
CCCP-65851 TU134 23241
CCCP-65852 TU134 23244
CCCP-65853 TU134 2324.?
CCCP-65854 TU134 23248
CCCP-65855 TU134 23252
CCCP-65856 TU134 2325.?
CCCP-65857 TU134 23255
CCCP-65858 TU134
CCCP-65859 TU134 23264
CCCP-65860 TU134 28265
CCCP-65861 TU134 28269
CCCP-65862 TU134 28270
CCCP-65863 TU134
CCCP-65864 TU134 28284

CCCP-65865 TU134 28286
CCCP-65866 TU134 28292
CCCP-65867 TU134
CCCP-65868 TU134
CCCP-65869 TU134 28306
CCCP-65870 TU134 28310
CCCP-65871 TU134 2.311?
CCCP-65872 TU134 29312
CCCP-65873 TU134 2931.?
CCCP-65874 TU134 29315
CCCP-65875 TU134 29317
CCCP-65876 TU134 31220
CCCP-65877 TU134 31250
CCCP-65878 TU134
CCCP-65879 TU134 31265
CCCP-65880 TU134 35200
CCCP-65881 TU134 35220
CCCP-65882 TU134 35270
CCCP-65883 TU134
CCCP-65884 TU134 36150
CCCP-65885 TU134 36160
CCCP-65886 TU134 36165
CCCP-65887 TU134 36170?
CCCP-65888 TU134 36175
CCCP-65889 TU134
CCCP-65890 TU134 38020
CCCP-65891 TU134 38030
CCCP-65892 TU134 38050
CCCP-65893 TU134 40120
CCCP-65894 TU134 40130
CCCP-65895 TU134 40140
CCCP-65896 TU134
CCCP-65897 TU134 42210
CCCP-65898 TU134
CCCP-65899 TU134 42225
CCCP-65900 TU134 63684
CCCP-65901 TU134 63731
CCCP-65902 TU134 63742
CCCP-65903 TU134 63750
CCCP-65904 TU134 63953
CCCP-65905 TU134 63965
CCCP-65906 TU134 66175
CCCP-65907 TU134 63996
CCCP-65908 TU134 63870
CCCP-65909 TU134 63970?
CCCP-65910 TU134 63971?
CCCP-65911 TU134 63972
CCCP-65912 TU134 63985
CCCP-65913 TU134 63986?
CCCP-65914 TU134 66109
CCCP-65915 TU134 66120
CCCP-65916 TU134 66152
CCCP-65917 TU134 63991
CCCP-65918 TU134 63993?
CCCP-65919 TU134 66168
CCCP-65921 TU134 63997
CCCP-65922 TU134
CCCP-65923 TU134
CCCP-65926 TU134 66101
CCCP-65927 TU134 66198
CCCP-65928 TU134
CCCP-65929 TU134
CCCP-65930 TU134 66500
CCCP-65931 TU134
CCCP-65932 TU134 66405
CCCP-65933 TU134
CCCP-65934 TU134 66143
CCCP-65935 TU134 66180
CCCP-65937 TU134
CCCP-65949 TU134 2351701?
CCCP-65950 TU134 2351702
CCCP-65951 TU134 2351703
CCCP-65952 TU134 235170.?
CCCP-65953 TU134 2351706
CCCP-65954 TU134 2351707
CCCP-65955 TU134 2351708
CCCP-65956 TU134 2351709
CCCP-65957 TU134 2351802
CCCP-65958 TU134 3351804
CCCP-65959 TU134 3351805
CCCP-65960 TU134 3351806
CCCP-65961 TU134 3351807
CCCP-65962 TU134
CCCP-65963 TU134
CCCP-65964 TU134
CCCP-65965 TU134 2351803
CCCP-65966 TU134 3351902
CCCP-65967 TU134 3351905
CCCP-65968 TU134 3351907
CCCP-65969 TU134 3351909
CCCP-65970 TU134 3351910?
CCCP-65971 TU134 3352001
CCCP-65972 TU134 3352002
CCCP-65973 TU134 3352003
CCCP-65974 TU134 3352004
CCCP-65975 TU134 3352006?
CCCP-65976 TU134 3352007
CCCP-65977 TU134 63245
CCCP-65978 TU134 63357
CCCP-65979 TU134
CCCP-65980 TU134
CCCP-65981 TU134
CCCP-65982 TU134
CCCP-65983 TU134
CCCP-65984 TU134
CCCP-65985 TU134
CCCP-65986 TU134
CCCP-65987 TU134 63505
CCCP-65988 TU134
CCCP-65989 TU134
CCCP-65990 TU134
CCCP-65991 TU134
CCCP-65992 TU134
CCCP-65993 TU134
CCCP-65994 TU134 66207
CCCP-65995 TU134 66400
CCCP-65996 TU134
CCCP-68001 TU144 044
CCCP-71052 AN-72
CCCP-72000 AN-72
CCCP-72002 AN-72
CCCP-72003 AN-72
CCCP-72004 AN-72
CCCP-72010 AN-72
CCCP-72019 AN-72
CCCP-72042 AN-72
CCCP-72502 IL-76
CCCP-72503 IL-76
CCCP-72598 AN-72
CCCP-72904 AN-72
CCCP-72905 AN-72
CCCP-72906 AN-72
CCCP-72907 AN-72
CCCP-72908 AN-72
CCCP-72909 AN-72
CCCP-72910 AN-72
CCCP-72915 AN-72
CCCP-72916 AN-72
CCCP-72918 AN-72
CCCP-72919 AN-72
CCCP-72920 AN-72
CCCP-72921 AN-72
CCCP-72922 AN-72
CCCP-72924 AN-72
CCCP-72925 AN-72
CCCP-72926 AN-72
CCCP-72927 AN-72
CCCP-72928 AN-72
CCCP-72929 AN-72
CCCP-72930 AN-72
CCCP-72931 AN-72
CCCP-72935 AN-72
CCCP-72938 AN-72
CCCP-72942 AN-72
CCCP-72943 AN-72
CCCP-72944 AN-72
CCCP-72946 AN-72
"CCCP-72948" AN-72
"CCCP-72949" AN-72 36572093819
"CCCP-72950" AN-72
CCCP-72958 AN-72
CCCP-72959 AN-72
CCCP-72960 AN-72 36572093865
CCCP-72961 AN-72
CCCP-72962 AN-72
CCCP-72963 AN-72
CCCP-72965 AN-72
CCCP-72966 AN-72
CCCP-72967 AN-72
CCCP-72970 AN-72
CCCP-72972 AN-72
CCCP-72974 AN-72
"CCCP-72976" AN-72
CCCP-72977 AN-72 36572094889
CCCP-72982 AN-72 36572096914
CCCP-74000 AN-74
CCCP-74001 AN-74
CCCP-74002 AN-74
CCCP-74003 AN-74
CCCP-74005 AN-74
CCCP-74006 AN-74
CCCP-74007 AN-74 36547095903
CCCP-74008 AN-74 36547095900
CCCP-74009 AN-74
CCCP-74010 AN-74
CCCP-74024 AN-74
CCCP-74025 AN-74 36547095905
CCCP-74026 AN-74 36547096919
CCCP-76012 IL-76
CCCP-76350 IL-76
CCCP-76361 IL-76 1033415497
CCCP-76400 IL-76 1023413438
CCCP-76401 IL-76 1023412399
CCCP-76402 IL-76 1023413430
CCCP-76403 IL-76 1023412414
CCCP-76419 IL-76 1023414470
CCCP-76420 IL-76 1023413446
CCCP-76421 IL-76 1033415504
CCCP-76422? IL-76 1023410348
CCCP-76423 IL-76 0053457720
CCCP-76425 IL-76 1003405167
CCCP-76426 IL-76 1013405184
CCCP-76428 IL-76
CCCP-76434 IL-76 1023412395
CCCP-76435 IL-76 1023413428
CCCP-76436 IL-76 1023411368
CCCP-76437 IL-76 0083484527
CCCP-76438 IL-76 0083483513
CCCP-76441 IL-76
CCCP-76442 IL-76 1023414450
CCCP-76443 IL-76 0043452534
CCCP-76445 IL-76
CCCP-76447 IL-76 1023412389
CCCP-76448 IL-76 1023413443
CCCP-76449 IL-76 1003403058
CCCP-76450 IL-76
CCCP-76451 IL-76
CCCP-76452 IL-76
CCCP-76453 IL-76 0063466995
CCCP-76454 IL-76
CCCP-76455 IL-76
CCCP-76456 IL-76 0073474208
CCCP-76457 IL-76
CCCP-76458 IL-76
CCCP-76459 IL-76
CCCP-76460 IL-76 0013431928
CCCP-76461 IL-76 0013431935
CCCP-76462 IL-76
CCCP-76463 IL-76 0013432960
CCCP-76464 IL-76
CCCP-76465 IL-76
CCCP-76466 IL-76
CCCP-76467 IL-76 0023440157
CCCP-76468 IL-76 0023441195
CCCP-76469 IL-76 0033444286
CCCP-76470 IL-76 0033445291
CCCP-76471 IL-76
CCCP-76472 IL-76 0033446350
CCCP-76473 IL-76 0033448404
CCCP-76474 IL-76 0033448407
CCCP-76475 IL-76 0043451523
CCCP-76476 IL-76 0043451528
CCCP-76477 IL-76 0043453575
CCCP-76478 IL-76 0053459788
CCCP-76479 IL-76 0053460790
CCCP-76480 IL-76 005346079.
CCCP-76481 IL-76 0053460795
CCCP-76482 IL-76 0053460832
CCCP-76483 IL-76 0063468042
CCCP-76484 IL-76 0063469081
CCCP-76485 IL-76 0063470088
CCCP-76486 IL-76 0073476281
CCCP-76487 IL-76 0073479367
CCCP-76488 IL-76 0073479371
CCCP-76489 IL-76 0083485554
CCCP-76490 IL-76 093416506
CCCP-76491 IL-76 093421630
CCCP-76492 IL-76 0043452549

CCCP-76493	IL-76	0043456700
CCCP-76494	IL-76	0063465965
CCCP-76495	IL-76	073410292
CCCP-76496	**IL-76**	
CCCP-76497	IL-76	073410320
CCCP-76498	IL-76	0023442218
CCCP-76499	IL-76	0023441186
CCCP-76500	**IL-76**	**01030104**
CCCP-76501	**IL-76**	
CCCP-76502	**IL-76**	
CCCP-76503	IL-76	
CCCP-76504	IL-76	073411328
CCCP-76505	IL-76	073411331
CCCP-76506	IL-76	073411334
CCCP-76507	IL-76	073411338
CCCP-76508	IL-76	
CCCP-76509	IL-76	
CCCP-76510	IL-76	083414432
CCCP-76511	**IL-76**	**083414444**
CCCP-76512	IL-76	083414447
CCCP-76513	IL-76	083414451
CCCP-76514	IL-76	083415453
CCCP-76515	IL-76	093417526
CCCP-76516	IL-76	
CCCP-76517	IL-76	
CCCP-76518	IL-76	093420594
CCCP-76519	IL-76	093420599
CCCP-76520	IL-76	093420605
CCCP-76521	IL-76	0003423699
CCCP-76522	IL-76	0003424707
CCCP-76523	IL-76	0003425732
CCCP-76524	IL-76	
CCCP-76525	IL-76	
CCCP-76526	IL-76	
CCCP-76527	IL-76	0003427796
CCCP-76528	IL-76	073410293
CCCP-76529	IL-76	073410308
CCCP-76532	IL-76	
CCCP-76533	IL-76	
CCCP-76534	IL-76	0023442210
CCCP-76535	IL-76	
CCCP-76536	**IL-76**	
CCCP-76537	IL-76	0033442225
CCCP-76538	**IL-76**	
CCCP-76539	IL-76	0033442234
CCCP-76540	IL-76	0033442238
CCCP-76541	IL-76	0033442241
CCCP-76542	**IL-76**	
CCCP-76543	**IL-76**	
CCCP-76544	IL-76	
CCCP-76545	IL-76	0033443266
CCCP-76546	IL-76	
CCCP-76547	IL-76	
CCCP-76548	IL-76	
CCCP-76549	IL-76	
CCCP-76550	IL-76	
CCCP-76551	IL-76	0033445309
CCCP-76552	IL-76	
CCCP-76553	**IL-76**	
CCCP-76554	**IL-76**	
CCCP-76555	IL-76	
CCCP-76556	IL-76	0033445294
CCCP-76557	IL-76	
CCCP-76558	IL-76	0033446333
CCCP-76559	**IL-76**	
CCCP-76561	**IL-76**	
CCCP-76566	**IL-76**	
CCCP-76567	**IL-76**	
CCCP-76568	IL-76	0033448420
CCCP-76569	IL-76	
CCCP-76570	IL-76	0033448427
CCCP-76571	IL-76	0033448429
CCCP-76572	IL-76	
CCCP-76573	IL-76	0043449437
CCCP-76574	**IL-76**	
CCCP-76576	IL-76	0043449449
CCCP-76577	IL-76	
CCCP-76578	IL-76	0043449468
CCCP-76579	IL-76	0043449471
CCCP-76580	IL-76	0043450476
CCCP-76581	IL-76	0043450484
CCCP-76582	IL-76	0043450487
CCCP-76583	IL-76	0043450491
CCCP-76584	IL-76	
CCCP-76585	**IL-76**	
CCCP-76586	IL-76	0043451508
CCCP-76587	IL-76	0043451517
CCCP-76588	IL-76	
CCCP-76589	IL-76	0043452534
CCCP-76590	IL-76	0043452544
CCCP-76591	IL-76	0043452546
CCCP-76592	IL-76	0043453562
CCCP-76594	IL-76	0043453568
CCCP-76595	IL-76	0043453571
CCCP-76596	IL-76	
CCCP-76598	**IL-76**	
CCCP-76599	IL-76	
CCCP-76600	**IL-76**	
CCCP-76601	IL-76	0043454606
CCCP-76602	IL-76	0043454611
CCCP-76603	IL-76	0043454623
CCCP-76604	IL-76	
CCCP-76605	IL-76	
CCCP-76606	IL-76	0043454633
CCCP-76609	IL-76	
CCCP-7661.?	IL-76	0043455653
CCCP-76610	**IL-76**	
CCCP-76611	**IL-76**	
CCCP-76612	**IL-76**	
CCCP-76613	**IL-76**	
CCCP-76614	IL-76	0043455665
CCCP-76615	IL-76	
CCCP-76616	IL-76	
CCCP-76617	**IL-76**	
CCCP-76618	IL-76	
CCCP-76619?	IL-76	0043455686
CCCP-7662.?	IL-76	0053457720
CCCP-76620	IL-76	
CCCP-76622	IL-76	0043457702
CCCP-76623	IL-76	
CCCP-76625	IL-76	
CCCP-76626	**IL-76**	
CCCP-76627	IL-76	0053458733
CCCP-76628	**IL-76**	**0053458741**
CCCP-76630	IL-76	0053458749
CCCP-76631	**IL-76**	
CCCP-76632	IL-76	
CCCP-76633	**IL-76**	
CCCP-76634	**IL-76**	**0053459770**
CCCP-76636	IL-76	
CCCP-76637	IL-76	0053460797
CCCP-76638	**IL-76**	
CCCP-76639	**IL-76**	**0053460805**
CCCP-76640	IL-76	
CCCP-76642	IL-76	0053460820
CCCP-76643	IL-76	
CCCP-76644	IL-76	0053460827
CCCP-76645	**IL-76**	**0053461834**
CCCP-76647	**IL-76**	
CCCP-76648	**IL-76**	
CCCP-76649	**IL-76**	
CCCP-76650	IL-76	0053462865
CCCP-76651	IL-76	0053462872
CCCP-76652	IL-76	0053462873
CCCP-76653	IL-76	
CCCP-76654	**IL-76**	
CCCP-76655	IL-76	0053463885
CCCP-76656	IL-76	0053463891
CCCP-76657	**IL-76**	
CCCP-76658	IL-76	
CCCP-76659	IL-76	0053463902
CCCP-76660	IL-76	0053463910
CCCP-76661	**IL-76**	
CCCP-76663	IL-76	0053464922
CCCP-76664	IL-76	0053464926
CCCP-76665	**IL-76**	
CCCP-76666	IL-76	0053464934
CCCP-76667	IL-76	
CCCP-76668	**IL-76**	
CCCP-76669	IL-76	
CCCP-76670	IL-76	0063465958
CCCP-76671	IL-76	0063465963
CCCP-76672	IL-76	0063466981
CCCP-76673	IL-76	0063466988
CCCP-76674	IL-76	0063466989
CCCP-76676	IL-76	
CCCP-76677	IL-76	0063467005
CCCP-76680	IL-76	0063467020
CCCP-76681	IL-76	0063467021
CCCP-76682	IL-76	0063467027
CCCP-76683	IL-76	
CCCP-76687	IL-76	0063469051
CCCP-76688	IL-76	0063469062
CCCP-76689	IL-76	
CCCP-76690	IL-76	
CCCP-76692	IL-76	0063470096
CCCP-76694	IL-76	0063470107
CCCP-76695	**IL-76**	
CCCP-76696	IL-76	0063470113
CCCP-76697	**IL-76**	**0063470118**
CCCP-76698	IL-76	0063471123
CCCP-76699	**IL-76**	
CCCP-76700	IL-76	0063471134
CCCP-76701	IL-76	
CCCP-76703	**IL-76**	
CCCP-76704	IL-76	
CCCP-76705	IL-76	0063472158
CCCP-76706	IL-76	0063472163
CCCP-76707	IL-76	
CCCP-76708	IL-76	0063473171
CCCP-76709	**IL-76**	
CCCP-76710	**IL-76**	**0063473183**
CCCP-76711	**IL-76**	**006347318.**
CCCP-76712	**IL-76**	**0063473190**
CCCP-76713	**IL-76**	
CCCP-76715	**IL-76**	
CCCP-76716	IL-76	
CCCP-76717	IL-76	
CCCP-76720	IL-76	0073475229
CCCP-76722	IL-76	0073475242
CCCP-76723	**IL-76**	
CCCP-76724	**IL-76**	
CCCP-76725	**IL-76**	
CCCP-76726	**IL-76**	
CCCP-76727	IL-76	0073475268
CCCP-76728	IL-76	0073475270
CCCP-76729	IL-76	0073476275
CCCP-76732	IL-76	0073476296
CCCP-76733	IL-76	0073476304
CCCP-76734	**IL-76**	
CCCP-76735	**IL-76**	
CCCP-76736	**IL-76**	
CCCP-76737	**IL-76**	
CCCP-76738	IL-76	0073477326
CCCP-76739	**IL-76**	
CCCP-76740	IL-76	
CCCP-76743	**IL-76**	
CCCP-76744	IL-76	0073478359
CCCP-76745	IL-76	0073479362
CCCP-76748	IL-76	
CCCP-76749	**IL-76**	**0073479392**
CCCP-76750	IL-76	0083485561
CCCP-76751	IL-76	0083487610
CCCP-76752	IL-76	0093498967
CCCP-76753	IL-76	0073481461
CCCP-76753	IL-76	1013406206
CCCP-76754	IL-76	093421637
CCCP-76755	IL-76	0013433984
CCCP-76756	IL-76	0013428839
CCCP-76757	IL-76	0013433990
CCCP-76758	IL-76	0073474203
CCCP-76759	IL-76	093418543
CCCP-76760	IL-76	0073479400
CCCP-76761	IL-76	0073479401
CCCP-76762	IL-76	
CCCP-76763	IL-76	0073480413
CCCP-76764	IL-76	
CCCP-76765	**IL-76**	
CCCP-76766	IL-76	0073481431
CCCP-76767	IL-76	
CCCP-76768	**IL-76**	
CCCP-76769	**IL-76**	
CCCP-76770	**IL-76**	
CCCP-76771	**IL-76**	
CCCP-76772	IL-76	
CCCP-76773	**IL-76**	
CCCP-76774	**IL-76**	
CCCP-76775	IL-76	0083481440
CCCP-76776	IL-76	0083482486
CCCP-76777	**IL-76**	
CCCP-76778	IL-76	0083482502
CCCP-76779	**IL-76**	
CCCP-76780	IL-76	
CCCP-76781	IL-76	
CCCP-76782	IL-76	0093498971
CCCP-76783	IL-76	0093498974
CCCP-76784	IL-76	0093494835
CCCP-76785	IL-76	0093495863

CCCP-76786 IL-76 0093496923
CCCP-76787 IL-76 0093495854
CCCP-76788 IL-76 0013433996
CCCP-76789 IL-76 0013433999
CCCP-76790 IL-76 0093496903
CCCP-76791 IL-76 0093497936
CCCP-76792 IL-76 0093497942
CCCP-76793 IL-76 0093498951
CCCP-76794 IL-76 0093498954
CCCP-76795 IL-76 0093498962
CCCP-76796 IL-76
CCCP-76797 IL-76 1003403052
CCCP-76798 IL-76 1003403063
CCCP-76799 IL-76 1003403075
CCCP-76800 IL-76
CCCP-76801 IL-76
CCCP-76802 IL-76
CCCP-76803 IL-76
CCCP-76804 IL-76
CCCP-76805 IL-76 1003403105
CCCP-76806 IL-76 1003403121
CCCP-76807 IL-76 1013405176
CCCP-76808 IL-76 1013405177
CCCP-76809 IL-76 1013408252
CCCP-76810 IL-76 1013409282
CCCP-76811 IL-76 1013407223
CCCP-76812 IL-76 1013407230
CCCP-76813 IL-76 1013408246
CCCP-76814 IL-76 1013408269
CCCP-76815 IL-76 1013409310
CCCP-76816 IL-76
CCCP-76817 IL-76
CCCP-76818 IL-76 1013408264
CCCP-76819 IL-76 1013409274
CCCP-76820 IL-76 1013409295
CCCP-76821 IL-76
CCCP-76822 IL-76 0093499982
CCCP-76823 IL-76 0023441189
CCCP-76824 IL-76 1023410327
CCCP-76827 IL-76
CCCP-76828 IL-76 1003405164
CCCP-76830 IL-76
CCCP-76831 IL-76 1013409287
CCCP-76832 IL-76 1023410360
CCCP-76833 IL-76
CCCP-76834 IL-76 1023409319
CCCP-76835 IL-76 1013408244
CCCP-76836 IL-76 1013409305
CCCP-76837 IL-76 1023409316
CCCP-76838 IL-76 1023411370
CCCP-76839 IL-76 1023411375
CCCP-76841 IL-76 1033418601
CCCP-76842 IL-76 1033418616
CCCP-76855 IL-76
CCCP-77101 TU144 01-1
CCCP-77102 TU144 01-2
CCCP-77103 TU144 02-1
CCCP-77105 TU144 03-1
CCCP-77106 TU144 04-1
CCCP-77107 TU144 05-1
CCCP-77108 TU144 04-2
CCCP-77109 TU144 05-2
CCCP-77110 TU144 06-1
CCCP-77111 TU144 06-2
CCCP-77112 TU144 07-1
CCCP-77113 TU144 08-1
CCCP-77114 TU144 08-2
CCCP-77115 TU144 09-1
CCCP-77116 TU144 09-2
CCCP-77144 TU144 02-2
CCCP-78711 IL-76
CCCP-78730 IL-76
CCCP-78731 IL-76
CCCP-78734 IL-76 1013409303
CCCP-78736 IL-76 1013408257
CCCP-78738 IL-76 0033442247
CCCP-78751 IL-76
CCCP-78752 IL-76 0083483519
CCCP-78753 IL-76 0083484522
CCCP-78754 IL-76 0083484527
CCCP-78755 IL-76 0083484531
CCCP-78756 IL-76 0083484536
CCCP-78757 IL-76
CCCP-78758 IL-76 0083484551
CCCP-78759 IL-76
CCCP-78760 IL-76 0083485566
CCCP-78761 IL-76
CCCP-78763 IL-76 0083486582
CCCP-78764 IL-76
CCCP-78765 IL-76 0083486590
CCCP-78766 IL-76 0083486595
CCCP-78767 IL-76
CCCP-78768 IL-76 0083487603
CCCP-78769 IL-76 0083487607
CCCP-78770 IL-76 0083487617
CCCP-78772 IL-76
CCCP-78774 IL-76 0083488643
CCCP-78775 IL-76 0083489647
CCCP-78776 IL-76 0083489652
CCCP-78777 IL-76
CCCP-78778 IL-76 0083490703
CCCP-78779 IL-76 0083489662
CCCP-78780 IL-76
CCCP-78781 IL-76
CCCP-78782 IL-76
CCCP-78783 IL-76
CCCP-78784 IL-76
CCCP-78785 IL-76 0083489691
CCCP-78786 IL-76
CCCP-78787 IL-76 0083490698
CCCP-78788 IL-76
CCCP-78789 IL-76 0083490706
CCCP-78791 IL-76
CCCP-78792 IL-76
CCCP-78794 IL-76 0093490726
CCCP-78795 IL-76
CCCP-78796 IL-76 0093491735
CCCP-78797 IL-76
CCCP-78798 IL-76
CCCP-78799 IL-76 0093491754
CCCP-78801 IL-76 0093492763
CCCP-78802 IL-76 0093492771
CCCP-78803 IL-76
CCCP-78804 IL-76
CCCP-78805 IL-76 0093492783
CCCP-78806 IL-76 0093492786
CCCP-78807 IL-76
CCCP-78808 IL-76 0093493794
CCCP-78809 IL-76
CCCP-78811 IL-76
CCCP-78812 IL-76
CCCP-78813 IL-76
CCCP-78814 IL-76
CCCP-78815 IL-76 0093495842
CCCP-78816 IL-76 0093495846
CCCP-78817 IL-76 0093495851
CCCP-78818 IL-76 0093495858
CCCP-78819 IL-76 0093495883
CCCP-78820 IL-76 0093496907
CCCP-78824 IL-76
CCCP-78825 IL-76 1013495871
CCCP-78826 IL-76 1003499991
CCCP-78827 IL-76 1003499997
CCCP-78828 IL-76 1003401004
CCCP-78829 IL-76
CCCP-78831 IL-76
CCCP-78833 IL-76 1003401025
CCCP-78834 IL-76
CCCP-78835 IL-76
CCCP-78836 IL-76 0093499986
CCCP-78837 IL-76 1003401024
CCCP-78838 IL-76 1003402044
CCCP-78839 IL-76 1003402047
CCCP-78840 IL-76 1003403056
CCCP-78842 IL-76 1003403069
CCCP-78843 IL-76 1003403082
CCCP-78844 IL-76
CCCP-78845 IL-76
CCCP-78846 IL-76
CCCP-78847 IL-76
CCCP-78848 IL-76 1003405159
CCCP-78849 IL-76 1013405192
CCCP-78850 IL-76 1003405196
CCCP-78851 IL-76
CCCP-78852 IL-76 1013407212
CCCP-78854 IL-76 1013407220
CCCP-78878 IL-76
CCCP-82001 AN124
CCCP-82002 AN124 19530501003?
CCCP-82003 AN124
CCCP-82004 AN124
CCCP-82005 AN124 9773054516003
CCCP-82006 AN124 19530501004
CCCP-82007 AN124 19530501005
CCCP-82008 AN124 19530501006
CCCP-82009 AN124 19530501007
CCCP-82010 AN124 9773053616017
CCCP-82011 AN124 9773054616023
CCCP-82012 AN124
CCCP-82013 AN124
CCCP-82014 AN124 9773054732039
CCCP-82020 AN124 19530502001
CCCP-82021 AN124 19530502002?
CCCP-82022 AN124 19530502003
CCCP-82023 AN124 195305020.4?
CCCP-82024 AN124 19530502035
CCCP-82025 AN124 19530502106
CCCP-82027 AN124 19530502288
CCCP-82028 AN124 19530502..9?
CCCP-82029 AN124 19530502630
CCCP-82030 AN124 9773054732045
CCCP-82031 AN124 9773051832049
CCCP-82032 AN124
CCCP-82033 AN124 977305..32161
CCCP-82034 AN124 9773051932162
CCCP-82035 AN124
CCCP-82036 AN124
CCCP-82037 AN124 9773052955071
CCCP-82038 AN124 9773054955077
CCCP-82039 AN124
CCCP-82040 AN124
CCCP-82041 AN124
CCCP-82042 AN124 9773054055093
CCCP-82043 AN124 9773054155101
CCCP-82044 AN124 9773054155109
CCCP-82045 AN124 9773052255113
CCCP-82060 AN225
CCCP-82066 AN124 19530502761
CCCP-82067 AN124 9773052255117
CCCP-82068 AN124 9773053259121
CCCP-82069 AN124
CCCP-83961 TU124
CCCP-83966 AN-72
CCCP-85000 TU154 H1
CCCP-85001 TU154 01
CCCP-85002 TU154 02
CCCP-85003 TU154 03
CCCP-85004 TU154 04
CCCP-85005 TU154 05
CCCP-85006 TU154 06
CCCP-85007 TU154 07
CCCP-85008 TU154 08
CCCP-85009 TU154 09
CCCP-85010 TU154 010
CCCP-85011 TU154 011
CCCP-85012 TU154 012
CCCP-85013 TU154 013
CCCP-85014 TU154 014
CCCP-85016 TU154 015
CCCP-85016 TU154 016
CCCP-85017 TU154 017
CCCP-85018 TU154 018
CCCP-85019 TU154 019
CCCP-85020 TU154 020
CCCP-85021 TU154 021
CCCP-85022 TU154 022
CCCP-85023 TU154 023
CCCP-85024 TU154 024
CCCP-85025 TU154 025
CCCP-85028 TU154 028
CCCP-85029 TU154 029
CCCP-85030 TU154 030
CCCP-85031 TU154 031
CCCP-85032 TU154 032
CCCP-85033 TU154 033
CCCP-85034 TU154 034
CCCP-85035 TU155 72A-035
CCCP-85035 TU154 035
CCCP-85037 TU154 037
CCCP-85038 TU154 038
CCCP-85039 TU154 039
CCCP-85040 TU154 040
CCCP-85041 TU154 041
CCCP-85042 TU154 042
CCCP-85043 TU154 043
CCCP-85044 TU154 044
CCCP-85049 TU154 049
CCCP-85050 TU154 050

CCCP-85051 TU154 051
CCCP-85052 TU154 052
CCCP-85053 TU154 053
CCCP-85054 TU154 054
CCCP-85055 TU154 055
CCCP-85056 TU154 056
CCCP-85057 TU154 057
CCCP-85059 TU154 059
CCCP-85060 TU154 060
CCCP-85061 TU154 061
CCCP-85062 TU154 062
CCCP-85063 TU154 063
CCCP-85064 TU154 064
CCCP-85065 TU154 065
CCCP-85066 TU154 066
CCCP-85067 TU154 067
CCCP-85068 TU154 068
CCCP-85069 TU154 069
CCCP-85070 TU154 070
CCCP-85071 TU154 071
CCCP-85072 TU154 072
CCCP-85074 TU154 074
CCCP-85075 TU154 075
CCCP-85076 TU154 076
CCCP-85078 TU154 078
CCCP-85079 TU154 079
CCCP-85080 TU154 080
CCCP-85081 TU154 081
CCCP-85082 TU154 082
CCCP-85083 TU154 083
CCCP-85084 TU154 084
CCCP-85085 TU154 085
CCCP-85087 TU154 086
CCCP-85087 TU154 087
CCCP-85088 TU154 088
CCCP-85089 TU154 089
CCCP-85090 TU154 090
CCCP-85091 TU154 091
CCCP-85092 TU154 092
CCCP-85093 TU154 093
CCCP-85094 TU154 094
CCCP-85096 TU154 096
CCCP-85097 TU154 097
CCCP-85098 TU154 098
CCCP-85099 TU154 099
CCCP-85100 TU154 100
CCCP-85101 TU154 101
CCCP-85102 TU154 102
CCCP-85103 TU154 103
CCCP-85104 TU154 104
CCCP-85105 TU154 105
CCCP-85106 TU154 106
CCCP-85107 TU154 107
CCCP-85108 TU154 108
CCCP-85109 TU154 109
CCCP-85110 TU154 110
CCCP-85111 TU154 111
CCCP-85112 TU154 112
CCCP-85113 TU154 113
CCCP-85114 TU154 114
CCCP-85115 TU154 115
CCCP-85116 TU154 116
CCCP-85117 TU154 117
CCCP-85118 TU154 118
CCCP-85119 TU154 119
CCCP-85120 TU154 120
CCCP-85121 TU154 121
CCCP-85122 TU154 122
CCCP-85123 TU154 123
CCCP-85124 TU154 124
CCCP-85125 TU154 125
CCCP-85130 TU154 130
CCCP-85131 TU154 131
CCCP-85132 TU154 132
CCCP-85133 TU154 133
CCCP-85134 TU154 134
CCCP-85135 TU154 135
CCCP-85136 TU154 136
CCCP-85137 TU154 137
CCCP-85138 TU154 138
CCCP-85139 TU154 139
CCCP-85140 TU154 140
CCCP-85141 TU154 141
CCCP-85142 TU154 142
CCCP-85145 TU154 145
CCCP-85146 TU154 146
CCCP-85147 TU154 147
CCCP-85148 TU154 148
CCCP-85149 TU154 149
CCCP-85150 TU154 150
CCCP-85151 TU154 151
CCCP-85152 TU154 152
CCCP-85153 TU154 153
CCCP-85154 TU154 154
CCCP-85155 TU154 155
CCCP-85156 TU154 156
CCCP-85157 TU154 157
CCCP-85158 TU154 158
CCCP-85160 TU154 160
CCCP-85162 TU154 162
CCCP-85163 TU154 163
CCCP-85164 TU154 164
CCCP-85165 TU154 165
CCCP-85166 TU154 166
CCCP-85167 TU154 167
CCCP-85168 TU154 168
CCCP-85169 TU154 169
CCCP-85170 TU154 170
CCCP-85171 TU154 171
CCCP-85172 TU154 172
CCCP-85173 TU154 173
CCCP-85174 TU154 174
CCCP-85176 TU154 176
CCCP-85177 TU154 177
CCCP-85178 TU154 178
CCCP-85179 TU154 179
CCCP-85180 TU154 180
CCCP-85181 TU154 181
CCCP-85182 TU154 182
CCCP-85183 TU154 183
CCCP-85184 TU154 184
CCCP-85185 TU154 185
CCCP-85186 TU154 186
CCCP-85187 TU154 187
CCCP-85188 TU154 188
CCCP-85189 TU154 189
CCCP-85190 TU154 190
CCCP-85192 TU154 192
CCCP-85193 TU154 193
CCCP-85194 TU154 194
CCCP-85195 TU154 195
CCCP-85196 TU154 196
CCCP-85197 TU154 197
CCCP-85198 TU154 198
CCCP-85199 TU154 199
CCCP-85200 TU154 200
CCCP-85201 TU154 201
CCCP-85202 TU154 202
CCCP-85203 TU154 203
CCCP-85204 TU154 204
CCCP-85205 TU154 205
CCCP-85206 TU154 206
CCCP-85207 TU154 207
CCCP-85210 TU154 210
CCCP-85211 TU154 211
CCCP-85212 TU154 212
CCCP-85213 TU154 213
CCCP-85214 TU154 214
CCCP-85215 TU154 215
CCCP-85216 TU154 216
CCCP-85217 TU154 217
CCCP-85218 TU154 218
CCCP-85219 TU154 219
CCCP-85220 TU154 220
CCCP-85221 TU154 221
CCCP-85222 TU154 222
CCCP-85223 TU154 223
CCCP-85226 TU154 226
CCCP-85227 TU154 227
CCCP-85228 TU154 228
CCCP-85229 TU154 229
CCCP-85230 TU154 230
CCCP-85231 TU154 231
CCCP-85232 TU154 232
CCCP-85233 TU154 233
CCCP-85234 TU154 234
CCCP-85235 TU154 235
CCCP-85236 TU154 236
CCCP-85237 TU154 237
CCCP-85238 TU154 238
CCCP-85240 TU154 240
CCCP-85241 TU154 241
CCCP-85242 TU154 242
CCCP-85243 TU154 243
CCCP-85244 TU154 244
CCCP-85245 TU154 245
CCCP-85246 TU154 246
CCCP-85247 TU154 247
CCCP-85248 TU154 248
CCCP-85249 TU154 249
CCCP-85250 TU154 250
CCCP-85251 TU154 251
CCCP-85252 TU154 252
CCCP-85253 TU154 253
CCCP-85254 TU154 254
CCCP-85255 TU154 255
CCCP-85256 TU154 256
CCCP-85257 TU154 257
CCCP-85259 TU154 259
CCCP-85260 TU154 260
CCCP-85261 TU154 261
CCCP-85263 TU154 263
CCCP-85264 TU154 264
CCCP-85265 TU154 265
CCCP-85266 TU154 266
CCCP-85267 TU154 267
CCCP-85268 TU154 268
CCCP-85269 TU154 269
CCCP-85271 TU154 271
CCCP-85272 TU154 272
CCCP-85273 TU154 273
CCCP-85274 TU154 274
CCCP-85275 TU154 275
CCCP-85276 TU154 276
CCCP-85279 TU154 279
CCCP-85280 TU154 280
CCCP-85281 TU154 281
CCCP-85282 TU154 282
CCCP-85283 TU154 283
CCCP-85284 TU154 284
CCCP-85285 TU154 285
CCCP-85286 TU154 286
CCCP-85287 TU154 287
CCCP-85288 TU154 288
CCCP-85289 TU154 289
CCCP-85290 TU154 290
CCCP-85291 TU154 291
CCCP-85292 TU154 292
CCCP-85293 TU154 293
CCCP-85294 TU154 294
CCCP-85295 TU154 295
CCCP-85296 TU154 296
CCCP-85297 TU154 297
CCCP-85298 TU154 298
CCCP-85299 TU154 299
CCCP-85300 TU154 300
CCCP-85301 TU154 301
CCCP-85302 TU154 302
CCCP-85303 TU154 303
CCCP-85304 TU154 304
CCCP-85305 TU154 305
CCCP-85306 TU154 306
CCCP-85307 TU154 307
CCCP-85308 TU154 308
CCCP-85309 TU154 309
CCCP-85310 TU154 310
CCCP-85311 TU154 311
CCCP-85312 TU154 312
CCCP-85313 TU154 313
CCCP-85314 TU154 314
CCCP-85315 TU154 315
CCCP-85316 TU154 316
CCCP-85317 TU154 317
CCCP-85318 TU154 318
CCCP-85319 TU154 319
CCCP-85321 TU154 321
CCCP-85322 TU154 322
CCCP-85323 TU154 323
CCCP-85324 TU154 324
CCCP-85327 TU154 327
CCCP-85328 TU154 328
CCCP-85329 TU154 329
CCCP-85330 TU154 330
CCCP-85331 TU154 331
CCCP-85332 TU154 332
CCCP-85333 TU154 333
CCCP-85334 TU154 334
CCCP-85335 TU154 335

CCCP-85336 TU154 336
CCCP-85337 TU154 337
CCCP-85338 TU154 338
CCCP-85339 TU154 339
CCCP-85340 TU154 340
CCCP-85341 TU154 341
CCCP-85343 TU154 343
CCCP-85344 TU154 344
CCCP-85345 TU154 345
CCCP-85346 TU154 346
CCCP-85347 TU154 347
CCCP-85348 TU154 348
CCCP-85349 TU154 349
CCCP-85350 TU154 350
CCCP-85351 TU154 351
CCCP-85352 TU154 352
CCCP-85353 TU154 353
CCCP-85354 TU154 354
CCCP-85355 TU154 355
CCCP-85356 TU154 356
CCCP-85357 TU154 357
CCCP-85358 TU154 358
CCCP-85359 TU154 359
CCCP-85360 TU154 360
CCCP-85361 TU154 361
CCCP-85362 TU154 362
CCCP-85363 TU154 363
CCCP-85364 TU154 364
CCCP-85365 TU154 365
CCCP-85366 TU154 366
CCCP-85367 TU154 367
CCCP-85368 TU154 368
CCCP-85369 TU154 369
CCCP-85370 TU154 370
CCCP-85371 TU154 371
CCCP-85372 TU154 372
CCCP-85373 TU154 373
CCCP-85374 TU154 374
CCCP-85375 TU154 375
CCCP-85376 TU154 376
CCCP-85377 TU154 377
CCCP-85378 TU154 378
CCCP-85379 TU154 379
CCCP-85380 TU154 380
CCCP-85381 TU154 381
CCCP-85382 TU154 382
CCCP-85383 TU154 383
CCCP-85384 TU154 384
CCCP-85385 TU154 385
CCCP-85386 TU154 386
CCCP-85387 TU154 387
CCCP-85388 TU154 388
CCCP-85389 TU154 389
CCCP-85390 TU154 390
CCCP-85391 TU154 391
CCCP-85392 TU154 392
CCCP-85393 TU154 393
CCCP-85394 TU154 394
CCCP-85395 TU154 395
CCCP-85396 TU154 396
CCCP-85397 TU154 397
CCCP-85398 TU154 398
CCCP-85399 TU154 399
CCCP-85400 TU154 400
CCCP-85401 TU154 401
CCCP-85402 TU154 402
CCCP-85403 TU154 403
CCCP-85404 TU154 404
CCCP-85405 TU154 405
CCCP-85406 TU154 406
CCCP-85407 TU154 407
CCCP-85409 TU154 409
CCCP-85410 TU154 410
CCCP-85411 TU154 411
CCCP-85412 TU154 412
CCCP-85413 TU154 413
CCCP-85414 TU154 414
CCCP-85416 TU154 416
CCCP-85417 TU154 417
CCCP-85418 TU154 418
CCCP-85419 TU154 419
CCCP-85421 TU154 421
CCCP-85423 TU154 423
CCCP-85424 TU154 424
CCCP-85425 TU154 425
CCCP-85426 TU154 426
CCCP-85427 TU154 427
CCCP-85429 TU154 429
CCCP-85430 TU154 430
CCCP-85431 TU154 431
CCCP-85432 TU154 432
CCCP-85433 TU154 433
CCCP-85434 TU154 434
CCCP-85435 TU154 435
CCCP-85436 TU154 436
CCCP-85437 TU154 437
CCCP-85438 TU154 438
CCCP-85439 TU154 439
CCCP-85440 TU154 440
CCCP-85441 TU154 441
CCCP-85442 TU154 442
CCCP-85443 TU154 443
CCCP-85444 TU154 444
CCCP-85445 TU154 445
CCCP-85446 TU154 446
CCCP-85448 TU154 448
CCCP-85449 TU154 449
CCCP-85450 TU154 450
CCCP-85451 TU154 451
CCCP-85452 TU154 452
CCCP-85453 TU154 453
CCCP-85454 TU154 454
CCCP-85455 TU154 455
CCCP-85456 TU154 456
CCCP-85457 TU154 457
CCCP-85458 TU154 458
CCCP-85459 TU154 459
CCCP-85460 TU154 460
CCCP-85461 TU154 461
CCCP-85462 TU154 462
CCCP-85463 TU154 463
CCCP-85464 TU154 464
CCCP-85465 TU154 465
CCCP-85466 TU154 466
CCCP-85467 TU154 467
CCCP-85468 TU154 468
CCCP-85469 TU154 469
CCCP-85470 TU154 470
CCCP-85472 TU154 472
CCCP-85475 TU154 475
CCCP-85476 TU154 476
CCCP-85477 TU154 477
CCCP-85478 TU154 478
CCCP-85479 TU154 479
CCCP-85480 TU154 480
CCCP-85481 TU154 481
CCCP-85482 TU154 482
CCCP-85485 TU154 485
CCCP-85486 TU154 486
CCCP-85487 TU154 487
CCCP-85489 TU154 489
CCCP-85490 TU154 490
CCCP-85491 TU154 491
CCCP-85492 TU154 492
CCCP-85494 TU154 494
CCCP-85495 TU154 495
CCCP-85496 TU154 496
CCCP-85497 TU154 497
CCCP-85498 TU154 498
CCCP-85499 TU154 499
CCCP-85500 TU154 500
CCCP-85502 TU154 502
CCCP-85503 TU154 503
CCCP-85504 TU154 504
CCCP-85505 TU154 505
CCCP-85506 TU154 506
CCCP-85507 TU154 507
CCCP-85508 TU154 508
CCCP-85509 TU154 509
CCCP-85510 TU154 510
CCCP-85511 TU154 511
CCCP-85512 TU154 512
CCCP-85513 TU154 513
CCCP-85514 TU154 514
CCCP-85515 TU154 515
CCCP-85516 TU154 516
CCCP-85518 TU154 518
CCCP-85519 TU154 519
CCCP-85520 TU154 520
CCCP-85521 TU154 521
CCCP-85522 TU154 522
CCCP-85523 TU154 523
CCCP-85524 TU154 524
CCCP-85525 TU154 525
CCCP-85526 TU154 526
CCCP-85527 TU154 527
CCCP-85528 TU154 528
CCCP-85529 TU154 529
CCCP-85530 TU154 530
CCCP-85531 TU154 531
CCCP-85532 TU154 532
CCCP-85533 TU154 533
CCCP-85534 TU154 534
CCCP-85535 TU154 535
CCCP-85536 TU154 536
CCCP-85537 TU154 537
CCCP-85538 TU154 538
CCCP-85539 TU154 539
CCCP-85541 TU154 540
CCCP-85542 TU154 542
CCCP-85544 TU154 544
CCCP-85545 TU154 545
CCCP-85546 TU154 546
CCCP-85547 TU154 547
CCCP-85548 TU154 548
CCCP-85549 TU154 549
CCCP-85550 TU154 550
CCCP-85551 TU154 551
CCCP-85552 TU154 552
CCCP-85553 TU154 553
CCCP-85554 TU154 554
CCCP-85555 TU154 555
CCCP-85556 TU154 556
CCCP-85557 TU154 557
CCCP-85558 TU154 558
CCCP-85559 TU154 559
CCCP-85560 TU154 560
CCCP-85561 TU154 561
CCCP-85562 TU154 562
CCCP-85563 TU154 563
CCCP-85564 TU154 564
CCCP-85565 TU154 565
CCCP-85565? TU154 565
CCCP-85566 TU154 566
CCCP-85567 TU154 567
CCCP-85568 TU154 568
CCCP-85570 TU154 570
CCCP-85571 TU154 571
CCCP-85572 TU154 572
CCCP-85573 TU154 573
CCCP-85574 TU154 574
CCCP-85575 TU154 575
CCCP-85577 TU154 577
CCCP-85578 TU154 578
CCCP-85579 TU154 579
CCCP-85580 TU154 580
CCCP-85581 TU154 581
CCCP-85582 TU154 582
CCCP-85583 TU154 583
CCCP-85585 TU154 585
CCCP-85586 TU154 586
CCCP-85587 TU154 587
CCCP-85588 TU154 588
CCCP-85589 TU154 589
CCCP-85590 TU154 590
CCCP-85591 TU154 591
CCCP-85592 TU154 592
CCCP-85593 TU154 593
CCCP-85594 TU154 594
CCCP-85595 TU154 595
CCCP-85596 TU154 596
CCCP-85597 TU154 597
CCCP-85598 TU154 598
CCCP-85600 TU154 600
CCCP-85602 TU154 602
CCCP-85603 TU154 603
CCCP-85604 TU154 604
CCCP-85605 TU154 605
CCCP-85606 TU154 606
CCCP-85607 TU154 607
CCCP-85608 TU154 608
CCCP-85609 TU154 609
CCCP-85610 TU154 705
CCCP-85611 TU154 715
CCCP-85612 TU154 721
CCCP-85613 TU154 722
CCCP-85614 TU154 723
CCCP-85615 TU154 731

CCCP-85616 TU154 732
CCCP-85617 TU154 736
CCCP-85618 TU154 737
CCCP-85619 TU154 738
CCCP-85620 TU154 739
CCCP-85621 TU154 742
CCCP-85622 TU154 746
CCCP-85623 TU154 749
CCCP-85624 TU154 750
CCCP-85625 TU154 752
CCCP-85626 TU154 753
CCCP-85627 TU154 756
CCCP-85628 TU154 757
CCCP-85629 TU154 758
CCCP-85630 TU154 759
CCCP-85631 TU154 760
CCCP-85632 TU154 761
CCCP-85633 TU154 762
CCCP-85634 TU154 763
CCCP-85635 TU154 764
CCCP-85636 TU154 766
CCCP-85637 TU154 767
CCCP-85638 TU154 768
CCCP-85639 TU154 771
CCCP-85640 TU154 772
CCCP-85641 TU154 773
CCCP-85642 TU154 778
CCCP-85643 TU154 779
CCCP-85644 TU154 780
CCCP-85645 TU154 782
CCCP-85646 TU154 784
CCCP-85647 TU154 785
CCCP-85648 TU154 786
CCCP-85649 TU154 787
CCCP-85650 TU154 788
CCCP-85651 TU154 793
CCCP-85652 TU154 794
CCCP-85653 TU154 795
CCCP-85654 TU154 796
CCCP-85655 TU154 798
CCCP-85656 TU154 801
CCCP-85657 TU154 802
CCCP-85658 TU154 808
CCCP-85659 TU154 809
CCCP-85660 TU154 810
CCCP-85661 TU154 811
CCCP-85662 TU154 816
CCCP-85663 TU154 817
CCCP-85664 TU154 818
CCCP-85665 TU154 819
CCCP-85666 TU154 820
CCCP-85667 TU154 825
CCCP-85668 TU154 826
CCCP-85669 TU154 827
CCCP-85670 TU154 828
CCCP-85671 TU154 829
CCCP-85672 TU154 830
CCCP-85673 TU154 833
CCCP-85674 TU154 834
CCCP-85675 TU154 835
CCCP-85676 TU154 836
CCCP-85677 TU154 839
CCCP-85678 TU154 841
CCCP-85679 TU154 842
CCCP-85680 TU154 843
CCCP-85681 TU154 848
CCCP-85682 TU154 849
CCCP-85683 TU154 850
CCCP-85684 TU154 851
CCCP-85685 TU154 853
CCCP-85686 TU154 854
CCCP-85687 TU154 857
CCCP-85688 TU154 859
CCCP-85689 TU154 860
CCCP-85690 TU154 861
CCCP-85691 TU154 864
CCCP-85692 TU154 865
CCCP-85693 TU154 866
CCCP-85694 TU154 867
CCCP-85695 TU154 868
CCCP-85696 TU154 869
CCCP-85697 TU154 870
CCCP-85698 TU154 871
CCCP-85699 TU154 874
CCCP-85700 TU154 875
CCCP-85701 TU154 876
CCCP-85702 TU154 877
CCCP-85703 TU154 878
CCCP-85704 TU154 879
CCCP-85705 TU154 880
CCCP-85706 TU154 881
CCCP-85707 TU154 882
CCCP-85708 TU154 883
CCCP-85709 TU154 884
CCCP-85710 TU154 885
CCCP-85711 TU154 887
CCCP-85712 TU154 888
CCCP-85713 TU154 889
CCCP-85714 TU154 890
CCCP-85715 TU154 891
CCCP-85716 TU154 892
CCCP-85717 TU154 893?
CCCP-85718 TU154 894?
CCCP-85719 TU154 901
CCCP-85720 TU154 902
CCCP-85721 TU154 903
CCCP-85722 TU154 904
CCCP-85723 TU154 905
CCCP-85724 TU154 906
CCCP-85725 TU154 907?
CCCP-85726 TU154 908
CCCP-85727 TU154 909
CCCP-85728 TU154 910
CCCP-85729 TU154 911
CCCP-85730 TU154 912
CCCP-85731 TU154 913
CCCP-85732 TU154 914
CCCP-85733 TU154 915
CCCP-85735 TU154 917
CCCP-85737 TU154 920
CCCP-85738 TU154 921?
CCCP-85739 TU154 922
CCCP-85740 TU154 895
CCCP-85741 TU154 896
CCCP-85743 TU154 926
CCCP-85744 TU154 927
CCCP-85745 TU154 928
CCCP-85746 TU154 929
CCCP-85748 TU154 924
CCCP-85750 TU154 933
CCCP-85759 TU154 943?
CCCP-85763 TU154 946
CCCP-85765 TU154 919?
(CCCP-85765) TU154 765
(CCCP-85770) TU154 770
(CCCP-85774) TU154 774
(CCCP-85775) TU154 775
(CCCP-85776) TU154 776
(CCCP-85789) TU154 789
CCCP-85801 TU154 960
CCCP-85803 TU154 822
CCCP-86000 IL-86 0101?
CCCP-86001 IL-86 0102?
CCCP-86002 IL-86 0103?
CCCP-86003 IL-86 51483200001
CCCP-86004 IL-86 51483200002
CCCP-86005 IL-86 51483200003
CCCP-86006 IL-86 51483200004
CCCP-86007 IL-86 51483200005
CCCP-86008 IL-86 51483200006
CCCP-86009 IL-86 51483200007
CCCP-86010 IL-86 51483200008
CCCP-86011 IL-86 51483200009
CCCP-86012 IL-86 51483202010
CCCP-86013 IL-86 51483202011
CCCP-86014 IL-86 51483202012
CCCP-86015 IL-86 51483202013
CCCP-86016 IL-86 51483202014
CCCP-86017 IL-86 51483202015
CCCP-86018 IL-86 51483202016
CCCP-86020 IL-76
CCCP-86021 IL-76
CCCP-86022 IL-76
CCCP-86023 IL-76
CCCP-86024 IL-76
CCCP-86025 IL-76
CCCP-86026 IL-76
CCCP-86027 IL-76
CCCP-86028 IL-76
CCCP-86029 IL-76
CCCP-86030 IL-76
CCCP-86031 IL-76
CCCP-86032 IL-76
CCCP-86033 IL-76
CCCP-86034 IL-76
CCCP-86035 IL-76
CCCP-86037 IL-76
CCCP-86038 IL-76
CCCP-86039 IL-76
CCCP-86040 IL-76
CCCP-86041 IL-76
CCCP-86042 IL-76
CCCP-86043 IL-76 093418539
CCCP-86044 IL-76
CCCP-86045 IL-76
CCCP-86046 IL-76
CCCP-86047 IL-76
CCCP-86048 IL-76
CCCP-86049 IL-76
CCCP-86050 IL-86 51483202017
CCCP-86051 IL-86 51483202018
CCCP-86052 IL-86 51483202019
CCCP-86053 IL-86 51483203020
CCCP-86054 IL-86 51483203021
CCCP-86055 IL-86 51483203022
CCCP-86056 IL-86 51483203023
CCCP-86057 IL-86 51483203024
CCCP-86058 IL-86 51483203025
CCCP-86059 IL-86 51483203026
CCCP-86060 IL-86 51483203027
CCCP-86061 IL-86 51483203028
CCCP-86062 IL-86 51483203029
CCCP-86063 IL-86 51483203030
CCCP-86064 IL-86 51483203031
CCCP-86065 IL-86 51483203032
CCCP-86066 IL-86 51483203033
CCCP-86067 IL-86 51483204034
CCCP-86068 IL-86 51483204035
CCCP-86069 IL-86 51483204036
CCCP-86070 IL-86 51483204037
CCCP-86071 IL-86 51483204038
CCCP-86072 IL-86 51483204039
CCCP-86073 IL-86 51483204040
CCCP-86074 IL-86 51483205041
CCCP-86075 IL-86 51483205044
CCCP-86076 IL-86 51483205045
CCCP-86077 IL-86 51483205047
CCCP-86078 IL-86 51483205049
CCCP-86079 IL-86 51483206050
CCCP-86080 IL-86 51483206051
CCCP-86081 IL-86 51483206052
CCCP-86082 IL-86 51483206053
CCCP-86083 IL-86 51483206054
CCCP-86084 IL-86 51483206055
CCCP-86085 IL-86 51483206056
CCCP-86086 IL-86 51483206057
CCCP-86087 IL-86 51483206058
CCCP-86088 IL-86 51483206059
CCCP-86089 IL-86 51483207060
CCCP-86090 IL-86 51483207061
CCCP-86091 IL-86 51483207062
CCCP-86092 IL-86 51483207063
CCCP-86093 IL-86 51483207064
CCCP-86094 IL-86 51483207065
CCCP-86095 IL-86 51483207066
CCCP-86096 IL-86 51483207067
CCCP-86097 IL-86 51483207068
CCCP-86098 IL-86 514832.....
CCCP-86101 IL-86 51483207069
CCCP-86102 IL-86 51483207070
CCCP-86103 IL-86 51483208071
CCCP-86104 IL-86 51483208072
CCCP-86105 IL-86 51483208073
CCCP-86106 IL-86 51483208074
CCCP-86107 IL-86 51483208075
CCCP-86108 IL-86 51483208076
CCCP-86109 IL-86 51483208077
CCCP-86110 IL-86 51483208078
CCCP-86111 IL-86 51483208079
CCCP-86112 IL-86 51483208080
CCCP-86113 IL-86 51483209081
CCCP-86114 IL-86 51483209082
CCCP-86115 IL-86 51483209083
CCCP-86116 IL-86 51483209084
CCCP-86117 IL-86 51483209085
CCCP-86118 IL-86 51483209086
CCCP-86119 IL-86 51483209087
CCCP-86120 IL-86 51483209088

CCCP-86121 IL-86 51483209089
CCCP-86122 IL-86 51483210090
CCCP-86123 IL-86 51483210091
CCCP-86124 IL-86 51483210092
CCCP-86125 IL-86 51483210093
CCCP-86132 IL-62 1034152
CCCP-86133 IL-62 1138234
CCCP-86134 IL-62 1138546
CCCP-86135 IL-62 1748445
CCCP-86136 IL-86 51483210094
CCCP-86137 IL-86 51483210095
CCCP-86138 IL-86 51483210096
CCCP-86139 IL-86 51483210097
CCCP-86141 IL-86 514832.....
CCCP-86145 IL-86 51483211101
CCCP-86146 IL-86 51483205042
CCCP-86147 IL-86 51483205043
CCCP-86148 IL-86 51483205046
CCCP-86149 IL-86 51483205048
CCCP-86450 IL-62 52104
CCCP-86451 IL-62 52105
CCCP-86452 IL-62 62201
CCCP-86453 IL-62 62202
CCCP-86454 IL-62 62203
CCCP-86455 IL-62 62205
CCCP-86456 IL-62 62301
CCCP-86457 IL-62 62302
CCCP-86458 IL-62 62303
CCCP-86459 IL-62 62304
CCCP-86460 IL-62 62305
CCCP-86461 IL-62 62401
CCCP-86462 IL-62 62402
CCCP-86463 IL-62 62403
CCCP-86464 IL-62 62405
CCCP-86465 IL-62 62501
CCCP-86466 IL-62 2749316
CCCP-86467 IL-62 3749733
CCCP-86468 IL-62 4749857
CCCP-86469 IL-62 72502
CCCP-86470 IL-62 72503
CCCP-86471 IL-62 72504
CCCP-86472 IL-62 2726517
CCCP-86473 IL-62 3726841
CCCP-86474 IL-62 3726952
CCCP-86475 IL-62 3727113
CCCP-86476 IL-62 4728229
CCCP-86477 IL-62 4727435
CCCP-86478 IL-62 4727657
CCCP-86479 IL-62 4728118
CCCP-86480 IL-62 2828354
CCCP-86481 IL-62 2829415
CCCP-86482 IL-62 2829526
CCCP-86483 IL-62 2829637
CCCP-86484 IL-62 4727324
CCCP-86484 IL-62 3829859
CCCP-86485 IL-62 3830912
CCCP-86486 IL-62 3830123
CCCP-86487 IL-62 3830234
CCCP-86488 IL-62 4830345
CCCP-86489 IL-62 4830456
CCCP-86490 IL-62 4831739
CCCP-86491 IL-62 1931142
CCCP-86492 IL-62 4140324
CCCP-86493 IL-62 4140748
CCCP-86494 IL-62 4140952
CCCP-86495 IL-62 2726628
CCCP-86497 IL-62 1931253
CCCP-86498 IL-62 1932314
CCCP-86499 IL-62 2932637
CCCP-86500 IL-62 2932859
CCCP-86501 IL-62 3933121
CCCP-86502 IL-62 3933345
CCCP-86503 IL-62 4934512
CCCP-86504 IL-62 4934621
CCCP-86505 IL-62 4934847
CCCP-86506 IL-62 1035324
CCCP-86507 IL-62 2035546
CCCP-86508 IL-62 2036718
CCCP-86509 IL-62 2036829
CCCP-86510 IL-62 1035213
CCCP-86511 IL-62 3036142
CCCP-86512 IL-62 3037314
CCCP-86513 IL-62 4037536
CCCP-86514 IL-62 4037647
CCCP-86515 IL-62 2138657
CCCP-86516 IL-62 2139524
CCCP-86517 IL-62 3139732
CCCP-86518 IL-62 3139956
CCCP-86519 IL-62 4140212
CCCP-86520 IL-62 1241314
CCCP-86521 IL-62 1241425
CCCP-86522 IL-62 2241536
CCCP-86523 IL-62 2241647
CCCP-86524 IL-62 3242321
CCCP-86525 IL-62 4851612
CCCP-86526 IL-62 2951447
CCCP-86527 IL-62 4037758
CCCP-86528 IL-62 4038111
CCCP-86529 IL-62 4038625
CCCP-86530 IL-62 4242543
CCCP-86531 IL-62 4242654
CCCP-86532 IL-62 4243111
CCCP-86533 IL-62 1343123
CCCP-86534 IL-62 1343332
CCCP-86535 IL-62 4344851
CCCP-86536 IL-62 4445948
CCCP-86537 IL-62 3546733
CCCP-86538 IL-62 00605
CCCP-86539 IL-62 2344615
CCCP-86540 IL-62 3546548
CCCP-86541 IL-62 3951359
CCCP-86542 IL-62 3952714
CCCP-86544 IL-62
CCCP-86552 IL-62 2052435
CCCP-86553 IL-62 3052657
CCCP-86554 IL-62 4053514
CCCP-86555 IL-62 4547315
CCCP-86556 IL-62 31401
CCCP-86557 IL-62 2725456
CCCP-86558 IL-62 1052128
CCCP-86559 IL-62 2153258
CCCP-86560 IL-62 .53.4.
CCCP-86561 IL-62 4154841
CCCP-86562 IL-62 4831517
CCCP-86563 IL-62 3036931
CCCP-86564 IL-62 4934734
CCCP-86565 IL-62 2546812
CCCP-86573 IL-62 4140536
CCCP-86574 IL-62 3344833
CCCP-86575 IL-62 1647928
CCCP-86576 IL-62 4546257
CCCP-86577 IL-62 2748552
CCCP-86578 IL-62 1951525
CCCP-86579 IL-62 2951636
CCCP-86580 IL-62 2343554
CCCP-86581 IL-62 2932526
CCCP-86582 IL-62 3036253
CCCP-86600 IL-76 033401022
CCCP-86604 IL-76
CCCP-86605 IL-62 41701
CCCP-86606 IL-62 41702
CCCP-86607 IL-62 41703
CCCP-86608 IL-62 41704
CCCP-86609 IL-62 41705
CCCP-86610 IL-62 41801
CCCP-86611 IL-62 41803
CCCP-86612 IL-62 41804
CCCP-86613 IL-62 51901
CCCP-86614 IL-62 51903
CCCP-86615 IL-62 51904
CCCP-86616 IL-62 51905
CCCP-86617 IL-62 52001
CCCP-86618 IL-62 52002
CCCP-86619 IL-62 52003
CCCP-86620 IL-62 52004
CCCP-86621 IL-62 52005
CCCP-86622 IL-62 52101
CCCP-86623 IL-62 52102
CCCP-86624 IL-62 52103
CCCP-86624 IL-76
CCCP-86625 IL-76
CCCP-86626 IL-76
CCCP-86627 IL-76 063405137
CCCP-86629 IL-76
CCCP-86635 IL-76
CCCP-86637 IL-76
CCCP-86640 IL-76 073409237
CCCP-86642 IL-76
CCCP-86644 IL-76
CCCP-86648 IL-62 90605
CCCP-86649 IL-62 00703
CCCP-86650 IL-62 00705
CCCP-86651 IL-62 00801
CCCP-86652 IL-62 00802
CCCP-86653 IL-62 00803
CCCP-86654 IL-62 00804
CCCP-86655 IL-62 00805
CCCP-86656 IL-62 10901
CCCP-86657 IL-62 10904
CCCP-86658 IL-62 10905
CCCP-86659 IL-62 31404
CCCP-86661 IL-62 50001
CCCP-86662 IL-62 50102
CCCP-86663 IL-62 50103
CCCP-86664 IL-62 50104
CCCP-86665 IL-62 50105
CCCP-86666 IL-62 60201
CCCP-86667 IL-62 60202
CCCP-86668 IL-62 60203
CCCP-86669 IL-62 60204
CCCP-86670 IL-62 70205
CCCP-86671 IL-62 70301
CCCP-86672 IL-62 70302
CCCP-86673 IL-62 70303
CCCP-86674 IL-62 70304
CCCP-86675 IL-62 80305
CCCP-86676 IL-62 80401
CCCP-86677 IL-62 80402
CCCP-86678 IL-62 80403
CCCP-86679 IL-62 80404
CCCP-86680 IL-62 80405
CCCP-86681 IL-62 90501
CCCP-86682 IL-62 90502
CCCP-86683 IL-62 90503
CCCP-86684 IL-62 90504
CCCP-86685 IL-62 90505
CCCP-86686 IL-62 90601
CCCP-86687 IL-62 90604
CCCP-86688 IL-62
CCCP-86689 IL-62 11001
CCCP-86690 IL-62 11002
CCCP-86691 IL-62 11003
CCCP-86692 IL-62 11102
CCCP-86693 IL-62 11103
CCCP-86694 IL-62 11104
CCCP-86695 IL-62 21204
CCCP-86696 IL-62 21205
CCCP-86697 IL-62 21301
CCCP-86698 IL-62 21303
CCCP-86699 IL-62 21304
CCCP-86700 IL-62 31503
CCCP-86701 IL-62 31504
CCCP-86702 IL-62 31505
CCCP-86703 IL-62 41601
CCCP-86704 IL-62 41603
CCCP-86705 IL-62 41605
CCCP-86706 IL-62 21105
CCCP-86707 IL-62 41604
CCCP-86708 IL-62 41802
CCCP-86709 IL-62 62204
CCCP-86710 IL-62 2647646
CCCP-86711 IL-62 4648414
CCCP-86711 IL-76 01300103
CCCP-86712 IL-62 4648339
CCCP-86712 IL-76 01300101
CCCP-86713 IL-76
CCCP-86714 IL-76
CCCP-86715 IL-76
CCCP-86717 IL-76
CCCP-86719 IL-76
CCCP-86720 IL-76 073409267
CCCP-86721 IL-76
CCCP-86722 IL-76
CCCP-86724 IL-76 073410284
CCCP-86725 IL-76
CCCP-86726 IL-76 083412380
CCCP-86727 IL-76
CCCP-86728 IL-76
CCCP-86729 IL-76
CCCP-86731 IL-76
CCCP-86733 IL-76
CCCP-86734 IL-76
CCCP-86735 IL-76
CCCP-86736 IL-76
CCCP-86737 IL-76
CCCP-86738 IL-76
CCCP-86739 IL-76
CCCP-86740 IL-76

CCCP-86741	**IL-76**	
CCCP-86742	**IL-76**	
CCCP-86744	**IL-76**	
CCCP-86745	**IL-76**	
CCCP-86746	**IL-76**	
CCCP-86747	IL-76	063407170
CCCP-86748	**IL-76**	
CCCP-86749	**IL-76**	
CCCP-86786	**IL-76**	
CCCP-86806	**IL-76**	
CCCP-86807	**IL-76**	
CCCP-86808	**IL-76**	
CCCP-86809	**IL-76**	
CCCP-86810	IL-76	
CCCP-86811	**IL-76**	
CCCP-86812	**IL-76**	**053404103**
CCCP-86813	**IL-76**	
CCCP-86815	**IL-76**	
CCCP-86817	IL-76	063407191
CCCP-86819	IL-76	
CCCP-86822	**IL-76**	
CCCP-86823	**IL-76**	**053405124**
CCCP-86824	**IL-76**	
CCCP-86825	IL-76	
CCCP-86826	**IL-76**	
CCCP-86827	IL-76	
CCCP-86828	**IL-76**	
CCCP-86829	**IL-76**	
CCCP-86830	IL-76	
CCCP-86831	**IL-76**	
CCCP-86832	IL-76	
CCCP-86833	IL-76	
CCCP-86834	**IL-76**	
CCCP-86835	IL-76	
CCCP-86836	**IL-76**	**0003422661**
CCCP-86837	**IL-76**	
CCCP-86838	**IL-76**	
CCCP-86839	IL-76	
CCCP-86840	**IL-76**	
CCCP-86841	**IL-76**	
CCCP-86842	IL-76	
CCCP-86843	IL-76	
CCCP-86844	**IL-76**	**0003424711**
CCCP-86845	**IL-76**	**0003426762**
CCCP-86846	IL-76	0003426765
CCCP-86848	**IL-76**	
CCCP-86849	**IL-76**	
CCCP-86850	IL-76	0003427782
CCCP-86851	IL-76	0003424715
CCCP-86852	**IL-76**	
CCCP-86853	IL-76	
CCCP-86855	**IL-76**	
CCCP-86856	**IL-76**	
CCCP-86857	IL-76	0003425744
CCCP-86858	IL-76	
CCCP-86859	**IL-76**	
CCCP-86860	**IL-76**	
CCCP-86861	**IL-76**	
CCCP-86862	**IL-76**	
CCCP-86863	IL-76	0003428809
CCCP-86864	**IL-76**	**0003428816**
CCCP-86865	**IL-76**	
CCCP-86866	IL-76	0003428821
CCCP-86867	**IL-76**	
CCCP-86868	IL-76	
CCCP-86869	IL-76	0013428844
CCCP-86871	**IL-76**	
CCCP-86872	IL-76	
CCCP-86873	IL-76	
CCCP-86874	IL-76	0013429853
CCCP-86875	**IL-76**	
CCCP-86876	IL-76	
CCCP-86877	**IL-76**	
CCCP-86880	**IL-76**	
CCCP-86881	**IL-76**	
CCCP-86882	**IL-76**	
CCCP-86883	**IL-76**	
CCCP-86884	**IL-76**	
CCCP-86885	**IL-76**	
CCCP-86886	**IL-76**	
CCCP-86887	**IL-76**	
CCCP-86888	**IL-76**	
CCCP-86889	**IL-76**	
CCCP-86891	IL-76	093421628
CCCP-86893	**IL-76**	
CCCP-86895	**IL-76**	
CCCP-86896	IL-76	0013434018
CCCP-86897	**IL-76**	
CCCP-86898	IL-76	
CCCP-86899	**IL-76**	
CCCP-86901	**IL-76**	
CCCP-86902	IL-76	
CCCP-86904	**IL-76**	
CCCP-86905	**IL-76**	
CCCP-86906	IL-76	
CCCP-86907	IL-76	
CCCP-86908	IL-76	
CCCP-86909	IL-76	0023437076
CCCP-86910	IL-76	
CCCP-86911	**IL-76**	**0023437093**
CCCP-86912	**IL-76**	
CCCP-86913	**IL-76**	
CCCP-86914	**IL-76**	
CCCP-86915	**IL-76**	
CCCP-86916	**IL-76**	
CCCP-86917	**IL-76**	
CCCP-86918	IL-76	0023437127
CCCP-86919	IL-76	0013438129
CCCP-86921	IL-76	
CCCP-86924	IL-76	0023441174
CCCP-86925	IL-76	
CCCP-86926	**IL-76**	
CCCP-86927	**IL-76**	
CCCP-87001	TU154	01
CCCP-87002	TU154	02
CCCP-87003	TU154	03
CCCP-87004	TU154	04
CCCP-87200	YAK40	9811956
CCCP-87201	YAK40	9..2056
CCCP-87202	YAK40	9..0157
CCCP-87203	YAK40	9741456
CCCP-87204	YAK40	9..1556
CCCP-87205	YAK40	9..0257
CCCP-87206	YAK40	9..0357
CCCP-87207	**YAK40**	**9..0457**
CCCP-87208	**YAK40**	**9..0557**
CCCP-87209	YAK40	9810657
CCCP-87210	YAK40	9810757
CCCP-87211	YAK40	
CCCP-87212	YAK40	
CCCP-87213	YAK40	9641050
CCCP-87214	YAK40	9640851
CCCP-87215	YAK40	9510540
CCCP-87216	YAK40	9510440
CCCP-87217	YAK40	9510340
CCCP-87218	YAK40	9440937
CCCP-87219	YAK40	9932059
CCCP-87223	YAK40	9840359
CCCP-87224	YAK40	9841259
CCCP-87225	YAK40	9841359
CCCP-87226	YAK40	9841459
CCCP-87227	YAK40	9841559
CCCP-87228	**YAK40**	**9841659**
CCCP-87229	**YAK40**	**9841759**
CCCP-87230	YAK40	9541542
CCCP-87231	**YAK40**	**9..1642**
CCCP-87232	YAK40	9531742
CCCP-87233	YAK40	9..1842
CCCP-87234	YAK40	9..1942
CCCP-87235	YAK40	9530143
CCCP-87236	**YAK40**	**9..0243**
CCCP-87237	YAK40	9530343
CCCP-87238	YAK40	9530643
CCCP-87239	YAK40	9530743
CCCP-87240	YAK40	9530843
CCCP-87241	YAK40	9530943
CCCP-87242	YAK40	9531043
CCCP-87243	YAK40	9531143
CCCP-87244	YAK40	9531243
CCCP-87245	YAK40	9531343
CCCP-87246	YAK40	9541443
CCCP-87247	YAK40	9531543
CCCP-87248	YAK40	9541743
CCCP-87249	**YAK40**	**9..0144**
CCCP-87250	YAK40	9310726
CCCP-87251	YAK40	9310826
CCCP-87253	YAK40	9310926
CCCP-87254	YAK40	9311026
CCCP-87255	YAK40	9..1226
CCCP-87256	YAK40	9311326
CCCP-87257	YAK40	9311426
CCCP-87258	YAK40	9311526
CCCP-87259	**YAK40**	**9311626**
CCCP-87260	YAK40	9311126
CCCP-87261	YAK40	9311726
CCCP-87262	YAK40	9321826
CCCP-87263	YAK40	9311926
CCCP-87264	YAK40	9312026
CCCP-87265	YAK40	9310127
CCCP-87266	YAK40	9310227
CCCP-87267	YAK40	9310327
CCCP-87268	YAK40	9310427
CCCP-87269	YAK40	9310527
CCCP-87270	YAK40	9310627
CCCP-87271	YAK40	9310727
CCCP-87272	YAK40	9330827
CCCP-87273	YAK40	9310927
CCCP-87274	YAK40	9311027
CCCP-87275	YAK40	9311127
CCCP-87276	YAK40	9311227
CCCP-87277	YAK40	9321327
CCCP-87278	YAK40	9311427
CCCP-87280	**YAK40**	**9..1527**
CCCP-87281	YAK40	9311627
CCCP-87282	YAK40	9..1727
CCCP-87283	YAK40	9321827
CCCP-87284	YAK40	9..1927
CCCP-87285	**YAK40**	**9..2027**
CCCP-87286	YAK40	9..0128
CCCP-87287	YAK40	9320228
CCCP-87288	YAK40	9320328
CCCP-87289	YAK40	9320428
CCCP-87290	YAK40	9320528
CCCP-87291	YAK40	9..0628
CCCP-87292	YAK40	9320728
CCCP-87293	YAK40	9320828
CCCP-87294	YAK40	9..0928
CCCP-87295	YAK40	9321228
CCCP-87296	YAK40	9321328
CCCP-87297	YAK40	9321428
CCCP-87298	YAK40	9321528
CCCP-87299	YAK40	9..1628
CCCP-87300	YAK40	9..1728
CCCP-87301	YAK40	9..1828
CCCP-87303	YAK40	9..1928
CCCP-87304	YAK40	9..2028
CCCP-87305	YAK40	9320129
CCCP-87306	YAK40	9320229
CCCP-87307	YAK40	9320329
CCCP-87308	YAK40	9320429
CCCP-87309	YAK40	9320529
CCCP-87310	YAK40	
CCCP-87311	YAK40	9320629
CCCP-87312	YAK40	9320729
CCCP-87313	YAK40	9330829
CCCP-87314	**YAK40**	**9..0929**
CCCP-87315	YAK40	9331429
CCCP-87316	**YAK40**	**9..1529**
CCCP-87317	YAK40	9331629
CCCP-87318	**YAK40**	**9..1729**
CCCP-87319	YAK40	9331829
CCCP-87320	YAK40	9331929
CCCP-87321	YAK40	9332029
CCCP-87322	YAK40	9330130
CCCP-87323	YAK40	9..0230
CCCP-87324	YAK40	9..0330
CCCP-87325	YAK40	9..0430
CCCP-87326	YAK40	9..0530
CCCP-87327	YAK40	9330630
CCCP-87328	YAK40	9..0730
CCCP-87329	YAK40	9..0830
CCCP-87330	YAK40	9510139
CCCP-87331	YAK40	9510239
CCCP-87332	YAK40	9..0339
CCCP-87333	YAK40	9510439
CCCP-87334	YAK40	9510738
CCCP-87336	YAK40	9510539
CCCP-87337	YAK40	9510639
CCCP-87338	YAK40	9510739
CCCP-87339	YAK40	9510839
CCCP-87340	YAK40	9510939
CCCP-87341	YAK40	9511039
CCCP-87342	YAK40	9511139
CCCP-87343	YAK40	9511239
CCCP-87344	YAK40	9511339
CCCP-87345	YAK40	9511439
CCCP-87346	YAK40	9..1539
CCCP-87347	YAK40	9511639

CCCP-87348 YAK40 9511739
CCCP-87349 YAK40 9511839
CCCP-87350 YAK40
CCCP-87351 YAK40 9412030
CCCP-87352 YAK40 9330131
CCCP-87353 YAK40 9330231
CCCP-87354 YAK40 9330331
CCCP-87355 YAK40 9340431
CCCP-87356 YAK40 9340531
CCCP-87357 YAK40 9340631
CCCP-87358 YAK40 9340731
CCCP-87359 YAK40 9340831
CCCP-87360 YAK40 9..0931
CCCP-87361 YAK40 9341031
CCCP-87362 YAK40 9341131
CCCP-87363 YAK40 9341231
CCCP-87364 YAK40 9341331
CCCP-87365 YAK40 9341531
CCCP-87366 YAK40 9341631
CCCP-87367 YAK40 9341731
CCCP-87368 YAK40 9341831
CCCP-87369 YAK40 9..1931
CCCP-87370 YAK40 9340132
CCCP-87371 YAK40 9340232
CCCP-87372 YAK40 9340332
CCCP-87373 YAK40 9410732
CCCP-87374 YAK40 9410832
CCCP-87375 YAK40 9410932
CCCP-87376 YAK40 9411032
CCCP-87377 YAK40 9..1325
CCCP-87378 YAK40 9241425
CCCP-87379 YAK40
CCCP-87380 YAK40 9..1132
CCCP-87381 YAK40 9411232
CCCP-87382 YAK40 9411332
CCCP-87383 YAK40 9411432
CCCP-87384 YAK40 9..1532
CCCP-87385 YAK40 9411632
CCCP-87386 YAK40 9411732
CCCP-87387 YAK40 9411832
CCCP-87388 YAK40 9412032
CCCP-87389 YAK40 9410133
CCCP-87390 YAK40 9..0233
CCCP-87391 YAK40 9..0333
CCCP-87392 YAK40 9410433
CCCP-87393 YAK40 9..0533
CCCP-87394 YAK40 9..0633
CCCP-87395 YAK40 9410733
CCCP-87396 YAK40 9410833
CCCP-87397 YAK40 9..0933
CCCP-87398 YAK40 9..1033
CCCP-87399 YAK40 9411133
CCCP-87400 YAK40 9411233
CCCP-87401 YAK40 9411333
CCCP-87402 YAK40 9411433
CCCP-87403 YAK40 9411533
CCCP-87404 YAK40 9411633
CCCP-87405 YAK40 9421733
CCCP-87406 YAK40 9421833
CCCP-87407 YAK40 9421933
CCCP-87408 YAK40 9422033
CCCP-87409 YAK40 9420134
CCCP-87410 YAK40 9420234
CCCP-87411 YAK40 9420334
CCCP-87412 YAK40 9420434
CCCP-87413 YAK40 9420534
CCCP-87414 YAK40 9420634
CCCP-87415 YAK40 9420734
CCCP-87416 YAK40 9420834
CCCP-87417 YAK40 9420934
CCCP-87418 YAK40 9421034
CCCP-87419 YAK40 9421134
CCCP-87420 YAK40 9..1234
CCCP-87421 YAK40 9421734
CCCP-87422 YAK40 9421834
CCCP-87423 YAK40 9..1934
CCCP-87424 YAK40 9422034
CCCP-87425 YAK40 9..0135
CCCP-87426 YAK40 9..0235
CCCP-87427 YAK40 9420335
CCCP-87428 YAK40 9420435
CCCP-87429 YAK40 9420535
CCCP-87430 YAK40 9420635
CCCP-87431 YAK40 9420735
CCCP-87432 YAK40 9420835
CCCP-87433 YAK40 9420935
CCCP-87434 YAK40 9431035
CCCP-87435 YAK40 9431135
CCCP-87436 YAK40 9431235
CCCP-87437 YAK40 9..1335
CCCP-87438 YAK40 9..1435
CCCP-87439 YAK40 9431535
CCCP-87440 YAK40 9431635
CCCP-87441 YAK40 9..1735
CCCP-87442 YAK40 9431935
CCCP-87443 YAK40 9..2035
CCCP-87444 YAK40 9430136
CCCP-87445 YAK40 9430236
CCCP-87446 YAK40 9430336
CCCP-87447 YAK40 9430436
CCCP-87448 YAK40 9430536
CCCP-87449 YAK40 9430636
CCCP-87450 YAK40 9..0736
CCCP-87451 YAK40 9..0836
CCCP-87452 YAK40 9..0936
CCCP-87453 YAK40 9..1036
CCCP-87454 YAK40 9..1136
CCCP-87455 YAK40 9..1236
CCCP-87456 YAK40 9..1336
CCCP-87457 YAK40 9431636
CCCP-87458 YAK40 9..1736
CCCP-87459 YAK40 9431836
CCCP-87460 YAK40 9431936
CCCP-87461 YAK40 9432036
CCCP-87462 YAK40 9430137
CCCP-87463 YAK40 9..0237
CCCP-87464 YAK40 9430337
CCCP-87465 YAK40 9430437
CCCP-87466 YAK40 9430537
CCCP-87467 YAK40 9440637
CCCP-87468 YAK40 9..1337
CCCP-87469 YAK40 9441437
CCCP-87470 YAK40 9441537
CCCP-87471 YAK40 9441637
CCCP-87472 YAK40 9441737
CCCP-87473 YAK40 9441837
CCCP-87474 YAK40 9441937
CCCP-87475 YAK40 9..2037
CCCP-87476 YAK40 9..0438
CCCP-87477 YAK40 9..0538
CCCP-87478 YAK40 9440638
CCCP-87479 YAK40 9441838
CCCP-87480 YAK40 9..0838
CCCP-87481 YAK40 9440938
CCCP-87482 YAK40 9441038
CCCP-87483 YAK40 9441138
CCCP-87484 YAK40 9441238
CCCP-87485 YAK40 9..1338
CCCP-87486 YAK40 9441438
CCCP-87487 YAK40 9441538
CCCP-87488 YAK40 9441638
CCCP-87489 YAK40 9512038
CCCP-87490 YAK40 9110117
CCCP-87491 YAK40 9621345
CCCP-87492 YAK40 9..1545
CCCP-87493 YAK40 9..1645
CCCP-87494 YAK40 9..1745
CCCP-87495 YAK40 9..1845
CCCP-87496 YAK40 9541945
CCCP-87497 YAK40 9542045
CCCP-87498 YAK40 9540146
CCCP-87499 YAK40 9610246
CCCP-87500 YAK40 9511939
CCCP-87501 YAK40 9..2039
CCCP-87502 YAK40 9510140
CCCP-87503 YAK40 9520240
CCCP-87504 YAK40 9510640
CCCP-87505 YAK40 9510740
CCCP-87506 YAK40 9..0840
CCCP-87507 YAK40 9520940
CCCP-87508 YAK40 9521040
CCCP-87509 YAK40 9521140
CCCP-87510 YAK40 9521240
CCCP-87511 YAK40 9521340
CCCP-87512 YAK40 9521440
CCCP-87513 YAK40 9521540
CCCP-87514 YAK40 9521640
CCCP-87515 YAK40 9521740
CCCP-87516 YAK40 9521840
CCCP-87517 YAK40 9521940
CCCP-87518 YAK40 9..2040
CCCP-87519 YAK40 9..0141
CCCP-87520 YAK40 9520241
CCCP-87521 YAK40 9520341
CCCP-87522 YAK40 9510441
CCCP-87523 YAK40 9520541
CCCP-87524 YAK40 9520641
CCCP-87525 YAK40 9520741
CCCP-87526 YAK40 9520841
CCCP-87527 YAK40 9520941
CCCP-87528 YAK40 9521041
CCCP-87529 YAK40 9521141
CCCP-87530 YAK40 9521241
CCCP-87531 YAK40 9521341
CCCP-87532 YAK40 9..1641
CCCP-87533 YAK40 9511741
CCCP-87534 YAK40 9521841
CCCP-87535 YAK40 9521941
CCCP-87536 YAK40 9..2041
CCCP-87537 YAK40 9520242
CCCP-87538 YAK40 9..0342
CCCP-87539 YAK40 9530442
CCCP-87540 YAK40 9530542
CCCP-87541 YAK40 9530642
CCCP-87542 YAK40 9530742
CCCP-87543 YAK40 9530842
CCCP-87544 YAK40 9..0942
CCCP-87545 YAK40 9531042
CCCP-87546 YAK40 9531142
CCCP-87547 YAK40 9531242
CCCP-87548 YAK40 9531342
CCCP-87549 YAK40 9531442
CCCP-87550 YAK40 9210121
CCCP-87551 YAK40 9210221
CCCP-87552 YAK40 9210321
CCCP-87553 YAK40 9210421
CCCP-87554 YAK40 9210521
CCCP-87555 YAK40 9210621
CCCP-87556 YAK40 9210721
CCCP-87557 YAK40 9210821
CCCP-87558 YAK40 9210921
CCCP-87559 YAK40 9211021
CCCP-87560 YAK40 9211121
CCCP-87561 YAK40 9..1221
CCCP-87562 YAK40 9211321
CCCP-87563 YAK40 9..1.21
CCCP-87564 YAK40 9211621
CCCP-87565 YAK40 9211721
CCCP-87566 YAK40 9211821
CCCP-87567 YAK40 9211921
CCCP-87568 YAK40 9212021
CCCP-87569 YAK40 9220222
CCCP-87570 YAK40 9220322
CCCP-87571 YAK40
CCCP-87572 YAK40 9220422
CCCP-87573 YAK40 9220522
CCCP-87574 YAK40 9220622
CCCP-87575 YAK40 9220722
CCCP-87576 YAK40 9220822
CCCP-87577 YAK40 9220922
CCCP-87578 YAK40 9221022
CCCP-87579 YAK40 9221122
CCCP-87580 YAK40 9221222
CCCP-87581 YAK40 9221322
CCCP-87582 YAK40 9221422
CCCP-87583 YAK40 9221522
CCCP-87584 YAK40 9..1622
CCCP-87585 YAK40 9..1722
CCCP-87586 YAK40 9221822
CCCP-87587 YAK40 9221922
CCCP-87588 YAK40 9222022
CCCP-87589 YAK40 9..0123
CCCP-87590 YAK40 9..0416
CCCP-87591 YAK40 9..0516
CCCP-87592 YAK40 9110616
CCCP-87593 YAK40 9..0716
CCCP-87594 YAK40 9..0816
CCCP-87595 YAK40 9..0916
CCCP-87596 YAK40 9..1016
CCCP-87597 YAK40 9110117
CCCP-87598 YAK40 9..0217
CCCP-87599 YAK40 9..0317
CCCP-87600 YAK40 9..0917
CCCP-87601 YAK40 9..1017
CCCP-87602 YAK40 9..0118
CCCP-87603 YAK40 9..0218
CCCP-87604 YAK40 9..0318
CCCP-87605 YAK40 9..0418

CCCP-87606 YAK40 9120518
CCCP-87607 YAK40 9..0618
CCCP-87608 YAK40 9..0718
CCCP-87609 YAK40 9..0918
CCCP-87610 YAK40 9..0918
CCCP-87611 YAK40 9..1018
CCCP-87612 YAK40 9..1118
CCCP-87613 YAK40 9..1218
CCCP-87614 YAK40 9..1318
CCCP-87615 YAK40 9131618
CCCP-87616 YAK40 9..1718
CCCP-87617 YAK40 9..1818
CCCP-87618 YAK40 9131918
CCCP-87619 YAK40 9..2018
CCCP-87619 YAK40 9230324
CCCP-87620 YAK40 9130119
CCCP-87621 YAK40 9130219
CCCP-87622 YAK40 9130319
CCCP-87623 YAK40 9130419
CCCP-87624 YAK40 9140519
CCCP-87625 YAK40 9140619
CCCP-87626 YAK40 9..0719
CCCP-87627 YAK40 9..0819
CCCP-87628 YAK40 9..0919
CCCP-87629 YAK40 9..1019
CCCP-87630 YAK40 9141119
CCCP-87631 YAK40 9141219
CCCP-87632 YAK40 9141319
CCCP-87633 YAK40 9..1419
CCCP-87634 YAK40 9..1519
CCCP-87635 YAK40 9141619
CCCP-87636 YAK40 9141719
CCCP-87637 YAK40 9..1819
CCCP-87638 YAK40 9141919
CCCP-87639 YAK40 9142019
CCCP-87640 YAK40 9140120
CCCP-87641 YAK40 9..0220
CCCP-87642 YAK40 9..0320
CCCP-87643 YAK40 9140420
CCCP-87644 YAK40 9140520
CCCP-87645 YAK40 9140620
CCCP-87646 YAK40 9140720
CCCP-87647 YAK40 9140820
CCCP-87648 YAK40 9140920
CCCP-87649 YAK40 9141020
CCCP-87650 YAK40 9..1120
CCCP-87651 YAK40 9141220
CCCP-87652 YAK40 9141320
CCCP-87653 YAK40 9..1620
CCCP-87654 YAK40 9211720
CCCP-87655 YAK40 9211820
CCCP-87656 YAK40 9211920
CCCP-87658 YAK40 9240225
CCCP-87659 YAK40 9240325
CCCP-87660 YAK40 9240425
CCCP-87661 YAK40 9240525
CCCP-87662 YAK40 9240625
CCCP-87663 YAK40 9..0725
CCCP-87664 YAK40 9..0825
CCCP-87665 YAK40 9..0925
CCCP-87666 YAK40 9241025
CCCP-87667 YAK40 9241525
CCCP-87668 YAK40 9021460
CCCP-87669 YAK40 9021760
CCCP-87672 YAK40 9....00
CCCP-87673 YAK40
CCCP-87675 YAK40 9831100
CCCP-87676 YAK40 9831200
CCCP-87678 YAK40 9840201
CCCP-87679 YAK40 9840301
CCCP-87680 YAK40 9840401
CCCP-87681 YAK40 9840501
CCCP-87682 YAK40 9..0102
CCCP-87684 YAK40 9840402
CCCP-87685 YAK40 9840502
CCCP-87686 YAK40 9..0103
CCCP-87687 YAK40
CCCP-87688 YAK40
CCCP-87689 YAK40 9..0403
CCCP-87690 YAK40 9..0503
CCCP-87691 YAK40 9..0104
CCCP-87692 YAK40 9..0204
CCCP-87693 YAK40 9..0304
CCCP-87694 YAK40 9..0404
CCCP-87695 YAK40 9..0504
CCCP-87696 YAK40 9910105
CCCP-87697 YAK40 9910205
CCCP-87698 YAK40 9..0305
CCCP-87699 YAK40 9220405
CCCP-87700 YAK40 9..0505
CCCP-87701 YAK40 9920106
CCCP-87702 YAK40 9920206
CCCP-87703 YAK40 9920306
CCCP-87704 YAK40 9920406
CCCP-87705 YAK40 9920506
CCCP-87706 YAK40 9930107
CCCP-87707 YAK40 9930207
CCCP-87708 YAK40 9930307
CCCP-87709 YAK40 9930407
CCCP-87710 YAK40 9940507
CCCP-87711 YAK40 9940607
CCCP-87712 YAK40 9..0707
CCCP-87713 YAK40 9..0807
CCCP-87714 YAK40 9..0907
CCCP-87715 YAK40 9..1007
CCCP-87716 YAK40 9..0108
CCCP-87717 YAK40 9..0208
CCCP-87718 YAK40 9330308
CCCP-87719 YAK40 9..0408
CCCP-87720 YAK40 9..0508
CCCP-87721 YAK40 9..0608
CCCP-87722 YAK40 9..0708
CCCP-87723 YAK40 9..0808
CCCP-87724 YAK40 9..0908
CCCP-87725 YAK40 9..1008
CCCP-87726 YAK40 9..0109
CCCP-87727 YAK40 9..0209
CCCP-87728 YAK40 9..0309
(CCCP-87729) YAK40 9020409
CCCP-87730 YAK40 9..0509
CCCP-87731 YAK40 9..0609
CCCP-87732 YAK40 9940709
CCCP-87733 YAK40 9..0809
CCCP-87734 YAK40 9..0909
CCCP-87735 YAK40 9..1009
CCCP-87736 YAK40 9..0110
CCCP-87737 YAK40 9..0210
CCCP-87738 YAK40 9010310
CCCP-87739 YAK40 9010410
CCCP-87740 YAK40 9..0510
CCCP-87741 YAK40 9010610
CCCP-87742 YAK40 9..0710
CCCP-87743 YAK40 9010810
CCCP-87744 YAK40 9..0910
CCCP-87745 YAK40 9011010
CCCP-87746 YAK40 9..0111
CCCP-87747 YAK40 9..0211
CCCP-87748 YAK40 9..0311
CCCP-87749 YAK40 9020411
CCCP-87750 YAK40 9..0511
CCCP-87751 YAK40 9..0611
CCCP-87752 YAK40 9020711
CCCP-87753 YAK40 9020811
CCCP-87754 YAK40 9..0911
CCCP-87755 YAK40 9021011
CCCP-87756 YAK40 9020112
CCCP-87757 YAK40 9020212
CCCP-87758 YAK40 9..0312
CCCP-87759 YAK40 9030412
CCCP-87760 YAK40 9..0512
CCCP-87761 YAK40 9030612
CCCP-87762 YAK40 9..0712
CCCP-87763 YAK40 9030812
CCCP-87764 YAK40 9030912
CCCP-87765 YAK40 9031012
CCCP-87766 YAK40 9..0113
CCCP-87767 YAK40 9030213
CCCP-87768 YAK40 9030313
CCCP-87769 YAK40 9030413
CCCP-87770 YAK40 9030513
CCCP-87771 YAK40 9030613
CCCP-87772 YAK40 9..0713
CCCP-87773 YAK40 9..0813
CCCP-87774 YAK40 9030913
CCCP-87775 YAK40 9031013
CCCP-87776 YAK40 9..0114
CCCP-87777 YAK40 9..0214
CCCP-87778 YAK40 9..0314
CCCP-87779 YAK40 9..0414
CCCP-87780 YAK40 9..0514
CCCP-87781 YAK40 9..0614
CCCP-87782 YAK40 9..0714
CCCP-87783 YAK40 9..0814
CCCP-87784 YAK40 9..0914
CCCP-87785 YAK40 9..1014
CCCP-87786 YAK40 9..0115
CCCP-87787 YAK40 9..0215
CCCP-87788 YAK40 9..0315
CCCP-87789 YAK40 9..0415
CCCP-87790 YAK40 9..0515
CCCP-87791 YAK40 9920203
CCCP-87792 YAK40 9910303
CCCP-87793 YAK40 9..0615
CCCP-87794 YAK40 9..0715
CCCP-87795 YAK40 9..0815
CCCP-87796 YAK40 9040915
CCCP-87797 YAK40 9..0116
CCCP-87798 YAK40 9..0216
CCCP-87799 YAK40 9040316
CCCP-87800 YAK40 9220223
CCCP-87801 YAK40 9230423
CCCP-87802 YAK40 9230523
CCCP-87803 YAK40 9..0923
CCCP-87804 YAK40 9231023
CCCP-87805 YAK40 9231123
CCCP-87807 YAK40 9231723
CCCP-87808 YAK40 9..1823
CCCP-87809 YAK40 9..1923
CCCP-87810 YAK40 9..2023
CCCP-87811 YAK40 9230124
CCCP-87812 YAK40 9230424
CCCP-87814 YAK40 9230524
CCCP-87815 YAK40 9230624
CCCP-87816 YAK40 9..0724
CCCP-87817 YAK40 9230824
CCCP-87818 YAK40 9231024
CCCP-87819 YAK40 9230122
CCCP-87819 YAK40 9..1124
CCCP-87820 YAK40 9..1224
CCCP-87821 YAK40 9241324
CCCP-87822 YAK40 9241424
CCCP-87823 YAK40 9..1524
CCCP-87824 YAK40 9241624
CCCP-87825 YAK40 9241724
CCCP-87826 YAK40 9..1824
CCCP-87827 YAK40 9241924
CCCP-87828 YAK40 9242024
CCCP-87829 YAK40 9..0125
CCCP-87830 YAK40 9241625
CCCP-87831 YAK40 9241725
CCCP-87832 YAK40 9241825
CCCP-87833 YAK40 9241925
CCCP-87834 YAK40 9242025
CCCP-87835 YAK40 9240126
CCCP-87836 YAK40 9240226
CCCP-87837 YAK40 9240326
CCCP-87838 YAK40 9..0426
CCCP-87839 YAK40 9240526
CCCP-87840 YAK40 9240626
CCCP-87841 YAK40 9320930
CCCP-87842 YAK40 9321030
CCCP-87843 YAK40 9331130
CCCP-87844 YAK40 9331330
CCCP-87845 YAK40 9331430
CCCP-87846 YAK40 9331530
CCCP-87847 YAK40 9331630
CCCP-87848 YAK40 9331730
CCCP-87849 YAK40 9..1830
CCCP-87850 YAK40 9..1930
CCCP-87854 YAK40
CCCP-87883 YAK40
CCCP-87891 YAK40
CCCP-87892 YAK40
CCCP-87893 YAK40
CCCP-87900 YAK40 9720254
CCCP-87901 YAK40 9720354
CCCP-87902 YAK40 9..0.54
CCCP-87903 YAK40 9..0.54
CCCP-87904 YAK40 9720854
CCCP-87905 YAK40 9720954
CCCP-87906 YAK40 9731054
CCCP-87907 YAK40 9731254
CCCP-87908 YAK40 9..1354
CCCP-87909 YAK40 9731454
CCCP-87910 YAK40 9731654
CCCP-87911 YAK40 9..1854
CCCP-87912 YAK40 9732054
CCCP-87913 YAK40 9..0.55

CCCP-87914 YAK40 9..0.55
CCCP-87915 YAK40 9..0.55
CCCP-87916 YAK40 9..0.55
CCCP-87917 YAK40 9..0.55
CCCP-87918 YAK40 9730855
CCCP-87919 YAK40 9..0955
CCCP-87920 YAK40 9731055
CCCP-87921 YAK40 9..1155
CCCP-87922 YAK40 9731355
CCCP-87923 YAK40 9741455
CCCP-87924 YAK40 9..1555
CCCP-87925 YAK40 9731655
CCCP-87926 YAK40 9741755
CCCP-87927 YAK40 9741855
CCCP-87928 YAK40 9..1955
CCCP-87929 YAK40 9..2055
CCCP-87930 YAK40 9..0156
CCCP-87931 YAK40 9..0256
CCCP-87932 YAK40 9..0356
CCCP-87933 YAK40 9740456
CCCP-87934 YAK40 9..0556
CCCP-87935 YAK40 9740656
CCCP-87935 YAK40 9811856
CCCP-87936 YAK40 9..0756
CCCP-87937 YAK40 9..0856
CCCP-87938 YAK40 9..0153
CCCP-87940 YAK40 9540445
CCCP-87941 YAK40 9540545
CCCP-87942 YAK40 9610645
CCCP-87943 YAK40 9..0745
CCCP-87944 YAK40 9..0845
CCCP-87945 YAK40 9..0945
CCCP-87946 YAK40 9611045
CCCP-87947 YAK40 9621145
CCCP-87949 YAK40
CCCP-87950 YAK40 9810857
CCCP-87951 YAK40 9810957
CCCP-87952 YAK40 9821057
CCCP-87953 YAK40 9811157
CCCP-87954 YAK40 9811357
CCCP-87955 YAK40 9811457
CCCP-87956 YAK40 9821757
CCCP-87957 YAK40 9821857
CCCP-87958 YAK40 9..1957
CCCP-87959 YAK40 9..2057
CCCP-87960 YAK40 9..0358
CCCP-87961 YAK40 9820458
CCCP-87962 YAK40 9820558
CCCP-87963 YAK40 9831058
CCCP-87964 YAK40 9830758
CCCP-87965 YAK40 9820858
CCCP-87966 YAK40 9820958
CCCP-87967 YAK40 9831158
CCCP-87968 YAK40 9841258
CCCP-87969 YAK40 9841358
CCCP-87970 YAK40 9831458
CCCP-87971 YAK40 9831558
CCCP-87972 YAK40 9..1658
CCCP-87973 YAK40 9041860
CCCP-87974 YAK40 9041960
CCCP-87980 YAK40 9530344
CCCP-87981 YAK40 9540444
CCCP-87982 YAK40 9540544
CCCP-87983 YAK40 9540644
CCCP-87984 YAK40 9540744
CCCP-87985 YAK40 9540844
CCCP-87986 YAK40 9540944
CCCP-87987 YAK40 9541144
CCCP-87988 YAK40 9..1244
CCCP-87989 YAK40 9541344
CCCP-87990 YAK40 9541444
CCCP-87991 YAK40 9541544
CCCP-87992 YAK40 9541644
CCCP-87993 YAK40 9541744
CCCP-87994 YAK40 9541844
CCCP-87995 YAK40 9541944
CCCP-87996 YAK40 9542044
CCCP-87997 YAK40 9540145
CCCP-87998 YAK40 9540245
CCCP-87999 YAK40 9540345
CCCP-88109 YAK40
CCCP-88151 YAK40 9610546
CCCP-88152 YAK40 9610646
CCCP-88153 YAK40 9610746
CCCP-88154 YAK40 9..0846
CCCP-88155 YAK40 9610946
CCCP-88156 YAK40 9611046
CCCP-88157 YAK40 9..1146
CCCP-88158 YAK40 9611246
CCCP-88159 YAK40 9611346
CCCP-88160 YAK40 9611446
CCCP-88161 YAK40 9611546
CCCP-88162 YAK40 9..1646
CCCP-88163 YAK40 9611746
CCCP-88164 YAK40 9..1846
CCCP-88165 YAK40 9611946
CCCP-88166 YAK40 9..2046
CCCP-88167 YAK40 9..0147
CCCP-88168 YAK40 9610647
CCCP-88169 YAK40 9610747
CCCP-88170 YAK40 9620847
CCCP-88171 YAK40 9620947
CCCP-88172 YAK40 9..1047
CCCP-88173 YAK40 9621147
CCCP-88174 YAK40 9621247
CCCP-88175 YAK40 9..1347
CCCP-88176 YAK40 9621447
CCCP-88177 YAK40 9621747
CCCP-88178 YAK40 9631847
CCCP-88179 YAK40 9621947
CCCP-88180 YAK40 9..2047
CCCP-88181 YAK40 9620148
CCCP-88182 YAK40 9620248
CCCP-88183 YAK40 9620348
CCCP-88184 YAK40 9620448
CCCP-88185 YAK40 9620548
CCCP-88186 YAK40 9620648
CCCP-88187 YAK40 9620748
CCCP-88188 YAK40 9620848
CCCP-88189 YAK40 9620948
CCCP-88190 YAK40 9..1048
CCCP-88191 YAK40 9621148
CCCP-88192 YAK40 9..1248
CCCP-88193 YAK40 9621348
CCCP-88194 YAK40 9621448
CCCP-88195 YAK40 9..1548
CCCP-88196 YAK40 9631648
CCCP-88197 YAK40 9631948
CCCP-88198 YAK40 9..2048
CCCP-88199 YAK40 9..0149
CCCP-88200 YAK40 9630249
CCCP-88201 YAK40 9630349
CCCP-88202 YAK40 9630449
CCCP-88203 YAK40 9630549
CCCP-88204 YAK40 9630649
CCCP-88205 YAK40 9630749
CCCP-88206 YAK40 9....49
CCCP-88207 YAK40 9..1.49
CCCP-88208 YAK40 9..1.49
CCCP-88209 YAK40 9..1549
CCCP-88210 YAK40 9631649
CCCP-88211 YAK40 9631749
CCCP-88212 YAK40 9..1849
CCCP-88213 YAK40 9631949
CCCP-88214 YAK40 9632049
CCCP-88215 YAK40 9630150
CCCP-88216 YAK40 9630250
CCCP-88217 YAK40 9630350
CCCP-88218 YAK40 9630450
CCCP-88219 YAK40 9..0550
CCCP-88220 YAK40 9..0650
CCCP-88221 YAK40 9..0750
CCCP-88222 YAK40 9..0850
CCCP-88223 YAK40 9..0950
CCCP-88224 YAK40 9641150
CCCP-88225 YAK40 9641250
CCCP-88226 YAK40 9641350
CCCP-88227 YAK40 9641550
CCCP-88228 YAK40 9641750
CCCP-88229 YAK40 9..1850
CCCP-88230 YAK40 9641950
CCCP-88231 YAK40 9..2050
CCCP-88232 YAK40 9640151
CCCP-88233 YAK40 9..0251
CCCP-88234 YAK40 9640351
CCCP-88235 YAK40 9..0451
CCCP-88236 YAK40 9640551
CCCP-88237 YAK40 9640751
CCCP-88238 YAK40 9640951
CCCP-88239 YAK40 9641051
CCCP-88240 YAK40 9641151
CCCP-88241 YAK40 9641351
CCCP-88242 YAK40 9641551
CCCP-88243 YAK40 9641651
CCCP-88244 YAK40 9641751
CCCP-88245 YAK40 9641851
CCCP-88246 YAK40 9641951
CCCP-88247 YAK40 9642051
CCCP-88248 YAK40 9..0.52
CCCP-88249 YAK40 9..0.52
CCCP-88250 YAK40 9..0.52
CCCP-88251 YAK40 9710552
CCCP-88252 YAK40 9..0652
CCCP-88253 YAK40 9..0852
CCCP-88254 YAK40 9710952
CCCP-88255 YAK40 9..1052
CCCP-88256 YAK40 9..1152
CCCP-88257 YAK40 9711252
CCCP-88258 YAK40 9711352
CCCP-88259 YAK40 9..1452
CCCP-88260 YAK40 9..1552
CCCP-88261 YAK40 9711652
CCCP-88262 YAK40 9..1752
CCCP-88263 YAK40 9711852
CCCP-88264 YAK40 9711952
CCCP-88265 YAK40 9722052
CCCP-88266 YAK40 9710453
CCCP-88267 YAK40 9720553
CCCP-88268 YAK40 9..0653
CCCP-88269 YAK40 9720753
CCCP-88270 YAK40 9720853
CCCP-88271 YAK40 9720953
CCCP-88272 YAK40 9..1053
CCCP-88273 YAK40 9721153
CCCP-88274 YAK40 9721253
CCCP-88275 YAK40 9721353
CCCP-88276 YAK40 9721453
CCCP-88277 YAK40 9721953
CCCP-88278 YAK40 9722053
CCCP-88279 YAK40 9720154
CCCP-88280 YAK40 9820658
CCCP-88286 YAK40
CCCP-88287 YAK40 9940360
CCCP-88290 YAK40 9840459
CCCP-88293 YAK40 9510138
CCCP-88652 IL-62 00802
CCCP-93927 TU134 2351508
CCCP-93929 TU134 1351206
CCCP-96000 IL-96 0101
CCCP-96001 IL-96 30000103
CCCP-96002 IL-96
CCCP-96005 IL-96 74393201002
CCCP-96006 IL-96 74393201003
CCCP-98102 YAK40
CCCP-98106 YAK40
CCCP-98109 YAK40 9740956
CCCP-98110 YAK40
CCCP-98111 YAK40 9741656
CCCP-98113 YAK40 9710253
CCCP-98114 YAK40 9..0353
CCCP-480182 AN225
CCCP-680125 AN124 19530501001?
CCCP-680210 AN124 19530501002?
CCCP-780151 AN-74
CCCP-780334 AN-74
ROSSIA-64007 TU204 1450743164007

Canada

CF-ASF B737 20221
CF-CPB B737 19884
CF-CPC B737 19885
CF-CPD B737 19886
CF-CPE B737 19887
CF-CPF DC-8 45620
CF-CPG DC-8 45623
CF-CPH DC-8 45621
CF-CPI DC-8 45622
CF-CPJ DC-8 45661
CF-CPK B727 20328
CF-CPK DC-8 45761
CF-CPL DC-8 46095
CF-CPM DC-8 45809
CF-CPN B727 20327
CF-CPN DC-8 45252
CF-CPO DC-8 45926
CF-CPP DC-8 45927

CF-CPQ	DC-8	45928
CF-CPS	DC-8	45929
CF-CPT	DC-8	45858
CF-CPU	B737	19888
CF-CPV	B737	20196
CF-CPZ	B737	20197
CF-CUM	COMET	06013
CF-CUN	COMET	06014
CF-CUR	B727	20512
CF-CUS	B727	20513
CF-DJC	B747	20208
CF-EJD-X	**C-102**	
CF-EPL	B737	20396
CF-EPO	B737	20300
CF-EPP	B737	20681
CF-EPR	B737	20397
CF-EPU	B737	20776
CF-FAN	B707	19789
CF-FUN	B727	19242
CF-FUN	B747	20305
(CF-FUN)	B747	20208
CF-NAB	B737	19847
(CF-NAD)	B737	19848
(CF-NAD)	B737	20521
(CF-NAF)	B737	19849
CF-NAH	B737	19848
CF-NAI	B737	19945
CF-NAP	B737	19946
CF-NAP	B737	20496
CF-NAQ	B737	20455
CF-NAW	B737	20521
CF-PWC	B737	20142
CF-PWD	B737	19742
CF-PWE	B737	19743
CF-PWJ	B707	18746
CF-PWM	B737	19921
CF-PWP	B737	20588
CF-PWV	B707	17696
CF-PWW	B707	17700
CF-PWW	B737	20670
CF-PWZ	B707	18826
CF-PXB	B727	19174
(CF-QBG)	C-137	20043
(CF-QBK)	B737	19989
CF-QBN	1-11	BAC.110
(CF-QBN)	B737	19990
CF-QBO	1-11	BAC.112
CF-QBR	1-11	094
CF-SVR	COMET	06018
CF-TAI	B707	19410
CF-TAN	B737	20206
CF-TAO	B737	20205
CF-TAR	B737	20223
CF-TIH	DC-8	45933
CF-TII	DC-8	45934
CF-TIJ	DC-8	45962
CF-TIK	DC-8	46033
CF-TIL	DC-8	46034
CF-TIM	DC-8	46035
CF-TIN	DC-8	46036
CF-TIO	DC-8	46076
CF-TIP	DC-8	46100
CF-TIQ	DC-8	46123
CF-TIR	DC-8	46124
CF-TIS	DC-8	46125
(CF-TIT)	DC-8	46113
CF-TIU	DC-8	46113
(CF-TIU)	DC-8	46126
CF-TIV	DC-8	46126
(CF-TIV)	DC-8	46114
CF-TIW	DC-8	46114
(CF-TIW)	DC-8	46115
CF-TIX	DC-8	46115
CF-TJA	DC-8	45442
CF-TJB	DC-8	45443
CF-TJC	DC-8	45444
CF-TJD	DC-8	45445
CF-TJE	DC-8	45565
CF-TJF	DC-8	45566
CF-TJG	DC-8	45609
CF-TJH	DC-8	45610
CF-TJI	DC-8	45611
CF-TJJ	DC-8	45612
CF-TJK	DC-8	45638
CF-TJL	DC-8	45640
CF-TJM	DC-8	45653
CF-TJN	DC-8	45654
CF-TJO	DC-8	45655
CF-TJP	DC-8	45679
CF-TJQ	DC-8	45686
CF-TJR	DC-8	45860
CF-TJS	DC-8	45861
CF-TJT	DC-8	45890
CF-TJU	DC-8	45891
CF-TJV	DC-8	45892
CF-TJW	DC-8	45893
CF-TJX	DC-8	45963
CF-TJY	DC-8	45964
CF-TJZ	DC-8	45980
CF-TLB	DC-9	45711
CF-TLC	DC-9	45712
CF-TLD	DC-9	45713
CF-TLE	DC-9	45725
CF-TLF	DC-9	45726
CF-TLG	DC-9	45727
CF-TLH	DC-9	45845
CF-TLI	DC-9	45846
CF-TLJ	DC-9	47019
CF-TLK	DC-9	47020
CF-TLL	DC-9	47021
CF-TLM	DC-9	47022
CF-TLN	DC-9	47023
CF-TLO	DC-9	47024
CF-TLP	DC-9	47068
CF-TLQ	DC-9	47069
CF-TLR	DC-9	47070
CF-TLS	DC-9	47071
CF-TLT	DC-9	47195
CF-TLU	DC-9	47196
CF-TLV	DC-9	47197
CF-TLW	DC-9	47198
CF-TLX	DC-9	47199
CF-TLY	DC-9	47200
CF-TLZ	DC-9	47265
CF-TMA	DC-9	47266
CF-TMB	DC-9	47289
CF-TMC	DC-9	47290
CF-TMD	DC-9	47292
CF-TME	DC-9	47293
CF-TMF	DC-9	47294
CF-TMG	DC-9	47340
CF-TMH	DC-9	47341
CF-TMI	DC-9	47342
CF-TMJ	DC-9	47348
CF-TMK	DC-9	47349
CF-TML	DC-9	47350
CF-TMM	DC-9	47351
CF-TMN	DC-9	47041
CF-TMN	DC-9	47352
CF-TMO	DC-9	47353
CF-TMP	DC-9	47354
CF-TMQ	DC-9	47422
CF-TMR	DC-9	47423
CF-TMS	DC-9	47424
CF-TMT	DC-9	47546
CF-TMU	DC-9	47554
CF-TMV	DC-9	47557
CF-TMW	DC-9	47560
CF-TMX	DC-9	47485
CF-TMY	DC-9	47592
CF-TMZ	DC-9	47598
CF-TNA	L1011	1019
CF-TNB	L1011	1021
CF-TNC	L1011	1023
CF-TND	L1011	1025
CF-TNE	L1011	1027
CF-TNF	L1011	1047
CF-TNG	L1011	1048
CF-TNH	L1011	1049
CF-TNI	L1011	1058
CF-TOA	B747	20013
CF-TOB	B747	20014
CF-TOC	B747	20015
CF-TOD	B747	20767
CF-TOE	B747	20881
CF-TON	DC-9	45826
CF-TOO	DC-9	47010
CF-TOP	DC-9	47011
CF-TOQ	DC-9	47012
CF-TOR	DC-9	47013
CF-TOS	DC-9	47014
CF-TOT	DC-9	47015
CF-TOU	DC-9	47152
CF-ZYP	C-137	20043

Morocco

CN-CCF	B727	20304
CN-CCG	**B727**	**20471**
CN-CCH	B727	20705
CN-CCT	CRVL	254
CN-CCV	CRVL	32
CN-CCX	**CRVL**	**57**
CN-CCY	CRVL	154
CN-CCZ	**CRVL**	**195**
CN-RGA	**B747**	**25629**
CN-RMA	B707	18375
CN-RMB	**B707**	**19773**
CN-RMC	**B707**	**19774**
CN-RMD	B707	17619
CN-RME	**B747**	**21615**
CN-RMF	**B737**	**24807**
CN-RMG	**B737**	**24808**
CN-RMH	B737	22632
CN-RMI	**B737**	**21214**
CN-RMJ	**B737**	**21215**
CN-RMK	**B737**	**21216**
CN-RML	B737	21112
CN-RML	**B737**	**22767**
CN-RMM	**B737**	**23049**
CN-RMN	**B737**	**23050**
CN-RMO	**B727**	**21297**
CN-RMP	**B727**	**21298**
CN-RMQ	**B727**	**21299**
CN-RMR	**B727**	**22377**
CN-RMS	B747	21253
CN-RMT	**B757**	**23686**
CN-RMU	B737	24922
CN-RMV	**B737**	**25317**
CN-RMW	**B737**	**25364**
CN-RMX	B737	22632
CN-RMX	**B737**	**26526**
CN-RMY	**B737**	**26525**
CN-RMZ	**B757**	**23687**
CN-RNA	**B737**	**26531**
CN-RNB	**B737**	**26527**
CN-RNC	**B737**	**26529**
CN-RND	**B737**	**26530**
(CN-RNE)	B737	27678
CN-RNF	**B737**	**27678**
(CN-RNF)	B737	27679
CN-RNG	**B737**	**27679**

Bolivia

CP-861	**B727**	**20279**
CP-1070	**B727**	**19860**
CP-1223	**B727**	**18795**
CP-1276	**B727**	**21082**
CP-1339	B727	20512
CP-1365	B707	18692
CP-1366	**B727**	**21494**
CP-1367	**B727**	**21495**
CP-1698	**B707**	**19586**
CP-1741	B727	22770
CP-2217	**DC-8**	**45668**
CP-2232	**A310**	**562**
CP-2247	146	E1104
CP-2249	146	E1017
CP-2254	146	E2055
CP-2260	146	E2060
CP-2273	**A310**	**475**
CP-2274	**B727**	**19132**
CP-2277	**B727**	**19429**
(CP-2338)	A310	562

Mozambique

CR-BAA	B737	20280
CR-BAB	B737	20281
CR-BAC	B737	20536
CR-BAD	B737	20786
(CR-LOR)	B737	21172
(CR-LOS)	B737	21173

Portugal

CS-DGI	B707	20514
CS-DGJ	B707	20515
CS-MAA	**A321**	**0550**
CS-MAB	**A321**	**0557**
CS-MAD	**A320**	**0573**
CS-TBA	B707	18961
CS-TBB	B707	18962
CS-TBC	B707	19740
CS-TBD	B707	19969
CS-TBE	B707	20136
CS-TBF	B707	20297
CS-TBG	B707	20298
CS-TBH	B707	19415
CS-TBI	B707	19767
CS-TBJ	B707	19179
CS-TBK	B727	19404
CS-TBL	B727	19405
CS-TBM	B727	19406
CS-TBN	B727	19597
CS-TBO	B727	19968
CS-TBP	B727	20489
CS-TBQ	B727	19665
CS-TBR	B727	20972
CS-TBS	B727	20973
CS-TBT	B707	20514
CS-TBU	B707	20515
CS-TBV	B727	19618
CS-TBW	B727	21949
CS-TBX	B727	21950
CS-TBY	B727	22430
CS-TCA	CRVL	117
CS-TCB	CRVL	125
CS-TCC	CRVL	137
CS-TCH	B727	20866
CS-TCI	B727	20867
CS-TCJ	B727	21018
CS-TEA	**L1011**	**1239**
CS-TEB	L1011	1240
CS-TEC	**L1011**	**1241**
CS-TED	**L1011**	**1242**
CS-TEE	**L1011**	**1243**
CS-TEF	L1011	1246
CS-TEG	L1011	1248
CS-TEH	**A310**	**483**
CS-TEI	**A310**	**495**
CS-TEJ	**A310**	**494**
CS-TEK	B737	23041
CS-TEL	B737	23042
CS-TEM	**B737**	**23043**
CS-TEN	**B737**	**23044**
CS-TEO	**B737**	**23045**
CS-TEP	**B737**	**23046**
CS-TEQ	**B737**	**23051**
(CS-TEQ)	B737	23047
CS-TER	B737	22636
CS-TES	**B737**	**22637**
CS-TET	B737	22415
CS-TEU	B737	22416
CS-TEV	B737	22402
CS-TEW	**A310**	**541**
CS-TEX	**A310**	**565**
CS-TEY	A310	573
CS-TGP	**B737**	**24131**
CS-TIA	B737	24364
(CS-TIA)	B737	24203
CS-TIB	**B737**	**24365**
(CS-TIB)	B737	24204
CS-TIC	**B737**	**24366**
(CS-TIC)	B737	24205
CS-TID	**B737**	**24449**
(CS-TID)	B737	24206
CS-TIE	**B737**	**24450**
(CS-TIE)	B737	24207
CS-TIF	B737	24212
CS-TIG	**B737**	**24213**
CS-TIH	**B737**	**24214**
CS-TII	B737	24986
CS-TIJ	B737	24987
CS-TIK	**B737**	**25161**
CS-TIL	**B737**	**25162**
(CS-TIM)	B737	24988
CS-TIN	**B737**	**23827**
CS-TIO	**B737**	**23830**
CS-TIR	B737	23411

CS-TIS	B737	23024
CS-TJA	B747	20501
CS-TJB	B747	20502
CS-TJC	B747	20928
CS-TJD	B747	21035
CS-TKA	B727	20765
CS-TKB	B727	20764
CS-TKC	B737	23830
CS-TKD	B737	23827
CS-TKE	B737	24905
CS-TKF	B737	27284
CS-TKG	B737	27285
CS-TMA	B737	22640
CS-TMB	B737	23023
CS-TMC	B737	23024
CS-TMD	B737	22699
CS-TME	B737	22600
CS-TNA	**A320**	**0185**
CS-TNB	**A320**	**0191**
CS-TNC	**A320**	**0234**
CS-TND	**A320**	**0235**
CS-TNE	**A320**	**0395**
CS-TNF	**A320**	**0407**
CS-TOA	**A340**	**041**
CS-TOB	**A340**	**044**
CS-TOC	**A340**	**079**
CS-TOD	**A340**	**091**
CS-TPA	**F-100**	**11257**
CS-TPB	**F-100**	**11262**
CS-TPC	**F-100**	**11287**
CS-TPD	**F-100**	**11317**
CS-TPE	**F-100**	**11342**
CS-TPF	**F-100**	**11258**

Cuba

(CU-...)	B707	17903
(CU-...)	B707	17904
CU-T992	IL-62	21202
CU-T994	IL-62	11001
CU-T1200	DC-8	45638
CU-T1201	DC-8	45611
CU-T1202	YAK40	9631449
CU-T1203	**YAK40**	**9641450**
CU-T1204	**YAK40**	**9641650**
CU-T1207	**YAK40**	
CU-T1208	**IL-62**	**3726739**
CU-T1209	**IL-62**	**1828132**
CU-T1210	DC-8	45612
CU-T1211	**YAK40**	**9731554**
CU-T1212	**YAK40**	**9731754**
CU-T1213	**YAK40**	**9731954**
CU-T1215	**IL-62**	**1828243**
CU-T1216	**IL-62**	**3829748**
CU-T1217	**IL-62**	**3933232**
CU-T1218	**IL-62**	**2035657**
CU-T1219	YAK40	9840959
CU-T1220	**YAK40**	**9841059**
CU-T1221	**YAK40**	**9841159**
CU-T1222	**TU154**	**447**
CU-T1224	**TU154**	**493**
CU-T1225	**IL-62**	**3139845**
CU-T1226	**IL-62**	**3242219**
CU-T1227	TU154	541
CU-T1232	**YAK40**	**9011060**
CU-T1233	**YAK40**	
CU-T1252	**IL-62**	**2343341**
CU-T1253	**TU154**	**576**
CU-T1256	**TU154**	**599**
CU-T1258	**IL-76**	**0043454615**
CU-T1259	**IL-62**	**3445111**
CU-T1264	**TU154**	**720**
CU-T1265	**TU154**	**751**
CU-T1271	**IL-76**	**0053459767**
CU-T1275	**TU154**	**777**
CU-T1276	TU154	719
CU-T1277	**YAK42**	**4520423016238**
CU-T1278	**YAK42**	**4520423016269**
CU-T1279	**YAK42**	**4520424914057**
CU-T1280	**IL-62**	**3749648**
CU-T1281	IL-62	3850453
CU-T1282	**IL-62**	**2052546**
CU-T1283	**IL-62**	**4053823**
CU-T1284	**IL-62**	**4053732**
CU-T1285	**YAK42**	**4520424914068**
CU-T1440	YAK40	9631249
"CU-t-1440"	**YAK40**	**9631249**
CU-T1441	**YAK40**	
CU-T1442	**YAK40**	**9541445**
CU-T1443	**YAK40**	**9710752**
CU-T1448	**YAK40**	**9011160**
CU-T1449	**YAK40**	**9021360**
CU-T1450	**YAK40**	**9021260**

Uruguay

CX-	**B737**	**23786**
CX-BHM	B737	20299
CX-BJV	B707	19212
CX-BKA	B727	19793
CX-BKB	B727	19010
CX-BLN	DC-8	45804
CX-BML	B707	17605
CX-BNT	B727	19314
CX-BNU	**B707**	**19239**
CX-BOH	B707	19240
CX-BON	**B737**	**22737**
CX-BOO	**B737**	**22738**
CX-BOP	**B737**	**22739**
CX-BPL	B707	19435
CX-BPQ	B707	18716
CX-BPZ	B707	19210
CX-BQG	**B720**	**18829**
CX-BQN	DC-8	45925
CX-BQN-F	DC-8	45925

Nauru

C2-RN1	F-28	11041
C2-RN2	F-28	11056
C2-RN3	B737	21073
C2-RN4	B727	20370
C2-RN5	B727	19252
C2-RN6	B737	21616
C2-RN7	B727	20278
C2-RN8	B737	22070
C2-RN9	B737	22072
C2-RN10	**B737**	**26960**
C2-RN11	B737	26961

Gambia

C5-	**B707**	**20172**
C5-	**B707**	**20176**
C5-DSZ	**B727**	**20470**
C5-GOA	B707	20177
C5-GOB	B707	19335
C5-GOC	B707	18839

Bahamas

C6-BDG	B707	18084
(C6-BDG)	B707	18085
C6-BDJ	1-11	089
C6-BDN	1-11	062
C6-BDP	1-11	063
C6-BDZ	B737	21231
C6-BEC	B737	20413
C6-BEH	B737	22531
C6-BEI	B737	20128
C6-BEK	B737	20956
C6-BEQ	B737	21279
C6-BES	B737	19921
C6-BEX	B737	21528
C6-BFB	B737	20221
C6-BFC	B737	21278
C6-BFJ	**B737**	**20211**

Mozambique

(C9-)	B767	26471
C9-ARF	B707	17593
C9-ARG	B720	18013
C9-BAA	**B737**	**20280**
C9-BAB	B737	20281
C9-BAC	**B737**	**20536**
C9-BAD	B737	20786
C9-BAE	IL-62	3344724
C9-CAA	TU134	63457

Germany/West Germany

D-	A321	0586
D-	A321	0591
D-	A321	0593
D-	A321	0595
D-	A321	0599
D-AASL	B737	24377
D-AAST	**CRVL**	**230**
D-ABAB	**B737**	**24769**
D-ABAC	**B737**	**24687**
D-ABAD	**B737**	**25178**
D-ABAE	**B737**	**27171**
D-ABAF	B737	26081
D-ABAF	CRVL	21
D-ABAF	CRVL	263
D-ABAG	**B737**	**27213**
D-ABAH	**B737**	**27826**
D-ABAI	**B737**	**28038**
D-ABAK	**B737**	**28271**
D-ABAK	CRVL	232
D-ABAL	**B737**	**28334**
D-ABAM	CRVL	214
D-ABAM	F-28	11030
D-ABAN	F-28	11029
D-ABAP	CRVL	235
D-ABAQ	F-28	11004
(D-ABAS)	F-28	11031
(D-ABAS)	F-28	11048
D-ABAV	CRVL	243
D-ABAW	CRVL	239
D-ABAX	F-28	11006
D-ABBE	B737	20253
D-ABBI	B727	19793
D-ABCE	B737	20254
"D-ABCE"	B707	17587
D-ABCI	B727	20430
D-ABDE	B737	20255
D-ABDF	**B737**	**24571**
D-ABDI	B727	20431
D-ABEA	B737	19013
D-ABEA	**B737**	**24565**
D-ABEB	B737	19014
D-ABEB	**B737**	**25148**
D-ABEC	B737	19015
D-ABEC	**B737**	**25149**
D-ABED	B737	19016
D-ABED	**B737**	**25215**
D-ABEE	**B737**	**25216**
D-ABEF	B737	19017
D-ABEF	**B737**	**25217**
D-ABEG	B737	19018
D-ABEH	B737	19019
D-ABEH	**B737**	**25242**
D-ABEI	B737	19020
D-ABEI	**B737**	**25359**
(D-ABEJ)	B737	19796
D-ABEK	B737	19021
D-ABEK	**B737**	**25414**
D-ABEL	B737	19022
D-ABEL	**B737**	**25415**
D-ABEM	B737	19023
D-ABEM	**B737**	**25416**
D-ABEN	B737	19024
D-ABEN	**B737**	**26428**
D-ABEO	B737	19025
D-ABEO	**B737**	**26429**
D-ABEP	B737	19026
D-ABEP	**B737**	**26430**
D-ABEQ	B737	19027
D-ABER	B737	19028
D-ABER	**B737**	**26431**
D-ABES	B737	19029
D-ABES	**B737**	**26432**
D-ABET	B737	19030
D-ABET	**B737**	**27903**
D-ABEU	B737	19031
D-ABEU	**B737**	**27904**
D-ABEV	B737	19032
D-ABEW	B737	19033
D-ABEW	**B737**	**27905**
D-ABEY	B737	19794
(D-ABEZ)	B737	19795
D-ABFA	**B737**	**22114**
D-ABFB	**B737**	**22113**
D-ABFC	**B737**	**22115**
D-ABFD	B737	22116
D-ABFE	B737	20256
D-ABFF	B737	22117
D-ABFH	B737	22118
D-ABFI	B727	20525
D-ABFK	B737	22119
D-ABFL	B737	22120
D-ABFM	B737	22121
D-ABFN	B737	22122
D-ABFP	**B737**	**22123**
D-ABFR	**B737**	**22124**
D-ABFS	B737	22125
D-ABFT	B737	22402
(D-ABFT)	B737	22126
D-ABFU	**B737**	**22126**
(D-ABFU)	B737	22127
D-ABFW	**B737**	**22127**
(D-ABFW)	B737	22128
D-ABFX	**B737**	**22128**
(D-ABFX)	B737	22129
D-ABFY	B737	22129
(D-ABFY)	B737	22130
D-ABFZ	B737	22130
(D-ABFZ)	B737	22131
D-ABGE	B737	20257
D-ABGI	B727	20526
D-ABHA	B737	22131
(D-ABHA)	B737	22132
D-ABHB	B737	22132
(D-ABHB)	B737	22133
D-ABHC	**B737**	**22133**
(D-ABHC)	B737	22134
D-ABHD	B737	22635
(D-ABHD)	B737	22134
(D-ABHD)	B737	22135
D-ABHE	B737	20258
D-ABHF	**B737**	**22134**
(D-ABHF)	B737	22135
(D-ABHF)	B737	22136
D-ABHH	1-11	084
D-ABHH	**B737**	**22135**
(D-ABHH)	B737	22136
(D-ABHH)	B737	22137
D-ABHI	B727	20560
D-ABHK	B737	22136
(D-ABHK)	B737	22137
(D-ABHK)	B737	22138
D-ABHL	B737	22137
(D-ABHL)	B737	22138
(D-ABHL)	B737	22139
D-ABHM	**B737**	**22138**
(D-ABHM)	B737	22139
(D-ABHM)	B737	22140
D-ABHN	**B737**	**22139**
(D-ABHN)	B737	22140
(D-ABHN)	B737	22141
D-ABHP	B737	22140
(D-ABHP)	B737	22141
(D-ABHP)	B737	22142
D-ABHR	B737	22141
(D-ABHR)	B737	22142
(D-ABHR)	B737	22143
D-ABHS	B737	22142
(D-ABHS)	B737	22143
(D-ABHS)	B737	22144
D-ABHT	B737	22636
(D-ABHT)	B737	22144
(D-ABHT)	B737	22634
D-ABHU	B737	22143
(D-ABHU)	B737	22635
D-ABHW	B737	22634
(D-ABHW)	B737	22636
D-ABHX	B737	22637
D-ABIA	B727	19011
D-ABIA	**B737**	**24815**
D-ABIB	B727	18360
D-ABIB	**B737**	**24816**
D-ABIC	B727	18361
D-ABIC	**B737**	**24817**
D-ABID	B727	18362
D-ABID	**B737**	**24818**

Registration	Type	c/n
D-ABIE	B727	19012
D-ABIE	**B737**	**24819**
D-ABIF	B727	18363
D-ABIF	**B737**	**24820**
D-ABIG	B727	18364
D-ABIH	B727	18365
D-ABIH	**B737**	**24821**
D-ABII	B727	19310
D-ABII	**B737**	**24822**
D-ABIJ	B727	19314
D-ABIK	B727	18366
D-ABIK	**B737**	**24823**
D-ABIL	B727	18367
D-ABIL	**B737**	**24824**
D-ABIM	B727	18368
D-ABIM	**B737**	**24937**
D-ABIN	B727	18369
D-ABIN	**B737**	**24938**
D-ABIO	B727	19311
D-ABIO	**B737**	**24939**
D-ABIP	B727	18370
D-ABIP	**B737**	**24940**
D-ABIQ	B727	18371
D-ABIR	B727	18933
D-ABIR	**B737**	**24941**
D-ABIS	B727	18934
D-ABIS	**B737**	**24942**
D-ABIT	B727	18935
D-ABIT	**B737**	**24943**
D-ABIU	B727	19312
D-ABIU	**B737**	**24944**
D-ABIV	B727	18936
D-ABIW	B727	19008
D-ABIW	**B737**	**24945**
D-ABIX	B727	19009
D-ABIX	**B737**	**24946**
D-ABIY	B727	19313
D-ABIY	**B737**	**25243**
D-ABIZ	B727	19010
D-ABIZ	**B737**	**25244**
D-ABJA	**B737**	**25270**
D-ABJB	**B737**	**25271**
D-ABJC	**B737**	**25272**
D-ABJD	**B737**	**25309**
D-ABJE	**B737**	**25310**
D-ABJF	**B737**	**25311**
D-ABJH	**B737**	**25357**
D-ABJI	**B737**	**25358**
(D-ABJK)	B737	25359
(D-ABJL)	B737	25414
(D-ABJM)	B737	25415
(D-ABJN)	B737	25416
D-ABKA	B727	20899
D-ABKA	**B737**	**27000**
D-ABKB	B727	20900
D-ABKB	**B737**	**27001**
D-ABKC	B727	20901
D-ABKC	**B737**	**27002**
D-ABKD	B727	20902
D-ABKD	**B737**	**27003**
D-ABKE	B727	20903
(D-ABKE)	B737	27004
D-ABKF	B727	20904
D-ABKF	**B737**	**27004**
(D-ABKF)	B737	27005
D-ABKG	B727	20905
D-ABKH	B727	20906
(D-ABKH)	B737	27007
D-ABKI	B727	20673
D-ABKJ	B727	20918
D-ABKK	B727	21113
D-ABKK	**B737**	**27005**
(D-ABKK)	B737	27004
D-ABKL	B727	21114
D-ABKL	B737	27007
D-ABKM	B727	21442
(D-ABKM)	B737	25796
D-ABKN	B727	21618
(D-ABKN)	B737	27231
D-ABKP	B727	21619
(D-ABKP)	B737	25800
D-ABKQ	B727	21620
D-ABKR	B727	21621
D-ABKS	B727	21622
D-ABKT	B727	21623
D-ABLI	B727	20674
D-ABMA	**B737**	**23153**
D-ABMB	**B737**	**23154**
D-ABMC	**B737**	**23155**
D-ABMD	**B737**	**23156**
D-ABME	**B737**	**23157**
D-ABMF	**B737**	**23158**
D-ABMI	B727	20675
D-ABNA	**B757**	**24737**
D-ABNB	**B757**	**24738**
D-ABNC	**B757**	**24747**
D-ABND	**B757**	**24748**
D-ABNE	**B757**	**24749**
D-ABNF	**B757**	**25140**
D-ABNH	**B757**	**25436**
D-ABNI	B727	20676
D-ABNI	**B757**	**25437**
D-ABNK	**B757**	**25438**
D-ABNL	**B757**	**25439**
D-ABNM	**B757**	**25440**
D-ABNN	**B757**	**25441**
D-ABNO	**B757**	**25901**
D-ABNP	**B757**	**26433**
D-ABNR	**B757**	**26434**
D-ABNS	**B757**	**26435**
D-ABNT	**B757**	**26436**
D-ABNX	**B757**	**24838**
D-ABNY	B757	22781
D-ABNZ	B757	22960
D-ABOB	B707	17718
D-ABOC	B707	17719
D-ABOD	**B707**	**17720**
D-ABOF	B707	17721
D-ABOG	B707	18056
D-ABOH	B720	18057
D-ABOK	B720	18058
D-ABOL	B720	18059
D-ABOM	B720	18060
D-ABON	B720	18248
D-ABOP	B720	18249
D-ABOQ	B720	18250
D-ABOR	B720	18251
D-ABOS	B707	18462
D-ABOT	B707	18463
D-ABOV	B707	18462
D-ABOX	B707	18819
D-ABPI	B727	20677
D-ABQI	B727	20757
D-ABRI	B727	20788
D-ABSI	B727	20789
D-ABTA	**B747**	**24285**
D-ABTB	**B747**	**24286**
D-ABTC	**B747**	**24287**
D-ABTD	**B747**	**24715**
D-ABTE	**B747**	**24966**
D-ABTF	**B747**	**24967**
D-ABTH	**B747**	**25047**
D-ABTI	B727	20790
D-ABUA	B707	18937
D-ABUA	**B767**	**26991**
(D-ABUA)	B767	26983
D-ABUB	B707	18923
D-ABUB	**B767**	**26987**
(D-ABUB)	B767	26984
(D-ABUB)	B767	26992
D-ABUC	B707	18926
D-ABUC	**B767**	**26992**
D-ABUD	B707	18927
D-ABUD	**B767**	**26983**
D-ABUE	B707	18932
D-ABUE	**B767**	**26984**
D-ABUF	B707	18928
D-ABUF	**B767**	**26985**
D-ABUG	B707	18929
D-ABUH	B707	18930
D-ABUH	**B767**	**26986**
D-ABUI	B707	19317
D-ABUI	**B767**	**26988**
D-ABUJ	B707	20123
D-ABUK	B707	18931
(D-ABUK)	B767	26989
D-ABUL	B707	19315
(D-ABUL)	B767	26990
D-ABUM	B707	19316
D-ABUO	B707	20124
D-ABUX	B767	25137
D-ABUY	B707	20395
D-ABUY	B767	25208
D-ABUZ	B767	25209
D-ABVA	**B747**	**23816**
D-ABVB	**B747**	**23817**
D-ABVC	**B747**	**24288**
D-ABVD	**B747**	**24740**
D-ABVE	**B747**	**24741**
D-ABVF	**B747**	**24761**
D-ABVH	**B747**	**25045**
D-ABVI	B727	20791
D-ABVK	**B747**	**25046**
D-ABVL	**B747**	**26425**
(D-ABVM)	B747	26426
D-ABVN	**B747**	**26427**
D-ABVO	**B747**	**28086**
D-ABWA	**B737**	**23833**
(D-ABWA)	B737	19679
D-ABWB	**B737**	**23834**
(D-ABWB)	B737	19680
D-ABWC	**B737**	**23835**
D-ABWD	**B737**	**23836**
D-ABWE	**B737**	**23837**
D-ABWF	**B737**	**24283**
D-ABWH	**B737**	**24284**
D-ABWI	B727	20792
D-ABWS	**B737**	**23811**
D-ABXA	**B737**	**23522**
D-ABXB	**B737**	**23523**
D-ABXC	**B737**	**23524**
D-ABXD	**B737**	**23525**
D-ABXE	**B737**	**23526**
D-ABXF	**B737**	**23527**
D-ABXH	**B737**	**23528**
D-ABXI	**B737**	**23529**
D-ABXK	**B737**	**23530**
D-ABXL	**B737**	**23531**
D-ABXM	**B737**	**23871**
D-ABXN	**B737**	**23872**
D-ABXO	**B737**	**23873**
D-ABXP	**B737**	**23874**
D-ABXR	**B737**	**23875**
D-ABXS	**B737**	**24280**
D-ABXT	**B737**	**24281**
D-ABXU	**B737**	**24282**
D-ABXW	**B737**	**24561**
D-ABXX	**B737**	**24562**
D-ABXY	**B737**	**24563**
D-ABXZ	**B737**	**24564**
D-ABYA	B747	19746
D-ABYB	B747	19747
D-ABYC	B747	19748
D-ABYD	B747	20372
D-ABYE	B747	20373
D-ABYF	B747	20493
D-ABYG	B747	20527
D-ABYJ	B747	21220
D-ABYK	B747	21221
D-ABYL	B747	21380
(D-ABYL)	B727	20675
D-ABYM	**B747**	**21588**
(D-ABYM)	B727	20676
D-ABYN	B747	21589
(D-ABYN)	B727	20677
D-ABYO	**B747**	**21592**
D-ABYP	**B747**	**21590**
D-ABYQ	**B747**	**21591**
D-ABYR	**B747**	**21643**
D-ABYS	B747	21644
D-ABYT	**B747**	**22363**
D-ABYU	**B747**	**22668**
D-ABYW	**B747**	**22669**
D-ABYX	**B747**	**22670**
D-ABYY	**B747**	**22671**
D-ABYZ	**B747**	**23286**
D-ABZA	**B747**	**23287**
D-ABZB	B747	23348
D-ABZC	**B747**	**23393**
D-ABZD	**B747**	**23407**
D-ABZE	**B747**	**23509**
D-ABZF	**B747**	**23621**
D-ABZH	**B747**	**23622**
D-ABZI	**B747**	**24138**
D-ACBA	B737	24652
D-ACBB	B737	24828
D-ACBC	B737	24273
(D-ACCA)	DC-8	45667
(D-ACCB)	DC-8	45684
D-ACEB	DC-9	47218
D-ACEC	DC-9	47219
D-ACFA	**146**	**E2200**
D-ACIP	B720	18162
D-ACIQ	B720	18163
D-ACIR	B720	18240
D-ACIS	B720	18242
D-ACIT	B720	18244
D-ACLA	**RJ100**	**7004**
D-ACLB	**RJ100**	**7005**
D-ACLC	**RJ100**	**7006**
D-ACLD	**RJ100**	**7009**
D-ACLE	**RJ100**	**7010**
D-ACLF	**RJ100**	**7015**
D-ACLG	**RJ100**	**7016**
(D-ACLG)	RJ100	7007
D-ACLH	**RJ100**	**7007**
(D-ACLH)	RJ100	7016
D-ACLI	**RJ100**	**7019**
D-ACLJ	**RJ100**	**7021**
D-ACLK	**RJ100**	**7023**
D-ACLL	**RJ100**	**7024**
D-ACLM	**RJ100**	**7025**
D-ACLN	**RJ100**	**7039**
D-ACLO	**RJ100**	**7041**
D-ACLP	**RJ100**	**7064**
D-ACLQ	**RJ100**	**7073**
D-ACLR	**RJ100**	**7086**
D-ACLS	**RJ100**	**7090**
D-ACLT	**RJ100**	**7093**
D-ACLU	RJ100	7104
D-ACLV	RJ100	7113
D-ACLW	RJ100	7114
D-ACLX	RJ100	7119
(D-ACLX)	RJ100	7036
D-ACVK	**CRVL**	**176**
D-ADAM	**VFW614G-017**	
D-ADAO	DC-10	47921
D-ADAP	B707	17697
D-ADAQ	B707	17701
D-ADBA	**B737**	**26441**
D-ADBB	**B737**	**26440**
D-ADBC	**B737**	**26442**
D-ADBD	**B737**	**27061**
D-ADBE	**B737**	**24569**
D-ADBG	**B737**	**25125**
D-ADBH	**B737**	**27336**
D-ADBI	**B737**	**27337**
D-ADBO	**DC-10**	**47922**
D-ADCO	DC-10	47923
(D-ADDA)	B737	22070
(D-ADDB)	B737	22726
(D-ADDC)	B737	22727
D-ADDO	**DC-10**	**47924**
D-ADEI	**146**	**E2086**
D-ADFA	**F-100**	**11307**
D-ADFB	**F-100**	**11311**
D-ADFC	**F-100**	**11315**
D-ADFD	**F-100**	**11344**
D-ADFE	**F-100**	**11363**
D-ADFO	**DC-10**	**47925**
D-ADGO	DC-10	47926
D-ADHO	DC-10	47927
D-ADIM	DC-8	45416
D-ADIR	DC-8	45526
D-ADIS	DC-9	47459
D-ADIT	DC-9	47450
D-ADIU	DC-9	47457
D-ADIX	DC-8	46137
D-ADIY	DC-8	46143
D-ADIZ	DC-8	46145
D-ADJO	**DC-10**	**47928**
D-ADKO	DC-10	47929
D-ADLO	**DC-10**	**46917**
D-ADMO	DC-10	46965
D-ADPO	**DC-10**	**46595**
D-ADQO	**DC-10**	**46596**
D-ADSO	**DC-10**	**48252**
D-ADUA	**DC-8**	**46003**
D-ADUC	**DC-8**	**46106**
D-ADUE	**DC-8**	**46044**
D-ADUI	**DC-8**	**45991**
D-ADUO	**DC-8**	**46047**
D-AERA	L1011	1033
D-AERB	**MD-11**	**48484**

D-AERC	L1011	1085
D-AERE	L1011	1120
D-AERF	**A330**	**082**
D-AERG	**A330**	**072**
D-AERH	**A330**	**087**
D-AERI	L1011	1114
D-AERJ	**A330**	**095**
D-AERK	**A330**	**120**
D-AERL	**L1011**	**1196**
D-AERM	L1011	1153
D-AERN	L1011	1158
D-AERO	L1011	1008
D-AERP	**L1011**	**1152**
D-AERQ	**A330**	**127**
D-AERT	**L1011**	**1183**
D-AERU	L1011	1125
D-AERV	L1011	1195
D-AERW	**MD-11**	**48485**
D-AERX	**MD-11**	**48486**
D-AERY	L1011	1008
D-AERZ	**MD-11**	**48538**
D-AEWA	**146**	**E3163**
D-AFGK	B727	19314
(D-AFWA)	1-11	BAC.161
(D-AFWB)	1-11	094
(D-AFWC)	1-11	091
D-AGAB	F-28	11046
D-AGAC	F-28	11050
D-AGAD	F-28	11051
D-AGAE	F-28	11052
D-AGEA	**B737**	**23970**
D-AGEB	**B737**	**23971**
D-AGEC	**B737**	**23972**
D-AGED	**B737**	**24269**
(D-AGED)	B737	24237
D-AGEE	**B737**	**24238**
D-AGEF	**B737**	**25069**
(D-AGEF)	B737	24269
D-AGEG	**B737**	**24237**
D-AGEH	**B737**	**23717**
D-AGEI	**B737**	**24220**
D-AGEJ	**B737**	**24221**
D-AGWA	MD-83	49845
D-AGWB	**MD-83**	**49846**
D-AGWC	**MD-83**	**49847**
D-AGWD	MD-83	49848
D-AGWE	MD-83	49788
D-AGWF	MD-83	49793
D-AHLA	**A310**	**520**
D-AHLA	F-28	11027
(D-AHLA)	A300	64
(D-AHLA)	B737	24776
D-AHLB	A300	83
D-AHLB	**A310**	**528**
D-AHLB	F-28	11031
(D-AHLB)	B737	24926
D-AHLC	A300	17
D-AHLC	**A310**	**620**
D-AHLC	F-28	11034
(D-AHLC)	B737	24927
D-AHLD	B737	22596
D-AHLD	**B737**	**24926**
D-AHLD	F-28	11032
D-AHLE	B737	22597
D-AHLE	**B737**	**24776**
D-AHLF	B737	22598
D-AHLF	**B737**	**24927**
D-AHLG	B737	22599
D-AHLG	**B737**	**26316**
(D-AHLG)	B737	27074
D-AHLH	B737	22600
D-AHLI	B737	22601
D-AHLI	**B737**	**25037**
D-AHLJ	A300	169
D-AHLJ	**B737**	**24125**
D-AHLK	A300	174
D-AHLK	**B737**	**24126**
D-AHLL	B727	18823
D-AHLL	**B737**	**24127**
D-AHLM	B727	18919
D-AHLM	**B737**	**27102**
D-AHLN	B727	18952
D-AHLN	**B737**	**25062**
D-AHLO	B727	19401
D-AHLO	**B737**	**24128**
D-AHLP	B727	18990
D-AHLP	**B737**	**24129**
D-AHLQ	B727	19282
D-AHLQ	**B737**	**24130**
D-AHLR	B727	19138
D-AHLR	**B737**	**24901**
D-AHLS	B727	19139
D-AHLS	**B737**	**27074**
D-AHLT	B727	21851
D-AHLT	**B737**	**27830**
D-AHLU	B727	21852
D-AHLU	**B737**	**27831**
D-AHLV	**A310**	**430**
D-AHLV	B727	21853
D-AHLW	**A310**	**427**
D-AHLX	**A310**	**487**
D-AHLZ	A300	25
D-AHLZ	**A310**	**468**
D-AHOI	**146**	**E3187**
D-AIAA	A300	21
D-AIAB	A300	22
D-AIAC	A300	26
D-AIAD	A300	48
D-AIAE	A300	52
D-AIAF	A300	132
D-AIAH	**A300**	**380**
D-AIAI	**A300**	**391**
D-AIAK	**A300**	**401**
D-AIAL	**A300**	**405**
D-AIAM	**A300**	**408**
D-AIAN	**A300**	**411**
D-AIAP	**A300**	**414**
D-AIAR	**A300**	**546**
D-AIAS	**A300**	**553**
D-AIAT	**A300**	**618**
D-AIAU	**A300**	**623**
D-AIAW	**A300**	**764**
D-AIBA	A300	53
D-AIBA	**A340**	**008**
D-AIBB	A300	57
D-AIBB	A340	009
D-AIBC	A300	75
D-AIBC	**A340**	**011**
D-AIBD	A300	76
D-AIBD	**A340**	**018**
D-AIBE	**A340**	**019**
D-AIBF	A300	77
D-AIBF	**A340**	**006**
D-AIBH	**A340**	**021**
D-AICA	A310	191
D-AICB	A310	201
D-AICC	A310	230
D-AICD	A310	233
D-AICF	A310	237
D-AICH	A310	254
D-AICK	A310	257
D-AICL	A310	273
D-AICM	A310	356
D-AICN	A310	359
D-AICP	A310	360
D-AICR	A310	397
D-AICS	A310	400
D-AIDA	**A310**	**434**
D-AIDB	**A310**	**484**
D-AIDC	**A310**	**485**
D-AIDD	**A310**	**488**
D-AIDE	**A310**	**522**
D-AIDF	**A310**	**524**
D-AIDH	**A310**	**527**
D-AIDI	**A310**	**523**
D-AIDK	**A310**	**526**
D-AIDL	**A310**	**547**
D-AIDM	**A310**	**595**
D-AIDN	**A310**	**599**
D-AIGA	**A340**	**020**
D-AIGB	**A340**	**024**
D-AIGC	**A340**	**027**
D-AIGD	**A340**	**028**
D-AIGF	**A340**	**035**
(D-AIGF)	A340	032
D-AIGH	**A340**	**052**
(D-AIGH)	A340	033
D-AIGI	**A340**	**053**
(D-AIGI)	A340	034
D-AIGK	**A340**	**056**
(D-AIGK)	A340	036
D-AIGL	**A340**	**135**
D-AILA	A319	609
D-AILB	A319	610
D-AILC	A319	616
D-AILD	A319	623
D-AILE	A319	627
D-AILF	A319	634
D-AILY	1-11	BAC.163
D-AIPA	**A320**	**0069**
D-AIPB	**A320**	**0070**
D-AIPC	**A320**	**0071**
D-AIPD	**A320**	**0072**
D-AIPE	**A320**	**0078**
D-AIPF	**A320**	**0083**
D-AIPH	**A320**	**0086**
D-AIPK	**A320**	**0093**
D-AIPL	**A320**	**0094**
D-AIPM	**A320**	**0104**
D-AIPN	A320	0105
D-AIPP	**A320**	**0110**
D-AIPR	**A320**	**0111**
D-AIPS	**A320**	**0116**
D-AIPT	**A320**	**0117**
D-AIPU	**A320**	**0135**
D-AIPW	**A320**	**0137**
D-AIPX	**A320**	**0147**
D-AIPY	**A320**	**0161**
D-AIPZ	**A320**	**0162**
D-AIQA	**A320**	**0172**
D-AIQB	**A320**	**0200**
D-AIQC	**A320**	**0201**
D-AIQD	**A320**	**0202**
D-AIQE	**A320**	**0209**
D-AIQF	**A320**	**0216**
D-AIQH	**A320**	**0217**
D-AIQK	**A320**	**0218**
D-AIQL	**A320**	**0267**
D-AIQM	**A320**	**0268**
D-AIQN	**A320**	**0269**
D-AIQP	**A320**	**0346**
D-AIQR	**A320**	**0382**
D-AIQS	**A320**	**0401**
D-AIRA	**A321**	**0458**
D-AIRB	**A321**	**0468**
D-AIRC	**A321**	**0473**
D-AIRD	**A321**	**0474**
D-AIRE	**A321**	**0484**
D-AIRF	**A321**	**0493**
D-AIRH	**A321**	**0412**
D-AIRK	**A321**	**0502**
D-AIRL	**A321**	**0505**
D-AIRM	**A321**	**0518**
D-AIRN	**A321**	**0560**
D-AIRO	**A321**	**0563**
D-AIRP	**A321**	**0564**
D-AIRR	**A321**	**0567**
D-AIRS	**A321**	**0595**
D-AISY	1-11	BAC.158
D-AITA	A300	134
D-AITB	A300	151
D-AIZV	A321	0520
D-AJAA	B727	18951
(D-AJAA)	B737	22025
D-AJET	**146**	**E2201**
D-ALAA	**A320**	**0565**
D-ALAB	**A320**	**0575**
D-ALAC	**A320**	**0580**
D-ALAL	B707	17638
D-ALAM	B707	17637
D-ALAQ	1-11	BAC.229
D-ALAR	1-11	BAC.207
D-ALAS	1-11	BAC.208
D-ALAT	1-11	BAC.187
D-ALFA	1-11	BAC.234
D-ALLA	DC-9	47673
D-ALLB	DC-9	47680
D-ALLC	DC-9	47672
D-ALLD	DC-9	47639
D-ALLD	**MD-83**	**49402**
D-ALLE	**MD-83**	**49449**
D-ALLF	**MD-83**	**49602**
D-ALLG	**MD-87**	**49670**
D-ALLH	MD-87	49671
D-ALLI	1-11	BAC.116
D-ALLI	MD-87	49767
D-ALLJ	**MD-87**	**49768**
D-ALLK	**MD-83**	**49769**
D-ALLL	**MD-83**	**49854**
D-ALLM	**MD-83**	**49856**
D-ALLN	**MD-83**	**49857**
D-ALLO	**MD-83**	**53012**
D-ALLP	**MD-83**	**53013**
D-ALLQ	**MD-83**	**53014**
D-ALLR	**MD-83**	**53015**
D-ALLS	**MD-82**	**49379**
(D-ALLS)	MD-83	53016
D-ALLT	**MD-82**	**49440**
(D-ALLT)	MD-83	53063
D-ALLU	**MD-83**	**49619**
D-ALLV	**MD-83**	**49620**
D-ALLW	MD-83	49792
D-ALOA	**146**	**E2066**
D-AMAM	1-11	BAC.229
D-AMAP	A300	09
D-AMAS	1-11	BAC.187
D-AMAT	1-11	BAC.235
D-AMAX	A300	12
D-AMAY	A300	20
D-AMAZ	A300	25
D-AMIE	1-11	BAC.190
D-AMOR	1-11	BAC.197
D-AMOR	DC-9	45787
D-AMUC	1-11	BAC.227
D-AMUH	**B757**	**27812**
D-AMUI	**B757**	**28112**
D-AMUJ	**B767**	**28111**
D-AMUK	**B757**	**22689**
D-AMUL	B757	25597
D-AMUM	**B757**	**24451**
D-AMUN	**B767**	**24259**
D-AMUP	**B767**	**25531**
D-AMUQ	**B757**	**26278**
D-AMUR	1-11	BAC.195
D-AMUR	B757	23118
D-AMUR	**B767**	**24257**
D-AMUS	B757	23119
D-AMUS	**B767**	**24258**
D-AMUT	B757	23651
D-AMUU	**B757**	**22688**
D-AMUV	**B757**	**23928**
D-AMUW	**B757**	**23929**
D-AMUX	**B757**	**23983**
D-AMUY	**B757**	**24176**
D-AMUZ	**B757**	**24497**
(D-ANDI)	1-11	BAC.158
D-ANDY	1-11	BAC.127
D-ANNO	1-11	BAC.160
D-ANTJ	**146**	**E2100**
D-ANUE	1-11	BAC.238
D-ANYL	CRVL	247
D-AOAA	A310	498
D-AOAB	A310	499
D-AOAC	A310	503
D-AOAD	IL-62	3036931
D-AOAE	IL-62	4831517
D-AOAF	IL-62	4934734
D-AOAG	IL-62	4140536
D-AOAH	IL-62	3344833
D-AOAI	IL-62	2546812
D-AOAJ	IL-62	1647928
D-AOAK	IL-62	4546257
D-AOAL	IL-62	2748552
D-AOAM	IL-62	1951525
D-AOAN	IL-62	2951636
D-AOBA	TU134	3351903
D-AOBB	**TU134**	**1351304**
D-AOBC	TU134	3352102
D-AOBD	TU134	3352106
D-AOBE	TU134	4352205
D-AOBF	TU134	4352206
D-AOBG	TU134	4352207
D-AOBH	TU134	4308068
D-AOBI	TU134	09070
D-AOBJ	TU134	12095
D-AOBK	TU134	31218
D-AOBL	TU134	6348320
D-AOBM	TU134	60495
D-AOBN	TU134	35180
D-AOBO	TU134	5338040
D-AOBP	TU134	40150
D-AOBQ	TU134	46155
D-AOBR	TU134	46300
D-AOBS	TU134	6348560

(D-AOEB)	B757	24122
(D-AOUP)	B737	22070
D-APOL	A310	447
D-APOM	**A310**	**448**
D-APON	**A310**	**472**
D-APOO	A310	475
D-APOP	A310	481
D-APOQ	A310	475
(D-ARJA)	RJ100	7004
(D-ARJB)	RJ100	7005
(D-ARJC)	RJ100	7006
(D-ARJD)	RJ100	7013
(D-ARJE)	RJ100	7014
(D-ARJF)	RJ100	7015
(D-ARJG)	RJ100	7023
(D-ARJH)	RJ100	7024
(D-ARJI)	RJ100	7025
(D-ARJJ)	RJ100	7028
(D-ARJK)	RJ100	7034
(D-ARJL)	RJ100	7037
(D-ARJM)	RJ100	7038
D-AVRA	**146**	**E2256**
D-AVRB	**146**	**E2253**
D-AVRC	**146**	**E2251**
D-AVRD	**146**	**E2257**
D-AVRE	**146**	**E2261**
D-AVRF	**146**	**E2269**
D-AVRG	**146**	**E2266**
D-AVRH	**146**	**E2268**
D-AVRI	**146**	**E2270**
D-AVRJ	**146**	**E2277**
D-AVRK	**146**	**E2278**
D-AVRL	**146**	**E2285**
D-AVRO	**146**	**E2246**
D-AVYA	A319	578
D-AVZA	A321	0412
D-AVZA	A321	0529
D-AVZB	A321	0434
D-AVZB	A321	0532
D-AVZC	A321	0473
D-AVZC	A321	0535
D-AVZD	A321	0474
D-AVZD	A321	0538
D-AVZE	A321	0477
D-AVZE	A321	0541
D-AVZF	A321	0484
D-AVZF	A321	0544
D-AVZG	A321	0488
D-AVZG	A321	0550
D-AVZH	A321	0493
D-AVZH	A321	0552
D-AVZI	A321	0494
D-AVZI	A321	0555
D-AVZJ	A321	0495
D-AVZJ	A321	0557
D-AVZK	A321	0498
D-AVZK	A321	0560
D-AVZL	A321	0502
D-AVZL	A321	0564
D-AVZM	A321	0505
D-AVZM	A321	0567
D-AVZN	A321	0509
D-AVZN	A321	0563
D-AVZO	A321	0513
D-AVZP	A321	0514
D-AVZQ	A321	0515
D-AVZQ	A321	0570
D-AVZR	A321	0516
D-AVZR	A321	0576
D-AVZS	A321	0517
D-AVZS	A321	0581
D-AVZT	A321	0518
D-AVZT	A321	0583
D-AVZU	A321	0519
D-AVZW	A321	0521
D-AVZX	A321	0522
D-AVZY	A321	0524
D-AVZZ	A321	0526
D-AZUR	**146**	**E2060**
D-BABA	VFW614G-001	
D-BABB	VFW614G-002	
D-BABC	VFW614G-003	
D-BABD	VFW614G-004	
D-BABE	VFW614G-005	
D-BABF	VFW614G-006	
D-BABG	VFW614G-007	
D-BABH	VFW614G-008	
D-BABI	VFW614G-009	
D-BABJ	VFW614G-010	
D-BABK	VFW614G-011	
D-BABL	VFW614G-012	
D-BABM	VFW614G-013	
D-BABN	VFW614G-015	
D-BABO	VFW614G-016	
D-BABP	VFW614G-017	
D-BABQ	VFW614G-020	
D-BABR	VFW614G-021	
D-BABS	VFW614G-022	
D-BABT	VFW614G-023	
D-BOBA	YAK40	9211420
D-BOBB	YAK40	9211520
D-BOBC	YAK40	9230122
D-BOBD	YAK40	9230323
D-BOBE	YAK40	9230623
D-COBA	YAK40	9211420
D-COBB	YAK40	9211520
D-COBC	YAK40	9230122
D-COBD	YAK40	9230323
D-COBE	YAK40	9230623

East Germany

DDR-ABA	A310	498
DDR-ABB	A310	499
DDR-ABC	A310	503
DDR-SCB	**TU134**	**8350503**
DDR-SCE	TU134	9350904
DDR-SCF	**TU134**	**9350905**
DDR-SCG	**TU134**	**9350912**
DDR-SCH	TU134	9350906
DDR-SCI	TU134	3351903
DDR-SCK	TU134	1351304
DDR-SCL	**TU134**	**1351305**
DDR-SCN	TU134	3352102
DDR-SCO	TU134	3352106
DDR-SCP	TU134	4352205
DDR-SCR	TU134	4352206
DDR-SCS	TU134	4352207
DDR-SCT	TU134	4308068
DDR-SCU	TU134	09070
DDR-SCV	TU134	12095
DDR-SCW	TU134	31218
DDR-SCX	TU134	6348320
DDR-SCY	TU134	60495
DDR-SCZ	**TU134**	**9350913**
DDR-SDC	TU134	35180
DDR-SDE	TU134	5338040
DDR-SDF	TU134	40150
DDR-SDG	TU134	46155
DDR-SDH	TU134	46300
DDR-SDI	TU134	6348560
DDR-SDK	TU134	49900
DDR-SDL	TU134	60108
DDR-SDM	TU134	60435
DDR-SDN	TU134	60612
DDR-SDO	TU134	62259
DDR-SDP	TU134	63260
DDR-SDR	TU134	63967
DDR-SDS	TU134	63952
DDR-SDT	TU134	63998
DDR-SDU	TU134	66135
DDR-SEB	IL-62	00704
DDR-SEC	**IL-62**	**10903**
DDR-SEF	**IL-62**	**31402**
DDR-SEG	**IL-62**	**31403**
DDR-SEH	**IL-62**	**31405**
DDR-SEI	IL-62	3036931
DDR-SEK	IL-62	4831517
DDR-SEL	IL-62	4934734
DDR-SEM	IL-62	4140536
DDR-SEN	IL-62	3242432
DDR-SEO	IL-62	3344833
DDR-SEP	IL-62	4445827
DDR-SER	IL-62	2546812
DDR-SES	IL-62	1647928
DDR-SET	IL-62	4546257
DDR-SEU	IL-62	2748552
DDR-SEV	IL-62	3749224
DDR-SEW	IL-62	2850324
DDR-SEY	IL-62	1951525
DDR-SEZ	IL-62	2951636
DDR-SFA	TU154	799
DDR-SFB	TU154	813
(DDR-SZA)	A310	498
(DDR-SZB)	A310	499
(DDR-SZC)	A310	503

East Germany

DM-SCA	BB152	6
DM-SCA	TU134	8350502
DM-SCB	BB152	7
DM-SCB	TU134	8350503
DM-SCC	BB152	8
DM-SCD	TU134	9350702
DM-SCE	TU134	9350904
DM-SCF	TU134	9350905
DM-SCG	TU134	9350912
DM-SCH	TU134	9350906
DM-SCI	TU134	3351903
DM-SCK	TU134	1351304
DM-SCL	TU134	1351305
DM-SCM	TU134	3351904
DM-SCN	TU134	3352102
DM-SCO	TU134	3352106
DM-SCP	TU134	4352205
DM-SCR	TU134	4352206
DM-SCS	TU134	4352207
DM-SCT	TU134	4308068
DM-SCU	TU134	09070
DM-SCV	TU134	12095
DM-SCW	TU134	31218
DM-SCX	TU134	6348320
DM-SCY	TU134	60495
DM-SCZ	TU134	9350913
DM-SDA	TU124	4351508
DM-SDB	TU124	5351708
DM-SDC	TU124	
DM-SDE	TU134	5338040
DM-SDF	TU134	40150
DM-SDG	TU134	46155
DM-SDH	TU134	46300
DM-SDI	TU134	6348560
DM-SDK	TU134	49900
DM-SDL	TU134	60108
DM-SDM	TU134	60435
DM-SDN	TU134	60612
DM-SDO	TU134	62259
DM-SDP	TU134	63260
DM-SEA	IL-62	00702
DM-SEB	IL-62	00704
DM-SEC	IL-62	10903
DM-SEF	IL-62	31402
DM-SEG	IL-62	31403
DM-SEH	IL-62	31405
DM-SEI	IL-62	3036931
DM-SEK	IL-62	4831517
DM-SEL	IL-62	4934734
DM-VBA	TU124	4351505
DM-VBB	TU134	9350913
DM-VBC	TU124	5351708
DM-VBC	TU134	1351305
DM-VBD	TU134	35180
DM-ZYA	BB152	1
DM-ZYB	BB152	3
DM-ZYC	BB152	5

Fiji

DQ-FBQ	1-11	BAC.245
DQ-FBV	1-11	BAC.250
DQ-FCR	1-11	BAC.116
DQ-FDM	B737	22679
DQ-FJA	B767	23058
DQ-FJB	**B737**	**26067**
DQ-FJC	**B767**	**26260**
DQ-FJD	**B737**	**27285**

Angola

D2-EAG	**YAK40**	**9230122**
D2-ECC	**TU134**	**49830**
D2-ESU	**B727**	**19431**
D2-FAS	**B727**	**20773**
D2-FAT	**B727**	**19497**
D2-FLY	**B727**	**19839**
D2-FLZ	**B727**	**19833**
D2-TAA	B737	21172
D2-TAB	B737	21173
D2-TAC	B707	18975
D2-TAD	B707	19355
D2-TAG	B707	18583
D2-TAH	B737	21723
(D2-TAL)	B707	19965
(D2-TAM)	B707	19963
D2-TBC	**B737**	**21173**
D2-TBD	**B737**	**21723**
D2-TBI	**B737**	**19681**
D2-TBN	B737	22775
D2-TBO	**B737**	**22776**
D2-TBP	**B737**	**23220**
D2-TBT	B737	21278
D2-TBU	B737	21279
D2-TBV	B737	22626
D2-TBX	**B737**	**23351**
D2-TIF	**IL-62**	**4648525**
D2-TIG	**IL-62**	**4750919**
D2-TJA	**B727**	**19813**
D2-TJB	**B727**	**19005**
D2-TJC	**B727**	**19180**
D2-TOB	B707	18975
D2-TOC	B707	19355
D2-TOG	**B707**	**18583**
D2-TOI	B707	18975
D2-TOJ	**B707**	**19355**
D2-TOK	**B707**	**19869**
D2-TOL	**B707**	**19963**
D2-TOM	B707	19965
D2-TON	**B707**	**19871**
D2-TOP	**B707**	**20136**
D2-TOR	**B707**	**18748**
D2-TOU	**B707**	**18964**
D2-TOV	B707	18881
D2-TPR	B707	20715
D2-TYA	**YAK40**	**9721553**
D2-TYB	**YAK40**	**9721653**
D2-TYC	YAK40	9721753
D2-TYD	YAK40	9721853

Cape Verde Islands

D4-CBG	**B757**	**27599**

Comoro Islands

D6-CAJ	B737	22581

Spain

EC-	**B737**	**24376**
EC-	**B737**	**25071**
EC-	**B767**	**24457**
EC-102	MD-83	49575
EC-113	MD-83	49631
EC-116	B757	23119
EC-117	A310	638
EC-117	B737	23506
EC-117	B757	22176
EC-129	B737	23331
EC-135	B737	23636
EC-135	B737	23750
EC-136	B737	23808
EC-136	B747	24071
EC-138	B737	23941
EC-147	MD-83	49577
EC-148	MD-83	49579
EC-149	MD-83	49621
EC-150	MD-83	49672
EC-151	B737	23922
EC-152	B737	23923
EC-153	B737	23766
EC-154	**A340**	**125**
EC-155	**A340**	**134**
EC-155	B737	23787
EC-156	**A340**	**145**
EC-157	**A340**	**146**
EC-157	B757	24119

EC-159 B737 24131
EC-159 MD-83 49710
EC-160 B737 24132
EC-163 MD-83 49668
EC-166 MD-83 49791
EC-167 B737 23752
EC-178 MD-83 49624
EC-179 MD-83 49622
EC-188 B737 24211
EC-189 B737 24299
EC-190 MD-83 49642
EC-198 146 E2102
EC-202 B757 24120
EC-203 B757 24122
EC-204 B737 24256
EC-204 B757 24118
EC-206 MD-83 49622
EC-211 B757 22781
EC-213 B737 23064
EC-214 DC-8 45905
EC-215 MD-83 49627
EC-216 MD-83 49630
EC-217 DC-8 46023
EC-223 MD-83 49626
EC-230 DC-8 45921
(EC-231) 146 E2112
EC-239 B737 23979
EC-244 B737 24462
EC-245 B737 24463
EC-246 DC-9 47656
EC-247 B757 24289
EC-248 B757 24290
EC-251 B737 23981
EC-255 B737 23684
EC-256 B757 23651
EC-257 MD-83 49642
EC-260 MD-83 49628
EC-261 MD-83 49631
EC-265 B757 22185
EC-269 MD-83 49629
EC-273 A300 76
EC-274 A300 77
EC-276 B737 23787
EC-277 B737 23788
EC-278 B757 24398
EC-279 B737 23809
EC-279 MD-83 49624
EC-281 146 E2089
EC-287 B747 20137
EC-288 DC-8 45895
EC-289 MD-83 49668
EC-290 MD-87 49827
EC-291 MD-87 49828
EC-292 MD-87 49829
EC-293 MD-87 49830
EC-294 MD-87 49831
EC-295 MD-87 49832
EC-296 MD-87 49833
EC-297 MD-87 49834
EC-298 MD-87 49835
EC-299 MD-87 49836
EC-300 MD-87 49837
EC-301 MD-87 49838
EC-302 MD-87 49839
EC-303 MD-87 49840
EC-304 MD-87 49841
EC-305 MD-87 49842
EC-306 MD-87 49843
EC-307 MD-83 49790
EC-308 B737 24345
EC-321 B757 22176
EC-326 B727 20606
EC-327 B727 20607
EC-328 B727 20593
EC-348 MD-83 49574
EC-349 B757 24397
EC-350 B757 24119
EC-355 B737 23712
EC-356 B737 23332
EC-356 B737 23748
EC-375 B737 23810
EC-376 B737 23826
EC-377 B737 23747
EC-382 MD-83 49622
EC-389 MD-83 49396
EC-390 B757 22689
EC-390 MD-83 49578
EC-401 B737 24545
EC-402 B737 24685
EC-403 B737 24689
EC-420 B757 26239
EC-421 B757 26240
EC-421 MD-82 49661
EC-422 B757 26241
EC-429 B737 23713
EC-432 B757 24772
EC-438 MD-83 49663
EC-439 MD-83 53050
EC-440 MD-83 53051
EC-446 B757 24792
EC-451 B757 22176
EC-457 B737 25858
EC-463 MD-83 49577
EC-479 MD-83 49398
EC-479 MD-83 49621
EC-485 MD-83 49622
EC-487 MD-83 49672
EC-489 DC-9 47061
EC-490 B757 24793
EC-495 MD-82 48022
EC-516 B757 24120
EC-520 B737 26293
EC-524 MD-83 49628
EC-525 MD-83 49629
EC-529 DC-8 45945
EC-531 MD-83 49620
EC-542 B737 24256
EC-544 B757 24121
EC-546 MD-83 49791
EC-546 MD-83 49826
EC-547 B737 26301
EC-547 B767 24999
EC-548 B767 25000
EC-575 A320 0134
EC-576 A320 0136
EC-577 A320 0143
EC-578 A320 0146
EC-579 A320 0158
EC-580 A320 0173
EC-581 A320 0176
EC-582 A320 0177
EC-583 A320 0199
EC-584 A320 0207
EC-585 A320 0223
EC-586 A320 0224
EC-587 A320 0240
EC-588 A320 0241
EC-589 A320 0246
EC-591 B737 23752
EC-591 MD-83 49574
EC-592 B737 24131
EC-592 MD-83 49938
EC-593 B737 24132
EC-594 B737 24299
EC-597 B757 24398
EC-597 B757 25597
EC-603 B737 24690
EC-607 MD-83 49708
EC-608 B757 26242
EC-609 B757 26243
EC-610 B757 26244
EC-611 B757 26245
EC-612 B757 26246
EC-615 146 E2117
EC-616 B757 26240
EC-618 B757 26241
EC-622 DC-9 45695
EC-633 MD-87 53207
EC-634 MD-87 53208
EC-635 B737 23495
EC-635 MD-87 53209
EC-636 MD-87 53210
EC-637 MD-87 53211
EC-638 MD-83 49630
EC-638 MD-87 53212
EC-639 MD-87 53213
EC-640 A310 638
EC-642 MD-83 49619
EC-642 MD-87 49779
EC-644 B737 24706
EC-645 B737 24707
EC-646 MD-83 49627
EC-655 B737 24124
EC-667 B737 23747
EC-667 B757 25053
(EC-668) B757 25054
EC-669 B757 24794
EC-703 B737 25159
EC-704 B737 25256
EC-705 B737 25263
EC-706 B737 25264
EC-711 B737 24059
EC-712 146 E3154
EC-714 MD-83 49401
EC-719 146 E2105
EC-733 MD-83 49792
EC-737 B737 24682
EC-738 B737 24688
EC-742 MD-83 49790
EC-744 B757 24122
EC-749 MD-83 49401
EC-751 MD-88 53193
EC-752 MD-88 53194
EC-753 MD-88 53195
EC-754 MD-88 53196
EC-755 MD-88 53197
EC-765 B747 20137
EC-772 B737 24686
EC-781 B737 23749
EC-782 B737 23707
EC-783 B737 23331
EC-784 B737 23332
EC-786 B757 24792
EC-793 MD-82 48022
EC-796 B737 26315
EC-797 B737 26317
EC-798 B737 26322
EC-805 MD-83 49626
EC-807 146 E3165
EC-807 MD-83 49642
EC-835 MD-83 49709
EC-839 146 E3169
EC-843 B757 22185
EC-847 B757 23227
EC-850 B737 24906
EC-851 B737 24912
EC-876 146 E3163
EC-880 A320 0264
EC-881 A320 0266
EC-882 A320 0274
EC-883 A320 0303
EC-884 A320 0312
EC-885 A320 0323
EC-886 A320 0356
EC-892 DC-8 46105
EC-893 MD-82 49900
EC-894 MD-82 53165
EC-896 B757 22688
EC-897 B737 24462
EC-897 B757 25597
EC-898 B737 23923
EC-898 MD-83 49668
EC-899 146 E3187
EC-936 B737 25180
EC-945 MD-88 53303
EC-946 MD-88 53304
EC-963 DC-8 46069
EC-964 MD-88 53305
EC-965 MD-88 53306
EC-966 MD-88 53307
EC-969 146 E1007
EC-970 B737 25743
EC-971 146 E1015
EC-987 MD-88 53308
EC-988 MD-88 53309
EC-989 MD-88 53310
EC-991 B737 25190
EC-994 MD-82 49144
EC-996 B737 24569
EC-997 B737 25116
EC-ARA DC-8 45617
EC-ARB DC-8 45618
EC-ARC DC-8 45619
EC-ARI CRVL 107
EC-ARJ CRVL 108
EC-ARK CRVL 109
EC-ARL CRVL 110
EC-ASN DC-8 45659
EC-ATP DC-8 45658
EC-ATV CRVL 163
EC-ATX CRVL 165
EC-AUM DC-8 45657
EC-AVY CRVL 173
EC-AVZ CRVL 159
EC-AXU CRVL 138
EC-AYD CRVL 197
EC-AYE CRVL 198
EC-BAV DC-8 45814
(EC-BAX) DC-9 45797
(EC-BAY) DC-9 45798
(EC-BAZ) DC-9 45799
EC-BBR CRVL 171
EC-BDC CRVL 176
EC-BDD CRVL 202
EC-BIA CRVL 226
EC-BIB CRVL 223
EC-BIC CRVL 225
EC-BID CRVL 228
EC-BIE CRVL 230
EC-BIF CRVL 232
EC-BIG DC-9 47037
EC-BIH DC-9 47076
EC-BII DC-9 47077
EC-BIJ DC-9 47079
EC-BIK DC-9 47080
EC-BIL DC-9 47084
EC-BIM DC-9 47088
EC-BIN DC-9 47089
EC-BIO DC-9 47090
EC-BIP DC-9 47091
EC-BIQ DC-9 47092
EC-BIR DC-9 47093
EC-BIS DC-9 47312
EC-BIT DC-9 47313
EC-BIU DC-9 47314
EC-BJC CV990 30-10-22
EC-BJD CV990 30-10-23
EC-BMV DC-8 45965
EC-BMX DC-8 45930
EC-BMY DC-8 45931
EC-BMZ DC-8 45988
EC-BNM CV990 30-10-32
EC-BPF DC-9 47364
EC-BPG DC-9 47365
EC-BPH DC-9 47368
EC-BQA CV990 30-10-36
EC-BQF 1-11 BAC.161
EC-BQQ CV990 30-10-34
EC-BQS DC-8 46079
EC-BQT DC-9 47446
EC-BQU DC-9 47447
EC-BQV DC-9 47453
EC-BQX DC-9 47454
EC-BQY DC-9 47455
EC-BQZ DC-9 47456
EC-BRJ CRVL 250
EC-BRO B747 19957
EC-BRP B747 19958
EC-BRQ B747 20137
EC-BRX CRVL 261
EC-BRY CRVL 264
EC-BSD DC-8 46116
EC-BSE DC-8 46155
EC-BTE CV990 30-10-21
EC-BVA F-28 11017
EC-BVB F-28 11019
EC-BVC F-28 11023
EC-BXI CV990 30-10-35
EC-BXR DC-8 45422
EC-BYD DC-9 47522
EC-BYE DC-9 47504
EC-BYF DC-9 47542
EC-BYG DC-9 47543
EC-BYH DC-9 47556
EC-BYI DC-9 47452
EC-BYJ DC-9 47461
EC-BYK DC-9 47428
EC-BYL DC-9 47545
EC-BYM DC-9 47496
EC-BYN DC-9 47565
EC-BZO CV990 30-10-30
EC-BZP CV990 30-10-18
EC-BZQ DC-8 45426
EC-BZR CV990 30-10-25

EC-CAD	DC-8	45423
EC-CAE	CRVL	176
EC-CAI	B727	20592
EC-CAJ	B727	20593
EC-CAK	B727	20594
EC-CAM	DC-8	45427
EC-CBA	**B727**	**20595**
EC-CBB	B727	20596
EC-CBC	B727	20597
EC-CBD	B727	20598
EC-CBE	B727	20599
EC-CBF	**B727**	**20600**
EC-CBG	**B727**	**20601**
EC-CBH	B727	20602
EC-CBI	B727	20603
EC-CBJ	B727	20604
EC-CBK	B727	20605
EC-CBL	B727	20606
EC-CBM	**B727**	**20607**
EC-CBN	DC-10	46925
EC-CBO	**DC-10**	**46926**
EC-CBP	**DC-10**	**46927**
EC-CCF	DC-8	45897
EC-CCG	DC-8	45898
EC-CCN	DC-8	45569
EC-CDA	DC-8	45429
EC-CDB	DC-8	45424
EC-CDC	DC-8	45567
EC-CEZ	**DC-10**	**47980**
EC-CFA	**B727**	**20811**
EC-CFB	**B727**	**20812**
EC-CFC	**B727**	**20813**
EC-CFD	**B727**	**20814**
EC-CFE	**B727**	**20815**
EC-CFF	**B727**	**20816**
EC-CFG	**B727**	**20817**
EC-CFH	**B727**	**20818**
EC-CFI	**B727**	**20819**
EC-CFJ	B727	20820
EC-CFK	**B727**	**20821**
EC-CGN	**DC-9**	**47637**
EC-CGO	**DC-9**	**47640**
EC-CGP	**DC-9**	**47642**
EC-CGQ	**DC-9**	**47643**
EC-CGR	**DC-9**	**47644**
EC-CGS	DC-9	47645
EC-CGY	DC-9	45696
EC-CGZ	DC-9	45699
EC-CID	**B727**	**20974**
EC-CIE	**B727**	**20975**
EC-CIZ	CRVL	247
EC-CLB	**DC-10**	**47981**
EC-CLD	**DC-9**	**47675**
EC-CLE	DC-9	47678
EC-CMS	CRVL	238
EC-CMT	DC-8	45568
EC-CNF	**CV990**	**30-10-8**
EC-CNG	**CV990**	**30-10-7**
EC-CNH	**CV990**	**30-10-17**
EC-CNJ	**CV990**	**30-10-14**
EC-CPI	CRVL	236
EC-CQM	DC-8	45668
EC-CSJ	**DC-10**	**46922**
EC-CSK	DC-10	46953
EC-CTR	**DC-9**	**47702**
EC-CTS	**DC-9**	**47704**
EC-CTT	**DC-9**	**47706**
EC-CTU	**DC-9**	**47707**
EC-CUM	CRVL	212
EC-CUS	DC-8	45265
EC-CYI	CRVL	263
EC-CZE	DC-8	45913
EC-DBE	DC-8	45824
EC-DCC	**B727**	**21609**
EC-DCD	**B727**	**21610**
EC-DCE	**B727**	**21611**
EC-DCN	CRVL	199
EC-DDU	B727	21777
EC-DDV	**B727**	**21778**
EC-DDX	**B727**	**21779**
EC-DDY	**B727**	**21780**
EC-DDZ	**B727**	**21781**
EC-DEA	**DC-10**	**47982**
EC-DEG	DC-10	46962
EC-DEM	DC-8	45856
EC-DFP	CRVL	257
EC-DGB	**DC-9**	**48103**
EC-DGC	**DC-9**	**48104**
EC-DGD	**DC-9**	**48105**
EC-DGE	**DC-9**	**48106**
EC-DHZ	**DC-10**	**47834**
EC-DIA	**B747**	**22238**
EC-DIB	**B747**	**22239**
EC-DIH	DC-8	45753
EC-DIR	DC-9	45698
EC-DKH	DC-8	45412
EC-DLC	**B747**	**22454**
EC-DLD	**B747**	**22455**
EC-DLE	**A300**	**130**
EC-DLF	**A300**	**133**
EC-DLG	**A300**	**135**
EC-DLH	**A300**	**136**
EC-DNP	**B747**	**22764**
EC-DNQ	**A300**	**156**
EC-DNR	**A300**	**170**
(EC-DNS)	A300	171
(EC-DNT)	A300	179
EC-DQP	DC-9	45792
EC-DQQ	DC-9	47531
EC-DQT	DC-9	47613
EC-DSF	DC-10	46992
EC-DSV	DC-9	47458
EC-DTI	DC-9	47639
EC-DTR	B737	22597
EC-DUB	B737	22598
EC-DUG	DC-10	46576
EC-DUL	B737	22369
EC-DVB	DC-8	46037
EC-DVC	DC-8	46016
EC-DVE	B737	22639
EC-DVN	B737	22296
EC-DXE	B747	20014
EC-DXK	B737	22638
EC-DXV	B737	22407
EC-DYA	DC-8	45885
EC-DYB	DC-8	46011
EC-DYY	DC-8	45888
EC-DYZ	B737	22703
EC-DZA	DC-8	46032
EC-DZB	B737	20218
EC-DZC	DC-8	46015
EC-DZH	B737	20336
EC-EAK	B737	23535
EC-EAM	DC-8	45908
EC-EAZ	DC-10	46727
EC-EBX	B737	23747
EC-EBY	B737	23748
EC-EBZ	B737	23712
EC-ECA	B737	23713
EC-ECM	B737	23787
EC-ECN	MD-83	49401
EC-ECO	MD-83	49442
EC-ECQ	B737	23788
EC-ECR	B737	23749
EC-ECS	B737	23707
EC-ECU	DC-9	47201
EC-EDM	B737	23388
EC-EEG	**B737**	**20910**
EC-EEK	**B747**	**24071**
EC-EFJ	MD-83	49575
EC-EFK	MD-83	49576
(EC-EFL)	MD-83	49642
EC-EFU	MD-83	49574
EC-EFX	**B757**	**23118**
EC-EGH	**B757**	**23119**
EC-EGI	B757	22176
EC-EGQ	B737	23506
EC-EHA	B737	23331
EC-EHJ	B737	23636
EC-EHM	B737	23766
EC-EHT	MD-83	49577
EC-EHX	B737	23752
EC-EHY	B757	24119
EC-EHZ	B737	23922
EC-EIA	B737	23923
EC-EID	B737	23941
EC-EIG	**MD-83**	**49579**
EC-EII	B737	24131
EC-EIK	MD-83	49668
EC-EIR	B737	24132
EC-EJQ	MD-83	49672
EC-EJU	MD-83	49621
EC-EJZ	MD-83	49622
EC-EKM	MD-83	49624
EC-EKT	MD-83	49642
EC-ELA	B757	24120
EC-ELJ	B737	24299
EC-ELM	DC-8	45905
EC-ELS	B757	24122
EC-ELT	**146**	**E2102**
EC-ELV	B737	23064
EC-ELY	**B737**	**24211**
EC-EMA	B757	24118
EC-EMD	**DC-8**	**46023**
EC-EMG	MD-83	49626
EC-EMI	B737	23979
EC-EMT	MD-83	49642
EC-EMU	B757	24290
EC-EMV	B757	24289
EC-EMX	**DC-8**	**45921**
EC-EMY	B737	23981
EC-ENQ	**B757**	**23651**
EC-ENS	B737	24462
EC-ENT	B737	24463
EC-ENZ	DC-9	47656
EC-EOK	B757	22185
EC-EOL	B757	24398
EC-EOM	MD-83	49628
EC-EON	**A300**	**76**
EC-EOO	**A300**	**77**
EC-EOY	MD-83	49629
EC-EOZ	MD-83	49627
EC-EPA	**146**	**E2089**
EC-EPL	MD-83	49630
EC-EPM	MD-83	49631
EC-EPN	B737	24345
EC-EQI	DC-8	45895
EC-ESC	B757	24397
EC-ESJ	MD-83	49790
EC-EST	B737	23332
EC-ETB	**B737**	**24545**
EC-ETZ	B757	22689
EC-EUC	**MD-87**	**49829**
EC-EUD	**MD-87**	**49828**
EC-EUE	**MD-87**	**49827**
EC-EUF	MD-83	49663
EC-EUL	**MD-87**	**49830**
EC-EUZ	MD-83	53050
EC-EVB	**MD-87**	**49831**
EC-EVC	B757	24792
EC-EVD	B757	24772
EC-EVE	**B737**	**24685**
EC-EVU	MD-83	53051
EC-EVY	MD-82	49661
EC-EXF	**MD-87**	**49832**
EC-EXG	**MD-87**	**49833**
EC-EXH	B757	24121
EC-EXM	**MD-87**	**49835**
EC-EXN	**MD-87**	**49836**
EC-EXR	**MD-87**	**49834**
EC-EXT	**MD-87**	**49837**
EC-EXX	MD-83	49398
EC-EXY	**B737**	**24689**
EC-EYB	**MD-87**	**49838**
EC-EYP	MD-82	48022
EC-EYS	DC-9	47061
EC-EYX	**MD-87**	**49839**
EC-EYY	**MD-87**	**49840**
EC-EYZ	**MD-87**	**49841**
EC-EZA	**MD-87**	**49842**
EC-EZR	MD-83	49826
EC-EZS	**MD-87**	**49843**
EC-EZU	MD-83	49620
EC-FAS	**A320**	**0134**
EC-FBP	B737	24690
EC-FBQ	**A320**	**0136**
EC-FBR	**A320**	**0146**
EC-FBS	**A320**	**0143**
EC-FCB	**A320**	**0158**
EC-FCQ	DC-9	45695
EC-FCU	**B767**	**24999**
EC-FDA	**A320**	**0176**
EC-FDB	**A320**	**0173**
EC-FEB	MD-83	49619
EC-FEE	**B757**	**25053**
EC-FEF	**B757**	**24794**
EC-FEO	**A320**	**0177**
EC-FEP	MD-83	49792
EC-FEQ	MD-83	49401
EC-FER	**B737**	**24299**
EC-FET	B737	24132
EC-FEY	**MD-87**	**53208**
EC-FEZ	**MD-87**	**53207**
EC-FFA	**MD-87**	**53209**
EC-FFB	B737	23752
EC-FFC	B737	24131
EC-FFH	**MD-87**	**53211**
EC-FFI	**MD-87**	**53210**
EC-FFK	**B757**	**24122**
EC-FFN	**B737**	**25159**
EC-FFY	**146**	**E3154**
EC-FGG	B737	24059
EC-FGH	**A320**	**0223**
EC-FGM	**MD-88**	**53193**
EC-FGQ	MD-82	48022
EC-FGR	**A320**	**0224**
EC-FGT	146	E3165
EC-FGU	**A320**	**0199**
EC-FGV	**A320**	**0207**
EC-FHA	**B767**	**25000**
EC-FHD	**MD-87**	**53212**
EC-FHG	**MD-88**	**53194**
EC-FHK	**MD-87**	**53213**
EC-FHR	**B737**	**25256**
EC-FHU	146	E3169
EC-FIA	**A320**	**0240**
EC-FIC	**A320**	**0241**
EC-FIG	**MD-88**	**53195**
EC-FIH	**MD-88**	**53196**
EC-FIU	146	E3163
EC-FIX	MD-83	49396
EC-FIY	B757	22688
EC-FJE	**MD-88**	**53197**
EC-FJQ	MD-82	49900
EC-FJR	**B737**	**24462**
EC-FJZ	B737	23923
EC-FKC	B737	23332
EC-FKD	**A320**	**0264**
EC-FKF	146	E3187
EC-FKH	**A320**	**0246**
EC-FKI	**B737**	**23707**
EC-FKJ	**B737**	**23749**
EC-FKS	B737	23331
EC-FLD	**B737**	**25180**
EC-FLF	**B737**	**25263**
EC-FLG	**B737**	**25264**
EC-FLK	**MD-88**	**53304**
EC-FLN	**MD-88**	**53303**
EC-FLP	**A320**	**0266**
EC-FLQ	**A320**	**0274**
EC-FLY	B757	25597
EC-FMJ	B737	25190
EC-FML	**A320**	**0303**
EC-FMN	**A320**	**0312**
EC-FMO	MD-82	49144
EC-FMP	B737	25743
EC-FMQ	B757	24792
EC-FMS	B737	24569
EC-FMY	MD-83	49631
EC-FND	**MD-88**	**53305**
EC-FNI	A310	638
EC-FNR	**A320**	**0323**
EC-FNU	MD-83	49622
EC-FOF	**MD-88**	**53306**
EC-FOG	**MD-88**	**53307**
EC-FOZ	**MD-88**	**53308**
EC-FPD	**MD-88**	**53309**
EC-FPJ	**MD-88**	**53310**
EC-FQB	B737	23684
EC-FQP	B737	23809
EC-FQY	**A320**	**0356**
EC-FRP	B737	23748
EC-FRZ	B737	23747
EC-FSA	B737	23826
EC-FSC	B737	23810
EC-FSY	**MD-83**	**49577**
EC-FSZ	**MD-83**	**49578**
EC-FTL	**B757**	**22176**
EC-FTR	**B757**	**26239**
EC-FTS	**MD-83**	**49621**
EC-FTT	**MD-83**	**49622**
EC-FTU	**MD-83**	**49672**
EC-FUA	B757	26240
EC-FUB	B757	26241

EC-FUT	**B737**	**26293**
EC-FVA	**DC-8**	**45945**
EC-FVB	**MD-83**	**49628**
EC-FVC	**MD-83**	**49629**
EC-FVJ	B737	24256
EC-FVR	**MD-83**	**49574**
EC-FVT	B737	23495
EC-FVV	**MD-83**	**49708**
EC-FVX	MD-83	49791
EC-FVY	**146**	**E2117**
EC-FXA	**MD-83**	**49938**
EC-FXB	**A310**	**638**
EC-FXI	**MD-83**	**49630**
EC-FXJ	B737	25858
EC-FXP	**B737**	**24706**
EC-FXQ	**B737**	**24707**
EC-FXU	**B757**	**26240**
EC-FXV	**B757**	**26241**
EC-FXX	MD-87	49779
EC-FXY	**MD-83**	**49627**
EC-FYE	B737	23747
EC-FYF	**B737**	**26301**
EC-FYG	B737	24124
EC-FYJ	**B757**	**26242**
EC-FYK	**B757**	**26243**
EC-FYL	**B757**	**26244**
EC-FYM	**B757**	**26245**
EC-FYN	**B757**	**26246**
EC-FZC	**MD-83**	**49790**
EC-FZE	**146**	**E2105**
EC-FZQ	**MD-83**	**49401**
EC-FZT	**B737**	**24688**
EC-FZX	B737	24682
EC-FZZ	**B737**	**24686**
EC-GAG	**B747**	**20137**
EC-GAP	**B737**	**26315**
EC-GAT	**MD-83**	**49709**
EC-GAZ	**B737**	**24906**
EC-GBA	**MD-83**	**49626**
EC-GBN	**B737**	**24912**
EC-GBU	**B737**	**26317**
EC-GBV	**MD-83**	**49668**
EC-GBX	**B757**	**25597**
EC-GBY	**MD-83**	**49642**
EC-GCA	**B757**	**22185**
EC-GCB	**B757**	**23227**
EC-GCI	**B727**	**20598**
EC-GCJ	**B727**	**20602**
EC-GCK	**B727**	**20603**
EC-GCL	**B727**	**20604**
EC-GCM	**B727**	**20606**
EC-GCV	**MD-82**	**53165**
EC-GCY	**DC-8**	**46105**
EC-GEE	**DC-8**	**46069**
EC-GEO	**146**	**E1007**
EC-GEP	**146**	**E1015**
EC-GEQ	**B737**	**23750**
EC-GEU	**B737**	**23808**
EC-GFE	**B737**	**25116**

Ireland

EI-ALA	B720	18041
EI-ALB	B720	18042
EI-ALC	B720	18043
EI-AMW	B707	18737
EI-ANE	1-11	049
EI-ANF	1-11	050
EI-ANG	1-11	051
EI-ANH	1-11	052
EI-ANO	B707	18880
EI-ANV	B707	19001
EI-APG	B707	19410
(EI-APP)	B737	19424
(EI-APS)	B737	19425
EI-ASA	B737	19424
EI-ASB	B737	19425
EI-ASC	B737	20218
EI-ASD	B737	20219
EI-ASE	B737	20220
EI-ASF	B737	20221
EI-ASG	B737	20222
EI-ASH	B737	20223
EI-ASI	**B747**	**19744**
EI-ASJ	**B747**	**19745**
EI-ASK	B737	19947
EI-ASL	B737	21011
EI-ASM	B707	19263
EI-ASN	B707	18976
EI-ASO	B707	19354
(EI-ATR)	CRVL	110
(EI-AVY)	CRVL	108
(EI-B)	B737	22396
EI-BCC	B737	21131
EI-BCR	**B737**	**20276**
EI-BDY	B737	21112
(EI-BEA)	B737	21112
EI-BEB	B737	21714
EI-BEC	B737	21715
EI-BED	**B747**	**19748**
EI-BEE	B737	20413
EI-BEF	B737	20449
EI-BER	B707	19212
EI-BFC	B737	20336
EI-BFN	B707	17719
EI-BFU	B707	17929
EI-BII	B737	21279
EI-BJE	B737	19742
EI-BJP	B737	19743
EI-BKQ	B707	18832
EI-BLC	B707	19964
(EI-BMB)	B737	22071
EI-BMY	B737	21278
EI-BNA	**DC-8**	**45989**
EI-BNS	B737	20521
EI-BOC	B737	20455
(EI-BOG)	B737	22071
EI-BOJ	B737	22071
EI-BOM	B737	22368
EI-BON	B737	22369
EI-BOS	B747	19898
EI-BOU	B747	20013
EI-BPF	DC-8	45897
EI-BPG	DC-8	45898
EI-BPH	B747	20013
EI-BPR	B737	21775
EI-BPV	B737	22024
EI-BPW	B737	21776
EI-BPY	B737	21774
EI-BRA	B727	20580
EI-BRB	B737	22279
EI-BRD	B727	20580
EI-BRF	B727	20710
EI-BRN	B737	22529
EI-BRR	B747	20014
EI-BRZ	B737	22703
EI-BSS	1-11	BAC.402
EI-BSY	1-11	BAC.266
EI-BSZ	1-11	BAC.272
EI-BTA	MD-83	49391
EI-BTB	MD-83	49392
EI-BTC	MD-83	49393
EI-BTD	MD-83	49394
EI-BTF	B737	23684
EI-BTG	DC-8	46001
EI-BTL	MD-83	49399
EI-BTM	B737	23826
EI-BTN	**L1011**	**1046**
EI-BTQ	B747	21650
EI-BTR	B737	21735
EI-BTS	**B747**	**22381**
EI-BTT	B737	23921
EI-BTU	MD-83	49619
EI-BTV	MD-83	49620
EI-BTW	B737	21960
EI-BTX	**MD-82**	**49660**
EI-BTY	**MD-82**	**49667**
(EI-BTY)	MD-82	49661
EI-BTZ	B737	22576
EI-BUD	B737	23809
EI-BUE	B737	23810
EI-BUI	B727	19249
EI-BUP	B727	18877
(EI-BVD)	B707	18873
EI-BVG	1-11	BAC.255
EI-BVH	1-11	BAC.407
EI-BVI	1-11	BAC.256
EI-BVO	B727	20381
EI-BWB	MD-82	49661
EI-BWC	B737	23024
EI-BWC	MD-83	49668
EI-BWD	MD-83	49575
EI-BWE	MD-83	49576
EI-BWF	**B747**	**21575**
EI-BWG	DC-8	46099
EI-BWI	1-11	007
EI-BWJ	1-11	009
EI-BWK	1-11	011
EI-BWL	1-11	012
EI-BWM	1-11	013
EI-BWN	1-11	020
EI-BWO	1-11	041
EI-BWP	1-11	043
EI-BWQ	1-11	057
EI-BWR	1-11	061
EI-BWS	1-11	085
EI-BWT	1-11	BAC.127
EI-BWY	B737	22744
EI-BWZ	B737	23023
(EI-BX.)	B737	23066
EI-BXA	**B737**	**24474**
EI-BXB	**B737**	**24521**
EI-BXC	**B737**	**24773**
EI-BXD	**B737**	**24866**
EI-BXE	B737	24878
EI-BXF	B737	24919
EI-BXG	B737	24968
EI-BXH	B737	24989
EI-BXI	**B737**	**25052**
(EI-BXJ)	B737	25115
EI-BXK	**B737**	**25736**
(EI-BXM)	B737	23065
EI-BXV	B737	20492
EI-BXW	B737	22743
EI-BXY	B737	22278
EI-BZA	**B747**	**22496**
EI-BZB	A300	83
EI-BZD	DC-10	46976
EI-BZE	**B737**	**24464**
EI-BZF	**B737**	**24465**
EI-BZG	B737	24466
EI-BZH	**B737**	**24546**
EI-BZI	**B737**	**24547**
EI-BZJ	**B737**	**24677**
EI-BZK	**B737**	**24678**
EI-BZL	**B737**	**24680**
EI-BZM	**B737**	**24681**
EI-BZN	**B737**	**24770**
EI-BZO	B737	23922
EI-BZP	B737	23923
EI-BZQ	B737	24462
EI-BZR	B737	24463
EI-BZS	B737	23747
EI-BZT	B737	23748
EI-BZU	DC-8	45994
EI-BZV	MD-83	49784
EI-BZW	DC-9	47126
EI-BZX	DC-9	47059
EI-BZY	DC-9	47085
EI-BZZ	DC-9	47122
(EI-CAG)	B767	25421
EI-CAI	B747	20108
EI-CAK	DC-8	46121
EI-CAL	**B767**	**24952**
EI-CAM	**B767**	**24953**
EI-CAS	1-11	BAC.406
EI-CBA	DC-9	47123
EI-CBB	DC-9	45785
EI-CBE	MD-83	49398
EI-CBG	**DC-9**	**47742**
EI-CBH	**DC-9**	**47796**
EI-CBI	**DC-9**	**48122**
EI-CBL	B737	20957
(EI-CBM)	L1011	1068
EI-CBN	MD-83	49401
EI-CBO	MD-83	49442
EI-CBP	B737	24905
EI-CBQ	B737	24907
EI-CBR	**MD-83**	**49939**
EI-CBS	**MD-83**	**49942**
EI-CBT	B737	24692
(EI-CBU)	MD-87	49673
EI-CBW	A300	269
EI-CBX	MD-83	49943
EI-CBY	**MD-83**	**49944**
EI-CBZ	**MD-83**	**49945**
EI-CCC	**MD-83**	**49946**
EI-CCE	**MD-83**	**49947**
EI-CCU	1-11	BAC.237
EI-CCW	1-11	BAC.186
EI-CCX	1-11	BAC.211
EI-CDA	**B737**	**24878**
EI-CDB	**B737**	**24919**
EI-CDC	**B737**	**24968**
EI-CDD	**B737**	**24989**
EI-CDE	**B737**	**25115**
EI-CDF	**B737**	**25737**
EI-CDG	**B737**	**25738**
EI-CDH	**B737**	**25739**
EI-CDI	**MD-11**	**48499**
EI-CDJ	MD-11	48500
EI-CDK	**MD-11**	**48501**
(EI-CDL)	MD-11	48502
(EI-CDM)	MD-11	48503
(EI-CDN)	MD-11	48504
EI-CDO	1-11	BAC.201
EI-CDS	**B737**	**26287**
EI-CDT	B737	25165
EI-CDY	**MD-83**	**49948**
(EI-CEA)	B767	25411
EI-CEB	**A300**	**240**
EI-CEE	B737	23923
EI-CEH	MD-83	49950
EI-CEK	**MD-83**	**49631**
EI-CEM	B767	25421
EI-CEO	**B747**	**21730**
EI-CEP	**MD-83**	**53122**
EI-CEQ	**MD-83**	**53123**
EI-CER	**MD-83**	**53125**
EI-CEU	B737	24345
EI-CEV	B737	23979
EI-CEW	B737	23981
EI-CEY	**B757**	**26152**
EI-CEZ	**B757**	**26154**
EI-CFQ	B737	24255
EI-CFR	B767	25865
(EI-CFS)	B737	26065
(EI-CFT)	B737	25288
(EI-CFU)	B737	25289
EI-CFZ	**MD-82**	**53120**
EI-CGA	MD-83	49668
EI-CGI	**MD-83**	**49624**
EI-CGO	**DC-8**	**45924**
EI-CGR	MD-83	49642
EI-CGS	MD-83	49626
(EI-CGX)	B737	23177
EI-CGY	DC-8	45976
EI-CGZ	B737	21685
EI-CHA	B737	23747
EI-CHB	B737	21206
EI-CHC	B737	21686
EI-CHD	B737	23176
EI-CHE	B737	23826
EI-CHH	**B737**	**23177**
EI-CHQ	B737	23173
EI-CHU	B737	23175
EI-CIB	1-11	BAC.191
EI-CIC	1-11	BAC.177
EI-CID	1-11	BAC.174
EI-CIE	1-11	BAC.176
EI-CIW	**MD-83**	**49785**
EI-CIX	B737	24911
EI-CIY	**B767**	**25208**
EI-CJA	**B767**	**26387**
EI-CJB	**B767**	**26388**
EI-CJC	**B737**	**22640**
EI-CJD	**B737**	**22966**
EI-CJE	**B737**	**22639**
EI-CJF	**B737**	**22967**
EI-CJG	**B737**	**22058**
EI-CJH	**B737**	**22057**
EI-CJI	**B737**	**22875**
EI-CJK	**A300**	**20**
EI-CJP	146	E1160
EI-CJW	**B737**	**21355**
EI-CJX	**B757**	**26160**
EI-CJY	**B757**	**26161**
EI-CKB	MD-83	49400
EI-CKD	**B767**	**26205**
EI-CKE	**B767**	**26208**
EI-CKK	**B737**	**21612**
EI-CKL	**B737**	**21356**

EI-CKM MD-83 49792
EI-CKP B737 22296
EI-CKQ B737 22906
EI-CKR B737 22025
EI-CKS B737 22023
EI-CKV B737 23747
EI-CKW B737 21677
EI-CLG 146 E3131
EI-CLG 146 E3155
EI-CLH 146 E3146
EI-CLI 146 E3159
EI-CLJ 146 E3155
EI-CLK B737 21733
EI-CLM B757 24367
EI-CLN B737 21443
EI-CLO B737 21444
EI-CLP B757 25268
EI-CLR B767 25411
EI-CLS B767 26262
EI-CLU B757 26274
EI-CLV B757 26275
EI-CLW B737 25187
EI-CLZ B737 25179
EI-CMA B757 25054
EI-CMD B767 27392
EI-CME B767 27393
EI-CMH B767 27568
EI-CMM MD-83 49937
EI-CMO B737 23866
EI-CMP DC-9 47089
EI-CMQ B767 27993
EI-CRK A330 070
EI-CTY 146 E2072
EI-DLA DC-10 46958
EI-DUB A330 055
EI-EWW B727 21269
EI-HCA B727 20382
EI-HCB B727 19492
EI-HCC B727 19480
EI-HCD B727 20185
EI-HCI B727 20183
EI-JET 146 E2073
EI-JFK A330 086
EI-LCH B727 20466
(EI-NYC) A330 070
EI-SHN A330 054
EI-SKY B727 20571
EI-TL. A300 07
EI-TLA DC-8 45973
(EI-TLB) DC-8 45993
EI-TLB A300 12
EI-TLC DC-8 45995
EI-TLD DC-8 45812
EI-TLE A320 0429
EI-TLF A320 0476
EI-TLG A320 0428
EI-TLH A320 0247
EI-TLI A320 0405
EI-TLJ A320 0257
EI-TNT B727 20725
EI-VIR A320 0449

Armenia

EK65072 TU134 49972
EK65650 TU134 0351006
EK65731 TU134 23515127
EK65822 TU134 09071
EK65831 TU134 17102
EK65848 TU134 23136
EK65884 TU134 36150
EK65975 TU134 33520067
EK85162 TU154 162
EK85166 TU154 166
EK85196 TU154 196
EK85200 TU154 200
EK85210 TU154 210
EK85279 TU154 279
EK85403 TU154 403
EK85442 TU154 442
EK85536 TU154 536
EK85566 TU154 566
EK85607 TU154 607
EK86117 IL-86 51483209085
EK86118 IL-86 51483209086
EK86724 IL-76 073410284
EK86817 IL-76 063407191
EK87908 YAK40 9..1354
EKA001 B737 26855

Liberia

EL- B707 20029
(EL-...) B727 18877
EL-AAG CRVL 254
EL-AAS CRVL 154
EL-AIL B737 21538
EL-AIW CRVL 106
EL-AIY B707 19986
EL-AIY B727 18892
(EL-AIY) B707 19377
EL-AIZ B727 18895
EL-AJA B707 19377
EL-AJC B707 17721
EL-AJK DC-8 46012
EL-AJO DC-8 45683
EL-AJQ DC-8 45686
EL-AJR B707 19247
EL-AJS B707 18873
EL-AJT B707 18891
EL-AJU B707 19315
EL-AJV B707 17635
EL-AJW B707 17631
EL-AKA B707 19335
EL-AKB B707 20035
EL-AKC B707 20177
EL-AKD B720 18030
EL-AKE B727 18877
EL-AKF B707 18922
EL-AKG L1011 1068
EL-AKH B707 19296
EL-AKI B707 18925
EL-AKJ B707 19375
EL-AKK B707 20177
EL-AKL B707 18839
EL-AKU B707 19964
EL-ALD 1-11 011
EL-GNU B707 19582
EL-GOL B727 18253
EL-JNS B707 18689
EL-LAT B707 19350
EL-OSZ CRVL 254
EL-SKD B707 18586
EL-TBA B707 20283
EL-ZGS B707 20261

Iran

EP-AGA B737 21317
EP-AMU B727 19011
EP-AMV B727 19314
EP-AMW B727 19314
EP-ARG TU154
EP-CPA YAK42 4520423219102
EP-CPB YAK42
EP-CPC YAK42
EP-CPE YAK42
EP-GAY TU154
EP-GDS B727 19557
EP-HIM B707 21396
EP-IAA B747 20998
EP-IAB B747 20999
EP-IAC B747 21093
EP-IAD B747 21758
EP-IAG B747 21217
EP-IAH B747 21218
EP-IAM B747 21759
(EP-IAN) B747 21760
(EP-IAP) B747 21761
(EP-IAR) B747 21762
EP-IBA A300 723
EP-IBB A300 727
EP-IBR A300 61
EP-IBS A300 80
EP-IBT A300 185
EP-IBU A300 186
EP-IBV A300 187
EP-IBZ A300 226
EP-ICA B747 21487
EP-ICB B747 21507
EP-ICC B747 21514
EP-IDA F-100 11292
EP-IDB F-100 11299
(EP-IDB) F-100 11267
EP-IDC F-100 11267
(EP-IDC) F-100 11299
EP-IDD F-100 11294
(EP-IDD) F-100 11287
(EP-IDE) F-100 11294
(EP-IDE) F-100 11298
EP-IDF F-100 11298
(EP-IDF) F-100 11302
EP-IDG F-100 11302
(EP-IDH) F-100 11304
(EP-IDI) F-100 11305
EP-IDJ F-100 11309
EP-IDK F-100 11317
(EP-IDL) F-100 11319
EP-IRA B727 19171
EP-IRB B727 19172
EP-IRC B727 19816
EP-IRD B727 19817
EP-IRF B737 20498
EP-IRG B737 20499
EP-IRH B737 20500
EP-IRI B737 20740
EP-IRJ B707 18958
EP-IRK B707 19267
EP-IRL B707 20287
EP-IRM B707 20288
EP-IRN B707 20741
EP-IRP B727 20945
EP-IRR B727 20946
EP-IRS B727 20947
EP-IRT B727 21078
EP-IRU B727 21079
EP-ITA TU154 902
EP-ITB TU154 880
EP-ITC TU154
EP-ITD TU154 903
EP-ITF TU154 860
EP-ITG TU154 866
EP-ITI TU154 941?
EP-ITJ TU154 883
EP-ITK TU154 877
EP-ITL TU154 810
EP-ITM TU154 884
EP-ITN TU154 942
EP-ITS TU154 859
EP-ITS TU154 867
EP-ITT TU154
EP-JAY IL-76 1013409297
EP-JAZ IL-76 1013409321
EP-LAD TU154 929
EP-LAH TU154 904
EP-LAH YAK42 4520423303016
EP-LAI TU154 891
EP-LAM YAK42 4520423304016
EP-LAN? YAK42 4520421402018
EP-LAO TU154 841
EP-LAP TU154 842
EP-LAQ TU154 850
EP-LAS TU154
EP-MKA IL-76
EP-MRP B727 19557
EP-NHA B707 21123
EP-NHD B747 19668
EP-NHJ B747 19667
EP-NHK B747 19669
EP-NHN B747 21486
EP-NHP B747 20082
EP-NHR B747 20081
EP-NHS B747 20080
EP-NHT B747 19678
EP-NHV B747 19667
EP-NHW B707 20834
EP-NHY B707 21396
EP-PAS F-28 11027
EP-PAT F-28 11164
EP-PAU F-28 11166
EP-PAV F-28 11070
EP-PAX F-28 11102
EP-PAZ F-28 11104
EP-PBA F-28 11052
EP-PBB F-28 11093

EP-PBF F-28 11003
EP-PLN B727 18363
EP-SHA B747 21507
EP-SHB B747 21486
EP-SHC B747 20080
EP-SHD B747 20081
EP-SHE B707 21128
EP-SHF B707 21123
EP-SHG B707 21125
EP-SHJ B707 21127
EP-SHP B727 18363

Moldova

ER-65036 TU134 48700
ER-65050 TU134 49756
ER-65051 TU134 49758
ER-65071 TU134 49915
ER-65094 TU134 60255
ER-65140 TU134 60932
ER-65707 TU134 63435
ER-65736 TU134 2351517?
ER-65741 TU134 2351602?
ER-65791 TU134 63110
ER-65897 TU134 42210
ER-72933 AN-72
ER-72935 AN-72
ER-72975 AN-72 36572094888
ER-72977 AN-72 36572094889
ER-85044 TU154 044
ER-85090 TU154 090
ER-85285 TU154 285
ER-85324 TU154 324
ER-85332 TU154 332
ER-85384 TU154 384
ER-85405 TU154 405
ER-85409 TU154 409
ER-85565 TU154 565
ER-87359 YAK40 9340831
ER-88202 YAK40 9630449
ER-ACA AN-72
ER-AGN AN-74

Estonia

(ES-AAC) TU154 895
(ES-AAD) TU154 896
ES-AAE TU134 48395
ES-AAF TU134 48565
ES-AAG TU134 49907
ES-AAH TU134 35270
ES-AAI TU134 60350
ES-AAJ TU134 60627
ES-AAK TU134 60977
ES-AAL TU134 62350
ES-AAM TU134 60380
ES-AAN TU134 60560
ES-AAO TU134 62239
ES-AAP TU134 38020
ES-AAR YAK40 9510439
ES-AAS YAK40 9632049
ES-AAT YAK40 9511639
ES-AAU YAK40 9411333
ES-ABC B737 26324
ES-ABD B737 26323
ES-LAI TU154 895
ES-LTP TU154 909
ES-LTR TU154 896
ES-NIT IL-76
ES-NOE AN-74 36547097932

Ethiopia

ET-AAG B720 18454
(ET-AAG) B720 18165
ET-AAH B720 18455
(ET-AAH) B720 18166
ET-ABP B720 18977
ET-ACD B707 19736
ET-ACQ B707 19820
ET-AFA B720 18418
ET-AFB B720 18419
ET-AFK B720 18417
ET-AHK B727 22759
ET-AHL B727 21978
ET-AHM B727 21979
ET-AIE B767 23106
ET-AIF B767 23107
ET-AIV B707 19531
ET-AIZ B767 23916
ET-AJA B737 23914
ET-AJB B737 23915
ET-AJS B757 24845
ET-AJU B727 21851
ET-AJX B757 25014
ET-AJZ B707 19433
ET-AKC B757 25353
ET-AKE B757 26057
ET-AKF B757 26058

Belarus

EW-65049 TU134 49755
EW-65082 TU134 60081
EW-65085 TU134 60123
EW-65106 TU134 60315
EW-65108 TU134 60332
EW-65133 TU134 60645
EW-65145 TU134 60985
EW-65149 TU134 61033
EW-65565 TU134 63998
EW-65605 TU134 09070
EW-65664 TU134 1351110
EW-65669 TU134 1351210
EW-65676 TU134 1351502
EW-65754 TU134 62154
EW-65772 TU134 62472
EW-65803 TU134 3352103
EW-65821 TU134 08060
EW-65832 TU134 17106
EW-65861 TU134 28269
EW-65892 TU134 38050
EW-65957 TU134 2351802
EW-65974 TU134 3352004
EW-76836 IL-76 1013409305
EW-76837 IL-76 1023409316
EW-78765 IL-76 0083486590
EW-78769 IL-76 0083487607
EW-78779 IL-76 0083489662
EW-78787 IL-76 0083490698
EW-78799 IL-76 0093491754
EW-78801 IL-76 0093492763
EW-78808 IL-76 0093493794
EW-78819 IL-76 0093495883
EW-78826 IL-76 1003499991
EW-78827 IL-76 1003499997
EW-78828 IL-76 1003401004
EW-78836 IL-76 0093499986
EW-78839 IL-76 1003402047
EW-78843 IL-76 1003403082
EW-78848 IL-76 1003405159
EW-78849 IL-76 1013405192
EW-85059 TU154 059
EW-85260 TU154 260
EW-85331 TU154 331
EW-85339 TU154 339
EW-85352 TU154 352
EW-85372 TU154 372
EW-85411 TU154 411
EW-85419 TU154 419
EW-85465 TU154 465
EW-85509 TU154 509
EW-85538 TU154 538
EW-85580 TU154 580
EW-85581 TU154 581
EW-85582 TU154 582
EW-85583 TU154 583
EW-85591 TU154 591
EW-85593 TU154 593
EW-85703 TU154 878
EW-85706 TU154 881
EW-85724 TU154 906
EW-85725 TU154 907?
EW-85748 TU154 924
EW-85815 TU154 1010
EW-86062 IL-86 51483203029
EW-87320 YAK40 9331929
EW-87330 YAK40 9510139
EW-87419 YAK40 9421134
EW-87577 YAK40 9220922
EW-87658 YAK40 9240225
EW-87669 YAK40 9021760
EW-88161 YAK40 9611546
EW-88187 YAK40 9620748
EW-88202 YAK40 9630449

Kyrgyzstan

EX-65111 TU134 60346
EX-65119 TU134 60475
EX-65125 TU134 60575
EX-65778 TU134 62590
EX-65779 TU134 62602
EX-65789 TU134 62850
EX-76815 IL-76 1013409310
EX-85021 TU154 021
EX-85252 TU154 252
EX-85257 TU154 257
EX-85259 TU154 259
EX-85294 TU154 294
EX-85313 TU154 313
EX-85369 TU154 369
EX-85444 TU154 444
EX-85491 TU154 491
EX-85497 TU154 497
EX-85519 TU154 519
EX-85590 TU154 590
EX-85718 TU154 894?
EX-87250 YAK40 9310726
EX-87293 YAK40 9320828
EX-87331 YAK40 9510239
EX-87354 YAK40 9330331
EX-87366 YAK40 9341631
EX-87379 YAK40
EX-87412 YAK40 9420434
EX-87426 YAK40 9..0235
EX-87442 YAK40 9431935
EX-87445 YAK40 9430236
EX-87538 YAK40 9..0342
EX-87561 YAK40 9..1221

Tajikistan

EY-1251 YAK40 9641251
EY-65003 TU134 44040
EY-65127 TU134 60627
EY-65730 TU134 2351511?
EY-65763 TU134 62299
EY-65788 TU134 62835
EY-65814 TU134 4352208
EY-65820 TU134 08056
EY-65835 TU134 17112
EY-65875 TU134 29317
EY-65876 TU134 31220
EY-65895 TU134 40140
EY-85247 TU154 247
EY-85251 TU154 251
EY-85281 TU154 281
EY-85385 TU154 385
EY-85406 TU154 406
EY-85440 TU154 440
EY-85466 TU154 466
EY-85469 TU154 469
EY-85475 TU154 475
EY-85487 TU154 487
EY-85511 TU154 511
EY-85691 TU154 864
EY-85692 TU154 865
EY-85717 TU154 893?
EY-87196 YAK40 9631648
EY-87214 YAK40 9640851
EY-87217 YAK40 9510340
EY-87269 YAK40 9310527
EY-87310 YAK40
EY-87313 YAK40 9330829
EY-87356 YAK40 9340531
EY-87434 YAK40 9431035
EY-87446 YAK40 9430336
EY-87461 YAK40 9432036
EY-87522 YAK40 9510441
EY-87554 YAK40 9210521
EY-87666 YAK40 9241025

EY-87697 YAK40 9910205
EY-87827 YAK40 9241924
EY-87835 YAK40 9240126
EY-87922 YAK40 9731355
EY-87963 YAK40 9831058
EY-87967 YAK40 9831158
EY-88267 YAK40 9720553

Turkmenistan

EZ-42404 YAK42 4520422116617
EZ-85241 TU154 241
EZ-85246 TU154 246
EZ-85250 TU154 250
EZ-85345 TU154 345
EZ-85383 TU154 383
EZ-85394 TU154 394
EZ-85410 TU154 410
EZ-85492 TU154 492
EZ-85507 TU154 507
EZ-85532 TU154 532
EZ-85549 TU154 549
EZ-85560 TU154 560
EZ-87338 YAK40 9510739
EZ-87387 YAK40 9411832
EZ-87409 YAK40 9420134
EZ-87427 YAK40 9420335
EZ-87531 YAK40 9521341
EZ-87548 YAK40 9531342
EZ-87668 YAK40 9021460
EZ-88169 YAK40 9610747
EZ-88178 YAK40 9631847
EZ-88230 YAK40 9641950
EZ-A001 B737 26855
EZ-A002 B737 25994
EZ-A003 B737 25995
EZ-A010 B757 25345
EZ-A011 B757 28336
EZ-A012 B757 28337
EZ-F421 IL-76 1023498978
EZ-F422 IL-76 1023410348
EZ-F423 IL-76 1033418608
EZ-F424 IL-76 1033418592
EZ-F425 IL-76 1023410336
EZ-F426 IL-76 1033418609
EZ-F427 IL-76 1033418620
EZ-F428 IL-76 1043418624
EZ-F429 IL-76
EZ-J672 YAK42 4520421316562
EZ-J673 YAK42 4520421316574
EZ-J674 YAK42 4520421319020

France

F- A319 588
F- A340 145
F- A340 146
F- B737 24132
(F-BDHC) A300 08
F-BGNX COMET 06020
F-BGNY COMET 06021
F-BGNZ COMET 06022
F-BGSA COMET 06015
F-BGSB COMET 06016
F-BGSC COMET 06019
F-BHHH CRVL 01
F-BHHI CRVL 02
F-BHOR CRVL 11
F-BHRA CRVL 1
F-BHRB CRVL 2
F-BHRC CRVL 5
F-BHRD CRVL 8
F-BHRE CRVL 9
F-BHRF CRVL 12
F-BHRG CRVL 13
F-BHRH CRVL 16
F-BHRI CRVL 17
F-BHRJ CRVL 23
F-BHRK CRVL 26
F-BHRL CRVL 31
F-BHRM CRVL 37
F-BHRN CRVL 39
F-BHRO CRVL 41
F-BHRP CRVL 45
F-BHRQ CRVL 46
F-BHRR CRVL 50
F-BHRS CRVL 54
F-BHRT CRVL 55
F-BHRU CRVL 58
F-BHRV CRVL 59
F-BHRX CRVL 60
F-BHRY CRVL 61
F-BHRZ CRVL 52
F-BHSA B707 17613
F-BHSB B707 17614
F-BHSC B707 17615
F-BHSD B707 17616
F-BHSE B707 17617
F-BHSF B707 17618
F-BHSG B707 17619
F-BHSH B707 17620
F-BHSI B707 17621
F-BHSJ B707 17622
F-BHSK B707 17918
F-BHSL B707 17919
F-BHSM B707 17920
F-BHSN B707 17921
F-BHSO B707 17922
F-BHSP B707 17923
F-BHSQ B707 17924
F-BHSR B707 18245
F-BHSS B707 18246
F-BHST B707 18247
F-BHSU B707 18375
F-BHSV B707 18456
F-BHSX B707 18457
F-BHSY B707 18458
F-BHSZ B707 18459
F-BIUY DC-8 45569
F-BIUZ DC-8 45570
F-BJAK CRVL 219
F-BJAO CRVL 42
F-BJAP CRVL 62
F-BJAQ CRVL 19
F-BJAU CRVL 70
F-BJCB DC-8 45671
F-BJCM B707 19986
F-BJEN CRVL 185
(F-BJGY) CRVL 258
F-BJLA DC-8 45567
F-BJLB DC-8 45568
F-BJSO CRVL 143
F-BJTA CRVL 53
F-BJTB CRVL 68
F-BJTC CRVL 83
F-BJTD CRVL 84
F-BJTD CRVL 162
F-BJTE CRVL 111
F-BJTF CRVL 113
F-BJTG CRVL 115
F-BJTH CRVL 124
F-BJTI CRVL 105
F-BJTJ CRVL 119
F-BJTK CRVL 141
F-BJTL CRVL 142
F-BJTM CRVL 144
F-BJTN CRVL 145
F-BJTO CRVL 148
F-BJTP CRVL 152
F-BJTQ CRVL 177
F-BJTR CRVL 22
F-BJTS CRVL 27
F-BJTU CRVL 189
F-BJUV DC-8 45627
F-BKGZ CRVL 83
F-BLCA B707 18685
F-BLCB B707 18686
F-BLCC B707 18881
F-BLCD B707 18941
F-BLCE B707 19291
F-BLCF B707 19292
F-BLCG B707 19521
F-BLCH B707 19522
F-BLCI B707 19723
F-BLCJ B707 19724
F-BLCK B707 19916
F-BLCL B707 19917
F-BLCZ CRVL 51
F-BLHY CRVL 158
F-BLKF CRVL 42
F-BLKI CRVL 136
F-BLKJ CRVL 169
F-BLKS CRVL 176
F-BLKX DC-8 45820
F-BLLB B707 18686
F-BLLC DC-8 45604
(F-BMKO) B707 19351
F-BMKS CRVL 181
F-BNFE CRVL 200
F-BNGE CRVL 10
F-BNKA CRVL 206
F-BNKB CRVL 208
F-BNKC CRVL 217
F-BNKD CRVL 220
F-BNKE CRVL 224
F-BNKF CRVL 227
F-BNKG CRVL 229
F-BNKH CRVL 248
F-BNKI CRVL 214
F-BNKJ CRVL 252
F-BNKK CRVL 256
F-BNKL CRVL 260
F-BNLD DC-8 45819
F-BNLE DC-8 45917
F-BNOG CRVL 271
F-BNOH CRVL 269
F-BNRA CRVL 201
F-BNRB CRVL 222
F-BOEE CRVL 212
F-BOHA CRVL 242
F-BOHB CRVL 244
F-BOHC CRVL 245
F-BOJA B727 19543
F-BOJB B727 19544
F-BOJC B727 19545
F-BOJD B727 19546
F-BOJE B727 19861
F-BOJF B727 19862
F-BOLF DC-8 45918
F-BOLG DC-8 45987
F-BOLH DC-8 46028
F-BOLI DC-8 45754
F-BOLJ DC-8 45927
F-BOLK DC-8 45803
F-BOLL DC-8 46096
F-BOLM DC-8 46058
(F-BOLN) DC-8 45862
F-BPJG B727 19863
F-BPJH B727 19864
F-BPJI B727 19865
F-BPJJ B727 20075
F-BPJK B727 20202
F-BPJL B727 20203
F-BPJM B727 20204
F-BPJN B727 20409
F-BPJO B727 20410
F-BPJP B727 20411
F-BPJQ B727 20470
F-BPJR B727 20538
F-BPJS B727 20539
F-BPJT B727 20540
F-BPJU B727 19683
F-BPJV B727 19684
F-BPVA B747 19749
F-BPVB B747 19750
F-BPVC B747 19751
F-BPVD B747 19752
F-BPVE B747 20355
F-BPVF B747 20376
F-BPVG B747 20377
F-BPVH B747 20378
(F-BPVI) B747 20541
F-BPVJ B747 20541
(F-BPVJ) B747 20542
F-BPVK B747 20543
F-BPVL B747 20798
F-BPVM B747 20799
F-BPVN B747 20800
F-BPVO B747 20887
F-BPVP B747 20954
F-BPVQ B747 21141
F-BPVR B747 21255
F-BPVS B747 21326
F-BPVT B747 21429
F-BPVU B747 21537
F-BPVV B747 21576
F-BPVX B747 21731
F-BPVY B747 21745
F-BPVZ B747 21787
F-BRGU CRVL 237
F-BRGX CRVL 234
F-BRIM CRVL 193
F-BRUJ CRVL 209
F-BSEL CRVL 167
F-BSGT B707 18837
F-BSGZ CRVL 83
F-BSRD CRVL 38
F-BSRR CRVL 21
F-BSRY CRVL 258
(F-BTDA) DC-10 46850
F-BTDB DC-10 46850
(F-BTDB) DC-10 46851
F-BTDC DC-10 46851
(F-BTDC) DC-10 46852
F-BTDD DC-10 46963
(F-BTDD) DC-10 46852
(F-BTDD) DC-10 46853
F-BTDE DC-10 46853
F-BTDF DC-10 46852
(F-BTDF) DC-10 46854
F-BTDG B747 22514
F-BTDH B747 22515
F-BTDL CRVL 136
F-BTMD MERC 02
F-BTMD MERC 11
F-BTOA CRVL 274
F-BTOB CRVL 277
F-BTOC CRVL 278
F-BTOD CRVL 279
F-BTOE CRVL 280
F-BTON CRVL 97
F-BTSC CNCRD 203
F-BTSD CNCRD 213
F-BTTA MERC 1
F-BTTB MERC 2
F-BTTC MERC 3
F-BTTD MERC 4
F-BTTE MERC 5
F-BTTF MERC 6
F-BTTG MERC 7
F-BTTH MERC 8
F-BTTI MERC 9
F-BTTJ MERC 10
(F-BTTX) MERC 11
F-BUAD A300 03
F-BUAE A300 04
F-BUAF A300 08
F-BUAG A300 15
F-BUAH A300 27
F-BUAI A300 62
F-BUAJ A300 97
F-BUAK A300 112
F-BUAL A300 29
F-BUAM A300 21
F-BUAN A300 132
F-BUAO A300 48
F-BUAP A300 52
F-BUAQ A300 57
F-BUAR A300 20
F-BUFC CRVL 161
F-BUFF CRVL 101
F-BUFH CRVL 123
F-BUFM CRVL 209
F-BUOE CRVL 170
F-BUOR DC-8 45862
F-BUTE F-28 11031
F-BUTI F-28 11034
F-BUZC CRVL 94
F-BUZJ B707 17658
F-BVFA CNCRD 205
F-BVFB CNCRD 207
F-BVFC CNCRD 209
F-BVFD CNCRD 211
F-BVFF CNCRD 215
F-BVGA A300 05
F-BVGB A300 06
F-BVGC A300 07
F-BVGD A300 10
F-BVGE A300 11
F-BVGF A300 13
F-BVGG A300 19
F-BVGH A300 23

Registration	Type	No.
F-BVGI	A300	45
F-BVGJ	A300	47
F-BVGK	A300	70
F-BVGL	A300	74
F-BVGM	A300	78
F-BVGN	A300	100
F-BVGO	A300	129
F-BVGP	A300	145
F-BVGQ	A300	146
F-BVGR	A300	175
F-BVGS	A300	178
F-BVGT	A300	183
F-BVPU	CRVL	196
F-BVPY	CRVL	271
F-BVPZ	CRVL	218
F-BVSF	CRVL	241
(F-BVTB)	CRVL	270
F-BXOO	CRVL	76
F-BYAI	CRVL	139
F-BYAT	CRVL	205
F-BYAU	CRVL	192
F-BYCA	CRVL	66
F-BYCB	CRVL	175
F-BYCD	CRVL	67
F-BYCN	B707	19370
F-BYCO	B707	19373
F-BYCP	B707	19377
F-BYCY	CRVL	233
F-BYFM	DC-8	45664
F-G	B737	23926
F-GAPA	CRVL	99
F-GATG	VFW614G-005	
F-GATH	VFW614G-013	
F-GATI	VFW614G-015	
(F-GATN)	B747	21515
F-GATO	DC-8	46106
F-GATP	CRVL	259
F-GATZ	CRVL	175
F-GBBR	F-28	11051
F-GBBS	F-28	11050
F-GBBT	F-28	11052
F-GBBX	F-28	11027
F-GBEA	A300	50
F-GBEB	A300	102
F-GBEC	A300	104
F-GBMI	CRVL	19
F-GBMJ	CRVL	149
F-GBMK	CRVL	180
F-GBNA	A300	65
F-GBNB	A300	66
F-GBNC	A300	67
F-GBND	A300	68
F-GBNE	A300	86
F-GBNF	A300	87
F-GBNG	A300	91
F-GBNH	A300	92
F-GBNI	A300	49
F-GBNI	A300	204
F-GBNJ	A300	51
F-GBNJ	A300	207
F-GBNK	A300	108
F-GBNL	A300	118
F-GBNM	A300	119
F-GBNN	A300	120
F-GBNO	A300	124
F-GBNP	A300	152
F-GBNQ	A300	153
F-GBNR	A300	154
F-GBNS	A300	155
F-GBNT	A300	158
F-GBNU	A300	161
F-GBNV	A300	211
F-GBNX	A300	216
F-GBNY	A300	220
F-GBNZ	A300	259
F-GBOX	B747	21835
F-GBYA	B737	23000
F-GBYB	B737	23001
F-GBYC	B737	23002
F-GBYD	B737	23003
F-GBYE	B737	23004
F-GBYF	B737	23005
F-GBYG	B737	23006
F-GBYH	B737	23007
F-GBYI	B737	23008
F-GBYJ	B737	23009
F-GBYK	B737	23010
F-GBYL	B737	23011
F-GBYM	B737	23349
F-GBYN	B737	23503
F-GBYO	B737	23504
F-GBYP	B737	23792
F-GBYQ	B737	23793
(F-GBYR)	B737	25118
F-GCBA	B747	21982
F-GCBB	B747	22272
F-GCBC	B747	22427
F-GCBD	B747	22428
F-GCBE	B747	22678
F-GCBF	B727	22287
F-GCBF	B747	22794
F-GCBG	B747	22939
F-GCBH	B747	23611
F-GCBI	B747	23676
F-GCBJ	B747	24067
F-GCBK	B747	24158
F-GCBL	B747	24735
F-GCBM	B747	24879
F-GCBN	B747	25266
F-GCDA	B727	22081
F-GCDB	B727	22082
F-GCDC	B727	22083
F-GCDD	B727	22084
F-GCDE	B727	22085
F-GCDG	B727	22288
F-GCDH	B727	22289
F-GCDI	B727	22290
F-GCGQ	B727	20609
F-GCGR	B737	21278
F-GCGS	B737	21279
F-GCJL	B737	19067
F-GCJT	CRVL	249
F-GCLL	B737	19064
F-GCMV	B727	22608
F-GCMX	B727	22609
F-GCSL	B737	19066
F-GCVI	CRVL	272
F-GCVJ	CRVL	275
F-GCVK	CRVL	276
F-GCVL	CRVL	273
F-GCVM	CRVL	270
F-GDFC	F-28	11133
F-GDFD	F-28	11135
F-GDFY	CRVL	182
F-GDFZ	CRVL	211
F-GDJK	DC-10	47849
F-GDJM	DC-8	45960
F-GDJU	CRVL	183
F-GDPM	DC-8	45662
F-GDPS	DC-8	45981
F-GDRM	DC-8	46063
F-GDSK	F-28	11179
F-GDUA	B747	22870
(F-GDUB)	B747	22871
(F-GDUE)	B747	23413
F-GDUS	F-28	11053
F-GDUT	F-28	11091
(F-GDUT)	B747	22870
F-GDUU	F-28	11108
F-GDUV	F-28	11109
F-GDUX	F-28	11110
F-GDUY	F-28	11142
F-GDUZ	F-28	11144
F-GDVA	A300	261
F-GDVB	A300	271
F-GDVC	A300	274
F-GECK	F-28	11004
F-GELP	CRVL	187
F-GELQ	CRVL	169
F-GEMA	A310	316
F-GEMB	A310	326
F-GEMC	A310	335
F-GEMD	A310	355
F-GEME	A310	369
F-GEMF	A310	172
F-GEMG	A310	454
F-GEMN	A310	502
F-GEMO	A310	504
F-GEMP	A310	550
F-GEMQ	A310	551
F-GEPC	CRVL	184
(F-GEQL)	CRVL	199
F-GESM	DC-8	46091
F-GETA	B747	23413
F-GETB	B747	23480
F-GETM	DC-8	46038
F-GEXA	B747	24154
F-GEXB	B747	24155
F-GEXI	B737	22406
F-GEXJ	B737	22760
F-GEXT	F-28	11060
F-GEXU	F-28	11070
F-GEXX	F-28	11102
F-GFBA	CRVL	243
F-GFBH	CRVL	199
F-GFBI	CRVL	236
F-GFCN	DC-8	46159
F-GFKA	A320	0005
F-GFKB	A320	0007
F-GFKC	A320	0009
F-GFKD	A320	0014
F-GFKE	A320	0019
F-GFKF	A320	0020
F-GFKG	A320	0021
F-GFKH	A320	0061
F-GFKI	A320	0062
F-GFKJ	A320	0063
F-GFKK	A320	0100
F-GFKL	A320	0101
F-GFKM	A320	0102
F-GFKN	A320	0128
F-GFKO	A320	0129
F-GFKP	A320	0133
F-GFKQ	A320	0002
F-GFKR	A320	0186
F-GFKS	A320	0187
F-GFKT	A320	0188
F-GFKU	A320	0226
F-GFKV	A320	0227
F-GFKX	A320	0228
F-GFKY	A320	0285
F-GFKZ	A320	0286
F-GFLV	B737	22597
F-GFLX	B737	22598
F-GFUA	B737	23635
F-GFUB	B737	24025
F-GFUC	B737	24026
F-GFUD	B737	24027
F-GFUE	B737	24387
F-GFUF	B737	24388
F-GFUG	B737	24750
F-GFUH	B737	24751
(F-GFUI)	B737	24789
F-GFUJ	B737	25118
F-GFUK	B747	21251
F-GFUU	MD-83	49826
F-GFVI	B737	20256
F-GFVJ	B737	20254
F-GFVK	B737	19848
(F-GFVK)	B737	19847
F-GFVR	B737	21538
(F-GFVR)	B737	19848
F-GFYL	B737	20205
F-GFZB	MD-83	49707
F-GGEA	A320	0010
F-GGEB	A320	0012
F-GGEC	A320	0013
F-GGED	A320	0015
F-GGEE	A320	0016
F-GGEF	A320	0004
(F-GGEF)	A320	0033
F-GGEG	A320	0003
(F-GGEG)	A320	0036
(F-GGEH)	A320	0044
F-GGFI	B737	20138
F-GGFJ	B737	20218
F-GGGR	B727	20822
F-GGKC	F-28	11073
F-GGKD	CRVL	255
(F-GGLC)	DC-8	46110
F-GGMA	MD-83	49399
F-GGMB	MD-83	49617
F-GGMC	MD-83	49709
F-GGMD	MD-83	49618
F-GGME	MD-83	49855
(F-GGME)	MD-83	49793
F-GGMF	MD-83	53463
F-GGML	B737	24785
F-GGMZ	DC-10	46990
F-GGPA	B737	19847
F-GGPB	B737	20389
(F-GGPB)	B737	19848
F-GGPC	B737	20282
F-GGTP	B737	20196
F-GGVP	B737	20943
F-GGVQ	B737	20944
F-GGZA	B737	20836
F-GHBM	B747	20120
F-GHEB	MD-83	49822
F-GHEC	MD-83	49662
F-GHED	MD-83	49576
F-GHEF	A300	555
F-GHEG	A300	559
F-GHEH	MD-83	49663
F-GHEI	MD-83	49968
F-GHEJ	A310	535
(F-GHEJ)	A300	555
F-GHEK	MD-83	49823
F-GHFT	B707	19587
F-GHGD	B767	24832
F-GHGE	B767	24854
F-GHGF	B767	24745
F-GHGG	B767	24746
F-GHGH	B767	25077
F-GHGI	B767	27135
F-GHGJ	B767	27136
F-GHGK	B767	27212
(F-GHGL)	B767	27427
(F-GHGM)	A310	545
(F-GHGO)	B767	27428
F-GHHO	MD-83	49985
F-GHHP	MD-83	49986
F-GHKM	CRVL	262
F-GHKN	CRVL	265
(F-GHKN)	CRVL	257
(F-GHKO)	CRVL	212
F-GHKP	CRVL	268
F-GHML	B737	19424
F-GHMU	CRVL	249
F-GHOI	DC-10	46870
(F-GHOJ)	DC-10	46854
F-GHOL	B737	24825
F-GHPC	B747	20137
F-GHQA	A320	0033
F-GHQB	A320	0036
F-GHQC	A320	0044
F-GHQD	A320	0108
F-GHQE	A320	0115
F-GHQF	A320	0130
F-GHQG	A320	0155
F-GHQH	A320	0156
F-GHQI	A320	0184
F-GHQJ	A320	0214
F-GHQK	A320	0236
F-GHQL	A320	0239
F-GHQM	A320	0237
(F-GHQN)	A320	0258
F-GHQO	A320	0278
F-GHQP	A320	0337
F-GHQQ	A320	0352
F-GHQR	A320	0377
F-GHUC	A310	418
F-GHUD	A310	444
F-GHUL	B737	24826
F-GHVM	B737	24026
F-GHVN	B737	25138
F-GHVO	B737	24025
(F-GHXH)	B737	22453
F-GHXK	B737	21599
F-GHXL	B737	21775
F-GHXM	B737	24788
F-GHXN	B737	24877
F-GHYM	A310	571
F-GIAH	F-28	11012
F-GIAI	F-28	11013
F-GIAJ	F-28	11070
F-GIAK	F-28	11104
F-GIDM	F-100	11273
F-GIDN	F-100	11272
F-GIDO	F-100	11271
F-GIDP	F-100	11270
F-GIDQ	F-100	11269
F-GIDT	F-100	11268
F-GIJS	A300	17

F-GIJT	A300	09
F-GIJU	A300	12
F-GIMG	F-28	11003
F-GIMH	**F-28**	**11003**
F-GIMJ	B747	19658
F-GINL	**B737**	**24827**
F-GIOA	**F-100**	**11261**
F-GIOB	F-100	11307
F-GIOC	F-100	11311
F-GIOD	F-100	11315
F-GIOE	F-100	11344
F-GIOF	F-100	11363
F-GIOG	**F-100**	**11364**
F-GIOH	**F-100**	**11424**
F-GIOI	**F-100**	**11433**
F-GIOJ	**F-100**	**11454**
F-GIOK	**F-100**	**11455**
F-GIOV	F-100	11248
F-GIOX	F-100	11249
F-GISA	**B747**	**25238**
F-GISB	**B747**	**25302**
F-GISC	**B747**	**25599**
F-GISD	**B747**	**25628**
F-GISE	**B747**	**25630**
F-GITA	**B747**	**24969**
F-GITB	**B747**	**24990**
F-GITC	**B747**	**25344**
F-GITD	**B747**	**25600**
F-GITE	**B747**	**25601**
F-GITF	**B747**	**25602**
(F-GITG)	B747	25629
F-GITH	**B747**	**25631**
(F-GIUA)	B747	25632
(F-GIVJ)	B707	19789
F-GIXA	**B737**	**20836**
F-GIXB	**B737**	**24789**
F-GIXC	**B737**	**25124**
F-GIXD	**B737**	**25744**
F-GIXE	**B737**	**26850**
F-GIXF	**B737**	**26851**
F-GIXG	**B737**	**24364**
F-GIXH	**B737**	**23788**
F-GIXI	**B737**	**23809**
F-GIXJ	**B737**	**23685**
F-GIXK	**B737**	**24028**
F-GIXL	**B737**	**23810**
F-GIYQ	**B767**	**27429**
F-GJAO	F-100	11327
F-GJDL	**B737**	**20440**
F-GJDM	CRVL	188
F-GJNA	**B737**	**25206**
F-GJNB	**B737**	**25227**
F-GJNC	**B737**	**25228**
F-GJND	**B737**	**25229**
F-GJNE	**B737**	**25230**
F-GJNF	**B737**	**25231**
F-GJNG	**B737**	**25232**
F-GJNH	**B737**	**25233**
F-GJNI	**B737**	**25234**
F-GJNJ	**B737**	**25235**
F-GJNK	**B737**	**25236**
(F-GJNL)	B737	25237
F-GJNM	**B737**	**25237**
F-GJNN	**B737**	**27304**
F-GJNO	**B737**	**27305**
(F-GJNP)	B737	27424
(F-GJNR)	B737	27426
F-GJVA	**A320**	**0144**
F-GJVB	**A320**	**0145**
F-GJVC	**A320**	**0204**
F-GJVD	**A320**	**0211**
F-GJVE	**A320**	**0215**
F-GJVF	**A320**	**0244**
F-GJVG	**A320**	**0270**
F-GJVV	**A320**	**0525**
F-GJVW	**A320**	**0491**
F-GJVX	**A320**	**0420**
F-GJVY	**A320**	**0436**
F-GJVZ	**A320**	**0085**
(F-GKCI)	B707	20546
(F-GKCS)	B707	20085
(F-GKCT)	B707	20084
F-GKDY	**B727**	**22438**
F-GKDZ	**B727**	**22441**
F-GKLJ	**B747**	**19660**
F-GKLX	F-100	11328

(F-GKLX)	F-100	11375
F-GKLY	**F-100**	**11332**
(F-GKMO)	MD-11	48742
(F-GKMP)	MD-11	48526
(F-GKMQ)	MD-11	48482
(F-GKMR)	DC-10	46872
(F-GKMR)	MD-11	48481
(F-GKMR)	MD-11	48625
(F-GKMS)	DC-10	46954
F-GKMY	**DC-10**	**47815**
(F-GKPZ)	B727	21988
F-GKTA	**B737**	**24413**
F-GKTB	**B737**	**24414**
F-GKTD	**A310**	**552**
F-GKTE	A310	562
(F-GKTE)	B737	24021
(F-GKTF)	B737	24376
F-GKTK	B737	21011
F-GKXA	**A320**	**0287**
F-GLGE	A320	0348
F-GLGG	**A320**	**0203**
F-GLGH	**A320**	**0220**
F-GLGI	**A320**	**0221**
F-GLGJ	**A320**	**0222**
F-GLGM	**A320**	**0131**
F-GLGN	**A320**	**0132**
F-GLIJ	**RJ100**	**7081**
F-GLIK	**RJ100**	**7084**
F-GLIR	**F-100**	**11509**
(F-GLIS)	F-70	11540
(F-GLIT)	F-70	11541
(F-GLIU)	F-70	11543
(F-GLIV)	F-70	11556
F-GLIX	F-70	11558
F-GLIY	**RJ100**	**7053**
F-GLIZ	**RJ100**	**7057**
F-GLLE	**B737**	**23927**
F-GLMX	**DC-10**	**47814**
F-GLNA	**B747**	**20399**
F-GLNI	**146**	**E2188**
F-GLTF	B737	23684
F-GLTT	B737	23921
F-GLXF	**B737**	**22657**
F-GLXG	**B737**	**21736**
F-GLXH	**B737**	**20544**
F-GLZA	**A340**	**005**
F-GLZB	**A340**	**007**
F-GLZC	**A340**	**029**
F-GLZD	**A340**	**031**
F-GLZE	**A340**	**038**
F-GLZF	**A340**	**043**
F-GLZG	**A340**	**049**
F-GLZH	**A340**	**078**
F-GLZI	**A340**	**084**
(F-GLZJ)	A340	114
F-GMAI	A320	0258
F-GMCD	MD-83	49642
F-GMDA	**A330**	**030**
F-GMDB	**A330**	**037**
F-GMDC	**A330**	**045**
F-GMDD	**A330**	**059**
F-GMDE	A330	086
F-GMFM	DC-8	46099
F-GMJD	**B737**	**22599**
F-GMMP	**146**	**E2176**
F-GMOL	F-28	11003
F-GMPG	**F-100**	**11362**
F-GMPP	MD-83	49668
F-GMZA	**A321**	**0498**
F-GMZB	**A321**	**0509**
F-GMZC	**A321**	**0521**
F-GMZD	**A321**	**0529**
F-GMZE	**A321**	**0544**
F-GNBB	DC-10	46981
F-GNDC	**DC-10**	**47849**
F-GNEM	**DC-10**	**46892**
F-GNFM	DC-8	45945
F-GNFS	B737	23981
F-GNIA	A340	010
F-GNIB	**A340**	**014**
F-GNIC	**A340**	**022**
F-GNID	**A340**	**047**
F-GNIE	**A340**	**051**
(F-GNJQ)	B737	27425
F-GNME	**RJ100**	**7020**
F-GNMN	**RJ100**	**7003**

F-GNZB	**F-28**	**11073**
F-GOBR	B727	20601
F-GOCJ	**A310**	**217**
F-GOMA	**146**	**E2211**
F-GPAN	**B747**	**21515**
F-GPDJ	**A310**	**162**
F-GPJM	**B747**	**20427**
F-GPVB	**DC-10**	**47957**
F-GPVD	**DC-10**	**47865**
F-GPVE	**DC-10**	**46981**
F-GPXA	**F-100**	**11487**
F-GPXB	**F-100**	**11492**
F-GPXC	**F-100**	**11493**
F-GPXD	**F-100**	**11494**
F-GPXE	**F-100**	**11495**
F-GRJA	**RJ100**	**7070**
F-GRJB	**RJ100**	**7076**
F-GRJC	**RJ100**	**7085**
F-GRJD	**RJ100**	**7088**
F-GRMC	**MD-83**	**53466**
F-GRMG	**MD-83**	**53464**
F-GRMH	**MD-83**	**53465**
(F-GRMR)	DC-10	46854
F-GRSA	**B737**	**25011**
F-GSKY	B747	23245
F-GSTA	**SA300**	**655/001**
F-GSTB	**SA300**	**751/002**
F-GSTC	**SA300**	**765/003**
F-GSTD	SA300	776/004
F-GSUN	**B747**	**23030**
F-GTDF	**DC-10**	**46854**
F-GTDG	**DC-10**	**46997**
F-GTDH	**DC-10**	**46851**
F-GTNT	146	E2117
(F-GTNT)	146	E2089
F-GTNU	146	E2112

France d'Outremer

F-OBNG	CRVL	18
F-OBNH	CRVL	20
F-OBNI	CRVL	28
F-OBNJ	CRVL	51
F-OBNK	CRVL	73
F-OBNL	CRVL	75
F-OCAZ	A300	01
F-OCHS	B737	23810
F-OCKH	CRVL	263
F-OCPJ	CRVL	258
(F-ODCX)	A300	03
F-ODCY	A300	09
F-ODGX	**B737**	**24094**
F-ODHC	A300	08
F-ODHY	A300	49
F-ODHZ	A300	51
F-ODJG	**B747**	**21468**
F-ODJU	A300	29
F-ODLX	**DC-10**	**46872**
F-ODLY	**DC-10**	**46954**
F-ODLZ	**DC-10**	**46869**
(F-ODOV)	DC-10	47849
F-ODRD	A300	22
F-ODRE	A300	26
F-ODRF	A300	48
F-ODRG	A300	52
F-ODRM	A300	374
(F-ODRM)	A300	354
(F-ODSU)	B737	24021
F-ODSV	**A310**	**473**
F-ODSX	**A300**	**530**
F-ODTK	**A300**	**252**
F-ODTN	MD-83	49791
F-ODVD	A310	421
F-ODVE	A310	422
F-ODVF	**A310**	**445**
F-ODVG	**A310**	**490**
F-ODVH	**A310**	**491**
F-ODVI	**A310**	**531**
F-ODZB	F-28	11073
F-ODZJ	**B737**	**24877**
F-ODZY	**B737**	**27452**
F-OGIV	B707	18837
F-OGIW	B707	18840
F-OGJD	CRVL	136
F-OGJE	CRVL	167
F-OGQA	F-100	11272
F-OGQB	F-100	11273
F-OGQC	DC-10	47886
F-OGQI	F-100	11268
(F-OGQN)	A310	418
(F-OGQO)	A310	444
F-OGQQ	**A310**	**592**
F-OGQR	**A310**	**593**
F-OGQS	**A310**	**596**
F-OGQT	**A310**	**622**
F-OGQU	**A310**	**646**
F-OGQY	**A310**	**574**
F-OGQZ	**A310**	**576**
F-OGRT	B737	25138
(F-OGRT)	B737	26854
F-OGSD	B737	24789
F-OGSS	B737	25124
F-OGSX	B737	24364
F-OGSY	B737	23809
F-OGTA	A300	126
F-OGTB	A300	117
F-OGTC	A300	121
F-OGTG	B747	25629
F-OGYA	**A320**	**0087**
F-OGYB	**A320**	**0088**
F-OGYC	A320	0123
F-OGYC	**A320**	**0569**
F-OGYD	A320	0181
F-OGYE	A320	0182
F-OGYF	A320	0195
F-OGYM	**A310**	**457**
F-OGYN	**A310**	**458**
F-OGYP	**A310**	**442**
F-OGYQ	**A310**	**453**
F-OGYR	**A310**	**456**
F-OGYS	**A310**	**467**
(F-OHCN)	F-28	11149
(F-OHCO)	F-28	11159
F-OHKA	B737	22074
F-OHLH	**A310**	**447**
F-OHLI	**A310**	**481**
F-OHMA	**A320**	**0368**
F-OHMB	A320	0376
F-OHMC	A320	0386
F-OHMD	**A320**	**0433**
F-OHME	**A320**	**0252**
F-OHMF	**A320**	**0259**
F-OHMG	**A320**	**0260**
F-OHMH	**A320**	**0261**
F-OHMI	**A320**	**0275**
F-OHMJ	**A320**	**0276**
F-OHMK	**A320**	**0296**
F-OHML	**A320**	**0320**
F-OHMM	**A320**	**0321**
F-OHMN	**A320**	**0353**
F-OHOA	**B727**	**22083**
F-OHPA	**A300**	**234**
F-OHPB	**A300**	**235**
F-OHPC	**A300**	**304**
F-OHPD	**A300**	**305**
F-OHPE	**A310**	**267**
F-OHPP	**A310**	**278**
F-OHPQ	**A310**	**318**
F-OKAI	**A320**	**0258**
F-OKBB	DC-10	46981
F-OLGA	F-100	11290
F-OLGB	**F-100**	**11296**
(F-OMOJ)	B727	22081
(F-OMOK)	B727	22082
(F-OMOL)	B727	22084
(F-OMOM)	B727	22085

France - Test Marks

F-W	A300	18
F-WAST	SA300	655/001
F-WAYB	A310	276
F-WBNG	CRVL	18
F-WBNI	CRVL	28
F-WBNK	CRVL	73
F-WGTP	B737	20196
F-WGYM	A310	267
F-WGYN	A310	276
F-WGYN	A310	458
F-WGYO	A310	276

Registration	Type	No.
F-WGYP	A310	278
F-WGYQ	A310	318
F-WGYR	**A310**	**331**
F-WGYT	A310	331
F-WGYU	A320	0344
F-WGYZ	A321	0538
F-WGYZ	A321	0555
F-WHHH	CRVL	01
F-WHHI	CRVL	02
F-WHRA	CRVL	1
F-WHRB	CRVL	2
F-WHRJ	CRVL	23
F-WHRK	CRVL	26
F-WJAK	CRVL	19
F-WJAK	CRVL	20
F-WJAK	CRVL	21
F-WJAK	CRVL	64
F-WJAK	CRVL	67
F-WJAK	CRVL	70
F-WJAK	CRVL	71
F-WJAK	CRVL	120
F-WJAK	CRVL	135
F-WJAK	CRVL	219
F-WJAK	CRVL	249
F-WJAK	CRVL	263
F-WJAL	CRVL	32
F-WJAL	CRVL	38
F-WJAL	CRVL	65
F-WJAL	CRVL	78
F-WJAL	CRVL	107
F-WJAL	CRVL	153
F-WJAL	CRVL	161
F-WJAL	CRVL	175
F-WJAL	CRVL	182
F-WJAL	CRVL	196
F-WJAL	CRVL	203
F-WJAL	CRVL	215
F-WJAL	CRVL	234
F-WJAL	CRVL	275
F-WJAM	CNCRD	213
F-WJAM	CRVL	24
F-WJAM	CRVL	33
F-WJAM	CRVL	38
F-WJAM	CRVL	42
F-WJAM	CRVL	66
F-WJAM	CRVL	108
F-WJAM	CRVL	235
F-WJAM	CRVL	243
F-WJAM	CRVL	247
F-WJAN	CNCRD	215
F-WJAN	CRVL	69
F-WJAN	CRVL	117
F-WJAN	CRVL	126
F-WJAN	CRVL	156
F-WJAN	CRVL	174
F-WJAN	CRVL	263
F-WJAN	CRVL	269
F-WJAO	CRVL	35
F-WJAO	CRVL	63
F-WJAO	CRVL	76
F-WJAO	CRVL	118
F-WJAO	CRVL	131
F-WJAP	CRVL	10
F-WJAP	CRVL	62
F-WJAQ	CRVL	19
F-WJAQ	CRVL	140
F-WJAQ	CRVL	167
F-WJAQ	CRVL	181
F-WJAQ	CRVL	204
F-WJAQ	CRVL	223
F-WJSO	CRVL	143
F-WJTH	**CRVL**	**124**
F-WKPZ	B727	21988
F-WLGA	A300	09
F-WLGA	A300	32
F-WLGA	A300	35
F-WLGA	CRVL	21
F-WLGA	CRVL	78
F-WLGA	CRVL	134
F-WLGB	A300	14
F-WLGB	A300	16
F-WLGB	A300	17
F-WLGB	A300	27
F-WLGB	A300	34
F-WLGB	A300	39
F-WLGB	A300	46
F-WLGB	CRVL	231
F-WLGB	CRVL	238
(F-WLGB)	A300	20
(F-WLGB)	A300	36
F-WLGC	A300	12
F-WLGC	A300	15
F-WLGC	A300	27
F-WLGC	A300	31
F-WLGC	CRVL	239
F-WLHY	CRVL	158
F-WLKF	CRVL	42
F-WLKI	CRVL	136
F-WLKJ	CRVL	128
F-WLKJ	CRVL	169
F-WLKS	CRVL	176
F-WNBB	DC-10	46981
F-WNDA	A300	21
F-WNDA	A300	25
F-WNDA	A300	45
F-WNDB	A300	08
F-WNDB	A300	26
F-WNDB	A300	30
F-WNDB	A300	48
F-WNDB	A300	50
F-WNDC	A300	22
F-WNDC	A300	28
F-WNDC	A300	33
F-WNDC	A300	52
F-WNDD	A300	24
F-WNDD	A300	29
F-WQAE	B737	24345
F-WQAX	A320	0347
F-WQAY	A320	0354
F-WQAZ	A320	0357
F-WQBA	A320	0411
F-WQBB	A320	0424
F-WQBC	A320	0441
F-WQBD	A320	0373
F-WQCK	B727	22608
F-WTCC	MERC	01
F-WTMD	MERC	02
F-WTMD	MERC	11
F-WTOA	CRVL	274
F-WTSA	**CNCRD**	**02**
F-WTSB	**CNCRD**	**201**
F-WTSC	CNCRD	203
F-WTSS	**CNCRD**	**001**
F-WTTA	MERC	1
F-WUAA	A300	04
F-WUAB	A300	01
F-WUAC	A300	02
F-WUAD	A300	03
F-WUAT	A300	36
F-WUAT	A300	43
F-WUAU	A300	37
F-WUAU	A300	42
F-WUAV	A300	38
F-WUAV	A300	49
F-WUAX	A300	40
F-WUAX	A300	44
F-WUAX	A300	47
F-WUAY	A300	31
F-WUAZ	A300	41
F-WVGA	A300	05
F-WVGB	A300	06
F-WVGC	A300	07
F-WVGH	A300	23
F-WW	A300	761
F-WW	A320	0572
F-WWA.	A300	770
F-WWAA	A300	380
F-WWAA	A300	470
F-WWAA	A300	516
F-WWAA	A300	563
F-WWAA	A300	606
F-WWAA	A300	621
F-WWAA	A300	746
F-WWAA	A300	768
F-WWAB	A300	388
F-WWAB	A300	536
F-WWAB	A300	566
F-WWAB	A300	607
F-WWAB	A300	631
F-WWAB	A300	681
F-WWAB	A300	719
F-WWAB	A300	739
F-WWAB	A300	756
F-WWAC	A300	462
F-WWAC	A300	512
F-WWAD	A300	463
F-WWAD	A300	517
F-WWAD	A300	569
F-WWAD	A300	608
F-WWAD	A300	627
F-WWAD	A300	670
F-WWAD	A300	709
F-WWAD	A300	736
F-WWAD	A300	753
F-WWAE	A300	361
F-WWAE	A300	466
F-WWAE	A300	518
F-WWAE	A300	572
F-WWAE	A300	609
F-WWAE	A300	628
F-WWAE	A300	675
F-WWAE	A300	711
F-WWAE	A300	734
F-WWAE	A300	752
F-WWAF	A300	365
F-WWAF	A300	469
F-WWAF	A300	521
F-WWAF	A300	575
F-WWAF	A300	610
F-WWAF	A300	629
F-WWAF	A300	677
F-WWAF	A300	713
F-WWAF	A300	737
F-WWAF	A300	757
F-WWAG	A300	138
F-WWAG	A300	368
F-WWAG	A300	577
F-WWAG	A300	611
F-WWAG	A300	632
F-WWAG	A300	685
F-WWAG	A300	721
F-WWAG	A300	740
F-WWAG	A300	759
F-WWAH	A300	371
F-WWAH	A300	471
F-WWAH	A300	532
F-WWAH	A300	578
F-WWAH	A300	612
F-WWAH	A300	633
F-WWAH	A300	688
F-WWAH	A300	722
F-WWAH	A300	743
F-WWAH	A300	763
F-WWAI	A300	377
F-WWAI	A320	0001
F-WWAI	**A340**	**001**
F-WWAJ	A300	374
F-WWAJ	A300	477
F-WWAJ	A300	525
F-WWAJ	A300	579
F-WWAJ	A300	616
F-WWAJ	A300	657
F-WWAJ	A300	683
F-WWAJ	A300	728
F-WWAJ	A300	742
F-WWAJ	A300	764
F-WWAK	A300	384
F-WWAK	A300	474
F-WWAK	A300	529
F-WWAK	A300	580
F-WWAK	A300	617
F-WWAK	A300	659
F-WWAK	A300	696
F-WWAK	A300	731
F-WWAK	A300	744
F-WWAL	A300	391
F-WWAL	A300	464
F-WWAL	A300	530
F-WWAL	A300	581
F-WWAL	A300	630
F-WWAL	A300	679
F-WWAL	A300	723
F-WWAL	A300	760
F-WWAM	A300	395
F-WWAM	A300	465
F-WWAM	A300	533
F-WWAM	A300	582
F-WWAM	A300	618
F-WWAM	A300	641
F-WWAM	A300	699
F-WWAM	A300	729
F-WWAM	A300	748
F-WWAM	A300	769
F-WWAN	A300	192
F-WWAN	A300	398
F-WWAN	A300	479
F-WWAN	A300	561
F-WWAN	A300	613
F-WWAN	A300	643
F-WWAN	A300	701
F-WWAN	A300	735
F-WWAN	A300	749
F-WWAO	A300	401
F-WWAO	A300	505
F-WWAO	A300	543
F-WWAO	A300	583
F-WWAO	A300	615
F-WWAO	A300	645
F-WWAO	A300	703
F-WWAO	A300	766
F-WWAP	A300	405
F-WWAP	A300	506
F-WWAP	A300	546
F-WWAP	A300	601
F-WWAP	A300	635
F-WWAP	A300	690
F-WWAP	A300	726
F-WWAP	A300	745
F-WWAQ	A300	408
F-WWAQ	A300	507
F-WWAQ	A300	557
F-WWAQ	A300	625
F-WWAQ	A300	673
F-WWAQ	A300	724
F-WWAR	A300	411
F-WWAR	A300	508
F-WWAR	A300	558
F-WWAR	A300	626
F-WWAR	A300	692
F-WWAR	A300	725
F-WWAR	**A300**	**758**
F-WWAS	A300	414
F-WWAS	A300	509
F-WWAS	A300	559
F-WWAS	**A319**	**572**
F-WWAS	**A340**	**002**
F-WWAT	A300	417
F-WWAT	A300	540
F-WWAT	A300	602
F-WWAT	A300	623
F-WWAT	A300	662
F-WWAT	A300	705
F-WWAT	A300	732
F-WWAT	A300	747
F-WWAU	A300	420
F-WWAU	A300	510
F-WWAU	A300	554
F-WWAU	A300	584
F-WWAU	A300	619
F-WWAU	A300	664
F-WWAU	A300	707
F-WWAU	A300	733
F-WWAU	A300	750
F-WWAV	A300	423
F-WWAV	A300	511
F-WWAV	A300	555
F-WWAV	A300	603
F-WWAV	A300	639
F-WWAV	A300	694
F-WWAV	A300	730
F-WWAX	A300	459
F-WWAX	A300	513
F-WWAX	A300	553
F-WWAX	A300	604
F-WWAX	A300	638
F-WWAX	A300	715
F-WWAX	A300	738
F-WWAX	**A300**	**755**
F-WWAY	A300	460
F-WWAY	A300	514
F-WWAY	A300	556
F-WWAY	A300	605
F-WWAY	A300	666
F-WWAY	A300	717

F-WWAY A300 741
F-WWAY A300 754
F-WWAZ A300 461
F-WWAZ A300 515
F-WWAZ A300 560
F-WWAZ A300 614
F-WWAZ A300 668
F-WWAZ A300 727
F-WWAZ A300 762
F-WWBA A310 375
F-WWBA A340 004
F-WWBB A310 379
F-WWBB A320 0250
F-WWBB A320 0315
F-WWBB A320 0394
F-WWBB A320 0466
F-WWBC A310 386
F-WWBC A320 0251
F-WWBC A320 0316
F-WWBC A320 0467
F-WWBC A320 0534
F-WWBD A310 394
F-WWBD A320 0252
F-WWBD A320 0317
F-WWBD A320 0401
F-WWBD A320 0469
F-WWBE A310 397
F-WWBE A320 0253
F-WWBE A340 006
F-WWBF A310 400
F-WWBF A320 0254
F-WWBF A320 0318
F-WWBF A320 0383
F-WWBF A320 0452
F-WWBG A310 389
F-WWBG A320 0255
F-WWBG A320 0319
F-WWBG A320 0384
F-WWBG A320 0453
F-WWBH A310 390
F-WWBH A320 0256
F-WWBH A320 0357
F-WWBH A320 0430
F-WWBH A320 0486
F-WWBI A310 415
F-WWBI A320 0257
F-WWBI A320 0320
F-WWBI A320 0386
F-WWBI A320 0551
F-WWBJ A310 419
F-WWBJ A320 0258
F-WWBJ A320 0333
F-WWBJ A320 0373
F-WWBJ A320 0395
F-WWBJ A320 0454
F-WWBK A310 427
F-WWBK A320 0259
F-WWBK A320 0321
F-WWBK A320 0396
F-WWBK A320 0455
F-WWBL A310 430
F-WWBL A320 0260
F-WWBL A320 0322
F-WWBL A320 0415
F-WWBM A310 468
F-WWBM A320 0261
F-WWBM A320 0323
F-WWBM A320 0397
F-WWBM A320 0470
F-WWBN A310 486
F-WWBN A320 0264
F-WWBN A320 0334
F-WWBN A320 0402
F-WWBN A320 0536
F-WWBO A310 487
F-WWBO A320 0266
F-WWBO A320 0335
F-WWBO A320 0403
F-WWBO A320 0504
F-WWBP A320 0272
F-WWBP A320 0339
F-WWBP A320 0416
F-WWBP A320 0475
F-WWBQ A320 0271
F-WWBQ A320 0340
F-WWBQ A320 0431
F-WWBQ A320 0506
F-WWBR A320 0274
F-WWBR A320 0341
F-WWBR A320 0417
F-WWBR A320 0476
F-WWBS A320 0281
F-WWBS A320 0347
F-WWBS A320 0432
F-WWBS A320 0491
F-WWBT A320 0283
F-WWBT A320 0348
F-WWBT A320 0507
F-WWBU A320 0284
F-WWBU A320 0349
F-WWBU A320 0426
F-WWBU A320 0492
F-WWBV A320 0288
F-WWBV A320 0387
F-WWBV A320 0443
F-WWBV A320 0496
F-WWBX A320 0289
F-WWBX A320 0363
F-WWBX A320 0478
F-WWBX A320 0537
F-WWBY A320 0290
F-WWBY A320 0360
F-WWBY A320 0444
F-WWBY A320 0508
F-WWBZ A320 0291
F-WWBZ A320 0365
F-WWBZ A320 0445
F-WWBZ A320 0510
F-WWCA A310 378
F-WWCA A310 524
F-WWCA A310 562
F-WWCA A340 005
F-WWCB A310 392
F-WWCB A310 472
F-WWCB A310 501
F-WWCB A310 564
F-WWCB A310 600
F-WWCB A310 656
F-WWCC A310 399
F-WWCC A310 434
F-WWCC A310 473
F-WWCC A310 526
F-WWCC A310 565
F-WWCC A310 620
F-WWCC A310 651
F-WWCC A310 669
F-WWCD A310 404
F-WWCD A310 435
F-WWCD A310 457
F-WWCD A310 502
F-WWCD A310 527
F-WWCD A310 622
F-WWCD A310 672
F-WWCD A310 691
F-WWCE A310 409
F-WWCE A310 438
F-WWCE A310 488
F-WWCE A310 528
F-WWCE A310 568
F-WWCE A310 624
F-WWCE A310 661
F-WWCE A310 687
F-WWCF A310 410
F-WWCF A310 440
F-WWCF A310 458
F-WWCF A310 504
F-WWCF A310 570
F-WWCF A310 634
F-WWCF A310 660
F-WWCG A310 406
F-WWCG A310 449
F-WWCG A310 467
F-WWCG A310 519
F-WWCG A310 573
F-WWCG A310 636
F-WWCG A310 689
F-WWCH A310 407
F-WWCH A310 450
F-WWCH A310 497
F-WWCH A310 585
F-WWCH A310 591
F-WWCH A310 652
F-WWCH A310 674
F-WWCI A310 412
F-WWCI A310 439
F-WWCI A310 484
F-WWCI A310 520
F-WWCI A310 574
F-WWCI A310 650
F-WWCI A310 693
F-WWCJ A310 413
F-WWCJ A310 452
F-WWCJ A310 485
F-WWCJ A310 522
F-WWCJ A310 576
F-WWCJ A310 654
F-WWCJ A310 684
F-WWCK A310 416
F-WWCK A310 453
F-WWCK A310 489
F-WWCK A310 523
F-WWCK A310 586
F-WWCK A310 638
F-WWCK A310 663
F-WWCK A310 697
F-WWCL A310 418
F-WWCL A310 475
F-WWCL A310 503
F-WWCL A310 544
F-WWCL A310 640
F-WWCL A310 665
F-WWCM A310 424
F-WWCM A310 446
F-WWCM A310 494
F-WWCM A310 534
F-WWCM A310 588
F-WWCM A310 671
F-WWCN A310 421
F-WWCN A310 447
F-WWCN A310 493
F-WWCN A310 535
F-WWCN A310 592
F-WWCN A310 682
F-WWCO A310 422
F-WWCO A310 448
F-WWCO A310 495
F-WWCO A310 537
F-WWCO A310 589
F-WWCO A310 644
F-WWCO A310 695
F-WWCP A310 425
F-WWCP A310 492
F-WWCP A310 538
F-WWCP A310 593
F-WWCP A310 676
F-WWCQ A310 426
F-WWCQ A310 441
F-WWCQ A310 481
F-WWCQ A310 539
F-WWCQ A310 594
F-WWCQ A310 647
F-WWCR A310 428
F-WWCR A310 444
F-WWCR A310 482
F-WWCR A310 541
F-WWCR A310 595
F-WWCR A310 648
F-WWCS A310 429
F-WWCS A310 443
F-WWCS A310 483
F-WWCS A310 542
F-WWCS A310 596
F-WWCT A310 431
F-WWCT A310 476
F-WWCT A310 499
F-WWCT A310 587
F-WWCT A310 646
F-WWCT A310 680
F-WWCU A310 432
F-WWCU A310 455
F-WWCU A310 498
F-WWCU A310 547
F-WWCU A310 597
F-WWCU A310 678
F-WWCV A310 436
F-WWCV A310 456
F-WWCV A310 496
F-WWCV A310 548
F-WWCV A310 598
F-WWCV A310 649
F-WWCW A310 589
F-WWCX A310 433
F-WWCX A310 478
F-WWCX A310 500
F-WWCX A310 549
F-WWCX A310 590
F-WWCX A310 642
F-WWCX A310 686
F-WWCY A310 437
F-WWCY A310 451
F-WWCY A310 545
F-WWCY A310 658
F-WWCZ A310 442
F-WWCZ A310 480
F-WWCZ A310 552
F-WWCZ A310 599
F-WWCZ A310 653
F-WWCZ A310 667
F-WWDA A320 0002
F-WWDA A340 003
F-WWDB A319 546
F-WWDB A320 0003
F-WWDB A320 0103
F-WWDB A320 0135
F-WWDB A320 0182
F-WWDB A320 0185
F-WWDB A320 0342
F-WWDB A320 0406
F-WWDB A320 0456
F-WWDC A310 567
F-WWDC A320 0004
F-WWDC A320 0073
F-WWDC A320 0136
F-WWDC A320 0189
F-WWDC A320 0238
F-WWDC A320 0324
F-WWDC A320 0388
F-WWDC A320 0433
F-WWDC A320 0511
F-WWDC A320 0568
F-WWDD A320 0006
F-WWDD A320 0027
F-WWDD A320 0040
F-WWDD A320 0137
F-WWDD A320 0190
F-WWDD A320 0241
F-WWDD A320 0300
F-WWDD A320 0366
F-WWDD A320 0435
F-WWDD A320 0512
F-WWDE A320 0008
F-WWDE A320 0028
F-WWDE A320 0083
F-WWDE A320 0138
F-WWDE A320 0196
F-WWDE A320 0245
F-WWDE A320 0305
F-WWDE A320 0373
F-WWDE A320 0436
F-WWDE A320 0523
F-WWDF A320 0011
F-WWDF A320 0029
F-WWDF A320 0085
F-WWDF A320 0139
F-WWDF A320 0197
F-WWDF A320 0234
F-WWDF A320 0350
F-WWDF A320 0404
F-WWDF A320 0497
F-WWDF A320 0558
F-WWDG A320 0017
F-WWDG A320 0046
F-WWDG A320 0105
F-WWDG A320 0140
F-WWDG A320 0198
F-WWDG A320 0306
F-WWDG A320 0367
F-WWDG A320 0418
F-WWDG A320 0457
F-WWDG A320 0569
F-WWDH A320 0018
F-WWDH A320 0091
F-WWDH A320 0141
F-WWDH A320 0191

F-WWDH	A320	0343
F-WWDH	A320	0407
F-WWDH	A320	0479
F-WWDH	A320	0571
F-WWDI	A320	0005
F-WWDI	A320	0030
F-WWDI	A320	0059
F-WWDI	A320	0142
F-WWDI	A320	0199
F-WWDI	A320	0230
F-WWDI	A320	0262
F-WWDI	A320	0325
F-WWDI	A320	0389
F-WWDI	A320	0527
F-WWDJ	A320	0007
F-WWDJ	A320	0031
F-WWDJ	A320	0086
F-WWDJ	A320	0143
F-WWDJ	A320	0200
F-WWDJ	A320	0242
F-WWDJ	A320	0307
F-WWDJ	A320	0374
F-WWDJ	A320	0446
F-WWDJ	A320	0487
F-WWDJ	A320	0573
F-WWDK	A320	0009
F-WWDK	A320	0032
F-WWDK	A320	0092
F-WWDK	A320	0144
F-WWDK	A320	0206
F-WWDK	A320	0247
F-WWDK	A320	0326
F-WWDK	A320	0405
F-WWDK	A320	0459
F-WWDK	A320	0540
F-WWDL	A320	0010
F-WWDL	A320	0034
F-WWDL	A320	0099
F-WWDL	A320	0145
F-WWDL	A320	0201
F-WWDL	A320	0243
F-WWDL	A320	0308
F-WWDL	A320	0390
F-WWDL	A320	0528
F-WWDM	A320	0012
F-WWDM	A320	0039
F-WWDM	A320	0087
F-WWDM	A320	0146
F-WWDM	A320	0202
F-WWDM	A320	0235
F-WWDM	A320	0351
F-WWDM	A320	0437
F-WWDM	A320	0489
F-WWDM	A320	0561
F-WWDN	A320	0013
F-WWDN	A320	0037
F-WWDN	A320	0088
F-WWDN	A320	0147
F-WWDN	A320	0203
F-WWDN	A320	0292
F-WWDN	A320	0361
F-WWDN	A320	0408
F-WWDN	A320	0460
F-WWDN	A320	0574
F-WWDO	A320	0014
F-WWDO	A320	0043
F-WWDO	A320	0068
F-WWDO	A320	0148
F-WWDO	A320	0205
F-WWDO	A320	0249
F-WWDO	A320	0314
F-WWDO	A320	0391
F-WWDO	A320	0447
F-WWDO	A320	0499
F-WWDO	A320	0575
F-WWDP	A320	0015
F-WWDP	A320	0047
F-WWDP	A320	0084
F-WWDP	A320	0149
F-WWDP	A320	0195
F-WWDP	A320	0419
F-WWDP	A320	0461
F-WWDP	A320	0530
F-WWDQ	A320	0016
F-WWDQ	A320	0052
F-WWDQ	A320	0093
F-WWDQ	A320	0150
F-WWDQ	A320	0207
F-WWDQ	A320	0263
F-WWDQ	A320	0327
F-WWDQ	A320	0398
F-WWDQ	A320	0462
F-WWDQ	A320	0562
F-WWDR	A320	0022
F-WWDR	A320	0050
F-WWDR	A320	0094
F-WWDR	A320	0151
F-WWDR	A320	0216
F-WWDR	A320	0265
F-WWDR	A320	0328
F-WWDR	A320	0392
F-WWDR	A320	0448
F-WWDR	A320	0565
F-WWDS	A320	0023
F-WWDS	A320	0041
F-WWDS	A320	0095
F-WWDS	A320	0162
F-WWDS	A320	0197
F-WWDS	A320	0217
F-WWDS	A320	0273
F-WWDS	A320	0344
F-WWDT	A320	0024
F-WWDT	A320	0042
F-WWDT	A320	0089
F-WWDT	A320	0152
F-WWDT	A320	0208
F-WWDT	A320	0248
F-WWDT	A320	0303
F-WWDT	A320	0375
F-WWDT	A320	0438
F-WWDT	A320	0490
F-WWDT	**A320**	**0577**
F-WWDU	A320	0025
F-WWDU	A320	0048
F-WWDU	A320	0096
F-WWDU	A320	0163
F-WWDU	A320	0279
F-WWDU	A320	0345
F-WWDU	A320	0409
F-WWDU	A320	0480
F-WWDU	**A320**	**0579**
F-WWDV	A320	0026
F-WWDV	A320	0053
F-WWDV	A320	0097
F-WWDV	A320	0165
F-WWDV	A320	0231
F-WWDV	A320	0280
F-WWDV	A320	0353
F-WWDV	A320	0410
F-WWDV	A320	0463
F-WWDV	A320	0580
F-WWDX	A320	0035
F-WWDX	A320	0090
F-WWDX	A320	0153
F-WWDX	A320	0218
F-WWDX	A320	0277
F-WWDX	A320	0346
F-WWDX	A320	0411
F-WWDX	A320	0464
F-WWDY	A320	0045
F-WWDY	A320	0098
F-WWDY	A320	0154
F-WWDY	A320	0209
F-WWDY	A320	0267
F-WWDY	A320	0329
F-WWDY	A320	0379
F-WWDY	A320	0531
F-WWDZ	A320	0038
F-WWDZ	A320	0160
F-WWDZ	A320	0219
F-WWDZ	A320	0293
F-WWDZ	A320	0354
F-WWDZ	A320	0500
F-WWDZ	**A320**	**0584**
F-WWFT	**A320**	**0001**
F-WWHB	A320	0430
F-WWIA	A320	0049
F-WWIA	A320	0106
F-WWIA	A320	0161
F-WWIA	A320	0223
F-WWIA	A320	0282
F-WWIA	**A321**	**0364**
F-WWIB	A320	0051
F-WWIB	A320	0107
F-WWIB	A320	0157
F-WWIB	A320	0213
F-WWIB	A320	0268
F-WWIB	A320	0330
F-WWIB	**A321**	**0385**
F-WWIC	A320	0056
F-WWIC	A320	0109
F-WWIC	A320	0158
F-WWIC	A320	0210
F-WWIC	A320	0269
F-WWIC	A320	0332
F-WWID	A320	0058
F-WWID	A320	0110
F-WWID	A320	0166
F-WWID	A320	0294
F-WWID	A321	0434
F-WWIE	A320	0060
F-WWIE	A320	0111
F-WWIE	A320	0164
F-WWIE	A320	0167
F-WWIE	A320	0295
F-WWIE	A320	0355
F-WWIE	A320	0420
F-WWIE	A320	0481
F-WWIE	A320	0553
F-WWIE	A321	0412
F-WWIF	A320	0057
F-WWIF	A320	0112
F-WWIF	A320	0168
F-WWIF	A320	0304
F-WWIF	A320	0368
F-WWIF	A320	0533
F-WWIG	A320	0066
F-WWIG	A320	0104
F-WWIG	A320	0159
F-WWIG	A320	0212
F-WWIG	A320	0275
F-WWIG	A320	0336
F-WWIG	A320	0399
F-WWIG	A320	0449
F-WWIG	A320	0554
F-WWIH	A320	0054
F-WWIH	A320	0113
F-WWIH	A320	0169
F-WWIH	A320	0296
F-WWIH	A320	0356
F-WWIH	A320	0427
F-WWIH	**A320**	**0542**
F-WWII	A320	0069
F-WWII	A320	0114
F-WWII	A320	0170
F-WWII	A320	0246
F-WWII	A320	0331
F-WWII	A320	0450
F-WWII	A320	0545
F-WWII	A340	061
F-WWIJ	A320	0070
F-WWIJ	A320	0119
F-WWIJ	A320	0171
F-WWIJ	A320	0220
F-WWIJ	A320	0309
F-WWIJ	A320	0381
F-WWIJ	A320	0439
F-WWIJ	A320	0548
F-WWIK	A320	0064
F-WWIK	A320	0116
F-WWIK	A320	0172
F-WWIK	A320	0221
F-WWIK	A320	0310
F-WWIK	A320	0376
F-WWIL	A320	0065
F-WWIL	A320	0117
F-WWIL	A320	0173
F-WWIL	A320	0222
F-WWIL	A320	0311
F-WWIL	A320	0369
F-WWIL	A320	0428
F-WWIL	A320	0556
F-WWIM	A320	0055
F-WWIM	A320	0118
F-WWIM	A320	0174
F-WWIM	A320	0224
F-WWIM	A320	0276
F-WWIM	A320	0338
F-WWIM	A320	0413
F-WWIM	A320	0465
F-WWIN	A320	0067
F-WWIN	A320	0120
F-WWIN	A320	0175
F-WWIN	A320	0229
F-WWIN	A320	0362
F-WWIN	A320	0451
F-WWIN	A320	0501
F-WWIN	A320	0566
F-WWIO	A320	0071
F-WWIO	A320	0121
F-WWIO	A320	0176
F-WWIO	A320	0225
F-WWIO	A320	0297
F-WWIO	A320	0358
F-WWIO	A320	0421
F-WWIO	A320	0482
F-WWIP	A320	0072
F-WWIP	A320	0122
F-WWIP	A320	0177
F-WWIP	A320	0240
F-WWIP	A320	0298
F-WWIP	A320	0370
F-WWIP	A320	0422
F-WWIP	A320	0559
F-WWIQ	A320	0074
F-WWIQ	A320	0178
F-WWIQ	A320	0233
F-WWIQ	A320	0299
F-WWIQ	A320	0371
F-WWIQ	A320	0440
F-WWIQ	A321	0458
F-WWIR	A320	0075
F-WWIR	A320	0123
F-WWIR	A320	0393
F-WWIR	A320	0471
F-WWIS	A320	0076
F-WWIS	A320	0124
F-WWIS	A320	0179
F-WWIS	A320	0312
F-WWIS	A320	0380
F-WWIS	A320	0441
F-WWIS	A321	0468
F-WWIT	A320	0077
F-WWIT	A320	0125
F-WWIT	A320	0180
F-WWIT	A320	0359
F-WWIT	A320	0400
F-WWIT	A320	0423
F-WWIT	A320	0483
F-WWIT	A320	0549
F-WWIU	A320	0078
F-WWIU	A320	0126
F-WWIU	A320	0181
F-WWIU	A320	0414
F-WWIU	A320	0472
F-WWIU	A320	0547
F-WWIV	A320	0079
F-WWIV	A320	0127
F-WWIV	A320	0182
F-WWIV	A320	0424
F-WWIV	A320	0503
F-WWIX	A320	0080
F-WWIX	A320	0131
F-WWIX	A320	0183
F-WWIX	A320	0193
F-WWIX	A320	0301
F-WWIX	A320	0372
F-WWIX	A320	0425
F-WWIX	A320	0539
F-WWIY	A320	0081
F-WWIY	A320	0132
F-WWIY	A320	0192
F-WWIY	A320	0232
F-WWIY	A320	0302
F-WWIY	A320	0378
F-WWIY	A320	0442
F-WWIY	**A320**	**0543**
F-WWIZ	A320	0082
F-WWIZ	A320	0134
F-WWIZ	A320	0194
F-WWIZ	A320	0313
F-WWIZ	A320	0382
F-WWIZ	A320	0429
F-WWIZ	A320	0485

F-WWJA	A340	008
F-WWJA	A340	040
F-WWJA	A340	089
F-WWJA	A340	091
F-WWJA	**A340**	**139**
F-WWJB	A340	009
F-WWJB	A340	041
F-WWJB	A340	125
F-WWJC	A340	010
F-WWJC	A340	046
F-WWJC	A340	080
F-WWJD	A340	011
F-WWJD	A340	048
F-WWJD	A340	093
F-WWJE	A340	013
F-WWJE	A340	058
F-WWJE	A340	101
F-WWJF	A340	014
F-WWJF	A340	057
F-WWJF	A340	094
F-WWJG	A340	015
F-WWJG	A340	076
F-WWJG	A340	103
F-WWJH	A340	016
F-WWJH	A340	117
F-WWJI	A340	018
F-WWJI	**A340**	**114**
F-WWJJ	A340	019
F-WWJJ	A340	053
F-WWJJ	A340	104
F-WWJK	A340	020
F-WWJK	A340	056
F-WWJL	A340	021
F-WWJL	A340	074
F-WWJL	**A340**	**126**
F-WWJM	A340	022
F-WWJM	A340	063
F-WWJN	A340	023
F-WWJN	A340	044
F-WWJN	A340	115
F-WWJO	A340	024
F-WWJO	A340	081
F-WWJO	A340	131
F-WWJP	A340	025
F-WWJP	A340	085
F-WWJP	**A340**	**133**
F-WWJQ	A340	026
F-WWJQ	A340	052
F-WWJQ	**A340**	**129**
F-WWJR	A340	027
F-WWJR	A340	075
F-WWJR	A340	134
F-WWJS	A340	028
F-WWJS	A340	079
F-WWJS	A340	135
F-WWJT	A340	032
F-WWJT	A340	097
F-WWJU	A340	033
F-WWJV	A340	035
F-WWJV	A340	088
F-WWJV	**A340**	**136**
F-WWJX	A340	036
F-WWJX	A340	089
F-WWJX	A340	137
F-WWJY	A340	034
F-WWJZ	A340	034
F-WWJZ	A340	090
F-WWJZ	**A340**	**128**
F-WWKA	**A330**	**012**
F-WWKB	**A330**	**017**
F-WWKD	A330	030
F-WWKD	A330	082
F-WWKD	A330	109
F-WWKE	A330	037
F-WWKE	A330	083
F-WWKE	A330	110
F-WWKF	A330	087
F-WWKF	A330	118
F-WWKG	A330	098
F-WWKG	A330	122
F-WWKH	A330	042
F-WWKH	A330	095
F-WWKI	A330	050
F-WWKI	A330	106
F-WWKJ	A330	054
F-WWKJ	A330	066

F-WWKJ	A330	119
F-WWKJ	**A340**	**123**
F-WWKK	A330	121
F-WWKL	A330	068
F-WWKL	A330	111
F-WWKM	A330	069
F-WWKM	A330	112
F-WWKN	A330	073
F-WWKN	A330	120
F-WWKO	A330	077
F-WWKO	A330	127
F-WWKP	A330	055
F-WWKP	A330	096
F-WWKQ	A330	060
F-WWKQ	A330	099
F-WWKQ	**A330**	**132**
F-WWKR	A330	062
F-WWKR	A330	102
F-WWKS	A330	064
F-WWKS	A330	113
F-WWKT	A330	065
F-WWKT	A330	116
F-WWKU	A330	071
F-WWKV	A330	070
F-WWKV	A330	107
F-WWKX	A330	067
F-WWKY	A330	072
F-WWKZ	A330	100
F-WWTA	A319	578
F-WWYM	A310	571
F-WWZI	A320	0194
F-WZEA	A300	51
F-WZEA	A300	68
F-WZEA	A300	101
F-WZEA	A300	135
F-WZEA	A310	224
F-WZEA	A310	283
F-WZEA	A310	329
F-WZEB	A300	52
F-WZEB	A300	69
F-WZEB	A300	110
F-WZEB	A300	133
F-WZEB	A310	230
F-WZEB	A310	285
F-WZEC	A300	55
F-WZEC	A300	71
F-WZEC	A300	85
F-WZEC	A300	103
F-WZEC	A300	126
F-WZEC	A310	233
F-WZEC	A310	288
F-WZED	A300	54
F-WZED	A300	72
F-WZED	A300	88
F-WZED	A300	105
F-WZED	A300	127
F-WZED	A300	143
F-WZED	A310	237
F-WZED	A310	291
F-WZED	A310	360
F-WZEE	A300	53
F-WZEE	A300	73
F-WZEE	A300	106
F-WZEE	A300	128
F-WZEE	A310	241
F-WZEE	A310	293
F-WZEF	A300	56
F-WZEF	A300	89
F-WZEF	A300	140
F-WZEF	A310	248
F-WZEF	A310	295
F-WZEF	A310	339
F-WZEF	A310	362
F-WZEG	A300	57
F-WZEG	A300	75
F-WZEG	A300	90
F-WZEG	A300	144
F-WZEG	A310	245
F-WZEG	A310	300
F-WZEG	A310	333
F-WZEH	A300	58
F-WZEH	A300	122
F-WZEH	A300	141
F-WZEH	A310	251
F-WZEH	A310	297
F-WZEH	A310	340

F-WZEI	A300	59
F-WZEI	A300	76
F-WZEI	A300	93
F-WZEI	A300	111
F-WZEI	A300	130
F-WZEI	A310	254
F-WZEI	A310	303
F-WZEI	A310	342
F-WZEI	A310	363
F-WZEJ	A300	60
F-WZEJ	A300	77
F-WZEJ	A300	94
F-WZEJ	A300	113
F-WZEJ	A300	134
F-WZEJ	A310	257
F-WZEJ	A310	311
F-WZEK	A300	61
F-WZEK	A300	121
F-WZEK	A310	260
F-WZEK	A310	306
F-WZEK	A310	343
F-WZEL	A300	63
F-WZEL	A300	107
F-WZEL	A300	131
F-WZEL	A310	264
F-WZEL	A310	318
F-WZEL	A310	345
F-WZEM	A300	64
F-WZEM	A300	95
F-WZEM	A300	109
F-WZEM	A300	132
F-WZEM	A310	267
F-WZEM	A310	309
F-WZEM	A310	346
F-WZEM	A310	364
F-WZEN	A300	65
F-WZEN	A300	79
F-WZEN	A300	114
F-WZEN	A300	136
F-WZEN	A310	270
F-WZEN	A310	372
F-WZEO	A300	66
F-WZEO	A300	80
F-WZEO	A300	125
F-WZEO	A310	273
F-WZEO	A310	331
F-WZEO	A310	347
F-WZEO	A310	352
F-WZEP	A300	67
F-WZEP	A300	81
F-WZEP	A300	96
F-WZEP	A300	115
F-WZEP	A300	137
F-WZEP	A300	197
F-WZEP	A310	276
F-WZEP	A310	313
F-WZEP	A310	349
F-WZEP	A310	367
F-WZEQ	A300	31
F-WZEQ	A300	82
F-WZEQ	A300	138
F-WZEQ	A300	198
F-WZER	A300	46
F-WZER	A300	98
F-WZER	A300	117
F-WZER	A300	194
F-WZER	A310	278
F-WZER	A310	320
F-WZES	A300	49
F-WZES	A300	83
F-WZES	A300	116
F-WZES	A300	139
F-WZES	A300	195
F-WZET	A300	50
F-WZET	A300	84
F-WZET	A300	99
F-WZET	A300	123
F-WZET	A300	142
F-WZET	A300	196
F-WZET	A310	281
F-WZET	A310	338
F-WZLH	A310	162
F-WZLH	A310	350
F-WZLH	A310	370
F-WZLI	A310	172
F-WZLJ	A310	191

F-WZLJ	A310	353
F-WZLK	A310	201
F-WZLK	A310	356
F-WZLL	A310	217
F-WZLL	A310	357
F-WZLR	A300	252
F-WZLS	A300	284
F-WZLS	A310	359
F-WZMA	A300	147
F-WZMA	A300	184
F-WZMA	A300	222
F-WZMA	A300	256
F-WZMB	A300	22
F-WZMB	A300	148
F-WZMB	A300	185
F-WZMB	A300	225
F-WZMB	A300	269
F-WZMC	A300	149
F-WZMC	A300	186
F-WZMC	A300	227
F-WZMD	A300	150
F-WZMD	A300	187
F-WZMD	A300	232
F-WZMD	A300	304
F-WZME	A300	151
F-WZME	A300	188
F-WZME	A300	226
F-WZME	A300	277
F-WZMF	A300	156
F-WZMF	A300	199
F-WZMF	A300	234
F-WZMG	A300	157
F-WZMG	A300	189
F-WZMG	A300	235
F-WZMH	A300	159
F-WZMH	A300	209
F-WZMH	A300	262
F-WZMI	A300	160
F-WZMI	A300	190
F-WZMI	A300	236
F-WZMJ	A300	26
F-WZMJ	A300	163
F-WZMJ	A300	202
F-WZMJ	A300	243
F-WZMK	A300	164
F-WZMK	A300	210
F-WZML	A300	165
F-WZML	A300	192
F-WZML	A300	239
F-WZML	A300	282
F-WZMM	A300	166
F-WZMM	A300	193
F-WZMM	A300	240
F-WZMM	A300	289
F-WZMN	A300	167
F-WZMN	A300	200
F-WZMN	A300	238
F-WZMO	A300	168
F-WZMO	A300	203
F-WZMO	A300	265
F-WZMP	A300	169
F-WZMP	A300	205
F-WZMP	A300	247
F-WZMQ	A300	170
F-WZMQ	A300	208
F-WZMR	A300	171
F-WZMS	A300	173
F-WZMS	A300	212
F-WZMS	A300	244
F-WZMS	A300	292
F-WZMT	A300	174
F-WZMT	A300	213
F-WZMT	A300	249
F-WZMU	A300	176
F-WZMU	A300	214
F-WZMU	A300	250
F-WZMV	A300	177
F-WZMV	A300	219
F-WZMV	A300	268
F-WZMV	A300	305
F-WZMW	A300	179
F-WZMX	A300	180
F-WZMX	A300	221
F-WZMX	A300	253
F-WZMX	A300	299
F-WZMY	A300	181

F-WZMY	A300	215
F-WZMY	A300	255
F-WZMY	A300	302
F-WZMZ	A300	182
F-WZMZ	A300	218
F-WZXP	A300	282
F-WZYA	A300	294
F-WZYA	A300	354
F-WZYB	A300	301
F-WZYB	A300	351
F-WZYC	A300	307
F-WZYC	A300	358
F-WZYD	A300	312
F-WZYE	A300	317
F-WZYF	A300	321
F-WZYG	A300	327
F-WZYH	A300	332
F-WZYI	A300	336
F-WZYJ	A300	341
F-WZYK	A300	344
F-WZYL	A300	348

France -State Owned

F-ZACE	**CRVL**	**116**
F-ZACF	**CRVL**	**193**
F-ZACQ	**CRVL**	**234**
F-ZARK	DC-8	45570
F-ZBCA	**E-3**	**24115**
F-ZBCB	**E-3**	**24116**
F-ZBCC	**E-3**	**24117**
F-ZBCD	**E-3**	**24510**

United Kingdom

G-	**A320**	**0203**
G-	**A320**	**0220**
G-	**A320**	**0221**
G-	**A320**	**0222**
G-	**A340**	**114**
G-	146	E1230
G-	146	E1249
G-	146	E1252
G-	146	E3281
G-	146	E3282
(G-)	B757	25597
(G-)	B757	25598
(G-....)	B737	25594
(G-....)	B737	25595
G-3-163	146	E3163
G-5-001	146	E2052
G-5-002	146	E2049
G-5-003	146	E2051
G-5-004	146	E2050
G-5-005	146	E1002
G-5-01	146	E1015
G-5-0120	146	E3120
G-5-019	146	E1019
G-5-02	146	E1005
G-5-02	146	E1017
G-5-02	146	E1021
G-5-02	146	E1026
G-5-03	146	E1029
G-5-03	146	E1032
G-5-035	146	E1035
G-5-04	146	E1004
G-5-053	146	E2053
G-5-054	146	E2054
G-5-055	146	E2055
G-5-056	146	E2056
G-5-057	146	E2057
G-5-058	146	E2058
G-5-059	146	E2059
G-5-060	146	E2060
G-5-061	146	E2061
G-5-062	146	E2062
G-5-063	146	E1063
G-5-064	146	E2064
G-5-065	146	E2065
G-5-066	146	E2066
G-5-067	146	E2067
G-5-068	146	E1068
G-5-069	146	E2069
G-5-070	146	E2070
G-5-071	146	E1071
G-5-072	146	E2072
G-5-073	146	E2073
G-5-074	146	E2074
G-5-075	146	E2075
G-5-076	146	E1076
G-5-077	146	E2077
G-5-078	146	E2078
G-5-079	146	E2079
G-5-080	146	E2080
G-5-081	146	E1081
G-5-082	146	E2082
G-5-083	146	E1083
G-5-084	146	E2084
G-5-085	146	E1085
G-5-086	146	E2086
G-5-087	146	E2087
G-5-088	146	E2088
G-5-090	146	E2090
G-5-091	146	E1091
G-5-092	146	E2092
G-5-093	146	E2093
G-5-094	146	E2094
G-5-095	146	E1095
G-5-096	146	E2096
G-5-097	146	E2097
G-5-098	146	E2098
G-5-099	146	E2099
G-5-1	COMET	06001
G-5-1	COMET	6476
G-5-1	NIMROD	6476
G-5-100	146	E2100
G-5-101	146	E1101
G-5-102	146	E2102
G-5-103	146	E2103
G-5-104	146	E1104
G-5-105	146	E2105
G-5-106	146	E2106
G-5-107	146	E2107
G-5-108	146	E2108
G-5-110	146	E2110
G-5-111	146	E2111
G-5-112	146	E2112
G-5-115	146	E2115
G-5-116	146	E2116
G-5-122	146	E3122
G-5-123	146	E3123
G-5-124	146	E1124
G-5-125	146	E3125
G-5-127	146	E2127
G-5-129	146	E3129
G-5-130	146	E2130
G-5-132	146	E3132
G-5-133	146	E2133
G-5-134	146	E3134
G-5-135	146	E3135
G-5-136	146	E2136
G-5-137	146	E3137
G-5-138	146	E2138
G-5-139	146	E2139
G-5-14	146	E1003
G-5-141	146	E3141
G-5-143	146	E3143
G-5-145	146	E3145
G-5-146	146	E1002
G-5-146	146	E2008
G-5-147	146	E3147
G-5-159	146	E3159
G-5-2	COMET	06002
G-5-23	COMET	06022
G-5-300	146	E3001
G-5-507	146	E1021
G-5-512	146	E1010
G-5-513	146	E1011
G-5-517	146	E2050
G-5-523	146	E1019
G-5-537	146	E1004
G-52-1	1-11	005
G-52-19	L1011	1249
G-6-002	146	E1002
G-6-009	146	E1009
G-6-013	146	E1013
G-6-118	146	E3118
G-6-124	146	E1124
G-6-144	146	E1144
G-6-146	146	E3146
G-6-147	146	E3147
G-6-148	146	E2148
G-6-152	146	E1152
G-6-154	146	E3154
G-6-155	146	E3155
G-6-157	146	E3157
G-6-158	146	E3158
G-6-159	146	E3159
G-6-160	146	E1160
G-6-161	146	E3161
G-6-162	146	E3162
G-6-163	146	E3163
G-6-164	146	E2164
G-6-165	146	E3165
G-6-166	146	E3166
G-6-167	146	E2167
G-6-169	146	E3169
G-6-171	146	E3171
G-6-172	146	E2172
G-6-173	146	E3173
G-6-174	146	E3174
G-6-175	146	E3175
G-6-177	146	E3177
G-6-178	146	E2178
G-6-179	146	E3179
G-6-180	146	E2180
G-6-181	146	E3181
G-6-183	146	E3183
G-6-184	146	E2184
G-6-185	146	E3185
G-6-186	146	E3186
G-6-187	146	E3187
G-6-189	146	E3189
G-6-190	146	E3190
G-6-191	146	E3191
G-6-192	146	E2192
G-6-193	146	E3193
G-6-194	146	E3194
G-6-195	146	E3195
G-6-196	146	E2196
G-6-197	146	E3197
G-6-200	146	E2200
G-6-201	146	E2201
G-6-202	146	E3202
G-6-203	146	E3203
G-6-204	146	E2204
G-6-205	146	E3205
G-6-206	146	E3206
G-6-207	146	E3207
G-6-209	146	E3209
G-6-210	146	E2210
G-6-211	146	E2211
G-6-212	146	E3212
G-6-213	146	E3213
G-6-214	146	E3214
G-6-215	146	E3215
G-6-216	146	E3216
G-6-217	146	E3217
G-6-218	146	E3218
G-6-219	146	E3219
G-6-220	146	E2211
G-6-220	146	E2220
G-6-222	146	E3222
G-6-223	146	E1223
G-6-224	146	E1224
G-6-225	146	E1225
G-6-227	146	E1227
G-6-228	146	E1228
G-6-231	146	E2231
G-6-232	146	E3232
G-6-233	146	E2233
G-6-234	146	E3234
G-6-236	146	E3236
G-6-237	146	E3237
G-6-238	146	E3238
G-6-239	146	E2239
G-6-240	146	E3240
G-6-241	146	E3241
G-6-242	146	E3242
G-6-243	146	E3243
G-6-244	146	E3244
G-6-245	146	E3245
G-6-246	146	E2246
G-6-247	146	E3247
G-6-248	146	E3248
G-6-250	146	E3250
G-6-251	146	E2251
G-6-253	146	E2253
G-6-255	146	E3255
G-6-256	146	E2256
G-6-257	146	E2257
G-6-258	146	E1258
G-6-258	146	E2268
G-6-259	146	E3259
G-6-260	146	E1260
G-6-261	146	E2261
G-6-262	146	E3262
G-6-263	146	E3263
G-6-264	146	E3264
G-6-265	146	E3265
G-6-266	146	E2266
G-6-267	146	E1267
G-6-270	146	E2270
G-6-271	146	E2271
G-6-272	146	E3272
G-6-273	146	E2273
G-6-274	146	E3274
G-6-275	146	E2275
G-6-276	146	E3276
G-6-277	146	E2277
G-6-278	146	E2278
G-6-279	146	E2279
G-6-280	146	E3280
G-6-285	146	E2285
G-11-111	146	E2111
G-11-115	146	E2115
G-11-121	146	E2121
G-11-127	146	E2127
G-11-128	146	E3128
G-11-131	146	E3131
G-11-134	146	E3134
G-11-137	146	E3137
G-11-140	146	E2140
G-11-144	146	E1144
G-11-147	146	E3147
G-11-149	146	E3149
G-11-156	146	E2156
G-16-1	1-11	094
G-16-2	1-11	BAC.118
G-16-3	1-11	BAC.127
G-16-4	1-11	BAC.130
G-16-5	1-11	BAC.121
G-16-6	1-11	BAC.162
G-16-7	1-11	BAC.192
G-16-8	1-11	BAC.193
G-16-9	1-11	BAC.194
G-16-10	1-11	BAC.196
G-16-11	1-11	BAC.197
G-16-12	1-11	BAC.198
G-16-13	1-11	BAC.212
G-16-14	1-11	BAC.157
G-16-15	1-11	BAC.236
G-16-16	1-11	BAC.241
G-16-17	1-11	BAC.239
G-16-19	1-11	066
G-16-22	1-11	BAC.230
G-16-23	1-11	BAC.199
G-16-24	1-11	BAC.166
G-16-25	1-11	BAC.260
G-16-32	1-11	BAC.131
G-41-174	B707	17593
G-41-274	B707	17603
G-41-372	B707	18085
G-ALVG	COMET	06001
G-ALYP	COMET	06003
G-ALYR	COMET	06004
G-ALYS	COMET	06005
G-ALYT	COMET	06006
G-ALYU	COMET	06007
G-ALYV	COMET	06008
G-ALYW	COMET	06009
G-ALYX	COMET	06010
G-ALYY	COMET	06011
G-ALYZ	COMET	06012
G-ALZB	COMET	06014
G-ALZK	COMET	06002
G-AMXA	COMET	06023
G-AMXB	COMET	06024
G-AMXC	COMET	06025
G-AMXD	COMET	06026
G-AMXE	COMET	06027
G-AMXF	COMET	06028

G-AMXG	COMET	06029
G-AMXH	COMET	06030
G-AMXI	COMET	06031
G-AMXJ	COMET	06032
G-AMXK	COMET	06033
G-AMXL	COMET	06034
G-ANAV	COMET	06013
G-ANLO	COMET	06100
G-AOJT	COMET	06020
G-AOJU	COMET	06021
G-AOVU	COMET	6424
G-AOVV	COMET	6425
G-APAS	COMET	06022
G-APDA	COMET	6401
G-APDB	**COMET**	**6403**
G-APDC	COMET	6404
G-APDD	COMET	6405
G-APDE	COMET	6406
G-APDF	COMET	6407
G-APDG	COMET	6427
(G-APDG)	COMET	6408
G-APDH	COMET	6409
G-APDI	COMET	6428
(G-APDI)	COMET	6410
G-APDJ	COMET	6429
(G-APDJ)	COMET	6411
G-APDK	COMET	6412
G-APDL	COMET	6413
G-APDM	**COMET**	**6414**
G-APDN	COMET	6415
G-APDO	COMET	6416
G-APDP	COMET	6417
G-APDR	COMET	6418
G-APDS	COMET	6419
G-APDT	COMET	6420
G-APFB	B707	17703
G-APFC	B707	17704
G-APFD	B707	17705
G-APFE	B707	17706
G-APFF	B707	17707
G-APFG	B707	17708
G-APFH	B707	17709
G-APFI	B707	17710
G-APFJ	**B707**	**17711**
G-APFK	B707	17712
G-APFL	B707	17713
G-APFM	B707	17714
G-APFN	B707	17715
G-APFO	B707	17716
G-APFP	B707	17717
G-APMA	COMET	6421
G-APMB	COMET	6422
G-APMC	COMET	6423
G-APMD	COMET	6435
(G-APMD)	COMET	6424
G-APME	COMET	6436
(G-APME)	COMET	6425
G-APMF	COMET	6426
G-APMG	COMET	6442
G-APYC	COMET	6437
G-APYD	**COMET**	**6438**
G-APZM	COMET	6440
G-ARBB	COMET	6443
G-ARCO	COMET	6449
G-ARCP	COMET	6451
G-ARDI	COMET	6447
(G-AREI)	COMET	6453
G-ARGM	COMET	6453
(G-ARJE)	COMET	6452
(G-ARJF)	COMET	6455
(G-ARJG)	COMET	6456
(G-ARJH)	COMET	6446
(G-ARJH)	COMET	6459
G-ARJK	COMET	6452
G-ARJL	COMET	6455
G-ARJM	COMET	6456
G-ARJN	COMET	6459
G-AROV	COMET	6460
G-ARPA	TRDNT	2101
G-ARPB	TRDNT	2102
G-ARPC	TRDNT	2103
G-ARPD	**TRDNT**	**2104**
G-ARPE	TRDNT	2105
G-ARPF	TRDNT	2106
G-ARPG	TRDNT	2107
G-ARPH	**TRDNT**	**2108**
G-ARPI	TRDNT	2109
G-ARPJ	TRDNT	2110
G-ARPK	**TRDNT**	**2111**
G-ARPL	**TRDNT**	**2112**
G-ARPM	TRDNT	2113
G-ARPN	**TRDNT**	**2115**
G-ARPO	**TRDNT**	**2116**
G-ARPP	**TRDNT**	**2117**
G-ARPR	**TRDNT**	**2119**
G-ARPS	TRDNT	2120
G-ARPT	TRDNT	2121
G-ARPU	TRDNT	2122
G-ARPW	**TRDNT**	**2123**
G-ARPX	**TRDNT**	**2124**
G-ARPY	TRDNT	2126
G-ARPZ	**TRDNT**	**2128**
G-ARRA	B707	18411
G-ARRB	B707	18412
G-ARRC	B707	18413
G-ARTA	VC-10	803
G-ARVA	VC-10	804
G-ARVB	VC-10	805
G-ARVC	VC-10	806
G-ARVE	VC-10	807
G-ARVF	**VC-10**	**808**
G-ARVG	VC-10	809
G-ARVH	VC-10	810
G-ARVI	VC-10	811
G-ARVJ	VC-10	812
G-ARVK	VC-10	813
G-ARVL	VC-10	814
G-ARVM	**VC-10**	**815**
(G-ARVN)	VC-10	816
(G-ARVO)	VC-10	817
(G-ARVP)	VC-10	818
G-ARWD	B707	18372
G-ARWE	B707	18373
G-ASDZ	COMET	6457
G-ASGA	VC-10	851
G-ASGB	VC-10	852
G-ASGC	**VC-10**	**853**
G-ASGD	VC-10	854
G-ASGE	VC-10	855
G-ASGF	VC-10	856
G-ASGG	VC-10	857
G-ASGH	VC-10	858
G-ASGI	VC-10	859
G-ASGJ	VC-10	860
G-ASGK	VC-10	861
G-ASGL	VC-10	862
G-ASGM	VC-10	863
G-ASGN	VC-10	864
G-ASGO	VC-10	865
G-ASGP	VC-10	866
G-ASGR	VC-10	867
(G-ASGS)	VC-10	868
(G-ASGT)	VC-10	869
(G-ASGU)	VC-10	870
(G-ASGV)	VC-10	871
(G-ASGW)	VC-10	872
(G-ASGX)	VC-10	873
(G-ASGY)	VC-10	874
(G-ASGZ)	VC-10	875
G-ASHG	1-11	004
G-ASIW	VC-10	819
G-ASIX	VC-10	820
G-ASJA	1-11	005
G-ASJB	1-11	006
G-ASJC	1-11	007
G-ASJD	1-11	008
G-ASJE	1-11	009
G-ASJF	1-11	010
G-ASJG	1-11	011
G-ASJH	1-11	012
G-ASJI	1-11	013
G-ASJJ	1-11	014
G-ASTJ	1-11	085
G-ASUF	1-11	015
(G-ASVT)	1-11	BAC.095
G-ASWU	TRDNT	2114
G-ASWV	TRDNT	2118
G-ASYD	**1-11**	**053**
G-ASYE	1-11	054
G-ASZF	B707	18924
G-ASZG	B707	18925
G-ATDJ	VC-10	825
G-ATNA	TRDNT	2130
G-ATPH	1-11	BAC.110
G-ATPI	1-11	BAC.112
G-ATPJ	1-11	033
G-ATPK	1-11	034
G-ATPL	1-11	035
G-ATTP	1-11	039
G-ATVH	1-11	040
G-ATVU	1-11	074
G-ATWV	B707	19498
G-ATZC	B707	19416
G-ATZD	B707	19590
G-AVBW	1-11	BAC.107
G-AVBX	1-11	BAC.109
G-AVBY	1-11	BAC.113
G-AVEJ	1-11	094
G-AVFA	TRDNT	2140
G-AVFB	**TRDNT**	**2141**
G-AVFC	TRDNT	2142
G-AVFD	TRDNT	2143
G-AVFE	**TRDNT**	**2144**
G-AVFF	TRDNT	2145
G-AVFG	**TRDNT**	**2146**
G-AVFH	TRDNT	2147
G-AVFI	TRDNT	2148
G-AVFJ	**TRDNT**	**2149**
G-AVFK	**TRDNT**	**2150**
G-AVFL	TRDNT	2151
G-AVFM	**TRDNT**	**2152**
G-AVFN	TRDNT	2153
G-AVFO	TRDNT	2156
(G-AVFO)	TRDNT	2154
G-AVGP	**1-11**	**BAC.114**
G-AVKA	B707	19415
G-AVMH	**1-11**	**BAC.136**
G-AVMI	**1-11**	**BAC.137**
G-AVMJ	1-11	BAC.138
G-AVMK	**1-11**	**BAC.139**
G-AVML	**1-11**	**BAC.140**
G-AVMM	**1-11**	**BAC.141**
G-AVMN	**1-11**	**BAC.142**
G-AVMO	**1-11**	**BAC.143**
G-AVMP	**1-11**	**BAC.144**
G-AVMR	**1-11**	**BAC.145**
G-AVMS	**1-11**	**BAC.146**
G-AVMT	**1-11**	**BAC.147**
G-AVMU	**1-11**	**BAC.148**
G-AVMV	**1-11**	**BAC.149**
G-AVMW	**1-11**	**BAC.150**
G-AVMX	**1-11**	**BAC.151**
G-AVMY	**1-11**	**BAC.152**
G-AVMZ	**1-11**	**BAC.153**
G-AVOE	1-11	BAC.129
G-AVOF	1-11	BAC.131
G-AVPB	B707	19843
G-AVRL	B737	19709
G-AVRM	B737	19710
G-AVRN	B737	19711
G-AVRO	B737	19712
G-AVTF	1-11	BAC.122
G-AVTW	B707	19767
G-AVYA	TRDNT	2135
G-AVYB	TRDNT	2136
G-AVYC	TRDNT	2137
G-AVYD	TRDNT	2138
G-AVYE	**TRDNT**	**2139**
G-AVYZ	1-11	BAC.133
G-AVZZ	B707	17699
G-AWBL	**1-11**	**BAC.132**
G-AWDF	1-11	BAC.134
G-AWDG	B707	17702
G-AWEJ	1-11	BAC.115
G-AWGG	1-11	BAC.116
G-AWHU	B707	19821
G-AWKJ	1-11	BAC.128
G-AWNA	**B747**	**19761**
G-AWNB	**B747**	**19762**
G-AWNC	**B747**	**19763**
G-AWND	B747	19764
G-AWNE	**B747**	**19765**
G-AWNF	**B747**	**19766**
G-AWNG	**B747**	**20269**
G-AWNH	**B747**	**20270**
G-AWNI	B747	20271
G-AWNJ	**B747**	**20272**
G-AWNK	B747	20273
G-AWNL	**B747**	**20284**
G-AWNM	**B747**	**20708**
G-AWNN	**B747**	**20809**
G-AWNO	**B747**	**20810**
G-AWNP	**B747**	**20952**
G-AWSY	B737	20236
G-AWTK	B707	18975
G-AWWD	B707	19355
G-AWWX	1-11	BAC.184
G-AWWY	1-11	BAC.185
G-AWWZ	1-11	BAC.186
G-AWXJ	1-11	BAC.166
G-AWYR	**1-11**	**BAC.174**
G-AWYS	**1-11**	**BAC.175**
G-AWYT	1-11	BAC.176
G-AWYU	1-11	BAC.177
G-AWYV	**1-11**	**BAC.178**
G-AWYZ	TRDNT	2301
G-AWZA	TRDNT	2302
G-AWZB	TRDNT	2303
G-AWZC	TRDNT	2304
G-AWZD	TRDNT	2305
G-AWZE	TRDNT	2306
G-AWZF	TRDNT	2307
G-AWZG	TRDNT	2308
G-AWZH	TRDNT	2309
G-AWZI	TRDNT	2310
G-AWZJ	**TRDNT**	**2311**
G-AWZK	**TRDNT**	**2312**
G-AWZL	TRDNT	2313
G-AWZM	**TRDNT**	**2314**
G-AWZN	**TRDNT**	**2315**
G-AWZO	**TRDNT**	**2316**
G-AWZP	TRDNT	2317
G-AWZR	**TRDNT**	**2318**
G-AWZS	**TRDNT**	**2319**
G-AWZT	**TRDNT**	**2320**
G-AWZU	**TRDNT**	**2321**
G-AWZV	TRDNT	2322
G-AWZW	TRDNT	2323
G-AWZX	**TRDNT**	**2324**
(G-AWZY)	TRDNT	2325
G-AWZZ	**TRDNT**	**2326**
G-AXBB	1-11	BAC.162
G-AXCK	1-11	090
G-AXCP	1-11	087
G-AXDN	**CNCRD**	**13522/01**
G-AXGW	B707	20374
G-AXGX	B707	20375
G-AXJK	1-11	BAC.191
G-AXJL	1-11	BAC.209
G-AXJM	1-11	BAC.214
G-AXLL	**1-11**	**BAC.193**
G-AXLM	1-11	BAC.199
G-AXLN	1-11	BAC.211
G-AXLR	VC-10	829
G-AXMF	1-11	BAC.200
G-AXMG	1-11	BAC.201
G-AXMH	1-11	BAC.202
G-AXMI	1-11	BAC.203
G-AXMJ	1-11	BAC.204
G-AXMK	1-11	BAC.205
G-AXML	1-11	BAC.206
G-AXMU	1-11	BAC.157
G-AXNA	B737	20282
G-AXNB	B737	20389
G-AXNC	B737	20417
G-AXOX	1-11	BAC.121
G-AXPH	1-11	BAC.194
G-AXRS	B707	19664
G-AXSY	1-11	BAC.195
G-AXVO	1-11	BAC.197
G-AXXY	B707	20456
G-AXXZ	B707	20457
G-AXYD	1-11	BAC.210
G-AYAG	B707	18085
G-AYBJ	B707	17597
G-AYEX	C-137	19417
G-AYHM	1-11	BAC.161
G-AYKN	1-11	BAC.215
G-AYLT	B707	20517
G-AYOP	**1-11**	**BAC.233**
G-AYOR	1-11	BAC.232
G-AYOS	1-11	BAC.213
G-AYRZ	B707	18084
(G-AYSC)	1-11	BAC.235

Registration	Type	Number
G-AYSI	B707	18707
G-AYSL	B707	17599
G-AYUW	1-11	BAC.239
G-AYVE	B707	18083
G-AYVF	TRDNT	2325
G-AYVG	B707	17598
G-AYVS	COMET	6474
G-AYWB	1-11	BAC.237
G-AYWX	COMET	6465
G-AYXB	1-11	BAC.192
G-AYXR	B707	17608
G-AYZZ	B707	20089
(G-AZDG)	1-11	BAC.127
G-AZEB	1-11	BAC.188
G-AZEC	1-11	BAC.189
G-AZED	1-11	BAC.127
G-AZFB	B720	18381
G-AZFT	TRDNT	2157
G-AZFU	TRDNT	2158
G-AZFV	TRDNT	2159
G-AZFW	TRDNT	2160
G-AZFX	TRDNT	2161
G-AZFY	TRDNT	2162
G-AZIY	COMET	6434
G-AZJM	B707	18886
G-AZKM	B720	18382
G-AZLW	COMET	6432
G-AZMF	**1-11**	**BAC.240**
G-AZMI	1-11	066
G-AZND	TRDNT	2134
G-AZNX	B720	18383
G-AZNZ	B737	19074
(G-AZOI)	B707	17602
G-AZPE	1-11	BAC.208
G-AZPW	B707	20275
G-AZPY	1-11	BAC.187
G-AZPZ	1-11	BAC.229
G-AZRO	B707	20488
G-AZTG	B707	17600
G-AZUK	1-11	BAC.241
G-AZWA	B707	17605
G-AZXM	TRDNT	2154
G-AZZC	DC-10	46905
G-AZZD	DC-10	46906
G-BAAA	L1011	1024
G-BAAB	L1011	1032
G-BABP	TRDNT	2163
G-BABR	TRDNT	2164
G-BABS	TRDNT	2165
G-BABT	TRDNT	2166
G-BABU	TRDNT	2167
G-BABV	TRDNT	2168
G-BADP	B737	20632
G-BADR	B737	20633
G-BAEF	B727	18879
G-BAEL	B707	17602
G-BAFZ	B727	18877
G-BAJF	TRDNT	2169
G-BAJG	TRDNT	2170
G-BAJH	TRDNT	2171
G-BAJI	TRDNT	2172
G-BAJJ	TRDNT	2173
G-BAJK	TRDNT	2174
G-BAJL	TRDNT	2327
G-BAJM	TRDNT	2328
G-BAJW	B727	18878
G-BAWP	B707	19354
G-BAZG	B737	20806
G-BAZH	B737	20807
G-BAZI	B737	20808
G-BBAE	**L1011**	**1083**
G-BBAF	**L1011**	**1093**
G-BBAG	L1011	1094
G-BBAH	**L1011**	**1101**
G-BBAI	**L1011**	**1102**
G-BBAJ	**L1011**	**1106**
G-BBDG	**CNCRD**	**13523/202**
G-BBME	**1-11**	**066**
G-BBMF	1-11	074
G-BBMG	**1-11**	**BAC.115**
G-BBPU	**B747**	**20953**
G-BBSZ	DC-10	46727
G-BBUV	COMET	6451
G-BBVS	TRDNT	2175
G-BBVT	TRDNT	2176
G-BBVU	TRDNT	2177
G-BBVV	TRDNT	2178
G-BBVW	TRDNT	2179
G-BBVX	TRDNT	2180
G-BBVY	TRDNT	2181
G-BBVZ	TRDNT	2182
G-BBWA	TRDNT	2183
G-BBWB	TRDNT	2184
G-BBWD	TRDNT	2185
G-BBWE	TRDNT	2186
G-BBWF	TRDNT	2187
G-BBWG	TRDNT	2188
G-BBWH	TRDNT	2189
G-BBZG	B720	18792
G-BCAL	B707	19297
G-BCBA	B720	18014
G-BCBB	B720	18013
G-BCCV	1-11	BAC.198
G-BCDA	B727	19281
G-BCLZ	B707	18710
G-BCRS	B707	17603
G-BCWA	1-11	BAC.205
G-BCWG	1-11	BAC.204
G-BCXR	1-11	BAC.198
G-BDAE	1-11	BAC.203
G-BDAN	B727	19279
G-BDAS	1-11	BAC.202
G-BDAT	1-11	BAC.232
G-BDCN	B707	18975
G-BDCW	L1011	1131
G-BDCX	L1011	1133
G-BDCY	L1011	1138
G-BDCZ	L1011	1140
G-BDDE	DC-8	45684
G-BDEA	B707	19296
G-BDHA	DC-8	45667
G-BDIF	COMET	6463
G-BDIT	COMET	6467
G-BDIU	COMET	6468
G-BDIV	COMET	6469
G-BDIW	**COMET**	**6470**
G-BDIX	**COMET**	**6471**
G-BDKE	B707	19623
G-BDLM	B707	19629
G-BDPV	**B747**	**21213**
G-BDPZ	B747	19745
G-BDSJ	B707	19630
G-BDXA	**B747**	**21238**
G-BDXB	**B747**	**21239**
G-BDXC	**B747**	**21240**
G-BDXD	**B747**	**21241**
G-BDXE	**B747**	**21350**
G-BDXF	**B747**	**21351**
G-BDXG	**B747**	**21536**
G-BDXH	**B747**	**21635**
G-BDXI	**B747**	**21830**
G-BDXJ	**B747**	**21831**
G-BDXK	**B747**	**22303**
(G-BDXK)	B747	22306
G-BDXL	**B747**	**22305**
(G-BDXL)	B747	22304
G-BDXM	**B747**	**23711**
(G-BDXM)	B747	22305
G-BDXN	B747	22442
G-BDXN	**B747**	**23735**
G-BDXO	**B747**	**23799**
G-BDXP	**B747**	**24088**
G-BEAF	B707	18591
G-BEAK	**L1011**	**1132**
G-BEAL	L1011	1145
G-BEAM	**L1011**	**1146**
G-BEBL	**DC-10**	**46949**
G-BEBM	**DC-10**	**46921**
G-BEBP	B707	18579
G-BECG	**B737**	**21335**
G-BECH	**B737**	**21336**
G-BEEX	COMET	6458
G-BEEY	COMET	6462
G-BEEZ	COMET	6466
G-BEGZ	B727	19620
G-BEJM	**1-11**	**BAC.118**
G-BEJW	1-11	BAC.154
G-BEKA	1-11	BAC.230
G-BELO	DC-10	46501
G-BETJ	DC-8	45379
G-BEVN	B707	19271
G-BEZT	B707	18765
G-BFBS	B707	18693
G-BFBZ	B707	18585
G-BFCA	L1011	1157
G-BFCB	L1011	1159
G-BFCC	L1011	1164
G-BFCD	L1011	1165
G-BFCE	L1011	1168
G-BFCF	L1011	1174
G-BFEO	**B707**	**18691**
G-BFGI	DC-10	46590
G-BFGM	B727	19249
G-BFGN	B727	19251
G-BFHW	DC-8	45879
G-BFIH	DC-9	47048
G-BFKW	CNCRD	214
G-BFKX	CNCRD	216
G-BFLD	B707	19625
G-BFLE	B707	19293
G-BFMC	1-11	BAC.160
G-BFMI	B707	17632
G-BFVA	B737	21693
G-BFVB	B737	21694
G-BFWN	1-11	BAC.261
G-BFZF	B707	18718
G-BGAT	DC-10	46591
G-BGBB	L1011	1178
G-BGBC	**L1011**	**1182**
G-BGCT	B707	18054
G-BGDA	**B737**	**21790**
G-BGDB	**B737**	**21791**
G-BGDC	B737	21792
G-BGDD	B737	21793
G-BGDE	**B737**	**21794**
G-BGDF	**B737**	**21795**
G-BGDG	**B737**	**21796**
G-BGDH	B737	21797
G-BGDI	**B737**	**21798**
G-BGDJ	**B737**	**21799**
G-BGDK	**B737**	**21800**
G-BGDL	**B737**	**21801**
G-BGDN	B737	21802
G-BGDO	**B737**	**21803**
G-BGDP	**B737**	**21804**
G-BGDR	**B737**	**21805**
G-BGDS	**B737**	**21806**
G-BGDT	**B737**	**21807**
G-BGDU	**B737**	**21808**
(G-BGFA)	B707	17721
(G-BGFB)	B707	18056
G-BGFS	B737	21359
(G-BGIR)	B707	19270
G-BGIS	B707	18717
G-BGJE	**B737**	**22026**
G-BGJF	**B737**	**22027**
G-BGJG	B737	22028
G-BGJH	**B737**	**22029**
G-BGJI	**B737**	**22030**
G-BGJJ	**B737**	**22031**
G-BGJK	B737	22032
G-BGJL	B737	22033
G-BGJM	B737	22034
G-BGKE	1-11	BAC.263
G-BGKF	1-11	BAC.264
G-BGKG	1-11	BAC.265
G-BGNW	B737	21131
(G-BGRU)	B737	22057
(G-BGRV)	B737	22058
(G-BGRW)	B737	22059
G-BGTU	1-11	BAC.108
G-BGTV	B737	22024
G-BGTW	B737	22023
G-BGTY	B737	21960
G-BGXE	DC-10	47811
G-BGXF	DC-10	47812
G-BGXG	DC-10	47813
G-BGXH	DC-10	47814
G-BGXI	DC-10	47815
G-BGYJ	B737	22057
G-BGYK	B737	22058
G-BGYL	B737	22059
G-BHBL	L1011	1193
G-BHBM	L1011	1198
G-BHBN	**L1011**	**1204**
G-BHBO	**L1011**	**1205**
G-BHBP	L1011	1211
G-BHBR	L1011	1212
G-BHCL	B737	21955
G-BHDH	**DC-10**	**47816**
G-BHDI	**DC-10**	**47831**
G-BHDJ	**DC-10**	**47840**
G-BHGE	B720	18421
G-BHNE	B727	21676
G-BHNF	B727	21438
G-BHOX	B707	17640
G-BHOY	B707	17651
G-BHVG	B737	22395
G-BHVH	B737	22396
G-BHVI	B737	22397
G-BHVT	B727	21349
G-BHWE	B737	22364
G-BHWF	B737	22365
G-BIAD	146	E1001
(G-BIAE)	146	E1002
(G-BIAF)	146	E1003
(G-BIAG)	146	E1004
(G-BIAJ)	146	E1005
G-BIAS	DC-8	45816
G-BICV	B737	21528
G-BIII	1-11	BAC.128
G-BIKA	**B757**	**22172**
G-BIKB	**B757**	**22173**
G-BIKC	**B757**	**22174**
G-BIKD	**B757**	**22175**
G-BIKF	**B757**	**22177**
(G-BIKF)	B757	22176
G-BIKG	**B757**	**22178**
(G-BIKG)	B757	22177
G-BIKH	**B757**	**22179**
(G-BIKH)	B757	22178
G-BIKI	**B757**	**22180**
(G-BIKI)	B757	22179
G-BIKJ	**B757**	**22181**
(G-BIKJ)	B757	22180
G-BIKK	**B757**	**22182**
(G-BIKK)	B757	22181
G-BIKL	**B757**	**22183**
(G-BIKL)	B757	22182
G-BIKM	**B757**	**22184**
(G-BIKM)	B757	22183
G-BIKN	**B757**	**22186**
(G-BIKN)	B757	22184
G-BIKO	**B757**	**22187**
(G-BIKO)	B757	22185
G-BIKP	**B757**	**22188**
(G-BIKP)	B757	22186
G-BIKR	**B757**	**22189**
(G-BIKR)	B757	22187
G-BIKS	**B757**	**22190**
(G-BIKS)	B757	22188
G-BIKT	**B757**	**23398**
(G-BIKT)	B757	22189
G-BIKU	**B757**	**23399**
(G-BIKU)	B757	22190
G-BIKV	**B757**	**23400**
G-BIKW	**B757**	**23492**
G-BIKX	**B757**	**23532**
G-BIKY	**B757**	**23495**
G-BIKZ	**B757**	**23533**
G-BIMA	A300	127
G-BIMB	A300	131
G-BIMC	A300	144
(G-BIMD)	A300	177
(G-BIME)	A300	180
(G-BIMF)	A300	190
(G-BIMG)	A300	229
(G-BIMH)	A300	238
(G-BIMI)	A300	282
(G-BIMJ)	A300	305
G-BIUR	B727	19619
G-BJBJ	B737	22632
G-BJCT	B737	22638
G-BJCU	B737	22639
G-BJCV	B737	22640
G-BJFH	B737	22278
G-BJMV	1-11	BAC.244
G-BJRT	1-11	BAC.234
G-BJRU	1-11	BAC.238
G-BJSO	B737	22071
G-BJXJ	B737	22657
G-BJXL	B737	22054
G-BJXM	B737	22055
G-BJXN	B747	20527

G-BJYL	1-11	BAC.208
G-BJYM	1-11	BAC.242
G-BJZD	DC-10	46970
G-BJZE	DC-10	46973
G-BJZV	B737	22277
G-BJZW	B737	22516
G-BKAG	B727	21055
G-BKAP	B737	21685
G-BKAU	1-11	BAC.107
G-BKAV	1-11	BAC.109
G-BKAW	1-11	BAC.113
G-BKAX	1-11	BAC.133
G-BKBT	B737	20943
G-BKCG	B727	20328
(G-BKGU)	B737	22966
(G-BKGV)	B737	22967
G-BKHE	B737	22966
G-BKHF	B737	22967
G-BKHO	B737	22979
G-BKHT	146	E1007
G-BKMN	146	E1006
G-BKMS	B737	22453
G-BKNG	B727	21056
G-BKNH	B737	21820
G-BKPW	B767	22980
G-BKRM	B757	22176
G-BKRO	B737	21278
G-BKVZ	B767	22981
G-BKWT	A310	295
G-BKWU	A310	306
G-BKXZ	146	E1010
G-BKYA	**B737**	**23159**
G-BKYB	**B737**	**23160**
G-BKYC	**B737**	**23161**
G-BKYD	B737	23162
G-BKYE	**B737**	**23163**
G-BKYF	**B737**	**23164**
G-BKYG	**B737**	**23165**
G-BKYH	**B737**	**23166**
G-BKYI	**B737**	**23167**
G-BKYJ	**B737**	**23168**
G-BKYK	**B737**	**23169**
G-BKYL	**B737**	**23170**
G-BKYM	**B737**	**23171**
G-BKYN	**B737**	**23172**
G-BKYO	**B737**	**23225**
G-BKYP	**B737**	**23226**
G-BLDE	B737	22876
G-BLDH	1-11	BAC.262
G-BLEA	B737	21397
G-BLHD	1-11	BAC.260
G-BLKB	B737	23060
G-BLKC	B737	23061
G-BLKD	B737	23062
G-BLKE	B737	23063
G-BLKV	B767	23072
G-BLKW	B767	23250
(G-BLPS)	A310	370
G-BLRA	146	E1017
G-BLUS	L1011	1235
G-BLUT	L1011	1236
G-BLVE	B747	21097
G-BLVF	B747	21098
G-BLVH	B757	23227
(G-BLVO)	1-11	041
(G-BLVP)	1-11	043
G-BMAA	DC-9	47048
G-BMAB	DC-9	45738
G-BMAC	DC-9	45739
G-BMAG	DC-9	45719
G-BMAH	DC-9	45712
G-BMAI	DC-9	45713
G-BMAK	DC-9	47430
G-BMAM	DC-9	47468
G-BMAN	1-11	BAC.131
G-BMAZ	B707	19270
G-BMDF	B737	22875
G-BMEC	B737	21776
G-BMFM	146	E2042
G-BMGS	B747	20121
G-BMHG	B737	21774
G-BMJE	B707	18954
G-BMLP	B727	20710
(G-BMMP)	B737	22633
G-BMMZ	B737	20544
G-BMNA	A300	169
G-BMNB	A300	09
G-BMNC	A300	12
G-BMON	B737	22416
G-BMOR	B737	21775
G-BMRA	**B757**	**23710**
G-BMRB	**B757**	**23975**
G-BMRC	**B757**	**24072**
G-BMRD	**B757**	**24073**
G-BMRE	**B757**	**24074**
G-BMRF	**B757**	**24101**
G-BMRG	**B757**	**24102**
G-BMRH	**B757**	**24266**
G-BMRI	**B757**	**24267**
G-BMRJ	**B757**	**24268**
G-BMSM	B737	22279
(G-BMSR)	B737	22660
G-BMTE	B737	23712
G-BMTF	B737	23713
G-BMTG	B737	23733
G-BMTH	B737	23734
G-BMUE	B727	18951
G-BMWD	DC-9	47570
(G-BMXK)	B747	21517
G-BMYE	146	E2008
G-BMYT	B727	18802
G-BMZK	A300	76
G-BMZL	A300	77
G-BMZU	B727	18365
G-BNAX	B767	23057
G-BNCT	B737	23766
G-BNCW	**B767**	**23807**
(G-BNDR)	146	E2062
(G-BNEP)	B757	22185
G-BNGH	B707	18718
G-BNGK	B737	22406
G-BNGL	B737	23924
G-BNGM	B737	23925
(G-BNHG)	B757	23227
G-BNIA	B737	22737
G-BNIH	1-11	BAC.406
G-BNJI	146	E2072
G-BNKJ	146	E2069
G-BNKK	146	E2070
G-BNLA	**B747**	**23908**
G-BNLB	**B747**	**23909**
G-BNLC	**B747**	**23910**
G-BNLD	**B747**	**23911**
G-BNLE	**B747**	**24047**
G-BNLF	**B747**	**24048**
G-BNLG	**B747**	**24049**
G-BNLH	**B747**	**24050**
G-BNLI	**B747**	**24051**
G-BNLJ	**B747**	**24052**
G-BNLK	**B747**	**24053**
G-BNLL	**B747**	**24054**
G-BNLM	**B747**	**24055**
G-BNLN	**B747**	**24056**
G-BNLO	**B747**	**24057**
G-BNLP	**B747**	**24058**
G-BNLR	**B747**	**24447**
G-BNLS	**B747**	**24629**
G-BNLT	**B747**	**24630**
G-BNLU	**B747**	**25406**
G-BNLV	**B747**	**25427**
G-BNLW	**B747**	**25432**
G-BNLX	**B747**	**25435**
(G-BNLX)	B747	25433
G-BNLY	**B747**	**27090**
(G-BNLY)	B747	25434
(G-BNLY)	B747	25811
G-BNLZ	**B747**	**27091**
(G-BNLZ)	B747	25435
(G-BNLZ)	B747	25812
G-BNND	146	E2074
G-BNNI	**B727**	**20950**
G-BNNJ	B737	24068
G-BNNK	**B737**	**24069**
G-BNNL	**B737**	**24070**
G-BNPA	B737	23811
G-BNPB	B737	24059
G-BNPC	B737	24060
G-BNPJ	146	E2078
G-BNRT	B737	23064
G-BNSA	MD-83	49643
G-BNSB	MD-83	49658
G-BNSD	B757	24118
G-BNSE	B757	24121
G-BNSF	B757	24122
G-BNUA	146	E2086
G-BNWA	**B767**	**24333**
G-BNWB	**B767**	**24334**
G-BNWC	**B767**	**24335**
G-BNWD	**B767**	**24336**
G-BNWE	**B767**	**24337**
G-BNWF	**B767**	**24338**
G-BNWG	**B767**	**24339**
G-BNWH	**B767**	**24340**
G-BNWI	**B767**	**24341**
G-BNWJ	**B767**	**24342**
G-BNWK	**B767**	**24343**
G-BNWL	**B767**	**25203**
G-BNWM	**B767**	**25204**
G-BNWN	**B767**	**25444**
G-BNWO	**B767**	**25442**
G-BNWP	**B767**	**25443**
G-BNWR	**B767**	**25732**
G-BNWS	**B767**	**25826**
G-BNWT	**B767**	**25828**
G-BNWU	**B767**	**25829**
G-BNWV	**B767**	**27140**
G-BNWW	**B767**	**25831**
G-BNWX	**B767**	**25832**
G-BNWY	**B767**	**25834**
G-BNXP	B737	23787
G-BNXW	B737	23827
G-BNYC	146	E2089
G-BNYS	**B767**	**24013**
G-BNYT	B737	21112
G-BNZT	B737	22703
(G-BNZU)	B737	21775
G-BOAA	**CNCRD**	**206**
G-BOAB	**CNCRD**	**208**
G-BOAC	**CNCRD**	**204**
G-BOAD	**CNCRD**	**210**
G-BOAE	**CNCRD**	**212**
G-BOAF	**CNCRD**	**216**
G-BOAG	**CNCRD**	**214**
G-BOEA	146	E1095
G-BOHC	B757	24120
G-BOHK	146	E2100
G-BOJJ	146	E3146
G-BOKV	B727	20739
G-BOKZ	146	E2102
G-BOLM	B737	23942
G-BOMA	146	E1091
G-BOMI	146	E2105
G-BOMJ	146	E2109
G-BOMK	146	E2112
G-BONM	B737	22738
G-BOPB	**B767**	**24239**
G-BOPJ	B737	24123
G-BOPK	B737	24124
G-BOSA	B737	20808
G-BOSL	B737	22161
G-BOWR	B737	23401
G-BOWW	146	E3120
G-BOXD	146	E2113
G-BOXE	146	E2114
G-BOYN	B737	23788
G-BOZA	B737	23718
G-BOZB	B737	24219
(G-BOZC)	B737	24220
(G-BOZD)	B737	24221
G-BPAT	B707	19367
G-BPBS	146	E2117
G-BPBT	146	E2119
G-BPEA	**B757**	**24370**
G-BPEB	**B757**	**24371**
G-BPEC	**B757**	**24882**
G-BPED	**B757**	**25059**
G-BPEE	**B757**	**25060**
G-BPEF	**B757**	**24120**
G-BPEH	B757	24121
G-BPEI	**B757**	**25806**
G-BPEJ	**B757**	**25807**
G-BPEK	**B757**	**25808**
G-BPFV	B767	24457
G-BPGW	B757	22185
G-BPKA	B737	24163
G-BPKB	B737	24164
G-BPKC	B737	24165
G-BPKD	B737	24166
G-BPKE	B737	24167
G-BPLA	B737	22906
G-BPND	**B727**	**21021**
G-BPNP	146	E1002
G-BPNS	B727	20550
G-BPNT	**146**	**E3126**
G-BPNX	1-11	BAC.110
G-BPNY	B727	20675
(G-BPNY)	B737	22161
G-BPNZ	B737	24332
G-BPSC	MD-83	49823
G-BPSD	MD-83	49826
G-BPSN	B757	24119
(G-BPUV)	146	E2133
G-BRAB	146	E3131
G-BRDR	B720	18688
G-BRGK	146	E3150
G-BRGM	146	E3151
G-BRIF	**B767**	**24736**
G-BRIG	**B767**	**24757**
G-BRJD	B757	24397
G-BRJE	B757	24398
G-BRJF	B757	24772
G-BRJG	B757	24771
G-BRJH	B757	24794
G-BRJI	B757	24792
G-BRJJ	B757	24793
G-BRJP	B737	22660
G-BRJS	146	E1004
G-BRKF	B737	24795
G-BRKG	B737	24796
G-BRLM	146	E1144
G-BRLN	146	E1152
G-BRNG	146	E2077
G-BROC	B737	24573
G-BRPW	146	E3153
(G-BRSA)	A320	0006
(G-BRSB)	A320	0008
G-BRUC	146	E1009
G-BRXI	146	E3154
G-BRXJ	B737	23830
G-BRXT	146	E2115
G-BSGI	146	E3168
G-BSKY	DC-8	45858
G-BSLP	146	E1144
(G-BSLS)	146	E3155
G-BSLZ	146	E3166
G-BSMR	146	E3158
(G-BSNA)	B757	25053
(G-BSNB)	B757	25054
(G-BSNC)	B757	25133
G-BSNR	**146**	**E3165**
G-BSNS	**146**	**E3169**
G-BSNV	**B737**	**25168**
G-BSNW	**B737**	**25169**
G-BSOC	146	E3161
G-BSOH	146	E2170
(G-BSRA)	B737	25116
(G-BSRB)	B737	25134
G-BSRU	146	E2018
G-BSRV	146	E2020
(G-BSSG)	146	E2172
G-BSST	**CNCRD**	**13520/002**
G-BSTA	146	E1002
(G-BSUA)	B757	24291
(G-BSUB)	B757	24137
G-BSUY	146	E3182
(G-BSXJ)	1-11	063
(G-BSXK)	1-11	089
G-BSXL	146	E3186
(G-BSXU)	1-11	093
(G-BSXV)	1-11	BAC.106
G-BSXZ	146	E3174
G-BSYN	1-11	BAC.186
G-BSYR	146	E3181
G-BSYS	146	E3183
G-BSYT	146	E3187
G-BSZA	B707	18586
G-BSZE	A300	192
(G-BSZZ)	146	E2180
G-BTAC	DC-8	45768
G-BTCP	146	E2178
G-BTDO	146	E2188
G-BTEB	B737	21736
G-BTEC	B737	20908
G-BTED	B737	20909

Registration	Type	No.
G-BTEJ	B757	25085
G-BTHT	146	E3194
G-BTIA	146	E2148
G-BTJG	146	E3163
G-BTJT	146	E3128
G-BTKC	146	E2184
G-BTLD	146	E3198
G-BTMI	146	E3193
G-BTNU	146	E3155
G-BTTP	**146**	**E3203**
G-BTUY	146	E3202
G-BTVO	146	E3205
G-BTVT	146	E2200
G-BTXN	146	E3129
G-BTXO	**146**	**E1104**
G-BTZF	B737	22967
G-BTZN	**146**	**E3149**
G-BUDX	B757	25592
G-BUDZ	B757	25593
G-BUFI	146	E1229
G-BUHB	**146**	**E3183**
G-BUHC	**146**	**E3193**
(G-BUHI)	B737	26284
G-BUHJ	**B737**	**25164**
G-BUHK	**B737**	**26289**
G-BUHL	**B737**	**25134**
G-BUHV	146	E3207
G-BUHW	146	E3217
G-BUSB	**A320**	**0006**
G-BUSC	**A320**	**0008**
G-BUSD	**A320**	**0011**
G-BUSE	**A320**	**0017**
G-BUSF	**A320**	**0018**
G-BUSG	**A320**	**0039**
G-BUSH	**A320**	**0042**
G-BUSI	**A320**	**0103**
G-BUSJ	**A320**	**0109**
G-BUSK	**A320**	**0120**
G-BUSL	B737	24096
G-BUSM	B737	24097
G-BVAE	146	E2239
G-BVBY	B737	25844
G-BVBZ	B737	25858
G-BVCD	146	E2211
G-BVCE	146	E3209
G-BVFV	146	E2073
G-BVHA	B737	25859
G-BVHB	B737	25860
G-BVJA	**F-100**	**11489**
G-BVJB	**F-100**	**11488**
G-BVJC	**F-100**	**11497**
G-BVJD	**F-100**	**11503**
G-BVJV	A320	0437
G-BVJW	A320	0467
G-BVKA	**B737**	**24694**
G-BVKB	**B737**	**27268**
G-BVKC	**B737**	**24695**
G-BVKD	**B737**	**26421**
G-BVLJ	146	E1160
G-BVMP	146	E2210
G-BVMS	146	E1227
G-BVMT	146	E2220
G-BVNM	**B737**	**24163**
G-BVNN	**B737**	**24164**
G-BVNO	**B737**	**24167**
G-BVPE	146	E3213
G-BVRJ	146	E1254
G-BVSA	146	E3159
G-BVTE	**F-70**	**11538**
G-BVTF	**F-70**	**11539**
G-BVTG	**F-70**	**11551**
G-BVTH	F-70	11577
G-BVUW	146	E1035
G-BVUX	**146**	**E1068**
G-BVUY	146	E1071
(G-BVWD)	146	E2253
G-BVYA	**A320**	**0354**
G-BVYB	**A320**	**0357**
G-BVYC	**A320**	**0411**
G-BVYS	146	E3259
G-BVZE	**B737**	**26422**
G-BVZF	**B737**	**25038**
G-BVZG	**B737**	**25160**
G-BVZH	**B737**	**25166**
G-BVZI	**B737**	**25167**
G-BVZU	**A320**	**0280**
G-BWCP	A320	0189
G-BWES	1-11	BAC.259
G-BWIN	**DC-10**	**46936**
G-BWJA	**B737**	**23923**
G-BWKN	**A320**	**0190**
G-BWKO	**A320**	**0343**
G-BWKY	146	E2277
G-BWLG	146	E2176
G-BWTI	F-70	11578
G-BYAA	**B767**	**25058**
G-BYAB	**B767**	**25139**
G-BYAC	**B757**	**26962**
G-BYAD	**B757**	**26963**
G-BYAE	**B757**	**26964**
G-BYAF	**B757**	**26266**
G-BYAG	**B757**	**26965**
G-BYAH	**B757**	**26966**
G-BYAI	**B757**	**26967**
G-BYAJ	**B757**	**25623**
G-BYAK	**B757**	**26267**
G-BYAL	**B757**	**25626**
G-BYAM	**B757**	**23895**
G-BYAN	**B757**	**27219**
G-BYAO	**B757**	**27235**
G-BYAP	**B757**	**27236**
G-BYAR	**B757**	**27237**
G-BYAS	**B757**	**27238**
G-BYAT	**B757**	**27208**
G-BYAU	**B757**	**27220**
G-BYAW	**B757**	**27234**
"G-BZBO"	B747	19745
G-CBIA	1-11	BAC.166
G-CDHW	B707	21096
(G-CHGN)	B707	18718
G-CITB	B747	22579
G-CIVA	**B747**	**27092**
G-CIVB	**B747**	**25811**
G-CIVC	**B747**	**25812**
G-CIVD	**B747**	**27349**
G-CIVE	**B747**	**27350**
G-CIVF	**B747**	**25434**
G-CIVG	**B747**	**25813**
(G-CJIG)	B757	23227
G-CLHX	146	E2270
G-CMMP	B737	24220
G-CMMR	B737	24221
G-CNMF	146	E2079
G-COES	MD-83	49937
G-CPEL	**B757**	**24398**
G-CROS	146	E2226
G-CRPH	**A320**	**0424**
G-CSHR	146	E2088
G-CSJH	146	E2094
G-CSVS	**B757**	**25620**
G-DACR	**A320**	**0349**
(G-DAIO)	MD-83	49400
G-DAJB	**B757**	**23770**
G-DAJC	**B767**	**27206**
G-DBAF	1-11	011
G-DCAC	MD-83	49935
G-DCIO	**DC-10**	**48277**
G-DDDV	B737	22633
G-DEVR	**MD-83**	**49941**
G-DFUB	B737	22415
G-DGDP	B737	22762
G-DHSW	B737	23495
G-DIAR	B737	23811
G-DJOS	1-11	BAC.237
G-DMCA	**DC-10**	**48266**
G-DOCA	**B737**	**25267**
G-DOCB	**B737**	**25304**
G-DOCC	**B737**	**25305**
G-DOCD	**B737**	**25349**
G-DOCE	**B737**	**25350**
G-DOCF	**B737**	**25407**
G-DOCG	**B737**	**25408**
G-DOCH	**B737**	**25428**
G-DOCI	**B737**	**25839**
G-DOCJ	**B737**	**25840**
G-DOCK	**B737**	**25841**
G-DOCL	**B737**	**25842**
G-DOCM	**B737**	**25843**
G-DOCN	**B737**	**25848**
G-DOCO	**B737**	**25849**
G-DOCP	**B737**	**25850**
G-DOCR	**B737**	**25851**
G-DOCS	**B737**	**25852**
G-DOCT	**B737**	**25853**
G-DOCU	**B737**	**25854**
G-DOCV	**B737**	**25855**
G-DOCW	**B737**	**25856**
G-DOCX	**B737**	**25857**
(G-DOCY)	B737	25844
G-DOCZ	**B737**	**25858**
G-DRJC	B757	23895
G-DWHH	B737	22761
G-ECAL	146	E2058
G-EKPT	1-11	BAC.211
G-ELDG	**DC-9**	**47484**
G-ELDH	DC-9	47555
G-ELDI	**DC-9**	**47559**
G-EOCO	**B707**	**19294**
G-EURP	B737	24237
G-EURR	B737	23717
G-EXPM	1-11	BAC.124
(G-FIOA)	F-100	11330
G-FIOO	F-100	11316
G-FIOR	F-100	11318
G-FIOS	F-100	11321
(G-FIOT)	F-100	11323
(G-FIOU)	F-100	11324
(G-FIOV)	F-100	11325
(G-FIOW)	F-100	11326
(G-FIOX)	F-100	11327
(G-FIOY)	F-100	11328
(G-FIOZ)	F-100	11329
G-FLRU	1-11	BAC.201
G-GBTA	**B737**	**25859**
(G-GBTB)	B737	25860
G-GCAL	DC-10	46501
G-GFAL	DC-10	46970
G-GLYN	B747	21516
G-GMJM	MD-83	49951
G-GNTZ	**146**	**E2036**
G-GPAA	B737	22368
G-GPAB	B737	22071
G-GSKY	DC-10	46973
G-HAGT	A320	0294
G-HBAP	**A320**	**0294**
G-HCRP	MD-83	49936
G-HEVY	B707	19350
G-HIHO	B747	20108
G-HUGE	B747	21252
G-HWPB	146	E2018
G-IBTW	B737	21960
G-IBTX	B737	21736
G-IBTY	B737	22703
G-IBTZ	B737	22576
G-IEAA	B737	24098
G-IEAB	B757	24636
G-IEAC	B757	25620
G-IEAD	B757	24771
G-IEAE	B737	24795
G-IEAF	A320	0362
G-IEAG	A320	0363
G-ILFC	B737	22161
G-ISEE	**146**	**E2208**
G-JALC	**B757**	**22194**
G-JANM	**A320**	**0301**
G-JAYV	146	E2269
G-JCWW	F-28	11135
G-JDFW	**A320**	**0299**
G-JEAJ	**146**	**E2099**
G-JEAK	**146**	**E2103**
G-JEAL	**146**	**E3129**
G-JEAM	**146**	**E3128**
G-JEAO	**146**	**E1010**
G-JEAR	**146**	**E2018**
G-JEAS	**146**	**E2020**
G-JSMC	MD-83	49941
G-KILO	B747	22306
G-KKUH	B737	24300
G-KMAM	A320	0301
G-KROO	1-11	BAC.125
G-LCRC	**B757**	**24636**
(G-LOGI)	MD-83	49398
G-LUXE	**146**	**E3001**
G-MAJS	**A300**	**604**
(G-MALE)	A320	0422
G-MANS	**146**	**E2088**
G-MCEA	**B757**	**22200**
G-MCKE	**B757**	**24368**
(G-MDII)	MD-11	48411
G-MEDA	A320	0480
G-MIMA	**146**	**E2079**
G-MONB	**B757**	**22780**
G-MONC	**B757**	**22781**
G-MOND	**B757**	**22960**
G-MONE	**B757**	**23293**
G-MONF	B737	23497
G-MONG	**B737**	**23498**
G-MONH	B737	23685
G-MONJ	**B757**	**24104**
G-MONK	**B757**	**24105**
G-MONL	B737	24255
G-MONM	B737	24256
G-MONN	B737	24029
G-MONP	B737	24028
G-MONR	**A300**	**540**
G-MONS	**A300**	**556**
G-MONT	B737	24026
(G-MONT)	A300	604
G-MONU	B737	24025
(G-MONU)	A300	605
G-MONV	B737	25033
G-MONW	**A320**	**0391**
G-MONX	**A320**	**0392**
G-MONY	A320	0279
G-MONZ	**A320**	**0446**
G-MPCD	A320	0379
G-MULL	**DC-10**	**47888**
G-N81AC	CNCRD	204
G-N94AA	CNCRD	206
G-N94AB	CNCRD	208
G-N94AD	CNCRD	210
G-N94AE	CNCRD	212
G-N94AF	CNCRD	216
G-NAFH	B737	23788
G-NIGB	B747	21517
G-NIII	1-11	BAC.128
G-NIUK	**DC-10**	**46932**
G-NROA	B727	21056
G-OAHF	**B757**	**24136**
G-OAHI	B757	24137
G-OAHK	B757	24291
G-OAJF	146	E3118
G-OALA	**A320**	**0247**
G-OBAF	146	E1004
G-OBMA	B737	23831
G-OBMB	B737	23832
G-OBMC	B737	24030
G-OBMD	**B737**	**24092**
G-OBME	B737	23867
G-OBMF	**B737**	**23868**
G-OBMG	**B737**	**23870**
G-OBMH	**B737**	**24460**
(G-OBMI)	B737	24461
G-OBMJ	**B737**	**24461**
G-OBMK	**B737**	**25596**
G-OBML	**B737**	**24300**
G-OBMM	**B737**	**25177**
G-OBMN	**B737**	**24123**
G-OBMO	**B737**	**26280**
G-OBMP	**B737**	**24963**
G-OBMX	**B737**	**25065**
G-OBMY	**B737**	**26419**
G-OBMZ	**B737**	**24754**
G-OBOZ	B757	24971
G-OBWA	**1-11**	**BAC.232**
G-OBWB	**1-11**	**BAC.202**
G-OBWC	**1-11**	**BAC.230**
G-OBWD	**1-11**	**BAC.203**
G-OBWE	**1-11**	**BAC.242**
(G-OBWF)	1-11	BAC.210
(G-OBWG)	1-11	BAC.184
(G-OBWH)	1-11	BAC.208
(G-OBWI)	1-11	BAC.205
(G-OBWJ)	1-11	BAC.244
(G-OBWK)	1-11	BAC.198
G-OBYA	**B767**	**28039**
G-OBYB	**B767**	**28040**
G-OBYC	**B767**	**28041**
G-OBYD	**B767**	**28042**
G-OCHA	B737	24068
G-OCLH	146	E2268
G-OCNW	1-11	012
(G-ODAN)	146	E1006
G-OEXC	A320	0349

G-OHAP	146	E2061
(G-OHAP)	146	E2008
G-OIII	146	E3221
G-OITA	**B767**	**27376**
G-OITB	**B767**	**27377**
G-OITC	**B767**	**27468**
G-OITF	**B767**	**27908**
G-OITG	**B767**	**27918**
G-OJET	146	E1004
G-OJMR	**A300**	**605**
(G-OLAN)	MD-11	48412
G-OLCA	146	E2099
G-OLCB	146	E2103
G-OLHB	146	E2020
G-OLXX	146	E1228
G-OOAA	**A320**	**0291**
(G-OOAA)	B737	24686
G-OOAB	**A320**	**0292**
(G-OOAB)	B737	24688
G-OOAC	**A320**	**0327**
G-OOAD	**A320**	**0336**
G-OOOA	**B757**	**23767**
G-OOOB	B757	23822
G-OOOC	B757	24017
G-OOOD	**B757**	**24235**
G-OOOG	B757	24292
G-OOOH	B757	24293
G-OOOI	**B757**	**24289**
G-OOOJ	**B757**	**24290**
G-OOOM	**B757**	**22612**
G-OOOS	**B757**	**24397**
G-OOOT	**B757**	**24793**
G-OOOU	**B757**	**25240**
G-OOOV	**B757**	**22211**
G-OOOW	**B757**	**22611**
G-OOOX	**B757**	**26158**
G-OPSA	146	E1002
G-OSAS	146	E2204
G-OSKI	146	E2018
G-OSLA	B737	22576
G-OSUN	146	E2020
G-OUTA	B737	23635
G-OUZO	**A320**	**0449**
G-OZBA	**A320**	**0422**
G-OZBB	A320	0389
G-OZRH	**146**	**E2047**
G-PATA	MD-83	49398
G-PATB	MD-83	49400
G-PATC	MD-83	49662
G-PATD	MD-83	49663
G-PATE	B737	24093
G-PIDS	**B757**	**22195**
G-PKBD	DC-9	47666
G-PKBE	DC-9	47523
G-PKBM	DC-9	47648
G-PRCS	146	E2176
G-PRIN	146	E2148
G-PROC	B737	23256
G-PROK	B737	23506
G-RAES	**B777**	**27853**
G-RJER	**MD-83**	**49949**
G-RJET	146	E1199
G-RJGR	**B757**	**22197**
G-SAIL	**B707**	**18690**
G-SBEA	**B737**	**21694**
G-SBEB	**B737**	**20807**
G-SCHH	146	E1005
G-SCSR	A320	0299
G-SCUH	B737	23254
G-SJMC	**B767**	**27205**
G-SRJG	B757	24771
G-SSCH	146	E1003
(G-SSCH)	146	E1004
G-SSHH	146	E1002
G-SSSH	146	E1001
G-SUEE	**A320**	**0363**
G-SURE	1-11	BAC.129
G-TARO	1-11	BAC.272
G-TEAA	B737	24462
G-TEAB	B737	23923
(G-TEAD)	B737	23636
G-TJAA	B707	17903
G-TJAB	B707	17640
G-TJAC	B707	17651
G-TJPM	**146**	**E3150**
G-TKYO	B747	21939

G-TNTA	**146**	**E2056**
G-TNTB	**146**	**E2067**
G-TNTD	146	E2109
G-TNTE	**146**	**E3153**
G-TNTF	146	E3154
G-TNTG	**146**	**E3182**
G-TNTH	146	E2089
G-TNTJ	146	E2100
G-TNTK	**146**	**E3186**
G-TNTL	**146**	**E3168**
G-TNTM	**146**	**E3166**
G-TNTP	146	E2105
G-TNTR	**146**	**E3151**
G-TOMO	1-11	BAC.267
G-TONW	MD-83	49952
G-TPTT	**A320**	**0348**
G-TRAD	B707	18717
G-TREN	**B737**	**24796**
G-TTPT	MD-83	49940
G-UKAC	**146**	**E3142**
G-UKAG	**146**	**E3162**
G-UKFA	**F-100**	**11246**
G-UKFB	**F-100**	**11247**
G-UKFC	**F-100**	**11263**
G-UKFD	**F-100**	**11259**
G-UKFE	**F-100**	**11260**
G-UKFF	**F-100**	**11274**
G-UKFG	**F-100**	**11275**
G-UKFH	**F-100**	**11277**
G-UKFI	**F-100**	**11279**
G-UKFJ	**F-100**	**11248**
G-UKFK	**F-100**	**11249**
G-UKHP	**146**	**E3123**
G-UKID	**146**	**E3157**
G-UKJF	**146**	**E1011**
G-UKLA	B737	23865
G-UKLB	B737	24344
G-UKLC	**B737**	**24231**
G-UKLD	**B737**	**24232**
G-UKLE	B737	24468
G-UKLF	**B737**	**24813**
G-UKLG	**B737**	**24814**
G-UKLH	**B767**	**26256**
G-UKLI	**B767**	**26257**
G-UKLJ	**A320**	
G-UKLK	A320	0190
G-UKLL	A320	0343
G-UKLN	146	E2069
G-UKPC	146	E1010
G-UKRC	**146**	**E3158**
G-UKRH	146	E2077
G-UKSC	**146**	**E3125**
G-VAEL	**A340**	**015**
G-VBIG	**B747**	**26255**
G-VBUS	**A340**	**013**
G-VFAB	**B747**	**24958**
G-VFLY	**A340**	**058**
G-VGIN	**B747**	**19732**
G-VHOT	**B747**	**26326**
G-VIIA	**B777**	**27843**
G-VIIB	**B777**	**27844**
G-VIIC	**B777**	**27845**
G-VIID	**B777**	**27846**
G-VIIE	**B777**	**27847**
G-VIIF	**B777**	**27848**
G-VIIG	**B777**	**27849**
G-VIIH	**B777**	**27850**
G-VIIJ	**B777**	**27851**
G-VIRG	**B747**	**21189**
G-VJFK	**B747**	**20842**
G-VLAX	**B747**	**20921**
G-VMIA	**B747**	**20108**
G-VOYG	**B747**	**20121**
G-VRGN	B747	21937
G-VSKY	**A340**	**016**
G-WAUS	146	E2008
G-WGEL	B737	22161
G-WIND	B707	18689
G-WISC	146	E2008
G-WLAD	1-11	BAC.112
G-WLCY	**146**	**E2030**
G-WWJC	F-28	11133
G-XAIR	146	E2235
G-XIAN	146	E1019
G-YJBM	**A320**	**0362**
G-YMRU	1-11	BAC.110

G-ZAPK	**146**	**E2148**
G-ZZZA	**B777**	**27105**
G-ZZZB	**B777**	**27106**
G-ZZZC	**B777**	**27107**
G-ZZZD	**B777**	**27108**
G-ZZZE	**B777**	**27109**
(G-ZZZF)	B777	27843
(G-ZZZG)	B777	27844
(G-ZZZH)	B777	27845
(G-ZZZI)	B777	27846
(G-ZZZJ)	B777	27847
(G-ZZZK)	B777	27848
(G-ZZZL)	B777	27849
(G-ZZZM)	B777	27850
(G-ZZZN)	B777	27851
(G-ZZZP)	B777	27853

Georgia

GR-65080	TU134	60065
GR-85547	TU154	547
GR-87754	YAK40	9..0911

Hungary

HA-	**F-70**	**11583**
HA-924	TU134	0350924
HA-925	TU134	0350925
HA-926	TU134	12096
HA-927	TU134	17103
HA-LBA	TU134	8350604
HA-LBB	TU134	8350605
HA-LBC	TU134	8350605
HA-LBD	TU134	8350801
HA-LBE	**TU134**	**8350802**
HA-LBF	**TU134**	**0350923**
HA-LBG	**TU134**	**0350924**
HA-LBH	**TU134**	**0350925**
HA-LBI	**TU134**	**1351301**
HA-LBK	**TU134**	**1351302**
HA-LBN	**TU134**	**12096**
HA-LBO	**TU134**	**17103**
HA-LBP	**TU134**	**63560**
HA-LBR	**TU134**	**63580**
HA-LBS	TU134	09074
HA-LCA	**TU154**	**045**
HA-LCB	**TU154**	**046**
HA-LCE	**TU154**	**047**
HA-LCF	TU154	126
HA-LCG	**TU154**	**127**
HA-LCH	**TU154**	**128**
HA-LCI	TU154	053
HA-LCK	TU154	054
HA-LCL	TU154	051
HA-LCM	**TU154**	**325**
HA-LCN	**TU154**	**326**
HA-LCO	**TU154**	**473**
HA-LCP	**TU154**	**474**
HA-LCR	**TU154**	**543**
HA-LCS	TU154	530
HA-LCT	TU154	542
HA-LCU	**TU154**	**531**
HA-LCV	**TU154**	**544**
HA-LEA	**B737**	**21735**
HA-LEB	**B737**	**22090**
HA-LEC	**B737**	**22979**
HA-LED	**B737**	**24909**
HA-LEF	**B737**	**24914**
HA-LEG	**B737**	**24916**
HA-LEH	B737	22453
HA-LEI	**B737**	**22803**
HA-LEJ	**B737**	**26303**
HA-LEK	**B737**	**23404**
HA-LEM	**B737**	**22804**
HA-LEN	**B737**	**26069**
HA-LEO	**B737**	**26071**
HA-LHA	**B767**	**27048**
HA-LHB	**B767**	**27049**
HA-LHC	B767	25864
HA-LIA	IL-62	4933456
HA-LJA	YAK40	9510340
HA-LJB	**YAK40**	**9640851**
HA-LJC	YAK40	9440937
HA-LMA	**F-70**	**11564**
HA-LMB	**F-70**	**11565**
HA-LMC	**F-70**	**11569**
HA-LRA	**YAK40**	**9440837**
HA-TAB	146	E2105
HA-TCA	IL-76	1013409303
HA-TCB	**IL-76**	**1013408257**
HA-YLR	**YAK40**	**9541044**
HA-YSA	TU134	12096
HA-YSB	TU134	17103

Switzerland

HB-	**A320**	**0577**
HB-AAS	**F-28**	**11110**
HB-IAA	DC-9	45702
HB-IBF	DC-8	46141
HB-ICA	CV990	30-10-7
HB-ICB	CV990	30-10-11
HB-ICC	**CV990**	**30-10-12(2)**
HB-ICD	CV990	30-10-15
HB-ICE	CV990	30-10-14
HB-ICF	CV990	30-10-6
HB-ICG	CV990	30-10-8
HB-ICH	CV990	30-10-17
HB-ICI	CRVL	250
HB-ICJ	**CRVL**	**169**
HB-ICK	CRVL	200
HB-ICL	CV880	22-00-43M
HB-ICM	CV880	22-00-45M
HB-ICN	CRVL	253
HB-ICO	CRVL	255
HB-ICP	CRVL	234
HB-ICQ	CRVL	222
HB-ICR	CRVL	119
HB-ICS	CRVL	121
HB-ICT	CRVL	122
HB-ICU	CRVL	123
HB-ICV	CRVL	147
HB-ICW	CRVL	33
HB-ICX	CRVL	38
HB-ICY	CRVL	43
HB-ICZ	CRVL	48
HB-IDA	DC-8	45416
HB-IDB	DC-8	45417
HB-IDC	DC-8	45526
HB-IDD	DC-8	45656
"HB-IDD"	B707	18457
HB-IDE	DC-8	45919
HB-IDF	DC-8	45920
HB-IDG	DC-8	45925
HB-IDH	DC-8	45984
HB-IDI	DC-8	46077
HB-IDK	DC-8	46078
HB-IDL	DC-8	46134
HB-IDM	DC-8	46001
HB-IDN	DC-9	47465
HB-IDO	DC-9	47480
HB-IDP	DC-9	47523
HB-IDR	DC-9	47535
HB-IDS	DC-8	45968
HB-IDT	DC-9	47711
HB-IDU	DC-8	45817
HB-IDV	DC-9	47116
(HB-IDV)	DC-9	47114
HB-IDW	DC-9	47115
HB-IDX	DC-9	47117
HB-IDY	DC-9	47395
HB-IDZ	DC-8	46074
HB-IEE	**B757**	**24527**
HB-IEF	DC-9	45702
HB-IEG	B707	17671
HB-IEH	**B737**	**22431**
HB-IEI	B707	19521
HB-IFA	DC-9	45731
HB-IFB	DC-9	45732
HB-IFC	DC-9	45785
HB-IFD	DC-9	45786
HB-IFE	DC-9	45787
HB-IFF	DC-9	45788
HB-IFG	DC-9	45789
HB-IFH	DC-9	45790
HB-IFI	DC-9	45791
HB-IFK	DC-9	45792
HB-IFL	DC-9	45793
HB-IFM	DC-9	45847

HB-IFN	DC-9	47094
HB-IFO	DC-9	47110
HB-IFP	DC-9	47111
HB-IFR	DC-9	47112
HB-IFS	DC-9	47113
HB-IFT	DC-9	47281
HB-IFU	DC-9	47282
HB-IFV	DC-9	47383
HB-IFW	DC-9	47384
HB-IFX	DC-9	47218
HB-IFY	DC-9	47219
HB-IFZ	DC-9	47479
HB-IGA	B747	20116
HB-IGB	B747	20117
HB-IGC	**B747**	**22704**
(HB-IGC)	B747	20118
HB-IGD	**B747**	**22705**
(HB-IGD)	B747	20119
HB-IGE	**B747**	**22995**
(HB-IGE)	B747	22706
HB-IGF	**B747**	**22996**
(HB-IGF)	B747	22707
HB-IGG	**B747**	**23751**
(HB-IGG)	B747	22708
(HB-IGG)	B747	22997
(HB-IGI)	DC-10	46577
(HB-IGL)	DC-10	46579
(HB-IGM)	DC-10	46580
HB-IHA	DC-10	46575
HB-IHB	DC-10	46576
HB-IHC	DC-10	46577
HB-IHD	DC-10	46578
HB-IHE	DC-10	46579
HB-IHF	DC-10	46580
HB-IHG	DC-10	46581
HB-IHH	DC-10	46582
HB-IHI	DC-10	46969
HB-IHK	DC-10	46998
HB-IHL	DC-10	46583
HB-IHM	DC-10	46584
HB-IHN	DC-10	48292
HB-IHO	DC-10	48293
HB-IHP	DC-10	46868
HB-IHU	B757	24527
HB-IIA	**B737**	**24023**
HB-IIB	**B737**	**24024**
HB-IIC	**B737**	**25016**
HB-IID	**B737**	**24255**
HB-IIE	**B737**	**26307**
HB-IJA	**A320**	**0533**
HB-IJB	**A320**	**0545**
HB-IJC	**A320**	**0548**
HB-IJD	**A320**	**0553**
HB-IJE	**A320**	**0559**
HB-IJF	**A320**	**0562**
HB-IJG	**A320**	**0566**
HB-IJH	**A320**	**0574**
HB-IKB	DC-9	47430
HB-IKC	DC-9	47468
HB-IKD	CRVL	249
HB-IKF	DC-9	47714
HB-IKG	DC-9	47715
HB-IKH	DC-9	47713
HB-IKK	MD-82	49247
HB-IKL	MD-82	49248
HB-IKM	**MD-83**	**49935**
HB-IKN	**MD-83**	**49951**
HB-INA	**MD-81**	**49100**
(HB-INA)	MD-81	48000
HB-INB	**MD-82**	**49101**
(HB-INB)	MD-81	48001
HB-INC	**MD-81**	**48002**
HB-IND	**MD-81**	**48003**
HB-INE	**MD-81**	**48004**
HB-INF	**MD-81**	**48005**
HB-ING	MD-81	48006
HB-INH	MD-81	48007
HB-INI	MD-81	48008
HB-INK	MD-81	48009
HB-INL	MD-81	48010
HB-INM	**MD-81**	**48011**
HB-INN	**MD-81**	**48012**
HB-INO	**MD-81**	**48013**
HB-INP	**MD-81**	**48014**
HB-INR	**MD-81**	**49277**
HB-INS	**MD-81**	**49356**
HB-INT	**MD-81**	**49357**
HB-INU	**MD-81**	**49358**
HB-INV	**MD-81**	**49359**
HB-INW	**MD-82**	**49569**
HB-INX	**MD-81**	**49570**
HB-INY	**MD-81**	**49571**
HB-INZ	**MD-81**	**49572**
HB-IOA	**A321**	**0517**
HB-IOB	**A321**	**0519**
HB-IOC	**A321**	**0520**
HB-IOD	**A321**	**0522**
HB-IOE	**A321**	**0535**
HB-IOF	**A321**	**0541**
HB-IPA	A310	224
HB-IPB	A310	251
HB-IPC	A310	217
HB-IPD	A310	260
HB-IPE	A310	162
HB-IPF	**A310**	**399**
(HB-IPF)	A310	172
HB-IPG	**A310**	**404**
HB-IPH	**A310**	**409**
HB-IPI	**A310**	**410**
HB-IPK	**A310**	**412**
HB-IPL	**A310**	**640**
HB-IPM	**A310**	**642**
HB-IPN	**A310**	**672**
HB-IPX	**A319**	**578**
HB-IPY	**A319**	**588**
HB-ISK	DC-9	47654
HB-ISL	DC-9	47655
HB-ISM	DC-9	47656
HB-ISN	DC-9	47657
HB-ISO	DC-9	47658
HB-ISP	DC-9	47659
HB-ISR	DC-9	47660
HB-ISS	DC-9	47661
HB-IST	DC-9	47662
HB-ISU	DC-9	47663
HB-ISV	DC-9	47783
HB-ISW	DC-9	47784
HB-ISX	**MD-81**	**49844**
HB-ISZ	**MD-83**	**49930**
HB-ITK	1-11	BAC.166
HB-ITL	1-11	BAC.212
HB-IUA	MD-87	49585
HB-IUB	MD-87	49586
HB-IUC	MD-87	49587
HB-IUD	MD-87	49641
HB-IUG	**MD-81**	**53149**
HB-IUH	**MD-81**	**53150**
HB-IUI	MD-83	49710
HB-IUK	**MD-83**	**49398**
HB-IUL	**MD-83**	**49442**
HB-IVA	**F-100**	**11244**
HB-IVB	**F-100**	**11250**
HB-IVC	**F-100**	**11251**
HB-IVD	**F-100**	**11252**
HB-IVE	**F-100**	**11253**
HB-IVF	**F-100**	**11254**
HB-IVG	**F-100**	**11255**
HB-IVH	**F-100**	**11256**
HB-IVI	**F-100**	**11381**
HB-IVK	**F-100**	**11386**
HB-IWA	**MD-11**	**48443**
HB-IWB	**MD-11**	**48444**
HB-IWC	**MD-11**	**48445**
HB-IWD	**MD-11**	**48446**
HB-IWE	**MD-11**	**48447**
HB-IWF	**MD-11**	**48448**
HB-IWG	**MD-11**	**48452**
HB-IWH	**MD-11**	**48453**
HB-IWI	**MD-11**	**48454**
HB-IWK	**MD-11**	**48455**
HB-IWL	**MD-11**	**48456**
HB-IWM	**MD-11**	**48457**
HB-IWN	**MD-11**	**48539**
HB-IWO	**MD-11**	**48540**
HB-IWP	**MD-11**	**48541**
HB-IXB	146	E2036
HB-IXC	146	E2072
HB-IXD	146	E2073
HB-IXF	**146**	**E2226**
HB-IXG	**146**	**E2231**
HB-IXH	**146**	**E2233**
HB-IXK	**146**	**E2235**
HB-IXQ	**146**	**E3282**
HB-IXR	**146**	**E3281**
HB-IXS	**146**	**E3280**
HB-IXT	**146**	**E3259**
HB-IXU	**146**	**E3276**
HB-IXV	**146**	**E3274**
HB-IXW	**146**	**E3272**
HB-IXX	**146**	**E3262**
HB-IXY	146	E3163
HB-IXZ	**146**	**E3118**

Ecuador

HC-ALT	COMET	6428
HC-AZP	B720	18036
HC-AZQ	B720	18037
HC-BAD	**CRVL**	**35**
HC-BAE	CRVL	40
HC-BAI	CRVL	82
HC-BAJ	**CRVL**	**117**
HC-BAT	CRVL	125
HC-BCT	**B707**	**19265**
HC-BDP	B720	18033
HC-BDS	CRVL	146
HC-BEI	**DC-8**	**45606**
HC-BFC	B707	19277
HC-BFM	CRVL	156
HC-BFN	CRVL	137
HC-BFN	**CRVL**	**166**
HC-BGP	**B707**	**19273**
HC-BHM	**B727**	**22078**
HC-BHY	**B707**	**20033**
HC-BIB	B727	20513
HC-BIC	B727	20328
HC-BIG	B737	22607
HC-BJL	**B727**	**19596**
HC-BJT	DC-8	45858
HC-BKN	DC-8	45754
HC-BKO	**DC-10**	**46575**
HC-BLE	**B727**	**19691**
HC-BLF	**B727**	**19692**
HC-BLM	DC-8	45640
HC-BLU	DC-8	45668
HC-BLV	**B727**	**20328**
HC-BLY	**B707**	**18709**
HC-BMC	DC-8	45640
HC-BMD	**F-28**	**11220**
HC-BPL	**B727**	**18753**
HC-BPV	**DC-8**	**45651**
HC-BQH	DC-8	45860
HC-BRA	A310	574
HC-BRB	A310	576
HC-BRF	B727	19388
HC-BRG	**B727**	**20973**
(HC-BRG)	B727	20268
HC-BRI	**B727**	**20560**
HC-BRP	**A310**	**598**
HC-BSC	**B727**	**20788**
HC-BSF	**A310**	**661**
HC-BSP	B727	19393
HC-BSU	**B727**	**21622**
HC-BTB	**B707**	**18937**
HC-BTI	B737	21130
HC-BTV	A320	0405
HC-BUH	**A320**	**0425**
HC-BUI	**A320**	**0527**
HC-BUM	**A320**	**0530**

Haiti

HH-JEC	B727	18743
HH-JJD	B727	19393
HH-PRI	B727	18742
HH-SMA	**CV880**	**22-00-17**

Dominican Republic

(HI-148)	1-11	BAC.114
HI-177	DC-9	47500
HI-212	B727	20426
HI-212CT	**B727**	**20426**
HI-242	B727	21036
HI-242CT	**B727**	**21036**
HI-312	B727	19505
HI-312CT	B727	19505
HI-372	B720	17915
HI-384	B707	17610
HI-384HA	**B707**	**17610**
HI-401	B720	18049
HI-413	DC-8	45387
HI-415	B720	18072
HI-426	DC-8	45667
HI-426CA	DC-8	45667
HI-426CT	DC-8	45667
HI-427	DC-8	45684
HI-435	DC-8	45416
HI-442	B707	19767
HI-442CT	**B707**	**19767**
HI-452	B727	21021
HI-452	DC-8	45410
HI-452CA	DC-8	45410
HI-459	DC-8	45640
HI-472	B747	20104
HI-499	**CRVL**	**154**
HI-573CA	DC-8	45765
HI-576CT	DC-8	46110
HI-588CA	DC-8	45685
HI-588CT	DC-8	45685
HI-596CA	B707	18716
HI-606CA	B727	20267
HI-612CA	B727	20302
HI-616CA	B727	20726
HI-617CA	B727	20726
HI-629CA	B727	22441
HI-630CA	B727	19991
HI-637CA	B727	20267
HI-656CA	**B727**	**19970**
HI-659	A310	594
HI-659CA	**A310**	**594**
HI-660CA	**B767**	**23280**

Colombia

HK-	**DC-9**	**45712**
HK-676	B720	18059
HK-677	B720	18057
HK-723	B720	18061
HK-724	B720	18086
HK-725	B720	18087
HK-726	B720	18831
HK-727	**B727**	**19127**
HK-749	**B720**	**18248**
HK-1271	**B727**	**19524**
HK-1272	B727	19525
HK-1273	**B727**	**19526**
HK-1337	**B727**	**19303**
HK-1400	B727	19662
HK-1400X	B727	19662
HK-1401	B727	19663
HK-1401X	B727	19663
HK-1402	B707	19741
HK-1403	B737	19679
HK-1404	B737	19680
HK-1410	B707	20340
HK-1709X	**CRVL**	**133**
HK-1716	B727	18999
HK-1717	**B727**	**18993**
HK-1718	B707	18714
HK-1718X	B707	18714
HK-1773	B707	17671
HK-1778	CRVL	140
HK-1779	**CRVL**	**164**
HK-1780	**CRVL**	**160**
HK-1802	B707	17638
HK-1802X	B707	17638
HK-1803	B727	19035
HK-1804	**B727**	**19037**
HK-1810	CRVL	165
HK-1811	**CRVL**	**138**
HK-1811X	CRVL	138
HK-1812	**CRVL**	**109**
HK-1812X	CRVL	109
HK-1818	B707	17637
HK-1818X	B707	17637
HK-1849	B707	18766
HK-1854	**DC-8**	**45636**
HK-1855X	DC-8	45665
HK-1942	B707	17643

HK-1942X	B707	17643
HK-1973	B720	18023
HK-1974	B720	18028
HK-2000	B747	19734
HK-2000X	B747	19734
HK-2015	B707	19361
HK-2016	B707	19276
HK-2057	A300	29
HK-2057X	A300	29
HK-2070	B707	19266
HK-2070X	B707	19266
HK-2151X	**B727**	**21343**
HK-2152X	**B727**	**21344**
HK-2212	**CRVL**	**131**
HK-2212X	CRVL	131
HK-2287X	**CRVL**	**168**
HK-2300	B747	21730
HK-2380	DC-8	45879
HK-2400X	B747	19735
HK-2401X	B707	18707
HK-2402X	**CRVL**	**161**
HK-2410	B707	17605
HK-2410X	B707	17605
HK-2420X	B727	18874
HK-2421X	B727	18875
HK-2422X	B727	18876
HK-2473	B707	19375
HK-2473X	B707	19375
HK-2474	B727	19099
(HK-2474)	B727	22474
HK-2475	B727	19094
(HK-2475)	B727	22475
HK-2476	B727	19102
(HK-2476)	B727	22476
HK-2477X	B707	17602
HK-2541	**B727**	**18281**
HK-2558	B720	18060
HK-2558X	B720	18060
HK-2559	B727	18994
HK-2560X	B727	18996
HK-2587X	**DC-8**	**45635**
HK-2597X	**CRVL**	**136**
HK-2598X	**CRVL**	**167**
HK-2600	B707	18886
HK-2600X	B707	18886
HK-2604	B727	18287
HK-2604X	B727	18287
HK-2605X	B727	20217
HK-2606	B707	18709
HK-2606X	B707	18709
HK-2632X	**DC-8**	**45768**
HK-2637	B727	19815
HK-2667	DC-8	45651
HK-2705	B727	18282
HK-2705X	B727	18282
HK-2717	B727	18252
HK-2717X	B727	18252
HK-2744X	B727	18266
HK-2833	B727	18321
HK-2833X	B727	18321
HK-2842	C-137	19575
HK-2845	B727	19005
HK-2846X	B727	19007
HK-2850X	CRVL	261
HK-2860	**CRVL**	**223**
HK-2864X	DC-9	45721
HK-2865X	**DC-9**	**45722**
HK-2900	B747	19733
HK-2910	B747	21381
HK-2910X	B747	21381
HK-2957	B727	18896
HK-2957X	B727	18896
HK-2960	B727	19249
HK-2960X	B727	19249
HK-2980X	B747	21730
HK-3030X	**B707**	**18808**
HK-3125X	**DC-8**	**45809**
HK-3126X	F-28	11085
HK-3133X	B727	18895
HK-3151	B727	19122
HK-3151X	B727	19122
HK-3168X	B727	18858
HK-3178X	**DC-8**	**45416**
HK-3201X	B727	18877
HK-3203	B727	18845
HK-3203X	B727	18845
HK-3212X	B727	18846
HK-3229X	B727	18814
HK-3232X	**B707**	**18717**
HK-3246X	**B727**	**19280**
HK-3270X	B727	18877
HK-3288X	CRVL	219
HK-3325X	CRVL	215
HK-3333X	**B707**	**18714**
HK-3355X	**B707**	**18886**
HK-3384X	B727	18879
HK-3396X	B727	18997
HK-3421X	B727	20432
HK-3442X	B727	18742
HK-3458X	B727	18877
HK-3480X	**B727**	**20739**
HK-3483X	B727	19499
HK-3486X	DC-9	47125
HK-3490X	DC-8	46041
HK-3564X	DC-9	47127
HK-3588X	B727	18743
HK-3599X	B727	18879
HK-3604X	B707	19352
HK-3605X	B727	20434
HK-3606X	B727	20433
HK-3612X	B727	19281
HK-3618X	B727	22702
HK-3651X	B727	18743
HK-3667X	**B727**	**19430**
HK-3676X	CRVL	232
HK-3710X	DC-9	45780
HK-3720X	**DC-9**	**45783**
HK-3738X	**B727**	**21997**
HK-3739X	**B727**	**20418**
HK-3745	**B727**	**20420**
HK-3745X	B727	20420
HK-3746X	**DC-8**	**45632**
HK-3752X	**DC-9**	**45781**
HK-3753X	**DC-8**	**45765**
HK-3756X	**CRVL**	**259**
HK-3770X	**B727**	**19242**
HK-3771X	B727	19595
HK-3785X	**DC-8**	**46066**
HK-3786X	**DC-8**	**45849**
HK-3795X	DC-9	45776
HK-3798X	**B727**	**18969**
HK-3803X	B727	19122
HK-3806	**CRVL**	**257**
HK-3808X	AN-72	36572094889
HK-3809X	AN-74	36547095903
HK-3810X	AN-74	36547096919
HK-3814X	**B727**	**19281**
HK-3816X	**DC-8**	**45685**
HK-3827X	**DC-9**	**47048**
HK-3830X	DC-9	45715
HK-3832X	DC-9	45735
HK-3833X	**DC-9**	**45716**
HK-3834X	B727	22759
HK-3835X	CRVL	182
HK-3836	**CRVL**	**211**
HK-3836X	CRVL	211
HK-3837X	**CRVL**	**250**
HK-3839X	DC-9	45742
HK-3840X	**B727**	**18879**
HK-3841X	**B727**	**18270**
HK-3842X	**DC-8**	**45985**
HK-3843X	B727	19499
HK-3845X	**B727**	**19534**
HK-3855X	CRVL	265
HK-3857X	**CRVL**	**268**
HK-3858X	**CRVL**	**212**
HK-3867X	DC-9	45735
HK-3869X	**CRVL**	**232**
HK-3870X	**B727**	**20422**
HK-3871X	**B727**	**19973**
HK-3872X	**B727**	**20303**
HK-3891X	**DC-9**	**45843**
HK-3905X	**DC-9**	**47399**
HK-3906X	**DC-9**	**47401**
HK-3914X	CRVL	188
HK-3926X	**DC-9**	**47231**
HK-3927X	**DC-9**	**47519**
HK-3928X	**DC-9**	**47311**
HK-3932X	**CRVL**	**201**
HK-3933X	**B727**	**19165**
HK-3947X	**CRVL**	**188**
HK-3948X	**CRVL**	**255**
HK-3955X	**CRVL**	**189**
HK-3958X	**DC-9**	**45738**
HK-3962X	CRVL	184
HK-3963X	**DC-9**	**47437**
HK-3964X	**DC-9**	**47434**
HK-3973X	**B727**	**19838**
HK-3977X	**B727**	**20548**
HK-3979X	DC-8	45882
HK-3984X	**DC-8**	**45862**
HK-3998X	**B727**	**20620**
HK-4010X	**B727**	**21267**
HK-4047	**B727**	**21458**

South Korea

HL	**MD-83**	**53485**
HL7201	DC-9	45827
HL7203	**MD-82**	**53147**
HL7204	**MD-82**	**53148**
HL7205	DC-9	45787
HL7206	**F-100**	**11378**
HL7207	**F-100**	**11387**
HL7208	**F-100**	**11388**
HL7209	**F-100**	**11432**
HL7210	**F-100**	**11438**
HL7211	**F-100**	**11439**
HL7212	**F-100**	**11476**
HL7213	**F-100**	**11504**
HL7214	**F-100**	**11513**
HL7215	**F-100**	**11519**
HL7216	**F-100**	**11522**
HL7217	**F-100**	**11523**
HL7218	**A300**	**14**
HL7219	**A300**	**16**
HL7220	**A300**	**18**
HL7221	**A300**	**24**
HL7223	**A300**	**28**
HL7224	**A300**	**30**
HL7225	**MD-82**	**53467**
HL7227	**B737**	**25764**
HL7228	**B737**	**25765**
HL7229	B737	24805
HL7230	**B737**	**24778**
HL7231	**B737**	**25766**
HL7232	**B737**	**25767**
HL7233	**B737**	**25768**
HL7235	**B737**	**26308**
HL7236	**MD-82**	**53468**
HL7237	**MD-82**	**53469**
HL7238	**A300**	**31**
HL7239	**A300**	**627**
HL7240	**A300**	**631**
HL7241	**A300**	**662**
HL7242	**A300**	**685**
HL7243	**A300**	**692**
HL7244	**A300**	**722**
HL7245	**A300**	**731**
HL7246	**A300**	**81**
HL7247	**B767**	**25757**
HL7248	**B767**	**25758**
HL7249	**B767**	**26265**
HL7250	**B737**	**25769**
HL7251	**B737**	**23869**
HL7252	**B737**	**23976**
HL7253	**B737**	**23977**
HL7254	**B737**	**23978**
HL7255	**B737**	**23980**
HL7256	**B737**	**24314**
HL7257	**B737**	**24469**
HL7258	**B737**	**24493**
HL7259	**B737**	**24494**
HL7260	**B737**	**24520**
HL7261	**B737**	**24786**
HL7262	**B737**	**24787**
HL7263	**B767**	**24797**
HL7264	**B767**	**24798**
HL7265	F-28	11203
HL7266	**B767**	**25347**
HL7267	**B767**	**25404**
HL7268	**B767**	**25132**
HL7269	**B767**	**26206**
HL7270	F-28	11219
HL7271	MD-83	49785
HL7272	**MD-82**	**49373**
HL7273	**MD-82**	**49374**
HL7274	MD-83	49787
HL7275	**MD-82**	**49416**
HL7276	**MD-82**	**49417**
HL7278	**A300**	**277**
HL7279	**A300**	**292**
HL7280	**A300**	**361**
HL7281	**A300**	**365**
HL7282	**MD-82**	**49418**
HL7283	**MD-82**	**49419**
HL7284	F-28	11223
HL7285	F-28	11221
HL7286	**B767**	**26207**
HL7287	**A300**	**358**
HL7288	**A300**	**477**
HL7289	**A300**	**479**
HL7290	**A300**	**388**
HL7291	**A300**	**417**
HL7292	**A300**	**543**
HL7293	**A300**	**554**
HL7294	**A300**	**560**
HL7295	**A300**	**582**
HL7296	A300	583
HL7297	**A300**	**609**
HL7298	**A300**	**614**
HL7299	**A300**	**717**
HL7307	B727	18875
HL7308	B727	18874
HL7309	B727	18876
HL7315	**DC-10**	**46934**
HL7316	**DC-10**	**46912**
HL7317	**DC-10**	**46915**
HL7328	DC-10	47887
HL7329	DC-10	48316
HL7336	B727	18321
HL7337	B727	18323
HL7339	DC-10	46960
HL7348	B727	20435
HL7349	B727	20468
HL7350	B727	20469
HL7351	B727	20572
HL7352	B727	20573
HL7353	B727	20728
HL7354	**B727**	**21455**
HL7355	B727	20466
HL7356	**B727**	**21456**
HL7357	**B727**	**21474**
HL7366	B727	20725
HL7367	B727	20571
HL7371	**MD-11**	**48407**
HL7372	**MD-11**	**48408**
HL7373	**MD-11**	**48409**
HL7374	**MD-11**	**48410**
HL7375	**MD-11**	**48523**
HL7401	**B747**	**22245**
HL7402	**B720**	**18160**
HL7403	B720	18164
HL7406	B707	20522
HL7410	B747	20770
HL7411	B747	20771
HL7412	B707	19715
HL7413	**B747**	**25405**
HL7414	**B747**	**25452**
HL7415	**B747**	**25777**
HL7416	**B747**	**25778**
HL7417	**B747**	**25779**
HL7418	**B747**	**25780**
HL7419	**B747**	**25781**
HL7420	**B747**	**25783**
HL7421	**B747**	**25784**
HL7425	B707	19716
HL7427	B707	19372
HL7429	B707	19363
HL7430	B707	18337
HL7431	B707	19369
HL7432	E-8	19626
HL7433	B707	19628
HL7435	B707	19366
HL7440	B747	20372
HL7441	**B747**	**20373**
HL7442	B747	20559
HL7443	**B747**	**21772**
HL7445	B747	21773
HL7447	B747	20493
HL7451	**B747**	**22480**
HL7452	**B747**	**22481**
HL7453	**B747**	**21938**

HL7454	**B747**	**22482**
HL7456	**B747**	**22483**
HL7457	**B747**	**22484**
HL7458	**B747**	**22485**
HL7459	**B747**	**22486**
HL7463	**B747**	**20770**
HL7464	**B747**	**20771**
(HL7466)	B747	22487
(HL7467)	B747	22489
HL7468	**B747**	**22487**
HL7469	**B747**	**22489**
HL7470	**B747**	**24194**
HL7471	**B747**	**20652**
HL7474	**B747**	**22169**
HL7475	**B747**	**24195**
HL7476	**B747**	**24196**
HL7477	**B747**	**24198**
HL7478	**B747**	**24199**
HL7479	**B747**	**24200**
HL7480	**B747**	**24619**
HL7481	**B747**	**24621**
HL7482	**B747**	**25205**
(HL7482)	B747	24620
HL7483	**B747**	**25275**
HL7484	**B747**	**26392**
HL7485	**B747**	**26395**
HL7486	**B747**	**26396**
HL7487	**B747**	**26393**
HL7488	**B747**	**26394**
HL7489	**B747**	**27072**
HL7490	**B747**	**27177**
HL7491	**B747**	**27341**
HL7492	**B747**	**26397**
HL7493	**B747**	**26398**
HL7494	**B747**	**27662**
HL7495	**B747**	**28096**
HL7496	**B747**	**26400**
HL7497	**B747**	**26401**
HL7498	**B747**	**26402**
HL7505	**B767**	**27394**
HL7507	**B767**	**25761**
HL7508	**B737**	**25772**
HL7509	**B737**	**28198**
HL7510	**B737**	**25771**
HL7580	**A300**	**756**
HL7581	**A300**	**762**

Panama

HP-	**B727**	**18435**
HP-	**B727**	**20465**
HP-500	B727	19815
HP-500A	**B727**	**18894**
HP-500A	B727	19815
HP-505	DC-9	45786
HP-619	B727	18920
HP-619API	**B727**	**18920**
HP-620	B727	18951
HP-661	B727	19280
(HP-679)	B720	18080
HP-685	B720	18044
HP-756	B707	17591
HP-760	B707	17589
HP-768	DC-8	45806
HP-792	B707	17589
HP-793	B707	17589
HP-794	B707	17591
HP-807	B707	17590
HP-807	DC-8	45660
HP-821	CV880	22-00-41
HP-826	DC-8	45298
HP-855	B707	17928
(HP-870)	B707	17587
HP-873	B737	19768
HP-873CMP	**B737**	**19768**
HP-876	CV880	22-00-52
HP-876P	**CV880**	**22-00-52**
HP-927	DC-8	45804
HP-950	DC-8	45678
HP-1001	B727	19815
HP-1027	B707	18709
HP-1028	C-137	19575
HP-1038	B737	19771
HP-1048	DC-8	45259
HP-1063	B727	19110
HP-1088	DC-8	45817
HP-1134	B737	20253
HP-1134CMP	**B737**	**20253**
HP-1163CMP	**B737**	**21693**
HP-1166TCA	DC-8	45272
HP-1169TLN	DC-8	45992
HP-1179TLN	B727	18742
HP-1187LTN	B727	19393
HP-1195CMP	**B737**	**20806**
HP-1205CMP	B737	22059
HP-1216CMP	B737	20588
HP-1218CMP	B737	20670
HP-1229PFC	**B727**	**18429**
HP-1234CMP	**B737**	**22660**
HP-1235CTH	B707	19210
HP-1245	B737	22620
HP-1245CMP	**B737**	**22620**
HP-1255CMP	**B737**	**21359**
HP-1261PVI	**B727**	**18965**
HP-1288CMP	**B737**	**22088**
HP-1297CMP	**B737**	**21645**

Honduras

(HR-)	B737	22340
HR-ALZ	B727	18879
HR-AMA	B707	19964
HR-AMC	L1011	1029
HR-AME	B707	18922
HR-AMF	**B707**	**20316**
HR-AMG	B707	19335
HR-AMG	**B727**	**18849**
HR-AMI	**B727**	**19182**
HR-AMN	B707	20315
HR-AMO	**1-11**	**086**
HR-AMP	B707	20172
HR-AMQ	B707	20176
HR-AMR	**B727**	**19836**
HR-AMU	DC-8	45882
HR-AMV	B707	18839
HR-AMW	B707	20177
HR-AMX	B707	18716
HR-AMZ	**B707**	**18766**
HR-ANG	B707	19210
(HR-ANU)	B707	18766
HR-SHA	B737	20957
HR-SHD	B737	20222
HR-SHE	B727	18823
HR-SHF	B727	18919
HR-SHG	B737	19921
HR-SHH	B737	20956
HR-SHI	B737	20956
HR-SHJ	B737	20492
HR-SHK	B737	24691
HR-SHL	B737	24683
(HR-SHM)	B737	24692
HR-SHO	**B737**	**20299**
HR-SHP	B737	20582
HR-SHQ	B737	21359
HR-SHU	**B737**	**20128**
HR-TNR	B737	20299
HR-TNS	B737	20223

Thailand

HS-	**B737**	**20300**
(HS-BBA)	B707	17593
(HS-BBB)	B707	17603
HS-PTA	**B727**	**21246**
HS-PTB	**B727**	**20448**
HS-RTA	**B737**	**27906**
HS-TAA	**A300**	**368**
HS-TAB	**A300**	**371**
HS-TAC	**A300**	**377**
HS-TAD	**A300**	**384**
HS-TAE	**A300**	**395**
HS-TAF	**A300**	**398**
HS-TAG	**A300**	**464**
(HS-TAG)	A300	417
HS-TAH	**A300**	**518**
HS-TAK	**A300**	**566**
HS-TAL	**A300**	**569**
HS-TAM	**A300**	**577**
HS-TAN	**A300**	**628**
HS-TAO	**A300**	**629**
HS-TAP	**A300**	**635**
HS-TAR	**A300**	**681**
HS-TAS	**A300**	**705**
HS-TAX	A300	33
HS-TAY	A300	65
HS-TAZ	A300	66
HS-TBA	B737	21440
HS-TBB	B737	21810
HS-TBC	B737	22267
HS-TBD	B737	22667
HS-TBE	**B737**	**23113**
HS-TBJ	**146**	**E3191**
HS-TBK	146	E3128
HS-TBK	**146**	**E3185**
HS-TBL	146	E3131
HS-TBL	**146**	**E3181**
HS-TBM	146	E3129
HS-TBM	**146**	**E3206**
HS-TBN	146	E3149
HS-TBO	146	E1104
HS-TBO	**146**	**E3189**
HS-TBQ	146	E2074
HS-TDA	**B737**	**24830**
HS-TDB	**B737**	**24831**
HS-TDC	**B737**	**25321**
HS-TDD	**B737**	**26611**
HS-TDE	**B737**	**26612**
HS-TDF	**B737**	**26613**
HS-TDG	**B737**	**26614**
HS-TEA	**A330**	**050**
(HS-TEA)	A330	042
HS-TEB	**A330**	**060**
HS-TEC	**A330**	**062**
HS-TED	**A330**	**064**
HS-TEE	**A330**	**065**
HS-TEF	**A330**	**066**
HS-TEG	**A330**	**112**
HS-TEH	**A330**	**122**
HS-TGA	**B747**	**21782**
HS-TGA	DC-10	46851
HS-TGB	**B747**	**21783**
HS-TGB	DC-10	46892
HS-TGC	**B747**	**21784**
HS-TGC	DC-10	46952
HS-TGD	**B747**	**23721**
HS-TGD	DC-10	46959
(HS-TGD)	B747	22472
HS-TGE	**B747**	**23722**
HS-TGE	CV990	30-10-17
HS-TGE	DC-10	46961
HS-TGF	**B747**	**22337**
HS-TGF	CRVL	56
HS-TGF	DC-8	45949
HS-TGG	**B747**	**22471**
HS-TGG	CRVL	49
HS-TGG	DC-8	45952
HS-TGH	A300	33
HS-TGH	**B747**	**24458**
HS-TGH	CRVL	29
HS-TGI	CRVL	25
HS-TGJ	**B747**	**24459**
HS-TGK	A300	35
HS-TGK	**B747**	**24993**
HS-TGK	CRVL	34
HS-TGL	A300	54
HS-TGL	**B747**	**25366**
HS-TGL	CRVL	30
HS-TGM	A300	55
HS-TGM	**B747**	**27093**
HS-TGM	DC-9	47395
HS-TGN	A300	71
HS-TGN	**B747**	**26615**
HS-TGN	DC-9	47396
HS-TGO	A300	72
HS-TGO	**B747**	**26609**
HS-TGO	DC-8	45386
HS-TGP	A300	84
HS-TGP	**B747**	**26610**
HS-TGP	DC-8	45390
HS-TGQ	B737	24480
HS-TGQ	DC-8	45922
HS-TGQ	DC-8	46129
HS-TGQ	DC-8	46150
HS-TGR	A300	85
HS-TGR	**B747**	**27723**
HS-TGR	DC-8	45389
HS-TGS	**B747**	**22472**
HS-TGS	DC-8	45385
HS-TGS	DC-8	46150
HS-TGT	A300	141
HS-TGT	DC-8	45384
HS-TGU	DC-8	45526
HS-TGW	A300	149
HS-TGW	DC-8	45416
HS-TGX	A300	249
HS-TGX	DC-8	45923
HS-TGY	A300	265
HS-TGY	DC-8	46054
HS-TGZ	DC-8	45924
HS-TGZ	DC-8	46129
HS-THH	**A300**	**33**
HS-THK	**A300**	**35**
HS-THL	**A300**	**54**
HS-THM	**A300**	**55**
HS-THN	**A300**	**71**
HS-THO	**A300**	**72**
HS-THP	**A300**	**84**
HS-THR	**A300**	**85**
HS-THT	**A300**	**141**
HS-THW	**A300**	**149**
HS-THX	**A300**	**249**
HS-THY	**A300**	**265**
HS-TIA	**A310**	**415**
HS-TIC	**A310**	**424**
HS-TID	A310	438
HS-TIF	A310	441
HS-TJA	**B777**	**27726**
HS-TJB	**B777**	**27727**
HS-TJC	**B777**	**27728**
HS-TJD	**B777**	**27729**
HS-TMA	**DC-10**	**48267**
HS-TMB	**DC-10**	**48290**
HS-TMC	DC-10	46959
HS-TMC	**DC-10**	**48319**
HS-TMD	DC-10	46961
HS-TMD	**MD-11**	**48416**
HS-TME	**MD-11**	**48417**
HS-TMF	**MD-11**	**48418**
HS-TMG	**MD-11**	**48451**
HS-TYQ	**A310**	**591**
HS-VGA	B707	17666
HS-VGB	B747	19744
HS-VGC	B707	17663
HS-VGD	A300	08
HS-VGE	DC-10	47887
HS-VGF	B747	19745
(HS-VGF)	A300	09
HS-VGG	B747	20399

Saudi Arabia

HZ-122	B727	20533
HZ-123	**B707**	**17696**
HZ-AB1	1-11	BAC.158
HZ-AB3	**B727**	**22362**
HZ-ACA	B720	18165
HZ-ACB	B720	18166
HZ-ACC	B707	19809
HZ-ACD	B707	19810
HZ-ACE	B707	18582
HZ-ACF	B707	18583
HZ-ACG	B707	21103
HZ-ACH	B707	21104
HZ-ACJ	B707	21367
HZ-ACK	B707	21368
HZ-AEA	DC-9	47000
HZ-AEB	DC-9	47001
HZ-AEC	DC-9	47002
HZ-AGA	**B737**	**20574**
HZ-AGB	**B737**	**20575**
HZ-AGC	**B737**	**20576**
HZ-AGD	**B737**	**20577**
HZ-AGE	**B737**	**20578**
HZ-AGF	**B737**	**20882**
HZ-AGG	**B737**	**20883**
HZ-AGH	**B737**	**21275**
HZ-AGI	**B737**	**21276**
HZ-AGJ	**B737**	**21277**
HZ-AGK	**B737**	**21280**
HZ-AGL	**B737**	**21281**

HZ-AGM B737 21282
HZ-AGN B737 21283
HZ-AGO B737 21360
HZ-AGP B737 21361
HZ-AGQ B737 21362
HZ-AGR B737 21653
HZ-AGS B737 21654
HZ-AGT B737 22050
HZ-AHA L1011 1110
HZ-AHB L1011 1116
HZ-AHC L1011 1137
HZ-AHD L1011 1144
HZ-AHE L1011 1124
HZ-AHF L1011 1130
HZ-AHG L1011 1148
HZ-AHH L1011 1149
HZ-AHI L1011 1160
HZ-AHJ L1011 1161
HZ-AHK L1011 1169
HZ-AHL L1011 1170
HZ-AHM L1011 1171
HZ-AHN L1011 1175
HZ-AHO L1011 1187
HZ-AHP L1011 1190
HZ-AHQ L1011 1192
HZ-AHR L1011 1214
HZ-AIA B747 22498
HZ-AIB B747 22499
HZ-AIC B747 22500
HZ-AID B747 22501
HZ-AIE B747 22502
HZ-AIF B747 22503
HZ-AIG B747 22747
HZ-AIH B747 22748
HZ-AII B747 22749
HZ-AIJ B747 22750
HZ-AIK B747 23262
HZ-AIL B747 23263
HZ-AIM B747 23264
HZ-AIN B747 23265
HZ-AIO B747 23266
HZ-AIP B747 23267
HZ-AIQ B747 23268
HZ-AIR B747 23269
HZ-AIS B747 23270
HZ-AIT B747 23271
HZ-AIU B747 24359
HZ-AJA A300 284
HZ-AJB A300 294
HZ-AJC A300 301
HZ-AJD A300 307
HZ-AJE A300 312
HZ-AJF A300 317
HZ-AJG A300 321
HZ-AJH A300 336
HZ-AJI A300 341
HZ-AJJ A300 348
HZ-AJK A300 351
(HZ-AJL) A300 366
HZ-AMB 1-11 069
HZ-AMB2 1-11 060
HZ-AMH 1-11 BAC.158
HZ-AMH 1-11 BAC.183
HZ-AMH B727 19620
HZ-AMK 1-11 054
HZ-BL1 1-11 080
HZ-DA5 B727 21460
HZ-DAT B707 17644
HZ-DG1 B727 19124
HZ-GP2 1-11 060
(HZ-GP2) B727 20228
HZ-GRP 1-11 060
HZ-GRP 1-11 067
HZ-GRP B727 20228
HZ-HE4 B727 19987
HZ-HE5 L1011 1250
HZ-HM1 B707 21081
HZ-HM1 B747 21652
HZ-HM11 DC-8 46084
HZ-HM1B B747 21652
HZ-HM2 B707 21081
HZ-HM3 B707 21368
HZ-HM4 B737 22050
HZ-HM5 L1011 1250
(HZ-HM5) B707 21104
HZ-HM6 L1011 1249
HZ-HMED B757 25495
HZ-HMIA B747 23070
HZ-HR1 1-11 081
HZ-HR1 B727 21853
HZ-HR3 B727 22968
HZ-JAM 1-11 BAC.111
HZ-KA1 B720 18451
(HZ-KA1) B707 18740
HZ-KA4 B720 18453
HZ-KA7 1-11 BAC.260
HZ-KB1 1-11 BAC.158
HZ-MAA 1-11 060
HZ-MAJ 1-11 088
HZ-MAM 1-11 BAC.259
HZ-MF1 1-11 BAC.158
HZ-MFA 1-11 080
HZ-MIS B737 22600
HZ-MO1 1-11 BAC.135
HZ-MS11 DC-8 46084
HZ-NAA B720 18451
HZ-NB2 1-11 064
HZ-NB3 1-11 060
(HZ-ND1) 1-11 BAC.183
HZ-NIR 1-11 088
HZ-OCV B727 19006
HZ-RH1 1-11 081
HZ-RH3 B727 22968
HZ-SAK1 B707 18586
HZ-SIR B737 22601
HZ-TA1 1-11 078
HZ-TA1 B727 18365
HZ-TAS B707 18338
HZ-TBA B737 23468
HZ-TFA B727 19006
HZ-WBT B727 19252

Solomon Islands

H4-SAL B737 22395
H4-SOL B737 25163

Italy

(I-) B737 19594
I-AEJA B757 25133
I-AEJB B767 24358
I-AEJC B767 24357
(I-AEJD) B767 26387
(I-AEJE) B767 26388
I-ALEC DC-8 45682
I-ATIA DC-9 47431
I-ATIE DC-9 47436
I-ATIH DC-9 47553
I-ATIJ DC-9 47544
I-ATIK DC-9 47477
I-ATIO DC-9 47437
I-ATIQ DC-9 47591
I-ATIU DC-9 47438
I-ATIW DC-9 47533
I-ATIX DC-9 47474
I-ATIY DC-9 47575
I-ATJA DC-9 47641
I-ATJB DC-9 47653
I-ATJC DC-9 47667
I-ATSC 146 E3146
I-ATSD 146 E3159
(I-BIX.) A321 0586
(I-BIX.) A321 0593
(I-BIX.) A321 0599
I-BIXA A321 0477
I-BIXB A321 0524
I-BIXC A321 0526
I-BIXD A321 0532
I-BIXE A321 0488
I-BIXF A321 0515
I-BIXG A321 0516
I-BIXI A321 0494
I-BIXL A321 0513
I-BIXM A321 0514
I-BIXN A321 0576
I-BIXO A321 0495
I-BIXP A321 0583
I-BIXU A321 0434
I-BRJF B757 24772
I-BUSB A300 101
I-BUSC A300 106
I-BUSD A300 107
I-BUSF A300 123
I-BUSG A300 139
I-BUSH A300 140
I-BUSJ A300 142
I-BUSL A300 173
I-BUSM A300 49
I-BUSN A300 51
I-BUSP A300 67
I-BUSQ A300 118
I-BUSR A300 120
I-BUST A300 68
I-DABA CRVL 71
I-DABE CRVL 72
I-DABF CRVL 179
I-DABG CRVL 205
I-DABI CRVL 74
I-DABL CRVL 132
I-DABM CRVL 143
I-DABP CRVL 192
I-DABR CRVL 81
I-DABS CRVL 106
I-DABT CRVL 85
I-DABU CRVL 77
I-DABV CRVL 146
I-DABW CRVL 150
I-DABZ CRVL 82
I-DACM MD-82 49971
I-DACN MD-82 49972
I-DACP MD-82 49973
I-DACQ MD-82 49974
I-DACR MD-82 49975
I-DACS MD-82 53053
I-DACT MD-82 53054
I-DACU MD-82 53055
I-DACV MD-82 53056
I-DACW MD-82 53057
I-DACX MD-82 53060
I-DACY MD-82 53059
I-DACZ MD-82 53058
I-DAND MD-82 53061
I-DANF MD-82 53062
I-DANG MD-82 53176
I-DANH MD-82 53177
I-DANL MD-82 53178
I-DANM MD-82 53179
I-DANP MD-82 53180
I-DANQ MD-82 53181
I-DANR MD-82 53203
I-DANU MD-82 53204
I-DANV MD-82 53205
I-DANW MD-82 53206
I-DATA MD-82 53216
I-DATB MD-82 53221
I-DATC MD-82 53222
I-DATD MD-82 53223
I-DATE MD-82 53217
I-DATF MD-82 53224
I-DATG MD-82 53225
I-DATH MD-82 53226
I-DATI MD-82 53218
I-DATJ MD-82 53227
I-DATK MD-82 53228
I-DATL MD-82 53229
I-DATM MD-82 53230
I-DATN MD-82 53231
I-DATO MD-82 53219
I-DATP MD-82 53232
I-DATQ MD-82 53233
I-DATR MD-82 53234
I-DATS MD-82 53235
I-DATU MD-82 53220
I-DAVA MD-82 49215
I-DAVB MD-82 49216
I-DAVC MD-82 49217
I-DAVD MD-82 49218
I-DAVF MD-82 49219
I-DAVG MD-82 49220
I-DAVH MD-82 49221
I-DAVI MD-82 49430
I-DAVJ MD-82 49431
I-DAVK MD-82 49432
I-DAVL MD-82 49433
I-DAVM MD-82 49434
I-DAVN MD-82 49435
I-DAVP MD-82 49549
I-DAVR MD-82 49550
I-DAVS MD-82 49551
I-DAVT MD-82 49552
I-DAVU MD-82 49794
I-DAVV MD-82 49795
I-DAVW MD-82 49796
I-DAVX MD-82 49969
I-DAVZ MD-82 49970
I-DAWA MD-82 49192
I-DAWB MD-82 49197
I-DAWC MD-82 49198
I-DAWD MD-82 49199
I-DAWE MD-82 49193
I-DAWF MD-82 49200
I-DAWG MD-82 49201
I-DAWH MD-82 49202
I-DAWI MD-82 49194
I-DAWJ MD-82 49203
I-DAWL MD-82 49204
I-DAWM MD-82 49205
I-DAWO MD-82 49195
I-DAWP MD-82 49206
I-DAWQ MD-82 49207
I-DAWR MD-82 49208
I-DAWS MD-82 49209
I-DAWT MD-82 49210
I-DAWU MD-82 49196
I-DAWV MD-82 49211
I-DAWW MD-82 49212
I-DAWY MD-82 49213
I-DAWZ MD-82 49214
I-DAXA CRVL 35
I-DAXE CRVL 36
I-DAXI CRVL 40
I-DAXO CRVL 44
I-DAXT CRVL 80
I-DAXU CRVL 79
I-DEMA B747 19729
I-DEMB B747 20520
I-DEMC B747 22506
I-DEMD B747 22507
I-DEME B747 19730
I-DEMF B747 22508
I-DEMG B747 22510
I-DEML B747 22511
I-DEMN B747 22512
I-DEMO B747 19731
I-DEMP B747 22513
I-DEMR B747 22545
I-DEMS B747 22969
I-DEMT B747 23300
I-DEMU B747 19732
I-DEMV B747 23301
I-DEMW B747 23476
I-DEMX B747 23286
I-DEMY B747 21589
I-DIBA DC-9 47038
I-DIBC DC-9 47233
I-DIBD DC-9 47234
I-DIBE DC-9 47046
I-DIBI DC-9 47129
I-DIBJ DC-9 47235
I-DIBK DC-9 47355
I-DIBL DC-9 47101
I-DIBM DC-9 47223
I-DIBN DC-9 47339
I-DIBO DC-9 47237
I-DIBP DC-9 47222
I-DIBQ DC-9 47236
I-DIBR DC-9 47038
I-DIBS DC-9 47039
I-DIBT DC-9 47046
I-DIBU DC-9 47047
I-DIBV DC-9 47101
I-DIBW DC-9 47129
I-DIBX DC-9 47283
I-DIBY DC-9 47223
I-DIBZ DC-9 47222
I-DIKA DC-9 47038
I-DIKB DC-9 47118
I-DIKC DC-9 47128
I-DIKD DC-9 47129
I-DIKE DC-9 47039
I-DIKF DC-9 47220

Reg.	Type	c/n
I-DIKG	DC-9	47221
I-DIKI	DC-9	47046
I-DIKJ	DC-9	47222
I-DIKL	DC-9	47223
I-DIKM	**DC-9**	**47224**
I-DIKN	DC-9	47225
I-DIKO	DC-9	47047
I-DIKP	DC-9	47226
I-DIKQ	DC-9	47227
I-DIKR	**DC-9**	**47228**
I-DIKS	DC-9	47229
I-DIKT	DC-9	47230
(I-DIKT)	DC-9	47283
I-DIKU	DC-9	47101
I-DIKV	DC-9	47231
(I-DIKV)	DC-9	47311
I-DIKW	DC-9	47283
(I-DIKW)	DC-9	47230
I-DIKY	DC-9	47232
I-DIKZ	DC-9	47311
(I-DIKZ)	DC-9	47231
I-DIRA	B727	21264
I-DIRB	B727	21268
I-DIRC	B727	21269
I-DIRD	B727	21661
I-DIRE	B727	21265
I-DIRF	B727	21662
I-DIRG	B727	21663
I-DIRI	B727	21265
I-DIRJ	B727	21270
I-DIRL	B727	21664
I-DIRM	B727	22052
I-DIRN	B727	22053
I-DIRO	B727	21266
I-DIRP	B727	22165
I-DIRQ	B727	22166
I-DIRR	B727	22167
I-DIRS	B727	22168
I-DIRT	B727	22702
I-DIRU	B727	21267
I-DIWA	DC-8	45598
I-DIWB	DC-8	45625
I-DIWC	DC-8	45960
I-DIWD	DC-8	45631
I-DIWE	DC-8	45599
I-DIWF	DC-8	45630
I-DIWG	DC-8	45660
I-DIWH	DC-8	46132
I-DIWI	DC-8	45600
I-DIWJ	DC-8	45986
I-DIWK	DC-8	46082
I-DIWL	DC-8	45682
I-DIWM	DC-8	45755
I-DIWN	DC-8	45909
I-DIWO	DC-8	45601
I-DIWP	DC-8	45636
I-DIWQ	DC-8	45961
I-DIWR	DC-8	45637
I-DIWS	DC-8	45665
I-DIWT	DC-8	45666
I-DIWU	DC-8	45624
I-DIWV	DC-8	45910
I-DIWW	DC-8	46098
I-DIWX	DC-8	46142
I-DIWY	DC-8	46027
I-DIWZ	DC-8	46026
I-DIZA	DC-9	47238
I-DIZB	DC-9	47434
I-DIZC	DC-9	47435
I-DIZE	DC-9	47239
I-DIZE	**DC-9**	**47502**
I-DIZF	DC-9	47519
(I-DIZF)	DC-9	47436
(I-DIZG)	DC-9	47437
I-DIZI	DC-9	47432
(I-DIZI)	DC-9	47431
(I-DIZL)	DC-9	47438
I-DIZO	DC-9	47518
I-DIZU	DC-9	47433
I-DUPA	**MD-11**	**48426**
I-DUPB	**MD-11**	**48431**
I-DUPC	**MD-11**	**48581**
I-DUPD	**MD-11**	**48630**
I-DUPE	**MD-11**	**48427**
I-DUPI	**MD-11**	**48428**
I-DUPO	**MD-11**	**48429**
I-DUPU	**MD-11**	**48430**
I-DYNA	DC-10	47861
I-DYNB	DC-10	47866
I-DYNC	DC-10	47867
I-DYND	DC-10	47868
I-DYNE	DC-10	47862
I-DYNI	DC-10	47863
I-DYNO	DC-10	47864
I-DYNU	DC-10	47865
I-FLRA	146	E2204
I-FLRE	**146**	**E2210**
I-FLRI	**146**	**E2220**
I-FLRO	**146**	**E1227**
I-FLRU	**146**	**E2204**
I-FLRV	146	E2184
I-FLRW	146	E2178
I-FLRX	146	E2170
(I-FLRZ)	146	E2200
I-FLYY	**DC-9**	**47754**
I-FLYZ	**DC-9**	**47697**
I-GISA	CRVL	21
I-GISE	CRVL	208
I-GISI	CRVL	188
I-GISO	CRVL	187
I-GISU	CRVL	169
I-JAKA	YAK40	9020409
I-JAKE	YAK40	9141418
I-JAKI	**YAK40**	**9141518**
I-JAKO	YAK40	9230122
I-JETA	**B737**	**21839**
I-LAUD	B767	25273
I-REJA	**F-70**	**11563**
I-REJB	**F-70**	**11571**
I-REJC	**F-70**	**11579**
I-REJD	F-70	11581
I-REJE	**F-70**	**11573**
I-REJI	**F-70**	**11574**
I-REJO	**F-70**	**11570**
I-REJU	**F-70**	**11575**
I-RIBC	DC-9	47233
I-RIBD	DC-9	47234
I-RIBJ	DC-9	47235
I-RIBN	DC-9	47339
I-RIBQ	DC-9	47236
I-RIFB	DC-9	47432
I-RIFC	DC-9	47233
I-RIFD	DC-9	47234
I-RIFE	**DC-9**	**47518**
I-RIFG	DC-9	47225
I-RIFH	**DC-9**	**47128**
I-RIFJ	**DC-9**	**47235**
I-RIFL	DC-9	47435
I-RIFM	**DC-9**	**47544**
I-RIFP	DC-9	47438
I-RIFS	**DC-9**	**47229**
I-RIFT	**DC-9**	**47591**
I-RIFU	**DC-9**	**47433**
I-RIFV	**DC-9**	**47533**
I-RIFW	**DC-9**	**47575**
I-RIFY	DC-9	47232
I-RIFZ	DC-9	47436
I-RIKS	DC-9	47229
I-RIKT	DC-9	47230
I-RIKV	DC-9	47231
I-RIKZ	DC-9	47311
I-RIZA	DC-9	47238
I-RIZB	DC-9	47432
I-RIZC	DC-9	47435
I-RIZF	DC-9	47519
I-RIZG	DC-9	47225
I-RIZH	DC-9	47128
I-RIZJ	DC-9	47434
I-RIZK	DC-9	47436
I-RIZL	DC-9	47437
I-RIZN	DC-9	47653
I-RIZP	DC-9	47438
I-RIZQ	DC-9	47518
I-RIZR	DC-9	47544
I-RIZS	DC-9	47553
I-RIZT	DC-9	47591
I-RIZU	DC-9	47433
I-RIZV	DC-9	47533
I-RIZW	DC-9	47575
I-RIZX	DC-9	47237
I-RIZY	DC-9	47232
I-SARJ	DC-9	45702
I-SARV	DC-9	45706
I-SARW	DC-9	47430
I-SARZ	DC-9	47468
I-SAVA	B707	17664
I-SMEA	**DC-9**	**47713**
I-SMEE	**DC-9**	**47656**
I-SMEI	**DC-9**	**47714**
I-SMEJ	**DC-9**	**47657**
I-SMEL	**MD-82**	**49247**
I-SMEM	**MD-82**	**49248**
I-SMEO	**DC-9**	**47655**
I-SMEP	**MD-82**	**49740**
I-SMER	**MD-82**	**49901**
I-SMES	**MD-82**	**49902**
I-SMET	**MD-82**	**49531**
I-SMEU	**DC-9**	**47715**
I-SMEV	**MD-82**	**49669**
I-STAE	CRVL	93
I-TEAA	**B737**	**24020**
(I-TEAB)	A310	588
I-TEAE	**B737**	**24022**
I-TEAI	**B737**	**25015**
I-TIAN	**DC-9**	**47010**
I-TIAP	F-28	11009
I-TIAR	**DC-9**	**47015**
I-TIBB	**F-28**	**11010**
I-TIDA	F-28	11014
I-TIDB	F-28	11006
I-TIDE	F-28	11015
I-TIDI	F-28	11991
(I-TIDO)	F-28	11037
I-TIDU	F-28	11004
I-TIGA	DC-9	45728
I-TIGB	DC-9	47002
I-TIGE	DC-9	45717
I-TIGI	DC-9	45724
I-TIGU	DC-9	45718
I-TNTC	**146**	**E2078**
I-VAFE	F-28	11994
I-VAGA	F-28	11032

Japan

Reg.	Type	c/n
JA8001	**DC-8**	**45418**
JA8002	DC-8	45419
JA8003	DC-8	45420
JA8004	**MD-90**	**53359**
JA8005	DC-8	45421
JA8006	DC-8	45626
JA8007	DC-8	45647
JA8008	DC-8	45420
JA8009	DC-8	45662
JA8010	DC-8	45651
JA8011	DC-8	45664
JA8012	DC-8	45680
JA8013	DC-8	45681
JA8014	DC-8	45678
JA8015	DC-8	45763
JA8016	DC-8	45764
JA8017	DC-8	45854
JA8018	DC-8	45882
JA8019	DC-8	45916
JA8020	**MD-90**	**53360**
JA8021	CV880	22-7-5-57
JA8022	CV880	22-7-6-58
JA8023	CV880	22-7-7-59
JA8024	CV880	22-7-8-60
JA8025	CV880	22-7-9-61
JA8026	CV880	22-00-46M
JA8027	CV880	22-00-48M
JA8028	CV880	22-00-49M
JA8029	**MD-90**	**53361**
JA8030	CV880	22-00-45M
JA8031	DC-8	45953
JA8032	DC-8	45954
JA8033	DC-8	45955
JA8034	DC-8	45956
JA8035	DC-8	46023
JA8036	DC-8	46022
JA8037	DC-8	46024
JA8038	DC-8	46031
JA8039	DC-8	46032
JA8040	DC-8	46057
JA8041	DC-8	46099
JA8042	DC-8	46127
JA8043	DC-8	46128
JA8044	DC-8	46139
JA8045	DC-8	46157
JA8046	DC-8	46158
JA8047	DC-8	46159
JA8048	DC-8	46160
JA8049	DC-8	45887
JA8050	DC-8	45848
JA8051	DC-8	46152
JA8052	DC-8	46153
JA8053	DC-8	46161
JA8054	DC-8	46148
JA8055	DC-8	46154
JA8056	DC-8	46162
JA8057	DC-8	45982
(JA8057)	DC-8	46164
JA8058	DC-8	45942
JA8059	DC-8	45943
JA8060	DC-8	45888
JA8061	DC-8	45889
JA8062	**MD-90**	**53352**
JA8063	**MD-90**	**53353**
JA8064	**MD-90**	**53354**
JA8065	**MD-90**	**53355**
JA8066	**MD-90**	**53356**
JA8067	DC-8	45992
JA8068	DC-8	45983
JA8069	**MD-90**	**53357**
JA8070	**MD-90**	**53358**
JA8071	**B747**	**24423**
JA8072	**B747**	**24424**
JA8073	**B747**	**24425**
JA8074	**B747**	**24426**
JA8075	**B747**	**24427**
JA8076	**B747**	**24777**
JA8077	**B747**	**24784**
JA8078	**B747**	**24870**
JA8079	**B747**	**24885**
JA8080	**B747**	**24886**
JA8081	**B747**	**25064**
JA8082	**B747**	**25212**
JA8083	**B747**	**25213**
JA8084	**B747**	**25214**
JA8085	**B747**	**25260**
JA8086	**B747**	**25308**
JA8087	**B747**	**26346**
JA8088	**B747**	**26341**
JA8089	**B747**	**26342**
JA8090	**B747**	**26347**
JA8091	B747	24730
JA8092	B747	24731
JA8094	**B747**	**24801**
JA8095	**B747**	**24833**
JA8096	**B747**	**24920**
JA8097	**B747**	**25135**
JA8098	**B747**	**25207**
JA8099	**B747**	**25292**
JA8101	B747	19725
JA8102	B747	19726
JA8103	B747	19727
JA8104	**B747**	**19823**
JA8105	**B747**	**19824**
JA8106	**B747**	**19825**
JA8107	B747	20332
JA8108	**B747**	**20333**
JA8109	B747	20503
JA8110	**B747**	**20504**
JA8111	**B747**	**20505**
JA8112	B747	20528
JA8113	**B747**	**20529**
JA8114	**B747**	**20530**
JA8115	**B747**	**20531**
JA8116	**B747**	**20532**
JA8117	B747	20781
JA8118	B747	20782
JA8119	B747	20783
JA8120	B747	20784
JA8121	B747	20923
JA8122	B747	20924
JA8123	**B747**	**21034**
JA8124	B747	21032
(JA8124)	B747	21030
JA8125	**B747**	**21030**
(JA8125)	B747	21032
JA8126	B747	21033
JA8127	**B747**	**21031**

JA8128	**B747**	**21029**
JA8129	**B747**	**21678**
JA8130	**B747**	**21679**
JA8131	**B747**	**21680**
JA8132	**B747**	**21681**
JA8133	B747	21604
JA8134	B747	21605
JA8135	**B747**	**21606**
JA8136	**B747**	**21922**
JA8137	**B747**	**21923**
JA8138	**B747**	**21924**
JA8139	**B747**	**21925**
JA8140	**B747**	**22064**
JA8141	**B747**	**22065**
JA8142	**B747**	**22066**
JA8143	**B747**	**22067**
JA8144	B747	22063
JA8145	**B747**	**22291**
JA8146	**B747**	**22292**
JA8147	**B747**	**22293**
JA8148	**B747**	**22294**
JA8149	**B747**	**22478**
JA8150	**B747**	**22479**
JA8151	B747	22477
JA8152	**B747**	**22594**
JA8153	**B747**	**22595**
JA8154	**B747**	**22745**
JA8155	**B747**	**22746**
JA8156	**B747**	**22709**
JA8157	**B747**	**22710**
JA8158	**B747**	**22711**
JA8159	**B747**	**22712**
JA8160	**B747**	**21744**
(JA8160)	B747	22989
JA8161	**B747**	**22990**
JA8162	**B747**	**22991**
JA8163	**B747**	**23149**
(JA8163)	B747	23067
JA8164	**B747**	**23150**
(JA8164)	B747	23068
JA8165	**B747**	**21743**
JA8166	**B747**	**23151**
JA8167	**B747**	**23138**
JA8168	**B747**	**23139**
JA8169	**B747**	**23389**
JA8170	**B747**	**23390**
JA8171	**B747**	**23391**
JA8172	**B747**	**23350**
JA8173	**B747**	**23482**
JA8174	**B747**	**23501**
JA8175	**B747**	**23502**
JA8176	**B747**	**23637**
JA8177	**B747**	**23638**
JA8178	**B747**	**23639**
JA8179	**B747**	**23640**
JA8180	**B747**	**23641**
JA8181	**B747**	**23698**
JA8182	**B747**	**23813**
JA8183	**B747**	**23967**
JA8184	**B747**	**23968**
JA8185	**B747**	**23969**
JA8186	**B747**	**24018**
JA8187	**B747**	**24019**
JA8188	**B747**	**23919**
JA8189	**B747**	**24156**
JA8190	**B747**	**24399**
JA8191	**B747**	**24576**
JA8192	**B747**	**22579**
JA8193	**B747**	**21940**
JA8194	**B747**	**25171**
JA8195	**B737**	**27433**
JA8196	**B737**	**27966**
JA8197	**B777**	**27027**
JA8198	**B777**	**27028**
JA8199	**B777**	**27029**
JA8231	**B767**	**23212**
JA8232	**B767**	**23213**
JA8233	**B767**	**23214**
JA8234	**B767**	**23216**
JA8235	**B767**	**23217**
JA8236	**B767**	**23215**
JA8237	**A300**	**256**
JA8238	**B767**	**23140**
JA8239	**B767**	**23141**
JA8240	**B767**	**23142**
JA8241	**B767**	**23143**
JA8242	**B767**	**23144**
JA8243	**B767**	**23145**
JA8244	**B767**	**23146**
JA8245	**B767**	**23147**
JA8250	**B737**	**23481**
JA8251	**B767**	**23431**
JA8252	**B767**	**23432**
JA8253	**B767**	**23645**
JA8254	**B767**	**23433**
JA8255	**B767**	**23434**
JA8256	**B767**	**23756**
JA8257	**B767**	**23757**
JA8258	**B767**	**23758**
JA8259	**B767**	**23759**
JA8260	**MD-81**	**49461**
JA8261	**MD-81**	**49462**
JA8262	**MD-81**	**49463**
JA8263	**A300**	**151**
JA8264	**B767**	**23965**
JA8265	**B767**	**23961**
JA8266	**B767**	**23966**
JA8267	**B767**	**23962**
JA8268	**B767**	**23963**
JA8269	**B767**	**23964**
JA8271	**B767**	**24002**
JA8272	**B767**	**24003**
JA8273	**B767**	**24004**
JA8274	**B767**	**24005**
JA8275	**B767**	**24006**
JA8276	**A300**	**169**
JA8277	**A300**	**174**
JA8278	**MD-87**	**49464**
JA8279	**MD-87**	**49465**
JA8280	**MD-87**	**49466**
JA8281	**MD-87**	**49467**
JA8282	**B737**	**24103**
JA8285	**B767**	**24350**
JA8286	**B767**	**24400**
JA8287	**B767**	**24351**
JA8288	**B767**	**24415**
JA8289	**B767**	**24416**
JA8290	**B767**	**24417**
JA8291	**B767**	**24755**
JA8292	**A300**	**110**
JA8293	**A300**	**194**
JA8294	**MD-81**	**49820**
JA8295	**MD-81**	**49821**
JA8296	**MD-81**	**49907**
JA8297	**MD-81**	**49908**
JA8299	**B767**	**24498**
JA8300	**A320**	**0549**
JA8301	B727	18821
JA8302	B727	18822
JA8303	B727	18823
JA8304	**A320**	**0531**
JA8305	B727	18919
JA8306	B727	18920
JA8307	B727	18874
JA8308	B727	18875
JA8309	B727	18876
JA8310	B727	18877
JA8311	B727	18878
JA8312	B727	18879
JA8313	**A320**	**0534**
JA8314	B727	19138
JA8315	B727	19139
JA8316	B727	18951
JA8317	B727	18952
JA8318	B727	19279
JA8319	B727	19280
JA8320	B727	19281
JA8321	B727	19557
JA8322	**B767**	**25618**
JA8323	**B767**	**25654**
JA8324	**B767**	**25655**
JA8325	B727	19282
JA8326	B727	19283
JA8327	B727	20078
JA8328	B727	20435
(JA8328)	B727	20079
JA8329	B727	20436
JA8330	B727	20468
JA8331	B727	20469
JA8332	B727	20466
JA8333	B727	20467
JA8334	B727	20509
JA8335	B727	20285
(JA8335)	B727	20510
JA8336	B727	20286
JA8337	B727	20510
JA8338	B727	20568
JA8339	B727	20569
JA8340	B727	20570
JA8341	B727	20571
JA8342	B727	20572
JA8342	**B767**	**27445**
JA8343	B727	20572
JA8343	B727	20573
JA8344	B727	20573
JA8345	B727	20724
JA8346	B727	20725
JA8347	B727	20726
JA8348	B727	20727
JA8349	B727	20728
JA8350	B727	20876
JA8351	B727	20877
JA8352	B727	20878
JA8353	B727	21455
JA8354	B727	21456
JA8355	B727	21474
JA8356	**B767**	**25136**
JA8357	**B767**	**25293**
JA8358	**B767**	**25616**
JA8359	**B767**	**25617**
JA8360	**B767**	**25055**
JA8362	**B767**	**24632**
JA8363	**B767**	**24756**
JA8364	**B767**	**24782**
JA8365	**B767**	**24783**
JA8366	**B737**	**23469**
JA8368	**B767**	**24880**
JA8369	**A300**	**239**
JA8370	**MD-87**	**53039**
JA8371	**MD-87**	**53040**
JA8372	**MD-87**	**53041**
JA8373	**MD-87**	**53042**
JA8374	**MD-81**	**53043**
JA8375	**A300**	**602**
JA8376	**A300**	**617**
JA8377	**A300**	**621**
JA8381	**A320**	**0138**
JA8382	**A320**	**0139**
JA8383	**A320**	**0148**
JA8384	**A320**	**0151**
JA8385	**A320**	**0167**
JA8386	**A320**	**0170**
JA8387	**A320**	**0196**
JA8388	**A320**	**0212**
JA8389	**A320**	**0219**
JA8390	**A320**	**0245**
JA8391	**A320**	**0300**
JA8392	**A320**	**0328**
JA8393	**A320**	**0365**
JA8394	**A320**	**0383**
JA8395	**A320**	**0413**
JA8396	**A320**	**0482**
JA8397	**B767**	**27311**
JA8398	**B767**	**27312**
JA8399	**B767**	**27313**
JA8400	**A320**	**0554**
JA8401	B737	20226
JA8402	B737	20227
JA8403	B737	20276
JA8404	**B737**	**27381**
JA8405	B737	20277
JA8406	B737	20413
JA8407	B737	20414
JA8408	B737	20449
JA8409	B737	20450
JA8410	B737	20451
JA8411	B737	20452
JA8412	B737	20506
JA8413	B737	20507
JA8414	B737	20508
JA8415	**B737**	**20561**
JA8416	**B737**	**20562**
JA8417	**B737**	**20563**
(JA8418)	B737	20564
JA8419	**B737**	**27430**
(JA8419)	B737	20565
(JA8419)	B737	24103
(JA8420)	B737	20566
(JA8421)	B737	20567
JA8423	DC-9	47603
JA8424	DC-9	47604
JA8425	DC-9	47605
JA8426	DC-9	47606
JA8427	DC-9	47608
JA8428	DC-9	47612
JA8429	DC-9	47613
JA8430	DC-9	47614
JA8432	DC-9	47615
JA8433	DC-9	47616
JA8434	DC-9	47617
JA8435	DC-9	47618
JA8436	DC-9	47619
JA8437	DC-9	47620
JA8439	DC-9	47759
JA8440	**DC-9**	**47760**
JA8441	**DC-9**	**47761**
JA8442	**DC-9**	**47762**
JA8443	B737	21476
JA8444	B737	21477
JA8445	**B737**	**21478**
JA8448	DC-9	47767
JA8449	**DC-9**	**47768**
JA8450	**DC-9**	**47780**
JA8451	**DC-9**	**47781**
JA8452	**B737**	**21766**
JA8453	**B737**	**21767**
JA8454	**B737**	**21768**
JA8455	**B737**	**21769**
JA8456	**B737**	**21770**
JA8457	**B737**	**21771**
JA8458	**MD-81**	**48029**
JA8459	**MD-81**	**48030**
JA8460	**MD-81**	**48031**
JA8461	**MD-81**	**48032**
JA8462	**MD-81**	**48033**
JA8464	**A300**	**82**
JA8465	**A300**	**89**
JA8466	**A300**	**90**
JA8467	**B737**	**22367**
JA8468	**MD-81**	**48070**
JA8469	**MD-81**	**48071**
JA8470	**MD-81**	**48072**
JA8471	**A300**	**160**
JA8472	**A300**	**163**
JA8473	**A300**	**176**
JA8475	**B737**	**22736**
JA8476	**A300**	**209**
JA8477	**A300**	**244**
JA8478	**A300**	**253**
JA8479	**B767**	**22785**
JA8480	**B767**	**22786**
JA8481	**B767**	**22787**
JA8482	**B767**	**22788**
JA8483	**B767**	**22789**
JA8484	**B767**	**22790**
JA8485	**B767**	**23016**
JA8486	**B767**	**23017**
JA8487	**B767**	**23018**
JA8488	**B767**	**23019**
JA8489	**B767**	**23020**
JA8490	**B767**	**23021**
JA8491	**B767**	**23022**
JA8492	**B737**	**23117**
JA8496	**MD-81**	**49280**
JA8497	**MD-81**	**49281**
JA8498	**MD-81**	**49282**
JA8499	**MD-81**	**49283**
JA8500	**B737**	**27431**
JA8501	L1011	1053
JA8502	L1011	1061
JA8503	L1011	1062
JA8504	**B737**	**27432**
JA8505	L1011	1068
JA8506	L1011	1070
JA8507	L1011	1082
JA8508	L1011	1099
JA8509	L1011	1100
JA8510	L1011	1103
JA8511	L1011	1105
JA8512	L1011	1112
JA8513	L1011	1113
JA8514	L1011	1117
JA8515	L1011	1119
JA8516	L1011	1127

JA8517	**L1011**	**1128**
JA8518	L1011	1129
JA8519	L1011	1134
JA8520	L1011	1154
JA8521	**L1011**	**1155**
JA8522	L1011	1156
JA8523	**B737**	**26603**
JA8524	**B737**	**26604**
JA8525	**B737**	**26605**
JA8527	**A300**	**724**
JA8528	**B737**	**23464**
JA8529	**A300**	**729**
JA8530	**DC-10**	**46920**
JA8531	**DC-10**	**46923**
JA8532	**DC-10**	**46660**
JA8533	**DC-10**	**46661**
JA8534	**DC-10**	**46913**
JA8535	**DC-10**	**46662**
JA8536	**DC-10**	**46966**
JA8537	**DC-10**	**46967**
JA8538	**DC-10**	**46974**
JA8539	**DC-10**	**47822**
JA8540	**DC-10**	**47823**
JA8541	**DC-10**	**47824**
JA8542	**DC-10**	**47825**
JA8543	**DC-10**	**47826**
JA8544	**DC-10**	**47852**
JA8545	**DC-10**	**47853**
JA8546	**DC-10**	**47855**
JA8547	**DC-10**	**47856**
JA8548	**DC-10**	**47857**
JA8549	**DC-10**	**48301**
JA8550	**DC-10**	**48315**
JA8551	**DC-10**	**48316**
JA8552	**MD-81**	**53297**
JA8553	**MD-81**	**53298**
JA8554	**MD-81**	**53299**
JA8555	**MD-81**	**53300**
JA8556	**MD-81**	**53301**
JA8557	**MD-81**	**53302**
JA8558	**A300**	**638**
JA8559	**A300**	**641**
JA8560	**A300**	**178**
JA8561	**A300**	**670**
JA8562	**A300**	**679**
JA8563	**A300**	**683**
JA8564	**A300**	**703**
JA8565	**A300**	**711**
JA8566	**A300**	**730**
JA8567	**B767**	**25656**
JA8568	**B767**	**25657**
JA8569	**B767**	**27050**
JA8573	**A300**	**737**
JA8574	**A300**	**740**
JA8577	**B737**	**23467**
JA8578	**B767**	**25658**
JA8579	**B767**	**25659**
JA8580	**MD-11**	**48571**
JA8581	**MD-11**	**48572**
JA8582	**MD-11**	**48573**
JA8583	**MD-11**	**48574**
JA8584	**MD-11**	**48575**
JA8585	**MD-11**	**48576**
JA8586	**MD-11**	**48577**
JA8587	**MD-11**	**48578**
JA8588	**MD-11**	**48579**
JA8589	**MD-11**	**48774**
(JA8589)	MD-11	48580
JA8609	**A320**	**0501**
JA8654	**A320**	**0507**
JA8657	**A300**	**753**
JA8659	**A300**	**770**
JA8664	**B767**	**27339**
JA8669	**B767**	**27444**
JA8670	**B767**	**25660**
JA8674	**B767**	**25661**
JA8677	**B767**	**25662**
JA8901	**B747**	**26343**
JA8902	**B747**	**26344**
JA8903	**B747**	**26345**
JA8904	**B747**	**26348**
JA8905	**B747**	**26349**
JA8906	**B747**	**26350**
JA8907	**B747**	**26351**
JA8908	**B747**	**26352**
JA8909	**B747**	**26353**
JA8910	**B747**	**26354**
JA8911	**B747**	**26355**
JA8912	**B747**	**27099**
(JA8913)	B747	26356
(JA8913)	B747	27827
(JA8914)	B747	26357
(JA8914)	B747	27828
JA8955	**B747**	**25639**
JA8956	**B747**	**25640**
JA8957	**B747**	**25642**
JA8958	**B747**	**25641**
JA8959	**B747**	**25646**
JA8960	**B747**	**25643**
JA8961	**B747**	**25644**
JA8962	**B747**	**25645**
JA8963	**B747**	**25647**
JA8964	**B747**	**27163**
JA8965	**B747**	**27436**
JA8966	**B747**	**27442**
JA8967	**B777**	**27030**
JA8968	**B777**	**27031**
JA8969	**B777**	**27032**
JA8975	**B767**	**27658**
JA8977	**B777**	**27636**
JA8978	**B777**	**27637**
JA8979	**B777**	**27638**
JA8981	**B777**	**27364**
JA8982	**B777**	**27365**
JA8983	**B777**	**27366**
JA8991	**B737**	**27916**
JA8992	**B737**	**27917**

Jordan

JY-ACS	CRVL	199
JY-ACT	CRVL	200
JY-ADG	CRVL	236
JY-ADO	B707	20494
JY-ADP	B707	20495
JY-ADR	B727	20885
JY-ADS	B720	18250
JY-ADT	B720	18251
JY-ADU	B727	20886
JY-ADV	B727	21021
JY-AEB	B707	18948
JY-AEC	B707	18949
JY-AED	B707	18716
JY-AEE	B707	18767
JY-AES	B707	20017
JY-AFA	B747	21251
JY-AFB	B747	21252
JY-AFD	B707	20283
JY-AFL	B707	19353
JY-AFR	B707	19706
JY-AFS	B747	22579
JY-AFT	B727	22268
JY-AFU	**B727**	**22269**
JY-AFV	**B727**	**22270**
JY-AFW	B727	22271
JY-AGA	**L1011**	**1217**
JY-AGB	**L1011**	**1219**
JY-AGC	**L1011**	**1220**
JY-AGD	**L1011**	**1229**
JY-AGE	**L1011**	**1238**
JY-AGH	L1011	1249
JY-AGI	L1011	1246
JY-AGJ	L1011	1248
JY-AHS	B727	18934
JY-AJK	**B707**	**18948**
JY-AJM	**B707**	**19590**
JY-AJN	**B707**	**20720**
JY-AJO	**B707**	**20723**
JY-CAB	B707	18716
JY-CAC	B707	20890
JY-CAD	A310	421
(JY-CAE)	A310	422
(JY-CAS)	A320	0569
JY-HKJ	**L1011**	**1247**
JY-HMH	B727	18934
JY-HNH	B727	22362
JY-HS1	**B727**	**20228**

Djibouti

J2-KAD	B727	19135
J2-KAF	B737	20893
J2-KBG	B727	20470
J2-KBH	**B727**	**20411**

St. Lucia

J6-SLF	B707	18689
J6-SLR	B707	18716

St Vincent

J8-VBA	146	E1068
J8-VBB	**146**	**E1071**
J8-VBC	**146**	**E1035**

orway

LN-AEO	B747	20121
(LN-AEQ)	B737	23923
LN-AET	B747	20120
LN-ALN	DC-10	46554
LN-BRA	**B737**	**24270**
LN-BRB	**B737**	**24271**
LN-BRC	**B737**	**24650**
LN-BRD	**B737**	**24651**
LN-BRE	**B737**	**24643**
LN-BRF	**B737**	**24652**
LN-BRG	**B737**	**24272**
LN-BRH	**B737**	**24828**
LN-BRI	**B737**	**24644**
LN-BRJ	**B737**	**24273**
LN-BRK	**B737**	**24274**
LN-BRL	B737	22277
LN-BRM	**B737**	**24645**
LN-BRN	**B737**	**24646**
LN-BRO	**B737**	**24647**
LN-BRP	**B737**	**25303**
LN-BRQ	**B737**	**25348**
LN-BRR	**B737**	**24648**
LN-BRS	**B737**	**24649**
LN-BRT	**B737**	**25789**
LN-BRU	**B737**	**25790**
LN-BRV	**B737**	**25791**
LN-BRV	**B737**	**25971**
LN-BRW	B737	25792
LN-BRW	**B737**	**25972**
LN-BRX	**B737**	**25797**
LN-BRY	B737	27155
LN-BRZ	B737	27153
(LN-BSC)	CRVL	169
LN-BSE	CRVL	259
LN-BUA	**B737**	**25794**
LN-BUA	B737	26297
LN-BUB	**B737**	**24703**
LN-BUC	**B737**	**26304**
LN-BUE	**B737**	**27627**
LN-KLH	**CRVL**	**3**
LN-KLI	CRVL	7
(LN-KLJ)	CRVL	24
LN-KLN	CRVL	209
LN-KLP	**CRVL**	**24**
LN-KLR	CRVL	30
(LN-LMA)	CV990	30-10-6
LN-MOA	DC-8	45385
LN-MOC	DC-8	46150
LN-MOF	DC-8	46097
LN-MOG	DC-8	46102
LN-MOH	DC-8	45767
LN-MOO	DC-8	45822
LN-MOT	DC-8	45388
LN-MOU	DC-8	45923
LN-MOW	DC-8	46131
LN-MOY	DC-8	46054
LN-MTC	B737	20453
LN-MTD	B737	20454
LN-NOR	B737	23827
LN-NOS	B737	23830
LN-NPB	B737	21763
LN-PIP	DC-8	45256
LN-RCA	A300	79
LN-RCB	B767	24357
LN-RCC	B767	24728
LN-RCD	**B767**	**24847**
(LN-RCD)	B767	24729
LN-RCE	**B767**	**24846**
LN-RCG	**B767**	**24475**
LN-RCH	**B767**	**24318**
LN-RCI	**B767**	**24476**
LN-RCK	**B767**	**24729**
LN-RCL	**B767**	**25365**
LN-RKA	DC-10	46868
LN-RKB	DC-10	46871
LN-RKC	DC-10	47814
LN-RKD	DC-10	46961
LN-RLA	**DC-9**	**47599**
LN-RLB	DC-9	47497
LN-RLC	DC-9	47179
LN-RLD	DC-9	47396
LN-RLE	**MD-82**	**49382**
LN-RLF	**MD-82**	**49383**
LN-RLG	**MD-82**	**49423**
LN-RLH	**DC-9**	**47748**
(LN-RLI)	MD-81	49554
LN-RLJ	DC-9	47287
LN-RLK	DC-9	47116
LN-RLL	DC-9	47301
LN-RLM	DC-9	47304
LN-RLN	**DC-9**	**47630**
LN-RLO	DC-9	47307
LN-RLP	**DC-9**	**47778**
LN-RLR	DC-9	47396
LN-RLR	**MD-82**	**49437**
LN-RLS	DC-9	47111
LN-RLS	**DC-9**	**47623**
LN-RLT	**DC-9**	**47626**
LN-RLU	DC-9	47511
LN-RLW	DC-9	47414
LN-RLX	DC-9	47513
LN-RLZ	**DC-9**	**47634**
LN-RMA	**MD-81**	**49554**
LN-RMB	MD-83	49557
LN-RMC	DC-9	47655
LN-RMD	**MD-82**	**49555**
LN-RMF	**MD-83**	**49556**
LN-RMG	**MD-87**	**49611**
LN-RMH	**MD-87**	**49612**
LN-RMJ	**MD-81**	**49912**
LN-RMK	**MD-87**	**49610**
LN-RML	**MD-81**	**53002**
LN-RMM	**MD-81**	**53005**
LN-RMN	**MD-82**	**53295**
LN-RMO	**MD-81**	**53315**
LN-RMP	**MD-87**	**53337**
LN-RMR	**MD-81**	**53365**
LN-RMS	**MD-81**	**53368**
LN-RMT	MD-81	53001
(LN-RMT)	MD-81	53407
LN-RMU	**MD-87**	**53340**
LN-RMX	**MD-87**	**49585**
LN-RMY	**MD-87**	**49586**
LN-RNA	B747	21381
(LN-RNB)	B747	22496
(LN-RTB)	DC-9	47111
LN-SUA	B737	20458
LN-SUA	B737	23464
LN-SUB	B737	21765
LN-SUC	F-28	11009
LN-SUD	B737	20711
LN-SUG	B737	20412
LN-SUH	B737	21219
LN-SUI	B737	21184
LN-SUJ	B737	23468
LN-SUK	B737	21729
LN-SUM	B737	21445
LN-SUM	F-28	11003
LN-SUM	F-28	11032
LN-SUN	F-28	11012
LN-SUO	F-28	11013
LN-SUP	B737	19409
LN-SUQ	B737	23467
LN-SUS	B737	19408
LN-SUT	B737	22022
LN-SUU	B737	23465
LN-SUV	B737	23469
LN-SUV	B767	23057
LN-SUW	B767	23058

LN-SUX F-28 11010
LN-SUY F-28 11011
LN-SUZ B737 23466
(LN-TEC) CRVL 263
LN-TUU B720 18041
LN-TUV B720 18043
LN-TUW B720 18158

Argentina

(LV-) B737 20330
(LV-) B737 20331
LV-AHN COMET 6408
LV-AHO COMET 6410
LV-AHP COMET 6411
LV-AHR COMET 6430
LV-AHS COMET 6432
LV-AHU COMET 6434
LV-AIB COMET 6460
LV-HGX CRVL 19
LV-HGY CRVL 127
LV-HGZ CRVL 149
LV-III CRVL 180
LV-ISA B707 19238
LV-ISB B707 19239
LV-ISC B707 19240
LV-ISD B707 19241
LV-IZR 1-11 BAC.122
LV-IZS 1-11 BAC.123
LV-JGP B707 19962
LV-JGR B707 19961
LV-JGX 1-11 BAC.117
LV-JGY 1-11 BAC.155
LV-JMW B737 20403
LV-JMX B737 20404
LV-JMY B737 20405
LV-JMZ B737 20406
LV-JND B737 20407
LV-JNE B737 20408
LV-JNR 1-11 BAC.192
LV-JNS 1-11 BAC.194
LV-JNT 1-11 BAC.196
LV-JNU 1-11 BAC.185
LV-JTD B737 20523
LV-JTO B737 20537
LV-LEB B737 20768
(LV-LEE) B737 20769
LV-LGO B707 20076
LV-LGP B707 20077
LV-LHT 1-11 BAC.185
LV-LIU B737 20964
LV-LIV B737 20965
LV-LIW B737 20966
LV-LOA F-28 11085
LV-LOB F-28 11086
LV-LOC F-28 11083
LV-LOX 1-11 BAC.212
LV-LRG B747 19896
LV-LRG F-28 11046
LV-LTP DC-8 45255
LV-LZD B747 21189
LV-LZN F-28 11048
LV-MCD B727 21457
LV-MDB B737 20836
LV-MEX 1-11 BAC.200
LV-MIM B727 21688
LV-MIN B727 21689
LV-MIO B727 21690
LV-MLO B747 21725
LV-MLP B747 21726
LV-MLR B747 21727
LV-MRZ 1-11 BAC.206
LV-MSG B707 18591
LV-MZD F-28 11127
LV-MZE B707 19297
LV-MZM 1-11 BAC.187
LV-OAX 1-11 BAC.197
LV-OAY 1-11 BAC.227
LV-ODY B727 21823
LV-OEP B747 22297
LV-OHV B747 21786
LV-OLN B727 22603
LV-OLO B727 22604
LV-OLP B727 22605
LV-OLR B727 22606
LV-OOZ B747 22592
LV-OPA B747 22593
LV-PBJ CRVL 180
LV-PEW 1-11 BAC.187
LV-PFR 1-11 BAC.197
LV-PHT B737 22278
LV-PID 1-11 BAC.122
LV-PIF 1-11 BAC.123
LV-PKA 1-11 BAC.155
LV-PKB 1-11 BAC.117
LV-PLM COMET 6408
LV-PLO COMET 6410
LV-PLP COMET 6411
LV-POY COMET 6430
LV-POZ COMET 6432
LV-PPA COMET 6434
LV-PRQ B737 20523
LV-PRR CRVL 19
LV-PSW 1-11 BAC.185
LV-PTS COMET 6460
LV-PVT CRVL 127
LV-PVU CRVL 149
LV-RAO B737 22296
LV-RBH B737 22296
LV-RCS F-28 11074
LV-RRA F-28 11145
LV-VAG MD-83 53117
LV-VBX MD-88 53047
LV-VBY MD-88 53048
LV-VBZ MD-88 53049
LV-VCB MD-88 53351
LV-VCS F-28 11018
LV-VFJ B727 20593
LV-VFL B727 20606
LV-VFM B727 20607
LV-VGB MD-88 53446
LV-VGC MD-88 53447
LV-VGF B737 20913
LV-WAW DC-9 47260
LV-WAX DC-9 47262
LV-WBO B737 20330
LV-WDS B727 20169
LV-WEG DC-9 47446
LV-WEH DC-9 47447
LV-WFC B727 20678
LV-WFN MD-81 48025
LV-WFT DC-9 47365
LV-WFX B737 21357
LV-WGM MD-83 49784
LV-WGN MD-83 49934
LV-WGU DC-9 47454
LV-WGX B737 21358
LV-WHL DC-9 47368
LV-WIS DC-9 47312
LV-WJH DC-9 47079
LV-WJS B737 22278
LV-WMH B757 26332
LV-WNA B737 22368
LV-WNB B737 22369

Luxembourg

LX-ACO B747 21253
LX-ACV B747 21964
LX-ACV DC-8 45989
LX-BCV B747 22403
LX-BCV DC-8 46002
LX-BJV B707 19212
LX-DCV B747 20887
LX-DCV B747 21650
LX-ECV B747 21965
LX-ECV B747 22390
LX-FCV B707 18925
LX-FCV B707 19212
LX-FCV B747 19658
LX-FCV B747 25866
LX-GCV B747 19660
LX-GCV B747 25867
LX-GCV DC-8 45640
LX-ICV B747 25632
LX-IDB DC-8 45417
LX-III DC-8 45659
LX-IRA B727 22081
LX-IRB B727 22082
LX-IRC B727 22084
LX-IRD B727 22085
LX-KCV B747 20102
LX-LCV B747 20105
LX-LGE CRVL 234
LX-LGF B737 25429
LX-LGF CRVL 166
LX-LGG B737 26437
LX-LGG CRVL 156
LX-LGH B737 21443
LX-LGI B737 21444
LX-LGN B737 20907
LX-LGO B737 26438
LX-LGP A300 269
LX-LGP B737 26439
(LX-LGP) A300 299
LX-LGR B737 27424
LX-LGS B707 20283
LX-LGS B737 27425
LX-LGT B707 19706
LX-LGU B707 19133
LX-LGV B707 18737
LX-LGW B707 17930
LX-LGX B747 21133
LX-LGY B747 21263
LX-LTM B747 21132
(LX-LTM) B747 21263
LX-MAM 1-11 BAC.259
LX-MCV B747 20106
LX-MJM B727 21853
LX-MMM B727 21853
LX-NCV B747 20103
LX-NCV B747 20108
LX-OCV B747 21575
LX-OOO B737 21839
LX-SAL B747 20116
(LX-TAM) DC-8 46002
LX-TAP B747 22169
LX-TLA DC-8 45960
LX-TLB DC-8 45925
LX-ZCV B747 21252

Lithuania

LY-AAA YAK40 9720154
LY-AAB YAK40 9520940
LY-AAC YAK40 9530344
LY-AAD YAK40 9412032
LY-AAM YAK42 4520423606235
LY-AAN YAK42 4520423606256
LY-AAO YAK42 4520423606267
LY-AAP YAK42 4520421706302
LY-AAQ YAK42 4520422708295
LY-AAR YAK42 4520422708304
LY-AAS YAK42 4520421811395
LY-AAT YAK42 4520424711396
LY-AAU YAK42 4520424711397
LY-AAV YAK42 4520424711399
LY-AAW YAK42 4520423811417
LY-AAX YAK42 4520424811431
LY-AAY YAK40 9720753
LY-AAZ YAK40 9641851
LY-ABA TU134 3352003
LY-ABB TU134 48415
LY-ABC TU134 49100
LY-ABD TU134 60054
LY-ABE TU134 60076
LY-ABF TU134 60172
LY-ABG TU134 60195
LY-ABH TU134 60308
LY-ABI TU134 60628
(LY-ABL) B737 22453
LY-BSD B737 22701
LY-BSG B737 22793
LY-GBA B737 22034
LY-GPA B737 22453

Bulgaria

LZ-ABA A320 0257
LZ-ABB A320 0271
LZ-ABC A320 0308
LZ-ABD A320 0314
LZ-BOA B737 24881
LZ-BOB B737 24921
LZ-BOC B737 25425
LZ-BTA TU154 026
LZ-BTB TU154 027
LZ-BTC TU154 036
LZ-BTD TU154 058
LZ-BTE TU154 073
LZ-BTF TU154 077
LZ-BTG TU154 095
LZ-BTH TU154 754
LZ-BTI TU154 706
LZ-BTJ TU154 270
LZ-BTK TU154 144
LZ-BTL TU154 051
LZ-BTL TU154 208
LZ-BTM TU154 054
LZ-BTM TU154 209
LZ-BTN TU154 054
LZ-BTN TU154 832
LZ-BTO TU154 258
LZ-BTP TU154 278
LZ-BTQ TU154 743
LZ-BTR TU154 051
LZ-BTR TU154 320
LZ-BTS TU154 422
LZ-BTT TU154 483
LZ-BTU TU154 484
LZ-BTV TU154 569
LZ-BTW TU154 707
LZ-BTX TU154 744
LZ-BTY TU154 800
LZ-BTZ TU154 781
LZ-DOA YAK40 9341431
LZ-DOB YAK40 9340432
LZ-DOC YAK40 9340532
LZ-DOD YAK40 9340632
LZ-DOE YAK40 9521441
LZ-DOF YAK40 9521541
LZ-DOK YAK40 9620247
LZ-DOL YAK40 9620347
LZ-DOM YAK40 9620447
LZ-DON YAK40 9620547
LZ-DOR YAK40 9231623
LZ-DOS YAK40 9231423
LZ-FEB B707 19584
LZ-INK IL-76 0093494835
LZ-JXA A310 378
LZ-JXB A310 419
LZ-JXC A310 573
LZ-MIF TU154
LZ-MIG TU154 840
LZ-MIK TU154 844
LZ-MIL TU154 845
LZ-MIR TU154 852
LZ-MIS TU154 863
LZ-MIV TU154 920
LZ-MNA TU154 908
LZ-NAL B737 22408
LZ-PVA B707 18937
LZ-PVB B707 19570
LZ-TUA TU134 8350405
LZ-TUB TU134 8350501
LZ-TUC TU134 9350807
LZ-TUD TU134 9350808
LZ-TUE TU134 9350914
LZ-TUF TU134 9350918
LZ-TUG TU134 49858
LZ-TUK TU134 1351209
LZ-TUL TU134 4352303
LZ-TUM TU134 3351906
LZ-TUN TU134 4352307
LZ-TUO TU134 0350922
LZ-TUP TU134 1351303
LZ-TUR TU134 4352308
LZ-TUS TU134 60642
LZ-TUT TU134
LZ-TUU TU134 1351409
LZ-TUV TU134 1351408
LZ-TUZ TU134 1351503

Mongolia

MPR-85644	TU154	780
MT-1036	**B727**	**20572**
MT-1037	**B727**	**20573**
(MT-1044)	B757	26153
MT-1054	**B727**	**20435**
bHMAY85564	TU154	564

NASA

NASA	C-141	6110
NASA515	**B737**	**19437**
NASA711	CV990	30-10-1
NASA930	**C-135**	**17969**
NASA931	C-135	18615

United States of America

N	**B727**	**20539**
N	**B727**	**23052**
(N)	B707	17610
(N)	B707	20720
(N)	B707	20723
(N)	B727	20203
(N)	B727	20410
(N)	B737	20689
(N)	B737	20692
(N)	B737	20693
(N)	B757	24072
(N)	B757	24073
(N)	B757	24074
N1CC	B727	18998
N1JR	1-11	055
N1PC	**B737**	**21613**
N1R	**B720**	**18022**
N1RN	CV880	22-7-5-57
N2CC	B727	19006
N2H	DC-9	45731
N3E	1-11	068
N5LC	1-11	015
N5LC	1-11	073
N5LG	1-11	015
N5NE	DC-9	45706
N8LG	1-11	015
N9DC	DC-9	45695
N9KR	DC-9	45775
N9MD	DC-9	47696
N9WP	1-11	078
N10DC	DC-10	46500
N10DC	DC-10	46501
N10DC	DC-8	45610
N10HM	1-11	080
N10MB	**DC-10**	**47907**
N10VG	B720	18156
N10XY	B727	19254
"N011JS"	B720	18044
N11AB	B737	24769
N11FQ	**MD-88**	**49759**
N11RV	B707	17606
N12CZ	1-11	056
N12FQ	**MD-88**	**49766**
N13FE	**DC-9**	**45706**
N14AZ	**B707**	**19498**
N15NP	DC-9	45702
N15VG	B720	18163
N17MK	**1-11**	**054**
N17VK	1-11	054
N18AZ	B707	18748
N18G	B727	18935
N18HD	1-11	068
N18HH	1-11	068
N18HH	**B727**	**18936**
N18KM	B720	18019
N19B	DC-10	46661
N19B	DC-10	46662
N19B	DC-10	46934
N19B	DC-10	47840
N19B	DC-10	47889
N19B	DC-10	48258
N19B	DC-8	45927
N19B	DC-8	45929
N19B	DC-9	47702
N19B	MD-82	48087
N19B	MD-83	49252
N19B	MD-82	49380
N19B	MD-87	49403
N19B	MD-81	49603
N19B	MD-87	49605
N19B	MD-83	49643
N19B	MD-83	49968
N19B	MD-88	53193
N20SW	B737	20369
N20SW	**B737**	**21337**
N20UA	DC-8	45890
N21AZ	**B707**	**18747**
N21CX	**DC-8**	**45955**
N21FE	B727	21102
N21SW	B737	20345
N21UA	DC-8	45891
N21UC	B727	18990
N22RB	1-11	080
N22SW	B737	20336
N22UA	DC-8	45892
N23	B720	18066
N23SW	B737	20346
N23SW	**B737**	**21338**
N23UA	DC-8	45893
N24SW	**B737**	**20925**
N24UA	**DC-8**	**45963**
N25AB	B737	24687
N25AS	DC-9	45725
N25AZ	**B727**	**18370**
N25SW	B737	20095
N25UA	DC-8	46127
N26SW	**B737**	**21117**
N26UA	DC-8	45887
N27	B727	19176
N27KA	B727	18859
N27SW	**B737**	**21262**
N27UA	**DC-8**	**45942**
N27W	F-28	11016
N28JS	B720	18044
N28KA	B727	18320
N28SW	**B737**	**21339**
(N28SW)	B737	21337
N28UA	DC-8	46031
N29	DC-9	45732
N29AF	**DC-9**	**45826**
N29AZ	**B707**	**19517**
N29KA	B727	18803
N29LR	DC-9	47519
N29SW	**B737**	**21340**
(N29SW)	B737	21338
N29UA	**DC-8**	**46159**
N30KA	B727	18857
(N30SW)	B737	21339
N30UA	**DC-8**	**45888**
N31CX	**DC-8**	**45911**
N31EK	DC-8	46052
N31KA	B727	18856
(N31SW)	B737	21340
N31TR	**B727**	**21948**
N31UA	**DC-9**	**45720**
N32UA	DC-9	47462
N33AW	B737	25402
N33UA	DC-9	47191
N33UT	B727	18936
N34AW	B737	25426
N35UA	DC-9	47192
N36KA	B727	18850
N36UA	DC-8	46022
N37KA	B727	18858
N37RT	F-28	11009
N39KA	B727	18324
N40	**B727**	**19854**
N40AF	B727	18741
N40AF	B737	19769
N40AS	1-11	061
N40KA	DC-10	46727
N40SH	**DC-9**	**45775**
(N41AF)	B737	19955
N41CX	**DC-8**	**46129**
(N41UA)	DC-8	45675
N42	CV880	22-7-3-55
N42AF	B737	19770
N42UA	DC-8	45676
N43UA	DC-8	45677
N44MD	**B727**	**19318**
(N44Q)	B727	18366
N44R	1-11	BAC.120
N44R	B727	18366
N44UA	**DC-8**	**45800**
(N45AF)	B737	22054
N45RT	C-18	18961
N45SB	CRVL	19
N45UA	DC-8	45801
N46	**B727**	**18360**
N46AF	B737	19768
(N46AF)	B737	22055
N46D	B707	18739
N46RT	C-18	18962
N46SB	CRVL	149
N46UA	DC-8	45802
N47AF	B737	19771
N47UA	DC-8	45964
N48AF	B737	19772
N48CA	DC-8	45422
N48UA	DC-8	45980
N49SB	CRVL	180
N49UA	DC-8	45886
N50AF	DC-9	47010
N50SW	**B737**	**21447**
N50UA	DC-8	45884
N51AF	B737	22529
N51CX	**DC-8**	**46027**
(N51FB)	DC-8	45935
N51SW	**B737**	**21448**
N51UA	DC-8	46032
N52AF	B737	22368
N52AW	**B757**	**25489**
N52SW	**B737**	**21533**
N52UA	DC-10	46905
N53AF	B737	22054
N53AF	DC-8	45637
N53AW	**B757**	**25490**
N53CA	**DC-8**	**45377**
N53FA	DC-8	45666
N53KM	DC-8	45604
N53SW	**B737**	**21534**
N54AF	B737	22055
N54CP	CV880	22-00-46M
N54FA	**DC-8**	**45637**
N54SW	**B737**	**21535**
N54UA	DC-9	47697
N55AJ	B727	18951
N55FB	**DC-8**	**45678**
N55JT	1-11	075
N55NW	CV880	22-00-7
N55SW	**B737**	**21593**
N56AF	B737	22369
N56B	1-11	055
N56FA	DC-8	46011
N56SW	**B737**	**21721**
N56UA	DC-9	47754
N57AF	B737	22370
N57AJ	DC-8	45619
N57FB	**DC-8**	**45669**
N57JE	B737	20693
N57SW	**B737**	**21722**
N58AF	B737	22371
N58AW	B757	25345
N58RD	B707	18694
N58RD	CV880	22-00-48M
N59AJ	DC-8	45272
N59AW	B757	25493
N59RD	B707	17905
N59SW	**B737**	**21811**
N59T	DC-9	47041
N60AF	DC-9	47011
N60AJ	DC-8	45618
N60FM	**B727**	**19535**
N60FM	DC-9	45731
N60NA	DC-10	46700
N60SW	**B737**	**21812**
N61AF	B737	19552
N61CX	**DC-8**	**46142**
N61FB	DC-8	46159
N61NA	DC-10	46701
N61SW	**B737**	**21970**
N61TA	**B707**	**17651**
N62AF	B737	19556
N62SW	**B737**	**22060**
N62TA	**B707**	**17640**
N62WH	**1-11**	**078**
N63AF	B737	19553
N63NA	DC-10	46703
N63SW	**B737**	**22061**
N64AF	B737	19549
N64NA	DC-10	46706
N64RD	DC-8	46017
N64SW	**B737**	**22062**
N65AF	DC-9	47152
N65NA	DC-10	46707
(N65SW)	B737	22356
N66AF	**DC-9**	**47152**
N66NA	DC-10	46708
N67AB	B737	23496
N67AF	B737	19554
N67AW	B767	25533
N67NA	DC-10	46709
N67SW	**B737**	**22356**
(N67SW)	B737	22357
N68AF	B737	19058
N68NA	DC-10	46710
N68SW	**B737**	**22357**
(N68SW)	B737	22358
N69AF	B737	19059
N69HM	1-11	061
N69NA	DC-10	46942
N70AF	DC-9	47014
N70NA	146	E1063
N70NA	DC-10	46943
N71MA	1-11	BAC.111
N71SW	**B737**	**22358**
N71UA	DC-8	45381
N72AF	DC-9	47015
N73AF	B737	21186
N73AF	B737	21720
N73AF	DC-9	47013
N73AF	DC-9	47152
N73FS	**B737**	**21765**
N73GQ	B737	19770
N73SW	**B737**	**22673**
N73TH	**B737**	**21729**
N74SW	**B737**	**22674**
N75AF	DC-9	47012
N76GW	1-11	065
N77	B727	18360
N77AZ	B727	19813
N77CS	1-11	054
N77QS	1-11	054
N78	B727	18362
N79SL	**DC-9**	**47011**
N80AF	B737	20223
(N80AF)	B737	22697
N80CC	B737	21957
N80GM	1-11	BAC.126
N80ME	**DC-9**	**45795**
N80NA	DC-10	46711
N80SW	**B737**	**22675**
N80UA	MD-82	48022
N81AC	CNCRD	204
N81AF	B737	22697
(N81AF)	B737	22698
N81NA	DC-10	46712
(N81R)	B720	18022
N81SW	**B737**	**22730**
N82AF	B737	22698
(N82AF)	B737	22699
N82MV	MD-83	49826
N82NA	DC-10	46713
N82SW	**B737**	**22731**
N82TF	B707	18922
N83AF	B737	22699
(N83AF)	B737	22700
N83MV	MD-83	49823
N83NA	DC-10	46714
N83SW	**B737**	**22732**
N84AF	B737	22700
(N84AF)	B737	22701
N84NA	DC-10	47837
N85AF	B737	22701
N85AS	DC-9	45711
(N85NA)	DC-10	46954
N85SW	**B737**	**22826**
(N86AF)	B737	22800
N86SW	**B737**	**22827**
(N87AF)	B737	22801
N87MD	**MD-87**	**49388**
N87SW	**B737**	**22903**
N87WA	B737	20794

(N88AF)	B737	22802
N88CH	**CV880**	**22-7-6-58**
N88NB	1-11	005
N88TF	B707	18964
N88ZL	**B707**	**18928**
(N89AF)	B737	22803
N89S	**DC-9**	**47042**
N89SM	DC-9	45775
N89SW	**B737**	**22904**
(N90AF)	B737	22804
N90AM	1-11	BAC.111
N90AX	**B727**	**20040**
(N90MJ)	B707	17697
N90S	**DC-9**	**47244**
N90SW	**B737**	**22905**
N90TF	1-11	080
N91S	**DC-9**	**47063**
N91SW	**B737**	**22963**
N92GS	B720	18452
N92GS	B727	18892
(N92JF)	B737	19606
N92S	**DC-9**	**47064**
N92SW	**B737**	**22964**
N92TA	L1011	1201
N92TB	L1011	1203
N93GS	B727	18893
N93S	**DC-9**	**47078**
N93SW	**B737**	**22965**
N94AA	CNCRD	206
N94AB	CNCRD	208
N94AD	CNCRD	210
N94AE	CNCRD	212
N94AF	CNCRD	216
N94FA	CNCRD	205
N94FB	CNCRD	207
N94FC	CNCRD	209
N94FD	CNCRD	211
N94GS	**B727**	**18892**
N94S	**DC-9**	**47204**
N94SD	CNCRD	213
N94SW	**B737**	**23053**
N95GS	B727	18895
N95S	**DC-9**	**47205**
N95SW	**B737**	**23054**
N96	C-135	18006
N96AC	B767	25536
N96B	**B727**	**18365**
N96S	**DC-9**	**47206**
N96SW	**B737**	**23055**
N97	B727	18360
(N97GA)	1-11	058
N97JF	1-11	089
N97KR	1-11	005
N97S	DC-9	47245
N98	C-135	17969
N98KT	**CRVL**	**102**
N98WS	B707	18338
N99WT	B707	17606
N99YA	DC-9	45702
N100CC	1-11	059
N100FS	B757	25054
N100JJ	DC-8	45763
N100ME	DC-9	47309
N100MU	B727	19534
N101AA	**DC-10**	**46500**
N101AA	DC-10	46501
N101DA	**B767**	**22213**
N101EX	1-11	007
N101FE	**B727**	**19197**
N101GU	B737	23766
N101MU	B727	18858
(N101MU)	B727	18255
(N101MU)	B727	18802
N101RW	146	E1002
N101TV	DC-10	46800
N102AA	**DC-10**	**46502**
N102AN	B737	27285
N102CK	**L1011**	**1198**
N102DA	**B767**	**22214**
N102EX	1-11	009
N102FE	**B727**	**19193**
N102GP	1-11	060
N102GU	**B737**	**23535**
N102ME	1-11	067
(N102RW)	146	E1010
N102SW	**B737**	**23108**
N102TV	DC-10	46801
N102UA	DC-10	46905
N103AA	**DC-10**	**46503**
N103CK	**L1011**	**1212**
N103DA	**B767**	**22215**
N103EV	**MD-11**	**48415**
N103EX	1-11	010
N103FE	**B727**	**19199**
N103ML	**F-100**	**11444**
N103MU	B727	18324
(N103RW)	146	E1011
N103SW	**B737**	**23109**
N103TV	DC-10	46802
N103WA	DC-10	46975
N104AA	DC-10	46504
N104CK	**L1011**	**1193**
N104DA	**B767**	**22216**
N104EX	1-11	011
N104FE	**B727**	**19198**
N104ML	**F-100**	**11445**
N104SW	**B737**	**23110**
N104WA	**DC-10**	**46727**
N104WA	DC-10	46986
N105AA	**DC-10**	**46505**
N105BN	B707	18068
N105BV	B707	20297
N105CK	**L1011**	**1178**
N105DA	**B767**	**22217**
N105EV	**MD-11**	**48544**
N105EX	1-11	012
N105FE	**B727**	**19194**
N105ML	**F-100**	**11475**
N105RK	B727	19122
N105SW	**B737**	**23249**
N105UA	**B747**	**26473**
N105WA	**DC-10**	**46891**
N105WP	**DC-8**	**46095**
N106AA	**DC-10**	**46506**
N106BN	B707	18069
N106BV	B707	19415
N106CK	**L1011**	**1211**
N106DA	**B767**	**22218**
N106EX	1-11	013
N106FE	**B727**	**19201**
N106ML	**F-100**	**11477**
N106UA	**B747**	**26474**
N106UR	F-28	11149
N106WA	DC-10	46835
N107AA	**DC-10**	**46507**
N107BN	B707	18739
N107BV	B707	19321
N107DL	**B767**	**22219**
(N107EV)	MD-11	48546
N107EX	1-11	085
N107FE	**B727**	**19202**
N107ML	**F-100**	**11450**
N107PY	**MD-87**	**49671**
N107UR	F-28	11159
N107WA	**DC-10**	**46836**
N108AA	**DC-10**	**46508**
N108BN	B707	18740
N108BV	B707	18940
N108DL	**B767**	**22220**
N108FE	B727	19204
N108ML	**F-100**	**11484**
N108RA	**B707**	**20315**
N108RD	DC-8	45663
N108UR	F-28	11173
N108WA	DC-10	46837
N109AA	DC-10	46509
N109BV	B707	19433
N109DL	**B767**	**22221**
N109FE	B727	19205
N109HT	B727	18998
N109ML	**F-100**	**11485**
N109RD	DC-8	45674
N109TH	1-11	067
N109UR	F-28	11181
N109WA	DC-10	46933
N109WA	DC-10	47819
N110AA	DC-10	46510
N110AC	B727	19253
N110BV	B707	19177
N110DL	**B767**	**22222**
N110DS	**B720**	**18063**
N110FE	B727	19806
N110HM	**MD-83**	**49787**
N110KC	DC-10	48200
N110ML	**F-100**	**11486**
N110NE	**B727**	**18952**
(N110TA)	1-11	BAC.236
N110UR	F-28	11182
N111AA	DC-10	46511
N111AC	**1-11**	**BAC.111**
N111AK	B727	21010
N111DN	**B767**	**22223**
N111EK	B727	19253
N111FE	B727	19805
N111FL	1-11	073
N111GS	1-11	BAC.126
N111JL	B727	18998
N111LP	**1-11**	**068**
N111MD	MD-11	48401
N111MF	B707	18338
(N111MF)	B727	22687
N111NA	1-11	055
N111NA	1-11	060
N111NA	1-11	065
N111NA	1-11	086
N111NS	1-11	078
N111QA	1-11	015
(N111UR)	F-28	11185
N112	CV880	22-7-3-55
N112AA	**DC-10**	**46512**
N112AK	DC-9	47151
(N112BV)	B707	19350
N112DL	**B767**	**22224**
N112FE	**B727**	**19890**
N112HM	B707	19869
N112NA	1-11	059
N112NA	1-11	088
N112PS	**DC-9**	**47013**
(N112TA)	B707	17696
(N112UR)	F-28	11185
N112WA	DC-10	47820
N113	B720	18066
N113	**B727**	**18935**
N113AA	**DC-10**	**46513**
N113AW	B737	24302
N113CA	B727	19243
N113DA	**B767**	**22225**
N113FE	**B727**	**19894**
N113WA	DC-10	47821
N114AA	**DC-10**	**46514**
N114AW	B737	24304
N114DL	**B767**	**22226**
N114FE	**B727**	**19527**
N114HM	B707	19871
N114M	**1-11**	**BAC.119**
N114WA	DC-10	46999
N115AA	**DC-10**	**46515**
N115AW	B737	24305
N115DA	**B767**	**22227**
N115FE	**B727**	**19814**
N115FS	B757	25155
N115TA	B727	20327
N115WA	DC-10	47818
N116AA	**DC-10**	**46516**
(N116AW)	B737	24462
N116DL	**B767**	**23275**
(N116DL)	B767	22228
N116FE	**B727**	**19298**
N116KB	B747	23027
N116TA	B727	20328
N116WA	DC-10	47906
N117AA	**DC-10**	**46517**
(N117AW)	B737	23923
N117DF	B737	23800
N117DL	**B767**	**23276**
(N117DL)	B767	22229
N117FE	**B727**	**19299**
N117KC	B747	23028
N117MR	1-11	065
N117TA	B727	20513
N117UR	F-28	11222
N117WA	**DC-10**	**48318**
N118AA	**DC-10**	**46518**
N118DL	**B767**	**23277**
(N118DL)	B767	22230
N118FE	**B727**	**19300**
N118KD	B747	23029
N118UR	F-28	11224
N119	DC-9	45732
N119AA	**DC-10**	**46519**
N119DL	**B767**	**23278**
(N119DL)	B767	22231
N119FE	**B727**	**19301**
N119GA	**1-11**	**072**
N119KE	B747	23030
N119UR	F-28	11226
N120AA	**DC-10**	**46520**
N120DL	**B767**	**23279**
(N120DL)	B767	22232
N120FE	**B727**	**19356**
N120KF	B747	23031
N120NE	**DC-9**	**45731**
N120TA	1-11	056
N120UR	F-28	11231
N121AA	**DC-10**	**46521**
N121DE	**B767**	**23435**
N121FE	B727	19357
N121GA	DC-8	45632
N121GU	**B737**	**20583**
N121KG	**B747**	**23032**
N121UR	F-28	11237
N122AA	**DC-10**	**46522**
N122DL	**B767**	**23436**
N122FE	B727	19358
N122GU	**B737**	**20586**
N122KH	**B747**	**23033**
(N122NA)	B737	23121
N122UR	F-28	11238
N123AA	**DC-10**	**46523**
N123AF	DC-8	46108
N123DN	**B767**	**23437**
N123FE	B727	19359
N123GU	**B737**	**20587**
N123H	**1-11**	**BAC.163**
N123KJ	**B747**	**23243**
N124	B727	18821
N124AA	**DC-10**	**46524**
N124AF	DC-8	46140
N124AJ	DC-8	45626
N124AS	B727	18821
N124DE	**B767**	**23438**
N124FE	**B727**	**19360**
N124GU	**B737**	**21109**
N124KK	**B747**	**23244**
N125AA	**DC-10**	**46525**
N125DL	**B767**	**24075**
N125DT	**L1011**	**1079**
N125FE	B727	19717
N125GU	B737	23849
N125KL	**B747**	**23245**
N125NK	**DC-9**	**47302**
(N125TW)	B747	20271
N126AA	**DC-10**	**46947**
N126AW	B737	20959
N126DL	**B767**	**24076**
N126FE	B727	19718
N126GU	**B737**	**20582**
N126NK	**DC-9**	**47303**
(N126TW)	B747	20273
N127	B727	19176
N127AA	**DC-10**	**46948**
N127AW	B737	20922
N127DL	**B767**	**24077**
N127FE	**B727**	**19719**
N127GU	**B737**	**22074**
N127MA	B757	25133
N127NK	**DC-9**	**47361**
N128AA	**DC-10**	**46984**
N128AW	B737	20958
N128DL	**B767**	**24078**
N128FE	**B727**	**19720**
N128GA	1-11	BAC.117
N128NA	**B727**	**20879**
N128NK	**DC-9**	**47307**
N128TA	1-11	BAC.117
N129AA	**DC-10**	**46996**
N129AW	B737	21115
N129CA	B727	19501
N129DL	**B767**	**24079**
N129JK	B727	18933
N129NA	**B727**	**20880**
N129NK	**DC-9**	**47305**
N129SW	**B737**	**22340**
N130AA	**DC-10**	**46989**

N130AW	B737	20521
N130DL	**B767**	**24080**
N130FA	DC-10	46554
N130FE	B727	19721
N130KR	**B707**	**18071**
N130SW	**B737**	**22699**
N131AA	**DC-10**	**46994**
N131AW	B737	20956
N131DN	**B767**	**24852**
N131EA	C-18	18713
N131FE	B727	19722
N131LF	A320	0491
N131ML	**F-100**	**11323**
N132AA	**DC-10**	**47827**
N132AW	B737	21186
N132DN	**B767**	**24981**
N132EA	C-18	19566
N132FE	B727	19850
N132ML	**F-100**	**11321**
N133AA	**DC-10**	**47828**
N133AW	B737	21735
N133CA	B727	18844
N133DN	**B767**	**24982**
N133FE	**B727**	**19851**
N133JC	**DC-10**	**46752**
N133ML	**F-100**	**11330**
(N133NA)	B737	23122
N133TW	**B747**	**19957**
N134AA	**DC-10**	**47829**
N134AW	B737	22576
N134CA	B727	18744
N134DL	**B767**	**25123**
N134FE	**B727**	**19852**
N134TW	**B747**	**19958**
N135AA	**DC-10**	**47830**
N135AW	B737	19940
N135CA	B727	19393
N135DL	**B767**	**25145**
N135FE	**B727**	**19853**
N135TA	**B737**	**19940**
N136AA	DC-10	47846
N136AA	DC-9	47553
N136AW	B737	19708
N136DL	**B767**	**25146**
N136FE	**B727**	**19855**
N136TR	**146**	**E2136**
N137AA	**DC-10**	**47847**
N137AW	B737	23148
N137DL	**B767**	**25306**
(N137FE)	B727	19856
N138AA	DC-10	46911
N138AW	**B737**	**22792**
N138DL	**B767**	**25409**
(N138FE)	B727	19857
N138MJ	B707	17696
N138SR	**B707**	**17697**
N138TA	B707	17696
N138TR	**146**	**E2138**
N139AA	DC-10	46711
N139AW	B737	22370
N139DL	**B767**	**25984**
N140AA	**DC-10**	**46712**
N140AW	B737	22371
N140LL	**B767**	**25988**
N140SC	**L1011**	**1067**
N140UA	B747	21022
N141AA	**DC-10**	**46713**
N141AC	146	E2051
N141AW	**B737**	**21955**
N141LF	A320	0405
N141RD	DC-8	45669
N141UA	B747	21023
N141US	**DC-10**	**46750**
N142AA	**DC-10**	**46714**
N142AC	146	E2053
N142AW	B737	20449
N142UA	B747	21024
N142US	DC-10	46751
N143AA	**DC-10**	**46555**
N143AW	B737	22453
N143CA	B727	18743
(N143DA)	B767	25992
N143FE	**B727**	**19136**
N143UA	B747	21025
N143US	DC-10	46752
N144AA	**DC-10**	**47848**
N144AC	146	E2054
N144AW	**B737**	**19074**
(N144DA)	B767	25993
N144FE	**B727**	**19137**
N144JC	**DC-10**	**46753**
(N144NA)	B737	23123
N144SP	B707	19209
N144UA	**B747**	**21026**
N144US	DC-10	46753
N145AA	**DC-10**	**46700**
N145AC	146	E2055
N145AW	**B737**	**20194**
N145FE	**B727**	**19109**
N145SP	B707	20174
N145UA	**B747**	**21441**
N145US	**DC-10**	**46754**
N146AA	**DC-10**	**46701**
N146AC	146	E2057
N146AP	146	E1013
N146AW	B737	20195
N146FE	**B727**	**19110**
N146FT	146	E2056
N146PZ	146	E3149
N146QT	146	E2056
N146SB	146	E2074
N146SP	B707	20016
N146UA	**B747**	**21547**
N146UK	146	E3120
N146US	**DC-10**	**46755**
N147AA	**DC-10**	**46702**
N147AW	**B737**	**22630**
N147FE	**B727**	**19080**
N147SP	B707	20085
N147UA	**B747**	**21548**
N147US	**DC-10**	**46756**
N148AA	**DC-10**	**46703**
N148AC	146	E2058
N148AW	B737	22340
N148FE	**B727**	**19086**
N148UA	B747	21648
N148US	**DC-10**	**46757**
N149AW	**B737**	**22575**
N149FE	**B727**	**19087**
N149FN	B727	18814
N149UA	B747	21649
N149US	**DC-10**	**46758**
N150AW	**B737**	**23218**
N150FE	**B727**	**19141**
N150FN	B727	19166
N150UA	B747	21992
N150US	**DC-10**	**46759**
N151AA	**DC-10**	**46706**
N151AW	**B737**	**23219**
N151FE	**B727**	**19147**
N151FN	B727	18805
N151LF	B757	26275
N151SY	**DC-10**	**48295**
N151UA	**B747**	**23736**
N151US	**DC-10**	**46760**
N152AA	**DC-10**	**46707**
N152AW	B737	23387
N152FE	**B727**	**18285**
N152FN	B727	19167
N152LM	B707	19210
N152SY	**DC-10**	**48289**
N152UA	**B747**	**23737**
N152US	**DC-10**	**46761**
N153AA	**DC-10**	**46708**
N153AF	DC-8	45682
N153AW	B737	23406
N153FA	DC-8	45755
N153FE	B727	18286
N153FN	B727	18846
N153UA	**B747**	**20102**
N153US	**DC-10**	**46762**
N154AA	**DC-10**	**46709**
N154AW	**B737**	**23776**
N154FE	**B727**	**18287**
N154FN	B727	18815
N154UA	**B747**	**20103**
N154US	**DC-10**	**46763**
N155AW	**B737**	**23777**
N155FE	**B727**	**18288**
(N155FN)	B727	18816
(N155MA)	B737	23124
(N155PA)	B737	20440
N155UA	**B747**	**20104**
N155US	**DC-10**	**46764**
N156AW	**B737**	**23778**
N156FE	**B727**	**18289**
N156FN	B727	18943
N156PL	MD-88	49759
N156TR	**146**	**E2156**
N156UA	**B747**	**20105**
N156US	**DC-10**	**46765**
N157AW	**B737**	**23779**
N157FE	B727	18314
(N157FN)	B727	18804
N157PL	MD-88	49760
N157UA	**B747**	**20106**
N157US	**DC-10**	**46766**
N158AW	**B737**	**23780**
(N158FE)	B727	18315
N158FN	B727	18812
N158PL	**MD-88**	**49761**
N158UA	**B747**	**21054**
N158US	**DC-10**	**46767**
N159AW	B737	23781
(N159FE)	B727	18316
(N159FN)	B727	18811
N159PL	**B737**	**21186**
(N159PL)	MD-88	49762
N159UA	**B747**	**21140**
N159US	**DC-10**	**46768**
N160AA	**DC-10**	**46710**
N160AW	**B737**	**23782**
(N160FE)	B727	18317
N160FN	B727	18942
N160GL	**B707**	**20026**
N160PL	**MD-88**	**49763**
N160UA	**B747**	**21237**
N160US	**DC-10**	**46769**
N161AA	**DC-10**	**46942**
N161AW	B737	23783
N161DB	**DC-8**	**45980**
N161FN	**B737**	**20521**
N161GL	B707	20172
N161LF	B757	26274
N161PL	**MD-88**	**49764**
N161UA	**B747**	**21352**
N161US	**DC-10**	**46770**
N162AA	**DC-10**	**46943**
N162AW	B737	23784
N162CA	DC-8	45956
(N162FE)	B727	18318
N162GL	B707	20089
N162PL	**MD-88**	**49765**
N162QS	DC-8	45956
N162US	**DC-10**	**46771**
N162W	**1-11**	**087**
N163AA	**DC-10**	**46914**
N163AW	B737	23785
N163CA	DC-8	45955
(N163FE)	B727	18319
(N163GL)	B707	20179
N163PL	MD-88	49766
N163PM	F-28	11163
N163UA	**B747**	**21353**
N163US	**146**	**E2022**
N164AA	**DC-10**	**46950**
N164AW	**B737**	**23625**
(N164FE)	B727	18861
(N164GL)	B707	20069
N164PL	B737	22735
N164UA	**B747**	**21657**
N164W	**1-11**	**090**
N165AW	**B737**	**23626**
(N165FE)	B727	18862
N165PL	A300	584
N165UA	**B747**	**21658**
N165US	**146**	**E2023**
N165W	B737	19605
N166AA	**DC-10**	**46908**
N166AW	**B737**	**23627**
N166FE	**B727**	**18863**
N166PL	A300	603
N166PL	MD-88	49928
N166US	**146**	**E2024**
N167AA	**DC-10**	**46930**
N167AW	**B737**	**23628**
N167FE	**B727**	**18864**
N167PL	B737	22531
N167US	**146**	**E2025**
N168AA	**DC-10**	**46938**
N168AW	**B737**	**23629**
N168FE	**B727**	**18865**
N168PL	**MD-88**	**53174**
N169AW	**B737**	**23630**
N169FE	**B727**	**18866**
N169PL	**MD-88**	**53175**
(N170AW)	B737	23122
N170FE	1-11	057
N170PL	**B737**	**22733**
N170RJ	146	E1199
N171AA	**DC-10**	**46906**
N171AW	B737	21599
N171DN	**B767**	**24759**
N171FE	1-11	061
N171G	**B727**	**21071**
N171LF	B767	26262
N171PL	**B737**	**22734**
N171UA	**B747**	**24322**
N171US	**146**	**E2028**
N172AW	**B737**	**23631**
N172DN	**B767**	**24775**
N172FE	1-11	056
N172PL	B737	19711
N172UA	**B747**	**24363**
N172US	146	E2030
N173AW	**B737**	**23632**
N173DN	**B767**	**24800**
N173FE	1-11	087
N173PL	B737	20236
N173UA	**B747**	**24380**
N173US	**146**	**E2031**
N174AW	**B737**	**23633**
N174DN	**B767**	**24802**
(N174FE)	1-11	BAC.127
N174GM	**B747**	**21141**
N174UA	**B747**	**24381**
N174US	**146**	**E2034**
N175AW	**B737**	**23634**
N175DN	**B767**	**24803**
N175UA	**B747**	**24382**
N175US	146	E2036
N176DN	**B767**	**25061**
N176UA	**B747**	**24383**
N177DN	**B767**	**25122**
N177UA	**B747**	**24384**
N177US	**146**	**E2039**
N178AT	**L1011**	**1008**
N178AW	**B737**	**22645**
N178DN	**B767**	**25143**
N178EE	B737	22728
N178UA	**B747**	**24385**
N178US	**146**	**E2040**
N179AT	**L1011**	**1120**
N179AW	**B737**	**22646**
N179DN	**B767**	**25144**
N179FE	1-11	075
N179UA	**B747**	**25158**
N179US	**146**	**E2041**
N180AW	**B737**	**22647**
N180AX	**B727**	**20041**
N180DN	**B767**	**25985**
N180FE	B727	18867
N180RN	B737	22628
N180UA	**B747**	**25224**
N181AT	**L1011**	**1125**
N181AW	**B737**	**22648**
N181DN	**B767**	**25986**
N181FE	**B727**	**18868**
N181LF	B767	26261
N181SK	**DC-8**	**45910**
N181UA	**B747**	**25278**
N181US	**146**	**E2042**
N182AW	**B737**	**22649**
N182DN	**B767**	**25987**
N182UA	**B747**	**25279**
N183AT	DC-10	46501
N183AT	**L1011**	**1153**
N183AW	**B737**	**22650**
N183DN	**B767**	**27110**
N183NA	**MD-83**	**49808**
N183UA	**B747**	**25379**
N183US	**146**	**E2043**
N184AT	DC-10	46751
N184AW	**B737**	**22651**

N184DN	**B767**	**27111**
N184FE	**B727**	**18870**
N184UA	**B747**	**25380**
N184US	**146**	**E2044**
N185AT	**L1011**	**1052**
N185AW	**B737**	**22652**
N185DN	**B767**	**27961**
N185FE	**B727**	**18871**
N185UA	**B747**	**25395**
N185US	**146**	**E2045**
N186AT	**L1011**	**1074**
N186AW	**B737**	**22653**
N186DN	**B767**	**27962**
N186FE	**B727**	**18872**
N186UA	**B747**	**26875**
N187AT	**L1011**	**1077**
N187AW	**B737**	**22654**
N187DN	**B767**	**27582**
N187FE	**B727**	**19079**
N187UA	**B747**	**26876**
N187US	**146**	**E2046**
N188AT	**L1011**	**1078**
N188AW	**B737**	**22655**
N188CL	B727	18893
N188DN	**B767**	**27583**
N188FE	**B727**	**19081**
N188LF	B737	23766
N188UA	**B747**	**26877**
N188US	146	E2047
N189AT	**L1011**	**1081**
N189AW	**B737**	**22656**
N189CB	B727	20739
N189FE	**B727**	**19082**
N189UA	**B747**	**26878**
N189US	**146**	**E2048**
N190AJ	**B727**	**18878**
N190AT	**L1011**	**1086**
(N190AW)	B737	20364
(N190CB)	B727	20545
N190FE	**B727**	**19083**
N190PL	A300	709
N190UA	**B747**	**26879**
N190US	146	E2072
N191AT	**L1011**	**1084**
N191CB	B727	20822
N191FE	**B727**	**19084**
(N191FS)	B727	19262
N191G	B737	25191
N191LF	B737	24332
N191PL	A300	713
N191UA	**B747**	**26880**
N191US	146	E2073
N192AT	**L1011**	**1057**
N192FE	B727	19085
N192GP	B737	21192
N192PL	A300	715
N192SA	DC-9	47418
N192UA	**B747**	**26882**
N192US	146	E2074
N193AT	**L1011**	**1071**
N193FE	**B727**	**19142**
N193UA	**B747**	**26883**
N193US	146	E2075
N194AT	**L1011**	**1230**
(N194AW)	B737	19552
N194CA	B707	17663
N194FE	**B727**	**19143**
N194US	**DC-9**	**47016**
N195AT	**L1011**	**1041**
N195AW	B737	21500
N195CA	B707	17668
N195FE	**B727**	**19144**
N195US	**DC-9**	**47017**
N196AJ	**B727**	**20838**
N196AT	**L1011**	**1076**
N196AW	B737	21501
N196CA	B707	17610
N196FE	**B727**	**19145**
N196US	**DC-9**	**47155**
N197AL	B737	20300
N197AT	**L1011**	**1082**
N197AW	B737	19709
N197CA	B707	17672
(N197FE)	B727	19146
N197JQ	B737	20196
N197QQ	B737	21184
N197SS	B737	20711
N197US	**DC-9**	**47154**
N198AW	B737	19710
N198CA	**B707**	**17661**
N198FE	**B727**	**19154**
N198US	**DC-9**	**47045**
N199AM	B727	19262
N199AW	B737	19712
N199FE	B727	19509
N200AU	**B737**	**19418**
N200AV	B727	21930
N200CC	1-11	068
N200LR	B727	21945
N200NE	B737	20440
N201EA	**A300**	**41**
N201FE	**B727**	**22924**
N201FE	B737	21926
N201US	**B727**	**22154**
N202AE	**B747**	**21097**
N202AU	B737	19419
N202AV	B727	21931
(N202BN)	F-100	11257
N202DJ	B707	20017
N202EA	**A300**	**42**
N202ME	**DC-9**	**47672**
N202PA	A300	195
N202PH	B747	20888
N202UA	**B737**	**24717**
N202US	**B727**	**22155**
N203AA	**MD-82**	**49145**
N203AE	**B747**	**21098**
N203AU	**B737**	**19420**
N203AV	**B727**	**22474**
N203EA	**A300**	**43**
N203FE	**B727**	**22925**
N203FE	B737	21927
N203ME	**DC-9**	**47673**
N203PA	A300	227
N203UA	**B737**	**24718**
N203US	**B727**	**22543**
N204AE	**B747**	**21099**
N204AU	**B737**	**19603**
N204AV	B727	22475
N204EA	**A300**	**44**
N204FE	**B727**	**22926**
N204FE	B737	21928
N204ME	**DC-9**	**47680**
N204P	F-28	11227
N204PA	A300	198
N204US	**B727**	**22544**
N205AA	**MD-82**	**49155**
N205AU	**B737**	**19421**
N205AV	B727	22476
N205EA	A300	65
N205FE	**B727**	**22927**
N205FE	B737	21929
N205P	F-28	11228
N205PA	A300	247
N205US	B727	20392
N206AU	**B737**	**19422**
N206EA	A300	66
N206FE	**B727**	**22928**
N206FE	B737	21959
N206ME	**DC-9**	**47791**
N206P	F-28	11229
N206PA	A300	234
N206US	B727	20393
N207AA	**MD-82**	**49158**
N207AE	**B747**	**21516**
N207AU	**B737**	**19423**
N207EA	A300	67
N207FE	**B727**	**22929**
N207ME	**DC-9**	**47794**
N207P	F-28	11230
N207PA	A300	236
N207US	B727	20302
N207US	**B727**	**21699**
N208AA	**MD-82**	**49159**
N208AE	**B747**	**21517**
N208AU	**B737**	**19547**
N208EA	A300	68
N208FE	**B727**	**22930**
N208P	F-28	11233
N208PA	A300	304
N208UP	**B727**	**21701**
N208US	B727	20303
N209EA	A300	86
N209FE	**B727**	**22931**
N209ME	**DC-9**	**47730**
N209P	F-28	11234
N209PA	A300	305
N209UP	**B727**	**21698**
N209US	**B737**	**19548**
N210AA	**MD-82**	**49161**
N210DS	B720	18167
N210EA	A300	87
N210FE	**B727**	**22932**
N210G	CRVL	138
N210NE	**B727**	**18903**
(N210NE)	B727	18905
N210PA	A300	238
N210UP	**B727**	**21697**
N210US	B737	19555
N211FE	**B727**	**22933**
N211JL	**B747**	**22989**
N211MD	MD-11	48402
N211NW	**DC-10**	**46868**
N211PA	A300	235
N211PL	B737	20681
N211UP	**B727**	**21700**
N211US	B737	20211
N212EA	A300	91
N212FE	**B727**	**22934**
N212JL	**B747**	**23067**
N212PA	A300	208
N212PL	B737	20776
N212UP	**B727**	**21392**
N212US	**B737**	**20212**
N213EA	A300	92
N213FE	**B727**	**22935**
N213JL	**B747**	**23068**
N213PA	A300	210
N213UP	**B727**	**21341**
N213US	**B737**	**20213**
N214AA	**MD-82**	**49162**
N214AU	**B737**	**20214**
N214P	F-28	11235
N214UP	**B727**	**21342**
N215AA	**MD-82**	**49163**
N215EA	A300	108
N215FE	**B727**	**22936**
N215P	F-28	11240
N215US	**B737**	**20095**
N216AA	**MD-82**	**49167**
N216EA	A300	118
N216FE	**B727**	**22937**
N216PA	A300	204
N216US	**B737**	**19954**
N217CA	1-11	063
N217EA	A300	119
N217FE	**B727**	**22938**
N217US	**B737**	**20215**
N218AA	**MD-82**	**49168**
N218CA	1-11	089
N218FE	**B727**	**21101**
N218TT	**B727**	**19684**
N218US	**B737**	**20216**
N219AA	**MD-82**	**49171**
N219EA	A300	120
N219FE	**B727**	**21102**
N219US	**B737**	**20414**
N220AM	B707	17696
N220AU	**DC-10**	**46501**
N220EA	A300	124
N220FE	**B727**	**20934**
N220NE	**B727**	**18905**
N220NW	**DC-10**	**46577**
N220RB	**DC-8**	**45280**
N220US	**B737**	**20453**
N221AA	**MD-82**	**49172**
N221AL	B727	22044
N221AU	B737	20125
N221CN	1-11	BAC.111
N221EA	**A300**	**152**
N221FE	B727	20764
N221FE	**B727**	**20932**
N221GE	B747	22995
N221GF	B747	22996
N221MP	B747	20120
N221NW	**DC-10**	**46579**
N221US	**B737**	**20454**
N222AW	B737	23789
N222AW	B737	24791
N222EA	A300	153
N222FE	B727	20765
N222FE	**B727**	**20933**
N222KW	**A300**	**236**
N223AA	**MD-82**	**49173**
N223AW	B737	24790
N223EA	A300	154
N223FB	DC-8	45985
N223FE	**B727**	**20935**
(N223FE)	B727	20766
N223KW	**A300**	**227**
N223NW	**DC-10**	**46580**
N223US	**B737**	**21665**
N224AA	**MD-82**	**49174**
N224EA	A300	155
N224KW	**A300**	**73**
N224NW	**DC-10**	**46581**
N224US	**B737**	**21666**
N225AA	**MD-82**	**49175**
N225EA	A300	158
N225GE	**A300**	**158**
N225KW	**A300**	**93**
N225NW	**DC-10**	**46582**
N225RX	A320	0225
N225US	**B737**	**21667**
N225VV	DC-8	45765
N226AA	**MD-82**	**49176**
N226AW	B737	25010
N226EA	A300	161
N226GE	**A300**	**161**
N226KW	**A300**	**95**
N226NW	**DC-10**	**46583**
N226US	**B737**	**21815**
N226VV	DC-8	45766
N227AA	**MD-82**	**49177**
N227AU	**B737**	**21816**
N227AW	B737	25011
N227EA	A300	204
N227JL	**B727**	**20875**
N227NW	**DC-10**	**46969**
N227VV	B707	19212
N228AA	**MD-82**	**49178**
N228AW	B737	25032
N228EA	A300	207
N228G	B727	20533
N228NW	**DC-10**	**46578**
N228US	**B737**	**21817**
N228VV	B707	18714
N228Z	DC-9	47151
N229EA	A300	211
N229NW	**DC-10**	**46551**
N229US	**B737**	**21818**
N230AU	**B737**	**21975**
N230EA	A300	216
N230NE	**B727**	**18907**
N230NW	**DC-10**	**46552**
N230RX	A320	0230
N231EA	A300	220
N231US	**B737**	**21976**
N232AA	**MD-82**	**49179**
N232EA	A300	259
N232NW	DC-10	46961
N232TA	**B737**	**22277**
N232US	**B737**	**22018**
N233AA	**MD-82**	**49180**
N233EA	A300	261
N233FE	**B727**	**21327**
N233US	**B737**	**22273**
N234AA	**MD-82**	**49181**
N234DC	DC-10	46940
N234EA	A300	271
N234FA	B707	20069
N234FE	B727	21328
N234US	**B737**	**22274**
N235EA	A300	274
N235FE	B727	21329
N235US	**B737**	**22275**
N235WA	**B737**	**22859**
N236AA	**MD-82**	**49251**
(N236DH)	B727	19191
N236FE	**B727**	**21330**
N236TA	**B737**	**19708**
N236US	**B737**	**22352**
N236WA	**B737**	**23184**
N237AA	**MD-82**	**49253**

Registration	Type	c/n
(N237DH)	B727	19192
N237FE	B727	21331
N237G	B707	19133
N237TA	B737	21645
N237US	**B737**	**22353**
N237WA	**B737**	**23185**
N238AT	B727	19150
N238RX	A320	0238
N238TA	**B737**	**22075**
(N238TZ)	B727	19150
N238US	**B737**	**22398**
N238WA	**B737**	**23186**
N239TA	**B737**	**23789**
N239US	**B737**	**22354**
N239WA	**B737**	**23187**
N240AU	**B737**	**22355**
N240FE	**B727**	**20978**
N240LA	B757	24367
N240NE	**B727**	**18906**
(N240RC)	CRVL	87
N240WA	B737	23188
N241AA	**MD-82**	**49254**
N241FE	**B727**	**20979**
N241LF	**B737**	**24132**
N241TC	DC-9	45775
N241US	**B737**	**22443**
N241WA	B737	23189
N242AA	**MD-82**	**49255**
N242FE	**B727**	**21178**
N242US	**B737**	**22444**
N242WA	**B737**	**23516**
N243FE	**B727**	**21480**
N243US	**B737**	**22445**
N243WA	**B737**	**23517**
N244AA	**MD-82**	**49256**
N244FE	**B727**	**21647**
N244US	**B737**	**22752**
N244WA	**B737**	**23518**
N245AA	**MD-82**	**49257**
N245AC	B707	18068
N245FE	**B727**	**22016**
N245HG	**DC-8**	**45662**
N245US	**B737**	**22751**
N245WA	**B737**	**23519**
N246AA	**MD-82**	**49258**
N246FE	**B727**	**22068**
N246SS	**146**	**E1003**
N246US	**B737**	**22753**
N246WA	B737	23520
N247JM	**A300**	**247**
N247RX	A320	0247
N247SP	B747	21023
N247US	**B737**	**22754**
N247WA	B737	23521
N248AA	**MD-82**	**49259**
N248US	**B737**	**22755**
N248WA	B737	23602
N249AA	**MD-82**	**49269**
N249US	**B737**	**22756**
N249WA	B737	23603
N250LA	B757	24291
N250NE	B727	20112
N251AA	**MD-82**	**49270**
N251DH	B727	19968
N251LF	**B737**	**22408**
N251US	B727	19970
N251US	**B737**	**22757**
N252AU	**B737**	**22758**
N252US	**B727**	**19971**
N253AA	**MD-82**	**49286**
N253AU	**B737**	**22795**
N253DV	**B737**	**23800**
N253FA	DC-8	45660
N253US	B727	19972
N254AU	**B737**	**22796**
N254FE	**B727**	**20936**
N254US	B727	19973
(N254WA)	B737	23604
N255AA	**MD-82**	**49287**
N255AU	**B737**	**22797**
N255US	**B727**	**19974**
(N255WA)	B737	23605
N256AU	**B737**	**22798**
N256US	**B727**	**19975**
(N256WA)	B737	23606
N257AU	**B737**	**22799**
N257FE	**B727**	**20939**
N257RX	A320	0257
N257US	B727	19976
(N257WA)	B737	23607
N258AA	**MD-82**	**49288**
N258FE	**B727**	**20940**
N258KP	B727	19977
N258US	**B727**	**19977**
(N258WA)	B737	23608
N259AA	**MD-82**	**49289**
N259AU	**B737**	**22806**
N259US	**B727**	**19978**
(N259WA)	B737	23609
N260AU	**B737**	**22866**
N260GS	**B727**	**19261**
N260NE	B727	20113
N260US	B727	19979
N261AU	**B737**	**22867**
N261LF	B737	26294
N261LR	**B737**	**22402**
N261US	**B727**	**19980**
N262AA	**MD-82**	**49290**
N262AU	**B737**	**22868**
N262FE	**B727**	**21624**
N262US	B727	19981
N263AU	**B737**	**22869**
N263FE	**B727**	**21625**
N263US	**B727**	**19982**
N264AU	**B737**	**22961**
N264FE	**B727**	**21626**
N264US	**B727**	**19983**
N265AU	**B737**	**22962**
N265FE	**B727**	**21671**
N265US	B727	19984
N266AA	**MD-82**	**49291**
N266AU	**B737**	**22878**
N266FE	**B727**	**21672**
N266US	**B727**	**19985**
N267AU	**B737**	**22879**
N267FE	**B727**	**21673**
N267US	**B727**	**20289**
N268AU	**B737**	**22880**
N268FE	**B727**	**21674**
N268US	**B727**	**20290**
N269AA	**MD-82**	**49292**
N269AU	**B737**	**22881**
N269FE	**B727**	**21675**
N269US	**B727**	**20291**
N270AE	B757	22185
N270AU	**B737**	**22882**
N270AX	**B727**	**19170**
N270E	1-11	BAC.120
N270FE	**B727**	**22035**
N270US	**B727**	**20292**
N271AA	**MD-82**	**49293**
N271AE	B757	23227
N271AF	B727	22003
N271AU	**B737**	**22883**
N271FE	**B727**	**22036**
N271LF	B737	23788
N271LR	**B737**	**22636**
N271N	F-28	11105
N271US	B727	20293
N271WA	**MD-11**	**48518**
N272AF	B727	22004
N272AU	**B737**	**22884**
N272FE	**B727**	**22037**
N272N	F-28	11095
N272US	**B727**	**20294**
N272WA	**MD-11**	**48437**
N273AF	B727	22005
N273AU	**B737**	**22885**
N273FE	**B727**	**22038**
N273N	F-28	11106
N273US	B727	20295
N273WA	**MD-11**	**48519**
N274AA	**MD-82**	**49271**
N274AF	B727	22091
N274AU	B737	22886
N274AW	DC-9	47236
(N274BN)	B727	20548
N274FE	**B727**	**22039**
N274N	F-28	11107
N274US	B727	20296
N274US	**B737**	**22886**
N274WA	**MD-11**	**48633**
N274WC	B727	20548
N275AA	**MD-82**	**49272**
N275AF	**B727**	**22092**
N275AU	**B737**	**22887**
N275AW	B757	25495
N275B	B707	20060
(N275BN)	B727	20549
N275FE	**B727**	**22040**
N275US	**B727**	**21154**
N275WA	**MD-11**	**48631**
N275WC	**B727**	**20549**
N276AA	**MD-82**	**49273**
N276AU	**B737**	**22888**
N276AW	B767	27376
(N276BN)	B727	20550
N276C	DC-8	45641
N276FE	**B727**	**22041**
N276US	**B727**	**21155**
N276WA	**MD-11**	**48632**
N276WC	B727	20550
N277AU	**B737**	**22889**
N277AW	DC-9	47230
N277FE	**B727**	**22042**
N277NS	1-11	057
N277US	**B727**	**21156**
N277WA	**MD-11**	**48743**
N278AA	**MD-82**	**49294**
N278AU	**B737**	**22890**
N278C	DC-8	45643
N278FE	**B727**	**22345**
N278US	**B727**	**21157**
N279AA	**MD-82**	**49295**
N279AU	**B737**	**22891**
N279FE	**B727**	**22346**
N279US	**B727**	**21158**
N280AU	**B737**	**22892**
N280FE	**B727**	**22347**
N280FH	F-28	11048
(N280FH)	F-28	11049
N280N	F-28	11061
N280NE	**B727**	**18971**
N280RX	A320	0280
N280US	**B727**	**21159**
N280WA	**MD-11**	**48458**
N281AU	**B737**	**23114**
N281FE	**B727**	**22348**
N281FH	F-28	11016
N281LF	**B737**	**22071**
N281MP	F-28	11221
N281N	F-28	11075
N281SC	B727	21949
N281US	**B727**	**21160**
N281ZV	B727	19281
N282AU	**B737**	**23115**
N282FE	**B727**	**22349**
N282FH	F-28	11018
N282MP	F-28	11223
N282N	F-28	11032
N282SC	**B727**	**22558**
N282US	**B727**	**21161**
N282WA	**B727**	**21484**
N283AA	**MD-82**	**49296**
N283AT	B727	19150
N283AU	**B737**	**23116**
N283DH	B727	18275
N283FE	**B727**	**22350**
N283FH	F-28	11020
(N283MP)	F-28	11226
N283N	F-28	11035
N283SC	**B727**	**22559**
N283US	**B727**	**21322**
N283WA	**B727**	**21485**
N284AT	B727	19151
N284AU	**B737**	**23131**
N284FE	**B727**	**22621**
N284FH	F-28	11024
(N284MP)	F-28	11231
N284N	F-28	11036
N284SC	**B727**	**21438**
(N284TZ)	B727	19151
N284US	**B727**	**21323**
N284WA	B727	21697
N285AA	**MD-82**	**49297**
N285AT	B727	19152
N285AU	**B737**	**23132**
N285AW	DC-9	47231
N285FE	**B727**	**22622**
N285FH	F-28	11033
(N285FH)	F-28	11032
N285SC	**B727**	**21676**
(N285TZ)	B727	19152
N285US	**B727**	**21324**
N286AA	**MD-82**	**49298**
N286AT	B727	19153
N286AU	**B737**	**23133**
N286AW	DC-9	47311
N286FE	**B727**	**22623**
N286FH	F-28	11038
N286N	F-28	11044
N286SC	**B727**	**21601**
N286US	**B727**	**21325**
N286WA	B727	21698
N287AA	**MD-82**	**49299**
N287AT	B727	18805
N287AU	**B737**	**23134**
N287FE	**B727**	**21849**
N287FH	F-28	11043
N287MD	MD-87	49389
N287N	F-28	11087
N287SC	**B727**	**21345**
N287US	**B727**	**21375**
N287WA	B727	21699
N288AA	**MD-82**	**49300**
N288AS	B727	22003
N288AT	B727	18943
N288AU	**B737**	**23135**
N288FE	**B727**	**21850**
N288FH	F-28	11044
N288N	F-28	11054
N288SC	**B727**	**20765**
N288US	**B727**	**21376**
N288WA	B727	21700
N289AA	**MD-82**	**49301**
N289AS	B727	22004
N289AT	B727	18942
N289FH	F-28	11047
N289N	F-28	11064
N289SC	**B727**	**22475**
(N289SC)	B727	21979
N289US	**B727**	**21377**
N289WA	B727	21701
N290AA	**MD-82**	**49302**
N290AS	B727	21510
N290AT	B727	18812
N290N	F-28	11063
N290NE	**B727**	**18972**
N290UE	146	E2080
N290US	**B727**	**21378**
N290WA	**B727**	**22108**
N291AA	**MD-82**	**49303**
N291AS	B727	21511
N291EA	A300	49
N291N	F-28	11043
N291UE	146	E2084
N291US	**B727**	**21379**
N291WA	**B727**	**22109**
N292AA	**MD-82**	**49304**
N292AS	B727	21458
N292EA	A300	51
N292UE	146	E2087
N292US	**B727**	**21503**
N292WA	**B727**	**22110**
N293AA	**MD-82**	**49305**
N293AS	B727	19534
N293AS	**B727**	**21348**
N293N	F-28	11037
N293UE	**146**	**E2097**
N293US	**B727**	**21504**
N293WA	**B727**	**22111**
N294AA	**MD-82**	**49306**
N294AS	**B727**	**22146**
N294N	F-28	11101
N294UE	**146**	**E2107**
N294US	**B727**	**21505**
N294WA	**B727**	**22112**
N295AA	**MD-82**	**49307**
N295AS	**B727**	**22147**
N295UE	**146**	**E2108**
N295US	**B727**	**21506**
N295WA	**B727**	**22532**
N296AA	**MD-82**	**49308**
N296AS	**B727**	**21459**

N296N	F-28	11096
N296US	**B727**	**21788**
N296WA	**B727**	**22533**
N297AA	**MD-82**	**49309**
N297AS	B727	21608
N297BN	B727	19391
N297N	F-28	11098
N297US	**B727**	**21789**
N297WA	**B727**	**22534**
N298AA	**MD-82**	**49310**
N298AS	B727	21426
N298BN	B727	19392
N298N	F-28	11103
N298US	**B727**	**22152**
N299AS	**B727**	**21427**
N299BN	B727	19393
N299LA	**B727**	**19121**
N299US	**B727**	**22153**
N300AA	B727	18856
N300AU	**B737**	**23228**
N300AW	**L1011**	**1134**
N300BN	B727	19394
N300DK	B727	18998
N300ME	**DC-9**	**45718**
N300ML	**A320**	**0317**
N300NE	**B727**	**18974**
N300SW	**B737**	**22940**
N301AA	**B767**	**22307**
N301AC	B737	23288
N301AL	B737	23841
N301AS	B720	18376
N301AU	**B737**	**23229**
N301AW	B737	24008
N301BN	B727	19395
N301DE	B737	25994
N301DL	**B737**	**23073**
N301EA	L1011	1003
(N301EA)	L1011	1002
N301FE	**DC-10**	**46800**
(N301FE)	DC-10	47807
N301ME	**DC-9**	**47190**
N301ML	**A320**	**0315**
N301P	B737	23228
N301RC	**MD-82**	**48054**
N301SA	A320	0354
N301SW	**B737**	**22941**
N301TW	B747	20501
N301UA	**B737**	**23642**
N301UP	**B767**	**27239**
N301US	**A320**	**0031**
(N301US)	B747	23719
N301XV	B737	20253
N302AA	**B767**	**22308**
N302AL	B737	23943
N302AS	B720	18377
N302AU	B737	23230
N302AW	**B737**	**24009**
N302BN	B727	19242
N302DE	B737	25995
N302DL	**B737**	**23074**
N302EA	L1011	1003
N302FE	**DC-10**	**46801**
(N302FE)	DC-10	47808
N302MB	**L1011**	**1129**
N302ME	**DC-9**	**47102**
N302ML	**A320**	**0338**
N302RC	**MD-82**	**48055**
(N302RP)	MD-82	48054
N302SA	A320	0357
N302SW	**B737**	**22942**
N302TW	B747	20502
N302UA	**B737**	**23643**
N302UP	**B767**	**27240**
N302US	**A320**	**0032**
(N302US)	B747	23720
N302VA	**B737**	**20126**
N302WA	**B737**	**23182**
N302XV	B737	20254
N303AA	**B767**	**22309**
N303AC	B737	23289
N303AL	**B737**	**23499**
N303AS	B720	18042
(N303AU)	B737	25265
N303AW	**B737**	**24010**
N303BN	B727	18897
N303DE	B737	25996
N303DL	**B737**	**23075**
N303EA	**L1011**	**1004**
N303FE	**DC-10**	**46802**
(N303FE)	DC-10	47809
N303ML	**A320**	**0304**
N303P	B737	23229
(N303RP)	MD-82	48055
N303SA	A320	0411
N303SW	**B737**	**22943**
N303TW	**B747**	**20116**
N303UA	**B737**	**23644**
N303UP	**B767**	**27241**
N303US	**A320**	**0034**
(N303US)	B747	23818
N303VA	**B737**	**20125**
N303WA	**B737**	**23183**
N303XV	B737	20255
N304AA	**B767**	**22310**
N304AC	B737	23290
N304AL	**B737**	**23500**
N304AS	B727	22005
(N304AU)	B737	25282
N304AW	**B737**	**24011**
N304BN	B727	20217
N304DE	B737	25997
N304DL	**B737**	**23076**
N304EA	**L1011**	**1005**
N304FE	**DC-10**	**46992**
(N304FE)	DC-10	47810
N304ML	**A320**	**0373**
N304P	B737	23230
N304RC	MD-82	48056
(N304RP)	MD-82	48056
N304RX	A320	0304
N304S	B720	18049
N304SW	**B737**	**22944**
N304TW	B747	20117
N304UA	**B737**	**23665**
N304UP	**B767**	**27242**
N304US	**A320**	**0040**
(N304US)	B747	23819
N304VA	**B737**	**19617**
N304WA	**B737**	**23345**
N304XV	B737	20256
N305AA	**B767**	**22311**
N305AS	B727	22091
(N305AU)	B737	25326
N305AW	**B737**	**24012**
N305BN	B727	18794
N305DE	B737	25998
N305DL	**B737**	**23077**
N305EA	L1011	1006
N305FE	**DC-10**	**47870**
N305GB	**L1011**	**1127**
N305P	B737	23257
(N305RP)	MD-82	48057
N305SW	**B737**	**22945**
N305TW	**B747**	**20742**
N305UA	**B737**	**23666**
N305UP	**B767**	**27243**
N305US	**A320**	**0041**
(N305US)	B747	23820
N305VA	**B737**	**19606**
N305WA	**B737**	**23346**
N306AA	B737	23291
N306AA	**B767**	**22312**
N306AS	B727	21997
(N306AU)	B737	25327
N306AW	**B737**	**24633**
N306BN	B727	18795
(N306DE)	B737	25999
N306DL	**B737**	**23078**
N306EA	L1011	1007
N306FE	**DC-10**	**48287**
N306GB	**L1011**	**1138**
N306P	B737	23258
N306RC	MD-82	48057
(N306RP)	MD-82	48086
N306SW	**B737**	**22946**
N306TW	**B747**	**20398**
(N306TW)	B747	19655
N306UA	**B737**	**23667**
N306US	**A320**	**0060**
(N306US)	B747	23821
N306VA	B737	19609
N306WA	**B737**	**23347**
N307AA	**B767**	**22313**
N307AC	B737	23251
N307AS	**B727**	**22000**
(N307AU)	B737	25328
N307AW	**B737**	**24634**
N307BN	B727	18796
(N307DE)	B737	26000
N307DL	**B737**	**23079**
N307EA	L1011	1008
N307FE	**DC-10**	**48291**
N307GB	**L1011**	**1131**
N307P	B737	23259
N307RC	**MD-82**	**48086**
(N307RP)	MD-82	48087
N307SW	**B737**	**22947**
N307UA	**B737**	**23668**
N307US	**A320**	**0106**
(N307US)	B747	24222
N307VA	**B737**	**19600**
N307WA	**B737**	**23440**
N308AA	**B767**	**22314**
N308AC	B737	23252
N308AS	**B727**	**22002**
(N308AU)	B737	25329
N308AW	**B737**	**24710**
N308BN	B727	19827
(N308DE)	B737	26001
N308DL	**B737**	**23080**
N308EA	L1011	1009
N308FE	**DC-10**	**48297**
N308GB	**L1011**	**1133**
(N308RC)	MD-82	48087
N308UA	**B737**	**23669**
N308US	**A320**	**0107**
(N308US)	B747	24223
N308VA	**B737**	**19613**
N308WA	**B737**	**23441**
N309AC	B737	23253
N309AS	**B727**	**21947**
(N309AU)	B737	25330
N309AW	**B737**	**24711**
N309BN	B727	19808
(N309DE)	B737	26002
N309DL	**B737**	**23081**
N309EA	L1011	1010
N309EL	B707	18692
N309FE	**DC-10**	**48298**
N309GB	**L1011**	**1156**
N309P	B737	23260
N309RC	**MD-82**	**48088**
N309SW	**B737**	**22948**
N309UA	**B737**	**23670**
N309US	**A320**	**0118**
(N309US)	B747	24224
N309VA	**B737**	**19614**
N309WA	**B737**	**23442**
N310AC	B737	23505
N310AS	B727	21948
N310AU	B737	22878
N310BN	B727	19008
N310DA	**B737**	**23082**
(N310DE)	B737	26003
N310EA	L1011	1011
N310EL	1-11	072
N310FE	**DC-10**	**48299**
N310MJ	DC-9	45740
N310NE	**B727**	**20241**
N310NW	**A320**	**0121**
N310SW	**B737**	**22949**
N310UA	**B737**	**23671**
(N310US)	B737	23257
N310VA	**B737**	**21501**
(N311AC)	B737	23752
N311AG	**B727**	**20512**
N311AU	B737	22879
N311AW	**B737**	**24712**
N311BN	B727	19012
(N311DE)	B737	26004
N311DL	**B737**	**23083**
N311EA	**L1011**	**1012**
N311FE	**DC-10**	**46871**
N311MD	MD-11	48458
N311NE	**B727**	**19703**
N311RC	**MD-82**	**48089**
N311SW	**B737**	**23333**
N311UA	**B737**	**23672**
N311US	**A320**	**0125**
(N311US)	B747	24225
N311VA	**B737**	**21500**
N311WA	**B737**	**23597**
N311XV	B737	19709
N312AA	**B767**	**22315**
(N312AC)	B737	23753
N312AU	B737	22880
N312AW	B737	24060
N312DL	**B737**	**23084**
N312EA	L1011	1019
N312FE	**DC-10**	**48300**
N312GB	**L1011**	**1100**
N312NE	**B727**	**20193**
N312P	B737	23261
(N312RC)	MD-82	48090
N312SW	**B737**	**23334**
N312UA	**B737**	**23673**
N312US	**A320**	**0152**
N312VA	**B737**	**20236**
N312WA	**B737**	**23598**
N312XV	B737	19710
N313AA	**B767**	**22316**
(N313AC)	B737	23754
N313AU	B737	22881
N313AW	**B737**	**23712**
N313DL	**B737**	**23085**
N313EA	**L1011**	**1020**
N313FE	**DC-10**	**48311**
N313NE	**B727**	**19702**
N313P	B737	23231
N313RC	**MD-82**	**48091**
N313SW	**B737**	**23335**
N313UA	**B737**	**23674**
N313US	**A320**	**0153**
N313VA	**B737**	**19711**
N313WA	**B737**	**23599**
N313XV	B737	19712
(N314AC)	B737	23755
N314AS	B727	18992
N314AU	B737	22882
N314AW	**B737**	**23733**
N314DA	**B737**	**23086**
N314EA	L1011	1022
N314FE	**DC-10**	**48312**
N314NE	**B727**	**19495**
N314P	B737	23232
N314PA	B727	18992
N314RC	**MD-82**	**49110**
N314SW	**B737**	**23336**
N314UA	**B737**	**23675**
N314US	**A320**	**0160**
N315AA	**B767**	**22317**
N315AU	B737	22883
N315AW	**B737**	**23734**
N315DL	**B737**	**23087**
N315EA	L1011	1023
N315FE	**DC-10**	**48313**
N315NE	**B727**	**20190**
N315P	B737	23233
N315PA	B727	18993
N315RX	A320	0315
N315SC	B737	23766
N315SW	**B737**	**23337**
N315UA	**B737**	**23947**
N315US	**A320**	**0171**
N316AA	**B767**	**22318**
N316AS	B727	18994
N316AU	B737	22884
N316AW	**B737**	**23713**
N316DL	**B737**	**23088**
N316EA	L1011	1037
N316FE	**DC-10**	**48314**
N316P	B737	23234
N316PA	B727	18994
N316SW	**B737**	**23338**
N316UA	**B737**	**23948**
N316US	**A320**	**0192**
N317AA	**B767**	**22319**
N317AU	B737	22885
N317AW	B737	23388
N317DL	**B737**	**23089**
N317EA	L1011	1038
N317F	B707	19004
N317FE	**DC-10**	**46835**
(N317FE)	DC-10	48317

Registration	Type	c/n
(N317NE)	B727	19489
N317P	B737	23235
N317PA	B727	18995
N317RX	A320	0317
N317UA	**B737**	**23949**
N317US	**A320**	**0197**
N318AS	B727	18996
N318AU	B737	22886
N318AW	B737	23506
N318CM	B737	22088
N318DL	**B737**	**23090**
N318EA	L1011	1039
N318F	B707	18880
N318FE	**DC-10**	**46837**
(N318FE)	DC-10	48318
N318PA	B727	18996
N318SW	**B737**	**23339**
N318UA	**B737**	**23950**
N318US	**A320**	**0206**
N319AA	**B767**	**22320**
N319AU	B737	22887
N319AW	B737	23838
N319DL	**B737**	**23091**
N319EA	**L1011**	**1040**
N319F	B707	19415
N319FE	**DC-10**	**47820**
N319P	B737	23236
N319PA	B727	18997
N319SW	**B737**	**23340**
N319UA	**B737**	**23951**
N319US	**A320**	**0208**
N320AA	**B767**	**22321**
N320AS	B727	18998
N320AU	B737	22888
N320AW	B737	23942
N320DL	**B737**	**23092**
N320EA	L1011	1042
N320FE	**DC-10**	**47835**
N320HG	B727	20533
N320MJ	B707	20028
N320P	B737	23237
N320PA	B727	18998
N320SW	**B737**	**23341**
N320UA	**B737**	**23952**
N320US	**A320**	**0213**
N321AA	**B767**	**22322**
N321AU	B737	22889
N321DL	**B737**	**23093**
N321E	B720	18423
N321EA	L1011	1043
N321FE	**DC-10**	**47836**
N321LF	**B757**	**26269**
N321P	B737	23510
N321PA	B727	18999
N321SW	**B737**	**23342**
N321UA	**B737**	**23953**
N321US	**A320**	**0262**
N321XV	B737	19929
N322AA	**B767**	**22323**
N322AS	B727	21364
N322AU	B737	22890
N322AW	**B737**	**25400**
N322DL	**B737**	**23094**
N322EA	L1011	1044
N322F	B707	18975
N322FE	**DC-10**	**47908**
N322K	**F-70**	**11521**
N322P	B737	23511
N322SW	**B737**	**23343**
N322UA	**B737**	**23954**
N322US	**A320**	**0263**
N322XV	B737	19930
N323AA	**B767**	**22324**
N323AS	B727	21365
N323AU	B737	22891
N323AW	**B737**	**23684**
N323DL	**B737**	**23095**
N323EA	L1011	1045
N323F	B707	18976
N323P	B737	23512
N323PA	B727	19005
N323SW	**B737**	**23344**
N323UA	**B737**	**23955**
N323US	**A320**	**0272**
N323XV	B737	20156
N324AA	**B767**	**22325**
N324AS	B727	19006
N324AS	B727	20264
N324AU	B737	22892
N324AW	**B737**	**23261**
N324DL	**B737**	**23096**
N324EA	L1011	1050
N324F	B707	19354
N324K	**F-70**	**11545**
N324P	B737	23513
N324PA	B727	19006
N324SW	**B737**	**23414**
N324UA	**B737**	**23956**
N324US	**A320**	**0273**
N325AA	**B767**	**22326**
N325AS	B727	20267
N325AU	B737	23114
N325AW	**B737**	**23260**
N325DL	**B737**	**23097**
N325EA	L1011	1051
N325F	B707	19355
N325P	B737	23514
N325PA	B727	19007
N325SW	**B737**	**23689**
N325UA	**B737**	**23957**
N325US	**A320**	**0281**
N326AS	B727	20268
N326AU	B737	23115
N326AW	B737	23258
N326DL	**B737**	**23098**
N326EA	L1011	1054
N326P	B737	23515
N326PA	B727	19035
N326SW	**B737**	**23690**
N326UA	**B737**	**23958**
N326US	**A320**	**0282**
N327AA	**B767**	**22327**
N327AS	B727	21345
N327AU	B737	23116
N327AW	B737	23507
N327DL	**B737**	**23099**
N327EA	L1011	1055
N327JL	**B727**	**20513**
N327NW	**A320**	**0297**
N327P	B737	23550
N327PA	B727	19036
N327SW	**B737**	**23691**
N327UA	**B737**	**24147**
N327US	B737	23255
N328AA	**B767**	**22328**
N328AS	B727	21601
N328AU	B737	23131
N328AW	B737	23377
N328DL	**B737**	**23100**
N328EA	L1011	1056
N328NW	**A320**	**0298**
N328P	B737	23551
N328PA	B727	19037
N328SW	**B737**	**23692**
N328UA	**B737**	**24148**
(N328US)	B737	23258
N329AA	**B767**	**22329**
N329AS	B727	22295
N329AU	B737	23132
N329DL	**B737**	**23101**
N329EA	L1011	1085
N329K	B727	19557
N329NW	**A320**	**0306**
N329PA	B727	19038
N329QS	**B727**	**19038**
N329SN	L1011	1085
N329SW	**B737**	**23693**
N329UA	**B737**	**24149**
N329US	B737	23256
N330AA	**B767**	**22330**
N330AU	B737	23133
N330DL	**B737**	**23102**
N330DS	**B720**	**18455**
N330EA	L1011	1087
N330NW	**A320**	**0307**
N330SW	**B737**	**23694**
N330UA	**B737**	**24191**
(N330US)	B737	23259
N331AU	B737	23134
N331DL	**B737**	**23103**
N331EA	L1011	1121
N331NW	**A320**	**0318**
N331SW	**B737**	**23695**
N331UA	**B737**	**24192**
(N331US)	B737	23260
N331XV	B737	19743
N332AA	**B767**	**22331**
N332AU	B737	23135
N332DL	**B737**	**23104**
N332EA	L1011	1123
N332NW	**A320**	**0319**
N332SW	**B737**	**23696**
N332UA	**B737**	**24193**
(N332US)	B737	23261
(N332XV)	B737	20336
N333EA	L1011	1126
N333GB	1-11	076
N333NW	**A320**	**0329**
N333RN	B737	19770
(N333RN)	B737	19682
N333SW	**B737**	**23697**
N333UA	**B737**	**24228**
N334AA	**B767**	**22332**
N334DL	**B737**	**23105**
N334EA	L1011	1141
N334NW	**A320**	**0339**
N334P	B737	23552
N334SW	**B737**	**23938**
N334UA	**B737**	**24229**
N334US	**B737**	**23231**
N335AA	**B767**	**22333**
N335EA	L1011	1142
N335NW	**A320**	**0340**
N335P	B737	23553
N335SW	**B737**	**23939**
N335UA	**B737**	**24230**
N335US	**B737**	**23232**
N336AA	**B767**	**22334**
N336EA	L1011	1143
N336NW	**A320**	**0355**
N336P	B737	23554
N336SW	**B737**	**23940**
N336UA	**B737**	**24240**
N336US	**B737**	**23233**
N337EA	L1011	1152
N337NW	**A320**	**0358**
N337P	B737	23555
N337SW	**B737**	**23959**
N337UA	**B737**	**24241**
N337US	**B737**	**23234**
N338AA	**B767**	**22335**
N338EA	L1011	1153
N338NW	**A320**	**0360**
N338RX	A320	0338
N338SW	**B737**	**23960**
N338UA	**B737**	**24242**
N338US	**B737**	**23235**
N339AA	**B767**	**22336**
N339EA	L1011	1158
N339NW	**A320**	**0367**
N339PA	B727	19134
N339SW	**B737**	**24090**
N339UA	**B737**	**24243**
N339US	**B737**	**23236**
N340DR	B727	19253
N340LA	A320	0425
N340NW	**A320**	**0372**
N340P	B737	23556
N340PA	B727	19135
N340UA	**B737**	**24244**
N340US	**B737**	**23237**
N341A	B720	18014
N341NW	**A320**	**0380**
N341P	B737	23557
N341PA	B727	19136
N341SW	**B737**	**24091**
N341TC	1-11	BAC.126
N341TC	**B727**	**19148**
N341UA	**B737**	**24245**
N341US	**B737**	**23510**
N342A	B707	18953
N342NW	**A320**	**0381**
N342P	B737	23558
N342PA	B727	19137
N342SP	B747	21024
N342SW	**B737**	**24133**
N342UA	**B737**	**24246**
N342US	**B737**	**23511**
N343A	B707	20456
N343NW	**A320**	**0387**
N343SW	**B737**	**24151**
N343UA	**B737**	**24247**
N343US	B737	23512
N344NW	**A320**	**0388**
N344SW	**B737**	**24152**
N344UA	**B737**	**24248**
N344US	B737	23513
N345AW	MD-83	53093
N345FA	B707	20069
N345HC	**DC-10**	**48265**
N345JW	**DC-8**	**46042**
N345NW	**A320**	**0399**
N345UA	**B737**	**24249**
N345US	B737	23514
N346NW	**A320**	**0400**
N346PS	146	E2022
(N346SS)	146	E1004
N346SW	**B737**	**24153**
N346UA	**B737**	**24250**
N346US	**B737**	**23515**
N347NW	**A320**	**0408**
N347PS	146	E2023
N347SW	**B737**	**24374**
N347UA	**B737**	**24251**
N347US	B737	23550
N348AU	B737	23507
N348NW	**A320**	**0410**
N348P	B737	23559
N348PS	146	E2024
N348SW	**B737**	**24375**
N348UA	**B737**	**24252**
N348US	B737	23551
N349NW	**A320**	**0417**
N349P	B737	23560
N349PS	146	E2025
N349SW	**B737**	**24408**
N349UA	**B737**	**24253**
N349US	**B737**	**23552**
N350AU	B737	22950
N350NA	**A320**	**0418**
N350P	B737	23739
(N350P)	B737	23561
(N350P)	B737	23646
N350PS	146	E2027
N350SW	**B737**	**24409**
N350UA	**B737**	**24301**
N350US	**B737**	**23553**
N351AA	**B767**	**24032**
N351AS	B747	21785
N351AU	B737	22951
N351LF	B737	26293
N351PA	**B727**	**20614**
N351PS	146	E2028
N351SR	B707	18586
N351SW	**B737**	**24572**
N351UA	**B737**	**24319**
N351US	B707	18584
N351US	**B737**	**23554**
N352AA	**B767**	**24033**
N352AU	B737	22952
N352BA	146	E2060
N352P	B737	23740
(N352P)	B737	23562
(N352P)	B737	23647
N352PA	**B727**	**20616**
N352PS	146	E2030
N352SW	**B737**	**24888**
N352UA	**B737**	**24320**
N352US	B707	18585
N352US	**B737**	**23555**
N353AA	**B767**	**24034**
N353AS	DC-8	45924
N353AU	B737	22953
N353FA	**DC-8**	**45624**
N353P	B737	23741
(N353P)	B737	23563
(N353P)	B737	23648
N353PA	**B727**	**20622**
N353PS	146	E2031
N353SW	**B737**	**24889**
N353UA	**B737**	**24321**
N353US	B707	18586
N353US	**B737**	**23556**
N354AA	**B767**	**24035**

N354AS B747 21189
N354AU B737 22954
N354P B737 23742
(N354P) B737 23564
(N354P) B737 23649
N354PA B727 20624
N354PS 146 E2034
N354SW B737 25219
N354UA B737 24360
N354US B707 18693
N354US B737 23557
N355AA B767 24036
N355AS B747 19729
N355AU B737 22955
N355P B737 23743
(N355P) B737 23565
(N355P) B737 23650
N355PA B727 19257
N355PA B727 20625
N355PS 146 E2036
N355Q DC-8 45668
N355QS B727 19257
N355SW B737 25250
N355UA B737 24361
N355US B707 18710
N355US B737 23558
N356AS B747 19730
N356AU B737 22956
N356BA 146 E2066
N356PA B727 19258
N356PA B727 20626
N356PS 146 E2039
N356QS B727 19258
N356SW B737 25251
N356UA B737 24362
N356US B707 18746
N356US B737 23559
N356WS DC-8 45668
N357AA B767 24038
N357AS B747 19731
N357AT L1011 1221
N357AU B737 22957
N357KP B727 20675
N357P B737 23930
N357PA B727 19259
N357PA B727 20627
N357PS 146 E2040
N357QS B727 19259
N357SW B737 26594
N357UA B737 24378
N357US B707 18747
N357US B737 23560
N358AA B767 24039
N358AS B737 21278
N358AS B747 19732
N358AU B737 22958
N358P B737 23931
N358PA B727 19260
N358PA B727 20674
"N358PA" B727 20676
N358PS 146 E2041
N358QS B727 19005
N358SW B737 26595
N358UA B737 24379
N358US B707 18748
N358US B737 23739
N359AA B767 24040
N359AS B737 21528
N359AS B747 20520
N359AU B737 22959
N359P B737 23932
N359PA B727 19261
N359PA B727 20789
N359PS 146 E2042
N359QS B727 19007
N359SW B737 26596
N359UA B737 24452
N359US B707 18888
N359US B737 23740
N360AA B767 24041
N360AU B737 23310
(N360P) B737 23933
N360PA B727 19262
N360PA B727 20676
N360PS 146 E2043
N360SW B737 26571
N360UA B737 24453
N360US B707 18889
N360US B737 23741
N361AA B767 24042
N361AU B737 23311
N361AW B767 27377
N361KP B727 20627
(N361P) B737 23934
N361PA B727 21849
N361PS 146 E2044
N361SW B737 26572
N361UA B737 24454
N361US B707 18921
N361US B737 23742
N362AA B767 24043
N362AU B737 23312
(N362P) B737 23935
N362PA B727 21850
N362PS 146 E2045
N362SW B737 26573
N362UA B737 24455
N362US B707 18922
(N362US) B737 23743
N363AA B767 24044
N363AU B737 23313
N363PA B727 22535
N363PS 146 E2046
N363SW B737 26574
N363UA B737 24532
N363US B707 18964
N364AU B737 23314
(N364P) B737 23936
N364PA B727 22536
N364PS 146 E2047
N364SW B737 26575
N364UA B737 24533
N364US B707 19034
N365AU B737 23315
(N365P) B737 23937
N365PA B727 22537
N365PS 146 E2048
N365SW B737 26576
N365UA B737 24534
N365US B707 19163
N366AA B767 25193
N366AU B737 23316
N366PA B727 22538
N366PS 146 E2072
N366SW B737 26577
N366UA B737 24535
N366US B707 19164
N367AU B737 23317
N367DL B737 21774
N367PA B727 22539
N367PS 146 E2073
N367SW B737 26578
N367UA B737 24536
N367US B707 19168
N368AA B767 25195
N368AU B737 23318
N368DE B737 22279
N368DL B737 21776
N368PA B727 22540
N368PS 146 E2074
N368SW B737 26579
N368UA B737 24537
N368US B707 19209
N368WA B707 19716
N369AA B767 25196
N369AU B737 23319
N369DL B737 21776
N369PA B727 22541
N369PS 146 E2075
N369SW B737 26580
N369UA B737 24538
N369US B707 19210
N369WA B707 19715
N370AA B767 25197
N370AU B737 23376
N370PA B727 22542
N370SW B737 26597
N370UA B737 24539
N370US B707 19263
N370WA B707 19442
N371AA B767 25198
N371AU B737 23377
N371EA B747 20012
N371EA L1011 1008
N371PA B727 20248
N371SW B737 26598
N371TA B737 24834
N371UA B737 24540
N371US B707 19411
N371US B737 22950
N371WA B707 19441
N372AA B767 25199
N372AU B737 23378
N372EA L1011 1033
(N372EA) B747 20011
N372PA B727 20249
N372SW B737 26599
N372TA B737 24856
N372UA B737 24637
N372US B707 19412
N372US B737 22951
N372WA B707 19179
N373AA B767 25200
N373AU B737 23379
N373DL B737 23520
N373PA B727 20678
N373S COMET 06018
N373SW B737 26581
N373TA B737 26283
N373UA B737 24638
N373US B707 19434
N373US B737 22952
N373WA B707 18582
N374AA B767 25201
N374AU B737 23380
N374DL B737 23521
N374PA B727 20679
N374SW B737 26582
N374TA B737 26286
N374UA B737 24639
N374US B707 19443
N374US B737 22953
N374WA B707 18583
N375AU B737 23381
N375DL B737 23602
N375NE B727 19405
N375PA B727 20875
N375SW B737 26583
N375TA B737 23787
N375UA B737 24640
N375US B707 19631
N375US B737 22954
N375WA B707 18707
N376AN B767 25445
N376AU B737 23382
N376DL B737 23603
N376PA B727 20169
N376SW B737 26584
N376UA B737 24641
N376US B707 19632
N376US B737 22955
N376WA B707 18991
N377AN B767 25446
N377AU B737 23383
N377DL B737 23604
N377PA B727 19992
N377UA B737 24642
N377US B707 19633
N378AN B767 25447
N378AU B737 23384
N378DL B737 23605
N378PA B727 20392
N378PS B737 19681
N378SW B737 26585
N378UA B737 24653
N378US B707 19634
N379AA B767 25448
N379AU B737 23385
N379DL B737 23606
N379PA B727 20302
N379PS B737 19682
N379SW B737 26586
N379UA B737 24654
N379US B707 19635
N380AN B767 25449
N380AU B737 23594
N380DL B737 23607
N380KP B727 21453
N380PA B737 20670
N380PS B737 19920
N380SW B737 26587
N380UA B737 24655
N380US B707 19636
N381AN B767 25450
N381AU B737 23595
N381DL B737 23608
N381KP B727 21578
N381LF B757 24367
(N381LF) B737 23506
N381PA B737 20588
N381PS B737 19921
N381UA B737 24656
N381US B707 19872
N382AN B767 25451
N382AU B737 23699
N382DL B737 23609
N382KP B727 21579
N382PA B737 19921
N382PS B737 20155
N382SW B737 26588
N382UA B737 24657
N382US B707 19773
N383AN B767 26995
N383AU B737 23700
N383KP B727 21580
N383PA B737 20205
N383SW B737 26589
N383UA B737 24658
N383US B707 19774
N383US B737 22956
N384AA B767 26996
N384AU B737 23701
N384PA B727 20303
(N384PA) B737 21231
N384PS B727 20437
N384SW B737 26590
N384UA B737 24659
N384US B707 19775
N384US B737 22957
N385AM B767 27059
N385AU B737 23702
N385PA B727 20393
N385PA B737 21719
N385SW B737 26600
N385UA B737 24660
N385US B707 19776
N385US B737 22958
N386AA B767 27060
N386AU B737 23703
N386PA B727 19973
(N386PA) B737 20785
N386SW B737 26601
N386UA B737 24661
N386US B707 19777
(N386US) B707 19872
N387AM B767 27184
N387AU B737 23704
N387PA B737 22276
N387SW B737 26602
N387UA B737 24662
N387US B737 22959
N388AA B767 27448
N388AU B737 23705
N388PA B727 19818
N388PA B727 19976
N388PA B737 22277
N388SW B737 26591
N388UA B737 24663
N388US B737 23310
N389AA B767 27449
N389AU B737 23706
N389PA B727 19819
N389PA B727 20293
N389PA B737 22516
N389SW B737 26592
N389UA B737 24664
N389US B737 23311
N390AA B767 27450
N390AU B737 23856
N390BA 1-11 BAC.129
N390EA DC-10 47862
N390PA B727 20899
N390SW B737 26593
N390UA B737 24665

N390US	**B737**	**23312**
N391AA	**B767**	**27451**
N391AU	B737	23857
N391EA	DC-10	47866
N391LF	A320	0428
N391PA	**B727**	**20900**
N391SW	**B737**	**27378**
N391UA	**B737**	**24666**
N391US	**B737**	**23313**
N392AU	B737	23858
N392BA	1-11	BAC.131
N392EA	**DC-10**	**47867**
N392PA	**B727**	**20901**
N392SW	**B737**	**27379**
N392UA	**B737**	**24667**
N392US	**B737**	**23314**
N393AU	B737	23859
N393PA	**B727**	**20902**
N393PA	DC-9	47392
N393SW	**B737**	**27380**
N393UA	**B737**	**24668**
N393US	**B737**	**23315**
N394AU	B737	23860
N394PA	DC-9	47376
(N394PA)	B727	20903
N394UA	**B737**	**24669**
N394US	**B737**	**23316**
N395AJ	**B727**	**21100**
N395AU	B737	23861
(N395PA)	B727	20906
N395SW	**B737**	**27689**
N395UA	**B737**	**24670**
N395US	**B737**	**23317**
N396AU	B737	23862
N396SW	**B737**	**27690**
N396UA	**B737**	**24671**
N396US	**B737**	**23318**
N397P	B737	23256
N397PA	B727	20918
N397SW	**B737**	**27691**
N397UA	**B737**	**24672**
N397US	**B737**	**23319**
N398SW	**B737**	**27692**
N398UA	**B737**	**24673**
N398US	**B737**	**23507**
N399P	B737	23255
N399UA	**B737**	**24674**
N399WN	**B737**	**27693**
N400AA	**MD-82**	**49311**
N400DA	**B727**	**21144**
N400KL	B757	25268
N400ME	**DC-9**	**45727**
N400RG	**B727**	**19149**
N401	B707	18832
N401AL	**B737**	**25663**
N401AW	B737	25603
N401BN	B727	20392
N401DA	**B727**	**21145**
N401EA	**DC-9**	**47682**
N401FE	**A310**	**191**
N401FE	DC-8	46117
N401KW	**B737**	**26281**
N401ME	**DC-9**	**47133**
N401MG	B737	21763
N401PA	B707	18832
(N401PA)	B727	20615
N401PE	B737	19018
N401PW	B747	23719
N401SH	B737	20584
N401SK	**1-11**	**073**
N401UA	A300	118
N401UA	**A320**	**0435**
N401UP	**B757**	**23723**
(N401US)	B727	18797
N401XV	146	E2059
N402A	**MD-82**	**49313**
N402AL	**B737**	**25664**
N402AW	B737	25505
N402BN	B727	20393
N402DA	**B727**	**21146**
N402EA	DC-9	47683
N402FE	**A310**	**201**
N402FE	DC-8	46073
(N402FE)	DC-8	46059
N402KW	**B737**	**26285**
(N402P)	B737	23886
N402PA	**B707**	**18833**
(N402PD)	B707	18833
N402PE	B737	19019
N402UA	A300	120
N402UA	**A320**	**0439**
N402UP	**B757**	**23724**
(N402US)	B727	18798
N402XV	146	E2060
N403A	**MD-82**	**49314**
(N403AL)	B737	25665
(N403AL)	B737	27187
N403AW	B737	25506
N403BN	B727	20394
N403DA	**B727**	**21147**
N403EA	DC-9	47685
N403EV	**B747**	**27141**
N403FE	**A310**	**230**
N403KW	**B737**	**24234**
(N403P)	B737	23885
N403PA	B707	18834
(N403PA)	B727	20617
N403PE	**B737**	**19020**
N403SW	**RJ100**	**7028**
N403UA	A300	68
N403UA	**A320**	**0442**
N403UP	**B757**	**23725**
(N403US)	B727	18799
N403XV	146	E2061
(N404AL)	B737	25666
(N404AL)	B737	27188
N404AW	B737	25507
N404BN	B727	20302
N404DA	**B727**	**21148**
N404EA	DC-9	47665
N404FE	**A310**	**233**
N404FE	DC-8	46001
N404KW	**B737**	**25371**
(N404P)	B737	23876
N404PA	**B707**	**18835**
(N404PB)	B707	18835
N404PE	B737	19021
N404UA	A300	65
N404UA	**A320**	**0450**
N404UP	**B757**	**23726**
N404US	**B737**	**23886**
(N404US)	B727	18800
N404XV	146	E2064
N405A	**MD-82**	**49316**
N405AW	B737	25508
N405BN	B727	20303
N405DA	**B727**	**21149**
N405EA	**DC-9**	**47688**
N405EV	**B747**	**27142**
N405FE	**A310**	**237**
N405FE	DC-8	46090
N405KW	**B737**	**24704**
(N405P)	B737	23877
N405PA	B707	18836
(N405PA)	B727	20618
N405PE	B737	19022
N405SW	**RJ100**	**7029**
N405UA	A300	66
N405UA	**A320**	**0452**
N405UP	**B757**	**23727**
N405US	**B737**	**23885**
(N405US)	B727	18801
N405XV	146	E2066
N406A	**MD-82**	**49317**
N406BN	**B727**	**19991**
N406DA	**B727**	**21150**
N406EA	**DC-9**	**47686**
N406EV	**B747**	**27898**
N406KW	**B737**	**24709**
(N406P)	B737	23878
N406PA	B707	18837
(N406PA)	B727	20619
N406PE	B737	19023
N406SW	**RJ100**	**7030**
N406UA	**A320**	**0454**
N406UP	**B757**	**23728**
N406US	**B737**	**23876**
(N406US)	B727	18802
N406XV	146	E2062
N407AA	**MD-82**	**49318**
N407BN	B727	19992
N407DA	**B727**	**21151**
N407EA	DC-9	47692
N407EV	**B747**	**27899**
N407FE	**A310**	**254**
N407FE	DC-8	46089
(N407P)	B737	23879
N407PA	B707	18838
(N407PA)	B727	20620
N407PE	B737	19024
N407SW	**RJ100**	**7034**
N407U	**A300**	**124**
N407UA	A300	124
N407UA	**A320**	**0456**
N407UP	**B757**	**23729**
N407US	**B737**	**23877**
(N407US)	B727	18803
N407XV	146	E2069
N408AA	**MD-82**	**49319**
N408BN	B727	19993
N408CE	B737	19408
N408DA	**B727**	**21152**
N408EA	**DC-9**	**47693**
N408EV	**B747**	**28092**
N408FE	**A310**	**257**
(N408P)	B737	23880
N408PA	B707	18839
(N408PA)	B727	20621
N408PE	**B737**	**19025**
N408SW	**RJ100**	**7055**
N408UA	**A320**	**0457**
N408UP	**B757**	**23730**
N408US	**B737**	**23878**
(N408US)	B727	18804
N408XV	146	E2077
N409AA	**MD-82**	**49320**
N409BN	**B727**	**20162**
N409DA	**B727**	**21153**
N409EA	**DC-9**	**47728**
N409EV	**B747**	**28093**
N409FE	**A310**	**273**
(N409P)	B737	23881
N409PA	B707	18840
N409PE	B737	19026
N409SW	**RJ100**	**7056**
N409UA	**A320**	**0462**
N409UP	**B757**	**23731**
N409US	**B737**	**23879**
(N409US)	B727	18805
N410AA	**MD-82**	**49321**
N410BN	B727	20608
N410DA	**B727**	**21222**
N410EA	**DC-9**	**47731**
N410FE	**A310**	**356**
(N410P)	B737	23882
N410PA	B707	18841
N410PE	B737	19027
N410SW	**RJ100**	**7066**
N410UA	**A320**	**0463**
N410UP	**B757**	**23732**
(N410US)	B727	18806
N411AA	**MD-82**	**49322**
N411BN	B727	20609
N411DA	**B727**	**21223**
N411EA	**DC-9**	**47732**
N411FE	**A310**	**359**
N411MD	MD-11	48419
N411PE	B737	19028
N411SW	**RJ100**	**7067**
N411UA	**A320**	**0464**
N411UP	**B757**	**23851**
N411US	**B737**	**23880**
(N411US)	B727	18807
N412AA	**MD-82**	**49323**
N412BN	B727	20610
N412CE	**B737**	**20412**
N412DA	**B727**	**21232**
N412EA	**DC-9**	**47733**
N412FE	**A310**	**360**
(N412P)	B737	23883
N412PA	B707	18842
N412PE	B737	19029
N412SW	**RJ100**	**7101**
N412UA	**A320**	**0465**
N412UP	**B757**	**23852**
N412US	**B737**	**23881**
N413AA	**MD-82**	**49324**
N413BN	B727	20611
N413DA	**B727**	**21233**
N413EA	DC-9	47745
N413EX	**B727**	**19206**
N413FE	**A310**	**397**
N413PE	B737	19030
N413SW	**RJ100**	**7102**
N413UA	**A320**	**0470**
N413UP	**B757**	**23853**
N413US	**B737**	**23882**
N414BN	B727	20612
N414DA	**B727**	**21256**
N414EA	**DC-9**	**47746**
N414EX	**B727**	**18899**
N414FE	**A310**	**400**
(N414P)	B737	23884
N414PA	B707	18956
N414PE	B737	19031
N414UA	**A320**	**0472**
N414UP	**B757**	**23854**
N415AA	**MD-82**	**49326**
N415BN	B727	20613
N415DA	**B727**	**21257**
N415EA	**DC-9**	**47749**
N415EX	B727	18945
N415FE	**A310**	**349**
N415PA	B707	18957
N415PE	B737	19032
N415UA	**A320**	**0475**
N415UP	**B757**	**23855**
N415US	**B737**	**23883**
N416AA	**MD-82**	**49327**
N416BN	B727	20729
N416DA	**B727**	**21258**
N416EA	**DC-9**	**47751**
N416EX	**B727**	**19287**
N416FE	**A310**	**288**
N416PA	B707	18958
N416PE	B737	19033
N416UA	**A320**	**0479**
N416UP	**B757**	**23903**
N416US	B737	23884
N417AA	**MD-82**	**49328**
N417BN	B727	20730
N417DA	**B727**	**21259**
N417DG	DC-10	46936
N417EA	**DC-9**	**47753**
N417EX	**B727**	**19290**
N417FE	**A310**	**333**
N417MA	B720	18082
N417PA	B707	18959
N417PE	B737	19794
N417UA	**A320**	**0483**
N417UP	**B757**	**23904**
N417US	**B737**	**23984**
N418AA	**MD-82**	**49329**
N418BN	B727	20731
N418DA	**B727**	**21271**
N418EA	**DC-9**	**47676**
N418EX	B727	18946
N418FE	**A310**	**343**
N418PA	B707	18960
N418UA	**A320**	**0485**
N418UP	**B757**	**23905**
N418US	**B737**	**23985**
N419AA	**MD-82**	**49331**
N419B	B707	19351
N419BN	B727	20732
N419DA	**B727**	**21272**
N419EA	DC-9	47677
N419EX	B727	18947
N419FE	**A310**	**345**
N419MA	**B720**	**18082**
N419PA	B707	19264
N419UA	**A320**	**0487**
N419UP	**B757**	**23906**
N419US	**B737**	**23986**
N420AA	**MD-82**	**49332**
N420AJ	DC-8	45419
N420BN	B727	20733
N420DA	**B727**	**21273**
N420EA	**DC-9**	**47689**
N420EX	B727	19102
N420FE	**A310**	**339**
N420GE	CRVL	42
N420PA	B707	19265
N420UA	**A320**	**0489**

N420UP B757 23907
N420US B737 23987
N421AJ DC-8 45421
N421BN B727 20734
N421DA B727 21274
N421EA DC-9 47679
N421EX B727 19099
N421FE A310 342
N421MA B720 18049
N421PA B707 19266
N421UA A320 0500
N421UP B757 25281
N421US B737 23988
N422AA MD-82 49334
N422BN B727 20735
(N422DA) B727 21303
N422EX B727 19094
N422FE A310 346
N422PA B707 19275
N422UA A320 0503
N422UP B757 25324
N422US B737 23989
N423AA MD-82 49335
N423BN B727 20736
(N423DA) B727 21304
N423EX B727 19314
N423FE A310 281
N423MA B707 18083
N423PA B707 19276
N423UA A320 0504
N423UP B757 25325
N423US B737 23990
N424AA MD-82 49336
N424BN B727 20737
(N424DA) B727 21305
N424EX B727 20042
N424FE A310 241
N424PA B707 19277
N424UA A320 0506
N424UP B757 25369
N424US B737 23991
N425BN B727 20738
(N425DA) B727 21306
N425FE A310 264
N425MA B707 17689
N425PA B707 19278
N425UA A320 0508
N425UP B757 25370
N425US B737 23992
N426AA MD-82 49338
N426BN B727 20772
(N426DA) B727 21307
N426EX B727 19089
N426FB DC-8 45667
N426PA B707 19361
N426UA A320 0510
N426UP B757 25457
N426US B737 24548
N427AA MD-82 49339
N427BN B727 20773
(N427DA) B727 21308
N427EX B727 19090
N427FB DC-8 45684
N427MA B707 17607
N427PA B707 19362
N427UA A320 0512
N427UP B757 25458
N427US B737 24549
N428AA MD-82 49340
N428BN B727 20774
(N428DA) B727 21309
N428EX B727 19097
N428FE A310 248
N428PA B707 19363
N428UA A320 0523
N428UP B757 25459
N428US B737 24550
N429AA MD-82 49341
N429BN B727 20775
(N429DA) B727 21310
N429EX B727 19100
N429RX A320 0429
N429UA A320 0539
N429UP B757 25460
N429US B737 24551
N430AA MD-82 49342
N430BN B727 20837
(N430DA) B727 21311
N430EX B727 19101
N430UA A320 0568
N430UP B757 25461
N430US B737 24552
N431AA MD-82 49343
N431BN B727 20838
(N431DA) B727 21312
N431EX B727 19103
N431LF A320 0361
N431MA B707 17597
N431PE B737 19884
N431UA A320 0571
N431UP B757 25462
N431US B737 24553
N432AA MD-82 49350
N432BN B727 20839
(N432DA) B727 21313
N432EX B727 19867
N432PE B737 19885
N432UA A320 0572
N432UP B757 25463
N432US B737 24554
N433AA MD-83 49451
N433BN B727 20840
(N433DA) B727 21314
N433EX B727 19868
N433MA B707 18084
N433PA B707 19364
N433PE B737 19886
N433UP B757 25464
N433US B737 24555
N433ZV B727 20433
N434AA MD-83 49452
N434BN B727 21041
(N434DA) B727 21315
N434EX B727 18898
N434KC DC-10 48201
N434PA B707 19365
N434PE B737 19887
N434UP B757 25465
N434US B737 24556
(N434ZV) B727 20434
N435AA MD-83 49453
N435BN B727 21042
N435EX B727 19095
N435EX B727 19288
(N435MA) B707 18085
N435PA B707 19366
N435PE B737 19888
N435UP B757 25466
N435US B737 24557
N436AA MD-83 49454
N436BN B727 21043
N436EX B727 19289
N436UP B757 25467
N436US B737 24558
N437AA MD-83 49455
N437BN B727 21044
N437RX A320 0437
N437UP B757 25468
N437US B737 24559
N438AA MD-83 49456
N438BN B727 21045
N438UP B757 25469
N438US B737 24560
N439AA MD-83 49457
N439BN B727 21118
N439UP B757 25470
N439US B737 24781
N440AA MD-82 49459
N440BN B727 21119
N440DR B727 19253
N440DS B720 18977
N440UP B757 25471
N440US B737 24811
N441AA MD-82 49460
N441BN B727 21242
N441J DC-8 45988
N441KA A320 0441
N441LF A320 0405
N441UP B757 27386
N441US B737 24812
N442AA MD-82 49468
N442BN B727 21243
N442UP B757 27387
N442US B737 24841
N443AA MD-82 49469
N443BN B727 21244
N443UP B757 27388
N443US B737 24842
N444BN B727 21245
(N444CM) B727 19665
N444RX A320 0444
N444SA B727 19987
N444UP B757 27389
N444US B737 24862
N445AA MD-82 49471
N445BN B727 21246
N445PA B707 19267
N445UP B757 27390
N445US B737 24863
N446AA MD-82 49472
N446BN B727 21247
N446FE A310 224
N446PA B707 19268
N446UP B757 27735
N446US B737 24873
N447AA MD-82 49473
N447BN B727 21248
N447FE A310 251
N447PA B707 19269
N447UP B757 27736
N447US B737 24874
N448AA MD-82 49474
N448BN B727 21249
N448DR B727 19253
N448FE A310 260
N448M B707 19270
N448PA B707 19270
N448UP B757 27737
N448US B737 24892
(N448WA) B707 19271
N449AA MD-82 49475
N449BN B727 21363
N449J B707 18954
N449PA B707 19271
N449RX A320 0449
N449UP B757 27738
N449US B737 24893
N450AA MD-82 49476
N450BN B727 21364
N450PA B707 19272
N450UP B757 25472
N450US F-28 11101
N451AA MD-82 49477
N451BN B727 21365
N451LF A320 0525
N451PA B707 19273
N451RN B707 19273
N451UP B757 27739
N451US F-28 11103
N452AA MD-82 49553
N452BN B727 21366
N452DA B727 20634
N452PA B707 19274
N452UP B757 25473
N452US F-28 11105
N453AA MD-82 49558
N453AC B737 19931
N453BN B727 21394
N453DA B727 20635
N453FA DC-8 45601
N453PA B707 19374
N453UP B757 25474
N453US F-28 11106
N454AA MD-82 49559
N454BN B727 21395
N454DA B727 20636
N454PA B707 19376
N454PC B707 18839
N454UP B757 25475
N454US F-28 11107
N455AA MD-82 49560
N455BN B727 21461
N455DA B727 20637
N455PA B707 19378
N455UP B757 25476
N456AA MD-82 49561
N456AW MD-83 53182
N456BN B727 21462
N456DA B727 20638
N456TM B737 20336
N456US F-28 11035
N457AA MD-82 49562
(N457AC) B737 19598
N457BN B727 21463
N457DA B727 20639
N457PA B707 19367
N457PC B707 20178
N457TM B737 20156
N457US F-28 11036
N458AA MD-82 49563
N458AC B707 18068
N458AC B737 21720
N458BN B727 21464
N458DA B727 20640
N458PA B707 19368
(N458TM) B737 21355
N458US F-28 11037
N459AA MD-82 49564
N459AC B737 19072
N459BN B727 21465
N459DA B727 20641
N459PA B707 19369
N459US F-28 11043
N460AA MD-82 49565
N460AC B737 20158
N460AT B737 20158
N460AU F-28 11044
N460BN B727 21466
N460DA B727 20642
N460PA B707 19370
N461AA MD-82 49566
N461AC B737 20976
(N461AC) B737 19306
N461AP 146 E1015
N461AT B737 20976
N461AU F-28 11032
N461BN B727 21488
N461DA B727 20643
(N461DA) B727 20634
N461EA 146 E2097
N461FE B727 22548
N461GB B737 19306
N461PA B707 19371
N461US B727 18797
N462AA MD-82 49592
N462AC B737 19307
N462AP 146 E1017
N462AT B737 22631
N462AU F-28 11054
N462BN B727 21489
N462DA B727 20644
(N462DA) B727 20635
N462EA 146 E2107
N462FE B727 22550
N462GB B737 19307
N462PA B707 19372
N462US B727 18798
N463AA MD-82 49593
(N463AC) B737 19308
N463AP 146 E1063
N463AU F-28 11061
N463BN B727 21490
N463DA B727 20645
(N463DA) B727 20636
N463FE B727 22551
N463GB B737 19308
N463PA B707 19373
N463US B727 18799
N464AA MD-82 49594
N464AC B737 19309
N464AT B737 21278
N464BN B727 21491
N464DA B727 20646
(N464DA) B727 20637
N464FE B727 21288
N464GB B737 19309
N464US B727 18800
N464US F-28 11063
N465AA MD-82 49595
N465AC B737 19713
N465AU F-28 11064
N465BN B727 21492
N465DA B727 20647
(N465DA) B727 20638

Registration	Type	No.
N465FE	**B727**	**21289**
N465GB	B737	19713
N465US	B727	18801
N466AA	**MD-82**	**49596**
N466AC	B737	19601
N466AT	**B737**	**21279**
N466BN	B727	21493
N466DA	**B727**	**20743**
(N466DA)	B727	20639
N466FE	**B727**	**21292**
N466US	B727	18802
N466US	**F-28**	**11075**
N467AA	**MD-82**	**49597**
N467AT	**B737**	**22055**
N467BN	B727	21529
N467DA	**B727**	**20744**
(N467DA)	B727	20640
N467FE	**B727**	**21449**
N467GB	B737	19714
N467US	B727	18803
N467US	F-28	11087
N468AA	**MD-82**	**49598**
N468AC	B737	20334
N468AT	B737	19074
N468BN	B727	21530
N468DA	**B727**	**20745**
(N468DA)	B727	20641
N468FE	**B727**	**21452**
N468US	B727	18804
N468US	F-28	11095
N469AA	**MD-82**	**49599**
N469AC	B737	20335
N469AT	B737	21613
N469BN	B727	21531
N469DA	**B727**	**20746**
(N469DA)	B727	20642
N469FE	**B727**	**21581**
N469US	B727	18805
N469US	**F-28**	**11096**
N470AA	**MD-82**	**49600**
N470AC	B737	20126
(N470AC)	B737	20336
N470BN	B727	21532
N470DA	**B727**	**20747**
(N470DA)	B727	20643
N470EV	**B747**	**20653**
N470PC	B707	18839
N470TA	B737	19611
N470US	B727	18806
N470US	F-28	11098
N471AA	**MD-82**	**49601**
N471BN	B727	21669
N471DA	**B727**	**20748**
(N471DA)	B727	20644
N471EV	**B747**	**20651**
N471GB	B737	19680
N471LF	B737	26288
N471US	B727	18807
N472AA	**MD-82**	**49647**
N472BN	B727	21670
N472DA	**B727**	**20749**
(N472DA)	B727	20645
N472EV	**B747**	**20320**
N472GB	B737	19679
N472US	B727	18942
N473AA	**MD-82**	**49648**
N473AC	B737	19614
N473BN	B727	21996
N473DA	B727	20750
(N473DA)	B727	20646
N473EV	**B747**	**19657**
N473PA	B707	19375
N473RN	B707	19375
N473US	B727	18943
N474	**MD-82**	**49649**
N474BN	B727	21997
N474DA	**B727**	**20751**
(N474DA)	B727	20647
N474EV	**B747**	**19637**
N474PA	B707	19377
N474US	**B727**	**18944**
N475AA	**MD-82**	**49650**
N475AC	MD-81	48027
N475AU	**F-28**	**11222**
N475BN	B727	21998
N475DA	**B727**	**20752**
N475EV	B747	19638
N475PA	B707	19379
N475US	B727	19121
N476AA	**MD-82**	**49651**
N476AC	MD-81	48028
N476BN	B727	21999
N476DA	**B727**	**20753**
N476EV	B747	19655
N476US	B727	19122
N476US	**F-28**	**11224**
N477AA	**MD-82**	**49652**
N477AC	**MD-82**	**48062**
N477AU	**F-28**	**11226**
N477BN	B727	22000
N477DA	**B727**	**20754**
N477EV	B747	20784
N477FE	**B727**	**21394**
N477US	B727	19123
N478AA	**MD-82**	**49653**
N478AC	**MD-82**	**48063**
N478BN	B727	22001
N478DA	**B727**	**20755**
N478EV	B747	21033
N478FE	**B727**	**21395**
N478RX	A320	0478
N478US	B727	19124
N478US	**F-28**	**11227**
N479AA	**MD-82**	**49654**
N479AC	MD-82	48066
N479AU	**F-28**	**11228**
N479BN	B727	22002
N479DA	**B727**	**20756**
N479EV	**B747**	**19898**
N479FE	**B727**	**21461**
N479US	B727	19125
N480AA	**MD-82**	**49655**
N480AC	MD-82	49112
N480AU	**F-28**	**11229**
N480BN	B727	22003
N480DA	**B727**	**20860**
N480EV	B747	20348
N480FE	**B727**	**21462**
N480GX	B747	19746
N480RX	**A320**	**0480**
N480US	B727	19126
N480US	F-28	11229
N481AA	**MD-82**	**49656**
N481AC	MD-82	49113
N481BN	B727	22004
N481DA	**B727**	**20861**
N481EV	**B747**	**19896**
N481FE	**B727**	**21463**
N481GX	A320	0131
N481US	**F-28**	**11230**
N482AA	**MD-82**	**49675**
N482AC	MD-82	49126
N482BN	B727	22005
N482DA	**B727**	**20862**
N482EV	**B747**	**20713**
N482FE	**B727**	**21464**
N482GX	A320	0132
N482US	**F-28**	**11231**
N483AA	**MD-82**	**49676**
N483AC	MD-82	49127
(N483AS)	B727	18331
N483BN	B727	22091
N483DA	**B727**	**20863**
N483EV	B747	20351
N483FE	**B727**	**21465**
N483GX	A320	0189
N483GX	B767	24973
N483US	**F-28**	**11233**
N484AA	**MD-82**	**49677**
N484BN	B727	22092
N484DA	**B727**	**20864**
N484EV	B747	20352
N484FE	**B727**	**21466**
N484GX	A320	0190
N484US	**F-28**	**11234**
N485AA	**MD-82**	**49678**
(N485BN)	B727	22093
N485DA	**B727**	**20865**
N485EV	**B747**	**20712**
N485FE	**B727**	**21488**
N485GX	A320	0343
N485US	F-28	11235
N486AA	**MD-82**	**49679**
(N486BN)	B727	22094
N486DA	B727	20866
N486FE	**B727**	**21489**
N486GX	A320	0420
N486US	**F-28**	**11237**
N487AA	**MD-82**	**49680**
(N487BN)	B727	22095
N487DA	B727	20867
N487FE	**B727**	**21490**
N487GS	B737	19600
N487GX	**B747**	**20493**
N487US	**F-28**	**11238**
N488AA	**MD-82**	**49681**
(N488AS)	B727	18852
(N488BN)	B727	22096
N488DA	B727	21018
N488FE	**B727**	**21491**
N488GX	**B747**	**20372**
N488US	B727	19867
N488US	**F-28**	**11240**
N489AA	**MD-82**	**49682**
(N489BN)	B727	22097
N489DA	**B727**	**21019**
N489FE	**B727**	**21492**
N489GX	MD-11	48458
N489US	B727	19868
N489US	**F-28**	**11149**
N490AA	**MD-82**	**49683**
(N490BN)	B727	22098
N490DA	**B727**	**21020**
N490FE	**B727**	**21493**
N490GX	B747	19650
N490SA	**DC-9**	**45798**
N490ST	**1-11**	**083**
N490US	B727	18898
N490US	**F-28**	**11152**
N490W	B727	19091
N491AA	**MD-82**	**49684**
(N491BN)	B727	22099
N491DA	**B727**	**21060**
N491FE	**B727**	**21529**
N491GX	B747	19641
N491PA	B707	19693
N491SA	**DC-9**	**45799**
N491ST	**1-11**	**056**
N491US	B727	18899
N491US	**F-28**	**11156**
N491WC	B737	21820
N492AA	**MD-82**	**49730**
(N492BN)	B727	22100
N492DA	**B727**	**21061**
N492FE	**B727**	**21530**
N492FE	**B727**	**21532**
N492GX	**B747**	**20350**
N492PA	B707	19694
N492US	B727	18945
N492US	**F-28**	**11159**
N492WC	B737	21821
N493AA	**MD-82**	**49731**
(N493BN)	B727	22101
N493DA	**B727**	**21062**
N493FE	**B727**	**21531**
N493GX	A320	0234
N493GX	B747	19647
N493PA	B707	19695
N493US	B727	18946
N493US	**F-28**	**11161**
N493WC	B737	21822
N494AA	**MD-82**	**49732**
(N494BN)	B727	22102
N494DA	**B727**	**21074**
N494GX	A320	0235
N494GX	B747	19648
N494PA	B707	19696
N494US	B727	18947
N494US	**F-28**	**11167**
N495	B707	19697
N495AA	**MD-82**	**49733**
N495AJ	**B727**	**20937**
(N495BN)	B727	22103
N495DA	**B727**	**21075**
N495FE	**B727**	**21669**
N495PA	**B707**	**19697**
N495US	B727	19206
N495US	**F-28**	**11168**
N495WC	B727	19092
N496AA	**MD-82**	**49734**
(N496BN)	B727	22104
N496DA	**B727**	**21076**
N496FE	**B727**	**21670**
N496PA	**B707**	**19698**
N496US	B727	19287
N496US	**F-28**	**11169**
N496WC	B727	19098
N497AA	**MD-82**	**49735**
(N497BN)	B727	22417
N497DA	**B727**	**21077**
N497FE	**B727**	**20866**
N497PA	**B707**	**19699**
N497PJ	MD-87	49777
N497US	B727	19288
N497US	**F-28**	**11173**
N497WC	B727	19096
N498AA	**MD-82**	**49736**
(N498BN)	B727	22418
N498DA	**B727**	**21142**
N498FE	**B727**	**20867**
N498GA	B707	19695
N498US	B727	19289
N498US	**F-28**	**11181**
N498WC	B727	19093
N499AA	**MD-82**	**49737**
N499BN	B727	20162
(N499BN)	B727	22419
N499DA	**B727**	**21143**
N499FE	**B727**	**21018**
N499US	B727	19290
N499US	**F-28**	**11182**
N500AV	B727	21021
N500CS	1-11	086
N500JJ	B707	17699
N500JJ	B727	18951
N500LS	**B727**	**20115**
N500ME	**DC-9**	**45711**
N500MH	B737	23174
N500MH	**DC-8**	**45812**
N500TR	**MD-82**	**49144**
N501AA	**MD-82**	**49738**
N501AM	**MD-82**	**49188**
N501AU	B737	23376
N501AV	B737	20128
(N501BN)	B747	20207
N501DA	**B727**	**21303**
N501DC	B727	20739
N501EA	B757	22191
N501ME	**DC-9**	**47132**
N501MH	B757	22176
N501NG	**B737**	**22395**
N501PA	L1011	1176
(N501PE)	B727	20634
N501SR	DC-8	45994
N501SW	**B737**	**24178**
N501UA	**B757**	**24622**
N501US	**B757**	**23190**
N502AU	**B737**	**23377**
N502AV	B727	20580
N502DA	**B727**	**21304**
N502EA	B757	22192
N502FE	**B727**	**18271**
N502MD	DC-9	47363
N502ME	**DC-9**	**48132**
N502MG	**B727**	**19391**
(N502PE)	B727	20635
N502RA	B727	19391
N502SR	B747	20208
N502SW	**B737**	**24179**
N502T	1-11	083
N502UA	**B757**	**24623**
N502US	**B757**	**23191**
N503AU	B737	23378
N503AV	B737	20227
N503DA	**B727**	**21305**
N503EA	B757	22193
N503FE	**B727**	**18273**
N503MD	DC-9	47430
N503MG	**B727**	**19392**
N503PA	L1011	1177
(N503PE)	B727	20636
N503RA	B727	19392
N503SW	**B737**	**24180**
N503T	1-11	BAC.183

N503UA	**B757**	**24624**
N503US	**B757**	**23192**
N504	F-28	11152
N504AU	**B737**	**23379**
N504AV	B727	20726
N504DA	**B727**	**21306**
N504DC	B747	21316
N504EA	B757	22194
N504FE	**B727**	**18274**
N504MD	DC-9	47468
N504MG	**B727**	**19395**
N504MM	**146**	**E3221**
N504PA	L1011	1181
(N504PE)	B727	20637
N504RA	B727	19395
N504SW	**B737**	**24181**
N504T	1-11	084
N504UA	**B757**	**24625**
N504US	**B757**	**23193**
N505	F-28	11156
N505AA	**MD-82**	**49799**
N505AU	**B737**	**23380**
N505AV	B737	20277
N505C	B727	20115
N505DA	**B727**	**21307**
N505EA	B757	22195
N505FE	**B727**	**18276**
N505MC	**B747**	**21251**
(N505MC)	B747	21048
N505MD	**MD-82**	**49149**
N505MM	**146**	**E3242**
N505PA	L1011	1184
(N505PE)	B727	20638
N505SW	**B737**	**24182**
N505T	B727	20115
N505UA	**B757**	**24626**
N505US	**B757**	**23194**
N506AU	**B737**	**23381**
N506DA	**B727**	**21308**
N506DC	B747	21251
N506EA	B757	22196
N506FE	**B727**	**18277**
N506MC	**B747**	**21252**
N506MD	DC-9	47431
N506MM	**146**	**E3244**
(N506PE)	B727	20639
N506SW	**B737**	**24183**
N506UA	**B757**	**24627**
N506US	**B757**	**23195**
N507AU	**B737**	**23382**
N507DA	**B727**	**21309**
N507DC	**DC-8**	**45855**
N507EA	B757	22197
N507FE	**B727**	**18278**
N507MC	**B747**	**21380**
N507MD	DC-9	47474
N507MM	**146**	**E3245**
N507PA	L1011	1185
(N507PE)	B727	20640
N507SW	**B737**	**24184**
N507UA	**B757**	**24743**
N507US	**B757**	**23196**
N508AU	**B737**	**23383**
N508DA	**B727**	**21310**
N508DC	DC-8	45935
N508EA	B757	22198
N508FE	**B727**	**18279**
N508MC	**B747**	**21644**
N508MD	DC-9	47477
N508MM	**146**	**E3247**
N508PA	L1011	1186
(N508PE)	B727	20641
N508SW	**B737**	**24185**
N508UA	**B757**	**24744**
N508US	**B757**	**23197**
N509	F-28	11161
N509AU	B737	23384
N509DA	**B727**	**21311**
N509DC	**B737**	**23636**
N509EA	B757	22199
N509FE	**B727**	**18280**
N509MC	**B747**	**21221**
N509MD	MD-83	49784
N509MM	**146**	**E3248**
N509PA	L1011	1188
(N509PE)	B727	20642
N509SW	**B737**	**24186**
N509UA	**B757**	**24763**
N509US	**B757**	**23198**
N510	F-28	11167
N510AM	**MD-82**	**49804**
N510AU	**B737**	**23385**
N510DA	**B727**	**21312**
N510EA	B757	22200
N510FE	**B727**	**18282**
N510FP	B757	24290
N510MD	MD-11	48421
N510MM	**146**	**E3250**
N510PA	L1011	1194
(N510PE)	B727	20643
N510SK	B757	24289
N510SW	**B737**	**24187**
N510UA	**B757**	**24780**
N511AM	**146**	**E3255**
N511AU	**B737**	**23594**
N511DA	**B727**	**21313**
N511DB	**B727**	**19139**
N511EA	B757	22201
N511FE	**B727**	**18283**
N511MD	MD-11	48420
N511P	B747	21162
N511PA	L1011	1195
N511PE	**B727**	**20634**
(N511PE)	B727	20644
N511RP	MD-83	49793
N511SW	**B737**	**24188**
N511UA	**B757**	**24799**
N511US	**B757**	**23199**
N512	F-28	11168
N512AT	**B757**	**25493**
N512AU	**B737**	**23595**
N512DA	**B727**	**21314**
N512DC	B747	21252
N512EA	B757	22202
N512FE	B727	19131
(N512FE)	B727	18435
(N512FE)	B727	19389
N512FP	DC-8	46075
N512MC	**B747**	**21220**
N512MM	**146**	**E3263**
N512PA	L1011	1197
N512PE	B727	20635
(N512PE)	B727	20645
N512SW	**B737**	**24189**
N512UA	**B757**	**24809**
N512US	**B757**	**23200**
N513	F-28	11169
N513AA	**MD-82**	**49890**
N513AU	B737	23699
N513DA	**B727**	**21315**
N513EA	B757	22203
N513FE	B727	19388
(N513FE)	B727	18847
N513PA	L1011	1208
N513PE	B727	20636
(N513PE)	B727	20646
N513SW	**B737**	**24190**
N513UA	**B757**	**24810**
N513US	**B757**	**23201**
N514AT	**B757**	**27971**
N514AU	**B737**	**23700**
N514DA	**B727**	**21430**
N514DC	B747	21162
N514EA	B757	22204
N514FE	B727	19389
(N514FE)	B727	19131
N514MD	MD-11	48411
N514PA	L1011	1210
N514PE	B727	20637
(N514PE)	B727	20647
N514SW	**B737**	**25153**
N514UA	**B757**	**24839**
N514US	**B757**	**23202**
N515AT	**B757**	**27598**
N515AU	**B737**	**23701**
N515DA	**B727**	**21431**
N515EA	B757	22205
N515FE	B727	19428
(N515FE)	B727	19180
N515MD	DC-9	47225
N515NA	**B737**	**19437**
N515PE	B727	20638
N515SW	**B737**	**25154**
N515UA	**B757**	**24840**
N515US	**B757**	**23203**
N516AM	**MD-82**	**49893**
N516AT	**B757**	**27972**
N516AU	**B737**	**23702**
N516DA	**B727**	**21432**
N516EA	B757	22206
N516FE	B727	19431
(N516FE)	B727	19182
N516MC	**B747**	**22507**
N516MD	DC-9	47128
N516PE	B727	20639
N516UA	**B757**	**24860**
N516US	**B757**	**23204**
N517AT	**B757**	**27973**
N517AU	**B737**	**23703**
N517DA	**B727**	**21433**
N517EA	B757	22207
N517FE	B727	18429
(N517FE)	B727	19166
N517MA	B707	20017
N517MC	**B747**	**23300**
N517PE	B727	20640
N517UA	**B757**	**24861**
N517US	**B757**	**23205**
N518AT	**B757**	**27974**
N518AU	**B737**	**23704**
N518DA	**B727**	**21469**
N518EA	B757	22208
N518FE	B727	18435
(N518FE)	B727	19167
N518MC	**B747**	**23476**
N518MD	DC-10	46999
N518PE	B727	20641
N518PM	B727	18435
N518UA	**B757**	**24871**
N518US	**B757**	**23206**
N519AU	**B737**	**23705**
N519DA	**B727**	**21470**
N519EA	B757	22209
(N519FE)	B727	19387
N519GA	B707	17646
N519MD	DC-10	47818
N519PE	B727	20642
N519SW	**B737**	**25318**
N519UA	**B757**	**24872**
N519US	**B757**	**23207**
N520AU	**B737**	**23706**
N520DA	**B727**	**21471**
N520EA	B757	22210
(N520FE)	B727	19388
N520L	B737	20194
N520PE	B727	20643
N520SW	**B737**	**25319**
N520UA	**B757**	**24890**
N520US	**B757**	**23208**
(N521)	F-28	11175
N521AU	**B737**	**23856**
N521DA	**B727**	**21472**
N521DB	**B727**	**21266**
N521EA	B757	22211
N521LF	B737	24234
N521MD	DC-9	47428
N521PE	B727	20644
N521SW	**B737**	**25320**
N521TX	DC-9	47521
N521UA	**B757**	**24891**
N521US	**B757**	**23209**
(N522)	F-28	11176
N522AU	**B737**	**23857**
N522DA	**B727**	**21582**
N522EA	B757	22611
(N522FE)	B727	19390
N522MD	DC-9	47323
N522PE	B727	20645
N522SW	**B737**	**26564**
N522TX	DC-9	47524
N522UA	**B757**	**24931**
N522US	**B757**	**23616**
(N523)	F-28	11177
N523AC	1-11	015
N523AU	**B737**	**23858**
N523DA	**B727**	**21583**
N523EA	B757	22612
(N523FE)	B727	19428
N523MD	DC-9	47320
N523NY	DC-9	47520
N523PE	B727	20646
N523SJ	B707	20546
N523SW	**B737**	**26565**
N523TX	DC-9	47520
N523UA	**B757**	**24932**
N523US	**B757**	**23617**
(N524)	F-28	11184
N524AC	**1-11**	**BAC.120**
N524AU	**B737**	**23859**
N524DA	**B727**	**21584**
N524EA	B757	22688
(N524FE)	B727	19430
N524MD	**DC-10**	**46999**
N524PE	B727	20647
N524SJ	B707	19789
N524SW	**B737**	**26566**
N524TX	DC-9	47539
N524UA	**B757**	**24977**
N524US	**B757**	**23618**
N525AU	**B737**	**23860**
N525DA	**B727**	**21585**
N525EA	B757	22689
N525EJ	B707	19417
(N525FE)	B727	19431
N525MD	**DC-10**	**46550**
N525NY	DC-9	47531
N525SJ	B707	20084
N525SW	**B737**	**26567**
N525TX	DC-9	47531
N525UA	**B757**	**24978**
N525US	**B757**	**23619**
N526AU	**B737**	**23861**
N526DA	**B727**	**21586**
(N526EA)	B757	22690
N526EJ	B707	19664
(N526FE)	B727	19834
N526MD	B727	20725
N526MD	DC-10	46998
N526PC	**B727**	**20370**
N526SJ	B707	19621
N526SW	**B737**	**26568**
N526UA	**B757**	**24994**
N526US	**B757**	**23620**
N527AU	**B737**	**23862**
(N527AU)	B737	24410
N527DA	**B727**	**21587**
(N527EA)	B757	22691
N527EJ	B707	19986
(N527FE)	B727	19836
N527MD	B727	20466
N527MD	**DC-9**	**47274**
N527PC	**B727**	**19665**
N527SJ	B707	20016
N527SW	**B737**	**26569**
N527UA	**B757**	**24995**
N527US	**B757**	**23842**
N528AU	**B737**	**24410**
(N528AU)	B737	24411
N528D	B727	21426
N528DA	**B727**	**21702**
N528E	B727	21427
(N528FE)	B727	18429
N528MD	B727	20468
N528MD	DC-9	47284
N528PC	**B727**	**19597**
N528PS	B727	19683
N528SJ	B707	20085
N528SW	**B737**	**26570**
N528UA	**B757**	**25018**
N528US	**B757**	**23843**
N528YV	**F-70**	**11528**
N529AC	**B727**	**20327**
N529AU	**B737**	**24411**
(N529AU)	B737	24412
N529DA	**B727**	**21703**
N529MD	DC-9	47262
N529PA	B747	21992
N529PS	B727	19684
N529UA	**B757**	**25019**
N529US	**B757**	**23844**
N530AU	**B737**	**24412**
(N530AU)	B737	24478
N530DA	B727	21813
N530EA	B727	19685

N530EJ B727 19618
N530KF B727 19176
N530MD B727 20571
N530MD DC-9 47260
N530PA B747 21022
N530PS B727 19685
N530UA B757 25043
N530US B757 23845
N531AU B737 24478
(N531AU) B737 24479
N531AW B747 19922
N531DA B727 21814
N531EA B727 19686
N531EJ B727 19619
N531LF A320 0371
N531MD B727 20728
N531PA B747 21023
N531PS B727 19686
N531TX DC-9 45847
N531UA B757 25042
N531US B757 23846
N532AU B737 24479
(N532AU) B737 24515
N532AW B747 19923
N532DA B727 22045
N532EA B727 19687
N532MD MD-83 53121
N532PA B747 21024
N532PS B727 19687
N532TX DC-9 45791
N532UA B757 25072
N532US B757 24263
N533AU B737 24515
(N533AU) B737 24516
N533AW B747 19924
N533DA B727 22046
N533MD DC-10 46553
N533PA B747 21025
N533PS B727 19688
N533TX DC-9 47281
N533UA B757 25073
N533US B757 24264
N534AU B737 24516
N534AW B747 20398
N534DA B727 22047
N534EA B727 19689
N534MD DC-9 47065
N534PA B747 21026
N534PS B727 19689
N534TX DC-9 47110
N534UA B757 25129
N534US B757 24265
N535DA B727 22048
N535MD DC-9 47003
N535PA B747 20651
(N535PA) B747 21027
N535PS B727 20161
N535TX DC-9 47111
N535UA B757 25130
N535US B757 26482
N536DA B727 22049
N536EA B727 20438
N536MD DC-9 47496
N536PA B747 21441
(N536PA) B747 21028
N536PS B727 20162
N536PS B727 20438
N536TX DC-9 47113
N536UA B757 25156
N536US B757 26483
N537DA B727 22073
N537MD DC-9 47004
N537PA B747 21547
N537PS B727 20163
N537TX DC-9 47112
N537UA B757 25157
N537US B757 26484
N537YV F-70 11537
N538DA B727 22076
N538MD DC-9 47545
N538PA B747 21548
N538PS B727 20164
N538TX DC-9 47218
N538UA B757 25222
N538US B757 26485
N539DA B727 22385
N539MD DC-9 47565
N539NY DC-9 45792
N539PA B747 21648
N539PS B727 20165
N539TX DC-9 45792
N539UA B757 25223
N539US B757 26486
N540DA B727 22386
N540MD DC-9 47325
N540PA B747 21649
N540PS B727 20166
N540UA B757 25252
N540US B757 26487
N541BN 1-11 015
N541DA B727 22387
N541LF A320 0397
N541NY DC-9 45793
N541PS B727 20167
N541TX DC-9 45793
N541UA B757 25253
N541US B757 26488
N542DA B727 22391
N542PS B727 20168
N542TX DC-9 47535
N542UA B757 25276
N542US B757 26489
N543DA B727 22392
N543NY DC-9 45789
N543TX DC-9 45789
N543UA B757 25698
N543US B757 26490
N544DA B727 22493
N544PS B727 20367
N544TX DC-9 47219
N544UA B757 25322
N544US B757 26491
N545DA B727 22494
N545NY DC-9 47094
N545PS B727 20169
N545TX DC-9 47094
N545UA B757 25323
N545US B757 26492
N546DA B727 22677
N546PS B727 20366
N546UA B757 25367
N546US B757 26493
N547EA B727 20250
N547PS B727 20250
N547UA B757 25368
N547US B757 26494
N548EA B727 20251
N548EA B727 20437
N548PS B727 20251
N548UA B757 25396
N548US B757 26495
N549EA B727 20252
N549PS B727 20252
N549UA B757 25397
N549US B757 26496
N550DS B720 18417
N550PS B727 20678
N550SW B747 20924
N550UA B757 25398
N551LF B737 24986
N551PA B727 20679
N551PE B727 20772
N551UA B757 25399
N552AA MD-82 53034
N552NA B727 20706
N552PE B727 20773
N552PS B727 20706
N552UA B757 26641
N553AA MD-83 53083
N553NA B727 20707
N553PE B727 20774
N553PS B727 20707
N553UA B757 25277
N554AA MD-83 53084
N554PE B727 20775
N554PS B727 20875
N554UA B757 26644
N555AN MD-83 53085
N555BN B727 20370
N555PE B727 20837
N555PS B727 21512
N555SL CRVL 102
N555UA B757 26647
N556AA MD-83 53086
N556NY DC-9 47423
N556PE B727 20838
N556PS B727 21513
N556UA B757 26650
N557AN MD-83 53087
N557AS DC-9 47013
N557NA B757 22191
N557NY DC-9 47424
N557PE B727 20839
N557PS B727 21691
N557UA B757 26653
N558AA MD-83 53088
N558AU B737 23512
N558HA DC-9 47045
N558PE B727 20840
N558PS B727 21692
N558UA B757 26654
N559AA MD-83 53089
N559AU B737 23513
N559PE B727 21041
N559PS B727 21958
N559UA B757 26657
N560AA MD-83 53090
N560AU B737 23514
N560MD MD-81 48000
N560PE B727 21042
N560UA B757 26660
N561AA MD-83 53091
N561LF B737 24987
N561PC DC-9 47014
N561PE B727 21043
N561UA B757 26661
N562AA MD-83 49344
N562AU B737 23550
N562PC DC-9 47012
N562PE B727 21044
N562UA B757 26664
N563AA MD-83 49345
N563AU B737 23551
N563PC DC-9 47055
N563PE B727 21045
N563UA B757 26665
N564AA MD-83 49346
N564PC DC-9 47062
N564PE B727 21118
N564UA B757 26666
N565AA MD-83 49347
N565PC DC-9 47240
N565PE B727 21119
N565UA B757 26669
N566AA MD-83 49348
N566PC DC-9 45828
N566PE B727 21242
N566UA B757 26670
N567AM MD-83 53293
N567AW MD-83 53183
N567PC DC-9 47153
N567PE B727 21243
N567UA B757 26673
N568AA MD-83 49349
N568BA 146 E1015
N568PC DC-9 47086
N568PE B727 21244
N568UA B757 26674
N569AA MD-83 49351
N569PE B727 21245
N569UA B757 26677
N570AA MD-83 49352
N570GB B737 20070
N570PE B727 21246
N570UA B757 26678
N571AA MD-83 49353
N571CA B757 24456
N571GB B737 20071
N571LF B737 26284
N571PE B727 21264
N571SC DC-10 46645
N571UA B757 26681
N572AA MD-83 49458
N572CA B757 24868
N572GB B737 20072
N572PE B727 21265
N572SC DC-10 46977
N572UA B757 26682
N573AA MD-83 53092
N573CA B757 24971
N573FB DC-8 45765
N573GB B737 20073
N573PE B727 21266
N573SC DC-10 46905
N573UA B757 26685
N573US B737 23560
N574AA MD-82 53151
N574GB B737 20074
N574PE B727 21267
N574PJ MD-83 49574
N574UA B757 26686
N574US B737 23739
N575AM MD-82 53152
N575PE B727 21268
N575UA B757 26689
N575US B737 23740
N576AA MD-82 53153
N576PE B727 21269
N576UA B757 26690
N576US B737 23741
N577AA MD-82 53154
N577JB B727 19401
N577PE B727 21270
N577UA B757 26693
N577US B737 23742
N578AA MD-82 53155
N578JC DC-8 45275
N578PE B727 21661
N578UA B757 26694
N578US B737 23257
N579AA MD-82 53156
N579JC DC-8 45289
N579PE B727 21662
N579UA B757 26697
N579US B737 23258
N580AA MD-82 53157
N580CR B727 20580
N580JC DC-8 45594
N580PE B727 21663
N580UA B757 26698
N581AA MD-82 53158
N581LF DC-10 46970
N581PE B727 22052
(N581PE) B727 21664
N581UA B757 26701
N581US B737 23259
N582AA MD-82 53159
N582PE B727 22053
N582UA B757 26702
N582US B737 23260
N583AA MD-82 53160
N583CC 1-11 015
N583PE B727 22165
N583UA B757 26705
N583US B737 23261
N584AA MD-82 53247
N584PE B727 22166
N584UA B757 26706
N584US B737 23743
N585AA MD-82 53248
N585PE B727 22167
N585UA B757 26709
N585US B737 23930
N586AA MD-82 53249
N586PE B727 22168
N586UA B757 26710
N586US B737 23931
N587A B720 18023
N587AA MD-82 53250
N587UA B757 26713
N587US B737 23932
N588AA MD-83 53251
N588UA B757 26717
N588US B737 23933
N589AA MD-83 53252
(N589UA) B757 26721
N589US B737 23934
N590AA MD-83 53253
N590CA B727 20098
(N590UA) B757 26722
N590US B737 23935
N591AA MD-83 53254
N591LF DC-10 46973
N591UA B757 28142

N591US B737 23936
N592AA MD-83 53255
(N592KA) B757 25592
N592UA B757 28143
N592US B737 23937
N593AA MD-83 53256
N593KA B757 25593
N593UA B757 28144
N594AA MD-83 53284
N594UA B757 28145
N595AA MD-83 53285
N596AA MD-83 53286
N597AA MD-83 53287
N598AA MD-83 53288
N599AA MD-83 53289
N599MP 146 E3194
N600AU B757 22192
N600CS B707 19739
N600DF MD-83 49619
N600GC DC-10 46965
N600JJ B707 17702
N600ME DC-9 45725
N600SK B737 25261
N600TR DC-9 47783
N600WN B737 27694
N601AA B747 21962
N601AN B757 27052
N601AP DC-9 47658
N601AR B727 19865
N601AU B757 22193
N601AW 146 E2012
N601BN B747 20207
(N601DA) DC-10 47965
N601DL B757 22808
N601EV B767 25076
N601FE MD-11 48401
N601FF B747 20207
N601GC DC-10 47921
N601ME MD-88 49762
N601NW DC-9 47038
N601RC B757 23321
N601TR B737 25178
N601TW B767 22564
N601UA B767 21862
N601US B747 19778
N601WN B737 27695
N602AA B747 21963
N602AN B757 27053
N602AR B727 20075
N602AU B757 22196
N602AW 146 E2014
N602BN B747 20208
N602BN B747 21682
(N602DA) DC-10 47966
N602DC DC-10 46976
N602DF B757 24398
N602DG F-100 11263
N602DL B757 22809
N602EV B767 25117
N602FE MD-11 48402
N602FF B747 19734
N602GC DC-10 47923
N602ME DC-9 48133
N602NW DC-9 47046
N602PE B747 21682
N602PR B747 19779
N602RC B757 23322
N602RP F-100 11246
N602SW B737 27953
N602TR F-100 11247
N602TW B767 22565
N602UA B767 21863
N602US B747 19779
N603AA B757 27054
N603AR B727 19862
N603AU B757 22198
N603AW 146 E2018
N603BN B747 21785
(N603DA) DC-10 47967
N603DC DC-9 47784
N603DJ B737 19955
N603DL B757 22810
N603FE MD-11 48459
N603FF B747 19746
N603NW DC-9 47101
N603P B767 23897
N603PE B747 19729
N603RC B757 23323
N603SW B737 27954
N603TW B767 22566
N603UA B767 21864
N603US B747 19780
N604AA B757 27055
N604AR B727 20409
N604AU B757 22199
N604AW 146 E2020
N604BN B747 21786
(N604DA) DC-10 47968
N604DL B757 22811
N604FE MD-11 48460
N604FF B747 19659
N604NA B727 19124
(N604NA) B727 18807
N604NW DC-9 47222
N604P B767 23898
N604PE B747 19731
N604RC B757 23566
N604SW B737 27955
N604TW B767 22567
N604UA B767 21865
N604US B747 19781
N605AA B757 27056
N605AR B727 19545
N605AU B757 22201
N605AW 146 E2016
N605BN B747 21991
(N605DA) DC-10 47969
N605DL B757 22812
N605FE MD-11 48514
N605FF B747 20271
N605NW DC-9 47223
N605PE B747 20520
N605RC B757 23567
N605SW B737 27956
N605TW B767 22568
N605UA B767 21866
N605US B747 19782
N606AA B757 27057
N606AR B727 19544
N606AU B757 22202
N606AW 146 E2033
N606BN B747 21992
N606DL B757 22813
N606FE MD-11 48602
N606FF B747 20273
N606NW DC-9 47225
N606PB B747 19783
N606PE B747 19730
N606RC B757 23568
N606SW B737 27926
N606TW B767 22569
N606UA B767 21867
N606US B747 19783
N607AM B757 27058
N607AU B757 22203
N607AW 146 E2052
(N607BN) B747 22234
N607DL B757 22814
N607FE MD-11 48547
N607NW DC-9 47232
N607P B767 23899
N607PE B747 20011
N607SW B737 27927
N607TW B767 22570
N607UA B767 21868
N607US B747 19784
N608AA B757 27446
N608AU B757 22204
N608AW 146 E2049
(N608BN) B747 22302
N608DA B757 22815
N608FE MD-11 48548
N608FF B747 19672
N608NW DC-9 47233
N608P B767 23900
N608PE B747 20012
N608SW B737 27928
N608TW B767 22571
N608UA B767 21869
N608US B747 19785
N609AA B757 27447
N609AG B727 20705
N609AU B757 22205
N609AW 146 E2070
(N609BN) B747 22235
N609DL B757 22816
N609FE MD-11 48549
N609FF B747 20354
N609HA DC-9 47676
N609KW B727 21950
N609NW DC-9 47234
N609PE B747 20534
N609SW B737 27929
N609TW B767 22572
N609UA B767 21870
N609US B747 19786
N610AA B757 24486
N610AG B727 21068
N610AR B747 20800
N610AU B757 27122
N610AW 146 E2082
N610BN B747 19746
N610DL B757 22817
N610FE MD-11 48603
N610FF B747 20501
N610NW DC-9 47432
N610PE B747 20535
N610PH DC-10 46584
N610TW B767 22573
N610UA B767 21871
N610US B747 19787
N610WN B737 27696
N611AM B757 24487
N611AR B747 19749
N611AU B757 27123
N611AW 146 E3120
N611BN B747 20527
N611DL B757 22818
N611FE MD-11 48604
N611FF B747 20502
N611NA DC-9 47435
(N611PE) B747 19732
N611SW B737 27697
N611UA B767 21872
N611US B747 20356
N612AA B757 24488
N612AR B747 19752
N612AU B757 27124
N612AW 146 E3122
(N612BN) B747 22236
N612DL B757 22819
N612FE MD-11 48605
N612NW DC-9 47436
N612SW B737 27930
N612UA B767 21873
N612US B747 20357
N613AA B757 24489
N613AU B757 27144
N613DL B757 22820
N613FE MD-11 48749
(N613FE) MD-11 48606
N613FF B747 19647
N613NW DC-9 47438
N613SW B737 27931
N613UA B767 21874
N613US B747 20358
N614AA B757 24490
N614AR B747 20009
N614AU B757 27145
N614AW 146 E3132
N614DL B757 22821
N614FE MD-11 48528
N614FF B747 20534
N614P B767 23901
N614SW B737 28033
N614UA B767 21875
N614US B747 20359
N615AM B757 24491
(N615AR) B747 20543
N615AU B757 27146
N615AW 146 E3141
N615DL B757 22822
N615FE MD-11 48767
(N615FE) MD-11 48622
N615FF B747 19638
N615SW B737 27698
N615UA B767 21876
N615US B747 20360
N616AA B757 24524
N616AU B757 27147
N616AW 146 E3145
N616DL B757 22823
N616FE MD-11 48747
N616FF B747 21939
N616SW B737 27699
N616US B747 21120
N617AM B757 24525
N617AU B757 27148
N617DL B757 22907
N617FE MD-11 48748
N617FF B747 19650
N617P B767 23902
N617SW B737 27700
N617UA B767 21877
N617US B747 21121
N618AA B757 24526
N618AU B757 22210
N618DL B757 22908
N618FE MD-11 48754
N618FF B747 21937
(N618SW) B737 28034
N618UA B767 21878
N618US B747 21122
N618WN B737 28034
N619AA B757 24577
N619AU B757 27198
N619DL B757 22909
N619FF B747 21316
N619HA DC-9 47677
N619SW B737 28035
N619UA B767 21879
N619US B747 21321
N620AA B757 24578
N620AU B757 27199
N620AW A320 0052
N620BN B747 20927
N620DL B757 22910
(N620FE) B747 19733
(N620FE) B747 20013
N620FF B747 21162
N620SW B737 28036
N620UA B767 21880
N620US B747 19918
N621AM B757 24579
N621AU B757 27200
N621AW A320 0053
N621DL B757 22911
N621FE B747 20014
(N621FE) B747 19661
N621FF B747 19729
N621LF B737 24705
N621SW B737 28037
(N621UA) B767 21881
N621US B747 19919
N622AA B757 24580
N622AU B757 27201
N622AW A320 0054
N622DH B727 20896
N622DL B757 22912
N622SW B737 27932
(N622UA) B767 21882
N622US B747 21704
N623AA B757 24581
N623AU B757 27244
N623DH B727 20895
N623DL B757 22913
N623FE B747 19897
N623SW B737 27933
(N623UA) B767 21883
N623US B747 21705
N624AA B757 24582
N624AU B757 27245
N624AW A320 0055
N624DH B727 20709
N624DL B757 22914
N624FE B747 20246
(N624FE) B747 20349
N624FT DC-8 45929
N624PL B747 20246
N624SW B737 27934
(N624UA) B767 21884
N624US B747 21706
N625AA B757 24583
(N625AU) B757 27246

Registration	Type	C/n
N625AW	A320	0064
N625DH	B727	20780
N625DL	B757	22915
N625FE	B747	20247
(N625FE)	B747	20353
N625FT	DC-8	45928
N625PL	B747	20247
N625SA	L1011	1125
N625SW	B737	27701
(N625UA)	B767	21885
N625US	B747	21707
N625VJ	B757	27246
N626AA	B757	24584
N626AU	B757	27303
N626AW	A320	0065
N626DL	B757	22916
N626FE	B747	20349
(N626FE)	B747	20391
N626SW	B737	27702
N626TX	DC-9	45726
(N626UA)	B767	21886
N626US	B747	21708
N627AA	B757	24585
N627AU	B757	27805
N627AW	A320	0066
N627DL	B757	22917
N627FE	B747	20353
(N627FE)	B747	20246
N627SW	B737	27935
(N627UA)	B767	21887
N627US	B747	21709
N628AA	B757	24586
N628AU	B757	27806
N628AW	A320	0067
N628DL	B757	22918
N628FE	B747	19661
(N628FE)	B747	20247
(N628GA)	B737	19945
N628SW	B737	27703
N628TX	DC-9	45727
(N628UA)	B767	21888
N628US	B747	22389
N629AA	B757	24587
N629AU	B757	27807
N629AW	A320	0076
N629DL	B757	22919
(N629F)	B747	20013
N629FE	B747	20391
N629HA	DC-9	47679
N629SW	B737	27704
(N629UA)	B767	21889
N629US	B747	22388
N630AA	B757	24588
N630AU	B757	27808
N630DL	B757	22920
N630FE	B747	19733
(N630FE)	B747	20653
N630SJ	B747	19733
N630SW	B737	27705
(N630UA)	B767	21890
N630US	B747	21668
N631AA	B757	24589
N631AU	B757	27809
N631AW	A320	0077
N631AW	146	E1003
N631DL	B757	23612
N631FE	B747	21827
(N631FF)	B747	20826
N631LF	B737	24708
N631SW	B737	27706
(N631UA)	B767	21891
N631US	B747	23111
N632AA	B757	24590
N632AU	B757	27810
N632AW	A320	0081
N632AW	146	E1063
N632DL	B757	23613
N632FE	B747	22245
(N632FE)	B747	20827
N632SW	B737	27707
(N632UA)	B767	22713
N632US	B747	23112
N633AA	B757	24591
N633AU	B757	27811
N633AW	A320	0082
N633DL	B757	23614
N633FE	B747	22237
(N633FE)	B747	21650
N633SW	B737	27936
(N633UA)	B767	22714
N633US	B747	21991
N634AA	B757	24592
N634AW	A320	0091
N634DL	B757	23615
N634FE	B747	22150
(N634FE)	B747	21764
N634SW	B737	27937
N634TW	B767	25209
(N634UA)	B767	22715
N634US	B747	22234
N635AA	B757	24593
N635AW	A320	0092
N635DL	B757	23762
N635FE	B747	22151
(N635FE)	B747	21841
N635SW	B737	27708
(N635UA)	B767	22716
N635US	B747	21682
N636AM	B757	24594
N636AW	A320	0098
N636DL	B757	23763
N636FE	B747	21764
(N636FE)	B747	21827
N636SW	B737	27709
(N636UA)	B767	22717
N636US	B747	23547
N637AM	B757	24595
N637AW	A320	0099
N637DL	B757	23760
N637SW	B737	27710
(N637UA)	B767	22718
N637US	B747	23548
N638AA	B757	24596
N638AW	A320	0280
N638AW	A320	0455
N638DL	B757	23761
N638FE	B747	21841
(N638FE)	B747	22245
N638SW	B737	27711
(N638UA)	B767	22719
N638US	B747	23549
N639AA	B757	24597
N639AW	A320	0471
N639DL	B757	23993
N639FE	B747	21650
(N639FE)	B747	22237
N639HA	DC-9	47689
N639SW	B737	27712
(N639UA)	B767	22720
N639US	B747	23887
N640A	B757	24598
N640DL	B757	23994
N640FE	B747	20826
(N640FE)	B747	22150
N640SW	B737	27713
(N640UA)	B767	22721
N640US	B747	23888
N641AA	B757	24599
(N641AA)	B737	19680
N641AW	A320	0453
N641DL	B757	23995
N641FE	B747	20827
(N641FE)	B747	22151
N641SW	B737	27714
N641UA	B767	25091
N642AA	B757	24600
N642DL	B757	23996
N642UA	B767	25092
N642WN	B737	27715
N643AA	B757	24601
(N643AA)	B737	19598
N643DL	B757	23997
N643UA	B767	25093
N644AA	B757	24602
(N644AA)	B737	19601
N644DL	B757	23998
N644UA	B767	25094
N645AA	B757	24603
(N645AA)	B737	19614
(N645AM)	B757	24603
N645DL	B757	24216
N645UA	B767	25280
N645US	B767	23897
N646AA	B757	24604
(N646AA)	B737	20126
N646DL	B757	24217
N646UA	B767	25283
N646US	B767	23898
(N647AA)	B757	24605
N647AM	B757	24605
N647DL	B757	24218
N647UA	B767	25284
N647US	B767	23899
N648AA	B757	24606
(N648AA)	B737	19307
N648DL	B757	24372
N648UA	B767	25285
N648US	B767	23900
N649AA	B757	24607
(N649AA)	B737	19308
N649DL	B757	24389
N649HA	DC-9	47712
N649UA	B767	25286
N649US	B767	23901
N650AA	B757	24608
(N650AA)	B737	19309
N650DH	1-11	059
N650DL	B757	24390
N650FE	A300	726
N650TW	B767	23057
N650UA	B767	25287
N650UG	DC-9	47418
N650US	B767	23902
N651AA	B757	24609
(N651AA)	B737	19713
N651DL	B757	24391
N651FE	A300	728
N651TF	B707	18586
N651TW	B767	23058
N651TX	DC-9	45714
N651UA	B767	25389
N651US	B767	24764
N652AA	B757	24610
(N652AA)	B737	19714
N652DL	B757	24392
N652FE	A300	735
N652PA	B747	20347
N652SJ	B747	20347
N652TX	DC-9	45715
N652UA	B767	25390
N652US	B767	24765
N653A	B757	24611
(N653A)	B737	20335
N653DL	B757	24393
N653FE	A300	736
N653PA	B747	20348
N653TX	DC-9	45716
N653UA	B767	25391
N653US	B767	24894
N654A	B757	24612
(N654A)	B737	19707
N654DL	B757	24394
N654FE	A300	738
N654PA	B747	20349
N654TX	DC-9	45735
N654UA	B767	25392
N654US	B767	25225
N655AA	B757	24613
(N655AA)	B737	19931
N655DL	B757	24395
N655FE	A300	742
N655PA	B747	20350
N655TX	DC-9	45736
N655UA	B767	25393
N655US	B767	25257
N656AA	B757	24614
(N656AA)	B737	20158
N656DL	B757	24396
N656FE	A300	745
N656PA	B747	20351
N656UA	B767	25394
N656US	B767	26847
N657AM	B757	24615
N657DL	B757	24419
N657FE	A300	748
N657PA	B747	20352
N657UA	B767	27112
N658AA	B757	24616
N658DL	B757	24420
N658FE	A300	752
N658PA	B747	20353
N658UA	B767	27113
N659AA	B757	24617
N659DL	B757	24421
N659FE	A300	757
N659HA	DC-9	47713
N659PA	B747	20354
N659UA	B767	27114
N660AM	B757	25294
N660DL	B757	24422
N660FE	A300	759
N660UA	B767	27115
N661AA	B757	25295
(N661AA)	B737	21066
N661AV	DC-8	45969
N661DN	B757	24972
N661FE	A300	760
N661UA	B767	27158
N661US	B747	23719
N662AA	B747	20101
N662AA	B757	25296
(N662AA)	B737	19072
(N662AA)	B737	21067
N662DN	B757	24991
N662FE	A300	761
N662SW	B737	23255
N662UA	B767	27159
N662US	B747	23720
N663AM	B757	25297
N663DN	B757	24992
N663FE	A300	766
N663SW	B737	23256
N663UA	B767	27160
N663US	B747	23818
N664AA	B757	25298
N664DN	B757	25012
N664FE	A300	768
(N664UA)	B767	27161
N664US	B747	23819
N664WN	B737	23495
N665AA	B757	25299
N665DN	B757	25013
N665FE	A300	769
(N665UA)	B767	27162
N665US	B747	23820
N665WN	B737	23497
N666A	B757	25300
N666DN	B757	25034
(N666UA)	B767	27186
N666US	B747	23821
N667DN	B757	25035
N667SW	B737	23063
(N667UA)	B767	27209
N667US	B747	24222
N668AA	B757	25333
N668DN	B757	25141
N668SW	B737	23060
(N668UA)	B767	27210
N668US	B747	24223
N669AA	B757	25334
N669DN	B757	25142
N669HA	DC-9	47654
N669HA	DC-9	47714
N669SW	B737	23752
(N669UA)	B767	27211
N669US	B747	24224
N670AA	B757	25335
N670DN	B757	25331
N670MA	B737	23121
N670MC	DC-9	47659
N670SW	B737	23784
N670US	B747	24225
N671	B737	23122
N671AA	B757	25336
N671AW	B737	23122
N671DN	B757	25332
N671MA	B737	23122
N671MC	DC-9	47660
N671SW	B737	23785
N671UP	B747	20323
(N671US)	B747	26473
N672AA	B757	25337
N672DL	B757	25977
N672MA	B737	23123

Reg	Type	No.
N672MC	**DC-9**	**47661**
N672SW	**B737**	**23406**
N672UP	**B747**	**20324**
(N672US)	B747	26474
N673AA	**B737**	**23251**
N673DL	**B757**	**25978**
N673MA	**B737**	**23124**
N673MC	**DC-9**	**47726**
N673UP	**B747**	**20325**
N674AA	**B737**	**23252**
N674DL	**B757**	**25979**
N674MA	B737	23292
N674MC	DC-9	47735
(N674PA)	B747	20326
N674UP	**B747**	**20100**
N675AA	**B737**	**23253**
N675DL	**B757**	**25980**
N675MA	**B737**	**23065**
N675MC	**DC-9**	**47651**
N675UP	**B747**	**20390**
N676AA	B737	23288
N676DL	**B757**	**25981**
N676MA	B737	23066
N676MC	**DC-9**	**47652**
N676SW	**B737**	**23288**
N676UP	**B747**	**20101**
N677AA	**B737**	**23289**
N677DL	**B757**	**25982**
N677MC	**DC-9**	**47756**
N677UP	**B747**	**20391**
N678AA	**B737**	**23290**
N678DL	**B757**	**25983**
N679AA	**B737**	**23291**
N679DA	**B757**	**26955**
N679HA	**DC-9**	**47662**
N679HA	DC-9	47715
N680AA	**B737**	**23505**
N680AM	B727	18970
N680DA	**B757**	**26956**
N680EM	B757	24923
N680FM	B727	18970
N680FM	**B757**	**24923**
N680UP	**B747**	**20923**
N681AA	**B757**	**25338**
(N681AA)	B737	23752
N681DA	**B757**	**26957**
N681MA	B737	24376
N681UP	**B747**	**19661**
N682AA	**B757**	**25339**
(N682AA)	B737	23753
N682DA	**B757**	**26958**
N682FM	B727	18970
N682G	**B727**	**19254**
N682MA	B737	25071
N682RW	**1-11**	**061**
N682SH	B767	22682
N682SW	**B737**	**23496**
N682UP	**B747**	**20349**
N683A	**B757**	**25340**
(N683AA)	B737	23754
N683DA	**B757**	**27103**
N683SW	**B737**	**24008**
N683UP	**B747**	**20353**
N684AA	**B757**	**25341**
(N684AA)	B737	23755
N684DA	**B757**	**27104**
N684WN	**B737**	**23941**
N685AA	**B757**	**25342**
N685DA	**B757**	**27588**
N685MA	**B737**	**23791**
N685SW	**B737**	**23401**
N686AA	**B757**	**25343**
N686DA	**B757**	**27589**
(N686DA)	B757	27207
N686MA	B737	24795
N686SW	**B737**	**23175**
N687AA	**B757**	**25695**
(N687DA)	B757	27172
N687SW	**B737**	**23388**
N688AA	**B757**	**25730**
N688SW	**B737**	**23254**
N688UP	**B747**	**20784**
N689AA	**B757**	**25731**
N689HA	DC-9	47663
N689MA	B737	24124
N689SW	**B737**	**23387**
N689UP	**B747**	**21033**
N690AA	**B757**	**25696**
N690MA	**B737**	**24165**
N690SW	**B737**	**23783**
N690UP	**B747**	**20348**
N690WA	**B727**	**19504**
N691AA	**B757**	**25697**
N691LF	**B767**	**25137**
N691MA	**B737**	**24166**
N691UP	**B747**	**19641**
N691WA	B727	19505
N691WN	**B737**	**23781**
N692AA	**B757**	**26972**
N692SW	**B737**	**23062**
N692WA	B727	19506
(N693)	B727	19507
N693AA	**B757**	**26973**
N693SW	**B737**	**23174**
N693WA	B727	19507
N694AA	146	E2051
N694AN	**B757**	**26974**
N694SW	**B737**	**23061**
N694WA	B727	19508
N695AA	146	E2053
N695AN	**B757**	**26975**
N695SW	**B737**	**23506**
N695WA	B727	19509
N696AA	146	E2054
N696AN	**B757**	**26976**
N696SW	**B737**	**23064**
N696WA	B727	19987
N697A	146	E2055
N697AN	**B757**	**26977**
N697SW	**B737**	**23838**
N698AA	146	E2057
N698AN	**B757**	**26980**
N698SW	**B737**	**23176**
N699AA	146	E2058
N699AN	**B757**	**27051**
N699HA	**DC-9**	**47763**
N699SW	**B737**	**23826**
N700FW	B707	18711
N700JA	1-11	059
N700ME	**DC-9**	**45696**
N700ML	B737	23404
N700NW	CV880	22-00-63
N700UP	**DC-8**	**45900**
N701AA	**B727**	**22459**
N701AW	B737	19013
N701CK	**B747**	**19725**
N701DA	L1011	1041
N701DH	**B727**	**19011**
N701EV	B727	19310
N701FT	DC-8	46117
N701ME	**MD-88**	**49760**
N701MG	B757	22197
N701ML	B737	23405
N701PA	B707	17674
N701PC	**B707**	**17639**
N701PJ	B737	19013
N701SW	B747	20826
N701TT	L1011	1041
N701UP	**DC-8**	**45938**
N701US	**B727**	**19444**
N702	B707	17677
N702AA	**B727**	**22460**
N702AW	B737	19015
N702CK	**B747**	**20332**
N702DA	L1011	1046
N702DH	**B727**	**19793**
N702FT	DC-8	46073
N702ML	**B737**	**22054**
N702PA	B707	17677
N702PC	B707	17645
N702PJ	B737	19015
N702PT	B707	17677
N702SW	B747	20827
N702TA	B707	17677
N702TT	L1011	1046
N702UP	**DC-8**	**45902**
N702US	**B727**	**19445**
N703	B707	17680
N703AA	**B727**	**22461**
N703AW	B737	19016
N703CK	**B747**	**19727**
N703DA	L1011	1052
N703DH	**B727**	**19010**
N703EV	B727	19311
N703FT	DC-8	46059
N703ML	B737	22529
(N703ML)	B737	22055
N703PA	B707	17680
N703PC	B707	19335
N703PJ	**B737**	**19016**
N703S	**B737**	**22529**
N703SW	B747	21764
(N703SW)	B747	20828
N703TT	L1011	1103
N703UP	**DC-8**	**45939**
N703US	**B727**	**19446**
N704CK	**B747**	**20528**
N704DA	L1011	1057
N704PA	B707	17683
N704SW	B747	21841
N705AA	**B727**	**22462**
N705CA	**B727**	**19479**
N705CK	B747	21032
N705DA	L1011	1071
N705DH	**B727**	**19191**
N705EV	B727	19009
N705FT	DC-8	46090
N705FW	B707	19270
N705ML	B737	22055
N705PA	B707	17686
N705PC	B707	19587
N705PS	DC-9	45846
(N705SW)	B747	22150
N705UP	**DC-8**	**45949**
N705US	**B727**	**19447**
N706AA	**B727**	**22463**
N706CA	**B727**	**19496**
N706CK	**B747**	**20010**
N706DA	L1011	1074
N706DH	**B727**	**19192**
N706FT	DC-8	46001
N706PA	B707	17689
N706PC	B707	20177
N706PS	DC-9	47020
(N706SW)	B747	22151
N706TA	B707	17689
N706UP	**DC-8**	**46056**
N707AA	**B727**	**22464**
N707AD	**B707**	**19529**
N707AR	B707	17634
N707CA	B727	20663
N707CK	**B747**	**21541**
N707DA	L1011	1077
N707DH	**B727**	**18321**
N707DY	B707	19412
N707EL	B707	19869
N707FT	DC-8	46089
N707GB	B707	18808
N707GE	**B707**	**17608**
N707GE	**B707**	**18840**
N707HD	B707	18084
N707HE	**B707**	**20124**
N707HG	B707	19353
N707HL	B707	19417
N707HP	**B707**	**18985**
N707HT	**B707**	**19271**
N707HW	B707	19294
N707JJ	B707	19352
N707KS	B707	17702
N707KS	**B707**	**20025**
N707KV	B707	19632
N707LE	**B707**	**19361**
N707MB	B707	19294
N707MB	B707	19986
N707ME	B707	19530
N707N	B707	20008
(N707NR)	B707	19574
N707PA	B707	17587
N707PD	B707	19964
N707PM	B707	19352
N707PS	DC-9	47023
N707QT	B707	21956
(N707R)	B707	17691
N707RZ	B707	18375
N707SH	B707	19353
N707SK	**B707**	**17702**
N707UM	**B707**	**24503**
N707UP	**DC-8**	**45907**
N707US	**B727**	**19448**
(N707V)	B707	17692
(N707W)	B707	17693
N707WJ	B707	20301
N707XX	**B707**	**18740**
(N707Y)	B707	17694
(N707Z)	B707	17695
N707ZS	B707	20261
N708A	B707	20060
N708AA	**B727**	**22465**
N708AW	**B737**	**19771**
N708CK	**B747**	**21543**
N708DA	L1011	1078
N708DH	**B727**	**18275**
N708PA	B707	17586
N708PS	DC-9	47068
N708SP	B737	19771
N708UP	**DC-8**	**46048**
N708US	**B727**	**19449**
N709AA	**B727**	**22466**
N709AW	B737	19770
N709CK	**B747**	**21542**
N709DA	L1011	1081
N709DH	**B727**	**19968**
N709HA	DC-9	47764
N709ML	B737	20336
N709PA	B707	17588
N709PC	**B707**	**20175**
N709SP	**B737**	**19770**
N709UP	**DC-8**	**45914**
N709US	B727	20139
N710AA	**B727**	**22467**
N710DA	L1011	1084
(N710EV)	B727	22078
N710FW	**B707**	**20017**
N710NA	**CV990**	**30-10-29**
N710PA	B707	17589
N711	B707	17590
N711BE	B727	20724
N711DA	L1011	1086
N711GN	B727	19401
N711LF	DC-8	45260
N711NA	CV990	30-10-1
N711PA	B707	17590
N711PC	B707	20172
(N711RC)	B727	22019
N711ST	1-11	058
N711SW	DC-9	45740
N711UT	B707	17601
N712AA	**B727**	**22468**
N712DA	**L1011**	**1088**
N712DH	**B727**	**19401**
N712NA	CV990	30-10-37
N712PA	B707	17591
N712PC	B707	20176
N712RC	**B727**	**22020**
N712UA	DC-8	45416
N713AA	**B727**	**22469**
N713DA	**L1011**	**1089**
N713NA	CV990	30-10-29
(N713RC)	B727	22021
N713UA	DC-8	45389
N713UP	**DC-8**	**46014**
N713US	B727	20140
N714	B707	17592
N714A	**B737**	**23405**
N714CK	B727	20187
N714DA	**L1011**	**1090**
N714FC	B707	17592
N714NA	**C-141**	**6110**
N714PA	B707	17592
N714PT	B707	17592
(N714RC)	B727	22344
N715A	**B737**	**21928**
N715AA	**B727**	**22470**
N715CL	DC-9	47068
N715DA	**L1011**	**1092**
N715DH	**B727**	**19618**
N715FW	**B707**	**19789**
(N715NA)	B737	19437
N715PA	B707	17593
N715RC	**B727**	**22019**
N715UA	DC-8	45386
N715UP	**DC-8**	**45915**
N715US	B727	19994
N716A	**B737**	**21929**

N716AA	**B727**	**20608**
N716DA	**L1011**	**1095**
N716HH	B707	17594
N716PA	B707	17594
N716RC	**B727**	**22021**
N716UA	DC-8	45385
N716US	B727	20141
N717AA	**B727**	**20610**
N717DA	**L1011**	**1096**
N717DH	**B727**	**19389**
N717NA	**DC-8**	**46082**
N717PA	B707	17595
N717QS	**B707**	**20717**
N717UA	DC-8	45390
N717US	B727	19995
N718AA	**B727**	**20611**
N718DA	**L1011**	**1097**
N718PA	B707	17596
N718RC	**B727**	**22344**
N718UA	DC-8	45384
N718UP	**DC-8**	**46018**
N718US	B727	20161
N719A	**B737**	**22679**
N719AA	**B727**	**20612**
N719CK	B727	19481
N719DA	**L1011**	**1135**
N719PA	B707	17597
N719QS	**B707**	**20719**
N719RC	**B727**	**22490**
(N719TA)	146	E2136
N719US	B727	20163
N720A	**B737**	**21926**
N720AA	**B727**	**20613**
N720AC	B720	18016
N720BA	146	E1002
N720BC	B720	18251
N720BG	B720	18033
N720CC	B720	17915
N720CK	B727	19487
N720DA	**L1011**	**1136**
N720DC	**B727**	**19253**
N720DH	**B727**	**19544**
N720FW	**B707**	**19263**
N720FW	B707	20085
N720GS	B707	19370
N720GT	**B720**	**18384**
N720JE	B727	19618
N720JR	**B720**	**18451**
N720PA	B707	17598
N720RC	**B727**	**22491**
N720US	B727	20164
N720V	B720	18376
N720W	B720	18377
N720ZK	B727	21849
N721AA	**B727**	**20729**
N721DA	**L1011**	**1139**
N721DH	**B727**	**19545**
N721EV	B727	18897
N721EW	**MD-87**	**49767**
N721GS	B707	19377
N721JE	B727	18843
N721LF	B737	26307
N721MF	**B727**	**22687**
N721ML	B737	22697
N721PA	B707	17599
N721PC	B727	18997
N721RC	**B727**	**22492**
N721RW	**B727**	**21200**
N721UA	DC-8	45753
N721US	B720	18351
N721US	B727	20165
N721WN	**B737**	**22697**
N721ZK	B727	21850
N722AA	**B727**	**20730**
N722CK	**B727**	**19485**
N722DA	**L1011**	**1147**
N722DH	**B727**	**19861**
N722EV	B727	19136
N722GS	**B707**	**19373**
N722JE	B727	19807
N722ML	B737	22698
N722PA	B707	17600
N722RW	**B727**	**21201**
N722S	B737	20449
N722UA	DC-8	45767
N722US	B720	18352
N722US	B727	20166
N722WN	**B737**	**22698**
N723GS	B707	19986
N723AA	**B727**	**20731**
N723CK	**B727**	**20191**
N723DA	**L1011**	**1150**
N723EV	B727	19137
N723GS	B707	19986
N723JE	**B727**	**18896**
N723ML	B737	23789
N723PA	B707	17601
N723PA	B747	21439
N723RW	**B727**	**21202**
N723US	B720	18353
N723US	B727	20167
N724DA	**L1011**	**1151**
N724DH	**B727**	**19862**
N724EV	B727	19109
N724JE	B727	19010
N724ML	B737	23790
N724PA	B707	17602
N724PA	B747	21316
N724PL	B727	19135
N724RW	B727	21457
N724US	B720	18354
N725AA	**B727**	**20732**
N725AL	B727	19665
N725AL	**B737**	**22051**
N725CA	B707	17603
N725CK	B727	19183
N725DA	**L1011**	**1162**
N725DT	B727	20046
N725EV	**B727**	**19112**
N725FW	**B707**	**20085**
N725JE	B727	19793
N725ML	B737	23791
N725PA	B707	17603
N725PA	B747	19898
N725PL	B727	19191
N725RW	**B727**	**21502**
N725US	B720	18355
N726AA	**B727**	**20733**
N726AL	B727	19666
N726AL	**B737**	**22426**
N726DA	L1011	1163
N726DH	**B727**	**20409**
N726EV	B727	19311
N726JE	B727	19815
N726PA	B707	17604
N726PA	B747	21048
N726PL	B727	19192
N726RW	B727	21655
N726US	B720	18356
N726VA	B727	20739
N727AA	**B727**	**20734**
N727AL	B727	19807
(N727AW)	B727	19401
N727BB	B727	19136
N727BE	**B727**	**18933**
N727BE	B727	20764
N727CD	B727	18849
N727CH	B727	18371
N727CH	B727	18933
N727CK	**B727**	**19195**
N727CR	B727	18894
N727DA	**L1011**	**1167**
N727DG	B727	19261
N727DH	**B727**	**20204**
N727EC	B727	19318
N727EV	B727	19500
N727FH	B727	20489
N727GB	B727	19136
N727GC	B727	20938
N727GS	B727	18893
N727HC	**B727**	**19835**
N727JE	B727	19011
N727JH	B727	20942
(N727KA)	B727	20371
N727KS	B727	20489
N727LA	**B727**	**19260**
N727LJ	B727	19137
N727LS	B727	20941
N727M	B727	19313
N727M	**B727**	**22541**
N727MB	B727	19318
N727MJ	B727	18365
N727MJ	B727	19313
N727NJ	**B727**	**18366**
N727PA	B707	17605
N727PA	B747	21162
N727PJ	B727	18752
N727PL	B727	19195
N727RE	B727	20228
N727RF	B727	19261
N727RL	B727	18253
N727RW	**B727**	**21656**
N727S	B727	18998
N727SG	B727	19260
N727SN	B727	21100
N727TA	B727	19122
N727TG	B727	19503
N727UD	B727	18367
N727US	B720	18420
N727VA	B727	20675
N727VA	B727	20765
N727VA	**B727**	**22536**
N727WE	B727	19262
N727WF	**B727**	**20045**
N727X	**B727**	**19394**
N727ZV	B727	19249
N728A	**DC-8**	**46081**
N728AA	**B727**	**20735**
N728AL	B737	21719
N728AL	**B737**	**22629**
N728BE	B727	20765
N728CK	**B727**	**18847**
N728DA	**L1011**	**1173**
N728EV	**B727**	**18794**
N728JE	B727	18368
N728JE	B737	19594
N728PA	B707	17606
N728PA	B747	20712
N728PL	**DC-8**	**45918**
N728Q	B707	20025
N728RW	**B727**	**21741**
N728U	B707	18689
N728US	B720	18421
N728US	B727	20168
N728VA	**B727**	**22537**
N728ZV	B727	20710
N729AA	**B727**	**20736**
N729AL	B737	22630
N729BE	B727	20766
N729CK	**B727**	**19482**
N729DA	**L1011**	**1180**
N729DH	B727	22080
N729EV	**B727**	**19116**
N729JP	B707	17607
N729PA	B707	17607
N729PA	B747	20713
N729PL	DC-8	45921
N729Q	B707	20029
N729RW	**B727**	**21742**
(N729TA)	146	E2138
N729UP	**DC-8**	**46029**
N729US	B720	18422
N729US	B727	20366
N730AA	**B727**	**20737**
N730AL	B737	22631
N730AS	**B737**	**22577**
N730DA	**L1011**	**1199**
N730EV	B727	19110
N730FW	B707	19212
N730JP	B707	17671
N730MA	B707	19212
N730MA	B737	23506
N730PA	B707	17608
N730PA	B747	20888
N730PL	DC-8	46161
N730Q	B707	20022
N730RW	B727	21823
N730S	B737	23506
N730T	B720	18154
N730TJ	**B737**	**20364**
N730UP	**DC-8**	**46030**
N730US	B720	18381
N730US	B727	20367
N731	B707	17607
N731AA	**B727**	**20738**
N731BA	B707	17607
N731EV	**B727**	**19113**
N731JP	B707	17607
N731L	DC-9	47326
N731PA	B747	19637
N731PL	DC-8	46023
N731Q	B707	20031
(N731RW)	B727	21824
N731T	B720	18423
N731TW	B707	17658
N731US	B720	18382
N731XL	B737	24095
N732AL	B727	19808
N732PA	B747	19638
N732Q	**B707**	**20034**
N732S	B737	23406
N732TW	B707	17659
N732US	B720	18383
N733AR	**B737**	**23466**
N733DS	**L1011**	**1224**
N733MA	B737	23062
N733PA	B747	19640
N733Q	B707	19621
N733T	B720	18581
N733TW	B707	17660
N733US	B720	18384
N734EB	1-11	005
N734MA	B737	23387
N734N	B737	19418
N734PA	B747	19641
(N734Q)	B707	18886
N734T	B720	18041
N734T	B720	18065
N734TW	B707	17661
N734US	B720	18687
N735D	**L1011**	**1226**
N735MA	B737	23289
N735N	B737	19419
N735PA	B747	19642
N735PL	**DC-8**	**46153**
N735SJ	B747	19642
N735T	B707	17662
N735TW	B707	17662
N735US	B720	18688
N736BP	**B737**	**23465**
N736DY	**L1011**	**1227**
N736N	B737	19420
N736PA	B747	19643
N736S	B737	23752
N736T	B720	18064
N736TW	B707	17663
N736US	B720	18792
N737AL	B707	19416
N737D	**L1011**	**1228**
(N737KD)	B737	19945
N737N	B737	19421
N737PA	B747	19644
N737Q	B737	19758
N737Q	B737	21279
N737RD	B737	20365
N737TW	B707	17664
N737US	B720	18793
N738AL	B707	20076
N738N	B737	19422
N738PA	B747	19645
N738TW	B707	17665
N739AL	B707	20077
N739BN	B727	20739
N739PA	B747	19646
N739TW	B707	17666
N740AS	**B737**	**22578**
N740DA	**L1011**	**1244**
N740DH	**B727**	**21930**
N740EV	B727	19252
N740FW	B707	19411
N740N	B737	19423
N740PA	B747	19647
N740RW	B727	21824
N740SJ	**B747**	**22477**
N740TW	B707	17667
N740US	B727	20467
N741AS	**B737**	**21959**
N741DA	**L1011**	**1245**
N741DH	**B727**	**21931**
N741L	DC-9	47418
N741N	B737	20211
N741PA	B747	19648
N741PR	**B747**	**21832**
N741RW	B727	21951

Reg.	Type	No.
N741SJ	B747	19648
N741SJ	**B747**	**22063**
N741TV	B747	21964
N741TW	B707	17668
N741US	B727	20509
N742AS	**B737**	**23136**
N742CK	B727	20184
N742DH	**B727**	**21290**
N742EV	**B727**	**19140**
N742MA	B737	23288
N742PA	B747	19649
N742PR	**B747**	**21833**
N742RW	**B727**	**21952**
N742SJ	**B747**	**21827**
N742TV	B747	21965
N742TW	B707	17669
N743AS	**B737**	**21821**
N743CK	B727	19486
N743EV	B727	19088
N743N	B737	20212
N743PA	B747	19650
N743PR	**B747**	**21834**
N743TV	B747	22403
N743TW	B707	17670
N743US	**B727**	**20285**
N744AS	**B737**	**21822**
N744CK	B727	19483
N744EV	B727	19827
N744MA	B737	23061
N744N	B737	20213
N744PA	B747	19651
N744PR	**B747**	**22382**
(N744TV)	B747	22404
N744TW	B707	17671
N744UP	**DC-8**	**45944**
N744US	B727	20286
N745AS	**B737**	**20794**
N745EV	**B727**	**19283**
N745N	B737	20214
N745SJ	**B747**	**20888**
(N745TV)	B747	22405
N745TW	B707	17672
N745US	B727	20510
N746AS	**B737**	**23123**
N746EV	B727	20078
N746N	B737	20215
N746TW	B707	18385
N746US	B727	20568
N747AV	B747	19734
N747BA	B747	19734
N747BA	B747	20770
N747BC	B747	20771
N747BC	B747	21048
N747BH	B737	23752
N747BH	B747	21162
N747BJ	B747	21316
N747BJ	B757	22209
(N747BJ)	B747	27141
N747BK	B747	21439
N747BK	B747	21604
N747BL	B747	19732
N747BL	B747	20781
N747BL	B747	21605
(N747BL)	B747	27142
N747BM	B747	20011
N747BN	B747	20012
N747BN	**B747**	**20782**
N747FT	B747	20712
N747GE	**B747**	**19651**
N747KS	B747	21133
N747MC	**B747**	**23348**
N747N	B737	20216
N747PA	**B747**	**19639**
N747QC	B747	19639
N747SP	B747	21022
N747TA	B747	20712
N747TW	B707	18386
N747US	B727	20569
N747WA	B747	20651
N747WR	B747	20651
N748EV	B727	19793
N748FT	B747	20713
N748MA	B737	23064
N748PA	B747	19652
N748TA	B747	20713
N748TW	B707	18387
N748UP	**DC-8**	**45948**
N748US	B727	20570
N748WA	B747	20652
N749FT	B747	20888
N749N	B737	19547
N749PA	B747	19653
N749R	B747	20013
N749TA	B747	20888
(N749TA)	146	E2156
N749TW	B707	18388
N749US	**B727**	**21393**
N749WA	B747	20653
N750AT	**B757**	**23126**
N750EV	B727	19010
N750FW	B707	19353
N750NA	**B757**	**26277**
N750NW	**DC-9**	**47114**
N750PA	B747	19654
N750RA	**MD-87**	**49777**
N750TW	B707	18389
N750UA	B727	19319
N750UP	**DC-8**	**45950**
N750US	**B727**	**21512**
N750VJ	B727	20302
N750WA	B747	19733
N751AT	**B757**	**23125**
N751DA	**L1011**	**1166**
N751L	B737	23507
N751MA	**B707**	**19582**
N751N	B737	19548
N751NW	**DC-9**	**47115**
N751PA	B747	19655
N751PR	**B747**	**27261**
N751RA	**MD-87**	**49779**
N751TA	B707	17649
N751TW	B707	18390
N751UA	DC-8	46139
N751US	**B727**	**21513**
N751VJ	B727	20303
N752AT	**B757**	**23128**
N752DA	**L1011**	**1172**
N752MA	B737	23063
N752N	B737	19073
N752NW	**DC-9**	**47116**
N752PA	B747	19656
N752PR	**B747**	**27262**
N752RA	**MD-87**	**49780**
N752TA	B707	17648
N752TW	**B707**	**18391**
N752UA	DC-8	45956
N752UP	**DC-8**	**45952**
N752US	**B727**	**21691**
N753AL	B727	19203
N753AS	**B727**	**19203**
N753DA	**L1011**	**1189**
N753MA	B737	23060
N753N	B737	20453
N753NW	**DC-9**	**47117**
N753PA	B747	19657
N753PR	**B747**	**27828**
N753RA	**MD-87**	**49587**
N753UA	DC-8	46024
N753US	**B727**	**21692**
N754AS	**B737**	**25095**
N754AT	**B757**	**24964**
N754DL	**L1011**	**1181**
N754N	B737	20454
N754NW	**DC-9**	**47178**
N754PA	B747	19658
N754PR	**B747**	**27663**
N754RA	**MD-87**	**49641**
N754TW	B707	18392
N754UA	B737	19707
N754US	**B727**	**21958**
N755AS	**B737**	**25096**
N755AT	**B757**	**24965**
N755DL	**L1011**	**1184**
N755MA	B737	23406
N755NW	**DC-9**	**47179**
N755PA	B747	19659
N755TW	B707	18393
N755UA	DC-8	45888
N755UP	**DC-8**	**46055**
N756AS	**B737**	**25097**
N756AT	**B757**	**27351**
N756DR	**L1011**	**1185**
N756NW	**DC-9**	**47180**
N756PA	B747	19660
N756TW	B707	18394
N756UA	DC-8	45921
N757A	**B757**	**22212**
N757AS	**B757**	**25155**
N757AT	**B757**	**23127**
(N757B)	B757	22172
(N757BC)	B757	22212
N757GA	**B757**	**24260**
N757NA	**B757**	**24567**
N757PA	B707	18083
N757TW	B707	18395
N758MA	B737	23752
N758N	B737	19603
N758NW	**DC-9**	**47286**
N758PA	B707	18084
N758TW	**B707**	**18396**
N759DA	**L1011**	**1176**
N759N	B737	19954
N759NW	**DC-9**	**47287**
N759PA	B707	18085
N759TW	B707	18397
N760AL	B727	21953
N760AS	**B737**	**25098**
N760AT	**B727**	**21954**
N760BE	B737	25017
N760DH	**L1011**	**1194**
N760FW	**B707**	**19442**
N760NC	**DC-9**	**47708**
N760NW	**DC-9**	**47288**
N760PA	B707	18335
N760TW	**B707**	**18913**
(N760TW)	B707	18398
N760US	B727	21954
N761DA	**L1011**	**1208**
N761N	B737	21665
N761NC	**DC-9**	**47709**
N761PA	B707	18336
N761TW	B707	17673
N761U	B707	19820
N762AL	B727	21954
N762AS	**B737**	**25099**
N762AT	**B727**	**22162**
N762BE	**L1011**	**1070**
(N762BT)	B767	24728
N762DA	**L1011**	**1210**
(N762HA)	L1011	1070
N762N	B737	21666
N762NC	**DC-9**	**47710**
N762NW	**DC-9**	**47395**
N762PA	B707	18337
N762TA	**B767**	**23623**
N762TB	B707	18337
N762TW	B707	17675
(N762TW)	B707	17674
N762U	B707	19821
N762UA	DC-8	45906
N762US	B727	22162
N763AB	B707	17676
N763AS	**B737**	**25100**
N763AT	**B727**	**22983**
N763BE	L1011	1082
(N763BT)	B767	24475
N763DL	**L1011**	**1197**
N763N	B737	21667
N763NC	**DC-9**	**47716**
N763NW	**DC-9**	**47396**
N763PA	B707	18338
N763TW	B707	17676
(N763TW)	B707	17675
N763U	B707	19822
N763US	B727	22983
N763W	B707	18338
N764AS	**B737**	**25101**
N764AT	**B727**	**22984**
N764BE	L1011	1103
N764BE	**L1011**	**1113**
N764DA	**L1011**	**1202**
(N764HA)	L1011	1113
N764MA	B737	23838
N764NC	**DC-9**	**47717**
N764PA	B707	18339
N764SE	B707	18339
N764TW	B707	17678
(N764TW)	B707	17676
N764US	B727	22984
(N765AB)	B707	17679
N765AS	B727	19534
N765AS	**B737**	**25102**
N765AT	**B727**	**23014**
N765B	**1-11**	**067**
N765BE	**L1011**	**1105**
N765DA	**L1011**	**1206**
(N765HA)	L1011	1105
N765NC	**DC-9**	**47718**
N765PA	B707	18579
N765TW	B707	17679
(N765TW)	B707	17677
N765US	B727	23014
N766AS	B727	19728
N766AT	**B727**	**21999**
N766BE	**L1011**	**1112**
N766DA	**L1011**	**1207**
(N766HA)	L1011	1112
N766NC	**DC-9**	**47739**
N766PA	B707	18580
N766RD	DC-8	46015
N766TW	B707	17681
(N766TW)	B707	17678
N766UA	**B777**	**26917**
N766US	B727	21999
N767AB	B707	17682
N767AS	**B737**	**27081**
N767AT	**B727**	**22001**
N767BA	**B767**	**22233**
N767BE	B767	23057
N767DA	**L1011**	**1209**
N767GE	B767	23764
N767JA	**B767**	**27385**
N767JB	**B767**	**27391**
N767JC	**B767**	**28016**
N767N	B737	20095
N767NC	**DC-9**	**47724**
N767PA	B707	18591
N767PW	B767	23765
N767RV	1-11	BAC.111
N767RV	B727	20512
N767S	B767	23215
N767TA	B767	23494
N767TW	B707	17682
(N767TW)	B707	17679
N767UA	**B777**	**26918**
N767US	B727	22001
N768AS	**B737**	**27082**
N768AT	**B727**	**21996**
N768BE	B767	23058
N768DL	**L1011**	**1216**
N768N	B737	21815
N768NC	**DC-9**	**47729**
N768TA	B767	25535
N768TW	B707	17684
(N768TW)	B707	17680
N768UA	**B777**	**26919**
N768US	B727	21996
N769AS	**B737**	**25103**
N769AT	**B727**	**21998**
N769BE	B720	18418
N769BE	**B757**	**24118**
N769DL	**L1011**	**1218**
(N769HA)	L1011	1091
N769N	B737	21816
N769NC	**DC-9**	**47757**
N769TA	**B767**	**26608**
N769TW	B707	17685
(N769TW)	B707	17681
N769UA	**B777**	**26921**
N769US	B727	21998
N770AL	B727	22162
N770AT	**B727**	**21953**
N770BE	B720	18419
N770BE	**B757**	**24119**
N770FW	**B707**	**20016**
N770JS	B707	19626
N770NC	**DC-9**	**47758**
N770TW	B707	17687
(N770TW)	B707	17682
N770UA	**B777**	**26925**
N771AL	B727	22163
N771AS	**B737**	**25104**
N771BE	B720	18793
N771CA	DC-8	46022

N771NC	**DC-9**	**47769**
N771PA	B747	19661
N771TW	B707	17688
(N771TW)	B707	17683
N771UA	**B777**	**26932**
(N772AB)	B707	17690
N772AL	B727	22164
N772AS	**B737**	**25105**
N772AT	**B727**	**22003**
N772BE	B727	20876
N772CA	**DC-8**	**46131**
N772FT	DC-8	46109
N772N	B737	21817
N772NC	**DC-9**	**47774**
N772TW	B707	17690
(N772TW)	B707	17684
N772UA	**B777**	**26930**
N772UP	**DC-8**	**46072**
N773AL	B727	22983
N773AS	**B737**	**25106**
N773AT	**B727**	**22004**
N773BE	B727	20877
N773FT	DC-8	45966
N773N	B737	21818
N773NC	**DC-9**	**47775**
N773TW	**B707**	**18405**
(N773TW)	B707	17685
N773UA	**B777**	**26929**
N774AL	B727	22984
N774AS	**B737**	**25107**
N774AT	**B727**	**21510**
N774BE	B727	20878
(N774BE)	B747	27828
N774C	DC-8	45634
N774FT	DC-8	46087
N774N	B737	21975
N774NC	**DC-9**	**47776**
N774TW	**B707**	**18406**
(N774TW)	B707	17686
N774UA	**B777**	**26936**
N775AL	B727	23014
N775AS	**B737**	**25108**
N775AT	**B727**	**21511**
N775AU	**B737**	**24933**
N775BE	B727	20727
N775MA	B737	23174
N775N	B737	21976
N775NC	**DC-9**	**47785**
N775TW	**B707**	**18407**
(N775TW)	B707	17687
N775UA	**B777**	**26947**
(N775UA)	B777	26926
N775US	B727	21953
N776AL	B727	22770
N776AS	**B737**	**25109**
N776AT	**B727**	**21608**
N776AU	**B737**	**24934**
N776FT	DC-8	46112
N776MA	B737	23252
N776N	B737	20414
N776NC	**DC-9**	**47786**
N776TW	B707	18408
(N776TW)	B707	17688
N776UA	**B777**	**26927**
N777AU	**B737**	**24979**
N777EC	B737	19309
N777FB	**B707**	**19210**
N777NC	**DC-9**	**47787**
N777NW	B707	17647
N777SJ	DC-10	46978
N777UA	**B777**	**26916**
(N777UA)	B777	26928
N777VV	**CRVL**	**87**
N777WA	**COMET**	**6443**
N778	B707	17903
N778AS	**B737**	**25110**
N778AT	**B727**	**22005**
N778AU	**B737**	**24980**
N778FT	DC-8	46049
N778JA	MD-82	48080
N778MA	B737	23785
N778N	B737	22018
N778NC	**DC-9**	**48100**
N778PA	B707	17903
N778TW	**B707**	**18409**
(N778TW)	B707	17689
N778UA	**B777**	**26931**
N778YY	B737	24970
N779AL	B727	23052
N779AS	**B737**	**25111**
N779AT	**B727**	**22091**
N779AU	**B737**	**24996**
N779C	DC-8	45644
N779FT	DC-8	45989
N779JA	MD-82	48079
N779MA	B737	23784
N779N	B737	22273
N779NC	**DC-9**	**48101**
N779PA	B707	17904
N779TW	**B707**	**18764**
(N779TW)	B707	17690
(N779TW)	B707	18410
N779UA	**B777**	**26933**
N779UP	**DC-8**	**45979**
N780AL	B727	21999
N780AL	DC-8	45928
N780AS	**B737**	**25112**
N780AT	**B727**	**22295**
N780AU	**B737**	**24997**
N780EC	B720	18033
N780EG	MD-87	49780
N780FT	DC-8	45990
N780JA	MD-82	49126
(N780JS)	B707	19574
N780MA	B737	23254
N780N	B737	22274
N780NC	**DC-9**	**48102**
N780PA	B720	18033
N780T	B747	19746
N780TW	**B707**	**18914**
(N780TW)	B707	18399
N780UA	**B777**	**26934**
N781AL	B727	22001
N781AL	**DC-8**	**45926**
N781AU	**B737**	**25020**
N781DL	**L1011**	**1003**
N781FT	DC-8	45991
N781JA	MD-82	49111
N781L	B737	23506
(N781L)	B737	23387
N781N	B737	22275
N781NC	**DC-9**	**48121**
N781PA	B720	18036
N781TW	B707	18400
N781UA	**B777**	**26928**
N782AL	B727	21996
N782AL	DC-8	45929
N782AS	**B737**	**25113**
N782AT	**B727**	**21972**
N782AU	**B737**	**25021**
N782DL	**L1011**	**1006**
N782FT	DC-8	46002
N782JA	MD-82	49103
N782N	B737	22352
N782NC	**DC-9**	**48107**
N782PA	B720	18037
N782TW	B707	18401
N782UA	**B777**	**26935**
N783AL	B727	21998
N783AL	DC-8	45927
N783AS	**B737**	**25114**
N783AU	**B737**	**25022**
N783DL	**L1011**	**1009**
N783FT	DC-8	46003
N783JA	MD-82	49104
N783N	B737	22353
N783NC	**DC-9**	**48108**
N783PA	B720	18057
N783TW	B707	18402
N783UA	**B777**	**26937**
N783UP	**DC-8**	**45973**
N784AL	**DC-8**	**46135**
N784AS	**B737**	**28199**
N784AU	**B737**	**25023**
N784DA	**L1011**	**1038**
N784FT	DC-8	46004
N784JA	MD-82	49386
(N784JA)	MD-82	49370
N784MA	B737	23781
N784N	B737	22354
N784NC	**DC-9**	**48109**
N784PA	B720	18059
N784TW	**B707**	**18403**
N784UA	**B777**	**26938**
N785AL	DC-8	46149
N785AS	**B737**	**27628**
N785AU	**B737**	**25024**
N785DL	**L1011**	**1121**
N785FT	DC-8	46005
N785JA	MD-82	49387
(N785JA)	MD-82	49371
N785MA	B737	23783
N785N	B737	22355
N785NC	**DC-9**	**48110**
N785PA	B720	18060
N785TW	B707	18404
N785UA	**B777**	**26939**
N786AL	**DC-8**	**46121**
(N786AU)	B737	25025
N786DL	**L1011**	**1123**
N786FT	DC-8	46006
N786JA	MD-82	49426
N786N	B737	22443
N786NC	**DC-9**	**48148**
N786PA	B720	18248
N786TW	B707	18711
N786UA	**B777**	**26940**
N787AL	DC-8	45999
(N787AU)	B737	25026
N787DL	**L1011**	**1126**
N787FT	DC-8	46007
N787JA	MD-82	49427
N787M	**L1011**	**1064**
N787N	B737	22444
N787NC	**DC-9**	**48149**
N787PA	B720	18250
N787TW	B707	18712
N787UA	**B777**	**26941**
N788AL	**DC-8**	**45999**
(N788AU)	B737	25027
N788BR	B727	20710
N788DA	**L1011**	**1141**
N788FT	DC-8	46008
N788N	B737	22445
N788PA	B720	18251
N788TW	C-18	18713
N788UA	**B777**	**26942**
N789AL	DC-8	46063
(N789AU)	B737	25028
N789DL	**L1011**	**1142**
N789FT	DC-8	45858
N789N	B737	22398
N789TW	B707	18709
N789UA	**B777**	**26943**
N790AL	DC-8	46093
(N790AU)	B737	25029
N790DL	**L1011**	**1143**
N790FA	B707	17697
N790FT	DC-8	46044
N790PA	B707	18714
N790SA	B707	17697
N790TW	B707	18738
N790UA	**B777**	**26944**
N791AL	**DC-8**	**46150**
(N791AL)	DC-8	45924
(N791AU)	B737	25030
N791FT	**DC-8**	**46045**
N791L	B727	21608
N791LF	B747	24956
N791N	B737	22752
(N791N)	B737	22751
N791PA	B707	18715
N791SA	B707	17698
N791TW	B720	18381
N791TW	B707	18756
N791UA	**B777**	**26945**
N792AL	DC-8	46041
(N792AU)	B737	25031
N792FT	**DC-8**	**46046**
N792N	B737	22753
(N792N)	B737	22752
N792PA	B707	18716
N792SA	B707	17701
N792TW	B720	18382
N792TW	B707	18757
N792UA	**B777**	**26946**
N793AL	DC-8	46097
N793DG	MD-83	49793
N793FT	DC-8	46047
N793N	B737	22754
(N793N)	B737	22753
N793NA	B707	17700
N793PA	B707	18717
N793SA	B707	17700
N793TW	B720	18383
N793TW	**B707**	**18915**
(N793UA)	B777	26947
N794	B707	18718
N794AJ	**B727**	**21243**
N794AL	DC-8	45923
N794EP	B707	18718
N794FT	DC-8	46086
N794N	B737	22755
(N794N)	B737	22754
N794PA	B707	18718
N794RN	B707	18718
N794TW	B707	20429
N794UA	**B777**	**26948**
N795AL	DC-8	46136
N795FT	**DC-8**	**46103**
N795N	B737	22756
(N795N)	B737	22755
N795PA	B707	18765
N795RN	B707	18765
N795TW	B720	18384
N795TW	**B707**	**18758**
N795UA	**B777**	**26950**
N796AL	**DC-8**	**46054**
N796FT	**DC-8**	**46104**
N796N	B737	22757
(N796N)	B737	22756
N796PA	B707	18766
N796TW	B707	18759
N796UA	**B777**	**26951**
N797AL	**DC-8**	**46163**
N797AS	B727	19169
N797FT	DC-8	46140
(N797FT)	DC-8	46138
N797N	B737	22758
(N797N)	B737	22757
N797PA	B707	18767
N797TW	B707	18760
N797UA	**B777**	**26952**
N797UP	**DC-8**	**45897**
N798AL	DC-8	46129
N798AS	B727	19170
N798FT	DC-8	46108
N798N	B737	22751
(N798N)	B737	22758
N798PA	B707	18790
(N798PA)	B707	18825
N798TW	B707	18761
N798UA	**B777**	**26953**
N798UP	**DC-8**	**45898**
N799AL	**DC-8**	**45922**
N799FT	DC-8	46001
N799N	B737	22795
N799PA	B707	18824
(N799PA)	B707	18826
N799TW	B707	18762
N799UA	**B777**	**26954**
N800CZ	**B767**	**26389**
N800DM	1-11	079
N800DM	**DC-9**	**47466**
N800EV	DC-8	45301
N800FT	B747	20100
N800MC	1-11	062
N800MC	1-11	078
N800ME	**DC-9**	**45842**
N800PA	DC-8	45253
N800PW	1-11	078
N800US	**MD-81**	**48034**
N800WA	B737	20255
N801AJ	**CV880**	**22-00-3**
N801AL	B737	19426
N801AL	DC-10	46933
N801AM	**B757**	**25624**
N801AX	**DC-8**	**46077**
N801BN	DC-8	46082
N801CK	**DC-8**	**45816**
N801DE	**MD-11**	**48472**
N801DH	**DC-8**	**46033**
N801E	DC-8	45408
N801EA	**B727**	**22432**

N801EV	DC-8	45750
N801FB	DC-8	45965
N801FT	B747	20101
N801GP	**DC-8**	**46039**
N801MG	DC-8	45986
N801ML	MD-87	49724
N801NY	MD-82	49127
N801PA	A310	288
N801PA	DC-8	45254
N801PH	**F-28**	**11097**
N801RW	146	E1002
N801SW	DC-8	45692
N801TW	CV880	22-00-1
N801TW	CV880	22-00-42
N801U	DC-8	45939
N801UP	**DC-8**	**46101**
N801US	DC-8	45602
N801US	**MD-81**	**48037**
N801VV	**MD-81**	**48046**
N801WA	B737	21763
N801WA	DC-8	46133
N802AJ	**CV880**	**22-00-6**
N802AL	**B737**	**22148**
(N802AL)	B737	20364
N802AM	**B757**	**26270**
N802AX	**DC-8**	**46134**
N802BN	**DC-8**	**45909**
N802CK	**DC-8**	**45679**
N802DE	**MD-11**	**48473**
N802DH	**DC-8**	**46076**
N802E	DC-8	45409
N802EA	**B727**	**22433**
N802FT	B747	20323
N802MG	**DC-8**	**46098**
N802ML	MD-87	49725
N802N	B737	22796
N802NY	MD-82	49222
N802PA	A310	333
N802PA	DC-8	45255
N802PH	**F-28**	**11017**
N802RW	146	E1010
N802SC	B727	18802
N802SW	DC-8	45818
N802TW	CV880	22-00-2
N802U	DC-8	45950
N802UP	**DC-8**	**46100**
N802US	DC-8	45603
N802US	**MD-81**	**48036**
N802VV	**MD-82**	**48048**
N802WA	DC-8	46146
N803AJ	**CV880**	**22-00-8**
N803AL	B737	20206
N803AM	**B757**	**26268**
N803AX	**DC-8**	**45917**
N803CK	B707	20315
N803CK	DC-8	45610
N803CK	**DC-8**	**46085**
N803DE	**MD-11**	**48474**
N803DH	**DC-8**	**46123**
N803E	DC-8	45410
N803EA	B727	22434
N803FT	B747	19897
N803MA	**B727**	**22434**
N803MG	DC-8	45910
N803ML	**MD-87**	**49726**
N803N	B737	22797
N803NY	MD-82	49229
N803PA	A310	343
N803PA	DC-8	45256
N803PH	**F-28**	**11031**
N803RW	146	E1011
N803SC	B727	19534
N803SW	DC-8	45821
N803TW	CV880	22-00-3
N803U	DC-8	45900
N803UP	**DC-8**	**46073**
N803US	DC-8	45604
N803US	**MD-81**	**48035**
N803VV	**MD-82**	**48087**
N803WA	DC-8	46149
N804AJ	CV880	22-00-10
N804AL	**B737**	**21719**
N804AM	**B757**	**26271**
N804AX	**DC-8**	**45987**
N804CK	**DC-8**	**45689**
N804DE	**MD-11**	**48475**
N804DH	**DC-8**	**46124**
N804DL	A310	345
N804E	DC-8	45411
N804EA	B727	22435
N804EV	**DC-8**	**45303**
N804FT	B747	20246
N804MA	**B727**	**22435**
N804ML	MD-87	49727
N804N	B737	22798
N804NY	MD-82	49246
N804PA	A310	345
N804PA	DC-8	45257
N804SW	DC-8	45816
(N804TW)	CV880	22-00-5
N804U	DC-8	45938
N804UP	**DC-8**	**46004**
N804US	DC-8	45605
N804US	**MD-81**	**48052**
N804WA	DC-8	46137
N805AL	**B737**	**21809**
N805AM	**B757**	**26272**
N805AX	**DC-8**	**45906**
N805CK	**DC-8**	**45649**
N805DE	**MD-11**	**48476**
N805DH	**DC-8**	**46125**
N805E	DC-8	45412
N805EA	**B727**	**22436**
N805FT	B747	20247
N805ML	MD-87	49777
N805N	B737	22799
N805NY	MD-82	49249
N805PA	A310	339
N805PA	DC-8	45258
N805SW	DC-8	45817
N805TW	CV880	22-00-6
N805U	DC-8	45817
N805UP	**DC-8**	**46117**
N805US	DC-8	45606
N805US	**MD-81**	**48053**
N805WA	DC-8	46143
N806AJ	CV880	22-00-12
N806AL	**B737**	**21927**
N806AM	**B757**	**26273**
N806BN	DC-8	45911
N806CK	DC-8	45808
N806CK	DC-8	45932
N806DE	**MD-11**	**48477**
N806E	DC-8	45413
N806EA	B727	22437
N806FT	B747	21827
N806MA	**B727**	**22437**
N806ML	MD-87	49778
N806N	B737	22806
N806NY	MD-82	49260
N806PA	A310	342
N806PA	DC-8	45259
N806SW	DC-8	45883
N806TW	CV880	22-00-8
N806UP	**DC-8**	**46006**
N806US	**MD-81**	**48038**
(N806US)	DC-8	45628
N806WA	DC-8	46145
N807AJ	**CV880**	**22-00-13**
N807AL	**B737**	**23443**
(N807AM)	B767	26261
N807AX	DC-8	45953
N807CK	**DC-8**	**45767**
N807DE	**MD-11**	**48478**
N807E	DC-8	45645
N807EA	B727	22438
N807FT	B747	21828
N807ML	MD-87	49779
N807N	B737	22866
N807NY	MD-82	49261
N807PA	A310	346
N807PA	DC-8	45260
N807TW	CV880	22-00-9
N807UP	**DC-8**	**46007**
N807US	**MD-81**	**48039**
(N807US)	DC-8	45629
N808AJ	**CV880**	**22-00-15**
N808AL	**B737**	**23445**
(N808AM)	B767	26262
N808AX	**DC-8**	**45954**
N808CK	**DC-8**	**45817**
N808DE	**MD-11**	**48479**
N808E	DC-8	45646
N808EA	B727	22439
N808FT	B747	22245
N808MA	**B727**	**21988**
N808MC	**B747**	**21048**
N808ML	MD-87	49780
N808NY	MD-82	49262
N808PA	DC-8	45261
N808TW	CV880	22-00-10
N808UP	**DC-8**	**46008**
N808US	**MD-81**	**48040**
(N808US)	DC-8	45630
N808ZS	**B707**	**19695**
N809AJ	**CV880**	**22-00-19**
N809AL	**B737**	**21720**
N809CK	**DC-8**	**45803**
N809CK	DC-8	46095
N809DE	**MD-11**	**48480**
N809E	DC-8	45649
N809EA	B727	22440
N809FT	B747	19733
N809FT	B747	21650
(N809FT)	B747	22237
N809HA	MD-81	48044
N809M	1-11	BAC.126
N809ML	MD-82	49931
N809N	B737	22867
N809NY	**MD-82**	**49263**
N809PA	DC-8	45262
N809TW	CV880	22-00-12
N809UP	**DC-8**	**46109**
N809US	**MD-81**	**48041**
(N809US)	DC-8	45631
N810AJ	**CV880**	**22-00-20**
N810AL	**B737**	**24031**
N810AS	146	E2062
N810BN	**DC-8**	**45905**
N810CK	**DC-8**	**45814**
N810DE	**MD-11**	**48565**
N810E	DC-8	45650
N810EA	B727	22441
N810EV	DC-8	45902
N810FT	B747	22237
N810GB	DC-8	45878
N810ML	MD-82	49932
N810N	B737	22868
N810NY	MD-82	49264
N810PA	DC-8	45263
N810TW	CV880	22-00-13
N810U	B737	20208
N810UP	**DC-8**	**46001**
N810US	**MD-81**	**48042**
(N810US)	DC-8	45632
N810ZA	DC-8	46162
N811AJ	**CV880**	**22-00-22**
N811AL	**DC-8**	**46099**
N811AX	**DC-8**	**46113**
N811BN	DC-8	45634
N811CK	**DC-8**	**46147**
N811DE	**MD-11**	**48566**
N811E	DC-8	45672
N811EA	B727	22548
N811EV	DC-8	46051
N811FT	B747	20826
N811GB	DC-8	46038
N811ML	MD-82	49889
N811N	B737	22869
N811NY	MD-82	49265
N811PA	A310	439
N811PA	DC-8	45264
N811TC	**DC-8**	**45883**
N811TW	CV880	22-00-14
N811UP	**DC-8**	**46089**
N811US	**MD-81**	**48043**
N811UT	B707	17692
N811ZA	DC-8	46154
N812AJ	**CV880**	**22-00-23**
N812AS	**146**	**E2074**
N812AX	**DC-8**	**46126**
N812BN	DC-8	45635
N812CK	**DC-8**	**45890**
N812DE	**MD-11**	**48600**
N812E	DC-8	45673
N812EA	B727	22549
N812FT	B747	20827
N812ML	MD-82	53017
(N812ML)	MD-82	53064
N812NY	MD-82	49250
N812PA	A310	442
N812PA	DC-8	45265
N812TC	**DC-8**	**45764**
N812TW	CV880	22-00-15
N812UP	**DC-8**	**46112**
N812US	**MD-81**	**48092**
N812ZA	DC-8	46028
N813AJ	**CV880**	**22-00-24**
N813AX	**DC-8**	**46136**
N813BN	DC-8	45642
N813CK	**DC-8**	**45893**
N813DE	**MD-11**	**48601**
N813E	DC-8	45688
N813EA	B727	22550
N813FT	B747	21764
N813N	B737	22961
N813NY	MD-82	48066
N813PA	A310	449
N813PA	DC-8	45266
N813TL	**DC-9**	**45732**
N813TW	CV880	22-00-18
N813UP	**DC-8**	**46059**
N813US	**MD-81**	**48093**
N813ZA	DC-8	46139
N814AJ	**CV880**	**22-00-32**
N814AS	**146**	**E2080**
N814AX	**DC-8**	**46041**
N814BN	DC-8	45644
N814CK	DC-8	46127
N814DE	**MD-11**	**48623**
N814E	**DC-8**	**45687**
N814EA	B727	22551
N814FT	B747	21841
N814GB	**DC-8**	**45913**
(N814ML)	MD-82	53065
N814N	B737	22962
N814NY	MD-82	49112
N814PA	A310	450
N814PA	DC-8	45267
N814TW	CV880	22-00-19
N814UP	**DC-8**	**46090**
N814US	**MD-81**	**48094**
N814ZA	DC-8	45956
N815AJ	**CV880**	**22-00-35**
N815AS	**146**	**E2084**
N815AX	**DC-8**	**46097**
N815CK	**DC-8**	**46151**
N815DE	**MD-11**	**48624**
N815DE	**MD-11**	**48751**
N815E	DC-8	45689
N815EA	**B727**	**22552**
N815EV	DC-8	46002
N815FT	B747	22150
(N815ML)	MD-82	53066
N815NY	MD-82	49113
N815PA	A310	451
N815PA	DC-8	45268
N815TW	CV880	22-00-20
N815UP	**DC-8**	**46002**
N815US	**MD-82**	**48095**
N815ZA	DC-8	46024
N816AJ	**CV880**	**22-00-40**
N816AL	**B737**	**23122**
N816AS	**146**	**E2087**
N816AX	**DC-8**	**46093**
N816CK	**DC-8**	**45892**
N816E	DC-8	45690
N816EA	**B727**	**22553**
N816EV	DC-8	45990
N816FT	B747	22151
(N816ML)	MD-82	53067
N816NY	MD-82	49370
N816PA	**A310**	**452**
N816PA	DC-8	45269
N816TW	CV880	22-00-22
N816UP	**DC-8**	**45990**
N816US	**MD-82**	**48096**
N816ZA	DC-8	46068
N817AJ	**CV880**	**22-00-4**
N817AL	**B737**	**23292**
N817AX	**DC-8**	**45928**
N817CK	**DC-8**	**45887**
N817E	DC-8	45807
N817EA	**B727**	**22554**

Registration	Type	c/n
N817EV	**DC-8**	**46022**
N817FT	B747	20349
(N817ML)	MD-82	53068
N817NY	MD-82	49371
N817PA	A310	453
N817PA	DC-8	45270
N817RA	**MD-83**	**49788**
N817SJ	**MD-81**	**48051**
N817TW	CV880	22-00-23
N817US	**MD-82**	**48097**
N818AJ	CV880	22-00-9
N818AX	**DC-8**	**46075**
N818CK	DC-8	45961
N818E	DC-8	45808
N818EA	**B727**	**22555**
N818EV	DC-8	46113
N818FT	B747	20353
(N818ML)	MD-82	53069
N818NY	MD-82	49478
N818PA	A310	455
N818PA	DC-8	45271
N818SJ	**MD-81**	**48058**
N818TW	CV880	22-00-24
N818UP	**DC-8**	**46108**
N818US	**MD-82**	**48098**
N819AJ	**CV880**	**22-00-36**
N819AL	B737	23791
N819AX	**DC-8**	**45927**
N819E	DC-8	45806
N819EA	B727	22556
N819EV	DC-8	46126
N819F	DC-8	45437
N819FT	B747	19661
N819HA	MD-81	48045
(N819ML)	MD-82	53070
N819NY	**MD-82**	**49479**
N819PA	A310	456
N819PA	DC-8	45272
N819SL	DC-8	45854
N819TW	CV880	22-00-25
N819UP	**DC-8**	**46019**
N819US	**MD-82**	**48099**
N820AJ	CV880	22-00-39
N820AX	**DC-8**	**46155**
N820BX	**DC-8**	**46065**
N820E	DC-8	45815
N820EA	**B727**	**22557**
N820F	DC-8	45435
N820FT	B747	20391
(N820ML)	MD-82	53071
N820NY	MD-82	49480
N820PA	A310	457
N820PA	DC-8	45273
N820TC	DC-8	45999
N820TW	CV880	22-00-26
N820US	**MD-82**	**49119**
N821AX	**DC-8**	**46116**
N821BX	**DC-8**	**45811**
N821CC	DC-10	46554
N821E	DC-8	45877
N821EA	B727	22558
N821F	**DC-8**	**45433**
N821L	B737	21687
N821L	DC-10	47848
N821LF	B747	24957
(N821ML)	MD-82	53072
N821PA	A310	458
N821RA	**MD-82**	**49931**
N821TC	DC-8	46127
N821TW	CV880	22-00-27
N821US	**MD-82**	**49138**
N822AL	**B747**	**20402**
N822AX	**DC-8**	**46079**
N822BX	**DC-8**	**45813**
N822E	DC-8	45907
N822EA	B727	22559
N822FT	B747	19733
N822PA	A310	467
N822RA	**MD-82**	**49932**
N822TW	CV880	22-00-28
N822US	**MD-82**	**49139**
N823AX	**DC-8**	**46122**
N823BX	**DC-8**	**46064**
N823E	DC-8	45914
(N823EA)	B727	22560
(N823ML)	MD-82	53073
N823PA	A310	539
N823RA	**MD-82**	**49889**
N823TW	CV880	22-00-30
N823US	**MD-82**	**49142**
N824AX	**DC-8**	**46141**
N824BX	**DC-8**	**45946**
N824E	DC-8	45915
(N824EA)	B727	22561
(N824ML)	MD-82	53100
N824PA	A310	542
N824RA	**MD-82**	**53017**
N824TW	CV880	22-00-31
N824US	**MD-82**	**49143**
N825AC	1-11	065
N825AQ	1-11	065
N825AX	**DC-8**	**46115**
N825BX	**DC-8**	**45978**
N825E	DC-8	45944
(N825ML)	MD-82	53101
(N825PA)	A310	574
N825TW	CV880	22-00-32
N825US	**MD-82**	**49237**
N826AX	**DC-8**	**46061**
N826BX	**DC-8**	**45998**
N826E	DC-8	45979
(N826ML)	MD-82	53102
(N826PA)	A310	576
N826TW	CV880	22-00-33
N826US	**MD-81**	**48026**
N827BX	**DC-8**	**45971**
(N827ML)	MD-82	53103
N827TW	CV880	22-00-34
N827US	**MD-81**	**48049**
N828BX	**DC-8**	**45993**
(N828ML)	MD-82	53104
N828TW	CV880	22-00-35
N828US	**MD-81**	**48028**
N829BX	**DC-8**	**45994**
N829HA	MD-81	48051
(N829ML)	MD-82	53105
(N829TW)	CV880	22-00-39
N829US	**MD-82**	**49429**
N830FT	**B747**	**19642**
(N830ML)	MD-82	53106
N830TW	CV880	22-00-40
N830US	**MD-82**	**49443**
N830VV	**MD-83**	**49397**
N831F	DC-8	45606
N831FT	**B747**	**19648**
N831L	**B727**	**21826**
N831LA	DC-10	46936
N831LF	**MD-83**	**53050**
(N831ML)	MD-82	53107
N831PC	B737	19306
N831RV	**B727**	**19093**
N831TW	**B727**	**18902**
(N831TW)	CV880	22-00-42
N831US	MD-82	53162
N831WA	**B727**	**21483**
N832AU	MD-82	53163
N832BE	146	E1223
N832FT	**B747**	**20347**
N832LA	**DC-10**	**46931**
(N832ML)	MD-82	53108
N832PC	B737	19307
N832RA	**MD-83**	**53044**
N832RV	**B727**	**19098**
N833AU	MD-82	53164
N833BE	146	E1224
N833DA	DC-8	45380
N833FA	DC-8	45378
N831LA	**DC-10**	**46937**
(N833ML)	MD-82	53109
N833N	B727	18935
N833NA	B720	18066
N833PC	B737	19308
N833RA	**MD-83**	**53045**
N833TW	B727	18903
N834AC	B737	19309
N834AU	MD-82	53165
N834BE	146	E1225
(N834ML)	MD-82	53110
N834N	B727	18858
N834RA	**MD-83**	**53124**
N835AB	**A310**	**650**
N835AU	MD-82	53166
(N835ML)	MD-82	53111
(N835N)	B727	19252
(N835PC)	B737	19713
N836AB	**A310**	**660**
(N836AB)	A310	676
N836AU	MD-82	53167
N836EV	DC-8	46051
(N836ML)	MD-82	53112
N836N	B727	18850
(N836PC)	B737	19714
N836RA	**MD-83**	**53046**
N836UP	**DC-8**	**45936**
N837AB	**A310**	**674**
(N837AB)	A310	676
N837AU	MD-82	53168
(N837ML)	MD-82	53113
N837N	B727	18802
N838AB	**A310**	**676**
N838AU	MD-82	53169
(N838ML)	MD-82	53114
N838N	B727	18803
N839AD	**A310**	**678**
N839AU	MD-82	53170
N839HA	MD-81	48058
N839TW	**B727**	**18904**
N840AB	**A310**	**682**
N840AU	MD-82	53171
N840RA	**MD-82**	**49424**
N840TW	B727	18905
N840UP	**DC-8**	**46140**
N841AB	**A310**	**686**
N841AX	**DC-8**	**45908**
N841L	B737	19955
N841L	B737	23255
N841LF	B737	23811
N841LF	B737	24988
(N841LF)	B737	26301
N841MM	B727	18368
N841N	B727	18324
N841RA	**MD-82**	**49421**
N841TW	B727	18906
N842AB	**A310**	**687**
N842AX	**DC-8**	**46015**
(N842L)	B737	19940
N842RA	**MD-82**	**49604**
N842TW	B727	18907
N843AA	**B727**	**20984**
N843AB	**A310**	**689**
N843AX	**DC-8**	**46017**
N843RA	**MD-82**	**49615**
N844AA	**B727**	**20985**
N844AX	**DC-8**	**45848**
N844RA	MD-82	49423
N844TW	**B727**	**18755**
N845AA	**B727**	**20986**
N845AX	**DC-8**	**46157**
N845CP	MD-83	49845
N845RA	MD-82	49380
N845TW	B727	18754
N846AA	**B727**	**20987**
N846AX	**DC-8**	**46158**
N846TW	B727	18753
N847AA	**B727**	**20988**
N847AX	**DC-8**	**46031**
N847TW	B727	18752
N848AA	**B727**	**20989**
N848AX	**DC-8**	**46032**
(N848AX)	DC-8	45912
N848CP	MD-83	49848
N848TW	**B727**	**18751**
N849AA	**B727**	**20990**
N849AX	**DC-8**	**45891**
N849AX	DC-8	45981
N849HA	MD-81	48073
N849TW	B727	18750
N850AA	**B727**	**20991**
N850AX	**DC-8**	**45894**
N850FT	**B747**	**19755**
N850SY	B727	21114
N850TW	B727	18569
N850US	**F-100**	**11276**
N851AA	B727	20992
N851AL	B727	21851
N851AX	**DC-8**	**45940**
N851F	DC-8	45824
N851FT	**B747**	**19756**
N851JB	**B707**	**20084**
N851L	B737	22657
N851LF	B737	23788
N851MA	B707	19212
N851MA	B707	19411
N851MA	**L1011**	**1158**
N851SY	B727	20792
N851TW	**B727**	**18570**
N851UP	**DC-8**	**46051**
N851US	**F-100**	**11278**
N852AA	B727	20993
N852AX	**DC-8**	**46016**
N852F	DC-8	45856
N852FT	**B747**	**19757**
N852SY	B727	20790
N852TW	B727	18571
N852UP	**DC-8**	**46052**
N852US	**F-100**	**11280**
N853AA	B727	20994
N853AX	**DC-8**	**46037**
N853FT	**B747**	**19753**
N853SY	B727	21113
N853TW	B727	18572
N853US	**F-100**	**11281**
N854AA	**B727**	**20995**
N854FT	**B747**	**19754**
N854SY	B727	20791
N854TW	**B727**	**18573**
N854US	**F-100**	**11282**
N854WT	B737	26850
N855AA	**B727**	**20996**
N855BC	DC-8	45804
N855FT	**B747**	**19733**
N855N	B727	20163
N855TW	**B727**	**18574**
N855US	**F-100**	**11283**
N856AA	**B727**	**20997**
N856N	B727	20164
N856TW	**B727**	**18575**
N856US	**F-100**	**11286**
N857AA	B727	21084
N857FT	**B747**	**20246**
N857N	B727	20165
N857TW	**B727**	**18576**
N857US	**F-100**	**11289**
N858AA	**B727**	**21085**
N858FT	**B747**	**20109**
N858N	B727	20161
N858TW	B727	18577
N858US	**F-100**	**11291**
N859AA	**B727**	**21086**
N859FT	**B747**	**20326**
N859HA	MD-81	48074
N859N	B727	20366
N859TW	B727	18578
N859US	**F-100**	**11293**
N860AA	**B727**	**21087**
N860FT	DC-8	45938
N860N	B727	20166
N860SY	B727	20905
N860US	**F-100**	**11295**
N861AA	**B727**	**21088**
N861BX	**B707**	**19293**
N861FT	DC-8	45900
N861L	B737	22760
N861LF	**MD-83**	**49826**
N861N	B727	20167
N861PL	**DC-8**	**45964**
N861SY	**B737**	**20588**
N861US	**F-100**	**11297**
N862AA	**B727**	**21089**
N862BX	B707	19625
N862FT	DC-8	45948
N862N	B727	20568
N862SY	B737	20670
N862US	**F-100**	**11300**
N863AA	**B727**	**21090**
N863BX	B707	19270
N863E	DC-8	45999
N863F	DC-8	46001
N863FT	DC-8	45949
N863N	B727	20510
N863SY	B727	18323
N863US	**F-100**	**11303**
N864AA	**B727**	**21369**
N864BX	B707	19375

Registration	Type	C/n
N864F	DC-8	46087
N864FT	DC-8	45952
N864N	B727	20286
N864US	**F-100**	**11306**
N865AA	**B727**	**21370**
N865BX	B707	18766
N865F	**DC-8**	**46088**
N865N	B727	20570
N865US	**F-100**	**11308**
N866AA	**B727**	**21371**
N866F	DC-8	46112
N866N	B727	20569
N866SY	B727	20905
N866UP	**DC-8**	**45966**
N866US	**F-100**	**11310**
N867AA	**B727**	**21372**
N867BX	**DC-8**	**46049**
N867F	DC-8	45939
N867FT	DC-8	45939
N867N	B727	20509
N867UP	**DC-8**	**45967**
N867US	**F-100**	**11312**
N868AA	**B727**	**21373**
N868BX	**DC-8**	**46034**
N868F	DC-8	45950
N868FT	DC-8	45950
N868UP	**DC-8**	**45968**
N868US	**F-100**	**11313**
N869AA	**B727**	**21374**
N869BX	**DC-8**	**46035**
N869F	DC-8	45913
(N869HA)	MD-82	49119
N869N	B727	20467
N869US	**F-100**	**11314**
N870AA	**B727**	**21382**
N870BX	**DC-8**	**46036**
N870N	B727	20285
N870PA	B707	20016
N870SJ	DC-8	46039
N870TV	**DC-8**	**46086**
N871AA	**B727**	**21383**
N871L	B737	23256
N871LF	B757	24543
N871PA	B707	20017
N871SJ	DC-8	45977
N871TV	DC-8	45968
N871TW	CV880	22-00-1
N871UM	DC-9	47434
N872AA	**B727**	**21384**
(N872BX)	B707	19584
N872PA	B707	20018
N872RA	**MD-83**	**49793**
N872SJ	**DC-8**	**46040**
N872TV	DC-8	46001
N872UM	DC-9	47437
N873AA	**B727**	**21385**
(N873BX)	B707	19585
N873RA	**MD-83**	**53093**
N873SJ	**DC-8**	**46091**
N873UM	DC-9	47436
N874AA	**B727**	**21386**
N874BX	B727	19134
N874SJ	**DC-8**	**46149**
N874UM	B747	20014
(N874UM)	B727	19863
N874UP	**DC-8**	**46074**
N875AA	**B727**	**21387**
N875BX	B727	19504
N875C	DC-8	45635
N875RA	**MD-83**	**53182**
N875SJ	**DC-8**	**46063**
N875UM	B747	20305
N876AA	**B727**	**21388**
N876RA	**MD-83**	**53183**
N876UM	B727	20430
N877AA	**B727**	**21389**
N877C	DC-8	45642
N877SE	**RJ100**	**7075**
N877UM	**B727**	**20525**
N878AA	**B727**	**21390**
N878RA	**MD-83**	**53184**
N878UM	B727	20431
N879AA	**B727**	**21391**
N879RA	**MD-83**	**53185**
N879UM	B727	20526
N880AA	**B727**	**21519**
N880AJ	CV880	22-00-1
N880DP	**1-11**	**079**
N880DV	**146**	**E2062**
N880EP	**CV880**	**22-00-38**
N880JT	CV880	22-7-8-60
N880NW	CV880	22-00-11
N880PA	**B707**	**20019**
N880RA	**MD-83**	**53186**
N880RB	**DC-9**	**47635**
N880SR	CV880	22-00-7
N880UP	**DC-8**	**46080**
N880US	**F-100**	**11331**
N880WA	CV880	22-00-51
N881AA	**B727**	**21520**
N881DV	146	E2074
N881LF	B737	23506
N881LF	**MD-83**	**53051**
N881PA	**B707**	**20020**
N881US	**F-100**	**11333**
N882AA	**B727**	**21521**
N882DV	146	E2136
N882PA	B707	20021
N882US	**F-100**	**11334**
N883AA	**B727**	**21522**
N883DV	146	E2138
N883PA	B707	20022
N883US	**F-100**	**11337**
N884AA	**B727**	**21523**
N884DV	146	E2156
N884PA	B707	20023
N884US	**F-100**	**11338**
N885AA	**B727**	**21524**
N885DV	146	E3163
N885PA	**B707**	**20024**
N885US	**F-100**	**11345**
N886AA	**B727**	**21525**
(N886DV)	146	E3165
N886MA	**B727**	**21855**
N886PA	B707	20025
N886US	**F-100**	**11346**
N887AA	**B727**	**21526**
(N887DV)	146	E3169
N887MA	**B727**	**21857**
N887PA	B707	20026
N887US	**F-100**	**11349**
N888AU	**F-100**	**11357**
N888NW	B707	17705
N888VT	B727	20371
N888WA	**COMET**	**6424**
N889AA	**B727**	**21527**
N889MA	B727	21854
N889TW	B727	19228
N889US	**F-100**	**11358**
N890AA	**B727**	**22006**
N890FS	B737	23467
N890FT	B747	20013
N890PA	B707	20027
N890TW	B727	19229
N890US	**F-100**	**11365**
N891AA	**B727**	**22007**
N891DL	MD-11	48411
N891FS	B737	23468
N891L	B737	23388
N891LF	B747	24896
N891PA	B707	20028
N891TW	B727	19230
N891US	**F-100**	**11366**
N892AA	**B727**	**22008**
(N892AF)	DC-8	45618
N892DL	MD-11	48412
N892PA	B707	20029
N892TW	B727	19231
N892US	**F-100**	**11372**
N893AA	**B727**	**22009**
N893AF	DC-8	45619
N893PA	**B707**	**20030**
N893TW	B727	19232
N893US	**F-100**	**11373**
N894AA	**B727**	**22010**
N894PA	B707	20031
N894TW	B727	19233
N894UP	**DC-8**	**46094**
N894US	**F-100**	**11379**
N895AA	**B727**	**22011**
N895AJ	**B727**	**20661**
N895N	B727	20168
N895PA	B707	20032
N895SY	**B707**	**20032**
N895TW	B727	19234
N895US	**F-100**	**11380**
N896AA	**B727**	**22012**
N896N	B727	20367
N896PA	B707	20033
N896US	**F-100**	**11391**
N897AA	**B727**	**22013**
N897PA	B707	20034
N897US	**F-100**	**11392**
N897WA	B707	18339
N898AA	**B727**	**22014**
N898PC	B727	19620
N898US	**F-100**	**11398**
N898WA	**B707**	**19502**
N899AA	**B727**	**22015**
N899US	**F-100**	**11399**
N900AX	**DC-9**	**47380**
N900CH	B727	19835
N900CL	**DC-8**	**45265**
N900DE	**MD-88**	**53372**
N900ME	**DC-9**	**45841**
N900ML	DC-9	45710
N900NW	**CV880**	**22-00-62**
N901AK	DC-9	45846
N901AW	**B757**	**23321**
N901AX	**DC-9**	**47381**
N901B	DC-9	45731
N901BN	A320	0052
N901CK	DC-9	47154
(N901CL)	DC-8	45274
N901DA	**MD-90**	**53381**
N901DC	DC-9	47038
N901DC	**MD-90**	**53367**
N901DE	**MD-88**	**53378**
N901DL	**MD-88**	**49532**
N901H	DC-9	45717
N901ML	DC-9	47104
N901MW	**CRVL**	**62**
N901PA	B747	20391
N901TS	B727	18257
N901TW	**MD-82**	**49166**
N901UA	**B737**	**25001**
N901VJ	**DC-9**	**47275**
N901WA	DC-10	46908
N902RQ	B707	18689
N902AK	DC-9	47020
N902AW	**B757**	**23322**
N902AX	**DC-9**	**47426**
N902BN	A320	0053
N902CK	DC-9	47045
N902CL	DC-10	46905
(N902CL)	DC-8	45276
N902DA	**MD-90**	**53382**
N902DC	DC-9	47039
N902DC	MD-90	53381
N902DE	**MD-88**	**53379**
N902DL	**MD-88**	**49533**
N902H	DC-9	45724
N902JW	DC-10	46905
N902ML	DC-9	47105
N902MW	**CRVL**	**88**
N902PA	B747	19896
N902PG	B727	20725
N902PJ	MD-83	49401
N902R	DC-8	45767
N902TS	**B727**	**18267**
N902TW	**MD-82**	**49153**
N902UA	**B737**	**25002**
N902UP	**B727**	**18898**
N902VJ	**DC-9**	**47177**
N902WA	DC-10	46928
N903AK	DC-9	47023
N903AW	**B757**	**23323**
N903AX	**DC-9**	**47427**
N903BN	A320	0054
N903CL	DC-8	45382
N903DA	**MD-90**	**53383**
N903DC	DC-9	47046
N903DE	**MD-88**	**53380**
N903DL	**MD-88**	**49534**
N903H	DC-9	47149
N903ML	MD-88	49759
N903MW	**CRVL**	**89**
N903PA	B747	20100
N903PG	B727	20466
N903R	DC-8	45647
N903TS	B727	18272
N903TW	**MD-82**	**49154**
N903UA	**B737**	**25003**
N903UP	**B727**	**18945**
N903VJ	**DC-9**	**47261**
N903WA	DC-10	46929
N904AK	DC-9	47068
N904AW	**B757**	**23566**
N904AX	**DC-9**	**47040**
N904BN	A320	0055
N904CL	DC-8	45376
N904DA	**MD-90**	**53384**
N904DC	DC-9	47047
N904DE	**MD-88**	**53409**
N904DL	**MD-88**	**49535**
N904ML	MD-88	49766
N904MW	CRVL	93
N904PA	B747	21743
N904PG	**B727**	**20468**
N904R	DC-8	46000
N904TS	B727	18291
N904TW	**MD-82**	**49156**
N904UA	**B737**	**25004**
N904UP	**B727**	**18946**
N904VJ	**DC-9**	**47377**
N904WA	DC-10	46930
N905AW	**B757**	**23567**
N905AX	**DC-9**	**47147**
N905BN	A320	0064
N905CL	**DC-8**	**45274**
N905DA	**MD-90**	**53385**
N905DC	DC-9	47101
N905DE	**MD-88**	**53410**
N905DL	**MD-88**	**49536**
N905H	DC-9	47150
N905ML	MD-83	53044
N905MW	CRVL	95
N905NA	**B747**	**20107**
N905PA	B747	21744
N905PG	B727	20571
N905TS	B727	18966
N905TW	**MD-82**	**49157**
N905UA	**B737**	**25005**
N905UP	**B727**	**18947**
N905VJ	**DC-9**	**47378**
N905WA	DC-10	46938
N906AW	**B757**	**23568**
N906AX	**DC-9**	**47072**
N906BN	A320	0065
N906CL	**DC-8**	**45276**
N906DA	**MD-90**	**53386**
N906DC	DC-9	47129
N906DE	**MD-88**	**53415**
N906DL	**MD-88**	**49537**
N906H	DC-9	47171
N906ML	MD-83	53045
N906PG	B727	20728
N906R	**DC-8**	**46087**
N906TS	B727	18967
N906TW	**MD-82**	**49160**
N906UA	**B737**	**25006**
N906UP	**B727**	**19314**
N906VJ	**DC-9**	**47379**
N906WA	DC-10	46939
N907AW	**B757**	**22691**
N907AX	**DC-9**	**47203**
(N907BN)	A320	0066
N907CL	DC-8	45967
N907DA	**MD-90**	**53387**
N907DC	DC-9	47476
N907DE	**MD-88**	**53416**
N907DL	**MD-88**	**49538**
N907GP	A320	0066
N907H	DC-9	47362
N907MD	MD-83	49934
N907ML	MD-83	53046
N907MW	**CRVL**	**129**
N907PG	B727	22164
N907R	DC-8	45764
N907TS	B727	18973
N907TW	**MD-82**	**49165**
N907UA	**B737**	**25007**
N907UP	**B727**	**19118**
N907VJ	**DC-9**	**47444**

Registration	Type	c/n
N907WA	**DC-10**	**46946**
N908AW	**B757**	**24233**
N908AX	**DC-9**	**47008**
(N908BN)	A320	0067
N908CL	DC-8	45903
(N908CL)	DC-8	45968
N908DA	**MD-90**	**53388**
N908DC	DC-9	45721
N908DE	**MD-88**	**53417**
N908DL	**MD-88**	**49539**
N908GP	A320	0067
N908H	**DC-9**	**47517**
N908PG	**B727**	**20951**
N908TS	B727	19685
N908TW	**MD-82**	**49169**
N908UA	**B737**	**25008**
N908UP	**B727**	**19114**
N908VJ	DC-9	47321
N908WA	DC-10	46977
N909AW	**B757**	**24522**
N909AX	**DC-9**	**47148**
(N909BN)	A320	0076
N909CH	1-11	067
N909DA	**MD-90**	**53389**
N909DC	DC-9	47410
N909DE	**MD-88**	**53418**
N909DL	**MD-88**	**49540**
(N909GP)	A320	0076
N909LH	B737	20195
N909PG	**B727**	**21852**
N909TS	B727	19686
N909TW	**MD-82**	**49170**
N909UA	**B737**	**25009**
N909UP	**B727**	**19115**
N909VJ	**DC-9**	**47322**
N909WA	DC-10	46983
N910AW	**B757**	**24523**
(N910BN)	A320	0077
N910CL	DC-8	46094
(N910DA)	MD-90	53390
N910DE	**MD-88**	**53419**
N910DL	**MD-88**	**49541**
N910DN	**MD-90**	**53390**
N910GP	A320	0076
N910PC	B707	20171
N910R	DC-8	45854
N910TS	B727	19687
N910UA	**B737**	**25254**
N910UP	**B727**	**19117**
N910VJ	**DC-9**	**47277**
N911AW	B757	24543
N911CL	DC-8	45981
N911DA	**MD-90**	**53391**
N911DE	**MD-88**	**49967**
N911DL	**MD-88**	**49542**
N911GP	A320	0077
N911KM	**DC-9**	**45740**
N911NA	**B747**	**20781**
N911R	DC-8	45817
N911RW	**DC-9**	**47149**
N911TS	B727	19689
N911TW	**MD-82**	**49182**
N911UA	**B737**	**25255**
N911UP	**B727**	**19119**
N911VV	**DC-9**	**47285**
(N912BN)	A320	0081
N912CA	**RJ100**	**7011**
N912CL	DC-8	45908
N912DE	**MD-88**	**49997**
N912DL	**MD-88**	**49543**
N912GP	A320	0081
N912R	DC-8	45908
N912RW	**DC-9**	**47150**
N912TS	**B727**	**20438**
N912TW	**MD-82**	**49183**
N912UA	**B737**	**25290**
N912UP	**B727**	**19244**
N912VJ	**DC-9**	**47020**
N912VV	**DC-9**	**47359**
N912WA	DC-10	46645
N913AW	**B757**	**22207**
(N913BN)	A320	0082
N913DE	**MD-88**	**49956**
N913DL	**MD-88**	**49544**
N913GP	A320	0082
N913R	DC-8	46128
N913RW	**DC-9**	**47171**
N913TS	**B727**	**20250**
N913TW	**MD-82**	**49184**
N913UA	**B737**	**25291**
N913UP	**B727**	**19245**
N913VJ	**DC-9**	**45846**
N913VV	**DC-9**	**47318**
N913WA	DC-10	46646
N914AW	**B757**	**22208**
(N914BN)	A320	0091
N914BV	**DC-8**	**45912**
N914CA	**RJ100**	**7012**
N914CL	DC-8	45912
N914DE	**MD-88**	**49957**
N914DL	**MD-88**	**49545**
N914GP	A320	0091
N914LF	**DC-9**	**45695**
N914RW	**DC-9**	**47362**
N914TS	**B727**	**20251**
N914TW	**MD-82**	**49185**
N914UA	**B737**	**25381**
N914UP	**B727**	**19246**
N914VJ	**DC-9**	**47068**
N914VV	**DC-9**	**47486**
N914WA	DC-10	47832
N915AW	**B757**	**22209**
(N915BN)	A320	0092
N915BV	**DC-8**	**45981**
N915CA	**RJ100**	**7013**
N915CL	DC-8	45894
N915DE	**MD-88**	**53420**
N915DL	**MD-88**	**49546**
N915F	**DC-9**	**47061**
N915GP	A320	0092
N915PJ	MD-83	49619
N915R	DC-8	45916
N915RW	**DC-9**	**47139**
N915TS	**B727**	**20252**
N915TW	**MD-82**	**49186**
(N915U)	DC-9	47407
N915UA	**B737**	**25382**
N915UP	**B727**	**19533**
N915VV	**DC-9**	**47443**
N915WA	DC-10	47833
N916AW	**B757**	**24291**
(N916BN)	A320	0098
N916CA	**RJ100**	**7014**
N916CL	DC-10	46906
N916DE	**MD-88**	**53421**
N916DL	**MD-88**	**49591**
N916F	**DC-9**	**47044**
N916GP	A320	0098
N916JW	DC-10	46906
N916R	DC-8	45753
N916RW	**DC-9**	**47144**
N916TS	**B727**	**20437**
N916TW	**MD-82**	**49187**
(N916U)	DC-9	47408
N916UA	**B737**	**25383**
N916UP	**B727**	**19808**
N916VJ	**DC-9**	**47023**
N916VV	**DC-9**	**47445**
(N917BN)	A320	0099
N917CA	**RJ100**	**7017**
N917CL	DC-10	46727
N917DE	**MD-88**	**49958**
N917DL	**MD-88**	**49573**
N917GP	A320	0099
N917JW	DC-10	46727
N917R	DC-8	46099
N917RW	**DC-9**	**47145**
N917TS	**B727**	**20149**
N917TW	**MD-82**	**49366**
(N917U)	DC-9	47409
N917UA	**B737**	**25384**
N917UP	**B727**	**19310**
N917VV	**DC-9**	**47323**
N918CA	**RJ100**	**7018**
N918CL	**DC-8**	**45648**
N918DE	**MD-88**	**49959**
N918DL	**MD-88**	**49583**
N918RW	**DC-9**	**47158**
N918TS	**B727**	**20445**
N918TW	**MD-82**	**49367**
(N918U)	DC-9	47410
N918UA	**B737**	**25385**
N918UP	**B727**	**19008**
N918VJ	**DC-9**	**48138**
N918VV	**DC-9**	**47320**
N919CL	DC-8	46106
N919DE	**MD-88**	**53422**
N919DL	**MD-88**	**49584**
N919JW	DC-8	46106
N919PJ	**DC-9**	**47663**
N919RW	**DC-9**	**47162**
N919TS	**B727**	**20447**
N919TW	**MD-82**	**49368**
N919UA	**B737**	**25386**
N919UP	**B727**	**19012**
N919VJ	**DC-9**	**48139**
N919VV	**DC-9**	**47260**
N919VV	DC-9	47723
N920CA	**RJ100**	**7022**
N920CL	DC-8	46058
N920DE	**MD-88**	**53423**
N920DL	**MD-88**	**49644**
N920L	**DC-9**	**47734**
N920PJ	**DC-9**	**47677**
N920PS	MD-81	48051
N920RW	**DC-9**	**47163**
N920TS	B727	20448
N920TW	**MD-82**	**49369**
N920UA	**B737**	**25387**
N920UP	**B727**	**19873**
N920VJ	DC-9	47682
N920VJ	**DC-9**	**48140**
N920VV	**DC-9**	**47262**
N920VV	DC-9	47674
N921CL	DC-8	45643
(N921DE)	MD-88	53424
N921DL	**MD-88**	**49645**
N921L	**DC-9**	**47107**
N921LF	A320	0453
N921R	**DC-8**	**46145**
N921RW	**DC-9**	**47164**
N921TS	**B727**	**22043**
N921UA	**B737**	**25388**
N921UP	**B727**	**19874**
N921VJ	DC-9	47683
N921VJ	**DC-9**	**48141**
N921VV	**DC-9**	**47284**
N921VV	DC-9	47451
N922AB	B737	23922
N922BV	DC-8	45925
N922CL	DC-8	45925
(N922DE)	MD-88	53425
N922DL	**MD-88**	**49646**
N922L	**DC-9**	**47108**
N922RW	**DC-9**	**47182**
N922TS	**B727**	**20415**
N922UA	**B737**	**26642**
N922UP	**B727**	**19231**
N922VJ	DC-9	47685
N922VJ	**DC-9**	**48142**
N922VV	DC-9	47274
N922VV	DC-9	47489
N923AX	**DC-9**	**47165**
N923CL	DC-8	45920
(N923DE)	MD-88	49960
N923DL	**MD-88**	**49705**
N923L	**DC-9**	**47109**
N923R	DC-8	46077
N923RW	**DC-9**	**47183**
N923TS	**B727**	**20441**
N923UA	**B737**	**26643**
N923UP	B727	19229
N923VJ	DC-9	47665
N923VJ	**DC-9**	**48143**
N923VV	DC-9	47488
N923VV	**DC-9**	**47529**
N924AX	**DC-9**	**47403**
N924BV	**DC-8**	**45920**
N924CA	**RJ100**	**7026**
N924CL	DC-8	46134
(N924DE)	MD-88	49961
N924DL	**MD-88**	**49711**
N924L	**DC-9**	**47324**
N924PS	MD-81	48034
N924RW	**DC-9**	**47185**
N924TS	**B727**	**21041**
N924UA	**B737**	**26645**
N924UP	**B727**	**19234**
N924VJ	DC-9	47688
N924VJ	**DC-9**	**48144**
N924VV	DC-9	47534
N925AX	**DC-9**	**45728**
N925BV	**DC-8**	**45885**
(N925DE)	MD-88	49962
N925DL	**MD-88**	**49712**
(N925DS)	B727	20046
N925L	**DC-9**	**47357**
N925PS	MD-81	48035
N925TS	**B727**	**21244**
N925UA	**B737**	**26646**
N925UP	**B727**	**19230**
N925US	**DC-9**	**47472**
N925VJ	DC-9	47686
N925VJ	**DC-9**	**48145**
N925VV	DC-9	47397
N926AX	DC-9	47002
N926CA	**RJ100**	**7027**
N926CL	DC-8	46092
N926DL	**MD-88**	**49713**
N926L	**DC-9**	**47172**
N926NW	**DC-9**	**47425**
N926PS	MD-81	48036
N926RC	**DC-9**	**47473**
N926UA	**B737**	**26648**
N926UP	**B727**	**19233**
N926VJ	DC-9	47692
N926VJ	**DC-9**	**48146**
N926VV	DC-9	45774
N927AX	**DC-9**	**45717**
N927CA	**RJ100**	**7031**
N927DA	**MD-88**	**49714**
N927DS	B727	20046
N927L	**DC-9**	**48123**
N927PS	MD-81	48037
N927RC	**DC-9**	**47469**
N927UA	**B737**	**26649**
N927UP	B727	19232
N927VJ	DC-9	47693
N927VJ	**DC-9**	**48154**
N927VV	DC-9	47442
N928AX	DC-9	45718
N928AX	**DC-9**	**47392**
N928DL	**MD-88**	**49715**
N928L	**DC-9**	**48124**
N928ML	**DC-9**	**47326**
N928PS	MD-81	48038
N928PS	MD-81	48052
N928UA	**B737**	**26651**
N928UP	**B727**	**19091**
N928VJ	**DC-9**	**48131**
N929AX	**DC-9**	**45874**
N929CA	**RJ100**	**7035**
N929DL	**MD-88**	**49716**
N929L	**DC-9**	**47174**
N929ML	DC-9	47418
N929PS	MD-81	48053
N929R	**DC-8**	**45901**
N929UA	**B737**	**26652**
N929UP	**B727**	**19092**
N929VJ	**DC-9**	**48118**
N930AS	**MD-82**	**49231**
N930AX	**DC-9**	**47363**
N930DL	**MD-88**	**49717**
N930EA	DC-9	45730
N930FT	**B727**	**19387**
N930MC	MD-82	48056
N930ML	DC-9	47527
N930NA	**C-135**	**17969**
N930RC	**DC-9**	**45729**
N930TL	F-28	11016
N930UA	**B737**	**26655**
N930UP	**B727**	**19096**
N930VJ	**DC-9**	**45868**
N930VV	**DC-9**	**47723**
N931AS	**MD-82**	**49232**
N931AX	**DC-9**	**47384**
N931CA	**RJ100**	**7037**
N931DL	**MD-88**	**49718**
N931EA	DC-9	45698
N931F	DC-9	47040
N931F	DC-9	47192
N931FT	B727	19390
N931L	**DC-9**	**47173**
N931LF	**A320**	**0448**

Registration	Type	c/n
N931MC	**MD-82**	**48057**
N931ML	**DC-9**	**47202**
N931NA	**C-135**	**18615**
N931PS	MD-81	48039
N931TW	**MD-82**	**49527**
N931UA	**B737**	**26656**
N931UP	**B727**	**19858**
N931VJ	**DC-9**	**47188**
N931VV	**DC-9**	**47674**
N932AS	**MD-82**	**49233**
N932AX	**DC-9**	**47465**
N932CA	**RJ100**	**7038**
N932DL	**MD-88**	**49719**
N932EA	DC-9	45699
N932F	DC-9	47041
N932F	**DC-9**	**47355**
N932FT	B727	19834
N932L	**DC-9**	**47669**
N932MC	MD-82	49120
N932ML	**DC-9**	**47547**
N932PS	MD-81	48040
N932UA	**B737**	**26658**
N932UP	**B727**	**19856**
N932VJ	**DC-9**	**47189**
N932VV	**DC-9**	**47451**
N933AS	**MD-82**	**49234**
N933AX	**DC-9**	**47291**
N933CA	**RJ100**	**7040**
N933DL	**MD-88**	**49720**
N933F	DC-9	47147
N933F	**DC-9**	**47191**
N933FT	B727	19182
N933L	**DC-9**	**47617**
N933MC	MD-82	49121
N933ML	DC-9	47548
N933PS	MD-81	48041
N933UA	**B737**	**26659**
N933UP	**B727**	**19857**
N933VJ	**DC-9**	**47216**
N933VV	**DC-9**	**47489**
N934AS	**MD-83**	**49235**
N934AX	**DC-9**	**47462**
N934CA	**RJ100**	**7042**
N934DL	**MD-88**	**49721**
N934F	DC-9	47148
N934FT	B727	19430
(N934FT)	B727	18429
N934L	**DC-9**	**47618**
N934MC	MD-82	49122
N934ML	**DC-9**	**47526**
N934PS	MD-81	48042
N934UA	**B737**	**26662**
N934UP	**B727**	**19135**
N934VJ	**DC-9**	**48114**
N934VV	**DC-9**	**47488**
N935AS	**MD-83**	**49236**
N935AX	**DC-9**	**47413**
N935DL	**MD-88**	**49722**
N935F	**DC-9**	**47220**
N935F	DC-9	47407
N935FT	B727	19180
N935L	**DC-9**	**47603**
N935MC	MD-82	49125
N935ML	**DC-9**	**47549**
N935PS	MD-81	48043
N935UA	**B737**	**26663**
N935UP	**B727**	**20143**
N935VJ	**DC-9**	**48115**
N935VV	**DC-9**	**47534**
N936AS	**MD-83**	**49363**
N936AX	**DC-9**	**47269**
N936CA	**RJ100**	**7043**
N936DL	**MD-88**	**49723**
N936F	DC-9	47408
N936FT	B727	19836
N936L	**DC-9**	**47711**
N936MC	MD-82	49444
N936ML	**DC-9**	**47501**
N936PS	MD-81	48092
N936UA	**B737**	**26667**
N936UP	**B727**	**19503**
N936VJ	**DC-9**	**48116**
N936VV	**DC-9**	**47397**
N937AS	**MD-82**	**49364**
N937AX	**DC-9**	**47074**
N937CA	**RJ100**	**7044**
N937DL	**MD-88**	**49810**
N937F	**DC-9**	**47409**
N937FT	B727	18847
N937MC	**MD-82**	**49450**
N937ML	**DC-9**	**47005**
N937PS	MD-81	48093
N937UA	**B737**	**26668**
N937UP	**B727**	**19302**
N937VJ	**DC-9**	**48117**
N937VV	**DC-9**	**45774**
N938AS	**MD-83**	**49365**
N938AX	**DC-9**	**47009**
N938CA	**RJ100**	**7046**
N938DL	**MD-88**	**49811**
N938F	DC-9	47221
(N938FT)	B727	19131
N938MC	**MD-83**	**49525**
(N938MC)	MD-82	49375
N938ML	DC-9	47007
N938PR	DC-9	47098
N938PS	MD-81	48094
N938UA	**B737**	**26671**
N938UP	**B727**	**19506**
N938VJ	**DC-9**	**48119**
N938VV	**DC-9**	**47442**
N939AS	**MD-83**	**49657**
N939AX	**DC-9**	**47201**
N939DL	**MD-88**	**49812**
N939F	DC-9	47413
N939FT	B727	19388
N939MC	MD-83	49526
(N939MC)	MD-82	49376
N939ML	DC-9	45710
N939PR	DC-9	47120
N939PS	MD-82	48099
N939UA	**B737**	**26672**
N939UP	**B727**	**19532**
N939VJ	**DC-9**	**48120**
N939VV	**DC-9**	**47089**
N940AS	**MD-83**	**49825**
N940CA	**RJ100**	**7048**
N940DL	**MD-88**	**49813**
N940F	**DC-9**	**47414**
(N940FT)	B727	19389
N940JW	DC-8	46155
(N940MC)	MD-82	49377
(N940MC)	MD-83	49662
N940ML	DC-9	47102
N940N	**DC-9**	**47572**
N940PS	MD-82	48095
N940UA	**B737**	**26675**
N940UP	**B727**	**19826**
N940VJ	**DC-9**	**47053**
N940VV	**DC-9**	**47523**
N941AS	**MD-83**	**49925**
N941AX	**DC-9**	**47419**
N941CA	**RJ100**	**7050**
N941DL	**MD-88**	**49814**
N941F	DC-9	47193
N941FT	B727	19428
N941JW	DC-8	45988
N941LF	**A320**	**0461**
(N941MC)	MD-82	49378
(N941MC)	MD-83	49663
N941ML	**DC-9**	**47131**
N941N	**DC-9**	**47450**
N941PS	MD-82	48096
N941UA	**B737**	**26676**
N941UP	**B727**	**19196**
N941VJ	**DC-9**	**47054**
N941VV	**DC-9**	**47666**
N942AS	**MD-83**	**53052**
N942AX	**DC-9**	**47552**
N942DL	**MD-88**	**49815**
N942FT	B727	19431
N942ML	DC-9	47190
N942ML	**DC-9**	**47478**
N942N	**DC-9**	**47459**
N942PS	MD-82	48097
N942UA	**B737**	**26679**
N942UP	**B727**	**19101**
N942VJ	**DC-9**	**47057**
N942VV	**DC-9**	**47648**
N943AS	**MD-83**	**53018**
N943AX	**DC-9**	**47528**
N943CA	**RJ100**	**7062**
N943DL	**MD-88**	**49816**
N943ML	DC-9	47133
N943N	**DC-9**	**47647**
N943PS	MD-82	48098
N943U	DC-9	48132
N943UA	**B737**	**26680**
N943UP	B727	19102
N943VJ	**DC-9**	**47058**
N944AS	**MD-83**	**53019**
N944AX	**DC-9**	**47550**
N944DL	**MD-88**	**49817**
N944F	**DC-9**	**47194**
(N944FT)	B727	18435
N944JW	**B707**	**18336**
N944ML	DC-9	47132
N944PS	MD-82	49119
N944U	DC-9	48133
N944UA	**B737**	**26683**
N944UP	B727	19103
N945AS	**MD-83**	**49643**
N945AX	**DC-9**	**47551**
N945CA	**RJ100**	**7069**
N945DL	**MD-88**	**49818**
N945F	**DC-9**	**47279**
N945L	DC-9	45728
N945ML	**DC-9**	**47168**
N945N	**DC-9**	**47664**
N945PS	MD-82	49138
N945UA	**B737**	**26684**
N945UP	B727	19094
N945VJ	**DC-9**	**47066**
N945VV	**DC-9**	**47238**
N945WP	**B737**	**24212**
N946AS	**MD-83**	**49658**
N946AX	**DC-9**	**47003**
N946CA	**RJ100**	**7072**
N946DL	**MD-88**	**49819**
N946L	DC-9	45729
N946ML	DC-9	47170
N946PS	MD-82	49139
N946UA	**B737**	**26687**
N946UP	**B727**	**19721**
N946VJ	**DC-9**	**47026**
N946VV	**DC-9**	**47226**
N946WP	**B737**	**23173**
N947AS	**MD-83**	**53020**
N947AX	**DC-9**	**47004**
N947CA	**RJ100**	**7077**
N947DL	**MD-88**	**49878**
N947L	DC-9	45730
N947ML	**DC-9**	**47514**
N947PS	MD-82	49142
(N947PS)	MD-82	49140
N947UA	**B737**	**26688**
N947UP	**B727**	**19722**
N947WP	**B737**	**23376**
N948AS	**MD-83**	**53021**
N948AX	**DC-9**	**47065**
N948CA	**RJ100**	**7079**
N948DL	**MD-88**	**49879**
N948L	**DC-9**	**47049**
N948ML	**DC-9**	**47169**
N948PS	MD-82	49143
(N948PS)	MD-82	49141
N948UA	**B737**	**26691**
N948UP	**B727**	**19357**
N948WP	**B737**	**23259**
N949AS	**MD-83**	**53022**
N949AX	**DC-9**	**47325**
N949CA	**RJ100**	**7080**
N949DL	**MD-88**	**49880**
N949L	**DC-9**	**45844**
N949N	**DC-9**	**47566**
N949PS	MD-82	49237
N949UA	**B737**	**26692**
N949UP	**B727**	**19717**
N949WP	**B737**	**23230**
N950AS	**MD-83**	**53023**
N950CC	1-11	086
N950DL	**MD-88**	**49881**
N950JW	DC-8	46058
(N950L)	DC-9	47246
N950PB	DC-9	47394
N950PS	MD-81	48028
N950R	**DC-8**	**45903**
N950U	**MD-82**	**49230**
N950UA	**B737**	**26695**
N950UP	**B727**	**19718**
N950VJ	**DC-9**	**47564**
N950WP	B737	23229
N951AS	**MD-82**	**49111**
N951AX	**DC-9**	**47616**
N951CA	**RJ100**	**7091**
N951DL	**MD-88**	**49882**
N951LF	**A320**	**0460**
N951N	DC-9	47067
N951PS	MD-82	49429
N951R	**DC-8**	**46092**
N951U	**MD-82**	**49245**
N951UA	**B737**	**26696**
N951UP	**B727**	**19850**
N951VJ	**DC-9**	**47576**
N951WP	**B737**	**22951**
N952AX	**DC-9**	**47615**
N952CA	**RJ100**	**7092**
N952DL	**MD-88**	**49883**
N952N	**DC-9**	**47073**
N952PS	MD-82	49443
N952R	DC-8	46061
N952U	**MD-82**	**49266**
N952UA	**B737**	**26699**
N952VJ	**DC-9**	**47574**
N952WP	**B737**	**23378**
N953AS	**MD-82**	**49386**
N953AX	**DC-9**	**47608**
N953DL	**MD-88**	**49884**
N953N	**DC-9**	**47083**
N953U	**MD-82**	**49267**
N953UA	**B737**	**26700**
N953VJ	**DC-9**	**47583**
N953WP	**B737**	**23384**
N954AS	**MD-82**	**49387**
N954AX	**DC-9**	**47612**
N954CA	**RJ100**	**7100**
N954DL	**MD-88**	**49885**
N954N	DC-9	47159
N954R	DC-8	45908
N954U	**MD-82**	**49426**
N954UA	**B737**	**26739**
N954UP	**B727**	**19827**
N954VJ	DC-9	47590
N955AS	**MD-82**	**48080**
N955AX	**DC-9**	**47619**
N955DL	**MD-88**	**49886**
N955N	**DC-9**	**47160**
N955U	**MD-82**	**49427**
N955UA	**B737**	**26703**
N955VJ	**DC-9**	**47593**
N956AS	**MD-82**	**48079**
N956AX	**DC-9**	**47620**
N956CA	**RJ100**	**7105**
N956DL	**MD-88**	**49887**
N956N	**DC-9**	**47252**
N956U	**MD-82**	**49701**
N956UA	**B737**	**26704**
N956VJ	**DC-9**	**47588**
N957AS	**MD-82**	**49126**
N957AX	**DC-9**	**47759**
N957DL	**MD-88**	**49976**
N957HA	DC-9	47784
N957N	**DC-9**	**47253**
N957R	**DC-8**	**46137**
N957U	**MD-82**	**49702**
N957UA	**B737**	**26707**
N958AS	**MD-83**	**53024**
N958DL	**MD-88**	**49977**
N958N	**DC-9**	**47254**
N958U	**MD-82**	**49703**
(N958UA)	B737	26708
N958VJ	**DC-9**	**47351**
N959DL	**MD-88**	**49978**
N959HA	DC-9	47658
N959N	**DC-9**	**47255**
N959R	**DC-8**	**46143**
N959U	**MD-82**	**49704**
(N959UA)	B737	26711
N959VJ	**DC-9**	**47352**
N960AS	**MD-83**	**53074**
N960CC	**B707**	**17634**
N960DL	**MD-88**	**49979**
N960N	**DC-9**	**47256**
(N960UA)	B737	26712

Registration	Type	c/n
N960VJ	**DC-9**	**47505**
N960VV	**DC-9**	**47067**
N960WP	**B737**	**23331**
N961AS	**MD-83**	**53075**
N961DL	**MD-88**	**49980**
N961GF	**DC-10**	**46961**
N961LF	**A320**	**0453**
N961N	**DC-9**	**47405**
N961R	**DC-8**	**46133**
(N961UA)	B737	26714
N961VJ	DC-9	47506
N961WP	**B737**	**23332**
N962AS	**MD-83**	**53076**
N962DL	**MD-88**	**49981**
N962GF	**DC-10**	**46640**
N962ML	DC-9	45871
N962N	**DC-9**	**47406**
N962VJ	**DC-9**	**47507**
N962WP	**B737**	**23748**
N963AS	**MD-83**	**53077**
N963DL	**MD-88**	**49982**
(N963HA)	DC-9	47735
N963ML	DC-9	45872
N963N	**DC-9**	**47415**
N963VJ	**DC-9**	**47508**
N964AS	**MD-83**	**53078**
N964DL	**MD-88**	**49983**
N964HA	DC-9	47726
N964ML	**DC-9**	**45873**
N964N	**DC-9**	**47416**
N964R	**DC-8**	**46000**
N964VJ	DC-9	47373
N964VV	**DC-9**	**47555**
N965AS	**MD-83**	**53079**
N965AX	**DC-9**	**47498**
N965DL	**MD-88**	**49984**
N965HA	DC-9	47661
N965ML	DC-9	45874
N965N	**DC-9**	**47417**
N965VJ	**DC-9**	**47374**
N966AS	**MD-82**	**49104**
N966AX	**DC-9**	**47510**
N966C	A300	117
N966DL	**MD-88**	**53115**
N966HA	DC-9	47654
N966ML	DC-9	47217
N966VJ	**DC-9**	**47420**
N966VV	DC-9	47168
N967AS	**MD-82**	**49103**
N967AX	**DC-9**	**47509**
N967C	A300	121
N967DL	**MD-88**	**53116**
N967ML	DC-9	45875
N967N	**DC-9**	**47573**
N967PR	DC-9	47121
N967VJ	**DC-9**	**47375**
N967VV	**DC-9**	**47170**
N968AS	**MD-83**	**53016**
N968AX	**DC-9**	**47499**
N968C	A300	126
N968DL	**MD-88**	**53161**
N968E	DC-9	45786
N968ML	**DC-9**	**45876**
N968VJ	**DC-9**	**47429**
N969AS	**MD-83**	**53063**
N969AX	**DC-9**	**47464**
N969DL	**MD-88**	**53172**
N969HA	DC-9	47763
N969ML	**DC-9**	**47268**
N969VJ	**DC-9**	**47421**
N969Z	**DC-9**	**47001**
N970AX	**DC-9**	**47494**
N970C	A300	250
N970DL	**MD-88**	**53173**
(N970HA)	DC-9	47764
N970ML	DC-9	47269
N970NE	DC-9	47053
N970PS	B727	18908
N970VJ	**DC-9**	**47050**
N970Z	**DC-9**	**45772**
N971AX	**DC-9**	**47497**
N971C	A300	262
N971DL	**MD-88**	**53214**
N971ML	**DC-9**	**47270**
N971NE	DC-9	47054
N971PS	B727	18909
N971VJ	**DC-9**	**47051**
N971Z	**DC-9**	**45773**
N972AS	**MD-88**	**53448**
N972C	**A300**	**289**
N972DL	**MD-88**	**53215**
N972ML	DC-9	47036
N972NE	DC-9	47057
N972PS	**B727**	**18910**
N972VJ	**DC-9**	**47052**
N972Z	DC-9	45841
N973AS	**MD-88**	**53449**
N973AX	**DC-9**	**47511**
N973DL	**MD-88**	**53241**
N973ML	DC-9	47074
N973NE	DC-9	47058
N973PS	B727	18797
N973PS	B727	18911
N973VJ	**DC-9**	**47099**
N973Z	**DC-9**	**47033**
N974AS	**MD-88**	**53450**
N974AX	**DC-9**	**47512**
N974C	A300	126
N974DL	**MD-88**	**53242**
N974ML	**DC-9**	**47119**
N974NE	DC-9	47066
N974PS	B727	18798
N974PS	B727	18912
N974UA	**B737**	**21597**
N974VJ	**DC-9**	**47130**
N974Z	DC-9	47034
N975AS	**MD-88**	**53451**
N975DL	**MD-88**	**53243**
N975ML	DC-9	47271
N975NE	DC-9	47075
N975PS	B727	18990
N975UA	**B737**	**21598**
N975VJ	**DC-9**	**47146**
N975Z	**DC-9**	**47035**
N976AS	**MD-88**	**53452**
N976DL	**MD-88**	**53257**
N976ML	DC-9	47272
N976NE	DC-9	47082
N976PS	B727	18799
N976PS	B727	19398
N976VJ	**DC-9**	**48147**
N976Z	**DC-9**	**47248**
N977AS	**MD-88**	**53453**
N977AX	**DC-9**	**47513**
N977DL	**MD-88**	**53258**
N977ML	**DC-9**	**47329**
N977MP	B737	21518
N977NE	DC-9	47095
N977PS	B727	18800
N977PS	B727	19815
N977UA	**B737**	**21508**
N977VJ	**DC-9**	**48155**
N977Z	**DC-9**	**47249**
N978AL	B727	21978
N978DL	**MD-88**	**53259**
N978NE	DC-9	47096
N978PS	B727	18801
N978UA	**B737**	**21509**
N978VJ	**DC-9**	**47371**
N978Z	**DC-9**	**47250**
N979AL	**B727**	**21979**
N979AX	**DC-9**	**47492**
N979DL	**MD-88**	**53266**
N979NE	DC-9	47097
N979UA	**B737**	**21544**
N979VJ	**DC-9**	**47372**
N979Z	**DC-9**	**47343**
N980AL	**B727**	**22759**
N980AX	**DC-9**	**47176**
(N980C)	A300	86
N980DC	MD-81	48000
N980DL	**MD-88**	**53267**
N980NE	DC-9	47134
N980UA	**B737**	**21545**
N980VJ	**DC-9**	**48156**
N980Z	**DC-9**	**47344**
N981AX	**DC-9**	**47273**
(N981C)	A300	87
N981DL	**MD-88**	**53268**
N981LR	**A320**	**0558**
N981NE	DC-9	47135
N981PS	DC-9	47006
N981UA	**B737**	**21546**
N981VJ	**DC-9**	**48157**
N981Z	**DC-9**	**47345**
N982AX	**DC-9**	**47317**
(N982C)	A300	91
N982DL	**MD-88**	**53273**
N982NE	DC-9	47136
N982PS	**DC-9**	**47251**
N982UA	**B737**	**21640**
N982US	**DC-9**	**45790**
N982VJ	**DC-9**	**48158**
(N982Z)	DC-9	47561
N983AX	**DC-9**	**47257**
(N983C)	A300	92
N983DL	**MD-88**	**53274**
N983NE	DC-9	47137
N983PS	B737	20156
N983UA	**B737**	**21641**
N983US	**DC-9**	**47282**
N983VJ	**DC-9**	**48159**
N983Z	**DC-9**	**47411**
N984AN	**B767**	**24357**
N984AX	**DC-9**	**47258**
(N984C)	A300	108
N984DL	**MD-88**	**53311**
N984PS	B737	20157
N984UA	**B737**	**21642**
N984US	**DC-9**	**47383**
N984VJ	**DC-9**	**47207**
N984Z	**DC-9**	**47412**
N985AN	**B767**	**24618**
N985AX	**DC-9**	**47522**
(N985C)	A300	119
N985DL	**MD-88**	**53312**
N985PS	B737	20158
N985UA	**B737**	**21747**
N985US	**DC-9**	**47479**
N985VJ	**DC-9**	**47208**
N985Z	**DC-9**	**47491**
N986AN	**B767**	**24835**
N986AX	**DC-9**	**47543**
(N986C)	A300	154
N986DL	**MD-88**	**53313**
N986PS	B737	20159
N986UA	**B737**	**21748**
N986US	**DC-9**	**47480**
N986VJ	**DC-9**	**47209**
N986Z	**DC-9**	**47589**
N987AA	B707	18825
N987AN	**B757**	**25494**
N987AS	CV990	30-10-13
N987AX	**DC-9**	**47364**
(N987C)	A300	155
N987DL	**MD-88**	**53338**
N987PS	B737	20160
N987UA	**B737**	**21749**
N987US	**DC-9**	**47458**
N987VJ	**DC-9**	**47210**
N987Z	**DC-9**	**47137**
N988AX	**DC-9**	**47084**
(N988C)	A300	216
N988DL	**MD-88**	**53339**
N988PS	B737	20368
N988UA	**B737**	**21750**
N988US	DC-9	47480
N988VJ	DC-9	47211
N988Z	**DC-9**	**47134**
N989AN	B757	24293
N989AX	**DC-9**	**47314**
(N989C)	A300	220
N989DL	**MD-88**	**53341**
N989PS	B737	20369
N989UA	**B737**	**21751**
N989VJ	**DC-9**	**47212**
N989Z	**DC-9**	**47135**
N990AB	**CV990**	**30-10-2**
N990AC	**CV990**	**30-10-5**
N990AX	**DC-9**	**47493**
(N990C)	A300	259
N990CF	**DC-8**	**46068**
N990DL	**MD-88**	**53342**
N990E	CV990	30-10-16
N990UA	**B737**	**21980**
N990Z	**DC-9**	**47136**
N991CF	**DC-8**	**45801**
N991DL	**MD-88**	**53343**
N991EA	DC-9	47728
N991LR	**A320**	**0561**
N991UA	**B737**	**21981**
N991VJ	**DC-9**	**47310**
N991Z	**DC-9**	**47096**
N992AJ	**B727**	**19428**
N992CF	**DC-8**	**45884**
N992DL	**MD-88**	**53344**
N992EA	DC-9	47731
N992UA	**B737**	**22089**
N992Z	**DC-9**	**47095**
N993CF	**DC-8**	**46028**
N993DL	**MD-88**	**53345**
N993EA	DC-9	47732
N993UA	**B737**	**22383**
N993VJ	**DC-9**	**47332**
N993Z	**DC-9**	**47082**
N994AJ	**B727**	**20942**
N994CF	**DC-8**	**45956**
N994DL	**MD-88**	**53346**
N994EA	DC-9	47733
N994UA	**B737**	**22384**
N994VJ	DC-9	47333
N994Z	**DC-9**	**47097**
N995CF	**DC-8**	**46024**
N995DL	**MD-88**	**53362**
N995EA	DC-9	47745
N995UA	**B737**	**22399**
N995VJ	**DC-9**	**47334**
N995WL	DC-8	45603
N995Z	**DC-9**	**47027**
N996CF	**DC-8**	**46162**
N996DL	**MD-88**	**53363**
N996EA	DC-9	47746
N996UA	**B737**	**22456**
N996VJ	**DC-9**	**47335**
N996Z	**DC-9**	**47028**
N997CF	**DC-8**	**46154**
N997DL	**MD-88**	**53364**
N997EA	DC-9	47749
N997UA	**B737**	**22457**
N997VJ	**DC-9**	**47336**
N997Z	**DC-9**	**47029**
N998CF	**DC-8**	**46139**
N998DL	**MD-88**	**53370**
N998EA	DC-9	47751
N998R	**DC-9**	**47030**
N998UA	**B737**	**22741**
N999CZ	**B737**	**25604**
N999DN	**MD-88**	**53371**
N999EA	DC-9	47753
N999UA	B737	22742
N999WA	**COMET**	**6425**
N1001U	**CRVL**	**86**
N1002D	DC-10	46970
N1002G	MD-81	48001
N1002N	DC-9	47782
N1002U	CRVL	87
N1002W	MD-81	48015
N1002X	DC-10	46583
N1002Y	DC-10	46584
N1003G	MD-81	48050
N1003L	**DC-10**	**48258**
N1003N	**DC-10**	**48276**
N1003P	**DC-9**	**48150**
N1003U	CRVL	88
N1003U	**DC-9**	**48151**
N1003W	DC-10	48289
N1003X	**MD-82**	**48067**
N1003Y	**MD-82**	**48068**
N1003Z	MD-82	48069
N1004A	**DC-10**	**48294**
N1004B	DC-10	48295
N1004D	MD-82	48089
N1004F	MD-82	48090
N1004G	MD-82	48091
N1004L	MD-82	49110
N1004N	MD-82	49111
N1004S	MD-82	48088
N1004S	MD-82	49140
N1004U	CRVL	89
N1004U	MD-82	49102
N1004W	MD-82	48022
N1004Y	MD-82	49373
N1005A	MD-82	49103
N1005B	MD-82	49104

N1005G	MD-82	49142
N1005J	MD-82	49143
N1005N	MD-82	49374
N1005S	MD-82	49355
N1005T	MD-82	49425
N1005U	CRVL	90
N1005U	MD-82	49428
N1005V	MD-82	49149
N1005W	MD-83	49662
N1006U	CRVL	91
N1007U	CRVL	92
N1008U	CRVL	93
N1009U	CRVL	94
N1010U	CRVL	95
N1011	L1011	1001
N1011U	CRVL	96
N1012U	CRVL	97
N1013U	CRVL	98
N1014U	CRVL	99
N1015U	CRVL	100
N1016U	CRVL	101
N1017U	CRVL	102
N1018U	CRVL	103
N1019U	CRVL	104
N1020U	CRVL	114
N1031F	DC-10	46825
N1032F	DC-10	46826
N1033F	DC-10	46960
(N1033F)	DC-10	46827
N1034F	DC-10	46962
N1035F	DC-10	46992
N1041W	DC-8	45669
N1051T	DC-9	45714
N1052T	DC-9	45715
N1053T	DC-9	45716
N1054T	DC-9	45735
N1055T	DC-9	45736
N1056T	DC-9	45737
N1057T	DC-9	45738
N1058T	DC-9	45739
N1059T	DC-9	45740
N1060T	DC-9	45741
N1061T	DC-9	45775
N1062T	DC-9	45776
N1063T	DC-9	45777
N1064T	**DC-9**	**45778**
N1065T	DC-9	45779
N1066T	DC-9	45780
N1067T	DC-9	45781
N1068T	**DC-9**	**45782**
N1069T	DC-9	45783
N1070T	**DC-9**	**45784**
N1074T	**MD-87**	**49727**
N1075T	**MD-87**	**49724**
N1112J	1-11	030
N1113J	1-11	031
N1114J	1-11	032
N1115J	1-11	082
N1116J	1-11	BAC.098
N1117J	**1-11**	**BAC.099**
N1118J	1-11	BAC.100
N1119J	1-11	BAC.101
N1120J	1-11	BAC.102
N1122J	1-11	BAC.103
N1123J	1-11	BAC.104
N1124J	1-11	BAC.134
N1125J	1-11	BAC.135
N1126J	1-11	BAC.179
N1127J	1-11	BAC.180
N1128J	1-11	BAC.181
N1129J	1-11	BAC.182
N1130J	1-11	BAC.096
N1131J	**1-11**	**BAC.097**
N1132J	1-11	BAC.105
N1134J	**1-11**	**045**
N1135J	**1-11**	**046**
N1136J	**1-11**	**071**
N1181L	L1011	1033
N1181Z	**B707**	**19693**
N1186Z	**B727**	**19134**
N1187Z	B727	18323
N1236E	B727	21270
N1238E	B737	21296
N1239E	B727	22078
N1239E	B747	21251
N1243E	B737	21283
N1246E	B727	21297
N1248E	B747	21468
N1252E	B747	21537
N1261L	DC-9	47317
N1262E	B737	21716
N1262L	DC-9	47257
N1263L	DC-9	47258
N1264L	DC-9	47259
N1265L	DC-9	47260
N1266L	DC-9	47261
N1267L	DC-9	47262
N1268L	DC-9	47284
N1269E	B737	21723
N1269E	B737	21763
N1269L	DC-9	47285
N1270L	DC-9	47318
N1271L	**DC-9**	**47319**
N1272L	DC-9	47320
N1273E	B727	21930
N1273L	DC-9	47321
N1274E	B737	21599
N1274L	DC-9	47322
N1275E	B737	21790
N1275L	DC-9	47323
N1276L	DC-9	47324
N1277L	DC-9	47356
N1278L	DC-9	47357
N1279E	**B727**	**21971**
N1279L	DC-9	47358
N1280E	B727	21972
N1280L	DC-9	47359
N1281L	DC-9	47377
N1282L	DC-9	47378
N1283L	DC-9	47379
N1284L	DC-9	47380
N1285E	B737	21790
N1285L	DC-9	47381
N1286L	DC-9	47426
N1287L	DC-9	47427
N1288	B737	20195
N1288E	B747	21668
(N1288E)	B747	21832
N1288L	DC-9	47443
N1289E	B747	22272
(N1289E)	B727	21971
(N1289E)	B747	21833
N1289L	DC-9	47444
N1290E	B747	22107
(N1290E)	B727	21972
(N1290E)	B747	21834
N1290L	DC-9	47445
N1291L	DC-9	47466
N1292L	DC-9	47529
N1293L	DC-9	47486
N1294L	DC-9	47516
N1295E	B747	22376
N1295L	**DC-9**	**47525**
N1298E	B747	22379
N1300L	DC-8	46014
N1301E	B747	22302
(N1301E)	B747	22380
N1301L	DC-8	46018
N1301L	L1011	1002
N1301T	DC-9	45695
N1302L	DC-8	46029
N1302T	DC-9	47043
N1303L	DC-8	46030
N1303T	DC-9	47044
N1304E	B747	21934
N1304L	DC-8	46048
N1304T	DC-9	47045
N1305E	B747	22428
N1305L	DC-8	46072
N1305T	DC-9	47055
N1306L	DC-8	46055
N1306T	DC-9	47061
N1307L	DC-8	46056
N1307T	DC-9	47062
N1308T	**DC-9**	**47315**
N1309E	B747	22380
N1309T	**DC-9**	**47316**
N1310T	DC-9	47487
N1311T	DC-9	47490
N1330U	DC-9	47411
N1331U	DC-9	47412
N1332U	**DC-9**	**47404**
N1334U	**DC-9**	**47280**
N1335U	DC-9	47393
N1336U	DC-9	47522
N1337U	DC-10	46704
N1338U	DC-10	46705
N1339U	DC-10	46550
N1340U	DC-10	46575
N1341U	DC-10	46850
N1342U	DC-10	46551
N1343U	DC-9	47570
N1345U	DC-9	47562
N1346U	DC-9	47563
N1346U	F-28	11173
N1347U	DC-9	47567
N1348U	DC-10	46727
N1349U	DC-10	46554
N1350U	DC-10	46851
N1352B	B747	20235
N1355B	B727	19527
N1355B	B727	20465
N1359B	B737	19758
N1400H	**F-100**	**11340**
N1401G	**F-100**	**11352**
N1402A	**B767**	**25989**
N1402K	**F-100**	**11353**
N1403M	**F-100**	**11354**
N1404D	**F-100**	**11355**
N1405J	**F-100**	**11356**
N1406A	**F-100**	**11359**
N1407D	**F-100**	**11360**
N1408B	**F-100**	**11361**
N1409B	**F-100**	**11367**
N1410E	**F-100**	**11368**
N1411G	**F-100**	**11369**
N1412A	**F-100**	**11370**
N1413A	**F-100**	**11376**
N1414D	**F-100**	**11377**
N1415K	**F-100**	**11385**
N1416A	**F-100**	**11395**
N1417D	**F-100**	**11396**
N1418A	**F-100**	**11397**
N1419D	**F-100**	**11402**
N1420D	**F-100**	**11403**
N1421K	**F-100**	**11404**
N1422J	**F-100**	**11405**
N1423A	**F-100**	**11406**
N1424M	**F-100**	**11407**
N1425A	**F-100**	**11408**
N1426A	**F-100**	**11411**
N1427A	**F-100**	**11412**
N1428D	**F-100**	**11413**
N1429G	**F-100**	**11414**
N1430D	**F-100**	**11415**
N1431B	**F-100**	**11416**
N1432A	**F-100**	**11417**
N1433B	**F-100**	**11418**
N1434A	**F-100**	**11419**
N1435D	**F-100**	**11425**
N1436A	**F-100**	**11426**
N1437B	**F-100**	**11427**
N1438H	**F-100**	**11428**
N1439A	**F-100**	**11434**
N1440A	**F-100**	**11435**
N1441A	**F-100**	**11436**
N1442E	**F-100**	**11437**
N1443A	**F-100**	**11446**
N1444N	**F-100**	**11447**
N1444Z	B737	20227
N1445B	**F-100**	**11448**
N1446A	**F-100**	**11449**
N1447L	**F-100**	**11456**
N1448A	**F-100**	**11457**
N1449D	**F-100**	**11458**
N1450A	**F-100**	**11459**
N1450Z	B737	20277
N1451N	**F-100**	**11460**
N1451Z	B737	20226
N1452B	**F-100**	**11464**
N1453D	**F-100**	**11465**
N1454D	**F-100**	**11466**
N1455K	**F-100**	**11467**
N1456D	**F-100**	**11468**
N1456K	**F-100**	**11491**
N1457B	**F-100**	**11469**
N1458H	**F-100**	**11478**
N1459A	**F-100**	**11479**
N1460A	**F-100**	**11480**
N1461C	**F-100**	**11481**
N1462C	**F-100**	**11482**
N1463A	**F-100**	**11483**
N1464A	**F-100**	**11490**
N1466A	**F-100**	**11498**
N1467A	**F-100**	**11499**
N1468A	**F-100**	**11501**
N1469D	**F-100**	**11502**
N1470K	**F-100**	**11506**
N1471K	**F-100**	**11507**
N1472B	**F-100**	**11514**
N1473K	**F-100**	**11515**
N1474D	**F-100**	**11520**
N1486B	B707	19809
N1501U	DC-8	45822
N1501W	B707	19963
N1502U	DC-8	45823
N1502W	B707	19964
N1503U	DC-8	45903
N1503W	B707	19965
N1504U	DC-8	45901
N1504W	B707	19966
N1505U	DC-8	45909
N1505W	B707	19967
N1506W	B707	20315
N1507W	B707	20316
N1508W	B707	20317
N1509U	DC-8	45858
N1509W	B707	20318
N1510W	B707	20319
N1541	1-11	015
N1542	1-11	016
N1543	**1-11**	**017**
N1544	**1-11**	**018**
N1545	**1-11**	**019**
N1546	1-11	020
N1547	1-11	041
N1548	**1-11**	**042**
N1549	1-11	043
N1550	1-11	044
N1551	1-11	045
N1552	1-11	046
N1553	1-11	070
N1554	1-11	071
N1607B	B747	22234
N1608B	B747	22302
N1631	B727	18850
N1632	B727	18858
N1633	B727	19249
N1634	B727	19250
N1635	B727	19251
N1636	B727	19252
N1637	B727	19595
N1638	B727	19596
N1639	B727	19444
N1640	B727	19445
(N1640A)	B737	19679
N1641	B727	19446
N1642	B727	19447
N1643	B727	19448
N1644	B727	19449
N1645	B727	20139
N1646	B727	20140
N1647	B727	20141
N1648	B727	19994
N1649	B727	19995
N1650	B727	20248
N1673B	B707	19810
N1709B	B707	20830
N1716B	B737	23766
N1727T	B727	19859
N1728T	B727	19860
N1731D	**L1011**	**1200**
N1732D	**L1011**	**1213**
N1733B	B737	20300
N1734D	**L1011**	**1225**
N1738D	**L1011**	**1234**
N1739D	**L1011**	**1237**
N1748B	B727	19994
N1750B	**MD-11**	**48419**
N1751A	**MD-11**	**48420**
N1752K	**MD-11**	**48421**
N1753	**MD-11**	**48487**
N1754	**MD-11**	**48489**
N1755	**MD-11**	**48490**

N1756 MD-11 48491
N1757A MD-11 48505
N1758B MD-11 48527
N1759 MD-11 48481
(N1759) MD-11 48528
N1760A MD-11 48550
N1761R MD-11 48551
N1762B MD-11 48552
N1763 MD-11 48553
N1764B MD-11 48554
N1765B MD-11 48596
N1766A MD-11 48597
N1767A MD-11 48598
N1768D MD-11 48436
(N1768D) MD-11 48599
(N1769B) MD-11 48611
N1776Q B720 18041
N1776R DC-8 45602
N1779B B727 20525
N1779B B727 20552
N1779B B727 20764
N1779B B727 22664
N1779B B737 22777
N1779B B737 22793
N1779B B737 24463
N1780B B727 20217
N1780B B727 20286
N1780B B727 20432
N1780B B727 20608
N1780B B727 22263
N1780B B727 22665
N1780B B737 19679
N1780B B737 22638
N1780B B747 21515
N1780B B747 21652
N1781B B727 19524
N1781B B727 19525
N1781B B727 19526
N1781B B727 19527
N1781B B727 20243
N1781B B727 20421
N1781B B727 20426
N1781B B727 20463
N1781B B727 20464
N1781B B727 20465
N1781B B727 20468
N1781B B727 20469
N1781B B727 20540
N1781B B737 19680
N1781B B747 23071
N1781B B747 23150
N1781B B767 22682
N1781B B767 23018
N1782B B727 20244
N1782B B727 22605
N1782B B737 20779
N1782B B737 22114
N1782B B737 22776
N1782B B737 24790
N1782B B747 21681
N1782B B747 22502
N1782B B747 22614
N1783B B727 20245
N1783B B747 21255
N1783B B747 22479
N1783B B767 22527
N1784B B727 18464
N1784B B737 25603
N1784B B737 25604
N1784B B737 26071
N1784B B747 22705
N1784B B747 23070
N1784B B747 23222
N1784B B767 22523
N1784B B767 22785
N1784B B767 22788
N1784B B767 23020
N1785B B707 20741
N1785B B707 20761
N1785B B727 19995
N1785B B727 20430
N1785B B727 20753
N1785B B737 20396
N1785B B737 23443
N1785B B747 21516
N1785B B747 22547
N1785B B747 22616
N1785B B747 22668
N1785B B747 25866
N1785B B747 27163
N1785B B767 22981
N1785B B767 23021
N1785B B767 23178
N1785B B767 27392
N1786B B707 20043
N1786B B727 20596
N1786B B727 22076
N1786B B727 22158
N1786B B737 20397
N1786B B737 20917
N1786B B737 21805
N1786B B737 22416
N1786B B737 22505
N1786B B737 22779
N1786B B737 23522
N1786B B737 23809
N1786B B737 24219
N1786B B737 24220
N1786B B737 24221
N1786B B737 24912
N1786B B737 24946
N1786B B737 25150
N1786B B737 25401
N1786B B737 27700
N1786B B747 21220
N1786B B747 23151
N1786B B757 25133
N1786B B757 25495
N1786B B757 26160
N1786E B737 25069
N1787B B727 20553
N1787B B727 20595
N1787B B727 20790
N1787B B727 21264
N1787B B737 20299
N1787B B737 20412
N1787B B737 21278
N1787B B737 21279
N1787B B737 21774
N1787B B737 23000
N1787B B737 26069
N1788B B727 20540
N1788B B727 20568
N1788B B727 20595
N1788B B727 20596
N1788B B727 20597
N1788B B727 20598
N1788B B727 20599
N1788B B727 20603
N1788B B727 20606
N1788B B727 20607
N1788B B737 20300
N1788B B737 20496
N1788B B737 20561
N1788B B737 20786
N1788B B747 23814
N1788B B747 23824
N1788B B767 23016
N1788B B767 23179
N1788B B767 24338
N1788B B767 26984
N1789B B727 20600
N1789B B737 23449
N1789B B737 23636
N1789B B737 24970
N1789B B737 25115
N1789B B747 21725
N1789B B757 25495
N1789B B767 23017
N1789B B767 23180
N1789B B767 24350
N1790 B737 20453
N1790B B727 20539
N1790B B727 20572
N1790B B727 20601
N1790B B737 20453
N1790B B737 23444
N1790B B737 23450
N1790B B737 24123
N1790B B737 25508
N1790B B737 26539
N1790B B737 27333
N1790B B747 21238
N1790B B757 26436
N1790U DC-9 45785
N1791 B737 20454
N1791B B727 20592
N1791B B737 20454
N1791B B737 23397
N1791B B737 23445
N1791B B737 23870
N1791B B747 21189
N1791B B747 22672
N1791B B757 24567
N1791B B767 22521
N1791B B767 22684
N1791B B767 22696
N1791B B767 23019
N1791U DC-9 45786
N1792B B737 23302
N1792B B737 23446
N1792B B737 25124
N1792B B737 27917
N1792B B747 21659
N1792B B747 21831
N1792B B757 24014
N1792B B757 24471
N1792B B757 25488
N1792B B757 27203
N1792B B767 23022
N1792B B767 23106
N1792N B767 22789
N1792U DC-9 45712
N1793T B707 20428
N1793U DC-9 45787
N1794B B747 20373
N1794B B747 20801
N1794B B767 27189
N1794B B767 27376
N1794B B767 27393
N1794U DC-9 47304
N1795B B747 20237
N1795B B747 20781
N1795U DC-9 47442
N1796B B747 19730
N1796B B747 20771
N1796U DC-9 47450
N1797B B737 20299
N1797U DC-9 47451
N1798B B747 19762
N1798B B747 20770
N1798U DC-9 47369
N1799B B737 20967
N1799B B737 25134
N1799B B747 19761
N1799B B747 20704
N1799U DC-9 47370
N1800 DC-8 45274
N1800B B737 22138
N1800B B737 22505
N1800B B737 22601
N1800B B747 19746
N1800B B747 20530
N1800B B747 21758
N1801 DC-8 45276
N1801U DC-10 46600
N1802 DC-8 45277
N1802U DC-10 46601
N1803 DC-8 45895
N1803U DC-10 46602
N1804 DC-8 45896
N1804U DC-10 46603
N1805 DC-8 45899
N1805U DC-10 46604
N1806 DC-8 45911
N1806U DC-10 46605
N1807 DC-8 45904
N1807U DC-10 46606
N1808E DC-8 46105
N1808U DC-10 46607
N1809E DC-8 46107
N1809U DC-10 46608
N1810U DC-10 46609
N1811U DC-10 46610
N1812U DC-10 46611
N1813U DC-10 46612
N1814U DC-10 46613
N1815U DC-10 46614
N1816U DC-10 46615
N1817U DC-10 46616
N1818U DC-10 46617
N1819U DC-10 46618
N1820U DC-10 46619
N1821U DC-10 46620
N1822U DC-10 46621
N1823U DC-10 46622
N1824U DC-10 46623
N1825U DC-10 46624
N1826U DC-10 46625
N1827U DC-10 46626
N1828U DC-10 46627
N1829U DC-10 46628
N1830U DC-10 46629
N1831U DC-10 46630
N1832U DC-10 46631
N1833U DC-10 47965
N1834U DC-10 47966
N1835U DC-10 47967
N1836U DC-10 47968
N1837U DC-10 47969
N1838U DC-10 46632
N1839U DC-10 46633
N1841U DC-10 46634
N1842U DC-10 46635
N1843U DC-10 46636
N1844U DC-10 48260
N1845U DC-10 48261
N1846U DC-10 48262
N1847U DC-10 48263
N1848U DC-10 48264
N1849U DC-10 46939
(N1849U) DC-10 46543
N1850U DC-10 48285
(N1851U) DC-10 48288
N1852U DC-10 47811
N1853U DC-10 47812
N1854U DC-10 47813
N1855U DC-10 47837
N1856U DC-10 46975
N1857U DC-10 46986
N1858U DC-10 46987
N1859U DC-10 47819
N1901 B727 19130
N1902 B727 19131
N1903 B727 19132
N1905 B727 19180
N1906 B727 19181
N1907 B727 19182
N1908 B727 19183
N1909 B727 19184
N1910 B727 19385
N1928 B727 19386
N1929 B727 19387
N1930 B727 19388
N1931 B727 19389
N1932 B727 19390
N1933 B727 19428
N1934 B727 19429
N1935 B727 19430
(N1938R) DC-9 47098
(N1939R) DC-9 47120
N1955 B727 19431
N1956 B727 19432
N1957 B727 19833
N1958 B727 19834
N1959 B727 19835
N1962 B727 19836
N1963 B727 19837
N1964 B727 19838
N1965 B727 19839
N1969 B727 20044
N1970 B727 18426
N1971 B727 18427
N1972 B727 18428
N1973 B727 18429
N1974 B727 18430
N1975 B727 18431
N1976 B727 18432
N1976P DC-8 45435
N1977 B727 18433
N1978 B727 18434
N1979 B727 18435
N1980 B727 18436
N1981 B727 18437

N1982 B727 18438
N1983 B727 18439
N1984 B727 18440
N1985 B727 18441
N1986 B727 18442
N1987 B727 18443
N1987B B707 21103
N1988 B727 18444
N1989 B727 18445
N1990 B727 18446
N1991 B727 18447
N1992 B727 18448
N1993 B727 18449
N1994 B727 18450
N1995 B727 18900
N1996 B727 18901
N1997 B727 19128
N1998 B727 19129
(N2001U) CRVL 62
N2090B B707 19291
N2111J 1-11 029
N2117X B737 19424
"N2138T" B707 18835
N2143H B707 17644
N2143J B720 18451
N2178F B707 19293
N2213E B707 20027
N2215Y B707 19631
N2235W B707 17631
N2276X B707 17602
N2282C B737 19013
N2286C B737 19014
N2289C B737 19015
(N2296N) CRVL 102
N2310 B737 23596
N2310B DC-8 45765
N2405T DC-9 47309
N2464C B720 18381
N2464K B720 18382
N2471 B727 19524
N2472 B727 19525
N2473 B727 19526
N2474 B727 19527
N2475 B727 19528
N2547R DC-8 46084
(N2550) B727 20045
N2606Z MD-83 49626
N2628Y B720 18165
(N2655Y) B737 21538
N2674U DC-8 46062
N2679T DC-9 47476
N2688Z B727 20476
N2689E B727 19318
N2697V B720 18066
(N2703J) B727 18367
N2703Y F-28 11223
N2711R B737 19426
(N2727) B727 19244
N2741A B727 18990
N2777 B727 19176
N2786 DC-9 47223
N2786S DC-9 47283
N2801W B727 20263
N2802W B727 20264
N2803W B727 20265
N2804W B727 20266
N2805W B727 20267
N2806W B727 20268
N2807W B727 20579
(N2807W) B727 20311
N2808W B727 20580
(N2808W) B727 20312
N2809W B727 20581
(N2809W) B727 20313
N2810W B727 20648
(N2810W) B727 20314
N2811W B727 20649
N2812W B727 20868
N2813W B727 20869
N2814W B727 20870
N2815W B727 20871
N2816W B727 20872
N2817W B727 20873
N2818W B727 20874
N2819W B727 21057
N2820W B727 21058
N2821W B727 21059
N2822W B727 21327
N2823W B727 21328
N2824W B727 21329
N2825W B727 21330
N2826W B727 21331
N2827W B727 21392
N2828W B727 21393
N2829W B727 21481
N2830W B727 21482
N2892Q DC-9 45841
N2896W DC-9 45722
N2913 B727 20045
N2914 B727 20046
N2915 B727 20143
N2919N DC-8 46052
N2920 CV990 30-10-35
N2941W B737 22596
N2969G B727 19304
N2969V B727 19137
N2977G B727 18897
N2978G B707 18924
N2979G B727 19305
N3001D MD-83 49936
N3002A MD-83 49941
N3004C MD-83 49935
N3010C MD-82 49903
N3010G MD-83 49808
N3016Z DC-10 48266
N3024W DC-10 48318
N3075A A300 606
N3124Z B720 18157
(N3126H) 1-11 BAC.122
(N3126Q) 1-11 BAC.123
N3127K B707 20028
N3128H DC-8 45672
N3140D L1011 1233
N3154 B720 18827
N3155 B720 18828
N3156 B720 18829
N3157 B720 18830
N3158 B720 18963
N3159 B720 19160
N3160 B720 19161
N3160M B737 20197
N3161 B720 19207
N3162 B720 19208
N3163 B720 19413
N3164 B720 19414
N3165 B720 19438
N3166 B720 19439
N3167 B720 19523
N3182B B727 19536
N3183B B720 18158
(N3201) B747 19676
(N3202) B747 19677
(N3203) B747 19678
N3203Y B747 19751
N3206T 146 E1144
N3209Y B727 20540
N3211M B727 18951
N3213T B737 25744
N3238N B707 19996
N3238S B707 20199
N3254D B727 19618
N3281G DC-9 47003
N3281K DC-9 47004
N3281N DC-9 47325
N3281R DC-9 47065
N3281U B737 23477
(N3281V) B737 23625
(N3281W) B737 23626
(N3281Y) B737 23627
(N3282G) B737 23628
(N3282N) B737 23629
(N3282P) B737 23630
(N3282R) B737 23631
(N3282V) B737 23632
(N3282W) B737 23633
(N3282X) B737 23634
N3282Y B737 23635
N3283G B737 23636
N3301 B737 23181
N3301L DC-9 45696
N3302L DC-9 45697
N3303L DC-9 45698
N3304L DC-9 45699
N3305L DC-9 45700
N3306L DC-9 45701
N3307L DC-9 45702
N3308L DC-9 45703
N3309L DC-9 45704
N3310L DC-9 45705
N3311L DC-9 45706
N3312L DC-9 45707
N3313L DC-9 45708
N3314L DC-9 45709
N3315L DC-9 45710
N3316L DC-9 47025
N3317L DC-9 47026
N3318L DC-9 47027
N3319L DC-9 47028
N3320L DC-9 47029
N3321L DC-9 47030
N3322L DC-9 47031
N3323L DC-9 47032
N3324L DC-9 47103
N3325L DC-9 47104
N3325T DC-8 45754
N3326L DC-9 47105
N3327L DC-9 47106
N3328L DC-9 47107
N3329L DC-9 47108
N3330L DC-9 47109
N3331L DC-9 47172
N3332L DC-9 47173
N3333L DC-9 47174
N3333M B737 20194
N3334L DC-9 47175
N3335L DC-9 47176
N3336L DC-9 47177
N3337L DC-9 47273
N3338L DC-9 47274
N3339L DC-9 47275
N3340L DC-9 47276
N3459D B727 20554
N3502P B757 24635
N3502P B757 25054
N3502P B757 26436
N3504T DC-9 47638
N3505T DC-9 45788
N3506T DC-9 47765
N3507A MD-82 49801
N3507T DC-9 47788
N3508T DC-9 47797
N3509J B737 26069
N3509T DC-9 47798
N3510T DC-9 47799
N3512T DC-9 48111
N3513T DC-9 48112
N3514T DC-9 48113
N3515 MD-82 49892
N3519L B737 25743
N3519L B757 24845
N3519M B757 26160
N3521N B737 24815
N3521N B737 25179
N3521N B757 26161
N3605 B727 18942
N3606 B727 18943
(N3727) B727 19245
N3746E B720 18060
N3751X DC-8 45619
(N3751Y) B707 18707
N3756F 1-11 005
N3791G B707 17598
N3831X B720 18059
N3833L B720 19523
N3842X B707 17692
N3878F DC-10 47864
N3878M DC-10 47863
N3878P DC-10 47861
N3931A DC-8 45961
N3931G DC-8 45986
N3939V 1-11 054
N3946A B727 19394
N3951A B707 17647
N3951B DC-8 45417
N3991C DC-9 47175
N4002M B727 20327
N4003G L1011 1177
N4003G L1011 1194
N4005X L1011 1176
N4039W B737 21112
N4094 B707 20342
(N4111X) 1-11 054
N4113D B737 25788
N4115J B707 19295
N4131G B707 19622
N4141A C-141 6110
N4157A DC-9 47039
N4225J B707 18809
N4245S B727 19282
N4249R B737 25116
N4264Y B737 20158
(N4278L) B737 21763
N4292P DC-8 45985
N4320B B737 25124
N4339D CV880 22-7-9-61
N4361V B737 26851
(N4367J) B727 18796
N4408F B707 18839
N4450Z B720 18831
N4465C B707 18413
N4465D B707 18411
(N4466C) B720 18963
N4489M DC-8 45618
N4501Q B747 22381
N4501W B737 19598
N4502R B747 22496
N4502W B737 19599
N4503W B737 19600
N4504 B737 19601
N4504W B737 19601
N4505W B737 19602
N4506H B747 22794
N4506W B737 19603
N4507W B737 19604
N4508E B747 22678
N4508H B747 22547
N4508W B737 19605
N4509 B727 19242
N4509W B737 19606
N4510W B737 19607
N4511W B737 19608
N4512W B737 19609
N4513W B737 19610
N4514W B737 19611
N4515W B737 19612
N4516W B737 19613
N4517W B737 19614
N4518W B737 19615
N4519W B737 19616
N4520W B737 19617
N4521W B737 20125
N4522 B737 20126
N4522V B747 22805
N4522W B737 20126
N4523W B737 20127
N4524W B737 20128
N4525W B737 20129
N4526W B737 20130
N4527W B737 20131
N4528W B737 20132
N4528Y B767 23624
(N4528Y) B767 23623
N4529T B767 23623
(N4529T) B767 23624
N4529W B737 20133
N4529W B737 20785
N4529W B737 22504
N4530W B737 20134
(N4530W) B737 22505
N4532N B727 22687
N4544F B747 22939
N4546U B727 19597
N4548M B747 23056
N4549V DC-9 47639
N4550T 1-11 BAC.135
N4551N B747 23137
N4554N B727 22982
N4555E B727 22983
N4555W B727 19793
N4556L B737 22800
N4556W B727 18282
N4558L B737 22801
N4561B DC-8 45610
N4562N B737 22859

N4563H B737 22700
N4569N B737 22701
N4570B B737 22875
N4571A B737 22876
N4571M B737 22793
N4574M B767 22921
N4574P DC-8 46116
N4575L B767 22923
N4578C DC-8 45943
N4582N DC-8 45982
N4585L B727 19010
(N4591Y) B707 17591
N4593U B707 17590
(N4594A) B707 17589
N4602D B727 18843
N4605D B707 18335
N4610 B727 18811
N4611 B727 18812
N4612 B727 18813
N4613 B727 18814
N4614 B727 18815
N4615 B727 18816
N4616 B727 18817
N4617 B727 18845
N4618 B727 18846
N4619 B727 18847
N4620 B727 19165
N4621 B727 19166
N4622 B727 19167
(N4646S) B727 18933
N4655Y DC-10 46551
N4655Z DC-10 46552
N4703U B747 19753
N4704U B747 19754
N4710U B747 19755
N4711U B747 19756
N4712U B747 19757
N4713U B747 19875
N4714U B747 19876
N4716U B747 19877
N4717U B747 19878
N4718U B747 19879
N4719U B747 19880
N4720U B747 19881
N4723U B747 19882
N4724U B747 19875
(N4727) B727 19246
N4727U B747 19883
N4728U B747 19925
N4729U B747 19926
N4730 B727 19450
N4731 B727 19451
N4732 B727 19452
N4732U B747 19927
N4733 B727 19453
N4734 B727 19454
N4735 B727 19455
N4735U B747 19928
N4736 B727 19456
N4737 B727 19457
N4738 B727 19458
N4739 B727 19459
N4740 B727 19460
N4741 B727 19461
N4742 B727 19462
N4743 B727 19463
N4744 B727 19464
N4745 B727 19465
N4746 B727 19466
N4747 B727 19467
N4748 B727 19468
N4749 B727 19469
N4750 B727 19470
N4751 B727 19471
N4752 B727 19472
N4753 B727 19473
N4754 B727 19474
N4761G DC-8 45917
N4768G DC-8 45679
N4769F DC-8 45686
N4769G DC-8 45860
N4805J DC-8 46063
N4809E DC-8 45762
N4863T DC-8 45951
N4864T DC-8 46059
N4865T DC-8 46073

N4866T DC-8 46089
N4867T DC-8 46090
N4868T DC-8 46091
N4869T DC-8 46117
N4901C DC-8 45274
N4902C DC-8 45276
N4902W B737 20440
(N4903C) DC-8 45277
N4904C DC-8 45668
N4905C DC-8 45805
N4905W B737 20917
N4906 B737 20138
N4906C DC-8 45862
N4907 B737 19594
N4907C DC-8 45967
N4908C DC-8 45968
N4909C DC-8 46060
N4910C DC-8 46094
N4929U DC-8 45296
N4934Z DC-8 46079
N4935C DC-8 45931
N4936S B727 19311
N4951W B737 21066
N4952W B737 21067
N5002K B757 24971
N5002K B757 25054
N5014K B777 27107
N5015 1-11 055
N5016 1-11 056
N5016R B777 27027
N5017 1-11 057
N5017V B777 27358
N5018 1-11 058
N5019 1-11 059
(N5019K) CRVL 146
N5020 1-11 060
N5021 1-11 061
N5022 1-11 062
N5023 1-11 063
N5024 1-11 064
N5025 1-11 065
N5026 1-11 066
N5027 1-11 067
N5028 1-11 068
N5029 1-11 069
N5030 1-11 072
N5031 1-11 073
N5032 1-11 074
N5033 1-11 075
N5034 1-11 076
N5035 1-11 077
N5036 1-11 078
N5037 1-11 079
N5038 1-11 080
N5038 B707 17652
N5039 1-11 081
N5040 1-11 086
N5041 1-11 087
N5042 1-11 088
N5043 1-11 089
N5044 1-11 090
N5055 B727 19173
N5065T B707 19519
N5073L B727 18936
N5088K B707 17704
N5089K B707 17722
N5090K B707 17905
N5091K B707 17705
N5092 B727 19174
N5092K B707 17706
N5093 B727 19175
N5093K B707 17619
N5094K B707 17708
N5094Q DC-8 46009
N5095K B707 17918
N5100X RJ100 7008
N5111Y B727 18270
N5129K L1011 1250
N5175U B737 20689
N5176Y B737 20692
N5177C B737 20693
N5294E B737 20691
N5294M B737 20694
N5341L DC-9 47277
N5342L DC-9 47278
N5366Y B707 19377

N5375S B737 23273
N5381X B707 18928
N5458E B727 18896
N5463Y DC-10 47814
N5464M DC-10 47815
N5472 B727 19525
N5473 B727 19526
N5474 B727 19527
N5475 B727 19524
N5487N B720 18380
(N5517U) B707 18842
N5517Z B707 18842
N5519U B707 18836
N5519V B707 18834
N5573B B737 22598
N5573B B737 23303
N5573B B737 23447
N5573B B737 23654
N5573B B737 24237
N5573B B747 22709
N5573B B747 23120
N5573B B747 23149
N5573B B747 24061
N5573B B757 24015
N5573B B757 24472
N5573B B757 24923
N5573B B767 22790
N5573E B727 22621
N5573F B747 22481
N5573K B737 22113
N5573K B737 22127
N5573K B737 23396
N5573K B737 23451
N5573K B737 23830
N5573K B737 24462
N5573K B737 24650
N5573K B737 27179
N5573K B747 22991
N5573K B757 23863
N5573K B757 24016
N5573K B767 22980
N5573K B767 23141
N5573L B737 22660
N5573P B737 23448
N5573P B747 21759
N5573P B747 23223
N5573P B757 25598
N5573S B747 23817
N5573S B747 27163
N5573S B767 27394
N5573X B737 22667
N5601 CV990 30-10-33
(N5601) CV990 30-10-1
N5601G CV990 30-10-1
N5602 CV990 30-10-34
(N5602) CV990 30-10-2
N5602G CV990 30-10-2
N5603 CV990 30-10-13
N5603 CV990 30-10-35
(N5603) CV990 30-10-3
N5603G CV990 30-10-3
N5604 CV990 30-10-36
(N5604) B727 19124
(N5604) CV990 30-10-4
N5604G CV990 30-10-4
N5605 CV990 30-10-9
N5606 CV990 30-10-10
N5606 CV990 30-10-34
N5607 B727 18804
N5607 CV990 30-10-16
N5608 B727 18805
N5608 CV990 30-10-18
N5609 B727 18806
N5609 CV990 30-10-21
N5610 CV990 30-10-22
N5611 CV990 30-10-23
N5612 CV990 30-10-24
N5612 CV990 30-10-36
N5613 CV990 30-10-25
N5614 CV990 30-10-26
N5615 CV990 30-10-27
N5616 CV990 30-10-25
N5616 CV990 30-10-28
N5617 CV990 30-10-29
N5618 CV990 30-10-30
N5619 CV990 30-10-31

N5620 CV990 30-10-32
N5623 CV990 30-10-20
N5625 CV990 30-10-19
N5700N B737 21800
N5700T B747 22616
N5701E B737 22397
(N5710) C-18 19566
N5711E B727 22084
N5726 DC-9 45726
N5728 DC-9 45727
N5768X DC-8 45768
N5771T B707 19212
N5772T B707 19213
N5772T B727 21655
N5773T B707 19214
N5774T B707 19435
N5791 B707 18756
N5824A DC-8 45824
N5828B 146 E1002
N5858 CV880 22-00-46M
N5863 CV880 22-00-48M
N5865 CV880 22-7-5-57
N5866 CV880 22-7-9-61
N5879X DC-8 45879
N5973L B747 22293
N6005C B747 22616
N6005C B747 22704
N6005C B747 22725
N6005C B747 23224
N6005C B747 23262
N6005C B747 23266
N6005C B747 23268
N6005C B747 23392
N6005C B747 23394
N6005C B747 23407
N6005C B747 23439
N6005C B747 23688
N6005C B747 23769
N6005C B747 23823
N6005C B747 23824
N6005C B747 23864
N6005C B747 23967
N6005C B747 23969
N6005C B747 24062
N6005C B747 24071
N6005C B747 24108
N6005C B747 24138
N6005C B747 24226
N6005C B747 24447
N6005C B747 24885
N6005C B747 25068
N6005C B747 25278
N6005C B747 25544
N6005C B747 25546
N6005C B747 25632
N6005C B767 23145
N6005C B767 23147
N6005C B767 23216
N6005C B767 23432
N6005C B767 23756
N6005C B767 23805
N6005C B767 23807
N6005C B767 23961
N6005C B767 24143
N6005C B767 24145
N6005C B767 24316
N6005C B767 24317
N6005C B767 24340
N6005C B767 24948
N6005F B747 23348
N6006C B747 23026
N6009F B737 22802
N6009F B747 22489
N6009F B747 23263
N6009F B747 23300
N6009F B747 23390
N6009F B747 23395
N6009F B747 23413
N6009F B747 23482
N6009F B747 23638
N6009F B747 23639
N6009F B747 23640
N6009F B747 23676
N6009F B747 23919
N6009F B747 24053
N6009F B747 24055

Registration	Type	c/n
N6009F	B747	24088
N6009F	B747	24134
N6009F	B747	24227
N6009F	B747	24619
N6009F	B747	24779
N6009F	B747	24836
N6009F	B747	24850
N6009F	B747	24887
N6009F	B747	24896
N6009F	B747	24976
N6009F	B747	24990
N6009F	B747	25046
N6009F	B747	25075
N6009F	B747	25315
N6009F	B747	25641
N6009F	B747	25813
N6009F	B747	26426
N6009F	B747	27663
N6009F	B747	27915
N6009F	B767	23305
N6009F	B767	23306
N6009F	B767	23328
N6009F	B767	23431
N6009F	B767	23745
N6009F	B767	23764
N6009F	B767	23765
N6009F	B767	23801
N6009F	B767	23804
N6009F	B767	23896
N6009F	B767	23916
N6009F	B767	24013
N6009F	B767	24085
N6009F	B767	24142
N6009F	B767	24239
N6009F	B767	24323
N6009F	B767	24324
N6009F	B767	24333
N6009F	B767	24407
N6009F	B767	24768
N6009F	B767	25533
N6009F	B767	26208
N6009F	B767	26913
N6009F	B767	27048
N6009F	B767	27377
N6018N	B737	22803
N6018N	B747	23221
N6018N	B747	23301
N6018N	B747	23350
N6018N	B747	23389
N6018N	B747	23709
N6018N	B747	23746
N6018N	B747	23911
N6018N	B747	23999
N6018N	B747	24018
N6018N	B747	24067
N6018N	B747	24107
N6018N	B747	24159
N6018N	B747	24162
N6018N	B747	24359
N6018N	B747	24761
N6018N	B747	24855
N6018N	B747	24883
N6018N	B747	24955
N6018N	B747	24998
N6018N	B747	25045
N6018N	B747	25547
N6018N	B747	25780
N6018N	B747	26344
N6018N	B747	27178
N6018N	B747	27442
N6018N	B747	27899
N6018N	B767	22786
N6018N	B767	22923
N6018N	B767	22973
N6018N	B767	22974
N6018N	B767	23058
N6018N	B767	23143
N6018N	B767	23309
N6018N	B767	23326
N6018N	B767	23402
N6018N	B767	23802
N6018N	B767	23806
N6018N	B767	23965
N6018N	B767	23966
N6018N	B767	23974
N6018N	B767	24006
N6018N	B767	24144
N6018N	B767	24157
N6018N	B767	24336
N6018N	B767	24727
N6018N	B767	24854
N6018N	B767	25316
N6018N	B767	25363
N6018N	B767	25535
N6018N	B767	25536
N6018N	B767	25826
N6018N	B767	26915
N6038E	B737	22804
N6038E	B747	23269
N6038E	B747	23287
N6038E	B747	23391
N6038E	B747	23509
N6038E	B747	23534
N6038E	B747	23652
N6038E	B747	23920
N6038E	B747	23982
N6038E	B747	24019
N6038E	B747	24161
N6038E	B747	24194
N6038E	B747	24195
N6038E	B747	24196
N6038E	B747	24198
N6038E	B747	24215
N6038E	B747	24731
N6038E	B747	25705
N6038E	B747	26547
N6038E	B747	27828
N6038E	B767	22524
N6038E	B767	22921
N6038E	B767	23142
N6038E	B767	23144
N6038E	B767	23213
N6038E	B767	23214
N6038E	B767	23280
N6038E	B767	23433
N6038E	B767	23645
N6038E	B767	23757
N6038E	B767	23759
N6038E	B767	23962
N6038E	B767	24003
N6038E	B767	24084
N6038E	B767	24087
N6038E	B767	24150
N6038E	B767	24325
N6038E	B767	27205
N6038N	B747	23271
N6046B	B747	22990
N6046P	B747	22750
N6046P	B747	23139
N6046P	B747	23264
N6046P	B747	23265
N6046P	B747	23270
N6046P	B747	23393
N6046P	B747	23611
N6046P	B747	23621
N6046P	B747	23622
N6046P	B747	23721
N6046P	B747	23735
N6046P	B747	24106
N6046P	B747	24156
N6046P	B747	24160
N6046P	B747	24177
N6046P	B747	24201
N6046P	B747	24202
N6046P	B747	24354
N6046P	B747	24777
N6046P	B747	24966
N6046P	B747	25546
N6046P	B767	22975
N6046P	B767	23212
N6046P	B767	23403
N6046P	B767	23434
N6046P	B767	23964
N6046P	B767	23973
N6046P	B767	24005
N6046P	B767	24083
N6046P	B767	24257
N6046P	B767	24318
N6046P	B767	24334
N6046P	B767	24716
N6046P	B767	24733
N6046P	B767	24742
N6046P	B767	24983
N6046P	B767	25273
N6046P	B767	26205
N6046P	B767	26986
N6055C	B747	23698
N6055X	B747	23267
N6055X	B747	23286
N6055X	B747	23408
N6055X	B747	23410
N6055X	B747	23501
N6055X	B747	23508
N6055X	B747	23711
N6055X	B747	23751
N6055X	B747	23799
N6055X	B747	23816
N6055X	B747	23968
N6055X	B747	24158
N6055X	B747	24730
N6055X	B747	25544
N6055X	B747	25647
N6055X	B747	27827
N6055X	B767	22525
N6055X	B767	23146
N6055X	B767	23304
N6055X	B767	23327
N6055X	B767	23758
N6055X	B767	23963
N6055X	B767	24004
N6055X	B767	24082
N6055X	B767	24086
N6055X	B767	24146
N6055X	B767	24498
N6055X	B767	25532
N6055X	B767	25534
N6055X	B767	26544
N6055X	B767	27569
N6055X	B767	27908
N6056X	B747	27175
N6063S	B767	25865
N6065S	B767	27427
N6065Y	B747	23409
N6065Y	B767	23107
N6065Y	B767	23307
N6066B	B747	24052
N6066U	B747	22472
N6066U	B747	23048
N6066U	B767	22528
N6066U	B767	23250
N6066Z	B737	22657
N6066Z	B747	23138
N6066Z	B767	22972
N6067B	B737	25714
N6067B	B747	22870
N6067B	B757	24401
N6067B	B767	22922
N6067B	B767	23140
N6067E	B767	23072
N6067U	B737	23274
N6067U	B757	23454
N6069D	B737	24692
N6069D	B737	25289
N6069D	B747	22487
N6069D	B757	24402
N6069P	B737	23635
N6108N	B747	22791
N6108N	B747	23480
N6108N	B747	26549
N6108N	B767	24349
N6140A	DC-9	47049
(N6141A)	DC-9	47050
(N6142A)	DC-9	47051
(N6143A)	DC-9	47052
(N6144A)	DC-9	47099
(N6145A)	DC-9	47130
(N6146A)	DC-9	47146
N6150Z	DC-10	47889
N6161A	DC-8	45969
N6161C	**DC-8**	**45856**
N6161M	**DC-8**	**45762**
N6162A	DC-8	46061
N6163A	DC-8	46062
N6164A	DC-8	46144
(N6165A)	DC-8	46133
(N6166A)	DC-8	46146
(N6167A)	DC-8	46149
N6167D	**B727**	**22430**
N6186	**B747**	**21439**
N6200N	DC-10	48292
N6200N	MD-11	48439
N6200N	MD-83	49399
N6200N	MD-83	49401
N6200N	MD-82	49417
N6200N	MD-82	49439
N6200N	MD-82	49483
N6200N	MD-82	49604
N6200N	MD-83	49807
N6202D	MD-11	48555
N6202D	MD-82	49441
N6202D	MD-82	49900
N6202D	MD-87	53010
N6202D	MD-83	53117
N6202S	MD-11	48601
N6202S	MD-82	49901
N6202S	MD-82	53118
N6203D	MD-11	48743
N6203D	MD-83	49442
N6203D	MD-82	53064
N6203D	MD-82	53119
N6203U	DC-10	48267
N6203U	**MD-11**	**48766**
N6203U	MD-87	49612
N6203U	MD-83	49708
N6204N	DC-10	48310
N6206F	MD-83	49945
N6206F	MD-82	53120
N6241	B737	19847
N6504K	B707	20035
N6546L	B707	19296
N6571C	DC-8	45391
N6572C	**DC-8**	**45392**
N6573C	DC-8	45393
(N6574C)	DC-8	45394
(N6575C)	DC-8	45395
(N6576C)	DC-8	45396
N6577C	DC-8	45442
N6578C	DC-8	45443
N6598W	**B707**	**19133**
N6658Y	B737	20221
N6666U	B757	23452
N6720	B707	18986
N6721	B707	18987
N6722	B707	18988
N6723	B707	18989
N6724	B707	19215
N6726	B707	19216
N6727	B707	19217
N6728	**B707**	**19218**
N6729	B707	19219
(N6757A)	B737	21720
N6763T	B707	19220
N6764T	B707	19221
N6771T	B707	19222
N6789T	**B707**	**19223**
N6790T	B707	19436
N6800	**B727**	**19475**
N6801	B727	19476
N6802	B727	19477
N6803	B727	19478
N6804	B727	19479
N6805	B727	19480
N6806	**B727**	**19481**
N6807	B727	19482
N6808	**B727**	**19483**
N6809	**B727**	**19484**
N6810	B727	19485
N6811	**B727**	**19486**
N6812	**B727**	**19487**
N6813	**B727**	**19488**
N6814	B727	19489
N6815	**B727**	**19490**
N6816	**B727**	**19491**
N6817	B727	19492
N6818	**B727**	**19493**
N6819	**B727**	**19494**
N6820	B727	19495
N6821	B727	19496
N6822	**B727**	**19700**
N6823	**B727**	**19701**
N6824	B727	19702
N6825	B727	19703
N6826	**B727**	**19704**
N6827	**B727**	**20180**

N6828	B727	20181
N6829	B727	20182
N6830	B727	20183
N6831	**B727**	**20184**
N6832	B727	20185
N6833	**B727**	**20186**
N6834	**B727**	**20187**
N6835	**B727**	**20188**
N6836	B727	20189
N6837	B727	20190
N6838	B727	20191
N6839	**B727**	**20192**
N6841	B727	20193
N6842	B727	20241
N6842	DC-8	45803
N6843	CV990	30-10-30
N6844	CV990	30-10-18
N6845	CV990	30-10-25
N6846	CV990	30-10-24
(N7000Y)	B707	18891
N7001U	**B727**	**18293**
N7002U	**B727**	**18294**
N7003U	B727	18295
N7003U	B727	18791
N7004U	**B727**	**18296**
N7005U	B727	18297
N7006U	B727	18298
N7007U	B727	18299
N7008U	B727	18300
N7009U	B727	18301
N7010U	B727	18302
N7011U	B727	18303
N7012U	B727	18304
N7013U	B727	18305
N7014U	B727	18306
N7015Q	DC-8	45882
N7015U	**B727**	**18307**
N7016U	B727	18308
N7017U	**B727**	**18309**
N7018U	B727	18310
N7019U	B727	18311
N7020U	**B727**	**18312**
N7021U	B727	18313
N7022U	B727	18314
N7023U	B727	18315
N7024U	B727	18316
N7025U	B727	18317
N7026U	B727	18318
N7027U	B727	18319
N7028U	B727	18320
N7029U	B727	18321
N7030U	B727	18322
N7031A	B737	21219
N7031F	B737	21445
N7031U	B727	18323
N7032U	B727	18324
N7033U	B727	18325
N7034E	DC-8	45658
N7034U	B727	18326
N7035T	L1011	1231
N7035U	B727	18327
N7036T	**L1011**	**1232**
N7036U	B727	18328
N7037U	B727	18329
N7038U	B727	18330
N7039U	B727	18331
N7040U	B727	18332
N7041U	B727	18848
N7042U	B727	18849
N7043U	B727	18850
N7043U	DC-8	46042
N7044U	B727	18851
N7045U	B727	18852
N7046A	B727	18877
N7046G	DC-8	45885
N7046H	**DC-8**	**46011**
N7046U	B727	18853
N7047U	B727	18854
N7048U	B727	18855
N7049U	B727	18856
N7050U	B727	18857
N7051U	B727	18858
N7052U	B727	18859
N7053U	B727	18860
N7054U	**B727**	**18861**
N7055A	**A300**	**462**
N7055U	**B727**	**18862**
N7056U	B727	18863
N7057U	B727	18864
N7058U	B727	18865
N7059U	B727	18866
N7060U	B727	18867
N7061U	B727	18868
N7062A	**A300**	**474**
N7062U	B727	18869
N7063U	B727	18870
N7064U	B727	18871
N7065U	B727	18872
N7066U	B727	19079
N7067U	B727	19080
N7068U	B727	19081
N7069U	B727	19082
N7070U	B727	19083
N7071	B707	17691
N7071U	B727	19084
N7072	B707	17692
N7072U	B727	19085
N7073	B707	17693
N7073U	B727	19086
N7074	B707	17694
N7074U	B727	19087
N7075	B707	17695
N7075U	B727	19088
N7076	B720	18064
N7076A	**A300**	**610**
N7076U	B727	19140
N7077	B720	18065
N7077U	B727	19141
N7078	B720	18066
N7078	B720	18154
N7078U	B727	19142
N7079	B720	18423
N7079S	B757	22206
N7079U	B727	19143
N7080	B720	18581
N7080U	B727	19144
N7081	B720	18042
N7081U	B727	19145
N7082A	**A300**	**643**
N7082U	B727	19146
N7083	B720	18041
N7083A	**A300**	**645**
N7083U	B727	19147
N7084U	B727	19148
N7085U	B727	19149
N7086U	B727	19150
N7087U	B727	19151
N7088U	B727	19152
N7089U	B727	19153
N7090U	B727	19154
(N7091U)	B727	19155
(N7092U)	B727	19156
(N7093U)	B727	19157
(N7094U)	B727	19158
N7095	B707	19104
(N7095U)	B727	19159
N7096	B707	19105
N7097	B707	19106
N7098	B707	19107
N7099	B707	19108
N7100	B707	19440
N7102	B707	19529
N7103	B707	19530
N7104	B707	19531
N7152J	B727	20937
N7158T	**B707**	**20036**
N7158Z	**B707**	**20179**
N7181C	DC-8	45602
N7182C	DC-8	45603
N7183C	DC-8	45605
N7184C	DC-8	45606
N7201U	B720	17907
N7202U	B720	17908
N7203U	B720	17909
N7204U	B720	17910
N7205U	B720	17911
N7206U	B720	17912
N7207U	B720	17913
N7208U	B720	17914
N7209U	B720	17915
N7210U	B720	17916
N7211U	B720	17917
N7212U	B720	18044
N7213U	B720	18045
N7214U	B720	18046
N7215U	B720	18047
N7216U	B720	18048
N7217U	B720	18049
N7218U	B720	18050
(N7219)	B720	18072
N7219U	B720	18072
N7220U	B720	18073
N7221U	B720	18074
N7222U	B720	18075
N7223U	B720	18076
N7224U	B720	18077
N7225U	B720	18078
N7226U	B720	18079
N7227U	B720	18080
N7228U	**B720**	**18081**
N7229L	B720	18159
N7229U	B720	18082
N7230T	B707	19572
N7231T	B707	19572
N7232X	**B707**	**19570**
N7251U	**B727**	**21398**
N7252U	**B727**	**21399**
N7253U	**B727**	**21400**
N7254U	**B727**	**21401**
N7255U	**B727**	**21402**
N7256U	**B727**	**21403**
N7257U	**B727**	**21404**
N7258U	**B727**	**21405**
N7259U	**B727**	**21406**
N7260U	**B727**	**21407**
N7261U	**B727**	**21408**
N7262U	**B727**	**21409**
N7263U	**B727**	**21410**
N7264U	**B727**	**21411**
N7265U	**B727**	**21412**
N7266U	**B727**	**21413**
N7267U	**B727**	**21414**
N7268U	**B727**	**21415**
N7269U	**B727**	**21416**
N7270	B727	19109
N7270C	B727	18897
N7270F	B727	19391
N7270L	B727	19536
(N7270Q)	B727	20250
N7270U	**B727**	**21417**
N7271	B727	19110
N7271F	B727	19392
N7271P	**B727**	**18998**
(N7271P)	B727	19243
(N7271Q)	B727	20251
N7271U	**B727**	**21418**
N7272	B727	19111
N7272F	B727	19393
(N7272Q)	B727	20252
N7272U	**B727**	**21419**
N7273	B727	19112
N7273F	B727	19394
N7273U	**B727**	**21420**
N7274	B727	19113
N7274F	B727	19395
N7274U	**B727**	**21421**
N7275	B727	19114
N7275F	B727	19995
N7275U	**B727**	**21422**
N7276	B727	19115
N7276F	B727	19991
N7276U	**B727**	**21423**
N7277	B727	19116
N7277F	B727	19992
N7277U	**B727**	**21424**
N7278	B727	19117
N7278F	B727	19993
N7278U	**B727**	**21425**
N7279	B727	19118
N7279F	B727	19994
N7279F	B727	20162
N7279U	**B727**	**21557**
N7279U	**B727**	**21567**
N7280	B727	19119
N7280U	**B727**	**21558**
N7281	B727	19120
N7281U	**B727**	**21559**
N7282	B727	19243
N7282U	**B727**	**21560**
N7283U	**B727**	**21561**
N7284	B727	19244
N7284U	**B727**	**21562**
N7285U	**B727**	**21563**
N7286	B727	19245
N7286U	**B727**	**21564**
N7287	B727	19246
N7287U	**B727**	**21565**
N7287V	B727	22080
N7288	B727	19497
N7288U	**B727**	**21566**
N7289	B727	19499
N7290	B727	19500
N7290U	**B727**	**21568**
N7291	B727	19501
N7291U	**B727**	**21569**
N7292U	**B727**	**21570**
N7293	B727	19534
N7293U	**B727**	**21571**
N7294	B727	19535
N7294U	**B727**	**21572**
N7295	B727	19532
N7295U	**B727**	**21573**
N7296	B727	19533
N7296U	**B727**	**21574**
N7297U	**B727**	**21892**
N7298U	**B727**	**21893**
N7299U	**B727**	**21894**
N7302F	B737	19758
N7310F	B737	20344
N7321S	B707	19840
N7322S	B707	19841
N7323S	B707	19842
N7340F	B737	21597
N7341F	B737	21598
N7342F	B737	21747
N7343F	B737	21748
N7344F	B737	21749
N7345F	B737	21750
N7346F	B737	21751
N7348F	B737	21981
N7349F	B737	22089
N7350F	B737	22383
N7351F	B737	22384
N7352F	B737	22399
N7353F	B737	22456
N7354F	B737	22457
N7355F	B737	22741
N7356F	B737	22742
N7357F	B737	22743
N7358F	B737	22744
N7359F	B737	23023
N7360F	B737	20222
N7361F	B737	20223
N7362F	B737	21131
N7363F	B737	20133
N7370F	B737	20073
N7371F	B737	20074
(N7371F)	B737	20070
N7372F	B737	20072
(N7372F)	B737	20071
N7373F	B737	20361
(N7373F)	B737	20072
N7374F	B737	20362
N7374F	B737	21980
(N7374F)	B737	20073
N7375A	**B767**	**25202**
N7375F	B737	20363
(N7375F)	B737	20074
N7376F	B737	20364
N7377F	B737	20365
N7378F	B737	20070
N7379F	B737	20071
N7380F	B737	19681
N7381	**B720**	**18977**
N7381F	B737	20369
N7382F	B737	20492
N7383F	B737	19075
N7384F	B737	20129
N7385F	B737	21069
N7386F	B737	20368
N7387F	B737	19682
N7388F	B737	19920
(N7388F)	B737	19758
N7389F	B737	19937

N7390F	B737	19945
N7391F	B737	21508
N7392F	B737	21509
N7393F	B737	21544
N7394F	B737	21545
N7395F	B737	21546
N7396F	B737	21640
N7397F	B737	21641
N7398F	B737	21642
N7399F	B737	23024
(N7401Q)	B747	20080
N7401U	B727	19089
(N7402Q)	B747	20081
N7402U	B727	19090
(N7403Q)	B747	20082
N7403U	B727	19091
(N7404Q)	B747	20083
N7404U	B727	19092
N7405U	B727	19093
N7406U	B727	19094
N7407U	B727	19095
N7408U	B727	19096
N7409U	B727	19097
N7410U	B727	19098
N7411U	B727	19099
N7412U	B727	19100
N7413U	B727	19101
N7414U	B727	19102
N7415U	B727	19103
N7416U	B727	19191
N7417U	B727	19192
N7418U	B727	19193
N7419U	B727	19194
N7420U	B727	19195
N7421U	B727	19196
N7422U	B727	19197
N7423U	B727	19198
N7424U	B727	19199
N7425U	B727	19200
N7426U	B727	19201
N7427U	B727	19202
N7428U	B727	19203
N7429U	B727	19204
N7430U	B727	19205
N7431U	B727	19805
N7432U	B727	19806
N7433U	B727	19890
N7434U	B727	19891
N7435U	B727	19892
N7436U	B727	19893
N7437U	B727	19894
N7438U	B727	19895
N7441U	**B727**	**21895**
N7442U	**B727**	**21896**
N7443U	**B727**	**21897**
N7444U	**B727**	**21898**
N7445U	**B727**	**21899**
N7446U	**B727**	**21900**
N7447U	**B727**	**21901**
N7448U	**B727**	**21902**
N7449U	**B727**	**21903**
N7450U	**B727**	**21904**
N7451U	**B727**	**21905**
N7452U	**B727**	**21906**
N7453U	**B727**	**21907**
N7454U	**B727**	**21908**
N7455U	**B727**	**21909**
N7456U	**B727**	**21910**
N7457U	**B727**	**21911**
N7458U	**B727**	**21912**
N7459U	**B727**	**21913**
N7460U	**B727**	**21914**
N7461U	**B727**	**21915**
N7462U	**B727**	**21916**
N7463U	**B727**	**21917**
N7464U	**B727**	**21918**
N7465B	DC-9	47465
N7465U	**B727**	**21919**
N7466U	**B727**	**21920**
N7467U	**B727**	**21921**
N7470	**B747**	**20235**
N7486B	B707	21261
N7501A	B707	17628
N7502A	B707	17629
N7503A	B707	17630
N7504A	B707	17631
N7505A	B707	17632
N7506	**MD-82**	**49800**
N7506A	B707	17633
N7507A	B707	17634
N7508	**MD-82**	**49802**
N7508A	B707	17635
N7509	**MD-82**	**49803**
N7509A	**B707**	**17636**
N7510A	B707	17637
N7511A	B707	17638
N7512A	B707	17639
N7512A	**MD-82**	**49806**
N7513A	B707	17640
N7514A	B707	17641
N7514A	**MD-82**	**49891**
N7515A	B707	17642
N7516A	B707	17643
N7517A	B707	17644
N7517A	**MD-82**	**49894**
N7518A	B707	17645
N7518A	**MD-82**	**49895**
N7519A	B707	17646
N7519A	**MD-82**	**49896**
N7520A	B707	17647
N7520A	**MD-82**	**49897**
N7521A	B707	17648
N7521A	**MD-82**	**49898**
N7522A	B707	17649
N7522A	**MD-82**	**49899**
N7523A	B707	17650
N7524A	B707	17651
N7525A	B707	17652
N7525A	**MD-82**	**49917**
N7526A	B707	18054
N7526A	**MD-82**	**49918**
(N7526A)	B707	17653
N7527A	B720	18013
N7527A	**MD-82**	**49919**
(N7527A)	B707	17654
N7528A	B720	18014
N7528A	**MD-82**	**49920**
(N7528A)	B707	17655
N7529A	B720	18015
(N7529A)	B707	17656
N7530	**MD-82**	**49922**
N7530A	B720	18016
(N7530A)	B707	17657
N7531A	B720	18017
N7531A	**MD-82**	**49923**
N7532A	B720	18018
N7532A	**MD-82**	**49924**
N7533A	B720	18019
N7533A	**MD-82**	**49987**
N7534A	B720	18020
N7534A	**MD-82**	**49988**
N7535A	B720	18021
N7535A	**MD-82**	**49989**
N7536A	B720	18022
N7536A	**MD-82**	**49990**
N7537A	B720	18023
N7537A	**MD-82**	**49991**
N7538A	B720	18024
N7538A	**MD-82**	**49992**
N7539A	B720	18025
N7539A	**MD-82**	**49993**
N7540A	B720	18026
N7540A	**MD-82**	**49994**
N7541A	B720	18027
N7541A	**MD-82**	**49995**
N7542A	B720	18028
N7542A	**MD-82**	**49996**
N7543A	B720	18029
N7543A	**MD-82**	**53025**
N7544A	B720	18030
N7544A	**MD-82**	**53026**
N7545A	B720	18031
N7546A	B720	18032
N7546A	**MD-82**	**53028**
N7547A	B720	18033
N7547A	**MD-82**	**53029**
N7548A	B720	18034
N7548A	**MD-82**	**53030**
N7549A	B720	18035
N7549A	**MD-82**	**53031**
N7550	**MD-82**	**53032**
N7550A	B720	18036
N7550A	**B707**	**18882**
N7551A	B720	18037
N7551A	B707	18883
N7552A	B707	18884
N7553A	B707	18885
N7554A	B707	19185
N7555A	B707	18689
N7556A	B707	18690
N7557A	B707	18691
N7558A	B707	18692
N7559A	B707	18938
N7560A	B707	18939
N7561A	B707	18940
N7562A	B707	19235
N7563A	B707	19236
N7564A	B707	19237
N7565A	C-18	19380
N7566A	C-18	19381
N7567A	C-18	19382
N7568A	**B707**	**19383**
N7569A	C-18	19384
N7570A	B707	19186
N7571A	B707	19187
N7572A	B707	19188
N7573A	B707	19323
N7574A	B707	19324
N7575A	**B707**	**19325**
N7576A	**B707**	**19326**
N7577A	**B707**	**19327**
N7578A	**B707**	**19328**
N7579A	**B707**	**19329**
N7580A	**B707**	**19330**
N7581A	**B707**	**19331**
N7582A	**B707**	**19332**
N7583A	**B707**	**19333**
N7584A	**B707**	**19334**
N7585A	B707	19335
N7586A	B707	19336
N7587A	B707	19337
N7588A	**B707**	**19338**
N7589A	B707	19339
N7590A	B707	19340
N7591A	B707	19341
N7592A	**B707**	**19342**
N7593A	B707	19343
N7594A	**B707**	**19344**
N7595A	B707	19515
(N7595A)	B707	19345
N7596A	B707	19516
(N7596A)	B707	19346
N7597A	B707	19517
(N7597A)	B707	19347
N7598A	C-18	19518
(N7598A)	B707	19348
N7599A	B707	19519
(N7599A)	B707	19349
N7620U	B727	19537
N7621U	**B727**	**19538**
N7622U	B727	19539
N7623U	B727	19540
N7624U	B727	19541
N7625U	B727	19542
N7626U	B727	19899
N7627U	B727	19900
N7628U	B727	19901
N7629U	B727	19902
N7630U	B727	19903
N7631U	B727	19904
N7632U	B727	19905
N7633U	B727	19906
N7634U	B727	19907
N7635U	**B727**	**19908**
N7636U	B727	19909
N7637U	B727	19910
N7638U	**B727**	**19911**
N7639U	**B727**	**19912**
N7640U	**B727**	**19913**
N7641U	B727	19914
N7642U	**B727**	**19915**
N7643U	**B727**	**20037**
N7644U	**B727**	**20038**
N7645U	**B727**	**20039**
N7646U	B727	20040
N7647U	B727	20041
(N7660A)	B737	22426
N7667A	**B757**	**25301**
N7667AB	B707	17682
N7667B	B707	21367
N7771	**B777**	**27116**
N7772	B777	26936
N7773	B777	26932
N7774	B777	26929
N7829A	**B727**	**20217**
N7876	CV990	30-10-4
N7878	CV990	30-10-37
(N7888)	C-18	18713
N7890	B727	20112
N7892	B727	20114
N7893	B727	20115
N8001U	DC-8	45278
N8002U	DC-8	45279
N8003U	DC-8	45280
N8004U	DC-8	45281
N8005U	DC-8	45282
N8006U	DC-8	45283
N8007U	1-11	054
N8007U	**DC-8**	**45284**
N8008D	**DC-8**	**45252**
N8008F	DC-8	45669
N8008U	DC-8	45285
N8009U	**DC-8**	**45286**
N8010U	DC-8	45287
N8011U	**DC-8**	**45288**
N8012U	DC-8	45289
N8013U	DC-8	45290
N8014U	DC-8	45588
N8015U	**DC-8**	**45589**
N8016	DC-8	45254
N8016U	DC-8	45590
N8017U	DC-8	45591
N8018D	DC-8	45278
N8018U	DC-8	45291
N8019U	DC-8	45592
N8020U	DC-8	45593
N8021U	DC-8	45594
N8021V	**DC-8**	**45612**
N8022U	DC-8	45595
N8023U	DC-8	45292
N8024U	DC-8	45293
N8025U	**DC-8**	**45294**
N8026U	DC-8	45295
N8027	DC-8	45255
N8027U	DC-8	45296
"N8027U"	B747	19883
N8028D	DC-8	45279
N8028U	DC-8	45297
N8029U	DC-8	45298
N8030U	DC-8	45596
N8031U	DC-8	45299
N8032M	B737	22022
N8032U	DC-8	45597
N8033U	DC-8	45300
N8034T	L1011	1230
N8034U	DC-8	45301
N8035U	**DC-8**	**45302**
N8036U	DC-8	45303
N8037U	DC-8	45304
N8038A	DC-8	45256
N8038D	DC-8	45280
N8038U	DC-8	45305
N8039U	**DC-8**	**45306**
N8040U	DC-8	45307
N8041U	**DC-8**	**45675**
N8042U	**DC-8**	**45676**
(N8043B)	B727	19254
N8043E	B727	20228
N8043U	DC-8	45677
N8044U	DC-8	45800
N8045U	DC-8	45801
N8046U	DC-8	45802
N8047U	DC-8	45880
N8048U	DC-8	45881
N8049U	DC-8	45886
N8050U	DC-8	45884
N8051U	DC-8	45885
N8052U	**DC-8**	**46009**
N8053U	DC-8	46010
N8054U	DC-8	46011
N8055U	DC-8	46012
N8060U	DC-8	45693
N8061U	DC-8	45694
N8062U	DC-8	45757

N8063U	DC-8	45758
N8064U	DC-8	45759
N8065U	DC-8	45756
N8066U	**DC-8**	**45850**
N8067A	**A300**	**510**
N8067U	DC-8	45851
N8068D	DC-8	45255
N8068U	DC-8	45852
N8069U	DC-8	45853
N8070U	DC-8	45810
N8071U	DC-8	45811
N8072U	DC-8	45812
N8073U	DC-8	45813
N8074U	DC-8	45849
N8075U	DC-8	45940
N8076U	**DC-8**	**45941**
N8077U	DC-8	45945
N8078U	DC-8	45946
N8079U	**DC-8**	**45947**
N8080U	DC-8	45970
N8081U	DC-8	45971
N8082U	DC-8	45972
N8083U	DC-8	45973
N8084U	**DC-8**	**45974**
N8085U	**DC-8**	**45975**
N8086U	DC-8	45976
N8087U	**DC-8**	**45977**
N8088U	DC-8	45978
N8089U	DC-8	45993
N8090P	B707	18921
N8090Q	B707	19434
N8090U	DC-8	45994
N8091J	B707	19776
N8091U	**DC-8**	**45995**
N8092U	DC-8	45996
N8093U	DC-8	45997
N8094U	DC-8	45998
N8095U	DC-8	46039
N8096U	DC-8	46040
N8097U	DC-8	46064
N8098U	DC-8	46065
N8099U	DC-8	46066
N8101N	B727	18252
N8102N	B727	18253
N8103N	B727	18254
N8104E	B727	18255
N8104N	**B727**	**18255**
N8105N	B727	18256
N8106N	B727	18257
N8107N	B727	18258
N8108N	B727	18259
N8109N	B727	18260
N8110N	B727	18261
N8111N	B727	18262
N8112N	B727	18263
N8113N	B727	18264
N8114N	B727	18265
N8115N	B727	18266
N8116N	B727	18267
N8117N	B727	18268
N8118N	B727	18269
N8119N	B727	18270
N8120N	B727	18271
N8121N	B727	18272
N8122N	B727	18273
N8123N	B727	18274
N8124N	B727	18275
N8125N	B727	18276
N8126N	B727	18277
N8127N	B727	18278
N8128N	B727	18279
N8129N	B727	18280
N8130N	B727	18281
N8131N	B727	18282
N8132N	B727	18283
N8133N	B727	18284
N8134N	B727	18285
N8135N	B727	18286
N8136N	B727	18287
N8137N	B727	18288
N8138N	B727	18289
N8139N	B727	18290
N8140G	B727	19393
N8140N	B727	18291
N8140P	B727	18744
N8140V	B727	18743
N8141N	B727	18965
N8142N	B727	18966
N8143N	B727	18967
N8144N	B727	18968
N8145N	B727	18969
N8146N	B727	18970
N8147N	B727	18971
N8148A	**DC-8**	**45267**
N8148N	B727	18972
N8149N	B727	18973
N8150N	B727	18974
N8151G	B727	19298
N8152G	B727	19299
N8153G	B727	19300
N8154G	B727	19301
N8155G	B727	19302
N8156G	B727	19356
N8157G	B727	19357
N8158G	B727	19358
N8159G	B727	19359
N8160C	CV990	30-10-9
N8160G	B727	19360
N8161G	B727	19717
N8162G	B727	19718
N8163G	B707	18746
N8163G	B727	19719
N8164G	B727	19720
N8165G	B727	19721
N8166A	DC-8	45269
N8166G	B727	19722
N8167G	B727	19850
N8168G	B727	19851
N8169G	B727	19852
N8170A	DC-8	45270
N8170G	B727	19853
N8171G	B727	19854
N8172G	B727	19855
N8173G	B727	19856
N8174G	B727	19857
N8175G	B727	19858
N8177U	**DC-8**	**45983**
(N8183E)	B727	19404
N8184A	**DC-8**	**45271**
N8207U	DC-8	45275
N8209U	DC-8	45260
N8215Q	**B720**	**18688**
N8215U	DC-8	45261
N8217U	DC-8	45263
N8228P	DC-10	46937
N8240U	**DC-8**	**45257**
N8243U	DC-8	45258
N8245U	DC-8	45259
N8246U	DC-8	45262
N8252U	DC-8	45264
N8258C	**CV990**	**30-10-19**
N8258U	DC-8	45387
N8259C	CV990	30-10-20
N8266U	DC-8	45388
N8270A	DC-9	47037
N8270H	DC-9	47089
N8274H	DC-8	45274
N8275H	DC-8	45275
N8276H	DC-8	45276
N8277H	DC-8	45277
N8277V	B737	21176
N8277V	B737	21443
N8277V	B747	21507
N8277V	B747	22704
N8277V	B767	22921
N8278V	B727	22349
N8278V	B727	22641
N8278V	B737	22057
N8278V	B747	22870
N8278V	B767	22692
N8279V	B737	22596
N8279V	B737	22635
N8279V	B747	22970
N8279V	B747	23026
N8280V	B727	22167
N8280V	B737	21804
N8280V	B737	22276
N8280V	B747	21239
N8280V	B747	22305
N8281V	B727	22394
N8281V	B747	22486
N8281V	B747	22498
N8282V	B737	22087
N8283V	B737	22607
N8284V	B727	22261
N8284V	B727	22268
N8284V	B747	21991
N8284V	B747	22502
N8285V	B727	21346
N8285V	B727	22430
N8285V	B737	22589
N8285V	B747	21241
N8285V	B747	22234
N8286V	B727	22262
N8286V	B727	22271
N8286V	B737	22602
N8286V	B747	21604
N8286V	B767	22923
N8287V	B767	22694
N8288V	B727	22081
N8288V	B727	22288
N8288V	B737	22160
N8288V	B737	22778
N8289V	B737	21791
N8289V	B747	19735
N8289V	B747	22969
N8289V	B767	22695
N8289V	B767	22980
N8290V	B727	21853
N8290V	B737	22283
N8291V	B727	22359
N8291V	B737	22281
N8291V	B737	22408
N8291V	B747	21590
N8292V	B727	22374
N8292V	B737	22282
N8292V	B737	22338
N8292V	B767	22693
N8293V	B727	20903
N8293V	B737	22031
N8293V	B737	22653
N8293V	B747	21514
N8293V	B757	22184
N8294V	B757	22185
N8295V	B727	22375
N8295V	B737	22406
N8295V	B737	22739
N8295V	B747	21352
N8296V	B737	22120
N8296V	B747	22614
N8296V	B747	22764
N8296V	B747	22971
N8297V	B737	22137
N8297V	B747	20977
N8297V	B747	21111
N8297V	B747	21134
N8298V	B737	22119
N8298V	B737	22132
N8320	B727	19526
N8356C	CV990	30-10-27
N8357C	**CV990**	**30-10-24**
N8400	B707	19433
N8401	C-18	19581
N8402	B707	19582
N8403	C-18	19583
N8404	B707	19584
N8405	B707	19585
N8406	B707	19586
N8408	B707	19587
N8409	B707	19588
N8410	B707	19589
N8411	B707	19574
N8412	B707	19575
N8413	B707	19576
N8414	B707	19577
N8415	B707	20087
N8416	B707	20088
(N8416)	B707	19578
N8416A	B707	20088
N8417	**B707**	**20089**
(N8417)	B707	19579
N8417A	B707	20089
N8418	DC-8	45600
(N8418)	B707	19580
N8418A	B707	17637
N8420A	B707	17638
(N8424)	B707	19578
(N8425)	B707	19579
(N8426)	B707	19580
N8431	B707	20170
N8432	B707	20171
N8433	B707	20172
N8434	B707	20173
N8434B	DC-8	45609
N8435	B707	20174
N8436	B707	20175
N8437	B707	20176
N8438	B707	20177
N8439	B707	20178
N8440	B707	20179
N8459	B707	20630
N8477H	CV880	22-7-2-54
N8478H	CV880	22-00-5
N8479H	CV880	22-00-8
N8480H	CV880	22-00-12
N8481H	CV880	22-00-20
N8482H	CV880	22-00-22
N8483H	CV880	22-00-23
N8484H	CV990	30-10-5
(N8484H)	CV990	30-10-14
N8485H	CV880	22-00-43M
N8485H	CV990	30-10-6
N8486H	CV880	22-00-44M
N8487H	CV880	22-00-45M
(N8487H)	CV880	22-00-37M
N8488H	CV880	22-00-46M
N8488H	CV880	22-7-4-56
N8489H	CV880	22-00-1
N8489H	CV880	22-00-47M
N8490H	CV880	22-00-48M
N8490H	CV880	22-7-1-53
N8491H	CV880	22-00-49M
N8492H	CV880	22-00-9
N8493H	**CV880**	**22-00-18**
N8494H	**CV880**	**22-00-34**
N8495H	CV880	22-00-39
N8497H	CV990	30-10-7
N8498H	CV990	30-10-8
N8498S	B720	18424
N8498T	B720	18425
N8499H	CV990	30-10-11
N8500	DC-9	45731
N8527S	B737	20194
N8536Z	B737	22075
N8596C	B727	21946
N8601	DC-8	45422
N8602	DC-8	45423
N8603	DC-8	45424
N8604	**DC-8**	**45425**
N8605	DC-8	45426
N8606	DC-8	45427
N8607	DC-8	45428
N8608	DC-8	45429
N8609	DC-8	45430
N8610	DC-8	45431
N8611	DC-8	45432
N8612	DC-8	45433
N8613	DC-8	45434
N8614	DC-8	45435
N8615	DC-8	45436
N8617	DC-8	45437
(N8618)	DC-8	45438
(N8619)	DC-8	45439
N8630	DC-8	46101
N8631	DC-8	45936
N8632	DC-8	45966
N8633	DC-8	46020
N8634	DC-8	46021
N8635	DC-8	46050
N8636	DC-8	46051
N8637	DC-8	46052
N8638	DC-8	46053
N8639	DC-8	46049
N8641	DC-8	46106
N8642	DC-8	46109
(N8647A)	B737	19306
N8700R	B727	18321
N8701E	B720	18155
N8702E	B720	18156
N8702Q	DC-10	46920
N8703E	B720	18157
N8703Q	DC-10	46923
N8704E	B720	18158
N8704Q	DC-10	46921

N8705E B720 18159
N8705Q DC-10 46660
N8705T B707 18916
N8706E B720 18160
N8706Q DC-9 47661
N8707E B720 18161
N8707Q DC-10 46959
N8708E B720 18162
N8708Q DC-10 46961
N8709E B720 18163
N8709Q DC-9 47697
N8710E B720 18164
N8710Q DC-9 47761
N8711E B720 18240
N8712E B720 18241
N8712Q DC-10 46976
N8713E B720 18242
N8713Q DC-9 47772
N8714E B720 18243
N8714Q DC-9 47773
N8715E B720 18244
N8715T B707 18917
(N8717U) DC-8 46118
(N8724U) DC-8 46119
N8725T B707 18918
N8729 B707 20058
N8730 B707 20059
N8731 B707 20060
N8731U DC-8 46130
(N8731U) DC-8 46120
N8732 B707 20061
N8733 B707 20062
N8734 B707 20063
N8735 B707 20064
N8736 B707 20065
N8737 B707 20066
N8738 B707 20067
(N8739) B707 18408
N8740 DC-8 45668
N8755 DC-8 46097
N8756 DC-8 46096
N8757 DC-8 46095
N8758 DC-8 46093
N8759 DC-8 46058
N8760 DC-8 46074
N8762 DC-8 46038
N8763 DC-8 46037
N8764 DC-8 46017
N8765 DC-8 46016
N8766 DC-8 46015
N8767 DC-8 45992
N8768 DC-8 45983
N8769 DC-8 45982
N8770 DC-8 45913
N8771 DC-8 45912
N8772 DC-8 45943
N8773 DC-8 45942
N8774 DC-8 45894
N8775 DC-8 45889
N8776 DC-8 45888
N8777 DC-8 45887
N8778 DC-8 45848
N8779R DC-8 45760
N8780B C-14
N8780R DC-8 45628
N8781R DC-8 45648
N8782R DC-8 45667
N8783R DC-8 45684
N8784R DC-8 45769
N8785R DC-8 45803
N8786R DC-8 45897
N8787R DC-8 45898
N8788R DC-8 45952
N8789R B707 19410
N8789R B727 20143
N8790R B720 18043
N8790R B727 20240
N8791R B727 20241
N8801E CV880 22-00-4
N8802E CV880 22-00-7
N8803E CV880 22-00-11
N8804E CV880 22-00-16
N8805E CV880 22-00-17
N8806E CV880 22-00-21
N8807E CV880 22-00-29
N8808E CV880 22-00-36
N8809E CV880 22-00-38
N8810E CV880 22-00-41
N8811E CV880 22-00-50
N8812E CV880 22-00-51
N8813E CV880 22-00-52
N8814E CV880 22-00-62
N8815E CV880 22-00-63
N8816E CV880 22-00-64
N8817E CV880 22-00-65
N8825E B727 20144
N8826E B727 20145
N8827E B727 20146
N8828E B727 20147
N8829E B727 20148
N8830E B727 20149
N8831E B727 20150
N8832E B727 20151
N8833E B727 20152
N8834E B727 20153
N8835E B727 20154
N8836E B727 20379
N8837E B727 20380
N8838E B727 20381
N8839E B727 20382
N8840A B707 19247
N8840E B727 20383
N8841E B727 20415
N8842E B727 20416
N8843E B727 20441
N8844E B727 20442
N8845E B727 20443
N8846E B727 20444
N8847E B727 20445
N8848E B727 20446
N8849E B727 20447
N8850E B727 20448
N8851E B727 20614
N8852E B727 20615
N8853E B727 20616
N8855E B727 20617
N8856E B727 20618
N8857E B727 20619
N8858E B727 20620
N8859E B727 20621
N8860 DC-9 45797
N8860E B727 20622
N8861E B727 20623
N8862E B727 20624
N8863E B727 20625
N8864E B727 20626
N8865E B727 20627
N8866E B727 20628
N8867E B727 20823
N8869E B727 20824
N8870A B707 18873
N8870Z B727 21288
N8871Z B727 21289
N8872Z B727 21290
N8873Z B727 21291
N8874Z B727 21292
N8875Z B727 21293
N8876Z B727 21449
N8877Z B727 21450
N8878Z B727 21451
N8879Z B727 21452
N8880A B707 18708
N8880Z B727 21453
N8881Z B727 21578
N8882Z B727 21579
N8883Z B727 21580
N8884Z B727 21581
N8885Z B727 21854
N8886Z B727 21855
N8887Z B727 21856
N8888B DC-8 45860
N8888Z B727 21857
N8889Z B727 21858
N8890Z B727 21859
N8891Z B727 21860
N8892Z B727 21861
(N8893Z) B727 22562
(N8894Z) B727 22563
N8901 DC-9 45826
N8901E DC-9 45742
N8902 DC-9 47010
N8902E DC-9 45743
N8903 DC-9 47011
N8903E DC-9 45744
N8904 DC-9 47012
N8904E DC-9 45745
N8905 DC-9 47013
N8905E DC-9 45746
N8906 DC-9 47014
N8906E DC-9 45747
N8907 DC-9 47015
N8907E DC-9 45748
N8908 DC-9 47152
N8908E DC-9 45749
N8909 DC-9 47016
N8909E DC-9 45770
N8910 DC-9 47153
N8910E DC-9 45771
N8911 DC-9 47017
N8911E DC-9 45825
N8912 DC-9 47154
N8912E DC-9 45829
N8913 DC-9 47018
N8913E DC-9 45830
N8914 DC-9 47155
N8914E DC-9 45831
N8915 DC-9 47086
N8915E DC-9 45832
N8916 DC-9 47087
N8916 DC-9 47156
N8916E DC-9 45733
N8917E DC-9 45734
N8918 DC-9 45828
N8918E DC-9 45833
N8919 DC-9 47240
N8919E DC-9 45834
N8920E DC-9 45835
N8921E DC-9 45836
N8922E DC-9 45837
N8923E DC-9 45838
N8924E DC-9 45839
N8925E DC-9 45840
N8926E DC-9 45863
N8927E DC-9 45864
N8928E DC-9 45865
N8929E DC-9 45866
N8930E DC-9 47139
N8931E DC-9 47140
N8932E DC-9 47141
N8933E DC-9 47142
N8934E DC-9 47143
N8935E DC-9 47144
N8936E DC-9 47145
N8937E DC-9 47158
N8938E DC-9 47161
N8939E DC-9 47162
N8940E DC-9 47163
N8941E DC-9 47164
N8942E DC-9 47165
N8943E DC-9 47166
N8944E DC-9 47167
N8945E DC-9 47181
N8946E DC-9 47182
N8947E DC-9 47183
N8948E DC-9 47184
N8949E DC-9 47185
N8950E DC-9 47186
N8951E DC-9 47187
N8952E DC-9 45867
N8953E DC-9 45868
N8953U DC-9 45797
N8954E DC-9 47188
N8954U DC-8 45878
N8955E DC-9 47189
N8955U DC-8 45948
N8956E DC-9 47214
N8956U DC-8 45949
N8957E DC-9 47215
N8958E DC-9 47216
N8959E DC-9 47157
N8960E DC-9 45869
N8960T DC-8 45938
N8960U DC-9 47114
N8961 DC-9 45842
N8961E DC-9 45870
N8961T DC-8 45902
N8961U DC-9 47115
N8962 DC-9 45843
N8962E DC-9 45871
N8962T DC-8 45900
N8963 DC-9 45844
N8963E DC-9 45872
N8963U DC-9 47192
N8964 DC-9 47048
N8964E DC-9 45873
N8964U DC-8 45961
N8965E DC-9 45874
N8965U DC-9 47301
N8966E DC-9 47217
N8966U DC-8 46067
N8967E DC-9 47267
N8967U DC-8 46068
N8968E DC-9 45875
N8968U DC-8 46069
N8969E DC-9 45876
N8969U DC-8 46070
N8970E DC-9 47268
N8970U DC-8 46071
N8971E DC-9 47269
N8971U DC-8 46081
N8972E DC-9 47270
N8972U DC-8 46084
N8973E DC-9 47036
N8973U DC-8 46085
N8974E DC-9 47074
N8974U DC-8 46110
N8975E DC-9 47119
N8975U DC-8 46111
N8976E DC-9 47271
N8977E DC-9 47272
N8978E DC-9 47327
N8979E DC-9 47328
N8980E DC-9 47329
N8981E DC-9 47330
N8982E DC-9 47331
N8983E DC-9 47399
N8984E DC-9 47400
N8985E DC-9 47401
N8985V B737 22059
N8986E DC-9 47402
N8987E DC-9 47403
N8988E DC-9 47098
N8989E DC-9 47121
N8990E DC-9 47120
N9001D MD-83 53138
N9001L MD-83 53137
N9001U B737 19039
N9002U B737 19040
N9003U B737 19041
N9004U B737 19042
N9005U B737 19043
N9006U B737 19044
N9007U B737 19045
N9008U B737 19046
N9009U B737 19047
N9010U B737 19048
N9011U B737 19049
N9012J MD-83 49952
N9012J MD-83 53121
N9012S MD-82 53065
N9012S MD-82 53479
N9012U B737 19050
N9013U B737 19051
N9014U B737 19052
N9015U B737 19053
N9016U B737 19054
N9017P MD-83 53124
N9017U B737 19055
N9018U B737 19056
N9019U B737 19057
N9020Q MD-11 48504
N9020Q MD-11 48746
N9020U B737 19058
N9020U MD-11 48428
N9020U MD-11 48503
N9020Z MD-11 48426
N9020Z MD-11 48427
N9020Z MD-11 48533
N9021U B737 19059
N9022U B737 19060
N9023U B737 19061
N9024U B737 19062
N9025U B737 19063
N9026U B737 19064

Registration	Type	c/n
N9027U	**B737**	**19065**
N9028U	B737	19066
N9029U	B737	19067
N9030U	B737	19068
N9031U	B737	19069
N9032U	**B737**	**19070**
N9033U	B737	19071
N9034U	B737	19072
N9035C	MD-83	53139
N9035U	B737	19073
N9036U	B737	19074
N9037U	B737	19075
N9038U	**B737**	**19076**
N9039U	**B737**	**19077**
N9040U	**B737**	**19078**
N9041U	B737	19547
N9042U	B737	19548
N9043U	B737	19549
N9044U	B737	19550
N9045U	**B737**	**19551**
N9046U	B737	19552
N9047F	DC-8	45445
N9047U	B737	19553
N9048U	B737	19554
N9049U	B737	19555
N9050U	B737	19556
N9051U	**B737**	**19932**
N9052U	**B737**	**19933**
N9053U	**B737**	**19934**
N9054U	**B737**	**19935**
N9055U	B737	19936
N9056U	B737	19937
N9057U	B737	19938
N9058U	B737	19939
N9059U	B737	19940
N9060U	**B737**	**19941**
N9061U	**B737**	**19942**
N9062U	**B737**	**19943**
N9063U	**B737**	**19944**
N9064U	B737	19945
N9065U	**B737**	**19946**
N9066U	**B737**	**19947**
N9067U	**B737**	**19948**
N9068U	B737	19949
N9069U	**B737**	**19950**
N9070U	**B737**	**19951**
N9071U	**B737**	**19952**
N9072U	**B737**	**19953**
N9073U	B737	19954
N9074U	B737	19955
N9075H	MD-83	53140
N9075U	**B737**	**19956**
N9076Y	MD-11	48502
N9093P	**MD-11**	**48532**
N9101	DC-9	45794
N9102	DC-9	45795
N9103	DC-9	45796
N9104	DC-9	47081
(N9105)	DC-9	47138
(N9106)	DC-9	47263
(N9107)	DC-9	47264
N9110V	DC-8	45817
N9115G	**L1011**	**1042**
N9134D	**MD-11**	**48768**
(N9149M)	B707	17713
N9166X	MD-11	48406
N9184X	**B727**	**20894**
N9230Z	B707	17683
N9233Z	B727	18366
N9234Z	B727	18368
N9302B	**MD-82**	**49528**
N9303K	**MD-82**	**49529**
N9304C	**MD-82**	**49530**
N9306T	**MD-83**	**49567**
N9307R	**MD-83**	**49663**
N9330	**DC-9**	**47138**
N9331	**DC-9**	**47263**
N9332	**DC-9**	**47264**
N9333	**DC-9**	**47246**
N9334	**DC-9**	**47247**
N9335	**DC-9**	**47337**
N9336	**DC-9**	**47338**
N9337	**DC-9**	**47346**
N9338	**DC-9**	**47347**
N9339	**DC-9**	**47382**
N9340	**DC-9**	**47389**
N9341	**DC-9**	**47390**
N9342	**DC-9**	**47391**
N9343	**DC-9**	**47439**
N9344	**DC-9**	**47440**
N9345	DC-9	47441
N9346	**DC-9**	**47376**
N9347	**DC-9**	**45827**
N9348	**DC-9**	**45787**
N9349	DC-9	47016
N9350	DC-9	47153
N9351	DC-9	47240
N9352	DC-9	47017
N9352	DC-9	47154
N9353	DC-9	47154
N9354	DC-9	47018
N9355	DC-9	47155
N9356	DC-9	47086
N9357	**DC-9**	**47156**
N9358	DC-9	47087
N9359	DC-9	45828
N9401W	**MD-83**	**53137**
N9402W	**MD-83**	**53138**
N9403W	**MD-83**	**53139**
N9404V	**MD-83**	**53140**
N9405T	**MD-83**	**53141**
N9406W	**MD-83**	**53126**
N9407R	**MD-83**	**49400**
N9409F	**MD-83**	**53121**
N9412W	**MD-83**	**53187**
N9413T	**MD-83**	**53188**
N9414W	**MD-83**	**53189**
N9515T	B727	19874
N9516T	B727	19873
N9601Z	DC-8	45567
N9603Z	DC-8	45383
N9604Z	DC-8	45623
N9605Z	DC-8	45614
N9607Z	DC-8	45607
N9608Z	DC-8	45608
N9609Z	DC-8	45640
N9612Z	DC-8	45653
N9661	B747	20100
N9662	B747	20101
N9663	B747	20102
N9664	B747	20103
N9665	B747	20104
N9666	B747	20105
N9667	B747	20106
N9668	B747	20107
N9669	B747	20108
N9670	B747	20109
N9671	B747	20323
N9672	B747	20324
N9673	B747	20325
N9674	B747	20326
N9675	B747	20390
N9676	B747	20101
N9676	B747	20391
N9683Z	DC-8	45750
N9684Z	DC-9	45711
N9727N	B747	21575
N9743Z	DC-9	47201
N9801F	MD-82	49116
N9802F	MD-82	49117
N9803F	MD-82	49118
N9804F	MD-82	49114
N9805F	MD-82	49102
N9806F	MD-82	49444
N9807F	MD-82	49450
N9896	B747	19896
N9897	B747	19897
N9898	B747	19898
N9899	B747	20246
N9900	B747	20247
N9985F	B707	18056
(N9986F)	B707	17718
N10022	**MD-81**	**48024**
(N10023)	B747	20012
N10024	B747	20534
N10027	MD-81	48025
N10028	DC-9	48137
N10028	MD-81	48026
N10029	MD-81	48049
N10033	**MD-82**	**48083**
N10034	MD-82	48056
N10035	MD-82	48057
N10037	MD-82	49114
N10038	**DC-10**	**48275**
N10045	**DC-10**	**48259**
N10046	MD-82	49141
(N10046)	MD-81	48026
N10060	**DC-10**	**46970**
N10112	L1011	1064
N10114	L1011	1079
N10115	L1011	1114
N10116	L1011	1120
N10117	L1011	1125
N10199	YAK40	9940360
N10236	**B737**	**19937**
(N10240)	B737	20368
N10242	**B737**	**20071**
N10248	**B737**	**20344**
(N10249)	B737	20369
N10251	**B737**	**20361**
N10323	**B737**	**23374**
(N10408)	B727	21661
N10409	B727	21662
N10556	**DC-9**	**47423**
N10756	**B727**	**21042**
N10791	**B727**	**20645**
N10801	**MD-82**	**49127**
N10834	**MD-82**	**49494**
N10970	**A300**	**250**
N11002	L1011	1014
N11003	**L1011**	**1015**
N11004	**L1011**	**1016**
N11005	**L1011**	**1017**
N11006	**L1011**	**1018**
N11060	**A300**	**470**
N11181	1-11	BAC.096
N11182	1-11	BAC.097
N11183	1-11	BAC.105
N11244	**B737**	**20073**
N11412	**B727**	**18874**
N11415	B727	19122
N11612	**B737**	**27325**
(N11612)	B737	27326
N11651	B727	20249
(N11843)	MD-82	49661
N11984	**A300**	**108**
N11985	**A300**	**119**
N12061	**DC-10**	**47851**
N12064	**DC-10**	**47862**
N12109	**B757**	**27299**
(N12109)	B757	27300
N12114	**B757**	**27556**
N12116	**B757**	**27558**
N12125	**B757**	**27567**
N12230	**B737**	**19884**
N12231	**B737**	**19885**
N12301	B727	19558
N12302	B727	19559
N12303	B727	19560
N12304	B727	19561
N12305	**B727**	**19562**
N12306	B727	19563
N12307	B727	19564
N12308	**B727**	**19565**
N12313	**B737**	**23364**
N12318	**B737**	**23369**
N12319	**B737**	**23370**
N12322	**B737**	**23373**
N12327	**B737**	**23457**
N12335	**B737**	**19758**
N12349	**B737**	**23587**
N12359	**B737**	**25905**
N12411	**B727**	**22052**
N12505	**DC-9**	**45788**
N12507	**DC-9**	**47788**
N12508	**DC-9**	**47797**
N12510	**DC-9**	**47799**
N12514	**DC-9**	**48113**
N12532	**DC-9**	**45791**
N12536	**DC-9**	**47113**
N12538	**DC-9**	**47218**
N12539	**DC-9**	**45792**
N12811	**MD-82**	**49265**
N12826	B727	19826
N12827	B727	19827
(N12844)	MD-82	49667
N13066	**DC-10**	**46591**
N13067	**DC-10**	**47866**
N13102	**B757**	**27292**
N13110	**B757**	**27300**
(N13110)	B757	27301
N13113	**B757**	**27555**
N13234	**B737**	**19888**
N13331	**B737**	**23569**
N13512	**DC-9**	**48111**
N13614	DC-9	45713
N13624	**B737**	**27528**
N13627	DC-10	47855
N13627	DC-10	48259
N13627	DC-9	47651
N13627	DC-9	47784
N13627	MD-81	48015
N13627	MD-82	49193
N13627	MD-83	49826
N13627	MD-83	53015
N13627	MD-83	53199
N13699	DC-9	45711
N13759	**B727**	**21044**
N13780	B727	20635
N13881	**MD-81**	**48045**
N13891	**MD-82**	**49102**
N13971	A300	262
N13972	A300	289
N13974	**A300**	**126**
N13983	**A300**	**92**
N14053	**A300**	**420**
N14056	**A300**	**463**
N14061	**A300**	**471**
N14062	**DC-10**	**47863**
N14063	**DC-10**	**47864**
N14065	**A300**	**508**
N14068	**A300**	**511**
N14074	**DC-10**	**46911**
N14077	**A300**	**612**
(N14102)	B757	27293
N14106	**B757**	**27296**
(N14106)	B757	27297
N14107	**B757**	**27297**
(N14107)	B757	27298
N14115	**B757**	**27557**
N14120	**B757**	**27562**
N14121	**B757**	**27563**
N14206	**B737**	**19023**
(N14208)	B737	19025
N14209	**B737**	**19026**
N14211	**B737**	**19028**
N14212	**B737**	**19029**
(N14216)	B737	19033
N14233	**B737**	**19887**
N14237	B737	19945
N14239	**B737**	**19920**
N14241	**B737**	**20070**
N14245	**B737**	**20074**
N14246	**B737**	**20129**
N14247	B737	20133
(N14250)	B737	20492
N14307	**B737**	**23358**
N14308	**B737**	**23359**
N14320	**B737**	**23371**
N14324	**B737**	**23375**
N14325	**B737**	**23455**
N14334	**B737**	**23572**
N14335	**B737**	**23573**
N14336	**B737**	**23574**
N14337	**B737**	**23575**
N14341	**B737**	**23579**
N14342	**B737**	**23580**
N14346	**B737**	**23584**
N14347	**B737**	**23585**
N14358	**B737**	**23943**
N14358	**B737**	**25904**
N14381	**B737**	**26310**
N14383	**B737**	**26312**
N14384	**B737**	**26313**
(N14405)	B727	21268
N14416	**B727**	**22168**
N14524	**DC-9**	**47539**
N14534	**DC-9**	**47110**
N14551	**MD-82**	**53033**
N14564	**DC-9**	**47490**
N14601	**B737**	**27314**
(N14601)	B737	27315
N14604	**B737**	**27317**
(N14604)	B737	27318

N14605	**B737**	**27318**
(N14605)	B737	27319
N14609	**B737**	**27322**
(N14609)	B737	27323
N14613	**B737**	**27326**
(N14613)	B737	27327
N14628	**B737**	**27532**
N14629	**B737**	**27533**
N14760	**B727**	**21118**
N14788	**B727**	**20642**
N14791	B707	18810
N14810	**MD-82**	**49264**
N14814	**MD-82**	**49112**
N14816	**MD-82**	**49370**
N14818	**MD-82**	**49478**
N14831	**MD-82**	**49491**
N14839	**MD-82**	**49635**
N14840	**MD-82**	**49580**
(N14845)	MD-83	49668
(N14846)	MD-82	49701
(N14847)	MD-82	49702
(N14848)	MD-82	49703
(N14849)	MD-82	49704
N14871	**MD-82**	**48022**
N14879	**MD-83**	**49526**
N14880	**MD-81**	**48044**
N14889	**MD-82**	**49118**
N14890	**MD-82**	**49114**
N14930	B747	20103
N14936	B747	20105
N14937	B747	20106
N14939	B747	20108
N14943	B747	20102
N14966	**A300**	**117**
N14968	A300	153
N14969	A300	207
N14973	A300	211
N14975	**A300**	**261**
N14976	**A300**	**271**
N14977	**A300**	**274**
N14980	A300	86
N15017	**L1011**	**1063**
N15069	**DC-10**	**46584**
N15255	**B737**	**21069**
N15335	DC-9	45725
N15512	B727	18897
N15525	**DC-9**	**47531**
N15710	C-18	19566
N15711	B707	19567
N15712	B707	20068
N15713	B707	20069
(N15772)	B727	21041
N15774	**B727**	**21242**
N15781	**B727**	**20636**
N15790	**B727**	**20644**
N15820	**MD-82**	**49480**
N15841	**MD-82**	**49581**
N15967	**A300**	**121**
N16201	**B737**	**19018**
N16203	B737	19020
N16232	**B737**	**19886**
N16254	B737	20365
N16301	**B737**	**23352**
N16310	**B737**	**23361**
N16339	**B737**	**23577**
N16521	**DC-9**	**47521**
N16545	**MD-82**	**53027**
N16607	**B737**	**27320**
(N16607)	B737	27321
N16617	**B737**	**27330**
(N16617)	B737	27331
N16618	**B737**	**27331**
(N16618)	B737	27332
N16632	**B737**	**27900**
N16648	B707	17661
N16649	B707	17668
N16738	B707	19568
N16739	B707	19569
N16758	**B727**	**21043**
N16761	**B727**	**21119**
N16762	**B727**	**21245**
N16764	B727	18936
N16765	B727	18361
N16766	B727	18364
N16767	B727	18365
N16768	B727	18363
(N16778)	B727	21246
N16784	**B727**	**20639**
N16802	**MD-82**	**49222**
N16804	**MD-82**	**49246**
N16806	**MD-82**	**49260**
N16807	**MD-82**	**49261**
N16808	**MD-82**	**49262**
N16813	**MD-82**	**48066**
N16815	**MD-82**	**49113**
N16883	**MD-81**	**48073**
N16884	**MD-81**	**48074**
N16887	**MD-82**	**49116**
N16892	**MD-83**	**49391**
N16893	**MD-83**	**49392**
N16894	**MD-83**	**49393**
N16895	**MD-83**	**49394**
N16982	**A300**	**91**
N17010	B747	19729
N17011	**B747**	**19730**
N17025	**B747**	**20535**
N17104	**B757**	**27294**
(N17104)	B757	27295
N17105	**B757**	**27295**
(N17105)	B757	27296
N17117	B737	19768
N17122	**B757**	**27564**
N17125	B747	20271
N17126	B747	20273
N17207	B720	19002
N17208	B720	19003
(N17217)	B737	19794
N17252	**B737**	**20362**
N17306	**B737**	**23357**
N17309	**B737**	**23360**
N17316	**B737**	**23367**
N17317	**B737**	**23368**
N17321	B707	18825
N17321	**B737**	**23372**
N17322	B707	18826
N17323	B707	18886
N17324	B707	18887
N17325	B707	19177
N17326	B707	19178
N17326	**B737**	**23456**
N17327	B707	19350
N17328	B707	19351
N17328	**B737**	**23458**
N17329	B707	19352
N17329	**B737**	**23459**
N17344	**B737**	**23582**
N17345	**B737**	**23583**
N17356	**B737**	**23942**
N17356	**B737**	**25902**
N17386	**B737**	**26321**
N17402	**B727**	**21265**
(N17403)	B727	21266
N17406	B727	21269
N17407	**B727**	**21270**
N17410	**B727**	**21663**
N17413	B727	22165
(N17418)	B727	21855
N17480	B727	21661
N17531	**DC-9**	**45847**
N17533	**DC-9**	**47281**
N17535	**DC-9**	**47111**
(N17541)	DC-9	45793
N17543	**DC-9**	**45789**
N17557	**DC-9**	**47424**
N17560	DC-9	47067
N17614	**B737**	**27327**
(N17614)	B737	27328
N17619	**B737**	**27332**
(N17619)	B737	27333
N17620	**B737**	**27333**
(N17620)	B737	27334
N17627	**B737**	**27531**
N17773	**B727**	**21045**
(N17775)	B727	21243
(N17776)	B727	21244
N17779	B727	20634
N17789	B727	20643
N17804	DC-10	47861
N17812	**MD-82**	**49250**
N18066	**A300**	**509**
N18112	**B757**	**27302**
N18119	**B757**	**27561**
N18350	**B737**	**23588**
N18359	B737	23841
(N18401)	B727	21264
N18476	B727	19173
N18477	B727	18361
N18479	B727	19174
N18480	B727	18741
N18513	**DC-9**	**48112**
N18544	**DC-9**	**47219**
N18563	**DC-9**	**47487**
N18611	**B737**	**27324**
(N18611)	B737	27325
N18622	**B737**	**27526**
N18701	B707	18978
N18702	B707	18979
N18703	**B707**	**18980**
N18704	**B707**	**18981**
N18706	**B707**	**18982**
N18707	**B707**	**18983**
N18708	**B707**	**18984**
N18709	B707	18985
N18710	**B707**	**19224**
N18711	**B707**	**19225**
N18712	**B707**	**19226**
N18713	**B707**	**19227**
N18748	**B727**	**18364**
N18786	**B727**	**20641**
N18813	1-11	BAC.126
N18814	1-11	BAC.119
N18815	B747	20887
N18833	**MD-82**	**49493**
N18835	MD-82	49439
N19059	**A300**	**469**
N19072	**DC-10**	**46576**
N19117	**B757**	**27559**
N19118	**B757**	**27560**
N19357	B737	23839
N19357	**B737**	**23841**
N19357	**B737**	**25903**
N19382	**B737**	**26311**
N19504	**DC-9**	**47638**
N19621	**B737**	**27334**
N19623	**B737**	**27527**
N19634	**B737**	**26319**
N19636	**B737**	**26340**
N20205	B737	19022
(N21037)	B707	20097
(N21100)	B757	27291
N21108	**B757**	**27298**
(N21108)	B757	27299
N21555	MD-87	49780
(N22055)	B707	20340
N22679	L1011	1008
N24213	**B737**	**19030**
N24343	**B727**	**21630**
(N24343)	B727	20848
N24633	**B737**	**27901**
N24666	B720	18383
N24728	**B727**	**20658**
(N24729)	B727	20659
(N24730)	B727	20660
N25071	**A300**	**514**
N25729	B727	20659
N26123	**B757**	**27565**
N26175	DC-9	47172
N26565	B727	18370
(N26600)	B737	27314
N26729	B727	21348
N26861	B747	19733
N26862	B747	19734
N26863	B747	19735
N26864	B747	20305
N26877	B727	19319
N26879	B727	20475
N27358	B737	23840
(N27417)	B727	21854
N27509	**DC-9**	**47798**
N27522	**DC-9**	**47524**
N27610	**B737**	**27323**
(N27610)	B737	27324
N27783	**B727**	**20638**
N28366	B747	20800
N28714	**B707**	**18408**
N28724	B707	19570
N28726	B707	19571
N28727	B707	19572
N28728	B707	19573
N28888	B747	20542
N28899	B747	20543
N28903	B747	20541
N29124	**B757**	**27566**
N29180	DC-8	46095
N29259	DC-9	45739
N29549	DC-8	45803
N29730	**B727**	**20660**
N29796	B707	19209
N29895	B727	19251
N29922	DC-8	45754
N29953	DC-8	45691
N29954	DC-8	45859
(N29959)	B707	17646
(N29967)	1-11	009
N29981	A300	87
N30008	MD-83	49663
N30010	MD-83	49937
N30016	MD-83	49940
N30075	MD-11	48474
N31001	L1011	1002
N31001	L1011	1013
N31007	L1011	1026
N31008	**L1011**	**1028**
N31009	L1011	1029
N31010	L1011	1030
N31011	**L1011**	**1031**
N31013	**L1011**	**1035**
N31014	**L1011**	**1036**
N31015	L1011	1059
N31018	L1011	1065
N31019	**L1011**	**1066**
N31021	L1011	1075
N31022	L1011	1076
N31023	**L1011**	**1080**
N31024	L1011	1091
N31029	**L1011**	**1109**
N31030	**L1011**	**1111**
N31031	**L1011**	**1115**
N31032	L1011	1215
(N31032)	L1011	1124
N31033	L1011	1221
(N31033)	L1011	1130
N31208	DC-10	47889
N31239	B707	17696
N31240	B707	17718
N31241	B707	17703
N32626	**B737**	**27530**
N32716	**B727**	**20385**
N32717	B727	20386
N32718	B727	20387
N32719	**B727**	**20388**
N32721	B727	20463
N32722	B727	20464
N32723	B727	20465
N32724	B727	20655
N32725	**B727**	**20656**
N32824	B707	18071
N32831	B757	23686
N32836	B737	23752
N33021	**B747**	**20520**
N33069	**A300**	**512**
N33103	**B757**	**27293**
(N33103)	B757	27294
N33202	**B737**	**19019**
(N33210)	B737	19027
N33414	**MD-82**	**49325**
N33502	**MD-82**	**49739**
N33506	**DC-9**	**47765**
N33608	**B737**	**27321**
(N33608)	B737	27322
N33635	**B737**	**26339**
N33637	**B737**	**27540**
N33785	**B727**	**20640**
N33805	**MD-82**	**49249**
N33817	**MD-82**	**49371**
N34078	**A300**	**615**
(N34256)	B737	22743
(N34257)	B737	22744
N34315	**B737**	**23366**
N34415	**B727**	**22167**
N34838	**MD-82**	**49634**
N35030	B737	25017
N35030	B757	26242
N35108	B737	26071

N35108 B737 26100
N35108 B757 25220
N35135 B737 24785
N35153 B757 24749
N35153 B757 25345
N35198 B737 27381
N35832 MD-82 49492
N35836 MD-82 49441
N35888 MD-82 49117
N37270 B727 19846
N37615 B737 27328
(N37615) B737 27329
N37681 B707 17608
N37777 B720 18044
N37882 MD-81 48027
N38641 DC-9 47060
N39305 DC-8 46098
N39307 DC-8 45910
N39340 B737 23578
N39343 B737 23581
N39356 B767 24037
N39360 B737 25906
N39364 B767 24045
N39365 B767 24046
N39367 B767 25194
N40061 DC-10 46973
N40064 A300 507
N40102 B720 18158
N40104 B727 21091
N40108 B747 19896
N40112 B737 21302
N40115 B727 21266
N40116 B747 21141
N40120 B737 21282
N40481 B727 18329
N40482 B727 18330
N40483 B727 18331
N40484 B727 18791
N40485 B727 18332
N40486 B727 18848
N40487 B727 18849
N40488 B727 18852
N40489 B727 18854
N40490 B727 18860
N40495 B737 24021
N41012 L1011 1034
N41016 L1011 1060
N41020 L1011 1072
N41033 B727 21269
N41035 B747 21025
N41063 A300 506
N41068 DC-10 47867
N41069 B737 25787
N42086 DC-8 46132
N42783 DC-10 47868
N42920 DC-8 45752
N43265 DC-9 47222
N43537 DC-9 47112
N44214 B737 19031
(N44253) B737 20363
N44316 B727 20049
N44503 MD-82 49797
N45090 DC-8 45908
N45191 DC-8 45981
N45224 B747 20520
N45498 B727 19665
N45733 B737 23059
N45742 B767 22922
N45793 B727 20647
N45814 DC-8 45814
N45908 DC-8 45416
N45914 DC-8 45389
N46625 B737 27529
N46793 B727 20489
N47142 B727 19135
N47330 B707 19353
N47331 B707 19869
N47332 B707 19870
N47332 B737 23570
(N47333) B707 19871
N47538 B727 18287
N47691 DC-8 45861
N47904 B767 27568
N47978 DC-8 46162
N48054 B727 21082
N48054 B727 21946
N48055 B707 21096
N48058 CV880 22-00-43M
N48059 CV880 22-00-44M
N48060 CV880 22-00-47M
N48062 CV880 22-7-2-54
N48063 CV880 22-7-4-56
N48075 DC-9 45723
N48200 DC-9 45721
N48354 L1011 1144
N48354 L1011 1157
N48354 L1011 1246
(N48901) B767 27392
(N50022) B747 20011
N50051 A300 459
N51307 1-11 BAC.126
N52309 B727 19828
N52310 B727 19829
N52311 B727 19830
N52312 B727 19831
N52313 B727 19832
N52616 B737 27329
(N52616) B737 27330
N52705 B720 18587
N52845 DC-8 45981
N52958 DC-8 45883
N53110 B747 19676
N53111 B747 19677
N53112 B747 19678
N53116 B747 20321
N53302 B707 19004
N54325 B727 20232
N54326 B727 20233
N54327 B727 20234
N54328 B727 20306
N54329 B727 20307
N54330 B727 20308
N54331 B727 20309
N54332 B727 20310
N54333 B727 20460
N54334 B727 20461
N54335 B727 20462
N54336 B727 20490
N54337 B727 20491
N54338 B727 20843
N54340 B727 20845
N54341 B727 21628
(N54341) B727 20846
N54342 B727 21629
(N54342) B727 20847
N54344 B727 21631
(N54344) B727 20849
N54345 B727 21632
(N54345) B727 20850
N54348 B727 21967
(N54348) B727 20853
N54349 B727 21968
(N54349) B727 20854
N54350 B727 21969
(N54350) B727 20855
N54351 B727 21983
(N54351) B727 20856
N54352 B727 21984
(N54352) B727 20857
N54353 B727 21985
(N54353) B727 20858
N54354 B727 21986
(N54354) B727 20859
N54627 DC-10 46925
N54629 DC-10 46852
N54630 DC-9 47588
N54631 DC-9 47597
N54633 DC-10 47886
N54634 DC-10 47887
N54635 DC-9 47600
N54637 DC-10 46931
N54638 DC-9 47649
(N54639) DC-10 46853
N54640 DC-10 46921
N54641 DC-9 47654
N54642 DC-9 47655
N54643 DC-10 46949
N54644 DC-10 47928
N54645 DC-9 47619
N54646 DC-10 46952
N54648 DC-9 45722
(N54649) DC-10 46854
N54652 DC-10 46661
N54652 DC-10 46913
N56807 B737 22265
N56807 B737 22648
N56807 B767 23017
N57000 B727 22038
N57001 B727 22270
N57001 B737 21710
N57001 B737 22277
N57001 B737 22365
N57002 B727 22036
N57002 B727 22039
N57002 B727 22642
N57004 B747 22376
N57008 B727 21950
N57008 B727 22040
N57008 B737 21957
N57008 B737 22267
N57008 B737 22431
N57008 B757 22176
N57008 B767 23057
N57111 B757 27301
(N57111) B757 27302
N57201 B720 18416
N57202 B720 18417
N57202 B747 21962
N57203 B720 18418
N57203 B747 21963
N57204 B720 18419
N57206 B720 18763
N57837 MD-82 49582
N58101 B757 27291
(N58101) B757 27292
N58201 B747 21961
N58414 B727 22166
N58541 DC-9 45793
N58545 DC-9 47094
N58606 B737 27319
(N58606) B737 27320
(N58902) B767 27393
N58937 B707 18334
N59081 A300 639
N59207 B737 19024
N59302 B737 23353
N59338 B737 23576
(N59404) B727 21267
N59412 B727 22053
N59523 MD-82 49915
N59630 B737 27534
N59792 B727 20646
(N59842) MD-82 49660
(N60279) B727 20161
(N60282) B727 20163
N60312 B737 23363
(N60362) B727 20164
(N60446) B727 20165
N60468 B747 27044
(N60471) B727 20166
(N60507) B727 20167
N60655 B747 23908
N60659 B747 23502
N60659 B747 23610
N60659 B747 23813
N60659 B747 23825
N60659 B747 26425
N60659 B747 26473
N60659 B747 26563
N60659 B767 22522
N60659 B767 23217
N60659 B767 23281
N60659 B767 23308
N60659 B767 23744
N60659 B767 24947
N60659 B767 25058
N60659 B767 26389
N60659 B767 27391
N60659 B767 27427
N60665 B747 25873
N60668 B747 23461
N60668 B747 23637
N60668 B747 23722
N60668 B747 24066
N60668 B747 24518
N60668 B747 24740
N60668 B747 25152
N60668 B747 25213
N60668 B767 22787
N60668 B767 23282
N60668 B767 23803
N60668 B767 24002
N60668 B767 24007
N60668 B767 27049
N60668 B767 27428
N60688 B747 26474
(N60690) B727 20168
N60697 B747 23610
N60697 B747 24870
N60697 B747 26056
N60697 B747 27117
N60697 B747 27137
N60697 B767 24846
N60697 B767 27385
(N60747) B727 20366
(N60819) B727 20367
N61304 B737 23355
N61699 B707 17661
(N61699) B707 17662
N62020 MD-83 49847
N62025 MD-81 49282
N62119 B727 18934
N62215 B720 18080
N62355 L1011 1103
N62357 L1011 1105
N62393 B707 21049
(N62510) MD-82 49804
N62631 B737 27535
N63305 B737 23356
N63305 B747 20799
N64315 B727 20048
N64319 B727 20052
N64320 B727 20053
N64321 B727 20054
N64322 B727 20055
N64323 B727 20098
N64324 B727 20099
N64339 B727 20844
N64346 B727 21633
(N64346) B727 20851
N64347 B727 21634
(N64347) B727 20852
N64739 B707 17719
N64740 B707 17694
(N64757) B707 17692
N64799 DC-8 45598
N64804 DC-8 45600
N64854 L1011 1058
N64854 L1011 1067
N64854 L1011 1069
N64854 L1011 1073
N64854 L1011 1110
N64854 L1011 1118
N64854 L1011 1247
N64911 L1011 1176
N64911 L1011 1250
N64959 L1011 1248
N64996 L1011 1249
N65010 B707 19163
N65358 DC-9 47048
N65516 DC-8 46143
N65517 DC-8 46145
N65518 DC-8 46137
N65894 B727 19501
N65910 B727 19243
N66480 MD-82 49900
N66510 B727 18742
N66651 B707 18716
N66656 DC-8 45953
N66726 B727 20657
N66731 B727 20661
N66732 B727 20662
N66733 B727 20663
N66734 B727 20664
(N67258) B737 23023
N67333 B707 19871
N68041 DC-10 46900
N68042 DC-10 46901
N68043 DC-10 46902
N68044 DC-10 46903
N68045 DC-10 46904
N68046 DC-10 47800
N68047 DC-10 47801
N68048 DC-10 47802

N68049	**DC-10**	**47803**
N68050	**DC-10**	**47804**
N68051	**DC-10**	**47805**
N68052	**DC-10**	**47806**
N68053	**DC-10**	**47807**
N68054	**DC-10**	**47808**
N68055	**DC-10**	**47809**
N68056	**DC-10**	**47810**
N68057	**DC-10**	**48264**
N68058	**DC-10**	**46705**
N68059	**DC-10**	**46907**
N68060	**DC-10**	**47850**
N68065	**DC-10**	**46590**
N68644	B727	18297
N68646	B720	18745
N68649	B727	18360
N68650	B727	18295
N68655	B707	18873
N68657	B707	19000
N68782	**B727**	**20637**
(N68903)	B767	27394
N69311	**B737**	**23362**
N69333	**B737**	**23571**
N69348	**B737**	**23586**
N69351	**B737**	**23589**
N69523	**DC-9**	**47520**
N69602	**B737**	**27315**
(N69602)	B737	27316
N69603	**B737**	**27316**
(N69603)	B737	27317
N69735	**B727**	**20665**
N69736	**B727**	**20666**
N69739	**B727**	**20668**
N69740	**B727**	**20669**
N69741	**B727**	**22250**
N69742	**B727**	**22251**
N69803	**MD-82**	**49229**
N69826	**MD-82**	**49486**
N70051	DC-8	45609
N70054	**A300**	**461**
N70072	**A300**	**515**
N70073	**A300**	**516**
N70074	**A300**	**517**
N70079	**A300**	**619**
N70330	**B737**	**23460**
N70352	**B737**	**23590**
N70353	**B737**	**23591**
N70401	**MD-82**	**49312**
N70404	**MD-82**	**49315**
N70425	**MD-82**	**49337**
N70504	**MD-82**	**49798**
N70524	**MD-82**	**49916**
N70529	**MD-82**	**49921**
N70542	**DC-9**	**47535**
N70611	1-11	083
N70700	**367-80**	**17158**
N70708	B727	19813
N70720	B737	21112
N70721	B737	21500
N70722	B737	21501
N70723	**B737**	**21739**
N70724	B737	21740
N70755	**B727**	**21366**
N70773	B707	17609
N70774	B707	17610
N70775	B707	17611
N70785	B707	17612
N70798	B707	17605
N71314	**B737**	**23365**
N71828	**MD-82**	**49488**
N72488	DC-8	45444
N72700	B727	18368
N72700	B727	18464
N72821	**MD-82**	**49481**
N72822	**MD-82**	**49482**
N72824	**MD-82**	**49484**
N72825	**MD-82**	**49485**
N72829	**MD-82**	**49489**
N72830	**MD-82**	**49490**
N72986	A300	154
N72987	A300	155
N72988	A300	216
N72990	A300	259
N73243	**B737**	**20072**
N73380	**B737**	**26309**
N73385	**B737**	**26314**

N73444	**MD-82**	**49470**
N73700	B737	19437
N73700	B737	22950
N73700	B737	23886
N73700	B737	24178
N73711	B737	20209
N73712	B737	20210
N73713	B737	20242
N73714	B737	19072
N73714	B737	19552
(N73714)	B737	20344
N73715	B737	19679
(N73715)	B737	20345
N73717	B737	19680
N73717	B737	20345
(N73717)	B737	20346
N73718	B737	20128
N73751	**B727**	**21247**
N74317	B727	20050
N74318	**B727**	**20051**
N74612	B707	18012
N74613	B707	17903
N74614	B707	17904
N74615	B707	17615
N74989	A300	220
N75356	B737	23838
N75429	B727	21427
N76073	**DC-10**	**46940**
N76200	**MD-83**	**53290**
N76201	**MD-83**	**53291**
N76202	**MD-83**	**53292**
N76354	**B737**	**23592**
N76355	**B737**	**23593**
N76360	B737	23941
N76361	B737	23942
N76362	B737	23943
(N76363)	B737	23944
N76752	**B727**	**21248**
N76753	**B727**	**21249**
N76823	**MD-82**	**49483**
N77080	**A300**	**626**
N77204	**B737**	**19021**
N77215	**B737**	**19032**
N77303	**B737**	**23354**
(N77364)	B737	23945
N77421	**MD-82**	**49333**
N77771	B777	27106
(N77771)	B777	27116
N77772	B747	19918
N77772	B777	27265
(N77772)	B777	26936
N77773	B747	19919
N77773	B777	27266
(N77773)	B777	26932
(N77774)	B777	26929
(N77775)	B777	26930
(N77776)	B777	26917
N77779	B777	27105
N77780	**B727**	**20635**
N77827	**MD-82**	**49487**
N78019	**B747**	**20527**
N78020	B747	19731
(N78365)	B737	23946
N79743	**B727**	**22252**
N79744	**B727**	**22253**
N79745	**B727**	**22448**
N79746	**B727**	**22449**
N79748	**B727**	**22450**
N79749	**B727**	**22451**
N79750	**B727**	**22452**
N79751	B727	21457
N79754	**B727**	**21363**
N79771	**B727**	**20840**
N80052	**A300**	**460**
N80057	**A300**	**465**
N80058	**A300**	**466**
N80084	**A300**	**675**
N80703	B707	17599
N81025	**L1011**	**1098**
N81026	**L1011**	**1104**
N81027	**L1011**	**1107**
N81028	**L1011**	**1108**
(N81826)	B727	19405
(N81827)	B727	19406
N81906	DC-8	45854
N82702	DC-9	47090

N83071	**DC-10**	**48293**
N83428	**B727**	**21426**
N83658	B707	18686
N83870	**MD-82**	**48056**
N83872	**MD-82**	**49120**
N83873	**MD-82**	**49121**
N84355	**B727**	**21987**
N84356	B727	21988
N84357	**B727**	**21989**
N84790	CV880	22-7-3-55
(N84905)	B767	27569
N86422	B727	21459
N86425	B727	21947
(N86425)	B727	21459
N86426	**B727**	**21364**
N86740	B707	20056
N86741	B707	20057
N87070	**DC-10**	**48292**
N87569	B737	21006
N87790	B727	20903
N88701	B727	19510
N88702	B727	19511
N88703	**B727**	**19512**
N88704	B727	19513
N88705	B727	19514
N88706	B727	19797
N88707	B727	19798
N88708	B727	19799
N88709	B727	19800
N88710	B727	19801
N88711	**B727**	**19802**
N88712	B727	19803
N88713	B727	19804
N88714	B727	20243
N88715	B727	20384
N88770	**B727**	**20839**
N88881	**A300**	**743**
N88931	B747	20798
N89427	**B727**	**21365**
N90070	**A300**	**513**
N90125	MD-81	53347
N90126	MD-87	53042
N90178	MD-11	48600
N90187	MD-11	48572
N90187	MD-11	48616
N90187	MD-11	48745
N90287	B707	17921
N90450	CV880	22-00-36
N90452	CV880	22-00-9
N90455	CV880	22-00-39
N90498	B707	17721
(N90498)	B707	17719
N90511	**MD-82**	**49805**
N90549	B767	23057
N90557	B727	18935
N90558	B727	18362
N90651	B707	17928
N91050	**A300**	**423**
N91392	**B727**	**18997**
(N91516)	MD-82	49893
N91566	MD-11	48559
N91566	MD-11	48571
N91891	B727	18741
(N92038)	B720	18792
N92874	**MD-82**	**49122**
N93101	B747	19667
N93102	B747	19668
N93103	B747	19669
N93104	**B747**	**19670**
N93105	**B747**	**19671**
N93106	B747	19672
N93107	**B747**	**19673**
N93108	**B747**	**19674**
N93109	**B747**	**19675**
(N93110)	B747	19676
(N93111)	B747	19677
(N93112)	B747	19678
N93113	B747	20080
N93114	B747	20081
N93115	B747	20320
N93117	**B747**	**20322**
N93118	B747	20082
N93119	**B747**	**20083**
N93134	B707	18067
N93135	B707	18069
N93136	B720	18165

N93137	B720	18250
N93138	B707	18245
N93141	B720	18061
N93142	B720	18062
N93143	B720	18063
N93144	B720	18167
N93145	B720	18451
N93146	B720	18452
N93147	B720	18453
N93148	B720	18588
N93149	B720	18589
N93150	B720	18590
N93151	B720	18749
N93152	B720	18818
N93153	B720	18820
N93738	**B727**	**20667**
N93875	**MD-82**	**49125**
N94280	CV990	30-10-12
N94284	CV880	22-00-43M
N94285	CV880	22-00-45M
N94314	**B727**	**20047**
N94454	DC-9	47291
N97891	B727	20113
N98876	**MD-82**	**49444**
N99548	B727	20512
N99763	**B727**	**20772**
N99862	DC-8	45303
N99890	B737	20693

Peru

OB-	**B737**	**19408**
(OB-)	B727	18744
(OB-)	B727	18844
(OB-)	B727	19243
(OB-)	B727	19501
OB-1018	**F-28**	**11065**
OB-1019	**F-28**	**11066**
OB-1141	B727	19312
OB-1210	DC-8	46142
OB-1222	**DC-8**	**45992**
OB-1244	**DC-8**	**45763**
OB-1248	DC-8	46027
OB-1249	DC-8	46132
OB-1256	B727	19305
OB-1260	**DC-8**	**46102**
OB-1267	**DC-8**	**45851**
OB-1268	**DC-8**	**45853**
OB-1277	B727	19400
OB-1287	DC-8	45759
OB-1288	**B737**	**19769**
OB-1296	**DC-8**	**45285**
OB-1300	**DC-8**	**45861**
OB-1301	**B727**	**20263**
OB-1303	B727	20266
OB-1314	B737	19425
OB-1316	**DC-8**	**45384**
OB-1317	**B737**	**19610**
OB-1323	DC-8	45953
OB-1344	**L1011**	**1002**
OB-1371	**B707**	**19575**
OB-1372	**DC-8**	**46078**
OB-1373	**DC-8**	**45984**
OB-1396	**F-28**	**11100**
OB-1400	**B707**	**19434**
OB-1401	**B707**	**18921**
OB-1407	DC-8	46038
OB-1421	DC-8	45752
OB-1438	DC-8	45985
OB-1451	B737	19072
OB-1452	**DC-8**	**46038**
OB-1456	DC-8	45272
OB-1465	**B727**	**18845**
OB-1476	**B737**	**20492**
OB-1485	**AN-72**	
OB-1486	**AN-72**	
OB-1487	AN-72	
OB-1489	**TU134**	**1351203**
OB-1490	TU134	60525
OB-1492	**TU134**	
OB-1493	**B737**	**19712**
OB-1504	**L1011**	**1087**
OB-1511	**B737**	**20277**
OB-1512	B727	19499
OB-1512	B727	20525

OB-1533	B727	19836
OB-1536	B737	20128
OB-1537	B727	21071
OB-1538	**B737**	**21206**
OB-1541	**B727**	**21072**
OB-1543	B727	18846
OB-1544	**B737**	**20956**
OB-1545	**L1011**	**1075**
OB-1546	**B727**	**19150**
OB-1547	**B727**	**19151**
OB-1548	**B727**	**19152**
OB-1552	TU134	60215
OB-1553	**TU134**	**60206**
(OB-1555)	TU134	60215
OB-1559	YAK40	9..0950
OB-1560	**B727**	**20903**
OB-1561	B737	19059
OB-1568	**YAK40**	
OB-1569	YAK40	
OB-1570	**B727**	**19153**
OB-1572	**B737**	**19714**
OB-1573	**B727**	**20728**
OB-1588	**B727**	**18942**
OB-1590	**B727**	**22164**
OB-1592	**B707**	**20301**
OB-1596	A300	204
OB-1601	**B727**	**18943**
OB-1611	**A300**	**216**
OB-1618	**DC-8**	**46132**
OB-1619	**B737**	**19616**
OB-1620	**B737**	**19615**
OB-1631	**A300**	**154**
OB-1634	**A300**	**259**
OB-1635	**B737**	**19554**
OB-1636	**F-28**	**11009**
OB-1637	**B737**	**19059**
OB-OAG-728	CV990	30-10-5
(OB-R-)	B737	19611
OB-R-231	F-28	11035
OB-R-390	F-28	11032
OB-R-397	F-28	11059
OB-R-398	F-28	11065
OB-R-399	F-28	11066
OB-R-728	CV990	30-10-5
OB-R-765	CV990	30-10-2
OB-R-902	B727	19846
OB-R-925	CV990	30-10-24
OB-R-931	DC-8	45619
OB-R-953	1-11	BAC.239
OB-R-962	DC-8	45629
OB-R-1018	F-28	11065
OB-R-1019	F-28	11066
OB-R-1020	F-28	11059
OB-R-1030	F-28	11032
OB-R-1080	1-11	BAC.241
OB-R-1081	B727	18269
OB-R-1083	DC-8	45768
OB-R-1084	DC-8	45879
OB-R-1115	B727	18897
OB-R-1115	B727	19115
OB-R-1116	DC-8	45629
OB-R-1123	DC-8	45760
OB-R-1124	DC-8	45648
OB-R-1125	DC-8	45643
OB-R-1135	B727	19506
OB-R1137	1-11	BAC.193
OB-R-1141	B727	19312
OB-R-1142	DC-8	45612
OB-R-1143	DC-8	45598
OB-R-1173	1-11	BAC.193
OB-R-1181	DC-8	45760
OB-R-1200	DC-8	45882
OB-R-1205	DC-8	45442
OB-R-1210	DC-8	46142
OB-R-1214	DC-8	45600
OB-R-1222	DC-8	45992
OB-R-1223	**DC-8**	**45420**
OB-R-1243	B707	19375
OB-R-1248	DC-8	46027
OB-R-1249	DC-8	46132
OB-R-1256	B727	19305
OB-R-1259	DC-8	45659
OB-R-1260	DC-8	46102
OB-R-1263	B737	20449
OB-R-1267	DC-8	45851
OB-R-1268	DC-8	45853
OB-R-1269	**DC-8**	**45852**
OB-R-1270	DC-8	45757
OB-R-1277	B727	19400
OB-R-1287	DC-8	45759
OB-R-1288	B737	19769
OB-R-1296	DC-8	45285
OB-R-1300	DC-8	45861
OB-R-1301	B727	20263
OB-R-1303	B727	20266
OB-R-1314	B737	19425
OB-R-1317	B737	19610
OB-R-1323	DC-8	45953
OB-T-1244	DC-8	45763
OB-T-1264	B707	19294
OB-T-1316	DC-8	45384

Lebanon

(OD-ADK)	COMET	6445
OD-ADQ	COMET	6446
OD-ADR	COMET	6445
OD-ADS	COMET	6448
OD-ADT	COMET	6450
OD-ADY	CRVL	83
OD-ADZ	CRVL	51
OD-AEE	CRVL	153
OD-AEF	CRVL	157
OD-AEM	CRVL	23
OD-AEO	CRVL	174
OD-AEV	COMET	6414
OD-AEW	CV990	30-10-31
OD-AEX	CV990	30-10-10
OD-AFA	VC-10	803
OD-AFB	B707	20224
OD-AFC	B707	20225
OD-AFD	**B707**	**20259**
OD-AFE	**B707**	**20260**
OD-AFF	CV990	30-10-18
OD-AFG	CV990	30-10-30
OD-AFH	CV990	30-10-25
OD-AFI	CV990	30-10-35
OD-AFJ	CV990	30-10-33
OD-AFK	CV990	30-10-26
OD-AFL	B720	18034
OD-AFM	B720	18027
OD-AFN	B720	18030
OD-AFO	B720	18035
OD-AFP	B720	18017
OD-AFQ	B720	18024
OD-AFR	B720	18018
OD-AFS	B720	18019
OD-AFT	B720	18020
OD-AFU	B720	18029
OD-AFW	B720	18026
OD-AFX	B707	19107
OD-AFY	B707	19108
OD-AFZ	B720	18025
OD-AGB	B720	18021
OD-AGC	B747	20391
OD-AGD	**B707**	**18939**
OD-AGE	B720	18963
OD-AGF	**B720**	**18830**
OD-AGG	B720	18828
OD-AGH	B747	21097
OD-AGI	B747	21098
OD-AGJ	B747	21099
OD-AGM	B747	20390
OD-AGN	B707	18938
OD-AGO	**B707**	**19269**
OD-AGP	**B707**	**19274**
OD-AGQ	B720	19160
OD-AGR	B720	19161
OD-AGS	**B707**	**19214**
OD-AGT	B707	19213
OD-AGU	**B707**	**19966**
OD-AGV	**B707**	**19967**
OD-AGW	B707	19440
OD-AGX	**B707**	**19104**
OD-AGY	**B707**	**19105**
OD-AGZ	B707	19531
OD-AHB	B707	19588
OD-AHC	**B707**	**19589**
OD-AHD	**B707**	**19515**
OD-AHE	**B707**	**19516**
OD-AHF	**B707**	**20170**
(OD-APA)	B707	19590

Austria

OE-	**F-70**	**11587**
(OE-BRL)	146	E1002
(OE-FGW)	B737	23601
OE-IBO	DC-8	46088
OE-IDA	B707	20043
OE-IEB	B707	18339
OE-ILC	1-11	BAC.255
OE-ILD	1-11	BAC.256
(OE-ILD)	DC-10	47870
OE-ILE	B737	22023
OE-ILF	**B737**	**23601**
OE-ILG	**B737**	**24081**
OE-INA	B707	18069
OE-IRA	B707	18068
OE-LAA	**A310**	**489**
(OE-LAA)	A310	387
(OE-LAA)	B767	23765
OE-LAB	**A310**	**492**
OE-LAC	**A310**	**568**
OE-LAD	**A310**	**624**
OE-LAG	**A340**	**075**
OE-LAH	**A340**	**081**
(OE-LAI)	A310	396
OE-LAS	**B767**	**27909**
OE-LAT	B767	25273
OE-LAU	**B767**	**23765**
OE-LAV	B767	24628
OE-LAW	**B767**	**26417**
OE-LAX	**B767**	**27095**
OE-LBA	**A321**	**0552**
OE-LBA	B707	18374
OE-LBB	**A321**	**0570**
OE-LBC	**A321**	**0581**
OE-LC.	**RJ100**	**7142**
OE-LCA	CRVL	161
OE-LCE	CRVL	156
OE-LCF	**RJ100**	**7094**
OE-LCG	**RJ100**	**7103**
OE-LCH	RJ100	7110
OE-LCI	CRVL	166
OE-LCK	RJ100	7133
OE-LCO	CRVL	167
OE-LCU	CRVL	136
OE-LDA	DC-9	47521
OE-LDB	DC-9	47524
OE-LDC	DC-9	47520
OE-LDD	DC-9	47539
OE-LDE	DC-9	47531
OE-LDF	DC-9	47458
OE-LDG	DC-9	47484
OE-LDH	DC-9	47555
OE-LDI	DC-9	47559
OE-LDK	DC-9	47651
OE-LDL	DC-9	47652
OE-LDM	DC-9	47726
OE-LDN	DC-9	47735
OE-LDO	DC-9	47756
OE-LDP	**MD-81**	**48015**
OE-LDR	**MD-81**	**48016**
OE-LDS	**MD-81**	**48017**
OE-LDT	**MD-81**	**48018**
OE-LDU	**MD-81**	**48019**
OE-LDV	**MD-81**	**48020**
OE-LDW	**MD-81**	**48059**
OE-LDX	**MD-82**	**48021**
OE-LDY	**MD-82**	**49115**
OE-LDZ	**MD-82**	**49164**
OE-LFG	**F-70**	**11549**
OE-LFH	**F-70**	**11554**
OE-LFK	**F-70**	**11555**
OE-LFO	**F-70**	**11559**
OE-LFP	**F-70**	**11560**
OE-LFQ	**F-70**	**11568**
OE-LFR	**F-70**	**11572**
OE-LMA	**MD-82**	**49278**
OE-LMB	**MD-82**	**49279**
OE-LMC	**MD-82**	**49372**
OE-LMD	**MD-83**	**49933**
OE-LME	**MD-83**	**53377**
OE-LMK	**MD-87**	**49411**
OE-LML	**MD-87**	**49412**
OE-LMM	**MD-87**	**49413**
OE-LMN	**MD-87**	**49414**
OE-LMO	**MD-87**	**49888**
OE-LNH	**B737**	**25147**
OE-LNI	**B737**	**27094**
OE-LRA	**RJ100**	**7032**
OE-LRB	**RJ100**	**7033**
OE-LRC	RJ100	7036
OE-LRD	**RJ100**	**7052**
OE-LRE	**RJ100**	**7059**
OE-LRF	**RJ100**	**7061**
OE-LRG	**RJ100**	**7063**
OE-LYM	MD-82	48022
OE-UNA	B707	18069
OE-URA	B707	18068

Finland

OH-KDM	DC-8	45628
OH-KSA	B747	20117
OH-LAA	**A300**	**299**
OH-LAB	**A300**	**302**
OH-LEA	CRVL	21
OH-LEB	CRVL	22
OH-LEC	CRVL	27
OH-LED	CRVL	116
OH-LER	CRVL	162
OH-LFR	DC-8	46013
OH-LFS	DC-8	46043
OH-LFT	DC-8	46013
OH-LFV	DC-8	46043
OH-LFY	DC-8	46130
OH-LFZ	DC-8	45987
OH-LGA	**MD-11**	**48449**
OH-LGB	**MD-11**	**48450**
OH-LGC	**MD-11**	**48512**
OH-LGD	**MD-11**	**48513**
OH-LHA	**DC-10**	**47956**
OH-LHB	DC-10	47957
(OH-LHC)	DC-10	48265
OH-LHD	DC-10	47865
OH-LHE	DC-10	46978
OH-LMA	**MD-87**	**49403**
OH-LMB	**MD-87**	**49404**
OH-LMC	**MD-87**	**49405**
(OH-LMD)	MD-87	49406
(OH-LME)	MD-83	49407
(OH-LMF)	MD-87	49408
OH-LMG	**MD-83**	**49625**
(OH-LMG)	MD-87	49409
OH-LMH	**MD-83**	**53245**
(OH-LMH)	MD-87	49410
OH-LMN	**MD-82**	**49150**
OH-LMO	**MD-82**	**49151**
OH-LMP	**MD-82**	**49152**
OH-LMR	**MD-83**	**49284**
OH-LMS	**MD-83**	**49252**
OH-LMT	**MD-82**	**49877**
OH-LMU	**MD-83**	**49741**
OH-LMV	**MD-83**	**49904**
OH-LMW	**MD-82**	**49905**
OH-LMX	**MD-82**	**49906**
OH-LMY	**MD-82**	**53244**
OH-LMZ	**MD-82**	**53246**
OH-LNA	DC-9	47603
OH-LNB	**DC-9**	**47604**
OH-LNC	**DC-9**	**47613**
OH-LND	**DC-9**	**47606**
OH-LNE	**DC-9**	**47605**
OH-LNF	**DC-9**	**47614**
OH-LPA	**MD-82**	**49900**
OH-LPB	**MD-83**	**49966**
OH-LPC	MD-83	49965
OH-LSA	CRVL	181
OH-LSB	CRVL	182
OH-LSC	CRVL	185
OH-LSD	CRVL	187
OH-LSE	CRVL	189
OH-LSF	CRVL	188
OH-LSG	CRVL	169
OH-LSH	CRVL	211
OH-LSI	CRVL	259
OH-LSK	CRVL	212
OH-LYA	DC-9	45713
OH-LYB	DC-9	45712
OH-LYC	DC-9	45711
OH-LYD	DC-9	45725
OH-LYE	DC-9	45729
OH-LYG	DC-9	45730
OH-LYH	DC-9	47044

OH-LYI	DC-9	47045
OH-LYK	DC-9	45841
OH-LYN	**DC-9**	**47694**
OH-LYO	**DC-9**	**47695**
OH-LYP	**DC-9**	**47696**
OH-LYR	**DC-9**	**47736**
OH-LYS	**DC-9**	**47737**
OH-LYT	**DC-9**	**47738**
OH-LYU	**DC-9**	**47771**
OH-LYV	**DC-9**	**47772**
OH-LYW	**DC-9**	**47773**
OH-LYX	**DC-9**	**48134**
OH-LYY	**DC-9**	**48135**
OH-LYZ	**DC-9**	**48136**
OH-SOA	DC-8	45606
OH-SOB	DC-8	45602

Czech Republic

OK-020	**YAK40**	**9431436**
OK-0420	TU154	420
OK-9522	**TU134**	**2351602**
OK-ABD	**IL-62**	**10902**
OK-AFA	TU134	1351406
OK-AFB	**TU134**	**1351410**
OK-AFD	TU134	1351407
OK-BYA	TU154	420
OK-BYB	TU154	488
OK-BYC	TU154	517
OK-BYD	TU154	601
OK-BYE	YAK40	9440338
OK-BYF	YAK40	9230823
OK-BYG	YAK40	9230723
OK-BYH	YAK40	9321128
OK-BYI	YAK40	9321028
OK-BYJ	**YAK40**	**9821257**
OK-BYK	**YAK40**	**9940260**
OK-BYL	YAK40	9940560
OK-BYO	TU154	803
OK-BYP	TU154	858
OK-BYQ	TU134	1351409
OK-BYR	TU134	1351408
OK-BYS	TU134	1351503
OK-BYT	TU134	49858
OK-BYV	IL-62	41805
OK-BYV	IL-62	3850145
OK-BYW	IL-62	4037425
OK-BYZ	IL-62	2647737
OK-BYZ	**TU154**	**1016**
OK-CFC	TU134	2351504
OK-CFD	TU134	2351505
OK-CFE	TU134	2351602
OK-CFF	**TU134**	**2351603**
OK-CFG	TU134	2351710
OK-CFH	**TU134**	**2351801**
OK-DBE	**IL-62**	**31501**
OK-DBF	IL-62	31502
OK-DFI	TU134	3351908
OK-DHA	**YAK40**	**9341230**
OK-EBG	IL-62	41602
OK-EEA	YAK40	9431436
OK-EEB	YAK40	9431536
OK-EEC	YAK40	9440737
OK-EED	YAK40	9440837
OK-EEF	YAK40	9440937
OK-EEG	YAK40	9441037
OK-EFJ	TU134	4323128
OK-EFK	TU134	4323130
OK-EGK	B727	21021
OK-EXB	YAK40	9431436
OK-FBF	**IL-62**	**41805**
OK-FEH	YAK40	9510340
OK-FEI	YAK40	9510440
OK-FEJ	YAK40	9510540
OK-GBH	**IL-62**	**62404**
OK-GEK	YAK40	9641050
OK-GEL	**YAK40**	**9640651**
OK-GEM	YAK40	9640851
OK-GEN	YAK40	9641251
OK-GEO	**YAK40**	**9641451**
OK-HEP	**YAK40**	**9730555**
OK-HEQ	**YAK40**	**9741056**
OK-HER	**YAK40**	**9741156**
OK-HFL	**TU134**	**7349913**
OK-HFM	**TU134**	**7360142**
OK-IFN	**TU134**	**8360282**
OK-JBI	**IL-62**	**2932748**
OK-JBJ	**IL-62**	**4933456**
OK-JGY	**B727**	**21623**
OK-KBK	**IL-62**	**1035435**
OK-KBN	**IL-62**	**4037425**
OK-LCP	TU154	488
OK-LCS	TU154	517
OK-LDA	**TU104**	**76600503**
OK-LDB	TU104	76600601
OK-LDC	**TU104**	**76600602**
OK-MDE	TU104	86601202
OK-NDD	TU104	96601803
OK-NDF	**TU104**	**9350801**
OK-OBL	**IL-62**	**4445032**
OK-PBM	IL-62	1545951
OK-RBZ	IL-62	2647737
OK-SCA	TU154	765
OK-TCB	TU154	770
OK-TCC	TU154	789
OK-TCD	**TU154**	**792**
OK-TEA	TU124	4351503
OK-TEB	TU124	4351504
OK-TGX	**B727**	**18798**
OK-UCE	**TU154**	**804**
OK-UCF	**TU154**	**807**
OK-UEC	TU124	5351607
(OK-UGA)	B727	18443
OK-UGZ	B727	18444
OK-VCG	**TU154**	**838**
OK-VCP	**TU154**	**858**
OK-WAA	**A310**	**564**
OK-WAB	**A310**	**567**
OK-WGF	**B737**	**24903**
OK-WGG	**B737**	**24693**
OK-XFJ	B707	19570
OK-XGA	**B737**	**26539**
OK-XGB	**B737**	**26540**
OK-XGC	**B737**	**26541**
OK-XGD	**B737**	**26542**
OK-XGE	**B737**	**26543**
OK-YBA	**IL-62**	**90602**
OK-YBB	**IL-62**	**90603**
OK-ZBC	IL-62	00701

Slovakia

OM-BYE	**YAK40**	**9440338**
OM-BYL	**YAK40**	**9940560**
OM-BYO	**TU154**	**803**
OM-CHD	**B727**	**20526**
OM-GAT	**TU134**	**48565**
OM-UFB	B707	18839
OM-WFA	B707	19335

Belgium

OO-ABA	B707	18746
OO-ABB	B737	21359
OO-AMI	DC-8	45376
OO-ATJ	B727	19011
(OO-BAI)	B707	18746
(OO-BTA)	B737	24020
(OO-BTB)	B737	24021
(OO-BTC)	B737	24022
(OO-BTD)	B737	24023
(OO-BTE)	B737	24024
OO-CAH	**B727**	**22609**
OO-CDE	B707	19590
OO-CMB	DC-8	45382
OO-CVA	CRVL	97
OO-CYE	B737	23787
OO-DHM	**B727**	**20114**
OO-DHN	**B727**	**20113**
OO-DHO	**B727**	**20112**
OO-DHP	**B727**	**19166**
OO-DHQ	**B727**	**19167**
OO-DHR	**B727**	**19834**
OO-DHS	**B727**	**20189**
OO-DHT	**B727**	**19489**
OO-DHU	**B727**	**20992**
OO-DHV	**B727**	**21084**
OO-DHW	**B727**	**20993**
OO-DHX	**B727**	**20994**
OO-DJA	**F-28**	**11163**
OO-DJB	**F-28**	**11184**
OO-DJC	**146**	**E2069**
(OO-DJC)	F-28	11092
OO-DJD	146	E2077
OO-DJE	**146**	**E2164**
OO-DJF	**146**	**E2167**
OO-DJG	**146**	**E2180**
OO-DJH	**146**	**E2172**
OO-DJJ	**146**	**E2196**
OO-DJK	**146**	**E2271**
OO-DJL	**146**	**E2273**
OO-DJN	**146**	**E2275**
OO-DJO	**146**	**E2279**
(OO-DJY)	146	E2069
(OO-DJZ)	146	E2077
OO-DTD	**146**	**E2077**
(OO-HVA)	DC-10	46891
OO-IID	B737	24255
(OO-IIE)	B737	23748
OO-ILF	B737	23401
OO-ILG	B737	23388
OO-ILH	B737	24234
OO-ILI	B757	24528
OO-ILJ	**B737**	**25262**
OO-ILK	**B737**	**23766**
OO-ING	A300	66
OO-JAA	B727	18951
OO-JOT	**DC-10**	**46850**
OO-LLS	**B727**	**22608**
OO-LRM	**DC-10**	**46998**
OO-LTA	B737	24020
OO-LTB	B737	24021
OO-LTC	B737	24022
OO-LTD	B737	24376
(OO-LTD)	B737	24023
OO-LTE	B737	24377
(OO-LTE)	B737	24024
OO-LTF	B737	25015
(OO-LTF)	B737	24376
OO-LTG	B737	25016
(OO-LTG)	B737	24377
(OO-LTH)	B737	24413
(OO-LTH)	B737	25017
(OO-LTI)	B737	24414
OO-LTJ	**B737**	**25039**
OO-LTK	B737	25040
OO-LTL	**B737**	**25041**
OO-LTM	**B737**	**25070**
OO-LTN	B737	25071
OO-LTO	B737	25011
OO-LTP	**B737**	**25032**
OO-LTQ	**B737**	**25844**
OO-LTR	B737	25116
OO-LTS	**B737**	**25860**
OO-LTT	B737	24708
OO-LTU	**B737**	**27455**
OO-LTV	**B737**	**23924**
OO-LTW	**B737**	**25010**
OO-LTX	B737	24131
OO-LTY	**B737**	**23925**
OO-MKO	A300	65
OO-NJE	**146**	**E2192**
OO-PHA	DC-8	45854
OO-PHC	B737	20221
OO-PHE	B737	19424
OO-PHF	B737	19549
OO-PHG	B737	19554
OO-PHN	**DC-10**	**46554**
OO-PLH	B737	20128
OO-PS1	B707	19378
OO-PSA	B707	19378
OO-PSI	B707	19378
OO-RVM	B737	22453
OO-SBJ	**B737**	**24573**
OO-SBM	**B737**	**25729**
OO-SBN	**B737**	**23979**
OO-SBQ	**B737**	**21596**
OO-SBQ	CRVL	123
OO-SBR	B707	17921
OO-SBS	B737	21839
OO-SBT	**B737**	**21840**
OO-SBU	B707	19442
OO-SBW	B707	17930
OO-SBY	**B767**	**27310**
OO-SBZ	**B737**	**23775**
OO-SCA	**A310**	**303**
OO-SCB	**A310**	**313**
OO-SCC	**A310**	**437**
OO-SCI	A310	331
OO-SDA	**B737**	**20907**
OO-SDB	B737	20908
OO-SDC	B737	20909
OO-SDD	B737	20910
OO-SDE	**B737**	**20911**
OO-SDF	**B737**	**20912**
OO-SDG	**B737**	**21135**
(OO-SDG)	B737	20913
OO-SDH	B737	20914
OO-SDJ	**B737**	**20915**
OO-SDK	**B737**	**20916**
OO-SDL	**B737**	**21136**
OO-SDM	**B737**	**21137**
OO-SDN	**B737**	**21176**
OO-SDO	**B737**	**21177**
OO-SDP	**B737**	**21139**
(OO-SDQ)	B737	21138
OO-SDR	**B737**	**21738**
OO-SDV	**B737**	**23771**
OO-SDW	**B737**	**23772**
OO-SDX	**B737**	**23773**
OO-SDY	**B737**	**23774**
OO-SGA	B747	20401
OO-SGB	B747	20402
OO-SGC	**B747**	**23439**
OO-SGD	**B747**	**24837**
OO-SJA	B707	17623
OO-SJB	B707	17624
OO-SJC	B707	17625
OO-SJD	B707	17626
OO-SJE	B707	17627
OO-SJF	B707	18374
OO-SJG	B707	18460
(OO-SJG)	B707	18375
OO-SJH	B707	18890
OO-SJJ	B707	19162
OO-SJK	B707	19211
OO-SJL	B707	19996
OO-SJM	B707	20198
OO-SJN	B707	20199
OO-SJO	B707	20200
OO-SJP	B707	17686
OO-SJR	B707	19706
OO-SLA	DC-10	47906
OO-SLB	DC-10	47907
OO-SLC	DC-10	47908
OO-SLD	DC-10	47835
OO-SLE	DC-10	47836
OO-SLF	A340	010
OO-SLG	A340	014
OO-SLG	**DC-10**	**47926**
OO-SLH	**DC-10**	**47927**
(OO-SQA)	B737	24355
(OO-SQB)	B737	24356
OO-SRA	**CRVL**	**64**
OO-SRB	CRVL	65
OO-SRC	CRVL	66
OO-SRD	CRVL	69
OO-SRE	CRVL	67
OO-SRF	CRVL	76
OO-SRG	CRVL	70
OO-SRH	CRVL	78
OO-SRI	CRVL	175
OO-SRK	CRVL	196
OO-STA	B727	19400
OO-STB	B727	19402
OO-STC	B727	19401
OO-STD	B727	19403
OO-STE	B727	19987
OO-STF	**B767**	**27212**
OO-SYA	**B737**	**24355**
OO-SYB	**B737**	**24356**
OO-SYC	**B737**	**25226**
OO-SYD	**B737**	**25247**
OO-SYE	**B737**	**25218**
OO-SYF	**B737**	**25248**
OO-SYG	**B737**	**25249**
OO-SYH	**B737**	**25418**
OO-SYI	**B737**	**25419**
OO-SYJ	**B737**	**26537**
OO-SYK	**B737**	**26538**
(OO-SYL)	B737	26539

(OO-SYM)	B737	26540
(OO-SYN)	B737	26541
(OO-SYO)	B737	26542
(OO-SYP)	B737	26543
OO-TBI	B757	25133
OO-TCP	DC-8	45265
OO-TEA	B720	18155
OO-TEB	B720	18043
OO-TEC	B707	17659
OO-TED	B707	17665
OO-TEE	B707	17666
OO-TEF	**A300**	**02**
OO-TEG	A300	17
OO-TEH	B737	21231
OO-TEJ	B737	21131
OO-TEK	B737	21719
OO-TEL	B737	21736
OO-TEM	B737	21735
OO-TEN	B737	21955
OO-TEO	B737	22090
(OO-TEZ)	B737	20908
OO-TJN	B727	19011
OO-TJO	A300	204
OO-TYA	B720	18384
OO-TYB	B737	21359
(OO-TYB)	B707	18832
OO-TYC	B707	19291
OO-TYD	B737	21774
OO-VDO	B737	24915
OO-VGM	**B720**	**18073**
OO-XTG	B737	25016
OO-YCK	B707	19621
OO-YCL	B707	19622

Denmark

OY-	**B737**	**25033**
OY-	**B737**	**28128**
OY-	**B737**	**28129**
OY-	**B737**	**28130**
OY-	**B737**	**28131**
OY-ANI	CV990	30-10-25
OY-ANL	CV990	30-10-36
OY-APA	B737	28083
OY-APB	B737	28084
OY-APG	B737	21278
OY-APH	B737	21279
OY-API	B737	21528
OY-APJ	B737	21685
OY-APK	B737	21686
OY-APL	B737	22070
OY-APN	B737	22071
(OY-APN)	B720	18421
OY-APO	B737	22072
(OY-APO)	B720	18422
OY-APP	B737	22406
(OY-APP)	B720	18384
OY-APR	B737	22407
OY-APS	B737	22408
OY-APU	B720	18792
OY-APV	B720	18793
OY-APW	B720	18422
OY-APY	B720	18421
OY-APZ	B720	18384
OY-ASA	VFW614G-008	
OY-BRM	F-28	11143
OY-BRN	F-28	11151
OY-CNA	**A300**	**79**
OY-CND	**A320**	**0163**
OY-CNE	**A320**	**0164**
OY-CNF	**A320**	**0168**
OY-CNG	**A320**	**0169**
OY-CNH	**A320**	**0179**
OY-CNI	**A320**	**0193**
OY-CNK	**A300**	**94**
OY-CNL	**A300**	**128**
OY-CNT	**DC-10**	**47833**
OY-CNU	**DC-10**	**47832**
OY-CNY	**DC-10**	**46983**
OY-CRG	**146**	**E2075**
OY-CTA	DC-9	47655
OY-CTB	DC-9	47657
OY-CTD	DC-9	47658
OY-DSK	B720	18157
OY-DSL	B720	18159
OY-DSM	B720	18161
OY-DSP	**B720**	**18241**
OY-DSR	B720	18243
OY-KAA	A300	122
OY-KDA	DC-10	46870
OY-KDB	DC-10	46933
OY-KDC	DC-10	46959
OY-KDH	**B767**	**24358**
OY-KDI	B767	24475
OY-KDK	B767	24476
OY-KDL	**B767**	**24477**
OY-KDM	**B767**	**25088**
OY-KDN	**B767**	**24848**
OY-KDO	**B767**	**24849**
(OY-KFA)	B747	20121
OY-KGA	DC-9	47115
OY-KGB	DC-9	47178
OY-KGC	DC-9	47286
OY-KGD	DC-9	47302
OY-KGE	DC-9	47305
OY-KGF	**DC-9**	**47308**
OY-KGG	DC-9	47395
OY-KGH	DC-9	47493
OY-KGI	DC-9	47494
OY-KGK	DC-9	47510
OY-KGL	**DC-9**	**47597**
OY-KGM	**DC-9**	**47624**
OY-KGN	**DC-9**	**47628**
OY-KGO	**DC-9**	**47632**
OY-KGP	**DC-9**	**47646**
OY-KGR	**DC-9**	**47725**
OY-KGS	**DC-9**	**47766**
OY-KGT	**MD-82**	**49380**
OY-KGU	DC-9	47110
OY-KGW	DC-9	47113
OY-KGY	**MD-81**	**49420**
OY-KGZ	**MD-81**	**49381**
OY-KHA	B747	20121
(OY-KHB)	B747	22381
OY-KHC	**MD-81**	**49436**
(OY-KHD)	MD-81	49555
OY-KHE	MD-82	49604
OY-KHF	**MD-87**	**49609**
OY-KHG	**MD-81**	**49613**
OY-KHI	**MD-87**	**49614**
OY-KHK	**MD-81**	**49910**
(OY-KHK)	MD-87	49610
OY-KHL	**MD-81**	**49911**
OY-KHM	**MD-81**	**49914**
OY-KHN	**MD-81**	**53000**
OY-KHO	MD-81	53003
OY-KHP	**MD-81**	**53007**
OY-KHR	**MD-81**	**53275**
OY-KHS	**MD-81**	**53001**
(OY-KHS)	MD-87	53010
OY-KHT	**MD-82**	**53296**
OY-KHU	**MD-81**	**53336**
OY-KHW	**MD-81**	**53348**
(OY-KHY)	MD-82	53412
(OY-KHZ)	MD-82	53414
OY-KIA	**DC-9**	**47301**
OY-KIB	DC-9	47307
OY-KIC	DC-9	47361
OY-KID	**DC-9**	**47360**
OY-KIE	**DC-9**	**47306**
OY-KIF	DC-9	47303
OY-KIG	**MD-81**	**48006**
OY-KIH	**MD-81**	**48007**
OY-KII	**MD-81**	**48008**
OY-KRA	CRVL	6
OY-KRB	CRVL	14
OY-KRC	CRVL	29
OY-KRD	**CRVL**	**47**
OY-KRE	CRVL	49
OY-KRF	CRVL	170
OY-KRG	CRVL	191
OY-KTA	DC-8	45384
OY-KTB	DC-8	45387
OY-KTC	DC-8	45804
OY-KTD	DC-8	45906
OY-KTE	DC-8	45922
OY-KTF	DC-8	46041
OY-KTG	DC-8	46093
OY-KTH	DC-8	46097
(OY-KVA)	CV990	30-10-5
(OY-KVA)	CV990	30-10-14
(OY-KVA)	CV990	30-10-17
OY-MAA	B737	24778
OY-MAB	B737	24805
OY-MAC	**B737**	**24859**
OY-MAD	**B737**	**24928**
OY-MAE	**B737**	**25066**
OY-MAK	B737	26440
OY-MAL	B737	26441
OY-MAM	B737	26442
OY-MAN	B737	27061
OY-MAO	B737	27336
OY-MAP	B737	27337
OY-MAR	**B737**	**27833**
OY-MAS	**B737**	**27834**
OY-MAT	**B737**	**27924**
OY-MAU	**B737**	**27925**
OY-MBK	B737	24911
OY-MBL	B737	25190
OY-MBV	B737	22735
OY-MBW	B737	22734
OY-MBZ	B737	22733
OY-MMD	B737	24569
OY-MME	B737	24570
OY-MMF	B737	24571
OY-MMK	B737	23331
OY-MML	B737	23332
OY-MMM	B737	23717
OY-MMN	B737	23718
OY-MMO	B737	24219
OY-MMO	B737	24569
(OY-MMO)	B737	24928
OY-MMP	B737	24220
OY-MMR	B737	24221
OY-MMW	B737	25125
(OY-MMW)	B737	24778
OY-MMY	**B737**	**25150**
(OY-MMY)	B737	24805
OY-MMZ	**B737**	**25360**
(OY-MMZ)	B737	24859
OY-SAA	CRVL	270
OY-SAB	CRVL	271
OY-SAC	CRVL	269
OY-SAD	CRVL	272
OY-SAE	CRVL	273
OY-SAF	CRVL	275
OY-SAG	CRVL	276
OY-SAH	CRVL	88
OY-SAJ	CRVL	104
OY-SAK	CRVL	99
OY-SAL	CRVL	89
OY-SAM	CRVL	95
OY-SAN	CRVL	98
OY-SAO	CRVL	101
OY-SAP	CRVL	90
OY-SAR	CRVL	103
OY-SAS	B727	20765
OY-SAT	B727	20766
OY-SAU	**B727**	**20764**
OY-SAY	CRVL	255
OY-SAZ	CRVL	263
OY-SBA	B727	20706
OY-SBB	B727	20707
OY-SBC	B727	21438
OY-SBD	B727	21676
OY-SBE	B727	22079
OY-SBF	B727	22080
OY-SBG	B727	22574
OY-SBH	B727	22164
OY-SBI	B727	23052
OY-SBJ	B727	21040
OY-SBK	DC-8	45923
OY-SBL	DC-8	46054
OY-SBM	DC-8	45924
OY-SBN	**B727**	**22163**
OY-SBO	**B727**	**22770**
OY-SBP	B727	21080
OY-SBV	CRVL	91
OY-SBW	CRVL	93
OY-SBY	CRVL	94
OY-SBZ	CRVL	114
OY-SCA	B727	20739
OY-SCB	B727	22536
OY-SCC	**B727**	**21945**
OY-SHA	B757	25155
OY-SHB	B757	25220
OY-SHE	B757	24135
OY-SHF	B757	24136
OY-SHI	B757	24137
OY-STA	CRVL	183
OY-STB	CRVL	186
OY-STC	CRVL	212
OY-STD	**CRVL**	**238**
OY-STE	CRVL	249
OY-STF	CRVL	257
OY-STG	CRVL	259
OY-STH	**CRVL**	**262**
OY-STI	CRVL	265
OY-STK	CRVL	266
OY-STL	CRVL	267
OY-STM	CRVL	268
OY-TOR	VFW614G-004	
OY-UPA	B727	19233
OY-UPD	**B727**	**19103**
OY-UPJ	**B727**	**19102**
OY-UPM	**B727**	**19229**
OY-UPS	**B727**	**19232**
OY-UPT	**B727**	**19094**

North Korea

885	IL-62	3933913
P-551	**TU154**	**129**
P-552	**TU154**	**143**
P-553	**TU154**	**191**
P-561	TU154	584?
P-618	**IL-62**	**2546624**
P-813	**TU134**	
P-814	**TU134**	
P-880?	**IL-62**	**41.5.**
P-881	**IL-62**	**3647853**
P-882	**IL-62**	**2850236**
P-885	**IL-62**	**3933913**
P-912	**IL-76**	**1003403104**
P-913	**IL-76**	**1003404126**
P-914	**IL-76**	**1003404146**

Netherlands

PH-	F-100	11496
PH-	F-100	11508
PH-	F-100	11510
PH-	F-100	11524
PH-	F-100	11525
PH-	F-100	11526
PH-	F-100	11530
PH-	F-70	11571
PH-	F-70	11576
PH-	F-70	11577
PH-	F-70	11578
PH-	F-70	11579
PH-	F-70	11580
PH-	F-70	11581
PH-	F-70	11583
PH-	F-70	11584
PH-	F-70	11585
PH-	F-70	11586
PH-	F-70	11587
(PH-...)	B737	23922
PH-AAI	DC-10	46971
PH-AAJ	DC-10	46972
PH-AAK	DC-10	46982
PH-ADA	DC-8	45750
PH-AGA	A310	241
PH-AGB	**A310**	**245**
PH-AGC	**A310**	**248**
PH-AGD	A310	264
PH-AGE	**A310**	**283**
PH-AGF	**A310**	**297**
PH-AGG	**A310**	**353**
PH-AGH	**A310**	**362**
PH-AGI	**A310**	**364**
PH-AGK	**A310**	**394**
PH-AHB	B727	20739
PH-AHD	B727	20822
PH-AHE	**B757**	**24135**
PH-AHF	B757	24136
PH-AHI	**B757**	**24137**
PH-AHK	B757	24291
PH-AHL	B757	24838
PH-AHM	B767	25058

Registration	Type	c/n
(PH-AHM)	B767	24736
PH-AHN	B757	24771
PH-AHN	B767	25139
PH-AHZ	B727	21021
PH-BBV	F-28	11127
PH-BDA	**B737**	**23537**
PH-BDB	**B737**	**23538**
PH-BDC	**B737**	**23539**
PH-BDD	**B737**	**23540**
PH-BDE	**B737**	**23541**
PH-BDG	**B737**	**23542**
PH-BDH	**B737**	**23543**
PH-BDI	**B737**	**23544**
PH-BDK	**B737**	**23545**
PH-BDL	**B737**	**23546**
PH-BDN	**B737**	**24261**
PH-BDO	**B737**	**24262**
PH-BDP	**B737**	**24404**
PH-BDR	**B737**	**24514**
PH-BDS	**B737**	**24529**
PH-BDT	**B737**	**24530**
PH-BDU	**B737**	**24857**
PH-BDW	**B737**	**24858**
PH-BDY	**B737**	**24959**
PH-BDZ	**B737**	**25355**
PH-BFA	**B747**	**23999**
PH-BFB	**B747**	**24000**
PH-BFC	**B747**	**23982**
PH-BFD	**B747**	**24001**
PH-BFE	**B747**	**24201**
PH-BFF	**B747**	**24202**
PH-BFG	**B747**	**24517**
PH-BFH	**B747**	**24518**
PH-BFI	**B747**	**25086**
PH-BFK	**B747**	**25087**
PH-BFL	**B747**	**25356**
PH-BFM	**B747**	**26373**
(PH-BFM)	B747	25673
PH-BFN	**B747**	**26372**
(PH-BFN)	B747	25672
PH-BFO	**B747**	**25413**
PH-BFP	**B747**	**26374**
PH-BFR	**B747**	**27202**
PH-BFS	**B747**	**28195**
(PH-BFS)	B747	26390
PH-BFT	**B747**	**28196**
(PH-BFT)	B747	26391
PH-BTA	**B737**	**25412**
PH-BTB	**B737**	**25423**
PH-BTC	**B737**	**25424**
PH-BTD	**B737**	**27420**
PH-BTE	**B737**	**27421**
PH-BTF	**B737**	**27232**
PH-BTG	**B737**	**27233**
PH-BUA	B747	19922
PH-BUB	B747	19923
PH-BUC	B747	19924
PH-BUD	B747	20398
PH-BUE	B747	20399
PH-BUF	B747	20400
PH-BUG	B747	20427
PH-BUH	**B747**	**21110**
PH-BUI	**B747**	**21111**
PH-BUK	**B747**	**21549**
PH-BUL	**B747**	**21550**
PH-BUM	**B747**	**21659**
PH-BUN	**B747**	**21660**
PH-BUO	**B747**	**21848**
PH-BUP	**B747**	**22376**
PH-BUR	**B747**	**22379**
PH-BUT	**B747**	**22380**
PH-BUU	**B747**	**23056**
(PH-BUU)	B747	23025
PH-BUV	**B747**	**23137**
PH-BUW	**B747**	**23508**
PH-BZA	**B767**	**27957**
PH-BZB	**B767**	**27958**
PH-BZC	**B767**	**26263**
PH-BZD	**B767**	**27610**
PH-BZE	**B767**	**28098**
PH-BZF	**B767**	**27959**
PH-BZG	**B767**	**27960**
PH-BZH	**B767**	**27611**
PH-BZJ	**B767**	**27612**
PH-BZK	**B767**	**27614**
PH-CDI	F-100	11245
PH-CFA	F-100	11323
PH-CFB	F-100	11324
PH-CFC	F-100	11325
PH-CFD	F-100	11326
PH-CFE	**F-100**	**11327**
PH-CFF	**F-100**	**11328**
PH-CFG	F-100	11329
PH-CFH	F-100	11330
PH-CHB	**F-28**	**11138**
PH-CHD	**F-28**	**11139**
PH-CHF	**F-28**	**11140**
PH-CHI	F-28	11141
PH-CHN	**F-28**	**11176**
(PH-CKA)	B747	26390
PH-DCA	DC-8	45376
PH-DCB	DC-8	45377
PH-DCC	DC-8	45378
PH-DCD	DC-8	45379
PH-DCE	DC-8	45380
PH-DCF	DC-8	45381
PH-DCG	DC-8	45382
PH-DCH	DC-8	45383
PH-DCI	DC-8	45613
PH-DCK	DC-8	45614
PH-DCL	DC-8	45615
PH-DCM	DC-8	45616
PH-DCN	DC-8	45629
PH-DCO	DC-8	45632
PH-DCP	DC-8	45608
PH-DCR	DC-8	45607
PH-DCS	DC-8	45683
PH-DCT	DC-8	45691
PH-DCU	DC-8	45859
PH-DCV	DC-8	45766
PH-DCW	DC-8	45762
PH-DCY	DC-8	45765
PH-DCZ	DC-8	45804
PH-DEA	DC-8	45903
PH-DEB	DC-8	45901
PH-DEC	DC-8	45999
PH-DED	DC-8	46000
PH-DEE	DC-8	46019
PH-DEF	DC-8	46080
PH-DEG	DC-8	46092
PH-DEH	DC-8	46075
PH-DEK	DC-8	46121
PH-DEL	DC-8	46122
PH-DEM	DC-8	46141
PH-DNA	DC-9	45718
PH-DNB	DC-9	45719
PH-DNC	DC-9	45720
PH-DND	DC-9	45721
PH-DNE	DC-9	45722
PH-DNF	DC-9	45723
PH-DNG	DC-9	47102
PH-DNH	DC-9	47131
PH-DNI	DC-9	47132
PH-DNK	DC-9	47133
PH-DNL	DC-9	47190
PH-DNM	DC-9	47191
PH-DNN	DC-9	47192
PH-DNO	DC-9	47193
PH-DNP	DC-9	47194
PH-DNR	DC-9	47279
PH-DNS	DC-9	47168
PH-DNT	DC-9	47169
PH-DNV	DC-9	47170
PH-DNW	DC-9	47201
PH-DNY	DC-9	47462
PH-DNZ	DC-9	47476
PH-DOA	DC-9	48132
PH-DOB	DC-9	48133
PH-DTA	DC-10	46550
PH-DTB	DC-10	46551
PH-DTC	DC-10	46552
PH-DTD	DC-10	46553
PH-DTE	DC-10	46554
PH-DTF	DC-10	46555
PH-DTG	DC-10	46556
PH-DTH	DC-10	46557
PH-DTI	DC-10	46933
PH-DTK	DC-10	46914
(PH-DTK)	DC-10	46934
PH-DTL	**DC-10**	**46952**
(PH-DTM)	DC-10	46958
PH-EXA	F-28	11013
PH-EXA	F-28	11023
PH-EXA	F-28	11026
PH-EXA	F-28	11028
PH-EXA	F-28	11992
PH-EXB	F-28	11056
PH-EXB	F-28	11079
PH-EXB	F-28	11994
PH-EXC	F-28	11024
PH-EXC	F-28	11080
PH-EXD	F-28	11049
PH-EXD	F-28	11061
PH-EXD	F-28	11064
PH-EXD	F-28	11081
PH-EXD	F-28	11106
PH-EXE	F-28	11037
PH-EXE	F-28	11063
PH-EXE	F-28	11107
PH-EXE	F-28	11993
PH-EXF	F-28	11025
PH-EXF	F-28	11035
PH-EXF	F-28	11041
PH-EXF	F-28	11048
PH-EXF	F-28	11053
PH-EXF	F-28	11108
PH-EXF	F-28	11209
PH-EXF	F-28	11992
PH-EXG	F-28	11049
PH-EXG	F-28	11074
PH-EXG	F-28	11101
PH-EXG	F-28	11109
PH-EXH	F-28	11056
PH-EXH	F-28	11090
PH-EXH	F-28	11096
PH-EXH	F-28	11103
PH-EXI	F-28	11047
PH-EXI	F-28	11068
PH-EXI	F-28	11088
PH-EXI	F-28	11098
PH-EXK	F-28	11069
PH-EXK	F-28	11112
PH-EXL	F-28	11067
PH-EXL	F-28	11089
PH-EXL	F-28	11099
PH-EXL	F-28	11110
PH-EXM	F-28	11038
PH-EXM	F-28	11043
PH-EXM	F-28	11075
PH-EXM	F-28	11115
PH-EXN	F-28	11035
PH-EXN	F-28	11065
PH-EXN	F-28	11082
PH-EXN	F-28	11118
PH-EXN	F-28	11136
PH-EXN	F-28	11140
PH-EXN	F-28	11146
PH-EXN	F-28	11158
PH-EXN	F-28	11173
PH-EXN	F-28	11182
PH-EXN	F-28	11188
PH-EXN	F-28	11199
PH-EXO	F-28	11066
PH-EXO	F-28	11083
PH-EXO	F-28	11095
PH-EXO	F-28	11121
PH-EXO	F-28	11133
PH-EXO	F-28	11160
PH-EXO	F-28	11167
PH-EXO	F-28	11174
PH-EXO	F-28	11184
PH-EXO	F-28	11195
PH-EXO	F-28	11201
PH-EXO	F-28	11205
PH-EXO	F-28	11210
PH-EXP	F-28	11070
PH-EXP	F-28	11084
PH-EXP	F-28	11122
PH-EXP	F-28	11125
PH-EXP	F-28	11141
PH-EXP	F-28	11149
PH-EXP	F-28	11168
PH-EXP	F-28	11185
PH-EXP	F-28	11198
PH-EXP	F-28	11203
PH-EXR	F-28	11044
PH-EXR	F-28	11071
PH-EXR	F-28	11113
PH-EXR	F-28	11128
PH-EXR	F-28	11135
PH-EXR	F-28	11152
PH-EXR	F-28	11164
PH-EXR	F-28	11171
PH-EXR	F-28	11177
PH-EXR	F-28	11193
PH-EXR	F-28	11204
PH-EXS	F-28	11072
PH-EXS	F-28	11097
PH-EXS	F-28	11129
PH-EXS	F-28	11137
PH-EXS	F-28	11144
PH-EXS	F-28	11161
PH-EXS	F-28	11165
PH-EXS	F-28	11169
PH-EXS	F-28	11181
PH-EXS	F-28	11186
PH-EXS	F-28	11197
PH-EXT	F-28	11073
PH-EXT	F-28	11085
PH-EXT	F-28	11091
PH-EXT	F-28	11127
PH-EXT	F-28	11138
PH-EXT	F-28	11148
PH-EXT	F-28	11159
PH-EXT	F-28	11162
PH-EXT	F-28	11169
PH-EXT	F-28	11175
PH-EXT	F-28	11202
PH-EXT	F-28	11208
PH-EXU	F-28	11077
PH-EXU	F-28	11086
PH-EXU	F-28	11104
PH-EXU	F-28	11114
PH-EXU	F-28	11130
PH-EXU	F-28	11139
PH-EXU	F-28	11151
PH-EXU	F-28	11162
PH-EXU	F-28	11170
PH-EXU	F-28	11176
PH-EXU	F-28	11190
PH-EXU	F-28	11196
PH-EXU	F-28	11206
PH-EXU	F-28	11211
PH-EXV	F-28	11044
PH-EXV	F-28	11075
PH-EXV	F-28	11087
PH-EXV	F-28	11105
PH-EXV	F-28	11116
PH-EXV	F-28	11126
PH-EXV	F-28	11145
PH-EXV	F-28	11153
PH-EXV	F-28	11165
PH-EXV	F-28	11200
PH-EXW	F-28	11018
PH-EXW	F-28	11032
PH-EXW	F-28	11117
PH-EXW	F-28	11131
PH-EXW	F-28	11147
PH-EXW	F-28	11154
PH-EXW	F-28	11163
PH-EXW	F-28	11178
PH-EXW	F-28	11187
PH-EXW	F-28	11192
PH-EXX	F-28	11020
PH-EXX	F-28	11119
PH-EXX	F-28	11132
PH-EXX	F-28	11150
PH-EXX	F-28	11155
PH-EXX	F-28	11172
PH-EXX	F-28	11179
PH-EXX	F-28	11189
PH-EXX	F-28	11207
PH-EXY	F-28	11036
PH-EXY	F-28	11076
PH-EXY	F-28	11094
PH-EXY	F-28	11100
PH-EXY	F-28	11120
PH-EXY	F-28	11124
PH-EXY	F-28	11142
PH-EXY	F-28	11156
PH-EXY	F-28	11162
PH-EXY	F-28	11166
PH-EXZ	F-28	11024
PH-EXZ	F-28	11078

PH-EXZ	F-28	11102
PH-EXZ	F-28	11111
PH-EXZ	F-28	11123
PH-EXZ	F-28	11134
PH-EXZ	F-28	11143
PH-EXZ	F-28	11157
PH-EXZ	F-28	11180
PH-EXZ	F-28	11183
PH-EXZ	F-28	11191
PH-EXZ	F-28	11194
PH-EXZ	F-28	11212
PH-EZA	F-100	11245
PH-EZA	F-100	11257
PH-EZA	F-100	11321
PH-EZA	F-100	11353
PH-EZA	F-100	11364
PH-EZA	F-100	11434
PH-EZA	F-100	11456
PH-EZA	F-100	11478
PH-EZA	F-100	11484
PH-EZA	F-28	11037
PH-EZA	F-28	11111
PH-EZA	F-28	11213
PH-EZA	F-28	11236
PH-EZA	F-70	11539
PH-EZA	F-70	11569
PH-EZB	F-100	11244
PH-EZB	F-100	11246
PH-EZB	F-100	11274
PH-EZB	F-100	11297
PH-EZB	F-100	11302
PH-EZB	F-100	11318
PH-EZB	F-100	11330
PH-EZB	F-100	11349
PH-EZB	F-100	11369
PH-EZB	F-100	11391
PH-EZB	F-100	11404
PH-EZB	F-100	11411
PH-EZB	F-100	11435
PH-EZB	F-100	11457
PH-EZB	F-100	11479
PH-EZB	F-100	11485
PH-EZB	F-28	11214
PH-EZB	F-28	11226
PH-EZB	F-70	11575
PH-EZC	F-100	11247
PH-EZC	F-100	11250
PH-EZC	F-100	11300
PH-EZC	F-100	11323
PH-EZC	F-100	11354
PH-EZC	F-100	11365
PH-EZC	F-100	11395
PH-EZC	F-100	11412
PH-EZC	F-100	11436
PH-EZC	F-100	11458
PH-EZC	F-100	11480
PH-EZC	F-100	11486
PH-EZC	F-28	11215
PH-EZC	F-28	11227
PH-EZC	F-70	11568
PH-EZD	F-100	11248
PH-EZD	F-100	11251
PH-EZD	F-100	11258
PH-EZD	F-100	11303
PH-EZD	F-100	11334
PH-EZD	F-100	11344
PH-EZD	F-100	11370
PH-EZD	F-100	11392
PH-EZD	F-100	11425
PH-EZD	F-100	11459
PH-EZD	F-100	11481
PH-EZD	F-100	11488
PH-EZD	F-28	11216
PH-EZD	F-28	11231
PH-EZD	F-70	11572
PH-EZE	F-100	11249
PH-EZE	F-100	11252
PH-EZE	F-100	11262
PH-EZE	F-100	11311
PH-EZE	F-100	11345
PH-EZE	F-100	11372
PH-EZE	F-100	11396
PH-EZE	F-100	11408
PH-EZE	F-100	11426
PH-EZE	F-100	11460
PH-EZE	F-100	11482
PH-EZE	F-100	11489
PH-EZE	F-28	11063
PH-EZE	F-28	11096
PH-EZE	F-28	11217
PH-EZE	F-28	11237
PH-EZF	F-100	11253
PH-EZF	F-100	11263
PH-EZF	F-100	11276
PH-EZF	F-100	11306
PH-EZF	F-100	11315
PH-EZF	F-100	11454
PH-EZF	F-100	11483
PH-EZF	F-100	11506
PH-EZF	F-100	11509
PH-EZF	F-28	11017
PH-EZF	F-28	11087
PH-EZG	F-100	11254
PH-EZG	F-100	11278
PH-EZG	F-100	11289
PH-EZG	F-100	11292
PH-EZG	F-100	11324
PH-EZG	F-100	11359
PH-EZG	F-100	11380
PH-EZG	F-100	11405
PH-EZG	F-100	11427
PH-EZG	F-100	11455
PH-EZG	F-100	11507
PH-EZG	F-100	11522
PH-EZG	F-28	11054
PH-EZG	F-28	11232
PH-EZH	F-100	11255
PH-EZH	F-100	11280
PH-EZH	F-100	11291
PH-EZH	F-100	11314
PH-EZH	F-100	11332
PH-EZH	F-100	11512
PH-EZH	F-28	11064
PH-EZH	F-28	11101
PH-EZH	F-70	11536
PH-EZH	F-70	11545
PH-EZI	F-100	11256
PH-EZI	F-100	11281
PH-EZI	F-100	11308
PH-EZI	F-100	11325
PH-EZI	F-100	11355
PH-EZI	F-100	11367
PH-EZI	F-100	11397
PH-EZI	F-100	11413
PH-EZI	F-100	11437
PH-EZI	F-100	11464
PH-EZI	F-100	11513
PH-EZI	F-28	11103
PH-EZI	F-28	11233
PH-EZJ	F-100	11259
PH-EZJ	F-100	11310
PH-EZJ	F-100	11326
PH-EZJ	F-100	11356
PH-EZJ	F-100	11368
PH-EZJ	F-100	11398
PH-EZJ	F-100	11414
PH-EZJ	F-100	11432
PH-EZJ	F-100	11465
PH-EZJ	F-100	11497
PH-EZJ	F-28	11105
PH-EZJ	F-28	11234
PH-EZK	F-100	11260
PH-EZK	F-100	11261
PH-EZK	F-100	11466
PH-EZK	F-100	11492
PH-EZK	F-100	11498
PH-EZK	F-100	11519
PH-EZK	F-28	11095
PH-EZK	F-28	11240
PH-EZK	F-70	11551
PH-EZL	F-100	11264
PH-EZL	F-100	11327
PH-EZL	F-100	11357
PH-EZL	F-100	11373
PH-EZL	F-100	11399
PH-EZL	F-100	11415
PH-EZL	F-100	11438
PH-EZL	F-100	11467
PH-EZL	F-100	11499
PH-EZL	F-28	11098
PH-EZL	F-28	11162
PH-EZL	F-28	11239
PH-EZL	F-70	11529
PH-EZM	F-100	11265
PH-EZM	F-100	11328
PH-EZM	F-100	11358
PH-EZM	F-100	11379
PH-EZM	F-100	11402
PH-EZM	F-100	11419
PH-EZM	F-100	11439
PH-EZM	F-100	11468
PH-EZM	F-100	11501
PH-EZM	F-100	11523
PH-EZM	F-28	11106
PH-EZM	F-70	11543
PH-EZN	F-100	11266
PH-EZN	F-100	11288
PH-EZN	F-100	11446
PH-EZN	F-100	11469
PH-EZN	F-100	11487
PH-EZN	F-100	11500
PH-EZN	F-100	11502
PH-EZN	F-100	11527
PH-EZN	F-28	11107
PH-EZN	F-70	11541
PH-EZN	F-70	11554
PH-EZO	F-100	11267
PH-EZO	F-100	11305
PH-EZO	F-100	11337
PH-EZO	F-100	11346
PH-EZO	F-100	11360
PH-EZO	F-100	11376
PH-EZO	F-100	11403
PH-EZO	F-100	11418
PH-EZO	F-100	11447
PH-EZO	F-100	11471
PH-EZO	F-100	11494
PH-EZO	F-100	11503
PH-EZO	F-28	11228
PH-EZP	F-100	11282
PH-EZP	F-100	11290
PH-EZP	F-100	11366
PH-EZP	F-100	11406
PH-EZP	F-100	11428
PH-EZP	F-100	11448
PH-EZP	F-100	11495
PH-EZP	F-100	11504
PH-EZP	F-28	11218
PH-EZP	F-28	11229
PH-EZP	F-70	11555
PH-EZR	F-100	11283
PH-EZR	F-100	11313
PH-EZR	F-100	11335
PH-EZR	F-100	11470
PH-EZR	F-28	11219
PH-EZR	F-28	11238
PH-EZR	F-70	11532
PH-EZR	F-70	11561
PH-EZR	F-70	11564
PH-EZS	F-100	11309
PH-EZS	F-100	11338
PH-EZS	F-100	11361
PH-EZS	F-100	11377
PH-EZS	F-100	11407
PH-EZS	F-100	11449
PH-EZS	F-28	11220
PH-EZS	F-70	11528
PH-EZS	F-70	11540
(PH-EZS)	F-100	11284
PH-EZT	F-100	11285
PH-EZT	F-100	11331
PH-EZT	F-100	11362
PH-EZT	F-100	11451
PH-EZT	F-100	11461
PH-EZT	F-28	11221
PH-EZT	F-28	11241
PH-EZT	F-70	11563
PH-EZU	F-100	11286
PH-EZU	F-100	11312
PH-EZU	F-100	11452
PH-EZU	F-100	11472
PH-EZU	F-100	11490
PH-EZU	F-28	11222
PH-EZU	F-28	11235
(PH-EZU)	F-100	11339
PH-EZV	F-100	11275
PH-EZV	F-100	11329
PH-EZV	F-100	11363
PH-EZV	F-100	11463
PH-EZV	F-100	11473
PH-EZV	F-100	11491
PH-EZV	F-100	11520
PH-EZV	F-28	11223
PH-EZV	F-70	11537
PH-EZV	F-70	11559
PH-EZW	F-100	11277
PH-EZW	F-100	11316
PH-EZW	F-100	11333
PH-EZW	F-100	11474
PH-EZW	F-28	11224
PH-EZW	F-70	11549
PH-EZW	F-70	11560
PH-EZW	F-70	11573
PH-EZX	F-100	11279
PH-EZX	F-100	11304
PH-EZX	F-100	11307
PH-EZX	F-100	11462
PH-EZX	F-100	11475
PH-EZX	F-100	11517
PH-EZX	F-28	11225
PH-EZX	F-70	11538
PH-EZX	F-70	11565
PH-EZY	F-100	11293
PH-EZY	F-100	11301
PH-EZY	F-100	11340
PH-EZY	F-100	11385
PH-EZY	F-100	11416
PH-EZY	F-100	11476
PH-EZY	F-100	11493
PH-EZY	F-100	11515
PH-EZY	F-28	11043
PH-EZY	F-70	11574
PH-EZZ	F-100	11295
PH-EZZ	F-100	11352
PH-EZZ	F-100	11417
PH-EZZ	F-100	11477
PH-EZZ	F-100	11514
PH-EZZ	F-28	11217
PH-EZZ	F-28	11230
PH-EZZ	F-70	11539
PH-EZZ	F-70	11553
PH-EZZ	F-70	11570
PH-FPT	F-28	11994
(PH-GCL)	A320	0436
(PH-GCX)	A320	0420
PH-HVF	B737	23411
PH-HVG	B737	23412
PH-HVI	B737	24098
PH-HVJ	**B737**	**23738**
PH-HVK	B737	23786
PH-HVM	**B737**	**24326**
PH-HVN	**B737**	**24327**
PH-HVT	**B737**	**24328**
PH-HVV	**B737**	**24329**
(PH-HVW)	B737	25420
(PH-HVX)	B737	25431
PH-INA	F-100	11249
PH-INC	F-100	11248
PH-JCA	F-100	11480
PH-JCB	F-100	11481
PH-JCC	F-100	11482
PH-JCD	F-100	11483
PH-JCH	F-70	11528
PH-JCJ	F-100	11505
PH-JCK	F-100	11511
PH-JCL	F-100	11516
PH-JCM	F-100	11518
PH-JCO	F-100	11500
PH-JCT	F-70	11537
PH-JHG	F-28	11001
PH-JPV	F-28	11130
PH-JXK	F-100	11386
PH-JXP	F-100	11371
PH-JXR	F-100	11375
PH-JXS	F-100	11382
PH-JXT	F-100	11383
PH-JXU	F-100	11384
(PH-JXU)	F-100	11383
PH-JXV	F-100	11389
PH-JXW	F-100	11390
PH-JXX	F-100	11374
PH-JXY	F-100	11381
PH-KBX	**F-70**	**11547**
PH-KCA	**MD-11**	**48555**

PH-KCB	**MD-11**	**48556**
PH-KCC	**MD-11**	**48557**
PH-KCD	**MD-11**	**48558**
PH-KCE	**MD-11**	**48559**
PH-KCF	**MD-11**	**48560**
PH-KCG	**MD-11**	**48561**
PH-KCH	**MD-11**	**48562**
PH-KCI	MD-11	48563
PH-KCK	**MD-11**	**48564**
PH-KLC	**F-100**	**11268**
PH-KLD	**F-100**	**11269**
PH-KLE	**F-100**	**11270**
PH-KLG	**F-100**	**11271**
PH-KLH	**F-100**	**11272**
PH-KLI	**F-100**	**11273**
(PH-KLK)	F-100	11274
(PH-KLL)	F-100	11275
(PH-KLN)	F-100	11277
(PH-KLO)	F-100	11279
PH-KXA	F-100	11378
PH-KXB	F-100	11387
PH-KXC	F-100	11388
PH-KXI	F-100	11394
PH-KXJ	F-100	11400
PH-KXK	F-100	11401
PH-KXL	F-100	11393
PH-KXP	F-100	11409
PH-KXR	F-100	11410
PH-KXZ	F-100	11423
PH-KZA	**F-70**	**11567**
PH-KZB	**F-70**	**11562**
PH-KZC	**F-70**	**11566**
PH-KZD	F-70	11582
PH-LEX	F-28	11179
PH-LMF	F-100	11257
PH-LMG	F-100	11292
PH-LMH	F-100	11267
PH-LMI	F-100	11284
PH-LMK	F-100	11285
PH-LML	F-100	11287
PH-LMM	F-100	11294
PH-LMN	F-100	11298
PH-LMO	F-100	11299
PH-LMU	F-100	11288
PH-LMV	F-100	11301
PH-LMW	F-100	11302
PH-LMX	F-100	11304
PH-LMY	F-100	11305
PH-LMZ	F-100	11309
PH-LNA	F-100	11317
PH-LNB	F-100	11319
PH-LND	F-100	11320
PH-LNE	F-100	11322
PH-LNF	F-100	11336
PH-LNG	F-100	11339
PH-LNH	F-100	11341
PH-LNI	F-100	11340
PH-LNJ	F-100	11342
PH-LNK	**F-100**	**11343**
PH-LNL	F-100	11347
PH-LNM	F-100	11348
PH-LNN	F-100	11350
PH-LNO	F-100	11351
(PH-LNP)	F-100	11323
(PH-LNR)	F-100	11324
(PH-LNT)	F-100	11325
PH-LXA	F-100	11429
PH-LXB	F-100	11430
PH-LXC	F-100	11431
PH-LXD	F-100	11440
PH-LXG	F-100	11420
PH-LXH	F-100	11421
PH-LXI	F-100	11422
PH-LXS	F-100	11441
PH-LXV	F-100	11424
PH-MAN	DC-9	47291
PH-MAO	DC-9	47363
PH-MAR	DC-9	47410
PH-MAS	DC-8	45824
PH-MAT	F-28	11008
PH-MAU	DC-8	45856
PH-MAX	DC-9	47514
PH-MBG	DC-10	46891
PH-MBH	DC-8	45818
PH-MBN	DC-10	46924
PH-MBP	DC-10	46956
PH-MBT	DC-10	46985
PH-MBY	MD-82	48048
PH-MBZ	MD-82	49144
PH-MCA	A310	281
PH-MCB	A310	349
(PH-MCC)	A310	433
PH-MCD	MD-82	48022
PH-MCE	**B747**	**23652**
PH-MCF	**B747**	**24134**
PH-MCG	**B767**	**24428**
PH-MCH	**B767**	**24429**
PH-MCI	**B767**	**25312**
PH-MCK	**B767**	**25273**
PH-MCL	**B767**	**26469**
PH-MCM	**B767**	**26470**
PH-MCN	**B747**	**25266**
PH-MCO	DC-10	46998
PH-MCP	**MD-11**	**48616**
PH-MCR	**MD-11**	**48617**
PH-MCS	**MD-11**	**48618**
PH-MCT	**MD-11**	**48629**
PH-MCU	**MD-11**	**48750**
PH-MCV	**B767**	**27619**
PH-MKC	F-100	11243
PH-MKC	**F-70**	**11243**
PH-MKH	F-100	11242
PH-MKS	F-70	11521
PH-MOL	F-28	11003
PH-MXA	F-100	11433
PH-MXB	F-100	11443
PH-MXC	F-100	11444
PH-MXD	F-100	11445
PH-MXK	F-100	11442
PH-MXL	F-100	11450
PH-MXM	F-70	11557
PH-MXN	F-70	11553
PH-MXO	F-100	11453
PH-MXW	F-100	11471
(PH-NMB)	B737	24377
PH-NXA	F-100	11433
PH-ONS	F-100	11517
PH-OZA	**B737**	**23718**
PH-OZB	**B737**	**23921**
PH-PBG	F-28	11092
PH-PBX	**F-28**	**11045**
PH-RAL	B737	21736
PH-RRA	**F-28**	**11219**
PH-RRB	F-28	11223
PH-RRC	F-100	11321
PH-RRC	**F-28**	**11203**
PH-RRG	F-100	11316
PH-RRH	F-100	11318
PH-RRJ	F-28	11118
PH-RRN	F-100	11452
PH-RRS	**F-70**	**11540**
PH-RRT	**F-70**	**11541**
PH-RRU	**F-70**	**11543**
PH-RRV	**F-70**	**11556**
PH-RRW	**F-70**	**11558**
PH-SEZ	**MD-82**	**49903**
PH-SIX	F-28	11092
PH-TAB	**F-100**	**11290**
PH-TAC	F-100	11296
(PH-TEV)	A300	17
PH-TIR	F-28	11124
PH-TKA	**B757**	**26633**
PH-TKB	**B757**	**26634**
PH-TKC	**B757**	**26635**
PH-TKY	B757	24118
PH-TKZ	B757	24119
PH-TRF	B707	19664
PH-TRH	CRVL	96
PH-TRM	CRVL	21
PH-TRN	CRVL	191
PH-TRO	CRVL	33
PH-TRP	CRVL	43
PH-TRR	CRVL	48
PH-TRS	CRVL	100
PH-TRU	CRVL	102
PH-TRV	B707	19107
PH-TRW	B707	19416
PH-TRX	CRVL	92
PH-TRY	CRVL	87
PH-TSA	B737	22738
PH-TSB	B737	22739
PH-TSD	B737	21797
PH-TSE	B737	21793
PH-TSI	B737	22737
PH-TSU	**B737**	**24905**
PH-TSW	**B737**	**24219**
PH-TSX	**B737**	**26318**
PH-TSY	**B737**	**28085**
PH-TSZ	**B737**	**27635**
PH-TVA	B707	17646
PH-TVC	B737	20836
PH-TVD	B737	20943
PH-TVE	B737	20944
PH-TVF	B737	20282
PH-TVG	B737	19711
(PH-TVG)	F-28	11124
PH-TVH	B737	19955
PH-TVI	B737	19940
PH-TVK	B707	20198
PH-TVL	A300	08
(PH-TVM)	B737	21131
PH-TVN	B737	21193
PH-TVO	B737	21196
PH-TVP	B737	21397
PH-TVR	B737	22025
PH-TVS	B737	22296
PH-TVT	CRVL	93
PH-TVU	B737	22906
PH-TVV	CRVL	44
PH-TVW	**CRVL**	**36**
PH-TVX	B737	22023
PH-TVZ	CRVL	91
PH-VAB	F-28	11099
PH-VGR	**F-28**	**11124**
PH-WEV	F-28	11002
PH-YAA	B737	25040
PH-ZAA	F-28	11004
PH-ZAB	F-28	11006
(PH-ZAC)	F-28	11008
PH-ZAD	F-28	11009
PH-ZAE	F-28	11010
PH-ZAF	F-28	11011
PH-ZAG	F-28	11012
PH-ZAH	F-28	11013
PH-ZAI	F-28	11014
PH-ZAK	F-28	11015
PH-ZAL	F-28	11016
PH-ZAM	F-28	11017
PH-ZAN	F-28	11018
(PH-ZAN)	F-28	11024
PH-ZAO	F-28	11019
PH-ZAP	F-28	11020
PH-ZAR	F-28	11991
PH-ZAS	F-28	11021
PH-ZAT	F-28	11022
PH-ZAU	F-28	11993
(PH-ZAU)	F-28	11992
PH-ZAV	F-28	11032
(PH-ZAV)	F-28	11023
PH-ZAW	F-28	11052
PH-ZAX	F-28	11053
(PH-ZAX)	F-28	11993
PH-ZBA	F-28	11057
PH-ZBB	F-28	11058
PH-ZBC	F-28	11060
PH-ZBD	F-28	11059
PH-ZBE	F-28	11062
PH-ZBF	F-28	11037
PH-ZBG	F-28	11027
PH-ZBH	F-28	11031
PH-ZBI	F-28	11034
PH-ZBJ	F-28	11163
PH-ZBK	F-28	11079
PH-ZBL	F-28	11093
PH-ZBM	F-28	11048
PH-ZBN	F-28	11097
PH-ZBO	F-28	11110
PH-ZBP	F-28	11125
PH-ZBR	F-28	11136
PH-ZBS	F-28	11137
PH-ZBT	F-28	11135
PH-ZBU	F-28	11133
PH-ZBV	F-28	11153
PH-ZBW	F-28	11157
PH-ZBX	F-28	11159
PH-ZBY	F-28	11169
PH-ZBZ	F-28	11167
PH-ZCA	F-28	11164
PH-ZCB	F-28	11166
PH-ZCC	F-28	11168
PH-ZCD	F-28	11177
PH-ZCE	F-28	11184
PH-ZCF	F-28	11185
PH-ZCG	F-28	11165
PH-ZCH	F-28	11220
PH-ZCI	F-100	11276
PH-ZCK	F-100	11274
PH-ZCL	F-100	11275
PH-ZCM	F-100	11277
PH-ZCN	F-100	11279

Philippines
(see also RP-)

PI-C801	DC-8	45607
PI-C801	DC-8	45608
PI-C802	DC-8	45762
PI-C803	DC-8	45937
PI-C804	DC-8	45607
PI-C827	DC-8	45378
(PI-C827)	DC-8	46121
PI-C829	DC-8	45380
(PI-C829)	DC-8	46122
PI-C969	CRVL	103
PI-C970	CRVL	90
PI-C1121	1-11	091
PI-C1131	1-11	092
PI-C1141	1-11	094
PI-C1151	1-11	BAC.157
PI-C1151	1-11	BAC.161
PI-C1161	1-11	BAC.213
PI-C1171	1-11	BAC.215
PI-C1181	1-11	BAC.226
PI-C1191	1-11	BAC.231
PI-C7071	B707	17661
PI-C7072	B707	17668
PI-C7073	B707	17680

Netherlands Antilles

PJ-BOA	B727	19506
PJ-DNA	DC-9	45722
PJ-DNB	DC-9	45723
PJ-DNC	DC-9	45721
PJ-SEF	**MD-82**	**49123**
PJ-SEG	**MD-82**	**49124**
PJ-SEH	**MD-82**	**49661**
PJ-SNA	DC-9	47648
PJ-SNB	DC-9	47666
PJ-SNC	DC-9	47669
PJ-SND	DC-9	47639
PJ-SNE	DC-9	47175

Indonesia

PK-	**A330**	**132**
PK-	**F-70**	**11576**
(PK-)	B727	18970
PK-DTA	146	E1144
(PK-DTC)	146	E1152
(PK-DTD)	146	E2170
PK-GAA	**A300**	**159**
PK-GAC	**A300**	**164**
PK-GAD	**A300**	**165**
PK-GAE	**A300**	**166**
PK-GAF	**A300**	**167**
PK-GAG	**A300**	**168**
PK-GAH	**A300**	**213**
PK-GAI	**A300**	**214**
PK-GAJ	**A300**	**215**
PK-GAK	**A300**	**611**
PK-GAL	**A300**	**613**
PK-GAM	**A300**	**625**
PK-GAN	**A300**	**630**
PK-GAO	**A300**	**633**
PK-GAP	**A300**	**657**
PK-GAQ	**A300**	**659**
PK-GAR	**A300**	**664**
PK-GAS	**A300**	**668**
PK-GAT	**A300**	**677**
PK-GAU	B707	21092

(PK-GBA)	B747	22246
(PK-GBB)	B747	22247
(PK-GBC)	B747	22248
(PK-GBD)	B747	22249
PK-GEA	DC-8	45765
PK-GEB	DC-8	45766
PK-GEC	DC-8	45632
PK-GFQ	**F-28**	**11117**
PK-GFR	**F-28**	**11113**
PK-GFS	**F-28**	**11119**
PK-GFT	**F-28**	**11129**
PK-GFU	F-28	11131
PK-GFV	F-28	11132
PK-GFW	**F-28**	**11134**
(PK-GHA)	F-28	11154
(PK-GHB)	F-28	11155
(PK-GHC)	F-28	11157
(PK-GHD)	F-28	11158
(PK-GHE)	F-28	11160
PK-GIA	**DC-10**	**46918**
PK-GIB	**DC-10**	**46919**
PK-GIC	**DC-10**	**46964**
PK-GID	**DC-10**	**46951**
PK-GIE	**DC-10**	**46685**
PK-GIF	**DC-10**	**46686**
PK-GIG	**MD-11**	**48502**
PK-GIH	**MD-11**	**48500**
PK-GII	**MD-11**	**48503**
PK-GIJ	**MD-11**	**48504**
PK-GJA	CV990	30-10-3
PK-GJB	CV990	30-10-4
PK-GJC	CV990	30-10-37
(PK-GJC)	DC-8	45766
PK-GJD	DC-8	45765
PK-GJE	DC-9	47385
PK-GJF	DC-9	47386
PK-GJG	DC-9	47481
PK-GJH	DC-9	47463
PK-GJI	DC-9	47561
PK-GJJ	DC-9	47569
PK-GJK	DC-9	47601
PK-GJN	DC-8	45766
PK-GJP	F-28	11078
PK-GJQ	F-28	11075
PK-GJR	F-28	11037
PK-GJS	F-28	11064
PK-GJT	F-28	11063
PK-GJU	F-28	11061
PK-GJV	F-28	11055
PK-GJW	F-28	11054
PK-GJX	F-28	11039
PK-GJY	F-28	11036
PK-GJZ	F-28	11035
PK-GKA	**F-28**	**11154**
PK-GKB	**F-28**	**11155**
PK-GKC	**F-28**	**11157**
PK-GKD	**F-28**	**11158**
PK-GKE	**F-28**	**11160**
PK-GKF	**F-28**	**11170**
PK-GKG	**F-28**	**11171**
PK-GKH	**F-28**	**11174**
PK-GKI	**F-28**	**11188**
PK-GKJ	**F-28**	**11189**
PK-GKK	**F-28**	**11193**
PK-GKL	**F-28**	**11175**
PK-GKM	**F-28**	**11177**
PK-GKN	**F-28**	**11196**
PK-GKO	**F-28**	**11198**
PK-GKP	**F-28**	**11199**
PK-GKQ	**F-28**	**11201**
PK-GKR	**F-28**	**11202**
PK-GKS	**F-28**	**11206**
PK-GKT	**F-28**	**11209**
PK-GKU	**F-28**	**11210**
PK-GKV	**F-28**	**11211**
PK-GKW	**F-28**	**11213**
PK-GKX	**F-28**	**11214**
PK-GKY	**F-28**	**11215**
PK-GKZ	**F-28**	**11216**
PK-GNA	**DC-9**	**47385**
PK-GNB	**DC-9**	**47386**
PK-GNC	**DC-9**	**47481**
PK-GND	DC-9	47463
PK-GNE	DC-9	47561
PK-GNF	**DC-9**	**47569**
PK-GNG	**DC-9**	**47601**
PK-GNH	DC-9	47635
PK-GNI	DC-9	47636
PK-GNJ	DC-9	47672
PK-GNK	DC-9	47673
PK-GNL	DC-9	47680
PK-GNM	**DC-9**	**47701**
PK-GNN	**DC-9**	**47722**
PK-GNO	DC-9	47730
PK-GNP	**DC-9**	**47740**
PK-GNQ	DC-9	47741
PK-GNR	**DC-9**	**47744**
PK-GNS	DC-9	47789
PK-GNT	DC-9	47790
PK-GNU	DC-9	47791
PK-GNV	DC-9	47792
PK-GNW	DC-9	47793
PK-GNX	DC-9	47794
PK-GNY	DC-9	47795
PK-GQA	**F-28**	**11217**
PK-GQB	**F-28**	**11218**
PK-GSA	**B747**	**22246**
PK-GSB	**B747**	**22247**
PK-GSC	**B747**	**22248**
PK-GSD	**B747**	**22249**
PK-GSE	**B747**	**22768**
PK-GSF	**B747**	**22769**
PK-GSG	**B747**	**25704**
PK-GSH	**B747**	**25705**
PK-GSI	**B747**	**24956**
PK-GVA	F-28	11035
PK-GVB	F-28	11036
PK-GVC	F-28	11039
PK-GVD	F-28	11054
PK-GVE	F-28	11055
PK-GVF	F-28	11061
PK-GVG	F-28	11063
PK-GVH	F-28	11064
PK-GVI	F-28	11037
PK-GVJ	F-28	11075
PK-GVK	F-28	11078
PK-GVL	F-28	11087
PK-GVM	F-28	11032
PK-GVN	F-28	11043
PK-GVO	F-28	11044
PK-GVP	F-28	11094
PK-GVQ	F-28	11096
PK-GVR	F-28	11098
PK-GVS	F-28	11101
PK-GVT	F-28	11095
PK-GVU	F-28	11103
PK-GVV	F-28	11105
PK-GVW	F-28	11106
PK-GVX	F-28	11107
PK-GWA	**B737**	**24403**
PK-GWA	DC-10	46918
(PK-GWA)	DC-10	46952
PK-GWB	DC-10	46919
PK-GWD	**B737**	**24470**
PK-GWE	**B737**	**24492**
PK-GWF	**B737**	**24698**
PK-GWG	**B737**	**24699**
PK-GWH	**B737**	**24700**
PK-GWI	**B737**	**24701**
PK-GWJ	**B737**	**24702**
PK-GWK	**B737**	**25713**
PK-GWL	**B737**	**25714**
PK-GWM	**B737**	**25715**
PK-GWN	**B737**	**25716**
PK-GWO	**B737**	**25717**
PK-GWP	**B737**	**25718**
PK-GWQ	**B737**	**25719**
PK-HHS	**B737**	**21957**
PK-IJA	B737	19408
PK-IJC	B737	20412
PK-IJD	**B737**	**20631**
PK-IJE	**B737**	**20926**
PK-IJF	**B737**	**21732**
PK-IJG	**B737**	**23320**
PK-IJH	**B737**	**21397**
PK-IJI	**B737**	**22125**
PK-IJJ	**B737**	**22130**
PK-IJK	**B737**	**22143**
PK-JGA	**F-100**	**11264**
PK-JGC	**F-100**	**11265**
PK-JGD	**F-100**	**11266**
PK-JGE	**F-100**	**11301**
PK-JGF	**F-100**	**11347**
PK-JGG	**F-100**	**11336**
(PK-JGG)	F-100	11339
(PK-JGG)	F-100	11348
PK-JGH	**F-100**	**11339**
(PK-JGH)	F-100	11336
(PK-JGH)	F-100	11350
PK-JGI	**F-70**	**11529**
PK-JGJ	**F-70**	**11532**
PK-JGK	F-70	11584
PK-JGL	F-70	11586
PK-JHA	**B737**	**20450**
PK-JHC	**B737**	**20506**
PK-JHD	**B737**	**20451**
PK-JHE	**B737**	**20452**
PK-JHF	B737	20508
PK-JHG	**B737**	**20507**
PK-JHH	**B737**	**22131**
PK-JHI	**B737**	**22132**
PK-JIA	**A300**	**198**
PK-JIC	**A300**	**195**
PK-JID	**A300**	**238**
PK-MBA	B707	18739
PK-MBC	**B737**	**22129**
PK-MBD	**B737**	**22141**
PK-MBE	**B737**	**22142**
PK-MJA	**F-100**	**11453**
PK-MJC	**F-100**	**11463**
PK-MJD	**F-100**	**11474**
PK-MJE	**F-100**	**11512**
PK-MJF	**F-100**	**11517**
PK-MJG	**F-100**	**11527**
PK-OCF	**B737**	**19601**
PK-OCG	**B737**	**20335**
PK-OCI	**B737**	**20255**
PK-PFE	**F-70**	**11553**
PK-PJC	1-11	BAC.166
PK-PJF	**1-11**	**065**
PK-PJJ	**146**	**E2239**
PK-PJK	**F-28**	**11192**
PK-PJL	**F-28**	**11111**
PK-PJM	**F-28**	**11178**
PK-PJN	**F-100**	**11288**
PK-PJP	**146**	**E2050**
PK-PJP	B727	21091
PK-PJQ	B707	21092
PK-PJS	**F-28**	**11030**
PK-PJT	F-28	11042
PK-PJU	F-28	11029
PK-PJV	F-28	11073
PK-PJW	F-28	11095
PK-PJW	F-28	11148
(PK-PJX)	F-28	11042
PK-PJY	**F-28**	**11146**
(PK-RI.)	B737	22875
PK-RII	**B737**	**22876**
PK-RIJ	**B737**	**21820**
PK-RIK	**B737**	**22531**
PK-RIL	**B737**	**22137**
PK-RIM	**B737**	**22136**
PK-RIQ	**B737**	**23023**
PK-RIR	**B737**	**22735**
PK-TAL	**1-11**	**BAC.259**
PK-TRU	**1-11**	**BAC.262**
PK-VBA	**B727**	**18970**
PK-YPJ	**F-28**	**11148**

Brazil

PP-	**B707**	**18922**
(PP-...)	B737	25787
(PP-...)	B737	25788
PP-AIU	B727	20580
PP-AIV	**B727**	**20874**
PP-AIW	**B727**	**22079**
PP-AIY	DC-8	46070
PP-AJM	**DC-10**	**47929**
PP-AJP	**B707**	**20069**
PP-BRB	**B707**	**18925**
PP-BRI	**B707**	**19776**
(PP-BRR)	B707	19375
PP-CJA	CRVL	129
PP-CJB	CRVL	133
PP-CJC	CRVL	62
PP-CJD	CRVL	168
PP-CJE	B727	20418
PP-CJF	B727	20419
PP-CJG	B727	20420
PP-CJH	B727	19305
PP-CJH	B727	20421
PP-CJI	B727	19242
PP-CJJ	B727	19400
PP-CJK	B727	18969
PP-CJL	B727	18968
PP-CJM	MD-82	49149
PP-CJN	**B737**	**21012**
PP-CJO	**B737**	**21013**
PP-CJP	**B737**	**21014**
PP-CJR	**B737**	**21015**
PP-CJS	**B737**	**21016**
PP-CJT	**B737**	**21017**
PP-CLA	A300	109
PP-CLB	A300	110
PP-DGX	**DC-8**	**45953**
PP-ITA	**B727**	**18968**
PP-ITL	**B727**	**20078**
PP-ITM	**B727**	**19507**
PP-ITP	**B727**	**19313**
PP-ITR	**B727**	**22549**
PP-ITV	**B727**	**22476**
PP-LBF	**B727**	**20705**
PP-LBN	B707	19239
PP-PDS	DC-8	45272
PP-PDT	DC-8	45273
PP-PDU	CRVL	118
PP-PDV	CRVL	120
PP-PDX	CRVL	126
PP-PDZ	CRVL	131
PP-PEA	DC-8	45253
PP-PEF	DC-8	45271
PP-PHB	**B707**	**18711**
PP-SDP	1-11	BAC.192
PP-SDQ	1-11	BAC.228
PP-SDR	1-11	BAC.230
PP-SDS	1-11	BAC.236
PP-SDT	1-11	BAC.193
PP-SDU	1-11	BAC.211
PP-SDV	1-11	BAC.199
PP-SLS	**B737**	**26104**
PP-SLT	**B737**	**26105**
PP-SMA	**B737**	**20092**
PP-SMB	**B737**	**20093**
PP-SMC	**B737**	**20094**
PP-SMD	B737	20095
PP-SME	B737	20096
PP-SMF	**B737**	**20589**
PP-SMG	**B737**	**20777**
PP-SMH	**B737**	**20778**
PP-SMK	B727	21348
PP-SMP	**B737**	**20779**
PP-SMQ	**B737**	**20155**
PP-SMR	**B737**	**20157**
PP-SMS	**B737**	**20159**
PP-SMT	**B737**	**20160**
PP-SMU	**B737**	**20967**
PP-SMV	**B737**	**20968**
PP-SMW	**B737**	**20346**
PP-SMX	B737	20969
PP-SMY	B737	20970
PP-SMZ	**B737**	**20971**
PP-SNA	**B737**	**21094**
PP-SNB	**B737**	**21095**
PP-SNC	B737	21187
PP-SND	B737	21188
PP-SNE	B727	21341
PP-SNF	B727	21342
PP-SNG	B727	21345
(PP-SNG)	B727	21343
PP-SNH	B727	21346
(PP-SNH)	B727	21344
PP-SNI	B727	21600
(PP-SNI)	B737	21597
PP-SNJ	B727	21601
(PP-SNJ)	B737	21598
PP-SNK	B737	21686
(PP-SNK)	B727	21345
(PP-SNK)	B737	21599
PP-SNL	**A300**	**202**
(PP-SNL)	B727	21346
PP-SNM	**A300**	**205**
(PP-SNM)	B727	21600

PP-SNN A300 225
(PP-SNN) B727 21601
PP-SNO B737 21685
PP-SNP B737 21206
PP-SNQ B737 23173
PP-SNR B737 23174
PP-SNS B737 23175
PP-SNT B737 23176
PP-SNU B737 23177
PP-SNV B737 23826
PP-SNW B737 22580
PP-SNW B737 24096
(PP-SNX) B737 24097
PP-SNY B737 20218
PP-SNY B737 23415
PP-SNZ B737 24097
PP-SOA B737 23747
PP-SOB B737 23748
PP-SOC B737 24790
PP-SOD B737 24791
PP-SOE B737 25010
PP-SOF B737 25011
PP-SOG B737 25032
PP-SOH B737 24683
PP-SOI B737 24691
PP-SOJ B737 24911
PP-SOK B737 25057
PP-SOL B737 25119
PP-SOM DC-10 46940
PP-SON DC-10 47868
PP-SOO DC-8 45974
PP-SOP DC-8 45976
PP-SOQ DC-8 45941
PP-SOR B737 25125
PP-SOT B737 25150
PP-SOU B737 25360
PP-SOV DC-10 47889
PP-SOW MD-11 48413
PP-SOZ MD-11 48414
PP-SPA B737 23464
PP-SPB B737 23465
PP-SPC B737 23466
PP-SPD MD-11 48411
PP-SPE MD-11 48412
PP-SPF B737 21073
PP-SPG B737 21616
PP-SPH B737 22070
PP-SPI B737 21476
PP-SPJ B737 21236
PP-SPK MD-11 48744
PP-SPL MD-11 48745
PP-SPM MD-11 48563
PP-SRK B727 21347
PP-SRT 1-11 BAC.119
PP-SRU 1-11 BAC.126
PP-SRV B737 22296
PP-SRW B737 22058
PP-SRX B737 19425
PP-SRY B727 19310
PP-SRZ B727 19311
PP-TLM B727 20580
PP-VJA B707 17905
PP-VJB B707 17906
PP-VJC CRVL 10
PP-VJD CRVL 15
PP-VJE CV990 30-10-13
PP-VJF CV990 30-10-19
PP-VJG CV990 30-10-20
PP-VJH B707 20008
PP-VJI CRVL 20
PP-VJJ B707 18694
PP-VJK B707 19822
PP-VJR B707 19320
PP-VJS B707 19321
PP-VJT B707 19322
PP-VJX B707 19842
PP-VJY B707 19840
PP-VJZ B707 19841
PP-VLA B727 20422
PP-VLB B727 20423
PP-VLC B727 20424
PP-VLD B727 20425
PP-VLE B727 19666
PP-VLE B727 20426
PP-VLF B727 20422
PP-VLG B727 20423
PP-VLH B727 20424
PP-VLI B707 19433
PP-VLJ B707 19106
PP-VLK B707 19870
PP-VLL B707 19871
PP-VLM B707 19869
PP-VLN B707 19177
PP-VLO B707 19350
PP-VLP B707 18940
PP-VLQ B727 19595
PP-VLR B727 19596
PP-VLS B727 19508
PP-VLT B727 19250
PP-VLU B707 19235
PP-VLV B727 19009
PP-VLW B727 19507
PP-VMA DC-10 46944
PP-VMB DC-10 46945
(PP-VMC) DC-10 46941
PP-VMD DC-10 46916
PP-VME B737 21000
PP-VMF B737 21001
PP-VMG B737 21002
PP-VMH B737 21003
PP-VMI B737 21004
PP-VMJ B737 21005
PP-VMK B737 21006
PP-VML B737 21007
PP-VMM B737 21008
PP-VMN B737 21009
PP-VMO DC-10 46540
PP-VMP DC-10 46541
PP-VMQ DC-10 46941
PP-VMR DC-10 47817
PP-VMS DC-10 47818
PP-VMT DC-10 47841
PP-VMU DC-10 47842
PP-VMV DC-10 47843
PP-VMW DC-10 47844
PP-VMX DC-10 47845
PP-VMY DC-10 48282
PP-VMZ DC-10 46999
PP-VNA B747 22105
PP-VNB B747 22106
PP-VNC B747 22107
PP-VND A300 143
PP-VNE A300 194
PP-VNF B737 22504
PP-VNG B737 22505
PP-VNH B747 23394
PP-VNI B747 23395
PP-VNL B767 23057
PP-VNM B767 23058
PP-VNN B767 23803
PP-VNO B767 23801
PP-VNP B767 23802
PP-VNQ B767 23804
PP-VNR B767 23805
PP-VNS B767 23806
PP-VNT B737 23828
PP-VNU B737 23797
PP-VNV B737 23798
PP-VNW B747 20238
PP-VNX B737 23829
PP-VNY B737 24864
PP-VNZ B737 24869
PP-VOA B747 24106
PP-VOB B747 24107
PP-VOC B747 24108
PP-VOD B737 24275
PP-VOE B737 24276
PP-VOF B737 24277
PP-VOG B737 24278
PP-VOH B737 24279
PP-VOI B767 24752
PP-VOJ B767 24753
PP-VOK B767 24843
PP-VOL B767 24844
PP-VOM B737 23922
PP-VON B737 24935
PP-VOO B737 24936
PP-VOP MD-11 48434
PP-VOQ MD-11 48435
PP-VOR B737 24093
PP-VOS B737 25048
PP-VOT B737 25049
PP-VOU B737 25050
PP-VOV B737 25051
PP-VOW B737 24961
PP-VOX B737 24962
PP-VOY B737 25210
PP-VOZ B737 25239
PP-VPA B737 26852
PP-VPB B737 26856
(PP-VPB) B737 26853
PP-VPC B737 26857
(PP-VPC) B737 26854
PP-VPD B737 26855
(PP-VPE) B737 26856
(PP-VPF) B737 26857
PP-VPG B747 24956
PP-VPH B747 24957
PP-VPI B747 24896
PP-VPJ MD-11 48404
PP-VPK MD-11 48405
PP-VPL MD-11 48406
PP-VPM MD-11 48439
PT- EMB145145003
PT- F-100 11525
PT- F-100 11526
PT- F-100 11530
PT-AIY DC-8 46070
PT-DUW CRVL 86
PT-LEP 146 E1010
PT-LEQ 146 E1011
PT-MCN F-100 11452
PT-MCO F-100 11471
PT-MDG B727 19319
PT-MNC B737 25165
PT-MRA F-100 11284
PT-MRB F-100 11285
PT-MRC F-100 11320
PT-MRD F-100 11322
PT-MRE F-100 11348
PT-MRF F-100 11351
PT-MRG F-100 11304
PT-MRH F-100 11305
PT-MRI F-100 11442
PT-MRJ F-100 11451
PT-MRK F-100 11440
PT-MRL F-100 11441
PT-MRM F-100 11422
PT-MRN F-100 11443
PT-MRO F-100 11470
PT-MRP F-100 11472
PT-MRQ F-100 11473
PT-MRR F-100 11461
PT-MRS F-100 11462
PT-MRT F-100 11505
PT-MRU F-100 11511
PT-MRV F-100 11516
PT-MRW F-100 11518
PT-MRX F-100 11508
PT-MRY F-100 11510
PT-MRZ F-100 11524
PT-SAV B727 19497
PT-SAW B727 19393
PT-SLM B737 25115
PT-SLN B737 26075
PT-SLP B737 26097
PT-SLU B737 25186
PT-SLV B737 25189
PT-SLW B737 24922
PT-TAA B767 22921
PT-TAB B767 22922
PT-TAC B767 22923
PT-TAD B767 24947
PT-TAE B767 24948
PT-TAF B767 25411
PT-TAG B767 24150
PT-TAH B767 23624
PT-TAI B767 24727
PT-TAJ B767 24728
PT-TAK B767 25421
PT-TAL B767 23764
PT-TAM B767 24349
PT-TCA B727 19136
PT-TCB B727 19137
PT-TCC B727 18844
PT-TCD B727 18744
PT-TCE B727 18743
(PT-TCE) B727 22424
PT-TCF B727 18742
(PT-TCF) B727 22425
PT-TCG B727 19136
PT-TCH B727 19088
PT-TCI B727 19140
PT-TCJ B707 19529
PT-TCK B707 19519
PT-TCL B707 19517
PT-TCM B707 19317
PT-TCN B707 20088
PT-TCO B707 18932
PT-TCP B707 19416
PT-TCQ B707 20456
PT-TCR B707 20018
PT-TCS B707 19354
"PT-TCT" B707 19296
PT-TCU B707 20316
PT-TDA B737 24690
(PT-TDA) B757 24635
(PT-TDB) B757 24868
PT-TDG B727 19319
(PT-TE.) B737 25190
PT-TEA B737 23499
PT-TEB B737 23500
PT-TEC B737 23708
PT-TED B737 23750
PT-TEE B737 23808
PT-TEF B737 24208
PT-TEG B737 24209
PT-TEH B737 24210
PT-TEI B737 23812
PT-TEJ B737 23926
PT-TEK B737 23927
PT-TEL B737 24467
PT-TEM B737 24511
PT-TEN B737 24513
(PT-TEN) B737 24512
PT-TEO B737 24692
(PT-TEO) B737 24676
(PT-TEP) B737 24790
PT-TEQ B737 25057
PT-TER B737 25119
PT-TYH B727 19497
PT-TYI B727 19827
PT-TYJ B727 19393
PT-TYK B727 19499
PT-TYL B727 19501
PT-TYM B727 19500
PT-TYN B727 19243
PT-TYO B727 19116
PT-TYP B727 19113
PT-TYQ B727 19110
PT-TYR B727 18794
PT-TYS B727 19111
PT-TYT B727 19112
PT-TYU B727 19109
PT-TYV 1-11 BAC.200
PT-TYW 1-11 BAC.206
PT-TYY 1-11 BAC.240
PT-WBA B737 21685
PT-WBB B737 21206
PT-WBC B737 21686
PT-WBD B737 23173
PT-WBE B737 23175
PT-WBF B737 23176
PT-WBG B737 23177
PT-WBH B737 23747
PT-WBI B737 23826
PT-WBJ B737 24911
PT-WBK DC-8 45941
PT-WBL DC-8 45974
PT-WBM DC-8 45976
PT-WHK F-100 11452
PT-WHL F-100 11471
PT-ZJA EMB145145801
PT-ZJB EMB145145001
PT-ZJC EMB145145002

Papua New Guinea

P2-ANA A310 378
P2-ANA B707 19622
P2-ANB B707 19621
P2-ANB F-28 11049
P2-ANC F-28 11089

P2-AND F-28 11118
P2-ANE F-28 11033
P2-ANF F-28 11038
P2-ANG A300 134
P2-ANG A310 549
P2-ANG B720 18014
P2-ANH B707 19294
P2-ANH F-28 11022
P2-ANI F-28 11223
P2-ANL F-28 11003
P2-ANU F-28 11041
P2-ANW F-28 11056
P2-ANY F-28 11070
P2-ANZ F-28 11034

Aruba

P4- B707 19585
P4-AAA B757 24771
P4-AFE B747 21962
P4-MDA MD-88 49759
P4-MDB MD-83 53045
P4-MDC MD-88 49766
P4-MDD DC-9 47271
P4-MDE MD-83 49950
P4-MDJ B707 21096
P4-TBN B707 21049

Russia

RA- IL-62 1545951
RA-10200 DC-10 46891
RA-21500 YAK40 9741356
RA-21501 YAK40 9741756
RA-21502 YAK40
RA-21503 YAK40 9832058
RA-21504 YAK40 9831758
RA-21505 YAK40 9830159
RA-21506 YAK40 9840259
RA-42316 YAK42 4520422202030
RA-42318 YAK42 452042..020..
RA-42320 YAK42 4520421302075
RA-42321 YAK42 4520423402088
RA-42322 YAK42 4520423402108
RA-42323 YAK42 4520423402116
RA-42324 YAK42 4520421402125
RA-42325 YAK42 452042.4021..
RA-42326 YAK42 4520424402154
RA-42328 YAK42 4520421505058
RA-42329 YAK42 4520422505093
RA-42330 YAK42 4520422505122
RA-42331 YAK42 452042..051..
RA-42332 YAK42 4520421605135
RA-42333 YAK42 4520422606156
RA-42335 YAK42 4520422606204
RA-42336 YAK42 452042.6062..
RA-42340 YAK42 4520424606270
RA-42341 YAK42 4520421706292
RA-42343 YAK42 4520421706305
RA-42346 YAK42 4520423708311
RA-42347 YAK42 4520423711322
RA-42350 YAK42 4520424711372
RA-42356 YAK42 4520422811400
RA-42357 YAK42 4520422811408
RA-42360 YAK42 4520423811421
RA-42361 YAK42 4520423811427
RA-42363 YAK42 4520424811438
RA-42364 YAK42 4520424811442
RA-42365 YAK42 4520424811447
RA-42367 YAK42 4520421914133
RA-42368 YAK42 4520422914166
RA-42370 YAK42 4520422914203
RA-42371 YAK42 4520422914225
RA-42373 YAK42 4520423914323
RA-42374 YAK42 4520423914340
RA-42375 YAK42 4520424914410
RA-42378 YAK42 4520421014494
RA-42379 YAK42 4520421014543
RA-42380 YAK42 4520422014549
RA-42382 YAK42 4520422016196
RA-42384 YAK42 4520423016230
RA-42385 YAK42 4520423016309
RA-42386 YAK42 4520424016310
RA-42387 YAK42 4520424016436
RA-42388 YAK42 4520424016510
RA-42389 YAK42 4520424016542
RA-42390 YAK42 4520424016557
RA-42391 YAK42 452042..165..
RA-42401 YAK42 4520421116567
RA-42402 YAK42 4520422116583
RA-42406 YAK42 4520424116638
RA-42408 YAK42 4520424116698
RA-42411 YAK42 4520421219043
RA-42412 YAK42 4520422219055
RA-42413 YAK42 4520422219066
RA-42414 YAK42 4520422219073
RA-42415 YAK42 4520422219089
RA-42417 YAK42 4520423.191..
RA-42421 YAK42 4520422303017
RA-42422 YAK42 4520424304017
RA-42423 YAK42 4520424216606
RA-42424 YAK42 4520421502016
RA-42425 YAK42 4520423303016
RA-42426 YAK42 4520423304016
RA-42427 YAK42 4520422305016
RA-42428 YAK42 4520422306016
RA-42429 YAK42 4520423407016
RA-42430 YAK42 4520423408016
RA-42432 YAK42 4520424410016
RA-42433 YAK42 4520421301017
RA-42434 YAK42 4520424305017
RA-42435 YAK42 4520424306017
RA-42436 YAK42
RA-42441 YAK42 4520421402018
RA-42524 YAK42 11030603
RA-42528 YAK42 11041003
RA-42538 YAK42 11130404
RA-42539 YAK42 11140504
RA-42541 YAK42 11140704
RA-42542 YAK42 11140804
RA-42543 YAK42 11250904
RA-42549 YAK42 11040105
RA-42550 YAK42 11140205
RA-42551 YAK42 11140305
RA-48110 YAK40 9230623
RA-48111 YAK40 9211420
RA-48112 YAK40 9211520
RA-64001 TU234 1450743164001
RA-64001 TU204 1450743164001
RA-64002 TU204 1450743164002
RA-64003 TU204 1450743164003
RA-64004 TU204 1450743164004
RA-64006 TU204 1450743164006
RA-64007 TU204 1450743164007
RA-64008 TU204 1450743164008
RA-64009 TU204 1450743164009
RA-64010 TU204 1450743164010
RA-64011 TU204 1450743164011
RA-64012 TU204 1450743164012
RA-64013 TU204 1450743164013
RA-64014 TU204 1450743164014
RA-64015 TU204 1450743164015
RA-64016 TU204 1450743164016
RA-64017 TU204 1450743164017
RA-64018 TU204 1450743164018
RA-64019 TU204 1450743164019
RA-64020 TU204 1450743164020
RA-64021 TU204 1450743164021
RA-64022 TU204 1450743164022
RA-64023 TU204 1450743164023
RA-64024 TU204 1450743164024
RA-64025 TU204 1450743164025
RA-64451 TU134 66550
RA-64454 TU134
RA-65002 TU134 44020
RA-65004 TU134 44060
RA-65005 TU134 44065
RA-65006 TU134 44080
RA-65007 TU134
RA-65008 TU134 46105
RA-65009 TU134 46120
RA-65010 TU134 46130
RA-65011 TU134 46140
RA-65012 TU134 46175
RA-65015 TU134
RA-65016 TU134
RA-65017 TU134 48360
RA-65018 TU134 48365
RA-65019 TU134 48375
RA-65020 TU134 48380
RA-65021 TU134 48390
RA-65024 TU134 48420
RA-65025 TU134 48450
RA-65026 TU134 48470
RA-65027 TU134 48485
RA-65028 TU134 48490
RA-65029 TU134 48500
RA-65032 TU134
RA-65033 TU134 48540
RA-65035 TU134 48590
RA-65037 TU134 48850
RA-65038 TU134 48950
RA-65039 TU134
RA-65040 TU134 49100
RA-65042 TU134 49350
RA-65043 TU134 49400?
RA-65045 TU134 49500?
RA-65046 TU134 49700
RA-65047 TU134 49600
RA-65052 TU134 49825
RA-65054 TU134 49840
RA-65055 TU134 49856
RA-65056 TU134
RA-65057 TU134 49865
RA-65059 TU134 49870
RA-65060 TU134 49872
RA-65062 TU134 49875
RA-65063 TU134 49880
RA-65064 TU134 49886
RA-65065 TU134 49890
RA-65066 TU134
RA-65067 TU134
RA-65068 TU134 49907
RA-65069 TU134 49908
RA-65070 TU134 49912
RA-65074 TU134 49987
RA-65078 TU134 60043
RA-65080 TU134 60065
RA-65083 TU134 60090
RA-65084 TU134 60115
RA-65086 TU134 60130
RA-65087 TU134 60155
RA-65090 TU134 60185
RA-65096 TU134 60257
RA-65097 TU134 60540
RA-65099 TU134 63700
RA-65100 TU134 60258
RA-65101 TU134 60260
RA-65102 TU134 60267
RA-65103 TU134 60297
RA-65104 TU134 60301
RA-65105 TU134 60308
RA-65106 TU134 60315
RA-65110 TU134 60343
RA-65113 TU134 60380
RA-65116 TU134 60420
RA-65117 TU134 60450
RA-65118 TU134 60462
RA-65122 TU134
RA-65126 TU134
RA-65127 TU134 60627
RA-65131 TU134 60637
RA-65132 TU134 60639
RA-65136 TU134 60885
RA-65137 TU134 60890
RA-65139 TU134
RA-65141 TU134 60945
RA-65143 TU134 60967
RA-65144 TU134 60977
RA-65148 TU134 61025
RA-65156 TU134
RA-65550 TU134 60321
RA-65552 TU134 66270
RA-65553 TU134 66300
RA-65554 TU134 66320
RA-65555 TU134 66350
RA-65557 TU134 66380
RA-65559 TU134 49909
RA-65562 TU134
RA-65563 TU134
RA-65564 TU134 63165
RA-65565 TU134 63998
RA-65566 TU134 63952
RA-65567 TU134 66135
RA-65568 TU134 63967
RA-65570 TU134

RA-65585 TU134
RA-65604 TU134 0101
RA-65606 TU134 46300
RA-65607 TU134 6348560
RA-65608 TU134 5338040
RA-65609 TU134 46155
RA-65610 TU134 40150
RA-65611 TU134 3351903
RA-65612 TU134 3352102
RA-65613 TU134 3352106
RA-65614 TU134 4352207
RA-65615 TU134 4352205
RA-65616 TU134 4352206
RA-65617 TU134 4308068
RA-65618 TU134 12095
RA-65619 TU134 31218
RA-65620 TU134 35180
RA-65621 TU134 6348320
RA-65622 TU134 60495
RA-65623 TU134 49985
RA-65624 TU134
RA-65626 TU134
RA-65647 TU134 0351002
RA-65651 TU134 0351007
RA-65653 TU134 0351009
RA-65661 TU134 351107
RA-65666 TU134 1351202
RA-65667 TU134 1351207
RA-65669 TU134 1351210
RA-65671 TU134 1351402?
RA-65676 TU134 1351502
RA-65679 TU134 23249
RA-65681 TU134 49760
RA-65682 TU134
RA-65684 TU134 62205
RA-65689 TU134
RA-65690 TU134
RA-65691 TU134 63195
RA-65697 TU134 63307
RA-65711 TU134 63972
RA-65716 TU134 63595
RA-65717 TU134 63657
RA-65719 TU134 63637
RA-65720 TU134 63820
RA-65721 TU134
RA-65722 TU134
RA-65723 TU134 66440
RA-65724 TU134 66445
RA-65725 TU134 66472
RA-65726 TU134 2351506
RA-65726 TU134 63720
RA-65738 TU134 2351519?
RA-65739 TU134 2351520?
RA-65740 TU134 2351510
RA-65751 TU134 61066
RA-65753 TU134
RA-65755 TU134 62165
RA-65756 TU134 62179
RA-65758 TU134
RA-65759 TU134 62239
RA-65760 TU134 62187
RA-65762 TU134 62279
RA-65769 TU134 62415
RA-65770 TU134 62430
RA-65771 TU134 62445
RA-65775 TU134 62530
RA-65776 TU134 62545
RA-65777 TU134 62552
RA-65780 TU134 62622
RA-65781 TU134 62645
RA-65783 TU134 62713
RA-65784 TU134 62715
RA-65785 TU134 62750
RA-65786 TU134 62775
RA-65792 TU134
RA-65793 TU134 63128
RA-65794 TU134
RA-65796 TU134 63150
RA-65797 TU134
RA-65800 TU134 3352009?
RA-65801 TU134 3352010
RA-65802 TU134 3352101
RA-65804 TU134 3352104?
RA-65805 TU134 3352105
RA-65811 TU134 352202
RA-65813 TU134 352204
RA-65815 TU134 4352209
RA-65819 TU134 4352304
RA-65823 TU134 0907.?
RA-65824 TU134 09074
RA-65825 TU134 09078
RA-65827 TU134 12084
RA-65828 TU134
RA-65829 TU134
RA-65830 TU134 12093
RA-65834 TU134 17109
RA-65837 TU134 17114
RA-65838 TU134 18116
RA-65840 TU134 18118
RA-65842 TU134 1812.?
RA-65843 TU134 18123
RA-65844 TU134
RA-65845 TU134 23131
RA-65846 TU134 2313.?
RA-65847 TU134 23135
RA-65851 TU134 23241
RA-65853 TU134 2324.?
RA-65854 TU134 23248
RA-65855 TU134 23252
RA-65858 TU134
RA-65859 TU134 23264
RA-65860 TU134 28265
RA-65861 TU134 28269
RA-65862 TU134 28270
RA-65863 TU134
RA-65865 TU134 28286
RA-65866 TU134 28292
RA-65867 TU134
RA-65868 TU134
RA-65869 TU134 28306
RA-65870 TU134 28310
RA-65872 TU134 29312
RA-65880 TU134 35200
RA-65881 TU134 35220
RA-65885 TU134 36160
RA-65887 TU134 36170?
RA-65889 TU134
RA-65891 TU134 38030
RA-65894 TU134 40130
RA-65898 TU134
RA-65899 TU134 42225
RA-65901 TU134 63731
RA-65902 TU134 63742
RA-65903 TU134 63750
RA-65904 TU134 63953
RA-65905 TU134 63965
RA-65906 TU134 66175
RA-65907 TU134 63996
RA-65908 TU134 63870
RA-65912 TU134 63985
RA-65914 TU134 66109
RA-65915 TU134 66120
RA-65916 TU134 66152
RA-65917 TU134 63991
RA-65918 TU134 63993?
RA-65919 TU134 66168
RA-65921 TU134 63997
RA-65926 TU134 66101
RA-65927 TU134 66198
RA-65928 TU134
RA-65929 TU134
RA-65930 TU134 66500
RA-65932 TU134 66405
RA-65933 TU134
RA-65934 TU134 66143
RA-65935 TU134 66180
RA-65939 TU134 1351409
RA-65940 TU134
RA-65941 TU134
RA-65950 TU134 2351702
RA-65954 TU134 2351707
RA-65955 TU134 2351708
RA-65956 TU134 2351709
RA-65958 TU134 3351804
RA-65960 TU134 3351806
RA-65961 TU134 3351807
RA-65963 TU134
RA-65966 TU134 3351902
RA-65967 TU134 3351905
RA-65969 TU134 3351909
RA-65970 TU134 3351910?
RA-65971 TU134 3352001
RA-65972 TU134 3352002
RA-65976 TU134 3352007
RA-65977 TU134 63245
RA-65978 TU134 63357
RA-65979 TU134
RA-65980 TU134
RA-65981 TU134
RA-65982 TU134
RA-65983 TU134
RA-65984 TU134
RA-65986 TU134
RA-65987 TU134 63505
RA-65988 TU134
RA-65989 TU134
RA-65990 TU134
RA-65991 TU134
RA-65992 TU134
RA-65993 TU134
RA-65994 TU134 66207
RA-65995 TU134 66400
RA-65996 TU134
(RA-71430) B737 22028
RA-72005 AN-72
RA-72024 AN-72
RA-72905 AN-72
RA-72908 AN-72
RA-72911 AN-72
RA-72914 AN-72
RA-72917 AN-72
RA-72922 AN-72
RA-72924 AN-72
RA-72925 AN-72
RA-72926 AN-72
RA-72930 AN-72
RA-72939 AN-72
RA-72940 AN-72
RA-72952 AN-72
RA-72955 AN-72
RA-72960 AN-72 36572093865
RA-72961 AN-72
RA-72962 AN-72
RA-72964 AN-72
RA-72965 AN-72
RA-72973 AN-72
RA-72982 AN-72 36572096914
RA-72983? AN-72
RA-73000 B737 21443
RA-73001 B737 21444
RA-73003 B737 19611
RA-74000 AN-74
RA-74003 AN-74
RA-74004 AN-74 36547094890
RA-74005 AN-74
RA-74006 AN-74
RA-74007 AN-74 36547095903
RA-74008 AN-74 36547095900
RA-74009 AN-74
RA-74024 AN-74
RA-74025 AN-74 36547095905
RA-74029 AN-74
RA-74030 AN-74
RA-74033 AN-74
RA-74034 AN-74
RA-74040 AN-74 36547097...
RA-74041 AN-74 36547096924
RA-74046 AN-74
RA-74047 AN-74 36547098943
RA-74048 AN-74 36547097941
RA-76347 IL-76
RA-76350 IL-76
RA-76352 IL-76 1023411378
RA-76354 IL-76
RA-76355 IL-76 1013408265
RA-76357 IL-76
RA-76360 IL-76 1033418578
RA-76361 IL-76 1033415497
RA-76362 IL-76 1033416533
RA-76363 IL-76 1033417540
RA-76367 IL-76 1033414474
RA-76369 IL-76 1033414480
RA-76370 IL-76 1023414458
RA-76371 IL-76 1033414485
RA-76379 IL-76 1033417569
RA-76380 IL-76
RA-76381 IL-76
RA-76382 IL-76 0013436048

RA-76383	IL-76	0023437076
RA-76386	IL-76	1033418600
RA-76388	IL-76	1013406204
RA-76389	IL-76	1013407212
RA-76400	IL-76	1023413438
RA-76401	IL-76	1023412399
RA-76402	IL-76	1023413430
RA-76403	IL-76	1023412414
RA-76404	IL-76	
RA-76405	IL-76	
RA-76406	IL-76	1023414463
RA-76409	IL-76	1023410355
RA-76411	IL-76	1023411384
RA-76412	IL-76	
RA-76413	IL-76	1013407215
RA-76416	IL-76	043402041
RA-76417	IL-76	043402046
RA-76418	IL-76	073409237
RA-76419	IL-76	1023414470
RA-76420	IL-76	1023413446
RA-76421	IL-76	1033415504
RA-76423	IL-76	0053457720
RA-76425	IL-76	1003405167
RA-76426	IL-76	1013405184
RA-76436	IL-76	1023411368
RA-76440	IL-76	
RA-76441	IL-76	
RA-76443	IL-76	0043452534
RA-76444	IL-76	0063470113
RA-76445	IL-76	
RA-76446	IL-76	
RA-76450	IL-76	
RA-76451	IL-76	
RA-76453	IL-76	0063466995
RA-76457	IL-76	
RA-76458	IL-76	
RA-76459	IL-76	
RA-76460	IL-76	0013431928
RA-76461	IL-76	0013431935
RA-76462	IL-76	
RA-76463	IL-76	0013432960
RA-76464	IL-76	
RA-76465	IL-76	
RA-76467	IL-76	0023440157
RA-76468	IL-76	0023441195
RA-76469	IL-76	0033444286
RA-76470	IL-76	0033445291
RA-76471	IL-76	
RA-76472	IL-76	0033446350
RA-76473	IL-76	0033448404
RA-76474	IL-76	0033448407
RA-76475	IL-76	0043451523
RA-76476	IL-76	0043451528
RA-76477	IL-76	0043453575
RA-76478	IL-76	0053459788
RA-76479	IL-76	0053460790
RA-76480	IL-76	005346079.
RA-76481	IL-76	0053460795
RA-76482	IL-76	0053460832
RA-76483	IL-76	0063468042
RA-76484	IL-76	0063469081
RA-76485	IL-76	0063470088
RA-76486	IL-76	0073476281
RA-76487	IL-76	0073479367
RA-76488	IL-76	0073479371
RA-76489	IL-76	0083485554
RA-76490	IL-76	093416506
RA-76491	IL-76	093421630
RA-76492	IL-76	093418548
RA-76493	IL-76	0043456700
RA-76494	IL-76	0063465965
RA-76495	IL-76	073410292
RA-76497	IL-76	073410320
RA-76498	IL-76	0023442218
RA-76499	IL-76	0023441186
RA-76503	IL-76	
RA-76504	IL-76	073411328
RA-76505	IL-76	073411331
RA-76506	IL-76	073411334
RA-76507	IL-76	073411338
RA-76508	IL-76	
RA-76509	IL-76	
RA-76510	IL-76	083414432
RA-76512	IL-76	083414447
RA-76513	IL-76	083414451
RA-76514	IL-76	083415453
RA-76515	IL-76	093417526
RA-76516	IL-76	
RA-76517	IL-76	
RA-76518	IL-76	093420594
RA-76519	IL-76	093420599
RA-76520	IL-76	093420605
RA-76521	IL-76	0003423699
RA-76522	IL-76	0003424707
RA-76523	IL-76	0003425732
RA-76524	IL-76	
RA-76525	IL-76	
RA-76526	IL-76	
RA-76527	IL-76	0003427796
RA-76528	IL-76	073410293
RA-76529	IL-76	073410308
RA-76533	IL-76	
RA-76540	IL-76	0033442238
RA-76544	IL-76	
RA-76545	IL-76	0033443266
RA-76546	IL-76	
RA-76547	IL-76	
RA-76548	IL-76	
RA-76549	IL-76	
RA-76550	IL-76	
RA-76551	IL-76	0033445309
RA-76552	IL-76	
RA-76556	IL-76	0033445294
RA-76557	IL-76	
RA-76558	IL-76	0033446333
RA-76572	IL-76	
RA-76577	IL-76	
RA-76588	IL-76	
RA-76591	IL-76	0043452546
RA-76592	IL-76	
RA-76599	IL-76	
RA-76604	IL-76	
RA-76605	IL-76	
RA-76615	IL-76	
RA-76620	IL-76	
RA-76623	IL-76	
RA-76625	IL-76	
RA-76632	IL-76	
RA-76635	IL-76	
RA-76640	IL-76	
RA-76643	IL-76	
RA-76650	IL-76	0053462865
RA-76655	IL-76	0053463885
RA-76659	IL-76	0053463902
RA-76666	IL-76	0053464934
RA-76669	IL-76	
RA-76672	IL-76	0063466981
RA-76692	IL-76	0063470096
RA-76693	IL-76	
RA-76701	IL-76	
RA-76706	IL-76	0063472163
RA-76708	IL-76	0063473171
RA-76720	IL-76	0073475229
RA-76722	IL-76	0073475242
RA-76727	IL-76	0073475268
RA-76731	IL-76	
RA-76733	IL-76	0073476304
RA-76738	IL-76	0073477326
RA-76745	IL-76	0073479362
RA-76746	IL-76	
RA-76750	IL-76	0083485561
RA-76751	IL-76	0083487610
RA-76752	IL-76	0093498967
RA-76753	IL-76	0073481461
RA-76753	IL-76	1013406206
RA-76754	IL-76	093421637
RA-76755	IL-76	0013433984
RA-76756	IL-76	0013428839
RA-76757	IL-76	0013433990
RA-76758	IL-76	0073474203
RA-76759	IL-76	093418543
RA-76761	IL-76	0073479401
RA-76762	IL-76	
RA-76763	IL-76	0073480413
RA-76764	IL-76	
RA-76766	IL-76	0073481431
RA-76772	IL-76	
RA-76776	IL-76	0083482486
RA-76780	IL-76	
RA-76781	IL-76	
RA-76783	IL-76	0093498974
RA-76785	IL-76	0093495863
RA-76786	IL-76	0093496923
RA-76787	IL-76	0093495854
RA-76788	IL-76	0013433996
RA-76789	IL-76	0013433999
RA-76790	IL-76	0093496903
RA-76791	IL-76	0093497936
RA-76792	IL-76	0093497942
RA-76795	IL-76	0093498962
RA-76796	IL-76	
RA-76797	IL-76	1003403052
RA-76798	IL-76	1003403063
RA-76799	IL-76	1003403075
RA-76800	IL-76	
RA-76801	IL-76	
RA-76803	IL-76	
RA-76806	IL-76	1003403121
RA-76807	IL-76	1013405176
RA-76808	IL-76	1013405177
RA-76809	IL-76	1013408252
RA-76812	IL-76	1013407230
RA-76814	IL-76	1013408269
RA-76817	IL-76	
RA-76818	IL-76	1013408264
RA-76819	IL-76	1013409274
RA-76820	IL-76	1013409295
RA-76822	IL-76	0093499982
RA-76823	IL-76	0023441189
RA-76825	IL-76	
RA-76832	IL-76	1023410360
RA-76833	IL-76	
RA-76834	IL-76	1023409319
RA-76835	IL-76	1013408244
RA-76838	IL-76	1023411370
RA-76839	IL-76	1023411375
RA-76840	IL-76	1033417553
RA-76841	IL-76	1033418601
RA-76842	IL-76	1033418616
RA-76843	IL-76	1033418584
RA-76844	IL-76	1033416525
RA-76845	IL-76	1043420696
RA-76872	IL-76	
RA-76896	IL-76	
RA-77114	TU144	08-2
RA-78...	IL-76	
RA-78731	IL-76	
RA-78738	IL-76	0033442247
RA-78750	IL-76	
RA-78757	IL-76	
RA-78764	IL-76	
RA-78766	IL-76	0083486595
RA-78768	IL-76	0083487603
RA-78770	IL-76	0083487617
RA-78776	IL-76	0083489652
RA-78778	IL-76	0083490703
RA-78783	IL-76	
RA-78784	IL-76	
RA-78785	IL-76	0083489691
RA-78789	IL-76	0083490706
RA-78794	IL-76	0093490726
RA-78795	IL-76	
RA-78796	IL-76	0093491735
RA-78797	IL-76	
RA-78805	IL-76	0093492783
RA-78807	IL-76	
RA-78809	IL-76	
RA-78811	IL-76	
RA-78815	IL-76	0093495842
RA-78816	IL-76	0093495846
RA-78817	IL-76	0093495851
RA-78818	IL-76	0093495858
RA-78820	IL-76	0093496907
RA-78825	IL-76	1013495871
RA-78829	IL-76	
RA-78831	IL-76	
RA-78833	IL-76	1003401025
RA-78834	IL-76	
RA-78835	IL-76	
RA-78838	IL-76	1003402044
RA-78840	IL-76	1003403056
RA-78842	IL-76	1003403069
RA-78844	IL-76	
RA-78845	IL-76	
RA-78846	IL-76	
RA-78847	IL-76	
RA-78850	IL-76	1003405196
RA-78851	IL-76	

RA-78852 IL-76 1013407212
RA-78854 IL-76 1013407220
RA-78878 IL-76
RA-82003 AN124
RA-82005 AN124 9773054516003
RA-82006 AN124 19530501004
RA-82010 AN124 9773053616017
RA-82011 AN124 9773054616023
RA-82012 AN124
RA-82013 AN124
RA-82020 AN124 19530502001
RA-82021 AN124 19530502002?
RA-82022 AN124 19530502003
RA-82023 AN124 195305020.4?
RA-82024 AN124 19530502035
RA-82025 AN124 19530502106
RA-82028 AN124 19530502..9?
RA-82030 AN124 9773054732045
RA-82033 AN124 977305..32161
RA-82034 AN124 9773051932162
RA-82035 AN124
RA-82036 AN124
RA-82037 AN124 9773052955071
RA-82038 AN124 9773054955077
RA-82039 AN124
RA-82041 AN124
RA-82042 AN124 9773054055093
RA-82043 AN124 9773054155101
RA-82044 AN124 9773054155109
RA-82045 AN124 9773052255113
RA-82046 AN124 9773052255117
RA-82047 AN124 9773053259121
RA-82067 AN124 9773052255117
RA-82069 AN124
RA-82070 AN124
RA-82071 AN124
RA-82072 AN124
RA-82073 AN124 9773054359139
RA-82074 AN124 9773051459142
RA-82075 AN124 9773053459147
RA-82077 AN124 9773054459151
RA-82078 AN124
RA-82079 AN124
RA-85007 TU154 07
RA-85013 TU154 013
RA-85016 TU154 016
RA-85018 TU154 018
RA-85019 TU154 019
RA-85024 TU154 024
RA-85025 TU154 025
RA-85028 TU154 028
RA-85031 TU154 031
RA-85033 TU154 033
RA-85034 TU154 034
RA-85037 TU154 037
RA-85038 TU154 038
RA-85041 TU154 041
RA-85042 TU154 042
RA-85043 TU154 043
RA-85051 TU154 051
RA-85052 TU154 052
RA-85056 TU154 056
RA-85057 TU154 057
RA-85060 TU154 060
RA-85061 TU154 061
RA-85062 TU154 062
RA-85063 TU154 063
RA-85064 TU154 064
RA-85069 TU154 069
RA-85070 TU154 070
RA-85075 TU154 075
RA-85078 TU154 078
RA-85080 TU154 080
RA-85081 TU154 081
RA-85082 TU154 082
RA-85084 TU154 084
RA-85089 TU154 089
RA-85091 TU154 091
RA-85092 TU154 092
RA-85094 TU154 094
RA-85096 TU154 096
RA-85098 TU154 098
RA-85099 TU154 099
RA-85101 TU154 101
RA-85104 TU154 104
RA-85106 TU154 106
RA-85107 TU154 107
RA-85108 TU154 108
RA-85109 TU154 109
RA-85110 TU154 110
RA-85112 TU154 112
RA-85114 TU154 114
RA-85115 TU154 115
RA-85117 TU154 117
RA-85119 TU154 119
RA-85123 TU154 123
RA-85124 TU154 124
RA-85130 TU154 130
RA-85131 TU154 131
(RA-85133) TU154 133
RA-85135 TU154 135
RA-85139 TU154 139
RA-85140 TU154 140
RA-85141 TU154 141
RA-85142 TU154 142
RA-85145 TU154 145
RA-85146 TU154 146
RA-85149 TU154 149
RA-85150 TU154 150
RA-85151 TU154 151
RA-85153 TU154 153
RA-85155 TU154 155
RA-85156 TU154 156
RA-85157 TU154 157
RA-85160 TU154 160
RA-85164 TU154 164
RA-85165 TU154 165
RA-85167 TU154 167
RA-85171 TU154 171
RA-85172 TU154 172
RA-85174 TU154 174
RA-85176 TU154 176
RA-85178 TU154 178
RA-85180 TU154 180
RA-85181 TU154 181
RA-85182 TU154 182
RA-85183 TU154 183
RA-85184 TU154 184
RA-85185 TU154 185
RA-85187 TU154 187
RA-85190 TU154 190
RA-85193 TU154 193
RA-85194 TU154 194
RA-85195 TU154 195
RA-85201 TU154 201
RA-85202 TU154 202
RA-85204 TU154 204
RA-85205 TU154 205
RA-85206 TU154 206
RA-85207 TU154 207
RA-85212 TU154 212
RA-85213 TU154 213
RA-85215 TU154 215
RA-85216 TU154 216
RA-85217 TU154 217
RA-85219 TU154 219
RA-85220 TU154 220
RA-85221 TU154 221
RA-85223 TU154 223
RA-85226 TU154 226
RA-85228 TU154 228
RA-85229 TU154 229
RA-85233 TU154 233
RA-85235 TU154 235
RA-85236 TU154 236
RA-85237 TU154 237
RA-85238 TU154 238
RA-85242 TU154 242
RA-85251 TU154 251
RA-85253 TU154 253
RA-85255 TU154 255
RA-85256 TU154 256
RA-85261 TU154 261
RA-85263 TU154 263
RA-85264 TU154 264
RA-85265 TU154 265
RA-85266 TU154 266
RA-85267 TU154 267
RA-85273 TU154 273
RA-85275 TU154 275
RA-85280 TU154 280
RA-85283 TU154 283
RA-85284 TU154 284
RA-85287 TU154 287
RA-85288 TU154 288
RA-85289 TU154 289
RA-85291 TU154 291
RA-85292 TU154 292
RA-85293 TU154 293
RA-85295 TU154 295
RA-85296 TU154 296
RA-85298 TU154 298
RA-85299 TU154 299
RA-85300 TU154 300
RA-85301 TU154 301
RA-85302 TU154 302
RA-85303 TU154 303
RA-85304 TU154 304
RA-85305 TU154 305
RA-85306 TU154 306
RA-85307 TU154 307
RA-85308 TU154 308
RA-85309 TU154 309
RA-85310 TU154 310
RA-85312 TU154 312
RA-85314 TU154 314
RA-85315 TU154 315
RA-85317 TU154 317
RA-85318 TU154 318
RA-85319 TU154 319
RA-85323 TU154 323
RA-85324 TU154 324
RA-85328 TU154 328
RA-85330 TU154 330
RA-85333 TU154 333
RA-85334 TU154 334
RA-85335 TU154 335
RA-85336 TU154 336
RA-85337 TU154 337
RA-85340 TU154 340
RA-85341 TU154 341
RA-85343 TU154 343
RA-85346 TU154 346
RA-85347 TU154 347
RA-85348 TU154 348
RA-85349 TU154 349
RA-85351 TU154 351
RA-85353 TU154 353
RA-85354 TU154 354
RA-85357 TU154 357
RA-85358 TU154 358
RA-85360 TU154 360
RA-85361 TU154 361
RA-85362 TU154 362
RA-85363 TU154 363
RA-85365 TU154 365
RA-85366 TU154 366
RA-85367 TU154 367
RA-85371 TU154 371
RA-85373 TU154 373
RA-85374 TU154 374
RA-85375 TU154 375
RA-85376 TU154 376
RA-85377 TU154 377
RA-85378 TU154 378
RA-85380 TU154 380
RA-85381 TU154 381
RA-85382 TU154 382
RA-85386 TU154 386
RA-85388 TU154 388
RA-85389 TU154 389
RA-85390 TU154 390
RA-85392 TU154 392
RA-85393 TU154 393
RA-85400 TU154 400
RA-85402 TU154 402
RA-85404 TU154 404
RA-85409 TU154 409
RA-85412 TU154 412
RA-85414 TU154 414
RA-85417 TU154 417
RA-85418 TU154 418
RA-85421 TU154 421
RA-85425 TU154 425
RA-85426 TU154 426
RA-85427 TU154 427
RA-85429 TU154 429
RA-85432 TU154 432

RA-85434 TU154 434
RA-85435 TU154 435
RA-85436 TU154 436
RA-85437 TU154 437
RA-85439 TU154 439
RA-85441 TU154 441
RA-85443 TU154 443
RA-85446 TU154 446
RA-85448 TU154 448
RA-85450 TU154 450
RA-85451 TU154 451
RA-85452 TU154 452
RA-85453 TU154 453
RA-85454 TU154 454
RA-85456 TU154 456
RA-85457 TU154 457
RA-85458 TU154 458
RA-85459 TU154 459
RA-85461 TU154 461
RA-85462 TU154 462
RA-85463 TU154 463
RA-85467 TU154 467
RA-85468 TU154 468
RA-85470 TU154 470
RA-85471 TU154 471
RA-85472 TU154 472
RA-85475 TU154 475
RA-85477 TU154 477
RA-85481 TU154 481
RA-85485 TU154 485
RA-85486 TU154 486
RA-85488 TU154 488
RA-85489 TU154 489
RA-85494 TU154 494
RA-85495 TU154 495
RA-85498 TU154 498
RA-85500 TU154 500
RA-85502 TU154 502
RA-85503 TU154 503
RA-85504 TU154 504
RA-85505 TU154 505
RA-85506 TU154 506
RA-85508 TU154 508
RA-85510 TU154 510
RA-85511 TU154 511
RA-85512 TU154 512
RA-85514 TU154 514
RA-85520 TU154 520
RA-85522 TU154 522
RA-85523 TU154 523
RA-85525 TU154 525
RA-85527 TU154 527
RA-85529 TU154 529
RA-85530 TU154 530
RA-85534 TU154 534
RA-85541 TU154 540
RA-85542 TU154 542
RA-85545 TU154 545
RA-85550 TU154 550
RA-85551 TU154 551
RA-85552 TU154 552
RA-85553 TU154 553
RA-85554 TU154 554
RA-85555 TU154 555
RA-85557 TU154 557
RA-85559 TU154 559
RA-85562 TU154 562
RA-85563 TU154 563
RA-85564 TU154 564
RA-85565 TU154 565
RA-85567 TU154 567
RA-85568 TU154 568
RA-85570 TU154 570
RA-85571 TU154 571
RA-85572 TU154 572
RA-85574 TU154 574
RA-85577 TU154 577
RA-85579 TU154 579
RA-85584 TU154 584?
RA-85585 TU154 585
RA-85586 TU154 586
RA-85587 TU154 587
RA-85588 TU154 588
RA-85592 TU154 592
RA-85594 TU154 594
RA-85595 TU154 595
RA-85596 TU154 596
RA-85597 TU154 597
RA-85602 TU154 602
RA-85603 TU154 603
RA-85604 TU154 604
RA-85605 TU154 605
RA-85606 TU154 606
RA-85607 TU154 607
RA-85609 TU154 609
RA-85610 TU154 705
RA-85611 TU154 715
RA-85612 TU154 721
RA-85613 TU154 722
RA-85614 TU154 723
RA-85615 TU154 731
RA-85616 TU154 732
RA-85617 TU154 736
RA-85618 TU154 737
RA-85619 TU154 738
RA-85620 TU154 739
RA-85621 TU154 742
RA-85622 TU154 746
RA-85623 TU154 749
RA-85624 TU154 750
RA-85625 TU154 752
RA-85626 TU154 753
RA-85627 TU154 756
RA-85628 TU154 757
RA-85629 TU154 758
RA-85630 TU154 759
RA-85631 TU154 760
RA-85632 TU154 761
RA-85633 TU154 762
RA-85634 TU154 763
RA-85635 TU154 764
RA-85636 TU154 766
RA-85637 TU154 767
RA-85638 TU154 768
RA-85639 TU154 771
RA-85640 TU154 772
RA-85641 TU154 773
RA-85642 TU154 778
RA-85643 TU154 779
RA-85644 TU154 780
RA-85645 TU154 782
RA-85646 TU154 784
RA-85647 TU154 785
RA-85648 TU154 786
RA-85649 TU154 787
RA-85650 TU154 788
RA-85651 TU154 793
RA-85652 TU154 794
RA-85653 TU154 795
RA-85654 TU154 796
RA-85655 TU154 798
RA-85656 TU154 801
RA-85657 TU154 802
RA-85658 TU154 808
RA-85659 TU154 809
RA-85660 TU154 810
RA-85661 TU154 811
RA-85662 TU154 816
RA-85663 TU154 817
RA-85665 TU154 819
RA-85666 TU154 820
RA-85667 TU154 825
RA-85668 TU154 826
RA-85669 TU154 827
RA-85670 TU154 828
RA-85672 TU154 830
RA-85673 TU154 833
RA-85674 TU154 834
RA-85675 TU154 835
RA-85676 TU154 836
RA-85677 TU154 839
RA-85678 TU154 841
RA-85679 TU154 842
RA-85680 TU154 843
RA-85681 TU154 848
RA-85682 TU154 849
RA-85683 TU154 850
RA-85684 TU154 851
RA-85685 TU154 853
RA-85686 TU154 854
RA-85687 TU154 857
RA-85688 TU154 859
RA-85689 TU154 860
RA-85690 TU154 861
RA-85692 TU154 865
RA-85693 TU154 866
RA-85694 TU154 867
RA-85695 TU154 868
RA-85696 TU154 869
RA-85697 TU154 870
RA-85699 TU154 874
RA-85702 TU154 877
RA-85704 TU154 879
RA-85705 TU154 880
RA-85708 TU154 883
RA-85709 TU154 884
RA-85710 TU154 885
RA-85712 TU154 888
RA-85713 TU154 889
RA-85714 TU154 890
RA-85715 TU154 891
RA-85716 TU154 892
RA-85720 TU154 902
RA-85722 TU154 904
RA-85723 TU154 905
RA-85726 TU154 908
RA-85728 TU154 910
RA-85730 TU154 912
RA-85731 TU154 913
RA-85733 TU154 915
RA-85736 TU154 918
RA-85737 TU154 920
RA-85739 TU154 922
RA-85742 TU154 320
RA-85745 TU154 928
RA-85746 TU154 929
RA-85747 TU154 930
RA-85749 TU154 931
RA-85750 TU154 933
RA-85751 TU154 934?
RA-85752 TU154 935
RA-85753 TU154 937?
RA-85754 TU154 936
RA-85755 TU154 938?
RA-85756 TU154 939?
RA-85757 TU154 941?
RA-85758 TU154 940
RA-85759 TU154 943?
RA-85760 TU154 942
RA-85761 TU154 944
RA-85762 TU154 945
RA-85763 TU154 946
RA-85764 TU154 947
RA-85766 TU154 948?
RA-85767 TU154 949?
RA-85768 TU154 950
RA-85769 TU154 951
RA-85770 TU154 952
RA-85771 TU154 953
RA-85772 TU154 954
RA-85773 TU154 955
RA-85774 TU154 956
RA-85775 TU154 957
RA-85777 TU154 959
RA-85778 TU154 962?
RA-85779 TU154 963
RA-85781 TU154 965
RA-85782 TU154 966
RA-85783 TU154 967
RA-85784 TU154 968
RA-85785 TU154 969
RA-85786 TU154 970
RA-85787 TU154 971
RA-85788 TU154 972
RA-85789 TU154 973
RA-85790 TU154 974
RA-85791 TU154 975
RA-85792 TU154 976
RA-85793 TU154 977
RA-85794 TU154 978
RA-85795 TU154 980?
RA-85796 TU154 986?
RA-85797 TU154 981
RA-85798 TU154 982
RA-85799 TU154 983
RA-85800 TU154 984
RA-85801 TU154 960
RA-85802 TU154 961

Registration	Type	c/n
RA-85803	TU154	822
RA-85804	TU154	517
RA-85805	TU154	979
RA-85806	TU154	987
RA-85807	TU154	988
RA-85808	TU154	989?
RA-85809	TU154	985
RA-85810	TU154	824
RA-85811	TU154	831
RA-85812	TU154	1005
RA-85813	TU154	991?
RA-85814	TU154	994
RA-85816	TU154	1006
RA-85817	TU154	1007
RA-85818	TU154	719
RA-85818	TU154	
RA-85821	TU154	805
RA-85822	TU154	806
RA-85823	TU154	775
RA-86002	IL-86	0103?
RA-86004	IL-86	51483200002
RA-86006	IL-86	51483200004
RA-86007	IL-86	51483200005
RA-86009	IL-86	51483200007
RA-86010	IL-86	51483200008
RA-86011	IL-86	51483200009
RA-86013	IL-86	51483202011
RA-86015	IL-86	51483202013
RA-86017	IL-86	51483202015
RA-86018	IL-86	51483202016
RA-86025	IL-76	
RA-86026	IL-76	
RA-86027	IL-76	
RA-86032	IL-76	
RA-86035	IL-76	
RA-86037	IL-76	
RA-86038	IL-76	
RA-86040	IL-76	
RA-86041	IL-76	
RA-86042	IL-76	
RA-86049	IL-76	
RA-86050	IL-86	51483202017
RA-86051	IL-86	51483202018
RA-86054	IL-86	51483203021
RA-86055	IL-86	51483203022
RA-86058	IL-86	51483203025
RA-86059	IL-86	51483203026
RA-86060	IL-86	51483203027
RA-86061	IL-86	51483203028
RA-86062	IL-86	51483203029
RA-86063	IL-86	51483203030
RA-86065	IL-86	51483203032
RA-86066	IL-86	51483203033
RA-86067	IL-86	51483204034
RA-86070	IL-86	51483204037
RA-86073	IL-86	51483204040
RA-86074	IL-86	51483205041
RA-86075	IL-86	51483205044
RA-86078	IL-86	51483205049
RA-86079	IL-86	51483206050
RA-86080	IL-86	51483206051
RA-86081	IL-86	51483206052
RA-86082	IL-86	51483206053
RA-86084	IL-86	51483206055
RA-86085	IL-86	51483206056
RA-86087	IL-86	51483206058
RA-86088	IL-86	51483206059
RA-86089	IL-86	51483207060
RA-86091	IL-86	51483207062
RA-86092	IL-86	51483207063
RA-86093	IL-86	51483207064
RA-86094	IL-86	51483207065
RA-86095	IL-86	51483207066
RA-86096	IL-86	51483207067
RA-86097	IL-86	51483207068
RA-86102	IL-86	51483207070
RA-86103	IL-86	51483208071
RA-86104	IL-86	51483208072
RA-86105	IL-86	51483208073
RA-86106	IL-86	51483208074
RA-86107	IL-86	51483208075
RA-86108	IL-86	51483208076
RA-86109	IL-86	51483208077
RA-86110	IL-86	51483208078
RA-86111	IL-86	51483208079
RA-86112	IL-86	51483208080
RA-86113	IL-86	51483209081
RA-86114	IL-86	51483209082
RA-86115	IL-86	51483209083
RA-86119	IL-86	51483209087
RA-86120	IL-86	51483209088
RA-86121	IL-86	51483209089
RA-86122	IL-86	51483210090
RA-86123	IL-86	51483210091
RA-86124	IL-86	51483210092
RA-86125	IL-86	51483210093
RA-86126	IL-62	4154535
RA-86127	IL-62	1254851
RA-86128	IL-62	2255719
RA-86129	IL-62	2255525
RA-86131	IL-62	2255637
RA-86136	IL-86	51483210094
RA-86137	IL-86	51483210095
RA-86138	IL-86	51483210096
RA-86139	IL-86	51483210097
RA-86140	IL-86	51483211102
RA-86145	IL-86	51483211101
RA-86146	IL-86	51483205042
RA-86147	IL-86	51483205043
RA-86148	IL-86	51483205046
RA-86149	IL-86	51483205048
RA-86451	IL-62	52105
RA-86452	IL-62	62201
RA-86453	IL-62	62202
RA-86454	IL-62	62203
RA-86455	IL-62	62205
RA-86457	IL-62	62302
RA-86458	IL-62	62303
RA-86459	IL-62	62304
RA-86460	IL-62	62305
RA-86461	IL-62	62401
RA-86462	IL-62	62402
RA-86463	IL-62	62403
RA-86464	IL-62	62405
RA-86465	IL-62	62501
RA-86466	IL-62	2749316
RA-86467	IL-62	3749733
RA-86468	IL-62	4749857
RA-86469	IL-62	72502
RA-86471	IL-62	72504
RA-86472	IL-62	2726517
RA-86473	IL-62	3726841
RA-86474	IL-62	3726952
RA-86475	IL-62	3727113
RA-86476	IL-62	4728229
RA-86478	IL-62	4727657
RA-86479	IL-62	4728118
RA-86480	IL-62	2828354
RA-86481	IL-62	2829415
RA-86482	IL-62	2829526
RA-86483	IL-62	2829637
RA-86484	IL-62	4727324
RA-86484	IL-62	3829859
RA-86485	IL-62	3830912
RA-86486	IL-62	3830123
RA-86487	IL-62	3830234
RA-86488	IL-62	4830345
RA-86489	IL-62	4830456
RA-86490	IL-62	4831739
RA-86491	IL-62	1931142
RA-86492	IL-62	4140324
RA-86493	IL-62	4140748
RA-86494	IL-62	4140952
RA-86495	IL-62	2726628
RA-86497	IL-62	1931253
RA-86498	IL-62	1932314
RA-86499	IL-62	2932637
RA-86501	IL-62	3933121
RA-86502	IL-62	3933345
RA-86503	IL-62	4934512
RA-86504	IL-62	4934621
RA-86505	IL-62	4934847
RA-86506	IL-62	1035324
RA-86507	IL-62	2035546
RA-86508	IL-62	2036718
RA-86509	IL-62	2036829
RA-86510	IL-62	1035213
RA-86511	IL-62	3036142
RA-86512	IL-62	3037314
RA-86514	IL-62	4037647
RA-86515	IL-62	2138657
RA-86516	IL-62	2139524
RA-86517	IL-62	3139732
RA-86518	IL-62	3139956
RA-86519	IL-62	4140212
RA-86520	IL-62	1241314
RA-86521	IL-62	1241425
RA-86522	IL-62	2241536
RA-86523	IL-62	2241647
RA-86524	IL-62	3242321
RA-86525	IL-62	4851612
RA-86526	IL-62	2951447
RA-86529	IL-62	4038625
RA-86530	IL-62	4242543
RA-86531	IL-62	4242654
RA-86532	IL-62	4243111
RA-86533	IL-62	1343123
RA-86534	IL-62	1343332
RA-86535	IL-62	4344851
RA-86536	IL-62	4445948
RA-86537	IL-62	3546733
RA-86538	IL-62	00605
RA-86539	IL-62	2344615
RA-86540	IL-62	3546548
RA-86541	IL-62	3951359
RA-86542	IL-62	3952714
RA-86551	IL-62	
RA-86552	IL-62	2052435
RA-86553	IL-62	3052657
RA-86554	IL-62	4053514
RA-86555	IL-62	4547315
RA-86556	IL-62	31401
RA-86557	IL-62	2725456
RA-86558	IL-62	1052128
RA-86559	IL-62	2153258
RA-86560	IL-62	.53.4.
RA-86561	IL-62	4154841
RA-86562	IL-62	4831517
RA-86563	IL-62	3036931
RA-86564	IL-62	4934734
RA-86565	IL-62	2546812
RA-86566	IL-62	3255859
RA-86567	IL-62	4256314
RA-86568	IL-62	4256223
RA-86569	IL-62	1356234
RA-86570	IL-62	5604
RA-86571	IL-62	
RA-86572	IL-62	5605
RA-86590	IL-62	2647737
RA-86600	IL-76	033401022
RA-86604	IL-76	
RA-86610	IL-76	
RA-86611	IL-62	41803
RA-86618	IL-62	52002
RA-86619	IL-62	52003
RA-86620	IL-62	52004
RA-86621	IL-62	52005
RA-86622	IL-62	52101
RA-86623	IL-62	52102
RA-86627	IL-76	063405137
RA-86632	IL-76	
RA-86649	IL-62	00703
RA-86656	IL-62	10901
RA-86657	IL-62	10904
RA-86673	IL-62	3154416
RA-86674	IL-62	70304
RA-86675	IL-62	80305
RA-86692	IL-62	11102
RA-86693	IL-62	11103
RA-86699	IL-62	21304
RA-86700	IL-62	31503
RA-86701	IL-62	31504
RA-86702	IL-62	31505
RA-86703	IL-62	41601
RA-86705	IL-62	41605
RA-86706	IL-62	21105
RA-86707	IL-62	41604
RA-86708	IL-62	41802
RA-86709	IL-62	62204
RA-86710	IL-62	2647646
RA-86711	IL-62	4648414
RA-86712	IL-62	4648339
RA-86715	IL-76	
RA-86720	IL-76	073409267
RA-86726	IL-76	083412380
RA-86747	IL-76	063407170
RA-86820	IL-76	
RA-86825	IL-76	

RA-86827 IL-76
RA-86830 IL-76
RA-86832 IL-76
RA-86833 IL-76
RA-86835 IL-76
RA-86839 IL-76
RA-86842 IL-76
RA-86843 IL-76
RA-86846 IL-76 0003426765
RA-86847 IL-76
RA-86850 IL-76 0003427782
RA-86851 IL-76 0003424715
RA-86853 IL-76
RA-86857 IL-76 0003425744
RA-86858 IL-76
RA-86863 IL-76 0003428809
RA-86866 IL-76 0003428821
RA-86868 IL-76
RA-86869 IL-76 0013428844
RA-86872 IL-76
RA-86873 IL-76
RA-86874 IL-76 0013429853
RA-86876 IL-76
RA-86891 IL-76 093421628
RA-86894 IL-76
RA-86896 IL-76 0013434018
RA-86898 IL-76
RA-86902 IL-76
RA-86906 IL-76
RA-86907 IL-76
RA-86908 IL-76
RA-86909 IL-76 0023437076
RA-86910 IL-76
RA-86925 IL-76
RA-86931 IL-62 3344724
RA-87200 YAK40 9811956
RA-87203 YAK40 9741456
RA-87204 YAK40 9..1556
RA-87205 YAK40 9..0257
RA-87206 YAK40 9..0357
RA-87209 YAK40 9810657
RA-87210 YAK40 9810757
RA-87211 YAK40
RA-87212 YAK40
RA-87216 YAK40 9510440
RA-87219 YAK40 9932059
RA-87221 YAK40 9831958
RA-87223 YAK40 9840359
RA-87224 YAK40 9841259
RA-87225 YAK40 9841359
RA-87226 YAK40 9841459
RA-87227 YAK40 9841559
RA-87232 YAK40 9531742
RA-87234 YAK40 9..1942
RA-87235 YAK40 9530143
RA-87238 YAK40 9530643
RA-87239 YAK40 9530743
RA-87240 YAK40 9530843
RA-87241 YAK40 9530943
RA-87243 YAK40 9531143
RA-87244 YAK40 9531243
RA-87247 YAK40 9531543
RA-87248 YAK40 9541743
RA-87251 YAK40 9310826
RA-87253 YAK40 9310926
RA-87254 YAK40 9311026
RA-87256 YAK40 9311326
RA-87260 YAK40 9311126
RA-87261 YAK40 9311726
RA-87262 YAK40 9321826
RA-87268 YAK40 9310427
RA-87270 YAK40 9310627
RA-87273 YAK40 9310927
RA-87277 YAK40 9321327
RA-87281 YAK40 9311627
RA-87284 YAK40 9..1927
RA-87286 YAK40 9..0128
RA-87287 YAK40 9320228
RA-87288 YAK40 9320328
RA-87290 YAK40 9320528
RA-87292 YAK40 9320728
RA-87294 YAK40 9..0928
RA-87295 YAK40 9321228
RA-87297 YAK40 9321428
RA-87299 YAK40 9..1628
RA-87300 YAK40 9..1728

RA-87303 YAK40 9..1928
RA-87304 YAK40 9..2028
RA-87307 YAK40 9320329
RA-87311 YAK40 9320629
RA-87315 YAK40 9331429
RA-87317 YAK40 9331629
RA-87319 YAK40 9331829
RA-87321 YAK40 9332029
RA-87324 YAK40 9..0330
RA-87325 YAK40 9..0430
RA-87326 YAK40 9..0530
RA-87332 YAK40 9..0339
RA-87334 YAK40 9510738
RA-87336 YAK40 9510539
RA-87339 YAK40 9510839
RA-87340 YAK40 9510939
RA-87341 YAK40 9511039
RA-87342 YAK40 9511139
RA-87343 YAK40 9511239
RA-87344 YAK40 9511339
RA-87348 YAK40 9511739
RA-87350 YAK40
RA-87351 YAK40 9412030
RA-87353 YAK40 9330231
RA-87357 YAK40 9340631
RA-87358 YAK40 9340731
RA-87359 YAK40 9340831
RA-87361 YAK40 9341031
RA-87362 YAK40 9341131
RA-87364 YAK40 9341331
RA-87365 YAK40 9341531
RA-87368 YAK40 9341831
RA-87371 YAK40 9340232
RA-87372 YAK40 9340332
RA-87373 YAK40 9410732
RA-87375 YAK40 9410932
RA-87376 YAK40 9411032
RA-87380 YAK40 9..1132
RA-87381 YAK40 9411232
RA-87382 YAK40 9411332
RA-87383 YAK40 9411432
RA-87386 YAK40 9411732
RA-87392 YAK40 9410433
RA-87393 YAK40 9..0533
RA-87395 YAK40 9410733
RA-87397 YAK40 9..0933
RA-87399 YAK40 9411133
RA-87400 YAK40 9411233
RA-87404 YAK40 9411633
RA-87405 YAK40 9421733
RA-87406 YAK40 9421833
RA-87408 YAK40 9422033
RA-87410 YAK40 9420234
RA-87414 YAK40 9420634
RA-87416 YAK40 9420834
RA-87417 YAK40 9420934
RA-87418 YAK40 9421034
RA-87422 YAK40 9421834
RA-87423 YAK40 9..1934
RA-87424 YAK40 9422034
RA-87425 YAK40 9..0135
RA-87428 YAK40 9420435
RA-87429 YAK40 9420535
RA-87431 YAK40 9420735
RA-87433 YAK40 9420935
RA-87436 YAK40 9431235
RA-87438 YAK40 9..1435
RA-87439 YAK40 9431535
RA-87440 YAK40 9431635
RA-87443 YAK40 9..2035
RA-87444 YAK40 9430136
RA-87447 YAK40 9430436
RA-87448 YAK40 9430536
RA-87449 YAK40 9430636
RA-87450 YAK40 9..0736
RA-87452 YAK40 9..0936
RA-87456 YAK40 9..1336
RA-87460 YAK40 9431936
RA-87462 YAK40 9430137
RA-87464 YAK40 9430337
RA-87465 YAK40 9430437
RA-87467 YAK40 9440637
RA-87468 YAK40 9..1337
RA-87472 YAK40 9441737
RA-87473 YAK40 9441837
RA-87474 YAK40 9441937

RA-87476 YAK40 9..0438
RA-87477 YAK40 9..0538
RA-87480 YAK40 9..0838
RA-87481 YAK40 9440938
RA-87482 YAK40 9441038
RA-87483 YAK40 9441138
RA-87484 YAK40 9441238
RA-87486 YAK40 9441438
RA-87487 YAK40 9441538
RA-87489 YAK40 9512038
RA-87493 YAK40 9..1645
RA-87494 YAK40 9..1745
RA-87495 YAK40 9..1845
RA-87496 YAK40 9541945
RA-87497 YAK40 9542045
RA-87499 YAK40 9610246
RA-87500 YAK40 9511939
RA-87502 YAK40 9510140
RA-87503 YAK40 9520240
RA-87505 YAK40 9510740
RA-87506 YAK40 9..0840
RA-87510 YAK40 9521240
RA-87511 YAK40 9521340
RA-87513 YAK40 9521540
RA-87514 YAK40 9521640
RA-87516 YAK40 9521840
RA-87517 YAK40 9521940
RA-87518 YAK40 9..2040
RA-87519 YAK40 9..0141
RA-87520 YAK40 9520241
RA-87523 YAK40 9520541
RA-87524 YAK40 9520641
RA-87527 YAK40 9520941
RA-87530 YAK40 9521241
RA-87533 YAK40 9511741
RA-87534 YAK40 9521841
RA-87535 YAK40 9521941
RA-87540 YAK40 9530542
RA-87541 YAK40 9530642
RA-87545 YAK40 9531042
RA-87546 YAK40 9531142
RA-87550 YAK40 9210121
RA-87551 YAK40 9210221
RA-87552 YAK40 9210321
RA-87556 YAK40 9210721
RA-87557 YAK40 9210821
RA-87558 YAK40 9210921
RA-87559 YAK40 9211021
RA-87560 YAK40 9211121
RA-87565 YAK40 9211721
RA-87568 YAK40 9212021
RA-87573 YAK40 9220522
RA-87575 YAK40 9220722
RA-87576 YAK40 9220822
RA-87578 YAK40 9221022
RA-87580 YAK40 9221222
RA-87581 YAK40 9221322
RA-87582 YAK40 9221422
RA-87583 YAK40 9221522
RA-87586 YAK40 9221822
RA-87588 YAK40 9222022
RA-87606 YAK40 9120518
RA-87611 YAK40 9..1018
RA-87625 YAK40 9140619
RA-87639 YAK40 9142019
RA-87640 YAK40 9140120
RA-87645 YAK40 9140620
RA-87646 YAK40 9140720
RA-87647 YAK40 9140820
RA-87651 YAK40 9141220
RA-87652 YAK40 9141320
RA-87653 YAK40 9..1620
RA-87655 YAK40 9211820
RA-87656 YAK40 9211920
RA-87662 YAK40 9240625
RA-87663 YAK40 9..0725
RA-87665 YAK40 9..0925
RA-87667 YAK40 9241525
RA-87669 YAK40 9021760
RA-87755 YAK40 9021011
RA-87791 YAK40 9920203
RA-87800 YAK40 9220223
RA-87801 YAK40 9230423
RA-87802 YAK40 9230523
RA-87805 YAK40 9231123
RA-87807 YAK40 9231723

RA-87809	**YAK40**	**9..1923**
RA-87810	**YAK40**	**9..2023**
RA-87811	**YAK40**	**9230124**
RA-87814	**YAK40**	**9230524**
RA-87815	**YAK40**	**9230624**
RA-87821	**YAK40**	**9241324**
RA-87822	**YAK40**	**9241424**
RA-87823	**YAK40**	**9..1524**
RA-87828	**YAK40**	**9242024**
RA-87829	**YAK40**	**9..0125**
RA-87837	**YAK40**	**9240326**
RA-87838	**YAK40**	**9..0426**
RA-87839	**YAK40**	**9240526**
RA-87840	**YAK40**	**9240626**
RA-87842	**YAK40**	**9321030**
RA-87843	**YAK40**	**9331130**
RA-87844	**YAK40**	**9331330**
RA-87845	**YAK40**	**9331430**
RA-87847	**YAK40**	**9331630**
RA-87849	**YAK40**	**9..1830**
RA-87900	**YAK40**	**9720254**
RA-87901	**YAK40**	**9720354**
RA-87903	**YAK40**	**9..0.54**
RA-87904	**YAK40**	**9720854**
RA-87905	**YAK40**	**9720954**
RA-87906	**YAK40**	**9731054**
RA-87907	**YAK40**	**9731254**
RA-87910	**YAK40**	**9731654**
RA-87912	**YAK40**	**9732054**
RA-87919	**YAK40**	**9..0955**
RA-87921	**YAK40**	**9..1155**
RA-87924	**YAK40**	**9..1555**
RA-87925	**YAK40**	**9731655**
RA-87932	**YAK40**	**9..0356**
RA-87936	**YAK40**	**9..0756**
RA-87938	**YAK40**	**9..0153**
RA-87940	**YAK40**	**9540445**
RA-87941	**YAK40**	**9540545**
RA-87942	**YAK40**	**9610645**
RA-87944	**YAK40**	**9..0845**
RA-87947	**YAK40**	**9621145**
RA-87949	**YAK40**	
RA-87950	**YAK40**	**9810857**
RA-87952	**YAK40**	**9821057**
RA-87953	**YAK40**	**9811157**
RA-87954	**YAK40**	**9811357**
RA-87956	**YAK40**	**9821757**
RA-87957	**YAK40**	**9821857**
RA-87959	**YAK40**	**9..2057**
RA-87962	**YAK40**	**9820558**
RA-87965	**YAK40**	**9820858**
RA-87966	**YAK40**	**9820958**
RA-87968	**YAK40**	**9841258**
RA-87969	**YAK40**	**9841358**
RA-87970	**YAK40**	**9831458**
RA-87971	**YAK40**	**9831558**
RA-87972	**YAK40**	**9..1658**
RA-87973	**YAK40**	**9041860**
RA-87977	**YAK40**	**9321128**
RA-87981	**YAK40**	**9540444**
RA-87983	**YAK40**	**9540644**
RA-87986	**YAK40**	**9540944**
RA-87991	**YAK40**	**9541544**
RA-87993	**YAK40**	**9541744**
RA-87994	**YAK40**	**9541844**
RA-87997	**YAK40**	**9540145**
RA-87999	**YAK40**	**9540345**
RA-88153	**YAK40**	**9610746**
RA-88155	**YAK40**	**9610946**
RA-88156	**YAK40**	**9611046**
RA-88159	**YAK40**	**9611346**
RA-88163	**YAK40**	**9611746**
RA-88165	**YAK40**	**9611946**
RA-88168	**YAK40**	**9610647**
RA-88170	**YAK40**	**9620847**
RA-88171	**YAK40**	**9620947**
RA-88176	**YAK40**	**9621447**
RA-88177	**YAK40**	**9621747**
RA-88179	**YAK40**	**9621947**
RA-88180	**YAK40**	**9..2047**
RA-88182	**YAK40**	**9620248**
RA-88184	**YAK40**	**9620448**
RA-88186	**YAK40**	**9620648**
RA-88188	**YAK40**	**9620848**
RA-88193	**YAK40**	**9621348**
RA-88200	**YAK40**	**9630249**

RA-88201	**YAK40**	**9630349**
RA-88205	**YAK40**	**9630749**
RA-88207	**YAK40**	**9..1.49**
RA-88209	**YAK40**	**9..1549**
RA-88210	**YAK40**	**9631649**
RA-88213	**YAK40**	**9631949**
RA-88215	**YAK40**	**9630150**
RA-88216	**YAK40**	**9630250**
RA-88218	**YAK40**	**9630450**
RA-88220	**YAK40**	**9..0650**
RA-88224	**YAK40**	**9641150**
RA-88225	**YAK40**	**9641250**
RA-88226	**YAK40**	**9641350**
RA-88227	**YAK40**	**9641550**
RA-88228	**YAK40**	**9641750**
RA-88229	**YAK40**	**9..1850**
RA-88231	**YAK40**	**9..2050**
RA-88232	**YAK40**	**9640151**
RA-88234	**YAK40**	**9640351**
RA-88236	**YAK40**	**9640551**
RA-88238	**YAK40**	**9640951**
RA-88239	**YAK40**	**9641051**
RA-88240	**YAK40**	**9641151**
RA-88241	**YAK40**	**9641351**
RA-88243	**YAK40**	**9641651**
RA-88246	**YAK40**	**9641951**
RA-88247	**YAK40**	**9642051**
RA-88251	**YAK40**	**9710552**
RA-88254	YAK40	9710952
RA-88257	**YAK40**	**9711252**
RA-88258	**YAK40**	**9711352**
RA-88261	**YAK40**	**9711652**
RA-88263	**YAK40**	**9711852**
RA-88264	**YAK40**	**9711952**
RA-88265	**YAK40**	**9722052**
RA-88270	**YAK40**	**9720853**
RA-88273	**YAK40**	**9721153**
RA-88274	**YAK40**	**9721253**
RA-88275	**YAK40**	**9721353**
RA-88276	**YAK40**	**9721453**
RA-88278	**YAK40**	**9722053**
RA-88280	**YAK40**	**9820658**
RA-88285	**YAK40**	
RA-88287	**YAK40**	**9940360**
RA-88291	**YAK40**	
RA-88293	**YAK40**	**9510138**
RA-88294	**YAK40**	**9331029**
RA-88295	**YAK40**	**9331329**
RA-88296	**YAK40**	**9421634**
RA-88297	**YAK40**	**9531243**
RA-88298	**YAK40**	**9930160**
RA-88300	**YAK40**	
RA-93926	**TU134**	**1351204**
RA-93927	**TU134**	**2351508**
RA-94001	**TU334**	**01001**
RA-96000	**IL-96**	**0101**
RA-96001	**IL-96**	**30000103**
RA-96002	**IL-96**	
RA-96005	**IL-96**	**74393201002**
RA-96006	**IL-96**	**74393201003**
RA-96007	**IL-96**	**74393201004**
RA-96008	**IL-96**	**74393201005**
RA-96009	**IL-96**	**74393201006**
RA-96010	**IL-96**	**74393201007**
RA-96011	**IL-96**	**74393201008**
RA-96012	**IL-96**	**74393201009**
RA-96013	**IL-96**	**74393201010**
RA-96014	**IL-96**	**74393201011**
RA-96015	**IL-96**	**74393201012**
RA-96016	**IL-96**	**74393201013**
RA-98101	**YAK40**	
RA-98106	**YAK40**	
RA-98109	**YAK40**	**9740956**
RA-98110	**YAK40**	
RA-98111	**YAK40**	**9741656**
RA-98113	**YAK40**	**9710253**

Croatia

RC-CTA	B737	22119
RC-CTB	B737	22116
RC-CTC	B737	22118

Laos

RDPL-34001	**YAK40**	
RDPL-34002	**YAK40**	
RDPL-34125	B737	20363
RDPL-34126	B737	19553
RDPL-34133	**B737**	**21440**

Russia

RF-87659	**YAK40**	**9240325**

Philippines
(see also PI-)

RP-1250	**F-28**	**11153**
RP-C	**DC-9**	**47789**
RP-C	**DC-9**	**47792**
RP-C	**DC-9**	**47795**
RP-C1	1-11	BAC.128
RP-C123	CRVL	257
RP-C345	DC-8	45807
RP-C348	**DC-8**	**45755**
RP-C349	**DC-8**	**45660**
RP-C479	146	E3168
RP-C480	146	E3166
RP-C481	**146**	**E2109**
RP-C482	**146**	**E2112**
RP-C801	DC-8	45608
RP-C803	DC-8	45937
RP-C804	DC-8	45607
RP-C827	DC-8	45378
RP-C829	DC-8	45380
RP-C830	DC-8	45688
RP-C831	DC-8	45690
RP-C832	DC-8	45806
RP-C837	DC-8	45646
RP-C840	DC-8	45645
RP-C843	DC-8	45683
RP-C911	**B707**	**17606**
RP-C970	CRVL	90
RP-C1161	1-11	BAC.213
RP-C1171	1-11	BAC.215
RP-C1177	F-28	11153
RP-C1181	1-11	BAC.226
RP-C1182	1-11	BAC.246
RP-C1183	1-11	BAC.248
RP-C1184	1-11	BAC.190
RP-C1185	1-11	BAC.195
RP-C1186	1-11	BAC.188
RP-C1187	1-11	BAC.189
RP-C1188	1-11	BAC.209
RP-C1189	1-11	BAC.204
RP-C1193	1-11	BAC.231
RP-C1194	1-11	BAC.199
RP-C1240	B727	19691
RP-C1241	B727	19692
(RP-C1383)	B737	22278
RP-C1505	**DC-9**	**47793**
RP-C1886	**B707**	**19034**
RP-C1938	**B737**	**19553**
RP-C2000	B737	25996
(RP-C2000)	DC-10	46958
RP-C2003	DC-10	46958
RP-C2114	**DC-10**	**47838**
RP-C3001	**A300**	**63**
RP-C3002	**A300**	**69**
RP-C3003	**A300**	**125**
RP-C3004	**A300**	**203**
RP-C3005	**A300**	**219**
RP-C3006	**A300**	**222**
RP-C3007	**A300**	**83**
RP-C3008	**A300**	**262**
RP-C4005	**B737**	**24060**
RP-C4006	**B737**	**24059**
RP-C4007	**B737**	**25996**
RP-C5475	B747	21941
RP-C5476	**B747**	**21943**
(RP-C5751)	B747	27261
(RP-C5752)	B747	27262
RP-C7073	B707	17680
RP-C7074	B707	17604
RP-C7075	B707	18336
RP-C7076	B707	18335

RP-C8881	**A300**	**09**
RP-C8882	**A300**	**46**
RP-C8886	**B737**	**20130**

Sweden

SE-	**F-100**	**11341**
(SE-)	L1011	1032
SE-DAA	CRVL	4
SE-DAB	CRVL	11
SE-DAC	CRVL	25
SE-DAD	CRVL	34
SE-DAE	CRVL	56
SE-DAF	**CRVL**	**112**
SE-DAG	CRVL	172
SE-DAH	CRVL	193
SE-DAI	CRVL	210
SE-DAK	DC-9	47492
SE-DAL	DC-9	47498
SE-DAM	DC-9	47499
SE-DAN	DC-9	47464
SE-DAO	DC-9	47509
SE-DAP	DC-9	47512
SE-DAR	**DC-9**	**47596**
SE-DAS	**DC-9**	**47610**
SE-DAT	DC-9	47625
SE-DAU	**DC-9**	**47627**
SE-DAW	**DC-9**	**47629**
SE-DAX	**DC-9**	**47631**
SE-DAY	CV990	30-10-8
SE-DAZ	CV990	30-10-17
SE-DBA	DC-8	45386
SE-DBB	DC-8	45389
SE-DBC	DC-8	45390
SE-DBD	DC-8	45753
SE-DBE	DC-8	45823
SE-DBF	DC-8	45905
SE-DBG	DC-8	45921
SE-DBH	DC-8	45924
SE-DBI	DC-8	46129
SE-DBK	DC-8	46136
SE-DBL	DC-8	46163
SE-DBM	**DC-9**	**47633**
SE-DBN	DC-9	47413
SE-DBO	DC-9	47361
SE-DBP	DC-9	47360
SE-DBR	DC-9	47306
SE-DBS	DC-9	47303
SE-DBT	DC-9	47288
SE-DBU	DC-9	47180
SE-DBW	DC-9	47117
SE-DBX	DC-9	47114
SE-DBY	DC-9	47112
SE-DBZ	DC-9	47094
SE-DCR	DC-8	45628
SE-DCT	DC-8	45648
SE-DDA	B727	19691
SE-DDB	B727	19692
SE-DDC	B727	20042
SE-DDD	B727	19313
SE-DDK	CV990	30-10-34
SE-DDL	B747	20120
SE-DDP	**DC-9**	**47747**
SE-DDR	**DC-9**	**47750**
SE-DDS	**DC-9**	**47777**
SE-DDT	**DC-9**	**47779**
SE-DDU	DC-8	45906
(SE-DEA)	DC-10	46869
SE-DEB	**CRVL**	**247**
(SE-DEB)	DC-10	46872
SE-DEC	CRVL	263
(SE-DEF)	B747	21575
SE-DEH	CRVL	188
SE-DEI	146	E2086
SE-DFD	DC-10	46869
SE-DFE	DC-10	46872
SE-DFF	DC-10	47815
SE-DFG	DC-10	46554
SE-DFH	DC-10	46954
SE-DFK	A300	94
SE-DFL	A300	128
SE-DFN	DC-9	47657
SE-DFO	DC-9	47658
(SE-DFP)	MD-83	49556
SE-DFR	**MD-81**	**49422**
SE-DFS	**MD-82**	**49384**
SE-DFT	**MD-82**	**49385**
SE-DFU	MD-82	49421
SE-DFV	MD-81	49422
(SE-DFW)	MD-81	49422
SE-DFX	MD-82	49424
SE-DFY	**MD-81**	**49438**
SE-DFZ	B747	21575
SE-DGA	**F-28**	**11067**
SE-DGB	**F-28**	**11068**
SE-DGC	**F-28**	**11069**
SE-DGD	F-28	11111
(SE-DGD)	F-28	11080
SE-DGE	**F-28**	**11112**
(SE-DGE)	F-28	11081
SE-DGF	**F-28**	**11115**
SE-DGG	**F-28**	**11116**
SE-DGH	**F-28**	**11120**
SE-DGI	**F-28**	**11122**
SE-DGK	**F-28**	**11123**
SE-DGL	**F-28**	**11126**
SE-DGM	**F-28**	**11128**
SE-DGN	**F-28**	**11130**
SE-DGO	**F-28**	**11190**
SE-DGP	**F-28**	**11191**
SE-DGR	**F-28**	**11204**
SE-DGS	**F-28**	**11236**
SE-DGT	**F-28**	**11239**
SE-DGU	**F-28**	**11241**
SE-DGX	**F-28**	**11225**
SE-DHA	CRVL	259
SE-DHB	**MD-83**	**49396**
SE-DHC	MD-83	49397
SE-DHD	MD-83	49578
SE-DHF	MD-83	49642
SE-DHG	**MD-87**	**49389**
SE-DHI	**MD-87**	**49706**
SE-DHM	146	E2109
SE-DHN	**MD-83**	**49623**
SE-DHS	**DC-10**	**46646**
SE-DHT	DC-10	47833
SE-DHU	DC-10	47832
SE-DHX	DC-10	46645
SE-DHY	DC-10	46983
SE-DHZ	DC-10	46977
SE-DIA	**MD-81**	**49603**
SE-DIB	**MD-87**	**49605**
SE-DIC	**MD-87**	**49607**
SE-DID	MD-82	49615
SE-DIF	**MD-87**	**49606**
SE-DIH	**MD-87**	**49608**
SE-DII	**MD-81**	**49909**
(SE-DII)	MD-82	49729
SE-DIK	**MD-82**	**49728**
SE-DIL	**MD-81**	**49913**
SE-DIM	146	E3150
(SE-DIM)	MD-81	49998
SE-DIN	**MD-81**	**49999**
SE-DIP	**MD-87**	**53010**
(SE-DIP)	MD-81	53001
SE-DIR	**MD-81**	**53004**
SE-DIS	**MD-81**	**53006**
SE-DIT	146	E3151
SE-DIU	**MD-87**	**53011**
SE-DIX	**MD-81**	**49998**
SE-DIY	**MD-81**	**53008**
SE-DIZ	**MD-82**	**53294**
SE-DKG	B737	19408
SE-DKH	B737	20412
SE-DKO	B767	24318
SE-DKP	B767	24727
SE-DKR	B767	24846
(SE-DKR)	B767	24477
SE-DKS	B767	24848
SE-DKT	B767	24849
SE-DKU	B767	24729
SE-DKX	B767	25365
SE-DLA	B737	24300
(SE-DLA)	B737	24694
(SE-DLB)	B737	24695
SE-DLC	DC-9	47493
SE-DLD	B737	20711
SE-DLG	B737	23388
SE-DLH	DC-8	45994
SE-DLM	DC-8	45971
SE-DLN	B737	23747
SE-DLO	B737	23748
SE-DLP	B737	19409
(SE-DLR)	B737	20197
SE-DLS	**MD-83**	**53198**
SE-DLU	**MD-83**	**53199**
SE-DLV	**MD-83**	**49965**
SE-DLX	MD-83	49966
SE-DMA	**MD-87**	**53009**
SE-DMB	**MD-81**	**53314**
SE-DMC	MD-87	53340
SE-DMD	**MD-81**	**53347**
SE-DME	**MD-81**	**53366**
(SE-DMF)	MD-81	53369
(SE-DMG)	MD-81	53408
(SE-DMH)	MD-82	53411
(SE-DMI)	MD-82	53413
SE-DMY	**MD-81**	**48010**
SE-DMZ	**MD-81**	**48009**
SE-DNA	B737	24694
SE-DNB	B737	24695
SE-DNC	B737	24754
(SE-DNC)	B737	25038
SE-DND	B737	25038
(SE-DND)	B737	25065
SE-DNE	B737	25065
SE-DNF	B737	25160
SE-DNG	B737	25166
SE-DNH	B737	25167
SE-DNI	B737	26419
SE-DNK	B737	26421
SE-DNL	B737	26422
SE-DNM	B737	27268
SE-DOA	B767	24475
SE-DOB	B767	24476
SE-DOC	**B767**	**26544**
(SE-DOF)	B767	24358
SE-DPA	**B737**	**25401**
SE-DPB	**B737**	**25402**
SE-DPC	**B737**	**25426**
SE-DPH	MD-83	49663
SE-DPI	**MD-83**	**49557**
SE-DPM	**L1011**	**1145**
SE-DPN	B737	23783
SE-DPO	B737	23784
SE-DPP	**L1011**	**1072**
SE-DPR	**L1011**	**1231**
SE-DPS	MD-83	49398
SE-DPU	MD-83	49938
SE-DPV	**L1011**	**1030**
SE-DPX	**L1011**	**1091**
SE-DRA	**146**	**E2115**
SE-DRB	**146**	**E2057**
SE-DRC	**146**	**E2053**
SE-DRD	**146**	**E2094**
SE-DRE	**146**	**E2051**
SE-DRF	**146**	**E2055**
SE-DRG	**146**	**E2054**
SE-DRH	**146**	**E1006**
SE-DRI	**146**	**E2058**
SE-DRU	MD-83	49442
SE-DSB	**L1011**	**1059**
SE-DSC	**L1011**	**1065**
SE-DSD	**L1011**	**1215**
SE-DSE	**L1011**	**1013**
SE-DSF	**A300**	**220**
SE-DSG	A300	259
SE-DSH	**A300**	**207**
SE-DSK	**B757**	**25592**
SE-DSL	**B757**	**25593**
SE-DSM	**B757**	**24528**
SE-DTB	**B737**	**24911**
SE-DTC	**L1011**	**1050**
SE-DTD	**L1011**	**1033**
SE-DTP	**B737**	**24068**
SE-DUA	F-100	11321
SE-DUB	F-100	11323
SE-DUC	**F-100**	**11324**
SE-DUD	**F-100**	**11325**
SE-DUE	**F-100**	**11326**
SE-DUF	**F-100**	**11329**
SE-DUG	F-100	11330
SE-DUH	**F-100**	**11350**
SE-DUI	**F-100**	**11371**
SE-DUK	**B757**	**25054**

Slovenia
(see also S5-)

SL-AAA	A320	0043
SL-AAB	A320	0113
SL-AAC	A320	0114
SL-ABA	MD-82	48048
SL-ABB	MD-82	48087
SL-ABC	MD-82	49379
SL-ABD	MD-82	49440
SL-ABE	MD-81	48046
SL-ABF	DC-9	47239
SL-ABG	DC-9	47530
SL-ABH	DC-9	47570

Poland

SP-GEA	**YAK40**	**9230224**
SP-LAA	IL-62	11004
SP-LAB	IL-62	21105
SP-LAC	IL-62	31401
SP-LAD	IL-62	41604
SP-LAE	IL-62	41802
SP-LAF	IL-62	62204
SP-LAG	IL-62	2725456
SP-LBA	IL-62	2932526
SP-LBB	IL-62	1034152
SP-LBC	IL-62	3036253
SP-LBD	IL-62	1138234
SP-LBE	IL-62	1138546
SP-LBF	IL-62	2343554
SP-LBG	IL-62	3344942
SP-LBH	IL-62	1748445
SP-LBI	IL-62	4831739
SP-LBR	IL-62	4727546
SP-LCA	TU154	727
SP-LCB	TU154	733
SP-LCC	**TU154**	**745**
SP-LCD	**TU154**	**755**
SP-LCE	**TU154**	**769**
SP-LCF	**TU154**	**774**
SP-LCG	TU154	775
SP-LCH	**TU154**	**776**
SP-LCI	TU154	805
SP-LCK	TU154	806
SP-LCL	**TU154**	**812**
SP-LCM	TU154	824
SP-LCN	TU154	831
SP-LCO	TU154	862
SP-LEA	YAK40	9021660
SP-LEB	YAK40	9541843
SP-LEC	YAK40	9541943
SP-LED	YAK40	9542043
SP-LEE	YAK40	9021560
SP-LGA	**TU134**	**8350602**
SP-LGB	TU134	8350603
SP-LGC	**TU134**	**9350804**
SP-LGD	**TU134**	**9350805**
SP-LGE	**TU134**	**9350806**
SP-LHA	**TU134**	**3351808**
SP-LHB	**TU134**	**3351809**
SP-LHC	**TU134**	**3351810**
SP-LHD	**TU134**	**48400**
SP-LHE	**TU134**	**48405**
SP-LHF	TU134	3352005
SP-LHG	TU134	3352008
SP-LHI	TU134	49985
SP-LKA	**B737**	**27416**
SP-LKB	**B737**	**27417**
SP-LKC	**B737**	**27418**
SP-LKD	**B737**	**27419**
SP-LKE	**B737**	**27130**
SP-LKF	**B737**	**27368**
SP-LLA	**B737**	**27131**
SP-LLB	**B737**	**27156**
SP-LLC	**B737**	**27157**
SP-LLD	**B737**	**27256**
SP-LLE	**B737**	**27914**
SP-LOA	**B767**	**24733**
SP-LOB	**B767**	**24734**
SP-LPA	**B767**	**24865**
SP-LPB	**B767**	**27902**
SP-PGA	YAK40	9331029
SP-PGA	YAK40	9510138

Sudan

ST-	**B707**	**19412**
ST-AAW	COMET	6457
ST-AAX	COMET	6463
ST-AFA	**B707**	**20897**
ST-AFB	**B707**	**20898**
ST-AFK	**B737**	**21169**
ST-AFL	**B737**	**21170**
ST-AHG	B707	17651
ST-AIB	B737	22859
ST-AIM	B707	19410
ST-AIX	B707	20086
ST-AJD	DC-8	45764
ST-AJR	DC-8	46009
ST-AKR	B707	19521
ST-AKW	**B707**	**20123**
ST-ALK	B707	18976
ST-ALL	B707	19622
ST-ALM	B707	19367
ST-ALP	B707	19295
ST-ALX	B707	18715
ST-AMF	**B707**	**19367**
ST-ANP	**B707**	**19632**
ST-DRS	**B707**	**21104**
ST-GLD	B707	19821
ST-NSR	B707	18931
ST-SAC	B707	19377
ST-SFT	IL-76	073410292

Egypt

SU-ALC	COMET	6439
SU-ALD	COMET	6441
SU-ALE	COMET	6444
SU-ALL	COMET	6454
SU-ALM	COMET	6458
SU-AMV	COMET	6462
SU-AMW	COMET	6464
SU-ANC	COMET	6466
SU-ANI	COMET	6475
SU-AOU	B707	19844
SU-AOW	B707	19845
SU-APD	B707	20341
SU-APE	B707	20342
SU-ARN	IL-62	00801
SU-ARO	IL-62	00705
SU-ARW	IL-62	90501
SU-ARX	IL-62	80305
SU-AVL	IL-62	00804
SU-AVU	IL-62	00802
SU-AVW	IL-62	00805
SU-AVX	**B707**	**20760**
SU-AVY	B707	20761
SU-AVZ	**B707**	**20762**
SU-AWJ	IL-62	00803
SU-AXA	B707	20763
SU-AXB	TU154	048
SU-AXC	TU154	049
SU-AXD	TU154	050
SU-AXE	TU154	051
SU-AXF	TU154	052
SU-AXG	TU154	053
SU-AXH	TU154	054
SU-AXI	TU154	055
SU-AXJ	**B707**	**20919**
SU-AXK	B707	20920
SU-AYH	B737	21191
SU-AYI	B737	21192
SU-AYJ	B737	21193
SU-AYK	**B737**	**21194**
SU-AYL	**B737**	**21195**
SU-AYM	B737	21196
SU-AYN	B737	21226
SU-AYO	**B737**	**21227**
SU-AYT	B737	20222
SU-AYX	B737	19425
SU-AZY	A300	25
SU-BAG	B707	18765
SU-BAO	B707	19775
SU-BBA	**B707**	**18810**
SU-BBS	A300	17
SU-BBU	CRVL	154
SU-BBV	CRVL	254
SU-BBW	B737	21196
SU-BBX	B737	21193
SU-BCA	A300	115
SU-BCB	**A300**	**116**
SU-BCC	**A300**	**150**
(SU-BCD)	A300	199
(SU-BCE)	A300	200
SU-BCJ	B737	22071
SU-BDF	**A300**	**199**
SU-BDG	**A300**	**200**
SU-BKK	DC-9	47656
SU-BLC	B737	23786
(SU-BLI)	B707	19001
(SU-BLJ)	B707	18880
(SU-BLK)	B707	19378
SU-BLL	B737	23981
SU-BLM	B737	24345
SU-BLN	B737	23252
SU-BLR	B737	23786
SU-DAA	**B707**	**19916**
SU-DAB	B707	19521
SU-DAC	**B707**	**19843**
SU-DAD	B707	20517
SU-DAE	B707	19622
(SU-DAF)	B707	19621
SU-DAI	B707	19590
SU-DAJ	B707	18686
SU-DAK	MD-82	49661
SU-DAL	MD-83	49845
SU-DAM	MD-83	49848
SU-DAN	A300	192
SU-DAO	MD-87	49779
SU-DAP	MD-87	49724
SU-DAQ	MD-87	49780
SU-DAR	**A300**	**175**
SU-DAS	**A300**	**145**
SU-EAA	**B707**	**19775**
SU-FAA	**B707**	**18069**
SU-FAB	B707	18068
SU-FAC	**B707**	**20087**
SU-GAA	A300	239
SU-GAB	A300	240
SU-GAC	**A300**	**255**
SU-GAH	**B767**	**23178**
SU-GAI	**B767**	**23179**
SU-GAJ	**B767**	**23180**
SU-GAK	B747	20117
SU-GAL	**B747**	**24161**
SU-GAM	**B747**	**24162**
SU-GAN	**B737**	**21226**
SU-GAO	**B767**	**24541**
SU-GAP	**B767**	**24542**
SU-GAR	**A300**	**557**
SU-GAS	**A300**	**561**
SU-GAT	**A300**	**572**
SU-GAU	**A300**	**575**
SU-GAV	**A300**	**579**
SU-GAW	**A300**	**581**
SU-GAX	**A300**	**601**
SU-GAY	**A300**	**607**
SU-GAZ	**A300**	**616**
SU-GBA	**A320**	**0165**
SU-GBB	**A320**	**0166**
SU-GBC	**A320**	**0178**
SU-GBD	**A320**	**0194**
SU-GBE	**A320**	**0198**
SU-GBF	**A320**	**0351**
SU-GBG	**A320**	**0366**
SU-GBH	**B737**	**25084**
SU-GBI	**B737**	**25307**
SU-GBJ	**B737**	**25352**
SU-GBK	**B737**	**26052**
SU-GBL	**B737**	**26051**
SU-GGG	**A340**	**061**
SU-OAA	IL-76	1013409297
SU-OAB	IL-76	1013409321
SU-OAC	**TU154**	**898**
SU-OAD	**TU154**	**899**
SU-RAA	**A320**	**0322**
SU-RAB	**A320**	**0326**
(SU-RAC)	B757	27203
(SU-RAD)	B757	27204
(SU-RAE)	B757	27215
(SU-RAF)	B757	27216
SU-RAG	A320	0344
SU-SAA	**B737**	**24124**

Greece

SX-BAQ	MD-83	49710
(SX-BAR)	1-11	BAC.096
SX-BAS	A320	0043
SX-BAT	A320	0113
SX-BAU	A320	0114
SX-BAV	MD-87	49706
SX-BAW	MD-87	49389
SX-BAX	A320	0361
SX-BAY	**A300**	**208**
SX-BAZ	**A300**	**210**
SX-BBU	**B737**	**25743**
SX-BBV	MD-82	48048
SX-BBW	MD-82	48087
SX-BBY	**B757**	**26151**
SX-BBZ	**B757**	**24792**
SX-BCA	**B737**	**21224**
SX-BCB	**B737**	**21225**
SX-BCC	**B737**	**21301**
SX-BCD	**B737**	**21302**
SX-BCE	**B737**	**22300**
SX-BCF	**B737**	**22301**
SX-BCG	**B737**	**22338**
SX-BCH	**B737**	**22339**
SX-BCI	**B737**	**22343**
SX-BCK	**B737**	**22400**
SX-BCL	**B737**	**22401**
SX-BEB	A300	46
SX-BEC	A300	56
SX-BED	**A300**	**58**
SX-BEE	**A300**	**103**
SX-BEF	**A300**	**105**
SX-BEG	**A300**	**148**
SX-BEH	**A300**	**184**
SX-BEI	**A300**	**189**
SX-BEK	**A300**	**632**
SX-BEL	**A300**	**696**
SX-BFI	**A300**	**204**
SX-BFM	**B727**	**21978**
SX-BFN	**B727**	**21851**
SX-BKA	**B737**	**25313**
SX-BKB	**B737**	**25314**
SX-BKC	**B737**	**25361**
SX-BKD	**B737**	**25362**
SX-BKE	**B737**	**25417**
SX-BKF	**B737**	**25430**
SX-BKG	**B737**	**27149**
SX-BSH	A320	0225
SX-BSJ	A320	0230
SX-BSV	A320	0449
SX-CBA	**B727**	**20003**
SX-CBB	**B727**	**20004**
SX-CBC	**B727**	**20005**
SX-CBD	**B727**	**20006**
SX-CBE	**B727**	**20201**
SX-CBF	**B727**	**19536**
SX-CBG	**B727**	**20918**
SX-CBH	**B727**	**20790**
SX-CBI	**B727**	**20791**
SX-DAK	COMET	6437
SX-DAL	COMET	6438
SX-DAN	COMET	6440
SX-DAO	COMET	6447
SX-DBA	B707	18948
SX-DBB	B707	18949
SX-DBC	B707	18950
SX-DBD	B707	19760
SX-DBE	B707	20035
SX-DBF	B707	20036
SX-DBG	B720	18352
SX-DBH	B720	18353
SX-DBI	B720	18355
SX-DBL	B720	18356
SX-DBL	B720	18420
SX-DBM	B720	18687
SX-DBN	B720	18688
SX-DBO	B707	19164
SX-DBP	B707	19163
(SX-ERA)	B767	24716
(SX-ERB)	B767	24742
(SX-ERC)	B767	24762
SX-OAA	B747	20742
SX-OAB	**B747**	**20825**
SX-OAC	**B747**	**21683**
SX-OAD	**B747**	**21684**
SX-OAE	**B747**	**21935**

Bangladesh

S2-AAL	B707	17903
S2-ABM	B707	17680
S2-ABN	B707	19168
S2-ABQ	B707	19441
S2-ACA	B707	19434
S2-ACA	B707	19776
S2-ACB	B707	19354
S2-ACF	B707	18921
S2-ACH	**F-28**	**11172**
(S2-ACI)	F-28	11180
S2-ACJ	**F-28**	**11180**
S2-ACK	B707	20018
S2-ACO	**DC-10**	**46993**
S2-ACP	**DC-10**	**46995**
S2-ACQ	**DC-10**	**47817**
S2-ACR	**DC-10**	**48317**
S2-ADA	DC-10	46999
S2-ADB	**DC-10**	**47818**

Slovenia

S5-AAA	**A320**	**0043**
S5-AAB	**A320**	**0113**
S5-AAC	**A320**	**0114**
S5-ABA	MD-82	48048
S5-ABB	MD-82	48087
S5-ABC	MD-82	49379
S5-ABD	MD-82	49440
S5-ABE	MD-81	48046
S5-ABF	**DC-9**	**47239**
S5-ABG	DC-9	47530
S5-ABH	**DC-9**	**47570**

Seychelles

(S7-1HM)	B767	24448
S7-2HM	B707	19869
S7-4HM	B707	19871
S7-AAQ	B767	26387
S7-AAS	**B767**	**24448**
S7-AAV	B767	26388
S7-AAX	**B757**	**25622**
S7-LAS	B707	20179
S7-RGA	A310	573
S7-RGU	**B767**	**27568**
S7-RGV	**B767**	**27392**
S7-RGW	**B767**	**27393**
S7-RGX	**A320**	**0238**
S7-SIA	DC-8	45629
S7-SIS	DC-8	46141

Saõ Tome Island

(S9-)	B727	18805
S9-NAB	DC-8	45421
S9-NAG	**DC-8**	**45259**
S9-NAN	DC-8	45433
S9-NAS	DC-8	45435
S9-NAZ	**B727**	**19404**
S9-TAE	1-11	084
S9-TAN	B727	18893
S9-TAO	**B727**	**19390**
S9-TBA	**B727**	**18801**

Turkey

TC-	**A321**	**0591**
TC-	**146**	**E1229**
TC-	**146**	**E1230**
TC-	**146**	**E1249**
TC-	**146**	**E1252**
(TC-...)	B737	23870
(TC-...)	B737	25124
TC-ABA	**CRVL**	**253**
TC-ACI	**TU154**	**834**
TC-ACT	**TU154**	**739**
TC-ACV	**TU154**	**833**
TC-ADA	B737	23866
(TC-ADA)	B737	24911
TC-AFA	**B737**	**26306**
TC-AFB	**B727**	**19864**

TC-AFC B727 19863
TC-AFD B727 21113
TC-AFE B727 21114
TC-AFG B727 21988
TC-AFK B737 24684
TC-AFL B737 24690
TC-AFM B737 26279
TC-AFN B727 21619
TC-AFO B727 21620
TC-AFP B727 21442
TC-AFR B727 21621
TC-AFT B727 21618
TC-AFU B737 26081
TC-AFV B727 20905
TC-AFY B737 24705
TC-AFZ B737 23981
TC-AGA B737 24512
TC-AHA B757 24121
TC-AJA B757 24771
TC-AJK B737 22090
TC-AJR B727 19393
TC-AJS B727 18744
TC-AJT B727 18743
TC-AJU B727 18951
TC-AJV B727 20265
TC-AJY B727 19993
TC-AJZ B727 18802
TC-AKA 1-11 BAC.255
TC-AKA CRVL 239
TC-AKB 1-11 BAC.253
TC-AKD B727 20930
TC-ALA B737 24519
TC-ALA CRVL 250
TC-ALB B727 20431
TC-ALC B737 19424
(TC-ALD) B727 20526
TC-ALF B727 20430
TC-ALK B727 20430
TC-ALM B727 20431
TC-ALN A300 65
TC-ALP A300 153
TC-ALR A300 155
TC-ALS A300 66
TC-ALS B737 25844
TC-ALT B737 20221
TC-ALU TU134 1351206
TC-ALV TU134 1351204
TC-ALY YAK42 4520424410016
TC-APA B737 25595
TC-ARI 1-11 BAC.253
TC-ARI CRVL 235
TC-ASA CRVL 222
TC-ASK B767 23280
TC-ATA B737 24687
TC-ATE B737 20521
TC-ATU B727 18742
TC-ATU B737 21736
TC-AVA B737 25594
TC-AYA B737 24683
TC-AZA B737 24691
TC-BIR B737 25040
TC-CYO B737 23415
TC-DEL B727 22439
TC-FAR YAK42 4520421014494
TC-GAA A320 0238
TC-GAB A320 0280
TC-GAC A310 278
TC-GEN B757 22206
TC-GHA B707 19869
TC-GHA B707 20069
TC-GHB B707 19871
TC-GRA TU154 739
TC-GRB TU154 833
TC-GRC TU154 834
TC-GRD TU134 66109
TC-GRE TU134 66120
TC-GUL B757 22209
(TC-GUL) DC-8 46159
TC-IHO B727 20430
TC-IKO B727 20431
TC-INA MD-83 49943
TC-INB MD-83 49936
TC-INC MD-83 49792
TC-IND MD-83 49940
TC-IYI YAK42 4520423304016
TC-JAA DC-9 47048
TC-JAB DC-9 45774
TC-JAC DC-9 47213
TC-JAD DC-9 47488
TC-JAE DC-9 47489
TC-JAF DC-9 47451
TC-JAG DC-9 47442
TC-JAH B707 17593
TC-JAJ B707 17603
TC-JAK DC-9 47397
TC-JAL DC-9 47534
TC-JAM B707 17607
TC-JAN B707 17594
TC-JAO F-28 11057
TC-JAP F-28 11058
TC-JAR F-28 11060
TC-JAS F-28 11070
TC-JAT F-28 11071
TC-JAU DC-10 46705
TC-JAV DC-10 46704
TC-JAY DC-10 46907
TC-JAZ F-28 11032
TC-JBA B707 17587
TC-JBA B727 20463
TC-JBB B707 17589
TC-JBB B727 20464
TC-JBC B707 17590
TC-JBC B727 20465
TC-JBD B707 17591
TC-JBE B707 17903
TC-JBF B727 20980
TC-JBG B727 20981
TC-JBH B727 20982
TC-JBJ B727 20983
TC-JBK DC-9 47674
TC-JBL DC-9 47723
TC-JBM B727 21260
TC-JBN B707 17697
TC-JBP B707 17697
TC-JBP B707 17701
TC-JBR B727 21603
TC-JBS B707 18834
TC-JBT B707 18836
TC-JBU B707 18842
TC-JBV DC-8 45429
TC-JBY DC-8 45694
TC-JBZ DC-8 45693
TC-JCA B727 22992
TC-JCB B727 22993
TC-JCC B707 18715
TC-JCD B727 22998
TC-JCE B727 22999
TC-JCF B707 17601
TC-JCF B707 19271
TC-JCK B727 21664
TC-JCL A310 338
TC-JCM A310 375
TC-JCN A310 379
TC-JCO A310 386
TC-JCP 1-11 BAC.254
TC-JCR A310 370
TC-JCS A310 389
TC-JCU A310 390
TC-JCV A310 476
TC-JCY A310 478
TC-JCZ A310 480
TC-JDA A310 496
TC-JDB A310 497
TC-JDC A310 537
TC-JDD A310 586
TC-JDE B737 24904
TC-JDF B737 24917
TC-JDG B737 25181
TC-JDH B737 25184
TC-JDI B737 25372
TC-JDJ A340 023
TC-JDK A340 025
TC-JDL A340 057
TC-JDM A340 115
TC-JDT B737 25261
TC-JDU B737 25288
TC-JDV B737 25289
TC-JDY B737 26065
TC-JDZ B737 26066
TC-JEA B737 27143
TC-JEC B727 22287
TC-JED B737 25740
TC-JEE B737 26290
TC-JEF B737 26291
TC-JEG B737 25374
TC-JEH B737 26320
TC-JEI B737 26298
TC-JEJ B737 25375
TC-JEK B737 26299
TC-JEL B737 26300
TC-JEM B737 26302
TC-JEN B737 25376
TC-JEO B737 25377
TC-JEP B737 25378
TC-JER B737 26073
TC-JES B737 26074
TC-JET B737 26077
TC-JEU B737 26078
TC-JEV B737 26085
TC-JEY B737 26086
TC-JEZ B737 26088
TC-JFA B727 20434
TC-JFB B727 20433
TC-JFO A310 257
TC-JKF A310 356
TC-JTB B737 23781
TC-JTC B737 23783
TC-JUC B727 20430
TC-JUH B727 20431
TC-JUN CRVL 259
TC-JUP B737 19408
TC-JUR B737 20412
TC-JUS B737 22453
TC-JUT B737 20197
TC-JUU B737 23404
TC-JUV A300 161
TC-JUY A300 158
TC-JYK A310 172
TC-MAB DC-8 46016
TC-MIO B737 23714
TC-ONA A320 0288
TC-ONB A320 0331
TC-ONC A320 0289
TC-OND A320 0371
TC-ONE A320 0453
TC-ONE A320 0528
TC-ONF A320 0444
TC-ONG A320 0361
TC-ONK A300 86
TC-RAA A300 17
TC-RAB A300 102
TC-RAC B727 20792
TC-RAD TU154 890
TC-RTU MD-83 49708
TC-RUT B727 20904
TC-SAL A320 0347
TC-SAN A320 0373
TC-SUN B737 24676
TC-SUP B737 24908
TC-SUR B737 24910
TC-SUS B737 27007
TC-SUT B737 25190
TC-TCA B727 21113
TC-TCB B727 21114
TC-THA 146 E3232
TC-THB 146 E3234
TC-THC 146 E3236
TC-THD 146 E3237
TC-THE 146 E3238
TC-THF 146 E3240
TC-THG 146 E3241
TC-THH 146 E3243
TC-THM 146 E3264
TC-THO 146 E3265
TC-TKA A300 86
TC-TKB A300 87
TC-TKC A300 91
TC-TRU MD-83 49442
TC-TUR B727 20792
TC-VAA B737 19424
TC-VAB B737 20221

Iceland

TF- B757 25625
TF-ABD B737 20417
TF-ABE B737 23122
TF-ABE L1011 1022
TF-ABF B737 20258
TF-ABF B737 21184
TF-ABG B737 21192
TF-ABG L1011 1005
TF-ABH B737 19553
TF-ABH L1011 1054
TF-ABI B737 23023
TF-ABI B747 20924
TF-ABJ B737 19594
TF-ABK B737 23922
TF-ABK B747 20116
TF-ABL B747 20117
TF-ABL L1011 1044
TF-ABM L1011 1221
TF-ABN B737 22278
TF-ABO B747 20208
TF-ABP L1011 1045
TF-ABQ B747 20543
TF-ABR B747 20014
TF-ABS B747 20305
TF-ABT B737 20458
TF-ABU B737 21686
TF-ABV B737 22137
TF-ABW B747 20376
TF-ABX B737 20257
TF-ABY B737 22136
TF-ABZ B747 21316
TF-AEA B707 18714
TF-AEB B707 19621
TF-AEC B707 19622
TF-AED DC-8 45817
TF-AIA B727 20951
TF-AIC B737 21184
TF-AIC B737 23253
TF-ANC B707 18746
TF-AVB CV880 22-00-48M
TF-AYA B720 18792
TF-AYB B720 18422
TF-AYC B720 18421
TF-AYE B707 18716
TF-AYF B707 20097
TF-AYG B707 19004
TF-BBA DC-8 45954
TF-BBB DC-8 46162
TF-BBC DC-8 46154
TF-BBD DC-8 46028
TF-BCV DC-8 45900
TF-BCV DC-8 46002
TF-CCV DC-8 45990
TF-ECV DC-8 45445
TF-FIA B727 19826
TF-FIA B737 24352
TF-FIB B737 24353
TF-FIC B737 24804
TF-FID B737 25063
TF-FIE B727 19503
TF-FIE B737 24795
TF-FIH B757 24739
TF-FII B757 24760
TF-FIJ B757 25085
TF-FIK B757 24771
TF-FIK B757 26276
TF-FLA DC-8 46020
TF-FLB DC-8 45753
TF-FLB DC-8 45936
TF-FLC DC-8 46049
TF-FLC DC-8 46088
TF-FLE DC-8 46042
TF-FLE DC-8 46101
TF-FLF DC-8 46062
TF-FLF DC-8 46112
TF-FLG B727 19826
TF-FLH B727 19503
TF-FLI B727 22295
TF-FLJ B727 19619
TF-FLK B727 20951
TF-FLT DC-8 46075
TF-FLU DC-8 45999
TF-FLV DC-8 46121
TF-GCV DC-8 45640
TF-ISA B737 20156
TF-ISA DC-8 45980
TF-ISB B737 20521
TF-ISB DC-8 45964
TF-IUC B707 19133

TF-IUD B707 19628
TF-IUE B707 18708
TF-IUE B707 19372
TF-IUF DC-8 46016
TF-IUG B707 19133
TF-LLK DC-8 45818
(TF-RMR) B727 21581
TF-VLA B720 18163
TF-VLB B720 18827
(TF-VLB) B720 18082
TF-VLC B720 18820
TF-VLG B707 19964
TF-VLJ B707 19351
TF-VLK B737 22453
TF-VLL B707 19270
TF-VLM B737 21715
TF-VLP B707 18964
TF-VLR B707 18881
TF-VLS B727 18893
TF-VLT B737 20458
TF-VLV C-18 18962
TF-VLW DC-8 45912
TF-VLX B707 19664
TF-VLY DC-8 46019
TF-VLZ DC-8 46080
TF-VVA B720 18082
TF-VVB B720 18075
(TF-VVC) B720 18073
TF-VVE B720 18163

Guatemala

TG-ALA B727 19302
TG-ALA B737 20583
TG-ALA B737 20586
TG-AMA B737 23388
TG-ANP B727 18742
TG-AOA B737 20582
TG-ARA 1-11 BAC.205
TG-AVA 1-11 BAC.206
TG-AYA 1-11 BAC.211
TG-AYA B727 19506
TG-AYA B737 20587
TG-AZA 1-11 BAC.231
TG-CAO F-28 11048
TG-LKA B727 19393
TG-TJF 1-11 089

Costa Rica

TI-1055C 1-11 BAC.162
TI-1056C 1-11 BAC.108
TI-1084C 1-11 BAC.237
TI-1095C 1-11 BAC.242
TI-1096C 1-11 BAC.244
TI-LRC B727 18856
TI-LRF 1-11 BAC.237
TI-LRI 1-11 BAC.242
TI-LRJ 1-11 BAC.244
TI-LRK 1-11 BAC.208
TI-LRL 1-11 BAC.237
TI-LRP DC-8 45672
TI-LRQ B727 21945
TI-LRR B727 21349
TI-VEL DC-8 45435

Cameroon

TJ-AAM B727 21636
TJ-CAA B707 20629
TJ-CAB B747 22378
TJ-CBA B737 20590
TJ-CBB B737 20591
TJ-CBD B737 21295
TJ-CBE B737 23386

Central African Republic

TL-AAI CRVL 10
TL-AAK DC-8 45803
TL-ABB CRVL 249
TL-AHI DC-8 45300
TL-FCA CRVL 42
(TL-KAB) CRVL 42

Congo

TN-ACP F-28 11072
TN-AEB B727 21655
TN-AEE B737 21538

Gabon

TR-LCR F-100 11258
TR-LQR DC-8 45821
TR-LST F-28 11080
TR-LSU F-28 11081
TR-LTR F-28 11104
TR-LTS F-28 11102
TR-LTZ DC-8 46053
TR-LVK DC-8 45805
TR-LWD CRVL 114
TR-LXK B747 21468
TR-LXL B737 21467

Tunisia

TS-IEB B737 22407
TS-IEC B737 23716
TS-IED B737 24141
TS-IKM CRVL 84
TS-IMA A300 188
TS-IMB A320 0119
(TS-IMB) A300 296
TS-IMC A320 0124
TS-IMD A320 0205
TS-IME A320 0123
TS-IMF A320 0370
TS-IMG A320 0390
TS-IMH A320 0402
TS-IMI A320 0511
TS-IOC B737 21973
TS-IOD B737 21974
TS-IOE B737 22624
TS-IOF B737 22625
TS-IOG B737 26639
TS-IOH B737 26640
TS-IOI B737 27257
TS-IOJ B737 27912
TS-ITU CRVL 246
TS-JEA B727 22665
TS-JEB B727 22666
TS-JHN B727 20545
TS-JHO B727 20739
TS-JHP B727 20822
TS-JHQ B727 20948
TS-JHR B727 21179
TS-JHS B727 21234
TS-JHT B727 21235
TS-JHU B727 21318
TS-JHV B727 21319
TS-JHW B727 21320
TS-MAC CRVL 207
TS-TAR CRVL 178

Tchad

TT-AAD CRVL 100
TT-AAM CRVL 100
TT-EAP B707 19964
TT-WAB B707 19964

Cote d'Ivoire

TU-TAC A310 571
TU-TAD A310 651
TU-TAE A310 652
TU-TAF A310 671
TU-TAH A300 744
TU-TAI A300 749
TU-TAL DC-10 46890
TU-TAM DC-10 46892
TU-TAN DC-10 46997
TU-TAO A300 137
TU-TAP B747 22169
TU-TAR A310 440
TU-TAS A300 243
TU-TAT A300 282
TU-TAU A310 435
TU-TAV B737 19848
(TU-TBD) DC-10 46892
TU-TBX DC-8 45604
TU-TBY B707 17922
TU-TCA DC-8 45670
TU-TCB DC-8 45671
TU-TCC DC-8 45857
TU-TCD DC-8 45627
TU-TCE DC-8 45569
TU-TCF DC-8 46135
TU-TCG DC-8 45669
(TU-TCG) DC-10 46890
TU-TCH DC-8 45883
TU-TCN CRVL 199
TU-TCO CRVL 215
TU-TCP DC-8 45568
TU-TCY CRVL 219
TU-TDB B707 18245
TU-TDC B707 17924
TU-TIJ F-28 11118
TU-TIK F-28 11121
TU-TIM F-28 11097
TU-TIN F-28 11099
TU-TIR F-28 11124
TU-TIS F-100 11318
TU-TIV F-100 11316
TU-TIZ F-28 11099
TU-TXA B707 18457
TU-TXB B707 18457
TU-TXF B707 18458
TU-TXG DC-8 45819
TU-TXI B707 18686
TU-TXJ B707 18458
TU-TXK DC-8 45819
TU-TXL B707 19291
TU-TXM B707 18686
TU-TXN B707 19291
TU-TXQ CRVL 201
TU-TXR CRVL 78
TU-TXT DC-8 46096
TU-VAA F-100 11245
TU-VAA F-28 11097
TU-VAB F-28 11099
TU-VAH F-28 11118
TU-VAJ F-28 11124
TU-VAN F-28 11121
(TU-VAZ) F-28 11124

Benin

TY-AAM B707 18084
TY-BBM B707 20457
TY-BBN F-28 11184
TY-BBR B707 20457
TY-BBW B707 18084

Mali

TZ-ADL B737 20544
TZ-ADR B727 19509
TZ-ADS CRVL 184
TZ-ADT 146 E1009

Kiribati

T3-ATB B727 19311
T3-VAL B737 20158

Uzbekistan

UK-75700	B757	28338
UK-76351	IL-76	1013408240
UK-76352	IL-76	1023411378
UK-76353	IL-76	1023414454
UK-76356	IL-76	
UK-76358	IL-76	1023410339
UK-76359	IL-76	1033414483
UK-76375	IL-76	
UK-76419	IL-76	1023414470
UK-76419	IL-76	
UK-76427	IL-76	
UK-76447	IL-76	1023412389
UK-76448	IL-76	1023413443
UK-76449	IL-76	1003403058
UK-76701	B767	28370
UK-76702	B767	28392
UK-76782	IL-76	0093498971
UK-76793	IL-76	0093498951
UK-76794	IL-76	0093498954
UK-76805	IL-76	1003403105
UK-76811	IL-76	1013407223
UK-76813	IL-76	1013408246
UK-76821	IL-76	
UK-76824	IL-76	1023410327
UK-76831	IL-76	1013409287
UK-76844	IL-76	1033416525
UK-85050	TU154	050
UK-85189	TU154	189
UK-85245	TU154	245
UK-85248	TU154	248
UK-85249	TU154	249
UK-85272	TU154	272
UK-85286	TU154	286
UK-85322	TU154	322
UK-85344	TU154	344
UK-85356	TU154	356
UK-85370	TU154	370
UK-85397	TU154	397
UK-85398	TU154	398
UK-85401	TU154	401
UK-85416	TU154	416
UK-85423	TU154	423
UK-85438	TU154	438
UK-85449	TU154	449
UK-85575	TU154	575
UK-85578	TU154	578
UK-85600	TU154	600
UK-85617?	TU154	736
UK-85711	TU154	887
UK-85764	TU154	947
UK-85776	TU154	958
UK-86012	IL-86	51483202010
UK-86016	IL-86	51483202014
UK-86052	IL-86	51483202019
UK-86053	IL-86	51483203020
UK-86056	IL-86	51483203023
UK-86057	IL-86	51483203024
UK-86064	IL-86	51483203031
UK-86072	IL-86	51483204039
UK-86083	IL-86	51483206054
UK-86090	IL-86	51483207061
UK-86569	IL-62	1356234
UK-86573	IL-62	4140536
UK-86574	IL-62	3344833
UK-86575	IL-62	1647928
UK-86576	IL-62	4546257
UK-86577	IL-62	2748552
UK-86578	IL-62	1951525
UK-86579	IL-62	2951636
UK-86610	IL-62	41801
UK-86659	IL-62	31404
UK-86694	IL-62	11104
UK-86704	IL-62	41603
UK-86932	IL-62	3242432
UK-86933	IL-62	3749224
UK-86934	IL-62	4445827
UK-87263	YAK40	9311926
UK-87264	YAK40	9312026
UK-87289	YAK40	9320428
UK-87296	YAK40	9321328
UK-87309	YAK40	9320529
UK-87349	YAK40	9511839
UK-87367	YAK40	9341731
UK-87378	YAK40	9241425
UK-87396	YAK40	9410833
UK-87430	YAK40	9420635
UK-87457	YAK40	9431636
UK-87515	YAK40	9521740
UK-87539	YAK40	9530442
UK-87540	YAK40	9530542
UK-87542	YAK40	9530742
UK-87564	YAK40	9211621
UK-87799	YAK40	9040316
UK-87830	YAK40	9241625
UK-87846	YAK40	9331530
UK-87848	YAK40	9331730
UK-87923	YAK40	9741455
UK-87985	YAK40	9540844
UK-87989	YAK40	9541344
UK-87996	YAK40	9542044
UK-88185	YAK40	9620548
UK-88194	YAK40	9621448
UK-88217	YAK40	9630350
UK-88242	YAK40	9641551

Kazakhstan

UN-001	B747	21962
(UN-002)	B757	23454
UN-170	YAK40	9640751
UN-171	YAK40	9630549
UN-185	IL-76	0023441174
(UN-186)	IL-76	0033442241
UN-189	IL-76	0053458749
UN-10200	DC-10	46891
UN-42407	YAK42	4520424116690
UN-42446	YAK42	
UN-42447	YAK42	4520424309017
UN-42448	YAK42	
UN-42557	YAK42	4520423302017
UN-42558	YAK42	4520423307017
UN-65115	TU134	
UN-65121	TU134	60505
UN-65130	TU134	60635
UN-65138	TU134	60907
UN-65147	TU134	61012
UN-65551	TU134	66212
UN-65683	TU134	62199
UN-65767	TU134	
UN-65776	TU134	62545
UN-65787	TU134	
UN-65900	TU134	63684
UN-72904	AN-72	
UN-76371	IL-76	1033414485
UN-76374	IL-76	1033416520
UN-76384	IL-76	1003401015
UN-76385	IL-76	1033416515
UN-76410	IL-76	1023412411
UN-76434	IL-76	1023412395
UN-76435	IL-76	1023413428
UN-76442	IL-76	1023414450
UN-76810	IL-76	1013409282
UN-76834	IL-76	1023409319
UN-78793	IL-76	
UN-85066	TU154	066
UN-85076	TU154	076
UN-85111	TU154	111
UN-85113	TU154	113
UN-85173	TU154	173
UN-85194	TU154	194
UN-85221	TU154	221
UN-85230	TU154	230
UN-85231	TU154	231
UN-85240	TU154	240
UN-85260	TU154	260
UN-85271	TU154	271
UN-85276	TU154	276
UN-85290	TU154	290
UN-85387	TU154	387
UN-85396	TU154	396
UN-85431	TU154	431
UN-85455	TU154	455
UN-85464	TU154	464
UN-85478	TU154	478
UN-85509	TU154	509
UN-85516	TU154	516
UN-85521	TU154	521
UN-85537	TU154	537
UN-85539	TU154	539
UN-85589	TU154	589
UN-85719	TU154	901
UN-85744	TU154	927
UN-85775	TU154	775
UN-85775	TU154	957
UN-85780	TU154	964?
UN-85781	TU154	965
UN-86068	IL-86	51483204035
UN-86069	IL-86	51483204036
UN-86071	IL-86	51483204038
UN-86077	IL-86	51483205047
UN-86086	IL-86	51483206057
UN-86101	IL-86	51483207069
UN-86116	IL-86	51483209084
UN-86130	IL-62	3255333
UN-87202	YAK40	9..0157
UN-87204	YAK40	9..1556
UN-87213	YAK40	9641050
UN-87233	YAK40	9..1842
UN-87246	YAK40	9541443
UN-87265	YAK40	9310127
UN-87267	YAK40	9310327
UN-87271	YAK40	9310727
UN-87272	YAK40	9330827
UN-87274	YAK40	9311027
UN-87275	YAK40	9311127
UN-87282	YAK40	9..1727
UN-87283	YAK40	9321827
UN-87296	YAK40	9741755
UN-87306	YAK40	9320229
UN-87312	YAK40	9320729
UN-87337	YAK40	9510639
UN-87352	YAK40	9330131
UN-87359	YAK40	9340831
UN-87363	YAK40	9341231
UN-87377	YAK40	9..1325
UN-87402	YAK40	9411433
UN-87403	YAK40	9411533
UN-87408	YAK40	9422033
UN-87471	YAK40	9441637
UN-87488	YAK40	9441638
UN-87489	YAK40	9512038
UN-87491	YAK40	9621345
UN-87498	YAK40	9540146
UN-87501	YAK40	9..2039
UN-87537	YAK40	9520242
UN-87567	YAK40	9211921
UN-87569	YAK40	9220222
UN-87592	YAK40	9110616
UN-87652	YAK40	9141320
UN-87654	YAK40	9211720
UN-87661	YAK40	9240525
UN-87824	YAK40	9241624
UN-87909	YAK40	9731454
UN-87920	YAK40	9731055
UN-87927	YAK40	9741855
UN-87933	YAK40	9740456
UN-87935	YAK40	9740656
UN-87935	YAK40	9811856
UN-87955	YAK40	9811457
UN-87990	YAK40	9541444
UN-88173	YAK40	9621147
UN-88181	YAK40	9620148
UN-88197	YAK40	9631948
UN-88249	YAK40	9..0.52
UN-88266	YAK40	9710453
UN-88271	YAK40	9720953
UN-88277	YAK40	9721953

Ukraine

UR-	AN-70	
(UR-)	B737	21616
UR-.....	AN-74	36547098970
UR-42308	YAK42	11040303
UR-42310	YAK42	11040403
UR-42317	YAK42	4520422202039
UR-42318	YAK42	452042..020..
UR-42319	YAK42	4520423402062
UR-42327	YAK42	4520424402161
UR-42334	YAK42	4520422606...
UR-42348	YAK42	4520423711342
UR-42358	YAK42	4520422811413
UR-42366	YAK42	4520421814047
UR-42369	YAK42	4520422914190
UR-42372	YAK42	4520423914266

UR-42376 YAK42 4520424914477
UR-42377 YAK42 4520421014479
UR-42381 YAK42 4520422014576
UR-42383 YAK42 4520422016201
UR-42403 YAK42 4520422116588
UR-42405 YAK42 4520423116624
UR-42409 YAK42 4520421216707
UR-42410 YAK42 4520421219029
UR-42416 YAK42 4520423219102
UR-42419 YAK42 4520423201016
UR-42449 YAK42 4520421401018
UR-42527 YAK42 11040903
UR-42530 YAK42 4253011120204
UR-42540 YAK42 11140604
UR-42544 YAK42 11151004
UR-65037 TU134 48850
UR-65048 TU134 49750
UR-65073 TU134 49980
UR-65076 TU134 60001
UR-65077 TU134 60028
UR-65089 TU134 60180
UR-65092 TU134 60206
UR-65093 TU134 60215
UR-65107 TU134 60328
UR-65109 TU134 60342
UR-65114 TU134 60395
UR-65123 TU134 60525
UR-65134 TU134 60647
UR-65135 TU134 60648
UR-65556 TU134 66372
UR-65718 TU134 63668
UR-65746 TU134 2351608
UR-65752 TU134 61079
UR-65757 TU134 62215
UR-65761 TU134 62244
UR-65764 TU134 62305
UR-65765 TU134 62315
UR-65773 TU134 62495
UR-65782 TU134 62672
UR-65790 TU134 63100
UR-65826 TU134 12083
UR-65841 TU134 18120
UR-65852 TU134 23244
UR-65864 TU134 28284
UR-65877 TU134 31250
UR-65888 TU134 36175
UR-72003 AN-72
UR-72004 AN-72
UR-72959 AN-72
UR-72966 AN-72
UR-74003 AN-74
UR-74004 AN-74 36547094890
UR-74010 AN-74
UR-74026 AN-74 36547096919
UR-74027 AN-74
UR-74028 AN-74
UR-74031 AN-74
UR-74032 AN-74
UR-74037 AN-74
UR-74038 AN-74 36547097936
UR-74043 AN-74
UR-74044 AN-74
UR-74053 AN-74
UR-74055 AN-74
UR-76316 IL-76 0043454633
UR-76317 IL-76 0053458733
UR-76318 IL-76 0023437127
UR-76319 IL-76 0013438129
UR-76320 IL-76 0043455686
UR-76321 IL-76 0053457713
UR-76322 IL-76 0053462873
UR-76323 IL-76 0063466988
UR-76345 IL-76
UR-76376 IL-76
UR-76382 IL-76 0013436048
UR-76389 IL-76
UR-76390 IL-76 0043453562
UR-76391 IL-76 0043453568
UR-76392 IL-76 0043454602
UR-76393 IL-76 0043455653
UR-76394 IL-76 0063466989
UR-76395 IL-76 0033443255
UR-76396 IL-76
UR-76397 IL-76
UR-76398 IL-76 0083484522
UR-76398 IL-76

UR-76399 IL-76 0083485566
UR-76408 IL-76 0053460820
UR-76412 IL-76
UR-76413 IL-76 1013407215
UR-76414 IL-76 0083482478
UR-76415 IL-76 0083481440
UR-76423 IL-76 0053457720
UR-76424 IL-76 0063470096
UR-76433 IL-76 0053460827
UR-76437 IL-76 0083484527
UR-76438 IL-76 0083483513
UR-76441 IL-76
UR-76443 IL-76 0043452534
UR-76444 IL-76 0063470113
UR-76532 IL-76
UR-76534 IL-76 0023442210
UR-76535 IL-76
UR-76537 IL-76 0033442225
UR-76539 IL-76 0033442234
UR-76541 IL-76 0033442241
UR-76555 IL-76
UR-76563 IL-76 0033447372
UR-76568 IL-76 0033448420
UR-76568 IL-76 0043449471
UR-76570 IL-76 0033448427
UR-76571 IL-76 0033448429
UR-76573 IL-76 0043449437
UR-76576 IL-76 0043449449
UR-76578 IL-76 0043449468
UR-76580 IL-76 0043450476
UR-76581 IL-76 0043450484
UR-76582 IL-76 0043450487
UR-76583 IL-76 0043450491
UR-76584 IL-76
UR-76586 IL-76 0043451508
UR-76587 IL-76 0043451517
UR-76590 IL-76 0043452544
UR-76595 IL-76 0043453571
UR-76596 IL-76
UR-76601 IL-76 0043454606
UR-76603 IL-76 0043454623
UR-76609 IL-76
UR-76614 IL-76 0043455665
UR-76618 IL-76
UR-76622 IL-76 0043457702
UR-76630 IL-76 0053458749
UR-76636 IL-76
UR-76637 IL-76 0053460797
UR-76651 IL-76 0053462872
UR-76655 IL-76 0053463885
UR-76656 IL-76 0053463891
UR-76658 IL-76
UR-76660 IL-76 0053463910
UR-76663 IL-76 0053464922
UR-76664 IL-76 0053464926
UR-76667 IL-76
UR-76670 IL-76 0063465958
UR-76671 IL-76 0063465963
UR-76676 IL-76
UR-76677 IL-76 0063467005
UR-76680 IL-76 0063467020
UR-76681 IL-76 0063467021
UR-76682 IL-76 0063467027
UR-76683 IL-76
UR-76684 IL-76
UR-76687 IL-76 0063469051
UR-76688 IL-76 0063469062
UR-76690 IL-76
UR-76694 IL-76 0063470107
UR-76698 IL-76 0063471123
UR-76700 IL-76 0063471134
UR-76704 IL-76
UR-76705 IL-76 0063472158
UR-76706 IL-76 0063472163
UR-76707 IL-76
UR-76716 IL-76
UR-76717 IL-76
UR-76721 IL-76 0073475239
UR-76728 IL-76 0073475270
UR-76729 IL-76 0073476275
UR-76730 IL-76 0073476277
UR-76732 IL-76 0073476296
UR-76740 IL-76
UR-76742 IL-76 0073478346
UR-76744 IL-76 0073478359
UR-76748 IL-76

UR-76759 IL-76
UR-76760 IL-76 0073479400
UR-76767 IL-76
UR-76778 IL-76 0083482502
UR-78734 IL-76 1013409303
UR-78736 IL-76 1013408257
UR-78752 IL-76 0083483519
UR-78755 IL-76 0083484531
UR-78756 IL-76 0083484536
UR-78758 IL-76 0083484551
UR-78772 IL-76
UR-78774 IL-76 0083488643
UR-78775 IL-76 0083489647
UR-78778 IL-76 0083490703
UR-78785 IL-76 0083489691
UR-78786 IL-76
UR-78820 IL-76 0093496907
UR-82007 AN124 19530501005
UR-82008 AN124 19530501006
UR-82009 AN124 19530501007
UR-82027 AN124 19530502288
UR-82029 AN124 19530502630
UR-82060 AN225
UR-82066 AN124 19530502761
UR-85068 TU154 068
UR-85074 TU154 074
UR-85093 TU154 093
UR-85116 TU154 116
UR-85118 TU154 118
UR-85132 TU154 132
UR-85137 TU154 137
UR-85148 TU154 148
UR-85152 TU154 152
UR-85154 TU154 154
UR-85179 TU154 179
UR-85218 TU154 218
UR-85232 TU154 232
UR-85244 TU154 244
UR-85269 TU154 269
UR-85288 TU154 288
UR-85316 TU154 316
UR-85350 TU154 350
UR-85362 TU154 362
UR-85368 TU154 368
UR-85379 TU154 379
UR-85395 TU154 395
UR-85399 TU154 399
UR-85407 TU154 407
UR-85424 TU154 424
UR-85445 TU154 445
UR-85460 TU154 460
UR-85476 TU154 476
UR-85482 TU154 482
UR-85490 TU154 490
UR-85499 TU154 499
UR-85513 TU154 513
UR-85526 TU154 526
UR-85535 TU154 535
UR-85561 TU154 561
UR-85585 TU154 585
UR-85700 TU154 875
UR-85701 TU154 876
UR-85707 TU154 882
UR-85710 TU154 885
UR-86132 IL-62 1034152
UR-86133 IL-62 1138234
UR-86134 IL-62 1138546
UR-86135 IL-62 1748445
UR-86451 IL-62 52105
UR-86527 IL-62 4037758
UR-86528 IL-62 4038111
UR-86529 IL-62 4038625
UR-86580 IL-62 2343554
UR-86581 IL-62 2932526
UR-86582 IL-62 3036253
UR-86903 IL-76 0013436048
UR-86921 IL-76
UR-86924 IL-76 0023441174
UR-87215 YAK40 9510540
UR-87230 YAK40 9541542
UR-87237 YAK40 9530343
UR-87245 YAK40 9531343
UR-87266 YAK40 9310227
UR-87276 YAK40 9311227
UR-87298 YAK40 9321528
UR-87308 YAK40 9320429

UR-87320	YAK40	9331929
UR-87327	**YAK40**	**9330630**
UR-87329	**YAK40**	**9..0830**
UR-87345	**YAK40**	**9511439**
UR-87421	**YAK40**	**9421734**
UR-87432	**YAK40**	**9420835**
UR-87435	**YAK40**	**9431135**
UR-87463	**YAK40**	**9..0237**
UR-87469	**YAK40**	**9441437**
UR-87479	**YAK40**	**9441838**
UR-87508	**YAK40**	**9521040**
UR-87512	**YAK40**	**9521440**
UR-87528	**YAK40**	**9521041**
UR-87547	**YAK40**	**9531242**
UR-87562	**YAK40**	**9211321**
UR-87566	**YAK40**	**9211821**
UR-87615	**YAK40**	**9131618**
UR-87624	**YAK40**	**9140519**
UR-87641	**YAK40**	**9..0220**
UR-87642	**YAK40**	**9..0320**
UR-87649	**YAK40**	**9141020**
UR-87660	**YAK40**	**9240425**
UR-87818	**YAK40**	**9231024**
UR-87832	**YAK40**	**9241825**
UR-87841	**YAK40**	**9320930**
UR-87918	**YAK40**	**9730855**
UR-87951	**YAK40**	**9810957**
UR-87961	**YAK40**	**9820458**
UR-87964	**YAK40**	**9830758**
UR-87987	**YAK40**	**9541144**
UR-87998	**YAK40**	**9540245**
UR-88151	**YAK40**	**9610546**
UR-88203	**YAK40**	**9630549**
UR-88203	YAK40	9630549
UR-88237	**YAK40**	**9640751**
UR-88237	YAK40	9640751
UR-88290	**YAK40**	**9840459**
UR-88299	**YAK40**	**9321028**
UR-98775	**IL-76**	
UR-ALC	**IL-76**	
UR-BFA	**B737**	**21685**
UR-GAA	B737	26069
UR-GAB	B737	26071
UR-GAC	**B737**	**23188**
UR-GAD	**B737**	**22802**
UR-GAE	**B737**	**24907**
UR-UAP	**AN124**	

Australia

VH-	**146**	**E1004**
VH-	**B737**	**20363**
VH-	**B737**	**20365**
(VH-...)	B747	21162
(VH-...)	B747	21316
"VH-AKK"	B707	20517
VH-ANA	**B727**	**22641**
VH-ANB	**B727**	**22642**
VH-ANE	**B727**	**22643**
VH-ANF	**B727**	**22644**
VH-ATD	**F-28**	**11047**
VH-ATE	F-28	11082
VH-ATG	**F-28**	**11084**
VH-AWE	**B757**	**24635**
VH-BZF	**B767**	**27569**
VH-CZA	**B737**	**23653**
VH-CZA	DC-9	47003
VH-CZB	**B737**	**23654**
VH-CZB	DC-9	47004
VH-CZC	**B737**	**23655**
VH-CZC	DC-9	47005
VH-CZD	**B737**	**23656**
VH-CZD	DC-9	47065
VH-CZE	**B737**	**23657**
VH-CZE	DC-9	47202
VH-CZF	**B737**	**23658**
VH-CZF	DC-9	47325
VH-CZG	**B737**	**23659**
VH-CZG	DC-9	47501
VH-CZH	**B737**	**23660**
VH-CZH	DC-9	47526
VH-CZI	**B737**	**23661**
VH-CZI	DC-9	47527
VH-CZJ	**B737**	**23662**
VH-CZJ	DC-9	47547

VH-CZK	**B737**	**23663**
VH-CZK	DC-9	47548
VH-CZL	**B737**	**23664**
VH-CZL	DC-9	47549
VH-CZM	B737	22645
VH-CZM	**B737**	**24302**
VH-CZN	B737	22646
VH-CZN	**B737**	**24303**
VH-CZO	B737	22647
VH-CZO	**B737**	**24304**
VH-CZP	B737	22648
VH-CZP	**B737**	**24305**
VH-CZQ	B737	22649
VH-CZR	B737	22650
VH-CZS	B737	22651
VH-CZS	B737	24030
VH-CZT	B737	22652
VH-CZT	**B737**	**27454**
VH-CZU	B737	22653
VH-CZU	**B737**	**27267**
VH-CZV	B737	22654
VH-CZV	**B737**	**23831**
VH-CZW	B737	22655
VH-CZW	**B737**	**23832**
VH-CZX	B737	22656
VH-CZX	**B737**	**24029**
VH-DHE	**B727**	**22080**
VH-EAA	B707	19621
VH-EAA	**B747**	**22495**
VH-EAB	B707	19622
VH-EAB	**B747**	**22672**
VH-EAC	B707	19623
VH-EAD	B707	19624
VH-EAE	B707	19625
VH-EAF	B707	19626
VH-EAG	B707	19627
VH-EAH	B707	19628
VH-EAI	B707	19629
VH-EAJ	B707	19630
VH-EAJ	**B767**	**23304**
VH-EAK	**B767**	**23305**
VH-EAL	**B767**	**23306**
VH-EAM	**B767**	**23309**
(VH-EAM)	B767	23307
VH-EAN	**B767**	**23402**
(VH-EAN)	B767	23308
VH-EAO	**B767**	**23403**
(VH-EAO)	B767	23309
VH-EAQ	**B767**	**23896**
VH-EBA	B707	17696
VH-EBA	B747	20009
VH-EBB	B707	17697
VH-EBB	B747	20010
VH-EBC	B707	17698
VH-EBC	B747	20011
VH-EBD	B707	17699
VH-EBD	B747	20012
VH-EBE	B707	17700
VH-EBE	B747	20534
VH-EBF	B707	17701
VH-EBF	B747	20535
VH-EBG	B707	17702
VH-EBG	B747	20841
VH-EBH	B707	18067
VH-EBH	B747	20842
VH-EBI	B707	18068
VH-EBI	B747	20921
VH-EBJ	B707	18069
VH-EBJ	B747	21054
VH-EBK	B707	18334
VH-EBK	B747	21140
VH-EBL	B707	18739
VH-EBL	B747	21237
VH-EBM	B707	18740
VH-EBM	B747	21352
VH-EBN	B707	18808
VH-EBN	B747	21353
VH-EBO	B707	18809
VH-EBO	B747	21657
VH-EBP	B707	18810
VH-EBP	B747	21658
VH-EBQ	B707	18953
VH-EBQ	**B747**	**22145**
VH-EBR	B707	18954
VH-EBR	**B747**	**22614**
VH-EBS	B707	18955

VH-EBS	**B747**	**22616**
VH-EBT	B707	19293
VH-EBT	**B747**	**23222**
(VH-EBT)	B747	22617
VH-EBU	B707	19294
VH-EBU	**B747**	**23223**
VH-EBV	B707	19295
VH-EBV	**B747**	**23224**
VH-EBW	B707	19296
VH-EBW	**B747**	**23408**
VH-EBX	B707	19297
VH-EBX	**B747**	**23688**
VH-EBY	**B747**	**23823**
VH-EBZ	B707	19354
VH-ECA	B747	21354
VH-ECB	**B747**	**21977**
VH-ECC	**B747**	**22615**
VH-EEI	B747	20108
VH-EWA	F-28	11195
(VH-EWA)	F-28	11173
VH-EWB	F-28	11205
(VH-EWB)	F-28	11181
VH-EWC	F-28	11207
VH-EWD	F-28	11208
VH-EWF	F-28	11143
VH-EWG	F-28	11151
VH-EWH	F-28	11186
VH-EWI	**146**	**E3171**
VH-EWJ	146	E3173
VH-EWK	146	E3175
VH-EWL	**146**	**E3177**
VH-EWM	**146**	**E3179**
VH-EWN	146	E3190
VH-EWR	**146**	**E3195**
VH-EWS	**146**	**E3197**
VH-FKA	**F-28**	**11021**
VH-FKB	F-28	11022
VH-FKC	**F-28**	**11025**
VH-FKD	**F-28**	**11026**
VH-FKE	**F-28**	**11040**
VH-FKF	**F-28**	**11008**
(VH-FKF)	F-28	11041
(VH-FKF)	F-28	11056
VH-FKG	F-28	11031
VH-FKI	**F-28**	**11183**
VH-FKJ	**F-28**	**11186**
VH-FKK	**F-28**	**11195**
VH-FKL	**F-28**	**11205**
VH-FKM	**F-28**	**11143**
VH-FKN	**F-28**	**11207**
VH-FKO	**F-28**	**11212**
VH-FKP	**F-28**	**11151**
VH-FKQ	**F-28**	**11208**
VH-HTC	B707	18937
VH-HYA	**A320**	**0022**
VH-HYB	**A320**	**0023**
VH-HYC	**A320**	**0024**
VH-HYD	**A320**	**0025**
VH-HYE	**A320**	**0026**
VH-HYF	**A320**	**0027**
VH-HYG	**A320**	**0029**
VH-HYH	**A320**	**0030**
VH-HYI	**A320**	**0140**
(VH-HYI)	A320	0059
VH-HYJ	**A320**	**0142**
(VH-HYJ)	A320	0068
VH-HYK	**A320**	**0157**
(VH-HYK)	A320	0073
VH-HYL	**A320**	**0229**
VH-HYO	**A320**	**0547**
VH-INH	**B747**	**23026**
VH-INJ	**B747**	**23029**
VH-INK	**B747**	**23028**
VH-IPC	**DC-9**	**47193**
VH-IPF	**DC-9**	**47408**
VH-ITA	B767	27376
VH-ITB	B767	27377
(VH-ITH)	B767	27468
VH-JJP	**146**	**E2037**
VH-JJQ	**146**	**E2038**
VH-JJS	**146**	**E2093**
VH-JJT	**146**	**E2098**
VH-JJU	**146**	**E2116**
VH-JJW	**146**	**E2110**
VH-JJX	**146**	**E2127**
VH-JJY	**146**	**E2113**

VH-JJZ	**146**	**E2114**
VH-JSF	146	E1160
VH-LAP	B727	18270
VH-LAR	F-28	11212
VH-LNH	MD-83	49938
VH-LNI	MD-83	53121
VH-LNJ	MD-82	49383
VH-LNK	MD-82	49423
VH-LNL	MD-82	49437
(VH-LNN)	MD-82	53118
VH-MMJ	F-28	11013
VH-NJC	**146**	**E1013**
VH-NJD	**146**	**E1160**
VH-NJE	B737	23766
VH-NJF	**146**	**E3198**
VH-NJG	**146**	**E2170**
VH-NJH	**146**	**E2178**
VH-NJJ	**146**	**E2184**
VH-NJL	**146**	**E3213**
VH-NJM	**146**	**E3194**
VH-NJN	**146**	**E3217**
VH-NJQ	146	E2176
VH-NJR	**146**	**E1152**
VH-NJT	**146**	**E1228**
VH-NJV	**146**	**E1002**
VH-NJY	**146**	**E1005**
VH-NJZ	**146**	**E1009**
VH-NOE	**B767**	**25535**
VH-OAM	B737	25010
VH-OAN	B737	25011
VH-OGA	**B767**	**24146**
VH-OGB	**B767**	**24316**
VH-OGC	**B767**	**24317**
VH-OGD	**B767**	**24407**
VH-OGE	**B767**	**24531**
VH-OGF	**B767**	**24853**
VH-OGG	**B767**	**24929**
VH-OGH	**B767**	**24930**
VH-OGI	**B767**	**25246**
VH-OGJ	**B767**	**25274**
VH-OGK	**B767**	**25316**
VH-OGL	**B767**	**25363**
VH-OGM	**B767**	**25575**
VH-OGN	**B767**	**25576**
VH-OGO	**B767**	**25577**
VH-OJA	**B747**	**24354**
VH-OJB	**B747**	**24373**
VH-OJC	**B747**	**24406**
VH-OJD	**B747**	**24481**
VH-OJE	**B747**	**24482**
VH-OJF	**B747**	**24483**
VH-OJG	**B747**	**24779**
VH-OJH	**B747**	**24806**
VH-OJI	**B747**	**24887**
VH-OJJ	**B747**	**24974**
VH-OJK	**B747**	**25067**
VH-OJL	**B747**	**25151**
VH-OJM	**B747**	**25245**
VH-OJN	**B747**	**25315**
VH-OJO	**B747**	**25544**
VH-OJP	**B747**	**25545**
VH-OJQ	**B747**	**25546**
VH-OJR	**B747**	**25547**
VH-RMA	**B767**	**24742**
VH-RMD	B727	18844
VH-RMD	**B767**	**22692**
VH-RME	B727	18743
VH-RME	**B767**	**22693**
VH-RMF	B727	18744
VH-RMF	**B767**	**22694**
VH-RMG	**B767**	**22695**
VH-RMH	**B767**	**22696**
VH-RMK	B727	21178
VH-RMK	**B767**	**22981**
VH-RML	B727	21480
VH-RML	**B767**	**22980**
VH-RMM	B727	21647
VH-RMM	**B767**	**24973**
VH-RMN	**B727**	**21695**
VH-RMO	B727	22016
VH-RMP	B727	22068
VH-RMR	B727	19253
VH-RMS	B727	20278
VH-RMT	B727	20370
VH-RMU	B727	20548
VH-RMV	B727	20549

VH-RMW	B727	20550
VH-RMX	**B727**	**20551**
VH-RMY	B727	20978
VH-RMZ	B727	20979
VH-TAA	**A300**	**134**
VH-TAB	A300	151
VH-TAC	**A300**	**157**
VH-TAD	**A300**	**196**
VH-TAE	**A300**	**218**
VH-TAF	**B737**	**23477**
VH-TAG	**B737**	**23478**
VH-TAH	**B737**	**23479**
VH-TAI	**B737**	**23483**
VH-TAJ	**B737**	**23484**
VH-TAK	**B737**	**23485**
VH-TAU	**B737**	**23486**
VH-TAV	**B737**	**23487**
VH-TAW	**B737**	**23488**
VH-TAX	**B737**	**23489**
VH-TAY	**B737**	**23490**
VH-TAZ	**B737**	**23491**
VH-TBG	B727	20552
VH-TBH	B727	20553
VH-TBI	B727	20554
VH-TBJ	B727	20555
VH-TBK	B727	20950
VH-TBL	B727	20951
VH-TBM	B727	21171
VH-TBN	B727	21479
VH-TBO	B727	21646
VH-TBP	B727	21696
VH-TBQ	B727	22017
VH-TBR	B727	22069
VH-TBS	**B727**	**20278**
VH-TJA	B727	18741
VH-TJA	**B737**	**24295**
VH-TJB	B727	18742
VH-TJB	**B737**	**24296**
VH-TJC	B727	18843
VH-TJC	**B737**	**24297**
VH-TJD	B727	19254
VH-TJD	**B737**	**24298**
VH-TJE	B727	20228
VH-TJE	**B737**	**24430**
VH-TJF	B727	20371
VH-TJF	**B737**	**24431**
VH-TJG	**B737**	**24432**
VH-TJH	**B737**	**24433**
VH-TJI	**B737**	**24434**
VH-TJJ	**B737**	**24435**
VH-TJJ	DC-9	47007
VH-TJK	**B737**	**24436**
VH-TJK	DC-9	47008
VH-TJL	**B737**	**24437**
VH-TJL	DC-9	47009
VH-TJM	**B737**	**24438**
VH-TJM	DC-9	47072
VH-TJN	**B737**	**24439**
VH-TJN	DC-9	47203
VH-TJO	**B737**	**24440**
VH-TJO	DC-9	47326
VH-TJP	**B737**	**24441**
VH-TJP	DC-9	47418
VH-TJQ	**B737**	**24442**
VH-TJQ	DC-9	47419
VH-TJR	**B737**	**24443**
VH-TJR	DC-9	47528
VH-TJS	**B737**	**24444**
VH-TJS	DC-9	47550
VH-TJT	**B737**	**24445**
VH-TJT	DC-9	47551
VH-TJU	**B737**	**24446**
VH-TJU	DC-9	47552
VH-TJV	**B737**	**25163**
VH-TJW	**B737**	**26961**
VH-TJX	**B737**	**28150**
VH-TJY	**B737**	**28151**
VH-YMA	A300	584
VH-YMB	A300	603
VH-YMI	A310	425
VH-YMJ	A300	540
VH-YMK	A300	556

Vietnam

VN-81416	B707	18832
VN-83415	B707	19821
VN-A102	TU134	
VN-A104	**TU134**	**61055**
VN-A106	**TU134**	**49752**
VN-A108	TU134	48430
VN-A110	**TU134**	**62144**
VN-A112	**TU134**	**62458**
VN-A114	**TU134**	**66220**
VN-A116	**TU134**	**66230**
VN-A118	**TU134**	**66250**
VN-A120	**TU134**	**66360**
VN-A122	**TU134**	**49900**
VN-A124	**TU134**	**60108**
VN-A126	TU134	60435
VN-A128	**TU134**	**60612**
VN-A130	**TU134**	**62259**
VN-A132	**TU134**	**63260**
VN-A304	**B707**	**17929**
VN-A441	**YAK40**	**9421334**
VN-A442	**YAK40**	**9211434**
VN-A443	**YAK40**	**9421534**
VN-A444	**YAK40**	
VN-A445	YAK40	9421634
VN-A446	**YAK40**	**9631748**
VN-A449	YAK40	9631848
VN-A450	**YAK40**	**9920960**
VN-A452	**YAK40**	**9920860**
VN-A502	F-70	11580
VN-A504	F-70	11585
VN-B1416	B707	18832

Bahamas

VP-BCN	1-11	BAC.188
VP-BCO	1-11	BAC.189
VP-BCP	1-11	034
VP-BCQ	1-11	BAC.198
VP-BCY	1-11	BAC.121
VP-BCZ	1-11	BAC.157
VP-BDE	B707	17700
VP-BDF	B707	18085
VP-BDG	B707	18084
VP-BDI	1-11	074
VP-BDJ	1-11	089
VP-BDN	1-11	062
VP-BDP	1-11	063

British Honduras

VP-HCM	B720	18046
VP-HCN	B720	18074
VP-HCO	B720	18045
VP-HCP	B720	17917
VP-HCQ	B720	18076

Kenya

VP-KPJ	COMET	6431
VP-KPK	COMET	6433
VP-KRL	COMET	6472

Bristish Virgin Islands

VP-LAK	1-11	BAC.205
VP-LAN	1-11	BAC.198
VP-LAP	1-11	BAC.188
VP-LAR	1-11	BAC.189

St Vincent & Grenadines

(see also J8-)

"VP-VNG"	B737	22505

Rhodesia

VP-WGA	B707	20110
VP-WKR	B707	18819
VP-WKS	B707	18923
VP-WKT	B707	18929
VP-WKU	B707	18930
VP-WKV	B707	18927
VP-WKW	B707	18891
VP-WMJ	DC-8	45821
VP-YNL	B720	18162
VP-YNM	**B720**	**18242**
VP-YNN	B720	18244
VP-YXA	1-11	039
VP-YXB	1-11	040

Fiji/Tonga

(see also DQ-)

(VQ-FBQ)	1-11	BAC.245

Bermuda

(VR-B)	B727	19088
(VR-B..)	B747	20305
VR-BAC	1-11	017
VR-BAT	B727	20371
VR-BAT	**B747**	**21648**
VR-BBW	B707	18372
VR-BBZ	B707	18373
VR-BCN	F-28	11016
VR-BCP	B707	19590
VR-BDJ	**B727**	**20046**
VR-BEA	**1-11**	**BAC.195**
VR-BEB	**1-11**	**BAC.226**
VR-BEG	B737	21957
VR-BEH	B737	20194
VR-BGW	B727	18366
VR-BHK	B727	18933
VR-BHM	**DC-8**	**46111**
VR-BHN	B727	18370
VR-BHO	B727	19251
VR-BHP	B727	18371
VR-BHS	1-11	076
VR-BIA	**DC-8**	**45658**
VR-BJR	**DC-8**	**46067**
VR-BKC	**B727**	**20533**
VR-BKO	B737	21957
(VR-BLC)	B757	24527
VR-BLG	**DC-8**	**46071**
VR-BMC	**B727**	**18323**
VR-BMG	DC-9	47006
VR-BMH	MD-83	49628
VR-BMI	MD-83	49629
VR-BMJ	MD-83	49791
VR-BMP	DC-10	46578
VR-BMR	DC-8	46071
VR-BMU	A310	594
VR-BMV	B707	18586
VR-BMX	B737	23404
VR-BNA	**B727**	**19262**
VR-BNC	F-28	11016
VR-BNK	A300	247
VR-BOC	**B737**	**24970**
VR-BOO	**MD-87**	**49778**
VR-BOP	**MD-87**	**49725**
VR-BOR	B707	18586
VR-BOU	A310	638
VR-BOX	B737	21206
VR-BRR	B727	20371
VR-BSA	B727	20046
VR-BZA	**B707**	**20375**

Cayman Islands

VR-C	**B727**	**20489**
VR-CAA	B737	25371
VR-CAB	1-11	BAC.237
VR-CAB	B737	24519
VR-CAL	1-11	BAC.211
VR-CAL	**B737**	**22022**
VR-CAL	B737	24512
VR-CAM	1-11	069
VR-CAM	**B727**	**20371**
VR-CAN	**B707**	**18067**
VR-CAO	B707	18586
VR-CAQ	1-11	005
VR-CAR	B707	18748
VR-CAU	**B757**	**25220**
VR-CBA	B727	18935
VR-CBE	B727	19282
VR-CBG	B727	19620
VR-CBI	1-11	057
VR-CBN	B707	20028
VR-CBQ	**B727**	**21460**
VR-CBV	B727	19620
VR-CBX	1-11	084
VR-CBY	1-11	BAC.183
VR-CBZ	1-11	083
VR-CBZ	B737	23800
VR-CCA	**B727**	**21010**
VR-CCB	B727	20228
VR-CCD	B737	23800
VR-CCG	**1-11**	**081**
VR-CCJ	1-11	BAC.126
VR-CCS	**1-11**	**069**
VR-CCW	B737	23387
VR-CDB	B727	19139
VR-CDL	**B727**	**21655**
VR-CEF	B737	23162
VR-CFG	**L1011**	**1195**
VR-CHS	B727	18934
VR-CHS	B727	20228
VR-CKA	DC-8	46095
VR-CKE	DC-9	47151
VR-CKL	B727	19253
VR-CKL	DC-8	46095
VR-CKO	**DC-9**	**47151**
VR-CKX	**B737**	**23162**
VR-CLM	B727	19282
VR-CMA	B727	21105
VR-CMB	B727	21106
VR-CMC	B727	21107
VR-CMD	B727	21108
VR-CMI	**1-11**	**BAC.183**
VR-CMM	**B727**	**18368**
VR-CMN	**B727**	**19282**
VR-CNN	B737	21518
VR-COJ	B727	21948
VR-CRB	B727	19139
VR-CRC	B737	25040
VR-CRK	**B757**	**23454**
VR-CTM	1-11	081
VR-CWC	**B727**	**19620**
VR-CYB	B737	22074
VR-CZZ	L1011	1249

Hong Kong

VR-H	**A340**	**136**
VR-H..	B747	22105
VR-H..	B747	22107
VR-HFS	CV880	22-00-47M
VR-HFT	CV880	22-00-43M
VR-HFX	CV880	22-00-37M
VR-HFY	CV880	22-7-2-54
VR-HFZ	CV880	22-7-1-53
VR-HGA	CV880	22-00-44M
VR-HGC	CV880	22-7-4-56
VR-HGF	CV880	22-7-6-58
VR-HGG	CV880	22-7-8-60
VR-HGH	B707	18584
VR-HGI	B707	18585
VR-HGN	B707	18693
VR-HGO	B707	18586
VR-HGP	B707	18922
(VR-HGP)	B707	18921
VR-HGQ	B707	18964
(VR-HGQ)	B707	18922
VR-HGR	B707	18921
(VR-HGR)	B707	18964
(VR-HGS)	B707	19034
VR-HGU	B707	19034
VR-HHB	B707	18747
VR-HHD	B707	18748
VR-HHE	B707	18888
VR-HHG	L1011	1056
VR-HHJ	B707	18889
VR-HHK	**L1011**	**1118**
(VR-HHK)	B707	19263
VR-HHL	**L1011**	**1122**
(VR-HHL)	B707	19412
VR-HHV	**L1011**	**1024**

VR-HHW	L1011	1032
VR-HHX	L1011	1054
VR-HHY	**L1011**	**1051**
VR-HIA	**B747**	**21966**
VR-HIB	**B747**	**22149**
VR-HIC	**B747**	**22429**
VR-HID	**B747**	**22530**
VR-HIE	**B747**	**22872**
VR-HIF	**B747**	**23048**
VR-HIH	**B747**	**23120**
VR-HII	**B747**	**23221**
VR-HIJ	**B747**	**23392**
(VR-HIJ)	B747	23221
VR-HIK	**B747**	**23534**
VR-HKB	B747	19642
(VR-HKC)	B707	20456
VR-HKG	**B747**	**21746**
VR-HKK	B707	20517
VR-HKL	B707	19367
VR-HKM	B747	20246
VR-HKN	**B747**	**19897**
VR-HKO	**B747**	**22237**
VR-HKP	B737	22071
VR-HL.	A330	012
VR-HLA	**A330**	**071**
VR-HLB	**A330**	**083**
VR-HLC	**A330**	**099**
VR-HLD	**A330**	**102**
VR-HLE	**A330**	**109**
VR-HLF	**A330**	**113**
VR-HLG	**A330**	**118**
VR-HLH	**A330**	**121**
VR-HME	B747	22106
VR-HMR	**A340**	**063**
VR-HMS	**A340**	**074**
VR-HMT	**A340**	**080**
VR-HMU	**A340**	**085**
VR-HMV	L1011	1033
VR-HMW	L1011	1094
VR-HNA	**B777**	**27265**
VR-HNB	**B777**	**27266**
VR-HNC	**B777**	**27263**
VR-HND	**B777**	**27264**
VR-HOA	L1011	1022
VR-HOB	**L1011**	**1037**
VR-HOC	L1011	1042
VR-HOD	**L1011**	**1043**
VR-HOE	**L1011**	**1021**
VR-HOF	**L1011**	**1027**
VR-HOG	L1011	1045
VR-HOH	L1011	1050
VR-HOI	**L1011**	**1039**
VR-HOJ	L1011	1044
VR-HOK	**L1011**	**1055**
VR-HOL	**B747**	**23709**
VR-HOM	**B747**	**23920**
VR-HON	**B747**	**24215**
VR-HOO	**B747**	**23814**
VR-HOP	**B747**	**23815**
VR-HOR	**B747**	**24631**
VR-HOS	**B747**	**24850**
VR-HOT	**B747**	**24851**
VR-HOU	**B747**	**24925**
VR-HOV	**B747**	**25082**
VR-HOW	**B747**	**25211**
VR-HOX	**B747**	**24955**
VR-HOY	**B747**	**25351**
VR-HOZ	**B747**	**25871**
VR-HTC	B707	18937
VR-HUA	**B747**	**25872**
VR-HUB	**B747**	**25873**
VR-HUD	**B747**	**25874**
VR-HUE	**B747**	**27117**
VR-HUF	**B747**	**25869**
VR-HUG	**B747**	**25870**
VR-HUH	**B747**	**27175**
VR-HUI	**B747**	**27230**
VR-HUJ	**B747**	**27595**
VR-HUK	**B747**	**27503**
VR-HVX	**B747**	**24568**
VR-HVY	**B747**	**22306**
VR-HVZ	**B747**	**23864**
VR-HXB	**A340**	**137**
VR-HYA	**A330**	**098**
VR-HYB	**A330**	**106**
VR-HYC	**A330**	**111**
VR-HYK	B737	22660
VR-HYL	B737	22408
VR-HYM	B737	22734
VR-HYN	B737	22733
VR-HYO	**A320**	**0393**
VR-HYP	**A320**	**0394**
VR-HYR	**A320**	**0414**
VR-HYS	**A320**	**0430**
VR-HYT	**A320**	**0443**
VR-HYU	**A320**	**0447**
VR-HYV	**A320**	**0415**
VR-HYZ	B737	22453

Tanganyika
(see also 5H-)

"VR-TBV"	B727	19620

Brunei
(see also VS-/V8-)

VR-UEB	B737	20913
VR-UEC	B737	21138
VR-UED	B737	21809
VR-UHM	B727	18371

Brunei
(see also VS-/V8-)

VS-1HB	B727	21010
VS-HB1	B727	21010
VS-UEB	B737	20913
VS-UEB	B737	21809
VS-UEC	B737	21138
VS-UHM	B727	18371

India

VT-DJI	B707	17722
VT-DJJ	B707	17723
VT-DJK	B707	17724
VT-DMN	B707	18055
VT-DNY	B707	18414
VT-DNZ	B707	18415
VT-DPA	**B737**	**22415**
VT-DPM	B707	18708
VT-DPN	CRVL	155
VT-DPO	CRVL	128
VT-DPP	CRVL	130
VT-DSB	CRVL	134
VT-DSI	B707	18873
VT-DUH	CRVL	203
VT-DUI	**CRVL**	**204**
VT-DVA	B707	19247
VT-DVB	B707	19248
VT-DVI	CRVL	213
VT-DVJ	CRVL	216
VT-DWN	CRVL	231
VT-DXT	B707	19988
VT-EAG	B737	20480
VT-EAH	B737	20481
VT-EAI	B737	20482
VT-EAJ	B737	20483
VT-EAK	B737	20484
VT-EAL	B737	20485
VT-EAM	B737	20486
VT-EBD	B747	19959
VT-EBE	**B747**	**19960**
VT-EBN	**B747**	**20459**
VT-EBO	B747	20558
VT-ECG	CRVL	70
VT-ECH	CRVL	78
VT-ECI	CRVL	237
VT-ECP	**B737**	**20960**
VT-ECQ	B737	20961
VT-ECR	B737	20962
VT-ECS	B737	20963
VT-EDR	**B737**	**21163**
VT-EDS	**B737**	**21164**
VT-EDU	**B747**	**21182**
VT-EDV	A300	34
VT-EDW	**A300**	**36**
VT-EDX	**A300**	**38**
VT-EDY	**A300**	**59**
VT-EDZ	**A300**	**60**
VT-EFJ	**B747**	**21446**
VT-EFK	**B737**	**21496**
VT-EFL	B737	21497
VT-EFM	**B737**	**21498**
VT-EFO	B747	21473
VT-EFU	**B747**	**21829**
VT-EFV	**A300**	**88**
VT-EFW	**A300**	**111**
VT-EFX	**A300**	**113**
VT-EGA	**B747**	**21993**
VT-EGB	**B747**	**21994**
VT-EGC	**B747**	**21995**
VT-EGD	**B737**	**22280**
VT-EGE	**B737**	**22281**
VT-EGF	**B737**	**22282**
VT-EGG	**B737**	**22283**
VT-EGH	**B737**	**22284**
VT-EGI	**B737**	**22285**
VT-EGJ	**B737**	**22286**
VT-EGM	**B737**	**22473**
VT-EHC	**A300**	**181**
VT-EHD	**A300**	**182**
VT-EHE	**B737**	**22860**
VT-EHF	**B737**	**22861**
VT-EHG	**B737**	**22862**
VT-EHH	**B737**	**22863**
VT-EHN	**A300**	**177**
VT-EHO	**A300**	**180**
VT-EHQ	**A300**	**190**
VT-EHW	B737	23036
VT-EHX	B737	23037
VT-EJG	**A310**	**406**
VT-EJH	**A310**	**407**
VT-EJI	**A310**	**413**
VT-EJJ	**A310**	**428**
(VT-EJJ)	A310	392
VT-EJK	**A310**	**429**
VT-EJL	**A310**	**392**
VT-EKC	B737	20943
VT-EKD	B737	20944
VT-ELV	A300	22
VT-ELW	**A300**	**26**
VT-ENQ	**B747**	**21936**
VT-EPB	**A320**	**0045**
VT-EPC	**A320**	**0046**
VT-EPD	**A320**	**0047**
VT-EPE	**A320**	**0048**
VT-EPF	**A320**	**0049**
VT-EPG	**A320**	**0050**
VT-EPH	**A320**	**0051**
VT-EPI	**A320**	**0056**
VT-EPJ	**A320**	**0057**
VT-EPK	**A320**	**0058**
VT-EPL	**A320**	**0074**
VT-EPM	**A320**	**0075**
VT-EPN	A320	0079
VT-EPO	**A320**	**0080**
VT-EPP	**A320**	**0089**
VT-EPQ	**A320**	**0090**
VT-EPR	**A320**	**0095**
VT-EPS	**A320**	**0096**
VT-EPT	**A320**	**0097**
VT-EPW	**B747**	**24159**
VT-EPX	**B747**	**24160**
VT-EQG	B737	20492
VT-EQH	B737	22744
VT-EQI	B737	23023
VT-EQJ	B737	23024
VT-EQS	**A310**	**538**
VT-EQT	**A310**	**544**
VT-ERN	B737	19553
VT-ERS	**B720**	**18159**
VT-ESA	**A320**	**0396**
VT-ESB	**A320**	**0398**
VT-ESC	**A320**	**0416**
VT-ESD	**A320**	**0423**
VT-ESE	**A320**	**0431**
VT-ESF	**A320**	**0432**
VT-ESG	**A320**	**0451**
VT-ESH	**A320**	**0469**
VT-ESI	**A320**	**0486**
VT-ESJ	**A320**	**0490**
VT-ESK	**A320**	**0492**
VT-ESL	**A320**	**0499**
VT-ESM	**B747**	**27078**
VT-ESN	**B747**	**27164**
VT-ESO	**B747**	**27165**
VT-ESP	**B747**	**27214**
VT-EVA	**B747**	**28094**
VT-EWA	B737	20956
VT-EWB	**B737**	**22703**
VT-EWC	**B737**	**22576**
VT-EWD	**B737**	**22633**
VT-EWF	**B737**	**22396**
VT-EWH	**B737**	**21714**
VT-EWI	**B737**	**21715**
VT-EWJ	**B737**	**22279**
VT-EWL	B737	23866
VT-JAA	**B737**	**24790**
VT-JAB	**B737**	**24791**
VT-JAC	**B737**	**24096**
VT-JAD	**B737**	**24097**
VT-JAE	**B737**	**27086**
VT-JAF	**B737**	**27168**
VT-JAG	**B737**	**24345**
VT-JAH	**B737**	**24682**
VT-MGA	**B737**	**22120**
VT-MGB	**B737**	**22121**
VT-MGC	**B737**	**22122**
VT-MGD	**B737**	**22117**
VT-MGE	**B737**	**23865**
VT-MGF	**B737**	**24344**
VT-MGG	**B737**	**24468**
VT-PDB	**B737**	**22416**
VT-PDC	**B737**	**23042**
VT-PDD	**B737**	**23041**
VT-SIA	B737	21763
VT-SIB	**B737**	**22161**
VT-SIC	**B737**	**24708**
VT-SID	**B737**	**24705**

Antigua

V2-LDT	B737	20582
V2-LDX	A300	204
V2-LDY	A300	65
V2-LEA	DC-10	46554
V2-LEC	**A310**	**539**
V2-LED	**A310**	**542**
V2-LEH	**DC-10**	**47861**
V2-LEJ	**L1011**	**1246**
V2-LEK	**L1011**	**1248**
V2-LEM	**L1011**	**1032**
V2-LEO	**L1011**	**1240**

St. Kitts Nevis

(V4-CGC)	B727	20679
(V4-THB)	B737	21184

Namibia

V5-ANA	**B737**	**23790**
V5-SPE	B747	21254
V5-SPF	**B747**	**21263**

Brunei

V8-AL1	**B747**	**26426**
V8-BG1	B727	18371
V8-BG1	B727	22362
V8-BG2	B727	18371
V8-BKH	**A340**	**009**
V8-DPD	**A310**	**431**
V8-HB1	B727	21010
V8-HB1	B757	23454
V8-HM1	A310	431
V8-HM1	B727	22362
V8-HM2	B727	22362
V8-JBB	**B747**	**21649**
V8-MJB	**B767**	**25537**
V8-PJB	**A340**	**046**
V8-RBA	**B757**	**23452**
V8-RBB	**B757**	**23453**
V8-RBC	B757	23454

V8-RBD B767 24742
V8-RBE B767 25346
V8-RBF B767 25530
V8-RBG B767 25532
V8-RBH B767 25534
V8-RBJ B767 25533
V8-RBK B767 25536
V8-RBL B767 27189
V8-RBM B767 27428
V8-UB1 B727 22362
V8-UEB B737 20913
V8-UEB B737 21809
V8-UEC B737 21138
V8-UHM B727 18371

Mexico

XA- DC-9 45702
XA- DC-9 45713
XA- DC-9 45719
XA- DC-9 45780
XA- DC-9 47039
XA- DC-9 47214
XA- DC-9 47283
XA- DC-9 47553
(XA-) B727 20383
(XA-) B727 22982
(XA-) B727 22983
(XA-) B727 22984
(XA-) B727 23014
(XA-...) B747 20402
XA-ADC 1-11 084
XA-AGS DC-9 45786
XA-AMA DC-9 48125
XA-AMB DC-9 48126
XA-AMC DC-9 48127
XA-AMD DC-9 48128
XA-AME DC-9 48129
XA-AMF DC-9 48130
(XA-AMG) DC-9 48150
(XA-AMH) DC-9 48151
(XA-AMI) DC-9 48152
(XA-AMI) MD-82 48067
(XA-AMJ) MD-82 48068
(XA-AMK) MD-82 48069
(XA-AML) MD-82 48083
(XA-AMM) DC-10 48275
(XA-AMN) DC-10 48276
XA-AMO MD-82 49149
XA-AMO MD-82 49188
XA-AMP DC-8 45687
XA-AMP MD-82 49189
(XA-AMP) MD-82 49150
XA-AMQ MD-82 49190
(XA-AMQ) MD-82 49151
XA-AMR DC-10 46931
XA-AMR DC-8 45955
(XA-AMR) MD-82 49191
XA-AMS DC-8 45911
XA-AMS MD-88 49926
(XA-AMS) MD-82 49152
XA-AMT DC-8 45909
XA-AMT MD-88 49927
XA-AMU MD-88 49928
XA-AMV MD-88 49929
XA-ASS B727 18800
XA-BBI B727 19528
XA-BCS DC-9 47043
XA-BCS DC-9 47061
XA-BDM DC-9 47087
XA-BTO B727 18853
XA-CSL DC-9 45743
XA-CUB B727 20709
XA-CUE B727 20710
XA-CUN B727 20780
XA-DAT B727 20787
XA-DEI DC-9 47650
XA-DEJ DC-9 47594
XA-DEK DC-9 47602
XA-DEL DC-9 47607
XA-DEM DC-9 47609
XA-DEN DC-9 47621
XA-DEO DC-9 47622
XA-DEV DC-9 47048
XA-DOD DC-8 45641
XA-DOE DC-8 45252
XA-DUG DC-10 46936
XA-DUH DC-10 46937
XA-DUI B727 20894
XA-DUJ B727 20895
XA-DUK B727 20896
XA-FAA B727 18911
XA-FAC B727 19427
XA-FAD B727 18912
XA-FAY B727 18908
XA-FAZ B727 18909
XA-FID B727 21071
XA-FIE B727 21072
XA-GBP B727 18252
XA-GDL DC-9 47085
XA-GOJ DC-9 45721
XA-GOK DC-9 45722
XA-GUU B727 20328
XA-GUV B727 20513
XA-HOH B727 21577
XA-HON B727 21617
XA-HOV B727 21637
XA-HOX B727 21638
XA-IEU B727 21836
(XA-IEV) B727 21837
(XA-IEW) B727 21838
XA-IOV DC-9 47006
XA-IUP B727 18910
XA-JEB DC-9 47394
XA-JEC DC-9 47106
XA-JED DC-9 47356
XA-JJA B727 18326
XA-KWK B757 26151
XA-LAC DC-9 47126
XA-LEX B727 18325
XA-LMM DC-9 45736
XA-LSA DC-8 45296
XA-MEB B727 21837
XA-MEC B727 21838
XA-MED B727 22156
XA-MEE B727 22157
XA-MEF B727 22158
XA-MEG B727 18743
XA-MEH B727 22409
XA-MEI B727 22410
XA-MEJ B727 22411
XA-MEK B727 22412
XA-MEL B727 22413
XA-MEM B727 22414
XA-MEN B727 18797
XA-MEP B727 18800
XA-MEQ B727 22424
XA-MER B727 22425
(XA-MET) DC-10 48259
(XA-MEU) DC-10 48289
XA-MEW DC-10 48294
XA-MEX DC-10 48295
(XA-MEX) DC-10 48258
XA-MEZ B727 22676
XA-MMX B757 25054
XA-MXA B727 22661
XA-MXB B727 22662
XA-MXC B727 22663
XA-MXD B727 22664
XA-MXE B727 21457
XA-MXF B727 21346
XA-MXG B727 21600
XA-MXH B727 20876
XA-MXI B727 21346
XA-MXJ B727 21600
XA-NAB COMET 6420
XA-NAD B727 19815
(XA-NAD) COMET 6457
(XA-NAE) COMET 6463
XA-NAP COMET 6418
XA-NAR COMET 6424
XA-NAS COMET 6425
XA-NAT COMET 6443
XA-NAZ COMET 6418
XA-NUS DC-8 45633
XA-PAL B727 18800
XA-PEI DC-8 45652
XA-PIK DC-8 45685
XA-POW COMET 6420
XA-RAN B727 19165
XA-RIY DC-10 47861
XA-RJP B737 24255
XA-RJR B737 25179
XA-RJS B737 25185
XA-RJT MD-87 49777
XA-RJV B727 20525
XA-RJW A320 0275
XA-RJX A320 0276
XA-RJY A320 0296
XA-RJZ A320 0320
XA-RKA A320 0321
XA-RKB A320 0353
XA-RKI B767 26200
XA-RKJ B767 26204
XA-RKM F-100 11341
XA-RKN F-100 11343
XA-RKP B737 25186
XA-RKQ B737 25189
XA-RKT DC-9 47122
XA-RLM B727 18326
XA-RLM B757 24566
XA-RMO 146 E2060
XA-RNQ DC-9 47059
XA-RPH MD-83 49792
XA-RRA B727 18911
XA-RRB B727 19427
XA-RRY DC-9 45785
XA-RSQ DC-9 45730
XA-RST 146 E1015
XA-RSW B737 19794
XA-RSY B737 19027
XA-RSZ B737 19033
XA-RTI 146 E2066
XA-RTK MD-83 49938
XA-RTN 1-11 085
XA-RUO MD-87 49673
XA-RVY B767 24762
XA-RVZ B767 24716
XA-RWG B727 18572
XA-RWW B767 24952
XA-RWX B767 24953
XA-RXG DC-9 45714
XA-RXI B727 20150
XA-RXJ B727 20154
XA-RYI B727 19228
XA-RYQ A320 0259
XA-RYS A320 0260
XA-RYT A320 0261
XA-RZI B727 20151
XA-RZU A320 0252
XA-SAB B737 25187
XA-SAC B737 25192
XA-SAD B757 25598
XA-SAS B737 25191
XA-SBH F-100 11350
XA-SCA B737 23979
XA-SCB B757 26151
XA-SCD F-100 11371
XA-SDF DC-9 47006
XA-SDH B727 18743
XA-SDL B720 18072
XA-SDR B727 20555
XA-SEA B727 18911
XA-SEB B727 18821
(XA-SED) B757 22691
XA-SEJ B727 19255
XA-SEK B727 18912
XA-SEL B727 19256
XA-SEM B727 19427
XA-SEM B737 23924
XA-SEN B727 19398
XA-SEO B737 23925
XA-SEP B727 18912
XA-SER B727 18908
XA-SEU B727 18909
XA-SEW B727 20217
XA-SFF B727 19462
XA-SFG B727 19474
XA-SFK MD-82 48068
XA-SFL MD-82 48069
XA-SFM MD-82 49149
XA-SFO MD-87 49673
XA-SFR B737 19707
(XA-SGA) A320 0368
(XA-SGB) A320 0376
(XA-SGC) A320 0386
XA-SGE F-100 11382
XA-SGF F-100 11384
XA-SGJ B737 24030
XA-SGS F-100 11390
XA-SGT F-100 11400
XA-SGY B727 19497
XA-SHG F-100 11410
XA-SHH F-100 11420
XA-SHI F-100 11309
XA-SHJ F-100 11319
XA-SHR DC-9 47284
XA-SHT B727 18742
XA-SHV DC-9 47214
XA-SHW DC-9 47166
XA-SIA DC-8 45878
XA-SIB DC-8 45855
XA-SID DC-8 45935
XA-SIE B727 22069
XA-SIH B737 23786
XA-SIJ B727 22017
XA-SIK B757 25624
XA-SIR B727 18743
XA-SIV B727 22424
XA-SIW B737 22370
XA-SIX B737 22371
XA-SIY B737 23747
XA-SIZ B737 23748
XA-SJD B757 26270
XA-SJE B727 21479
XA-SJI B737 20588
XA-SJK B727 20525
XA-SJM B727 20162
XA-SJU B727 20552
XA-SKA DC-9 47060
XA-SKC B727 19181
XA-SKQ B757 25490
XA-SKR B757 25489
XA-SKY B767 25411
XA-SLC B737 22055
XA-SLG B727 21171
XA-SLK B737 23412
XA-SLM B727 21696
XA-SLY B737 24098
XA-SMB B727 21646
XA-SMD B757 25490
XA-SME B757 25489
XA-SMI DC-9 47018
XA-SMJ B757 26268
XA-SMK B757 26271
XA-SML B757 26272
XA-SMM B757 26273
XA-SNC B737 24377
XA-SNR DC-9 45699
XA-SNW B727 18450
XA-SOA DC-9 47059
XA-SOB DC-9 47085
XA-SOC DC-9 47100
XA-SOD DC-9 47122
XA-SOE DC-9 47123
XA-SOF DC-9 47124
XA-SOG DC-9 47125
XA-SOH DC-9 47126
XA-SOI DC-9 47127
XA-SOJ DC-9 45785
XA-SOM B737 20197
XA-SOY DC-9 47085
XA-SPA DC-9 45698
XA-SPG B757 25155
XA-SPH B727 22146
XA-SPK B727 19497
XA-SPU B727 20181
XA-SQO B727 18752
XA-SSW DC-9 45735
XA-SSZ DC-9 45715
XA-STB B737 20128
XA-STE B737 20808
XA-STM B737 23411
XA-STN B737 23412
XA-SVQ B737 23786
XA-SVZ DC-9 47125
XA-SWG DC-9 47230
XA-SWH DC-9 47236
XA-SWL B737 20711
XA-SWO B737 27284
XA-SWW MD-83 49848
XA-SXC B727 20619
XA-SXE B727 20615

XA-SXJ MD-83 49845
XA-SXO B727 20268
XA-SXV DC-9 45715
XA-SXZ B727 18436
XA-SYA B727 19432
XA-SYE DC-10 46990
XA-SYG A300 211
XA-SYI B727 20264
XA-SYT B737 19409
XA-SYX B737 19059
XA-SZC DC-9 45739
XA-TAA B727 20432
XA-TAB B727 20433
XA-TAC B727 20434
XA-TAE B727 18800
XA-TAE B757 25268
(XA-TAY) B727 20524
XA-TCD B757 22691
XA-TCG F-100 11374
XA-TCH F-100 11375
XA-TCP B737 21278
XA-TCQ B737 21528
XA-TCT DC-9 47274
XA-TCW B727 20580
XA-TCX B727 22440
XA-TOR MD-83 49710
XA-TUR MD-83 49642
XA-TUR MD-83 49708
XA-TUY B727 19815
XA-TYT B727 19534
XA-XAX DC-8 45432
XB-GBP B727 18252
XB-IBV B737 19772
XB-LCR B737 19772
XB-MUO 1-11 005
XC-BCO DC-9 47087
XC-BDM DC-9 47154
XC-CBD B757 22690
XC-UJA B727 19123
XC-UJB B727 19121
XC-UJB B737 24095
XC-UJI B737 20127
XC-UJL B737 19772
XC-UJM B757 22690

Burkina Faso

XT-ABX B707 18925
XT-ABZ B707 18837
XT-BBE B727 18990
XT-BBF B707 19521
(XT-BBH) B707 18837
XT-FZP F-28 11163
XT-FZP F-28 11185

Kampuchea

XU-001 F-28 11012
XU-101 TU134 49890
XU-102 TU134 66550
XU-122 TU134
XU-JTA CRVL 145
XU-JTB CRVL 53

Vietnam

XV-NJA CRVL 10
XV-NJB B727 19818
XV-NJC B727 19819
XV-NJD B707 17683

Laos

XW-PNH CRVL 83
XY-ADR B727 19620
XY-ADU F-28 11019
XY-ADV F-28 11017
XY-ADW F-28 11114
XY-AGA F-28 11232

Afghanistan

"YA-.AA" IL-76 063406146
YA-FAR B727 19690
YA-FAU B727 20343
YA-FAW B727 19619
YA-FAX B727 22290
YA-FAY B727 22289
YA-FAZ B727 22288
YA-HBA B720 18060
YA-KAB YAK40 9120417
YA-KAD YAK40 9120517
YA-KAE YAK40 9441037
YA-KAF YAK40 9120617
YA-KAM YAK40 9..1226
YA-LAS DC-10 47888
YA-TAP TU154 747
YA-TAR TU154 748
YA-TAT TU154 600

Iraq

YI-AEA TRDNT 2125
YI-AEB TRDNT 2127
YI-AEC TRDNT 2129
YI-AED TU134 9350915
YI-AEL TU124 5351607
YI-AEY TU124 4351503
YI-AGE B707 20889
YI-AGF B707 20890
YI-AGG B707 20891
YI-AGH B737 20892
YI-AGI B737 20893
YI-AGJ B737 21183
YI-AGK B727 21197
YI-AGL B727 21198
YI-AGM B727 21199
YI-AGN B747 21180
YI-AGO B747 21181
YI-AGP B747 22366
YI-AGQ B727 22261
YI-AGR B727 22262
YI-AGS B727 22263
YI-AIK IL-76 073410292
YI-AIL IL-76 073410293
YI-AIM IL-76
YI-AIN IL-76
YI-AIO IL-76 073410315
YI-AIP IL-76 073410308
YI-AKO IL-76 093416506
YI-AKP IL-76 093421630
YI-AKQ IL-76 093421635
YI-AKS IL-76 093418543
YI-AKT IL-76 093418548
YI-AKU IL-76 093421637
YI-AKV IL-76
YI-AKW IL-76 0013428839
YI-AKX IL-76 0013433990
YI-ALL IL-76 0013433984
YI-ALM B747 22858
YI-ALO IL-76 0013433996
YI-ALP IL-76 0013433999
YI-ALQ IL-76 0023441189
YI-ALR IL-76 0023441200
YI-ALS IL-76 0033442247
YI-ALT IL-76 0033448393
YI-ALU IL-76 0033448398
YI-ALV IL-76 0033448409
YI-ALW IL-76 0033448416
YI-ALX IL-76 0043449455
YI-ANA IL-76 0063469055
YI-ANB IL-76 0063469071
YI-ANC IL-76 0063470102
YI-AND IL-76 0063471155
YI-ANE IL-76 0073474224
YI-ANF IL-76 0073475236
YI-ANG IL-76 0073476288
YI-ANH IL-76 0073476307
YI-ANI IL-76 0073481442
YI-ANJ IL-76
YI-ANK IL-76
YI-ANL IL-76 0083484542
YI-AOA A310 318
YI-AOB A310 276
YI-AOC A310 267
YI-AOD A310 331
YI-AOE A310 278
YI-AOQ TU134

Syria

YK-AFA CRVL 184
YK-AFB CRVL 190
YK-AFC CRVL 183
YK-AFD CRVL 186
YK-AGA B727 21203
YK-AGB B727 21204
YK-AGC B727 21205
YK-AGD B727 22360
YK-AGE B727 22361
YK-AGF B727 22763
YK-AHA B747 21174
YK-AHB B747 21175
YK-AIA TU154 708
YK-AIB TU154 709
YK-AIC TU154 710
YK-AQA YAK40 9341932
YK-AQB YAK40 9530443
YK-AQC YAK40 9..0543
YK-AQD YAK40 9830158
YK-AQE YAK40 9830258
YK-AQF YAK40 9931859
YK-AQG YAK40 9941959
YK-AQH YAK40 9930160
YK-ATA IL-76 093421613
YK-ATB IL-76 093421619
YK-ATC IL-76 0013431911
YK-ATD IL-76 0013431915
YK-AYA TU134 63992
YK-AYB TU134 63994
YK-AYC TU134 63989
YK-AYD TU134 2763990
YK-AYE TU134 66187
YK-AYF TU134 66190

Latvia

YL-BAA B737 22028
YL-BAA DC-9 47016
YL-BAB B737 22032
YL-BAC B737 22034
YL-BAE B727 18900
YL-BAF B727 18440
YL-BAK 146 E1223
YL-BAL 146 E1224
YL-BAN 146 E1225
YL-LAA TU154 133
YL-LAB TU154 515
YL-LAC B737 22034
YL-LAC TU154 516
YL-LAD TU154 556
YL-LAE TU154 546
YL-LAF TU154 539
YL-LAG TU154 524
YL-LAH TU154 558
YL-LAI TU154 895
YL-LAJ IL-76 083414432
YL-LAK IL-76 0003424707
YL-LBA TU134 61000
YL-LBB TU134 63215
YL-LBC TU134 63221
YL-LBD TU134 63235
YL-LBE TU134 63285
YL-LBF TU134 63295
YL-LBG TU134 63333
YL-LBH TU134 63340
YL-LBI TU134 63365
YL-LBJ TU134 63410
YL-LBK TU134 63425
YL-LBL TU134 63515
YL-LBM TU134 63536
YL-LBN TU134 63187

Nicaragua

YN-BSQ B727 18843
(YN-BWL) B707 17675
YN-BWX B727 18742
YN-BXW B727 18284
YN-BYI B720 18688
YN-CBT TU154 821
YN-CCN B707 18054
YN-CDE B707 19335

Romania

YR-ABA B707 20803
YR-ABB B707 20804
YR-ABC B707 20805
YR-ABD B707 21651
YR-ABM B707 19272
YR-ABN B707 19379
YR-BCA 1-11 BAC.130
YR-BCB 1-11 BAC.156
YR-BCC 1-11 BAC.167
(YR-BCC) 1-11 BAC.166
YR-BCD 1-11 BAC.159
YR-BCE 1-11 BAC.165
YR-BCF 1-11 BAC.168
YR-BCG 1-11 077
YR-BCH 1-11 BAC.161
YR-BCI 1-11 BAC.252
YR-BCJ 1-11 BAC.253
YR-BCK 1-11 BAC.254
YR-BCL 1-11 BAC.255
YR-BCM 1-11 BAC.256
YR-BCN 1-11 BAC.266
YR-BCO 1-11 BAC.272
YR-BCP 1-11 BAC.162
YR-BCR 1-11 BAC.267
YR-BGA B737 27179
YR-BGB B737 27180
YR-BGC B737 27181
YR-BGD B737 27182
YR-BGE B737 27395
YR-BRA 1-11 BAC.401
YR-BRB 1-11 BAC.402
YR-BRC 1-11 BAC.403
YR-BRD 1-11 BAC.404
YR-BRE 1-11 BAC.405
YR-BRF 1-11 BAC.406
YR-BRG 1-11 BAC.407
YR-BRH 1-11 BAC.408
YR-BRI 1-11 BAC.409
YR-IRA IL-62 21302
YR-IRB IL-62 21305
YR-IRC IL-62 51902
YR-IRD IL-62 4727546
YR-IRE IL-62 4831628
YR-JBA 1-11 BAC.234
YR-JBB 1-11 BAC.238
YR-JCA B707 19530
YR-JCB B707 20022
YR-LCA A310 636
YR-LCB A310 644
YR-LCC A310 450
YR-TPA TU154 159
YR-TPB TU154 161
YR-TPC TU154 175
YR-TPD TU154 224
YR-TPE TU154 225
YR-TPF TU154 239
YR-TPG TU154 262
YR-TPH TU154 277
YR-TPI TU154 342
YR-TPJ TU154 408
YR-TPK TU154 415
YR-TPL TU154 428

El Salvador

(YS-) B767 25221
YS-01C 1-11 BAC.108
YS-08C B737 21599
YS-17C 1-11 093
YS-18C 1-11 BAC.106

Yugoslavia

YU-A..? TU134
YU-AGA B707 17601

(YU-AGB) DC-8 45883
YU-AGD B707 19866
YU-AGE B707 19284
YU-AGF B707 19286
YU-AGG B707 19285
YU-AGH B707 17594
YU-AGI B707 19210
YU-AGJ B707 19411
YU-AHA CRVL 139
YU-AHB CRVL 135
YU-AHD CRVL 151
YU-AHE CRVL 194
YU-AHF CRVL 218
YU-AHG CRVL 233
YU-AHH TU134 9350701
YU-AHI TU134 9350705
YU-AHJ DC-9 47239
YU-AHK CRVL 237
YU-AHL DC-9 47425
YU-AHM DC-9 47469
YU-AHN DC-9 47470
YU-AHO DC-9 47472
YU-AHP DC-9 47473
YU-AHR DC-9 47503
YU-AHS TU134 0350921
YU-AHT DC-9 47482
YU-AHU DC-9 47532
YU-AHV DC-9 47460
YU-AHW DC-9 47530
YU-AHX TU134 1351203
YU-AHY TU134 1351204
YU-AHZ TU134 1351205
YU-AJA TU134 1351206
YU-AJB DC-9 47392
YU-AJD TU134 2351508
YU-AJE CRVL 209
YU-AJF DC-9 47570
YU-AJG CRVL 191
YU-AJH DC-9 47562
YU-AJI DC-9 47563
YU-AJJ DC-9 47567
YU-AJK DC-9 47568
YU-AJL DC-9 47571
YU-AJM DC-9 47582
YU-AJN DC-9 47579
YU-AJO DC-9 47457
YU-AJP DC-9 47408
YU-AJR DC-9 47649
YU-AJS TU134 48370
YU-AJT DC-9 47697
YU-AJU DC-9 47754
YU-AJV TU134 60035
YU-AJW TU134 60321
YU-AJX DC-9 47172
YU-AJY DC-9 47172
YU-AJZ MD-81 48046
YU-AKA B727 20930
YU-AKB B727 20931
YU-AKD B727 21040
YU-AKE B727 21037
YU-AKF B727 21038
YU-AKG B727 21039
YU-AKH B727 21080
YU-AKI B727 22393
YU-AKJ B727 22394
YU-AKK B727 22665
YU-AKL B727 22666
YU-AKM B727 22702
YU-AKN 1-11 BAC.266
YU-AKO B727 20951
YU-AKP YAK40 9120717
YU-AKR B727 20549
YU-AKV YAK40 9630849
YU-AMA DC-10 46981
YU-AMB DC-10 46988
YU-AMC DC-10 46578
YU-AMD DC-10 46554
(YU-AME) MD-11 48607
(YU-AMF) MD-11 48608
(YU-AMG) MD-11 48483
(YU-AMG) MD-11 48609
(YU-AMH) MD-11 48582
YU-ANA MD-82 48047
YU-ANB MD-82 48048
YU-ANC MD-82 48087
YU-AND B737 23329
YU-ANE TU134 63165
YU-ANF B737 23330
YU-ANG MD-82 49379
YU-ANH B737 23415
YU-ANI B737 23416
YU-ANJ B737 23714
YU-ANK B737 23715
YU-ANL B737 23716
YU-ANM 1-11 BAC.266
YU-ANN 1-11 BAC.272
YU-ANO MD-82 49440
YU-ANP B737 23912
YU-ANR 1-11 BAC.401
YU-ANS 1-11 BAC.403
YU-ANT 1-11 BAC.404
YU-ANU B737 24139
YU-ANV B737 24140
YU-ANW B737 24141
YU-ANX B737 20227
YU-ANY B737 20277
YU-ANZ B737 20956
YU-AOA A320 0043
YU-AOB A320 0028
YU-AOD A320 0113
YU-AOE A320 0114
YU-AOF B737 22596
YU-AOG B737 22601

Venezuela

YV-C-AAA DC-9 47309
YV-C-ANP DC-9 47000
YV-C-ANV DC-9 47002
YV-C-AVB DC-9 45703
YV-C-AVC DC-9 47048
YV-C-AVD DC-9 47243
YV-C-AVI CRVL 20
YV-C-AVM DC-9 47056
YV-C-AVR DC-9 47060
YV-C-LEV DC-9 47006
YV-C-VIA CV880 22-7-1-53
YV-C-VIA DC-8 46042
YV-C-VIB CV880 22-7-4-56
YV-C-VIB DC-8 46063
YV-C-VIC CV880 22-00-37M
YV-C-VIC DC-8 45879
YV-C-VID DC-8 45768
YV-C-VIE DC-8 45377
YV-C-VIF DC-8 45381
YV-C-VIG DC-8 45616
YV-C-VIM DC-8 45816
YV-C-VIN DC-8 46052
YV-01C DC-9 47309
YV-02C DC-9 47002
YV-03 DC-9 47000
YV-03C DC-9 47000
YV-18C DC-9 47001
YV-19C DC-9 47394
YV-20C DC-9 47705
YV-21C DC-9 47719
YV-22C DC-9 47703
YV-23C DC-9 47720
YV-24C DC-9 47727
YV-25C DC-9 47721
YV-32C DC-9 47770
YV-33C DC-9 47782
YV-35C DC-9 47712
YV-36C MD-83 49395
YV-37C DC-9 47752
YV-38C MD-83 49567
YV-39C MD-83 49659
YV-40C DC-9 47783
YV-41C DC-9 47784
YV-42C MD-83 49793
YV-43C MD-83 49788
YV-44C MD-83 53046
YV-51C DC-9 47006
YV-52C DC-9 47048
YV-57C DC-9 47060
YV-65C DC-9 45723
YV-66C DC-9 45710
YV-67C DC-9 47025
YV-68C DC-9 47031
YV-69C DC-9 47309
YV-70C DC-9 47103
YV-72C DC-9 47105
YV-73C DC-9 47106
YV-74C B727 22043
YV-74C B737 20909
YV-75C B727 22044
YV-76C B727 20394
YV-77C B727 21457
YV-77C B757 23227
YV-78C B757 22185
YV-79C B727 18800
YV-79C B737 20908
YV-80C B727 18326
YV-80C DC-9 47692
YV-81C B727 18327
YV-82C B727 18325
YV-82C DC-9 47121
YV-85C DC-9 47683
YV-87C B727 18853
YV-87C DC-9 47685
YV-88C B727 18855
YV-89C B727 18851
YV-90C B727 18856
YV-90C B727 19815
YV-90C DC-9 47665
YV-91C B727 19165
YV-92C B727 20724
YV-93C B727 20876
YV-94C B727 20877
YV-95C B727 20878
YV-96C B727 20727
YV-97C B727 20885
YV-99C B737 24463
YV-125C B727 20596
YV-125C DC-8 46042
YV-126C B727 20594
YV-126C DC-8 46063
YV-127C B727 20597
YV-127C DC-8 45377
YV-128C B727 20605
YV-128C DC-8 45381
YV-128C DC-8 45861
YV-129C B727 20599
YV-129C DC-8 45616
YV-130C DC-8 46052
YV-131C DC-8 45613
YV-132C B727 22604
YV-132C DC-8 45614
YV-133C DC-10 46555
YV-134C DC-10 46556
YV-135C DC-10 46971
YV-136C DC-10 46972
YV-137C DC-10 46982
YV-138C DC-10 46557
YV-139C DC-10 46953
YV-139C DC-9 47476
(YV-139C) DC-10 46952
YV-145C CV880 22-00-64
(YV-158C) MD-82 49103
(YV-159C) MD-82 49104
YV-160C A300 53
YV-161C A300 75
YV-392C DC-8 45603
YV-405C B737 19771
YV-406C B737 19016
YV-445C DC-8 45663
YV-447C DC-8 45684
YV-448C B727 18270
YV-458C DC-9 47527
YV-459C DC-9 47548
YV-460C DC-8 45640
YV-461C DC-8 45878
YV-462C B727 20303
YV-463C B727 20248
YV-464C B727 20392
YV-465C B727 19992
YV-466C B727 19973
YV-480C B727 18270
YV-495C DC-9 47047
YV-496C DC-9 47237
YV-497C DC-9 47653
YV-499C DC-8 45686
YV-505C DC-8 45410
YV-598C YAK42
YV-608C B727 20394
YV-612C DC-9 45710
YV-613C DC-9 47104
YV-614C DC-9 47105
YV-671C B707 19435
YV-705C DC-9 45867
YV-714C DC-9 47007
YV-715C DC-9 47320
YV-716C DC-9 47358
YV-717C DC-9 47323
YV-718C DC-9 47187
YV-719C DC-9 47157
YV-71C DC-9 47104
YV-720C DC-9 45837
YV-728C B727 18270
YV-760C DC-9 47098
YV-762C B727 22268
YV-763C B727 18327
YV-764C DC-9 47331
YV-765C B727 18855
YV-766C DC-9 47679
YV-767C DC-9 47745
YV-768C B727 21457
YV-770C DC-9 47330
YV-810C DC-8 45410
YV-813C B727 19393
YV-815C DC-9 45875
YV-816C DC-9 47272
YV-817C DC-9 47036
YV-818C DC-9 47399
YV-819C DC-9 47401
YV-820C DC-9 47743
YV-821C B727 19534
YV-830C DC-9 45699
(YV-837C) B727 18853
YV-838C B727 19165
YV-839C B727 18325
YV-840C B727 19815
YV-852C DC-9 45745
YV-855C B727 20905
YV-856C B727 20614
YV-909C B727 19561
YV-910C B727 19979
YV-937C MD-83 49567

Zimbabwe

Z-WKR B707 18819
Z-WKS B707 18923
Z-WKT B707 18929
Z-WKU B707 18930
Z-WKV B707 18927
Z-WMJ DC-8 45821
Z-WPA B737 23677
Z-WPB B737 23678
Z-WPC B737 23679
Z-WPD 146 E2065
Z-WPE B767 24713
Z-WPF B767 24867
Z-WSB DC-8 45805
Z-WST B707 18747
Z-WYY B727 18370
Z-WZL DC-8 45975
Z-YNL B720 18162
Z-YNN B720 18244

New Zealand

(ZK-ILF) B747 24896
ZK-NAA B737 22638
ZK-NAB B737 22364
ZK-NAC B737 19929
ZK-NAD B737 19930
ZK-NAD B737 23040
ZK-NAE B737 19931
ZK-NAF B737 23038
ZK-NAH B737 23039
ZK-NAI B737 22365
ZK-NAJ B737 20344
ZK-NAK B737 20156
ZK-NAL B737 20158
ZK-NAL B737 21138
ZK-NAM B737 19758
ZK-NAP B737 21130
ZK-NAQ B737 21131
ZK-NAQ B737 22022
ZK-NAR B737 21645

ZK-NAS	B737	22088
ZK-NAT	**B737**	**23470**
(ZK-NAT)	B737	22657
ZK-NAU	**B737**	**23471**
ZK-NAV	**B737**	**23472**
ZK-NAW	**B737**	**23473**
ZK-NAX	**B737**	**23474**
ZK-NAY	**B737**	**23475**
ZK-NAZ	B737	20913
ZK-NBA	**B767**	**23326**
ZK-NBB	**B767**	**23327**
ZK-NBC	**B767**	**23328**
ZK-NBD	B767	23058
ZK-NBE	B767	24150
ZK-NBF	B767	22681
ZK-NBH	B767	22682
ZK-NBI	**B767**	**23072**
ZK-NBJ	**B767**	**23250**
ZK-NBS	**B747**	**24386**
ZK-NBT	**B747**	**24855**
ZK-NBU	**B747**	**25605**
ZK-NCE	**B767**	**24875**
ZK-NCF	**B767**	**24876**
ZK-NCG	**B767**	**26912**
ZK-NCH	**B767**	**26264**
ZK-NCI	**B767**	**26913**
ZK-NCJ	**B767**	**26915**
ZK-NEA	B737	19013
ZK-NEB	B737	19015
ZK-NEC	B737	19016
ZK-NED	B737	19770
ZK-NEE	B737	20195
ZK-NEF	B737	22575
ZK-NQC	**B737**	**22994**
ZK-NZA	146	E2116
ZK-NZA	DC-8	45750
ZK-NZB	146	E2127
ZK-NZB	DC-8	45751
ZK-NZC	**146**	**E2119**
ZK-NZC	DC-8	45752
ZK-NZD	DC-8	45932
ZK-NZE	DC-8	45985
(ZK-NZE)	B747	24386
ZK-NZF	**146**	**E3134**
ZK-NZF	DC-8	45303
ZK-NZG	**146**	**E3135**
ZK-NZG	DC-8	45301
ZK-NZH	**146**	**E3137**
ZK-NZI	**146**	**E3143**
ZK-NZJ	**146**	**E3147**
ZK-NZK	**146**	**E3190**
ZK-NZL	**146**	**E3175**
ZK-NZL	DC-10	47846
ZK-NZM	**146**	**E3173**
ZK-NZM	DC-10	47847
ZK-NZN	DC-10	47848
ZK-NZP	DC-10	46910
ZK-NZQ	DC-10	46911
ZK-NZR	DC-10	47849
ZK-NZS	DC-10	46954
ZK-NZT	DC-10	46950
ZK-NZV	**B747**	**22722**
ZK-NZW	**B747**	**22723**
ZK-NZX	**B747**	**22724**
ZK-NZY	**B747**	**22725**
ZK-NZZ	**B747**	**22791**
ZK-POL	B737	22575
ZK-SHH	146	E1005
ZK-SUH	**B747**	**24896**
ZK-SUI	**B747**	**24957**

Paraguay

ZP-CAB	**B737**	**21130**
ZP-CAC	**B737**	**21518**
ZP-CCE	**B707**	**18841**
ZP-CCF	B707	18957
ZP-CCG	**B707**	**19264**
ZP-CCH	DC-8	46115
ZP-CCR	DC-8	46037

South Africa

ZS-CKC	B707	17928
ZS-CKD	B707	17929
ZS-CKE	B707	17930
ZS-DYL	B707	18891
ZS-DYM	B727	18892
ZS-DYN	B727	18893
ZS-DYO	B727	18894
ZS-DYP	B727	18895
ZS-DYR	B727	18896
ZS-EKV	B707	19133
ZS-EKW	B727	19318
ZS-EKX	B727	19319
ZS-EUW	B707	19705
ZS-EUX	B707	19706
(ZS-EUY)	B737	19707
(ZS-EUZ)	B737	19708
(ZS-FKG)	B707	20230
(ZS-FKH)	B737	20229
(ZS-FKT)	B707	20110
ZS-KAW	F-28	11027
ZS-LSF	B707	20283
(ZS-LSI)	B707	19575
ZS-LSJ	B707	19577
(ZS-LSJ)	B707	19723
(ZS-LSJ)	B707	19917
(ZS-LSK)	B707	19522
ZS-LSL	B707	19706
ZS-NCA	146	E1002
ZS-NCB	146	E2148
ZS-NGB	F-28	11219
ZS-NLJ	B707	19964
ZS-NLN	**B737**	**21686**
ZS-NMS	**1-11**	**BAC.186**
ZS-NMT	**1-11**	**BAC.201**
ZS-NMX	**B727**	**18426**
ZS-NMY	**B727**	**18447**
ZS-NMZ	**B727**	**19129**
ZS-NNG	**B737**	**21793**
ZS-NNH	**B737**	**21797**
ZS-NNM	**1-11**	**BAC.108**
ZS-NNN	**DC-9**	**47516**
ZS-NOU	**B727**	**21113**
ZS-NOV	**B727**	**21114**
ZS-NPX	**B727**	**19131**
(ZS-NPZ)	DC-10	46578
ZS-NRA	**DC-9**	**47430**
ZS-NRB	**DC-9**	**47468**
ZS-NRC	**DC-9**	**47090**
ZS-NRD	**DC-9**	**47037**
ZS-NSA	**B727**	**19130**
ZS-NUG	**1-11**	**BAC.237**
ZS-NUH	**1-11**	**BAC.257**
ZS-NUI	**1-11**	**BAC.258**
ZS-NUJ	**1-11**	**BAC.261**
(ZS-NVH)	B727	18443
ZS-NVR	**B727**	**20673**
ZS-NWA	**B727**	**20757**
ZS-NZP	A320	0203
ZS-NZR	A320	0220
ZS-NZS	A320	0221
ZS-NZT	A320	0222
ZS-SAA	B707	17928
ZS-SAA	B747	22170
ZS-SAB	B707	17929
(ZS-SAB)	B747	22171
ZS-SAC	B707	17930
ZS-SAC	**B747**	**23031**
ZS-SAD	B707	18891
ZS-SAE	B707	19133
ZS-SAF	B707	19706
ZS-SAG	B707	20110
ZS-SAH	B707	20230
ZS-SAI	B707	20283
ZS-SAJ	**B747**	**23027**
ZS-SAL	**B747**	**20237**
ZS-SAM	**B747**	**20238**
ZS-SAN	**B747**	**20239**
ZS-SAO	**B747**	**20556**
ZS-SAP	**B747**	**20557**
ZS-SAR	**B747**	**22170**
ZS-SAS	B747	22171
ZS-SAT	**B747**	**22970**
ZS-SAU	**B747**	**22971**
ZS-SAV	**B747**	**24976**
ZS-SAW	**B747**	**25152**
ZS-SAX	**B747**	**26637**
ZS-SAY	**B747**	**26638**
ZS-SBA	B727	18892
ZS-SBB	B727	18893
ZS-SBC	B727	18894
ZS-SBD	B727	18895
ZS-SBE	B727	18896
ZS-SBF	B727	19318
ZS-SBG	B727	19319
ZS-SBH	B727	20475
ZS-SBI	B727	20476
ZS-SBL	B737	19707
ZS-SBM	B737	19708
ZS-SBN	**B737**	**20229**
ZS-SBO	**B737**	**20329**
ZS-SBP	B737	20330
ZS-SBR	**B737**	**20331**
ZS-SDA	**A300**	**32**
ZS-SDB	**A300**	**37**
ZS-SDC	**A300**	**39**
ZS-SDD	**A300**	**40**
ZS-SDE	**A300**	**138**
ZS-SDF	**A300**	**192**
ZS-SDG	**A300**	**212**
ZS-SDH	A300	222
ZS-SDI	A300	269
ZS-SHA	**A320**	**0243**
ZS-SHB	**A320**	**0249**
ZS-SHC	**A320**	**0250**
ZS-SHD	**A320**	**0251**
ZS-SHE	**A320**	**0334**
ZS-SHF	**A320**	**0335**
ZS-SHG	**A320**	**0440**
ZS-SIA	**B737**	**22580**
ZS-SIB	**B737**	**22581**
ZS-SIC	**B737**	**22582**
ZS-SID	**B737**	**22583**
ZS-SIE	**B737**	**22584**
ZS-SIF	**B737**	**22585**
ZS-SIG	**B737**	**22586**
ZS-SIH	**B737**	**22587**
ZS-SII	**B737**	**22588**
ZS-SIJ	**B737**	**22589**
ZS-SIK	**B737**	**22590**
ZS-SIL	**B737**	**22591**
ZS-SIM	**B737**	**22828**
(ZS-SIN)	B707	20283
(ZS-SIO)	B707	19706
ZS-SPA	**B747**	**21132**
ZS-SPB	**B747**	**21133**
ZS-SPC	**B747**	**21134**
ZS-SPD	B747	21253
ZS-SPE	**B747**	**21254**
ZS-SPF	B747	21263
ZS-SRA	**B767**	**26471**

Macedonia

Z3-ARA	**DC-9**	**47530**

Mauritius

3B-NAE	B707	18891
3B-NAF	B707	19133
3B-NAG	B747	21134
3B-NAI	B747	20238
3B-NAJ	B747	21132
3B-NAK	**B767**	**23973**
3B-NAL	**B767**	**23974**
3B-NAO	B747	21263
3B-NAQ	B747	21786
3B-NAR	B747	21254
3B-NAS	B747	22170
3B-NAT	**A340**	**048**
3B-NAU	**A340**	**076**
3B-NAV	**A340**	**094**
3B-RGY	**A320**	**0376**
3B-RGZ	**A320**	**0386**
3B-SMC	**B747**	**24063**

Equatorial Guinea

3C-4GE	**YAK40**	**9940660**
3C-ABH	B707	18056
3C-ABT	B707	17721
3C-CGE	**YAK40**	**9821557**
3C-MNB	YAK40	9821557

Swaziland

3D-ADA	B737	19708
3D-ADV	DC-8	45858
3D-ADV	DC-8	46012
3D-AFR	**DC-8**	**45802**
3D-AFX	**DC-8**	**45886**
3D-AIA	**DC-8**	**45854**
3D-ALM	**F-100**	**11335**
3D-ALN	**F-28**	**11136**
3D-ASB	B707	19519
3D-ASC	B707	19706
3D-LLG	1-11	069

Guinea

3X-GAW	YAK40	9440637
3X-GAZ	B707	18748
3X-GCA	B727	19120
3X-GCB	**B737**	**22627**
3X-GCC	B707	19291
(3X-GCC)	B707	18685
3X-GCH	B727	19120

Azerbaijan

4K-401	B707	19584
4K-727	**TU154**	**727**
4K-733	**TU154**	**733**
4K-4201	B727	19460
4K-65702	**TU134**	**63375**
4K-65703	TU134	63383
4K-65705	**TU134**	**63415**
4K-65708	**TU134**	**63447**
4K-65709	**TU134**	**63484**
4K-65710	**TU134**	**63490**
4K-65711	**TU134**	**63498**
4K-65713	**TU134**	**63520**
4K-65714	**TU134**	**63527**
4K-65985	**TU134**	
4K-76130	**IL-76**	
4K-76671	**IL-76**	**0063465963**
4K-76677	**IL-76**	**0063467005**
4K-78030	**IL-76**	
4K-78129	IL-76	0083489683
4K-78130	**IL-76**	**0043454611**
4K-78710	**IL-76**	
4K-85147	**TU154**	**147**
4K-85158	**TU154**	**158**
4K-85177	**TU154**	**177**
4K-85192	**TU154**	**192**
4K-85199	**TU154**	**199**
4K-85211	**TU154**	**211**
4K-85214	**TU154**	**214**
4K-85274	**TU154**	**274**
4K-85329	**TU154**	**329**
4K-85364	**TU154**	**364**
4K-85391	**TU154**	**391**
4K-85395	**TU154**	**395**
4K-85524	**TU154**	**524**
4K-85548	**TU154**	**548**
4K-85698	**TU154**	**871**
4K-85729	**TU154**	**911**
4K-85732	**TU154**	**914**
4K-85734	**TU154**	**916**
4K-85738	**TU154**	**921?**
4K-87218	**YAK40**	**9440937**
4K-87257	**YAK40**	**9311426**
4K-87278	**YAK40**	**9311427**
4K-87413	**YAK40**	**9420534**
4K-87415	**YAK40**	**9420734**
4K-87478	**YAK40**	**9440638**
4K-87504	**YAK40**	**9510640**
4K-87643	**YAK40**	**9140420**
4K-87644	**YAK40**	**9140520**

4K-87812	**YAK40**	**9230424**
4K-87817	**YAK40**	**9230824**
4K-87946	**YAK40**	**9611045**
4K-88174	**YAK40**	**9621247**
4K-88211	**YAK40**	**9631749**
4K-AZ1	**B727**	**19460**
4K-AZ2	**B727**	**19461**
4K-AZ3	**B707**	**19321**
4K-AZ4	**B707**	**19415**

Georgia

4L-65053	**TU134**	**49838**
4L-65061	**TU134**	**49874**
4L-65750	**TU134**	**61042**
4L-65774	**TU134**	**62519**
4L-65798	**TU134**	**63179**
4L-65808	**TU134**	**352109**
4L-65810	**TU134**	**352201**
4L-65817	**TU134**	**4352301**
4L-65857	**TU134**	**23255**
4L-65865	**TU134**	**28286**
4L-65879	**TU134**	**31265**
4L-65886	**TU134**	**36165**
4L-65959	**TU134**	**3351805**
4L-85168	**TU154**	**168**
4L-85170	**TU154**	**170**
4L-85188	**TU154**	**188**
4L-85197	**TU154**	**197**
4L-85198	**TU154**	**198**
4L-85203	**TU154**	**203**
4L-85359	**TU154**	**359**
4L-85430	**TU154**	**430**
4L-85496	**TU154**	**496**
4L-85518	**TU154**	**518**
4L-85547	**TU154**	**547**
4L-87242	**YAK40**	**9531043**
4L-87258	**YAK40**	**9311526**
4L-87305	**YAK40**	**9320129**
4L-87322	**YAK40**	**9330130**
4L-87370	**YAK40**	**9340132**
4L-87374	**YAK40**	**9410832**
4L-87459	**YAK40**	**9431836**
4L-87466	**YAK40**	**9430537**
4L-87754	**YAK40**	**9..0911**
4L-87804	**YAK40**	**9231023**
4L-88152	**YAK40**	**9610646**
4L-88158	**YAK40**	**9611246**
4L-88183	**YAK40**	**9620348**
4L-AAA	**B737**	**23708**

Sri Lanka

4R-ABA	**A320**	**0374**
4R-ABB	**A320**	**0406**
4R-ACN	**TRDNT**	**2135**
4R-ACQ	DC-8	45604
4R-ACS	B720	18013
4R-ACT	DC-8	45445
4R-ADA	**A340**	**032**
4R-ADB	**A340**	**033**
4R-ADC	**A340**	**034**
4R-ALA	B707	19738
4R-ALB	B707	19737
4R-ALC	B737	21278
4R-ALD	B737	20913
4R-ALE	L1011	1047
4R-ALF	L1011	1053
4R-ALG	L1011	1025
4R-ALH	L1011	1061
4R-TNJ	L1011	1067
4R-TNK	L1011	1069
4R-TNL	L1011	1073
4R-ULA	**L1011**	**1235**
4R-ULB	**L1011**	**1236**
4R-ULC	**L1011**	**1053**
4R-ULD	L1011	1061
4R-ULE	**L1011**	**1062**
4R-ULF	B747	20009
4R-ULG	B747	20010
4R-ULH	B737	19742
4R-ULJ	L1011	1021
4R-ULK	L1011	1027
4R-ULL	B737	20195
4R-ULM	L1011	1211
4R-ULN	L1011	1178
4R-ULO	B737	21192

Yemen Arab Republic

4W-ABZ	B737	21296
4W-ACF	B727	21844
4W-ACG	B727	21845
4W-ACH	B727	21846
4W-ACI	B727	21847
4W-ACJ	B727	21842

Israel

4X-ABA	B720	18424
4X-ABB	B720	18425
(4X-ABK)	B737	21955
4X-ABL	B737	21736
4X-ABM	B737	22090
4X-ABN	**B737**	**22856**
4X-ABO	**B737**	**22857**
4X-ACN	B707	17666
(4X-ACN)	B707	18012
4X-ACU	B707	17665
4X-AGJ	B727	19011
4X-AGT	B707	17661
4X-AGU	B707	17668
4X-AOT	**B737**	**21740**
4X-AOX	B737	20794
4X-AOY	B707	19517
4X-ATA	B707	18070
4X-ATB	B707	18071
4X-ATC	B707	18357
4X-ATD	B707	18985
4X-ATE	B707	18456
4X-ATF	B707	19277
4X-ATG	B707	20174
4X-ATR	B707	19004
4X-ATS	B707	19502
4X-ATT	B707	20097
4X-ATU	B707	20122
4X-ATX	B707	20122
4X-ATY	B707	20301
4X-AXA	**B747**	**20135**
4X-AXB	**B747**	**20274**
4X-AXC	**B747**	**20704**
4X-AXD	**B747**	**21190**
4X-AXF	**B747**	**21594**
4X-AXG	B747	21737
4X-AXH	**B747**	**22254**
4X-AXK	**B747**	**22151**
4X-AXL	**B747**	**22150**
4X-AXQ	**B747**	**20841**
4X-AXZ	**B747**	**19735**
4X-BAA	B737	21820
4X-BAB	B737	22875
4X-BAC	B737	22876
4X-BAE	B727	19249
4X-BAF	**B737**	**20413**
4X-BAR	1-11	BAC.230
4X-BAS	1-11	BAC.199
4X-BMA	B720	18014
4X-BMB	B720	18013
4X-BMC	B707	20456
4X-BYA	B707	17610
4X-BYA	B707	18012
4X-BYB	B707	20429
4X-BYC	B707	19291
4X-BYD	B707	17612
4X-BYD	B707	17667
4X-BYH	B707	17668
4X-BYH	B707	20721
4X-BYI	B707	17661
4X-BYK	B707	18246
4X-BYL	B707	18374
4X-BYM	B707	18460
4X-BYN	B707	17619
4X-BYN	B707	20716
4X-BYQ	B707	20110
4X-BYS	B707	20230
4X-BYT	B707	17625
4X-BYU	**B707**	**20629**
4X-BYV	B707	17615
4X-BYW	B707	17617
4X-BYX	B707	17922
4X-BYY	B707	20428
4X-BYZ	B707	17596
4X-EAA	**B767**	**22972**
4X-EAB	**B767**	**22973**
4X-EAC	**B767**	**22974**
4X-EAD	**B767**	**22975**
4X-EBL	**B757**	**23917**
4X-EBM	**B757**	**23918**
4X-EBR	**B757**	**24254**
4X-EBS	**B757**	**24884**
4X-EBT	**B757**	**25036**
4X-EBU	**B757**	**26053**
4X-EBV	**B757**	**26054**
4X-ELA	**B747**	**26055**
4X-ELB	**B747**	**26056**
4X-ELC	**B747**	**27915**
(4X-JAA)	B707	18012
(4X-JAD)	B707	17667
4X-JYA	B707	17610
4X-JYA	B707	18012
4X-JYB	**B707**	**20429**
4X-JYC	**B707**	**19291**
4X-JYD	B707	17612
4X-JYD	**B707**	**17667**
4X-JYE	**B707**	**17612**
4X-JYH	B707	17668
4X-JYH	**B707**	**20721**
4X-JYI	B707	17661
4X-JYI	B707	19000
4X-JYK	B707	18246
4X-JYL	**B707**	**18374**
4X-JYM	**B707**	**18460**
4X-JYN	B707	20716
4X-JYN	B707	17619
4X-JYQ	**B707**	**20110**
4X-JYS	**B707**	**20230**
4X-JYT	**B707**	**17625**
4X-JYU	B707	20629
4X-JYV	**B707**	**17615**
4X-JYW	**B707**	**17617**
4X-JYX	**B707**	**17922**
4X-JYY	**B707**	**20428**
4X-JYZ	B707	17596

Jordan

4YB-CAB	B707	18716
4YB-CAC	B707	20890

Libya

5A-	**B707**	**19628**
5A-CVA	B707	17719
5A-DAA	**CRVL**	**158**
5A-DAB	**CRVL**	**162**
5A-DAE	**CRVL**	**221**
5A-DAH	B727	20244
5A-DAI	**B727**	**20245**
5A-DAK	**B707**	**21228**
5A-DGK	DC-8	45300
5A-DGL	DC-8	45417
5A-DGN	DC-8	45382
5A-DHL	B707	18765
5A-DHO	B707	17647
5A-DIA	B727	21050
5A-DIB	**B727**	**21051**
5A-DIC	**B727**	**21052**
5A-DID	**B727**	**21229**
5A-DIE	**B727**	**21230**
5A-DIF	**B727**	**21332**
5A-DIG	**B727**	**21333**
5A-DIH	**B727**	**21539**
5A-DII	**B727**	**21540**
5A-DIJ	B747	22105
5A-DIK	B707	18881
5A-DIK	B747	22106
(5A-DIL)	B747	22107
5A-DIX	**B707**	**18880**
5A-DIY	**B707**	**19001**
5A-DIZ	B707	18746
5A-DJD	DC-8	45417
5A-DJM	**B707**	**19378**
5A-DJO	B707	18955
5A-DJP	DC-8	45659
5A-DJS	B707	18964
5A-DJT	B707	18888
5A-DJU	**B707**	**18889**
5A-DJV	B707	19590
5A-DKA	B707	19212
5A-DKK	IL-76	
5A-DLA	A310	295
5A-DLB	A310	306
5A-DLL	**IL-76**	
5A-DLT	B707	18686
5A-DLU	**F-28**	**11197**
5A-DLV	**F-28**	**11200**
5A-DLW	**F-28**	**11194**
5A-DMM	**IL-76**	
5A-DNA	**IL-76**	**0023439140**
5A-DNB	**IL-76**	**0013437086**
5A-DNC	**IL-76**	
5A-DND	**IL-76**	
5A-DNE	**IL-76**	
5A-DNF	IL-76	
5A-DNG	**IL-76**	**0013432961**
5A-DNH	**IL-76**	
5A-DNI	**IL-76**	
5A-DNJ	**IL-76**	
5A-DNK	**IL-76**	
5A-DNL	**IL-76**	
5A-DNO	**IL-76**	
5A-DNP	**IL-76**	
5A-DNQ	**IL-76**	
5A-DNS	**IL-76**	
5A-DNT	**IL-76**	**0023439141**
5A-DNW	**IL-76**	
5A-DRR	**IL-76**	**083415469**
5A-DZZ	IL-76	

Cyprus

(5B-CAC)	DC-8	45303
5B-CIO	B737	23921
5B-DAA	TRDNT	2154
5B-DAB	TRDNT	2155
5B-DAC	TRDNT	2141
5B-DAD	TRDNT	2114
5B-DAE	TRDNT	2134
5B-DAF	1-11	BAC.201
5B-DAG	1-11	BAC.257
5B-DAH	1-11	BAC.258
5B-DAJ	1-11	BAC.261
5B-DAK	B707	17632
5B-DAL	B707	17631
5B-DAM	B707	17628
5B-DAO	B707	18054
5B-DAP	B707	17635
5B-DAQ	**A310**	**300**
5B-DAR	**A310**	**309**
5B-DAS	**A310**	**352**
5B-DAT	**A320**	**0028**
5B-DAU	**A320**	**0035**
5B-DAV	**A320**	**0037**
5B-DAW	**A320**	**0038**
5B-DAX	**A310**	**486**
5B-DAY	B707	19622
5B-DAZ	**B707**	**19521**
5B-DBA	**A320**	**0180**
5B-DBB	**A320**	**0256**
5B-DBC	**A320**	**0295**
5B-DBD	**A320**	**0316**
5B-DBE	**B727**	**18371**
5B-DBF	**B737**	**23040**

Tanzania

5H-AAF	COMET	6433
5H-ARS	**B727**	**19687**
5H-ATC	**B737**	**21710**
5H-CCM	**F-28**	**11137**
5H-MMT	VC-10	882
5H-MOG	VC-10	885
5H-MOI	DC-9	47430
(5H-MRF)	B737	21711
5H-MRK	**B737**	**21711**

Nigeria

5N-	**1-11**	**063**
5N-	**1-11**	**BAC.184**
5N-	**1-11**	**BAC.210**
5N-	**1-11**	**BAC.241**
5N-ABD	VC-10	804
5N-ABJ	**B707**	**20474**
5N-ABK	B707	20669
5N-AGN	F-28	11049
5N-AGY	B727	22825
5N-ANA	F-28	11993
5N-ANB	F-28	11053
5N-ANC	**B737**	**20671**
5N-AND	**B737**	**20672**
5N-ANF	F-28	11090
5N-ANH	F-28	11091
5N-ANI	F-28	11108
5N-ANJ	F-28	11109
5N-ANK	F-28	11110
5N-ANN	**DC-10**	**46957**
5N-ANO	**B707**	**21428**
(5N-ANO)	DC-10	46968
5N-ANP	B727	21426
5N-ANQ	B727	21427
5N-ANR	DC-10	46968
5N-ANU	F-28	11142
5N-ANV	F-28	11144
5N-ANW	**B737**	**22771**
5N-ANX	B737	22772
5N-ANY	**B737**	**22773**
5N-ANZ	**B737**	**22774**
5N-AOK	1-11	BAC.113
5N-AOM	1-11	BAC.122
5N-AON	DC-8	45954
5N-AOO	B707	19590
5N-AOP	**1-11**	**BAC.109**
5N-AOQ	**B707**	**19664**
5N-AOS	**1-11**	**BAC.123**
5N-AOT	1-11	BAC.133
5N-AOW	1-11	094
5N-AOY	**CRVL**	**180**
5N-AOZ	**1-11**	**BAC.107**
5N-ARH	DC-8	45859
5N-ARO	B707	18924
5N-ARQ	**B707**	**18809**
5N-ASY	B707	18922
5N-ATS	DC-8	45817
5N-ATY	**DC-8**	**45858**
5N-ATZ	DC-8	45965
5N-AUA	B737	22985
5N-AUB	**B737**	**22986**
(5N-AUC)	B737	22987
(5N-AUD)	B737	22988
5N-AUE	**A310**	**270**
5N-AUF	**A310**	**285**
5N-AUG	**A310**	**329**
5N-AUH	**A310**	**340**
(5N-AUI)	DC-10	48318
5N-AUS	DC-8	45854
5N-AVO	**CRVL**	**256**
5N-AVP	**CRVL**	**260**
5N-AVQ	**CRVL**	**220**
5N-AVR	DC-8	45758
5N-AVS	DC-8	45756
5N-AVX	**1-11**	**BAC.167**
5N-AVY	DC-8	45688
5N-AWE	DC-8	45753
5N-AWF	**CRVL**	**206**
5N-AWH	B727	19120
5N-AWK	CRVL	50
5N-AWO	B707	19372
5N-AWO	**CRVL**	**217**
5N-AWQ	CRVL	219
5N-AWT	CRVL	215
5N-AWV	**B727**	**18254**
5N-AWX	B727	18256
5N-AWY	**B727**	**18258**
5N-AWZ	DC-8	46012
5N-AXQ	**1-11**	**BAC.157**
5N-AXT	**1-11**	**BAC.121**
5N-AXV	**1-11**	**BAC.159**
5N-AYJ	B707	19168
5N-AYR	**1-11**	**BAC.162**
5N-AYS	1-11	BAC.129
5N-AYT	**1-11**	**BAC.131**
5N-AYU	**1-11**	**062**
5N-AYV	**1-11**	**BAC.128**
5N-AYW	**1-11**	**BAC.166**
5N-AYY	**1-11**	**043**
5N-AYZ	DC-8	45421
5N-BAA	**1-11**	**041**
5N-BAB	**1-11**	**BAC.127**
5N-BBA	DC-9	47217
5N-BBB	L1011	1068
5N-BBC	**DC-9**	**45871**
5N-BBD	**B707**	**19625**
5N-BBE	DC-9	45872
5N-BBG	**B727**	**20049**
5N-BBH	**B727**	**20050**
5N-BIN	**1-11**	**BAC.265**
5N-BLV	**DC-9**	**47276**
5N-CMB	B727	20757
5N-COE	DC-9	47276
5N-DDD	B727	20419
5N-DIO	B737	19549
5N-EDE	**B727**	**19972**
5N-EDO	**B747**	**19726**
5N-EEO	**B707**	**19270**
5N-EHI	**1-11**	**074**
5N-ENO	**1-11**	**BAC.208**
5N-EYI	**1-11**	**BAC.211**
5N-FGN	**B727**	**22825**
5N-GAB	B747	21141
5N-GBA	**B727**	**20677**
5N-GGG	**1-11**	**BAC.160**
5N-GIN	DC-9	47161
5N-HAS	DC-8	45912
5N-HHS	**B747**	**19644**
5N-HTA	1-11	051
5N-HTB	**1-11**	**052**
5N-HTC	**1-11**	**049**
5N-HTD	**1-11**	**050**
5N-IMO	1-11	BAC.229
5N-INZ	DC-9	47402
5N-JIL	B707	18922
5N-KAY	**DC-9**	**47259**
5N-KBA	1-11	BAC.179
5N-KBC	**1-11**	**BAC.104**
5N-KBD	**1-11**	**BAC.102**
5N-KBG	1-11	082
5N-KBM	**1-11**	**BAC.105**
5N-KBO	**1-11**	**BAC.180**
5N-KBR	1-11	093
5N-KBS	**1-11**	**031**
5N-KBT	**1-11**	**BAC.100**
5N-KBV	**1-11**	**032**
5N-KBW	**1-11**	**BAC.106**
5N-KBX	**B727**	**20444**
5N-KBY	**B727**	**20442**
5N-KGB	1-11	082
5N-KKK	**1-11**	**BAC.154**
5N-LLL	**B727**	**20655**
5N-MAM	B727	18801
5N-MAS	B707	18718
5N-MCI	B737	19554
5N-MKE	DC-8	45753
5N-MML	**B727**	**20906**
5N-MMM	**B727**	**20657**
5N-MXX	**B707**	**18940**
5N-MZE	**1-11**	**BAC.110**
5N-NEC	B727	20673
5N-NRC	**1-11**	**BAC.124**
5N-OAL	**1-11**	**BAC.214**
5N-OCL	**B707**	**19631**
5N-OCM	DC-8	45753
(5N-OGI)	DC-10	46928
5N-OKA	**1-11**	**BAC.168**
5N-OMO	**1-11**	**034**
5N-ONE	**B707**	**19353**
5N-ORI	B727	18330
5N-ORO	**1-11**	**BAC.264**
5N-OSA	1-11	BAC.153
5N-OVE	**1-11**	**BAC.112**
5N-PAL	**B727**	**20679**
5N-PAX	**B727**	**20678**
5N-QQQ	**B727**	**20659**
5N-SDP	**1-11**	**BAC.125**
5N-SKS	1-11	BAC.100
5N-SKS	**1-11**	**BAC.243**
5N-SMA	**B727**	**19388**
5N-SSS	**B727**	**20147**
5N-TAS	B707	19375
5N-THG	**B747**	**19640**
5N-TKE	**B727**	**19406**
5N-TOM	1-11	BAC.124
5N-TRT	**B727**	**18330**
5N-TTK	**B727**	**20432**
5N-TTT	**B727**	**20463**
5N-UDE	1-11	BAC.259
5N-USE	1-11	BAC.151
5N-USE	1-11	BAC.235
5N-VWE	DC-9	47259

Malagasy Republic

5R-MFA	**B737**	**20231**
5R-MFB	**B737**	**20680**
5R-MFH	**B737**	**26305**
5R-MFK	B707	18686
5R-MFT	**B747**	**21614**
5R-MUA	**YAK40**	**9840859**
5R-MUB	**YAK40**	

Mauritania

5T-CJW	CRVL	91
5T-CLF	F-28	11092
5T-CLG	**F-28**	**11093**
5T-MAL	CRVL	91
5T-RIM	**CRVL**	**91**

Niger

5U-BAG	**B737**	**21499**
(5U-MAF)	B737	21499

Togo

5V-MAB	F-28	11079
5V-SBB	**B727**	**22165**
5V-TAB	F-28	11079
5V-TAD	B720	19523
5V-TAF	DC-8	45692
5V-TAG	**B707**	**19739**
5V-TAI	**F-28**	**11079**

Samoa

5W-FAX	B737	23788
5W-ILF	**B737**	**26282**
5W-PAL	B737	22575
5W-TEA	B767	23280

Uganda

5X-AAO	COMET	6431
5X-CAU	**B707**	**17713**
5X-DAR	B707	18825
5X-JCR	**B707**	**18832**
5X-JEF	**B707**	**19821**
5X-JET	**B707**	**19411**
5X-JOE	**DC-10**	**47906**
5X-JON	**B707**	**20546**
5X-TRA	**B707**	**20722**
5X-UAC	B707	18747
5X-UAL	B707	18580
(5X-UAL)	B707	18765
5X-UBC	B707	19630
5X-UCM	B707	19177
5X-USM	**B737**	**24785**
5X-UVA	VC-10	881
5X-UVJ	VC-10	884
5X-UVY	DC-9	47478
5X-UWM	B707	18691

Kenya

5Y-AAA	COMET	6472
5Y-ADA	VC-10	883
5Y-ADD	COMET	6413
5Y-AKX	DC-9	45787
5Y-ALD	COMET	6412
5Y-ALF	COMET	6406
5Y-ALR	DC-9	47468
5Y-AMT	COMET	6405
(5Y-ANA)	B707	19521
5Y-ASA	DC-8	45379
5Y-AXA	B707	19621
5Y-AXC	B707	18746
5Y-AXG	B707	19369
5Y-AXI	**B707**	**18927**
5Y-AXM	**B707**	**18819**
5Y-AXS	B707	19133
5Y-AXW	**B707**	**19366**
5Y-BAS	DC-8	45629
5Y-BBH	DC-9	47430
5Y-BBI	**B707**	**19634**
5Y-BBJ	B707	19633
5Y-BBK	B707	19872
5Y-BBR	DC-9	47478
5Y-BBX	B720	18588
5Y-BEL	**A310**	**416**
5Y-BEN	**A310**	**426**
5Y-BFB	B707	18964
5Y-BFC	B707	18881
5Y-BFF	B707	20179
5Y-BFT	**A310**	**519**
5Y-BGI	B757	24566
(5Y-BHF)	B757	24923
(5Y-BHG)	B757	24924
5Y-BHV	**B737**	**21193**
5Y-BHW	**B737**	**21196**
5Y-LKL	B707	19133
(5Y-QSR)	DC-8	45629
5Y-SIM	**B707**	**20517**
5Y-ZEB	DC-8	46122

Somalia

6O-SAU	B720	18013
6O-SAW	B720	18015
6O-SAX	B720	18031
6O-SBM	B707	18953
6O-SBN	B707	18954
6O-SBS	B707	19315
6O-SBT	B707	19316
6O-SCG	B727	22430

Senegal

6V-AAR	CRVL	5
(6V-ACP)	CRVL	5
6V-AEF	**B727**	**21091**

Jamaica

6Y-JGA	DC-9	47351
6Y-JGB	DC-9	47352
6Y-JGC	DC-8	45963
6Y-JGD	**DC-8**	**45760**
6Y-JGE	DC-8	45648
6Y-JGF	DC-8	45643
6Y-JGG	DC-8	45894
6Y-JGH	DC-8	45912
6Y-JII	DC-8	46084
6Y-JIJ	DC-9	47639
6Y-JIP	B727	21105
6Y-JIQ	B727	21106
6Y-JIR	B727	21107
6Y-JIS	B727	21108
6Y-JMA	B727	21105
6Y-JMB	B727	21106
6Y-JMC	B727	21107
6Y-JMD	B727	21108
6Y-JME	DC-8	45442
6Y-JMF	DC-8	45612
6Y-JMG	B727	22036
6Y-JMH	B727	20936
6Y-JMJ	**A300**	**127**
6Y-JMK	**A300**	**131**
6Y-JML	B727	20978
6Y-JMM	**B727**	**21105**
6Y-JMN	**B727**	**21106**

6Y-JMO B727 21107
6Y-JMP B727 20935
6Y-JMP B727 21108
6Y-JMQ B727 22347
6Y-JMR A300 109
6Y-JMS A300 143

Yemen

7O-ABQ B720 18032
7O-ABY B707 19777
7O-ACI B737 21763
7O-ACJ B707 18737
7O-ACN TU154 501
7O-ACO B707 20374
7O-ACP B720 18016
7O-ACQ B737 23129
7O-ACR B737 23130
7O-ACS B707 20547
7O-ACT TU154 822
7O-ACU B737 21296
7O-ACV B727 21844
7O-ACW B727 21845
7O-ACX B727 21846
7O-ACY B727 21847
7O-ADA B727 21842
7O-ADF IL-76 1033418578
7O-ADG IL-76 1033415497
7O-ADH IL-76

Lesotho

7P-LAN B707 19517

Malawi

7Q-YKE 1-11 039
7Q-YKF 1-11 BAC.243
7Q-YKG 1-11 BAC.245
7Q-YKH VC-10 819
7Q-YKI 1-11 BAC.214
7Q-YKJ 1-11 BAC.240
7Q-YKK 1-11 BAC.235
7Q-YKL B747 21133
7Q-YKP B737 25056
(7Q-YKR) B737 25604

Algeria

(7T-V..) B747 21991
(7T-V..) B747 22234
7T-VAE CRVL 51
7T-VAG CRVL 18
7T-VAI CRVL 28
7T-VAK CRVL 73
7T-VAL CRVL 75
7T-VEA B727 20472
7T-VEB B727 20473
7T-VEC B737 20544
7T-VED B737 20650
7T-VEE B737 20758
7T-VEF B737 20759
7T-VEG B737 20884
7T-VEH B727 20955
7T-VEI B727 21053
7T-VEJ B737 21063
7T-VEK B737 21064
7T-VEL B737 21065
7T-VEM B727 21210
7T-VEN B737 21211
7T-VEO B737 21212
7T-VEP B727 21284
7T-VEQ B737 21285
7T-VER B737 21286
7T-VES B737 21287
7T-VET B727 22372
7T-VEU B727 22373
7T-VEV B727 22374
7T-VEW B727 22375
7T-VEX B727 22765
7T-VEY B737 22766
7T-VEZ B737 22700
7T-VJA B737 22800
7T-VJB B737 22801
7T-VJC A310 291
7T-VJD A310 293
7T-VJE A310 295
7T-VJF A310 306
7T-VJG B767 24766
7T-VJH B767 24767
7T-VJI B767 24768
(7T-VRA) L1011 1250
7T-WIA IL-76
7T-WIB IL-76
7T-WIC IL-76
7T-WID IL-76 1023414470
7T-WIE IL-76
7T-WIG IL-76 1023413435
7T-WIU IL-76

Barbados

8P-CAC B707 19412
8P-CAD B707 19632
8P-GUL B757 22206
8P-PLC DC-8 46042

Maldive Republic

8Q-CA003 DC-8 45649
8Q-CA004 DC-8 45808
8Q-CA005 DC-8 45689
8Q-PNB DC-8 45649
8Q-PNC DC-8 45808

Guyana

8R-GGA TU154 719

Croatia

9A-ADL TU134 63952
9A-ADP TU134 63967
9A-ADR TU134 66135
9A-CTA B737 22119
9A-CTB B737 22116
9A-CTC B737 22118
9A-CTD B737 22140
9A-CTE B737 22634

Ghana

9G-ABO VC-10 823
9G-ABP VC-10 824
(9G-ABQ) VC-10 825
(9G-ABU) VC-10 840
9G-ABZ F-28 11062
9G-ACA F-28 11077
9G-ACB B707 17593
(9G-ACB) F-28 11062
9G-ACD B707 17603
9G-ACG DC-8 45256
9G-ACJ B707 17903
9G-ACK B707 17721
9G-ACM DC-9 47755
9G-ACN B707 17640
9G-ACO B707 17651
9G-ACR B707 19001
9G-ACX B707 19498
9G-ACY B707 19212
9G-ACZ B707 19369
(9G-ACZ) B707 19843
9G-ADA F-28 11187
9G-ADB B707 20457
9G-ADL B707 19369
9G-ADM B707 19369
9G-ADN DC-9 47276
9G-ADS B707 19587
9G-ANA DC-10 48286
9G-EBK B707 19372
9G-ESI B707 19372
9G-MAN B707 19212
9G-MKA DC-8 45804
9G-MKB DC-8 45860
9G-MKC DC-8 45692
9G-MKD DC-8 45965
9G-MKE DC-8 45753
9G-MKF DC-8 45820
9G-OLF B707 19821
9G-OLU B707 19519
9G-ONE B707 19821
9G-RBO B707 18746
9G-RCA B707 18746
(9G-TOO) B707 20517
9G-TWO B707 20517
9G-WON B707 19821

Malta

9H-AAK B720 18063
9H-AAL B720 18167
9H-AAM B720 18378
9H-AAN B720 18380
9H-AAO B720 18829
9H-ABA B737 23038
9H-ABB B737 23039
9H-ABC B737 23040
9H-ABE B737 23847
9H-ABF B737 23848
9H-ABG B737 24031
9H-ABP A320 0112
9H-ABQ A320 0293
9H-ABR B737 25613
9H-ABS B737 25614
9H-ABT B737 25615
9H-ABX A320 0289
9H-ACM 146 E1254
9H-ACN 146 E1258
9H-ACO 146 E1260
9H-ACP 146 E1267
9H-ACS B737 23830
9H-ACT B737 23827

Zambia

9J- B737 19426
9J-ABR DC-8 45599
9J-ADY B707 18976
9J-ADZ B737 19424
(9J-AEA) B737 21236
9J-AEB B707 19263
9J-AEC B707 19354
9J-AEG B737 21236
9J-AEL B707 19295
9J-AEQ B707 19367
9J-AFL DC-8 46099
9J-AFM B737 22744
(9J-AFN) DC-10 47922
9J-AFO B757 24635
9J-AFT B707 19964
9J-AFU B737 19075
9J-RCH 1-11 039
9J-RCI 1-11 040

Kuwait

9K-ACA COMET 6465
9K-ACE COMET 6474
9K-ACF TRDNT 2114
9K-ACG TRDNT 2118
9K-ACH TRDNT 2134
9K-ACI COMET 6427
(9K-ACI) 1-11 033
9K-ACJ B707 20084
(9K-ACJ) 1-11 034
9K-ACK B707 20085
(9K-ACK) 1-11 035
9K-ACL B707 20086
9K-ACM B707 20546
9K-ACN B707 20547
9K-ACS B707 20016
9K-ACU B707 20018
9K-ACV B737 21206
9K-ACX B707 19789
9K-ADA B747 21541
9K-ADB B747 21542
9K-ADC B747 21543
9K-ADD B747 22740
9K-ADE B747 27338
(9K-ADF) B747 27663
9K-AFA B727 22359
9K-AFB B727 22360
9K-AFC B727 22361
9K-AFD B727 22763
9K-AHA A310 267
9K-AHB A310 276
9K-AHC A310 278
9K-AHD A310 318
9K-AHE A310 331
9K-AHF A300 327
9K-AHG A300 332
9K-AHH A310 339
9K-AHI A300 344
9K-AHJ A310 342
9K-AHK A310 346
9K-AIA B767 23280
9K-AIB B767 23281
9K-AIC B767 23282
9K-AKA A320 0181
9K-AKB A320 0182
9K-AKC A320 0195
9K-ALA A310 647
9K-ALB A310 649
9K-ALC A310 663
9K-ALD A310 648
9K-AMA A300 673
9K-AMB A300 694
9K-AMC A300 699
9K-AMD A300 719
9K-AME A300 721
9K-ANA A340 089
9K-ANB A340 090
9K-ANC A340 101
9K-AND A340 104

Sierra Leone

9L-LAZ B720 18251

Malaysia

(9M-...) B707 17594
9M-AOA COMET 6401
9M-AOB COMET 6403
9M-AOC COMET 6404
9M-AOD COMET 6405
9M-AOE COMET 6406
9M-AOT B707 19738
9M-AOU B737 19768
9M-AOV B737 19770
9M-AOW B737 19772
9M-AQB B707 19529
9M-AQC B737 20521
9M-AQD B707 17592
9M-AQL B737 20582
9M-AQM B737 20583
9M-AQN B737 20584
9M-AQO B737 20585
9M-AQP B737 20586
9M-AQQ B737 20587
9M-ARG B737 20631
9M-ASO B707 18955
9M-ASQ B707 18953
9M-ASR B737 20926
9M-ATR B707 18954
9M-CHG B737 27456
9M-EKC RJ100 7089
9M-LKY B737 27456
9M-MAS DC-10 46955
9M-MAT DC-10 46640
(9M-MAT) DC-10 46957
9M-MAV DC-10 48283
9M-MAW DC-10 46959
9M-MAX DC-10 46961
9M-MAZ DC-10 46933
9M-MBA B737 20582
9M-MBB B737 20583
9M-MBC B737 20584
9M-MBD B737 20585
9M-MBE B737 20586

9M-MBF B737 20587
9M-MBG B737 20631
9M-MBH B737 20926
9M-MBI B737 21109
9M-MBJ B737 21732
9M-MBK B737 22620
9M-MBL B737 23320
9M-MBM B737 23849
9M-MBN B737 21231
9M-MBO B737 22395
9M-MBP B737 21176
9M-MBQ B737 21138
9M-MBY B737 21686
9M-MBZ B737 21685
9M-MCQ B707 18953
9M-MCR B707 18954
9M-MCS B707 18955
9M-MFA B737 26445
9M-MFB B737 26446
9M-MFC B737 26448
9M-MFD B737 26450
(9M-MFD) B737 26449
9M-MFE B737 26454
(9M-MFE) B737 26450
9M-MFF B737 26456
(9M-MFF) B737 26451
9M-MFG B737 27354
9M-MFH B737 27355
9M-MFI B737 27356
(9M-MFZ) B737 27125
9M-MHA A300 73
9M-MHB A300 93
9M-MHC A300 95
9M-MHD A300 147
9M-MHG B747 22724
9M-MHH B747 22791
9M-MHI B747 22304
9M-MHJ B747 22442
9M-MHK B747 23600
9M-MHL B747 24315
9M-MHM B747 24405
9M-MHN B747 24836
9M-MHO B747 25126
(9M-MHP) B747 27042
9M-MJA B737 24703
9M-MJB B737 24704
9M-MJC B737 24705
9M-MJD B737 24706
9M-MJE B737 24707
9M-MJF B737 24708
9M-MJG B737 24709
9M-MJH B737 24686
9M-MJI B737 24688
9M-MJJ B737 24163
9M-MJK B737 24682
9M-MJL B737 24344
9M-MJM B737 24693
9M-MJN B737 24903
9M-MJO B737 24906
9M-MJP B737 24915
9M-MJQ B737 24912
9M-MJR B737 24683
9M-MJS B737 24691
9M-MJT B737 24915
9M-MKA A330 067
9M-MKB A330 068
9M-MKC A330 069
9M-MKD A330 073
9M-MKE A330 077
9M-MKF A330 100
9M-MKG A330 107
9M-MKH A330 110
9M-MKI A330 116
9M-MKJ A330 119
9M-MKZ A330 096
(9M-ML.) B737 25348
9M-MLA B737 24164
9M-MLB B737 24167
9M-MLC B737 23865
9M-MLD B737 24434
9M-MLE B737 24432
9M-MLF B737 25116
9M-MLG B737 25595
9M-MLH B737 25134
9M-MLI B737 24344
9M-MLJ B737 25594
9M-MLK B737 25303
9M-MLL B737 24644
9M-MMA B737 26443
9M-MMB B737 26444
9M-MMC B737 26453
9M-MMD B737 26464
9M-MME B737 26465
9M-MMF B737 26466
9M-MMG B737 26467
9M-MMH B737 27084
9M-MMI B737 27096
9M-MMJ B737 27097
9M-MMK B737 27083
9M-MML B737 27085
9M-MMM B737 27153
9M-MMM B737 27166
(9M-MMM) B737 27086
9M-MMN B737 27167
(9M-MMN) B737 27087
9M-MMO B737 27086
(9M-MMO) B737 26468
9M-MMP B737 27168
9M-MMQ B737 27087
(9M-MMQ) B737 26447
9M-MMR B737 26468
9M-MMS B737 27169
9M-MMT B737 27170
9M-MMU B737 26447
9M-MMV B737 26449
9M-MMW B737 26451
9M-MMX B737 26452
9M-MMY B737 26455
9M-MMZ B737 26457
(9M-MNA) B737 26458
(9M-MNB) B737 26459
(9M-MNC) B737 26460
(9M-MND) B737 26461
9M-MPA B747 27042
9M-MPB B747 25699
9M-MPC B747 25700
9M-MPD B747 25701
9M-MPE B747 25702
9M-MPF B747 27043
9M-MPG B747 25703
9M-MPH B747 27044
9M-MPQ B737 20254
9M-MQA B737 26458
9M-MQB B737 26459
9M-MQC B737 26460
9M-MQD B737 26461
9M-MQE B737 26462
9M-MQF B737 26463
9M-MQG B737 27190
9M-MQH B737 27352
9M-MQI B737 27353
9M-MQJ B737 27383
9M-MQK B737 27384
9M-MQL B737 27191
9M-MQM B737 27306
9M-MZA B737 27125
9M-MZB B737 27347
9M-PMM B737 20458
9M-PMP B737 20220
9M-PMR B737 19553
9M-SAS B727 18371
9M-SMV B747 27069
9M-TDM B707 21049
9M-TMS B707 21096

Nepal

(9N-ABA) B727 19813
9N-ABD B727 20421
9N-ABN B727 19813
9N-ABV B727 18879
9N-ABW B727 18878
9N-ABY B727 19113
9N-ACA B757 23850
9N-ACB B757 23863

Zaire

(9Q-...) B707 17905
(9Q-...) B737 19309
(9Q-ARW) B747 19637
9Q-CAR B727 18877
9Q-CAU B727 20424
9Q-CAV B727 18967
9Q-CBD B707 17658
9Q-CBF DC-8 45629
9Q-CBG B727 18367
9Q-CBL B707 19266
9Q-CBS B707 20200
9Q-CBS B727 19319
9Q-CBT B727 19138
9Q-CBW B707 20200
9Q-CCP CRVL 229
9Q-CDA B707 19294
9Q-CDJ B727 20424
9Q-CDM B727 18919
9Q-CDM DC-8 45686
9Q-CDZ B727 18934
9Q-CEH 1-11 057
9Q-CFN CRVL 254
9Q-CFT B720 18043
9Q-CGC CRVL 119
9Q-CGO B707 17602
9Q-CJM B707 20341
9Q-CJT B707 19335
9Q-CJW B707 17602
9Q-CJW B707 19844
9Q-CKB B707 19519
(9Q-CKF) B747 20829
9Q-CKG B707 19844
9Q-CKI 1-11 BAC.177
9Q-CKI B707 19821
9Q-CKI DC-8 45683
9Q-CKK B707 20761
(9Q-CKK) B707 19844
9Q-CKP 1-11 BAC.191
9Q-CKP B707 17658
9Q-CKY 1-11 BAC.176
9Q-CLC CRVL 240
9Q-CLD CRVL 251
9Q-CLE DC-8 45266
9Q-CLF DC-8 45268
9Q-CLG DC-8 46151
9Q-CLH DC-8 46147
9Q-CLI DC-10 47886
9Q-CLP CRVL 115
9Q-CLT DC-10 46932
9Q-CLV DC-8 45610
9Q-CLY B707 20517
9Q-CMA B707 17686
9Q-CMD B707 18694
9Q-CMD CRVL 74
9Q-CNI B737 20793
9Q-CNJ B737 20794
9Q-CNK B737 20795
9Q-CNL B737 20276
(9Q-CNL) B737 20796
(9Q-CNM) B737 20797
9Q-CPI CRVL 183
9Q-CPJ B727 19088
9Q-CPM B707 18357
9Q-CPS CRVL 21
9Q-CQM DC-8 45607
9Q-CRA B707 19844
9Q-CRA B727 18877
9Q-CRG B727 18361
9Q-CRT B707 17718
9Q-CRU CRVL 71
9Q-CRW B707 17713
9Q-CRY B707 17601
9Q-CSB B707 19179
9Q-CSF B727 18332
9Q-CSG B727 18369
9Q-CSH B727 19558
9Q-CSJ 1-11 013
9Q-CSJ DC-8 45686
9Q-CSS DC-10 46928
9Q-CSW B707 19375
9Q-CSY B727 19180
9Q-CSZ B707 19577
9Q-CTD B720 18162
9Q-CTD TRDNT 2308
9Q-CTI TRDNT 2305
9Q-CTK B707 18413
9Q-CTM TRDNT 2304
9Q-CTY TRDNT 2308
9Q-CTZ TRDNT 2307
9Q-CTZ TRDNT 2322
9Q-CUG 1-11 057
9Q-CVG B707 19162
9Q-CVG B707 20122
9Q-CVH DC-8 45862
9Q-CVO CRVL 209
9Q-CWA B727 20775
9Q-CWK CRVL 209
9Q-CWR B707 18357
9Q-CWT B727 18291
9Q-CZF B707 17930
9Q-CZK B707 17602
9Q-CZL CRVL 123
9Q-CZZ CRVL 105
9Q-MNS B707 19969

Burundi

9U-BTA CRVL 144

Singapore

9V- A340 123
9V- A340 126
9V- A340 128
9V- A340 139
9V-BAS COMET 6401
9V-BAT COMET 6404
9V-BAU COMET 6406
9V-BBA B707 19737
9V-BBB B707 19739
9V-BBC B737 19769
9V-BBE B737 19771
9V-BBH COMET 6417
9V-BBJ COMET 6414
9V-BCR B737 20492
9V-BDC B707 19530
9V-BEF 1-11 BAC.166
9V-BEH DC-8 45902
9V-BEW B707 19351
9V-BEX B707 19352
9V-BEY B707 19353
9V-BFB B707 19738
9V-BFC B707 19529
9V-BFD B737 19768
9V-BFE B737 19770
9V-BFF B737 19772
9V-BFN B707 18809
9V-BFW B707 18808
9V-SDA DC-10 46990
9V-SDB DC-10 46993
9V-SDC DC-10 46991
9V-SDD DC-10 46995
9V-SDE DC-10 46999
9V-SDF DC-10 47817
9V-SDG DC-10 47818
9V-SFA B747 26563
9V-SFB B747 26561
9V-SFC B747 26560
9V-SFD B747 26553
9V-SGA B727 21347
9V-SGB B727 21348
9V-SGC B727 21349
9V-SGD B727 21458
9V-SGE B727 21459
9V-SGF B727 21460
9V-SGG B727 21945
9V-SGH B727 21946
9V-SGI B727 21947
9V-SGJ B727 21948
9V-SGK B757 23125
9V-SGL B757 23126
9V-SGM B757 23127
9V-SGN B757 23128
9V-SIA B747 20712
9V-SIB B747 20713
9V-SJF A340 117
9V-SKA B747 23026
(9V-SKB) B747 23027

(9V-SKC)	B747	23028
9V-SKD	B747	23029
(9V-SKE)	B747	23030
(9V-SKF)	B747	23031
(9V-SKG)	B747	23032
(9V-SKH)	B747	23033
(9V-SKJ)	B747	23243
(9V-SKK)	B747	23244
(9V-SKL)	B747	23245
9V-SKM	**B747**	**23409**
9V-SKN	**B747**	**23410**
9V-SKP	**B747**	**23769**
9V-SKQ	**B747**	**24177**
9V-SLK	**F-70**	**11536**
9V-SLL	**F-70**	**11561**
9V-SMA	**B747**	**24061**
9V-SMB	**B747**	**24062**
9V-SMC	B747	24063
9V-SMD	**B747**	**24064**
9V-SME	**B747**	**24065**
9V-SMF	**B747**	**24066**
9V-SMG	**B747**	**24226**
9V-SMH	**B747**	**24227**
9V-SMI	**B747**	**24975**
9V-SMJ	**B747**	**25068**
(9V-SMJ)	B747	24975
9V-SMK	**B747**	**25127**
(9V-SMK)	B747	25068
9V-SML	**B747**	**25128**
(9V-SML)	B747	25127
9V-SMM	**B747**	**26547**
(9V-SMM)	B747	25128
9V-SMN	**B747**	**26548**
9V-SMO	**B747**	**27066**
9V-SMP	**B747**	**27067**
9V-SMQ	**B747**	**27132**
9V-SMR	**B747**	**27133**
9V-SMS	**B747**	**27134**
9V-SMT	**B747**	**27137**
9V-SMU	**B747**	**27068**
9V-SMW	**B747**	**27178**
9V-SMY	**B747**	**27217**
9V-SMZ	**B747**	**26549**
9V-SPA	**B747**	**26550**
9V-SPB	**B747**	**26551**
9V-SPC	**B747**	**27070**
9V-SPD	**B747**	**26552**
9V-SPE	**B747**	**26554**
9V-SPF	**B747**	**27071**
9V-SPG	**B747**	**26562**
9V-SPH	**B747**	**26555**
(9V-SQA)	B747	23033
9V-SQC	B747	20888
9V-SQD	B747	21048
9V-SQE	B747	21162
9V-SQF	B747	21316
9V-SQG	B747	21439
9V-SQH	B747	21683
9V-SQI	B747	21684
9V-SQJ	B747	21935
9V-SQK	B747	21936
9V-SQL	B747	21937
9V-SQM	B747	21938
9V-SQN	B747	21939
9V-SQO	B747	21940
9V-SQP	**B747**	**21941**
9V-SQQ	**B747**	**21942**
9V-SQR	B747	21943
9V-SQS	**B747**	**21944**
9V-SQT	B747	22150
(9V-SQT)	B747	23026
9V-SQU	B747	22151
(9V-SQU)	B747	23027
9V-SQV	B747	22245
(9V-SQV)	B747	23028
(9V-SQW)	B747	23029
(9V-SQX)	B747	23030
(9V-SQY)	B747	23031
9V-SQZ	**B737**	**24021**
(9V-SQZ)	B747	23032
9V-STA	A300	117
9V-STA	**A310**	**665**
9V-STB	A300	121
9V-STB	**A310**	**669**
9V-STC	A300	126
9V-STC	**A310**	**680**
9V-STD	A300	169
9V-STD	**A310**	**684**
9V-STE	A300	174
9V-STE	**A310**	**693**
9V-STF	A300	222
9V-STF	**A310**	**697**
9V-STG	A300	268
9V-STH	A300	269
9V-STI	**A310**	**347**
(9V-STI)	A300	308
9V-STJ	**A310**	**350**
(9V-STJ)	A300	310
9V-STK	**A310**	**357**
9V-STL	**A310**	**363**
9V-STM	**A310**	**367**
9V-STN	**A310**	**372**
9V-STO	**A310**	**433**
9V-STP	**A310**	**443**
9V-STQ	**A310**	**493**
9V-STR	**A310**	**500**
9V-STS	**A310**	**501**
9V-STT	**A310**	**534**
9V-STU	**A310**	**548**
9V-STV	**A310**	**570**
9V-STW	**A310**	**589**
9V-STY	**A310**	**634**
9V-STZ	**A310**	**654**
(9V-SXA)	B727	21347
(9V-SXB)	B727	21348
(9V-SXC)	B727	21349
(9V-SXD)	B727	21458
(9V-SXE)	B727	21459
(9V-SXF)	B727	21460
9V-TRA	**B737**	**24679**
9V-TRB	**B737**	**24902**
9V-TRC	**B737**	**24570**
9V-TRD	**B737**	**25017**
9V-TRE	**B737**	**27457**
9V-TRY	MD-87	49673
9V-WGA	B727	21946

Rwanda

9XR-CH	CRVL	209
9XR-JA	B707	19292
9XR-VO	**B707**	**19292**

Trinidad & Tobago

9Y-TCO	B727	18794
9Y-TCP	B727	18795
9Y-TCQ	B727	18796
9Y-TDB	B707	18334
9Y-TDC	B707	18067
9Y-TDO	B707	17692
9Y-TDP	B707	17694
9Y-TDQ	B707	17695
9Y-TDR	B707	17693
9Y-TED	B707	19209
9Y-TEE	B707	19412
9Y-TEJ	B707	19631
9Y-TEK	B707	19632
9Y-TEX	B707	20027
9Y-TEZ	B707	20028
9Y-TFF	DC-9	47737
9Y-TFG	DC-9	47742
9Y-TFH	DC-9	47743
9Y-TFI	DC-9	47752
9Y-TGC	DC-9	47796
9Y-TGJ	**L1011**	**1179**
9Y-TGN	**L1011**	**1191**
9Y-TGP	DC-9	48122
9Y-THA	**L1011**	**1222**
(9Y-THB)	L1011	1233
9Y-THN	**MD-83**	**49390**
9Y-THQ	**MD-83**	**49448**
9Y-THR	**MD-83**	**49568**
9Y-THT	MD-83	49575
9Y-THU	**MD-83**	**49824**
9Y-THV	**MD-83**	**49632**
9Y-THW	**MD-83**	**49786**
9Y-THX	**MD-83**	**49789**
9Y-THY	MD-83	49400

Odds and Ends

17563	IL-76	1053417563
"17696"	B707	17696
18925	B707	18925
IS-76900	**IL-76**	**1053417563**
"LT-AAS"	YAK42	4520421811395
MOLDOVA-74009	AN-74	
"VR-VZA"	B707	20375

NOTES

NOTES

Military Index

Angola

SG-104 TU134

Argentina

5-T-10 F-28 11147
5-T-20 F-28 11145
5-T-21 F-28 11150
0740 F-28 11147
0741 F-28 11145
0742 F-28 11150
T-01 B707 21070
T-01 F-28 11028
T-01 B757 25487
T-02 F-28 11028
T-02 F-28 11048
T-04 F-28 11028
T-91 CRVL 19
T-92 CRVL 149
T-93 CRVL 180
T-95 B707 19241
T-96 B707 19238
TC-51 F-28 11076
TC-52 F-28 11074
TC-53 F-28 11020
TC-54 F-28 11018
TC-55 F-28 11024
TC-91 B707 21070
TC-92 B707 20077
TC-93 B707 19962
TC-93 B707 20076
TC-94 B707 20076
VR-21 B707 19962

Australia

A12-124 1-11 BAC.124
A12-125 1-11 BAC.125
A20-103 B707 21103
A20-261 B707 21261
A20-623 B707 19623
A20-624 B707 19624
A20-627 B707 19627
A20-629 B707 19629
(A20-809) B707 19809

Belgium

CB-01 B727 19402
CB-02 B727 19403

Brazil

2401 C-137 19840
2402 C-137 19842
2403 C-137 20008
2404 C-137 19870
(2405) B707 19321
VC92-2110 1-11 BAC.154
VC92-2111 1-11 BAC.118
VC96-2115 B737 21165
VC96-2116 B737 21166

Bulgaria

050 TU134 0350922
050 TU134 1351303
060 YAK40 9621547
LZ D 050 TU134 1351303

Canada

5301 COMET 06017
5302 COMET 06018
13701 C-137 20315
13702 C-137 20316
13703 C-137 20317
13704 C-137 20318
13705 C-137 20319
15001 A310 446
15002 A310 482
15003 A310 425
15004 A310 444
15005 A310 441

Chile

01 B707 19000
901 B707 19374
901 B727 19196
902 B707 19443
903 B707 18926
904 B707 19374
905 B707 19000

China

50050 TRDNT 2132
50052 TRDNT 2171
50053 TRDNT 2189
50054 TRDNT 2186
50056 TRDNT 2130
50057 TRDNT 2327
50058 TRDNT 2328
50152 TRDNT 2133
50158 TRDNT 2174
50255 TU124 5351709?
50256 TU124 5351808
50257 TU124 6352002

CIS

01 IL-86 51483201026
15 TU124

Colombia

1201 B707 19716
FAC-001 F-28 11992
FAC-1140 F-28 11165
FAC-1141 F-28 11162
FAC-1142 DC-9 45722
FAC-1146 B727 19595

Czechoslovakia

0420 TU154 420
0601 TU154 601
608 TU124
0723 YAK40 9230723
0823 YAK40 9230823
1407 TU134 1351407

East Germany

108 IL-62 3749224
114 TU154 799
115 TU134 60108
116 TU134 60435
117 TU134 60612
118 TU134 62259
119 TU134 63260
120 IL-62 3242432
121 IL-62 4831517
121 TU154 813
122 IL-62 4934734
123 TU134 49900
170 TU134 3352102
171 TU134 3352106
175 TU134 4352205
176 IL-62 4445827
176 TU134 4352206
176 TU134 63967
177 TU134 9350913
178 TU134 4352207
179 TU134 31218
181 TU134 35180
182 TU134 1351305
183 TU134 9350904
183 TU134 63998
184 TU134 63952
185 TU134 40150
186 TU134 46155
193 TU134 66135
495 TU124 4351505
496 TU124 5351708

Ecuador

FAE-220 F-28 11220
FAE-788 B727 20788
FAE-8033 B720 18033
FAE-8036 B720 18036
FAE-8037 B720 18037
FAE-19255 B707 19265
FAE-19273 B707 19273
FAE-19277 B707 19277
FAE-19691 B727 19691
FAE-19692 B727 19692
FAE-20033 B707 20033
FAE-20328 B727 20328
FAE-20560 B727 20560
FAE-20788 B727 20788
FAE-21622 B727 21622
FAE-22078 B727 22078

Ethiopia

1601 YAK40

France

116 CRVL 116
141 CRVL 141
158 CRVL 158
193 CRVL 193
201 CRVL 201
201 E-3 24115
202 E-3 24116
203 E-3 24117
204 E-3 24510
234 CRVL 234
240 CRVL 240
251 CRVL 251
264 CRVL 264
12735 C-135 18695
12735 C-135 18695
12736 C-135 18696
12736 C-135 18696
12737 C-135 18697
12737 C-135 18697
12738 C-135 18698
12738 C-135 18698
12739 C-135 18699
12739 C-135 18699
12740 C-135 18700
12740 C-135 18700
38470 C-135 18679
38470 C-135 18679
38471 C-135 18680
38471 C-135 18680
38472 C-135 18681
38473 C-135 18681
38473 C-135 18682
38474 C-135 18683
38474 C-135 18683
38475 C-135 18684
38475 C-135 18684
45570 DC-8 45570
45692 DC-8 45692
45819 DC-8 45819
45820 DC-8 45820
46013 DC-8 46013
46043 DC-8 46043
46130 DC-8 46130
62-3516 C-135 18499
63-8033 C-135 18650

36-CA E-3 24115
36-CB E-3 24116
36-CC E-3 24117
36-CD E-3 24510
93-CA C-135 18679
93-CB C-135 18680
93-CC C-135 18681
93-CE C-135 18683
93-CF C-135 18684
93-CG C-135 18695
93-CH C-135 18696
93-CI C-135 18697
93-CJ C-135 18698
93-CK C-135 18699
93-CL C-135 18700
CA C-135 18679
CB C-135 18680
CC C-135 18681
CD C-135 18682
CE C-135 18683
CF C-135 18684
CG C-135 18695
CH C-135 18696
CI C-135 18697
CJ C-135 18698
CK C-135 18699
CL C-135 18700

F-RADA A310 421
F-RADB A310 422
F-RAFA CRVL 158
F-RAFA DC-8 45820
F-RAFB DC-8 45692
F-RAFC DC-8 45819
F-RAFD DC-8 46043
F-RAFE DC-8 45570
F-RAFF DC-8 46130
F-RAFG CRVL 141
F-RAFG DC-8 46013
F-RAFH CRVL 201
F-RBPR CRVL 240
F-RBPS CRVL 251
F-RBPT CRVL 264

F-ZACE CRVL 116
F-ZACF CRVL 193
F-ZACQ CRVL 234

Germany

10+01 B707 19997
10+02 B707 19998
10+03 B707 19999
10+04 B707 20000
10+21 A310 498
10+22 A310 499
10+23 A310 503
11+01 TU154 799
11+02 TU154 813
11+10 TU134 63967
11+11 TU134 63952
11+12 TU134 66135
11+13 TU134 9350906
11+14 TU134 46300
11+15 TU134 6348560
11+20 IL-62 3749224
11+21 IL-62 3242432
11+22 IL-62 4445827
1701 VFW614 G-014
1702 VFW614 G-018
1703 VFW614 G-019

Ghana

G530 F-28 11125

India

1642	TU124	6351902?
1643	TU124	6351903?
1644	TU124	6351904?
K-	**B737**	**20483**
K-	**B737**	**20484**
K-	B737	21164
K-2370	B737	21498
K-2371	B737	21497
K-2412	**B737**	**23036**
K-2413	**B737**	**23037**
K2661/A	**IL-76**	
K2662/B	**IL-76**	**....58725**
K2663/C	**IL-76**	
K2664/D	**IL-76**	
K2665/E	**IL-76**	
K2878	**IL-76**	
K2879/H	**IL-76**	
K-2899	**B707**	**19988**
K-2900	**B707**	**19248**
K2901	**IL-76**	
K2902/M	**IL-76**	
K2903	**IL-76**	
K2999/U	**IL-76**	
K3000	**IL-76**	
K3001	**IL-76**	
K3002	**IL-76**	
K3003	**IL-76**	
K3004	**IL-76**	
K3005/E	**IL-76**	
K3012	**IL-76**	
K3013	**IL-76**	
K3014	**IL-76**	
K3015	**IL-76**	
K3077/V	**IL-76**	
K3078/W	**IL-76**	**0093496912**
V642	TU124	6351902?
V643	TU124	6351903?
V644	TU124	6351904?
V642	TU124	6351902?
'VU-AVA'	TU124	6351902?
'VU-AVB'	TU124	6351903?
'VU-AVC'	TU124	6351904?

Indonesia

A-2801	**F-28**	**11042**
A-7002	**B707**	**21092**
AI-7301	**B737**	**22777**
AI-7302	**B737**	**22778**
AI-7303	**B737**	**22779**

Iran

1001	B707	21396
1002	B727	19557
1002	**B707**	**20890**
5-241	B707	20830
5-242	B707	20831
5-243	B707	20832
5-244	B707	20833
5-245	B707	20834
5-246	B707	20835
(5-247)	B707	21123
(5-248)	B707	21124
(5-249)	B707	21125
(5-250)	B707	21126
(5-251)	B707	21127
(5-252)	B707	21128
(5-253)	B707	21129
5-280	B747	19667
5-281	B747	19678
5-282	B747	19668
5-282	B747	20080
5-283	B747	19677
5-284	B747	20081
5-286	B747	20082
5-287	B747	19669
5-288	B747	20083
5-289	B747	19733
5-290	B747	19734
5-291	B747	19735
5-8101	**B747**	**19667**
5-8102	**B747**	**19678**
5-8103	B747	20080
5-8104	B747	19677
5-8105	B747	20081
5-8106	**B747**	**19668**
5-8107	B747	20082
5-8108	**B747**	**19669**
(5-8109)	B747	20083
5-8110	B747	19733
(5-8111)	B747	19734
5-8112	B747	19735
5-8113	B747	21486
5-8114	B747	21487
5-8115	B747	21507
5-8116	B747	21514
5-8117	B747	21668
5-8301	**B707**	**20830**
5-8302	**B707**	**20831**
5-8303	**B707**	**20832**
5-8304	**B707**	**20833**
5-8305	B707	20834
5-8306	**B707**	**20835**
5-8307	B707	21123
5-8308	**B707**	**21124**
5-8309	**B707**	**21125**
5-8310	**B707**	**21126**
5-8311	**B707**	**21127**
5-8312	**B707**	**21128**
5-8313	**B707**	**21129**
5-8314	**B707**	**21475**

Iraq

634	TU124	4351602?
635	TU124	4351603?
2068	IL-76	093418543
2803	IL-76	093416506
4600	IL-76	0013433984
4601	IL-76	0013433999
4660	IL-76	0013433996

Israel

001	**B707**	**17612**
004	B707	17668
006	B707	18012
008	B707	17612
008	**B707**	**17667**
009	B707	17610
115	**B707**	**17615**
116	**B707**	**17617**
117	**B707**	**17922**
118	B707	18246
119	B707	17619
128	**B707**	**18374**
137	B707	17625
137	**B707**	**18460**
140	**B707**	**17625**
2..	B707	20716
240	B707	17596
242	**B707**	**20110**
246	**B707**	**20230**
248	B707	20629
250	**B707**	**20428**
255	**B707**	**20429**
257	B707	19000
258	**B707**	**19291**
264	**B707**	**20721**
IAF001	**B707**	**20716**
(4X-JAA)	B707	18012
(4X-JAD)	B707	17667
4X-JYA	B707	17610
4X-JYA	B707	18012
4X-JYB	**B707**	**20429**
4X-JYC	**B707**	**19291**
4X-JYD	B707	17612
4X-JYD	**B707**	**17667**
4X-JYE	**B707**	**17612**
4X-JYH	B707	17668
4X-JYH	**B707**	**20721**
4X-JYI	B707	17661
4X-JYI	B707	19000
4X-JYK	B707	18246
4X-JYL	**B707**	**18374**
4X-JYM	**B707**	**18460**
4X-JYN	B707	17619
4X-JYN	B707	20716
4X-JYQ	**B707**	**20110**
4X-JYS	**B707**	**20230**
4X-JYT	**B707**	**17625**
4X-JYU	B707	20629
4X-JYV	**B707**	**17615**
4X-JYW	**B707**	**17617**
4X-JYX	**B707**	**17922**
4X-JYY	**B707**	**20428**
4X-JYZ	B707	17596

Italy

14-01	**B707**	**19740**
14-02	**B707**	**20298**
14-03	**B707**	**20514**
14-04	**B707**	**20515**
31-12	**DC-9**	**47595**
31-13	**DC-9**	**47600**
SM-12	DC-9	47595
SM-13	DC-9	47600
(MM.....)	B707	21103
(MM.....)	B707	21261
MM62012	**DC-9**	**47595**
MM62013	**DC-9**	**47600**
MM62148	**B707**	**19740**
MM62149	**B707**	**20298**
MM62150	**B707**	**20514**
MM62151	**B707**	**20515**

Japan

28-1001	**C-1**	**8001**
28-1002	**C-1**	**8002**
38-1003	**C-1**	**8003**
48-1004	**C-1**	**8004**
48-1005	**C-1**	**8005**
58-1006	**C-1**	**8006**
58-1007	**C-1**	**8007**
58-1008	**C-1**	**8008**
58-1009	C-1	8009
58-1010	C-1	8010
58-1011	**C-1**	**8011**
58-1012	**C-1**	**8012**
58-1013	**C-1**	**8013**
68-1014	**C-1**	**8014**
68-1015	C-1	8015
68-1016	**C-1**	**8016**
68-1017	**C-1**	**8017**
68-1018	**C-1**	**8018**
68-1019	**C-1**	**8019**
68-1020	**C-1**	**8020**
78-1021	**C-1**	**8021**
78-1022	**C-1**	**8022**
78-1023	**C-1**	**8023**
78-1024	**C-1**	**8024**
78-1025	**C-1**	**8025**
78-1026	**C-1**	**8026**
88-1027	**C-1**	**8027**
88-1028	**C-1**	**8028**
98-1029	**C-1**	**8029**
08-1030	**C-1**	**8030**
18-1031	**C-1**	**8031**
20-1101	**B747**	**24730**
20-1102	**B747**	**24731**

Kenya

KAF908	**F-70**	**11557**

Korea

85101	**B737**	**23152**

Kuwait

KAF-26	**MD-83**	**49809**
KAF 320	DC-9	47691
KAF 321	**DC-9**	**47690**

Laos

974	**YAK40**	
976	**YAK40**	

Malaysia

FM2101	F-28	11088
FM2102	F-28	11089
M28-01	**F-28**	**11088**
M28-02	F-28	11089

Mexico

TP-01	B727	19123
TP-01	**B757**	**22690**
TP-02	B727	19121
TP-02	**B737**	**24095**
TP-03	B737	19772
TP-03	B737	20127
TP-04	B737	19772
TP-05	**B727**	**19123**
TP-0201	1-11	005
TP-10501	B727	18912
TP-10502	B727	19427
TP-10503	**B727**	**18908**
TP-10504	**B727**	**18909**
TP-10505	B727	18911

Morocco

CNA-NR	**B707**	**21956**
CNA-NS	**B707**	**18334**

Mozambique

63457	TU134	63457

NATO

LX-N19996	**B707**	**19996**
LX-N20198	**B707**	**20198**
LX-N20199	**B707**	**20199**
LX-N90442	**E-3**	**22855**
LX-N90443	**E-3**	**22838**
LX-N90444	**E-3**	**22839**
LX-N90445	**E-3**	**22840**
LX-N90446	**E-3**	**22841**
LX-N90447	**E-3**	**22842**
LX-N90448	**E-3**	**22843**
LX-N90449	**E-3**	**22844**
LX-N90450	**E-3**	**22845**
LX-N90451	**E-3**	**22846**
LX-N90452	**E-3**	**22847**
LX-N90453	**E-3**	**22848**
LX-N90454	**E-3**	**22849**
LX-N90455	**E-3**	**22850**
LX-N90456	**E-3**	**22851**
LX-N90457	**E-3**	**22852**
LX-N90458	**E-3**	**22853**
LX-N90459	**E-3**	**22854**

Netherlands

T-235	**DC-10**	**46956**
T-264	**DC-10**	**46985**

New Zealand

NZ7271	**B727**	**19892**
NZ7272	**B727**	**19895**
NZ7273	B727	19893

North Korea

551	TU154	129
552	TU154	143
553	TU154	191

Oman

551	**1-11**	**BAC.247**
552	**1-11**	**BAC.249**
553	**1-11**	**BAC.251**
1001	1-11	BAC.247
1002	1-11	BAC.249
1003	1-11	BAC.251

Pakistan

65-18991	B707	18991
68-19635	**B707**	**19635**
68-19866	**B707**	**19866**

Panama

(FAP-400)	B727	18894
FAP-500	B727	19815

Paraguay

FAP-01	**B707**	**18957**

Peru

369	**AN-72**	
390	**F-28**	**11100**
FAP-319	**C-137**	**19575**
FAP-370	DC-8	46078
FAP-371	**DC-8**	**45984**
PRP-001	**B737**	**27426**

Poland

031	YAK40	9331029
032	**YAK40**	**9331129**
033	**YAK40**	
034	**YAK40**	**9331229**
035	YAK40	9331329
036	YAK40	9510138
037	**YAK40**	**9510238**
038	**YAK40**	**9441237**
039	**YAK40**	**9441137**
040	**YAK40**	**9541643**
041	**YAK40**	**9541843**
042	**YAK40**	**9541943**
043	**YAK40**	**9542043**
044	**YAK40**	**9840659**
045	**YAK40**	**9840759**
046	YAK40	9021460
047	**YAK40**	**9021560**
048	**YAK40**	**9021660**
049	YAK40	9021760
101	TU134	3352005
101	TU134	49909
102	TU134	3352008
102	TU134	49985
103	TU134	3351809
104	TU134	3351808
837/01	**TU154**	**837**
837/02	TU154	862
862/02	**TU154**	**862**
96102	TU134	49985

Portugal

8801	B707	20514
8802	B707	20515

Russia

01	**TU134**	**6350203?**
01	**TU134**	**9350705**
01	**YAK40**	**9530142**
01 black	**AN-72**	
01 red	**AN-72**	
01 red	**AN-74**	
01 red	**IL-76**	**1003401024**
02	**TU134**	
02 blue	**AN-72**	
02 red	**AN-72**	
03 black	**AN-72**	
03 blue	**AN-72**	
03 red	**AN-72**	
04 blue	**AN-72**	
05	TU104	1681302?
05	**TU134**	
05	**YAK40**	
06 yellow	**AN-72**	**36576096906?**
08 black	**AN124**	
08 red	**AN124**	**9773054516003**
09 black	AN124	9773054955077
09 blue	**AN-72**	
10	**TU134**	
10 black	**AN124**	**19530502..7?**
11	**TU134**	
11 red	**AN-74**	
12	**TU134**	
15	**TU134**	
16	**TU134**	
17	**TU134**	
20	**IL-76**	
21	IL-76	043402041
21	**IL-76**	
21	TU124	1350303
21	**TU134**	
21 black	AN124	977305..32161
22	TU124	0610
22 blue	**AN-72**	
23	**TU134**	
24 blue	**AN-72**	
25	**TU134**	**63761**
26	**TU134**	
27	**TU134**	**64400**
30	**TU134**	**64845**
31	**TU134**	
32	**IL-76**	
33	**IL-76**	
34 blue	**IL-76**	**1003404138**
38	**IL-76**	
40	**IL-76**	
40	**TU134**	
42	**IL-76**	
46	**TU104**	**8350705**
47	**TU104**	**8350704**
48	**TU134**	
50	**IL-76**	
50	TU124	4351601
51	**TU134**	
51 red	**IL-76**	**0083488634**
55	TU124	1350303
58 blue	**AN-72**	
59 blue	**AN-72**	
60 blue	**AN-72**	
74	**TU134**	
77	**TU134**	**7350304**
78	**TU134**	
82	**TU134**	
84	**TU134**	
86	**TU134**	
87	**TU134**	
88	**IL-76**	
92	**IL-76**	
97	**IL-76**	
101 blue	**TU134**	
948	**AN-72**	
949	**AN-72**	**36572093819**
950	**AN-72**	
976 black	**AN-72**	
"616"	**IL-76**	
"624"	**IL-76**	
"626"	**IL-76**	
"629"	**IL-76**	
"632"	**IL-76**	
"635"	**IL-76**	
"644"	**IL-76**	
"680"	**TU134**	
"681"	TU134	49760
"719"	**IL-76**	
"725"	**IL-76**	
"819"	**IL-76**	
"993"	TU134	
"RA-19"	**TU134**	
(unmarked)	TU134	64740

Saudi Arabia

1801	**E-3**	**23417**
1802	**E-3**	**23418**
1803	**E-3**	**23419**
1804	**E-3**	**23420**
1805	**E-3**	**23421**
1811	**E-3**	**23422**
1812	**E-3**	**23423**
1813	**E-3**	**23424**
1814	**E-3**	**23425**
1815	**E-3**	**23426**
1816	**E-3**	**23427**
1817	**E-3**	**23428**
1818	**E-3**	**23429**
SA-R-7	COMET	6461

South Africa

AF-615	**B707**	**19522**
AF-617	**B707**	**19723**
AF-619	**B707**	**19917**
AF-621	**B707**	**20283**
AF-623	**B707**	**19706**
1415	**B707**	**19522**
1417	**B707**	**19723**
1419	**B707**	**19917**
1421	**B707**	**20283**
1423	**B707**	**19706**

Senegal

(6W-SBC)	CRVL	5

Serbia

71501	**YAK40**	**9120717**
71502	**YAK40**	**9120817**
71503	**YAK40**	**9222020**
71504	**YAK40**	**9231523**
71505	**YAK40**	**9630849**
71506	**YAK40**	**9731255**

Slovak

0823	**YAK40**	**9230823**

Spain

45-10	**B707**	**20060**
45-11	**B707**	**18757**
45-12	**B707**	**21367**
45-13	**B707**	**19164**
401-01	DC-8	45814
401-07	DC-8	45658
401-30	DC-8	45814
T.15-1	DC-8	45814
T.15-2	DC-8	45658
T.17-1	**B707**	**20060**
T.17-2	**B707**	**18757**
T.17-3	**B707**	**21367**
T.17-4	**B707**	**19164**

Sweden

Fv85172	**CRVL**	**172**
Fv85210	**CRVL**	**210**

Taiwan

2721	**B727**	**19399**
2722	**B727**	**19520**
2723	**B727**	**20111**
2724	**B727**	**19818**
18351	**B720**	**18351**

Thailand

60109	DC-8	46150
60110	DC-8	46129
60112	DC-8	45922
22-222	**B737**	**23059**
33-333	B737	24480
44-444	**A310**	**591**
55-555	**B737**	**27906**

Turkey

23512	**C-135**	**18495**
23568	**C-135**	**18551**

Ukraine

01	**TU134**	
02	**TU134**	
03	**TU134**	**63892**
07 red	**AN-72**	**36576096915**
11 red	**AN-72**	
42	**TU134**	
71	**TU134**	
76742	**IL-76**	**0073478346**

United Kingdom

7610M	COMET	06006
7905M	COMET	06037
7926M	COMET	06028
7927M	COMET	06029
7958M	COMET	06045
7971M	**COMET**	**06035**
8031M	COMET	06034
8351M	**COMET**	**06022**
8700M	**VC-10**	**856**
8777M	**VC-10**	**825**
8882M	COMET	6468
8967M	**NIMROD**	**8038**
8986M	**NIMROD**	**8036**
9000M	NIMROD	8044
9140M	**NIMROD**	**8049**
XK655	COMET	06023
XK659	COMET	06025
XK663	COMET	06027
XK669	COMET	06024
XK670	COMET	06028
XK671	COMET	06029
XK695	**COMET**	**06030**
XK696	COMET	06031
XK697	COMET	06032
XK698	COMET	06034
XK699	**COMET**	**06035**
XK715	COMET	06037
XK716	COMET	06045
XM823	**COMET**	**06022**
XM829	COMET	06021
XN453	COMET	06026
XP915	**COMET**	**06100**
XR395	COMET	6467
XR396	COMET	6468
XR397	COMET	6469
XR398	COMET	6470
XR399	COMET	6471
XR806	**VC-10**	**826**
XR807	**VC-10**	**827**
XR808	**VC-10**	**828**
XR809	VC-10	829
XR810	**VC-10**	**830**
XS235	**COMET**	**6473**
XV101	**VC-10**	**831**
XV102	**VC-10**	**832**
XV103	**VC-10**	**833**
XV104	**VC-10**	**834**
XV105	**VC-10**	**835**
XV106	**VC-10**	**836**
XV107	**VC-10**	**837**
XV108	**VC-10**	**838**
XV109	**VC-10**	**839**
XV144	COMET	06033
XV147	COMET	6476
XV147	**NIMROD**	**6476**

XV148	COMET	6477
XV148	NIMROD	6477
XV226/26	NIMROD	8001
XV227/27	NIMROD	8002
XV228/28	NIMROD	8003
XV229/29	NIMROD	8004
XV230/30	NIMROD	8005
XV231/31	NIMROD	8006
XV232/32	NIMROD	8007
XV233/33	NIMROD	8008
XV234/34	NIMROD	8009
XV235/35	NIMROD	8010
XV236/36	NIMROD	8011
XV237/37	NIMROD	8012
XV238/38	NIMROD	8013
XV239/39	NIMROD	8014
XV240/40	NIMROD	8015
XV241/41	NIMROD	8016
XV242/42	NIMROD	8017
XV243/43	NIMROD	8018
XV244/44	NIMROD	8019
XV245/45	NIMROD	8020
XV246/46	NIMROD	8021
XV247/47	NIMROD	8022
XV248/48	NIMROD	8023
XV249/49	NIMROD	8024
XV250/50	NIMROD	8025
XV251/51	NIMROD	8026
XV252/52	NIMROD	8027
XV253/53	NIMROD	8028
XV254/54	NIMROD	8029
XV255/55	NIMROD	8030
XV256/56	NIMROD	8031
XV257/57	NIMROD	8032
XV258/58	NIMROD	8033
XV259/59	NIMROD	8034
XV260/60	NIMROD	8035
XV261/61	NIMROD	8036
XV262/62	NIMROD	8037
XV263/63	NIMROD	8038
XV814	COMET	6407
XW626	COMET	6419
XW664/64	NIMROD	8039
XW665/65	NIMROD	8040
XW666/66	NIMROD	8041
XX105	1-11	008
XX914	VC-10	825
XX919	1-11	091
XX944	COMET	6417
XZ280/80	NIMROD	8042
XZ281/81	NIMROD	8043
XZ282/82	NIMROD	8044
XZ283/83	NIMROD	8045
XZ284/84	NIMROD	8046
XZ285/85	NIMROD	8047
XZ286/86	NIMROD	8048
XZ287/87	NIMROD	8049
ZA140/A	VC-10	814
ZA141/B	VC-10	809
ZA142/C	VC-10	811
ZA143/D	VC-10	813
ZA144/E	VC-10	806
ZA147/F	VC-10	882
ZA148/G	VC-10	883
ZA149/H	VC-10	884
ZA150/J	VC-10	885
ZD230/K	VC-10	851
ZD231	VC-10	852
ZD232	VC-10	854
ZD233	VC-10	855
ZD234	VC-10	856
ZD235/L	VC-10	857
ZD236	VC-10	858
ZD237	VC-10	859
ZD238	VC-10	860
ZD239	VC-10	861
ZD240/M	VC-10	862
ZD241/N	VC-10	863
ZD242/P	VC-10	866
ZD243	VC-10	867
ZD493	VC-10	812
ZD695	146	E1004
ZD696	146	E1005
ZD948	L1011	1157
ZD949	L1011	1159
ZD950	L1011	1164
ZD951	L1011	1165
ZD952	L1011	1168
ZD953	L1011	1174
ZE432	1-11	BAC.250
ZE433	1-11	BAC.245
ZE700	146	E1021
ZE701	146	E1029
ZE702	146	E1124
ZE704	L1011	1186
ZE705	L1011	1188
ZE706	L1011	1177
ZH101	E-3	24109
ZH102	E-3	24110
ZH103	E-3	24111
ZH104	E-3	24112
ZH105	E-3	24113
ZH106	E-3	24114
ZH107	E-3	24499
ZH763	1-11	BAC.263

United States of America

159113	C-9	47577
159114	C-9	47584
159115	C-9	47587
159116	C-9	47580
159117	C-9	47581
159118	C-9	47585
159119	C-9	47578
159120	C-9	47586
160046	C-9	47684
160047	C-9	47687
160048	C-9	47681
160049	C-9	47698
160050	C-9	47699
160051	C-9	47700
160749	C-9	47691
160750	C-9	47690
161266	C-9	48137
161529	C-9	48165
161530	C-9	48166
161572	CV880	22-7-3-55
162390	C-9	47003
162391	C-9	47004
162392	C-9	47065
162393	C-9	47325
162753	C-9	47410
162754	C-9	47476
162782	E-6	23430
162783	E-6	23889
162784	E-6	23890
163036	C-9	47041
163037	C-9	47221
163050	DC-8	45881
163208	C-9	47639
163511	C-9	47431
163512	C-9	47474
163513	C-9	47477
163918	E-6	23891
163919	E-6	23892
163920	E-6	23893
164386	E-6	23894
164387	E-6	24500
164388	E-6	24501
164404	E-6	24502
164405	E-6	24504
164406	E-6	24505
164407	E-6	24506
164408	E-6	24507
164409	E-6	24508
164410	E-6	24509
164605	C-9	47545
164606	C-9	47496
164607	C-9	47428
164608	C-9	47565
165342	C-18	18961
165343	C-18	18962
553134	C-135	17250
563596	C-135	17345
"26000"	B707	17720
"26000"	B720	18065
53-1481	C-135	17969
55-3118	C-135	17234
55-3119	C-135	17235
55-3120	C-135	17236
55-3121	C-135	17237
55-3122	C-135	17238
55-3123	C-135	17239
55-3124	C-135	17240
55-3125	C-135	17241
55-3126	C-135	17242
55-3127	C-135	17243
55-3128	C-135	17244
55-3129	C-135	17245
55-3130	C-135	17246
55-3131	C-135	17247
55-3132	C-135	17248
55-3133	C-135	17249
55-3134	C-135	17250
55-3135	C-135	17251
55-3136	C-135	17252
55-3137	C-135	17253
55-3138	C-135	17254
55-3139	C-135	17255
55-3140	C-135	17256
55-3141	C-135	17257
55-3142	C-135	17258
55-3143	C-135	17259
55-3144	C-135	17260
55-3145	C-135	17261
55-3146	C-135	17262
56-3591	C-135	17340
56-3592	C-135	17341
56-3593	C-135	17342
56-3594	C-135	17343
56-3595	C-135	17344
56-3596	C-135	17345
56-3597	C-135	17346
56-3598	C-135	17347
56-3599	C-135	17348
56-3600	C-135	17349
56-3601	C-135	17350
56-3602	C-135	17351
56-3603	C-135	17352
56-3604	C-135	17353
56-3605	C-135	17354
56-3606	C-135	17355
56-3607	C-135	17356
56-3608	C-135	17357
56-3609	C-135	17358
56-3610	C-135	17359
56-3611	C-135	17360
56-3612	C-135	17361
56-3613	C-135	17362
56-3614	C-135	17363
56-3615	C-135	17364
56-3616	C-135	17365
56-3617	C-135	17366
56-3618	C-135	17367
56-3619	C-135	17368
56-3620	C-135	17369
56-3621	C-135	17370
56-3622	C-135	17371
56-3623	C-135	17372
56-3624	C-135	17373
56-3625	C-135	17374
56-3626	C-135	17375
56-3627	C-135	17376
56-3628	C-135	17377
56-3629	C-135	17378
56-3630	C-135	17379
56-3631	C-135	17380
56-3632	C-135	17381
56-3633	C-135	17382
56-3634	C-135	17383
56-3635	C-135	17384
56-3636	C-135	17385
56-3637	C-135	17386
56-3638	C-135	17387
56-3639	C-135	17388
56-3640	C-135	17389
56-3641	C-135	17390
56-3642	C-135	17391
56-3643	C-135	17392
56-3644	C-135	17393
56-3645	C-135	17394
56-3646	C-135	17395
56-3647	C-135	17396
56-3648	C-135	17397
56-3649	C-135	17398
56-3650	C-135	17399
56-3651	C-135	17400
56-3652	C-135	17401
56-3653	C-135	17402
56-3654	C-135	17403
56-3655	C-135	17404
56-3656	C-135	17405
56-3657	C-135	17406
56-3658	C-135	17407
57-1418	C-135	17489
57-1419	C-135	17490
57-1420	C-135	17491
57-1421	C-135	17492
57-1422	C-135	17493
57-1423	C-135	17494
57-1424	C-135	17495
57-1425	C-135	17496
57-1426	C-135	17497
57-1427	C-135	17498
57-1428	C-135	17499
57-1429	C-135	17500
57-1430	C-135	17501
57-1431	C-135	17502
57-1432	C-135	17503
57-1433	C-135	17504
57-1434	C-135	17505
57-1435	C-135	17506
57-1436	C-135	17507
57-1437	C-135	17508
57-1438	C-135	17509
57-1439	C-135	17510
57-1440	C-135	17511
57-1441	C-135	17512
57-1442	C-135	17513
57-1443	C-135	17514
57-1444	C-135	17515
57-1445	C-135	17516
57-1446	C-135	17517
57-1447	C-135	17518
57-1448	C-135	17519
57-1449	C-135	17520
57-1450	C-135	17521
57-1451	C-135	17522
57-1452	C-135	17523
57-1453	C-135	17524
57-1454	C-135	17525
57-1455	C-135	17526
57-1456	C-135	17527
57-1457	C-135	17528
57-1458	C-135	17529
57-1459	C-135	17530
57-1460	C-135	17531
57-1461	C-135	17532
57-1462	C-135	17533
57-1463	C-135	17534
57-1464	C-135	17535
57-1465	C-135	17536
57-1466	C-135	17537
57-1467	C-135	17538
57-1468	C-135	17539
57-1469	C-135	17540
57-1470	C-135	17541
57-1471	C-135	17542
57-1472	C-135	17543
57-1473	C-135	17544
57-1474	C-135	17545
57-1475	C-135	17546
57-1476	C-135	17547
57-1477	C-135	17548
57-1478	C-135	17549
57-1479	C-135	17550
57-1480	C-135	17551
57-1481	C-135	17552
57-1482	C-135	17553
57-1483	C-135	17554
57-1484	C-135	17555
57-1485	C-135	17556
57-1486	C-135	17557
57-1487	C-135	17558
57-1488	C-135	17559
57-1489	C-135	17560
57-1490	C-135	17561
57-1491	C-135	17562
57-1492	C-135	17563
57-1493	C-135	17564
57-1494	C-135	17565

57-1495 C-135 17566
57-1496 C-135 17567
57-1497 C-135 17568
57-1498 C-135 17569
57-1499 C-135 17570
57-1500 C-135 17571
57-1501 C-135 17572
57-1502 C-135 17573
57-1503 C-135 17574
57-1504 C-135 17575
57-1505 C-135 17576
57-1506 C-135 17577
57-1507 C-135 17578
57-1508 C-135 17579
57-1509 C-135 17580
57-1510 C-135 17581
57-1511 C-135 17582
57-1512 C-135 17583
57-1513 C-135 17584
57-1514 C-135 17585
57-2589 C-135 17725
57-2590 C-135 17726
57-2591 C-135 17727
57-2592 C-135 17728
57-2593 C-135 17729
57-2594 C-135 17730
57-2595 C-135 17731
57-2596 C-135 17732
57-2597 C-135 17733
57-2598 C-135 17734
57-2599 C-135 17735
57-2600 C-135 17736
57-2601 C-135 17737
57-2602 C-135 17738
57-2603 C-135 17739
57-2604 C-135 17740
57-2605 C-135 17741
57-2606 C-135 17742
57-2607 C-135 17743
57-2608 C-135 17744
57-2609 C-135 17745
58-0001 C-135 17746
58-0002 C-135 17747
58-0003 C-135 17748
58-0004 C-135 17749
58-0005 C-135 17750
58-0006 C-135 17751
58-0007 C-135 17752
58-0008 C-135 17753
58-0009 C-135 17754
58-0010 C-135 17755
58-0011 C-135 17756
58-0012 C-135 17757
58-0013 C-135 17758
58-0014 C-135 17759
58-0015 C-135 17760
58-0016 C-135 17761
58-0017 C-135 17762
58-0018 C-135 17763
58-0019 C-135 17764
58-0020 C-135 17765
58-0021 C-135 17766
58-0022 C-135 17767
58-0023 C-135 17768
58-0024 C-135 17769
58-0025 C-135 17770
58-0026 C-135 17771
58-0027 C-135 17772
58-0028 C-135 17773
58-0029 C-135 17774
58-0030 C-135 17775
58-0031 C-135 17776
58-0032 C-135 17777
58-0033 C-135 17778
58-0034 C-135 17779
58-0035 C-135 17780
58-0036 C-135 17781
58-0037 C-135 17782
58-0038 C-135 17783
58-0039 C-135 17784
58-0040 C-135 17785
58-0041 C-135 17786
58-0042 C-135 17787
58-0043 C-135 17788
58-0044 C-135 17789
58-0045 C-135 17790
58-0046 C-135 17791
58-0047 C-135 17792
58-0048 C-135 17793
58-0049 C-135 17794
58-0050 C-135 17795
58-0051 C-135 17796
58-0052 C-135 17797
58-0053 C-135 17798
58-0054 C-135 17799
58-0055 C-135 17800
58-0056 C-135 17801
58-0057 C-135 17802
58-0058 C-135 17803
58-0059 C-135 17804
58-0060 C-135 17805
58-0061 C-135 17806
58-0062 C-135 17807
58-0063 C-135 17808
58-0064 C-135 17809
58-0065 C-135 17810
58-0066 C-135 17811
58-0067 C-135 17812
58-0068 C-135 17813
58-0069 C-135 17814
58-0070 C-135 17815
58-0071 C-135 17816
58-0072 C-135 17817
58-0073 C-135 17818
58-0074 C-135 17819
58-0075 C-135 17820
58-0076 C-135 17821
58-0077 C-135 17822
58-0078 C-135 17823
58-0079 C-135 17824
58-0080 C-135 17825
58-0081 C-135 17826
58-0082 C-135 17827
58-0083 C-135 17828
58-0084 C-135 17829
58-0085 C-135 17830
58-0086 C-135 17831
58-0087 C-135 17832
58-0088 C-135 17833
58-0089 C-135 17834
58-0090 C-135 17835
58-0091 C-135 17836
58-0092 C-135 17837
58-0093 C-135 17838
58-0094 C-135 17839
58-0095 C-135 17840
58-0096 C-135 17841
58-0097 C-135 17842
58-0098 C-135 17843
58-0099 C-135 17844
58-0100 C-135 17845
58-0101 C-135 17846
58-0102 C-135 17847
58-0103 C-135 17848
58-0104 C-135 17849
58-0105 C-135 17850
58-0106 C-135 17851
58-0107 C-135 17852
58-0108 C-135 17853
58-0109 C-135 17854
58-0110 C-135 17855
58-0111 C-135 17856
58-0112 C-135 17857
58-0113 C-135 17858
58-0114 C-135 17859
58-0115 C-135 17860
58-0116 C-135 17861
58-0117 C-135 17862
58-0118 C-135 17863
58-0119 C-135 17864
58-0120 C-135 17865
58-0121 C-135 17866
58-0122 C-135 17867
58-0123 C-135 17868
58-0124 C-135 17869
58-0125 C-135 17870
58-0126 C-135 17871
58-0127 C-135 17872
58-0128 C-135 17873
58-0129 C-135 17874
58-0130 C-135 17875
(58-0131) C-135 17876
(58-0132) C-135 17877
(58-0133) C-135 17878
(58-0134) C-135 17879
(58-0135) C-135 17880
(58-0136) C-135 17881
(58-0137) C-135 17882
(58-0138) C-135 17883
(58-0139) C-135 17884
(58-0140) C-135 17885
(58-0141) C-135 17886
(58-0142) C-135 17887
(58-0143) C-135 17888
(58-0144) C-135 17889
(58-0145) C-135 17890
(58-0146) C-135 17891
(58-0147) C-135 17892
(58-0148) C-135 17893
(58-0149) C-135 17894
(58-0150) C-135 17895
(58-0151) C-135 17896
(58-0152) C-135 17897
(58-0153) C-135 17898
(58-0154) C-135 17899
(58-0155) C-135 17900
(58-0156) C-135 17901
(58-0157) C-135 17902
58-6970 C-137 17925
58-6971 C-137 17926
58-6972 C-137 17927
59-1443 C-135 17931
59-1444 C-135 17932
59-1445 C-135 17933
59-1446 C-135 17934
59-1447 C-135 17935
59-1448 C-135 17936
59-1449 C-135 17937
59-1450 C-135 17938
59-1451 C-135 17939
59-1452 C-135 17940
59-1453 C-135 17941
59-1454 C-135 17942
59-1455 C-135 17943
59-1456 C-135 17944
59-1457 C-135 17945
59-1458 C-135 17946
59-1459 C-135 17947
59-1460 C-135 17948
59-1461 C-135 17949
59-1462 C-135 17950
59-1463 C-135 17951
59-1464 C-135 17952
59-1465 C-135 17953
59-1466 C-135 17954
59-1467 C-135 17955
59-1468 C-135 17956
59-1469 C-135 17957
59-1470 C-135 17958
59-1471 C-135 17959
59-1472 C-135 17960
59-1473 C-135 17961
59-1474 C-135 17962
59-1475 C-135 17963
59-1476 C-135 17964
59-1477 C-135 17965
59-1478 C-135 17966
59-1479 C-135 17967
59-1480 C-135 17968
59-1481 C-135 17969
59-1482 C-135 17970
59-1483 C-135 17971
59-1484 C-135 17972
59-1485 C-135 17973
59-1486 C-135 17974
59-1487 C-135 17975
59-1488 C-135 17976
59-1489 C-135 17977
59-1490 C-135 17978
59-1491 C-135 17979
59-1492 C-135 17980
59-1493 C-135 17981
59-1494 C-135 17982
59-1495 C-135 17983
59-1496 C-135 17984
59-1497 C-135 17985
59-1498 C-135 17986
59-1499 C-135 17987
59-1500 C-135 17988
59-1501 C-135 17989
59-1502 C-135 17990
59-1503 C-135 17991
59-1504 C-135 17992
59-1505 C-135 17993
59-1506 C-135 17994
59-1507 C-135 17995
59-1508 C-135 17996
59-1509 C-135 17997
59-1510 C-135 17998
59-1511 C-135 17999
59-1512 C-135 18000
59-1513 C-135 18001
59-1514 C-135 18002
59-1515 C-135 18003
59-1516 C-135 18004
59-1517 C-135 18005
59-1518 C-135 18006
59-1519 C-135 18007
59-1520 C-135 18008
59-1521 C-135 18009
59-1522 C-135 18010
59-1523 C-135 18011
60-0313 C-135 18088
60-0314 C-135 18089
60-0315 C-135 18090
60-0316 C-135 18091
60-0317 C-135 18092
60-0318 C-135 18093
60-0319 C-135 18094
60-0320 C-135 18095
60-0321 C-135 18096
60-0322 C-135 18097
60-0323 C-135 18098
60-0324 C-135 18099
60-0325 C-135 18100
60-0326 C-135 18101
60-0327 C-135 18102
60-0328 C-135 18103
60-0329 C-135 18104
60-0330 C-135 18105
60-0331 C-135 18106
60-0332 C-135 18107
60-0333 C-135 18108
60-0334 C-135 18109
60-0335 C-135 18110
60-0336 C-135 18111
60-0337 C-135 18112
60-0338 C-135 18113
60-0339 C-135 18114
60-0340 C-135 18115
60-0341 C-135 18116
60-0342 C-135 18117
60-0343 C-135 18118
60-0344 C-135 18119
60-0345 C-135 18120
60-0346 C-135 18121
60-0347 C-135 18122
60-0348 C-135 18123
60-0349 C-135 18124
60-0350 C-135 18125
60-0351 C-135 18126
60-0352 C-135 18127
60-0353 C-135 18128
60-0354 C-135 18129
60-0355 C-135 18130
60-0356 C-135 18131
60-0357 C-135 18132
60-0358 C-135 18133
60-0359 C-135 18134
60-0360 C-135 18135
60-0361 C-135 18136
60-0362 C-135 18137
60-0363 C-135 18138
60-0364 C-135 18139
60-0365 C-135 18140
60-0366 C-135 18141
60-0367 C-135 18142
60-0368 C-135 18143
60-0369 C-135 18144
60-0370 C-135 18145
60-0371 C-135 18146
60-0372 C-135 18147
60-0373 C-135 18148
60-0374 C-135 18149

60-0375	C-135 18150	61-2672	C-135 18348	62-3575	C-135 18558	63-8035	C-135 18652
60-0376	C-135 18151	61-2673	C-135 18349	62-3576	C-135 18559	63-8036	C-135 18653
60-0377	C-135 18152	61-2674	C-135 18350	62-3577	C-135 18560	63-8037	C-135 18654
60-0378	C-135 18153	61-2775	C-141 6001	62-3578	C-135 18561	63-8038	C-135 18655
61-0261	C-135 18168	61-2776	C-141 6002	62-3579	C-135 18562	63-8039	C-135 18656
61-0262	C-135 18169	61-2777	C-141 6003	62-3580	C-135 18563	63-8040	C-135 18657
61-0263	C-135 18170	61-2778	C-141 6004	62-3581	C-135 18564	63-8041	C-135 18658
61-0264	C-135 18171	61-2779	C-141 6005	62-3582	C-135 18565	63-8042	C-135 18659
61-0265	C-135 18172	62-3497	C-135 18480	62-3583	C-135 18566	63-8043	C-135 18660
61-0266	C-135 18173	62-3498	C-135 18481	62-3584	C-135 18567	63-8044	C-135 18661
61-0267	C-135 18174	62-3499	C-135 18482	62-3585	C-135 18568	63-8045	C-135 18662
61-0268	C-135 18175	62-3500	C-135 18483	62-4125	C-135 18465	63-8046	C-135 18663
61-0269	C-135 18176	62-3501	C-135 18484	62-4126	C-135 18466	63-8047	C-135 18664
61-0270	C-135 18177	62-3502	C-135 18485	62-4127	C-135 18467	63-8048	C-135 18665
61-0271	C-135 18178	62-3503	C-135 18486	62-4128	C-135 18468	63-8049	C-135 18666
61-0272	C-135 18179	62-3504	C-135 18487	62-4129	C-135 18469	63-8050	C-135 18667
61-0273	C-135 18180	62-3505	C-135 18488	62-4130	C-135 18470	63-8051	C-135 18668
61-0274	C-135 18181	62-3506	C-135 18489	62-4131	C-135 18471	63-8052	C-135 18669
61-0275	C-135 18182	62-3507	C-135 18490	62-4132	C-135 18472	63-8053	C-135 18701
61-0276	C-135 18183	62-3508	C-135 18491	62-4133	C-135 18473	63-8054	C-135 18702
61-0277	C-135 18184	62-3509	C-135 18492	62-4134	C-135 18474	63-8055	C-135 18703
61-0278	C-135 18185	62-3510	C-135 18493	62-4135	C-135 18475	63-8056	C-135 18704
61-0279	C-135 18186	62-3511	C-135 18494	62-4136	C-135 18476	63-8057	C-135 18705
61-0280	C-135 18187	62-3512	C-135 18495	62-4137	C-135 18477	63-8058	C-135 18670
61-0281	C-135 18188	62-3513	C-135 18496	62-4138	C-135 18478	63-8059	C-135 18671
61-0282	C-135 18189	62-3514	C-135 18497	62-4139	C-135 18479	63-8060	C-135 18672
61-0283	C-135 18190	62-3515	C-135 18498	62-6000	C-137 18461	63-8061	C-135 18673
61-0284	C-135 18191	62-3516	C-135 18499	63-7976	C-135 18593	(63-8062)	C-135 18674
61-0285	C-135 18192	62-3517	C-135 18500	63-7977	C-135 18594	(63-8063)	C-135 18675
61-0286	C-135 18193	62-3518	C-135 18501	63-7978	C-135 18595	(63-8064)	C-135 18676
61-0287	C-135 18194	62-3519	C-135 18502	63-7979	C-135 18596	(63-8065)	C-135 18677
61-0288	C-135 18195	62-3520	C-135 18503	63-7980	C-135 18597	(63-8066)	C-135 18678
61-0289	C-135 18196	62-3521	C-135 18504	63-7981	C-135 18598	63-8075	C-141 6006
61-0290	C-135 18197	62-3522	C-135 18505	63-7982	C-135 18599	63-8076	C-141 6007
61-0291	C-135 18198	62-3523	C-135 18506	63-7983	C-135 18600	63-8077	C-141 6008
61-0292	C-135 18199	62-3524	C-135 18507	63-7984	C-135 18601	63-8078	C-141 6009
61-0293	C-135 18200	62-3525	C-135 18508	63-7985	C-135 18602	63-8079	C-141 6010
61-0294	C-135 18201	62-3526	C-135 18509	63-7986	C-135 18603	63-8080	C-141 6011
61-0295	C-135 18202	62-3527	C-135 18510	63-7987	C-135 18604	63-8081	C-141 6012
61-0296	C-135 18203	62-3528	C-135 18511	63-7988	C-135 18605	63-8082	C-141 6013
61-0297	C-135 18204	62-3529	C-135 18512	63-7989	C-135 18606	63-8083	C-141 6014
61-0298	C-135 18205	62-3530	C-135 18513	63-7990	C-135 18607	63-8084	C-141 6015
61-0299	C-135 18206	62-3531	C-135 18514	63-7991	C-135 18608	63-8085	C-141 6016
61-0300	C-135 18207	62-3532	C-135 18515	63-7992	C-135 18609	63-8086	C-141 6017
61-0301	C-135 18208	62-3533	C-135 18516	63-7993	C-135 18610	63-8087	C-141 6018
61-0302	C-135 18209	62-3534	C-135 18517	63-7994	C-135 18611	63-8088	C-141 6019
61-0303	C-135 18210	62-3535	C-135 18518	63-7995	C-135 18612	63-8089	C-141 6020
61-0304	C-135 18211	62-3536	C-135 18519	63-7996	C-135 18613	63-8090	C-141 6021
61-0305	C-135 18212	62-3537	C-135 18520	63-7997	C-135 18614	63-8470	C-135 18679
61-0306	C-135 18213	62-3538	C-135 18521	63-7998	C-135 18615	63-8471	C-135 18680
61-0307	C-135 18214	62-3539	C-135 18522	63-7999	C-135 18616	63-8472	C-135 18681
61-0308	C-135 18215	62-3540	C-135 18523	63-8000	C-135 18617	63-8473	C-135 18682
61-0309	C-135 18216	62-3541	C-135 18524	63-8001	C-135 18618	63-8474	C-135 18683
61-0310	C-135 18217	62-3542	C-135 18525	63-8002	C-135 18619	63-8475	C-135 18684
61-0311	C-135 18218	62-3543	C-135 18526	63-8003	C-135 18620	63-8871	C-135 18719
61-0312	C-135 18219	62-3544	C-135 18527	63-8004	C-135 18621	63-8872	C-135 18720
61-0313	C-135 18220	62-3545	C-135 18528	63-8005	C-135 18622	63-8873	C-135 18721
61-0314	C-135 18221	62-3546	C-135 18529	63-8006	C-135 18623	63-8874	C-135 18722
61-0315	C-135 18222	62-3547	C-135 18530	63-8007	C-135 18624	63-8875	C-135 18723
61-0316	C-135 18223	62-3548	C-135 18531	63-8008	C-135 18625	63-8876	C-135 18724
61-0317	C-135 18224	62-3549	C-135 18532	63-8009	C-135 18626	63-8877	C-135 18725
61-0318	C-135 18225	62-3550	C-135 18533	63-8010	C-135 18627	63-8878	C-135 18726
61-0319	C-135 18226	62-3551	C-135 18534	63-8011	C-135 18628	63-8879	C-135 18727
61-0320	C-135 18227	62-3552	C-135 18535	63-8012	C-135 18629	63-8880	C-135 18728
61-0321	C-135 18228	62-3553	C-135 18536	63-8013	C-135 18630	63-8881	C-135 18729
61-0322	C-135 18229	62-3554	C-135 18537	63-8014	C-135 18631	63-8882	C-135 18730
61-0323	C-135 18230	62-3555	C-135 18538	63-8015	C-135 18632	63-8883	C-135 18731
61-0324	C-135 18231	62-3556	C-135 18539	63-8016	C-135 18633	63-8884	C-135 18732
61-0325	C-135 18232	62-3557	C-135 18540	63-8017	C-135 18634	63-8885	C-135 18733
61-0326	C-135 18233	62-3558	C-135 18541	63-8018	C-135 18635	63-8886	C-135 18734
61-0327	C-135 18234	62-3559	C-135 18542	63-8019	C-135 18636	63-8887	C-135 18735
61-0328	C-135 18235	62-3560	C-135 18543	63-8020	C-135 18637	63-8888	C-135 18736
61-0329	C-135 18236	62-3561	C-135 18544	63-8021	C-135 18638	63-9792	C-135 18706
61-0330	C-135 18237	62-3562	C-135 18545	63-8022	C-135 18639	63-12735	C-135 18695
61-0331	C-135 18238	62-3563	C-135 18546	63-8023	C-135 18640	63-12736	C-135 18696
61-0332	C-135 18239	62-3564	C-135 18547	63-8024	C-135 18641	63-12737	C-135 18697
61-2662	C-135 18292	62-3565	C-135 18548	63-8025	C-135 18642	63-12738	C-135 18698
61-2663	C-135 18333	62-3566	C-135 18549	63-8026	C-135 18643	63-12739	C-135 18699
61-2664	C-135 18340	62-3567	C-135 18550	63-8027	C-135 18644	63-12740	C-135 18700
61-2665	C-135 18341	62-3568	C-135 18551	63-8028	C-135 18645	64-0609	C-141 6022
61-2666	C-135 18342	62-3569	C-135 18552	63-8029	C-135 18646	64-0610	C-141 6023
61-2667	C-135 18343	62-3570	C-135 18553	63-8030	C-135 18647	64-0611	C-141 6024
61-2668	C-135 18344	62-3571	C-135 18554	63-8031	C-135 18648	64-0612	C-141 6025
61-2669	C-135 18345	62-3572	C-135 18555	63-8032	C-135 18649	64-0613	C-141 6026
61-2670	C-135 18346	62-3573	C-135 18556	63-8033	C-135 18650	64-0614	C-141 6027
61-2671	C-135 18347	62-3574	C-135 18557	63-8034	C-135 18651	64-0615	C-141 6028

64-0616	C-141	6029
64-0617	C-141	6030
64-0618	C-141	6031
64-0619	C-141	6032
64-0620	C-141	6033
64-0621	C-141	6034
64-0622	C-141	6035
64-0623	C-141	6036
64-0624	C-141	6037
64-0625	C-141	6038
64-0626	C-141	6039
64-0627	C-141	6040
64-0628	C-141	6041
64-0629	C-141	6042
64-0630	C-141	6043
64-0631	C-141	6044
64-0632	C-141	6045
64-0633	C-141	6046
64-0634	C-141	6047
64-0635	C-141	6048
64-0636	C-141	6049
64-0637	C-141	6050
64-0638	C-141	6051
64-0639	C-141	6052
64-0640	C-141	6053
64-0641	C-141	6054
64-0642	C-141	6055
64-0643	C-141	6056
64-0644	C-141	6057
64-0645	C-141	6058
64-0646	C-141	6059
64-0647	C-141	6060
64-0648	C-141	6061
64-0649	C-141	6062
64-0650	C-141	6063
64-0651	C-141	6064
64-0652	C-141	6065
64-0653	C-141	6066
64-14828	C-135	18768
64-14829	C-135	18769
64-14830	C-135	18770
64-14831	C-135	18771
64-14832	C-135	18772
64-14833	C-135	18773
64-14834	C-135	18774
64-14835	C-135	18775
64-14836	C-135	18776
64-14837	C-135	18777
64-14838	C-135	18778
64-14839	C-135	18779
64-14840	C-135	18780
64-14841	C-135	18781
64-14842	C-135	18782
64-14843	C-135	18783
64-14844	C-135	18784
64-14845	C-135	18785
64-14846	C-135	18786
64-14847	C-135	18787
64-14848	C-135	18788
64-14849	C-135	18789
65-0216	C-141	6067
65-0217	C-141	6068
65-0218	C-141	6069
65-0219	C-141	6070
65-0220	C-141	6071
65-0221	C-141	6072
65-0222	C-141	6073
65-0223	C-141	6074
65-0224	C-141	6075
65-0225	C-141	6076
65-0226	C-141	6077
65-0227	C-141	6078
65-0228	C-141	6079
65-0229	C-141	6080
65-0230	C-141	6081
65-0231	C-141	6082
65-0232	C-141	6083
65-0233	C-141	6084
65-0234	C-141	6085
65-0235	C-141	6086
65-0236	C-141	6087
65-0237	C-141	6088
65-0238	C-141	6089
65-0239	C-141	6090
65-0240	C-141	6091
65-0241	C-141	6092
65-0242	C-141	6093
65-0243	C-141	6094
65-0244	C-141	6095
65-0245	C-141	6096
65-0246	C-141	6097
65-0247	C-141	6098
65-0248	C-141	6099
65-0249	C-141	6100
65-0250	C-141	6101
65-0251	C-141	6102
65-0252	C-141	6103
65-0253	C-141	6104
65-0254	C-141	6105
65-0255	C-141	6106
65-0256	C-141	6107
65-0257	C-141	6108
65-0258	C-141	6109
65-0259	C-141	6111
65-0260	C-141	6112
65-0261	C-141	6113
65-0262	C-141	6114
65-0263	C-141	6115
65-0264	C-141	6116
65-0265	C-141	6117
65-0266	C-141	6118
65-0267	C-141	6119
65-0268	C-141	6120
65-0269	C-141	6121
65-0270	C-141	6122
65-0271	C-141	6123
65-0272	C-141	6124
65-0273	C-141	6125
65-0274	C-141	6126
65-0275	C-141	6127
65-0276	C-141	6128
65-0277	C-141	6129
65-0278	C-141	6130
65-0279	C-141	6131
65-0280	C-141	6132
65-0281	C-141	6133
65-9397	C-141	6134
65-9398	C-141	6135
65-9399	C-141	6136
65-9400	C-141	6137
65-9401	C-141	6138
65-9402	C-141	6139
65-9403	C-141	6140
65-9404	C-141	6141
65-9405	C-141	6142
65-9406	C-141	6143
65-9407	C-141	6144
65-9408	C-141	6145
65-9409	C-141	6146
65-9410	C-141	6147
65-9411	C-141	6148
65-9412	C-141	6149
65-9413	C-141	6150
65-9414	C-141	6151
66-0126	C-141	6152
66-0127	C-141	6153
66-0128	C-141	6154
66-0129	C-141	6155
66-0130	C-141	6156
66-0131	C-141	6157
66-0132	C-141	6158
66-0133	C-141	6159
66-0134	C-141	6160
66-0135	C-141	6161
66-0136	C-141	6162
66-0137	C-141	6163
66-0138	C-141	6164
66-0139	C-141	6165
66-0140	C-141	6166
66-0141	C-141	6167
66-0142	C-141	6168
66-0143	C-141	6169
66-0144	C-141	6170
66-0145	C-141	6171
66-0146	C-141	6172
66-0147	C-141	6173
66-0148	C-141	6174
66-0149	C-141	6175
66-0150	C-141	6176
66-0151	C-141	6177
66-0152	C-141	6178
66-0153	C-141	6179
66-0154	C-141	6180
66-0155	C-141	6181
66-0156	C-141	6182
66-0157	C-141	6183
66-0158	C-141	6184
66-0159	C-141	6185
66-0160	C-141	6186
66-0161	C-141	6187
66-0162	C-141	6188
66-0163	C-141	6189
66-0164	C-141	6190
66-0165	C-141	6191
66-0166	C-141	6192
66-0167	C-141	6193
66-0168	C-141	6194
66-0169	C-141	6195
66-0170	C-141	6196
66-0171	C-141	6197
66-0172	C-141	6198
66-0173	C-141	6199
66-0174	C-141	6200
66-0175	C-141	6201
66-0176	C-141	6202
66-0177	C-141	6203
66-0178	C-141	6204
66-0179	C-141	6205
66-0180	C-141	6206
66-0181	C-141	6207
66-0182	C-141	6208
66-0183	C-141	6209
66-0184	C-141	6210
66-0185	C-141	6211
66-0186	C-141	6212
66-0187	C-141	6213
66-0188	C-141	6214
66-0189	C-141	6215
66-0190	C-141	6216
66-0191	C-141	6217
66-0192	C-141	6218
66-0193	C-141	6219
66-0194	C-141	6220
66-0195	C-141	6221
66-0196	C-141	6222
66-0197	C-141	6223
66-0198	C-141	6224
66-0199	C-141	6225
66-0200	C-141	6226
66-0201	C-141	6227
66-0202	C-141	6228
66-0203	C-141	6229
66-0204	C-141	6230
66-0205	C-141	6231
66-0206	C-141	6232
66-0207	C-141	6233
66-0208	C-141	6234
66-0209	C-141	6235
66-7944	C-141	6236
66-7945	C-141	6237
66-7946	C-141	6238
66-7947	C-141	6239
66-7948	C-141	6240
66-7949	C-141	6241
66-7950	C-141	6242
66-7951	C-141	6243
66-7952	C-141	6244
66-7953	C-141	6245
66-7954	C-141	6246
66-7955	C-141	6247
66-7956	C-141	6248
66-7957	C-141	6249
66-7958	C-141	6250
66-7959	C-141	6251
66-8303	C-5	500-0001
66-8304	C-5	500-0002
66-8305	C-5	500-0003
66-8306	C-5	500-0004
66-8307	C-5	500-0005
66-30052	B707	18949
67-0001	C-141	6252
67-0002	C-141	6253
67-0003	C-141	6254
67-0004	C-141	6255
67-0005	C-141	6256
67-0006	C-141	6257
67-0007	C-141	6258
67-0008	C-141	6259
67-0009	C-141	6260
67-0010	C-141	6261
67-0011	C-141	6262
67-0012	C-141	6263
67-0013	C-141	6264
67-0014	C-141	6265
67-0015	C-141	6266
67-0016	C-141	6267
67-0017	C-141	6268
67-0018	C-141	6269
67-0019	C-141	6270
67-0020	C-141	6271
67-0021	C-141	6272
67-0022	C-141	6273
67-0023	C-141	6274
67-0024	C-141	6275
67-0025	C-141	6276
67-0026	C-141	6277
67-0027	C-141	6278
67-0028	C-141	6279
67-0029	C-141	6280
67-0030	C-141	6281
67-0031	C-141	6282
67-0164	C-141	6283
67-0165	C-141	6284
67-0166	C-141	6285
67-0167	C-5	500-0006
67-0168	C-5	500-0007
67-0169	C-5	500-0008
67-0170	C-5	500-0009
67-0171	C-5	500-0010
67-0172	C-5	500-0011
67-0173	C-5	500-0012
67-0174	C-5	500-0013
67-19417	C-137	19417
67-22583	C-9	47241
67-22584	C-9	47242
67-22585	C-9	47295
67-22586	C-9	47296
68-0211	C-5	500-0014
68-0212	C-5	500-0015
68-0213	C-5	500-0016
68-0214	C-5	500-0017
68-0215	C-5	500-0018
68-0216	C-5	500-0019
68-0217	C-5	500-0020
68-0218	C-5	500-0021
68-0219	C-5	500-0022
68-0220	C-5	500-0023
68-0221	C-5	500-0024
68-0222	C-5	500-0025
68-0223	C-5	500-0026
68-0224	C-5	500-0027
68-0225	C-5	500-0028
68-0226	C-5	500-0029
68-0227	C-5	500-0030
68-0228	C-5	500-0031
68-8932	C-9	47297
68-8933	C-9	47298
68-8934	C-9	47299
68-8935	C-9	47300
68-10958	C-9	47366
68-10959	C-9	47367
68-10960	C-9	47448
68-10961	C-9	47449
69-0001	C-5	500-0032
69-0002	C-5	500-0033
69-0003	C-5	500-0034
69-0004	C-5	500-0035
69-0005	C-5	500-0036
69-0006	C-5	500-0037
69-0007	C-5	500-0038
69-0008	C-5	500-0039
69-0009	C-5	500-0040
69-0010	C-5	500-0041
69-0011	C-5	500-0042
69-0012	C-5	500-0043
69-0013	C-5	500-0044
69-0014	C-5	500-0045
69-0015	C-5	500-0046
69-0016	C-5	500-0047
69-0017	C-5	500-0048
69-0018	C-5	500-0049
69-0019	C-5	500-0050
69-0020	C-5	500-0051
69-0021	C-5	500-0052

69-0022	C-5	500-0053
69-0023	C-5	500-0054
69-0024	C-5	500-0055
69-0025	C-5	500-0056
69-0026	C-5	500-0057
69-0027	C-5	500-0058
70-0445	C-5	500-0059
70-0446	C-5	500-0060
70-0447	C-5	500-0061
70-0448	C-5	500-0062
70-0449	C-5	500-0063
70-0450	C-5	500-0064
70-0451	C-5	500-0065
70-0452	C-5	500-0066
70-0453	C-5	500-0067
70-0454	C-5	500-0068
70-0455	C-5	500-0069
70-0456	C-5	500-0070
70-0457	C-5	500-0071
70-0458	C-5	500-0072
70-0459	C-5	500-0073
70-0460	C-5	500-0074
70-0461	C-5	500-0075
70-0462	C-5	500-0076
70-0463	C-5	500-0077
70-0464	C-5	500-0078
70-0465	C-5	500-0079
70-0466	C-5	500-0080
70-0467	C-5	500-0081
71-0874	C-9	47467
71-0875	C-9	47471
71-0876	C-9	47475
71-0877	C-9	47495
71-0878	C-9	47536
71-0879	C-9	47537
71-0880	C-9	47538
71-0881	C-9	47540
71-0882	C-9	47541
71-1403	T-43	20685
71-1404	T-43	20686
71-1405	T-43	20687
71-1406	T-43	20688
71-1407	E-3	20518
71-1408	E-3	20519
71-1841	B707	20495
72-0282	T-43	20689
72-0283	T-43	20690
72-0284	T-43	20691
72-0285	T-43	20692
72-0286	T-43	20693
72-0287	T-43	20694
72-0288	T-43	20695
72-1873	C-14	
72-1874	C-14	
72-1875	C-15	
72-1876	C-15	
72-7000	C-137	20630
73-1149	T-43	20696
73-1150	T-43	20697
73-1151	T-43	20698
73-1152	T-43	20699
73-1153	T-43	20700
73-1154	T-43	20701
73-1155	T-43	20702
73-1156	T-43	20703
73-1674	E-3	21046
73-1675	E-3	21185
73-1676	E-4	20682
73-1677	E-4	20683
73-1681	C-9	47668
73-1682	C-9	47670
73-1683	C-9	47671
74-0787	E-4	20684
75-0125	E-4	20949
75-0556	E-3	21047
75-0557	E-3	21207
75-0558	E-3	21208
75-0559	E-3	21209
75-0560	E-3	21250
76-1704	E-3	21434
76-1705	E-3	21435
76-1706	E-3	21436
76-1707	E-3	21437
77-0351	E-3	21551
77-0352	E-3	21552
77-0353	E-3	21553

77-0354	E-3	21554
77-0355	E-3	21555
77-0356	E-3	21556
78-0576	E-3	21752
78-0577	E-3	21753
78-0578	E-3	21754
79-0001	E-3	21755
79-0002	E-3	21756
79-0003	E-3	21757
79-0433	KC-10	48200
79-0434	KC-10	48201
79-0442	E-3	22855
79-0443	E-3	22838
79-0444	E-3	22839
79-0445	E-3	22840
79-0446	E-3	22841
79-0447	E-3	22842
79-0448	E-3	22843
79-0449	E-3	22844
79-0450	E-3	22845
79-0451	E-3	22846
79-0452	E-3	22847
79-0453	E-3	22848
79-0454	E-3	22849
79-0455	E-3	22850
79-0456	E-3	22851
79-0457	E-3	22852
79-0458	E-3	22853
79-0459	E-3	22854
79-1710	KC-10	48202
79-1711	KC-10	48203
79-1712	KC-10	48204
79-1713	KC-10	48205
79-1946	KC-10	48206
79-1947	KC-10	48207
79-1948	KC-10	48208
79-1949	KC-10	48209
79-1950	KC-10	48210
79-1951	KC-10	48211
80-0137	E-3	22829
80-0138	E-3	22830
80-0139	E-3	22831
81-0004	E-3	22832
81-0005	E-3	22833
81-0891	C-18	19518
81-0892	C-18	19382
81-0893	C-18	19384
81-0894	C-18	19583
81-0895	C-18	19381
81-0896	C-18	19581
(81-0897)	C-18	19236
81-0898	C-18	19380
82-0006	E-3	22834
82-0007	E-3	22835
82-0008	E-3	22836
82-0009	E-3	22837
82-0067	E-3	23418
82-0068	E-3	23417
82-0068	E-3	23419
82-0069	E-3	23420
82-0070	E-3	23421
82-0071	E-3	23422
82-0072	E-3	23423
82-0073	E-3	23424
82-0074	E-3	23425
82-0075	E-3	23426
82-0076	E-3	23427
82-0190	KC-10	48212
82-0191	KC-10	48213
82-0192	KC-10	48214
82-0193	KC-10	48215
82-8000	C-25	23824
83-0075	KC-10	48216
83-0076	KC-10	48217
83-0077	KC-10	48218
83-0078	KC-10	48219
83-0079	KC-10	48220
83-0080	KC-10	48221
83-0081	KC-10	48222
83-0082	KC-10	48223
83-0510	E-3	23428
83-0511	E-3	23429
83-1285	C-5	500-0082
83-4610	C-22	18811
83-4612	C-22	18813
83-4615	C-22	18816

83-4616	C-22	18817
83-4618	C-22	21946
84-0059	C-5	500-0083
84-0060	C-5	500-0084
84-0061	C-5	500-0085
84-0062	C-5	500-0086
84-0185	KC-10	48224
84-0186	KC-10	48225
84-0187	KC-10	48226
84-0188	KC-10	48227
84-0189	KC-10	48228
84-0190	KC-10	48229
84-0191	KC-10	48230
84-0192	KC-10	48231
84-0193	C-22	18362
84-1398	C-18	18713
84-1399	C-18	19566
85-0001	C-5	500-0087
85-0002	C-5	500-0088
85-0003	C-5	500-0089
85-0004	C-5	500-0090
85-0005	C-5	500-0091
85-0006	C-5	500-0092
85-0007	C-5	500-0093
85-0008	C-5	500-0094
85-0009	C-5	500-0095
85-0010	C-5	500-0096
85-0027	KC-10	48232
85-0028	KC-10	48233
85-0029	KC-10	48234
85-0030	KC-10	48235
85-0031	KC-10	48236
85-0032	KC-10	48237
85-0033	KC-10	48238
85-0034	KC-10	48239
85-6973	C-137	20043
85-6974	C-137	20297
86-0011	C-5	500-0097
86-0012	C-5	500-0098
86-0013	C-5	500-0099
86-0014	C-5	500-0100
86-0015	C-5	500-0101
86-0016	C-5	500-0102
86-0017	C-5	500-0103
86-0018	C-5	500-0104
86-0019	C-5	500-0105
86-0020	C-5	500-0106
86-0021	C-5	500-0107
86-0022	C-5	500-0108
86-0023	C-5	500-0109
86-0024	C-5	500-0110
86-0025	C-5	500-0111
86-0026	C-5	500-0112
86-0027	KC-10	48240
86-0028	KC-10	48241
86-0029	KC-10	48242
86-0030	KC-10	48243
86-0031	KC-10	48244
86-0032	KC-10	48245
86-0033	KC-10	48246
86-0034	KC-10	48247
86-0035	KC-10	48248
86-0036	KC-10	48249
86-0037	KC-10	48250
86-0038	KC-10	48251
86-0416	E-8	19626
86-0417	E-8	19574
(86-8800)	C-25	23824
(86-8900)	C-25	23825
87-0025	C-17	T1
87-0027	C-5	500-0113
87-0028	C-5	500-0114
87-0029	C-5	500-0115
87-0030	C-5	500-0116
87-0031	C-5	500-0117
87-0032	C-5	500-0118
87-0033	C-5	500-0119
87-0034	C-5	500-0120
87-0035	C-5	500-0121
87-0036	C-5	500-0122
87-0037	C-5	500-0123
87-0038	C-5	500-0124
87-0039	C-5	500-0125
87-0040	C-5	500-0126
87-0041	C-5	500-0127
87-0042	C-5	500-0128

87-0043	C-5	500-0129
87-0044	C-5	500-0130
87-0045	C-5	500-0131
87-0117	KC-10	48303
87-0118	KC-10	48304
87-0119	KC-10	48305
87-0120	KC-10	48306
87-0121	KC-10	48307
87-0122	KC-10	48308
87-0123	KC-10	48309
87-0124	KC-10	48310
88-0265	C-17	P1
88-0266	C-17	P2
88-0322	E-8	24503
89-1189	C-17	P3
89-1190	C-17	P4
89-1191	C-17	P5
89-1192	C-17	P6
90-0175	E-8	19621
90-0532	C-17	P7
90-0533	C-17	P8
90-0534	C-17	P9
90-0535	C-17	P10
92-3289	E-8	19622
92-3291	C-17	P11
92-3292	C-17	P12
92-3293	C-17	P13
92-3294	C-17	P14
92-9000	C-25	23825
93-0599	C-17	P15
93-0600	C-17	P16
93-0601	C-17	P17
93-0602	C-17	P18
93-0603	C-17	P19
93-0604	C-17	P20
94-0065	C-17	P21
94-0066	C-17	P22
94-0067	C-17	P23
94-0068	C-17	P24
94-0069	C-17	P25
94-0070	C-17	P26

Venezuela

0001	B737	21167
(0002)	B737	21168
0003	DC-9	47000
6944	B707	19760
8747	B707	18950

Yugoslavia

7601	CRVL	241
14301	B727	21080
14302	B727	21040
71501	YAK40	9120717
71502	YAK40	9120817
71503	YAK40	9222020
71504	YAK40	9231523
71505	YAK40	9630849
71506	YAK40	9731255
73601	B707	19177
74101	CRVL	241
74301	B727	21080
74302	B727	21040

Zaire

9T-MSS	B707	19969

Zambia

AF604	YAK40	
AF605	YAK40	9532042
AF606	YAK40	

NOTES

NOTES

NOTES

NOTES

NOTES

AIR-BRITAIN SALES

Companion publications to the United Kingdom and Ireland Registers are also available by post-free mail order from

Air-Britain Sales Department (Dept JAW96)
5 Bradley Road
Upper Norwood
LONDON SE19 3NT

Visa / Mastercard accepted - please give full details of card number and expiry date.

* UNITED KINGDOM AND IRELAND REGISTERS HANDBOOK 1996 - £ 16.00
  Current registers of all the UK and Irish register Aircraft, including non-British aircraft based in the UK. Alphabetical index by type. 482 pages. 32nd annual edition. Available in ring-bound / hardback format.

* EUROPEAN REGISTERS HANDBOOK 1996 - £ 18.00
  Current registers of over 40 Western and Eastern European countries plus Middle East. Available in ring-bound / hardback format.

* CIVIL REGISTERS OF GERMANY 1996 (Available early July 1996) - £ 16.00
  Current registers in same format as United Kingdom & Ireland Register.

* AIRLINE FLEETS 1996 (Available June 1996) - £ 15.00
  Over 1600 fleets listed plus leasing companies and "airliners in limbo". Available in ring bound / hardback format.

* BUSINESS JETS INTERNATIONAL 1996 (Available June 1996) - £ 12.00
  Complete production lists of all purpose-built business jets with full 20,000+ cross-reference.

* BUSINESS TURBOPROPS INTERNATIONAL 1996 (Available June 1996) - £ 12.50
  In same format as above.

* COMPLETE CIVIL AIRCRAFT REGISTERS OF FINLAND SINCE 1926 - £ 11.00
  Fully researched and detailed history of all civilian aircraft in Finland.

* TURBOPROP AIRLINERS AND MILITARY TRANSPORTS OF THE WORLD 1994 - £ 12.50
  Detailed production lists of 80 turboprop airliner types including Eastern Europeans and military transports with full cross-reference index.

* COMPLETE RUSSIAN CIVIL REGISTERS - £ 11.00
  From WWII to 1994, 112 pages with both CCCP and RA registers.

* BAC ONE-ELEVEN - £ 20.00
  The complete development history and comprehensive production details, 240 A4 pages, hard cover.

* BEECH 17 - £ 11.00
  Comprehensive production history of every one of the 785 Staggerwings. Fully illustrated.

* MILITARY TITLES -
  Air-Britain also publishes a comprehensive range of military titles -

    * RAF Serial Registers
    * Detailed RAF Type "Files"
    * Squadron Histories
    * Royal Navy Aircraft Histories.

  Please write for details.

IMPORTANT NOTE - members receive substantial discounts on all of the above Air-Britain publications. For details of membership - see overleaf.

AIR-BRITAIN MEMBERSHIP

If you are not already a member of Air-Britain, why not join now?

Members can receive -

* Discounts on Air-Britain Monographs.

* Quarterly Air-Britain Digest A4 magazine containing articles of aviation interest and comprehensive black & white and colour photographic coverage.

* Monthly Air-Britain News

  A5 magazine with minimum of 100 pages, includes
  - complete coverage of UK civil and military aviation scene;
  - comprehensive updates on virtually all overseas registers, including USA;
  - sections on bizjets, bizprops and jet, turbine & piston commercial aircraft;
  - full coverage of air displays, UK and overseas.

* Quarterly - Archive and Aeromilitaria.
  Historical A4 magazines packed with previously unpublished information and photos.

* Access to our Information Services, Black and White Photo and Colour Slide Libraries, Air-Britain Travel to overseas airfields, museums and displays.

* Access to our expanding Branch network.

Basic Membership fee for 1996 is £22.00 (to include 4 Air-Britain Digests and 12 Air-Britain News).
(Visa / Mastercard accepted - please give full card details including number and expiry date.)

To join or for more information please write to:-

Air-Britain Membership Department (Dept JAW96)
36 Nursery Road
Taplow
Maidenhead
Berks SL6 0JZ

For sample Air-Britain Digest and News, please enclose £1.00; or include samples of Aeromilitaria and Archive for £2.00.